THE RACECOURSE ROBINS

from

ADAMS to YOUDS

THIS BOOK HAS BEEN PUBLISHED AS A LIMITED EDITION OF WHICH THIS IS NUMBER:

376

A LIST OF THE ORIGINAL SUBSCRIBERS TO THIS LIMITED EDITION MAY BE FOUND AT THE BACK OF THE PUBLICATION

A Who's Who of Wrexham Association Football Club

1921 to 1999

by Gareth M . Davies & Peter Jones

THE RACECOURSE ROBINS

from

ADAMS to YOUDS

ICH DIEN
1873 1873
WREXHAM A.F.C.

Sponsored by

GLASS MERCHANTS
JRB
GLAZING CONTRACTORS

J. R. Boyle (Wxm) Ltd.

A Who's Who of Wrexham Association Football Club
1921 to 1999

by Gareth M . Davies & Peter Jones

Published by Gareth M. Davies and Peter Jones,
27 St. Seiriol's Close, Holyhead, Ynys Mon. LL65 1RD.

ISBN 0 9524950 1 5

Designed and typeset by the authors,
Paul Atherton and Steve Trinick

Printed by Engraving Services Ltd.
Denhill House, Radnor Street, Manchester M15 5RD

Contents

Introduction and Acknowledgements 7

Foreword by Joey Jones 8

Brief History of Wrexham A.F.C. 9

Players Adams to Youds 11

The Robins Wartime Players 351

Managers at the Racecourse 390

Records and Reference 399

Subscribers 425

A Plea For Further Help

Without the help of many players, their families and fellow supporters then this book would just not have been possible. It is with this in mind that we would like to make a further plea for help. Due to the number of photographs that we have collected over the years, we are now continuing our work into the history of Wrexham Association Football Club by putting together a pictorial history of the club for publication next year. If you have any photographs, memorablia or anything to do with Wrexham Association Football Club, players or the Racecourse, then we would like to hear from you.

We also welcome your comments on the 'Racecourse Robins From Adams To Youds', and if you know the whereabouts of any player who we have been unable to trace, then please write to Gareth at 27 St.Seiriol's Close, Holyhead, Ynys Mon, LL65 1RD (01407) 760576.

FOR ALL YOUR GLASS & GLAZING REQUIREMENTS

JOHN R. BOYLE

(Wrexham Ltd) **Established over 40 years**

It is with great pleasure that we find John R.Boyle (Wrexham) Ltd., sponsoring 'The Racecourse Robins from Adams to Youds'. They have been loyal servants to Wrexham Association Football Club in sponsorship for many years now, with the firm's owner Mr.David Griffiths (pictured below with the current Wrexham management team) having been a loyal supporter of the club since the 1950s. We hope that you will support his firm in the way that he has supported your favourite Football Club.

John R.Boyle (Wrexham) Ltd. began business in 1956, and five years later the firm's current owner, Mr.David Griffiths, was taken on as an apprentice glazier. He has since seen the business expand beyond all recognition, and from being an apprentice he became a director, eventually buying the business after Mr.Boyle died in 1992.

When Mr.Griffiths began his association with the firm they didn't have one van on the road, it was just counter sales and supplying the odd builder with glass. The firm has now progressed to four vans fitted with specialist racks and is now situated in modern premises in Unit 4 on the Pandy Industrial Estate on the edge of the town.

The firm has built up its reputation on speed and efficiency, and have a 24-hour emergency call-out service for breakages of shop fronts in the town or even private houses. In his many years with the firm, Mr.Griffiths has seen many changes in the trade, and are now a lot more into the PVC market, but still remaining essentially as traditional glass merchants. No job is too big or too small from glazing a new house or factory to repairing a broken window.

Another big change in recent years has been the call for safety glass, shopkeepers, factories and schools all demanding stronger glass for their windows. In addition to the glazing work, the firm's work includes glass cutting, drilling, polishing, leaded windows, supply of mirrors and greenhouse glass, and as far as designs are concerned, J.R.Boyle will do any to the customers requirements.

For many years the firm has provided the glazing for the building of new houses on estates and is always in great demand because of its reputation for high quality work. Not only is the firm well known in the Wrexham area, but it has an excellent reputation throughout North Wales.

With such experience for high-quality work, speed and reliability, there can be no doubt that John R.Boyle (Wrexham) Ltd., will continue to grow in strength. But there will always be high on the list the outstanding service to the customer for which the firm has been noted for the past 40 odd years.

Please give your support to John R.Boyle (Wrexham) Ltd., as they support YOUR favourite team - Wrexham Association Football Club.

SHOP WINDOW REPLACEMENTS

24 HOUR CALL-OUT BOARDING UP SERVICE

For prompt action contact:

Unit 4, Pandy Industrial Estate, Pandy, Wrexham.

Tel: (01978) 266319 Fax: (01978) 361598

Introduction

When Wrexham Association Football Club overcame the mighty Arsenal in the F.A.Cup in January 1992, the unbelievable feeling the fans enjoyed on that never to be forgotten dull afternoon, epitomised what it really means to be a fan of the 'Racecourse Robins'.

No disrespect to fans of the 'Big Fish' in the higher echelons of our beloved game, but never in a million years will they encounter such euphoria. What is common place to them is what we Wrexham fans live for! There is a certain identity with a club like Wrexham which somehow bonds us together into one 'Happy Family', even through difficult times in the club's history.

This has no doubt transmitted to the players who have performed on the Racecourse since 1921 when the club entered the Football League for the first time, and in their non-league days since 1872 - The year of the formation of Wrexham Football Club.

The players are the ones who make the history of a football club, and when we embarked on this venture we both knew it could be a difficult task to do them justice. We need not have worried as it has been most rewarding in the vast majority of the numerous 'Robins' we made contact with, who have made our cause so worthwhile. It has been fascinating and enlightening receiving answers to the various requests they have been bombarded with, and we leave it to you to judge if we have been successful?

When Peter (whose enthusiasm for this club ensures Wrexham A.F.C. will never die) became a fan in the late 1960s, little did he realise that one day he would be compiling a 'tome' on his Racecourse favourites like Albert Kinsey, Billy Ashcroft and hundreds of others since who have graced the club.

Neither did I when travelling from Holyhead by train in the guard's van in the middle 1950s as a youngster (still do!!) who marvelled at the pace and shooting power of Don Weston, and the defensive art of Ally McGowan.

We are both so proud to be able to present this compilation to you and hope that you enjoy the read as much as we have had in putting it together.

Gareth M.Davies - on behalf of Peter Jones and myself. July 1999.

Dedication;
I would like to dedicate my part of the book to my late Father David Anderson Davies, a proud son of Rhosllanerchrugog who gave me my baptism as a Wrexham A.F.C. supporter in 1956 - little did I realise what he let himself or me in for!! G.M.D.

Acknowledgements

The authors would like to take this opportunity to thank the following for their invaluable contributions to this work, which has been a labour of love for us both over a number of years. To make this book possible many numerous individuals and organisations, have given considerable help in achieving our goal.

We would first of all I would like to thank the many former and current players and their families for so kindly giving their time to answer the many questions that we have put to them, and providing us with the information and photographs when required. Hopefully the reasons for the questions that we asked are shown in this publication. One prime example of this help was from ex-player Don Parrish, who gave us vital leads to the whereabouts of other 'Robins', one of these being Derek Hughes, who had previously been omitted in error from various Football League player records. Thankfully this is now remedied - if nothing else we have brought Derek back to life!!

Others deserving of a special mention are members of the Association of Football Statisticians and Scottish Football Historians, many of whom have their own particular interests, and whose help went along way to form part of this book. Many members have already compiled detailed volumes on their own particular clubs, and without the various cross references, life would have been a little more difficult. We invite historians of other clubs to use the information contained herein in the same spirit as we have put together this book, which will no doubt add to the further extension of the history of our game.

Among other major sources of information that we have used to obtain details of the careers of Wrexham players have been the many contemporary notes taken from newspapers of the time, the Wrexham Advertiser, Wrexham and North Wales Guardian, Wrexham Leader, Evening Leader, Daily Post and Western Mail. There have been many others where the smallest of snippets have been taken from - all have helped in some way or another. Not forgetting either the various telephone directories which have often brought us direct contact with certain players or their families, even if it resulted in tired eyes!!

Then there is the F.A.of Wales, whose staff gave us much needed assistance on our visits to Cardiff to seek player transfer details. Also the staff from the many libraries that have given time to answer the smallest of query, but a big thank you to the staff at the Wrexham Library.

One individual in particular we would like to thank for his work in assisting us to collate details of pre-World War Two players, is Jim Creasy, who has a vast knowledge of all inter-war players, and whose help has been unlimited. Many thanks Jim.

There have been many other individuals who have given us help in one way or another, but we feel that we should mention the following who have helped us greatly: Tony Bluff, Michael Braham, Eric Burns, Stephen Byrne, Mark Chapman, Mike Clarke, Bill Cook, Mike Davage, Mike Durkin, Leigh Edwards, Arthur Baird Ellis, Jim Evans, Joan Evans, Ian Garland, Marshall Gillespie, Steve Hobin, Gareth Hughes, Betty Jones, Colin Jose, Douglas Lamming, Gwyneth McLean, Geraint Lloyd Owen, Geraint Parry, David Roberts, Ceri Stennett, Harry Smith, Jim Stewart, Geoff Thelwell, Mel Thomas, Wyn Gray Thomas, Geoff Wilde and Greville Williams. We thank you all.

A big thank you to John Humphreys, whose undying love for Wrexham Association Football Club is as great as ours, and it is with this in mind that he has been of great assistance in the time consuming job of proof reading, but has enjoyed it all the more because of the subject. Many thanks John.

Finally, we would like to express our sincere thanks to Graham Atherton and the 'lads' at Engraving Services for their assistance in making this project possible. A big thank you to Steve and Paul whose knowledge of Wrexham Football Club must now rank with the best!!

We are sure that there have been many others over the years who we have not mentioned, but the omission of anyone reflects the size of the task undertaken, not on their contribution. To them and all those who we have mentioned. We are eternally grateful.

Last by no means least we would like to give our biggest thankyou of all to our respective families for putting up with this very time consuming project. They are special people.

Gareth M.Davies and Peter Jones.

July 1999.

Foreword

Foreword by Joey Jones.

I am very honoured to have been asked to provide the foreword for this book, as there have been so many great players who have worn the red shirt of Wrexham over the years. I know that both Gareth and Peter have worked extremely hard over a number of years to put together a book of this quality, and I am sure that everyone who reads it will have their own special memories of favourite players, or of those who may be recalled for other reasons.

My own memories of Wrexham Football Club began in my home town of Llandudno. I lived on the same council estate as Gareth Davies, who - by the time that I joined Wrexham - was a fully fledged member of the first team. I can remember going to the local shop on our estate and Gareth showing me and my mates the shirt that he wore for a Wales XI game against a Manchester United XI played at Bangor. It was Gareth's brother, Glyn, who I first accompanied to Wrexham with for trials, having been recommended by John Neal's North Wales scout Evan Williams, who has since passed away. Also at those trials was a certain Mickey Thomas.

I first joined Wrexham as a schoolboy when I was 14, having already had trials with Chester! I remained as a schoolboy until I was 15, when I left school. At the time I was deliberating what to do as I hadn't heard from Wrexham, and I had no qualifications. Evan Williams then visited my house and told me that John Neal wanted me to sign on the ground staff at the Racecourse in 1970.

It was a great honour to have joined Wrexham at that time, as the player that I respected, Gareth Davies, was a regular first team player. The club had just won promotion to the Third Division - with players like Albert Kinsey, Dave Gaskell, Eddie May, and Stuart Mason. I was a midfield player at that time, but that soon changed when Alan Bermingham was injured. John Neal would always have us playing a practice game on a Thursday, and he asked me to play at right-back in place of Alan. I told him that I was a midfield player, but he persuaded me to play that game at full-back. I never played in midfield again!

It was at right-back that I made my first team debut in January 1973 in a Welsh Cup match against......Chester! And, yes, you've guessed it, I got booked! In fact there were about nine bookings in that game, although we lost 1-0. I went on to become a regular in the team until I was asked to join Liverpool, the team that I had supported as a youngster. It was with the Anfield club that I achieved the highlight of my career when we won the European Cup in Rome, beating Borussia Monchengladbach in the Final.

I returned to Wrexham in October 1978, who had become a Second Division side by that time, although I also received offers from both Leeds United and Middlesbrough, but the choice as I saw it was simple. Stay at Liverpool or rejoin Wrexham. I came back on the understanding that the team would stay together, as the club had the nucleus of a great side. However, injuries stopped us from going any further in that first season, and the team then began to break up. I was eventually able to enjoy the fairly unique privilege of playing in the same side as my kid brother, Frank.

I remained at the Racecourse until October 1982, when I joined Chelsea. I'd already turned the move down a month or so previously, as I didn't want to leave Wrexham, but I was then told by the directors that the club would be bankrupt if I didn't move, so I reluctantly accepted the London club's offer. I spent three years at Stamford Bridge, although I remained living in Wrexham throughout that time. I then moved on to Huddersfield Town, who were a very similar club to Wrexham. I had two happy years at Leeds Road before Dixie brought me back to North Wales, when I was still only thirty years old. I went on to end my career with Wrexham, before Brian Flynn asked me to join the coaching staff.

Looking back I must say that John Neal was the biggest influence on my career, a man for whom I have the greatest respect. Arfon Griffiths was one of the best players ever to have played for the club. He was a different class and was a very good manager to play under. Of my career, I can honestly say that I was only ever booked once for dissent, the rest are debatable!!

I still hold out hope that Wrexham Football Club will one day achieve their goal of reaching the Premier League. I've always had ambition as a player - my aim was to get into the first team, which was followed by representing Wales, and to play at as higher level as possible. I've achieved all of those, now I want to see Wrexham Football Club go as far as it can. I'll never forget the Colchester game when the club was on the verge of going out of the Football League. I can honestly say that I would have given up my European Cup winners' medal at that time just for us to stay up!

Looking back on my time at the club I have so many special memories - all of which will be rekindled by reading through the pages of this book. From my days on the ground staff, when I came through the ranks with the likes of Billy Ashcroft, Alan Hill, Bob Scott, Graham Whittle, Dave Smallman, Mike McBurney, Roger Mostyn and Mickey Thomas, to those of more recent times, they're all here. I'm sure that you, too, will have your own particular favourites (and some least favourites!) from all the years that you have been following this wonderful club of ours. Regardless of your age, there's something within the covers of this book for everyone.

Joey Jones.
July 1999

...and a message from Mrs Amy Dexter (Staff Tea Lady at Wrexham A.F.C. from 1955 to 1986).

Mrs. 'D', as she was known by all, sadly passed away before this book could be published, but we're sure that she would have wished for her message to be printed here: "I would just like to simply say to all those players who came in for a cup of tea after training - I can probably remember every single one of you, and if you took sugar! They were happy days. Love from Mrs.D"

A Brief History of Wrexham Association Football Club

Wrexham Association Football Club may not be one of the biggest names in British football, but they are one of the oldest and a club with a proud and illustrious history. Based in the North-East of Wales, Wrexham are one of only six Welsh clubs to have played in the English Football League (The other five being Cardiff City, Swansea City, Newport County, Merthyr Town and Aberdare Athletic). The Club have competed for most of their history in an English League, but it was in 1921 that they were accepted into the Football League. Remaining loyal to their Welsh roots, the 'Robins' have won the Welsh Cup a record 23 times, representing Wales in Europe in eight campaigns, and reaching the Quarter-Finals of the Cup-Winners' Cup in 1976.

The origins of one of the pioneering clubs in Welsh football came about on the 28th September 1872 when Wrexham Football Club was formed from a meeting held at the Turf Hotel, which still stands to this day as the only Public House to be situated on a Football League ground. The meeting was formed by members of Wrexham Cricket Club for the 'purpose of starting a football team for the ensuing season'. Football at this time was a fast growing sport, and the cricket players wanted further activity when the cricket season came to a conclusion, and with this in mind the meeting had been called.

The attendance at the inaugural meeting was described as 'large', and from the gathering Wrexham Football Club was formed, with a management committee formed from the following gentlemen of the newly-formed club: President, F.Page; Honorary Secretary, W.H.Pritchard; Committee, T.Walker, N.Humphreys, D.Dale, E.Cross, G.Pritchard and E.Evans.

The initial match was arranged to be played on the Cricket (Racecourse) Ground on Saturday 5th October 1872, when two teams comprising members of the newly-formed football club, played a game between themselves, with the outcome of the first match ending in a 2-2 draw. It was not until 19th October 1872 that Wrexham Football Club played their first match against opposition other than themselves, when a team of past and present members of Grove Park School turned up to play a 12-a-side game on the Cricket Ground, which Wrexham won 2-0.

Wrexham continued to play several other teams during the inaugural season, although the number of players in each game varied, as both teams would agree the exact number prior to each game. Matches to be arranged were against Provincial Insurance Office (16-a-side), The Volunteer Fire Brigade (15-a-side), Ruabon, Chester College (16-a-side) and Plas Madoc. Not surprisingly, most of these games ended scoreless, due to the large numbers on each side. Over the next few years it was Wrexham who led the campaign in the area to reduce the numbers in each side to eleven. Those early encounters were to see the Denbighshire club criticised after a match with Chester College, played on 15th March 1873, when the Chester team described the Wrexham club as a 'nondescript outfit' and in 'both cricket and football matches, the Wrexham teams never present a neat and uniformed appearance'!

For a number of years following Wrexham's formation, the football season would begin in October, after the cricket campaign had been completed, and end in March in time for the new cricket season. With the rapid growth of football, the Cambrian Football Association was formed in 1876, although within a matter of weeks founder, Llewelyn Kendrick, was to change the name to the Football Association of Wales. The same year, Wales played their first ever international match against Scotland in Glasgow, with two Wrexham players representing the Welsh side, Edwin Cross and Alfred Davies.

With the forming of the F.A.W., their committee decided that the next step would be to organise a similar competition to the 'English Cup' (F.A.Cup), as they had noted how the competition had unified the English clubs, and felt a similar competition would be beneficial to the growing band of football clubs in Wales, and the Marches (English clubs that were situated in counties bordering Wales).

The inaugural season saw the competition formed by teams from North and Mid-Wales, as football had hardly taken off at the time in the rugby-orientated south of the country. A team from Swansea entered, but they withdrew before the competition had begun. Wrexham reached the Final of the inaugural competition meeting fellow pioneering club, Druids. The match was played at Acton Park by kind permission of the Welsh F.A. President, Sir Robert Cunliffe, who had arranged a playing area in the grounds of Acton Hall, after the famous Druids club stated they wished to play on a neutral venue, and not the Racecourse. Wrexham won the game 1-0, in front of a crowd described to have been in the region of 1,500. Despite Wrexham's victory, the club did not receive the trophy until the following year, as the Welsh F.A. had no funds to purchase one at that time.

Over the next twelve years, Wrexham would play friendly matches with opposition from both England and Wales, although they were still the team to beat in the Welsh Cup competition which they continued to enter, albeit only once during that time would they lift the trophy, in 1883. It the same year the club entered the English Cup for the first time, although the first match in the competition saw them receive a bye to the Second Round as Liverpool Ramblers scratched on the morning of the match, failing to raise a side. This left Oswestry as Wrexham's first ever opposition in the competition, thought the North Wales club suffered a 4-3 home defeat. The club's most successful season in the English Cup during the early years was when they reached the First Round proper in 1888/89. They were drawn away to play the London Swifts, Wrexham losing 3-1.

Other major chapters in Wrexham's history during this period would see the club leave the Racecourse for the 1881/82 season due to an increase of £10 in the rent by their landlords, the cricket club. The club then played all home matches on Rhosddu Recreation Ground, until the 1883/84 season when they returned to the Racecourse Ground, where they have played ever since. The move to the new ground also saw the club change it's name to 'Wrexham Athletic', but after just one season dropped the 'Athletic'. Another addition to the club's name was introduced for 1884/85, becoming known as 'Wrexham Olympic', and it was not until 1887/88 that Wrexham dropped the name 'Olympic' from the club's title. Ever since then the club has been known as 'Wrexham'.

Wrexham's application to join the newly-formed Football Combination League was accepted in 1890, kicking off their inaugural season in organised League football on 6th September 1890 against the Manchester based team, Gorton Villa. The result proved that League competition was not going to be easy, Wrexham losing 5-1! with the only goal scored by Arthur Lea, who played football with only one arm. In fact he was not the only member of the side to have played football with one arm, as James Roberts also had the same disability. Wrexham finished the season second from bottom in eighth place.

Wrexham remained in the Combination League for just four seasons, but increased expenditure, especially in travelling costs, and the lack of club funds resulted in the club withdrawing from the League and joining the Welsh League 1894/95. The club was to spend two campaigns in the League, winning the championship in both seasons. In 1896/97 saw the club rejoined the Combination League, after they were found to be losing more support than gaining it, due to the level of the opposition. The club remained in the Combination competition until 1905, during which time they claimed the title four times, finally gaining election to the Birmingham & District League for the 1905/06 season, following previous unsuccessful attempts.

Wrexham's first ever match in the Birmingham & District League was against Kidderminster Harriers on the Racecourse, in front of a crowd of around 2,000, Wrexham won 2-1 with goals from Robert Evans and a Ted Hughes penalty. Wrexham ended their inaugural season in a very respectable sixth place, remaining in the Birmingham & District League until 1921, although there were no League games played between 1915 and 1919 due to the Great War. Throughout their time in this competition, Wrexham never actually won a League title, but enjoyed successful times, especially their final two campaigns in the League, finishing in third place both times. During this period, Wrexham were also to earn much success in both the English and Welsh Cup's. The club again reached the First Round proper of the English Cup for only the second time, finally losing to Exeter City, 2-1 after extra-time, following a replay in the 1908/09 season. As for the Welsh Cup, Wrexham won the trophy six times during their time in the Birmingham & District League.

In 1921 Wrexham gained election to the newly organised Football League Division Three North. Playing in blue shirts, their first ever Football League match held on the Racecourse against Hartlepools United, but ended in disappointment for the 8,000 or so Wrexham fans who turned up as, they lost 2-0. The following week saw revenge extracted when Wrexham travelled to the North-East for the return match and won 1-0 with Reg Leck scoring the club's first ever goal in the Football League. That season was to be one of many 'first's', as Ted Regan scored the club's first ever hat-trick in a 6-1 home win over Chesterfield, and although Billy Cotton was also to score a hat-trick in the same match, Regan was the first to complete the feat. Brian Simpson received the unwanted record of the first Wrexham player to be sent-off in a Football League game, when receiving his marching orders at Southport in January 1922.

The 'Robins', as they were soon known because of Club secretary Ted Robinson, who had been attached to the club since 1894, went on to become an established Football League side over the next few years, with the team selected by committee until November 1924, when the Director's appointed the club's first ever manager. He was Charlie Hewitt, who had enjoyed success as manager of Mold Town. The 1926/27 season saw the club progress past the First Round of the English Cup for the first time, only to be beaten 3-1 by a North Wales non-league side, Rhyl! The following season the 'Robins' went even further, reaching the Fourth Round, losing 3-1 at home Birmingham, who happened to be Wrexham's first ever First Division opposition in the competition.

1928/29 saw the club enjoy their best season since joining the Football League, finishing in a very admirable third place, a record 32 League goals from Albert Mays being a major factor in Wrexham's dramatic fortunes, while the end of the season would see the emergence of a certain Thomas Bamford, who went on to smash Mays' goalscoring record and become the greatest ever goalscorer in the history of Wrexham Football Club with 201 League and Cup goals. The 1929/30 season saw Wrexham achieve their record Football League score, with a 8-0 win over Rochdale on the Racecourse.

In 1932/33 Wrexham achieved their best ever position in the Football League Division Three North, finishing as runners-up to Hull City, only two points adrift of the Humberside club. The campaign also saw the 'Robins' win 18 of their 21 League games at home, the only defeat suffered against local rivals, Chester. Following the departure of Bamford and Bill Bryant to Manchester United in October 1934, this left the club in the doldrums until the abandoned 1939/40 Football League season, the season when the club changed to play in red and white. During this period Wrexham clocked up a record breaking 11-1 victory over New Brighton in a Northern Section Cup match in 1934, and also set a new attendance record with 29,261 turning up for a Boxing Day match with Chester, who won 2-1.

The War saw the club placed in the Regional League (West) Division along with teams such as the Merseyside and Manchester clubs. During this period player registrations were relaxed to allow those serving in the forces to turn out for a club close to where they were stationed. These players were allowed to play as 'guests' and each club could field as many as they wished. Indeed, without the 'guest' player system, wartime football would have collapsed. Wrexham benefited more than most from this system, as players from the barracks in the town, and nearby Nesscliffe, Kinmel Bay and Chester were introduced. Famous players to have appeared for the club during this period included England internationals; Stanley Matthews, Stan Cullis, Johnny Hancocks, Neil Franklin Pongo Waring and Ronnie Dix. Welsh internationals; Tommy G. Jones, Tommy Griffiths, Ehud Rogers, Tommy Bamford and Don Dearson, as well as Scottish caps like Matt Armstrong and Gordon Bremner. Wrexham's most successful season during the war years was 1943/44, when finishing top of the North Regional Championship, enjoying the same record as Southern counterparts Bath City. The 'Robins' offered to play Bath City over two legs to decide an outright winner, but the West Country club refused due to the travelling involved. Nevertheless, it was regarded at the time that Wrexham were the outright winners due to the strength of opponents that they had overcome in comparison to Bath.

The first post-war Football League season, commenced in 1946/47, a campaign which also saw a dramatic rise in attendance's, and for a number of seasons which followed was described as the golden era of football. Wrexham reached their highest League position since 1933 when finishing in third place at the end of the 1947/48 season. The summer of 1949 would see the club make their first ever overseas tour when they travelled to Germany to play three games against teams from the British Army on the Rhine. The Welsh Cup was to see Wrexham achieve little success in the competition, they had last won in 1931, and further success eluded them until 1957, while the F.A.Cup brought Third Round involvement in 1953, where they were unlucky to lose 2-1 to Stoke City at the Victoria Ground. The same season Wrexham came the closest yet to promotion since 1933, when finishing in third place, missing out by just three points behind champions Oldham Athletic.

Wrexham reached the Fourth Round of the F.A.Cup in 1956/57 where they were to play the biggest match in the club's history to date, when drawn against Manchester United and the 'Busby Babes'. The largest ever crowd seen on the Racecourse of 34,445, larger than the population of the town of Wrexham at the time, turned up to see an exhibition performance from one of United's greatest ever team's as they strolled to a 5-0 win. Only a year later, the Munich air disaster was to rob football of some of this great team. The end of the season saw Wrexham regain the Welsh Cup for the first time since 1931.

The following campaign Wrexham finished in twelfth position in the final season of the Third Division North, which was just enough to see the North Wales club qualify for the newly organised Third Division. However, two seasons on the club were relegated in 1960, but following the appointment of player/manager, Ken Barnes, he took the club back to the Third Division in his first season in charge, which included the club's record Football League score of 10-1 over Hartlepool United. Relegation came again two seasons later, and the club hit it's lowest ebb since joining the Football League in 1966, finishing rock bottom of the Football League, having to apply for re-election for the first and only time in the clubs' history.

The next four seasons Wrexham made steady progress, and in 1969/70 finally gained success under manager John Neal, who led the club into the Third Division, and two years later into European football for another 'first'. The 'Robins' inaugural match in Europe was against Swiss side, F.C.Zurich, Wrexham gaining an aggregate 3-2 win. The 1973/74 season saw Wrexham reach the Quarter-Finals of the F.A.Cup, the furthest that the club had ever gone in this competition, eventually losing 1-0 to First Division Burnley. Two years later, and Wrexham reached the Quarter-Finals of the European Cup-Winners' Cup, beating Swedish side, Djurgardens, and Polish side, Stal Rzeszow before losing 2-1 on aggregate to the Belgian giants, Anderlecht, who went on to win the trophy.

In 1976/77 Wrexham were on the verge of promotion to the Second Division, but with only four matches left and requiring just three points to reach their goal, unbelievably missed out following two defeats by Crystal Palace, a draw at Oxford and a home defeat by champions Mansfield Town. The close season resulted in manager John Neal leaving the Racecourse to take up a similar position at Middlesbrough, while the 'Prince of Wales' himself, Arfon Griffiths, took charge of team affairs. Griffiths was to make three important signings, putting the final piece into the jigsaw, with Dixie McNeil, Dai Davies and Les Cartwright adding vital experience to the team which saw the 'Robins' storm to the Third Division championship, also reaching the Quarter-Finals of both the League Cup and F.A.Cup, and winning the Welsh Cup.

Wrexham spent four seasons in the Second Division, each time finishing in the bottom half of the table, although having more memorable cup wins, including the 3-1 away win over European Cup holders, Nottingham Forest, but the end of 1981/82 was to see Wrexham relegated. The following campaign was no better, as the club again suffered relegation, and by now were in great financial abyss. Over the next ten seasons the club was to struggled to survive, but their were some good times, especially the great European Cup-Winners' Cup win over Portuguese Cup winners, F.C.Porto. The club did reach the Fourth Division play-off's in 1989, losing in the Final to Leyton Orient, but the 'Robins' greatest ever cup win was to come in January 1992, when Wrexham, who had finished bottom of the Football League the previous season, met the reigning Football League champions, Arsenal, on the Racecourse in a F.A.Cup Third Round match. When the final whistle blew 'Flynn's Babes' set off the most ecstatic scenes ever seen on the Racecourse, while the news spread around the world of one of the greatest ever Cup shocks. The result was to lift the club from the financial insecurity that had dogged the club since the heady days of the Second Division.

The following season Wrexham were playing in the Third Division, but not through promotion, just a case of the renumbering of the League's following the introduction of the Premier League. It was also to see Wrexham step up another Division at the end of it, finishing runners-up to Cardiff City, winning promotion to the Second Division in 1993.

The club have remained in this Division ever since, coming close to reaching the end of season play-off's on a number of occasions, and only last season (1997/98) missing out on goals scored. The 'Robins' are now in a better financial situation than they have been for a number of years, with the Club now in possession of a 125 year lease on the Racecourse Ground, as well as proud owners of the new Colliers Park training complex. With work on the Mold Road side of the ground finally given the go ahead for the face lift that it has needed for a number of years, the future is looking good for Wrexham Association Football Club.

League Record

Combination League 1890-1894
Welsh League 1894-1896
Combination League 1896-1905
Birmingham & District League 1905-1921
Football League Division Three North (Wartime 1939-1946)..1921-1958
Football League Division Three 1958-1960
Football League Division Four 1960-1962
Football League Division Three 1962-1964
Football League Division Four 1964-1970
Football League Division Three 1970-1978
Football League Division Two 1978-1982
Football League Division Three 1982-1983
Football League Division Four 1983-1992
(N.B.Divisions renumbered 1992)
Football League Division Three 1992-1993
Football League Division Two 1993-

Major Honours

Welsh Cup Winners ....1878, 1883, 1893, 1897, 1903, 1905, 1909, 1910, 1911, 1914, 1915, 1921, 1924, 1925, 1931, 1957, 1958, 1960, 1972, 1975, 1978, 1986 & 1995 (23).
Welsh Cup runners-up ....1879, 1890, 1891, 1895, 1896, 1898, 1899, 1902, 1920, 1932, 1933, 1950, 1962, 1965, 1967, 1971, 1979, 1981, 1983, 1984, 1988, 1990 & 1991 (23).
Welsh Invitation Cup Winners 1998
Welsh Premier Cup runner-up 1999
Welsh League Champions..........1895 & 1896
Combination League Champions..........1901, 1902, 1903 & 1905
Football League Division Three North runners-up 1933
Football League Cup quarter-finalists ....1961 & 1978
Football League Division Four runners-up 1970
F.A.Cup Quarter-Finalists ....1974, 1978 & 1997
European Cup-Winners' Cup Quarter-finalists..........1976
Football League Division Three Champions..........1978
Football League Division Four play-off finalists..........1989
Football League Division Two runners-up..........1993

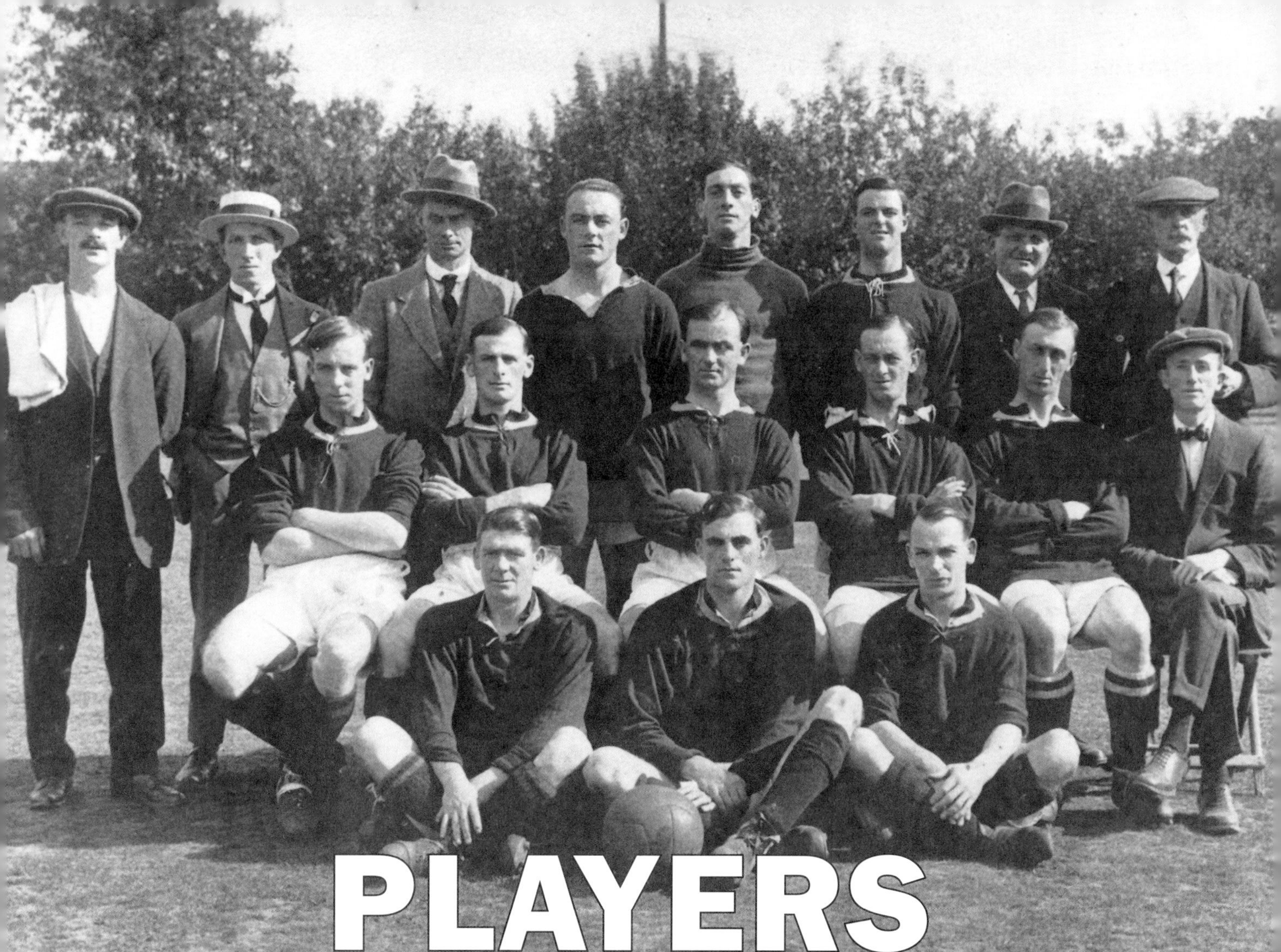

PLAYERS ADAMS to YOUDS

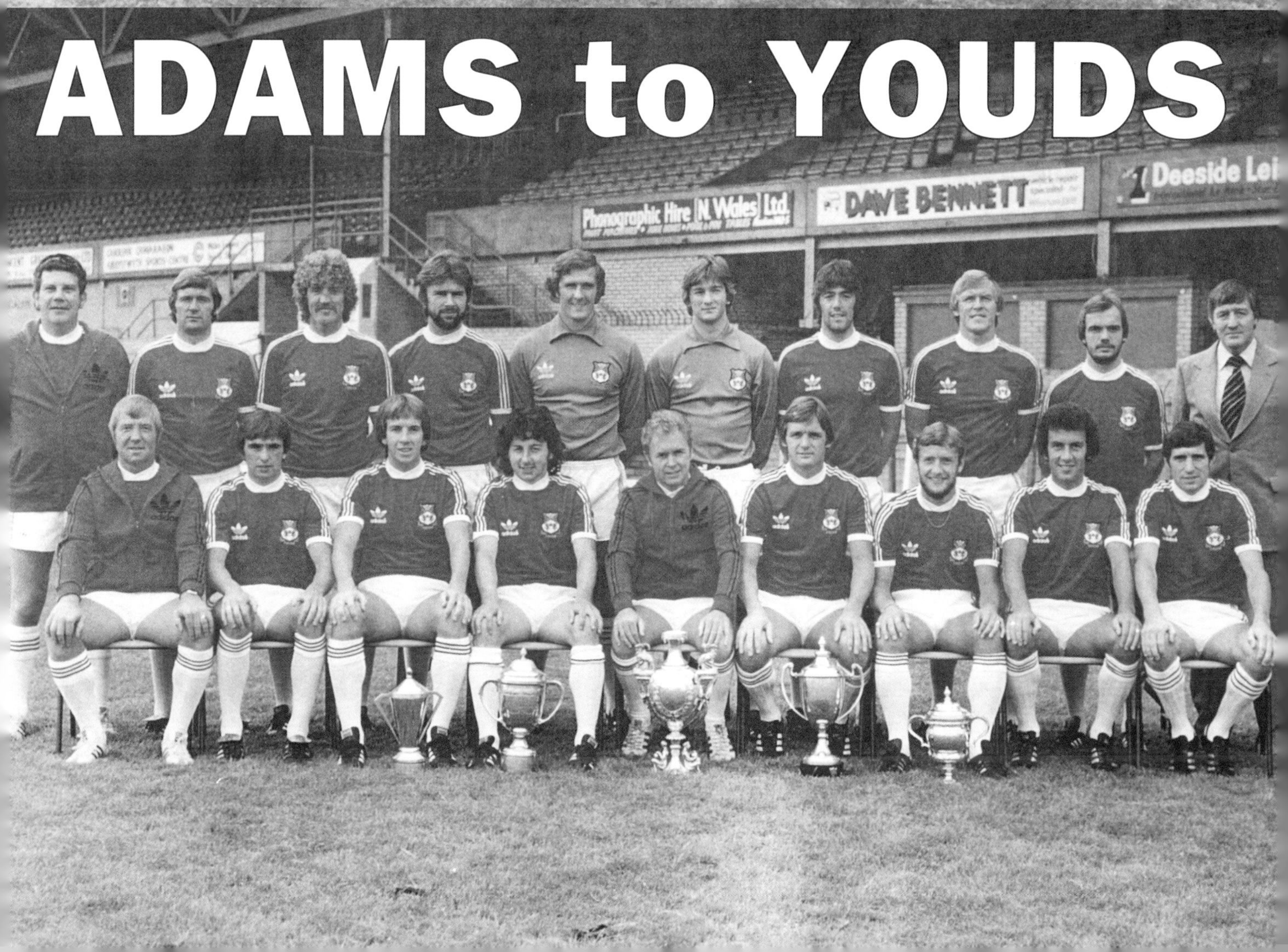

This section contains biographical details of over 700 players who have made a competitive first team appearance for Wrexham since 1921, when the Club first joined the Football League, until 1st July 1999, except those who appeared only in wartime games between 1939 and 1946 (see Wrexham Wartime Players Section). Friendly matches, Benefit & Testimonial games, mini-tournaments, e.g. the Isle of Man International Tournament, are not included in the appearance records. Please note that transfer fees are largely derived from the Press.

First team competitive matches are defined as those played in the following competitions only, which are regarded as first team fixtures.

- Football League 1921-1939 & 1946 to date, but not including abandoned matches, the three matches played in the aborted 1939/40 season or the matches against Wigan Borough (24/10/31), Accrington Stanley (08/10/61), or Aldershot (17/09/91). The competition has been known as the Canon League (1983-1986), Today League (1986/1987), Barclays League (1987-1993), Endsleigh Insurance League (1993-1996), Nationwide Football League (1996 to date).
- Barclays Football League Division Four Play-offs 1989.
- Football Association Challenge Cup 1921-1939 & 1945 to date. This section also includes appearances in this competition from players who played F.A.Cup games prior to 1921.
- The Football Association of Wales Challenge Cup 1921-1940 & 1946-1995. This section also includes appearances in this competition from players who played Welsh Cup games prior to 1921.
- Football League Cup 1960-1998. The competition has also been known as the Milk Cup (1982-1986), Littlewoods Challenge Cup (1986-1990), Rumbelows League Cup (1990-1992), the Coca Cola Cup (1992-1998) & Worthington Cup (1998 to date).
- Football League Associate Members Cup 1983-1998. The competition has also been known as the Freight Rover Trophy (1984-1987), Sherpa Van Trophy (1987-1989), Leyland Daf Cup (1989-1991), Autoglass Trophy (1991-1994), Auto Windscreens Shield 1994 to date).
- Football League Division Three North Section Cup, commonly known as the Northern Section Cup 1933-1939.
- European Cup-Winners' Cup 1972/73, 1975/76, 1978/79, 1979/80, 1984/85, 1986/87, 1990/91 & 1995/96
- Welsh Invitation/Premier Cup 1997- to date. A first team competition sponsored by BBC Wales for the top teams from the League of Wales, the three Nationwide Football League sides, Cardiff City, Swansea City and Wrexham, as well as Merthyr Tydfil from the Dr.Marten's Premier League.

Date of birth where known, (some shown as quarterly)

Position where he usually appeared for Wrexham

Player's full name where known

Wrexham career in years, not seasons

ADAMS, Edward Fairclough 1931 - 1935

Position; *Goalkeeper*
D.O.B; *30th November, 1906.*
Birthplace; *Anfield, Liverpool, Merseyside.*
Died; *Burnley, 30th November, 1991.*
Height; *5ft 10in* **Weight;** *12st 4lbs*
Debut v. *Lincoln City (h) 19th December, 1931.*
Total Appearances & Goals; *99 apps 0 gls*
Career; *Oakmere 1926/27; Earle; Liverpool 26th May 1927 0apps; Burscough Rangers cs1928; Manchester Central 1929; Connah's Quay & Shotton 28th Aug 1931; Barrow 5th Dec 1931 0apps; WREXHAM 18th December 1931; Southport 2nd Jul 1935 13apps 0gls; Cancelled 1st Jan 1936; Burnley 29th Feb 1936 111apps 0gls, (WW2 21apps 0gls); New Brighton (WW2 Guest) Nov 1941 12apps 0gls; Chester (WW2 Guest) Aug 1943 1app 0gls; WREXHAM (WW2 Guest) Sept 1943 1app 0gls;*
Honours; *Welsh Cup runner-up 1933;*

Season	League apps	League gls	F.A.Cup apps	F.A.Cup gls	Welsh Cup apps	Welsh Cup gls	N.S.C. apps	N.S.C. gls	Total apps	Total gls
1931/32	9	0	-	-	-	-	-	-	9	0
1932/33	25	0	-	-	6	0	-	-	31	0
1933/34	13	0	-	-	-	-	-	-	13	0
1934/35	40	0	2	0	2	0	2	0	46	0
	87	**0**	**2**	**0**	**8**	**0**	**2**	**0**	**99**	**0**

Place and date of death where known

Birthplace where known, with town and county shown

Player's height and weight where known. Measurements in feet and inches, stones and pounds

Debut first senior team game for Wrexham

Total Appearances & Goals in all competitions as defined above. Appearances as substitute shown in brackets

Career Full career details where known

Honours Player's honours from his football career where known

Wrexham career statistics Season by season, competition by competition. Appearances as substitute shown in brackets

A

Chris Armstrong

ADAMS, Edward Fairclough 1931 - 1935

Position; *Goalkeeper*
D.O.B; *30th November, 1906.*
Birthplace; *Anfield, Liverpool, Merseyside.*
Died; *Burnley, 30th November, 1991.*
Height; *5ft 10in* ***Weight;*** *12st 4lbs*
Debut v. *Lincoln City (h) 19th December, 1931.*
Total Appearances & Goals; *99 apps 0 gls*
Career; *Oakmere 1926/27; Earle; Liverpool 26th May 1927 0apps; Burscough Rangers cs1928; Manchester Central 1929; Connah's Quay & Shotton 28th Aug 1931; Barrow 5th Dec 1931 0apps; WREXHAM 18th December 1931; Southport 2nd Jul 1935 13apps 0gls; Cancelled 1st Jan 1936; Burnley 29th Feb 1936 111apps 0gls, (WW2 21apps 0gls); New Brighton (WW2 Guest) Nov 1941 12apps 0gls; Chester (WW2 Guest) Aug 1943 1app 0gls; WREXHAM (WW2 Guest) Sept 1943 1app 0gls;*
Honours; *Welsh Cup runner-up 1933;*

Ted Adams was a relative late comer to League Football, as he did not make his debut until the tender age of 25, although going on to play until he was nearly 37! Ted played for Liverpool Schoolboys at inside-left before switching to goalkeeper. After leaving school he played around the local leagues on his native Merseyside, for Earle, attracting the attention of Liverpool, having a 'blinder' in the Lancashire Amateur Cup final against Marine at Goodison Park in 1927. He was signed by Liverpool as an amateur, serving his time as a shipwright, and spending just over a season at Anfield before dropping back into non-league football with Burscough. Adams went on to play for both Manchester Central and Connah's Quay, returning to the Football League with Barrow in December 1931. However, two weeks later he was to leave Holker Street, without making a first team appearance, to join Wrexham. Caretaker manager, Roy Burkinshaw, needed a 'keeper urgently after Wilf Burrows had broken his arm in a League match at Darlington. Ted went straight into the Wrexham first team for his Football League debut at home to Lincoln City which ended in a 3-1 defeat. He spent a further three seasons at the Racecourse, during which time he was to compete for the goalkeeper's spot with both Dick Finnigan and Bob Foster. The 1932/33 campaign saw him make the 'keepers position his own as the club finished in its highest pre-war League position. In July 1935 Ted left the Racecourse, joining Southport, but by December was so disillusioned with football that he surprisingly announced that he was retiring from the game altogether, and his contract was cancelled. Whilst with Southport he had been described as being able to "deal brilliantly with difficult shots, but unreliable with easier tasks particularly from corner kicks." Despite his disillusionment with the game, Burnley Manager, Alf Boland, persuaded him to give his football career another go in February 1936, and he signed for the Turf Moor club, initially on trial, before going on to make over a hundred appearances for the 'Clarets'. Ted remained with Burnley until October 1940, later 'guesting' for New Brighton, Chester, Blackburn Rovers, and Wrexham during the war. He played his final match on the Racecourse against Liverpool in a Northern Regional match in September 1943 which saw him concede five goals! Adams later settled in the Burnley area, working for the Prestige Group for over twenty years. Ted died of pneumonia on his 85th birthday in 1991.

Season	League		F.A.Cup		Welsh Cup		N.S.C.		Total	
	apps	gls	apps	gls	apps	gls	apps	gls	apps	gls
1931/32	9	0	-	-	-	-	-	-	9	0
1932/33	25	0	-	-	6	0	-	-	31	0
1933/34	13	0	-	-	-	-	-	-	13	0
1934/35	40	0	2	0	2	0	2	0	46	0
	87	**0**	**2**	**0**	**8**	**0**	**2**	**0**	**99**	**0**

ADAMSON, Robert McLellan 1938 - 1939

Position; *Inside-Left*
D.O.B; *21st May, 1914*
Birthplace; *Balbeggie, Perthshire*
Died; *Perth Royal Infirmary, 27th August, 1995*
Height; *5ft 9in* ***Weight;*** *11st 7lbs*
Debut v. *Southport (a) 27th August, 1938*
Total Appearances & Goals; *40 apps 16 gls*
Career; *Perth Craigie; Dundee Violet Juniors; Hearts 1931; Dundee May 1935 10apps 3gls; WREXHAM 28th Jul 1938; Carlisle United May 1939 2apps 0gls; Dundee United; East Fife cs1946 8apps 2gls;*

Bert Adamson was playing for Dundee Violet Juniors when spotted by Hearts at the age of seventeen. He spent just over three seasons with the 'Jam Tarts' before signing for Dundee, making his first team debut in a Scottish Cup first round defeat at St.Johnstone in September 1935. Bert went on to make ten League appearances, scoring three goals, for the Dens Park Club, before moving south of the Border to join Wrexham in July 1938. In his one season at the Racecourse Adamson played at inside-left in a forward line that also featured George Burditt, George Snow, Albert Nelson, Archie Burgon and Jack Williams. In his 35 League games that season, Bert scored 13 goals, including one in a 3-0 win over Hartlepool on his home debut. One story that he loved to tell from his time with Wrexham described how, when accompanying one of the club's directors, Sam Clutton, to sign another player they ended up at a market! No new player was acquired, but they did buy some pigs! In the close season of 1939 Bert left the Racecourse and returned North, to sign for Carlisle United along with Archie Burgon, but both their football careers were to come to a swift halt when WW2 began a short time after they had joined the Brunton Park club. However, Bert continued to play football, appearing for both Dundee United and East Fife with whom he was playing when finally calling it a day in 1947. After retiring from football Adamson worked on the railways later finding employment with Scottish Brewers in Perth as a Drayman, a job which he did until retirement. His son-in-law, Tommy Campbell, has managed both Forfar Athletic and Montrose, where he was in charge during last season. Bert died in Perth aged 81.

Season	League		F.A.Cup		Welsh Cup		N.S.C.		Total	
	apps	gls	apps	gls	apps	gls	apps	gls	apps	gls
1938/39	35	13	1	0	2	2	2	1	40	16
	35	**13**	**1**	**0**	**2**	**2**	**2**	**1**	**40**	**16**

ALLEYNE, Robert Anthony 1987 - 1988

Position; *Forward*
D.O.B; *27th September, 1968*
Birthplace; *Dudley, West Midlands*
Height; *5ft 9in* ***Weight;*** *11st 3lbs*
Debut v. *Newport County (a) 24th October, 1987*
Total Appearances & Goals; *8/3 apps 2 gls*
Career; *Leicester City Jan 1987 1/2 apps 0gls; 24th WREXHAM Oct 1987 (Loan); Chesterfield 18th Mar 1988 32/8apps 5gls; Teilt (Belgium) Aug 1989; Telford United Mar 1992; Sutton Coldfield 1992; Tamworth 1993; Matlock Town cs1994;*

Robert Alleyne joined Wrexham on loan from Leicester City in October 1987, making his debut in a 1-0 defeat at Newport County. Rob was only 19 when he arrived at the Racecourse but he had already played in Leicester City's first team, having made his Football League debut as a substitute against West Ham United in a 4-1 defeat, without having played so much as a full reserve game due to an injury crisis. Rob's stay at the Racecourse lasted until January, when his final appearance for the club was as a substitute at home to Crewe in a 2-1 win on New Year's Day. The highlight of his time at the Racecourse must have been the 3-0 win against Wolves at Molineux, Graham Turner's first match as manager of the Midlands club, with Rob scoring one of the goals. He returned to Filbert Street, helping their youth side to the semi-finals of the F.A.Youth Cup, but never lived up to his early promise and was subsequently transferred to Chesterfield in March 1988. He made an immediate impression at Saltergate, scoring with a spectacular winning strike on his home debut against York City the same month. He remained in the side for the rest of the season as the 'Spireites' fought their way to safety. The following campaign saw a change of management, and Rob found it increasingly more difficult to earn a first team place. At the end of the season he was released by Chesterfield, but was soon fixed up with Belgian Third Division side, Teilt. Rob returned to England for a trial with Walsall, but it was pre-Bosman days and Teilt put a ridiculous price on his head, holding him to his contract which meant having to wait three years before he could play for anyone else. Alleyne returned to live in Birmingham, taking up work as the assistant manager of a Men's clothes shop for two years. Once free of his contract with Teilt he took up playing again, and had short spells with both Telford United and Sutton Coldfield. Alleyne eventually

moved back to Chesterfield, where he appeared for Matlock Town during the 1994/95 season. He later became a gym and aerobics instructor at the Brampton Manor Health and fitness club, which saw him put on two stones in weight due to body building.

Season	League		F.A.Cup		Welsh Cup		League Cup		F.R.T.		Total	
	apps	gls	apps	gls	apps	gls	apps	gls	apps	gls	apps	gls
1987/88	7/3	2	-	-	1	0	-	-	-	-	8/3	2
	7/3	**2**	**-**	**-**	**1**	**0**	**-**	**-**	**-**	**-**	**8/3**	**2**

AMBLER, Roy 1961 - 1962

Position; *Inside-Forward*
D.O.B; *2nd December, 1937*
Birthplace; *Wakefield, Yorkshire*
Height; *5ft 10in* ***Weight;*** *11st 6lb*
Debut v. *Stockport County (a) 11th November, 1961*
Total Appearances & Goals; *26 apps 14 gls*
Career; *Outwood Stormcocks; Leeds United 10th Dec 1954 0gls; Shrewsbury Town 8th Jan 1959 29apps 8gls; WREXHAM 6th May 1961; York City 5th Nov 1962 12apps 3gls; Southport 18th July 1963 11apps 0gls; Matlock Town cs1964; Buxton cs1966; Stalybridge Celtic 1968; Bradford Park Avenue 1970;*

Roy Ambler began playing football seriously while at Secondary School in Stanley, near to his native Wakefield. As well as representing his School team Roy was also selected to play for Yorkshire Schoolboys and North of England Schoolboys, appearing in the same team as Bobby Charlton. By this time he was playing for a Leeds United nursery team, the quaintly named Outwood Stormcocks, and after leaving school at 15, was signed by Leeds. At Elland Road he made his way through the youth ranks, as well as representing the Northern Intermediate League XI side, before signing professional in December 1954. Roy spent five years at Elland Road without making a first team appearance, although two years were lost due to National Service with the Royal Signals. During his last three seasons with the Yorkshire side Ambler averaged thirty goals a season for the reserves, but his only first team opportunities came in friendly games. In January 1959 he joined Shrewsbury Town, making his Football League debut at outside-right in a 4-2 home win over Watford, but in just over two years at the Gay Meadow Roy couldn't command a regular first team place, and in April 1961 he joined Wrexham. He had impressed Wrexham manager Billy Morris, who paid out a 'substantial fee' for the hard-working inside-forward. However, the week after Ambler moved to the Racecourse, Billy Morris was replaced by Ken Barnes in the manager's seat. Barnes, however, had planned to use Ambler in the forward line for the new season, before he was injured in pre-season training. It wasn't until November that Roy was to make his long awaited debut for Wrexham, at Stockport in a 2-1 win, in which he scored. His jinx continued as he struggled with injuries, and when fit found it difficult to command a regular first team place. Roy did manage to score eight goals in the 1961/62 season helping Wrexham to promotion back to the Third Division. Undoubtedly Ambler's most memorable moment at the Racecourse was when he became one of the three players, together with Wyn Davies and Ron Barnes, to score a hat-trick in the club's record 10-1 League win over Hartlepool United. Despite these goals Roy could not establish himself in a regular first team place the following season, and it came as no surprise when he was allowed to leave the Racecourse in November 1962 to join York City. Roy was once again in and out of the first team at Bootham Crescent and after scoring three goals in just twelve games, left the Minstermen at the end of the season to join Southport. At Haig Avenue Roy failed to score in eleven League games, but did find the net in the Liverpool Senior Cup semi-final against Tranmere Rovers, as well as hitting the bar in the final against Liverpool. Ambler became the reserve's top scorer with 17 goals in 30 Combination games, but failed to reproduce find that sort of form in the first team, and in the close season of 1964 left to join Cheshire League side Matlock Town. Roy spent two seasons here before joining rivals Buxton in 1966. Next step was Stalybridge Celtic in 1968, staying two years, before joining Bradford Park Avenue in 1970, soon after their relegation from the Football League. Appointed reserve team coach, at Park Avenue he also turned out on occasions for the Northern Premier League outfit. Roy spent three seasons with Bradford, managing the first team for the final seventeen games of the 1972/73 season. Ambler later scouted for West Bromwich Albion for a number of years, while working as a sales representative, selling kitchen and bedroom furniture. Today, he still lives in his native Yorkshire, near Leeds, where he is known to be working for a Mail Order Company.

Season	League		F.A.Cup		Welsh Cup		League Cup		Total	
	apps	gls	apps	gls	apps	gls	apps	gls	apps	gls
1961/62	13	8	1	0	3	1	-	-	17	9
1962/63	8	5	-	-	-	-	1	0	9	5
	21	**13**	**1**	**0**	**3**	**1**	**1**	**0**	**26**	**14**

ANDERSON, John Lockhart 1956-1959 & 1961-1962

Position; *Inside-Forward*
D.O.B; *5th April, 1928*
Birthplace; *Glasgow, Strathclyde*
Height; *5ft 8 1/2in* ***Weight;*** *10st 12lbs*
Debut v. *Chester (h) 18th August, 1956*
Total Appearances & Goals; *116 apps 30 gls*
Career; *Partick Thistle; Northampton Town Jun 1953 14apps 5gls; Exeter City Jul 1954 7apps 0gls; Dundee cs1955 3apps 1gls; WREXHAM 14th Jun 1956; Rochdale Jul 1959 28apps 5gls; Chester Jul 1960 17apps 2gls; WREXHAM 12th Aug 1961; Colwyn Bay 6th February 1965;*
Honours; *Welsh Cup Winner 1957 & 1958;*

After a glittering schoolboy career in his native Glasgow Johnny Anderson signed for Partick Thistle, before he chose to move south of the border and join Northampton Town in June 1953. John made his Football League debut for the 'Cobblers' at inside-left, in a 3-0 home win over Southampton. He then went on to make a further thirteen League appearances for the County ground outfit, scoring five goals, until joining Exeter City at the end of the 1953/54 season. Anderson had just seven League outings for the 'Grecians' before returning to Scotland, disillusioned. He joined Dundee, making his debut in a 4-0 Scottish League Cup defeat at Airdrie in August 1955, going on to spend a season at Dens Park until returning to the Football League with Wrexham having been persuaded by manager, Cliff Lloyd, to try again. Johnny made an immediate impact at the Racecourse, scoring in each of his first three games for his new club, his superb close control and tantalising runs soon making him a firm favourite with the Wrexham fans. John remained a regular in the first team throughout his first two seasons with Wrexham, winning two Welsh Cup winners' medals and helping the club qualify for the newly formed Third Division in 1958. However, the 1958/59 season saw his first team chances rather limited, due to new signing Brian Cripsey, and at the end of the campaign he was given a free transfer, joining Rochdale in the close season. John spent just one season at Spotland, scoring five goals in 28 League games until joining Chester in the summer of 1960. In his one term at Sealand Road Anderson scored twice in seventeen League appearances, before returning to the Racecourse at the end of the season. He was signed on trial with a 'view to being a useful coach/cum player for the reserves.' Under new manager Ken Barnes, the position of trainer soon became permanent following the departure of Jack Jones. However, in September 1961 John was called upon to play in the first team at Tranmere as a replacement for the injured Wyn Davies, which proved to be his final first team game for the club. Anderson stayed in his coaching position at the Racecourse until January 1965, when both he and Ken Roberts became part of the 'cost-cutting' the club needed at that time. He began playing again with Welsh League side, Colwyn Bay, before taking up a coaching position at Colchester United shortly afterwards which was quickly followed by a similar position at Aldershot in the summer of 1969. In 1972 he was on the point of leaving the 'Shots', when they were forced to axe their reserve team, but was persuaded to stay on by manager Tommy McAnearney, and he went on to keep his coaching position at the Recreation Ground for over twenty years, before retiring and returning to live in Wrexham. Johnny Anderson later returned to the Aldershot area, where his family are now rooted.

Season	League		F.A.Cup		Welsh Cup		Total	
	apps	gls	apps	gls	apps	gls	apps	gls
1956/57	44	18	7	2	4	0	55	20
1957/58	38	5	1	0	5	1	44	6
1958/59	16	4	-	-	-	-	16	4
1961/62	1	0	-	-	-	-	1	0
	99	**27**	**8**	**2**	**9**	**1**	**116**	**30**

ANDERSON, Thomas Cowan 1962 - 1963

Position; *Outside-Left/Utility Forward*
D.O.B; *24th September, 1934*
Birthplace; *Haddington, East Lothian.*
Height; *5ft 9in* **Weight;** *11st 7lbs*
Debut v. *Chesterfield (h) 28th March, 1962*
Total Appearances & Goals; *15 apps 3 gls*
Career; *Hearts (Am); Queen of the South (Pro) Sept 1955; Watford 17th Dec 1956 52apps 12gls; Bournemouth 14th Jun 1958 £1,000 5apps 1gls; Q.P.R. 5th Nov 1958 11apps 3gls; Torquay United 1st Jul 1959 9apps 4gls; Stockport County 10th Jun 1960 60apps 17gls; Doncaster Rovers 10th Nov 1961 16apps 3gls; WREXHAM 15th Mar 1962 £3,000; Hellas (Australia) 15th Feb 1963; Barrow 11th Dec 1963 11apps 3gls; Hellas (Australia) Feb 1964; Watford 16th Dec 1964 21 apps 2gls; St.Mirren Oct 1965; Melbourne George Cross (Australia) Dec 1965; Leyton Orient Jul 1967 8/1apps 0gls; Limerick Jan 1968; South Africa;*
Honours; *Scotland Schoolboy International; Welsh Cup runner-up 1962;*

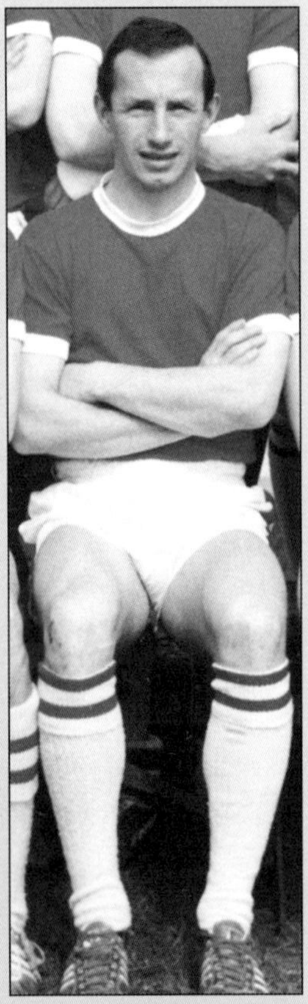

Once described as 'One of soccer's happy wanderers' Tommy Anderson came to Wrexham in March 1962, having experienced a rather nomadic footballing career before being signed by manager Ken Barnes to help out in the final push for promotion. Whilst at school Tommy was capped by Scotland Schoolboys and appeared at Wembley against England in the same side as Dave Mackay. After leaving school he went to Skerry's Commercial College in Edinburgh where, in-between studies, he played for Queen of the South. He was then enlisted for his National Service with the R.A.F., with whom he was stationed in the Middle-East. Upon being demobbed he was quickly signed up by Watford in December 1956, where he made his Football League debut. Tommy's 'wandering' finally led him to sign for Wrexham in March 1962 for £3,000, making his debut in a 4-2 home win over Chesterfield in which he scored in atrocious conditions. Tommy didn't miss a match for the rest of the season and helped the club gain promotion back to the Third Division, as well as playing in the three Welsh Cup Final matches which were eventually lost to Bangor City. The following season saw Anderson mainly playing reserve team football in the Cheshire County League, enjoying just two Third Division opportunities all season. In February 1963 he took up an offer in Australia to join Hellas, spending a few months before returning home to join Barrow, where he scored three goals in eleven games. Tommy returned to Australia in February 1964 to become player/coach with Melbourne George Cross, whilst also working as a P.T. instructor in a local school. He then returned home to Britain to join Leyton Orient in July 1967, making nine League appearances without scoring. Tommy is then believed to have gone to South Africa, before finally settling in Australia, becoming a Sydney soccer reporter, and later host of his own radio programme. During his football career Tommy Anderson was described as a 'nimble forward of blistering pace', an attribute which brought him second place in the 1957 Powderhill Sprint Race.

Season	League		F.A.Cup		Welsh Cup		Total	
	apps	gls	apps	gls	apps	gls	apps	gls
1961/62	10	2	-	-	3	0	13	2
1962/63	2	1	-	-	-	-	2	1
	12	**3**	**-**	**-**	**3**	**0**	**15**	**3**

APPLEYARD, George Charles 1926 - 1927

Position; *Centre-Forward*
D.O.B; *31st May, 1900*
Birthplace; *Rawmarsh, Yorkshire*
Died; *Rotherham, 7th August, 1967.*
Height; *5ft 9in* **Weight;** *11st 0lbs*
Debut v. *Chesterfield (h) 28th August, 1926*
Total Appearances & Goals; *5 apps 2 gls*
Career; *Rotherham Forge FC; Rotherham Town; Rawmarsh Athletic; Barnsley May 1923 4apps 2gls; Exeter City Jul 1924 8apps 1gls; Torquay United June 1925; WREXHAM 21st Jul 1926;*

George Appleyard first played local football for Rotherham Forge FC, which was followed by spells with Rotherham Town and Rawmarsh Athletic with whom he scored 42 goals in just 28 games. This kind of form brought him to the attention of Football League Division Two side, Barnsley, who signed George in May 1923. With Barnsley, he made his Football League debut in a 3-1 defeat at Leeds United, scoring the Oakwell club's consolation goal. Despite this early success Appleyard made just three more League appearances, scoring one goal before leaving to join Third Division South side Exeter City in the close season of 1924. At St.James Park George got off to another good start by scoring the only goal of the game on his debut at Bristol City, but after a further seven League appearances without scoring faded into their reserve side. In the close season of 1925 he joined neighbours Torquay United, a non-league club at that time playing in the Southern League Western Section. Appleyard spent one season at Torquay before returning to League football with Wrexham in the close season of 1926. He played in the first five matches of the 1926/27 campaign and scored two goals, including one in his last match for the Robins, a 2-2 draw at home to New Brighton.

Season	League		F.A.Cup		Welsh Cup		Total	
	apps	gls	apps	gls	apps	gls	apps	gls
1926/27	5	2	-	-	-	-	5	2
	5	**2**	**-**	**-**	**-**	**-**	**5**	**2**

ARCHIBALD, Murray John 1946 - 1947

Position; *Centre-Forward*
D.O.B; *19th March, 1917*
Birthplace; *Carron, Scotland*
Height; *5ft 9in* **Weight;** *11st 0lbs*
Debut v. *Barrow (h) 28th September, 1946*
Total Appearances & Goals; *1 apps 0 gls*
Career; *Bangor City; WREXHAM (Am) 6th Mar 1946, (Pro) 31st Aug 1946, Contract terminated 17th December 1946;*

Murray Archibald joined Wrexham in March 1946, having previously assisted Bangor City where 'he had scored a large number of goals' while serving in the armed forces. He made a number of reserve team appearances for 'The Robins' eventually making his first team debut in a Third Division North Cup match during World War Two, a 3-2 defeat at Tranmere Rovers. Murray made six more appearances for Wrexham before the end of the 1945/46 season, scoring two goals. He had done enough to impress manager Tom Williams and was signed as a professional towards the end of August 1946. Murray was eventually called up for his Football League debut the following month, in a 1-1 home draw with Barrow, but that proved to be his one and only Football League appearance.

Season	League		F.A.Cup		Welsh Cup		Total	
	apps	gls	apps	gls	apps	gls	apps	gls
1946/47	1	0	-	-	-	-	1	0
	1	**0**	**-**	**-**	**-**	**-**	**1**	**0**

ARKWRIGHT, Ian 1980 - 1984

Position; *Midfield*
D.O.B; *18th September, 1959*
Birthplace; *Shafton, Yorkshire*
Height; *5ft 8'1/4in* **Weight;** *10st 8lbs*
Debut v. *Fulham (h) 15th March, 1980*
Total Appearances & Goals; *132/3 apps 11 gls*
Career; *Wolves Sept 1977 3/1apps; WREXHAM 12th Mar 1980 (Loan), 7th May 1980 £100,000; Torquay United Mar 1984 2 apps (Loan); HIK Hanko (Finland) cs1984; Finn Harps Sept 1984;*

Ian Arkwright attended Willowgarth School in Brierley, near Barnsley, playing both football and Rugby Union for Barnsley and Yorkshire Schoolboys. He was also chosen for the England schoolboy football squad, but never actually made an appearance. It was whilst playing for Yorkshire schoolboys that he was spotted by Wolves, signing as an apprentice upon leaving school in 1976. Ian progressed rapidly at Molineux, signing professional on his eighteenth birthday. However, he had to wait almost a year before breaking into the first team; his chance coming in September 1978 at home to Q.P.R., when he came on as sub in a 1-0 win. He made four appearances for Wolves before a fit-again Kenny Hibbitt took over. His next appearance in the first team was at Wrexham in a testimonial match for Gareth

Davies, in which the legendary George Best guested for the 'Reds'. Back at Molineux Ian was to find his first team chances limited, with several good midfield players at the Black Country club at that time. In March 1980 Arkwright was given the chance of first team football with Second Division Wrexham on loan, having impressed 'Robins' manager Arfon Griffiths in a friendly match at Lilleshall for Wolves against the Racecourse club. He made his debut in a 1-1 draw with Fulham, remaining with the North Wales club until the end of the season. After making some impressive performances while on loan, Arfon Griffiths splashed out £100,000 for the promising 20 year-old midfielder. The following season Ian suffered with an ankle injury received in just the second match against Cardiff. He returned to the team in November, but was unable to recapture the confidence and form that he had displayed the previous campaign although the turn of the year he played an important part in beating the F.A.Cup holders, West Ham United in a 1-0 Third Round victory on the Racecourse. With a change of manager, Mel Sutton taking over from Arfon Griffiths for the 1981/82 season, Ian suffered another blow when breaking his leg in a pre-season training accident, and it was the following April before he returned to first team action, too late to help stave off relegation to the Third Division. The 1982/83 season once again saw a change of manager, with Bobby Roberts taking the helm. Ian was a regular in the first team throughout that campaign, showing glimpses of the form that everyone at the club knew he could produce. Despite his efforts the club found themselves relegated yet again, this time in the final match of the season at Reading. With relegation Ian was given a free transfer, mainly due to the high salary he was earning, but after agreeing to take a substantial pay-cut, he was re-signed. He began the new term in the first team, but by March was loaned out to Torquay United, making two League appearances before returning to Wrexham, only to be released at the end of the season. Ian then took up an offer to join Finnish side HIK Hanko, where he spent the summer break, before returning home to join Irish League side Finn Harps where he spent four seasons. Ian then returned to his native Barnsley, suffering from a persistent ankle injury, taking up work for a local firm as a screen printer. He played a couple of seasons for his works football team, PLM Redfearns, eventually having to give up playing altogether due to osteo arthritis in the ankle. Today, Ian still lives in the Barnsley area where he enjoys watching his local team.

Season	League		F.A.Cup		Welsh Cup		League Cup		A.M.C.		Total	
	apps	gls	apps	gls	apps	gls	apps	gls	apps	gls	apps	gls
1979/80	10	0	-	-	-	-	-	-	-	-	10	0
1980/81	16/1	0	5	0	5	0	2	0	-	-	28/1	0
1981/82	4	0	-	-	-	-	-	-	-	-	4	0
1982/83	44	6	2	0	5	0	2	0	-	-	53	6
1983/84	28/1	4	1	0	5	0	2	0	1/1	1	37/2	5
	102/2	**10**	**8**	**0**	**15**	**0**	**6**	**0**	**1/1**	**1**	**132/3**	**11**

ARMSTRONG, Christopher Peter

1988 - 1991

Position; *Forward*
D.O.B; *19th June, 1971*
Birthplace; *Newcastle-upon-Tyne, Tyne & Wear*
Height; *6ft 0in* ***Weight;*** *11st 0lbs*
Debut v. *Wigan Athletic (a) 29th August, 1989 (League Cup)*
Total Appearance & Goal; *62/27 apps 18gls*
Career; *Llay Welfare; WREXHAM 12th Oct 1988; Millwall 16th Aug 1991 11/17apps 5gls £125,000; Crystal Palace 1st Sept 1992 £1,000,000 118apps 45gls; Tottenham Hotspur 30th Jun 1995 £4,500,000 85/10apps 32gls;*
Honours; *Welsh Cup runner-up 1990; First Division Championship Winner 1994; One England 'B' International cap;*

Brought up by foster parents in the village of Llay, near Wrexham, Chris Armstrong surprisingly began playing football as a goalkeeper, representing Clwyd and North Wales Schools in that position. By the time he had left School no Football League clubs had shown any interest, and he took up work as a packer in a local factory while continuing to play football for Llay Welfare, converting to a forward in their Welsh National League side. It was whilst playing against Wrexham Reserves that 'The Robins' coach Joey Jones alerted Youth team coach, Cliff Sear, to the youngster's potential. This was just the springboard that his football career needed. Sear recommended that Chris should sign on for Wrexham on non-contract terms, so the club could have a better look at him. He again impressed, and in the summer of 1989 was offered a full-time contract, which was improved and extended after his elevation to first team status. Because of his inexperience, Chris found himself in and out of the first team, but his lightning acceleration and blistering pace was often called upon from the substitutes' bench to instil some life into the team. Initially he did struggle to find the net, but his first goal couldn't have come at a better time when he scored twice in a 3-2 win at Burnley, and once in a 2-1 home win over Gillingham in the following match to ensure Wrexham's Football League status was secure. Chris' most memorable moment for Wrexham must have been his goal in Denmark against Lyngby in a European Cup Winners' Cup match that earned Wrexham a second round draw with Manchester United. In the summer of 1991. Wrexham played a friendly with Millwall, and by the start of the new season, the lions manager Bruce Rioch had returned to the Racecourse and paid £125,000 for him, plus further instalments. Rioch knew that he had an investment for the future, which was quickly proved when, after just one season at the 'Den', Premier League club Crystal Palace signed Arsenal fan Armstrong for £1,000,000, of which Wrexham received a large percentage. He got off to a flying start at Selhurst Park, scoring twice on his debut in a 2-2 home draw with Oldham. Armstrong then went on to help the 'Eagles' to promotion in 1994 by scoring 22 League goals to take the First Division Championship. However, the following season was to see Palace relegated, despite Chris assisting them to the semi-finals of both the F.A. Cup and the Coca Cola Cup. He then made the national headlines, when a routine blood test found a banned substance in his blood, namely cannabis forcing him to miss the Coca-Cola Cup semi-final. Despite this setback, Chris came back and continued to score goals for Palace up to the end of the season. During the close season both Everton and Spurs offered £4,500,000 for his services. Chris chose to stay in London and signed for Gerry Francis at Tottenham. He was bought as a replacement for the departed Spurs favourite Jurgen Klinsmann and found it hard to win over the supporters at first, but he soon began a prolific goalscoring partnership with Teddy Sheringham. The next two years at White Hart Lane saw Chris missing because of injury, but he did return to help ensure 'Spurs' Premier League status towards the end of the 1997/98 season. The arrival of George Graham at White Hart Lane has seen the striker re-establish himself in the first team, scoring several vital goals, during the 1998/99 campaign including a hat-trick against Everton.

Season	League		F.A.Cup		Welsh Cup		League Cup		L.D.C.		E.C.W.C.		Total	
	apps	gls	apps	gls	apps	gls	apps	gls	apps	gls	apps	gls	apps	gls
1989/90	10/12	3	-	-	2/3	0	-	-	-	-	-	-	12/15	3
1990/91	30/8	10	0/1	0	3/2	2	2	0	2/1	2	3	1	40/12	15
	40/20	**13**	**0/1**	**0**	**5/5**	**2**	**2**	**0**	**2/1**	**2**	**3**	**1**	**62/27**	**18**

ASCROFT, John Herbert

1929 - 1930

Position; *Outside-Left*
D.O.B; *J/F/M 1909*
Birthplace; *Bebington, Merseyside*
Height; *5ft 8in* ***Weight;*** *11st 0lbs*
Debut v. *Stockport County (h) 31st August, 1929*
Total Appearances & Goals; *10 apps 6 gls*
Career; *Connah's Quay & Shotton; Flint Town 2nd Feb 1927; Oldham Athletic May 1927 0apps; Flint Town Aug 1927; Arsenal 7th March 1928 (trial) 0apps; Bangor City 4th Aug 1928; WREXHAM 14th Mar 1929 £250; Workington Aug 1930 (trial); Runcorn 1936/37;*

John Ascroft played his early football for Welsh League sides Connah's Quay & Shotton and Flint Town, but was with Flint only a short while before Oldham Athletic stepped in to sign him in May 1927. John's stay at Boundary Park was brief, and he returned to Flint for the start of the 1927/28 season, without having made a first team appearance for the 'Latics'. By March, he was invited for a trial by Arsenal, but failed to impress. It was during the close season of 1928 he joined Bangor City, but before season 1928/29 was over was signed by Third Division North side Wrexham for a £250 transfer fee. He made his Football League debut in the opening match of the 1929/30 campaign at outside-left, against Stockport County on the Racecourse, and scored Wrexham's goal in the 1-1 draw. Although making only nine more League appearances for the club he did notch a further five goals. Two of those were scored in the 8-0 win at home to Rochdale, which was a League record victory for the club at that time. Tommy Bamford hit the target in the same match. Despite his goalscoring record John was allowed to leave the club at the end of the 1929/30 season. Ashcroft later played for Runcorn during the 1936/37 season, during which he was also believed to have played for Workington.

Season	League		F.A.Cup		Welsh Cup		Total	
	apps	gls	apps	gls	apps	gls	apps	gls
1929/30	10	6	-	-	-	-	10	6
	10	**6**	**-**	**-**	**-**	**-**	**10**	**6**

***ASHCROFT,* William** 1970 - 1977

Position; *Centre-Forward*
D.O.B; *1st October, 1952*
Birthplace; *Garston, Liverpool, Merseyside.*
Height; *6ft 1in Weight; 12st 9lbs*
Debut v. *Reading (a) 3rd October, 1970*
Total Appearances & Goals; *246/26 apps 96 gls*
Career; *WREXHAM 10th Oct 1970; Middlesbrough 1st Sept 1977 139/20apps 21gls (£120,000); Twente Enschede (Holland) Aug 1981; Tranmere Rovers Aug 1985 16/7apps 2gls; Cheshire Lions cs1986;*
Honours; *Welsh Cup Winner 1972 & 1975; Northern Floodlit League Cup Winner 1970; Alves Cup Winner 1970; P.F.A.Third Division XI 1977; North Wales Coast XI 1972;*

Billy Ashcroft was born less than 100 yards away from South Liverpool's football ground. At school he never took football seriously until towards the end of his time there, but in less than a year had signed for Blackpool as an associate schoolboy. However, he left Bloomfield Road because of the travelling and his wish to concentrate on his studies. Although he had trials with both Everton and Tranmere, both of which came to nothing, it was only after switching from playing wing-half to centre forward that he came to Wrexham's attention. He made an immediate impact and signed for 'The Robins' straight from school in 1968, eventually signing professional terms for the club on his eighteenth birthday in October 1970. Indeed, just two days' later he made his Football League debut at Reading. Billy soon established himself in the first team at the Racecourse, making himself a firm favourite with the crowd. His bushy red hair and unshaven face earned him the nickname 'Yeti', while his robust style of play was enough to unsettle the best of defenders, and at the Racecourse he enjoyed many of the good times that the club experienced during the 1970s. These included playing in Wrexham's first ever matches in European competition against F.C.Zurich; the F.A.Cup run of the 1973/74 season when Wrexham reached the quarter finals; and the 1976/77 campaign, which was eventually to end in disappointment when the club unbelievably missed out on promotion, with Ashcroft scoring twenty goals in a prolific goalscoring partnership with Graham Whittle. However, Billy's most memorable match will always be the European Cup-Winners' Cup quarter-final match against Anderlecht, which saw Wrexham give the eventual winners a real run for their money, going out 2-1 on aggregate. The end of the 1976/77 campaign was to see manager John Neal leave the club for Middlesbrough. Neal had signed Billy from school, and in September 1977 he returned to the Racecourse to pay £120,000 to be re-united with his star pupil. With 'Boro' Billy found goals hard to come by, with Neal later switching him to centre-half, a position he had played for Wrexham during an injury crisis. Billy went on to make 159 League appearances at Ayresome Park, scoring 21 goals, before moving abroad to join Dutch side Twente Enschede in the close season of 1981. With Twente, he appeared alongside Dutch internationals (and former Ipswich stars) Frans Thijssen and Arnold Muhren, but in 1985 returned home. Billy first had a trial spell with Hull City, as well as being linked with Wrexham, he signed for Tranmere Rovers in the summer of 1985. Ashcroft enjoyed one season with the Birkenhead club, where injuries limited his appearances to just 23 outings, and at the end of the campaign he was given a free transfer. He turned out for a local side, Cheshire Lions, before finishing playing altogether, moving into the licensing trade, first taking over the Derby Arms in Halewood, Liverpool, followed by the 'The George' public house in Southport.

Season	League		F.A.Cup		Welsh Cup		League Cup		E.C.W.C.		Total	
	apps	gls	apps	gls	apps	gls	apps	gls	apps	gls	apps	gls
1970/71	18/1	8	-	-	2	0	-	-	-	-	20/1	8
1971/72	23/6	5	2	0	3	1	-	-	-	-	28/6	6
1972/73	35	14	2	0	-	-	2	0	4	1	43	15
1973/74	24/4	6	-	-	0/1	0	1/1	3	-	-	25/6	9
1974/75	17/6	4	-	-	3/1	4	1	0	-	-	21/7	8
1975/76	36/6	14	3	1	3	2	3	0	5	2	50/6	19
1976/77	40	20	6	5	3	2	5	2	-	-	54	29
1977/78	3	1	-	-	-	-	2	1	-	-	5	2
	196/23	**72**	**13**	**6**	**14/2**	**9**	**14/1**	**6**	**9**	**3**	**246/26**	**96**

***ATHERTON,* James Geoffrey** 1947 - 1948

Position; *Goalkeeper*
D.O.B; *2nd April, 1923*
Birthplace; *Queensferry, Flintshire*
Height; *ft in* ***Weight;*** *st lbs*
Debut v. *Darlington (h) 22nd November, 1947*
Total Appearances & Goals; *21 apps 0 gls*
Career; *Hawarden; Chester WW2 Mar 1943 2apps 0gls; Ewloe; WREXHAM Jul 1947; Ellesmere Port Town cs1949; Colwyn Bay; Connah's Quay Nomads cs1950- cs1952;*
Honours; *Three Welsh Amateur International caps; Welsh National League Championship Winner; North Wales Coast Amateur Cup Winner 1951;*

Geoff Atherton first began playing football at Deeside Central School, from where he was chosen to represent Flintshire Schoolboys. Upon leaving school he played for Hawarden in the Flintshire League, while beginning work as an apprentice fitter at Shotton Steelworks. Geoff's performances in goal soon began to attract the attention of Football League clubs, including Bolton Wanderers and Wolves, where he went on trial. However, any thoughts of a glittering football career were thwarted with the outbreak of the Second World War. Soon after he attended for a trial with Chester, and signed amateur forms immediately following a match in which Tommy Lawton also played. Lawton told Geoff, "keep at it, you've got potential." During WW2, he made his first team debut for Chester in a 3-1 home defeat by Crewe in March 1943. Atherton made one more appearance for Chester, a 4-1 home win over Crewe, before being called up for the Army. He then joined R.E.M.I., serving with them until WW2 was over. Geoff then played for Chester's reserve team at weekends, as an amateur, from where he was later approached by Doncaster Rovers. The Chester manager, Frank Brown, wouldn't agree to the move, but at the end of the season released him! Atherton then joined Flintshire League side, Ewloe, before joining Wrexham on trial. Signed by Wrexham on amateur terms in July 1947 by manager Tom Williams, he was seen as goalkeeping cover for both Frank Williams and Tom Bayley. Throughout his time with Wrexham, Atherton continued to work at Shotton Steelworks, but didn't have long to wait for his Football League debut, when he replaced Frank Williams in goal for the match with Darlington in November 1947 in a 2-1 home defeat. That season saw Geoff make a further sixteen League appearances, as well as being chosen to play for the Welsh Amateur International side against England at Shrewsbury in March 1948. Wales won 4-3, their first win at this level in 27 years! Towards the end of the season Atherton was one of four 'keepers recommended to play for Great Britain in the 1948 Olympic games, but wasn't chosen for the final squad, although playing two more matches for the Welsh amateur side against the Indian Olympic team. Despite missing out on the Olympics Geoff went on Wrexham's overseas tour to Germany in the close season of 1948, where he played in the club's three touring matches. 1948/49 saw a new goalkeeper signed, in the experienced Archie Ferguson. This meant that Geoff found himself again playing reserve team football, although he did make one further senior appearance for Wrexham when he was called upon at the 11th hour, coming straight off a night shift to face Rotherham at the Racecourse. Wrexham lost 4-0, and he never played another match in a Wrexham jersey, and at the end of the season joined Ellesmere Port Town for their initial stint in the Cheshire League. However, during the campaign he left to join Colwyn Bay, staying until the end of the season, when he signed for Connah's Quay Nomads. Geoff went on to help the 'Nomads' lift the North Wales Coast Amateur Cup, spending two seasons at the Halfway before finally hanging up his boots in 1952. Atherton continued to live in Hawarden, working at Shotton Steelworks until he retired. He then spent much of his spare time playing golf.

Season	League		F.A.Cup		Welsh Cup		Total	
	apps	gls	apps	gls	apps	gls	apps	gls
1947/48	17	0	1	0	2	0	20	0
1948/49	1	0	-	-	-	-	1	0
	18	**0**	**1**	**0**	**2**	**0**	**21**	**0**

B

Gary Bennett

BAILEY, Rowland Mills 1925

Position; *Outside-Left*
D.O.B; *10th August, 1903*
Birthplace; *Bradford, Yorkshire*
Died; *Leeds, A/M/J 1972*
Height; *5ft 9 1/2in* **Weight;** *11st 0lbs*
Debut v. *Southport (h) 29th August, 1925*
Total Appearances & Goals; *11 apps 2 gls*
Career; *Rotherham County; Harrogate Town; Doncaster Rovers Mar 1924 17apps 1gls; Barnsley 15th March 1925 0apps; WREXHAM 15th May 1925; Llandudno 16th Dec 1925;*

Rowland Bailey had played for Rotherham County and Harrogate Town attending trials with both Huddersfield Town and Halifax Town before eventually joining Doncaster Rovers in March 1924. It was with 'Rovers' that he finally made his Football League debut in a 3-1 home win over Hartlepool United in April. Rowland made one further League appearance that season for Doncaster, which was the clubs first in the Football League. The following season Bailey made fifteen first team appearances before his transfer to Barnsley in exchange for Ernie Smart in March 1925. However, he failed to make the senior side at Oakwell and at the end of the campaign was allowed to sign for Wrexham manager Charlie Hewitt. With Wrexham Rowland played in the first eleven matches of the 1925/26 season at outside-left, scoring on his debut at home to Southport in a 3-2 win, while his last match for the club turned out to be at Halifax, in October, in a 2-1 defeat. By December he was allowed to leave the Racecourse, signing for Welsh League side Llandudno.

Season	League		F.A.Cup		Welsh Cup		Total	
	apps	gls	apps	gls	apps	gls	apps	gls
1925/26	11	2	-	-	-	-	11	2
	11	**2**	**-**	**-**	**-**	**-**	**11**	**2**

BAINES, Peter Cecil 1943 - 1946

Position; *Inside-Forward*
D.O.B; *11th September, 1919.*
Birthplace; *Manchester, Lancashire*
Died; *Manchester, 6th January, 1997.*
Height; *5ft 6in* **Weight;** *st lbs*
Debut v. *Rochdale (a) 3rd September, 1946*
Total Appearances & Goals; *55 apps 34 gls*
Career; *Oldham Athletic 11th Nov 1937 0apps; WREXHAM 25th April 1943, (WW2) 52apps 35gls; Grimsby Town (WW2 Guest) Sept 1943 17apps 5gls, Halifax Town (WW2 Guest) 1943/44 2apps 0gls, Hartlepool United (WW2 Guest) 1943/44 10apps 8gls; Liverpool (WW2 Guest) Dec 1944 1app 1gls; Middlesbrough (WW2 Guest) Apr 1945 1app 0gls; WREXHAM (re-registered 12th June 1946); Crewe Alexandra 16th Nov 1946 (In exchange for Jack Boothway) 7apps 0gls; Hartlepool United 21st Jun 1947 9apps 1gls; New Brighton (trial) 17th Oct 1947 2apps 0gls; Carlisle United (trial) 13th December 1947 0apps;*

Peter Baines is believed to be the first coloured player to have played a first team game for Wrexham when he signed for the club during WW2, and during his time at the Racecourse was more popularly known by the nickname of 'Darkie' Baines. Peter was brought up in an orphanage in Manchester, which didn't deter him from excelling at football. It was for Oldham Athletic that he first signed as an amateur, turning professional in November 1937. However, his time with Oldham was spent mainly playing reserve team football as he failed to make a first team appearance for the 'Latics'. The outbreak of WW2 saw Peter's promising career come to a sudden halt, as he joined the Army in the latter part of 1939, and remained in the forces until 1946 when the War was over. He did play football as available, and when home on leave 'guested' for a number of clubs. It was during this period that he first signed for Wrexham in April 1943, and went on to make 52 War-time appearances for the club, scoring an amazing 35 goals, which included a hat-trick on his debut in a 6-3 home win over Stockport County, quickly making him a firm favourite with the crowd. That type of record helped him to earn a contract for Wrexham when the hostilities were over. During his time at the Racecourse he showed that he was a 'thrustful, scheming inside-forward who could use either foot successfully, which was his biggest strength'. Despite this, after only six matches in the Football League for Wrexham he was transferred to Crewe Alexandra, in a part-exchange deal with Jack Boothway arriving at the Racecourse. Peter's stay at Gresty Road was short, because at the end of the 1946/47 season he was allowed to sign for Hartlepool United after just seven League games. His time in the North-East was also to be limited, and played in just nine League games, scoring one goal before he was released. He then had trials with New Brighton and Carlisle United leaving the Football League scene and dropping into non-League football before retiring in 1954. Unfortunately, in the late 1950's Peter was sent to Prison at Manchester Crown Court for receiving stolen goods, the first of many appearances before the courts. After his professional football career had ended he had worked as a Cabinet maker, a Market Porter, and a door to door salesman. Peter died in Manchester in January 1997 aged 77.

Season	League		F.A.Cup		Welsh Cup		Total	
	apps	gls	apps	gls	apps	gls	apps	gls
1943/44	5	1	-	-	-	-	5	1
1944/45	35	27	-	-	-	-	35	27
1945/46	9	4	-	-	-	-	9	4
1946/47*	6	2	-	-	-	-	6	2
	55	**34**	**-**	**-**	**-**	**-**	**55**	**34**

* 1946/47 season is the only Football League season.

BAKER, Darren Spencer 1982 - 1984

Position; *Midfield*
D.O.B; *28th June, 1965*
Birthplace; *Wednesbury, West Midlands*
Height; *5ft 9in* **Weight;** *11st 0lbs*
Debut v. *Plymouth Argyle (a) 25th September, 1982*
Total Appearances & Goals; *21/8 apps 2 gls*
Career; *WREXHAM Aug 1983; Bangor City cs1984; Caernarfon Town Sept 1987; Bangor City 1989; Llangefni Town Sept 1990; Caernarfon Town Jan 1991; Conwy United Aug 1993 30/8apps 4gls; Porthmadog Oct 1994 7/5apps 0gls; Cemaes Bay Jul 1995 7/8apps 5gls; Llangefni Town 1996; Glantraeth 1998; Llangerni 1998/99;*
Honours; *Welsh Youth International; Welsh Schoolboy international; Welsh Intermediate Cup Winner; Welsh Alliance League Winner*

Although originally from the West Midlands Darren Baker's family moved to Anglesey while he was a youngster. It was whilst playing for a local junior side on the Island that he was capped at Welsh Schoolboy level, which resulted in him joining the groundstaff at Wrexham in the summer of 1981, having already signed for the club on schoolboy forms. With Wrexham, Baker became a member of Bobby Roberts' highly successful youth team which saw several other players go on to play first team football. Darren made his first team debut in the Third Division at the age of 17, substituting Dixie McNeil at Plymouth in September 1982. That season he went on to make a further 14 League appearances, scoring his only goal in a 1-1 draw at Doncaster Rovers in his first full start. August 1983 saw manager Bobby Roberts sign Darren on a professional contract, but he failed to fulfil his early promise and at the end of the season he was released. Baker then signed for Bangor City, but a broken leg was to interrupt his football career at Farrar Road. Darren went on to play for Caernarfon Town before joining League of Wales side Conwy United in the summer of 1993. In October 1994 he joined Porthmadog, who were managed at the time by former Wrexham striker Ian Edwards, but at the end of the 1994/95 season left 'Yr Traeth' to join newly promoted League of Wales side Cemaes Bay. He spent a season at the School Lane Club before joining his local side on Anglesey, Llangefni. Darren has, in fact, represented the Isle of Anglesey football team on a number of occasions in the World Island games, playing in Aaland, Gibralter and the Isle of Man. In 1998/99 he joined Glantraeth in the Cymru Alliance before rejoining his adopted Llangefni. Captaining them to the Fitlock Alliance Championship and promotion to the Cymru Alliance for season 1999/2000. Now employed as a Section Leader at a Chicken Factory in Llangefni.

Season	League		F.A.Cup		Welsh Cup		League Cup		A.M.C.		Total	
	apps	gls	apps	gls	apps	gls	apps	gls	apps	gls	apps	gls
1982/83	10/5	1	-	-	0/2	0	-	-	-	-	10/7	1
1983/84	8/1	0	-	-	1	0	-	-	2	1	11/1	1
	18/6	**1**	**-**	**-**	**1/2**	**0**	**-**	**-**	**2**	**1**	**21/8**	**2**

BAKER, Norman 1929 - 1930

Position; *Outside-Left*
D.O.B; *21st June 1909*
Birthplace; *Buckley, Flintshire*
Died; *Flint, 21st January 1980*
Height; *ft in* **Weight;** *st lbs*
Debut v. *Wigan Borough (h) 5th October, 1929*
Total Appearances & Goals; *1 app 0 gls*
Career; *Oak Alyn Rovers; Normal College, Bangor; Mold FC cs1929; WREXHAM Oct 1929; New Brighton Aug 1930 0apps; Connah's Quay & Shotton FC Sept 1931;*

Norman Baker played football for Oak Alyn Rovers after leaving school, and attended the Normal College in Bangor for whom he also played football. When he left College in the summer of 1929 his form attracted a number of clubs with Wrexham and Oswestry Town both interested in signing him. It was said, prior to trials with both of these clubs, "regarded as one of the best players in the college team. Whoever signs him will not regret it." Norman in fact signed for Mold F.C., but it was not long before he joined Wrexham, in October 1929. Baker made his Football League debut for Wrexham, when he replaced the injured John Ascroft, in a 2-1 home win over the now defunct Wigan Borough. However, that proved to be Norman`s one and only first team game for Wrexham, and in the close season of 1930 he joined New Brighton, for whom his brother Fred also played. Both had previously appeared for Mold, but Norman failed to impress for the 'Rakers', and the following summer was released without making a first team appearance for the club. Norman Baker joined Cheshire League side Connah's Quay & Shotton FC during the close season of 1931.

Season	League		F.A.Cup		Welsh Cup		Total	
	apps	gls	apps	gls	apps	gls	apps	gls
1929/30	1	0	-	-	-	-	1	0
	1	**0**	**-**	**-**	**-**	**-**	**1**	**0**

BAMFORD, Thomas 1929 - 1934

Position; *Centre-Forward*
D.O.B; *2nd September, 1905*
Birthplace; *Port Talbot, Glamorgan*
Died; *Wrexham, 12th December, 1967.*
Height; *5ft 9in* **Weight;** *11st 11lbs*
Debut v. *Accrington Stanley (h) 30th March, 1929*
Total Appearances & Goals; *245 apps 207 gls*
Career; *Cardiff Docks; Cardiff Wednesday; Bridgend Town; WREXHAM 4th Apr 1929; Manchester United 17th Oct 1934 98apps 53gls; Swansea Town 8th Jun 1938 36apps 14gls; WREXHAM (WW2 Guest) May 1940 17apps 8gls; Hartlepool Utd (WW2 Guest) 1943/44 13apps 6gls;*
Honours; *Five Welsh International caps 1930-3; Welsh Cup Winner 1931; Welsh Cup runner-up 1932, 1933, 1938 & 1940; Second Division Championship Winner 1936;*

Tommy Bamford's place in Wrexham Football Club's 'Hall of Fame' is assured. He holds a number of goalscoring records for the club, including a record tally of 174 League goals, and the most League goals in a season, 44, during 1933/34. His footballing career never really started until he was signed by Wrexham on amateur terms in April 1929, after playing most of his earlier football in the local leagues around South Wales. Tommy's League career with Wrexham began after journeying up to North Wales in search of work, but at the 'late' age of 23, he launched his Football League career in fine style by scoring six goals in just seven league games at the end of 1928/29. The 'Brylcream' haired centre forward was soon signed on professional terms, and although not very tall, he was just 5ft 9in, he quickly made his mark. His goals helped Wrexham to reach their highest pre-war League position in the 1932/33 season, when they finished runners-up in the Third Division North to Hull City. Bamford also earned himself a call-up to the Welsh international team in October 1930, against Scotland at Hampden Park in a 1-1 draw- and yes, you've guessed it, Tommy scored! In January 1932 he was suspended by the club for 14 days along with his brother, Walter, and a reserve team player named Pritchard, for 'breach of training ground regulations'. His goalscoring record soon began to attract the attention of the 'bigger' clubs, with both Birmingham and Sheffield United showing an interest in signing him. Tommy began the 1934/35 season as the club captain, but by October 1934 he was transferred to Manchester United, who were then a Second Division side. Bamford signed for United along with team-mate Billy Bryant. He spent four seasons at Old Trafford, winning a Second Division Championship medal in 1936, but was not always a regular in the United side, despite maintaining an excellent strike rate. In 1938 Tommy returned to his native South Wales, to join Swansea Town, where he stayed until the outbreak of WW2. During this period he did play for Wrexham once again, as a 'guest' player, making a further fourteen appearances (eight goals) between 1940 and 1941. He also 'guested' for Hartlepool, and played one match for the Northern Command. When WW2 ended, Bamford settled in Wrexham, and took up work in a local steelworks. Tommy Bamford died at his Queen's Park home in Wrexham during December 1967, aged 62.

Season	League		F.A.Cup		Welsh Cup		N.S.C.		Total	
	apps	gls	apps	gls	apps	gls	apps	gls	apps	gls
1928/29	7	6	-	-	-	-	-	-	7	6
1929/30	37	25	5	2	3	2	-	-	45	29
1930/31	35	34	3	4	4	7	-	-	42	45
1931/32	35	30	1	1	6	2	-	-	42	33
1932/33	40	31	3	3	6	6	-	-	49	40
1933/34	41	44	1	0	1	0	4	6	43	44
1934/35	9	4	-	-	-	-	-	-	9	4
	204	**174**	**13**	**10**	**20**	**17**	**4**	**6**	**245**	**207**

BAMFORD, Walter Phillip 1930 - 1931

Position; *Inside-Forward*
D.O.B;
Birthplace; *Port Talbot, Glamorgan*
Height; *5ft 9ins* **Weight;** *11st 5lbs*
Debut v. *Doncaster Rovers (h) 14th January, 1931*
Total Appearances & Goals; *1 app 0 gls*
Career; *Cardiff Wednesday FC; WREXHAM (Am) Oct 1930, (Pro) 19th Dec 1930; Carlisle United June 1932 0apps;*

Brother to the more famous Tommy, Walter joined Wrexham on trial as an amateur in October 1930 following Tommy's recommendation. Two months later, Bamford signed professional terms for Wrexham. The following month he was to make his one and only first team appearance, when playing at outside-right in place of Tommy Lewis, on the Racecourse against Doncaster Rovers during January 1931 in a 4-1 win. Walter was described in the local newspaper match report as 'not up to standard', but it wasn't until the end of the 1931/32 season that he was released by Wrexham. In June 1932, he was known to have joined Carlisle United, but never made the first team at Brunton Park.

Season	League		F.A.Cup		Welsh Cup		Total	
	apps	gls	apps	gls	apps	gls	apps	gls
1930/31	1	0	-	-	-	-	1	0
	1	**0**	**-**	**-**	**-**	**-**	**1**	**0**

BANNAN, Thomas Nelson 1951 - 1955 & 1957 - 1959

Position; *Centre-Forward*
D.O.B; *13th April, 1930*
Birthplace; *Darngavel, Lanarkshire*
Height; *5ft 7'1/2in* **Weight;** *10st 12lbs*
Debut v. *Chester (a) 18th August, 1951*
Total Appearances & Goals; *260 apps 104 gls*
Career; *Plains St.Davids; Airdrie 1946/47; WREXHAM 6th Jun 1951; Lincoln City 23rd Jun 1955 (£1,000 & Eric Littler in exchange) 67apps 19gls; WREXHAM 19th Sept 1957 £3,000; Barrow 21st Aug 1959 £1,500 45apps 15gls;*
Honours; *Welsh Cup Winner 1958;*

Tommy Bannan began his football career in his native Scotland with local side Plains St.Davids, joining local Scottish League side Airdrie, whom he had supported as a boy. Tommy went on to make his first team debut for Airdrie against Raith Rovers in a Scottish Second Division game, two hours after signing professional terms with the Lanarkshire club during the 1946/47 season. To cap it all Bannan scored the only goal of the game, which gave Airdrie two precious points, helping them to win promotion that same season as runners-up to Dundee. It was when he was 21 years-old that he was recommended to Wrexham manager Peter Jackson, who signed the Scottish centre-forward in June 1951. Tommy was not the biggest of forwards, but what he lacked in height made up for by being in the right place at the right time. His Football League debut came in the opening game of the 1951/52 season at Chester, scoring Wrexham's goal in a 2-1 defeat. Over the next four seasons Tommy became a prolific goalscorer with Wrexham, but in the summer of 1955 Lincoln manager Bill Anderson splashed out £1,000 for his services, with striker Eric Littler moving in the opposite direction to join Wrexham. Tommy had scored 60 League goals in 158 appearances during his time at the Racecourse. With Lincoln he remained a consistent goalscorer for two years, before he was to rejoin Wrexham by 'public demand', when

manager Cliff Lloyd paid out £3,000 for the man from Lanarkshire. The next two seasons again saw Tommy amongst the goals, including notching the winner in the 1958 Welsh Cup final replay against Chester on the Racecourse. He had scored in each of the previous rounds of that year's cup run, including a hat-trick against Flint. The following term he finished as the club's top scorer with 15 League goals, but at the end of the season was to reluctantly leave Wrexham and join Barrow, after his wife was taken ill. Tommy still lived in Airdrie at that time, so when Barrow offered £1,500 for his signature the club accepted his situation in allowing him to leave the Racecourse. Bannan made his debut for Barrow against Darlington in a 4-1 home win, in which he scored one of their goals. He went on to stay at Holker Street for one season, scoring fifteen goals in 45 league matches. At the end of the season he returned to Scotland, becoming a licensee in Airdrie.

			Season		League		F.A.Cup
Welsh Cup	Total						
apps	gls	apps	gls	apps	gls	apps	gls
1951/52	40	12	3	2	4	0	47	14
1952/53	45	18	3	3	1	1	49	22
1953/54	37	14	6	4	1	0	44	18
1954/55	36	16	3	0	3	3	42	19
1957/58	28	8	1	0	5	6	34	14
1958/59	40	15	1	0	3	2	44	17
	226	**83**	**17**	**9**	**17**	**12**	**260**	**104**

BANNISTER, Keith
1955

Position; *Right-Half*
D.O.B; *13th November, 1930*
Birthplace; *Sheffield, Yorkshire*
Height; *5ft 10in*
Weight; *11st 8lbs*
Debut v. *York City (a) 20th August, 1955*
Total Appearances & Goals; *14 apps 0 gls*
Career; *Rawcliffe Boys; Sheffield & Haslam Boys; Sheffield United 26th May 1948 0apps; Birmingham City 1st Aug 1950 22apps 0gls; Kings Lynn Aug 1954; WREXHAM 27th Jul 1955; Chesterfield 10th Dec 1955 21apps 1gls; Norwich City 3rd Jul 1956 7apps 0gls; Peterborough United Jul 1957; Kings Lynn Jul 1958;*
Honours; England Youth International;

Keith Bannister joined Sheffield United straight from School after the Second World War had ended, having played for Rawcliffe Boys and Sheffield & Haslam Boys. In May 1948 he was signed on professional terms by Sheffield United, after already representing the England Youth team. Keith completed a further two seasons at Bramall Lane, without breaking into the first team. In August 1950 he was allowed to leave the 'Blades', when he signed for Second Division side Birmingham City. At St.Andrews Bannister made his Football League debut at right-half, in a 5-0 home defeat against Nottingham Forest in November 1952. He was unable to command a regular first team place while at St.Andrews, and at the end of 1953/54 was released, having made 22 League appearances without scoring. In August of 1954, Keith signed for Kings Lynn, where he remained for a season before returning to the Football League when signing for Wrexham in July 1955. Bannister made his debut for 'The Robins' in their opening match of the season at York, which they won 3-1. He then went on to play in the following 13 League games at right-half, before losing his place in the side to Dennis Griffiths in October. Keith never played another first team game again for Wrexham, and after just five months at the Racecourse he joined Chesterfield. His stay at Saltergate was also short, despite making his debut in the first match after signing, a 2-1 home win over Carlisle, and keeping his place in the side although missing the final four matches of the season. In the summer of 1956 he joined Norwich City, and enjoyed a season at Carrow Road, although not making his debut until Christmas Day 1956 in a 1-1 draw at Colchester. Keith made just six more League appearances for the 'Canaries', without appearing on the winning side once, joining Midland League side Peterborough United at the end of the season. He enjoyed just one first team outing for the London Road club, at home to Grimsby Town Reserves, and in July 1958 returned to non-league football with Kings Lynn, where he is last known to have played.

Season	League		F.A.Cup		Welsh Cup		Total	
	apps	gls	apps	gls	apps	gls	apps	gls
1955/56	14	0	-	-	-	-	14	0
	14	**0**	**-**	**-**	**-**	**-**	**14**	**0**

BARNARD, Sidney
1937 - 1938

Position; *Inside-Forward*
D.O.B; *10th July, 1914*
Birthplace; *Aigburth, Liverpool, Merseyside*
Height; *5ft 8ins* ***Weight;*** *10st 0lbs*
Debut v. *Lincoln City (h) 1st September, 1937*
Total Appearances & Goals; *2 apps 1 gls*
Career; *Aigburth Parish Church FC; Blackburn Rovers Aug 1934; Stockport County Aug 1935 0apps; Bangor (Ireland) Aug 1936; WREXHAM 23rd Aug 1937 to 28th Sept 1937;*
Honours; *Central League Cup Winner 1935;*

Sidney Barnard initially played football for the St.Anne's School in his native Liverpool. After leaving school he appeared in local League football in Liverpool for Aigburth Parish Church FC, before being spotted by a scout from Blackburn Rovers for whom he signed in August 1934. Sid went on to spend twelve months at Ewood Park, without figuring in the first team, although he did help the reserves to win the Central League Cup. At the end of that season he was transferred to Stockport County. Sid again failed to made a Football League appearance leaving Edgeley Park to try his luck in Ireland, joining Bangor, County Down, in 1936/37. He spent a season over the water before returning home and joining Third Division North side, Wrexham, in August 1937, having been signed by manager Ernie Blackburn. Barnard made his Football League debut for Wrexham in the second match of the 1937/38 season on the Racecourse against Lincoln City, a 1-0 win in which Sid scored the Wrexham goal. He appeared in the following match, a 1-0 home defeat by New Brighton, which proved to be his final first team game for Wrexham as he played in the reserve side for the rest of his time at the Racecourse. With the outbreak of World War Two Sid was called up for the Army. He later played for and coached the Liverpool Police team at Mather Avenue, and was employed at Dunlops as a security officer before retiring. In his spare time he won many trophies in Crown Green Bowling, and was last known to be residing in the Liverpool area in 1998.

Season	League		F.A.Cup		Welsh Cup		Total	
	apps	gls	apps	gls	apps	gls	apps	gls
1937/38	2	1	-	-	-	-	2	1
	2	**1**	**-**	**-**	**-**	**-**	**2**	**1**

BARNES, Charles Ronald
1961 - 1963

Position; *Outside-Right*
D.O.B; *21st February, 1936*
Birthplace; *Bolton, Lancashire*
Died; *Darcy Lever, December 1991*
Height; *5ft 11in* ***Weight;*** *11st 0lbs*
Debut v. *Millwall (a) 19th August, 1961*
Total Appearances & Goals; *102 apps 29 gls*
Career; *Lomax FC; Blackpool (Pro) 6th May 1954 9apps 0gls; Rochdale 2nd Jun 1959 £1,000 91apps 7gls; WREXHAM 25th Jul 1961 £4,000; Norwich City 30th Aug 1963 £5,000 (plus Alan Jones) 21apps 1gls; Peterborough United 25th Jun 1964 £5,000 39apps 6gls; Torquay United 27th Jan 1966 114apps 25gls; Cape Town City (South Africa) May 1969 to Dec 1970;*
Honours; *Welsh Cup runner-up 1962;*

Ron Barnes joined Blackpool as a Junior in 1952, when spotted playing for Bolton Schoolboys and his local side, Lomax FC, who competed in the Lancashire Combination League and who he had joined upon leaving school at 15 years-old. With Blackpool, Ron progressed through the groundstaff to sign professional in May 1954, going on to stay at Bloomfield Road for over seven years, in which time he only amassed nine League appearances. This was mainly due to the fact that Barnes was the understudy to a certain Stanley Matthews! His Football League

debut came in August 1956, in a 5-2 win over Everton. Then, in 1957, he was called up for his two years' National Service in which he served with the R.A.F., mainly stationed at Cranwell. Upon being demobbed in May 1959, Ron returned to Bloomfield Road only to find that he was to be transferred to Rochdale for £1,000. He made his debut for 'Dale' in the opening match of the 1959/60 season in a 2-2 draw at Southport. He went on to become an ever-present in the Rochdale team for two seasons, missing just one game. In the close season of 1961 he was signed by Wrexham's new player/manager, Ken Barnes, for £4,000, becoming a firm favourite with the Racecourse crowd, his fast direct style of wing play helping the 'Robins' win promotion back to the Third Division, as well as reaching the Welsh Cup final. His most memorable match for Wrexham came in March 1962, when the club achieved their record Football League score of 10-1, trouncing Hartlepool United on the Racecourse with Ron scoring one of three hat-tricks! The following season saw him miss just one match as the club consolidated their position in the new Division. He was also voted the club's 'Player of the Year' for his consistency, but the new 1963/64 season was just weeks old when Second Division Norwich City stepped in to sign Barnes in exchange for £5,000 plus Wrexham born goalkeeper John Allan Jones. His time with Norwich passed without much incident, and after just 21 League games found himself out in the cold with Gerry Mannion preferred. The following summer Barnes was on the move again, this time to Third Division Peterborough United, where he was to spend eighteen months, making 39 League appearances, before signing for fellow Third Division side Torquay United. Ron enjoyed almost four years at Plainmoor, during which time he was a regular performer on the right wing, scoring 25 goals in 114 League games for the 'Gulls'. He left Devon in the close season of 1969 to take up an offer in South Africa, playing for a team called Cape Town City. He apparently settled in South Africa, and spent over twenty years working in the print trade. Ron Barnes later returned to Britain, but sadly passed away in December 1991 aged just 55.

Season	League		F.A.Cup		Welsh Cup		N.S.C.		Total	
	apps	gls	apps	gls	apps	gls	apps	gls	apps	gls
1961/62	41	11	2	0	5	2	-	-	48	13
1962/63	45	12	4	3	2	0	1	0	52	15
1963/64	2	1	-	-	-	-	-	-	2	1
	88	**24**	**6**	**3**	**7**	**2**	**1**	**0**	**102**	**29**

BARNES, Kenneth Herbert

1961 - 1965

Position; *Wing-Half*
D.O.B; *6th March, 1929*
Birthplace; *Birmingham, West Midlands*
Height; *5ft 11in Weight; 10st 13lbs*
Debut v. *Millwall (a) 19th August, 1961*
Total Appearances & Goals; *156 apps 30 gls*
Career; *Stafford Rangers; Manchester City 8th May 1950 258apps 18gls; WREXHAM 1st May 1961 (Registered as a player 12th May 1961); Witton Albion (player/manager) March 1965;*
Honours; *F.A.Cup Winner 1956; F.A.Cup runner-up 1955; Welsh Cup runner-up 1962;*

Having been born in St.Andrew's Road, Birmingham it really came as no surprise when Ken Barnes was signed by Birmingham City as a schoolboy. However, he progressed no further and joined local side Moor Green, while taking up work for the Post Office as an electrical engineer. At the age of 16 he was recommended to Bolton Wanderers, who he joined for training, but when they wanted him to sign he had enlisted for his National Service with the R.A.F. and his commanding officer would not sanction his release. When he eventually left the R.A.F. Ken joined non-league side, Stafford Rangers, as a part-time professional in the Birmingham Combination League. It was whilst with them that Manchester City beat off Sheffield Wednesday, Birmingham, West Brom and Bolton to sign him in May 1950. Not long after he had joined City they signed another wing-half, Welsh international Roy Paul, leaving Ken to wait until 5th January 1952 before making his first team debut at home to Derby County. Following his debut, he still didn't become a regular in the City first team until the 1954/55 season. Ken then went on to make over 250 league appearances for City, and was considered to be the best uncapped wing-half in the country at the time. He was, however, selected for the Football League in a representative match against Russia, but even then luck was against him as he couldn't play because of a broken toe. Ken spent 11 years at Maine Road before allowed to leave on a free transfer to join Fourth Division Wrexham as their new player-manager in May 1961. He appointed former players Ken Roberts, as his first team coach, and Johnny Anderson, as youth team coach. Ken's first season at the club was to be a success, as he took the club to promotion to the Third Division, finishing in third place behind Millwall and Colchester United. However, the success of promotion was to be shrouded in disappointment when Wrexham lost the Welsh Cup final replay to Bangor City, which meant that they missed out on European football. Ken's next season was to be one of consolidation, with the club finishing in 9th place, but 1963/64 was to see the club relegated back to the Fourth Division. The club's board stood by Barnes, but the following season the team failed to mount a promotion fight, and in February they suffered a 6-1 defeat by Chester at Sealand Road. A few days later he was relieved of his duties, with Cliff Lloyd put in charge until Billy Morris was appointed the new manager in March 1965. As for Ken, he joined Witton Albion as player-manager, which was later followed by a spell as manager of Bangor City. In August 1970 he was offered a job as Manchester City's trainer-coach, remaining at Maine Road up until his retirement. During that time he worked in a number of different jobs at City, including Chief Scout and Youth team coach. Ken was rewarded with two testimonials with City, the first being awarded in 1975. His son Peter also played for City and England, and had a trial period with Wrexham in July/August 1991. Ken was an expert penalty taker during his time at the Racecourse.

Season	League		F.A.Cup		Welsh Cup		N.S.C.		Total	
	apps	gls	apps	gls	apps	gls	apps	gls	apps	gls
1961/62	34	7	3	0	3	2	1	0	41	9
1962/63	40	8	4	0	2	1	1	0	47	9
1963/64	34	1	-	-	3	1	4	1	41	3
1964/65	24	8	2	1	1	0	-	-	27	9
	132	24	9	1	9	4	6	1	156	30

BARNES, Richard Ian

1994 - 1996

Position; *Forward*
D.O.B; *6th September, 1975*
Birthplace; *Wrexham, Denbighshire*
Height; *5ft 10in* ***Weight;*** *11st 6lbs*
Debut v. *Hull City (a) 29th April, 1995*
Total Appearances & Goals; *0/2 apps 0 gls*
Career; *WREXHAM 1992 31st May 1994 (pro); Holywell Town Jul 1996 0/1app 0gls; Exeter City (trial) Aug 1996; Porthmadog Sept 1996 7/16apps 1gls;*
Honours; *Two Wales Schoolboy International caps; Welsh Youth Cup Winner 1994; Welsh Youth Cup runner-up 1993;*

It was a dream come true when Richard Barnes joined his home town team as an apprentice. He had played youth football in the Wrexham area for the Gresford and Brickfield youth teams, and appeared for his school team, Groves, whilst also playing representative football for Wrexham Schoolboys, North Wales Under-15's and finally twice for the Welsh Under-16 Schoolboys team, both against Eire. At 14, Richard joined Wrexham on schoolboy terms progressing to full-time on YTS terms, when he left School in 1992. Barnes continued his progression, winning a Welsh Youth Cup Winners' medal in April 1993 when Wrexham beat Swansea City 4-1 in the final at Llanidloes. He worked his way through the ranks at the Racecourse until finally earning himself a professional contract in the summer of 1994. Richard then played regular reserve team football before finally making his first team debut at Hull City in the last match of the 1994/95 season, coming on as a substitute for the injured Tony Humes at left-back. The following campaign he made one further first team appearance, as sub for Steve Futcher in Romania, during a European Cup-Winners' Cup match against Petrolul Ploesti. Barnes then received a number of niggling injuries, but recovered to play regularly at right-back for the Pontin's League side. However, at the end of the 1995/96 season

Richard was released by the club, joining League of Wales side Holywell Town, but after just one friendly match was to join Third Division Exeter City on a months' trial. Nothing came of his trial with the 'Grecians', and he returned home, signing for another League of Wales side, Porthmadog, in September 1996.

Season	League apps	gls	F.A.Cup apps	gls	Welsh Cup apps	gls	League Cup apps	gls	Auto Tro apps	gls	E.C.W.C. apps	gls	Total apps	gls
1994/95	0/1	0	-	-	-	-	-	-	-	-	-	-	0/1	0
1995/96	-	-	-	-	-	-	-	-	-	-	0/1	0	0/1	0
	0/1	**0**	-	-	-	-	-	-	-	-	**0/1**	**0**	**0/2**	**0**

BARNES, Robert Alan

1989 - 1990

Position; *Right-Back*
D.O.B; *26th November, 1969*
Birthplace; *Stoke-on-Trent, Staffordshire*
Height; *5ft 8in* **Weight;** *10st 8lbs*
Debut v. *Rochdale (a) 2nd September, 1989*
Total Appearances & Goals; *8/1apps 0gls*
Career; *Manchester City Jun 1988; WREXHAM 20th Jun 1989; Northwich Victoria Nov 1990 (Loan) 5/1apps 0gls; WREXHAM Released Dec 1990; Stafford Rangers Jan 1991 4/1apps 0gls;*

Robbie Barnes had impressed a Manchester City Scout when he was playing at School and County levels in his native Stoke-on Trent. Following up on this City signed Robbie on Schoolboy forms, and after three years he was offered an apprenticeship with the Maine Road club upon leaving school. He was then offered a one year professional contract when his apprenticeship was completed, unfortunately, City chose to release the 19 year-old at the end of the term. Wrexham manager Dixie McNeil quickly stepped in to beat Walsall and Rotherham in snapping up the promising youngster's signature on a two year contract. He made his Football League debut for Wrexham in a 3-0 win at Rochdale, but his initial season at the Racecourse was mainly a frustrating time, as following his early promise, injuries saw him miss a number of matches, and they were followed by a loss of form. The following season he made just one substitute appearance, at home to Chesterfield, before allowed to join GM Conference League side Northwich Victoria on loan in November 1990. Upon his return to Wrexham the following month Robbie found he was to be released. It was a disappointing end to Barnes' promising Football League career. He later played for Stafford Rangers for a short spell, before retiring from the game completely to take up work as a professional dancer in his home City of Stoke-on-Trent with a group that included his brother. They called themselves 'Menergy', their act was similar to the more well known 'Chippendales'! Robbie also combined his work, doing some modelling.

Season	League apps	gls	F.A.Cup apps	gls	Welsh Cup apps	gls	League Cup apps	gls	L.D.C. apps	gls	Total apps	gls
1989/90	8	0	0/1	0	1	0	-	-	1	0	10/1	0
1990/91	0/1	0	-	-	-	-	-	-	-	-	0/1	0
	8/1	**0**	**0/1**	**0**	**1**	**0**	-	-	**1**	**0**	**10/1**	**0**

BARROW, William Henry

1936 - 1937

Position; *Outside-Right*
D.O.B; *29th January, 1911*
Birthplace; *Cardiff, Glamorgan*
Height; *5ft 7in* **Weight;** *10st 7lbs*
Debut v. *New Brighton (h) 21st October, 1936 (Football League Northern Section Cup)*
Total Appearances & Goals; *14 apps 2 gls*
Career; *Clapton Orient 1929 0apps; Margate Town Jun 1932; Southend United Feb 1934 £300 34apps 2gls; Bournemouth & Boscombe Jun 1935 26apps 4gls; WREXHAM 29th May 1936; Barry Town 11th Jun 1937;*
Honours; *Welsh Schoolboy international;*

Bill Barrow was brought up in the Grange area of Cardiff, not far from where Ninian Park stands today. He attended the Grange Council school, and was selected to play for Wales Schoolboys against Scotland at Ninian Park. That match brought his talents to the notice of a number of Football League sides from outside the South Wales area. On leaving school he was signed by Clapton Orient. At the time 'The O's' were struggling in the lower reaches of the Third Division South, and their plight was not helped by severe financial difficulties. Jimmy Seed, a former England international, took charge of Orient in April 1931, having previously guided Sheffield Wednesday to the First Division title in 1929 and 1930. Seed signed experienced players, and ignored the youngsters at the club- like Bill Barrow. Frustrated at not being able to gain a first team place he left Orient in the close season of 1932, and joined Kent League side Margate Town. Although they were a non-league side he remained as a professional throughout his time there. After some dazzling right-wing performances he was signed by Third Division South side Southend United, and thrust straight into the 'Shrimpers' first team at Bournemouth in February 1934 in a 4-1 win. The fairy-tale start continued as he scored on his home debut, in a 4-1 win over Swindon Town, and remained in the first team for the rest of the season. Barrow in fact played in Southend's last ever match at the Kursaal Ground, a goal-less draw with Norwich City, before they moved to the Southend Stadium. The 1934/35 season saw him out of favour, although he was soon to win his place back, making a total of twenty League appearances eventually losing his place in the side again in March. At the end of the season he left Southend and signed for Bournemouth. under new manager Bob Crompton, the former Blackburn and England international. Bill was one of his first signings, along with former Wrexham player George Bellis. He scored four goals in 26 League games for the 'Cherries', before returning to his native Wales in June 1936 to sign for Wrexham manager Ernie Blackburn. However, with Blackburn moving on to manage Hull City just after the season had begun, Barrow found that he had to be patient. He made his first team debut in October in a Football League Northern Section cup match against New Brighton, in a 1-0 home defeat. Due to the form of youngster Ron Jones, Barrow's next game did not arrive until New Year's Day, a League match against New Brighton, when Bill helped to gain revenge for the early season cup defeat by scoring Wrexham's third goal in the 4-1 win. His goal was described as 'a brilliant individual effort by the Wrexham outside-right, who took up a pass from Harold Lapham and raced on to score from a difficult angle'. Barrow turned out a further twelve times that season, but at the end of the campaign the 'Robins' manager, Captain James Logan, released him and he returned to his native Cardiff to play for Barry Town up to the outbreak of the Second World War. He was then enlisted with the R.A.F., and continued to play some football, representing his Station team. He was based at R.A.F. Gloucester, and the team played in a local League. At the end of the hostilities Bill and his brother started their own business with a ship store's in Cardiff Docks, which they ran until he retired in 1981. Bill was still living in Cardiff at the time of writing.

Season	League apps	gls	F.A.Cup apps	gls	Welsh Cup apps	gls	Total apps	gls
1936/37	13	2	-	-	1	0	14	2
	13	**2**	-	-	**1**	**0**	**14**	**2**

BASHAM, Steve

1998

Position; *Forward*
D.O.B; *2nd December, 1977.*
Birthplace; *Southampton, Hampshire*
Height; *5ft 11ins* **Weight;** *11st 3lbs*
Debut; v. *Luton Town (h) 7th February, 1998.*
Total Appearances & Goals; *4/1 apps 0 gls*
Career; *Southampton 24th May 1996 1/18apps 1gls; WREXHAM 5th Feb 1998 (Loan); Preston North End 6th Feb 1999 (Loan) 16/1apps 10 gls 15th Jun 1999;*

Steve Basham was signed on loan by Wrexham manager Brian Flynn in February 1998, a bid to strengthen his squad for the latter part of the 1997/98 season. He made his debut as a substitute for Dean Spink in a 2-1 home win over Luton Town, and got off to a flying start by setting up the winning goal for Neil Roberts, showing great control and awareness to force his way into the area and laying a perfect ball for Roberts. Steve then played in the next four matches, during which time he showed that he was 'strong, quick and has a good eye for goal'. Despite this, he failed to get on the score sheet, but it wasn't for the want of trying. Wrexham signed him for a second month on loan before he picked up a groin strain. However, he never made another first team

appearance for as soon as he regained his fitness he was recalled by Southampton on 25th March, to ease their injury problems. It was felt by many that Steve could have boosted Wrexham's fire power to help them qualify for the Second Division play-offs, which they eventually missed out on goals scored. As for Steve he returned to Southampton where he was to make seven substitute appearances before the end of the 1997/98 season. Basham had joined the 'Saints' as a trainee, and he made his way through the youth ranks to sign professional for Southampton in May 1996. He had a good strike rate for the 'Saints' reserve side, and must have been highly regarded at that time as he was called into the first team squad for the opening match of 1996/97 at Chelsea. Basham then came on to make his Premier League debut as a substitute for Matthew Oakley in the scoreless draw. Described at Southampton as a 'rather old fashioned type centre-forward who holds the ball up well, with a good shot in either foot and strong in the air. He can also play on either flank', Steve made his full Premier League debut against Manchester United at Old Trafford in February 1997 in a 2-1 defeat. Having returned to the Dell from Wrexham, he made a number of substitute appearances for the 'Saints'. In February 1999 he took up an offer of a further loan spell with Preston North End, which resulted in the move becoming permanent in the summer. The name 'Basham' is synonymous with the town of Wrexham and surrounding districts, as during the 1930's Johnny Basham a well known boxing champion of his era was a popular figure in the area although unlikely to be related to Steve!

Season	League		F.A.Cup		Welsh Cup		League Cup		L.D.C.		Total	
	apps	gls	apps	gls	apps	gls	apps	gls	apps	gls	apps	gls
1997/98	4/1	0	-	-	-	-	-	-	-	-	4/1	0
	4/1	**0**	**-**	**-**	**-**	**-**	**-**	**-**	**-**	**-**	**4/1**	**0**

BATER, Phillip Thomas 1981 - 1983

Position; *Left-Back*
D.O.B; *26th October, 1955*
Birthplace; *Cardiff, Glamorgan*
Height; *5ft 10'1/2in* ***Weight;*** *12st 12lbs*
Debut v. *Norwich City (h) 12th September, 1981*
Total Appearances & Goals; *92 apps 1 gls*
Career; *Bristol Rovers Oct 1973 211/1apps 2gls; WREXHAM 9th Sept 1981 £50,000; Bristol Rovers 15th Sept 1983 £10,000 90/8apps 1gls; Brentford 26th Jun 1986 19apps 2gls; Cardiff City July 1987 67/9apps; Gloucester City 1991;*
Honours; *Two Welsh under-21 International caps; Welsh Youth International; Welsh Cup Winner 1988; Welsh Cup runner-up 1983;*

Phil Bater slipped through the South Wales clubs' scouting nets, as Bristol Rovers were quick to snap him up on apprentice terms after he left school in 1971. Two years later Phil signed professional terms for the Eastville club, and it wasn't long before he made his Football League debut, at the age of 19 in a 2-0 win over Aston Villa in September 1974, the season after Rovers had won promotion to the Second Division. Over the next seven years he made a total of 212 League appearances for the 'Pirates', scoring twice. Following relegation to the Third Division in 1981 Phil wanted to continue at a higher level, and in September 1981 the new Wrexham manager, Mel Sutton, splashed out £50,000 on the experienced full-back and quickly installed him as the club captain. After the euphoria of the signing Phil and Wrexham found themselves struggling, and at the end of the season he was to experience relegation for the second time. The new season commenced with a change in management, as Bobby Roberts took charge. Dire financial problems off the field forced Roberts' to sell the club's best players, and relegation was to follow yet again. At the end of that term Phil did win a Welsh Cup runners-up medal, when Wrexham lost to Swansea City in the final. Throughout the two seasons Phil spent at the Racecourse he was arguably Wrexham's most consistent performer, but with his contract up in September 1983 and the club still in financial trouble, manager Roberts was forced to accept a cut-price £10,000 offer from his former club, Bristol Rovers. Phil went on to make a further 98 League appearances for the 'Rovers' before joining Brentford in June 1986, where he completed just one season at Griffin Park, turning out in the league on 19 occasions before moving back home to South Wales and Cardiff City in July 1987. Phil achieved an unwanted club record for Cardiff when he became the only 'Bluebirds' player to be sent-off on his League debut, in September 1987, in a 3-0 defeat at.......Wrexham! He made 76 League appearances at Ninian Park, helping the club to promotion to the Third Division in his first season, and also winning a Welsh Cup winners' medal when the 'Bluebirds' beat Wrexham 2-0 at Swansea's Vetch Field. Phil left Ninian Park at the end of the 1988/89 season, when he dropped down into non-league football, initially with Gloucester City, going on to play for several local amateur teams in the Bristol area where he worked as a landscape gardener. Bater later began helping out at the 'Pirates' own school of excellence, and in March 1997 was taken on full-time by the club's coaching staff. In the close season of 1997 Phil was appointed assistant to player/ manager Ian Holloway, who he helped lead 'Rovers' to the 1998 play-offs, where they lost to Northampton Town at the semi-final stage.

Season	League		F.A.Cup		Welsh Cup		League Cup		Total	
	apps	gls	apps	gls	apps	gls	apps	gls	apps	gls
1981/82	36	1	4	0	2	0	4	0	46	1
1982/83	37	0	2	0	4	0	2	0	45	0
1983/84	-	-	-	-	-	-	1	0	1	0
	73	**1**	**6**	**0**	**6**	**0**	**7**	**0**	**92**	**1**

BAYLEY, Thomas Kenneth 1947 - 1948

Position; *Goalkeeper*
D.O.B; *25th June, 1921*
Birthplace; *Wednesbury, West Midlands*
Died; *Stafford, March 1996*
Height; *ft in* ***Weight;*** *st lbs*
Debut v. *Hull City (a) 4th October, 1947*
Total Appearances & Goals; *6 apps 0 gls*
Career; *Darlaston; WREXHAM 31st Aug 1947; Darlaston cs1948;*

Tom Bayley joined Wrexham in August 1947, originally on a month's trial from Birmingham League side Darlaston. Due to some impressive performances for the reserves in the Cheshire League he was signed permanently for the rest of the 1947/48 season by manager Tom Williams. Tom got his chance of a first team place when regular custodian, Frank Williams, was on the injured list. He made a 'successful debut' in an away match at Boothferry Park, with Hull managing to score only once, and he kept the 'Tigers' forwards at bay in a one-sided second half. Tom kept his place for a five game spell which ended at Rotherham in a 6-0 defeat, leading to Geoff Atherton being given another first team opportunity. Bayley was to play only one more game for Wrexham that season, in a 1-1 draw at home to Crewe, before he was released at the end of 1947/48. He then rejoined his former club, Darlaston.

Season	League		F.A.Cup		Welsh Cup		Total	
	apps	gls	apps	gls	apps	gls	apps	gls
1947/48	6	0	-	-	1	0	7	0
	6	**0**	**-**	**-**	**1**	**0**	**7**	**0**

BEANLAND, Anthony 1967 - 1969

Position; *Wing-Half*
D.O.B; *11th January, 1944*
Birthplace; *Bradford, Yorkshire*
Height; *5ft 9in* ***Weight;*** *11st 3lb*
Debut v. *Luton Town (h) 19th August, 1967*
Total Appearances & Goals; *97 apps 5 gls*
Career; *Blackpool 10th Oct 1960, (Pro) 11th Jan 1962 0apps; Southport 6th Jul 1962 143apps 3gls; Southend United 15th Mar 1966 £5,000 57apps 3gls; WREXHAM 3rd Jul 1967; Bradford Park Avenue 26th Jun 1969 31apps 1gls; Kirkby Town Jan 1971; Morecambe cs1972;*

Tony Beanland first showed promise as a footballer at Belle Vue Grammar School in his native Bradford. He was chosen to play for Bradford Schoolboys as well as being invited for trials with the English Grammar Schools, for whom he later played against Scotland. Upon leaving school Tony had the choice of joining a number of clubs, including the two Bradford teams. However, it was to First Division Blackpool, that he turned, joining them in October 1960. He then progressed with the 'Seasiders', signing professional in January 1962 on his eighteenth birthday. With the maximum wage being abolished at the end of the 1961/62 season Tony and many other youngsters around the country found themselves released. Despite this setback he was recommended to Southport by Alan Ball's father, Alan Ball Senior, who had seen him playing at Blackpool. Beanland soon made an impact at Haig Avenue when, still only 18 years-old, he made his Football League debut for Southport in a 2-1 home win over Newport County. Beanland quickly established himself as a regular, going on to spend four seasons with Southport. At the age of 21 Tony became Southport's youngest ever first team captain, but in March 1966 he was reluctantly transferred to Southend United for £5,000, which was said to have financed the transfer of Jim Fryatt to Southport. Alvan Williams was the manager who signed Beanland, who he was to later recruit for Wrexham. He spent just over a season at Roots Hall, becoming a regular in midfield, but following Williams' departure to Wrexham he became part of the 'Southend' invasion of the 1960s. Williams was to bring with him a number of players, including John Neal as his first team coach. Tony signed for Wrexham on 3rd July 1967, the day before Steve Ingle and Ray Smith followed him. His stay at the Racecourse was to last for two seasons, playing in his favourite wing-half position where he was always an industrious player, distributing the ball to great effect. He had joined the club in the rebuilding period, after the disaster of having to apply for re-election in 1966, and his signing was to help form a new base in preparation for a promotion drive that was to come the season after he left for Bradford Park Avenue. That move came in June 1969, but in his only season with the Bradford club they finished bottom of the Football League, and were later to be voted out, with Tony playing in Bradford's last ever Football League match. In the summer of 1970 he continued to train with Southport, and might have rejoined them but for the arrival of a similar type of player to himself. He continued to play football for Kirkby Town before joining Morecambe in the close season of 1972. After his professional football career was over he took up work as a joiner/shop fitter in Preston, but a few years later became a publican, running several pubs in the Manchester area. Today, Tony is still in the licensing trade, running a pub in Adlington, near Chorley.

Season	League		F.A.Cup		Welsh Cup		League Cup		Total	
	apps	gls	apps	gls	apps	gls	apps	gls	apps	gls
1967/68	42	3	1	0	2	0	1	0	46	3
1968/69	42	2	2	0	4	0	3	0	51	2
	84	**5**	**3**	**0**	**6**	**0**	**4**	**0**	**97**	**5**

BEAUMONT, Nigel

1988 - 1992

Position; *Centre half*
D.O.B; *11th February, 1967*
Birthplace; *Pontefract, Yorkshire*
Height; *6ft 1in* **Weight;** *13st 5lbs*
Debut v. *Exeter City (a) 27th August, 1988*
Total Appearances & Goals; *150/5 apps 4 gls*
Career; *Bradford City Aug 1983 2apps 0gls; WREXHAM July 1988; Telford United Aug 1992 29/4apps 1gls; Brymbo cs1993; Oswestry Town Jul 1995; Gresford Athletic 1995/6; Lex XI Jul 1996; Flint Town United 1996/97 0/1app 0gls; Brymbo Broughton Dec 1996; Lex XI Jun 1997;*
Honours; *Welsh Cup runner-up 1990 and 1991; Welsh National League Championship Winner 1996;*

Nigel Beaumont was a big, rawboned centre-half affectionately nicknamed 'Garth' because of his size. Nigel began playing football while at school in Knottingly, in his native Yorkshire. It was here that he represented Wakefield & District Schoolboys. Despite trial offers with Leeds United and Huddersfield Town it was Bradford City who snapped him up as a schoolboy, leading to him signing, firstly as an apprentice and then as a professional for the Valley Parade club on his eighteenth birthday. His first team opportunities were limited, despite making his Football League debut in a 2-2 Yorkshire 'derby' draw at Barnsley in March 1986. He also played in the following match with Charlton Athletic at the Odsal Stadium, which was used following the horrific 'Bradford fire disaster' in May 1985, at which Nigel was present. In May 1988 Beaumont was released by Bradford having been limited to just those two first team appearances, but was not short of offers, as teams from South Africa and New Zealand showed interest. 'The Big Man' was delighted when Wrexham manager Dixie McNeil stepped in to sign him in July 1988, and he made his Wrexham debut in the opening game of the new 1988/89 season, a 2-0 win at Exeter, although he had to make way for Mike Williams once he was fit. Towards the end of that season he was back in the side to help Wrexham reach the play-offs, playing in all four play-off matches that nearly saw the 'Robins' promoted before losing to a late goal against Leyton Orient. The 1989/90 season would see 'Big Nige' miss only three matches, and at the end of the campaign was deservedly voted the club's 'Player of the Season' by the fans. The next season saw him play three matches in Europe, against Lyngby of Denmark and Manchester United, missing only the away trip to Denmark. The following campaign he would be out of favour, and from December until the end of the season did not appear in the first team. The summer break would see him discarded by manager Brian Flynn, but Nigel quickly fixed himself up with a club, GM Conference League side Telford United. Following his release at the end of the 1992/93 season he returned to the Wrexham area playing for Brymbo, Oswestry Town, and Gresford Athletic, with whom he won a Welsh National League Championship medal in 1996. In July 1996, Beaumont joined Cymru Alliance side, Lex XI, before switching to another local side, Brymbo Broughton. He returned to Lex XI in the close season of 1997, and not long after was appointed assistant manager.

Season	League		F.A.Cup		Welsh Cup		League Cup		E,C,W,C.		F.R.T.		Total	
	apps	gls	apps	gls	apps	gls	apps	gls	apps	gls	apps	gls	apps	gls
1988/89	20/1*	0	-	-	0/1	0	2	0	-	-	-	-	26/2*	0
1989/90	43	3	1	0	7	0	2	0	-	-	2	0	55	3
1990/91	36/1	1	1	0	4/1	0	4	0	3	0	3	0	51/2	1
1991/92	13/1	0	2	0	1	0	-	-	-	-	2	0	18/1	0
	112/3*	**4**	**4**	**0**	**12/2**	**0**	**8**	**0**	**3**	**0**	**7**	**0**	**150/5***	**4**

* = Includes 4 apps in play-off's.

BECK, Alfred Henry

1932 -1934

Position; *Half-Back*
D.O.B; *21st February, 1901*
Birthplace; *Walsall Wood, Staffordshire*
Died; *Walsall, J/F/M/ 1979.*
Height; *5ft 11in* **Weight;** *12st 6lbs*
Debut v. *Barnsley (h) 27th August, 1932*
Total Appearances & Goals; *35 apps 2 gls*
Career; *Rushall FC; Walsall Jul 1921 3apps 1gls; Darlaston Aug 1922; Cannock Town; Burton Town; Walsall May 1926 40apps 0gls; Stafford Rangers Feb 1928; Barrow Jun 1928 29apps 0gls; York City Jun 1929 119apps 12gls; WREXHAM 24th May 1932; Ards (trial) cs1934; Glentoran Oct 1934; Dudley Town 22nd Jul 1935;*
Honours; *England Junior international; Irish Cup Winner 1935.*

Harry Beck was playing for a local side, Rushall FC, before he was signed by Walsall in the summer of 1921 for their inaugural season in the Football League. He had to wait until December 1921 before making his Football League debut, which came in a home game against Wrexham, ending in a 2-2 draw with Harry scoring one of the Walsall goals. He made just two more League appearances for the 'Saddlers' before drifting back into non-league football with Birmingham League sides, Darlaston, Cannock, and Burton Town, but he rejoined Walsall in May 1926. In just under two seasons he made forty League appearances until dropping back into Birmingham League football once again, this time with Stafford Rangers in 1928. Despite this, by the end of the season Beck was back in the Football League with Barrow, where he was appointed club captain. He spent a season at Holker Street, before signing for York City at the

start of their initial season in the Football League. He made his debut in the opening game against Wigan Borough, and went on to be a virtual ever-present throughout the three terms that he spent with the 'Minstermen'. It came as a surprise when he was released at the end of the 1931/32 season, but was quickly snapped up by Wrexham. While at York, Beck had a stick of chewing gum placed in his mouth by a referee! 'He was apparently a rather argumentative player, who would persistently bait the referee, but was effectively quietened by the referee of the New Brighton away game, to whom he had chuntered over every decision'. At Wrexham Harry found the competition for a first team place very intense, with Hugh McMahon his main challenge. After two seasons with Wrexham he left the Racecourse in the close season of 1934 to travel over the water to Ireland, where he attended trials with Ards before signing for Glentoran in October. He was made captain of the Glens helping them lift the Irish Cup in his first and only season against Larne. In July 1935 he joined Birmingham League side, Dudley Town.

Season	League		F.A.Cup		Welsh Cup		N.S.C.		Total	
	apps	gls	apps	gls	apps	gls	apps	gls	apps	gls
1932/33	19	2	-	-	3	0	-	-	22	2
1933/34	11	0	1	0	-	-	1	0	13	0
	30	**2**	**1**	**0**	**3**	**0**	**1**	**0**	**35**	**2**

BEESLEY, Eric

1957 - 1959

Position; *Centre-Half*
D.O.B; *4th June, 1933*
Birthplace; *Wigan, Lancashire*
Height; *5ft 9in* ***Weight;*** *11st 6lbs*
Debut v. *Caernarvon Town (h) 28th January, 1959 (Welsh Cup)*
Total Appearances & Goals; *1 app 0 gls*
Career; *Wigan Technical College; Stubshaw Cross 1952; Corby Town; Crompton Recs; WREXHAM (Amateur) March 1957 (Pro) 9th May 1957; Skelmersdale Town cs1959;*
Honours; *Cheshire League Challenge Cup Winner;*

Eric Beesley was a centre-half with Wrexham, where his lack of first team football had mainly been due to the consistency of the club's regular centre-half, Alan Fox. Eric's father, Ernie, was an amateur with Portsmouth before World War Two, and would probably have turned professional had it not been for the War. As for Eric, he played football for his school teams in his native Wigan, and continued to play after he left. He was appearing for Wigan Technical College when signing for Lancashire Combination Second Division side Stubshaw Cross in 1952. However, his time was disrupted by being called up for his National Service, serving with the Royal Air Force mainly at R.A.F.Luffenham in Rutland, where he captained his station team. While here Eric signed for Corby Town, who played in the Midland League and managed a few games before his National Service was completed. He then returned home and began playing football for Crompton Recs in the Lancashire Combination League, which led to him signing for Wrexham at the age of 24, initially as an amateur in March 1957, having been recommended by a Wrexham supporter living in that area who had seen him playing for Recs. Eric played several Cheshire League matches for Wrexham reserves before signing professional terms in May 1957. He played second team football in the Cheshire League for almost two years before he was given his first team opportunity, in a Welsh Cup match against Caernarfon Town on the Racecourse in January 1959, which Wrexham won comfortably, 5-0. Eric appeared at centre-half instead of Alan Fox and was the only game that Fox missed throughout that campaign. Eric Beesley never made a

Football League appearance for Wrexham, and at the end of the season was released, but did win a Cheshire League Challenge Cup winners' medal playing for the reserve team. After leaving Wrexham he signed for Skemersdale Town, turning down two offers from Cheshire League sides Rhyl and Bangor City. However, after playing just five games for 'Skem' he tore a knee cartilage, which put an end to his playing career. After his playing days were over, Eric worked for British Aerospace as a Toolmaker, but for the past thirty years was employed with a plastics company in various middle management roles before retiring in June 1998. He still lives in his native Wigan.

Season	League		F.A.Cup		Welsh Cup		Total	
	apps	gls	apps	gls	apps	gls	apps	gls
1957/58	-	-	-	-	1	0	1	0
	-	-	-	-	**1**	**0**	**1**	**0**

BEEVER, Alfred

1925 - 1926

Position; *Wing-Half*
D.O.B; *7th September, 1899*
Birthplace; *Birley Carr, Sheffield, Yorkshire*
Died; *Sheffield, 5th October, 1982.*
Height; *5ft 10in* ***Weight;*** *11st 9lbs*
Debut v. *Southport (h) 29th August, 1925*
Total Appearances & Goals; *42 apps 1 gls*
Career; *Grenside FC; Sheffield United Feb 1923 0apps; Mid-Rhondda 23rd July 1924; WREXHAM 5th May 1925; Aberdare Athletic 4th May 1926 31apps 3gls; WREXHAM 5th May 1927; Merthyr Town 31st Jul 1928 8apps 0gls; Scunthorpe & Lindsey United Nov 1929;*
Honours; *Welsh League representative cap 1924/25;*

Alf Beever was brought up in the industrial City of Sheffield, where he took up playing football. While he was playing for local side Grenside FC he was spotted and signed by Sheffield United, eventually turning professional in February 1923. Alf never actually made a first team appearance for the 'Blades', and in the close season of 1924 was allowed to leave. He then signed for the South Wales side Mid-Rhondda, for one season, during which he made a representative appearance for the Welsh League against the Irish League. Due to this inter-league cap and his club form he attracted the attention of League sides, and Wrexham manager Charlie Hewitt signed him in the summer of 1925. Beever made his Football League debut at wing-half in a 3-2 home win over Southport in the opening match of the 1925/26 season. He played in the wing-half position regularly throughout the season, and it came as a surprise when he was allowed to move back to South Wales to join Third Division South side Aberdare Athletic at the end of the campaign. Alf spent one season down South before he made the return trip to North Wales and was re-signed by Wrexham in May 1927. Unfortunately, he never made the same impact the second time around, having just three outings, two of which were at left-back. This was mainly due to the consistent form of Robert Graham and Ted Regan. At the end of the season Alf was released by Wrexham, and returned once again to South Wales where he joined Third Division South side, Merthyr Town. Beever later played for Scunthorpe & Lindsey United in the Midland League. His brother, Lewis, also played League football for Rotherham United.

Season	League		F.A.Cup		Welsh Cup		Total	
	apps	gls	apps	gls	apps	gls	apps	gls
1925/26	35	1	1	0	3	0	39	1
1927/28	3	0	-	-	-	-	3	0
	38	1	1	0	3	0	42	1

BEIGHTON, Graham

1966 - 1967

Position; *Goalkeeper*
D.O.B; *1st July, 1939*
Birthplace; *Sheffield, Yorkshire*
Height; *5ft 10in* ***Weight;*** *11st 0lbs*
Debut v. *Barnsley (h) 8th January, 1966*
Total Appearances & Goals; *24 apps 0 gls*
Career; *Sheffield Wednesday Mar 1959 0apps; Stockport County Jun 1961 137apps 0gls; WREXHAM 7th Jan 1966; Barnsley Oct 1967 0apps;*

Graham Beighton played football for his School XI at Burngreave Secondary Modern until he left at 15. Graham immediately joined the groundstaff at Sheffield Wednesday, where he progressed to sign professional in March 1959. Without making a first team appearance at Hillsborough he signed for Stockport County in the close season of 1961, making his Football League debut at Hartlepool United in a 2-2 draw in September in place of regular 'keeper, Harry Lea. The following month Graham took over in goal from Lea on a regular basis, becoming the club's first choice 'keeper over the next four seasons. A solid and dependable stopper, he was unfortunate in that his period with County

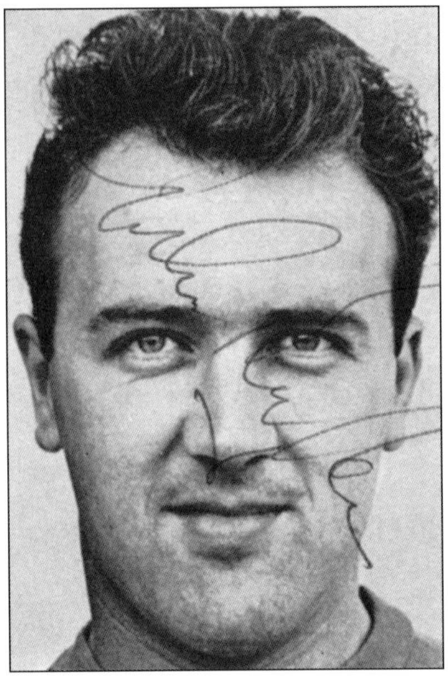

coincided with their worst ever spell as they hovered around the re-election zone. He lost his place in the County side to a young Ken Mulhearn, before he was signed by the new Wrexham manager Jack Rowley, in a part-exchange deal that involved Steve Fleet moving in the opposite direction during January 1966. In only his second match for Wrexham he returned to Edgeley Park, where Wrexham triumphed 4-2 over his former club. Beighton went on to play in every match up to the end of that season, but it ended in disappointment as the club finished 92nd in the Football League for the first time in the club's history, forcing them to apply for re-election. With the club re-elected, the following season saw him out of favour, as new signing Jonny Schofield took over the number one spot. Graham continued to play in the Cheshire League side up until October 1967, when he was allowed to leave the Racecourse and join Barnsley. He never actually made a first team appearance during his time at Oakwell, and at the end of the season dropped out of League football, still only 28 years-old.

Season	League		F.A.Cup		Welsh Cup		Total	
	apps	gls	apps	gls	apps	gls	apps	gls
1965/66	23	0	-	-	1	0	24	0
	23	**0**	**-**	**-**	**1**	**0**	**24**	**0**

BELL, Gordon
1929 - 1930

Position; *Outside Left*
D.O.B; *9th January, 1906.*
Birthplace; *Sunderland, Tyne & Wear*
Died; *Sunderland, A/M/J 1979*
Height; *5ft 8in* ***Weight;*** *10st 10lbs*
Debut v. *Chesterfield (h) 23rd November, 1929*
Total Appearances & Goals; *30 apps 7 gls*
Career; *Newcastle United Swifts; Chilton Colliery; Sunderland Jun 1922; Darlington Jun 1922; Durham City Sept 1925; Carlisle United Aug 1927; Leeds United Jun 1928; WREXHAM 21st Nov 1929; Swansea Town 23rd Jun 1930 £100 18apps 6gls; Carlisle United Apr 1931 1app 0gls; Consett Jan 1934;*
Honours; *England Schoolboy International;*

Gordon Bell showed plenty of early promise at school, turning out for Sunderland boys, and after impressing as captain of North and South Durham at County level was selected to represent England as a schoolboy on two occasions, against Scotland and Wales, in 1920. After leaving education he was signed by Newcastle United and played for their junior side, the 'Swifts', but nothing came of his time at St.James' Park and he returned home to play for Chilton Colliery. Not long after his local side, Sunderland, signed him on amateur forms, though this also was unproductive, and he joined Darlington the same month. In September 1925 Bell was signed by fellow Third Division North side Durham City, before joining North-Eastern League side, Carlisle United, who he helped to gain election to the Football League, at the expense of his former club at Durham. Gordon never actually got the chance to play in Carlisle's inaugural season in the Football League as he was signed by Leeds United in the summer, where he went on to spend just over one season. In November 1929 he was signed by Wrexham, after new manager Jack Baynes had spotted Gordon playing for Leeds United reserves in a Central League match against Everton. He made his League debut against Chesterfield in a 1-1 home draw when taking over from George Wynne. Bell went on to become the club's regular outside-left, providing the ammunition for prolific scorer Tommy Bamford, until the end of the 1929/30 season, when he was surprisingly allowed to join Swansea Town for a £100 fee. Gordon remained at the Vetch for a season, scoring six goals in eighteen League matches until released. He then returned North to rejoin Carlisle United in April 1931. He made just one League appearance during the 1931/32 season, in a 1-1 home draw with York City, before being released in April 1932.

Season	League		F.A.Cup		Welsh Cup		Total	
	apps	gls	apps	gls	apps	gls	apps	gls
1929/30	24	7	4	0	2	0	30	7
	24	**7**	**4**	**0**	**2**	**0**	**30**	**7**

BELLAMY, Ernest William
1937 - 1939

Position; *Left-Back*
D.O.B; *O/N/D 1912*
Birthplace; *Creswell, Derbyshire*
Height; *5ft 10in Weight; 12st 7lbs*
Debut v. *Lincoln City (h) 1st September, 1937*
Total Appearances & Goals; *104 apps 0 gls*
Career; *Creswell FC; Bristol City May 1934 0apps; Grimsby Town 0apps; WREXHAM 17th Jul 1936; Left club cs1939, WREXHAM Aug 1940 (WW2) 29apps 0gls;*

Bill Bellamy was signed from Grimsby Town in the close season of 1936. He never actually made a first team appearance for the 'Mariners' during his time at Blundell Park, and it was much the same at Wrexham. He spent his first season at The Racecourse playing for the club's reserves in the Birmingham & District League, but that was to change the following season when manager Captain James Logan plunged Bill, along with four other young debutants, into only the second match of the 1937/38 season at home to Lincoln City. It paid off with Wrexham winning 1-0. Bellamy then became the club's regular left-back for the following two seasons before he was allowed to leave the club in the close season of 1939. He served as a sergeant instructor in the Army during WW2, but did return to spend most of the 1940/41 season playing for Wrexham. He made a further nine appearances following that term, turning out for the Racecourse club when the opportunity arose.

Season	League		F.A.Cup		Welsh Cup		N.S.C.		Total	
	apps	gls	apps	gls	apps	gls	apps	gls	apps	gls
1937/38	34	0	1	0	-	-	1	0	36	0
1938/39	34	0	-	-	2	0	3	0	39	0
1940/41	20	0	-	-	-	-	-	-	20	0
1941/42	5	0	-	-	-	-	-	-	5	0
1943/44	4	0	-	-	-	-	-	-	4	0
	97	**0**	**1**	**0**	**2**	**0**	**4**	**0**	**104**	**0**
*F/League	68	0	1	0	2	0	4	0	75	0

BELLETT, Walter Ronald
1962 - 1963

Position; *Left-Back*
D.O.B; *14th November, 1933*
Birthplace; *Stratford, London.*
Height; *5ft 9in* ***Weight;*** *11st 10lbs*
Debut v. *Port Vale (a) 15th December, 1962.*
Total Appearances & Goals; *2 apps 0 gls*
Career; *Grays Athletic; Chelmsford City Feb 1954; Barking Town Mar 1954; Chelsea Sept 1954 35apps 1gls; Plymouth Argyle Dec 1958 (Combined fee of £12,000 with Len Casey) 41 apps 1 gls; Chelmsford City cs1960; Leyton Orient Jan 1961 0 apps; Chester July 1961 12 apps 1 gls; WREXHAM 4th July 1962; Tranmere Rovers Jul 1963 0apps; Gravesend & Northfleet Jun 1964; Canvey Island cs1966;*
Honours; *England Youth International; Third Division Championship Winner 1959; Combination League Championship Winner;*

A `True` Cockney - Wally Bellett was born within the sound of Bow Bells in East London. He showed tremendous promise as a schoolboy footballer, appearing for the Central Park school team in East Ham, from where he represented Essex schoolboys and Essex Youth. At the age of 15, while still at school, Wally was playing senior football for Grays Athletic, a top non-league side in Essex at that time. From there he was signed on amateur forms by Arsenal, during which time he was selected to play for the England Youth team against Ireland in Cliftonville. Shortly afterwards he was called up for his National Service. He joined the R.A.F., serving a lot of his time in Malaysia, and playing a few games for a local side named Pnang. He returned home in February 1954, and signed for Chelmsford City before completing the season with Barking Town. It was then that Bellet was taken on trial with Chelsea, impressing enough to sign professional in September 1954. For the next eighteen months he

played reserve team football in the Combination League, making his Football League debut in February 1956 in a 2-2 draw at Manchester City. Wally went on to make a further 34 League appearances for Chelsea, scoring one goal. He was described in his Stamford Bridge days as 'Hard tackling, rugged and quick off the mark.' During his time with 'The Pensioners' he also won two Combination League Championship medals' with the second string. In December 1958 he was to leave Stamford Bridge, moving to Plymouth Argyle in a £12,000 deal which also saw Len Casey transferred to Home Park. Bellet made his debut for the 'Pilgrims' in a top of the table clash with Hull City, a 1-1 draw, in front of a 20,000+ crowd at Home Park. Plymouth went on to win the Third Division Championship, but the following season Wally lost his place in the team as Plymouth struggled to get to grips with the higher grade of football. At the end of the term Wally was to leave Home Park, and drifted back into non-league football with Chelmsford City. His contract lasted until January 1960, when it was cancelled to allow him the chance to return to League football with Leyton Orient. However, he did not claim a first team slot with the 'O's and at the end of the season joined Chester, where he spent the 1961/62 season making twelve League appearances. A solidly built full-back, Wally Bellett arrived at the Racecourse from Chester in July 1962 for a three month trial period, with the prospect of having to take over the left back position from the man who had been playing in that position regularly for the past nine seasons -Aly McGowan. Wally got his first team chance in December, when he appeared in just two games, before McGowan returned to the side. In March, McGowan received a long term injury, when he broke his leg, but Wally was overlooked with Reg Holland being preferred. That proved enough for Bellett, and at the end of the season joined Tranmere Rovers, but failed to make a first team appearance. In the close season of 1964 he returned south, and joined Gravesend & Northfleet in the Southern League. Two years later he was on the coaching staff with the Essex club, Canvey Island. He went on to spend almost ten years with the Metropolitan League side and continued to play Sunday football well into his 50s, as well as coaching 10-15 year-olds near Benfleet. After retiring from professional football Wally was employed as a car mechanic, before working as a lorry driver at the King's Holiday Camp on Canvey Island, where he has settled.

Season	League apps	gls	F.A.Cup apps	gls	Welsh Cup apps	gls	League Cup apps	gls	Total apps	gls
1962/63	2	0	-	-	-	-	-	-	2	0
	2	**0**	**-**	**-**	**-**	**-**	**-**	**-**	**2**	**0**

BELLIS, George Alfred 1927 - 1929

Position; *Centre-Half*
D.O.B; *8th June, 1904*
Birthplace; *Kirkee (Khadki), India*
Died; *Seaforth, Liverpool, 6th January, 1969*
Height; *6ft 0'1/2in* ***Weight;*** *12st 5lbs*
Debut v. *Chesterfield (a) 27th August, 1927*
Total Appearances & Goals; *92 apps 5 gls*
Career; *Waterloo; LMS Railway United (Formby); Seaforth Fellowship; Southport (Am) 23rd Aug 1923, (Pro) 28th Aug 1924 41apps 4gls; WREXHAM 21st May 1927 £150; Wolves 1st Jun 1929 £600 42apps 0gls; Burnley 1st Dec 1932 86apps 0gls; Bournemouth June 1935 56apps 0gls; Wellington Town May 1937 to May 1939; Tranmere Rovers (WW2 Guest) 1939/40 7apps 0gls;*
Honours; *Second Division Championship Winner 1932.*

George Bellis was born in India, where his father was a Company Sergeant-Major in the Royal Engineers. From the age of 9 George lived in Waterloo, where he spent much of his early football years playing for his school team (St.John's) and in the local leagues around Liverpool for Waterloo, LMS Railway United (Formby) and Seaforth Fellowship. At the age of 19 he was given his first opportunity of League football when he signed amateur forms with Southport after applying for a trial. In the summer of 1924 George signed professional with Southport, and made his Football League debut in a 5-1 defeat at Accrington in November 1924. He went on to make 41 League appearances with Southport before signing for Wrexham in May 1927 for £150. It was with the Racecourse club that his career really took off, as he established himself as a strong tackling centre-half, becoming a great personal friend of fellow 'Robin' Ted Read. In his first season he helped Wrexham to reach the F.A.Cup fourth round, the farthest the club had progressed since they first entered the competition in 1883, before Birmingham won 3-1 at the Racecourse against a spirited Wrexham side. After being a virtual ever present at centre-half for two seasons with Wrexham (he had missed just two games), George came to the notice of Second Division side Wolves, who splashed out £600 for him. He spent two and a half seasons at Molineux, playing in the side that clinched promotion back to Division One. In December 1932 he joined Burnley, and was appointed club captain. His stay at Turf Moor saw him make 86 league appearances, including a change of position to full back. It was whilst he was still playing at full back that he was transferred to Bournemouth, in June 1935, at the age of 31. With the South coast club he made a further 56 league appearances before being released in the summer of 1937. George then joined Birmingham and District League side Wellington Town until the Second World War ended his football career, although he did appear as a 'guest' for Tranmere Rovers. George was described as a 'big and powerful fellow, who scarcely knew his own strength.' and 'a canny player of the third back type. Few could get the better of him.' In 1941 Bellis was employed at Napiers (English Electric), where he stayed until he retired. However, six days after his retirement George collapsed and died, on 6th January 1969.

Season	League apps	gls	F.A.Cup apps	gls	Welsh Cup apps	gls	Total apps	gls
1927/28	40	4	5	0	3	0	48	4
1928/29	42	1	1	0	1	0	44	1
	82	**5**	**6**	**0**	**4**	**0**	**9**	**5**

BELLIS, Thomas Gilbert 1938 - 1950

Position; *Half-Back*
D.O.B; *21st April, 1919*
Birthplace; *Mold, Flintshire*
Height; *5ft 8in* ***Weight;*** *10st 7lbs*
Debut v. *Hartlepool United (h) 29th August 1938*
Total Appearances & Goals; *103 apps 1 gls*
Career; *Buckley Town; WREXHAM 14th May 1938, WW2 70apps 1gls; Colwyn Bay 13th Jul 1949; Holywell Town 28th Jul 1951; Caernarfon Town 18th Sept 1952; Mold Alex 19th Aug 1955;*
Honours; *North Wales Coast FA Amateur Cup Winner 1937;*

'Gib' Bellis was playing for Welsh National League side Buckley Town, when taken on trial by Bolton Wanderers at the age of 18. However, when they came to offer him a contract Wrexham stepped in and offered him the same terms, meaning he could continue to work on his father's farm and milk round in his native Mold. It was with this in mind that 'Gib' chose Wrexham. He made his League debut in only the second game of the 1938/39 season in a 3-0 home win over Hartlepool United. He went on to make a further 13 appearances in the first team that season, while the following term saw him play in the second match of the season before the Football League was suspended due to a certain Austrian corporal! 'Gib' continued to play football, but managed only six games up to the 1944/45 season due to a bad knee injury. In the two seasons prior to the resumption of League football he was a virtual ever-present in the Wrexham side, playing against the likes of the two Manchester clubs, Liverpool, and Everton in the regional Leagues. After WW2 had ended 'Gib' was one of only three pre war Wrexham players to continue playing. In the 1947/48 season he missed only one match in a side that finished third in the League, the best position the club had achieved since finishing runners-up in 1933. In the close season of 1948 Bellis captained the Wrexham team that went on tour to Germany, playing three matches against British Army teams in Celle, Hanover, and Rothesan, with 'The Robins' winning all three games. The following season 'Gib' sustained another injury to his knee in a home game with Accrington Stanley in February, and after recovering found his first team chances

limited. He continued to battle for a first team place by playing for the reserves in the Cheshire League. However, in July 1949 he accepted the chance to become player/manager at Colwyn Bay, as well as working at the Smitt Diamond factory, which jointly were to match his wages at Wrexham. He spent two seasons with Colwyn Bay before joining Holywell Town, for one campaign later moving on to Mold Alex for a term where he eventually hung up his boots. After his playing days were over he worked for MANWEB, followed by employment at John Summers Steelworks for 16 years until retirement. 'Gib' was still residing in his native Town of Mold in 1998. A popular figure at the Racecourse and always known for the large amount of bandages strapped around his legs.

Season	League		F.A.Cup		Welsh Cup		Total	
	apps	gls	apps	gls	apps	gls	apps	gls
1938/39	14	0	-	-	-	-	14	0
1939/40	-	-	-	-	1	0	1	0
1946/47	15	1	-	-	-	-	15	1
1947/48	41	0	2	0	3	0	46	0
1948/49	25	0	-	-	2	0	27	0
	95	1	2	0	6	0	103	1

BENNETT, Edward Thomas — 1925 - 1926

Position; *Right/Left Back*
D.O.B; *10th August, 1904*
Birthplace; *Barton Regis, Bristol, Avon*
Died; *Southmead Hospital, Bristol 1957*
Height; *5ft 8in* ***Weight;*** *11st 6lbs*
Debut v. *Wigan Borough (h) 16th September, 1925*
Total Appearances & Goals; *41 apps 0 gls*
Career; *Bristol City 0apps; Swansea Town 30th March 1923 11apps 0gls; WREXHAM 6th May, 1925; Manchester City 4th May 1926 19apps 0gls; Norwich City 10th May 1929 11apps 0gls to May 1931;*
Honours; *North Wales Coast F.A.Challenge Cup runner-up 1926;*

Ted Bennett was spotted playing local football in his native Bristol by Bristol City. However, Ted failed to make an impact with 'The Robins' and was allowed to join Swansea Town in March 1923. Playing at right-back he made his Football League debut with the 'Swans' and enjoyed a total of eleven League appearances in his two seasons at the Vetch. At the end of the 1924/25 season he was allowed to move North and join Wrexham. Bennett made his debut at right-back, in place of the injured Alf Jones, in a 1-0 home win over Wigan Borough. Ted then went on to keep his place in the side for the rest of the season, playing in either full-back berths. His form must have impressed the watching scouts, because at the end of the season he was signed by Second Division side Manchester City. At Maine Road he made his League debut at left-back in October 1926, at Port Vale in a game City won 2-0. Ted had a run of twelve games for City before returning to the reserve team. The following season saw him make five more League appearances as City went on to win the second Division Championship. Bennett, became disenchanted with his limited first team opportunities, as he made just two appearances for City in their return to the top flight, and at the end of 1928/29 agreed to join Third Division South side Norwich City. He fared little better at Carrow Road as they were well blessed with full-backs at the time, and made just eleven League appearances for the 'Canaries' in two seasons. Ted later returned to live in Bristol where he worked as a Barman, which was followed by becoming a licensee of his own Public House. He was later employed as a Council Worker.

Season	League		F.A.Cup		Welsh Cup		Total	
	apps	gls	apps	gls	apps	gls	apps	gls
1925/26	37	0	1	0	3	0	41	0
	37	0	1	0	3	0	41	0

BENNETT, Gary Michael — 1992 - 1995 & 1997

Position; *Forward*
D.O.B; *20th September, 1963*
Birthplace; *Liverpool, Merseyside*
Height; *5ft 11in* ***Weight;*** *12st 0lbs*
Debut v. *York City (a) 29th August, 1992*
Total Appearances & Goals; *175/2 apps 114 gls*
Career; *Skelmersdale United; Kirkby Town; Wigan Athletic 9th Oct 1984 10/10apps 3gls; Chester City 22nd Aug 1985 109/17apps 36gls; Southend United 11th Nov 1988 £25,000 36/6apps 6gls; Chester City 1st Mar 1990 £20,000 71/9apps 15gls; WREXHAM 12th Aug 1992; Tranmere Rovers 10th Jul 1995 £300,000 26/3apps 9gls; Preston North End 27th Mar 1996 £200,000 5/3apps 1gls; WREXHAM 28th Feb 1997 £100,000; Chester City 11th Jul 1997 £50,000 42/6apps 13gls;*
Honours; *Fourth Division runner-up 1986; Third Division runner-up 1993; Freight Rover Trophy Winner 1985; Welsh Cup Winner 1995; PFA Second Division team 1995;*

The greatest goalscorer Wrexham have enjoyed since the legendary Tommy Bamford - and what a bargain! Gary's goalscoring exploits for Wrexham will be remembered in the same vein as those of the great Bamford, but his football career was not always a bed of roses. Liverpudlian Gary's football education began in Kirkby, before he went on to play as an amateur for Skelmersdale United, making his living working as a cloth-cutter in a factory that manufactured shirts. He was spotted playing in the Preston League for Kirkby by a Wigan Athletic scout and, after a trial period, was signed by Wigan manager Harry McNally, initially as a part-timer. He made his Football League debut for Wigan as a substitute in a 1-1 draw at Cambridge in October 1984. With the 'Latics' Gary went on to have considerable success as he helped them to Wembley, in the Freight Rover Trophy final, which led to him taking the plunge to sign full-time. Harry McNally, who had left Wigan, persuaded him to join Chester in August 1985. He spent three seasons at Sealand Road, becoming a firm favourite with their fans who christened him 'Psycho' after his no-nonsense style of play. Chester finished Fourth Division runners-up in 1986, but in November 1988 was signed by Third Division Southend United for £25,000. His first season with the Essex club ended in relegation, but they made a quick return the following year, although they clinched promotion without the services of Gary who had rejoined Chester in March for £20,000. His second spell with the Cestrians lasted just over two seasons before he was surprisingly released at the end of 1991/92. Wrexham manager Brian Flynn stepped

in to sign Bennett on a free transfer, and was not initially the most popular of signings at the time because of his Chester connections. However, Flynn played him as an out and out striker, going on to win over the fans by doing what he did naturally......... scoring goals! His ever dangerous direct style of play made things happen, especially when he was running at defenders and was also a great chaser of lost causes. In his first season Gary's goalscoring exploits helped Wrexham gain promotion to the new Second Division, scoring sixteen of the goals himself. The next two seasons were even better as he continued to improve his goal tally, proving along the way that he could also score goals against the best, such as cup games against Nottingham Forest, and Premier League side's Ipswich Town, and Coventry City. His goalscoring exploits attracted a great deal of interest from other clubs, and after turning down a move to Birmingham City joined Tranmere Rovers in the close season of 1995, equalling the club record fee received (at the time) of £300,000. Not bad for a free transfer signing! However, at Prenton Park Gary found life difficult with goals harder to come by, though to be fair to him he was deployed in a wider role. Nevertheless, he did score nine goals in 29 League games before he was transferred in March 1996, just prior to the transfer deadline, to promotion chasing Division Three side Preston North End. He went on to help them win the Third Division Championship, with one goal in eight League games. The following season Gary struggled with injury, which in turn made him unable to command a regular first team place, and in February, 1997, the Wrexham manager Brian Flynn resigned 'Benno' for a £100,000 fee. He returned prior to the F.A.Cup sixth round match with Chesterfield, but only a place amongst the subs could be found for him, and when he finally came off the bench couldn't find that golden touch to put Wrexham in the semi-finals for the first time in the club's history. He found goals more difficult to come by the second time around, and in the close season he was allowed to move on, rejoining Chester City for the third time for a £50,000 fee. Gary Bennett's goalscoring feats for Wrexham Football Club will never be forgotten.

Season	League		F.A.Cup		Welsh Cup		League Cup		Auto Tro.		Total	
	apps	gls	apps	gls	apps	gls	apps	gls	apps	gls	apps	gls
1992/93	34/1	16	1	1	4	2	1	2	3	2	43/1	23
1993/94	41	32	2	0	2	3	4	3	2	1	51	39
1994/95	45	29	4	2	8	8	4	2	4	6	65	47
1996/97	16	5	0/1	0	-	-	-	-	-	-	16/1	5
	136/1	**82**	**7/1**	**3**	**14**	**13**	**9**	**7**	**9**	**9**	**175/2**	**114**

BENNETT, Terence Randolph

1959 - 1961

Position; *Goalkeeper*
D.O.B; *15th July, 1940*
Birthplace; *Shrewsbury, Shropshire*
Height; *ft in* **Weight;** *st lbs*
Debut v. *Bangor City (a) 22nd March, 1961 (Welsh Cup)*
Total Appearances & Goals; *1 app 0 gls*
Career; *WREXHAM Sept 1960; Stafford Rangers Nov 1961; Welshpool cs1963;*
Honours; *Welsh Amateur Cup runner-up 1966 & 1968;Staffordshire Senior Cup Winner;*

Terry Bennett was the son of former Shrewsbury Town goalkeeper, Sid Bennett, so it was a natural progress for Terry to follow in his father's footsteps and become a custodian. This was despite attending the Rugby only Priory school in Shrewsbury. To overcome this Terry would play football for a local side, Rolls Royce reserves at 15. He then progressed into the first team, who competed in the Shropshire County League, soon attracting the scouts of Football League clubs. However, he opted to continue with his education and went to London, attending the Kings College University to take a degree in Civil Engineering. While there he played football for the College team, and also for the London Universities side, which at that time was coached by a certain Jimmy Hill who was playing for Fulham at the time. Terry had a trial at Craven Cottage, as well as with West Ham and Luton Town. His goalkeeping earned him a call up to the England Youth squad that included Terry Venables and Gordon West, but his chance to play never came as on arrival at Lilleshall, he was told that there had been a mix up and that he was too old! Bennett still harboured hopes of playing professional football, and wrote to Wrexham for a trial towards the end of his second year at University. Terry was then invited to play for the Wrexham 'A' team, followed by a reserve team match in the Cheshire League against Bangor City. He then played in a couple more matches before returning to University, with the offer of appearing for Wrexham during his breaks from college. By January 1961, Wrexham manager Billy Morris invited him to sign professional, but he turned the offer down to concentrate on his exams. Billy Morris said, 'The faired haired 'keeper has a great future in the game.' Two months after turning down the offer, Terry was called upon to step into the first team in place of Arthur Johnson for a Welsh Cup semi-final match against Bangor City at Farrar Road. Wrexham embarrassingly lost 3-0, but he was exonerated from any blame, as the newspaper report pointed out after the match, 'What a nerve-wracking debut it was for Terry, but he had no chance with any of the goals, and in fact saved Wrexham from a much heavier defeat with some brilliant saves.' Once his exams were completed Terry signed amateur forms at the beginning of the 1961/62 season, while taking up work with a Manchester based firm of consultant engineers. He never made another first team appearance for Wrexham, as Kevin Keelan had been signed in the mean time, and in November 1961 signed for Cheshire League side Stafford Rangers. He went on to spend almost two years with Stafford winning a Staffordshire Senior Cup winners' medal, before joining Welshpool in the close season of 1963. Bennett spent the rest of his playing career with Welshpool, winning many honours, including the Mid Wales League Championship and twice reaching the final of the Welsh Amateur Cup. Terry finished playing football in 1970, although he continued to play cricket for a number of years, having also played for Shropshire at Minor Counties level. He still works in the building trade, running his own family business in Baschurch near Shrewsbury.

Season	League		F.A.Cup		Welsh Cup		Total	
	apps	gls	apps	gls	apps	gls	apps	gls
1960/61	-	-	-	-	1	0	1	0
	-	**-**	**-**	**-**	**1**	**0**	**1**	**0**

BENNION, Stanley

1955 - 1963

Position; *Forward*
D.O.B; *9th February, 1938*
Birthplace; *Blacon, Chester, Cheshire*
Height; *5ft 7in* **Weight;** *10st 10lbs*
Debut v. *Swindon Town (h) 30th September, 1959*
Total Appearances & Goals; *64 apps 20 gls*
Career; *Saughall; WREXHAM (Am) 26th Jan 1955; Saltney Juniors cs1955; WREXHAM (Am) Oct 1958, (Pro) 5th Oct 1959; Halifax Town May 1963; Chester 8th Jun 1963 19apps 3gls; New Brighton cs1965; Rhyl 21st Aug 1969; Hoole 16th Apr 1973; Cheshire NALGO 1978/79; Cestrian Alex 1984/85;*
Honours; *Welsh Youth Cup Winner 1956; Cheshire League Championship Winner 1972; Welsh Amateur Cup Winner 1973; Cheshire League Cup Winner 1971;*

Although born and bred in Chester it was Wrexham who signed Stan Bennion as a youngster. He first played football at Chester Grammar School, but missed out on any representative honours as they wouldn't allow their pupils to play for anyone apart from the school. Upon leaving Stan began working as a site clerk for a local contracting firm, though he continued to play football for Saughall in the local league. It was whilst with them that he was spotted by a former Wrexham player, who was scouting for the club, Ted Regan, and he recommended Stan to manager Peter Jackson. Bennion was first signed by Wrexham on amateur terms, and began playing for Wrexham's team in the Welsh National League. The following season he was loaned out to Saltney Juniors, where he won a Welsh Youth Cup winners' medal. The 1956/57 season saw Stan allowed to leave the Racecourse to join Saltney permanently, before he was called up for his National Service in the Army, serving in Wiltshire and in Cyprus. Despite this, Stan still managed to continue playing football in regimental matches. On leaving the Army, he returned to play football for Saltney Juniors, but by October had re-signed for Wrexham on a part-time professional basis whilst continuing with his job as a clerk for Chester City Council. With Wrexham Stan progressed through the Cheshire League side to making his first team debut at the beginning of the 1959/60 season against Swindon Town, in a match that saw the switching on of the floodlights at the Racecourse for the very first time. Stan scored the Wrexham goal in a 2-1 defeat, and he went on to become a regular in the side up until March. During his time at Wrexham he was described as able to play in 'any forward position with credit'. His form during his time with the club was described as 'inconsistent', as he regularly found himself in and out of the team for either injury or loss of form. His best spell came at the start of the 1961/62 promotion season, when he scored 15 goals in 28 League matches, but again lost his place

towards the end of the season when Tommy Anderson was signed. Stan's most memorable match in his time at the Racecourse must have been the record 10-1 win over Hartlepool, in which three hat-tricks were scored with Stan scoring the odd goal! The 1962/63 season proved to be his last at Wrexham, as he was released in the summer, but was quickly snapped up by Halifax Town. However, his contract was soon cancelled because the Shay club would not pay any wages until the new season started! Bennion then signed for Chester a couple of weeks later, spending two seasons at Sealand Road, making just nineteen League appearances and scoring three goals. He left in the close season of 1965 to join Cheshire League side New Brighton, where he spent five seasons, leaving in 1970 when the club offered all the players just £1.00 contracts! He joined Rhyl, winning more honours, before going on to play for Hoole, Cheshire NALGO and Cestrian Alex. Stan, who is now in his sixties, was still playing local football in Chester, where he lives at the time of writing.

Season	League		F.A.Cup		Welsh Cup		League Cup		Total	
	apps	gls	apps	gls	apps	gls	apps	gls	apps	gls
1959/60	20	3	3	1	1	0	-	-	24	4
1960/61	4	0	-	-	-	-	-	-	4	0
1961/62	28	15	3	1	1	0	1	0	33	16
1962/63	3	0	-	-	-	-	-	-	3	0
	55	**18**	**6**	**2**	**2**	**0**	**1**	**0**	**64**	**20**

BENT, Graham William

1963 - 1965

Position; *Inside-Forward*
D.O.B; *6th October, 1945*
Birthplace; *Ruabon, nr.Wrexham, Denbighshire*
Height; *5ft 11ins* **Weight;** *11st 0lbs*
Debut v. *Coventry City (a) 12th October, 1963*
Total Appearances & Goals; *12 apps 2 gls*
Career; *Aston Villa April 1961; WREXHAM (Am) 6th July 1963, (Pro) 3rd Dec 1963; Rhyl; Hereford Town; Dudley Town 1965; Nuneaton Borough; Tamworth; Hednesford Town; Atherstone;*
Honours; *Welsh Amateur International; Welsh Schoolboy international;*

Graham Bent was educated at Llay Junior and Secondary Modern Schools and then at Grove Park School in Wrexham. At a very early age he showed plenty of ability at football, playing for his School XI's. During the 1960/61 season he was a prolific goalscorer in the Wrexham and District Schoolboys team, from where he went on to gain recognition with the Welsh Schoolboy international team against both England, at Swansea, and Scotland, at Kilmarnock. He missed the return match with England, which was played at Wembley, because of a broken leg he received while playing in the local Schools' Cup final on his last day of school! It was with his leg still in plaster, that he joined Aston Villa as an apprentice in April 1961, at the age of fifteen, despite having the opportunity to join Wrexham. With Aston Villa he managed only a few matches the following season because of the broken leg taking its time to mend. The 1962/63 season saw Graham play regularly in the 'Villa' Central League side at inside-right; however, he never really settled in the Midlands, and at the end of the season left Villa Park. At the start of 1963/64, Graham joined Wrexham for a trial period, and in December manager Ken Barnes signed him on a permanent basis. By that time he had already made his Football League debut against Jimmy Hill's, Coventry City side at Highfield Road, in a 3-0 defeat, when replacing the injured Clive Colbridge. Bent went on to make a further ten first team appearances for Wrexham that season, though the following season was to be one of disappointment. He figured in just one League game, and at the end of the season Wrexham's new manager, Billy Morris, released him, and he never played in the Football League again. During the summer period he returned to the Birmingham area from where his wife originated and signed for Birmingham League side, Dudley Town. He then went on to enjoy a prolonged career with several Midlands clubs including Hereford Town, Nuneaton Borough, Tamworth and Atherstone with whom he retired from playing in 1986 with knee trouble. He has since managed a number of local sides in the Atherstone area including Manor FC (Nuneaton) who he led to victory in the West Midlands Vase. On finishing with full time professional football, Graham started up his own engraving/sign making business in Coventry which he is still doing at present, having now settled in the Atherstone area, where he also coaches youngsters on Saturday mornings.

Season	League		F.A.Cup		Welsh Cup		Leagu Cup		Total	
	apps	gls	apps	gls	apps	gls	apps	gls	apps	gls
1963/64	9	2	2	0	-	-	-	-	11	2
1964/65	1	0	-	-	-	-	-	-	1	0
	10	**2**	**2**	**0**	-	-	-	-	**12**	**2**

BERMINGHAM, Alan

1967 - 1971

Position; *Left-Back*
D.O.B; *11th September, 1944*
Birthplace; *Liverpool, Merseyside*
Height; *5ft 9in* **Weight;** *11st 4lbs*
Debut v. *Brentford (h) 2nd October, 1967*
Total Appearances & Goals; *134/2 apps 2 gls*
Career; *Everton cs1960; Skelmersdale United; WREXHAM 29th May 1967; Durban City (South Africa) 4th Jun 1971; Enfield 1975/76; Bangor City 22nd May 1976; Buckley United; Conwy United;*
Honours; *Four England Schoolboy international caps; Division Four runner-up 1970;*

Alan Bermingham played his early football at Warbreck Secondary School and Evered Avenue High School in his native city of Liverpool. As well as playing for his school teams, Alan was also selected to play for both Liverpool and Lancashire schoolboys, appearing in the same side as former Liverpool player Chris Lawler. He was then picked to play for England schoolboys against Wales, Scotland, Ireland, and West Germany, although it wasn't just football at which he excelled at the time. During the summer months he played cricket, again representing England schoolboys and, also played at the home of cricket, Lord's, for the England Grammar Schools' team. He even spent one summer, when 17, on the groundstaff of Lancashire. However, it was football upon which Alan had set his mind by this time, having been on Everton's books as a schoolboy since he was 14. After leaving school he joined the groundstaff at Goodison Park, while still remaining in full-time education. Playing in midfield, Bermingham helped Everton beat Manchester United 2-0 in the Lancashire Youth Cup final. He made his way through the ranks with Everton, playing for the 'A' team, and now and again for the reserves, but became disillusioned with not making further progress and left Goodison to take up a teachers' training course in Prescot. He continued to play football for Skelmersdale United, and had a trial with Sheffield Wednesday around this time, and although he signed amateur forms them nothing actually came of it. He finished his teaching course and continued to play for 'Skem' in the Lancashire Combination League. Wrexham manager, Ken Barnes, then invited him along to the Racecourse for a trial during the 1964/65 season, though again there were no developments. He continued with Skelmersdale, and helped them reach Wembley in 1967 in the final of the F.A.Amateur Cup where they met Enfield. With the score at 0-0 Skelmersdale were awarded a penalty. Alan stepped up to take it... and missed! It was his biggest disappointment in football as, in the replay at Maine Road, Enfield won 3-0. During the close season of 1967, Wrexham manager Alvan Williams signed

the now 23 year-old. Although he was now playing at left-back he made his Football League debut at right-back, in place of Steve Ingle in a 2-1 defeat at Brentford in October 1967. Alan was vying for a place in either full-back position, with Ingle and Steve Stacey, but following Stacey's move to Ipswich the following season went on to make the left-back berth his own for the next two seasons, during which time he helped the club to promotion to the Third Division in 1970, as well as playing at Liverpool in the F.A.Cup, and Manchester United in the League Cup. Alan missed the promotion run-in, due to an Achilles' tendon injury. The following season saw him suffer a recurrence of the Achilles' problem: every time he tried to make a come-back it would flare up again and, when finally fully fit he found new signing Tommy Vansittart was playing well in his position. Not happy with reserve team football Alan decided to leave, and moved to South Africa in June 1971. He spent four and a half years playing for Durban City, who he helped win the League title twice, the Castle Cup once, and the Champions of Champions' Cup twice. Out in South Africa Alan also played cricket for Minor Old Boys, opening the batting with Test player Barry Richards. He returned home in 1976 and played a few games for Enfield in the Southern League, before settling in North Wales and appearing for Bangor City in the Northern Premier League for half a season. Alan then played local football for Buckley United and Conwy United before hanging up his boots. By this time cricket had become Alan's first love, playing for Colwyn Bay as a wicket keeper, although he did help out at Felinheli F.C., where he managed them for a short time. Alan, who still lives in Abergele, now works as a self-employed designer, specialising in Leisure complexes.

Season	League		F.A.Cup		Welsh Cup		Leagu Cup		Total	
	apps	gls	apps	gls	apps	gls	apps	gls	apps	gls
1967/68	32/2	0	-	-	1	0	-	-	33/2	0
1968/69	39	2	2	0	4	0	3	0	48	2
1969/70	40	0	4	0	2	0	4	0	50	0
1970/71	3	0	-	-	-	-	-	-	3	0
	114/2	**2**	**6**	**0**	**7**	**0**	**7**	**0**	**134/2**	**2**

BERTRAM, 1926 - 1927

Position; *Half-Back*
D.O.B;
Birthplace;
Height; *ft in* ***Weight;*** *st lbs*
Debut v. *Llandudno (a) 9th March, 1927 (Welsh Cup)*
Total Appearances & Goals; *1 app 0 gls*
Career; *Carlisle United; Oswestry Town Aug 1926; WREXHAM (Am) March 1927;*

Not much at all is known about our Mr.Bertram, except that he was playing for Oswestry Town during 1926/27 when he was given a chance with Wrexham in March 1927. He turned out at half-back, in place of Robert Graham, in a Welsh Cup match at Llandudno that Wrexham won 4-1 with Billie Rogers scoring all four goals, which proved to be his one and only appearance in a Wrexham shirt. He was described during his time with Oswestry as being 'ex-Carlisle', who would have been a non-league side at that time.

Season	League		F.A.Cup		Welsh Cup		Total	
	apps	gls	apps	gls	apps	gls	apps	gls
1926/27	-	-	-	-	1	0	1	0
	-	**-**	**-**	**-**	**1**	**0**	**1**	**0**

BETTS, Eric 1953 - 1956

Position; *Outside-Left*
D.O.B; *27th July, 1925*
Birthplace; *Coventry, Warwickshire*
Died; *Rochdale, 16th March, 1990*
Height; *5ft 10in* ***Weight;*** *11st 0lbs*
Debut v. *York City (h) 10th October, 1953*
Total Appearances & Goals; *62 apps 23 gls*
Career; *Mansfield Villa; Nottingham Forest Jul (Am) 1943 1app 0gls; Crystal Palace (WW2) Mar 1945 4apps 2gls; Mansfield Villa; Mansfield Town 25th Feb 1946 19apps 5gls; Coventry City 18th Aug 1947 1app; Nuneaton Borough 1948; Walsall 14th May 1949 30apps 3gls; West Ham United 15th April 1950 3apps 1gls; Nuneaton Borough cs1951; Rochdale 13th Oct 1951 52apps 8gls; Crewe Alexandra 12th Feb 1953 25apps 5gls; WREXHAM 9th Oct 1953; Oldham Athletic 23rd Feb 1956 26apps 5gls; Released 30th Jun 1957; Bangor City 8th Jul 1957 to August 1960;*

Eric Betts was a fast moving winger who possessed a hard shot. He enjoyed a nomadic career, totting up 208 Football League appearances, scoring 47 goals, nearly half of which were notched while he was at the Racecourse. Eric had played War-time football, firstly for his local side, Mansfield Villa, and then Nottingham Forest, for whom he had signed as an amateur, followed by a few games for Crystal Palace as a 'guest' player. After WW2 he was quickly snapped up by Mansfield Town in February 1946, and made his Football League debut, in a 1-1 draw at Crystal Palace, in December 1946. In the close season of 1947 Eric was signed by Coventry City, but his first team appearances for the 'Sky Blues' were limited to just one League game, at home to Fulham, in a 5-2 win. It came as no surprise when he was released in the New Year of 1948, and joined non-league side Nuneaton Borough. However, his Football League career was resurrected by joining Walsall in May 1949. Despite making his debut for the 'Saddlers' in a 3-1 home defeat at the hands of Northampton Town he went on to make a good enough impression for Second Division West Ham United to sign him in April 1950. He played in the opening three matches of the 1950/51 season, scoring in a 2-1 home win over Luton Town, but they were to be his only first team games for the 'Hammers', and at the end of the 1950/51 season he was released. Eric then returned to Nuneaton, but it was only for a short spell because in October 1951 he signed for Rochdale, making his debut in a 3-0 defeat at Bradford City. At Spotland Eric remained a first team regular on the left wing until February 1953, when he was transferred to Crewe Alexandra where he made 25 League appearances, scoring five goals. In October 1953 he was on the move again, this time to Wrexham. Eric made his debut in a 1-1 home draw with York City, and the tall winger went on to have the most successful period of his football career. His first season was mostly spent covering for Gordon Richards, but 54/5 finally saw him win a regular first team place. That was

to continue throughout the following campaign when he scored a hat-trick against Bradford City in only the second match, but he was to then receive an injury in the following game, a 3-1 home win over Derby. That kept him out of action, but when recovered he found Gordon Richards to be in fine form. Eric struggled to regain his place in the team, and he made just five more first team appearances before signing for Oldham Athletic for £350 in February 1956. He made his 'Latics' debut in a 2-2 home draw with Chesterfield, but made just one further appearance that season. The next season saw him 'share' the outside-left position with Ron Fawley, as Betts scored five goals in 24 League appearances. At the end of the season Eric left Boundary Park, and drifted back into non-league football with Bangor City helping them to reach the Welsh Cup semi-final in 1960, taking Cardiff City to a replay after a 1-1 draw at Ninian Park in which he scored the Bangor goal.

Season	League		F.A.Cup		Welsh Cup		Total	
	apps	gls	apps	gls	apps	gls	apps	gls
1953/54	13	8	1	0	1	0	15	8
1954/55	32	10	3	2	4	0	39	12
1955/56	8	3	-	-	-	-	8	3
	53	**21**	**4**	**2**	**5**	**0**	**62**	**23**

BEYNON, Edwin Rees 1946 - 1951

Position; *Inside-Forward*
D.O.B; *17th November, 1924*
Birthplace; *Aberdare, Glamorgan*
Height; *5ft 8 1/2in* ***Weight;*** *11st 8lbs*
Debut v. *Rotherham United (a) 3rd May, 1947*
Total Appearances & Goals; *82 apps 26 gls*
Career; *R.A.F.; WREXHAM Jan 1947; Shrewsbury Town 20th Oct 1951 91apps 6gls; Wellington Town cs1955; Bangor City 1st Aug 1957; Llandudno 27th Jul 1959; Holywell Town 18th Sept 1959- to Jan 1960;*
Honours; *Welsh Schoolboy International; North Wales Coast F.A.Cup Winner 1958;*

Eddie Beynon came to the Racecourse via an unusual route, namely Egypt. He had been recommended to the club by a supporter who had seen him playing for the Royal Air Force in Cairo, and this led to manager Tom Williams sending the signing-on forms out to the Middle-East! Before enlisting in the R.A.F. Eddie had played alongside Welsh international Alf Sherwood for Wales Schoolboys, but WW2 had interrupted any thoughts of a football career, like so many others at that time. Eddie had showed his potential while he was playing for the school team in his native Aberdare, where he also represented Aberdare schoolboys. After leaving school he found work in the local coal mines, followed by employment with the Co-op creamery department, before finally enlisting with the R.A.F. in April 1943. Eddie signed for Wrexham in February 1947 following his demobilisation from the services, and turned out to be a very reliable forward during his five year stay at the Racecourse, while his goalscoring creditably averaged a goal every third game. He still holds the record of scoring the fastest ever Wrexham goal, when he scored after just SIX seconds with a thirty five yard shot! Eddie played 18 games in 1947/48, a season which saw Wrexham finish in their highest League position since 1933. During his time at the Racecourse Eddie was often sidelined with niggling injuries, and when back to full fitness, had to wait for his chance of first team football. In October 1951 he was transferred to Shrewsbury Town, in a part-exchange deal that saw Peter Fisher arrive at the Racecourse. Eddie got off to the worst possible start with the 'Shrews', when his injury bogey returned in a pre-season friendly match. He broke his leg! Once recovered Eddie was switched to playing at wing-half, where he went on to make 91 League appearances for the Gay Meadow club, before moving to Wellington Town in the close season of 1955. Beynon spent two seasons with Wellington before he was persuaded by former Wrexham and Wales international Tommy Jones to join Bangor City. With Bangor he won a North Wales Coast F.A.Challenge Cup winners' medal in his first season at Farrar Road. Sadly, the following season saw him struck with an injury problem that was to finally end his playing career. At the end of the 1958/59 season Eddie was rewarded with a Benefit match by Bangor, with Wrexham sending a team to Farrar Road for an entertaining match that ended in a 4-4 draw. He then had two short spells with both Llandudno and Holywell Town before finishing with football. Shortly afterwards he moved to London in 1961 to work, firstly as a Security Officer with the City of London Authority, then as a driving instructor in the St.Pauls area of the Capital, which he continued to do until he retired in 1989. Eddie later returned to settle in his native Aberdare.

Season	League		F.A.Cup		Welsh Cup		Total	
	apps	gls	apps	gls	apps	gls	apps	gls
1946/47	5	2	-	-	1	0	6	2
1947/48	18	7	2	2	1	0	21	9
1948/49	25	9	1	0	2	1	28	10
1949/50	5	1	1	0	-	-	6	1
1950/51	18	3	2	1	-	-	20	4
1951/52	1	0	-	-	-	-	1	0
	72	**22**	**6**	**3**	**4**	**1**	**82**	**26**

BINGHAM, Harold 1927 - 1928

Position; *Outside-Left*
D.O.B; *1903*
Birthplace;
Height; *5ft 9in* ***Weight;*** *11st 7lb*
Debut v. *Lincoln City (h) 3rd December, 1927*
Total Appearances & Goals; *4 apps 0 gls*
Career; *Cardiff City 29th Sept 1923 0apps; Pembroke Dock 4th Sept 1924; Chester Jun 1925; WREXHAM 19th Nov 1927; Caernarvon Athletic 30th Jul 1928 to April 1929; Burton Town Aug 1932;*
Honours; *Cheshire County League Championship Winner 1926 & 1927; North Wales Coast F.A. Representative appearance; Welsh League Representative XI;*

Harold Bingham was playing for Cardiff City's reserve team when he signed for South Wales League side Pembroke Dock. He spent almost a season here before moving North to sign for Chester during the close season of 1925. He went on to spend just over two seasons with Chester, helping them win the Cheshire County League twice, in 1926 and 1927. Playing on the left-wing, Harry's form with Chester had attracted the attention of Football League sides. He was described as an 'impetuous, but hard working enthusiastic player, who caused much merriment among his comrades at Sealand Road with his racy humour' Harry had scored 28 goals in 90 Cheshire League games for Chester. In November 1927 Harry made the step up to the Football League, when he moved over the Border to join Third Division North side Wrexham. He had been signed as cover for the outside-left position which was, at the time, occupied by Gordon Gunson. He made a quick impression, scoring a hat-trick in his first match for Wrexham reserves in a 8-6 win over Holyhead Town. That type of form meant it wasn't long before Harry was to make his first team debut, when he replaced Gordon Gunson in a 1-0 home win over Lincoln City in December 1927. Even so, Harry was to make only two more League appearances for Wrexham, both in the outside-left position, as Gunson continued as the the first team regular. At the end of the season Harry left the Racecourse and joined Welsh National League side Caernarvon Athletic. With the 'Canaries' Harry was an ever-present prolific goalscorer throughout his time at the club, scoring 85 goals, which earned him representative appearances for the Welsh League XI and for the North Wales Coast F.A. against the Scottish Juniors. Harry remained an ever-present for the 'Canaries' until he left in April 1929, but He is later known to have played for Birmingham league side, Burton Town.

Season	League		F.A.Cup		Welsh Cup		Total	
	apps	gls	apps	gls	apps	gls	apps	gls
1927/28	3	0	-	-	1	0	4	0
	3	**0**	**-**	**-**	**1**	**0**	**4**	**0**

BIRD, Jesse Herbert 1923 - 1925

Position; *Outside-Right*
D.O.B; *J/F/M 1904*
Birthplace; *Hoylake, Merseyside*
Died; *Hoylake, 20th September, 1968*
Height; *5ft 6in* ***Weight;*** *10st 4lbs*
Debut v. *Bradford Park Avenue (h) 21st April, 1923*
Total Appearances & Goals; *8 apps 0 gls*
Career; *Hoylake; WREXHAM (Am) March 1924, (Pro) 9th Jul 1924; Mold Town 18th Jul 1925; Buckley Town 27th Aug 1927; Mold Town 26th Sept 1929; Connah's Quay & Shotton 25th Jan 1930;*

Jesse Bird was playing local football for Hoylake when given a trial by Wrexham in March 1924. His first game, for the reserves in a Welsh League fixture against Holyhead Town, must have impressed as he played in the very next first team game, taking over the outside-right position from Billy Harrison against Bradford Park Avenue on the Racecourse in a 2-2 home draw. This was followed by appearing in the next two games, both against Durham City. On his debut against Bradford Bird was described as 'having speed and a fine centre of the ball when on the run. Altogether his performance was creditable.' He signed professional terms during the close season of 1924. However, the following season Jesse found his first team opportunities limited as he made just five first team appearances, all in the middle of October, when he was called up in place of Eric Lovelady. At the end of that period he found himself out of favour, and never played in a first team match for Wrexham again. Bird was released at the end of the season, and joined Mold Town where he spent two seasons. Jesse then went on to play for Buckley Town, Mold Town (again) and Connah's Quay & Shotton. A real case of 'Bird on the wing!!'

Season	League		F.A.Cup		Welsh Cup		Total	
	apps	gls	apps	gls	apps	gls	apps	gls
1923/24	3	0	-	-	-	-	3	0
1924/25	5	0	-	-	-	-	5	0
	8	**0**	**-**	**-**	**-**	**-**	**8**	**0**

BLEW, Frank William Elford 1921 - 1927

Position; *Left-Back*
D.O.B; *J/F/M/ 1902*
Birthplace; *Wrexham, Denbighshire*
Died; *Wrexham, 13th February, 1968*
Height; *5ft 7in* ***Weight;*** *11st 4lbs*
Debut v. *Hednesford Town (h) 10th April, 1920*
League Debut v. *Chesterfield (a) 12th November, 1921*
Total Appearances & Goals; *50 apps 1 gls*
Career; *WREXHAM Jul 1921; Llandudno 6th Sept 1924; WREXHAM 21st Oct 1925;*
Honours; *Two Welsh Amateur international caps; Three Welsh Junior international caps; North Wales Coast F.A.Challenge Cup runner-up 1926;*

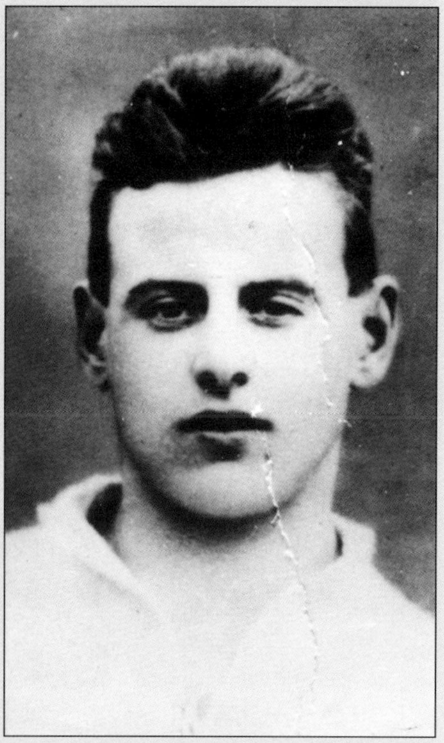

Frank Blew was the son of former Wales and Wrexham player Horace Blew. Throughout his football career, Frank was never a full time player, as he worked as a motor engineer and thus remained as an amateur throughout his career, only ever being called upon as cover in an emergency. He first played for Wrexham in the Birmingham and District League towards the end of the 1919/20 season in place of David Jardine. When not required by Wrexham, he would play for local teams like Llandudno for whom he signed in the 1922/23 season. Frank was described as a 'good full-back', who was honoured for Wales at Amateur level in three matches against England in 1922, 1923 and 1924, as well as being capped three times in Junior internationals for Wales, all against Ireland. He made his Football League debut for Wrexham in his usual position of Left-back against Chesterfield in November 1921 in a 3-0 defeat, but he would play wherever he was asked as he appeared at centre-forward in the last three matches of the 1921/22 season, scoring one goal in a 3-1 defeat at Tranmere. In September 1926 he even took over the goalkeepers' gloves when Ted Robson was injured just minutes into the second-half, after being 'rushed' by an oncoming Walsall forward. Frank was at one time `mine host` of the Green Man Hotel in Wrexham, before he went on to work at the Borough Surveyor's Depot in Wrexham as a Foreman Mechanic where he spent 31 years before retiring in 1966. Throughout that time he retained his interest in the game, and in later life was a very active member of the Wrexham Supporters' Association, of which he later became Chairman in 1951. In March 1959 he became a director of Wrexham Football Club, filling a vacancy caused by the death of Tom Stanley, a position he held for just over a season. Frank died at his home in Wrexham in February 1968.

Season	League		F.A.Cup		Welsh Cup		Total	
	apps	gls	apps	gls	apps	gls	apps	gls
1919/20	1	0	-	-	-	-	1	0
1920/21	12	0	-	-	1	0	13	0
1921/22	5	1	2	0	1	0	8	1
1923/24	7	0	-	-	-	-	7	0
1925/26	2	0	-	-	1	0	3	0
1926/27	14	0	4	0	-	-	18	0
	41	1	6	0	3	0	50	1

BOERSMA, Philip 1970

Position; *Forward*
D.O.B; *24th September, 1949*
Birthplace; *Liverpool, Merseyside*
Height; *5ft 10in* ***Weight;*** *11st 7lbs*
Debut v. *Lincoln City (a) 21st March, 1970*
Total Appearances & Goals; *4/3 apps 0 gls*
Career; *Liverpool (Am) 1966, (Pro) 24th Sept 1968; WREXHAM Mar 1970 (Loan); Liverpool May 1970 73/9apps 17gls; Middlesbrough 4th Dec 1975 £72,000 41/6apps 3gls; Luton Town 5th Aug 1977 £35,000 35/1apps 8gls; Swansea City 9th Sept 1978 £35,000 15/3apps 1gls;*
Honours; *Football League Championship Winner 1973; U.E.F.A.Cup Winner 1973; Charity Shield Winner 1974;*

Phil Boersma joined Wrexham from Liverpool on loan, after manager John Neal felt he needed a replacement for the injured Ian Moir. The club were making a final push for promotion to the Third Division at that time. Phil played in seven League matches, without scoring, as Wrexham clinched promotion in his fifth game for the club. At the end of the season he returned to Anfield. Boersma had joined Liverpool straight from school where he had represented both Kirkby and Lancashire schoolboys, and it was following those games that he was invited to Liverpool for trials. When he eventually left school Phil joined the Anfield groundstaff as an apprentice, making his way through the youth ranks to sign professional on his nineteenth birthday. He then made his first team debut in a League Cup tie at Manchester City in September 1969, coming on as a sub for Alun Evans in a 3-2 defeat. He went on to make nearly 100 appearances for Liverpool, winning a League Championship medal in 1973, and playing in the UEFA Cup final that same season when he came on as sub for Steve Heighway in the second leg of the match with Borussia Monchengladbach. Phil turned his back on Liverpool after he was left out of the 1974 F.A.Cup Final side against Newcastle, but returned to win a winners' medal in the infamous 'Bremner/Keegan' Charity Shield match in 1974. Phil then scored six goals in the opening eight games of the new campaign, but this type of form never lasted, and in December 1975 he was transferred to First Division Middlesbrough for £72,000. Boersma spent almost two years at Ayresome Park, switching to more of a midfield role alongside the emerging talents of Graeme Souness. It was here that they became firm friends, a factor which proved significant for Phil later in his career. He scored three goals in 47 League appearances at Ayresome Park, before he was transferred to Second Division Luton Town in August 1977 for £35,000. His stay at Kenilworth Road lasted for just over a season, scoring eight goals in 36 League games, before joining up with his former Anfield playing

colleague John Toshack, then player/manager at Third Division Swansea City, in September 1978. Boersma helped the 'Swans' to promotion to the Second Division in his first season at the Vetch, but that joy was overshadowed by a compound fracture and dislocation of the right ankle during a match against Swindon Town in April1979. Phil tried his best to regain his fitness, but he was forced to call it a day almost two years later, in 1981. By this time he had become involved with coaching, and he remained on the coaching staff under Toshack to help guide them to the First Division. In March 1984 Phil left the Vetch, and teamed up with Colin Murphy on the coaching staff at Lincoln City. Following Murphy's departure in the close season of 1985, Phil was appointed assistant manager to John Pickerill, but his time in that position was short, as Pickerill left in December and Phil with him. He then joined Doncaster Rovers as their physio for the rest of the 1985/86 season. At the end of the season Boersma was to join up with his former team-mate from his Middlesbrough days, Graeme Souness, who had just been appointed manager of Glasgow Rangers. Phil was appointed physiotherapist, later becoming first team coach, as the 'Gers' won four Scottish Championships, and the League Cup four times. With Rangers again on the verge of winning the League in 1991, Souness left Ibrox to take charge of Liverpool in April. He took Phil with him as first team trainer, and he stayed with Liverpool, winning the F.A.Cup in 1992, up until Souness' departure in 1994. Phil then took up a coaching position with Oldham Athletic where he spent six months before receiving a call from Souness. This time he followed him to Turkey, as coach at Galatasary, where they won the Turkish Cup in his one season with them. Souness then returned to England during the close season of 1996, taking up the manager's job at Southampton, again appointing Boersma as his first team coach. Boersma helped the 'Saints' to stave off the threat of relegation from the Premier League until Souness resigned in the close season of 1997. Phil remained at the Dell until a new manager was appointed, who then released him. He teamed up again with Souness at Torino in Italy, but his time there was short lived. He was then to go with Souness to Benfica where he remained until the end of the 1998/99 season.

Season	League		F.A.Cup		Welsh Cup		League Cup		Total	
	apps	gls	apps	gls	apps	gls	apps	gls	apps	gls
1969/70	4/3	0	-	-	-	-	-	-	4/3	0
	4/3	**0**	**-**	**-**	**-**	**-**	**-**	**-**	**4/3**	**0**

BONNER, Bernard
1952

Position; *Centre-Forward*
D.O.B; *22nd July, 1927*
Birthplace; *Motherwell, Lanarkshire*
Height; *ft in* ***Weight;*** *st lbs*
Debut v. *Southport (a) 8th March, 1952*
Total Appearances & Goals; *1 app 0 gls*
Career; *Dunfermline Athletic; WREXHAM 16th Feb 1952; Released cs1952;*

Bernard Bonner was another Scotsman who signed for Wrexham in the 1950s on the recommendation of the club's Scottish scout Bobbie Archibald. Bernard signed for Wrexham from Scottish Second Division side Dunfermline Athletic, in February 1952. Initially, he had joined Wrexham as a full-back, but after playing as an emergency centre-forward in a reserve game against Macclesfield Town, giving an impressive performance, he was chosen to play in the first team the following Saturday at Southport. However, a 2-1 defeat, and failure to get on the score sheet, meant that it was to be Bernard's one and only match for Wrexham in the Football League before being released at the end of the season.

Season	League		F.A.Cup		Welsh Cup		Total	
	apps	gls	apps	gls	apps	gls	apps	gls
1951/52	1	0	-	-	-	-	1	0
	1	**0**	**-**	**-**	**-**	**-**	**1**	**0**

BOOTH, Raymond
1967 - 1969

Position; *Outside-Left*
D.O.B; *5th September, 1949*
Birthplace; *Southsea, Wrexham, Denbighshire*
Height; *5ft 8in* ***Weight;*** *10st 3lbs*
Debut v. *Bradford City (a) 27th March, 1967*
Total Appearances & Goals; *5 apps 0 gls*
Career; *Brymbo Steelworks; WREXHAM 17th Oct 1967; Bethesda Athletic 13th Aug 1969; Rhyl 6th Sept 1969; Connahs Quay Nomads 1st Nov 1969; Holyhead Town 18th Sept 1971; Portmadoc 11th Jul 1972; Rhos Aelwyd 22nd Feb 1974; Connah's Quay Nomads 28th Jan 1975;*
Honours; *Welsh Youth International;*

A local Wrexham lad, Ray Booth first played football for his school teams at New Broughton Junior and Brynteg Secondary Modern, from where he also represented Wrexham & District schoolboys. It was through playing for them that the Wrexham Youth Coach of the period, Ken Roberts, invited him to join the groundstaff. Ray then made his way through the youth ranks at the Racecourse to make his Football League debut for Wrexham at the age of 17, even before he had signed professional. Booth got his chance very early, when manager Jack Rowley plunged him into the first team in place of David Carrick in a 3-3 draw at Bradford City during March 1967. He then played in the following two matches before being replaced by Dave Campbell, and shortly afterwards was called up into the Welsh Youth International squad for a match against Scotland in Dumfries during April of that year. The following term Ray did not figure in the first team but the 1968/69 season saw him given further opportunities, in March, against Southend United and Bradford City, both at home as cover for Arfon Griffiths. However, at the end of the season Ray was released by manager John Neal, drifting into non-league football in North Wales, having spells with Bethesda Athletic, Rhyl, Connahs Quay Nomads, Holyhead Town, Portmadoc, Rhos Aelwyd and back to Connah's Quay. Booth in fact continued playing football up until the 1994/95 season for local sides in the Wrexham area, and finished playing in the Wrexham Sunday League for the Squire Yorke team. After retiring from professional football Ray has worked for the same company in financial services since 1971.

Season	League		F.A.Cup		Welsh Cup		Legu Cup		Total	
	apps	gls	apps	gls	apps	gls	apps	gls	apps	gls
1966/67	3	0	-	-	-	-	-	-	3	0
1968/69	2	0	-	-	-	-	-	-	2	0
	5	**0**	**-**	**-**	**-**	**-**	**-**	**-**	**5**	**0**

BOOTHWAY, John
1946 - 1950

Position; *Centre-Forward*
D.O.B; *4th February, 1919*
Birthplace; *Sale, Manchester, Lancashire*
Died; *Runcorn, 7th April, 1979*
Height; *6ft 2 ½in* ***Weight;*** *13st 3lbs*
Debut *v. Tranmere Rovers (a) 2nd November, 1946*
Total Appearances & Goals; *113 apps 65 gls*
Career; *Manchester City (WW2) Apr 1941 76apps 57gls; Everton (WW2 Guest) Jan 1944 3apps 2gls; Crewe Alexandra (WW2) Jul 1944 68apps 67gls; Blackburn Rovers (WW2 Guest) 1945/46 1app 0gls; Stoke City (WW2 Guest) Apr 1946 1app 0gls; Crewe Alexandra 1946/47 11apps 5gls; WREXHAM 1st Nov 1946; Hyde United Aug 1950; Mossley Dec 1950 (Player/ manager);*

Jack Boothway, like so many other promising footballers of his time had his football career severely disrupted by World War Two. It was during the WW2 period that he was given the opportunity to sign for Manchester City. He made his first team debut for City in April 1941, and played for the Maine Road club up until 1944. During that time the 6ft 2in centre-forward scored a phenomenal 57 goals in only 76 matches, including all five goals in a 5-3 defeat of Wrexham in September 1941. Jack made a guest appearance for Crewe Alexandra in the 1943/44 season, who stepped in to sign him in the summer of 1944 and stayed at Gresty Road until the Football League was resumed in 1946. His War-time career with the Cheshire club saw him net 67 goals in just 68 matches! Jack then made his Football League debut for Crewe in the opening match of the 1946/47 season, a 2-1 defeat at Gateshead, but the kind of goalscoring form shown during the war period had deserted him, and in October 1946 he was to join Wrexham for a record fee and part-exchange deal that saw Peter Baines move in the opposite direction. Boothway played part-time for Wrexham while continuing to work as a Draughtsman for a Manchester firm. Although he failed to find the net on his debut at Tranmere he certainly made up for it on his home debut, scoring a hat-trick in the 7-1 win over Darlington. Jack's career at the Racecourse continued to be fruitful, as he recorded a goal every other game in his four seasons at the Racecourse, finishing up as the club's top scorer in three out of the four seasons. The 1947/48 season saw Wrexham attain their highest League position since 1933, with Boothway forming a formidable striking

partnership with Billy Tunnicliffe, Norman Sharp, Eddie Beynon and Dennis Grainger. He was regarded at the time as the best centre-forward at Wrexham since the legendary Tommy Bamford. He was to leave the Racecourse at the end of the 1949/50 campaign, after losing his place to Ronnie Wynn. Still involved with football after leaving Wrexham, he signed for non-league side Hyde United, for the start of the new term. However, his time was to be short, as he was offered a post as player/manager of fellow Cheshire League side Mossley in December 1950. He remained with Mossley for a number of seasons before joining Northwich Victoria as manager in July 1955. Boothway enjoyed almost three seasons at Drill Field before becoming manager at Buxton in January 1958. He then took over at Runcorn who he managed throughout the 1960's. Jack Boothway passed away in April 1979, aged 60.

Season	League		F.A.Cup		Welsh Cup		Total	
	apps	gls	apps	gls	apps	gls	apps	gls
1946/47	22	17	4	6	2	2	28	25
1947/48	27	13	2	0	3	0	32	13
1948/49	28	16	1	0	2	1	31	17
1949/50	18	9	3	1	1	0	22	10
	95	**55**	**10**	**7**	**8**	**3**	**113**	**65**

BOWDEN, Jonathan Lee

1987 - 1991

Position; *Midfield*
D.O.B; *21st January, 1963*
Birthplace; *Stockport, Cheshire*
Height; *6ft 0in* ***Weight;*** *11st 7lbs*
Debut v. *Hartlepool United (h) 22nd August, 1987*
Total Appearances & Goals; *185/11 apps 26 gls*
Career; *Oldham Athletic 22nd Jan 1980 73/9apps 5gls; Port Vale 6th Sept 1985 £5,000 64/6apps 7gls; WREXHAM 6th Aug 1987 £12,500; Rochdale 18th Sept 1991 £10,000 73/33apps 17gls;*
Honours; *Welsh Cup runner-up 1988, 1990 and 1991.*

Jon Bowden began his football career as a forward, playing for Goyt Bank Secondary School team, and for Stockport Boys. At this time, Jon also played for a local junior team called Grove United in Hazel Grove, near Stockport and after appearing against a Tottenham youth team was offered an apprenticeship at White Hart Lane, which he turned down due to the distance involved. Despite also playing for Oldham at schoolboy level Jon sought a career away from the game when he left school to begin work as an apprentice electrician. However, he continued to play for Oldham on a Saturday, and on his seventeenth birthday finally signed professional terms for the 'Latics'. Following his switch to the paid ranks he moved to midfield, which was said at the time to have 'suited his style of play, as his wholehearted determination and effort made him an ideal ball winner.' With Oldham, he made his Football League debut in February 1982, at Shrewsbury in a 2-1 defeat, when coming on as a sub for Paul Atkinson. His next match was again as sub for the same player, in another 2-1 defeat, this time at Grimsby in April, but on this occasion Jon scored the Oldham goal. 1982/83 saw him become a regular in the 'Latics' team and remain there up until the end of 1984/85. With no sign of a first team place at the start of the following campaign Bowden agreed a move to Division Four side Port Vale for £5,000 in September. At Vale Park he made his debut in a 4-1 home win over Cambridge United, when regarded as the 'architect of victory', but this was marred when he dislocated his shoulder three minutes from time. Jon missed just four games with the injury and returned to help Vale clinch promotion in his first season in the Potteries. The following term saw Vale make a quick return to the Fourth Division, which led to him losing his place to Ray Walker in the team. Jon left Vale Park in the summer of 1987, agreeing a £12,500 move to Wrexham. Bowden's hard-working and robust style of play quickly led to him being affectionately nicknamed 'Animal' at the Racecourse, making his debut against Hartlepool United for 'The Robins' in a 2-1 home win. Despite another mediocre season in the League he helped Wrexham to reach the Welsh Cup final, where they lost 2-0 to Cardiff City at the Vetch Field, Swansea. His second term with Wrexham the club reach the Fourth Division play-off final against Orient, with Jon scoring in the second leg to give Wrexham some hope, although it was not enough, as the 'O's' won 2-1. 1989/90 was a season of struggle, as the team fought hard to steer away from relegation to the GM Conference League, which looked very likely in March with the club lying six points adrift of the rest of the division. However, with safety assured Wrexham again reached the Welsh Cup Final. This was the first final to have been played at the National Stadium in Cardiff, but it was to be another disappointment as Jon could only pick up a runners'-up tankard in the 2-1 defeat. Even so, Wrexham qualified for Europe as the winners', Hereford, were an English side. The next season Jon played against Lyngby of Denmark, where a 1-0 aggregate win was rewarded with a tie against Jon's favourite 'other' team, Manchester United, although Wrexham lost 5-0 on aggregate. That same campaign saw 'The Robins again struggle suffering from mounting debts, as manager Brian Flynn gave his youngsters their opportunity with the knowledge that there was no relegation that season. As for Bowden, his experience in midfield helped nurture the young players, but at the end of the season the club finished bottom of the League. He did help the team reach his third Welsh Cup final, against Swansea City at the National Stadium. It didn't prove to be third time lucky as Wrexham lost 2-0. At the end of that term he turned down a new contract, but it wasn't until the following season that he was to move on, when Rochdale paid £10,000 for him. At Spotland he got off to a great start, helping 'Dale' to a 1-0 win over local rivals, Burnley, at Turf Moor. Bowden went on to make over 100 League appearances for Rochdale, playing in a number of positions, including centre-half, before retiring in the close season of 1995. He then joined Oldham Athletic as assistant physio, whilst also helping out with coaching duties. Jon, who still lives in the Stockport area, became physio at Doncaster Rovers in July '98 for their first season in the Football Conference.

Season	League		F.A.Cup		Welsh Cup		League Cup		E,C,W,C.		F.R.T.		Total	
	apps	gls	apps	gls	apps	gls	apps	gls	apps	gls	apps	gls	apps	gls
1987/88	21/5	1	1	0	5/1	1	2	0	-	-	-	-	29/6	2
1988/89	41/1	9	2	1	3	0	2	0	4*	1*	4	2	56/1	13
1989/90	31/2	1	-	-	6	1	2	0	-	-	-	-	39/2	2
1990/91	39/1	5	0/1	0	5	1	4	0	3	0	3	0	54/2	6
1991/92	6	3	-	-	-	-	2	0	-	-	-	-	8	3
	141/9	**20**	**3/1**	**1**	**19/1**	**3**	**12**	**0**	**3**	**0**	**7**	**2**	**185/11**	**26**

* Includes 4 Play off matches and 1 goal

BOYLE, Thomas Wilkinson 1923 - 1924

Position; *Centre-Half*
D.O.B; *29th January, 1889*
Birthplace; *Hoyland, nr Barnsley, Yorkshire.*
Died; *Whittingham Hospital, 5th January, 1940*
Height; *5ft 7in* **Weight;** *11st 10lbs*
Debut v. *Ashington (h) 5th August, 1923*
Total Appearances & Goals; *7 apps 0 gls*
Career; *Hoyland Star; Elsecar Athletic; Barnsley May 1906 160apps 18gls; Burnley Sept 1911 £1,150 210apps 36gls; WREXHAM 12th Jun 1923; Coach in Germany cs1924;*
Honours; *One England international Cap; Four Football League XI Representative appearances; Football League Championship Winner 1921; F.A.Cup winner 1914; F.A.Cup runner-up 1910; Second Division runner-up 1913;*

Tommy Boyle joined Wrexham when he was in his mid-thirties, having already enjoyed a distinguished playing career which had been interrupted by the First World War. He began his career in local football with Hoyland Star, followed by Elsecar Athletic, where he was spotted by his local Football League club Barnsley for whom he signed in May 1906. Tommy went on to captain Second Division Barnsley in the 1910 F.A.Cup final against Newcastle, losing 1-0 after a replay at Everton. In September 1911 he joined Burnley for a club record fee of £1,150, and within weeks was made the 'Clarets' captain, helping them to promotion in 1913 to the First Division as runners-up. The following season he won a F.A.Cup winners' medal when Burnley beat Liverpool 1-0 in the final at Crystal Palace. He won his one and only England cap whilst at Turf Moor against Ireland in 1913. During World War One Bombardier Boyle fought in France and suffered serious injuries in 1917. Such was the strength of the man that he made a complete recovery, and when League football resumed Tommy continued with the Turf Moor club leading them to the First Division championship in 1921. Boyle was highly respected at Burnley for his leadership and ability to motivate the players around him. He played his final match for 'The Clarets' in February 1922, and at the end of the season was appointed player/coach. The following season his appearances were limited to reserve team football, but in April 1923 he left Turf Moor joining Wrexham as player/coach, his player registration not being submitted until 12th June. With Burnley Tommy had been regarded as one of the all-time greats, as 'his timing in the air made him one of the most powerful headers of the ball during his era, and was strong in the tackle, whilst his distribution of the ball was first class'. At the Racecourse, Tommy played in the opening seven matches of the 1923/24 season for Wrexham, but he was suspended by the club after failing to turn out in two reserve games in October 1923. He later settled down to concentrate on his coaching, but left Wrexham in the close season to go and work in Germany as a football coach later returning to live in Blackpool. Tommy's health later began to deteriorate and financial difficulties led to a nervous breakdown. Tommy died at Whittingham Hospital on the 5th January 1940. During the peak of his playing days, Boyle was described as a 'Fine Pivot, strong physically and strong in all phases of half back play. He was especially good with his head. His greatest quality, however, was his leadership.'

Season	League		F.A.Cup		Welsh Cup		Total	
	apps	gls	apps	gls	apps	gls	apps	gls
1923/24	7	0	-	-	-	-	7	0
	7	**0**	**-**	**-**	**-**	**-**	**7**	**0**

BRACE, Deryn Paul John 1994 - 1998

Position; *Full-Back*
D.O.B; *15th March, 1975*
Birthplace; *Haverfordwest, Dyfed*
Height; *5ft 7in* **Weight;** *10st 6lbs*
Debut v. *Hartlepool United (h) 30th April 1994*
Total Appearances & Goals; *100/7 apps 2 gls*
Career; *Norwich City 6th Jul 1993; WREXHAM 28th April 1994;*
Honours; *Five Welsh under-21 International caps; One Welsh Youth international cap; Welsh Cup Winner 1995; Welsh Invitation Cup Winner 1998; Welsh Premier Cup runner-up 1999;*

A small, tenacious player who is equally at home in either of the full-back positions. Deryn can always be relied upon to give 100%, which makes him so popular with the Wrexham supporters. He was brought up on his father's farm in his native South West Wales near Haverfordwest, in a rugby playing community, and only played football occasionally with his friends. It was whilst appearing in one of these games that Deryn was spotted by a Norwich City scout; he was only fourteen at the time and was invited to spend a week at Great Yarmouth for trials, and told to "keep in touch". However, over the next two years he only played about ten games, and drifted back to the fifteen man game. Norwich City made contact again, and he went training with the 'Canaries' at weekends eventually being offered a YTS place, making his way through the youth team and reserves in the Combination League. He was a member of the Norwich team that reached the semi-finals of the F.A.Youth Cup, which they lost 4-3 to Leeds on aggregate, and also played in the final of the South East Counties League Cup, beaten by Spurs. By this time Deryn had represented Wales at Youth level, making his debut in a 1-1 draw against Israel at Cardiff. At the end of his YTS course in the summer of 1993 he was offered a one year professional contract at Carrow Road, and celebrated by breaking a toe! He played reserve team football for most of the 1993/94 season, but when Mike Walker left to join Everton John Deehan was put in charge and told Brace that he was not in his plans. A number of clubs showed interest in signing Deryn but he chose Wrexham, who he joined in April 1994, initially on trial. Following a couple of reserve games he was given clearance to play in the last League game of the 1993/94 season in a 2-0 win over Hartlepool. He was then awarded a professional contract, and went on to play fourteen League games the following season, a campaign which saw him make the first of his five Under-21 appearances against Austria in September 1994. At the end of the season he also played in the Welsh Cup final against Cardiff City at the National Stadium which Wrexham won 2-1. The 1995/96 season was to see him again hit by the injury jinx that has dogged his career to date, missing out on playing in a European Cup-Winners' Cup game in Romania after breaking his collarbone in a training accident, and then involved in a car crash while returning to Wrexham after a visit home. As if to add insult to injury, Brace was invited to a full Wales squad get-together, but went down with pneumonia! Once recovered he went on to help Wrexham to reach the quarter-finals of the F.A.Cup in 1997, before disappointingly losing 1-0 to Chesterfield. It was Deryn's best season to date, although he had still missed a number of games through injury. Injuries again played a part in restricting his appearances for the 1997/98 campaign, and once fit he found that a rejuvenated Phil Hardy was back to his best. It meant Deryn remained on the sidelines, although he did come on as a substitute to claim a winners' medal in the first ever Welsh Invitation Cup final. He still remains injury prone but more determined than ever to remain positive and beat the jinx.

Season	League		F.A.Cup		Welsh Cup		League Cup		Auto W.		E.C.W.C		Total	
	apps	gls	apps	gls	apps	gls	apps	gls	apps	gls	apps	gls	apps	gls
1993/94	1	0	-	-	-	-	-	-	-	-	-	-	1	0
1994/95	10/4	0	1	0	3	0	-	-	1	0	-	-	15/4	0
1995/96	16	1	-	-	-	-	1	0	-	-	1	0	18	1
1996/97	26	1	4	0	-	-	2	0	1	0	-	-	33	1
1997/98	8	0	-	-	2/1*	0*	2	0	-	-	-	-	12/1	0
1998/99	15/2	0	-	-	5*	0*	1	0	-	-	-	-	21/2	0
	76/6	**2**	**5**	**0**	**10/1**	**0**	**6**	**0**	**2**	**0**	**1**	**0**	**100/7**	**2**

*= Welsh Invitation/Premier Cup games

BRADBURY, Terence Eugene

1967 - 1969

Position; *Wing-Half*
Birthplace; *Paddington, London.*
Height; *5ft 11in* **Weight;** *11st 6lbs*
D.O.B; *15th November, 1939*
Debut v. *Luton Town (h) 19th August, 1967*
Total Appearances & Goals; *89/1 apps 4 gls*
Career; *Chelsea Jul 1957 29apps 1gls; Southend United Sept 1962 (£4,500) 160/1apps 19gls; Leyton Orient June 1966 25/2apps 0gls; WREXHAM 15th Jun 1967; Chester 20th June 1969 (Player/coach) 90apps 2gls; Weymouth cs1972 (Player/coach); Northwich Victoria cs1973 (Player/manager);*
Honours; *England Schoolboy international.*

Terry Bradbury began his footballing career with Chelsea as a junior in 1955. He had a very promising schoolboy career, playing for his school teams at Harrow and Willesden. He represented both Middlesex and London schoolboys, as well as playing four times for England at that level, including appearing in front of 90,000 at Wembley in a 4-0 win over Wales! Ted Drake, the Chelsea manager, was quick to spot Terry's early promise and signed him for 'The Pensioners' on schoolboy forms. Terry made his way through the youth ranks at Stamford Bridge, making his Football League debut against Aston Villa at Villa Park in August 1960. Bradbury emerged as a strongly built wing-half, and made a further 28 League appearances before being allowed to leave in September 1962 following a disagreement with Tommy Docherty. It was at this time that Chelsea were in a transitional period, and with the signing of Frank Upton, and the emergence of a young Terry Venables, he left to join Third Division Southend United. At Roots Hall he went straight into the first team for his debut at Port Vale. Southend lost 5-1! However, Terry went on to remain in the 'Shrimpers' team for the rest of the season, making 161 League appearances in almost four seasons and scoring 19 goals. In the summer of 1966 Bradbury was to join another Third Division side, Leyton Orient. At Brisbane Road he made his debut in a 3-1 defeat at Oldham in the opening match of the season, remaining a regular in the side for most of the term until losing his place towards the end of the season, which resulted in his release. However, his former manager at Southend United, Alvan Williams, who was now manager at Wrexham, stepped in and signed him. His League debut on the opening day of the 1967/68 season for Wrexham was marred by being sent-off following a scuffle with Luton Town's Graham French. 'A hard tackling, aggressive player, Terry formed a midfield partnership with Tony Beanland', as he soon settled in at the Racecourse, quickly establishing himself as a firm favourite with the Wrexham supporters. His first season saw him help the side to a very creditable eighth position, while the following year the side finished one position lower. Terry was an automatic choice for Wrexham up until February 1969, when Mickey Evans forced his way back into the League side, although Terry switched to playing in defence following an injury to Gareth Davies, but it still came as a shock when at the end of that season he was surprisingly released by new manager John Neal. Despite this set-back, he was quickly fixed up with another club when in June 1969, he joined local rivals Chester as player/coach to Ken Roberts He spent three seasons at Sealand Road making 90 League appearances and scoring twice, before joining Southern League side Weymouth in the close season of 1972 as player/ coach. Bradbury spent just one season on the south coast before joining Northwich Victoria as player/ manager enjoying another campaign at the Drill Field until a financial crisis and, a hurried pruning of the club's management was to see Terry leave football altogether. He then entered the licensing trade, initially working for Whitbreads before buying his own pub in Chapel-en-le-Frith in Derbyshire. He sold that in 1992, and became the steward at the Conservative club in Buxton, where he is still pulling pints.

Season	League		F.A.Cup		Welsh Cup		League Cup		Total	
	apps	gls	apps	gls	apps	gls	apps	gls	apps	gls
1967/68	38	3	1	0	2	0	1	0	42	3
1968/69	39/1	0	2	0	3	0	3	1	47/1	1
	77/1	**3**	**3**	**0**	**5**	**0**	**4**	**1**	**89/1**	**4**

BRAMMER, David

1992 - 1999

Position; *Midfield*
D.O.B; *28th February, 1975*
Birthplace; *Bromborough, Merseyside*
Height; *5ft 8in* **Weight;** *11st 0lb*
Debut v. *Bury (h) 10th October, 1992*
Total Appearances & Goals; *110/21 apps 12 gls*
Career; *WREXHAM 2nd Jul, 1993; Port Vale 24th Mar 1999 £350,000 9apps 0gls;*
Honours; *Welsh Invitation Cup Winner 1998; Welsh Youth Cup runner-up 1993;*

Dave Brammer was brought up on the Wirral, and was one of many young players from the area who went on to sign apprentice forms with Wrexham. He played for his school team at Bebington High School and via them was selected to play for Wirral Schoolboys, progressing to captain the side to victories in the Merseyside and Cheshire Cups. Although interesting both Tranmere Rovers and Everton, it was for Wrexham whom Dave decided to sign YTS forms upon leaving school. He then progressed through the ranks to make his League debut at 17, in a 4-2 home win over Bury in October 1992, deputising for an injured Gareth Owen. A hard tackling, industrious midfield player Brammer went on to sign professional for Wrexham in July 1993. It was the following season-1993/94 -that he began to figure more regularly in the Wrexham side, but struggled to find the kind of form that had earned him his debut. It wasn't until the 1995/96 season that Brammer began to pay back the faith manager Brian Flynn had shown in him with the kind of performances he had produced in his early days at the Racecourse. It did not last, unfortunately, as he suffered a hernia, which needed an operation, and once fit he was unable to regain a first team place. At the beginning of March, with not playing regular first team football, together with off field problems, frustration took over and he asked to be placed on the transfer list. With no incoming offers, Dave decided to settle down and fight for a first team place for the new 1996/97 season, but his efforts were not helped by niggling injuries. The following campaign he featured more often in 'The Robins' midfield, and almost helped the club to reach a much wanted play-off position, although the disappointment of missing out was cushioned with a Welsh Invitation Cup final win over Cardiff City in which David appeared. A strong midfield battler with a powerful right foot shot, he still has time on his side to become a top class midfield operator with fine passing of the ball a strong feature of his play. In 1998/99 he became a far more consistent performer showing the form all at the club knew him capable of, which did not go unnoticed as First Division Port Vale snapped up the promising midfielder on dead-line day for

£350,000. Dave went on to inspire the 'Valiants' to relegation safety.

Season	League		F.A.Cup		Welsh Cup		League Cup		Auto T		E.C.W.C		Total	
	apps	gls	apps	gls	apps	gls	apps	gls	apps	gls	apps	gls	apps	gls
1992/93	1/1	0	-	-	-	-	-	-	-	-	-	-	1/1	0
1993/94	16/6	2	1	0	1	0	-	-	1/1	0	-	-	19/7	2
1994/95	13/1	1	-	-	1/1	0	3	0	1	0	-	-	18/2	1
1995/96	11	2	2	0	-	-	1	0	2	0	-	-	16	2
1996/97	17/4	1	0/2	0	-	-	0/1	0	1	0	-	-	18/7	1
1997/98	29/4	4	-	-	7*	2*	1	0	1	0	-	-	38/4	6
1998/99	31/3	2	5	1	5*	0*	1/1	0	6	1	-	-	48/4	4
	118/19	**12**	**8/2**	**1**	**14/1**	**2**	**6/2**	**0**	**12/1**	**1**	**-**	**-**	**158/25**	**16**

* = Welsh Invitation/Premier Cup

***BRAND,* Andrew Scougal** 1982

Position; *Goalkeeper*
D.O.B; *8th November, 1957*
Birthplace; *Edinburgh, Lothian*
Height; *6ft 1in* ***Weight;*** *11st 1lbs*
Debut v. *Brentford (a) 4th December, 1982*
Total Appearances & Goals; *1 app 0 gls*
Career; *Everton Nov 1975 2apps 0gls; Crewe Alexandra 25th Feb 1977 14apps 0gls (Loan); Crewe Alexandra 2nd Aug 1978 1app 0apps (Loan); Sheffield United 23rd Aug 1979 0apps (Loan); Hereford United 23rd May 1980 54apps 0gls; WREXHAM 26th Nov 1982 (Loan); Winsford United; Leeds United 1983 0apps; Witton Albion; Blackpool Apr 1984 3apps 0gls; Flint Town United; Stalybridge Celtic Mar 1985;*

Wrexham manager Bobby Roberts signed Drew Brand on loan from Hereford United as goalkeeping cover for the suspended Eddie Niedzwiecki in November 1982. Drew was to play only one match for Wrexham, at Brentford, in which he conceded four goals in a 4-1 defeat after Wrexham had taken the lead through a Jake King goal. The match report stated that it was a 'nightmare debut for Drew'. The following game saw Eddie Niedzwiecki back, and he returned to Hereford at the end of the month. Brand had begun his career with Everton after impressing for Edinburgh Schools. At Goodison Park he made just two League appearances, his Football League debut coming in a 5-2 defeat at Leeds, replacing David Lawson in November 1975. His second outing was the final match of the 1976/77 season, a 2-0 home win over Newcastle United when standing in for former Wrexham 'keeper Dai Davies. Prior to that last appearance for 'The Toffees' Drew had made 15 League appearances, while on two loan spells with Crewe Alexandra and Sheffield United. In May 1980 he finally left Goodison Park when transferred to Hereford United, making his debut for the 'Bulls' in a 5-1 defeat at Doncaster Rovers in September 1980. He went on to make 54 League appearances in his two campaigns at Edgar Street, but a wrangle over terms was to eventually see him released by Hereford and move into non-league football with Winsford United shortly after his loan spell with Wrexham. In 1983 Leeds United signed him as cover for David Harvey, but he never made the senior side at Elland Road, eventually moving back into non-league football with Witton Albion. Blackpool signed him on non-contract terms in April 1984, and he played in the final three League games of the season for the Seaside club. Drew later had a spell in goal for Flint Town United.

Season	League		F.A.Cup		Welsh Cup		Total	
	apps	gls	apps	gls	apps	gls	apps	gls
1982/83	1	0	-	-	-	-	1	0
	1	**0**	**-**	**-**	**-**	**-**	**1**	**0**

***BREAKWELL,* Thomas** 1937 - 1938

Position; *Half-Back*
D.O.B; *3rd July, 1915*
Birthplace; *Stourport-on-Severn, Worcestershire*
Height; *5ft 10in* ***Weight;*** *11st 7lbs*
Debut v. *Lincoln City (h) 1st September, 1937*
Total Appearances & Goals; *3 apps 0 gls*
Career; *Lytham; Blackpool (Am) 1931; Bolton Wanderers Jun 1935; Bradford Park Avenue May 1936 18apps 1gls; WREXHAM 16th Jun 1937 to cs1938; Rochdale (WW2 Guest) 1942/3 & 43/4 20apps 0gls;*

Although Tom Breakwell was born in Stourport his family moved to Blackpool when he was just six months-old. Tom became a promising footballer whilst at school, and joined Blackpool at the age of sixteen as an amateur, but nothing came of his time with the 'Seasiders' and he began playing local football. It was while turning out for Lytham that he was spotted by Bolton Wanderers, signing professional for 'The Trotters' in June 1935. Tom spent one season at Burnden Park but failed to make an impression, and in the close season of 1936 joined Bradford Park Avenue. It was with Bradford that he made his breakthrough into the Football League, playing in his half-back position, making 18 League appearances and scoring one goal, but at the end of the season was allowed to leave and signed for Wrexham manager, Captain James Logan. Breakwell didn't have to wait long before he made the first team, along with four other debutants, in the second match of the season against Lincoln City on the Racecourse in a 1-0 win. He kept his place for the following match against New Brighton. Eventually, he found himself out of favour and had to wait until February before he was to have another chance. That came against Crewe Alexandra on the Racecourse when replacing the transferred Jack Lewis at centre-half. Wrexham won the match 1-0, but it proved to be Tom's last game in a Wrexham shirt as Tommy Matthias took over in the following matches and at the end of the season was released by the club. Tom then returned to Bradford where he joined the Bradford City Police Force. His wife found it difficult to settle in Bradford, and he left the Police in 1942 to return to Blackpool joining the R.A.F. He then trained as a Pilot in America, and eventually was flying Halifax Bombers. However, Tom was not to feature on any bombing missions, as his job was to go out after the raids and take aerial photographs of the damage that had been caused. He left the R.A.F. at the end of the War in 1945 with the rank of Flying Officer. During the War period he did play football when possible, and 'guested' for Rochdale between 1942 and 1944. On his return to Blackpool after the hostilities Tom's father-in-law taught him to become a butcher and he was to become very successful, eventually owning his own shop. Unfortunately, he had to give this up in 1960 due to the fact that he collapsed when carrying a side of beef. Breakwell then sold the business and became a traveller for Messrs. Wallace Cameron, selling Medical Supplies, which prompted him to begin his own company, called First Medical, in 1975. This was also a success, and upon reaching the age of 70 in 1985 Tom sold the business to his partner and retired. Tom was still living in Blackpool in 1998.

Season	League		F.A.Cup		Welsh Cup		Total	
	apps	gls	apps	gls	apps	gls	apps	gls
1937/38	3	0	-	-	-	-	3	0
	3	**0**	**-**	**-**	**-**	**-**	**3**	**0**

***BREMNER,* Kevin Johnston** 1982 - 1983

Position; *Forward*
D.O.B; *7th October, 1957*
Birthplace; *Banff, Scotland*
Height; *5ft 10in* ***Weight;*** *12st 6lbs*
Debut v. *Reading (h) 1st January, 1983*
Total Appearances & Goals; *4 apps 1 gls*
Career; *Deveronvale Jul 1976; Celtic (trial) Oct 1978; Keith Jul 1979; Colchester United 7th Oct 1980 £40,000 89/6apps 31gls; Birmingham City Oct 1982 3/1apps 1gls (Loan); WREXHAM Dec 1982 (Loan); Plymouth Argyle Jan 1983 5apps 1gls (Loan); Millwall Feb 1983 £25,000 87/9apps 32gls; Reading Aug 1985 £36,000 60/4apps 21gls; Brighton HA 8th Jul 1987 £65,000 125/3apps 36gls; Peterborough United 27th Jul 1990 £18,000 13/4apps 3gls; Dundee cs1991 15/9apps 6gls; Shrewsbury Town 27th Mar 1992 (Loan) 7apps 2gls; Brora Rangers Jul 1992; Deveronvale Jul 1994; Gillingham 1995;*
Honours; *Scottish First Division Championship Winner 1991; Third Division Championship Winner 1986; Third Division runner-up 1985 & 1988; Bells Cup Winner 1978; Highland League Championship Winner 1980; Aberdeenshire Cup Winner 1980; Highland League Cup Winner 1980; Aberdeenshire Shield Winner 1994;*

Kevin Bremner joined Wrexham on loan, from manager Bobby Roberts' former club Colchester United during Christmas 1982. He made his debut against Reading on New Year's Day 1983 and scored in the 4-0 win, which later helped him to an unusual record of scoring four times against 'Reading' for four different clubs that year. At the Racecourse, the fans, and Bobby Roberts, all wanted Kevin to sign on permanently but, due to the dire financial situation at the club, there were no funds available. That same problem also prevented the club from signing Jim Steel, who arrived on loan immediately after Kevin left. What a strike force that pair would have proved! Kevin had began playing football while at Aberchirder Primary, and Banff Academy Senior Schools. He also represented Banffshire County and North Scotland schoolboy XIs, and on leaving school he took up playing for a local side, Deveronvale, where he spent three years, winning a Bells Cup winners' medal in 1978. It was also around this period that he had trials with both Celtic and Aston Villa, but nothing came of them and in the close season of 1979 was transferred to Highland League side, Keith. He had a successful time, winning the League and Cup double in 1980, as well as helping Keith to the third round of the Scottish F.A.Cup. At the beginning of the 1980/81 season he was invited down to Colchester United for a trial on the recommendation of a former team mate of his, Willie Hunter, who was boss of Inverness Caley at the time. On his 23rd birthday (October 1980), Kevin finally signed professional terms for manager Bobby Roberts for a £25,000 fee. His Football League debut came in the following game, appearing as sub at half-time in a 2-2 draw with Barnsley. From then until the end of the season he never missed a match, soon becoming a crowd favourite with his enthusiastic approach to the game. Despite this, the Layer Road club suffered relegation, but the following season Kevin never missed a match as the 'U's' just missed out on a quick return. The 1982/83 season saw him refuse to sign a new contract with the Essex club, ending up having three loan spells at Birmingham, Wrexham, and Plymouth before George Graham of Millwall stepped in to sign him for £25,000 in February 1983. Bremner's signing contributed much to the 'Lions' successful fight against relegation as they won nine of the remaining17 games, with Kevin contributing six goals, including two against Wrexham at the Racecourse! He went on to remain at the 'Den' for two more seasons, assisting the 'Lions' to promotion in 1985 by finishing Third Division runners-up. He joined Reading during the summer, and went on to spend two years at Elm Park, in which time he helped the 'Royals' to promotion to the Second Division and to their highest Football League position of 13th. At the end of 1986/87 Bremner was on the move again, this time to the south coast and Third Division Brighton & Hove Albion, where he was to enjoy his longest and most successful spell, assisting the 'Seagulls' to promotion in his first season as runners-up. The following two seasons saw Kevin finish as top marksman at the Goldstone Ground, but in July 1990 he was allowed to leave Brighton and join Fourth Division Peterborough United. Once again success was to follow him around, as he helped the 'Posh' to promotion in his one and only season at London Road. In the close season of 1991 he returned to his native Scotland, joining Scottish First Division side, Dundee, tasting success once more as the 'Dark Blues' won the First Division Championship, although Kevin left before the end of the term for a seven game stint with Shrewsbury Town. On returning to his homeland he took up a job as player/manager and commercial manager of Brora Rangers, for two years before rejoining his first senior club, Deveronvale, to take up a similar position. In 1995, Kevin was invited to take over the Youth team manager's job at Gillingham by their owner, Paul Scally, an acquaintance from his time with Millwall. It was in that capacity that he was called upon to turn out for the Gillingham's first team as a substitute in a Auto Windscreen Shield match against Hereford United in November 1996 at the age of almost 39.

Season	League		F.A.Cup		Welsh Cup		League Cup		Total	
	apps	gls	apps	gls	apps	gls	apps	gls	apps	gls
1982/83	4	1	-	-	1	1	-	-	5	2
	4	**1**	**-**	**-**	**1**	**1**	**-**	**-**	**5**	**2**

BRIGNULL, Phillip Arthur 1985 - 1986

Position; *Central Defender*
D.O.B; *2nd October, 1960*
Birthplace; *Stratford, London*
Height; *6ft 0in* **Weight;** *12st 12lbs*
Debut v. *Colchester United (a) 20th December, 1985*
Total Appearances & Goals; *6 apps 1 gls*
Career; *West Ham United Sept 1978 0/1apps; Bournemouth Aug 1981 128/1apps 11gls; WREXHAM 19th Dec 1985 (Loan); Cardiff City 3rd Feb 1986 (Loan), 15th Mar 1986 £15,000 49apps; Newport County Aug 1987 3apps 0gls; Merthyr Tydfil cs1988; Newport County Sept 1988; Sully Mar 1989; AFC Cardiff cs1989; Weymouth Nov 1989;*
Honours; *England Schoolboy International; Associate Members Cup Winner 1984;*

Phil Brignull was signed by Wrexham manager Dixie McNeil on a month's loan in December 1985. He made his debut in a 5-2 defeat at Colchester, and also finished his loan period with a 5-2 defeat on New Years Day at Burnley! Phil did, however, score one of the Wrexham goals in that match. One significant point from his loan spell with Wrexham, was that he played in a Welsh Cup match against Bridgend in an 8-0 win, which meant that he was then cup-tied for a semi-final match against Wrexham when with Cardiff City, for whom he signed shortly after his loan spell at the Racecourse. Phil's Football career had began at West Ham United as an apprentice. However, in the five years he spent at Upton Park he only ever made one appearance for the 'Hammers'. That was against Cardiff City at Ninian Park, coming on as a substitute for John McDowall, in a scoreless draw. In August 1981 Brignull left Upton Park to join Bournemouth on a free transfer, and went on to make over one hundred appearances for the south coast club. During that time he helped them win promotion to Division Three in 1981, and also to success in the Associate Members' Cup in 1984. It was whilst he was with the 'Cherries' that he was loaned to Wrexham. In February 1986 Phil joined Cardiff City for £15,000, and went on to make 49 league appearances for the 'Bluebirds' before moving on to Newport County in August 1987 on a free transfer. At Somerton Park he was to make just three League appearances, before a bad knee injury forced him to retire prematurely from League Football. He did, however, start to play football again with Merthyr Tydfil, followed by another spell with Newport County, who by that time were playing in the GM Conference League, and stayed with until they were wound up in March 1989. He then played for local South Wales League sides, Sully and AFC Cardiff, finally having a spell with Weymouth. He later returned to the Cardiff area to settle, and worked for Allied Dunbar as a sales representative in Cardiff. Phil is a cousin of the Brentford manager, David Webb.

Season	League		F.A.Cup		Welsh Cup		League Cup		Total	
	apps	gls	apps	gls	apps	gls	apps	gls	apps	gls
1985/86	5	1	-	-	1	0	-	-	6	1
	5	**1**	**-**	**-**	**1**	**0**	**-**	**-**	**6**	**1**

BROWN, Albert Roy 1939 - 1947

Position; *Outside-Right*
D.O.B; *14th August, 1917*
Birthplace; *Sneinton, Nottinghamshire*
Height; *5ft 5ins* **Weight;** *10st 0lbs*
Debut v. *New Brighton (h) 31st August, 1946*
Total Appearances & Goals; *51 apps 8 gls*
Career; *Sneinton; Nottingham Forest Feb 1936 51apps 7gls; WREXHAM 28th Jun 1939 3apps 0gls, WW2 20apps 4gls; Watford (WW2 Guest) 10apps 4gls; Mansfield Town 2nd Aug 1947 17apps 2gls; Stafford Rangers 1948; Goole Town 48/49;*

Albert Brown was signed by Nottingham Forest from local club Sneinton.

He made over half a century of appearances for Forest, featuring regularly in their Second Division side, before signing for Wrexham in the close season of 1939. His Football League career in North East Wales Wrexham came to an abrupt halt when, after playing in the first three matches of the 1939/40 season all football was suspended due to the outbreak of the Second World War. Albert continued to play War-time football, and made nine appearances for Wrexham, scoring three goals up to the end of the 1939/40 season. He did not feature again for Wrexham until the conflict had ended and the Football League had recommenced. He made his 'debut' yet again in the opening match of that season in a 3-2 home win over New Brighton. Brown remained at the Racecourse until the end of the campaign when he joined Mansfield Town for a season, before dropping into non-League football with Stafford Rangers and Goole Town. During his career Albert was said to be "a midget, but feared nobody. He could shoot and centre well."

Season	League		F.A.Cup		Welsh Cup		War League		Total	
	apps	gls	apps	gls	apps	gls	apps	gls	apps	gls
1939/40	3	0	-	-	-	-	9	3	12	3
1945/46	-	-	-	-	-	-	11	1	11	1
1946/47*	24	3	3	1	1	0	-	-	28	4
	27	**3**	**3**	**1**	**1**	**0**	**20**	**4**	**51**	**8**
F/League	24	3	3	1	1	0	-	-	28	4

* Football League record only.

BROWN, Ambrose Robert 1936 - 1937

Position; *Inside-Foward*
D.O.B; *15th February, 1911*
Birthplace; *Burton-upon-Trent, Staffordshire*
Died; *East Staffs, January, 1989.*
Height; *5 ft 11 in* **Weight;** *12 st 0 lbs*
Debut v. *Chester (a) 29th August, 1936*
Total Appearances & Goals; *32 apps 5 gls*
Career; *Newhall Swifts; Chesterfield Oct 1933 27apps 10gls; Portsmouth Jun 1935 1app 0gls; WREXHAM 11th Jun 1936; T.W.R. Aug 1938;*

Ambrose Brown was playing local football for Newhall Swifts when he was signed by Third Division North side Chesterfield in October 1933. He had to wait a while before making his Football League debut, which came during the 1934/35 season in a 4-0 home win over Hartlepool United in October, when he scored one of the goals. Ambrose then went on to become a regular in the side, appearing in either of the centre-forward or Inside-Forward positions, scoring a total of ten League goals in 27 matches for the 'Spireites. It was this kind of form that made First Division Portsmouth sign him in the close season of 1935, but his time at Fratton Park was spent playing mainly reserve team football, as he made just one League appearance in his time there. That game was played in November 1935 against West Bromwich Albion at the Hawthorns, and 'Pompey' lost 2-0. At the end of the 1935/36 season Brown was allowed to leave Hampshire and return North. He was then signed by Wrexham manager Ernie Blackburn, making his debut in the first match of the 1936/37 season, a 4-1 defeat at Chester. He went on to become a regular in the Wrexham team throughout the season, in which time he was tarnished with the record of being the quickest player ever to be sent-off in a Football League match at Hull City on Christmas Day. It was claimed that he had been sent-off after just 20 seconds, but this wasn't the case, as newspaper reports of the time stated that he was sent-off after 'six minutes'. Still not that good, but enough to clear Ambrose`s name of this unwanted record! Brown lost his place in the Wrexham team towards the end of the season, when Dai Phillips took his place, with Ambrose eventually being released in the summer.

Season	League		F.A.Cup		Welsh Cup		N.S.C.		Total	
	apps	gls	apps	gls	apps	gls	apps	gls	apps	gls
1936/37	27	5	3	0	1	0	1	0	32	5
	27	**5**	**3**	**0**	**1**	**0**	**1**	**0**	**32**	**5**

BROWN, John Thomas 1931 - 1934

Position; *Left-Back*
D.O.B; *15th June, 1901*
Birthplace; *Eastwood, Nottinghamshire*
Died; *Eastwood, Notts J/F/M 1977*
Height; *5ft 10in* **Weight;** *11st 7lbs*
Debut v. *Rochdale (h) 5th September, 1931*
Total Appearances & Goals; *94 apps 0 gls*
Career; *Kirkby Colliery; Leicester City Aug 1922 114 apps 0gls; WREXHAM 2nd Sept 1931; Nuneaton Town Jul 1934; Heanor Town Sept 1936;* **Honours;** *Welsh Cup runner-up 1932 & 1933*

Jack Brown was signed by Leicester City in the summer of 1922, while working as a miner and playing football for Kirkby Colliery. He became a 'patient understudy' at Filbert Street, for nine years, making over 100 League appearances for the 'Foxes' before being signed by Wrexham manager Jack Baynes prior to his illness in August 1931. At Leicester Jack was described as 'clever with his head, strong in his kicking and daring to a degree.' He was a regular in the Leicester City side that finished Division One runners'-up to Sheffield Wednesday in the 1928/29 season, Leicester's best ever season in the Football League. With Wrexham, Jack made his Football League debut at left-back in the third match of the 1931/32 season at home to Rochdale in a 4-0 win. He then kept his place for the rest of the season, and also played in every League match the following term. During the time he played in two Welsh Cup finals, but on both occasions ended up on the losing side. The 1932 final was against Swansea Town, who beat Wrexham 2-0 after a replay, while the following year saw Wrexham lose 2-0 to rivals Chester. During his spell at the Racecourse he did help the club to their highest League placing in 1932/33, when Wrexham finished runners-up to Hull City. The 1933/34 season proved to be frustrating for Jack, as he lost his place to new signing Jimmy Hamilton. He made only five League appearances before his release in the summer of 1934. Brown then slipped into non-League football when he joined Nuneaton Town, for two seasons eventually joining Heanor Town in 1936.

Season	League		F.A.Cup		Welsh Cup		Total	
	apps	gls	apps	gls	apps	gls	apps	gls
1931/32	38	0	1	0	6	0	45	0
1932/33	42	0	3	0	4	0	49	0
1933/34	5	0	-	-	-	-	5	0
	85	**0**	**4**	**0**	**10**	**0**	**99**	**0**

BROWN, Peter Barry 1958 - 1960

Position; *Outside/Inside-Left*
D.O.B; *13th July, 1934*
Birthplace; *Andover, Hampshire.*
Height; *5ft 7in* **Weight;** *9st 3lbs*
Debut v. *Swindon Town (a) 23rd August, 1958*
Total Appearances & Goals; *33 apps 9 gls*
Career; *Andover; Southampton January 1952 16apps 3gls; WREXHAM 5th July 1958; Poole Town Jul 1960; Dorchester Town Apr 1962; Andover Jun 1963;*

Peter Brown was a product of the Southampton Youth policy, having signed for the club from his local side, Andover, in January 1952. He spent five years (in total) at the Dell, playing mainly for the reserve side, interrupted later in 1952 when he was called up for National Service, serving mainly at Crookham, where he was a member of the Royal Army Medical Corp, who he also represented at football. Upon his return to Southampton Peter went on to make his first team debut for the 'Saints' in the last game of the season at Norwich City, during April 1954, in a 1-0 defeat. He then went on to record a further fifteen League appearances, scoring three goals, for the 'Saints' before he was transferred to Wrexham in July 1958 for their initial campaign in the newly organised Third Division. At the Racecourse Peter went straight into the first team for the opening match of the 1958/59 season, playing at outside-left in a 1-0 defeat at Swindon. By the end of September, however, he found himself out of favour, with Brian Cripsey preferred on

the left wing and Ken Murray at inside-left. The rest of the season Brown only appeared as cover for injuries, playing in any of the left forward positions as required. The following season continued in much the same way, and a disillusioned Brown left the Racecourse on a free transfer. Whilst at Wrexham Peter had been described as 'on the small side, but a great-hearted worker who likes to be among the goals.' After leaving the North Wales club he returned south, to play non-league football for Poole Town, Dorchester, and Andover. Having finished playing professional football Brown became employed as a sign-writer in Hampshire. His son, Kevan, was also on the books of Southampton, but failed to make a first team appearance, although he did play League football for both Brighton and Aldershot.

Season	League		F.A.Cup		Welsh Cup		Total	
	apps	gls	apps	gls	apps	gls	apps	gls
1958/59	17	4	-	-	-	-	17	4
1959/60	16	5	-	-	-	-	16	5
	33	**9**	**-**	**-**	**-**	**-**	**33**	**9**

BROWN, William 1925 - 1926

Position; *Centre-Forward*
D.O.B;
Birthplace; *Liverpool, Merseyside*
Height; *5ft 6in* ***Weight;*** *9st 4lbs*
Debut v. *Durham City (a) 28th April, 1926*
Total Appearances & Goals; *1 apps 0 gls*
Career; *WREXHAM Nov 1925; Rhyl 20th Jan 1928;*

William Brown is another player from the 'One Game Wonder' brigade as he played in just a single Football League match for Wrexham at the end of the 1925/26 season. It came in a 2-1 defeat at Durham, when he stepped in at centre-forward to replace Frank Roberts. One description was 'almost scoring on his debut following a free-kick, but it was intercepted at the last moment.' Bill was also mentioned as an amateur signed 'from the Liverpool District'. His first game was a reserve match against Druids on the 2nd April 1926 in a 7-0 win. He distinguished himself by scoring four of the goals.' He was signed on professional forms in May 1926, following his first team debut, but that match at Durham proved to be his only first team outing. It is believed that he later played for Rhyl.

Season	League		F.A.Cup		Welsh Cup		Total	
	apps	gls	apps	gls	apps	gls	apps	gls
1925/26	1	0	-	-	-	-	1	0
	1	**0**	**-**	**-**	**-**	**-**	**1**	**0**

BRYANT, Clifford Samuel 1936 - 1937

Position; *Centre-Half*
D.O.B; *6th August 1913.*
Birthplace; *Kingswood, Bristol, Avon*
Died; *Bristol, 2nd December, 1997.*
Height; *5ft 10ins* ***Weight;*** *12st 0lbs*
Debut v. *Chester (a) 29th August, 1936*
Total Appearances & Goals; *8 apps 0 gls*
Career; *Wesley Rangers; Bristol Rovers Oct 1930 (pro May 1931) 1app 0gls; Blackburn Rovers 10th Jun 1932 4apps 0gls; WREXHAM May 1936; Cheltenham Town cs1937; Glastonbury 5th Sept 1938 (to 4th Sept 1939);*
Honours; *England Schoolboy International;*

Cliff Bryant was signed by Wrexham manager Ernie Blackburn in May 1936 from Blackburn Rovers. Cliff had made just four League appearances at Ewood Park in four years, including his debut away to Newcastle in April 1933, although he did tour Sweden and Denmark while at Blackburn. As a schoolboy Cliff represented Bristol Schools, and also won two caps for the England schoolboy team. After leaving school he played for a local side in Bristol, Wesley Rangers, from where he signed for Third Division South side, Bristol Rovers, initially as an amateur, in May 1932. With the West country outfit Cliff played at centre-half, making his Football League debut in March 1931 in a 2-1 home win over Fulham. Unfortunately, it proved to be his one and only League appearance for the Bristol club as he left in the close season of 1932, signing for Blackburn Rovers, which was followed by his move to The Racecourse Ground. He made his Wrexham debut in the opening match of the 1936/37 season in a disappointing 4-1 defeat at Chester. Following the defeat Cliff was replaced in the side by Jack Lewis, and didn't make another first team appearance until February, when he went on to play a further seven games before the end of the season. At the conclusion of the term Bryant was released by the club, and returned nearer to his native Bristol, joining Cheltenham Town. He spent a campaign here before playing for Glastonbury, where he remained up until the outbreak of WW2. After the conflict had ended he was too old to resume his football career and instead worked at his family off-licence and bakery in Queen Street, Kingswood, Bristol. He later worked for British Road Services and Rolls Royce, where he remained until his retirement. He didn't sever all links with football after he finished playing, as he became the West Country scout for West Bromwich Albion in 1947. Sadly, Cliff passed away on 2nd December 1997, just two weeks after his wife died. He was 84.

Season	League		F.A.Cup		Welsh Cup		Total	
	apps	gls	apps	gls	apps	gls	apps	gls
1936/37	8	0	-	-	-	-	8	0
	8	**0**	**-**	**-**	**-**	**-**	**8**	**0**

BRYANT, William 1933 - 1934

Position; *Outside-Right*
D.O.B; *26th November, 1913*
Birthplace; *Shildon, Durham*
Died; *County Durham, O/N/D 1975*
Height; *5ft 9'1/2in* ***Weight;*** *11st 6lbs*
Debut v. *Gateshead (h) 7th October, 1933.*
Total Appearances & Goals; *45 apps 17 gls*
Career; *Bishop Auckland Training Centre Juniors; Cockfield FC Aug 1931; Wolves Sept 1931 5apps 0gls; WREXHAM 4th Oct 1933; Manchester United 23rd Oct 1934 148apps 44gls; Chester (WW2 Guest) 1941/42 1app 1gls; Stockport County (WW2 Guest) 1945/46 1app 0gls; Bradford City 26th Nov 1945 (WW2) 22apps 2gls; Altrincham Aug 1946; Stalybridge Celtic;*
Honours; *Second Division Championship Winner 1936;*

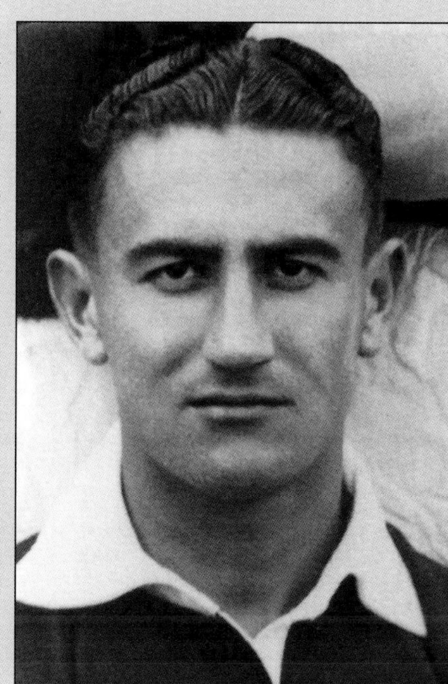

Although born in the North-East Bill Bryant was surprisingly signed by Wolves while playing for Durham Schools and local side Cockfield. He had previously played for his school, Timothy Huckworth, with whom he had picked up a County Durham Cup-winners' medal. Whilst representing Durham schoolboys he gained a Hyde Charity Shield winners' medal, and then won a Darlington Junior League Championship medal in 1931 with the Bishop Auckland Training Centre Juniors side. However, it was the Black Country club who gave him his first taste of League Football, signing professional in September 1931 and making his Football League debut in December 1932 in a 5-3 home win over Blackburn Rovers. Bill played in the following three matches, and then made one more appearance for Wolves at the beginning of the 1933/34 season before he was allowed to sign for Wrexham manager Ernie Blackburn in October 1933. At The Racecourse he teamed up with the club's prolific goalscorer, Tommy Bamford, and although Bill was to score his fair share of goals, including a hat-trick in the record 11-1 win over New Brighton in the Northern Section Cup, he was there mainly to provide the ammunition for Bamford, and they proved to be a successful combination. However, with the 1934/35 season only a month or two old Second Division Manchester United stepped in to sign both Bill and Tommy Bamford for a then club record fee. At Old Trafford Bryant made his debut in a 2-1 win at Blackpool, scoring United's first goal. He soon established himself in the United side and the following season helped them to the Second Division championship. He went on to make 148 League appearances for United, before WW2 was to interrupt League football. Bill was to continue playing for United in War-time football, turning out in well over 150 matches. He also 'guested' for Chester, Stockport County, and Bradford City during that period. With WW2 at an end was to make way for Johnny Delaney at United, and was released to join Bradford City, where he stayed for a brief spell before dropping into non-league football nine months later, playing for Altrincham in the Cheshire League, followed by a spell with Stalybridge Celtic. After he finished playing professional football Bill worked at I.C.I at Trafford Park in Manchester, in their standardising store. He later returned to live in his native County Durham where he died in 1975, aged 61. During his football career Bill had been described as 'A fast winger, with a fair shot. He rarely found the net, but provided his centre-forwards with fine openings.'

Season	League		F.A.Cup		Welsh Cup		N.S.C.		Total	
	apps	gls	apps	gls	apps	gls	apps	gls	apps	gls
1933/34	31	9	1	1	1	0	3	5	36	15
1934/35	9	2	-	-	-	-	-	-	9	2
	40	**11**	**1**	**1**	**1**	**0**	**3**	**5**	**45**	**17**

BULLING, James 1932 - 1936

Position; *Right-Half*
D.O.B; *12th February, 1909*
Birthplace; *West Bridgford, Nottinghamshire*
Died; *Wrexham, 13th October, 1992*
Height; *5ft 11'1/2in* ***Weight;*** *12st 0lbs*
Debut v. *Barnsley (h) 27th August, 1932*
Total Appearances & Goals; *133 apps 3 gls*
Career; *Nottingham Forest Feb 1928 0apps; Shirebrook Jul 1928; Leicester City Apr 1930 12apps 0gls; WREXHAM 18th Jun 1932; Shrewsbury Town Jun 1936 19apps 0gls;*
Honours; *Welsh Cup runner-up 1933;*

James Bulling's career never really got off the ground at Nottingham Forest, where he had first signed as a junior in 1928. He was the nephew of the Forest full-back, Harold Bulling, but found himself released by Forest without making a first team appearance. It was with local Notts side, Shirebrook, that Jim began to shine, First Division Leicester City taking notice and signing him in April 1930 along with another player, Charles Gellatly. With Leicester City he made his Football League debut at wing-half against Liverpool at Anfield in November 1930. However, after two seasons at Filbert Street, and eleven more League appearances, he found himself released. Jim soon fixed himself up with another club when he signed for Third Division North side Wrexham. Under the managership of Ernie Blackburn, Bulling missed only three matches in his first season at the Racecourse, which was to see the club just fail to secure promotion to the Second Division when they finished as runners'-up to Hull City, their highest pre-war position. That same season Bulling gained a Welsh Cup runners'-up medal when Wrexham lost 2-0 to Chester in the final. Over the next two seasons he was a regular in the team, but 1935/36 saw him face competition for his wing-half position from both Matt Lawrence and Dai Richards. At the end of the term he was released by the club, but was quickly snapped up by Birmingham & District League side Shrewsbury Town. He remained with the Shropshire club for one season, making his debut in a 3-0 win over Hereford. When his playing days were over he was to enlist in the Army when war broke out, joining the Royal Engineers with whom he saw service in Italy. After the hostilities had ended Jim worked as a plumber at Shotton Steelworks, where he stayed until his retirement in the 1970s. Jim died at his family home in Acton, Wrexham, in 1992. He was 83.

Season	League		F.A.Cup		Welsh Cup		Total	
	apps	gls	apps	gls	apps	gls	apps	gls
1932/33	39	1	3	0	6	0	48	1
1933/34	40	0	1	0	1	0	42	0
1934/35	32	2	-	-	1	0	33	2
1935/36	10	0	-	-	-	-	10	0
	121	**3**	**4**	**0**	**8**	**0**	**133**	**3**

BURDITT, George Leslie 1937 - 1939

Position; *Centre-Forward*
D.O.B; *27th February, 1910*
Birthplace; *Ibstock, Leicestershire*
Died; *Nottingham, O/N/D 1981*
Height; *5ft 10'1/2in* ***Weight;*** *11st 12lbs*
Debut v. *Bradford City (h) 13th November, 1937*
Total Appearances & Goals; *76 apps 44 gls*
Career; *Ibstock Penistone Rovers; Norwich City Apr 1931; Nottingham Forest Apr 1934 18apps 10gls; Millwall May 1936 1app 0gls; WREXHAM 12th Nov 1937; Doncaster Rovers 20th Apr 1939 0apps; Leeds United (WW2 Guest) 1940/41 9apps 3gls;*

George Burditt was signed by Nottingham Forest in April 1934 from Norwich City, with whom he had served as an apprentice since arriving from his local non-league side Ibstock Penistone Rovers in 1931. With Norwich, (for whom his brother, Fred, had also played, along with Millwall and Notts County), he failed to make a first team appearance, but at the City Ground scored 10 goals in just 18 League appearances during his only season at Forest, 1934/35, including a brace on his Football League debut, a 5-1 home win over Newcastle United. George struggled to keep his first team place throughout the season, and at the end of the term was transferred to Millwall. Whilst at Forest the Nottingham Post described him, 'As a marksman there is not much that he requires to learn.' His move to London to join his brother didn't work out as he had planned, and George made only one League appearance against Northampton Town on 2nd January 1937, a 1-0 home win. He stayed at 'The Den' until November 1937, when he was offered the chance of moving back North with Wrexham. Burditt went straight into the Wrexham team at centre-forward for his debut, a 2-1 home win over Bradford City in November 1937. He went on to play in every match until the end of the season, finishing as the club's second highest goalscorer behind his striking partner, Harold Lapham. The following season, 1938/39, George missed just three League games as he led the club's scoring charts with 29 goals in 45 League and Cup games. With just two games to go he was surprisingly allowed to leave The Racecourse, where he had been described as a 'strong, determined and enthusiastic player', joining Doncaster Rovers in April 1939. His time with Doncaster was to be short, although playing in their pre-season games, but when the 1939/40 season commenced he found himself in 'The Rovers' reserve side, and with the outbreak of war was to leave the Belle Vue club. During WW2 George played as a 'guest' for Leeds United.

Season	League		F.A.Cup		Welsh Cup		N.S.C.		Total	
	apps	gls	apps	gls	apps	gls	apps	gls	apps	gls
1937/38	28	13	2	1	1	1	-	-	31	15
1938/39	39	22	1	1	2	4	3	2	45	29
	67	**35**	**3**	**2**	**3**	**5**	**3**	**2**	**76**	**44**

BURGON, Frederick Archibald 1935 - 1939

Position; *Outside-Left*
D.O.B; *28th March, 1912*
Birthplace; *Nottingham, Nottinghamshire*
Died; *Metheringham, Lincs, 20th September, 1994*
Height; *5ft 10'1/2in* ***Weight;*** *11st 4lbs*
Debut v. *York City (a) 2nd November, 1935*
Total Appearances & Goals; *160 apps 43 gls*
Career; *West Bridgford Secondary School; Colwick FC; Burton Joyce FC; Grantham Town; Notts County (trial); Nottingham Forest (trial); Newark Town Nov 1931; Notts County Jun 1932 26apps 1gls; Grantham Town Aug 1934; Tottenham Hotspur Jan 1935 (£700) 4apps 0gls; WREXHAM 30th Oct 1935; Carlisle United cs1939 £150;*

After impressive performances playing in local non-league football for Newark Town and Grantham Town, plus trials with both Nottingham sides, Archie Burgon was finally signed by Notts County in the summer of 1932. County were a struggling Second Division side at the time, and Archie made his Football League debut for 'The Magpies' in a 2-2 home draw with Bury in October 1932. In spite of not appearing regularly in the County side his performances were still good enough for Tottenham Hotspur to come in and sign him for £700 in January 1935. The Spurs side at that time was fighting relegation, and Burgon made his debut in a 1-0 defeat at Aston Villa in February. He made just three more appearances for Spurs as they battled unsuccessfully to beat the drop. Archie found himself playing reserve team football at the start of the following season, and in October was allowed to leave White Hart Lane on a free transfer when he was signed by Wrexham manager Ernie Blackburn. Having played most of his football as a centre-forward, Archie was switched to outside-left, by Blackburn, a change which proved to be a good move, both for him and the club as he became a regular in the side for the next four seasons. Although Wrexham had a lack of success during this period Archie did have the honour of scoring against Manchester City in a 3-1 F.A.Cup defeat on the Racecourse in January 1937. This proved a successful season for him as he finished as the club's second top scorer to Harold Lapham, with twenty League and Cup goals. Archie remained at the Racecourse until the end of the 1938/39 season, when he was allowed to leave and join Carlisle United. He appeared in Carlisle's first two games of the 1939/40 season, before the outbreak of WW2. During the conflict he served in the R.A.F. as a fitter, continuing to play football for his R.A.F. station teams. After WW2 he became a partner in his family's Public House in Nottingham, before taking over as Landlord of the Star and Garter Pub in Metheringham, which is where he resided and passed away on 20th September 1994, aged 82. Noted as a first rate pianist often entertaining his team-mates.

Season	League		F.A.Cup		Welsh Cup		N.S.C.		Total	
	apps	gls	apps	gls	apps	gls	apps	gls	apps	gls
1935/36	29	6	1	0	2	0	2	2	34	8
1936/37	39	18	3	2	1	0	1	0	44	20
1937/38	36	6	2	1	1	0	1	0	40	7
1938/39	36	6	1	0	2	1	3	1	42	8
	140	**36**	**7**	**3**	**6**	**1**	**7**	**3**	**160**	**43**

***BURKINSHAW,* Ralph** 1930 - 1932

Position; *Centre-Half*
D.O.B; *26th March, 1898*
Birthplace; *Kilnhurst, Yorkshire.*
Died; *Mexborough, J/A/S 1951*
Height; *5ft 8'1/2in* ***Weight;*** *12st 7lbs*
Debut v. *Southport (a) 30th August, 1930*
Total Appearances & Goals; *73 apps 2 gls*
Career; *Mexborough Town Apr 1916; Barnsley (War-time player) Apr 1916; Sheffield Wednesday 1918 (War-time player) 10apps 1gls; Sheffield United Jan-Feb 1919; South Shields Aug 1919 2apps 0gls; Wath Athletic May 1920; Northampton Town Sept 1920 0apps; Gainsborough Trinity Oct 1920; Bury Nov 1920 105apps 20gls; Bradford City Jul 1925 166apps 30gls; WREXHAM 9th Jul 1930; Scarborough 13th Jul 1932; Mexborough Sept 1933; Denaby United Aug 1936;*
Honours; *Second Division runner-up 1924; Third Division North Championship Winner 1929; Welsh Cup Winner 1931;*

Ralph Burkinshaw began playing football during WW1 with Mexborough Town from where he was signed by Barnsley. He later joined Sheffield Wednesday during the 1918/19 season where his brothers, Jack and Laurie, were also on the club's books. Playing at centre-forward Ralph made his debut for 'The Owls' in a 2-0 defeat at Coventry City in a Midland Section Principal Tournament match. He made nine more appearances with Wednesday, together with a short spell at neighbours Sheffield United, before joining South Shields in the first season after WW1. A term with them was followed by a brief period with Wath Athletic, before trying his luck with Northampton Town in September 1920. He spent just one month with the 'Cobblers', without making a first team appearance, signing for Gainsborough Trinity for a month until recruited by Second Division Bury in November of the same year. At Gigg Lane he helped the club into the First Division in 1923/24 before joining Bradford City in July 1925, where he was quickly converted from his Inside-forward position to that of a right-half, due to of 'his shrewd positional sense and great anticipation of the game'. At Valley Parade the versatile performer helped Bradford to the Third Division North championship in 1929, before he was signed by Wrexham manager Jack Baynes in July 1930. He made his debut in the opening match of the 1930/31 season, at centre-half, in a 1-1 draw at Southport. In his first season at Wrexham his excellent reading of the game helped the club to reach a respectable fourth place, their second highest position since joining the Football League. In 1931 he was a member of the Welsh Cup winning side that beat Shrewsbury Town 7-0 in the final. In October of the following season Burkinshaw took over as caretaker manager when Jack Baynes became ill, and in December -when Baynes sadly passed away- Ralph was firm favourite to take over as club boss. It came as a big disappointment to him in January when the club announced that former Accrington manager, Ernie Blackburn, would be the new manager at Wrexham. Burkinshaw stepped down to continue in his playing role, but at the end of the season was released. He then dropped back into non-league football with Scarborough, for one season before joining his old club, Mexborough, until they were disbanded in 1936. He ended his playing career with Denaby United, having taken over the Wine Lodge public house in Mexborough after leaving Wrexham. He later worked as a baker at Bessimes Bakery in the town. Ralph died in 1951, whilst still in his early fifties.

Season	League		F.A.Cup		Welsh Cup		Total	
	apps	gls	apps	gls	apps	gls	apps	gls
1930/31	37	1	3	0	4	1	44	2
1931/32	27	0	1	0	1	0	29	0
	64	**1**	**4**	**0**	**5**	**1**	**73**	**2**

***BURROWS,* Wilfred** 1931 - 1933

Position; *Goalkeeper*
D.O.B; *16th February, 1902.*
Birthplace; *Castleford, Yorkshire.*
Died; *Leeds, July 1985*
Height; *5ft 9'1/2in* ***Weight;*** *11st 0lbs*
Debut v. *Chester (a) 30th September, 1931*
Total Appearances & Goals; *35 apps 0 gls*
Career; *Castleford; Selby Town; Tranmere Rovers Aug 1925 49apps 0gls; WREXHAM 16th Jul 1931; York City Sep 1933 3apps 0gls; Bangor City 27th Oct 1934; Bury Mar 1935 0apps; Colwyn Bay 20th Aug 1936; Shrewsbury Town Oct 1936;*
Honours; *Welsh Cup runner-up 1932;*

Wilf Burrows was keeping goal for Selby Town when Tranmere Rovers manager Bert Cooke signed the ex-Castleford custodian in August 1925. He remained six years at Prenton Park, and was a regular in the side until Bert Gray, the Welsh international 'keeper, took over. He was then signed by Jack Baynes, the Wrexham manager, in the summer of 1931 as cover

for Dick Finnigan. Burrows had to wait patiently before he could make his debut for 'The Robins', which came at the end of September. However, disaster was to strike when, after only five League games, he broke his arm in a League match at Darlington, which was to put him out of the side until the following April. He then stepped in for Ted Adams, who had joined the club following his injury. Wilf played in the last six matches of that season, as well as appearing in the Welsh Cup final, a 2-0 defeat at Swansea. He started the 1932/33 season as the club's first choice 'keeper, but following a 5-3 defeat at Accrington Ted Adams was chosen for the following game and kept his place in the side for the rest of the season. Wilf had to be content with reserve team football as the beginning of the 1933/34 season again saw Burrows playing second fiddle to Adams, and in September 1933 he decided to leave the Racecourse, signing for York City. He was to find himself again acting as first team cover at Bootham Crescent, this time for Des Fawcett. During his twelve months with York Wilf was to make just three League appearances, which included a home game against his former club, Wrexham, which York lost 4-2 on the last day of the season proving to be Wilf's final appearance for the Minstermen before he was released in the summer of 1934. He showed his liking for North Wales where he joined Bangor City, followed by a short spell with Bury, where he was signed as cover. He returned once again to North Wales, signing for Colwyn Bay for a short spell, until joining Birmingham & District League side Shrewsbury Town in October 1936, after the Shropshire club had sold their first choice 'keeper, Walter Rigby, to Aston Villa for £350. Wilf made his Shrewsbury debut in a 3-1 win over Brierley Hill Alliance, and stayed at the Gay Meadow until the end of the 1936/37 season.

Season	League		F.A.Cup		Welsh Cup		Total	
	apps	gls	apps	gls	apps	gls	apps	gls
1931/32	11	0	-	-	4	0	15	0
1932/33	17	0	3	0	-	-	20	0
	28	**0**	**3**	**0**	**4**	**0**	**35**	**0**

BURTON, Matthew 1921 - 1923

Position; *Outside-Left*
D.O.B; *8th February, 1897.*
Birthplace; *Grassmoor, Derbyshire*
Died; *Hasland, Nr.Grassmoor, 16th May, 1940*
Height; *5ft 9in* ***Weight;*** *12st 0lbs*
Debut v. *Hartlepool United (h) 27th August, 1921*
Total Appearances & Goals; *67 apps 13 gls*
Career; *Grassmoor Athletic; Everton during WW1; Stoke City 20th Jan 1920 (£75 fee) 8apps 1gls; WREXHAM 22nd August 1921; New Brighton 12th July 1923 16apps 6gls; Oswestry Town 6th Jun 1925; Rhos Athletic Mar 1926; Llandudno 28th Jun 1926; Rhos Athletic 24th Aug 1927; Connah's Quay & Shotton 10th Dec 1927 to 6th April, 1928;*
Honours; *Cheshire Senior Cup Winner 1924;*

Matthew Burton was playing for his local side, Grassmoor Athletic (which is near Chesterfield), as a left winger when spotted by Everton, for whom he duly signed during the WW1 period. However, he failed to make a first team appearance for the Goodison Park club, and in January 1920 was signed by Stoke City for a £75 fee. It was with the 'Potteries' club that Matt finally made his Football League debut in February 1920 in a 1-0 defeat at Bury. He made seven more League appearances for Stoke before being transferred to Third Division North founder members Wrexham in the summer of 1921. At Wrexham Matt figured in the club's first ever Football League match against Hartlepool United, and in the inaugural season was a first team regular, playing in either wing positions and even at centre-forward, ending the season as the club's leading goalscorer with nine goals. He was described as being 'a lively winger, who was not averse to a first time shot.' The following season, the goals dried up, and at the end of the campaign he found himself released. Burton then signed for New Brighton who had just been elected to the Third Division North. He was to remain with the Wirral club for two seasons, scoring the winning goal in the 1924 Cheshire Senior Cup final replay win over Tranmere Rovers. Following an injury in a Cheshire Cup match with Witton Albion in December 1924 he never made another first team appearance for the 'Rakers', and it was around this time that he was jailed for two months for an offence of bigamy. Matt joined Birmingham and District League side Oswestry Town, in June 1925. However, later that season he played in Welsh National League football for Rhos Athletic, before joining Connah's Quay in December 1927. He later returned to his native Chesterfield where he finally settled, continuing to work as a miner, a job that he had done since leaving school. Sadly, Matt died in tragic circumstances in May 1940 of hypothermia. He had been out with some friends and, due to drinking a little too much, fell asleep and was found the following morning.

Season	League		F.A.Cup		Welsh Cup		Total	
	apps	gls	apps	gls	apps	gls	apps	gls
1921/22	32	9	4	3	3	0	39	12
1922/23	22	1	3	0	3	0	28	1
	54	**10**	**7**	**3**	**6**	**0**	**67**	**13**

BUTT, Robert Edwin 1964 - 1965

Position; *Outside-Right*
D.O.B; *27th March, 1946*
Birthplace; *Chester, Cheshire*
Height; *5ft 3in* ***Weight;*** *9st 7lbs*
Debut v. *Southport (a) 19th April, 1965*
Total Appearances & Goals; *3 apps 0 gls*
Career; *WREXHAM (Am) 1961; Shotton Lane Youth Club Aug 1963; Shrewsbury Town Dec 1963 0apps; Wrexham Jan 1965; Ellesmere Port Town cs1966; Connah's Quay Nomads 1967/68; Pwllheli;*

Robert Butt joined Wrexham in 1961 at the age of fifteen having played for his school team, Aston County Secondary School in Queensferry, and also Flintshire schoolboys. When leaving school Bobby was invited for trials with Wrexham after both Ken Barnes and Ken Roberts had watched him playing for his school team. He was then offered the chance to join the groundstaff at the Racecourse. Butt remained with Wrexham until the end of 1962/63, when he was released. He began the new 1963/64 season with his local side, Shotton Lane Youth Club, but his time there was short as Bobby was signed by Shrewsbury Town manager Arthur Rowley. He stayed with the Gay Meadow club for just over twelve months but never made a first team appearance, playing for the reserve side for most of the time in the Combination League against the likes of Tottenham, Arsenal, and Chelsea's reserve teams. He felt that he wasn't making any progress with 'The Shrews', and left the Shropshire to rejoin Wrexham in January 1965, who were still managed by Ken Barnes. Shortly after he had returned to the Racecourse the club saw a change in manager, with Billy Morris installed. The management take over saw Bobby finally make his Football League debut on 19th April 1965, playing in place of Graham 'Flicka' Williams on the right wing in a 2-0 win at Southport, which was followed by two more appearances, both 1-0 defeats, at Hartlepool United and at home to Millwall. Those three games proved to be Bobby's only Football League experiences as he was released by the club at the end of the 1965/66 season. Butt then joined Ellesmere Port Town who at that time played in the Cheshire League. His first game ironically was against Wrexham reserves, and he went on to spend around eighteen months there before joining Connah's Quay Nomads, who had just won promotion to the Welsh League. Bobby spent a number of enjoyable seasons at the Halfway ground before he received a call from a former

Wrexham team mate, Barry Wright, who was manager of Welsh League side Pwllheli, to join him. After he had finished playing professional football Butt took up work at Shotton Steelworks, where he is still employed after 35 years. He is currently a Senior Union Official for the Transport and General Workers Union, and a Trustee of the company Pension Scheme, while also finding time to be a Magistrate since 1992. Bobby was still living in Shotton in 1998.

Season	League		F.A.Cup		Welsh Cup		League Cup		Total	
	apps	gls	apps	gls	apps	gls	apps	gls	apps	gls
1964/65	3	0	-	-	-	-	-	-	3	0
	3	**0**	-	-	-	-	-	-	**3**	**0**

BUXTON, Arthur

1930 - 1933

Position; *Left-Back*
D.O.B; *15th May, 1908*
Birthplace; *Barlborough, Derbyshire*
Died; *Wrexham, 8th January 1979.*
Height; *5ft 10'1/2in* ***Weight;*** *11st 10lbs*
Debut v. *Southport (a) 30th August, 1930*
Total Appearances & Goals; *22 apps 0 gls*
Career; *Worksop Town; WREXHAM 27th May 1930; Ripley Town (trial) cs1931; Lincoln City Mar 1932 0apps; WREXHAM 5th May 1932; Luton Town Sept 1932 (trial) Wellington Town 1932 (trial); Bangor City July 1933; Wellington Town Aug 1934; New Brighton 10th Aug 1937 54apps 0gls; WREXHAM (War-time Guest) Dec 1940 4apps 0gls;*
Honours; *Welsh Cup runner-up 1932; Birmingham League Championship Winner 1935 & 1936; North Wales Coast F.A.Challenge Cup runner-up 1934; Derbyshire League Cup Winner 1929;*

Derbyshire born, Arthur Buxton signed for Wrexham from non-league Worksop Town in May 1930 when still a teenager, having attended Barlborough school. He made his Football League debut in the opening match of the 1930/31 season, a 1-1 draw at Southport, and appeared in the next five games before Wynne Crompton stepped in to replace him. Arthur was to remain as an understudy to both Welsh international Crompton and Jack Brown during his three seasons at the Racecourse, although during that time he had trials with many clubs in order to secure regular first team football. His trial periods included stints with Ripley Town, Lincoln City, Luton Town, and Wellington Town, each time returning to the Racecourse. Buxton had come back to Wrexham at the beginning of May in time to deputise for the injured John Donoghue in the 1932 Welsh Cup final with Swansea Town, which Wrexham lost 2-0 after a replay. The beginning of the 1932/33 season turned out to be a disaster for Arthur as he broke an ankle in a pre-season trial match which sidelined him for most of that term. When he had finally recovered his fitness he found that he was to be released at the end of the campaign, though soon fixed up with another club when he signed for Bangor City. During the summer months Buxton was a keen cricketer, and played regularly throughout the 1930's and 1940's for Marchwiel, as well as representing Denbighshire. Arthur spent one season with Bangor City, before joining Birmingham & District League side Wellington Town, where he was to remain for three seasons, making over 140 appearances and winning two League Championship medals. In August 1937 he made a surprising return to the Football League when signing for New Brighton. He began life with the 'Rakers' in the reserves, but after a switch to centre-half he got his first team chance and became the pivot of the New Brighton defence for the rest of the term. The following season he reverted to his more familiar left-back position, and had accumulated 54 League appearances for New Brighton when World War Two was to disrupt his playing career. Buxton made a further 24 War-time appearances for New Brighton before leaving them in the close season of 1940. He made four 'guest' appearances for Wrexham the following term, finally retiring from playing. During WW2, Arthur was employed at the War Ammunitions factory in Marchwiel, near Wrexham, the town in which he settled. After the hostilities had ended he took up work at Bersham Colliery before going on to work at the Abenbury Brickworks, where he was employed for 27 years up until his retirement in 1974. Arthur died in Wrexham in January 1979, aged 70.

Season	League		F.A.Cup		Welsh Cup		Total	
	apps	gls	apps	gls	apps	gls	apps	gls
1930/31	14	0	1	0	-	-	15	0
1931/32	1	0	-	-	2	0	3	0
1940/41	4	0	-	-	-	-	4	0
	19	**0**	**1**	**0**	**2**	**0**	**22**	**0**

BUXTON, Steven Christopher

1977 - 1984 & 1986 - 1990

Position; *Forward*
D.O.B; *13th March, 1960*
Birthplace; *Birmingham, West Midlands*
Height; *5ft 5in* ***Weight;*** *11st 2lbs*
Debut v. *Sheffield Wednesday (a) 3rd May, 1978*
Total Appearances & Goals; *229/70 apps 65 gls*
Career; *WREXHAM Jul 1978; Sweden cs1984; Stockport County Jul 1984 12/6apps 1gls; Altrincham 1985; WREXHAM Oct 1985; Telford United Aug 1990 14apps 2gls; Northwich Victoria Jan 1991 13/3apps 3gls; Newtown Sept 1991; Mold Alex Aug 1992 13/1apps 8gls; Bangor City Feb 1993 44/22apps 21gls; Holywell Town Jul 1996 17/1apps 3gls; Flint Town United Jun 1997 30/4apps 5gls;*
Honours; *Welsh Cup Winner 1986; Wels*h Cup runner-up 1979, 1981, 1983 & 1988; League of Wales Championship Winner 1994 & 1995; Welsh Youth Cup Winner 1978; Welsh Schoolboy International;

Having been capped at Welsh Schoolboy level Wrexham were quick to recognise the potential of Steve Buxton, who they signed on apprentice terms in 1976. Steve was given his first team chance when he came on as substitute against Sheffield Wednesday at Hillsborough in the final game of the 1977/78 season, which had been the greatest in Wrexham's history. Over the four that Wrexham experienced in the Second Division Buxton was never a regular but was a vital member of the first team squad, someone who when called upon could guarantee that he would give 110%. Successive relegations saw the club finish up in the Fourth Division at the end of the 1983/84 season. A 'clash of personalities' with manager Bobby Roberts would see him leave Wrexham and go to play in Sweden for a short spell. He returned for the new season and joined Stockport County, but after only 18 League games and one goal, left Edgeley Park for Altrincham, while also taking up the offer of work at Tetra Pak as a machine operator. He kept in trim by training at the Racecourse, as former team-mate Dixie McNeil had become the new manager. During the 1985/86 season, with Dixie's squad beset by injury problems, Steve was signed on a non-contract basis. The following season the arrangement was extended, with the condition that Steve could still carry on working. He stayed at the Racecourse until the summer of 1990, by which time he had played in both European Cup-Winners' Cup matches against Real Zaragoza, coming on as substitute and scoring in the second leg match. He also gained a Welsh Cup winners medal in the 1986 final against Kidderminster Harriers, and added a runners-up medal in the same competition in 1988. Steve holds the unique record of having made more Football League substitute appearances than any other player for Wrexham, with 50. After his release in 1990 he joined Telford United,

along with Neil Salathiel, but later that season moved to Northwich Victoria, before trying his luck with Newtown in September 1991. In the summer of 1992 Buxton joined Mold Alexandra for their first season in the League of Wales. However, by February, he had left Mold to join Bangor City, winning a League of Wales Championship medal the following. Steve's time with Bangor saw him suffer with many injury problems, and in July 1996 he joined Holywell Town. Injuries again disrupted his appearances, and Holywell were relegated from the Welsh flagship League at the end of 1996/97. He then left the club to take up the post of assistant player/manager at Flint Town United in June 1997, who suffered relegation at the end of 1997/98 from the League of Wales, but continued in the same capacity in the Cymru Alliance in 1998/99 season. 'A busy player always liking to be in the thick of the action'.

Season	League		F.A.Cup		Welsh Cup		League Cup		F.R.T.		E.C.W.C.		Total	
	apps	gls	apps	gls	apps	gls	apps	gls	apps	gls	apps	gls	apps	gls
1977/78	0/1	0	-	-	-	-	-	-	-	-	-	-	0/1	0
1978/79	10/3	2	-	-	2/1	1	-	-	-	-	-	-	12/4	3
1979/80	9/4	1	0/1	0	0/1	0	1/1	0	-	-	0/2	1	10/9	2
1980/81	10/4	2	1	0	0/2	0	-	-	-	-	-	-	11/6	2
1981/82	7/2	3	1	0	2	0	0/1	0	-	-	-	-	10/3	3
1982/83	39	10	2	0	6	3	2	0	-	-	-	-	49	13
1983/84	18/2	3	-	-	3	0	-	-	2	0	-	-	23/2	3
1985/86	1/4	3	1	0	1	0	-	-	-	-	-	-	3/4	3
1986/87	17/12	8	1	1	2	1	0/2	1	5	2	0/3	1	25/17	14
1987/88	27/8	6	2	1	4/2	3	0/2	0	-	-	-	-	33/12	10
1988/89	25/7*	4	-	-	3	2	2	2	2	0	-	-	32/5*	8
1989/90	16/5	4	1	0	2	0	2	0	0/2	0	-	-	21/7	4
	179/50*	**46**	**9/1**	**2**	**25/6**	**10**	**7/6**	**3**	**9/2**	**2**	**0/5**	**2**	**229/70**	**65**

* = includes play-off matches apps.

C

Bob Connor

CAMPBELL, David 1965 - 1967

Position; *Forward*
D.O.B; *18th February, 1947*
Birthplace; *Wrexham, Denbighshire*
Height; *5ft 9in* **Weight;** *11st 2lbs*
Debut v. *Hartlepool United (a) 24th April, 1965*
Total Appearances & Goals; *46/3 apps 7 gls*
Career; *Druids United cs1962; Manchester United 1963; WREXHAM (Am) May 1964, (Pro) 1st Jul 1965; Corby Town cs1967; Bangor City 25th Mar 1968; Caernarfon Town 3rd Sept 1968; Prestatyn 25th Mar 1969; Overton 1972;*
Honours; *Welsh Cup runner-up 1965 & 1967;*

David Campbell played football for Rhosddu Junior and Victoria Secondary Modern schools, followed by Yale Grammar School. While at school he was also selected to represent Wrexham and District Schoolboys. At 15 Dave left school, and attended the Technical College in Wrexham on a Plumbers' course. As for football, he signed amateur forms for Druids United, who had a strong connection at that time with Manchester United. He had only played around eight or nine games for Druids when invited to join the groundstaff at Old Trafford in 1963. His first match for United was a 'B' game at Everton's Belfield training ground, with George Best playing in the same side. Dave progressed through the youth ranks with United, and also played one Central League match. However, at the end of the 1963/64 season he was told by Matt Busby that he did not consider him good enough, though Busby did contact Wrexham manager Ken Barnes to recommend Dave to him. Although disillusioned by his release, and still only seventeen years-old, Campbell joined the groundstaff at Wrexham in May 1964. He then progressed playing regular reserve team football, doing enough to earn a first team call up for his debut at Hartlepool United in April 1965, in a 1-0 defeat, a month before signing professional. Campbell made one more League appearance that season, and appeared in the 1965 Welsh Cup Final against Cardiff City, who included John Charles and Ivor Allchurch in their side, as they beat Wrexham 3-0 at Shrewsbury's Gay Meadow. 1965/66 saw Dave playing regularly on the left wing, but overall it was a disappointing period for Wrexham as the club finished 92nd in the Football League and had to seek re-election for the only time in the club's history. Dave did make club history that season when he became the first player to come on as a substitute in a Football League match, in a 2-0 defeat at Doncaster Rovers, when he replaced Martyn King. With the club re-elected and a new manager, Jack Rowley, at the helm Dave was to find his first team chances limited, as injury kept him sidelined for most of the season. It wasn't until March 1967 that he returned to action, which enabled him to play in the Welsh Cup Final, against Cardiff City again, which Wrexham lost 4-3 on aggregate. At the end of the season new manager, Alvan Williams, decided to release Campbell and his name was circulated around other clubs. He joined Corby Town of the Southern League, for one season playing alongside a young Dixie McNeil. Whilst there Dave worked on a building site, which he followed with employment at the local steelworks. He returned to the Wrexham area and signed for Bangor City towards the end of the season. His stay at Farrar Road was short, as he joined Caernarvon Town in September 1968, remaining until March 1969 moving to Prestatyn until the end of the season. Dave did not play football again for three years, until turning out for Overton in the Welsh National League, playing about five games before suffering a knee injury in a game that was to end his playing career. Campbell helped form the 'Acton' public house Sunday football team, later managing the 'Gate', Wrexham area Sunday XI. He took up coaching youngsters in Garden Village, going on to assist with the youths at Lex XI. Dave worked at a number of local factories in the Wrexham area before a car accident left him suffering with spondilos. He still lives in the Wrexham area.

Season	League apps	gls	F.A.Cup apps	gls	Welsh Cup apps	gls	League Cup apps	gls	Total apps	gls
1964/65	2	0	-	-	1	0	-	-	3	0
1965/66	34/1	6	1	0	1	0	1	0	37/1	6
1966/67	5/1	1	-	-	1/1	0	-	-	6/2	1
	41/2	**7**	**1**	**0**	**3/1**	**0**	**1**	**0**	**46/3**	**7**

CAPPER, John 1949 - 1955

Position; *Centre-Back*
D.O.B; *23rd July, 1931*
Birthplace; *Wrexham, Denbighshire*
Height; *6ft 1in* **Weight;** *11st 8lbs*
Debut v. *Grimsby Town (a) 23rd August, 1952*
Total Appearances & goals; *55 apps 0 gls*
Career; *Victoria Y.C; WREXHAM 1st Nov 1949; Headington United Jun 1955; Lincoln City Jan 1956 21apps 0gls; Chester Sept 1959 36apps 0gls;*

Although christened John he was always known as 'Jack' Capper. Jack joined Wrexham as a Junior in 1947 and went on to sign a professional contract in November 1949. A strapping six foot centre-half, he had begun playing football while at Victoria Junior School in Wrexham, continuing at Grove Park Grammar School. He played local football for New Broughton and Victoria Youth clubs. When first joining Wrexham Jack played in the 'A' team, in the Welsh National League Wrexham area, progressing to the reserves in the Cheshire League. Not long after signing professional Jack was called up for his National Service in the Army, serving with the Royal Artillery in Hong Kong, Malaysia, and Singapore. He did, however, play football when time allowed, appearing for the Army's Far East Land Forces team, and also the Hong Kong Colony XI. Capper finished his two year stint in the forces in October 1951 and, upon his return, resumed playing for Wrexham's Cheshire League side, appearing regularly until the start of the 1952/53 season. Manager Peter Jackson then played him in the opening two games of the season, after regular centre-half George Spruce had been sold to Barnsley. When Jack picked up an injury Ron Wynn took over, and he struggled to win back his place in the side. He reclaimed his position for the last sixteen matches of the season helping Wrexham to finish in third place in the League, the highest position since 1933. Over the next two seasons he found himself sharing the centre-half position with Ronnie Wynn, and at the end of 1954/55 a Benefit match was awarded for his loyal service to Wrexham with 'The Robins' entertaining a Football League XI. He was described in the match programme by Wrexham's secretary/manager, Cliff Lloyd, "A good club man and, although his career has been interrupted by National Service, and a fair share of injury, he is always ready to do what he can for the club." The following month Jack joined Southern League side, Headington United, who later became members of the Football League as Oxford United. His stay in Oxford lasted until January 1956, when Second Division Lincoln City stepped in to sign the 6ft 1in pivot as cover. His appearances were restricted at Sincil Bank to just 21 League games in over three years by the form of Tony Emery, a Lincoln stalwart of over 400 appearances. In September 1959 Jack was signed by Chester for £1,500, and made his debut in a 2-1 defeat at Carlisle United in place of George Spruce, who had kept Capper out of the side at Wrexham. He enjoyed two seasons with the Sealand Road club, before deciding to retire from football in May 1961, at the age of 29, when joining the Lincolnshire Police Force. He was later promoted to Detective Sergeant, and served with the Police up until his semi-retirement. Jack then returned to live in Wrexham, where he spent a short time as the Chief Security Officer at Prest Haven Holiday Camp in Prestatyn. Capper was still living in Wrexham in 1998.

Season	League apps	gls	F.A.Cup apps	gls	Welsh Cup apps	gls	Total apps	gls
1952/53	18	0	-	-	-	-	18	0
1953/54	13	0	5	0	-	-	18	0
1954/55	17	0	2	0	-	-	19	0
	48	**0**	**7**	**0**	**-**	**-**	**55**	**0**

CAREY, Brian Patrick 1991 - 1992 & 1996 -

Position; *Centre-Half*
D.O.B; *31st May, 1968*
Birthplace; *Cork, Republic of Ireland*
Height; *6ft 3in* ***Weight;*** *13st 9lbs*
Debut v. *Peterborough United (a) 19th January, 1991*
Total Appearances & Goals; *181apps 4 gls*
Career; *Albert Rovers; Cork City Sept 1987; Manchester United 2nd Sept 1989 £100,000 0apps; WREXHAM (Loan) 17th Jan 1991, (Loan) 24th Dec 1991; Leicester City 16th Jul 1993 £250,000 35/4apps 0gls; WREXHAM 8th Jul 1996 £100,000;*
Honours; *Three Eire International caps; One Eire Under-21 International cap; F.A.I. Cup runner-up 1989; Welsh Invitation Cup Winner 1998; Welsh Premier Cup runner-up 1999;*

Brian Carey first began playing football for a local junior side in his native Cork, Greenwood FC, as football had been overtaken by both Hurling and Gaelic football as the main participant sports at his school. Brian later joined Munster Senior League side, Albert Rovers, before he was signed by Cork City manager Eamonn O'Keefe in the close season of 1987. Like most players in the League of Ireland Brian was a part-timer, and he combined playing football with his college studies in Quantity Surveying. He went on to help Cork reach the Irish Cup final in 1989, losing to Derry City. At that match Brian was spotted by Manchester United manager, Alex Ferguson. He remained in Ireland taking his final exams at college before joining the Old Trafford club. Carey faced stiff opposition for a first team place, and in four years with United never made a first team appearance in a competitive match. Nonetheless, he caught Jack Charlton's eye and won the first of his three Irish international caps in April 1992 in a 4-1 home win over U.S.A. In January 1991 Brian began the first of two loan spells with Wrexham, making his Football League debut in a 2-2 draw at Peterborough. That first spell saw Brian make just three League appearances in total, but it was during his second loan period that both Brian and Wrexham really hit the headlines when he played in the club's memorable F.A.Cup giant-killing victory against the Football League Champions, Arsenal, in January 1992. Despite Brian's performances he was allowed to leave Old Trafford at the end of the season, and joined Leicester City for £250,000, where manager Brian Little was planning his third consecutive tilt at play-off assisted promotion. The 1993/94 season saw a number of defensive combinations tried at Filbert St, with Brian finding it hard to impose himself, but he did enough to help Leicester reach their goal, and at the end of the season played at Wembley in Leicester's play-off final win over Derby County. Carey made his Premier League debut against Wimbledon at Selhurst Park in the first game of the season, but suffered the ignominy of being sent-off! Brian then failed to win his place back in the side and asked for a transfer in January 1995. However, it wasn't until May and Leicester's relegation that Brian was made open to offers, and as none materialised, continued with Leicester throughout the following season on a weekly contract, helping them reach the Premier League via the play-offs once again beating Crystal Palace in the final. In July 1996, following the departure of Barry Hunter to Reading, Wrexham stepped in to sign him for £100,000 as the perfect replacement. He played a major part in his first season back at Wrexham, helping them reach the quarter-finals of the F.A.Cup for only the third time in the club's history, before losing 1-0 to Chesterfield, and missing out on a lucrative semi-final match with Middlesbrough. The 1997/98 season saw Brian inspire Wrexham towards the play-offs, just missing out on goals scored, although helping 'The Robins', win the Welsh Invitation Cup in its initial season, beating Cardiff City 2-1 in the final. He was then honoured when named as the club's 'Player of the Season' for the second successive campaign. One of Wrexham's best ever signings - organises the back division well with his assured displays at the heart of defence. One of his biggest assets is being able to use his height to great advantage in either penalty area.

Season	League		F.A.Cup		Welsh Cup		League Cup		A.G.T.		Total	
	apps	gls	apps	gls	apps	gls	apps	gls	apps	gls	apps	gls
1990/91	3	0	-	-	-	-	-	-	-	-	3	0
1991/92	13	1	3	0	1	1	-	-	-	-	17	2
1996/97	38	0	9	0	-	-	2	0	1	0	50	0
1997/98	43	1	3	0	8*	0*	2	0	1	0	57	2
1998/99	36	2	3	0	8*	0*	2	0	5	0	54	2
	133	**4**	**18**	**0**	**17**	**0**	**6**	**0**	**7**	**0**	**181**	**6**

* = Welsh Invitation/Premier Cup.

CARRICK, David Matthew 1966 - 1968

Position; *Inside-Forward*
D.O.B; *5th December, 1946*
Birthplace; *Ramshaw, Lancashire*
Died; *Manchester, 1st July, 1989*
Height; *5ft 7in* ***Weight;*** *10st 12lbs*
Debut v. *Exeter City (h) 20th August, 1966*
Total Appearances & Goals; *30/4 apps 4 gls*
Career; *Wolves Dec 1964 0apps; WREXHAM 1st Jul 1966; Altrincham cs1968; Port Vale Jan 1969 14/2apps 1gls; Stalybridge Celtic Apr 1969; Witton Albion Aug 1971; Preston North End Nov 1973 0/2apps 0gls; Rochdale Mar 1974 25/1apps 4gls; Droylsden 1975; Altrincham; Oswestry Town Jul 1979;*

David Carrick arrived at the Racecourse for a 'nominal' fee from Wolves. He was signed by Wrexham on the same day as Mickey Evans, who had also joined from Molineux. David made his debut at outside-left on the opening day of the 1966/67 season, against Exeter City in a scoreless home draw, but a defeat in the next game at Hartlepool United saw him fall out of favour. It wasn't until November that he regained his place in the team, when scoring the first goal in the 3-2 F.A.Cup win over Chesterfield on the Racecourse. By March he had lost his place once again, and missed out on the 1967 Welsh Cup final against Cardiff City having played in all the previous rounds. The following season Carrick again found his first team chances limited, making just a handful of League appearances before leaving the Racecourse at the end of the campaign to join Cheshire League side Altrincham. It wasn't long before he was back in League football, joining Port Vale in January 1969. He made 16 League appearances for Vale, but was released at the end of the season and once again returned to non-league football. Dave had spells with Stalybridge Celtic and Witton Albion before returning yet again to Football League action with Preston North End in November 1973. However, he only made two substitute appearances for the Deepdale club, and in March 1974 signed for Rochdale. At Spotland Dave made his debut in a 4-0 defeat at Aldershot, spending just over a season there, making 26 League appearances and scoring four goals. At the end of the 1974/75 season he once again drifted back into non-league football with Droylsden. Carrick went on to play for a number of non-league sides, which included both Altrincham and Oswestry Town. Sadly, Dave contacted Motor Neurone disease, and he died before his fortieth birthday at a Manchester Hospice in July 1989.

Season	League		F.A.Cup		Welsh Cup		League Cup		Total	
	apps	gls	apps	gls	apps	gls	apps	gls	apps	gls
1966/67	18/1	3	2	0	4	1	1	0	25/1	4
1967/68	2/3	0	1	0	1	0	1	0	5/3	0
	20/4	**3**	**3**	**0**	**5**	**1**	**2**	**0**	**30/4**	**4**

CARRODUS, Francis 1979 - 1982

Position; *Midfielder*
D.O.B; *31st May, 1949*
Birthplace; *Manchester, Lancashire*
Height; *5ft 9in* ***Weight;*** *10st 11lbs*
Debut v. *Luton Town (h) 15th December, 1979*
Total Appearances & Goals; *116/1 apps 8 gls*
Career; *Lymm Grammar School Old Boys; Old Altrinchiams Old Boys; Heyes Albion; Altrincham July 1964; Manchester City Nov 1969 33/9apps 1gls; Aston Villa 15th Aug 1974 £100,000 150apps 7gls; WREXHAM 12th Dec 1979 £70,000; Birmingham City Aug 1982 7/1apps; Bury Oct 1983 31/3apps 1gls; Witton Albion 1984/85; Runcorn cs1985; Altrincham cs1986; Macclesfield Town; Old Altrinchiams;*
Honours; *Second Division runner-up 1975; League Cup Winner 1975 & 1977; F.A.Trophy runner-up 1986; Champion Shield Winner 1985;*

Frank Carrodus began playing football at an early age in the town of Altrincham. Appearing for Heyes Primary, Wellington Secondary, and Lymm Grammar Schools, and later with Lymm Grammar School Old Boys, Old Altrinchiams and Heyes Albion. Early promise with these local sides led to Frank signing for Cheshire League Altrincham in July 1964. His performances for 'Alty' soon attracted Football League scouts to Moss Lane and in November 1969, at the age of 20, he was signed by

Manchester City following assistant manager, Malcolm Allison's, recommendation. Frank initially joined City as a part-timer, as he wished to complete his studies, but in February 1970 made his Football League debut in a 1-1 draw with Arsenal at Maine Road. In almost five years at Maine Road Frank found it difficult to sustain a regular first team place, especially with the likes of Colin Bell and Mike Summerbee in the side. After 42 League appearances he was sold to Aston Villa for £100,000 in July 1974. With Villa, Frank became a regular in the team assisting them to a promotion and League Cup double in 1975, adding another League Cup winners' medal in 1977. 1978/79 was a right-off for Carrodus, as he underwent three knee operations in fourteen months. With Villa wanting him to retire and take a testimonial he overcame his injury problems, and when Arfon Griffiths' Second Division Wrexham were keen to boost their midfield Villa agreed to let him go for a £70,000 fee. Frank's stay at the Racecourse lasted for nearly three seasons in which time he surprisingly missed only ten League matches. His most memorable match for Wrexham was the 3-1 F.A.Cup win over European Cup holders, Nottingham Forest, on the City Ground. He was also voted as runner-up to Eddie Niedzwiecki for the 'Player of the Season' award in 1981/82, which proved to be his final term with 'The Robins' as he joined Birmingham City for the start of the following campaign. Carrodus made his debut for 'The Blues' in a 3-0 defeat at Old Trafford, but just seven games later was out injured and another knee operation was required. Frank overcame that, and joined Fourth Division Bury for the 1983/84 season. He spent one season at Gigg Lane before returning to the non-league scene with Runcorn, winning a Champions' Shield Winners' medal as Bob Lord Trophy holders, beating Wealdstone, champions of the Gola League. At the end of 1985/86 he played at Wembley for Runcorn against his former club, Altrincham, in the F.A.Trophy final. Sadly for Frank the 'Linnets' lost 1-0. He later appeared for both Altrincham and Macclesfield Town, where he finished playing football seriously in 1987. However, he continued to play for his local side in Altrincham, Old Atrinchiams veterans, and also for the Manchester City veterans XI. Frank, who lives in Altrincham, now runs his own company organising corporate hospitality.

Season	League		F.A.Cup		Welsh Cup		League Cup		Total	
	apps	gls	apps	gls	apps	gls	apps	gls	apps	gls
1979/80	20	1	4	0	1	0	-	-	25	1
1980/81	36	1	-	-	3/1	1	1	0	40/1	2
1981/82	41	4	3	0	2	1	5	0	51	5
	97	**6**	**7**	**0**	**6/1**	**2**	**6**	**0**	**116/1**	**8**

CARTER, Michael

1987 - 1989

Position; *Midfielder*
D.O.B; *18th April, 1960*
Birthplace; *Warrington, Cheshire*
Height; *5ft 9in* ***Weight;*** *10st 7lbs*
Debut v. *Torquay United (a) 15th August, 1987*
Total Appearances & Goals; *32/13 apps 7 gls*
Career; *Bolton Wanderers Jul 1977 37/12apps 8gls; Mansfield Town Mar 1979 (Loan) 18apps 4gls; Swindon Town Mar 1982 (Loan) 4/1apps 0gls; Plymouth Argyle Aug 1982 6/6apps 1gls; Hereford United Mar 1983 91/6apps 11gls; WREXHAM Jun 1987; Colne Dynamoes 1989;*
Honours; *Welsh Cup runner-up 1988;*

Mike Carter began his footballing life as an out and out forward, playing mainly in the Runcorn area where he was spotted by First Division Bolton Wanderers. After trials he was signed on apprentice terms upon leaving school, turning professional for the 'Trotters' in July 1977. However, it wasn't with Bolton that Mike was to make his Football League debut, but with Third Division Mansfield Town, to whom he was loaned in March 1979, and where he made his bow in a 1-1 home draw with Blackpool. Mike remained with the Field Mill club until the end of the season, making 18 League appearances and scoring four goals. He returned to Burnden Park in readiness for the 1979/80 season, though it wasn't until December that he was given his first team chance, appearing as a substitute against Bristol City. He played a few more games up to the end of that season, which ended with Bolton being relegated. The next two terms saw him suffer with injuries, and he struggled to win back his first team place. In March 1982 he joined Swindon Town on loan, making five League appearances, before signing permanently for Plymouth Argyle manager, Bobby Moncur, in the close season of 1982. It didn't turn out to be a good move, as he failed to settle in the South West, making just twelve League appearances before being loaned to Hereford United in March 1983. After ten League games for the 'Bulls' he damaged his knee ligaments in a 2-1 defeat at Aldershot. Following his recovery, the move to Edgar Street was made permanent during the summer, although his first season was to be a disaster, as he broke down in pre-season training, which came close to ending his career prematurely. Despite this set-back Carter fought his way back to full fitness, and over the next three seasons featured regularly in the Hereford team. At the end of the 1986/87 season he was released, prompting Dixie McNeil to return to his old club to sign him in June 1987. He got off to a dazzling start with Wrexham, but it all ended with a bump.

He put Wrexham 1-0 ahead at Torquay in the opening game of the 1987/88 season, only to end up losing 6-1! In his two seasons at the Racecourse Mike struggled to establish a regular first team place, as he suffered a series of niggling injuries. He did make two substitute appearances for Wrexham in the club's play-off matches at the end of the 1988/89 season, but it came as no surprise when he was released at the end of the season, following the completion of his contract. Mike then joined the progressive non-league side, Colne Dynamoes, whose multi-millionaire Chairman was funding their rise towards League status. He signed Mike, and other players with Football League experience, to enable him to do this. However, he eventually withdrew his money from the club and they folded shortly afterwards.

Season	League		F.A.Cup		Welsh Cup		League Cup		E.C.W.C.		Play-off's		Total	
	apps	gls	apps	gls	apps	gls	apps	gls	apps	gls	apps	gls	apps	gls
1987/88	19/2	5	2	1	2/1	0	2	0	1	0	-	-	26/2	6
1988/89	6/7	1	-	-	-	-	0/1	0	0/1	0	0/2	0	6/11	1
	25/9	**6**	**2**	**1**	**2/1**	**0**	**2/1**	**0**	**1/1**	**0**	**0/2**	**0**	**32/13**	**7**

CARTWRIGHT, Leslie

1977 - 1982

Position; *Midfielder*
D.O.B; *4th March, 1952*
Birthplace; *Aberdare, Glamorgan*
Height; *5ft 9in* ***Weight;*** *10st 13lbs*
Debut v. *Stockport County (h) 13th August, 1977 League Cup*
Total Appearances & Goals; *150/4 apps 13 gls*
Career; *Hirwaun YMCA; Penywaun Welfare; Coventry City May 1970 50/18apps 4gls; WREXHAM 31st May 1977 £40,000; Bangor City Dec 1981; Cambridge United Mar 1982 52/8apps 1gls; Southend United Sept 1983 (Loan) 2/2apps 0gls; Worcester City Jun 1985; Coventry Sporting Nov 1985; Nuneaton Borough;*
Honours; *Seven full Welsh international caps; 4 Welsh under-23 caps; Third Division Championship Winner 1978; Welsh Cup Winner 1978;*

Les Cartwright attended a Rugby-only school in his native Aberdare, but he played football outside the school gates for local clubs Hirwaun YMCA and Penywaun Welfare. It was whilst he was playing for these teams that he was spotted by a Wolves scout, and invited for trials. However, as Wolves deliberated over signing him, Coventry City stepped in, and snapped up the promising youngster in May 1970. Because he had already turned eighteen Cartwright signed a professional contract. He made his way through the 'A' and reserve teams at Highfield Road finally making his Football League debut in September 1973, coming on as a substitute for Ernie Hunt in a 2-0 win at Leicester and scoring one of the goals. This led to a further 67 League appearances for the 'Sky Blues' and international honours for Wales, gaining four caps at under-23 level, and the first of his seven full Welsh caps. In June 1977 Les left Highfield Road when he became the new Wrexham manager Arfon Griffiths' first important signing, a £40,000 fee enticing him to the Racecourse. His signature, along with those of Dai Davies and Dixie McNeil, proved to be the inspiration the team required, having just missed out on promotion the previous season. Wrexham stormed to the Third Division title, and Les' gamble of dropping down two divisions paid off. He stayed with Wrexham for over three seasons, experiencing European football, and

playing in some dramatic cup matches against the likes of Spurs, West Ham and Wolves. However, he was dogged by injury problems throughout his last couple of terms at Wrexham, undergoing three operations in less than two years, and in December 1981 he was released by the club. Les then joined Bangor City on a non-contract basis, before returning to League football with Cambridge United in March 1982. He went on to stay at the Abbey Stadium for three years, making 60 League appearances, plus four more during a loan spell at Southend in September 1983. At the end of the 1984/85 season he left Cambridge, due to serious knee problems and moved to Wolvey in Leicestershire to run a Post Office business. He continued to play football, teaming up with Bobby Shinton at Worcester City for a short spell in June 1985, followed by a period with Nuneaton Borough finally calling it a day in 1986. Cartwright was not involved with football for a time, concentrating on his business, but he was then invited to help out with Coventry's youngsters on a part-time basis. Les appeared for a Coventry City veterans' side in a 'Past Masters' tournament at Molineux in July 1997. He sold his post office business in 1998 although continuing to live at the premises. Football remains important in his life and coaches primary schoolchildren, while also working for Leicester City's coaching academy.

Season	League		F.A.Cup		Welsh Cup		League Cup		E.C.W.C.		Total	
	apps	gls	apps	gls	apps	gls	apps	gls	apps	gls	apps	gls
1977/78	41	4	6	1	4	2	6	0	-	-	57	7
1978/79	23	0	3	1	2	0	3	1	2	1	33	3
1979/80	10/4	0	-	-	1	1	3	0	-	-	14/4	1
1980/81	33	2	5	0	2	0	2	0	-	-	42	2
1981/82	4	0	-	-	-	-	-	-	-	-	4	0
	111/4	**6**	**14**	**2**	**9**	**3**	**14**	**1**	**2**	**1**	**150/4**	**13**

CARTWRIGHT, Mark Neville

1994 -

Position; *Goalkeeper*
D.O.B; *13th January, 1973*
Birthplace; *Chester, Cheshire*
Height; *6ft 2in* ***Weight;*** *13st 6lbs*
Debut v. *Chesterfield (h) 2nd November, 1996*
Total Appearances & Goals; *66 apps 0 gls*
Career; *Cheadle Town; York City Jul 1989 0apps; Stockport County 17th Aug 1991 0apps; Florida Tech 1991; WREXHAM 5th Mar 1994; Runcorn Dec 1995 (Loan) 6apps 0gls; Weymouth 13th Jul 1999 (Loan); Luton Town Jul 1999 (Trial);*
Honours; *Welsh Invitation Cup Winner 1998;*

Mark Cartwright first played organised football at Primary school in Runcorn, before moving to Congleton. It was here that he began playing for a local youth club in the Town, turning out for a team called Vale Juniors, though this came to an abrupt end when the entire under-14s team received their marching orders during one match! He then joined Cheadle Town, from where he was recommended to York City by the under-15s manager, who had contacts with the club. Mark joined York on schoolboy forms, and went on to sign YTS forms for the Bootham Crescent club on leaving school. However, he was to be jinxed in his first year by catching hepatitis, which was to keep him out of action for three months, and then suffered a two footed challenge that shredded his cruciate ligament. Despite being advised to quit football Mark bravely fought on, and the second year of his apprenticeship saw him playing regularly in goal for York's Northern Intermediate side. However, at the end of that season he found himself released by the club, so took up a P.F.A. offer of a move to the U.S.A. This involved Mark studying for a four year Business degree at Florida Tech, and appearing for the University team. In his first season they won the local League and qualified for the play-offs, finally making it through to the final four in the country. Florida Tech were hosts for the final, and they won on home soil to become the U.S.National Champions. He continued to keep goal as they finished runners-up for the next two years. Following his third year Mark began to think seriously about returning home, and he joined Wrexham for training before being offered terms on a permanent basis as cover for Andy Marriott. His first three seasons at the Racecourse proved frustrating, as he did not get a first team opportunity due to Marriott's consistency. During that period Cartwright was called into the Welsh Under-21 squad, acting as cover for Danny Coyne, without making an appearance. In December 1995 he joined Runcorn for a two month loan period, making six appearances in place of another former Wrexham goalkeeper, Mark Morris, who was injured. The 1996/97 campaign saw Mark once again playing reserve team football, but in November he finally got his first big chance when Marriott suffered a broken jaw. He made his League debut on the Racecourse in a 3-2 win over Chesterfield, in which he did very well, being named 'Man of the Match'.

He played three more games, including a First round F.A.Cup match keeping Wrexham in the competition with some crucial saves, laying the foundation for a run that was to carry the club to the sixth round of the F.A.Cup that season. As soon as Marriott was fit again he returned to reserve team football, eventually leading him to request a transfer during 1997/98, a season which saw him play in the newly formed Welsh Invitation Cup competition, helping Wrexham win the inaugural final with a 2-1 win over Cardiff City. Throughout his time at the Racecourse, Mark had been unfortunate to be understudy to such a quality goalkeeper as Andrew Marriott, but that was to change in the summer of 1998, when Cartwright was given a regular first team opportunity, after Marriott fell out with the club's management. During his time with Wrexham, Mark kept himself busy in his spare time as a partner in a creative design business in Macclesfield, called 'Blue Creative Design & Print'.

Season	League		F.A.Cup		W.I.C.		League Cup		A.W.S.		Total	
	apps	gls	apps	gls	apps	gls	apps	gls	apps	gls	apps	gls
1996/97	3	0	1	0	-	-	-	-	-	-	4	0
1997/98	4	0	-	-	8	0	-	-	-	-	12	0
1998/99	30	0	5	0	7	0	2	0	6	0	50	0
	37	**0**	**6**	**0**	**15**	**0**	**2**	**0**	**6**	**0**	**66**	**0**

CASE, James Robert

1993

Position; *Midfield*
D.O.B; *18th May, 1954*
Birthplace; *Liverpool, Merseyside*
Height; *5ft 9in* ***Weight;*** *12st 5lbs*
Debut v. *Bury (a) 27th February, 1993*
Total Appearances & Goals; *1/3 apps 0 gls*
Career; *Garston Woodcutters; South Liverpool 1971; Liverpool 1st May 1973 170/16apps 23gls; Brighton & Hove Albion 19th Aug 1981 £350,000 124/3apps 10gls; Southampton 20th Mar 1985 £30,000 213/2apps 10gls; Bournemouth 25th Jul 1991 38/2apps 1gls; Halifax Town 16th May 1992 17/4apps 2gls; WREXHAM 26th Feb 1993; Darlington 22nd Oct 1993 1app 0gls; Sittingbourne Nov 1993; Brighton & Hove Albion 30th Dec 1993 30apps 0gls;*
Honours; *Football League Championship Winner 1976, 1977, 1979 & 1980; League Cup Winner 1978 & 1981; European Cup Winner 1977, 1978 & 1981; UEFA Cup Winner 1976; European Super Cup Winner 1977; F.A.Cup runner-up 1977 & 1983; F.A.Charity Shield Winner 1977, 1979 & 1980; One England under-21 International cap; Football League representative cap 1990;*

Jimmy Case began playing football for Garston Woodcutters in his home city of Liverpool. He spent two seasons with Northern Premier League side South Liverpool, whilst also serving his time as an apprentice electrician, before he was signed by Liverpool on amateur forms in 1972. Jimmy did enough to earn himself a professional contract in May 1973, but had to wait a further two years before making his first team debut in the final match of the 1974/75 season, a 3-1 home win over Q.P.R. The following campaign Jimmy held down a regular first team place, going on to win many honours in the game at both domestic and European levels, his only disappointment was not winning a full England cap. Case had a ferocious shot, scoring many spectacular goals for all the clubs he represented and his career progressed also developed great vision and finely polished passing skills. In August 1981 he was transferred to Brighton for £450,000, and during 1982/83 returned to Anfield to score

the winning goal for the visitors, who went on to reach Wembley that season before losing to Manchester United in the 1983 F.A.Cup final. In March 1985, Lawrie McMenemy paid out £30,000 to sign Jimmy for Southampton. It proved to be a bargain buy, confounding all those who were of the opinion that he was past his best. He proved them all wrong by spending six years at the Dell, making 216 League appearances, and winning the player of the season award in 1990. However, when Chris Nicholl departed, and Ian Branfoot took over, Case was allowed to leave the Dell. He resumed his travels by moving down the south coast to Bournemouth for one season before returning North to join Halifax Town. His stay at The Shay was short, and Jimmy signed for Wrexham on a free transfer in February 1993 after Mike Lake had returned to Sheffield United following his loan spell. Jimmy stepped into his shoes for a League match at Bury, which Wrexham lost 3-1, but was then left out of the team when Lake and Wrexham agreed terms the following week. Wrexham went on to win promotion to the Second Division with Jimmy making just three more appearances as a substitute, although his presence in the dressing room had been 'inspirational' according to manager Brian Flynn. At the end of the season he was released, and returned to his southern-based home. The following season he did some scouting for Wrexham before turning out for Sittingbourne, and when Liam Brady took charge at Brighton he brought back the 39 year-old to help steer away the club from the relegation zone and preserve their Second Division status. In November 1995 Jimmy, at the age of 41, announced his retirement from playing to concentrate on his coaching duties at the Goldstone Ground. During the same month Liam Brady resigned as manager, and Case was appointed as caretaker-boss. He was given the job on a permanent basis in December, but was unable to prevent the turmoiled club from sliding into the Third Division. In December 1996, with the 'Seagulls' nine points adrift at the bottom of the Football League, he was sacked. After a little scouting Jimmy returned to managership with Southern League side Bashley Town in May 1997, and was still managing the Hampshire club in recent times.

Season	League		F.A.Cup		Welsh Cup		League Cup		A.G.T.		Total	
	apps	gls	apps	gls	apps	gls	apps	gls	apps	gls	apps	gls
1992/93	1/3	0	-	-	-	-	-	-	-	-	1/3	0
	1/3	**0**	-	-	-	-	-	-	-	-	**1/3**	**0**

CEGIELSKI, Wayne 1976 - 1982

Position; *Centre-Half*
D.O.B; *11th January, 1956*
Birthplace; *Bedwellty, Gwent*
Height; *6ft 1in* ***Weight;*** *12st 4lbs*
Debut v. *Mansfield Town (a) 18th December, 1976*
Total Appearances & Goals; *149/14 apps 1 gls*
Career; *Tottenham Hotspur May 1973 0apps; Northampton Town 13th Mar 1975 (Loan) 11apps 0gls; VfB Stuttgart (Germany) cs1975; Tacoma Tides (USA) May 1976; WREXHAM Sept 1976; Port Vale 30th Jul 1982 91/1apps 5gls; Blackpool Mar 1985 5/1apps 1gls; Hereford United Jul 1985 46/4apps 2gls; Umes (Sweden) Mar 1987; Worcester City Sept 1987; Northwich Victoria 1987 31apps 1gls;*
Honours; *Two Welsh under-21 caps; Welsh Youth Cap; Third Division Championship Winner 1978; Welsh Cup runner-up 1979;*

Wayne Cegielski played his early football in his home town of Blackwood, in Gwent, where he appeared for Cefn Fforest Junior and Bedwellty Grammar Schools. He gained representative honours for his County, Monmouthshire, and played for the local Boy's team, Pengam. Wayne progressed well enough to sign apprentice forms for Tottenham Hotspur, after accepting an invitation to play in a South Wales trial match for the London club. At White Hart Lane Wayne progressed through the junior ranks, as well as being capped at youth level for Wales. He signed professional terms with the North London club in May 1973 and served as a deputy for Mike England, though never given his chance in the first team, spending most of his time playing for the second string in the Combination League. In March 1975 Wayne was given the opportunity of first team football on loan to Northampton Town, where he made his Football League debut at centre-half in a 2-0 defeat at Darlington. Cegielski went on to make ten more League appearances for the 'Cobblers' before returning to Tottenham, only to be told that he was to be released. Despite an offer of a contract by Northampton Wayne decided to try his luck abroad with German club Stuttgart, where he remained for a season making several appearances in the Bundesliga. In May 1976 he travelled to America to play for Tacoma Tides in Washington State. It was whilst he was living there he wrote to Wrexham manager John Neal, asking for a trial upon his return to Britain at the end of the American term, and impressed enough to earn a professional contract in September 1976. He had to wait for his first team chance due to the form of John Roberts and Gareth Davies, though within weeks of moving to the Racecourse he was called up into the Welsh under-21 squad, making two appearances against England and Scotland. Having finally made his Wrexham debut in December 1976 in a 2-0 defeat at Mansfield, replacing

Mickey Evans in the side, he went on to spend a total of six seasons at the Racecourse. He became an important member of the Third Division Championship squad of 1978, playing in many memorable cup matches against the likes of his old club Spurs; Wolves; Nottingham Forest; Chelsea; and Cup holders West Ham, where he actually played in goal due to Dai Davies' sending off. However, following relegation in 1982, the club's perilous financial situation forced the off-loading of a number of players. Wayne was one of these, and he was quickly snapped up by Port Vale where, in his first season at Vale Park he captained the side to promotion to the Third Division. His stay with Vale was to extend to March 1985, when he signed on loan for Blackpool. He appeared in six matches for the 'Seasiders', helping them to clinch promotion. At the end of the season he was released by Vale, and joined Hereford United in July 1985 on a free transfer. Wayne made his debut for the 'Bulls' in a 4-0 defeat at Mansfield in the opening game of the 1985/86 season, and went on to spend two seasons at Edgar Street, making 50 League appearances. In March 1986 he went to Sweden, to play for Umes in the Swedish League. He returned in September 1986 and joined Worcester City, combining playing with employment as a plumbing and heating engineer. Within a short time Wayne joined Northwich Victoria until the end of 1987/88, when retiring from football. Today, Wayne lives in the 'Potteries', whilst working as a sales representative for a Cardiff based company.

Season	League		F.A.Cup		Welsh Cup		League Cup		E.C.W.C.		Total	
	apps	gls	apps	gls	apps	gls	apps	gls	apps	gls	apps	gls
1976/77	8/1	0	1/2	0	3	0	-	-	-	-	12/3	0
1977/78	5/4	0	1	0	1	0	0/1	0	-	-	7/5	0
1978/79	24/5	0	3	1	5	0	1	0	1	0	34/5	1
1979/80	3	0	-	-	-	-	1	0	-	-	4	0
1980/81	38	0	5	0	5	0	-	-	-	-	48	0
1981/82	34/1	0	4	0	2	0	5	0	-	-	45/1	0
	112/11	**0**	**14/2**	**1**	**15**	**0**	**7/1**	**0**	**1**	**0**	**149/14**	**1**

CHADWICK, Simon Leslie 1985 - 1986

Position; *Forward*
D.O.B; *15th March, 1968*
Birthplace; *Liverpool, Merseyside*
Height; *5ft 11in* ***Weight;*** *10st 7lbs*
Debut v. *Port Vale (h) 8th March, 1986*
Total Appearances & Goals; *1/1 apps 0 gls*
Career; *WREXHAM 15th Aug 1985; Bury (Trial) cs1986 0apps;*
Honours; *Welsh Youth Cup Winner 1985;*

Simon Chadwick showed lots of promise as a schoolboy, playing for both School and District teams in his native Liverpool. He came to the attention of Wrexham playing for his Liverpool Sunday League side, and was invited to the Racecourse for a couple of trial matches before signing on Youth Training Scheme forms. His initial season at the Racecourse saw Simon make steady progress, helping Wrexham to lift the Welsh Youth Cup with a 3-1 win over Logan St.Patricks, in which he scored. At the end of the 1984/85 season Chadwick got his first taste of senior team football when he appeared in the Duke of Westminster Cup match, in aid of the Bradford Disaster Charity, against Chester. The following campaign he was given a place on the subs bench, before making his Football League debut in a 3-1 home defeat by Port Vale in March 1986, when he came on for the injured David Gregory after just seventeen minutes and supplied the pass for Andy Edwards' opening goal. The next game saw Simon given his first start, replacing Gregory, in a 2-0 home win over Rochdale. That proved to be his last first team game for Wrexham, as he was released by the club at the end of the season. He joined Bury on trial in the close season of 1986, but after doing enough to be offered a contract was forced to retire from playing football on Doctor's orders. Simon was last known to be residing in the Liverpool area.

Season	League		F.A.Cup		Welsh Cup		League Cup		Total	
	apps	gls	apps	gls	apps	gls	apps	gls	apps	gls
1985/86	1/1	0	-	-	-	-	-	-	1/1	0
	1/1	**0**	**-**	**-**	**-**	**-**	**-**	**-**	**1/1**	**0**

CHALK, Martyn Peter Glyn 1996 -

Position; *Right Wing/Midfield*
D.O.B; *30th August, 1969*
Birthplace; *Swindon, Wiltshire*
Height; *5ft 6in* ***Weight;*** *10st 0lbs*
Debut v. *Bristol Rovers (h) 20th February, 1996*
Total Appearances & Goals; *119/37apps 8gls*
Career; *Grimsby Amateurs; Louth United; Derby County 23rd Jan 1990 £10,000 4/3apps 1gls; Stockport County 30th Jun 1994 £40,000 29/14apps 6gls; WREXHAM 16th Feb 1996 £25,000;*
Honours; *Welsh Invitation Cup Winner 1998; Welsh Premier Cup runner-up 1999;*

Although born in Swindon Martyn was raised in the Norfolk seaside resort of Great Yarmouth, where he played football for Cliff Park School. He also represented both Great Yarmouth and Norfolk schoolboy teams, and it was during this period that the former Aston Villa pro, Sammy Morgan, took him under his wing and attempted to fix him up as an apprenticeship at Norwich City. It never worked out and he left school to join his Father's antique business in Grimsby. Martyn continued to play football for Grimsby Amateurs in the Lincolnshire League, after a spell in Sunday football with Kingsway. He progressed by signing for Louth United in the Central Midlands League, and before long Derby County took an interest. He was invited for training for two weeks in January 1990, and signed a two year contract upon completion of the trial, with Louth receiving £10,000. His first campaign was spent playing in the 'Rams' reserve team in the Pontin's League, but niggling injuries hampered his progress. However, on Boxing Day 1991, he made his Football League debut, coming on as a substitute for Phil Gee in a scoreless draw with Grimsby Town at the Baseball Ground. He came off the bench again in the following match, against Charlton Athletic, before starting his first full match on New Year's Day 1992, a 1-1 draw at Middlesbrough, when he celebrated with his first League goal. Big money signings saw Martyn pushed to the back of the queue for a first team place, and over the next two years he played reserve team football. A number of clubs showed an interest including Wrexham, and in July 1994 he moved to Stockport County for £40,000. Martyn made his debut for the 'Hatters' in the opening match of the 1994/95 season, a 4-1 home win over Cardiff City. It wasn't long before he was thrilling the 'County' fans with his jinking runs and dangerous crosses. 'Chalky' was a regular for Stockport throughout that campaign, but the following season found it difficult to retain a regular first team place. In February 1996 he was involved in a double deal, joining Wrexham for £25,000, with Kieron Durkan moving in the opposite direction for £100,000. He soon settled in at the Racecourse, making his League debut for 'The Robins' in a 3-2 home win over Bristol Rovers. 'Chalky' is no doubt a gifted player, who is at home on either flank, and who compensates for his slight build with his aggression. An avid collector of antiques in his spare time.

Season	League		F.A.Cup		League Cup		A.W.S		W.I.C.		Total	
	apps	gls	apps	gls	apps	gls	apps	gls	apps	gls	apps	gls
1995/96	19	4	-	-	-	-	-	-	-	-	19	4
1996/97	34/9	1	6	0	2	0	1	0	-	-	43/9	1
1997/98	15/11	1	1/2	0	0/1	0	-	-	6/2	1	22/16	2
1998/99	19/9	0	4/1	0	1	0	5	0	6/2	1	35/12	1
	87/29	**6**	**11/3**	**0**	**3/1**	**0**	**6**	**0**	**12/4**	**2**	**119/37**	**8**

CHARLES, Stephen 1984 - 1987

Position; *Midfielder*
D.O.B; *10th May, 1960.*
Birthplace; *Sheffield, Yorkshire*
Height; *5ft 9in* ***Weight;*** *10st 7lbs*
Debut v. *Hartlepool United (h) 3rd November, 1984*
Total Appearances & Goals; *146/4 apps 45 gls*
Career; *Sheffield University; Sheffield United 16th Jan 1980 112/11apps 10gls; WREXHAM 2nd Nov 1984 £10,000; Mansfield Town 3rd Aug 1987 £15,000 231/6apps 39gls; Scunthorpe United 20th Nov 1992 (loan) 4apps 0gls; Scarborough 26th Feb 1993 93apps 15gls; Stalybridge Celtic cs1996 38/4apps 10gls; Boston United Sept 1997;*
Honours; *Two England Schoolboy international caps; Welsh Cup Winner 1986; Division Four Championship Winner 1982;*

Steve Charles was a keen footballer while at Rowlinson school in Sheffield, appearing for Sheffield Schools and South Yorkshire Boys, and winning representative honours in two matches for England schoolboys, against Wales and Scotland. It was no surprise, therefore, that he was required by both Sheffield clubs. After trials with Wednesday he signed schoolboy forms with the 'Owls', and when he was sixteen they offered him an apprenticeship, only for him to turn it down to stay on at school. He was offered a full contract, when he passed his 'A' levels, but again declined, preferring to go on to Sheffield University to study mathematics. While studying for his degree Steve was offered a place on a soccer scholarship course in the United States, and he went to the Columbia University in New York. There, he played for his College in the Ivy League, a competition for all University football teams. He set the University all-time goalscoring record while on campus, prompting an offer to sign for New York Cosmos. Again he refused, due to the size and quality of the squad they had already assembled. After two years Charles returned to his Sheffield home, for Christmas 1979, and trained with Sheffield United to keep fit. They offered him a full-time contract and this time he accepted. He signed in January 1980, making his debut for the 'Blades' at Exeter in the same month. Steve continued with his studies, gaining two degrees in mathematics and marketing. He spent five seasons at Bramall Lane, in which time he made 123 League appearances, scoring ten goals. He also helped the 'Blades' to gain promotions from the Fourth to the Second Division. 1984/85 was to see Steve disillusioned with life at Bramall Lane, frustrated by the lack of regular first team football. Wrexham manager Bobby Roberts stepped in with a £10,000 bid, which was accepted. 'Biffo' as he was affectionately named at Wrexham, was immediately installed as the club captain, and made his debut in a 1-1 home draw with Hartlepool United, scoring the Wrexham goal from the penalty spot. Throughout his three seasons Steve at the Racecourse he was a regular, helping to win the Welsh Cup in 1986, and the following season played in Europe against FC Zurrieq of Malta and Real Zaragoza of Spain. At the end of 1986/87, he surprisingly decided to leave Wrexham, moving to Third Division Mansfield Town for £15,000 in August 1987. He went on to spend almost six seasons at Field Mill, in which time he won two Nottinghamshire County Cup winners' medals, and also played in the 'Stags' promotion side of 1992. The following term he was loaned to Scunthorpe United in November 1992, turning out four times for the 'Iron'. In February 1993 he joined Scarborough, for over three seasons, scoring 15 goals in 93 League games for the Yorkshire club. Steve left Scarborough at the end of the 1995/96 season, joining GM Conference side Stalybridge Celtic as a part-time pro and combining playing with lecturing at Wakefield College. He is the course co-ordinator for the HND (Higher National Diploma) in Sports Science. Steve had one season with Stalybridge, and was about to start the 1997/98 season with them when he joined Unibond League side Boston United.

Season	League		F.A.Cup		Welsh Cup		League Cup		F.R.T.		E.C.W.C.		Total	
	apps	gls	apps	gls	apps	gls	apps	gls	apps	gls	apps	gls	apps	gls
1984/85	32	7	1	0	3	0	-	-	2	0	-	-	38	7
1985/86	39/1	21	1	0	5	1	4	0	2	2	-	-	51/1	24
1986/87	40/1	10	2/1	1	4	0	4	0	4/1	2	3	1	57/3	14
	111/2	**38**	**4/1**	**1**	**12**	**1**	**8**	**0**	**8/1**	**4**	**3**	**1**	**146/4**	**45**

CHARNLEY, Raymond Ogden 1968 - 1969

Position; *Centre-Forward*
D.O.B; *29th May, 1935*
Birthplace; *Lancaster, Lancashire*
Height; *6ft 0in* ***Weight;*** *11st 7lbs*
Debut v. *Aldershot (a) 10th August, 1968*
Total Appearances & Goals; *22/2 apps 7 gls*
Career; *Red Rose Boys' Club; Bolton-le-Sands; Morecambe; Blackpool May 1957 £1,000 363apps 193gls; Preston North End Dec 1967 23apps 4gls; WREXHAM 24th Jul 1968 £10,000; Bradford Park Avenue 14th Jan 1969 59apps 15gls; Morecambe Jun 1970;*
Honours; *One England International Cap;*

Ray Charnley was signed by Wrexham manager Alvan Williams in July 1969, with the 'obvious intention of assisting in a strong promotion effort.' Ray had already made his mark in the game whilst with First Division Blackpool, who obtained his signature at the 'advanced' age of 22 from Morecambe in May 1957 for £1,000. Ray had first come to prominence as a footballer at the Greaves Secondary Modern school in his native Lancaster, from where he was chosen to play for the Lancaster schoolboys' team. Upon leaving school Ray began working as an apprentice painter and decorator, continuing to play football for Red Rose Boys Club in Lancaster, and appearing for North Lancashire and Lancashire Boys Clubs'. During his time with Red Rose he was granted trials with both Wolves and Bolton Wanderers but, with the large number of trialists attending at that time, he was overlooked. Charnley began playing for a local village side, north of Lancaster, Bolton-le-Sands, where he spent around two seasons before being offered the chance to sign for Blackpool. However, his father advised him to complete his apprenticeship as a painter and decorator, as there would be no going back if he had left at that time. It wasn't long before Ray was offered the chance to sign for Morecambe, of the Lancashire Combination League. Here Ray began to score goals on a regular basis. He spent almost three seasons with them, during which time he was offered the chance of League football with Gillingham. He declined the offer as it was too far away from his home. Not long after, First Division Blackpool made another bid; they were only 25 miles down the road, and he had now finished his apprenticeship, so couldn't refuse a second time, especially as they had Stanley Matthews and Stan Mortensen in their team at the time. He signed for Blackpool in May 1957 for a £1,000 fee, and made his Football League debut in a 2-0 defeat at Luton Town in September 1957. Ray went on to become Blackpool's top scorer for seven seasons, and is still Blackpool's third top goalscorer of all time, with 193 goals in 363 League appearances. Charnley, who, it was said, played his best football alongside Alan Ball, received a belated call-up for his one and only England cap in a European Championship match with France, in a 1-1 draw at Hillsborough in October 1962. He lined up alongside Jimmy Greaves. He had already been on a far East tour with an FA.XI, playing matches against Malaysia; New Zealand; and Hong Kong. Back at Bloomfield Road Ray continued to score goals, until a bad 4-1 home defeat by Millwall at the start of the 1967/68 season, and typically he scored the Blackpool goal. Manager Stan Mortensen made the unpopular decision to drop him, and he played just one more game for the 'Seasiders' before joining rivals Preston

North End, who had earlier rejected him in 1956. In all Ray had spent just over eleven years with the 'Seasiders'. With Second Division Preston looking doomed to relegation, Charnley helped to spearhead a rescue act by assisting the Deepdale club to avoid the drop. Despite this he was allowed to leave, and signed for Fourth Division Wrexham in July 1968. He arrived at the Racecourse at a very experimental time, with a lot of comings and goings, and the constant upheaval eventually prompted a change of manager in September, with John Neal taking over from Alvan Williams. Ray failed to score on his Wrexham debut at Aldershot, but he was on target in the next match at home to Bradford. By January 1969 John Neal had paid out a then club record fee for Brian Tinnion, and the 33 year-old was allowed to leave. Bradford Park Avenue stepped in to sign him, shortly after Tinnion's arrival, and he joined Bradford in a part-exchange deal which saw John Sykes move in the opposite direction. He remained at Park Avenue until the summer of 1970, when they failed to gain re-election to the Football League. Ray had scored 15 goals in 59 League appearances for the doomed club. In the close season of 1970 he returned to play for Morecambe, for just over a season before retiring from the game. He settled in Blackpool, setting up his own painting and decorating business, which he was still involved.

Season	League		F.A.Cup		Welsh Cup		League Cup		Total	
	apps	gls	apps	gls	apps	gls	apps	gls	apps	gls
1968/69	19/1	5	0/1	1	-	-	3	1	22/2	7
	19/1	**5**	**0/1**	**1**	**-**	**-**	**3**	**1**	**22/2**	**7**

CLAYTON, John

1930 - 1932

Position; *Left-Half*
D.O.B; *1907*
Birthplace; *Mansfield, Nottinghamshire*
Height; *5ft 9'1/2in* ***Weight;*** *12st 11lbs*
Debut v. *York City (h) 3rd September, 1930.*
Total Appearances & goals; *57 apps 1 gls*
Career; *Loughborough Corinthians 1927; Chesterfield May 1929 5apps 0gls; WREXHAM 20th May 1930; Carlisle United Jun 1932 24apps 0gls; Mansfield Town Jul 1933 15apps 1gls; Grantham Town Sept 1934; Gainsborough Trinity Aug 1935;*
Honours; *Welsh Cup Winner 1931;*

John Clayton was spotted by Chesterfield playing for Loughborough Corinthians and spent twelve months with the Saltergate side, making his Football League debut at left-half in October 1929 in a 5-1 home win over Crewe Alexandra. He made just four more League appearances for the 'Spireites' before being signed by Wrexham manager Jack Baynes in May 1930. John made his Wrexham debut in place of the injured Billie Rogers in September, starting a sequence of four matches. He then found himself in the reserve team until Boxing Day 1930 when stepping into the side in place of John Donoghue. He remained in the first team until the end of the season, helping the club to finish in fourth place in the Third Division North, and to victory in the Welsh Cup final with a 7-0 thrashing of Shrewsbury Town. He began the following campaign as the club's first choice left-half, but he was to end it in the reserves, as youngster Matt Lawrence took his place in the side. Clayton did however play in the final match of the season, in place of Tommy Bamford, at centre-forward! And Wrexham lost 5-0!! During the close season John left Wrexham, signing for Carlisle United. After appearing in the opening match of the 1932/33 season he failed to hold down a regular place and, following 24 League games and one season with 'The Cumbrians' joined his home town club Mansfield Town, a non-League side at that time competing in the Midland League. Clayton spent one season at Field Mill before joining fellow Midland League side, Grantham Town, for one term before moving on to join Gainsborough Trinity.

Season	League		F.A.Cup		Welsh Cup		Total	
	apps	gls	apps	gls	apps	gls	apps	gls
1930/31	25	1	-	-	4	0	29	1
1931/32	26	0	1	0	1	0	28	0
	51	**1**	**1**	**0**	**5**	**0**	**57**	**1**

COADY, Lewis

1994 - 1997

Position; *Forward*
D.O.B; *20th September, 1976*
Birthplace; *Liverpool, Merseyside*
Height; *6ft 1in* ***Weight;*** *11st 1lbs*
Debut v. *Stockport County (h) 17th April, 1995*
Total Appearances & Goals; *2 apps 0 gls*
Career; *WREXHAM (YTS) 1993, (Pro) 1995; Sligo Rovers Dec 1996 (Loan); Colwyn Bay Feb 1997; Doncaster Rovers Feb 1997 1app 0gls; Porthmadog Mar 1997 6apps 4gls; Caernarfon Town Sept 1997 2/1apps 0gls; Vauxhall G.M. Apr 1998;*
Honours; *Welsh Youth Cup Winner 1994; Welsh Youth Cup runner-up 1995;*

Although born in Skelmersdale Lewis Coady was brought up in Runcorn, and began playing football for his Primary School team, turning out for Murdershaw Athletic Youth Club at around the same time. At Brook Vale Secondary School in Runcorn Coady surprisingly only played football for the school team in his final year. However, it was out of school that his football career began to blossom, as he was also playing for Vale Athletic in the Runcorn Junior League, as well as attending training sessions with Crewe Alexandra from the age of 12 to 14. At 14 he was eligible to sign schoolboy forms for Crewe, but turned them down and opted for training with Liverpool under Steve Heighway. Due to the fact that it was only a training arrangement -no matches were actually played- Coady left, and joined Sporting Priory in the Runcorn Junior League. It was then that he was spotted by Wrexham, and invited to attend training at the club. A couple of months later the Youth Development Officer at Wrexham, Mike Buxton, invited Lewis to sign on YTS forms. He then progressed with the youth team at the Racecourse, winning a Welsh Youth Cup winners' medal in 1994, followed by a runners'-up medal in the same competition a year later, and appearing at Old Trafford in an F.A.Youth Cup match. Before the 1994/95 season had ended he found himself making his Football League debut against Stockport County in April 1995, playing in his usual position on the left-side of midfield. He had a reasonable match, looking composed and having time on the ball, as Wrexham won 1-0. He did enough to keep his place in the side the following week at Rotherham, in another 1-0 win, and at the end of the season he signed professional terms. However, his behaviour both on and off the field sometimes left a lot to be desired as he went before the courts, as well as the F.A.. Lewis failed to make another first team appearance for Wrexham as his form deteriorated. He moved to Ireland in December 1996, along with Steve Futcher, to try to rejuvenate his career with a loan spell at Sligo Rovers, but returned home after just a couple of games. He was then released by Wrexham in January 1997, joining Unibond League side Colwyn Bay for a short period at the beginning of 1997, before being offered a trial with Doncaster Rovers. He made one League appearance for the Belle Vue club, in a 1-0 win over Hereford United, but was released shortly afterwards. Following this, he joined League of Wales side Porthmadog, where he spent the rest of the season, eventually teaming up with his brother, Gary, from Warrington Town. In the close season of 1997, Lewis was on the verge of signing for Connahs Quay Nomads, but he started the season with Porthmadog, but with the campaign not even a month old, joined fellow League of Wales side, Caernarfon Town. He later moved to North West Counties League club, Vauxhall G.M. in April 1998.

Season	League		F.A.Cup		Welsh Cup		League Cup		Auto Tro		Total	
	apps	gls	apps	gls	apps	gls	apps	gls	apps	gls	apps	gls
1994/95	2	0	-	-	-	-	-	-	-	-	2	0
	2	**0**	**-**	**-**	**-**	**-**	**-**	**-**	**-**	**-**	**2**	**0**

COLBRIDGE, Clive

1962 - 1965

Position; *Outside-Left*
D.O.B; *27th April, 1934*
Birthplace; *Hull, Humberside*
Height; *5ft 7in* ***Weight;*** *10st 4lbs*
Debut v. *Chester (h) 17th February, 1962*
Total Appearances & Goals; *108 apps 33 gls*
Career; *Hull City (Am) 1950; Leeds United May 1952 0apps; York City May 1955 37apps 14gls; Workington Sept 1957 46apps 8gls; Crewe Alexandra 24th Oct 1958 29apps 8gls; Manchester City 13th May 1959 £10,000 62apps 12gls; WREXHAM 17th Feb 1962; Altrincham 29th Jul 1965; Rhyl 7th Aug 1967;*
Honours; *Welsh Cup runner-up 1962 & 1965;*

Clive Colbridge is the son of a noted Yorkshire athlete. He was a winger who could operate on either flank, but was most effective on the left side of the field. Clive had quickly impressed whilst at Hull's Maybury Road and Grammar Schools, also rerpresenting Yorkshire Boys. It was his home town club who signed him as a schoolboy upon leaving school. Clive completed amateur forms for Hull City in 1950, as well as taking up work as a trainee travelling salesman with a local timber firm. However, he gave that up at the age of 18 when offered a professional contract by Leeds United in May 1952. He played mainly in the Central and Intermediate League teams at Elland Road, but his time with Leeds was to be interrupted by two years' National Service in the R.A.F., which he spent stationed mainly in Liberia as a National Service Clerk. Upon being demobbed, things didn't really work out at Elland Road, and in May 1955 joined York City without having made a first team appearance at Leeds. He made his Football League debut for York in September 1955, a 3-0 home win over Hartlepool United in which he scored York's first goal. Clive went on to spend just over two seasons with the Bootham Crescent club joining Workington in September 1957, where he spent another term. He then joined Crewe Alexandra in October 1958, where he spent almost a season before being transferred to Second Division Manchester City in May 1959 for £10,000. Colbridge enjoyed three seasons at Maine Road, making 62 League appearances, with his most memorable moment coming when scoring for City at Spurs in front of a 65,000 crowd to end Spurs' record eleven match winning run from the start of the 1960/61 season. In February 1962, his former team-mate at City, Ken Barnes, who was now player/manager of Wrexham stepped in to sign Clive in Wrexham's final push for promotion back to the Third Division. However, an irritating ankle injury was to limit his appearances: after just two outings he was diagnosed as having a hairline fracture. Once recovered, Clive became a regular in the Wrexham side throughout the following two seasons who on his day he could destroy opposing defences with his wing play. Illustrated never more so than in 1963/64 v Barnsley at the Racecourse 2-1 down at half time he was the inspiration in Wrexham winning 7-2. 1964/65 saw him share the outside-left position with Graham Williams, and at the end of the campaign he was allowed to leave the club and join Cheshire League side Altrincham. He spent two years with 'Alty', before joining Rhyl in the close season of 1967. Clive is known to have later settled in Ellesmere Port and worked for an insurance company in the Chester area.

Season	League		F.A.Cup		Welsh Cup		League Cup		Total	
	apps	gls	apps	gls	apps	gls	apps	gls	apps	gls
1961/62	6	1	-	-	3	1	-	-	9	2
1962/63	40	11	4	0	1	0	1	0	46	11
1963/64	38	12	2	0	2	1	4	0	46	13
1964/65	24	9	2	0	5	1	1	0	32	10
	108	**33**	**8**	**0**	**11**	**3**	**6**	**0**	**133**	**36**

COLEMAN, Phil

1983

Position; *Central Defender*
D.O.B; *8th September, 1960*
Birthplace; *Woolwich, London*
Height; *5ft 11in* ***Weight;*** *12st 1lbs*
Debut v. *Peterborough United (h) 3rd September, 1983*
Total Appearances & Goals; *20 apps 2 gls*
Career; *Millwall Aug 1978 23/13apps 1gls; Colchester United Feb 1981 £15,000 82/4apps 6gls; WREXHAM 1st Sept 1983 (loan) 17apps 2gls; Chelmsford City cs1984; Exeter City Dec 1984 6apps 0gls; Aldershot Feb 1985 45apps 5gls; Dulwich Hamlet; Millwall Sept 1986 8/2apps 0gls; Mypa 45 (Finland) 1988; Colchester United Dec 1988 6/4apps 0gls; Wivenhoe Town (Player/Manager) 1989;*
Honours; *F.A.Youth Cup Winner 1979; Finnish League Division One Championship Winner 1988; Isthmian League Championship Winner 1989/90; English Schools U-19;*

Phil Coleman was signed by Millwall straight from Roans school in London where he had represented the England Schools under-19 side. At the Den, Phil became a member of Millwall's best ever youth side, reaching the 1979 F.A.Youth Cup Final against Manchester City. Millwall drew 0-0 at Maine Road, but won the home leg 2-0, with Phil scoring the second goal with a header from a corner. Coleman went on to sign professional for the 'Lions' in August 1978 and, playing in his usual central defensive position, made his debut at the Den in a London 'derby' against West Ham United in May 1979 when still only eighteen. Millwall won 2-1, and he kept his place in the side for the following match, a 2-2 home draw with Wrexham. Over the next two seasons Phil found himself in and out of the team at the Den on a regular basis, accumulating 36 League appearances and scoring one goal, before joining Colchester United in February 1981 for a £15,000 fee. He made his 'U's' debut in a goalless draw at Chester but, having already left one relegation-doomed club, he joined another, as both Colchester and Millwall were demoted at the end of the season. The next two campaigns saw Phil playing regularly in the 'U's' defence, but at the start of the 1983/84 season he was allowed to join Wrexham for a three months' loan period. Unfortunately, Coleman never had the best of times at the Racecourse, as Wrexham won just three of the seventeen games in which he appeared, and to cap it all was injured at Chesterfield, after which he was to return to Layer Road. After just eight more League games for the 'U's' that season he was allowed to leave. He then had a spell playing non-league football with Chelmsford City, before Exeter City stepped in to sign him in December 1984. At St.James' Park his stay was short, making his debut in a 4-3 'derby' win over Torquay, followed by another five League appearances before moving to Aldershot in February 1985. He made his 'Shots' debut in a 1-1 home draw with Chester, going on to spend just over a season at the Recreation Ground parting company with them at the end of 1985/86. He again began a new season with a non-league outfit, joining up with Dulwich Hamlet. However, he was soon back with a League club when his former club, Millwall, signed him as defensive cover in September 1986. Phil made ten more League appearances for the 'Lions' leaving at the end of the 1986/87 to try his luck in Finland with Mypa 45, with whom he won a Finnish League Division One championship medal. He later rejoined Colchester United in December 1988, and made ten more League appearances before his release at the end of the season. He was eventually appointed player/manager of Wivenhoe Town, with whom he won a Isthmian League championship medal in 1990, combining his duties with work as a PE teacher.

Season	League		F.A.Cup		Welsh Cup		League Cup		A.M.C.		Total	
	apps	gls	apps	gls	apps	gls	apps	gls	apps	gls	apps	gls
1983/84	17	2	1	0	1	0	1	0	-	-	20	2
	17	**2**	**1**	**0**	**1**	**0**	**1**	**0**	**-**	**-**	**20**	**2**

COMSTIVE, Paul Thomas

1984 - 1987

Position; *Midfield*
D.O.B; *25th November, 1961*
Birthplace; *Southport, Lancashire*
Height; *6ft 1in* ***Weight;*** *12st 7lbs*
Debut v. *Southend United (h) 24th November, 1984*
Total Appearances & Goals; *126/7 apps 11 gls*
Career; *Blackburn Rovers Oct 1979 3/3apps 0gls; Rochdale Sept 1982 (Loan) 9apps 2gls; Wigan Athletic Aug 1983 35apps 2gls; WREXHAM 22nd Nov 1984 £3,000; Burnley 7th Aug 1987 £8,000 81/1apps 17gls; Bolton Wanderers 20th Sept 1989 £37,000 42/7apps 3gls; Chester City 27th Nov 1991 £10,000 55/2apps 6gls; Southport cs1993 56/5apps 11gls; Morecambe cs1995; Chorley Mar 1996;*
Honours; *Welsh Cup Winner 1986; Sherpa Van Trophy runner-up 1988;*

Although born and bred in Southport Paul Comstive was snapped up as a schoolboy by Plymouth Argyle. Nothing came of his time at Home Park, and he under went trials nearer home with Blackpool and Blackburn

Rovers. He took his chance with the latter, although by this time he was too old for an apprenticeship, and in October 1979 signed a professional contract. Comstive went on to make his Football League debut with the Ewood Park club a year later, at Hillsborough against Sheffield Wednesday. However, Paul was to make just five more first team appearances for 'Rovers' before joining Rochdale on loan in September 1982. He then returned to Blackburn, as Rochdale could not afford the fee to sign him only to be released by 'Rovers' at the end of the season. He then joined Wigan Athletic in August 1983. Paul's stay at Springfield Park lasted twelve months, in which he notched up 35 League appearances, scoring twice. In November 1984 Wrexham manager Bobby Roberts signed Paul for a fee of £3,000. He played him at left-back for his debut, at home to Southend in a 2-1 defeat, Comstive scoring Wrexham's only goal. Paul kept his place in the team, and helped 'The Robins' steer clear of the re-election zone. The following term Comstive switched to midfield half way through the season, helping Wrexham lift the Welsh Cup for the first time since 1978. The 1986/87 season, saw him participate in all four European Cup-Winners' Cup matches for Wrexham against F.C.Zurrieq and Real Zaragoza, establishing himself as a crowd favourite. Despite this, he turned down a new contract offered in the close season by manager, Dixie McNeil, and joined Burnley. The fee of £8,000, fixed by tribunal, was a big disappointment to Wrexham, who considered him a much more valuable asset. Paul went straight into the Burnley first team, missing just two matches all season, and scored in a 3-0 League Cup over the 'Robins' at Turf Moor. He also hit the winning goal against Preston that took the 'Clarets' to Wembley for the Sherpa Van Trophy final in 1988. The following season he continued in the Burnley midfield, as they finished in a disappointing 16th place. Paul found himself in the reserves at the beginning of 1989/90, and in September left Turf Moor when Bolton Wanderers obtained his services. Paul was to remain at Burnden Park for just over two years during which time he made over fifty appearances before joining Chester City in November 1991. In his first season with 'City' Comstive missed just one match as they survived relegation by five points. The following season he returned to his original left-back position, but it ended in disappointment as Chester were relegated (No cheering, Wrexham fans!). Paul was released by Chester during the close season of 1993, and joined his home town team of Southport, who were playing in the GM Conference. He spent two seasons with the 'Sandgrounders' until joining another GM Conference side, Morecambe, in the close season of 1995. Paul played for most of the season with 'The Shrimpers', but joined Chorley just before the transfer deadline in March 1996. Today, Comstive still lives in Southport where he works for the Royal Mail as a Delivery Officer.

Season	League apps	League gls	F.A.Cup apps	F.A.Cup gls	Welsh Cup apps	Welsh Cup gls	League Cup apps	League Cup gls	F.R.T. apps	F.R.T. gls	E.C.W.C. apps	E.C.W.C. gls	Total apps	Total gls
1984/85	28	3	-	-	2	0	-	-	2	0	-	-	32	3
1985/86	33/2	3	3	0	6	1	2/1	0	1	0	-	-	45/3	4
1986/87	34/2	2	3	0	4	0	1/2	0	3	2	4	0	49/4	4
	95/4	**8**	**6**	**0**	**12**	**1**	**3/3**	**0**	**6**	**2**	**4**	**0**	**126/7**	**11**

CONDON, **Bernard Clive** 1927 - 1928

Position; *Centre Forward*
D.O.B; *14th October, 1902*
Birthplace; *Swansea, Glamorgan*
Died; *Newport, Gwent, November 1987*
Height; *5ft 9in* ***Weight;*** *11st 0lbs*
Debut v. *Rotherham United (h) 15th October, 1927*
Total Appearances & Goals; *2 apps 0 gls*
Career; *Barry Town 8th Nov 1924; Taunton; Barry Town Apr 1926; Swansea Town 11th Aug 1926; Merthyr Town 1926/27; Bridgend United 15th Feb 1927; Clapton Orient Jul 1927; WREXHAM 30th Sept 1927; Mold Town 14th Nov 1927; Bath City 1927/28; Barry Town 12th Apr 1928; Manchester City Aug 1928 (trial); Barry Town 19th Oct, 1928; Llanelly 31st Aug, 1929; Barry Town 15th Nov 1929 to 1931/32;*

A 'young amateur', Bernard Condon was playing for Southern League side Barry Town before enjoying a short spell with Taunton in the Western Competition. He returned to Jenner Park in April 1926, and shortly afterwards signed for Swansea Town in August. Bernard had a spell at the Vetch, without making a first team appearance, before signing for Merthyr Town and then Bridgend United in February 1927, remaining until the end of the season. He moved to London in the close season to try his luck with Football League side Clapton Orient, but after a couple of months with the 'O's' and failing to make the grade with the East London club, he took the trip up to North Wales to join Third Division North side, Wrexham. Bernard was with the Denbighshire club for just two months, though it was enough for him to be given his Football League debut, when he replaced Billie Rogers at centre-forward in a 3-2 home win over Rotherham United during October. He also played in the following match at Doncaster, a 2-1 defeat, which proved to be his last appearance in a Wrexham shirt as he was allowed to leave. Bernard then joined Welsh League neighbours, Mold Town in November for a short spell before heading south to Bath City in the New Year, and then back to South Wales and Barry Town. The close season saw him move to Manchester City for a trial period, but he failed to impress, and returned once again to his homeland. At the end of 1928/29, a season which had seen Condon score 22 league and cup goals for Barry, he left to join Llanelly, but the lure of the 'Linnets' was too strong and he returned to Barry Town in November 1929 where he remained until the end of 1931/32. During this time he formed a good attacking partnership with Dai Ward, who was a renowned goalscorer of the period.

Season	League apps	League gls	F.A.Cup apps	F.A.Cup gls	Welsh Cup apps	Welsh Cup gls	Total apps	Total gls
1927/28	2	0	-	-	-	-	2	0
	2	**0**	**-**	**-**	**-**	**-**	**2**	**0**

CONNELL, **William C.** 1926 - 1927

Position; *Goalkeeper*
D.O.B;
Birthplace; *Liverpool, Merseyside*
Height; *ft in* ***Weight;*** *st lbs*
Debut v. *Doncaster Rovers (a) 21st February, 1925*
Total Appearances & Goals; *10 apps 0 gls*
Career; *West Kirby; Port Sunlight; Flint Town cs1924; WREXHAM Feb 1925; Flint Town Apr 1925; Mold Town Jul 1925; WREXHAM (Am) Aug 1926, (Pro) 10th Nov 1926; Crewe Alexandra Aug 1927 2apps 0gls; New Brighton Sept 1929 0apps;Honours; Welsh Cup runner-up 1925; Wirral Senior Cup Winner 1922;*

Bill Connell was the son of a former Liverpool trainer. He began playing in Cheshire League football with West Kirby, captaining the side that won the Wirral Senior Cup in 1922. Connell later kept goal for Port Sunlight before crossing the North Wales border to appear for Flint Town United during the close season of 1924. At Welsh League side Flint he came to the notice of Wrexham, and in February 1925 joined 'The Robins' on amateur forms whilst remaining on Flint's books. This was allowed at the time, as an amateur player could be signed by both a Welsh League team and an English League club. Bill made his Football League debut for Wrexham in February 1925, at Doncaster in a 1-0 defeat, in place of George Godding. He made a further two League appearances that season, but at the end of the campaign had to play 'against' Wrexham, for Flint in 'a keenly contested' Welsh Cup final which Wrexham won 3-1. Bill continued on Wrexham's books as an amateur for the following two seasons, also playing for Flint, but he was not required again by Wrexham until September 1926 when Ted Robson was injured in a match against Walsall. Bill was called up, and made seven League appearances until Robson returned to fitness. He later signed for Crewe Alexandra in August 1927, where he made two Football League appearances. Connell was later on the books of New Brighton, but failed to make a first team appearance for the 'Rakers'.

Season	League apps	League gls	F.A.Cup apps	F.A.Cup gls	Welsh Cup apps	Welsh Cup gls	Total apps	Total gls
1924/25	3	0	-	-	-	-	3	0
1926/27	7	0	-	-	-	-	7	0
	10	**0**	**-**	**-**	**-**	**-**	**10**	**0**

CONNOLLY, Karl Andrew 1991 -

Position; *Forward*
D.O.B; *9th February, 1970*
Birthplace; *Liverpool, Merseyside*
Height; *5ft 11in* **Weight;** *11st 2lbs*
Debut v. *Hereford United (h) 17 August, 1991*
Total Appearances & Goals; *405/17 apps 111 gls*
Career; *Napoli (Liverpool Sunday League); WREXHAM 8th May 1991;*
Honours; *Third Division runner-up 1993; Welsh Cup Winner 1995; Welsh Invitation Cup Winner 1998; P.F.A. Second Division XI 1996; Welsh Premier Cup Runner Up 1999;*

Karl Connolly was playing local football in the Liverpool area when Wrexham scout Keith McKeown invited him along to the Racecourse for a trial. This was in March 1990, and after training with the other first team players he was selected to play in a reserve match. He was then asked back for extended trials, which led to non contract terms over the summer period followed by a three month contract at the beginning of the 1991/92 season. Much to Karl's surprise he made his debut in the first match of the season against Hereford United, and he has not looked back since. Connolly was on Tranmere Rovers books as a schoolboy, but was not offered an apprenticeship on leaving school at 16, although he continued to play for the 'Prentonians' on a casual basis whilst working at a chip shop! Karl then drifted into local football, playing for a team called 'Rockies' in the St.Helens Combination and also Napoli in the Warrington Sunday League. He had been deployed in his favourite position of centre-forward, but at Wrexham he was switched to a left sided midfielder-come-winger, as he is a naturally left footed player. Since making his Football League debut in August 1991 Connolly has gone on to become a first team regular throughout his time with the club, playing in the great F.A.Cup win over Football League Champions Arsenal, as well as assisting the side to promotion to Division Two in 1992/93. He won a Welsh Cup Winners medal in 1995, when Wrexham beat Cardiff City in the final at the National Stadium, and the 1995/96 season saw him selected by his fellow professionals for the P.F.A.'s Second Division team. This was after switching to play in his favourite position of centre-forward following the departure of Gary Bennett, when he finished the season as the club's leading scorer with 21 league and cup goals. His undoubted talents have prompted much speculation with talk of various offers from a number of interested parties. Karl's darting runs are a feature of his play, and an 'on-song' Connolly, would see the whole team respond around him. This was demonstrated during 'The Robins' 1996/97 F.A.Cup run, when the club reached the quarter-finals. However, a dip in form and niggling injuries saw his appearances restricted, which frustrated him to the point of asking for a move just prior to the transfer deadline to enable him to take up a "fresh challenge" elsewhere. Despite this, he remained at the Racecourse, finishing as leading scorer again in 1997/98, as the club were to just miss out on the Second Division play-offs on goals scored, although he did help 'The Robins' to win the Welsh Invitation Cup in its inaugural season. Although now deployed in his favourite position there are many fans who prefer to see him operate in the wide left role setting up chances as well as scoring.

Season	League		F.A.Cup		Welsh Cup		League Cup		Auto Tro		E.C.W.C.		Total	
	apps	gls	apps	gls	apps	gls	apps	gls	apps	gls	apps	gls	apps	gls
1991/92	33/3	8	5	1	2	0	2	0	3	1	-	-	45/3	10
1992/93	40/2	9	1	0	5	0	2	0	1/1	0	-	-	49/3	9
1993/94	38/1	2	2	0	2	1	4	1	3	0	-	-	49/1	4
1994/95	45	10	4	2	8	2	4	1	4	0	-	-	65	15
1995/96	45/1	18	4	1	-	-	2	0	3	2	2	0	56/1	21
1996/97	27/3	14	8	1	-	-	2	0	1	0	-	-	38/3	15
1997/98	31/4	7	4	5	3*	1*	2	1	1	0	-	-	41/4	14
1998/99	43/1	11	5	5	7/1*	5*	2	1	5	1	-	-	62/2	23
	302/15	**79**	**33**	**15**	**24/1**	**8**	**20**	**4**	**21/1**	**4**	**2**	**0**	**405/17**	**111**

* = Welsh Invitation/Premier Cup.

CONNOR, Robert 1951 - 1954

Position; *Goalkeeper*
D.O.B; *13th October, 1925.*
Birthplace; *Bradford, Yorkshire*
Height; *5ft 10'1/2ins* **Weight;** *11st 7lbs*
Debut v. *Barrow (h) 29th August, 1951*
Total Appearances & Goals; *88 apps 0 gls*
Career; *Farsley Celtic; Salts AFC; Bradford City Nov 1949 28apps 0gls; WREXHAM 28th Jul 1951; Bath City Jul 1954; Trowbridge Town cs1955;*
Honours; *Western League Championship Winner 1956;*

Bob Connor was a relative late comer to League football due to the Second World War. He had begun playing football while at Bradford Moor and Lapage Street Schools, turning out at either full-back or wing-half. It was only after leaving school that Bob was to become a goalkeeper; Swain Green, his Sunday School team, announced that they needed someone to play between the posts, and Bob obliged, showing rare talent. He was soon selected to play for Bradford youth before WW2 was to interrupt his progress. He worked in the Textile industry at the beginning of the War, and in 1941 was enlisted in the Royal Air Force, stationed mainly on the south coast. During his time in the R.A.F. Connor did manage to play some football for his station team, and also 2898 Squadron. In 1944 he joined the Military Police, with whom he remained until he was demobbed in 1946. Bob then took up playing for Farsley Celtic in the West Riding County League, and later Salts AFC who operated in the same League. At this time he had trials with both Halifax Town and Bradford Park Avenue. It was only after phoning the Bradford City manager, David Steele, requesting a trial that his career in football really took off. Bob had played just one reserve match, and was waiting to see if he was going to be offered another chance, when he was told that he was making his Football League debut for Bradford City at Crewe. That was in October 1949, and he went on to spend over one and a half seasons at Valley Parade before being snapped up by Wrexham manager Peter Jackson, upon his release. At Wrexham, Bob went on to replace the popular Archie Ferguson after the opening three matches of the season, making his debut in a 4-2 home win over Barrow. In his first season at the club, Connor finished runner-up to George Spruce in the 'Player of the Season' awards. In all, he spent three seasons at the Racecourse, sharing the 'keepers position with Pat Egglestone over the last two. At the end of 1953/54 he was released by Wrexham, joining Southern League side Bath City, but it turned out to be a frustrating move as he underwent a cartilage operation on his right knee which restricted his appearances. When recovered, he left Bath to join Western League First Division side Trowbridge, remaining there for the rest of his football career. In his first season Bob helped them to the Western League Championship, and they finished the following season as runners-up. Connor later returned to live in his native Bradford, taking up employment again in the textile industry as a foreman. In 1974, Bob was diagnosed as having cancer in his throat. He recovered after intensive treatment, and continued to work until his retirement in 1984, finally settling in Shipley, near Bradford.

Season	League		F.A.Cup		Welsh Cup		Total	
	apps	gls	apps	gls	apps	gls	apps	gls
1951/52	40	0	3	0	4	0	47	0
1952/53	17	0	2	0	1	0	20	0
1953/54	20	0	-	-	1	0	21	0
	77	**0**	**5**	**0**	**6**	**0**	**88**	**0**

CONROY, Michael George 1986 - 1987

Position; *Midfield*
D.O.B; *31st July, 1957*
Birthplace; *Johnstone, Strathclyde*
Height; *5ft 9in* **Weight;** *11st 2lbs*
Debut v. *Hereford United (a) 23rd August, 1986*
Total Appearances & Goals; *35/2 apps 3 gls*
Career; *Port Glasgow Juniors; Glasgow Celtic 10th Apr 1978 66apps 9gls; Hibernians 11th Oct 1982 31apps 2gls; Blackpool 1st Sept 1984 66apps 2gls; WREXHAM 15th Jul 1986; Leyton Orient Jul 1987 2/1apps 0gls; Cork City cs1988;*
Honours; *Scottish F.A.Cup Winner 1980;*

Mike Conroy began his football career playing for local Scottish Junior side, Port Glasgow Juniors. His form was such a revelation that his father's former club, Glasgow Celtic, were soon to offer him professional

terms. Mike made his way through the ranks at Parkhead, to make his debut in a 4-1 defeat at Hibs in April 1978. However, he achieved personal satifaction in scoring the Celtic goal. He kept his place for the last four matches of the season, but Celtic were very much in a transitional period at this time, as Kenny Dalglish had left to join Liverpool, and Billy McNeil had taken over the manager's job from Jock Stein. The highlight of Conroy's time with Celtic, was playing in the 1980 Scottish Cup final win over the 'auld' enemy, Rangers, at 'centre-half'! He had been forced to play out of position because both of Celtic's regular centre-backs were suspended, though he made such a good job of blotting out Rangers' Derek Johnstone that he was named 'Man of the Match'. Even so, Mike was unable to command a regular first team place at Parkhead over the next two seasons, and in August 1982 he joined Hibernians. Conroy's stay at Easter Road was not a happy one, as injuries restricted his appearances in his two years with the 'Hibee's'. He was released at the end of 1983/84 and moved south, to join Fourth Division Blackpool. His first season at Bloomfield Road was a great success, as his work-rate in midfield helped the 'Seasiders' finish runners-up in the League. The following season saw Mike struck once again with injury problems, missing three months of the campaign. Despite this, it came as quite a surprise when he was given a free transfer at the end of the season. With offers from Scunthorpe United, Chesterfield, Fulham, and Wrexham he decided to join the Welsh club in July 1986 as they prepared for another European escapade. He made his Wrexham debut in a scoreless draw at Hereford United in August 1986, and then played in the two European games with FC Zurrieq, but missed out on appearing against the Spanish side Real Zaragoza because of injury. Although accumulating 25 League appearances for 'The Robins', he never managed to show the consistency he had displayed for Blackpool in their promotion year, though problems with niggling injuries had much to do with this. At the end of the season Mike found himself released by Wrexham, and he joined Leyton Orient in July 1987. However, his time with the 'O's' was spent mainly on the sidelines, as he was injured before the season had commenced and he was not to make his debut until the following January, when he appeared as substitute in a 1-1 home draw with Stockport County. Conroy made just two more League appearances before being released in the summer. It was then that he took up an offer to go to Ireland, joining Cork City in the close season of 1988. He was appointed assistant manager of the club in 1991/92, but he was dismissed from that position in the summer of 1993.

Season	League		F.A.Cup		Welsh Cup		League Cup		S.V.T		E.C.W.C.		Total	
	apps	gls	apps	gls	apps	gls	apps	gls	apps	gls	apps	gls	apps	gls
1986/87	23/2	2	3	0	1	0	4	0	2	1	2	0	35/2	3
	23/2	**2**	**3**	**0**	**1**	**0**	**4**	**0**	**2**	**1**	**2**	**0**	**35/2**	**3**

COOKE, Joseph

1986 - 1988

Position; *Centre-Half*
D.O.B; *15th February, 1955*
Birthplace; *Leeward Islands, Dominica, West Indies.*
Height; *6ft 1in* ***Weight;*** *13st 0lbs*
Debut v. *Hereford United (a) 23rd August, 1986*
Total Appearances & Goals; *68/2 apps 5 gls*
Career; *Bradford City May 1972 184/20apps 62gls; Peterborough United 12th Jan 1979 £45,000 18apps 5gls; Oxford United 17th Aug 1979 £50,000 71/1apps 13gls; Exeter City Jun 1981 £25,000 17apps 3gls; Bradford City Jan 1982 £10,000 61/1apps 6gls; Rochdale Jul 1984 75apps 4gls; WREXHAM 15th Aug 1986 £8,000; Released May 1988;*
Honours; *Division Four runner-up 1982;*

Joe Cooke's family came to Britain when he was a child, uprooting from the Leeward Islands of Dominica to settle in the Bradford area. While at School he was chosen to play for Bradford Boys, where he was spotted by Bradford City who signed him on associate schoolboy forms in July 1970. Joe showed so much early promise that he made his Football League debut as a 16 year-old apprentice in September 1971, coming on as sub against Chesterfield. Cooke played in many positions at Valley Parade, where aerial dominance and physical presence enabled him to be comfortable in either centre-forward or centre-half positions. Despite this, it was not until the 1974/75 season that he finally became a regular with 'The Bantams'. Joe went on to make a total of 204 League appearances for the Valley Parade club, helping them to reach the F.A.Cup quarter-finals as a Fourth Division club in 1976, and then to promotion in 1977. Cooke finished that season as the club's leading scorer with 17 goals, playing the entire season at centre-forward. The following term saw Bradford go straight back down, and in January 1979 Joe left Valley Parade to join Third Division Peterborough United for a record £45,000, which also saw Lammie Robertson move the other way. At London Road he helped the 'Posh' to a 2-1 home win over Chester on his debut, but failed to save them from relegation. He was on his travels again in the close season, joining Oxford United for £50,000, and though he began up front, was switched midway through the season to centre-half, where he spent the rest of his time, apart from the odd game. At the end of 1980/81, a season that had seen him finish as Oxford's top scorer with six goals, Joe joined Exeter City for £25,000. He never really settled in the South West and, despite missing just three games, was allowed to return to Bradford in January 1982 for a £10,000 fee, following a month 'on loan'. Cooke's experience was just what Bradford required, and they went on to finish Fourth Division runners-up. Injuries restricted his appearances over the next two seasons, and at the end of the 1983/84 season he was released. Joe then signed for Rochdale, where he was appointed club captain, spending two seasons at Spotland before Wrexham manager 'Dixie' McNeil obtained his signature for £8,000 in July 1986 to replace the departed Jack Keay at centre-half. Joe was again given the captaincy for the new 1986/87 season, and went on to play in the four European Cup-Winners' Cup matches that same season against F.C.Zurrieq and Real Zaragoza. The following season was to be his last, as his appearances were limited because of an on-going knee injury, which finally took its toll and forced Joe to retire from professional football at the end of that season. He later began running his own Health and fitness gymnasium in the Bradford area where he had settled.

Season	League		F.A.Cup		Welsh Cup		League Cup		F.R.T.		E.C.W.C.		Total	
	apps	gls	apps	gls	apps	gls	apps	gls	apps	gls	apps	gls	apps	gls
1986/87	38	4	2	0	4	0	3	1	3	0	4	0	54	5
1987/88	11/2	0	-	-	1	0	2	0	-	-	-	-	14/2	0
	49/2	**4**	**2**	**0**	**5**	**0**	**5**	**1**	**3**	**0**	**4**	**0**	**68/2**	**5**

COOKE, Terence John

1998 - 1999

Position; *Outside-Right*
D.O.B; *5th August, 1976*
Birthplace; *Birmingham, West Midlands*
Height; *5ft 7in* ***Weight;*** *9st 9lbs*
Debut; ***v.*** *Burnley (a) 31st October, 1998*
Total Appearances & Goals; *13 apps 0 gls*
Career; *Manchester United 1st Jul 1994 1/3apps 0gls; Sunderland 29th Jan 1996 (Loan) 6apps 0gls; Birmingham City 29th Nov 1996 (Loan) 1/3apps 0gls; WREXHAM 29th Oct 1998 (Loan); Manchester City 14th Jan 1999 (Loan) 15th Apr 1999 £600,000 21apps 7gls;*
Honours; *Four England under-21 international caps; England Youth international caps; F.A.Youth Cup Winner 1995; Pontins League Championship Winner 1996 & 1997; Second Division Play-Off winner 1999;*

Terry Cooke was signed by Wrexham manager Brian Flynn in October 1998 in a bid to give the club some much needed firepower having failed to score in the four previous matches prior to his signing. Terry, who hails from Marston Green in Birmingham was signed by Manchester United's School of Excellence at the age of 13, and went on to sign apprentice terms in 1992 upon leaving school. He became a member of United's

1995 F.A.Youth Cup winning side when they beat Tottenham Hotspur 4-3 on penalties, after an aggregate score of 2-2, in which Terry scored both of United's goals. By that time he had already signed professional forms for the 'Red Devils' in the summer of 1994, and had also been capped by England at Youth level. He made his Premier League debut for United in a 3-0 home win over Bolton Wanderers in September 1995 when covering for Roy Keane, making three further appearances in the League that season. The signing of Karel Proborsky put Cooke back down the pecking order, and since then has languished mostly in United's reserve team, winning two championship medals in the Pontins League in 1996 and 1997. He accepted a loan spell to Sunderland in January 1996 and made six appearances for the Roker club, making his debut in a scoreless home draw with Tranmere Rovers. Having returned to Old Trafford, he accepted a further loan spell to Birmingham City in November 1996, making his debut in a 1-0 win at Norwich City as a substitute for Ricki Otto. He made three further League appearances for the 'Blues'. A right-winger, he is described as having 'lightening pace and excellent skills', as well as being 'comfortable with the ball, he sees things quickly and is a good crosser of the ball.' He made his England under-21 debut against Croatia in April 1996 in a 1-0 defeat, and has since won three further caps against Belgium, Angola and Portugal. A cruciate ligament injury saw him on the sidelines for most of 1998, and his loan move to the Racecourse was part of the recovery procedure that he had set himself. He made his debut for Wrexham in a 2-1 defeat against Burnley at Turf Moor.

Season	League apps	gls	F.A.Cup apps	gls	League Cup apps	gls	A.W.S. apps	gls	W.P.C. apps	gls	Total apps	gls
1998/99	10	0	-	-	-	-	1	0	2	0	13	0
	10	**0**	-	-	-	-	**1**	**0**	**2**	**0**	**13**	**0**

COOPER, Graham — 1988 - 1990

Position; *Forward*
D.O.B; *22nd May, 1962*
Birthplace; *Huddersfield, Yorkshire*
Height; *5ft 10in* ***Weight;*** *10st 9lbs*
Debut v. *Exeter City (a) 27th August, 1988*
Total Appearances & Goals; *69/20 apps 21 gls*
Career; *Emley; Huddersfield Town Mar 1984 61/13apps 13gls; WREXHAM 3rd Aug 1988 50/13apps 16gls; York City 8th Nov 1990 (Loan) 2apps 0gls; Northwich Victoria Dec 1990 Halifax Town Jan 1991 32/7apps 4gls; Kui-Tan (Hong Kong) May 1992;*

Born and bred in Huddersfield Graham Cooper showed plenty of ability as a youngster while playing at the Town's Newsome Secondary School, winning many trophies, and representing Huddersfield boys. Despite his early promise he left school and took up work as an apprentice engineer at 'David Brown's Gears'. He retained his interest in football, and turned out for Northern Premier League side Emley. It was from here that he was invited to play for Huddersfield Town's reserve side. He continued with his apprenticeship, although once completed he volunteered for redundancy and accepted Huddersfield's offer of a professional contract, signing for the 'Terriers' in March 1984. Graham impressed manager Mick Buxton sufficiently to make his Football League debut before the season had ended. That was in May, a 1-1 draw at Portsmouth when he stepped in for Steve Doyle. The following match, Huddersfield's last home fixture of the season, saw Graham pitted against Newcastle United. They had already won promotion, and included Peter Beardsley, Chris Waddle, and Terry McDermott in the team. However, Graham subdued the 'Geordies' celebrations by scoring for the 'Terriers' in a 2-2 draw. He was a regular in the side the following season until disaster struck, breaking his leg for a second time in a reserve match. This forced him to miss the entire 1985/86 season. He struggled to maintain a regular first team place upon his return to fitness, but he did play in some memorable Cup games against the likes of Arsenal, Norwich City, and Luton Town, although his most memorable match was against Barnsley, scoring the only goal of a game that Huddersfield needed to win to stay up in the final match of the 1986/87 season. Cooper was allowed to leave Leeds Road at the end of the following campaign, but was quickly signed by Wrexham manager Dixie McNeil. His first season at the Racecourse saw the club reach the final of the 1988/89 play-offs, only to lose to Leyton Orient 2-1 on aggregate. The following year he helped the club reach the final of the Welsh Cup, but missed the final against Hereford United at the National Stadium in Cardiff because of injury. Despite losing that game, Wrexham still qualified for Europe as Hereford were an English club. The 1990/91 season saw him struggle with injury problems again, but he was able to play in the four European matches against both Lyngby and Manchester United. It looked as though Cooper would miss out on those matches due to UEFA regulations then in force that restricted clubs to just four 'foreigners', but he suddenly announced that his father was Welsh! The likeable winger was to leave the Racecourse shortly after that European experience, moving to York City on loan where he played just two League games. He then assisted Northwich Victoria helping them out for one game, before signing for Halifax Town in January 1991. The move to the 'Shay' was to see Graham playing regular first team football again, but he left Yorkshire in the summer of 1992 to move to Hong Kong, joining up with a team called Kui-Tan. Upon returning he struggled with injury, and was later told by a specialist to stop playing due to osteo-arthritis in his hip joint. Graham, back in his native Huddersfield, took up working in engineering again while still keeping involved with football by helping out with coaching at Emley Reserves. During his time at the Racecourse, Graham endeared himself to the crowd and emerged as a great character. On and off the field!!

Season	League apps	gls	F.A.Cup apps	gls	Welsh Cup apps	gls	League Cup apps	gls	F.R.T. apps	gls	E.C.W.C. apps	gls	Total apps	gls
1988/89	29/8	12	1/1	1	1/2	0	2	1	2	0	-	-	35/11	14
1989/90	16/2	3	1	0	2/1	1	1/1	0	2	1	-	-	22/4	5
1990/91	5/4	2	-	-	-	-	2/1	0	1	0	4	0	12/5	2
	50/14	**17**	**2/1**	**1**	**3/3**	**1**	**5/2**	**1**	**5**	**1**	**4**	**0**	**69/20**	**21**

COPE, William Arthur — 1922 - 1923

Position; *Full Back*
Birthplace; *Stoke-on-Trent, Staffordshire*
Height; *5ft 8in* ***Weight;*** *11st 4lbs*
D.O.B; *25th November, 1884*
Died; *Hartshill, Stoke, 18th February, 1937*
Debut v. *Grimsby Town (a) 26th August, 1922.*
Total Appearances & Goals; *15 apps 0 gls*
Career; *Mount Pleasant; Burslem Port Vale 29th Aug 1904 73apps 1gls; Stoke 7th Jul 1907 25apps 0gls; Oldham Athletic 18th June 1908 £300 63apps 1gls; West Ham United 6th May 1914 £150 137apps 0gls (including 31 in Southern League); WREXHAM 20th Jul 1922; Retired cs1923;*

Bill Cope was playing for Mount Pleasant, a local side in the 'Potteries', when spotted by Football League Division Two side Burslem Port Vale. He joined them in August 1904, and made his League debut for Vale in a 2-0 home defeat by Barnsley in October 1904, playing in his usual full-back slot. He was a regular in the side over the next three seasons, playing in either of the full-back positions, but found himself without a team in June 1907 when the club were wound-up with crippling debts. Billy had played in their final League match, a 3-0 home win over Blackpool. He was soon snapped up by neighbours Stoke, but after one season he again found himself without a League club when the Potters themselves resigned from the competition. Undaunted, Billy then signed on the dotted line for Oldham Athletic in only their second season in League football for a £300 transfer fee. Cope spent six years with the 'Latics', but he was limited to just 63 League outings during that time due to the stiff competition for places in the side. Cope again proved to be a capable full-back, covering on either flank. His game was described as being characterised by 'some hefty clearances, despite the fact he wore only size-4 boots!' In May 1914 he moved south, to join Southern League side West Ham United for a £150 transfer fee. He had made 31 appearances for 'The Hammers' before the League was curtailed by the outbreak of WW1. Billy continued to play football for the East Enders in the regionalised Leagues, making 111 appearances between 1915 and 1919. When things returned to normal after the War, West Ham joined the Football League Second Division and Cope was made club captain, playing in their inaugural Football League match at home to Lincoln City on 30th August, 1919. At West Ham he was described as 'lacking speed, but kicked strongly' which seems to have been considered an admirable quality in the 1920s. Billy was also said to be known as a 'Hard man of his day, and a great disciple of the one-back game.' He was allowed to leave West Ham at the end of the 1921/22 season, when 37 years-old. However, he continued to play League football, signing for Third Division North side, Wrexham. He made his debut for 'The Robins' in the opening match of the 1922/23 season at Grimsby Town, but it was an inauspicious start as Wrexham lost 4-0! He went on to make a further twelve League appearances for the club, playing only when required, acting mainly as cover for regular full-backs Noel Edwards and George Holmes. At the end of the season Billy finally retired from League football at the age of 38. He later returned to live in his native City of Stoke-on-Trent, where he died in 1937, aged only 52.

Season	League		F.A.Cup		Welsh Cup		Total	
	apps	gls	apps	gls	apps	gls	apps	gls
1922/23	13	0	-	-	2	0	15	0
	13	**0**	**-**	**-**	**2**	**0**	**15**	**0**

COTTON, William Charles 1921 - 1924

Position; *Centre Forward*
D.O.B; *10th April, 1894.*
Birthplace; *Liverpool, Merseyside*
Died; *Blixworth, Northants A/M/J 1971*
Height; *5ft 11in* **Weight;** *13st 4lbs*
Debut v. *Hartlepool United (h) 27th August, 1921*
Total Appearances & Goals; *106 apps 47 gls*
Career; *Liverpool Boys; South Liverpool 1919/20; Everton (Trial); South Garston FC 1919/20; WREXHAM 28th May, 1921; Kettering Town Jul 1924; Port Vale Jul 1925 (trial) 0apps; Connahs Quay 10th Nov 1925; Buckley United 12th Feb 1926; Halifax Town 19th March 1926 5apps 3gls; Crewe Alexandra Jul 1926 13apps 3gls; Connahs Quay & Shotton 4th March 1927; Yeovil & Petters United Aug 1927; Buckley United 22nd October 1927; Prescott FC 1928; Brenka FC Aug 1929*
Honours; *Welsh Cup Winner 1924;*

Billy Cotton played for Liverpool Boys before WW1 was to disrupt any hope he had of a playing career. He joined the Army for the War period, leaving when it ended to take up playing again for South Liverpool. He followed this with a spell at near-neighbours South Garston FC, during which time he had a trial with Everton. Eventually, he was signed by Third Division North side Wrexham in the close season of 1921, to strengthen the squad for the start of the club's first season in the Football League. Billy played in the club's inaugural match against Hartlepool United on the Racecourse, but failed to get on the score sheet in a 2-0 defeat. However, he was soon to find the net, and went on to score many goals for the North Wales club. In fact, he became the first Wrexham player to score a Football League hat-trick, in a match against Chesterfield on the Racecourse in November 1921 which the home side won 6-1. Although Ted Regan also grabbed a hat-trick in the same match Billy was the first to complete the feat. In May 1924 he scored the winning goal against Merthyr Town in the Welsh Cup final. During the close season Cotton could not agree new terms with the Wrexham directors, and he quit the Racecourse to join Kettering Town, leaving behind trouble and controversy between the fans and the Club. Not surprisingly, Cotton continued to find the net on a regular basis for the Northamptonshire club, and in July 1925 joined Port Vale on trial. Surprisingly, he failed to make a first team appearance for Vale, and in November of the same year joined Welsh League side Connah's Quay. His stay with the 'Deesiders' was short, and it was followed by an even shorter spell with Buckley United early in 1926, from where he eventually returned to the Football League with Halifax Town in March. Bill remained at The Shay until the end of 1925/26, scoring three goals in five games before signing for Crewe Alexandra during the close season. Billy stayed at Gresty Road until March 1927, returning to play for Connah's Quay until the end of the season. In August 1927 he joined Yeovil and Petters on a month's trial, but he was not retained at the end of it, and returned to North Wales to rejoin Buckley United in October 1927. Billy is then believed to have had spells with Prescott and Brenka FC.

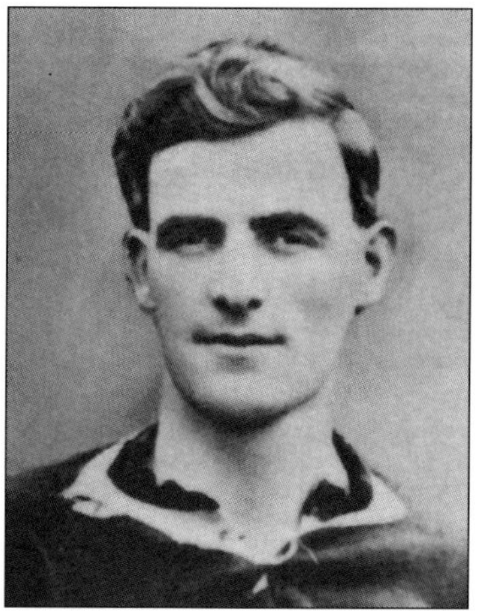

Season	League		F.A.Cup		Welsh Cup		Total	
	apps	gls	apps	gls	apps	gls	apps	gls
1921/22	26	8	4	2	2	2	32	12
1922/23	31	12	2	0	3	3	36	15
1923/24	31	14	2	3	5	3	38	20
	88	**34**	**8**	**5**	**10**	**8**	**106**	**47**

CRIPSEY, Brian Samuel 1958 - 1960

Position; *Outside-Left*
D.O.B; *26th June, 1931*
Birthplace; *Hull, Humberside.*
Height; *5ft 7in* **Weight;** *10st 3lbs*
Debut v. *Mansfield Town (a) 22nd September, 1958 (Scored)*
Total Appearances & Goals; *27 apps 3 gls*
Career; *Brunswick Institute; Hull City Nov 1951 145apps 19gls; WREXHAM 22nd Sept 1958 £4,000; Bridlington Trinity Jul 1960; Goole Town; North Shore United 1963*
Honours; *Third Division North Representative XI 1956/57;*

As a youngster Brian Cripsey played for Southcoats Lane School, representing Yorkshire Schoolboys, as well as assisting three junior clubs in his native Hull: Maybury Youth Club; Dansom Lane Police Boys' Club; and Bridlington Central United. After leaving school he trained as a Laboratory Technologist, working at the local Medical Research Centre, and continuing to play football for his local side, Brunswick Institute. In 1949, at the age of 18, he was called up for his two years' National Service, joining the Royal Army Medical Corps and stationed in Crookham, Hampshire. He turned out for the depot team, where he was invited to play for Brighton & Hove Albion reserves. He also appeared for local works' team Thorneycroft Athletic, and was selected to play for the Hampshire County side in the Southern Cup. Once Cripsey completed his National Service he received a number of offers to join Football League clubs, including Q.P.R., Leicester, and Aston Villa, but he decided to join his home town club, Hull City, in November 1951. It was not until January 1953 that Brian was to figure in 'The Tigers' first team, playing at outside-left in place of the injured Eddie Burbanks in a 1-0 defeat at Brentford. He kept his place for the next eleven games, but he had to wait until the 1955/56 season, before he was able to command a regular first team place. He became a virtual ever-present over the next three years, but in September 1958 was allowed to leave Boothferry Park to join Wrexham for a club record fee of

£4,500. With Hull, Cripsey had been described as a 'clever ball player, who is fast and elusive.' He made his Wrexham debut at Mansfield, scoring the goal in a 3-1 defeat. He played for most of 1958/59 in the newly reorganised Third Division, but was dogged by a knee injury, and unfortunately never quite hit the sort of form which persuaded manager John Love to break the bank to sign him. The 1959/60 season was a virtual write-off for Brian, as he suffered a recurrence of the knee injury in the opening match of the season against Newport, and was later rushed into hospital for a cartilage operation. He worked hard to regain his fitness, but made just one more first team appearance, at Shrewsbury in January 1960, a match which Brian felt he had been rushed back too soon. By the end of the term Brian had decided to retire from football, returning to live in Hull, where he worked as a salesman for four weeks before taking up employment with Northern Dairies in their Laboratory. He continued there for three and a half years, playing football when he could at non-league level for both Bridlington Trinity and Goole Town, eventually deciding to emigrate to New Zealand in 1963. He played for North Shore United for three years, combining this with work as a laboratory technician with the New Zealand Co-op Dairy. After three years he joined up with the New Zealand Blood Transfusion Service, with whom he spent 26 years before retiring at 61. Today, Brian lives in retirement in Auckland, New Zealand.

Season	League		F.A.Cup		Welsh Cup		Total	
	apps	gls	apps	gls	apps	gls	apps	gls
1958/59	25	3	-	-	-	-	25	3
1959/60	2	0	-	-	-	-	2	0
	27	**3**	**-**	**-**	**-**	**-**	**27**	**3**

CROMPTON, Wynne 1927 - 1932

Position; *Left Back*
D.O.B; *11th February, 1907*
Birthplace; *Cefn-y-Bedd, Denbighshire*
Died; *Wrexham, 28th May, 1988*
Height; *5ft 7in* **Weight;** *11st 6lbs*
Debut v. *Doncaster Rovers (h) 22nd October, 1927*
Total Appearances & Goals; *79 apps 0 glsCareer; Oak Alyn Rovers 1926; WREXHAM (Am) Jul 1927 (Pro) 24th Sept 1927; Tunbridge Wells Rangers Jun 1932; Leyton Orient July 1933 79apps 0gls; Crystal Palace May 1935 0apps; Exeter City Oct 1935 7apps 0gls; Oswestry Town Sept 1936-1937; Cross Street FC 2nd Dec1938 to 1939;*
Honours; *Three Welsh International caps; One Welsh Junior International cap; Welsh Cup Winner 1931;*

Wynne Crompton began his football career with Welsh League side Oak Alyn, where he soon began showing impressive enough form for Wrexham to sign him in the summer of 1927. Wynne made his Football League debut in October 1927, in a 2-1 home defeat at the hands of Doncaster Rovers. It was said of him at the time that 'he showed a neat, methodical approach to his work and a keenness in the tackle'. He went on to make a further six League appearances that season. Crompton could play in either full-back berth but, was not able to hold down a regular first team spot due to the consistency of Alf Jones and Albert Lumberg, at least not until the 1930/31 season when Lumberg left the club. Whilst waiting for his chance Wynne, an amateur, had gained representative honours for the Welsh League, against the League of Ireland, as well as for the Cheshire League, and he had also appeared for Wales in a Junior international fixture against Ireland in 1930. Once settled in the first team at the Racecourse he quietly developed a fine understanding with Alf Jones and became noted for his 'excellent covering, tenacious tackling and reliability under pressure'. He capped the season by picking up a Welsh Cup Winners' medal when Wrexham thrashed Shrewsbury Town 7-0 in the final, and he also represented Wales in the famous 'Unknowns' team that faced Scotland at Hampden Park. He acquitted himself well, and played in the other two Home International matches of 1930/31. The following season saw Crompton lose his place in the side to new signing, John Brown, making just four League appearances in a campaign that had seen his cousin, Matt Lawrence, become a regular in the Wrexham side, and at the end of it he was released. In June 1932 he joined Kent League side Tunbridge Wells Rangers, but just a day after signing received an offer from Carlisle United to remain with a Football League club. It was however, too late. Wynne did return to League football after a season, joining Leyton Orient. At Brisbane Road he made 79 League appearances in two seasons before joining Crystal Palace in May 1935. After just five months, and without having made a first team appearance for Palace, he joined Exeter City, where he completed his League career. In September 1936 he joined Birmingham & District League side, Oswestry Town, bringing a much needed steadiness to the team, but two years later a knee injury virtually ended his career. He did play for a local Wrexham side, Cross Street FC, before retiring from football altogether in 1939. After ending his career in the professional game Wynne worked as a miner at Llay near Wrexham, and was later employed at Shotton Steelworks until his retirement. His grandson, Steve, also played League football for both Wolves and Hereford United.

Season	League		F.A.Cup		Welsh Cup		Total	
	apps	gls	apps	gls	apps	gls	apps	gls
1927/28	7	0	3	0	-	-	10	0
1928/29	5	0	-	-	1	0	6	0
1929/30	19	0	3	0	2	0	24	0
1930/31	29	0	2	0	4	0	35	0
1931/32	4	0	-	-	-	-	4	0
	64	**0**	**8**	**0**	**7**	**0**	**79**	**0**

CROSBY, Malcolm 1984

Position; *Midfield*
D.O.B; *4th July, 1954.*
Birthplace; *South Shields, Tyne & Wear*
Height; *5ft 9in* **Weight;** *11st 0lbs*
Debut v. *Rochdale (a) 8th September, 1984*
Total Appearances & Goals; *5/1 apps 0 gls*
Career; *Aldershot Jul 1972 301/23apps 27gls; York City Nov 1981 99/4apps 4gls; WREXHAM 7th Sept-Oct 1984 (Loan);*
Honours; *England Youth International; Fourth Division Championship Winner 1984;*

The popular 'Geordie' began his Football League career far from home at Aldershot, having joined them as a groundstaff boy. Malcolm then graduated through the ranks before making his Football League debut as a substitute in a 4-2 defeat at Darlington in February 1972. At the end of that season he signed professional for the 'Shots', and in his first senior campaign Aldershot won promotion to the Third Division, although he made just one appearance. It was not until 1974/75 that he began to play regular first team football, going on to spend over ten years with the 'Hampshire Club', featuring mainly as an industrious midfield player, although he could also be depended upon to slot into any of the back four positions. In November 1981, he left the Recreation Ground to join York City, in an exchange deal with Ian McDonald moving in the opposite direction. Malcolm made his debut at Scunthorpe in a 3-0 win, and quickly settled into the side. The 1983/84 season saw him make 33 appearances, as York strolled to the Fourth Division championship, with an amazing 101 points. However, at the beginning of the following season he was allowed to join Wrexham on loan, making his debut in a 2-0 win at Rochdale. He was to play in the following five League games, although he missed out on the Club's two European Cup-Winners' Cup matches with F.C.Porto, as he hadn't signed in time to register. Despite this he did travel out to Portugal to give the team his support, as Wrexham triumphed against all the odds on the away goals rule. On completion of his loan spell, Crosby was allowed to return to York, where he was to end his playing career helping out with the coaching of the juniors at Bootham Crescent. It was said during his playing days at York that he was 'a big influence on the club during his stay.' He finally left the 'Minstermen' at the end of the 1985/86 season to take up a coaching appointment in Kuwait, where he remained until 1987 when rejoining his

former manager at York, Dennis Smith, who was in charge at Sunderland in Malcolm's native North-East. Crosby was appointed as youth team coach at Roker Park, later becoming assistant-manager to Smith, a position he held until Smith's dismissal in December 1991. Malcolm was then appointed caretaker manager at a difficult time, with the Club fighting against relegation to the Third Division. In addition to steering them to safety, Malcolm also led Sunderland to the 1992 F.A.Cup final, where they lost 2-0 to Liverpool. His permanent appointment as the Club's manager was confirmed just before the F.A.Cup final. However, less than a year later he was sacked by the North-East club, in February 1993. He later rejoined Dennis Smith at Oxford in September 1993, again as assistant-manager. Despite relegation to the Second Division in 1994, he helped Smith to lead 'The U's' to promotion back to the First Division two years later. Smith resigned in December 1997 to take up the manager's job at West Bromwich Albion and Malcolm was given the opportunity to become manager at the Manor Ground, although he was to spend just five games in charge before asking to step back down to coaching duties. Towards the end of February 1998 Malcolm left the Manor Ground, to rejoin his former boss at West Brom as first team coach. He then left the Hawthorns in June 1999 to join Derby County manager Jim Smith as first team coach.

Season	League		F.A.Cup		Welsh Cup		League Cup		E,C,W,C.		F.R.T.		Total	
	apps	gls	apps	gls	apps	gls	apps	gls	apps	gls	apps	gls	apps	gls
1984/85	5/1	0	-	-	-	-	-	-	-	-	-	-	5/1	0
	5/1	**0**	**-**	**-**	**-**	**-**	**-**	**-**	**-**	**-**	**-**	**-**	**5/1**	**0**

CROSS, Jonathan Neil

1991 - 1998

Position; *Forward*
D.O.B; *2nd March, 1975*
Birthplace; *Wallasey, Merseyside.*
Height; *5ft 10in* ***Weight;*** *11st 4lbs*
Debut v. *Crewe Alexandra (a) 9th November, 1991*
Total Appearances & Goals; *116/37 apps 17 gls*
Career; *WREXHAM July 1991, 15th Nov 1992 (Pro); Cliftonville (Loan) 27th Feb 1996; Hereford United (Loan) 2nd Dec 1996 to Jan 1997 5apps 1gls; Tranmere Rovers 26th Mar 1998 (Loan) 0apps; Connah's Quay Nomads Jul 1998; Chester City Aug 1998 33/2apps 1gls;*
Honours; *Third Division runner-up 1993; Northern Ireland Coca Cola Cup Winner 1996;*

Jonathan Cross was once tipped to become Wrexham's first ever £1 million player, following a sensational start to his career as a winger in Wrexham's promotion season of 1992/93. However, he couldn't maintain his swift rise to stardom; loss of form cost him a regular first team place, which he later tried win back by switching positions to play at both centre-forward and left-back. Jonathan was a tall youngster, and this led him to playing initially as a centre-half while at Plessington High School in Bebington. He was later converted to a winger because of his speed, in which position he appeared for both Wirral and Merseyside under-14s. In 1990, he played for the Merseyside under 16s Schoolboys team that captured the English Schools Trophy, beating Essex Schools 3-2 at Anfield Road. Jon was signed by Wrexham as a 14 year-old, which did not restrict him from being chosen for the Great Britain Schools Catholic team, playing in a tournament in Holland along with 15 other countries. The British side reached the final, but lost to France. Upon leaving school in the summer of 1991, Jon agreed to sign YTS terms for Wrexham, and within months he was making his first team debut in a 2-1 defeat at Crewe Alexandra at the age of 16 years 8 months and seven days. He went on to clock up seven more first team appearances that season before making a name for himself in that promotion season of 1992/93. He began the season playing on the right wing, but then had to play at left-back as emergency cover for the injured Phil Hardy. With Hardy fully fit Jon was reinstated on the wing, and he obliged with some exciting wing play that certainly whetted the appetite of the Racecourse regulars. Manager Brian Flynn soon noted his potential, and quickly signed him on a four year professional contract in December 1992. At around the same time, he was nominated by Welsh team manager Terry Yorath as the 'Barclays Young Eagle of the Month'. Despite this early promise, which resulted in him being linked with a number of big money transfers, his form was to take a dip over the next three seasons as he struggled to hold down a regular first team spot, and he was not helped by a series of niggling injuries and illness. In February 1996 Jon took up an offer of a loan spell with Northern Irish League side, Cliftonville, where he was to gain considerable success by scoring the winning goal in the Coca Cola Cup Final. He spent a month in Ireland before returning to Wrexham, where he again found it difficult to establish himself in the first team. In December 1996 he joined Hereford United for another loan spell, where he got off to a great start by scoring on his debut in a 1-1 draw at Exeter City. However, he was allowed to return to Wrexham after five League games, where he again found first team football opportunities limited, although he was called up into the side for the last five games of the season to cover at left-back, a position that he was to later regard as his best. He found a first team place even harder to secure the following season, and by March he was informed by manager Brian Flynn that he would be released in the summer. Jon then took up an offer of a trial period with Tranmere Rovers, with a view to earning a permanent contract with the Prenton Park club, but again he failed to impress and was released without making a first team appearance. He then appeared in a pre-season friendly for League of Wales side Connah's Quay Nomads, against Chester City, and following the game he was invited to join Chester for a trial period. He successfully completed that trial by signing a twelve months' contract with the Deva Stadium club in time for the beginning of the 1998/99 campaign, when he made his debut for Chester at left-back in their opening game, a 2-0 home defeat by Leyton Orient.

Season	League		F.A.Cup		Welsh Cup		League Cup		Auto Tro		E.C.W.C.		Total	
	apps	gls	apps	gls	apps	gls	apps	gls	apps	gls	apps	gls	apps	gls
1991/92	3/3	0	-	-	1	0	-	-	0/1	0	-	-	4/4	0
1992/93	35/3	7	-	-	3	2	1/1	0	3	0	-	-	42/4	9
1993/94	20/5	2	1	0	1/1	0	2	0	1	1	-	-	25/6	3
1994/95	18/6	1	3/1	1	1/1	0	1/1	1	2/2	0	-	-	25/11	3
1995/96	4/3	0	-	-	-	-	-	-	1/1	0	1	0	6/4	0
1996/97	11/7	2	-	-	-	-	0/1	0	-	-	-	-	11/8	2
1997/98	2	0	-	-	-	-	-	-	-	-	-	-	3*	0*
	93/27	**12**	**4/1**	**1**	**6/2**	**2**	**4/3**	**1**	**7/4**	**1**	**1**	**0**	**116/37**	**17**

* = Includes 1app 0gls in Welsh Invitation Cup.

CUNNINGTON, Shaun Gary

1984 - 1988

Position; *Midfield*
D.O.B; *4th January, 1966*
Birthplace; *Bourne, Lincolnshire*
Height; *5ft 9in* ***Weight;*** *11st 0lbs*
Debut v. *Bristol Rovers (a) 18th December, 1982*
Total Appearances & Goals; *267/2 apps 16 gls*
Career; *Bourne Town; WREXHAM 11th Jan 1984; Grimsby Town 19th Feb 1988 £55,000 182apps 13gls; Sunderland 17th Jul 1992 £650,000 52/6apps 8gls; West Bromwich Albion 11th Aug 1995 £220,000 8/5apps 0gls; Notts County 14th Mar 1997 £25,000 9/8apps 0gls; Kidderminster Harriers 1st Aug 1998 24/3apps 2gls;*
Honours; *Welsh Cup Winner 1986; Welsh Cup runner-up 1984;*

Brought up in the town of Bourne in Lincolnshire Shaun Cunnington played for his school team in the local Lincolnshire Leagues. At the age of 15 he was playing for Bourne Town's reserve XI when Terry Bates, who had been Youth Development Officer at Wrexham, recommended him to Wrexham manager Arfon Griffiths. He signed apprentice forms for Wrexham after leaving school in 1982, quickly progressing to be given his Football League debut by manager Bobby Roberts at Bristol Rovers in December 1982. He had been called up to replace the injured Phil Bater at left-back, whilst still only 16! He made two more appearances that season as a substitute. 1983/84 was to see the major breakthrough in Shaun's career, as he became the Racecourse club's regular left-back,

signing professional in January 1984. Wrexham qualified for Europe at the end of that season, despite losing to Shrewsbury Town in the Welsh Cup final, and the following campaign saw Shaun feature in the memorable away goals win over FC Porto, before going out to the Italian giants, AS Roma. 1985/86 saw him win a Welsh Cup winners' medal with Wrexham, and taste European action again in the 1986/87 season against FC Zurrieq of Malta and Real Zaragoza of Spain, who put Wrexham out of the competition on the away goals rule. Shaun left the Racecourse in February 1988, joining Grimsby Town for £55,000 -money that was desperately needed by Wrexham at that time. He had been a regular in the side throughout his time at the Racecourse, playing wherever he was asked; left-back; the centre of defence; or in midfield. He was still only 22 when he joined Third Division, Grimsby Town, yet he had made over 250 appearances in a Wrexham shirt. Shaun made his debut for the 'Mariners' in a scoreless home draw with Doncaster Rovers, but he was unable to help them to avoid relegation. Two seasons later he played in Grimsby's promotion winning side as they finished runners-up to Exeter City, and he followed that by helping the 'Mariners' to promotion for a second consecutive season. His contribution to the Blundell Park clubs success did not go unnoticed, and he was transferred to Sunderland for a Grimsby club record fee of £650,000 in the summer of 1992. Shaun made his debut for the 'Rokerites' at Swindon in a 1-0 defeat, and he went on to become a regular in the until injury was to disrupt his playing career over the next two seasons. He made the odd appearance as he battled to overcome his problems, but was unable to regain a regular place in the senior side. Shaun's former manager at Grimsby, Alan Buckley, then gave him a chance at West Bromwich Albion. After a trial in the friendly match against Real Oviedo at the Hawthorns in the close season of 1995 Cunnington proved his fitness, and a few days later he signed permanently. However, injuries continued to trouble him and he made just nine League appearances in 1995/96. He was restricted to just four more League appearances throughout the following season, before being allowed to join Second Division Notts County in March 1997. He was said to have had a nightmare debut at Rotherham, in a side that was already destined to relegation, but he was to overcome his early problems with some solid performances that saw him impress as a leader and ball winner in the middle of the park. The following season saw Notts County storm to the Third Division title in record time, although Shaun was to struggle with injuries yet again, making just nine League appearances all season. In the summer of 1998 he dropped into non-league football, signing for Conference League side Kidderminster Harriers.

Season	League		F.A.Cup		Welsh Cup		League Cup		F.R.T.		E.C.W.C.		Total	
	apps	gls	apps	gls	apps	gls	apps	gls	apps	gls	apps	gls	apps	gls
1982/83	1/2	0	-	-	1	0	-	-	-	-	-	-	1/2	0
1983/84	42	0	1	0	9	0	1	0	3	0	-	-	56	0
1984/85	41	6	1	0	3	1	2	0	2	0	4	0	53	7
1985/86	42	2	3	1	7	1	4	0	2	0	-	-	58	4
1986/87	46	1	3	0	5	0	4	0	5	0	4	0	67	1
1987/88	24	3	1	0	2	0	2	0	2	1	-	-	31	4
	196/2	**12**	**9**	**1**	**27**	**2**	**13**	**0**	**14**	**1**	**80**	**-**	**267/2**	**16**

D

Gareth Davies

DALLAS, William Robert Dempster 1957 - 1958

Position; *Centre-Half*
D.O.B; *6th March, 1931*
Birthplace; *Glasgow, Strathclyde*
Height; *ft in* **Weight;** *1st lbs*
Debut v. *Darlington (a) 24th August, 1957*
Total Appearances & Goals; *8 apps 0 gls*
Career; *Luton Town Dec 1952 0apps; St.Mirren; WREXHAM 24th Jul 1957 £2,000; Nuneaton Borough 19th Jul 1958;*

Willie Dallas was one of the many Scots who signed for Wrexham during the 1950s. He had been on the books of Luton Town, though never involved with their first team, returning to Scotland to join St.Mirren. It was when playing for the Paisley club that he was spotted by Wrexham's Scottish scout, Jimmy McGowan -Racecourse favourite Aly McGowan's brother. Willie had made 30 appearances in the Scottish First Division for the Love Street club. He signed for Wrexham in July 1957, along with another St.Mirren player, John McTurk, for a £2,000 fee. Willie was plunged straight into the first team for the initial game of the new season, at Darlington, which ended in a 2-1 defeat. He also featured in the next two matches before regular centre-half Alan Fox returned to the side. Dallas had made a further five League appearances by the end of the season, deputising for Fox, before he was transfer-listed at his own request at the end of the campaign. In July 1958 he joined non-league side Nuneaton Borough but, because of their non-league status, Wrexham never received back any of the £2,000 that they had forked out for him.

Season	League		F.A.Cup		Welsh Cup		Total	
	apps	gls	apps	gls	apps	gls	apps	gls
1957/58	8	0	-	-	-	-	8	0
	8	**0**	-	-	-	-	**8**	**0**

DARRACOTT, Terence Michael 1979 - 1980

Position; *Right-Back*
D.O.B; *6th December, 1950*
Birthplace; *Liverpool, Merseyside*
Height; *5ft 9in* **Weight;** *11st 6lbs*
Debut v. *Orient (h) 15th September, 1979*
Total Appearances & Goals; *27 apps 0 gls*
Career; *Everton (Am) cs1966, (Pro) Jul 1968 138/10apps 0gls; Tulsa Roughnecks cs1979; WREXHAM 11th Sept 1979 £25,000;*
Honours; *League Cup runner-up 1977; Central League Championship Winner 1968;*

'One of the most genuine and well loved characters Merseyside has ever produced', these words from the book, 'Everton - A Complete Record' by Gordon Smailes and Ian Ross, illustrate the high esteem in which this popular full-back was held by the Goodison faithful during his time with Everton. Terry had begun playing football at St.Anne's Roman Catholic school in the Edge Hill district of his native Liverpool, where he went on to represent Liverpool and District Schoolboys. It was not long before he was invited along for trials with Everton, and he signed amateur forms for the 'Toffeemen' in the summer of 1966. Terry gradually worked his way through the youth and reserve teams before he earned an unexpected first team call-up at the age of 18 in April 1968. He had been asked to deputise for the injured World Cup hero Ray Wilson against Arsenal at Goodison Park in front of a crowd of 40,000. Everton won 2-0, and went on to spend a total of thirteen years with the club, making 148 League appearances. His greatest memory was playing at Wembley in the 1977 League Cup Final against Aston Villa, to whom they eventually lost after a second replay. Terry left Everton at the end of the 1978/79 season, despite being offered a coaching post. He went to America to play for Tulsa Roughnecks in the North American Soccer League (NASL), during the summer of 1979, where he came up against the likes of Franz Beckenbaur, Johan Cruyff, Carlos Alberto, Johnny Neeskens, Gerd Muller, George Best and Teofilo Cubbilas. Terry returned home after their season had ended, and within a few days had received a call from the Wrexham manager Arfon Griffiths. He joined Second Division Wrexham in September 1979, and made his debut in a 2-1 home win over Leyton Orient, providing the cross that led to Wrexham's first goal scored by Alan Hill. Darracott held the right-back position for most of that season until he sustained a knee injury against Birmingham City, which eventually led to him having to hang up his boots. His biggest match for Wrexham was against Everton in a F.A.Cup fifth round match at Goodison Park, when he was made captain for the day. However, it was hardly a day he would want to remember as Wrexham lost 5-2! After retiring from the game he took up employment as Landlord of the Royal Oak Public House in Flint, keeping in touch with football by running his pub's team, and followed this by coaching Prescot. It wasn't long before he was to return to professional football as reserve team coach at Everton in 1984. Terry's close friendship with Mike Lyons, who was the opposing captain on the day Wrexham played at Everton, saw them join forces at Grimsby Town in October 1985, with Darracott installed as Lyons' assistant manager. Life at Blundell Park proved to be a struggle, and in 1987 he returned to Goodison Park as first team coach to Colin Harvey. He remained with Everton until Howard Kendall returned from Athletico Bilbao in Spain, to take over at Manchester City, and invited Terry to become his assistant manager in November 1989. Kendall's stay was short-lived, but Darracott remained at Maine Road and became the club's youth team coach until 1993, when he accepted a similar post at Blackburn Rovers.

Season	League		F.A.Cup		Welsh Cup		League Cup		Total	
	apps	gls	apps	gls	apps	gls	apps	gls	apps	gls
1979/80	22	0	4	0	1	0	-	-	27	0
	22	**0**	**4**	**0**	**1**	**0**	-	-	**27**	**0**

DAVIES, Gareth 1968 - 1982

Position; *Central-Defender*
D.O.B; *11th July, 1949*
Birthplace; *Bangor, Gwynedd*
Height; *5ft 10 1/2in* **Weight;** *11st 7lbs*
Debut v. *Bradford City (h) 24th February, 1968*
Total Appearances & Goals; *482/7 apps 9 gls*
Career; *Llandudno Town; Colwyn Bay 1966; WREXHAM 11th Apr 1967; Lex XI;*
Honours; *Three Full Welsh International caps; Four Welsh Under-23 International caps; Third Division Championship Winner 1978; Welsh Cup Winner 1972, 1975 & 1978; Division Four runner-up 1970;*

One of the most respected players ever to have represented Wrexham Football Club, Gareth Davies, first made a name for himself as an inside-forward for Craig-Y-Don Primary school in Llandudno. Later, when attending John Bright Grammar School, he found himself gaining honours with Caernarvonshire schoolboys. Gareth was also chosen as a substitute for the Welsh Grammar Schools under-18 side against England; at that time he was playing for his school in the mornings, and for Llandudno in the Welsh League North in the afternoon! He later joined Colwyn Bay of the same League at 17, from where he was invited for trials with Liverpool before Wrexham manager Alvan Williams stepped in to sign the promising youngster, having seen him playing in trials for the Welsh Youth team. It could so easily have been a different career for Gareth, as he attended an interview at Bangor Normal College to train to become a teacher, but the lure of professional football was too great, and he left his full-time studies to take up an apprenticeship at the Racecourse. It was a decision that he wouldn't regret. Gareth was playing initially as a centre-forward at Wrexham, but following Alvan Williams departure, new manager John Neal switched him to play in the centre of defence. It was as a central defender that David went on to enjoy a successful and distinguished playing career, making his Football League debut in a 2-0 home defeat by Bradford City in February 1968. He made seven more League appearances that season, before establishing himself in the heart of the defence in 1968/69. Gareth went on to become a regular in the Wrexham side until 1983, when he retired due to injury. During those sixteen years at the Racecourse he helped the club to promotion from the old Fourth Division in 1970; captained the side to the Third Division

Championship in 1978; won three Welsh Cup finals in 1972, 1975 and 1978; played in four European campaigns; (he still holds the record, along with Mel Sutton, of appearing in the most European matches for Wrexham -14.) and assisted the 'Robins' to the quarter-finals of the F.A.Cup in both 1974 and 1978, as well as the last eight of the League Cup in 1978, completing many giant-killing feats along the way. Gareth also won three full Welsh international caps to add to the four Under-23 caps he had gained previously. He was selected for his senior international debut against Iran in Tehran in 1978, and made two further appearances the same year against England and Northern Ireland. In 1971, he was called up to a Welsh F.A.XI tour of the Far East and Australasia and, in a 1-0 victory against New Zealand, scored the games only goal. In November 1979 Gareth was awarded a testimonial match by Wrexham; Wolves provided the opposition, and George Best turned out in a Wrexham shirt in honour of Gareth's loyalty to the North Wales club. He remained with Wrexham following the clubs relegation to the Third Division in 1982, staying long enough to see the beginning of the desperate financial struggle, a legacy of their Second Division days, which at one point saw the team having to travel to a League match at Walsall in four cars! Not long after that Davies decided to hang up his boots. He then moved into Hotel management in the Wrexham area, running the Cross Foxes in the Town, and then the Holt Lodge, which was followed by owning his own premises, The Trefor Park Hotel in Wrexham, where he still resides. During his playing days Gareth was described as a 'controlled, unhurried type of player, who could always be relied upon to 'sweep up' at the back (his best position). He was good in the air and a fine reader of the game.'

Season	League		F.A.Cup		Welsh Cup		League Cup		E.C.W.C.		Total	
	apps	gls	apps	gls	apps	gls	apps	gls	apps	gls	apps	gls
1967/68	8	0	-	-	-	-	-	-	-	-	8	0
1968/69	30	1	2	0	4	1	-	-	-	-	36	2
1969/70	45	3	4	0	1	0	4	0	-	-	54	3
1970/71	44	0	1	0	2	0	2	0	-	-	49	0
1971/72	25	2	1	0	4	0	3	2	-	-	33	4
1972/73	43	1	3	0	1	0	2	0	4	0	53	1
1973/74	23/6	0	2	0	1/1	0	2	0	-	-	28/7	0
1974/75	22	0	-	-	2	1	-	-	-	-	24	1
1975/76	42	0	3	0	3	0	3	1	6	1	57	2
1976/77	46	0	6	0	4	0	5	1	-	-	61	1
1977/78	46	2	8	1	5	0	6	0	-	-	65	3
1978/79	22	0	3	1	1	0	3	1	2	0	31	2
1979/80	40	0	4	0	1	0	4	0	2	0	51	0
1980/81	28	0	3	1	3	1	1	0	-	-	35	2
1981/82	13/1	0	-	-	-	-	1	1	-	-	14/1	1
1982/83	5	0	-	-	-	-	-	-	-	-	5	0
	482/7	**9**	**40**	**3**	**32/1**	**3**	**36**	**6**	**14**	**1**	**604/8**	**22**

DAVIES, Geoffrey Peter

1973 - 1976

Position; *Centre-Forward*
D.O.B; *1st July, 1947.*
Birthplace; *Ellesmere Port, Cheshire*
Height; *5ft 11'1/2in* ***Weight;*** *12st 8lbs*
Debut v. *Halifax Town (a) 20th October, 1973*
Total Appearances & Goals; *64/3 apps 15 gls*
Career; *Ellesmere Port Town; Northwich Victoria 1968; Wigan Athletic Aug 1970 £800 76apps 52gls; Chester Aug 1972 £2,000 18/14apps 5gls; WREXHAM 18th Oct 1973 £4,000; Boston Minutemen May-Aug 1975 (Loan); Boston Minutemen April 1976; Chicago Sting Jul 1976; Port Vale Aug 1976 7apps 0gls; Hartlepool United 4th Nov 1976 5apps 1gls (Loan); San Jose Earthquakes Apr 1977; Wimbledon Aug 1977 23apps 1gls; Los Angeles Skyhawks Feb 1978; San Francisco Fog Nov 1980; Northwich Victoria Sept 1984; Caernarfon Town Oct 1985;*
Honours; *Welsh Cup Winner 1975; Northern Premier League Championship Winner 1971; Northern Premier League Cup Winner 1972;*

A relative late-comer to League football Geoff Davies first played football at St.John's R.C. School in Bebington from where he represented Wirral Schoolboys. After leaving school to become an apprentice Vehicle Fitter at Calor Gas in Stanlow, Ellesmere Port. He continued playing football under the ex-Everton player, Jimmy Harris, at Ellesmere Port Town in the Cheshire County League, where he was to score many goals. He joined Northwich Victoria in 1968, and spent almost two seasons with the Drill Field club before he was signed by Northern Premier League side, Wigan Athletic, for a small fee in the close season of 1970. He made a flying start, scoring five hat-tricks in his first three months, going on to help Wigan Athletic claim the Northern Premier League Championship in his first season at Springfield Park. This in addition to scoring the winning goal against Peterborough United in a F.A.Cup Second round match, which earned them a tie with Manchester City. The 1971/72 season saw Davies find the goals harder to come by, although he did score 22! It was during this period that he played against Wrexham for Wigan in the Second Round of the F.A.Cup, a game which Wrexham won 4-0. However, he did help Wigan capture the N.P.L.Cup, and by the end of the season was offered the chance to turn professional at the age of 24 by Ken Roberts, the manager of Fourth Division Chester. Geoff signed in August 1972, and made his Football League debut in a 3-2 defeat at Newport County in the second match of the season. He did not maintain his prolific form at Sealand Road, scoring just five goals in his first season, although he spent most of the time on the sub's bench. This did not deter Wrexham manager, John Neal, who paid out £4,000 to bring him to the Racecourse in October 1973. He made an impressive start for Wrexham on his debut at Halifax in a 2-1 win.

The will-to-win and a never-say-die attitude were notable features of Geoff's play, and he played a big part in Wrexham's F.A.Cup run of 1973/74, when the 'Robins' reached the quarter-finals of the F.A.Cup before losing to First Division Burnley by a solitary deflected goal. That season also saw Geoff become the first player to score on a Sunday for Wrexham, when he the only goal of the game in a 1-0 Welsh Cup win over his former club, Chester. The following term Davies helped Wrexham reach the Final of the Welsh Cup against Cardiff City, although he only managed a substitute's appearance in that game. The summer of 1975, Geoff travelled to America to play in the North America Soccer League (NASL) for Boston Minutemen, where he played alongside the great Eusebio. He returned in time for the new season, and played in the away leg of the European Cup-Winners' Cup match in Djurgardens, Sweden, but by this time he was struggling to command a regular first team place, and before the season had ended left the Racecourse for America. He rejoined the Boston Minutemen, before being transferred to Chicago Sting. Geoff returned to Britain at the start of the following campaign, signing for Third Division Port Vale in August 1976. He made seven League appearances for the Burslem club, without scoring, and was then confined to the reserves until joining Hartlepool United on loan in November 1976. He played in five League games, scoring one goal, before returning to Vale, where he remained in their reserve team until another stint in America with San Jose Earthquakes in the summer of 1977. Geoff returned to Britain in August, joining Football League newcomers Wimbledon, for whom he appeared in their first ever match in the Football League. Davies made 23 League appearances for the 'Dons', scoring just one goal, before making yet another trip to the States at the end of the season, playing for Los Angeles Skyhawks, with whom he later became Head Coach, which also saw him appear on National Television promoting the League, and making three adverts for Puma, Michelob Beer and Matel Electronic Soccer games. The N.A.S.L. collapsed in 1979 due to financial problems. The Major Indoor League was then introduced and Geoff played the six-a-side game for San Francisco Fog for a season, until they sold the franchise to Kansas City. It was around this time that he decided to become a hairdresser, and after qualifying he was invited to work at Vidal Sassoon's Beverly Hills Salon by the man himself. Geoff was employed there for two months before returning to soccer as a coach at summer camps etc; He returned home in the summer of 1984 and began training with Wrexham, appearing in a couple of reserve team matches, and was on the substitutes' bench for a first team friendly at Northwich Victoria. He later signed for the Drill Field outfit in September 1984, before going on to join Caernarfon Town in October 1985. Geoff returned to America in 1986 where he has since resided in San Francisco. He has expanded his coaching work to become a Youth Development Officer for the San Francisco All-Stars team, who are a team comprising of the best junior players in the state.

Season	League		F.A.Cup		Welsh Cup		League Cup		E.C.W.C.		Total	
	apps	gls	apps	gls	apps	gls	apps	gls	apps	gls	apps	gls
1973/74	24/1	4	7	3	3	2	-	-	-	-	34/1	9
1974/75	32/1	10	1	0	2/1	0	1	0	-	-	36/2	10
1975/76	8/1	1	0/1	0	0/1	0	1/1	0	1	0	10/4	1
	64/3	**15**	**8/1**	**3**	**5/2**	**2**	**2/1**	**0**	**1**	**0**	**80/7**	**20**

DAVIES, Gordon John 1991 - 1992

Position; *Forward*
D.O.B; *8th August, 1955*
Birthplace; *Merthyr Tydfil, Glamorgan*
Height; *5ft 7in* **Weight;** *10st 12lbs*
Debut v. *Hereford United (h) 17th August, 1991*
Total Appearances & Goals; *26/3 apps 5 gls*
Career; *Manchester City 1972 (apprentice) 0apps; Merthyr Tydfil; Fulham Mar 1978 £5,000 244/3apps 114gls; Chelsea 15th Nov 1984 £90,000 11/2apps 6gls; Manchester City 11th Oct 1985 £70,000 31apps 9gls; Fulham 30th Oct 1986 £50,000 120/27apps 45gls; WREXHAM Aug 1991; Tornado (Norway) player/ manager Feb 1992; Northwich Victoria 1992 35/1apps 12gls;*
Honours; *18 Welsh International caps; Welsh Schoolboy International;*

Gordon Davies left school in Merthyr to join Manchester City as an apprentice, but things never worked out for him at Maine Road and he was released. He then had to look for alternative work, and embarked upon a teacher training course in geography. Despite his setback with City Gordon continued to play football in the Southern League with Merthyr Tydfil, as well as working as a Physical Education teacher at a local school. His goalscoring exploits at Penydarren Park soon began attracting the attention of Football League clubs and, in March 1978, he left Merthyr and teaching to turn professional with Second Division Fulham for a £5,000 transfer fee, at the relatively late age of 22. With the Craven Cottage club Davies, who became affectionately nicknamed 'Ivor' by the Fulham fans, after Welsh TV character Ivor the Engine, continued his prolific goalscoring form, helping Fulham rise from the depths of Division Three to the brink of the top flight. He was rewarded with international recognition in 1980, making his Welsh debut against Turkey in a World Cup qualifying match, where he was pelted with rotten oranges after the game. 'Ivor' went on to gain a further seventeen caps for Wales. Although on the small side Gordon was a determined player who had a good eye for the half chance, and, in November 1984, he joined Chelsea for a £90,000 transfer fee, scoring on his debut in a 1-1 draw at Sheffield Wednesday. However, life was far from easy for him at Stamford Bridge, as the consistency of Kerry Dixon and David Speedie limited his chances. In October 1985 Gordon, now 30, rejoined Manchester City for a £70,000 fee, and he made his debut in a 1-0 defeat against Chelsea at Stamford Bridge. He was enjoying his spell at Maine Road, until manager Billy McNeil decided to leave for Aston Villa and Jimmy Frizzell took over. The new manager had other plans, and in October 1986 Gordon was allowed to return to Craven Cottage. Although he had lost some of his sharpness his gift for goalscoring remained and, in 1988, he overtook Johnny Haynes' club record of 157 League and Cup goals, followed in 1991 by breaking Bedford Jezzard's club record of 154 League goals, eventually reaching 159. 'Ivor' was very popular with Fulham's fans, who were very aggrieved when he was given a free transfer in May 1991. He was awarded a testimonial by Fulham, who played the full Welsh team, before accepting an invitation to train with Wrexham by his former Welsh team mate, Brian Flynn. He impressed in pre-season friendlies, and in August 1991, was given a twelve month contract. Although never really producing the goalscoring form he had shown with Fulham, he was a great help to the many youngsters in the side, including the likes of Lee Jones, Steve Watkin and Karl Connolly. Gordon played a key role in Wrexham's greatest ever F.A.Cup win, over League Champions Arsenal at the Racecourse in January 1992, but by this time he was looking for a post in management, which eventually materialised with Norwegian First Division club, Tornado. Gordon postponed taking up the post until Wrexham's F.A.Cup run was over, which freed him to play in the two epic Fourth Round matches with West Ham United. His final game for Wrexham was against the 'Hammers' on the Racecourse, when he was given a rousing ovation by the Wrexham supporters when substituted towards the end of the game. Gordon Davies' first spell in management with Tornado did not prove fruitful, and he returned home to play in the Conference League with Northwich Victoria during 1992/93. Gordon, who is a keen golfer and squash player, later returned to live in London, taking up employment with Rentokil in 1993, for whom he now works as sales manager. Proving he still has the instinct to kill off opponents!!

Season	League		F.A.Cup		Welsh Cup		League Cup		E.C.W.C.		Total	
	apps	gls	apps	gls	apps	gls	apps	gls	apps	gls	apps	gls
1991/92	21/1	4	3	0	0/1	1	2	0	0/1	0	26/3	5
	21/1	**4**	**3**	**0**	**0/1**	**1**	**2**	**0**	**0/1**	**0**	**26/3**	**5**

DAVIES, Hywel 1924 - 1931

Position; *Centre-forward/Outside left*
D.O.B; *20th November, 1902*
Birthplace; *Llanddulas, Flintshire*
Died; *Denbigh, 16th August, 1976*
Height; *5ft 9in* **Weight;** *11st 6lbs*
Debut v. *Barrow (a) 6th December, 1924*
Total Appearances & Goals; *16 apps 0 gls*
Career; *Abergele GS; Oxford University (also Abergele and Llanddulas); WREXHAM Dec 1924-1931; Brynffordd FC 1931;*
Honours; *One Welsh international cap; Five Welsh Amateur International caps; Two North Wales Coast FA XI representative appearances;*

The Reverend Hywel Davies played for Wrexham in the Football League whilst a member of the clergy! The son of a blacksmith, he was educated at St.David's College in Lampeter, where he was a brilliant scholar. Hywel later took a second degree in theology, at Jesus College, Oxford, where he became a football 'Blue' in 1924. That same year Hywel toured Canada and the United States, with the Corinthians football team. The Vancouver Sun described him as 'a youngster with great speed', and also commented 'Davies is a Welsh amateur international, youthful, tall, clean-cut like all his fellows and easy to look at'. Upon his return home, it wasn't long before he joined Wrexham as an amateur, making his Football League debut for the club in December 1924 at Barrow, as he replaced Archie Longmuir at outside-left, in a 2-2 draw. That was his only first team outing that season but, over the following three years Davies, made a total of fifteen appearances for Wrexham. In 1925 he was ordained, and went on to serve as a curate in Wrexham until 1934, which included a spell in charge of St.John's Church, Hightown. It was rumoured that a League scout once turned up at the Racecourse and, liking the look of Hywel, suggested a transfer fee to a Wrexham director. It was flatly refused, but the scout upped the figure. When a third, substantial, offer was also rejected, the scout enquired "Why ever not?" to which the director replied, "Because he's a ——— Parson, that's why! And he'll be working tomorrow". "Well, I'll be at the church", said the scout, and he was! It was in 1928 that he made his one and only full international appearance for Wales against Ireland in Belfast, a game which Wales won 2-1. Between 1928 and 1931 Hywel made further amateur appearances for Wales, and also toured Yugoslavia with the Corinthians. From 1929, his duties largely kept him away from football, though he continued to act as secretary to the Welsh Dragons, an amateur side modelled on the Corinthians. Hywel later played for Brynffordd, near Holywell, who competed in the Dyserth area League. He also held several posts in soccer, including President of the North Wales Coast F.A., for whom he had twice gained representative honours as a player against the Scottish Junior League. In January 1934 Davies became Rector of Brynffordd, where he was always keen to help out youngsters at Church kick-abouts and frequently took to the field in clerical garb to play, and coach. From 1947 to 1973, Hywel was the Rector of Denbigh. Sadly, he passed away three years later.

Season	League		F.A.Cup		Welsh Cup		Total	
	apps	gls	apps	gls	apps	gls	apps	gls
1924/25	1	0	-	-	-	-	1	0
1925/26	7	0	-	-	3	0	10	0
1926/27	3	0	-	-	-	-	3	0
1927/28	2	0	-	-	-	-	2	0
	13	**0**	**-**	**-**	**3**	**0**	**16**	**0**

DAVIES, John 1922 - 1923

Position; *Centre-Half*
D.O.B;
Birthplace; *Rhosllanerchrugog, Denbighshire*
Height; *ft in* ***Weight;*** *st lbs*
Debut v. *Walsall (a) 10th February, 1923*
Total Appearances & Goals; *1 app 0 gls*
Career; *Rhos FC; WREXHAM Feb 1923;*

John was signed from local side Rhos FC as an amateur. He was brought in as emergency cover for the injured George Savage in a Football League match at Walsall in February 1923. Davies played the game at centre-half and, despite the 1-0 defeat, was described as having 'made a praiseworthy attempt to fulfil the heavy responsibility that rests upon the shoulders of a centre-half. He strove hard to fill the gap, being a tireless worker from start to finish, and he had one of the best scoring efforts, which came from his foot.' John remained with Wrexham as an amateur until the end of the season, when he returned to Rhos who were a successful side in the Welsh National League.

Season	League		F.A.Cup		Welsh Cup		Total	
	apps	gls	apps	gls	apps	gls	apps	gls
1922/23	1	0	-	-	-	-	1	0
	1	**0**	**-**	**-**	**-**	**-**	**1**	**0**

DAVIES, Jonathan 1924 - 1925

Position; *Outside-Left*
D.O.B; *21st September, 1904*
Birthplace; *Rhosllanerchrugog, Denbighshire*
Died; *Wrexham, 6th August 1978*
Height; *ft in* ***Weight;*** *st lbs*
Debut v. *Tranmere Rovers (h) 28th March, 1925*
Total Appearances & Goals; *1 apps 0 gls*
Career; *Rhos; WREXHAM Mar 1925; Rhos; Denbigh United cs1926; Bangor City cs1927; Blaenau Ffestiniog 1929; Llanerch Celts; Oswestry Town Oct 1930; Colwyn Bay United; Wellington Town May 1931; Macclesfield Town; Bangor City cs1932; Runcorn; Whitchurch;*
Honours; *Three Welsh Amateur International caps;*

Jonathan Davies attended Ruabon Grammar School from where he played for his local Welsh National League side, Rhosllanerchrugog. It was with Rhos Athletic that he joined Wrexham as an amateur during the 1924/25 season. He made just one first team appearance for Wrexham, in a Football League match on the Racecourse against Tranmere Rovers in March 1925, replacing Frank Jones at outside left in the 4-0 win. After returning to Rhos he went on to appear for Denbigh United, Blaenau Ffestiniog and Macclesfield Town. It was during this time that Jonathan won a Welsh Amateur international cap when he played against England at Aberystwyth towards the end of the 1929/30 season. He later made two more appearances, both against Scotland, on Partick Thistle's and Dundee's grounds. Davies remained as an amateur throughout his career, rejecting many offers to turn professional, preferring his chosen profession of schoolteacher at Rhos Junior school, where he stayed for a total of 44 years until his retirement in 1967. He later became a local councillor, as well as a member and secretary of the Rhos Male Voice Choir. He was also heavily involved with Urdd Gobaith Cymru (Welsh League of Youth), and attached to Rhos Aelwyd in their efforts in the Pontyfedwen Cup, the Urdd's football tournament, during the 1950s. His grandson, Mark Lewis Jones (Stage name) is a member of the 'Royal Shakespeare Company', and he has appeared in a number of Front Line film and T.V. productions, working alongside the likes of Sir Anthony Hopkins, Meryl Streep and Angela Lansbury etc. including more recently in I.T.V.'s The Knock. Jonathan Davies, passed away at Wrexham Maelor Hospital in August 1978. He was 73.

Season	League		F.A.Cup		Welsh Cup		Total	
	apps	gls	apps	gls	apps	gls	apps	gls
1924/25	1	0	-	-	-	-	1	0
	1	**0**	**-**	**-**	**-**	**-**	**1**	**0**

DAVIES, Ronald Wyn 1959 - 1962

Position; *Centre-Forward*
D.O.B; *20th March, 1942*
Birthplace; *Caernarfon, Gwynedd*
Height; *6ft 1in* ***Weight;*** *12st 5lbs*
Debut v. *Exeter City (h) 25th August, 1960*
Total Appearances & Goals; *67 apps 26 gls*
Career; *Deiniolen; Llanberis; Caernarvon Town 1959; WREXHAM (Am) 30th Dec 1959 £500, (Pro) 22nd Apr 1960; Bolton Wanderers 8th March 1962 £20,000 + Ernie Phythian 155apps 66gls; Newcastle United 28th Oct 1966 £80,000 181apps 40gls; Manchester City 3rd Aug 1971 £52,000 45apps 8gls; Manchester United 16th Sept 1972 £65,000 15/1apps 4gls; Blackpool 16th Jun 1973 34/2apps 5gls; Crystal Palace 19th Aug 1974 3apps 0gls (Loan); Stockport County Aug 1975 28/2apps 7gls; Arcadia Shepherds (South Africa) May 1976; Crewe Alexandra Aug 1976 50/5apps 13gls; Bangor City 1978;*
Honours; *34 Welsh Full International caps; Four Welsh Under-23 International caps; Two Welsh Youth International caps; Inter-Cities Fairs Cup Winner 1969; Welsh Youth Cup Winner 1960;*

Welsh speaking Wyn Davies began playing football at school in his native Caernarvon, where he also represented Caernarfon Boys' Club. He took up work at a quarry in Llanberis upon leaving school, and joined local village side, Deiniolen. He later signed for Llanberis in the local Caernarvon and District League, and it was whilst he was with them that Wyn was spotted by Arthur Lunn, the manager of Welsh League (North) side Caernarvon Town, who signed Davies as a left-half. It wasn't long before Wyn was switched to play in a forward position, and he responded by scoring eight goals in nineteen games for the 'Canaries'. His form soon attracted the likes of Aston Villa and Manchester United, who both invited him for trials. However, it was Wrexham who eventually secured his services in December 1959, for a £500 fee. Wyn found it difficult to settle at first, as he was unable to speak much English, due to having been brought up in a Welsh-speaking community. His football skills did the talking for him, however, and he was soon capped by Wales at Youth level, and gained a Welsh Youth Cup winners' medal in April 1960 following Wrexham's win over Newtown. At the beginning of 1960/61 he made a successful Football League debut for Wrexham at centre-forward, scoring one of the goals in a 3-1 home win over Exeter City. Despite that early success Wyn notched just eight goals in 26 League games that season, but it was his ability to win the ball in the air and to make chances for others that marked him out as a player with a great future. He continued to make rapid progress, and it was not long before the bigger clubs began to take notice. As 'The Robins' marched on to promotion Wyn was to miss the end of season celebrations, joining Bolton Wanderers for £20,000, plus Ernie Phythian, who was valued at £10,000. His last League game for the Racecourse club turned out to be the club's record 10-1 Football League win over Hartlepool United, in which he was one of three players to score a hat-trick. Wyn's debut for Bolton ended in disaster, as they lost 6-1 to Wolves! However, he went on to win the first of 34 full Welsh caps when playing against England at Wembley. He amassed 66 goals in 155 League games for Bolton, benefitting greatly from the coaching advice of Nat Lofthouse, before being transferred to Newcastle United in October 1966 for £80,000. The move proved to be a success, as the Geordie fans affectionately nicknamed him the 'Mighty Wyn' and 'Wyn the Leap' because of his ball-winning skills in the air. Although not a prolific goalscorer at Newcastle he was certainly an effective target man who created chances for others, and played a major part in helping Newcastle to win the Fairs Cup in 1969, beating the Hungarian side Ujpesti Dozsa. He scored 40 goals in 180 League games at St.James' Park before handing over the number nine shirt to Malcolm MacDonald, following his decision to join Manchester City in August 1971 in a £52,000 deal. In his first season at Maine Road Wyn came close to winning a League Championship medal, when City missed out by just one point. Having been replaced by Rodney Marsh he moved across the City to join United in September 1972, but his stay at Old Trafford was short and he joined Blackpool in the close season of 1973. Wyn spent two injury plagued years at Bloomfield Road, and had a loan spell with Crystal Palace, where he was again troubled with injuries. In August 1975 he joined Stockport County, completing a year before going to South Africa to play for Arcadia Shepherds in the summer. However, he was to return home early in August 1976 and join Crewe Alexandra, where he spent almost two seasons finally having to retire from professional football due to a knee injury received in a match against Torquay United. He did manage to fit in a few games for Bangor City before hanging up his boots. He then returned to settle in Bolton, taking up work as a Baker. A lover of the Welsh countryside, he now likes nothing better than taking his dogs for a walk.

Season	League		F.A.Cup		Welsh Cup		League Cup		Total	
	apps	gls	apps	gls	apps	gls	apps	gls	apps	gls
1960/61	26	8	-	-	2	0	4	1	32	9
1961/62	29	13	3	2	2	2	1	0	35	17
	55	**21**	**3**	**2**	**4**	**2**	**5**	**1**	**67**	**26**

DAVIES, Thomas S. 1938 - 1939

Position; *Outside-Left*
D.O.B;
Birthplace;
Height; *ft in* ***Weight;*** *st lbs*
Debut v. *Oldham Athletic (a) 10th December 1938*
Total Appearances & Goals; *1 app 0 gls*
Career; *Cross Street FC; WREXHAM May 1938; Shotton Athletic cs1939;*

Thomas Davies was serving in the Royal Air Force at Market Drayton in Shropshire when he was signed by Wrexham on amateur forms in the close season of 1938. However, he began the following season playing for Cross Street FC in the local Wrexham area 'Chums League', and he hadn`t even made a reserve team appearance for the Racecourse club when he was called upon at the last moment to make his Football League debut in December 1938 at Oldham. Davies had been summoned to replace injured regular outside-left Archie Burgon, who was said to have pulled a leg muscle. Wrexham lost the match 4-2, and it proved to be Tom's one and only first team outing for the club. He was later known to have signed for Shotton Athletic in the summer of 1939.

Season	League		F.A.Cup		Welsh Cup		Total	
	apps	gls	apps	gls	apps	gls	apps	gls
1938/39	1	0	-	-	-	-	1	0
	1	**0**	**-**	**-**	**-**	**-**	**1**	**0**

DAVIES, William David 1977 - 1981

Position; *Goalkeeper*
D.O.B; *1st April, 1948*
Birthplace; *Ammanford, Dyfed*
Height; *6ft 1in* ***Weight;*** *13st 4lbs*
Debut v. *Swindon Town (h) 24th September, 1977*
Total Appearances & Goals; *199 apps 0 gls*
Career; *Ammanford Town; Swansea Town Jul 1969 9apps 0gls; Everton 17th Dec 1970 £25,000 82apps 0gls; WREXHAM 22nd Sept 1977 £8,000; Swansea City Jul 1981 £45,000 71apps 0gls; Tranmere Rovers Jun 1983 42apps 0gls; Bangor City Aug 1985; WREXHAM Nov 1985;*
Honours; *52 Full Welsh International caps; 4 Welsh Under-23 International caps; Welsh Schoolboy International; Third Division Championship Winner 1978; Welsh Cup Winner 1978; Welsh Amateur Cup Winner 1969; P.F.A.Third Division XI 1978;*

Dai Davies was a late convert to football as he attended a rugby only school, Amman Valley Grammar, in his native South Wales. However, he did play in goal during his schooldays for his local side, Ammanford Town, who were managed at the time by Dean Saunders' father, Roy. It was Roy Saunders who recommended Dai to Swansea Town, and he played his part in taking the club to the quarter-finals of the English F.A. Youth Cup in 1964. Still on Swansea's books, Dai left school and went to Cardiff College of Education to qualify as a P.E.teacher, during which time he picked up a Welsh Amateur Cup winners' medal in 1969 with the college team. He returned to Swansea in July 1969, and signed professional forms, before going on to make his Football League debut in a scoreless draw at Chesterfield in the last game of 1969/70 after Swansea had won promotion. He made eight more League appearances with the 'Swans', and was selected for the Welsh under-23 side against England at Wrexham. It was enough to alert Everton to his potential and they signed him in December 1970 for £25,000, plus another £15,000 after thirty games. Dai found himself understudy to both Gordon West and Andy Rankin at Goodison Park, but made his Everton debut in March 1971 in a 2-1 defeat at Newcastle. He played in the following match at Nottingham Forest -another defeat 3-2- before spending three years in the reserves, during which time he did have a loan spell back at Swansea.

The 1974/75 season finally saw Dai established in the Everton first team, and regular first team football also brought international honours. He took over the Welsh keeper's jersey for his international debut in Hungary, the first of his 52 Welsh caps. However, Everton signed George Wood from Blackpool in August 1977, and they allowed Davies to leave Goodison having made 82 League appearances. Following offers to join Chester and Blackpool Dai's former international team mate, Arfon Griffiths, who was manager at Wrexham, stepped in to sign him in September 1977 for £8,000. Dai was one of three inspirational signings by Griffiths, the other two being Les Cartwright and Dixie McNeil, and they helped Wrexham to storm to the Third Division championship; win the Welsh Cup; and reach the quarter-finals of both the League Cup and F.A.Cup. During his time with the 'Robins' Dai was a very commanding figure, becoming the so called 'extra defender' with superb organisational skills and control of his area, proving there is more to life as a goalkeeper than just shot-stopping. He remained at the Racecourse until July 1981, playing in 144 League games, before rejoining Swansea City, who had by that time reached the First Division. Dai spent two seasons at the Vetch Field, finishing 6th in their initial season in the top flight, though they followed that by relegation at the end of 1982/83. It was then that he left the 'Swans', to join Tranmere Rovers in August 1983. He spent one season at Prenton Park before retiring from professional football to move into business with his Welsh shop he had already opened in Mold. However, in 1985 Dai answered an S.O.S. from Bangor City manager John Mahoney, to assist in his clubs European Cup-Winners' Cup matches against Athletico Madrid. Not long after that, Wrexham manager, and former team mate Dixie McNeil, asked him to appear in Wrexham's Welsh Cup matches as the 'Robins' regular 'keeper was cup-tied for the competition. Dai went on to help Wrexham to win the Welsh Cup, beating Kidderminster Harriers in the final. The following term he was named as Wrexham's substitute 'keeper for their European matches, as well as playing one more game in the Welsh Cup. Since retiring from the game Dai has always followed Wrexham's progress, and is often seen on match days at the Racecourse standing on the 'Kop'. Dai, a proud Welsh-speaking Welshman, was recipient of a rare Welsh honour in August 1978, when he became the first Welsh footballer to be admitted to the Gorsedd Circle of Bards at the National Eisteddfod in Cardiff. He chose the name 'Dai o'r Cwm' (Dai of the Valleys) after his native Amman Valley. He now works frequently for BBC Radio Wales and Radio Cymru, and appears regularly on 'Gol', a Welsh language football programme, as well as employed as a supply teacher in local schools, and running a Natural Healing Centre in Llangollen. As a T.V. pundit Dai is always interesting, while not affraid to air his views on topics in football, and could never be accused of sitting on the fence!

Season	League		F.A.Cup		Welsh Cup		League Cup		E.C.W.C.		Total	
	apps	gls	apps	gls	apps	gls	apps	gls	apps	gls	apps	gls
1977/78	30	0	8	0	4	0	3	0	-	-	45	0
1978/79	36	0	3	0	3	0	3	0	2	0	47	0
1979/80	36	0	4	0	2	0	2	0	2	0	46	0
1980/81	42	0	5	0	4	0	2	0	-	-	53	0
1985/86	-	-	-	-	7	0	-	-	-	-	7	0
1986/87	-	-	-	-	1	0	-	-	-	-	1	0
	144	**0**	**20**	**0**	**21**	**0**	**10**	**0**	**4**	**0**	**199**	**0**

DAVIS, Frederick James 1955 - 1961

Position; *Wing-Half*
D.O.B; *23rd May, 1929.*
Birthplace; *Walsall, West Midlands*
Died; *Surrey, 10th September, 1996*
Height; *5ft 10in* ***Weight;*** *12st 0lbs*
Debut v. *York City (a) 20th August, 1955*
Total Appearances & Goals; *264 apps 14 gls*
Career; *Bloxwich Strollers; Reading Dec 1952 63apps 1gls; WREXHAM 13th Jul 1955; Rhyl 21st July 1961; Colwyn Bay 2nd Sept 1966;*
Honours; *Welsh Cup Winner 1957, 1958 & 1960;*

Fred Davis was playing non-league football for local side Bloxwich Strollers when spotted by Third Division South team, Reading. He signed for the 'Royals' in December 1952, and went on to make 63 League appearances in almost three years for the Elm Park club, scoring one goal. In July 1955 Fred was signed by Third Division North side, Wrexham, where he went on to enjoy a distinguished career as a regular in the half-back line throughout the six years that he spent with the North Wales club. He made his debut for Wrexham in the opening match of the 1955/56 season at York City, in a 3-1 win, and totted up over 260 League and Cup appearances. They included the famous F.A.Cup match against Manchester United's 'Busby Babes', who had knocked out his old club, Reading, in the previous round. Fred led Wrexham into the newly-organised Third Division in 1958, when the Third Division's North and South Leagues were amalgamated. He also collected three Welsh Cup winners' medals with Wrexham in 1957, 1958 and 1960. Fred was described as a 'most stylish wing-half', during his time with the 'Robins'. He eventually left the Racecourse at the end of the 1960/61 season, following the departure of Billy Morris and the appointment of Ken Barnes as the new manager. Davis then signed for Cheshire League side Rhyl in July 1961, going on to play for Colwyn Bay in the Welsh League (North), and later working for Granada TV in Manchester. He finally settled in the Reading area, where he passed away in September 1996, aged 67.

Season	League		F.A.Cup		Welsh Cup		League Cup		Total	
	apps	gls	apps	gls	apps	gls	apps	gls	apps	gls
1955/56	40	1	1	0	1	0	-	-	42	1
1956/57	39	1	6	0	5	0	-	-	50	1
1957/58	41	2	-	-	4	0	-	-	45	2
1958/59	40	1	1	0	2	0	-	-	43	1
1959/60	24	0	-	-	4	0	-	-	28	0
1960/61	46	7	1	0	3	2	6	0	56	9
	230	**12**	**9**	**0**	**19**	**2**	**6**	**0**	**264**	**1**

DIAMOND, Barry 1987

Position; *Midfield*
D.O.B; *20th February, 1960*
Birthplace; *Dumbarton, Strathclyde*
Height; *5ft 7in* ***Weight;*** *11st 5lbs*
Debut v. *Torquay United (h) 24th January, 1987*
Total Appearances & Goals; *4/2 apps 0 gls*
Career; *Dumbarton; Barrow; Workington cs1981; Barrow 1981; Oulun P.S. (Finland); Rochdale Jul 1984 £3,500 50/2apps 16gls; Stockport County 17th Dec 1985 6apps 0gls (Loan); Halifax Town Feb 1986 17/5apps 3gls; WREXHAM 22nd Jan 1987 (Loan); Gainsborough Trinity; Morecambe Jan 1988; Hyde United 1989; Chorley 1989/90; Mossley; Colne Dynamoes;*
Honours; *Northern Premier League Championship Winner 1984;*

Barry Diamond joined his home town club of Dumbarton soon after leaving school. Though unable to command a regular first team place at Boghead Park he attracted many scouts from south of the border from the non-league circuit. It was Barrow manager Vic Halom who first signed Barry, and he became an instant success, scoring goals on a regular basis for the Holker Street club. However, he left Barrow after an internal wrangle and joined another former Football League side, Workington, in the close season of 1981. His stay with the 'Reds' was short-lived as, having played in just a handful of games, he returned to Barrow. He later travelled to Finland, where he played for Oulun P.S. during the summer season, before returning home to take up an offer from his ex-Barrow manager, Vic Halom who was then the manager of Football League side, Rochdale. He signed for the Spotland club in July 1984, and made his Football League debut in a 1-0 home defeat by Hereford United on the opening game of the season. He went on to complete that season as Rochdale's top scorer with 15 goals in 43 League games. The start of the following term saw Barry full of optimism, but following just nine League appearances he was made the scapegoat for Rochdale's slump from top of that Division to mid-table. In December he was loaned out to Stockport County, making six League appearances without scoring, before Halifax Town stepped in to sign him in February 1986. Barry scored twice in his second appearance for the 'Shaymen', a 3-0 win at Tranmere, and two days later hit the target at Southend United to spark an impressive run of results that also included a 5-2 win over Wrexham! However, he then hit a barren spell, and failed to find the net for the rest of the season. The new campaign saw Barry playing more in midfield than as a front runner, as once again he lost his place in the side. In January 1987 he was given the opportunity to join Wrexham on loan, making his debut in a 2-1 home win over Torquay United, but never really impressed during his month's stay at the Racecourse, and at the end of the loan period he was allowed to return to the 'Shay'. At the end of the season Barry was released by Halifax, and he drifted back into non-league football with Gainsborough Trinity, followed by spells with Morecambe, Hyde United, Chorley, Mossley and Colne Dynamoes among other non-league outfits.

Season	League		F.A.Cup		Welsh Cup		League Cup		E.C.W.C		Total	
	apps	gls	apps	gls	apps	gls	apps	gls	apps	gls	apps	gls
1986/87	2/2	0	-	-	-	-	-	-	2	0	4/2	0
	2/2	**0**	**-**	**-**	**-**	**-**	**-**	**-**	**2**	**0**	**4/2**	**0**

DICKIE, William Campbell 1929 - 1930

Position; *Half-Back*
D.O.B; *22nd November, 1903*
Birthplace; *Maryhill, Strathclyde*
Died; *Islington, London, 10th Dec 1977*
Height; *5ft 9'1/2in* ***Weight;*** *11st 7lbs*
Debut v. *Doncaster Rovers (a) 16th November, 1929*
Total Appearances & Goals; *25 apps 0 gls*
Career; *Poole Town 1926; Everton 27th April 1927 0apps; Southport 12th May 1928 31apps 1gls; Connah's Quay & Shotton FC 5th Oct 1929; WREXHAM 13th Nov 1929; Connah's Quay & Shotton FC 23rd Jul 1930; Llanelli 24th Dec 1931; Connah's Quay & Shotton FC; Worgret Wanderers (Wareham) 18th Sept 1934 (permit player); Poole Municipal Sports 23rd Sept 1935;*

Bill Dickie was a real mystery man! He came from a well-to-do Ayrshire family, and first made his mark as a footballer with Poole Town, while serving with Lawrence of Arabia in the Tank Corps at Bovington Camp in Dorset. Bill married at 19, and produced a son and daughter, though the former died tragically young when he fell over a tenement balcony in Glasgow. On 8th January 1927 Bill impressed when playing for Poole

Town in a F.A.Cup 3rd round cup-tie at Goodison Park against Everton, and before the season was over, Everton had signed him. The 1927/28 season saw him make twenty consecutive appearances in Everton's Central League side before breaking his leg. Once recovered Bill was allowed to leave Goodison Park and join Third Division North side, Southport, in May 1928. It was with Southport that the Scotsman finally made his Football League debut, at right-half in the first match of the 1928/29 season, a 2-1 win over Ashington. Bill became a regular in the Southport team throughout that season, and was described as 'possessing wonderful ball control' and as being 'above Third Division standard'. However, he managed just one League appearance in 1929/30, and in October left to join Welsh League side Connah's Quay and Shotton. After one month Wrexham stepped in to sign him, and he made his debut for the 'Robins' at Doncaster in a 4-2 defeat. Bill went on to make nineteen consecutive appearances in the Wrexham first team, during which time he was described as 'a clever and effective right-half'. He was also a 'big favourite with the Racecourse followers'. Despite these tributes Bill was to leave the Racecourse at the end of the season. He returned to Connah's Quay & Shotton, eventually playing non-league football for a number of other clubs that included Llanelli, Connah's Quay & Shotton (again), Worgret Wanderers (Wareham), and Poole Municipal Sports. At Poole Bill had spells running a pub, as well as working as a chauffeur in Bournemouth, before his marriage broke up. He was later known to have been a Sergeant-Major in the Catering Corps during World War Two. He subsequently remarried and had a son, (who he later took to watch Arsenal), continuing to work in a number of jobs until his retirement in the mid-seventies. Three months after his son's wedding, Bill died at his home in Holloway. His son, totally unaware of his father's first family, never even knew that he could drive a car!

Season	League		F.A.Cup		Welsh Cup		Total	
	apps	gls	apps	gls	apps	gls	apps	gls
1929/30	19	0	5	0	1	0	25	0
	19	**0**	**5**	**0**	**1**	**0**	**25**	**0**

DIGNAM, Joseph Colquhoun 1957 - 1958

Position; *Inside-Forward*
D.O.B; *10th January, 1931*
Birthplace; *Glasgow, Strathclyde*
Height; *5ft 8in* ***Weight;*** *10st 7lbs*
Debut v. Chesterfield *(h) 28th August, 1957*
Total Appearances & Goals; *8 apps 0 gls*
Career; *Bathgate Thistle; Alloa Athletic Aug 1955; WREXHAM 25th Jul 1957; Stirling Albion 31st Jul 1958 £500 2apps 1gls; Hamilton Academicals Nov 1958 12apps 4gls;*

Joe Dignam was one of many Scotsmen who made the move down to North Wales in the 1950s. He had shown lots of promise whilst playing for Scottish Junior League side Bathgate Thistle, before signing for Scottish Second Division side Alloa Athletic in the close season of 1955. He enjoyed much success with Alloa, scoring fifty five goals in the two seasons spent in the Scottish League, before he was signed by Wrexham manager Cliff Lloyd during the close season of 1957. Joe, was another player to have been recommended to Wrexham by the club's Scottish scout, Jimmy McGowan -brother of Aly, Wrexham's full-back at that time. Joe made his Football League debut in the second match of the season, a 2-2 home draw with Chesterfield. By the end of October he had made a total of eight League appearances without scoring a goal; they proved to be his only first team outings for the club, and he was released at the end of the season. Joe then returned to Scotland, signing for Stirling Albion for a £500 transfer fee. He made just two Scottish League appearances for Stirling, scoring one goal, before joining Hamilton Academicals in November 1958. Joe went on to make twelve League appearances for the 'Accies', hitting the target four times, including one appearance in the Scottish Cup. He was given a free transfer by Hamilton at the end of the 1958/59 season.

Season	League		F.A.Cup		Welsh Cup		Total	
	apps	gls	apps	gls	apps	gls	apps	gls
1957/58	8	0	-	-	-	-	8	0
	8	**0**	-	-	-	-	**8**	**0**

DONALDSON, Leslie Darcy Robert 1950 - 1952

Position; *Inside-Forward*
D.O.B; *30th July, 1922*
Birthplace; *Glasgow, Strathclyde*
Died; *Rhyl, 8th January, 1995.*
Height; *5ft 9in* ***Weight;*** *10st 0lbs*
Debut v. *Mansfield Town (h) 19th August, 1950*
Total Appearances & Goals; *32 apps 6 gls*
Career; *Provanside Hibs; Glasgow Perthshire; Hearts 1944; Clyde 1946; Rhyl 28th Feb 1948; WREXHAM 2nd June 1950; Northwich Victoria 25th Sept 1951; Holyhead Town 22nd Aug 1952; Holywell 12th Nov 1954; Caernarfon Town Dec 1954; Rhyl 29th Aug 1955; Llandudno 16th Aug 1958; Dolgellau 20th Aug 1960;*
Honours; *Cheshire League Championship Winner 1948; Cheshire League Cup Winner 1949; N.W.C.F.A.Challenge Cup Winner 1950; Welsh League Cookson Cup Winner 1954;*

Glasgow born, Les Donaldson initially played football for both Wellfield Junior and Albert Higher Grade Schools in his native City. After leaving school he took up work as an apprentice Lathe Turner, while turning out for local team Provanside Hibs. He then joined Glasgow Perthshire, for whom he played in the Scottish Junior League Cup Final. During World War Two he spent almost two seasons assisting Hearts, before joining Clyde for their first Post War season in 1946/47. The following campaign Les continued with the 'Bully Wee' before deciding to take up an offer to move south of the border and join Cheshire County League side Rhyl, in February 1948. The move had been negotiated following the recommendation of a Rhyl scout in Glasgow! Les went on to help the 'Seasiders' clinch the Cheshire County League Championship in his first season at Belle Vue, while the following campaign the 'Lilywhites' finished runners-up in the League, but claimed the Cheshire County League Cup. The 1949/50 term saw Rhyl finish runners-up in the Cup, but win the North Wales Coast F.A.'s Challenge Cup. On the back of some impressive displays Donaldson was signed by Wrexham in June 1950. He made an excellent start, scoring on his Football League debut in a 2-2 home draw with Mansfield Town in the opening match of the 1950/51 season. Comfortable in either of the inside-forward positions Donaldson was a regular in the Wrexham side throughout that first season, although his second year proved to be frustrating as he enjoyed just one outing due to the form of Len Wootton and Ron Hewitt. Les joined Northwich Victoria in September 1951, where he spent the rest of the season before returning to North Wales to join Welsh League (North) side, Holyhead Town, in August 1952. Donaldson spent just over two seasons with the Ynys Mon 'Harbourmen', collecting a Cookson Cup winners' medal in 1954, before joining Holywell in December of the same year and assisting them to runners'-up spot in the same competition. In the summer of 1955, Les returned to Rhyl for three more seasons. He joined Welsh League side Llandudno in August 1958, where he picked up both League and Cookson Cup runners'-up medals. He spent another two seasons with Dolgellau, before ending his playing career at the conclusion of 1960/61. Following his retirement as a full-time professional, Les had returned to working as a lathe turner at John

Summers Steelworks in Shotton, where he was employed for around fifteen years. He later worked at Courtaulds until it closed down. Les, who settled in his adopted Rhyl, passed away in January 1995. He was 72.

Season	League		F.A.Cup		Welsh Cup		Total	
	apps	gls	apps	gls	apps	gls	apps	gls
1950/51	29	6	1	0	1	0	31	6
1951/52	1	0	-	-	-	-	1	0
	30	**6**	**1**	**0**	**1**	**0**	**32**	**6**

DONOGHUE, John 1930 - 1932

Position; *Left-Half*
D.O.B; *22nd January, 1903*
Birthplace; *New York, U.S.A.*
Height; *5ft 7in* ***Weight;*** *10st 10lbs*
Died; *Scotland, 11th July, 1971*
Debut v. *Southport (a) 30th August, 1930*
Total Appearances & Goals; *77 apps 2 gls*
Career; *St.Francis Juniors; Shawfield Juniors; Glasgow Celtic 11th Jun 1926 42apps 1gls; Third Lanark 1927 (loan); Cowdenbeath 21st Sept 1927 (loan); Belfast Celtic 11th Oct 1929 to 30th Apr 1930 (loan); WREXHAM 14th Jul 1930; Glasgow Celtic 12th Aug 1932; Excelsior de Roubaix (France) 29th Sept 1932 to Jun 1933;*
Honours; *Welsh Cup Winner 1931; Scottish Cup runner-up 1928;*

Born of Irish parents in New York John Donoghue, moved to Scotland as a young boy. He played football for his school team, St.Francis Juniors, followed by a spell with Shawfield Juniors, where he was spotted and signed by Glasgow Celtic in the close season of 1926. John made his Celtic debut at centre-half in a 3-2 defeat at Hibernian towards the end of September 1927. He later played in the 1928 Scottish Cup final, which Celtic lost to Rangers 4-0, and also appeared in their following season's semi-final defeat at the hands of Kilmarnock. Those two campaigns had seen Celtic finish runners-up in the Scottish League on both occasions. Donoghue enjoyed four seasons at Parkhead, making a total of 42 Scottish League appearances, during which he completed three loan spells: the first, at Third Lanark, came towards the end of 1926/27; The second was with Cowdenbeath in September of the following campaign; and John then spent a period in Ireland from October 1929 to April 1930 with the now defunct Belfast Celtic. He was finally allowed to leave Glasgow Celtic in the close season of 1930, moving down to North Wales to join Wrexham. He made his Football League debut for 'The Robins' in the opening match of the 1930/31 season at Southport in a 1-1 draw, playing in his usual left-half position. He was a regular throughout that season, helping the club to win the Welsh Cup by beating Shrewsbury Town 7-0 in the Final. The following term saw Donoghue again playing regularly in the heart of the defence, taking the Racecourse club to their second successive Welsh Cup Final. Disappointingly, he missed the Final, and Wrexham lost to Swansea Town. At the end of the season he was released by the North Wales Club and returned to Scotland, re-signing for Glasgow Celtic. However, after just one month he was allowed to leave without having made a first team appearance. John then went overseas to France, playing for Excelsior De Roubaix, with whom he remained until June 1933.

Season	League		F.A.Cup		Welsh Cup		Total	
	apps	gls	apps	gls	apps	gls	apps	gls
1930/31	31	1	3	0	3	0	37	1
1931/32	36	1	1	0	3	0	40	1
	67	**2**	**4**	**0**	**6**	**0**	**77**	**2**

DOWMAN, Stephen John 1980 - 1983

Position; *Centre-Half*
D.O.B; *15th April, 1958*
Birthplace; *Manor Park, London*
Height; *5ft 11in* ***Weight;*** *12st 4lbs*
Debut v. *Swansea City (a) 6th March, 1981*
Total Appearances & Goals; *109 apps 6 gls*
Career; *Colchester United Apr 1976 150/4apps 21gls; WREXHAM 14th Jul 1980 £75,000; Charlton Athletic 26th Aug 1983 (Loan), 30th Jan 1984 £15,000 60/1apps 5gls; Newport County Aug 1985 9apps 1gls; Cambridge United Oct 1985 45apps 3gls; Brightlingsea United 1987; Wivenhoe Town cs1991; Heybridge Swifts 1993; Braintree Town 1994; Heybridge Swifts Oct 1994;*
Honours; *Welsh Cup runner-up 1983; Essex Senior League Championship Winners 1988/89 & 1989/90;*

Steve Dowman played his early football for Manor Park School in East Ham, London, just five minutes away from Upton Park, where he also represented Essex schoolboys. Despite trials with West Ham United, Chelsea, and Fulham no League club's offered him an apprenticeship, and he began working in a Bank upon leaving school. He continued to play local football, and eventually left his job in Banking to sign apprentice forms for Colchester United. Steve progressed through the clubs youth and reserve teams, until manager Bobby Roberts offered him professional terms in April 1976. He spent a further season in the reserves before making his Football League debut as a substitute in the second match of 1976/77, a 3-0 home win over Halifax Town. It was a season that saw the Layer Road Club win promotion to the Third Division, behind Cambridge United and Exeter City, and Steve crowned it by being voted the 'U's' Player of the Year. He went on to make 154 League appearances for the Essex side, before signing for Second Division Wrexham in July 1980 for a £75,000 fee. Steve was to endure a disastrous start to his career at the Racecourse, picking up a serious a knee injury during a pre-season friendly at Oxford United before the 1980/81 campaign had even begun. He had to undergo a cartilage operation, following which he suffered with a blood disorder, and these problems meant that he had to wait until March 1981 before making his League debut for Wrexham. Once fit Steve proved to be a strong central defender, becoming very popular with the Racecourse faithful. He played in Wrexham's shock 3-1 F.A.Cup win over Nottingham Forest in 1982, although that was to be one of very few bright spots in his time in North Wales as Wrexham were to drop from the Second to Fourth Divisions in successive seasons. Steve's former manager at Colchester, Bobby Roberts, had taken charge at the Racecourse by then; Dowman informed him that he did not wish to play in the Fourth Division, so he was loaned out to Charlton Athletic in August 1983. That loan was extended a number of times before he finally signed for the London club for £15,000 in January 1984. Steve remained a further eighteen months with the 'Valiants', making 61 League appearances, before leaving the Valley at the end of 1984/85. By this time he had launched a carpet business in Colchester, although he continued to play football by signing for Newport County in August 1985. However, after three months and only nine League appearances he joined Cambridge United, where he was to spend two further seasons before having to retire from full-time football at the age of 29 due to the persistent knee injury sustained during his Wrexham days. Steve was granted a testimonial match against Ipswich Town, played in August 1987. He retained his appetite for football, however, and began the 1987/88 season as player/manager of Brightlingsea United, where he was living. The following two terms saw him lead them to the Essex Senior League Championship, before signing as a player for Wivenhoe Town in 1991. Two years later was appointed player/manager of the same club, although he was soon departing to take over similar positions with both Heybridge Swifts and Braintree Town. In October 1994 he became player/manager back at Heybridge Swifts, although he was to later return to Wivenhoe Town as manager, a position he still held at the start of the 1998/99 season. Since ending his career as a professional footballer Steve has continued with his business as a carpet retailer.

Season	League		F.A.Cup		Welsh Cup		League Cup		Total	
	apps	gls	apps	gls	apps	gls	apps	gls	apps	gls
1980/81	4	0	-	-	-	-	-	-	4	0
1981/82	40	0	4	1	3	2	5	0	52	3
1982/83	43	2	2	0	6	1	2	0	53	3
	87	**2**	**6**	**1**	**9**	**3**	**7**	**0**	**109**	**6**

DUNCAN, Joseph James 1968 - 1969

Position; *Outside-Right*
D.O.B; *24th February, 1950*
Birthplace; *Huyton, Merseyside*
Height; *ft in* **Weight;** *st lbs*
Debut v. *Workington (h) 5th May, 1969*
Total Appearances & Goals; *1 app 0 gls*
Career; *WREXHAM 1968/69; Blaenau Ffestiniog Aug 1969;*
Honours; *Welsh League (North) Championship Winner 1972 & 1973; North Wales Coast F.A. Challenge Cup Winner 1972;*

Joey Duncan joined Wrexham as an amateur during the 1968/69 season. Having played a number of games for the reserve side, he was to make his Football League debut for the club in the last match of the 1968/69 season at home to Workington. He stepped into the side to replace Ian Moir, in a game that Wrexham went on to win 1-0. This proved to be Joey's one and only first team appearance in a Wrexham shirt, as he was released by the club at the end of the season. He then joined Welsh League North side, Blaenau Ffestiniog, where he went on to have considerable success winning both the League and North Wales Coast F.A.Challenge Cup in 1972, when they beat Porthmadog, 4-2, at Bangor City's Farrar Road ground, with Joey scoring one of the goals. He won a further championship medal with Blaenau Ffestiniog in 1973, having already been chosen to play for the North Wales Coast F.A.representative XI against the Scottish Juniors at Rhyl in 1970/71, in a 3-3 draw, and the following season at Kirkintilloch, the home of Kirkintilloch Rob Roy F.C., in which he scored one of the goals in the Coast F.A.'s 3-2 defeat. The Coast team also included Bob Scott and Billy Ashcroft. It is not known which clubs Joey joined after the left Blaenau Ffestiniog, but is understood to have played for Liverpool Sunday League side, St.Dominics until the late 1980's.

Season	League apps	League gls	F.A.Cup apps	F.A.Cup gls	Welsh Cup apps	Welsh Cup gls	League Cup apps	League Cup gls	Total apps	Total gls
1968/69	1	0	-	-	-	-	-	-	1	0
	1	**0**	**-**	**-**	**-**	**-**	**-**	**-**	**1**	**0**

DUNLOP, Albert 1963 - 1965

Position; *Goalkeeper*
D.O.B; *21st April, 1932*
Birthplace; *Liverpool, Merseyside*
Died; *Liverpool, 6th March, 1990*
Height; *5ft 8'1/2in* **Weight;** *12st 12lbs*
Debut v. *Crewe Alexandra (h) 2nd November, 1963*
Total Appearances & Goals; *18 apps 0 gls*
Career; *Everton Aug 1949 211apps 0gls; WREXHAM 1st November 1963 £3,000; Rhyl 14th Sept 1965 to May 1967;*

As a youngster Albert Dunlop signed for Bolton Wanderers on amateur terms, but his forms were immediately cancelled by the F.A. as he had committed an offence by signing on a Sunday! This was contrary to F.A. regulations. However, before he could put pen to paper again Everton stepped in, and he went to Goodison Park instead. Albert played in Everton's junior sides, gaining honours with them all, as well as representing the Liverpool County side that won the English Youth Championship. Dunlop signed professional for Everton in August 1949 at the age of seventeen. However, he had to wait seven years before making his Football League debut, which turned out to be a baptism of fire. He was thrust into Everton's desperate fight to avoid relegation, replacing Jimmy O'Neill for a match against Manchester United in front of more than 50,000 people at Old Trafford. It turned out to be the shock of the season, when Everton won 5-2 to end United's 26 match unbeaten run. Albert went on to keep his place in the side for the next five seasons, during which time he was described as being a 'dependable and reliable goalkeeper, who never really managed to fulfil his rich potential,' while 'his main attributes were a safe pair of hands and good vision, although prone to the occasional error as a direct result of lack of concentration. He was an effective last line of defence, and a larger than life character off the pitch.' During his time at Goodison Albert became a very good club cricketer in the summer months, playing for Liverpool Cricket Club as an able all rounder- a right hand batsman and a right medium fast bowler and appeared in four matches for Cheshire (Av. Batting, 1959). By 1962/63, Everton's championship winning season, he had been replaced in the side by Gordon West, although turning out in the final four matches of the season, which were all successful. In November of the following campaign Dunlop was to leave Goodison Park to join Wrexham for a £3,000 transfer fee, as the club looked to replace the departed Kevin Keelan. He went straight into the side for his debut, a 1-1 home draw with Crewe Alexandra, and played in the following match, before he was suspended. His career was put on hold following publication of a Sunday newspaper story in which he alleged that certain players in Everton's Championship side of 1963 had taken drugs. Albert was suspended by Wrexham Football Club from all club matches for a period of three weeks during this time, and it was not until the following season that he was to play first team football again. He then struggled to command a regular first team spot, mainly because of the form of new signing Steve Fleet, and at the end of the season was released. He then joined Cheshire League side Rhyl for the new season, before his appointment as player/manager of the club in March 1966, a position he held until May 1967. After quitting the game his personal life became overburdened with problems: he was placed on probation for two years in 1979 after being found guilty of three charges of deception; and he was jailed for fifteen months in February 1987 on charges of fraud involving the double glazing company that he worked for. Albert died in his native Liverpool three years later. He was only 57.

Season	League apps	League gls	F.A.Cup apps	F.A.Cup gls	Welsh Cup apps	Welsh Cup gls	League Cup apps	League Cup gls	Total apps	Total gls
1963/64	2	0	-	-	-	-	-	-	2	0
1964/65	13	0	-	-	2	0	1	0	16	0
	15	**0**	**-**	**-**	**2**	**0**	**1**	**0**	**18**	**0**

DURKAN, Kieron John 1990 - 1996

Position; *Forward*
D.O.B; *1st December, 1973*
Birthplace; *Chester, Cheshire*
Height; *5ft 11in* **Weight;** *12st 0lbs*
Debut v. *Mansfield Town (a) 3rd September, 1991*
Total Appearances & Goals; *65/10 apps 6 gls*
Career; *WREXHAM 16th Jul 1992; Stockport County 16th Feb 1996 £100,000 52/12apps 4gls; Macclesfield Town 25th Mar 1998 £15,000 25/5apps 3gls;*
Honours; *Three Republic of Ireland Under-21 International caps, 1 goal; Welsh Cup Winner 1995; Third Division runner-up 1993; Second Division runner-up 1997; Welsh Youth Cup Winner 1991 & 1992;*

'Kizza', as he was affectionately known at the Racecourse, will always be remembered at Wrexham for his goal in the 2-1 F.A.Cup win over Premier League side, Ipswich Town. He scored with a superb right-footed volley from an acute angle that nearly burst the net to set up a mouth-watering fourth round F.A.Cup match with Premier League Champions, Manchester United, at Old Trafford. He also scored in that match to give 'The Robins' a shock 1-0 lead. Kieron began playing football in Runcorn with local youth side, Weston Point, playing for all their under 9s to under 12s teams. He then appeared for St.Michael's in Widnes, from where he was invited for training with Crewe Alexandra at the age of 12. He also attended training with Manchester City before being approached by Wrexham's youth development officer Mike Buxton, who had spotted him playing for his school team, Heath, in Runcorn. Durkan then went on to play for Halton and Cheshire Schoolboys, winning the Cheshire Cup with Halton as a member of the same team as Robbie Lunt. Kieron signed YTS

forms for Wrexham when he left school in 1990, progressing with the youth and reserve teams, and collecting a Welsh Youth Cup winners' medal following a 1-0 win over Swansea. He then made his Football League debut at Mansfield in September 1991, as a second half substitute for Mickey Thomas. Kieron made two more first team appearances that season, both in the Autoglass Trophy. He also played in Wrexham's second successful Welsh Youth Cup Final, scoring one of the goals in a 2-1 victory over Cardiff City. 1992/93 saw 'Kizza' feature in only two first team games, while the following term he made around a dozen appearances. It was during the 1994/95 campaign that Kieron began to stake a serious claim for a first team spot, playing regularly on the right hand side of midfield. He was also capped twice at under-21 level by the Republic of Ireland, against both England and Austria. He was a fine crosser of the ball, with a strong right-foot, though he lacked the pace to become a top class player. With the signing of Craig Skinner during the close season of 1995 Kieron found himself out of favour, and in February was transferred to Stockport County for a £100,000 fee, a deal which also included Martyn Chalk moving to Wrexham. On his return to the Racecourse with his new club a few weeks later Kieron set up one of the goals in County's 3-2 win, much to his satisfaction. He went on to play a big part in Stockport's promotion season of 1996/97, as they finished runners-up in the Second Division to Bury. They also reached the semi-finals of the Coca Cola Cup, where they lost narrowly to Middlesbrough, after having beaten Premier League sides Blackburn Rovers and Southampton in earlier rounds. Despite this success 'Kizza' struggled to command a regular first team place for the 1997/98 campaign, and in March he was allowed to join Macclesfield Town, who gained promotion for the second successive season. Kieron returned to the Racecourse at the beginning of the 1998/99 season, only to see 'Macc' lose 2-1, although they had the consolation of scoring their first ever goal in Division Two.

Season	League		F.A.Cup		Welsh Cup		League Cup		Auto Tro.		E.C.W.C.		Total	
	apps	gls	apps	gls	apps	gls	apps	gls	apps	gls	apps	gls	apps	gls
1991/92	0/1	0	-	-	-	-	-	-	2	0	-	-	2/1	0
1992/93	0/1	0	-	-	-	-	-	-	1	0	-	-	1/1	0
1993/94	9/1	1	1	0	-	-	-	-	1	0	-	-	11/1	1
1994/95	28/2	2	2/1	2	7	1	2	0	3	0	-	-	42/3	5
1995/96	6/3	0	1	0	-	-	1/1	0	-	-	1	0	9/4	0
	43/8	**3**	**4/1**	**2**	**7**	**1**	**3/1**	**0**	**7**	**0**	**1**	**0**	**65/10**	**6**

DWYER, Alan Robert

1973 - 1981

Position; *Left-Back*
D.O.B; *5th October, 1952*
Birthplace; *Liverpool, Merseyside*
Height; *5ft 7in* ***Weight;*** *10st 7lbs*
Debut v. *Blaenau Ffestiniog (h) 23rd January, 1974 (Welsh Cup).*
Total Appearances & Goals; *226/13 apps 7 gls*
Career; *Halewood YC; WREXHAM 26th Oct 1973; Chesterfield Aug 1981 (trial) 0apps; Leicester City Sept 1981 (trial) 0apps; Stockport County Oct 1981 4apps 0gls; Bangor City 1981/82; Oswestry Town Mar 1982; Runcorn; Chirk AAA 1984; Lex XI 1987;*
Honours; *Third Division Championship Winner 1978; Welsh Cup Winner 1978; Welsh Cup runner-up 1979 & 1981; Northern Premier League Championship Winner 1982;*

Alan Dwyer was spotted when playing for Halewood Youth Club in his native Liverpool by the productive scouting network that Wrexham employed during the astute managership of John Neal. He was invited for trials to the Racecourse, and signed as an apprentice in 1971. Playing as a forward, Alan progressed through the youth ranks at the Racecourse, making his first team debut in a Welsh Cup match against Blaenau Ffestiniog in January 1974 and scoring in a 6-3 win. He made four League appearances the following season, going on to gain a regular first team place in the side after switching positions to play at left-back for the 1975/76 season as cover for Dave Fogg. It was following Fogg's departure in the summer of 1976 to Oxford United that Alan went on to make the position his own, helping the team to the verge of promotion, only to see Wrexham falter in the last five matches of the 1976/77 season. The following year Alan and Wrexham made up for the disappointment of the previous campaign, as they stormed to the Third Division Championship in style, as well as winning the Welsh Cup, and reaching the quarter-finals of both the F.A.Cup and League Cup. During his time at the Racecourse, it was said of him, 'he is one of the best distributors of the ball Wrexham have had in years'. Although Dwyer kept his place at left-back over the next three seasons, he was to struggle with a succession of niggling injuries, which cost him many appearances, and put paid to any interest from bigger clubs. He went on to play in two more Welsh Cup finals, in 1979 and 1981, losing to both Shrewsbury Town and Swansea City respectively. He also appeared in two European Cup-Winners' Cup campaigns in 1975/76, against Djurgardens of Sweden, and Stal Rzeszow of Poland, and 1979/80 against 1.F.C Magdeburg of East Germany. Alan was released by Wrexham at the end of 1980/81. He had a trial period with Chesterfield, but turned down the contract they offered him. He then had a trial with Leicester City, which came to nothing, before joining Stockport County in October 1981. At Edgeley Park, he had four more outings before joining Northern Premier League side Bangor City, who he assisted to the League championship that season. Having finished playing professional football Alan became a lorry driver, though he continued to play the game at non-league level with Oswestry Town, joining up with them towards the end of the 1981/82 season. He did however, miss their Welsh Cup match at Wrexham in November through injury. Dwyer then had a short spell at Runcorn before linking up with his former Wrexham team-mate, Dixie McNeil, at Chirk AAA during the 1984/85 campaign. Following McNeil's appointment as Wrexham manager in May 1985 Dwyer replaced him as player/manager of Chirk, before joining forces with Lex XI in 1987. Alan still lives in the Wrexham area. His son Kevin is a striker with Acton Park, who play in the Marstons Sunday League.

Season	League		F.A.Cup		Welsh Cup		League Cup		E.C.W.C.		Total	
	apps	gls	apps	gls	apps	gls	apps	gls	apps	gls	apps	gls
1973/74	-	-	-	-	1	1	-	-	-	-	1	1
1974/75	2/2	0	-	-	-	-	-	-	-	-	2/2	0
1975/76	29/3	2	3	1	-	-	3	2	2/1	0	37/4	5
1976/77	31	0	4	0	2	0	4	0	-	-	41	0
1977/78	45	0	9	0	5	1	6	0	-	-	65	1
1978/79	28/1	0	-	-	2/1	0	3	0	-	-	33/2	0
1979/80	13/5	0	-	-	2	0	3	0	2	0	20/5	0
1980/81	21	0	1	0	3	0	2	0	-	-	27	0
	169/11	**2**	**17**	**1**	**15/1**	**2**	**21**	**2**	**4/1**	**0**	**226/13**	**7**

E

Mickey Evans

EDWARDS, Andrew John 1982 - 1986

Position; *Forward*
D.O.B; *28th March, 1965*
Birthplace; *Wrexham, Denbighshire*
Height; *5ft 9in* ***Weight;*** *12st 0lbs*
Debut v. *Shrewsbury Town (h) 31st August, 1982 (Milk Cup)*
Total Appearances & Goals; *125/29 apps 35 gls*
Career; *WREXHAM Aug 1983; George Cross (Australia) cs1986; Western Suburbs (Australia) 1987; Morecambe Sept 1987; Colne Dynamoes 1987/88; Newtown; Caernarfon Town Jan 1989; Newtown; Colwyn Bay; Llansantffraid 1992/93; Conwy United Jan 1994 13/1apps 4gls; Flint Town United cs1994 19apps 10gls; Brymbo 1995/96; Llansantffraid Jul 1996 3apps 1gls; Flint Town United Sept 1996 23/1apps 5gls; Lex XI Jun 1997; Welshpool Town 1997/98 1app 0gls;*
Honours; *Welsh Youth international; Welsh Cup Winner 1986; Welsh Cup runner-up 1984; Cymru Alliance League Championship Winner 1993;*

Andy Edwards joined Wrexham straight from school, having already signed on schoolboy forms, after he had been spotted playing for the Queen's Park Youth Club side. Andy progressed through the various age levels of the Wrexham schoolboy teams, as well as representing both Clwyd and North Wales Schoolboys, and appearing for the Great Britain Catholic Schools side in Malta. Edwards joined Wrexham in their Second Division days in 1981, but following relegation in 1982 and the consequent big clear out of many of the club's senior professionals, the way was opened for some of the promising youngster's to prove themselves. Andy was one of those, and he was given his first team chance by manager Bobby Roberts in a 1-0 home win over Shrewsbury Town in a Milk Cup match in August 1982. By the end of that season Wrexham were once again relegated, although he had done enough to earn himself a professional contract by that time. They were bad times for Wrexham as a club, with very strict financial restraints placed upon the manager. At the end of 1983/84 Andy picked up a Welsh Cup runners'-up medal, when Wrexham lost to Shrewsbury Town 2-1 on aggregate, and scored the Wrexham goal. Wrexham qualified for Europe despite the defeat, as Shrewsbury were an English club, and the following season 'Ted', as he was affectionately known, played in the famous victory over F.C. Porto, and also in the Olympic Stadium against A.S.Roma. The 1985/86 season saw 'Ted' collect his first major honour when Wrexham won the Welsh Cup, but at the end of the campaign Wrexham manager Dixie McNeil informed him that he would not be retained. Andy then travelled to Australia for a short while, to play for Melbourne Sunshine, and Western Suburbs, before returning to the UK to play for Northern Premier League side, Morecambe. He followed this with a spell at Colne Dynamoes, and went on to play for a number of Welsh non-league clubs, including Newtown, Caernarfon Town -where he broke his leg, ironically against Colne- and Llansantffraid, helping them to promotion to the League of Wales in 1993. Working as a Milkman for Goodwins in Wrexham, Andy joined Conwy United in January 1994. He remained with the Morfa club until the end of the season, before signing in the summer for former manager, Dixie McNeil, by this time at Flint Town United. He stayed with Flint for just over a season before deciding to join Cymru Alliance League side, Brymbo, due to the travelling involved in the League of Wales. In the close season of 1996 he returned to Llansantffraid in the League of Wales, and appeared in both legs of their European Cup-Winners' Cup match with Ruch Chorzow of Poland. However, in September 1996 'Ted' was released by the 'Saints' after he failed to turn up for a League of Wales game with Caersws- because of his wife's birthday! He then rejoined Flint Town United, spending the rest of the season at 'Cae y Castell', joining Lex XI in the close season of 1997. Andy retired from playing football because of the condition of his knees, but he has since taken up playing rugby at Wrexham Rugby Club.

Season	League		F.A.Cup		Welsh Cup		League Cup		A.M.C.		E.C.W.C.		Total	
	apps	gls	apps	gls	apps	gls	apps	gls	apps	gls	apps	gls	apps	gls
1982/83	5/9	0	-	-	3/1	1	1	0	-	-	-	-	9/10	1
1983/84	22/7	7	1	0	7	1	2	0	2/1	1	-	-	34/8	9
1984/85	37	11	1	0	3	2	0/1	0	2	0	3	0	46/1	13
1985/86	25/9	9	2	0	6	3	2	0	1/1	0	-	-	36/10	12
	89/25	**27**	**4**	**0**	**19/1**	**7**	**5/1**	**0**	**5/2**	**1**	**3**	**0**	**125/29**	**35**

EDWARDS, David Arthur 1949 - 1950

Position; *Centre-Forward*
D.O.B; *1927*
Birthplace; *Llangollen, Denbighshire*
Height; *ft in* ***Weight;*** *st lbs*
Debut v. *New Brighton (a) 4th March 1950*
Total Appearances & Goals; *1 app 1 gls*
Career; *WREXHAM Nov 1949;*

A local lad from Llangollen, David Edwards joined Wrexham as an amateur whilst serving in the Army as a Lieutenant. He made his one and only League appearance for Wrexham at centre-forward, in March 1950 in a 3-1 defeat at New Brighton. It was said about David in the match report, that he 'revealed promise, distributed the ball well, and was a persistent raider, despite having something of a thankless job against the New Brighton player/manager, Jack Atkinson, a seasoned pivot and ex-Boltonian. A promising debut though.' Edwards in fact scored the Wrexham consolation goal when he 'collected a centre from Bobby McLaughlin, eluded a tackle, and drove the ball wide of the custodian.' Despite those comments, it proved to be David's one and only first team appearance for Wrexham.

Season	League		F.A.Cup		Welsh Cup		Total	
	apps	gls	apps	gls	apps	gls	apps	gls
1949/50	1	1	-	-	-	-	1	1
	1	**1**	**-**	**-**	**-**	**-**	**1**	**1**

EDWARDS, Ian Robert 1979 - 1982

Position; *Centre-Forward*
D.O.B; *30th January, 1955*
Birthplace; *Rossett, Denbighshire*
Height; *6ft 1in* ***Weight;*** *12st 5lbs*
Debut v. *West Ham United (a) 3rd November, 1979*
Total Appearances & Goals; *95/4 apps 30 gls*
Career; *Rhyl; West Bromwich Albion Feb 1973 13/3apps 3gls; Chester 26th Nov 1976 £20,000 104apps 36gls; WREXHAM 31st Oct 1979 £125,000; Crystal Palace 2nd Jul 1982 16/2apps 4gls; Mold Alexandra 1983; Porthmadog Feb 1989;*
Honours; *Four Full Welsh international caps.*

Ian showed a lot of promise during his schooldays at the Alun School in Mold. He turned down the offer of an apprenticeship with Wrexham, having played regularly for the club's junior teams, preferring to concentrate on his school work while continuing to play football with Cheshire League side, Rhyl. In February 1973 he was signed by West Bromwich Albion manager Don Howe, and worked his way through the youth ranks at the Hawthorns to make his Football League debut in a 4-0 home win over Sheffield Wednesday in March 1975. Despite scoring on his debut Ian was to find his first team opportunities limited at the Hawthorns, and after making fifteen further League appearances, scoring two goals, he left the 'Baggies' to join Chester in exchange for £20,000 in November 1976. Ian spent three years at Sealand Road, becoming a big favourite amongst the Chester fans, during which time he earned himself international recognition with Wales when capped in a friendly against Kuwait at Wrexham. He next played against Malta, again on the Racecourse, and hit the headlines when he equalled a Welsh record by scoring four goals in a 7-0 win. That sort of form persuaded Wrexham manager Arfon Griffiths to part with £100,000 for the big centre-forward in November 1979. Ian went on to spend three years with Wrexham but, during that time, injuries were to cost him many appearances. During his career he was described as 'an awkward gangling type of centre-forward, who never showed the type of consistency and ruthlessness to become a real success'. The highlights of his time at the Racecourse were the F.A.Cup victories over holders West Ham United (after two replays), and Brian Clough's Nottingham Forest, not forgetting his 30 yard match winning volley in a televised Second Division match at Derby. He stayed with Wrexham until the end of 1981/82, when the club were relegated. Ironically, his final match for the 'Robins' was against Crystal Palace, a 2-1 defeat in a game that saw him receive his marching orders, but he

was to sign for Palace only a week later! His stay at Selhurst Park was brief, due to a niggling knee injury that had consistently hindered his football career for so long. A specialist finally called a halt to his professional career, and Edwards returned to the Wrexham area where he took up work as a milkman, continuing to play local football with Mold Alexandra where he became player/manager. Ian later moved to Criccieth to run an hotel, also playing football for Porthmadog for a short while, but his knee injuries continued to give him trouble. A seventh operation on his knee was necessary, and this forced him to finally hang up his boots. After a long absence from the game, it came as a surprise when he returned to football on 18th May 1994 following his appointment as the new manager of League of Wales side, Porthmadog. Despite the signing of his former Welsh team mate, Mickey Thomas, Porthmadog struggled close to the bottom of the League, and although leading the club to the quarter-finals of the Welsh Cup and a meeting with Swansea City, he was dismissed before the game was played, in January 1995. He then left football and returned to concentrate upon running his Hotel and restaurant in Criccieth.

Season	League		F.A.Cup		Welsh Cup		League Cup		Total	
	apps	gls	apps	gls	apps	gls	apps	gls	apps	gls
1979/80	20	3	4	1	1	3	-	-	25	7
1980/81	23/3	6	5	0	2	1	2	1	32/3	8
1981/82	29/1	11	3	0	1	2	5	2	38/1	15
	72/4	**20**	**12**	**1**	**4**	**6**	**7**	**3**	**95/4**	**30**

EDWARDS, Jake

1998 -

Position; *Centre-Forward*
D.O.B; *11th May, 1976*
Birthplace; *Prestwich, Manchester, Lancashire*
Height; *5ft 11in* ***Weight;*** *11st 7lbs*
Debut v. *Swansea City (a) 1st December, 1998 (Welsh Premier Cup)*
Total Appearances & Goals; *6/11 apps 3 gls*
Career; *Union Lancers; Kearny Thistle; James Madison University; Tranmere Rovers (trial) Dec 1995; Tranmere Rovers (trial) Dec 1997; WREXHAM (trial) Jan 1998; WREXHAM Jul 1998:*

Although born at Prestwich in Manchester Jake Edwards' family moved to New Jersey in the United States in 1988 when he was just 12 years old. It was in America that he took an interest in 'soccer', and he began playing for Union Lancers, followed by Kearny Thistle - two clubs which had junior teams at different age levels. Jake then entered the James Madison University in Virginia, where he helped his side reach the Quarter-Finals of the National Tournament for two years in succession, and was selected as his region's 'All-American'. Jake's father, who was employed by British Airways, acted as a host during the 1994 World Cup, and Jake was a ball boy for the two Republic of Ireland games played at the Giants' Stadium in New York, against Italy and Norway. It was during the World's biggest soccer tournament that Jake was introduced to the former Liverpool and Scotland international Ian St.John, who offered help to arrange a trial in England. A year later he took up St.John's invitation, and took part in a trial at Tranmere Rovers at Christmas 1995. He then returned to the U.S.A., where he continued with his studies returning for a further three week trial with Tranmere Rovers at Christmas 1997. A week's trial with Wrexham then followed in the New Year, before he went back to the States with the offer of a further spell with the 'Robins' upon completing his degree in Exercise Science. In the summer of 1998 he returned to the Racecourse for a further trial and made a first team appearance during the pre-season friendly at Salisbury. He was then offered a six month professional contract with the Racecourse club, which he accepted. Jake had to wait until December 1998 before making his competitive senior debut, when he substituted Craig Skinner in a Welsh Premier Cup match at Swansea, the game ending in a 2-2 draw. His next appearance came a week later when he again turned out as a substitute, this time for Karl Connolly, in an Auto Windscreen Cup match at Macclesfield Town, scoring the only goal of the match.

Season	League		F.A.Cup		W.P.C.		League Cup		A.W.S.		Total	
	apps	gls	apps	gls	apps	gls	apps	gls	apps	gls	apps	gls
1998/99	4/5	1	-	-	1/2	0	-	-	1/4	2	6/11	3
	4/5	**1**	**-**	**-**	**1/2**	**0**	**-**	**-**	**1/4**	**2**	**6/11**	**3**

EDWARDS, James Elfyn

1978 - 1979

Position; *Defender*
D.O.B; *4th May, 1960*
Birthplace; *Aberystwyth, Dyfed*
Height; *5ft 11in* ***Weight;*** *12st 3lbs*
Debut v. *Shrewsbury Town (a) 24th May, 1979 (Welsh Cup final 2nd leg)*
Total Appearances & Goals; *1 app 0 gls*
Career; *WREXHAM Jul 1978; Tranmere Rovers Jul 1979 62apps 1gls; Runcorn cs1981; Altrincham cs1984; Macclesfield Town 1986/87; Halifax Town cs1993 26apps 1gls; Southport Mar 1994 15apps 0gls; Winsford United Oct 1994; TNS Llansantffraid Aug 1997 4apps 0gls;*
Honours; *Welsh Youth International; Welsh semi-professional international; Welsh Cup runner-up 1979; Welsh Youth Cup Winner 1978; Alliance League Championship Winner 1982; Northern Premier League Championship Winner 1987; Northern Premier League Challenge Cup Winner 1987; Northern Premier League Presidents Cup Winner 1987; F.A. Trophy runner-up 1989; Cheshire Senior Cup Winner 1991;*

Elfyn Edwards joined Wrexham straight from school in 1976, serving his apprenticeship to earn a professional contract in July 1978. He only made one first team appearance for Wrexham, deputising for the injured John Roberts at centre-half, in the Welsh Cup final second leg at Shrewsbury. The first leg had ended in a 1-1 draw, but Elfyn was unable to help Wrexham retain the trophy they had won the previous season as 'The Robins' lost the second leg by a solitary goal. Edwards was released by the club at the end of the season, although quickly fixed up when he signed for Tranmere Rovers in July. Elfyn made his first team debut for the Wirral club in a League Cup match at Port Vale in a 2-1 win, and went on to make 62 League appearances before being released in the summer of 1981. He then signed for Conference League side Runcorn, going on to play for Altrincham and Macclesfield Town. He won many honours with the Moss Rose club, and played at Wembley in the F.A.Trophy final, which 'Macc' lost 1-0 to Telford United. During this time Elfyn had become qualified as a Fireman with the Greater Manchester Fire Brigade. Coninuing to play football, he signed for Halifax Town in the close season of 1993 for their initial season in the Conference League following relegation from the Football League. In March 1994 he signed for fellow Conference League side, Southport, although he was to leave Haig Avenue at the beginning of the following season to join Winsford United. The summer of 1997 saw him return to Wales, when he signed for League of Wales side, Llansantffraid, but was to make only a handful of appearances. Elfyn is still employed by the Fire Service in Manchester. Edwards was once 'shot at' when playing for Winsford United. He was the victim of someone in the crowd with an air rifle and was hit in the leg with a pellet!

Season	League		F.A.Cup		Welsh Cup		League Cup		E.C.W.C.		Total	
	apps	gls	apps	gls	apps	gls	apps	gls	apps	gls	apps	gls
1978/79	-	-	-	-	1	0	-	-	-	-	1	0
	-	**-**	**-**	**-**	**1**	**0**	**-**	**-**	**-**	**-**	**1**	**0**

EDWARDS, John

1965 - 1966

Position; *Goalkeeper*
D.O.B; *23rd May, 1940*
Birthplace; *Wrexham, Denbighshire*
Height; *6ft 0'1/2in* ***Weight;*** *12st 7lbs*
Debut v. *Rochdale (a) 27th December, 1965*
Total Appearances & Goals; *1 app 0 gls*
Career; *Caergwrle Boys Brigade; Bradley Rangers; GKN Sankey 1964/65; Bradley Sports; WREXHAM Oct 1965; Rhyl (Loan) April 1968;*
Honours; *Five Welsh Amateur International caps;*

John Edwards first played football as an outside-right at Llay Secondary Modern school, who he represented in the Wrexham & District Schools final was played on the Racecourse when he was 13. However, it was whilst playing in goal in the school yard that he was to be switched to goalkeeper. John began working on his father's farm in Cefn-Y-Bedd upon leaving school, but continued to play football for the Caergwrle Boys' Brigade, until he was 18. John then signed for Bradley Rangers, who played in the Welsh National League, playing at either outside-right, or in goal. He spent one season with their reserve team before stepping up to the first team. It wasn't long before he was selected for trials with the Welsh Amateur side, initially playing for the Welsh National League against the Welsh League (North) at Rhyl under floodlights, before going on for a second trial match at Bala, when North Wales played against Mid Wales. However, a knee injury sustained in the above game meant that he missed out on representative honours on that occasion. In 1964, John finally won the first of his five Welsh Amateur international caps appeared playing against England at the Gay Meadow, Shrewsbury. He also appeared against England (again), Scotland, Ireland and Iceland in Reykjavik, when he came on as a substitute. It was at around this time that John played four games for GKN Sankeys in the Cheshire League, but it wasn't long before he finally signed for Wrexham on amateur terms in October 1965, following previous attempts by manager Billy Morris to lure him to the Racecourse. A couple of months later Edwards was plunged into the first team for his League debut at Rochdale in December 1965, replacing the injured Steve Fleet in goal. It was to turn out to be a big disappointment as Wrexham lost 6-0! That proved to be his only first team appearance for Wrexham, although he continued to play for the reserves until April 1968, when manager John Neal allowed him to go on loan to Cheshire County League side Rhyl. John played around six games for the Belle Vue club before twisting his knee in a match against Winsford United. It proved to be a cruciate ligament injury which was to end John's football career. Continuing to work on his father's farm, John Neal offered him the chance to become Wrexham's reserve team coach/trainer, running the Northern Floodlit League and Welsh League teams on a part-time basis. This involved training the amateurs on Tuesday and Thursday evenings, which he did up until 1973. John was then asked to take over from Aly McGowan as the club's full-time groundsman, whilst continuing with his coaching duties. He was to remain employed by Wrexham Football Club until June 1980, when he was informed that he was to be a victim of the club's cost-cutting drive. Edwards then took up employment at the Moss Valley Municipal Golf Course as green keeper. He worked there until the early 1990s when persuaded to return to the Racecourse as groundsman. He worked hard at restoring the Racecourse playing surface to it's previous high standard, as well as preparing the playing surfaces at the club's brand new training ground at Collier's Park. John still remains as the club's groundsman.

Season	League		F.A.Cup		Welsh Cup		League Cup		Total	
	apps	gls	apps	gls	apps	gls	apps	gls	apps	gls
1965/66	1	0	-	-	-	-	-	-	1	0
	1	**0**	**-**	**-**	**-**	**-**	**-**	**-**	**1**	**0**

EDWARDS, Joseph Noel

1919 - 1926

Position; *Inside-Left*
D.O.B; *26th November, 1898.*
Birthplace; *Johnstown, Denbighshire*
Died; *Wrexham, 26th November, 1952*
Height; *5ft 7in* ***Weight;*** *10st 7lbs*
Debut v. *Nuneaton Town (a) 20th September, 1919*
Football League debut v. *Hartlepool United (h) 27th August, 1921*
Total Appearances & Goals; *174 apps 42 gls*
Career; *Rhos; WREXHAM 3rd Oct 1919; Llandudno 2nd Jul 1926; Oswestry Town cs1927; Holywell Town 25th Aug 1928; Carlisle United cs1929 0apps;*
Honours; *Welsh Cup Winner 1921 & 1924; Welsh Cup runner-up 1920; One Welsh Junior International cap; North Wales Coast F.A.Challenge Cup runner-up 1926;*

Noel Edwards joined Wrexham during the first season following the end of World War One, and made his debut in Wrexham's Birmingham and District League side in a scoreless draw at Nuneaton. He became a very versatile player for the 'Robins', although he performed mainly at either left-back or inside-left. Noel made a total of over 170 appearances for Wrexham in his seven years with the club, during which time he helped them to achieve Football League status. He was described in May 1921 as 'young, speedy, wholehearted and worth his place in the team'. Noel, in fact, played in Wrexham's first ever Football League match against Hartlepool, but was to miss most of the remainder of the season after receiving a nasty injury against Accrington Stanley on the Racecourse in October. During his seven years with Wrexham Edwards -who was related to Welsh international Abel Hughes who played for Rhos Eagle Wanderers and Liverpool- also helped the 'Robins' win the Welsh Cup in 1921 and 1924. He was capped at Junior level for Wales against Ireland, at Holyhead, when he also captained the side. In March 1926 Edwards was rewarded for his loyalty to Wrexham Football Club with a well earned benefit match. It was said at the time, 'A more popular and faithful player it would not be possible to find. On the field he is clean and sure, and his speed is tremendous.' He was allowed to leave Wrexham at the end of the 1925/26 season, when he joined Welsh League side Llandudno. He later appeared for both Oswestry Town and Holywell Town, and is believed to have joined Carlisle United in the close season of 1929. He was thought to have joined them on trial, though never actually making a first team appearance for the 'Cumbrians'. Noel, who was a keen cricketer and member of Rhos Cricket Club, is known to have later worked for the National Assistance Board in Wrexham before he suddenly passed away at Wrexham War Memorial Hospital on his 54th birthday in 1952.

Season	League		F.A.Cup		Welsh Cup		Total	
	apps	gls	apps	gls	apps	gls	apps	gls
1919/20	28	12	5	6	5	1	38	19
1920/21	31	15	4	1	5	3	40	19
1921/22	12	0	-	-	2	1	14	1
1922/23	27	0	3	0	2	0	32	0
1923/24	18	1	2	0	6	0	26	1
1924/25	17	2	1	0	-	-	18	2
1925/26	6	0	-	-	-	-	6	0
	139	**30**	**15**	**7**	**20**	**5**	**174**	**42**
F/L total	**80**	**3**	**6**	**0**	**10**	**1**	**96**	**4**

EGGLESTONE, Pat

1953 - 1956

Position; *Goalkeeper*
D.O.B; *17th March, 1927*
Birthplace; *Penrith, Cumbria*
Height; *5ft 10in* **Weight;** *12st 7lbs*
Debut v. *Oldham Athletic (a) 7th February, 1953*
Total Appearances & Goals; *95 apps 0 gls*
Career; *Leeds United (Amateur) 1941; Bradford City (Amateur) 1943; Portsmouth (Amateur) 1946; Bradford City (Amateur) 1948 2apps 0gls; Halifax Town Sept 1949 20apps 0gls; Shrewsbury Town Aug 1950 109apps 0gls; WREXHAM 1st Feb 1953; Shelbourne Jul 1956; Corby Town Aug 1958;*

Although born in Penrith Pat was brought up in Bradford. He played football for his school team, Thorpe Modern, where he was chosen to play for both Bradford Boys and the West Riding Youth team. He also appeared in Bradford Junior football for both Swain House and Thackley. He left School at 14 and signed for Leeds United on amateur forms during the Second World War. After two years with the Elland Road club he signed for Bradford City, also on amateur forms, for whom he made five War-time appearances. Like so many other promising young footballers at that time, WW2 was to interrupt his footballing career, and Pat was enlisted in the Royal Armoured Corps, with whom he served until the war had ended. He then joined Portsmouth, close to the Bovington Army camp where he was based. Pat returned home to Bradford upon leaving the Army, where he re-signed for City on amateur forms in May 1948 . Egglestone finally made his Football League debut for Bradford City in a 1-1 draw with Halifax Town in September 1948. He made one more League appearance for the Valley Parade club before offered a professional contract with Halifax Town in September 1949. Pat spent one season at the Shay, making twenty League appearances, before joining Shrewsbury Town for their initial season in the Football League in August 1950. Pat, in fact, played in their first ever Football League match against Scunthorpe United. He spent almost three years at the Gay Meadow, making 109 League appearances, eventually losing his place in the side to Wilf Birkett. In February 1953 Wrexham manager Peter Jackson persuaded him to sign for 'The Robins' for a small fee of around £500. Pat didn't have it all his own way at the Racecourse, as he had to compete for the goalkeeping shirt with Bob Connor, Earl Godding and Billy Waters. He combined playing with working part-time at Brymbo Steelworks, as assistant groundsman to the former Wrexham player, Jackie Lloyd, who was the brother of the club secretary Cliff Lloyd. Pat was also a keen cricketer; playing for Brymbo Steelworks during the summer months, with whom he won the club's batting and bowling honours, and was selected to represent Denbighshire against Lancashire Seconds. He was released by Wrexham during the close season of 1956, and joined Irish League side Shelbourne, in Dublin. Pat would travel from his Wrexham home for each match while continuing to work at Brymbo Steelworks! He stayed with the Irish side for a season before joining Corby Town as a part-timer in the Southern League, remaining for three years before retiring from football altogether. However, Pat remained involved with the game by taking up refereeing, reaching a high standard in non-league circles in the London Combination League. He settled in the Kettering area after retiring from football, and worked as a compositor in the Print trade before retiring to make his home in Desborough, near Kettering. At the start of the 1998/99 season Pat was one of a number of former players who attended the Wrexham AFC players re-union dinner.

Season	League		F.A.Cup		Welsh Cup		Total	
	apps	gls	apps	gls	apps	gls	apps	gls
1952/53	17	0	-	-	-	-	17	0
1953/54	26	0	-	-	1	0	27	0
1954/55	24	0	6	0	4	0	34	0
1955/56	17	0	-	-	-	-	17	0
	84	**0**	**6**	**0**	**5**	**0**	**95**	**0**

ELLIS, Jonathan

1920 - 1922

Position; *Right-Back*
D.O.B; *20th November, 1890*
Birthplace; *Flint, Flintshire*
Died; *Denbigh, 12th December, 1941*
Height; *5ft 9in* **Weight;** *12st 4lbs*
Debut v. *Coventry City Res (a) 28th August, 1920*
Football League debut v. *Hartlepool United (h) 27th August, 1921*
Total Appearances & Goals; *58 apps 0 gls*
Career; *Flint Church Guild 1908; Flint Town Sept 1909; Connah's Quay FC Aug 1910; Flint Alliance Aug 1911; Connah's Quay & Shotton Alliance 14th Nov 1911; Tranmere Rovers Aug 1913; WREXHAM 9th June 1920; Rhos FC 25th Aug 1922;*
Honours; *Welsh Cup Winner 1921*

Jack Ellis first played football at school in his native Flint. He then appeared in the Flint Church Guild side, quickly followed by signing for Flint Town. He spent two seasons with Flint before joining neighbours Connah's Quay FC in August 1910. Although he helped Connah's Quay to the Welsh Cup Final of 1911, he was not selected for the match against Wrexham, and in the close season left to join Flint Alliance. It was during his time here that Jack was spotted by Tranmere Rovers, who signed him in August 1913. He went on to spend seven years with the 'Prentonians', although the First World War was to interrupt his playing career. Jack was a member of the Flint (RWF) Territorial Army when WW1 broke out, and was soon absorbed into the Regular Army with the Royal Welch Fusiliers, with whom he was sent out to Gallipoli. John was involved in the famous Suvia Bay landing, when troops effected a foothold under withering fire from the Turks. He was wounded in the Gallipoli campaign, and was eventually sent home. Once declared fit he was appointed Instructor of Musketry, with the rank of Colour-Sergeant, later becoming Company Sergeant-Major. After spending some time in this country he was drafted to German East Africa, attached to the King's African Rifles, and promoted to Regimental Sergeant-Major. It was in this campaign that he was 'Mentioned in Despatches for gallant and distinguished services in the field', a commendation that was signed by Winston Churchill. He remained in East Africa until May 1919. Following his return home Jack was eventually signed by Wrexham in the close season of 1920, when the club were still a Birmingham and District League outfit. During the 1920/21 season Ellis was selected as a 'probable' in a trial match in January 1921, for the Welsh National side, along with two other Wrexham players, Noel Edwards and E.D.Roberts, for which he received a cap. Although never selected for the Welsh side, he did collect a Welsh Cup Winners' medal at the end of 1920/21, having what was described as a 'fine game' in the Final against Pontypridd. That was to be Wrexham's last season in the Birmingham & District League as they were then elected to the Football League Division Three North, and Jack began the new season at right-back in the club's inaugural match in the Football League against Hartlepool United on the Racecourse. He went on to make a further 18 League appearances before leaving the club during the close season of 1922 to become player/manager of Rhos FC, who had just completed the previous season as Welsh National League Champions. It was with Rhos that Jack saw out his football career. He took over as landlord of the Eagles Hotel in Rhos in July 1921, running it for over twenty years and becoming very popular and well known in the Rhos area for his deeds of human kindness during the difficult times of the 1920s. He was nominated as a candidate in the District Council Elections and, after an unsuccessful first effort, won the seat for the Rhos Ward in 1931, and was re-elected in 1934. Ill health forced him to stand down, although he did continue to lead the Remembrance Parades through Rhos. He was a member of a talented musical family as his wife was a well-known local operatic singer

and his son, Arthur Ellis, who resides in Penycae, a double winner at the Royal National Eisteddfod of Wales.

Season	League		F.A.Cup		Welsh Cup		Total	
	apps	gls	apps	gls	apps	gls	apps	gls
1920/21	28	0	4	0	4	0	36	0
1921/22	19	0	2	0	1	0	22	0
	47	**0**	**6**	**0**	**5**	**0**	**58**	**0**

ELLIS, Kenneth 1949 - 1950

Position; *Inside-Right*
D.O.B; *22nd January, 1928*
Birthplace; *Buckley, Flintshire*
Height; *ft in* ***Weight;*** *st lbs*
Debut v. *Lincoln City (a) 24th December, 1949*
Total Appearances & Goals; *5 apps 0 gls*
Career; *Chester (Amateur) May 1946 1app 0gls; WREXHAM May 1949; Flint Town United cs1951; Connah's Quay Nomads cs1953;*

Ken Ellis signed for Chester as an amateur just after the Second World War, having played regularly for Chester Colts in the Cheshire and District League as a junior at the age of 17. Ken, who worked as an engineering apprentice at this time, continued to turn out for Chester, and it was during this period that he had one of his proudest moments in football. He also played for the local Air Training Corps, and he was chosen to represent the A.T.C. in a Youth tournament in Switzerland. As a preliminary to the main competition he played in a curtain raiser before the France v. England match, at the Colombes Stadium in Paris in front of a 60,000 crowd. Throughout the 1946/47 season Ken played for the Chester reserve team at Sealand Road at inside-right. He finally made his Football League debut for the 'Seals' in March 1947, when he was called up to replace the injured Dick Yates for the home game with Accrington Stanley. Tommy Burdon moved to centre-forward with Ellis alongside him at inside-right to help Chester to a 3-1 win. With Yates fit again for the next match Ken returned to the reserves. It proved to be his only first team game for Chester, despite remaining at Sealand Road for two more seasons, playing regularly for the reserve side. He was released at the end of the 1948/49 season, when he was snapped up by Wrexham on amateur forms. Once again he found himself playing reserve team football at first, but his League debut for Wrexham came on Christmas Eve 1949, when he deputised for Dennis Grainger at outside-right in a 2-0 defeat at Lincoln City. Ken appeared in the following three matches before Grainger returned to the side. He enjoyed one more outing for Wrexham before being replaced by Billy Tunnicliffe at outside-left in a 1-0 home defeat to Gateshead in March 1950. He spent the entire 1950/51 season playing in the reserve side in the Cheshire County League, before being released in the summer. He then joined Welsh League side Flint Town United, where he spent two seasons moving on to Connah's Quay Nomads in the close season of 1953, playing a few matches before leaving football altogether. Ken then took up work for British Steel at Shotton as a draughtsman,for thirty years before retiring in 1984 and settling in the Buckley area.

Season	League		F.A.Cup		Welsh Cup		Total	
	apps	gls	apps	gls	apps	gls	apps	gls
1949/50	5	0	-	-	-	-	5	0
	5	**0**	**-**	**-**	**-**	**-**	**5**	**0**

ELVIDGE, Christopher 1921 - 1922

Position; *Inside-Forward*
D.O.B; *A/M/J 1892*
Birthplace; *Stourbridge, West Midlands*
Height; *ft in* ***Weight;*** *st lbs*
Debut v. *Chesterfield (h) 5th November 1921*
Total Appearances & Goals; *15 apps 5 gls*
Career; *Hereford Town; WREXHAM (Am) Sept 1921, (Pro) 5th Oct 1921; Shrewsbury Town Aug 1922 98apps 65gls;*
Honours; *Birmingham & District League Championship Winner 1923; Shropshire Senior Cup Winner 1923 & 1925; Walsall Senior Cup Winner 1925;*

Chris Elvidge joined Wrexham in September 1921 from Hereford Town on trial. He played a number of reserve games before being signed permanently the following month, and was soon handed his Football League debut, when he replaced Reg Leck against Chesterfield in November 1921. It was a sensational start to his League career, as Wrexham won 6-1, although he didn't feature on the score sheet. Chris also played in the following match, the return game at Chesterfield, but was then replaced by the fit again Leck. He completed a further ten League games in what was Wrexham's inaugural season in the Football League, appearing in a variety of forward positions. He was released by Wrexham at the end of the season, joining Birmingham & District League side Shrewsbury Town. Chris became a great success in his three seasons at the Gay Meadow, scoring an incredible 65 goals in just 98 Birmingham League appearances. They included a hat-trick on his debut in a 3-1 win at Cradley Heath. He also once notched six goals in a 7-0 win over Cannock. Elvidge won a Birmingham & District League Championship medal with Shrewsbury in 1923, before retiring from football in September 1925. He became mine host of the Bull's Head Public House in Shrewsbury, where he remained as licensee until the the early 1930s.

Season	League		F.A.Cup		Welsh Cup		Total	
	apps	gls	apps	gls	apps	gls	apps	gls
1921/22	12	2	-	-	3	3	15	5
	12	**2**	**-**	**-**	**3**	**3**	**15**	**5**

EMERY, Steven Roger 1985 - 1986

Position; *Midfielder*
D.O.B; *7th February, 1956*
Birthplace; *Ledbury, Herefordshire*
Height; *5ft 10in* ***Weight;*** *11st 10lbs*
Debut v. *Swindon Town (a) 17th August, 1985*
Total Appearances & Goals; *10/1 apps 0 glsCareer; Hereford United Feb 1974 203/1apps 10gls; Derby County 21st Sept 1979 £100,000 73/2apps 4gls; Newport County Mar 1983 0apps; Hereford United Jun 1983 72/3apps 2gls; WREXHAM Aug 1985; Gloucester City Feb 1987; Westfields Apr 1987; Ledbury Town Nov 1994;*
Honours; *Third Division Championship Winner 1977; Welsh Cup runner-up 1976;*

Steve Emery became Hereford United's first ever apprentice signing after they had been elected to the Football League. He stepped up to the professional ranks on his eighteenth birthday, and that same month made his Football League debut for the 'Bulls' in a 2-0 defeat at Cambridge United. He went on to play in over 200 games for the Edgar Street club, winning a Third Division Championship medal in 1977, and having collected a Welsh Cup runners'-up medal the previous year, before his former manager at Hereford, Colin Addison, splashed out £100,000 to sign him for Derby County. Steve was unfortunate with injuries at the Baseball Ground, fracturing a cheekbone against Chelsea in 1980, and having his leg broken twice! The first of these came following a wild challenge by Gerry Gow of Rotherham in February 1982, and Steve did not appear in another senior match for the 'Rams' afterwards. However, he showed great courage by reviving his career in the lower divisions. Colin Addison once again signed him for Newport County in March 1983, but he failed to make the first team at Somerton Park, and returned to Hereford during the close season of 1983. He spent two seasons at Edgar Street before former

Hereford team-mate Dixie McNeil signed him for Wrexham in August 1985. Steve made his 'Robins' debut in the opening match of the 1985/86 season, a 1-0 win at Swindon Town, but had only managed a further ten games before tragedy struck again when he broke his leg in a 3-0 defeat at Southend, just as he had begun to rediscover his old form. He attempted a comeback, but finally decided to call it a day in December 1986. He left Wrexham, and went into the licensing trade,though he did take up playing football again at non-league level with both Gloucester City and Westfields, who he later managed. He was appointed player/manager of the Skol Combination side Ledbury Town in November 1994. They were bottom of the League at the time, but Steve succeeded in turning their fortunes around and he led them to safety.

Season	League		F.A.Cup		Welsh Cup		League Cup		F.R.T.		Total	
	apps	gls	apps	gls	apps	gls	apps	gls	apps	gls	apps	gls
1985/86	8/1	0	-	-	-	-	2	0	-	-	10/1	0
	8/1	**0**	-	-	-	-	**2**	**0**	-	-	**10/1**	**0**

***EMMERSON,* Mark William Ray** 1981 - 1983

Position; *Midfield*
D.O.B; *7th August, 1965*
Birthplace; *Nantwich, Cheshire*
Height; *5ft 10in* ***Weight;*** *11st 6lbs*
Debut v. *Preston North End (a) 28th September, 1982*
Total Appearances & Goals; *1/1 apps 0 gls*
Career; *WREXHAM Sept 1981; Oswestry Town Dec 1983; Blackpool Jan 1984; Northwich Victoria Sept 1984; Winsford United cs1986; Caernarfon Town Nov 1988; Rhyl cs1989; Barnton Rovers 1991;*
Honours; *Cheshire Senior Cup Winner; Two Mid-Cheshire Senior Cup Winner; Staffordshire Cup runner-up;*

Mark Emmerson was a product of Wrexham's youth policy of the early 1980s, becoming the third generation member of his family to progress through to football's professional ranks. His father, Arthur Emmerson, played for Burnley, before injury forced him to retire at the age of 17, while his Grandfather, Billy Chambers, won a Lancashire League Cup winners' medal with Blackburn Rovers, before moving on to both Northwich Victoria and Rhyl. Mark played organised football from an early age at Cuddington Primary and Weaverham High Schools, both near Northwich, from where he was chosen to play for Northwich Schoolboys, Mid-Cheshire Under-16s, and Cheshire Under-16s. His performances for these sides did not go unnoticed, and at fifteen was signed on schoolboy forms by Huddersfield Town. He spent four months at Leeds Road before told that he wouldn't be offered an apprenticeship. He then enrolled at the Sir John Dean College in Northwich to continue with his studies and while playing local football in Northwich for junior team, Castle under-16s was spotted by Wrexham scout Cliff Roberts. He was invited to the Racecourse for a trial, and appeared against Brymbo in a Welsh National League game, in which he acquitted himself well enough to be offered non-contract terms in September 1981, which he accepted. He signed apprentice terms shortly afterwards, following a reserve team game at Bolton. Mark must have made an immediate impression at Wrexham because, within a couple of months of his arrival at the Racecourse, he was selected to make his Football League debut at Preston in September 1982 -along with another teenager, John Muldoon. Despite a 3-0 defeat Wrexham manager Bobby Roberts said after the match, "I must give special mention to the three kids-Andy Edwards, John Muldoon and Mark Emmerson. They certainly did not let the side down. One has to take into consideration that they jumped from the Welsh National League into the Third Division of the Football League and both leagues are a million miles apart in terms of sharpness and technique, so they can be well pleased with their games." Not long after his debut Emmerson played in the successful Wrexham Youth side that reached the quarter-finals of the F.A.Youth Cup only to be beaten by Sheffield Wednesday. Mark then broke his foot, which kept him out of action for a while, though he earned another first team chance after his recovery, when he came on as substitute for Darren Baker in a 3-1 defeat at Wigan Athletic. This was to be his last game for Wrexham, despite having scored regularly for the reserves, and Emmerson left the Racecourse in December 1983 by 'mutual consent'. He then joined Oswestry Town before invited to join Blackpool on non-contract terms, where he remained for the rest of the season, playing for Oswestry on a Saturday while training with Blackpool in the week and appearing for their reserves in the Central League. At the end of the season he was released, but was quickly offered terms by his local side, Northwich Victoria, who were playing in the Conference League. He made his debut for Northwich at Yeovil, where a crowd of 10,000 turned up to see Ian Botham making his debut for Yeovil. He went on to win a Cheshire Senior Cup winners' medal, two Mid-Cheshire Senior Cup winners' medals, and a Staffordshire Cup runners'-up medal while at the Drill Field, where he also played against his boyhood hero, Bryan Robson, in a friendly match with Manchester United. Mark left the 'Vic's' at the end of the season to join Winsford United following the departure of manager Stuart Pearson. He went on to play for both Caernarfon Town and Rhyl, returning to the Racecourse with the latter for a Welsh Cup quarter-final match in February 1990. Mark helped the 'Lilywhites' to a deserved 1-1 draw, before losing the replay 2-0. He remained with Rhyl as they finished runners-up to Barrow in the Northern Premier League, until signing for West Cheshire League side Barnton Rovers, where he is still playing at the time of writing, as well as turning out for a Sunday League side, Thatched Tavern FC. Mark became an accounts clerk upon giving up the professional game, and is now self-employed, having set up his own Accountancy and book-keeping company. He is still living in the Northwich area.

Season	League		F.A.Cup		Welsh Cup		League Cup		Total	
	apps	gls	apps	gls	apps	gls	apps	gls	apps	gls
1982/83	1/1	0	-	-	-	-	-	-	1/1	0
	1/1	**0**	-	-	-	-	-	-	**1/1**	**0**

***EMSON,* Paul David** 1986 - 1988

Position; *Forward*
D.O.B; *22nd October, 1958*
Birthplace; *Grimsby, Humberside*
Height; *5ft 11in* ***Weight;*** *11st 3lbs*
Debut v. *Hereford United (a) 23rd August, 1986*
Total Appearances & Goals; *61/12 apps 10 gls*
Career; *Brigg Town; Derby County Sep 1978 £5,000 112/15apps 13gls; Grimsby Town Aug 1983 90/7apps 15gls; WREXHAM 15th Aug 1986; Darlington Aug 1988 39/9apps 5gls,(+ 28/6apps 7gls in Conference League); Kettering Town cs1990 10/2apps 1gls; Gateshead cs1991 2/2apps 1gls;*
Honours; *Conference League Championship Winner 1990;*

Paul Emson began his footballing career with local non-league side Brigg Town where he was spotted by Frank Blunstone, Tommy Docherty's assistant at Derby. The 'Doc' paid out a £5,000 fee to secure his services upon the recommendation of his right hand man. Paul had to wait until the end of the 1978/79 season to make his Football League debut for Derby in a 3-3 draw at Aston Villa in April 1979. He couldn't secure a regular first team place in the first team during the following season, due to new signing Gordon Hill, but regained his place when the 'Doc' left the Baseball Ground and Colin Addison was appointed as his successor. Emson eventually found a first team place hard to come by, due to a combination of injury and poor form, and when Peter Taylor took charge he found himself surplus to requirements at the end of the 1982/83 season. In August 1983 he signed for Grimsby Town, making 97 League appearances for the 'Mariners' in his three seasons with the club, but another change of manager, as Mike Lyons replaced Dave Booth, saw him on the move again. This time Wrexham manager Dixie McNeil signed the pacey winger, and he made his debut for the 'Robins' in the opening game of the 1986/87 season, a scoreless draw at Hereford United. Paul was able to experience European football in his first season at the Racecourse, when he played against both F.C.Zurrieq of Malta and the Spanish giants, Real Zaragoza, to which Wrexham lost narrowly on the away goals rule. He suffered a setback at the start of the following campaign, when he was injured in a pre-season friendly match at Mold, sustaining a broken collar bone. Having forced his way back into the first team, he then picked up a heel injury finally losing his place in the side to Mike Carter, and at the end of the 1987/88 season was released. Paul quickly fixed himself up with a move to Darlington but, at the end of his first season with 'The Quakers', they were relegated to the Conference League. He remained with the Feethams club, however, helping them to regain Football League status by winning the Conference championship at the first time of asking. Paul spent one further season with Darlington before leaving the club in the close season of 1990. He then joined Conference side Kettering Town where he spent one season, before joining Gateshead in the summer of 1991 for a short spell.

Season	League		F.A.Cup		Welsh Cup		League Cup		F.R.T.		E.C.W.C.		Total	
	apps	gls	apps	gls	apps	gls	apps	gls	apps	gls	apps	gls	apps	gls
1986/87	30/5	3	1/1	0	5	2	3/1	2	3/2	1	3	0	45/9	8
1987/88	12/2	2	1/1	0	1	0	-	-	2	0	-	-	16/3	2
	42/7	**5**	**2/2**	**0**	**6**	**2**	**3/1**	**2**	**5/2**	**1**	**3**	**0**	**61/12**	**10**

ESDAILLE, David

1992 - 1993

Position; *Midfielder*
D.O.B; *22nd July, 1963*
Birthplace; *Manchester, Lancashire*
Height; *5ft 9in* ***Weight;*** *11st 0lbs*
Debut v. *Bury (h) 18th August, 1992 (Coca Cola Cup)*
Total Appearances & Goals; *6/1 apps 0 gls*
Career; *Flixton; Chorley; Winsford United 1990; WREXHAM Aug 1992; Bury 1993 1/5apps 0gls; Witton Albion 1st Oct 1993 (Loan) 5apps 0gls; Altrincham (Loan) 4apps 0gls; Winsford United; Trafford; Hyde United; Flixton; Droylsden Nov 1996; Doncaster Rovers Jul 1997 10/3apps 0gls;*

David Esdaille was playing schoolboy football in his native Manchester when was chosen to represent both Trafford and Manchester Boys right up to under-19 level. The first interest to be shown in him by Football League clubs came from Oldham Athletic when he was 15. He was invited to training at Boundary Park on Monday evenings, but nothing came of this and he joined Manchester League side Flixton. Having completed his 'O' levels Dave went on to study for his 'A' levels at college, and it was at around this time that Preston North End began to take notice and, following a month's trial he was offered a contract. However, Dave decided to turn down the offer in order to go to Manchester University, where he was to achieve a B.A. degree in Physical Education. He continued to play local football during his University days, and another offer of a trial followed, this time with Blackpool. He spent a month with them before leaving. In the mean time, he had been turning out for a Manchester Sunday League side 'Astro', when they remained unbeaten in over five years. In 1989, Astro's manager, Mike McKenzie, was put in charge of Northern Premier League side Winsford United, and took most of the Astro team with him, including Dave, who at that time was playing his Saturday football for Chorley. He helped Winsford to win promotion to the First Division of the Northern Premier League in his first season, and the following term they finished runners-up to Colwyn Bay. 1991/92 Winsford embarked on an F.A.Cup run that saw them reach the First Round proper of the competition, where they met Wrexham. Despite a valiant effort by the Cheshire club Wrexham eventually ran out 5-2 winners, but Dave had done enough to impress Wrexham manager Brian Flynn to be invited along for trials with the Racecourse club. The 'Ruud Gullit' lookalike was then taken on tour with the first team squad to play in the Isle of Man international tournament, where he made an impressionable start. Following their return he was signed on a non-contract basis, and eventually made his first team debut as a substitute for Mickey Thomas in a Coca Cola Cup match with Bury in a 1-1 draw on the Racecourse. This was followed by his full League debut in October, a 2-0 win at Carlisle, and he went on to make five more first team appearances before a disastrous 6-1 defeat in the F.A.Cup at Crewe. Dave was released by the club at the end of the month, as Wrexham went on to win promotion to the Second Division. He joined Bury, where he managed six League outings before the end of that season, although he failed to make a further first team appearance the following year. He did have two loan spells, with both Witton Albion and Altrincham, before being released. Esdaille drifted back into non-league football, playing for Winsford United, Trafford, Hyde United, Flixton and Droyslden, until being given another chance in the Football League when he signed for Doncaster Rovers in the close season of 1997. He made his debut for the Yorkshire club as a substitute in the opening game of the 1997/98 season, a 2-1 defeat at Shrewsbury, but it was to be a dismal year for both David and Doncaster as he made an unlucky thirteen League appearances in a 'Rovers' side that was quickly doomed to relegation to the Conference League because of desperate financial implications. His brother Darren also played in the same Doncaster team.

Season	League		F.A.Cup		Welsh Cup		League Cup		F.R.T.		A.G.T.		Total	
	apps	gls	apps	gls	apps	gls	apps	gls	apps	gls	apps	gls	apps	gls
1992/93	4	0	1	0	1	0	0/1	0	-	-	-	-	6/1	0
	4	**0**	**1**	**0**	**1**	**0**	**0/1**	**0**	**-**	**-**	**-**	**-**	**6/1**	**0**

EVANS, Arthur Richard

1927 - 1928

Position; *Goalkeeper*
D.O.B; *1905*
Birthplace; *Wrexham, Denbighshire*
Height; *5ft 7in* ***Weight;*** *10st 0lbs*
Debut v. *Rotherham United (a) 25th February, 1928*
Total Appearances & Goals; *2 apps 0 gls*
Career; *Miners' Institute; Denbigh United cs1926; WREXHAM 19th May 1927; Denbigh United 1st Sept 1928; Bangor City 10th Aug 1929; Llanelly 9th Aug 1930; Whitchurch;*
Honours; *One Welsh Junior International cap;*

Wrexham-born Arthur Evans was a goalkeeper with the Miners' Institute in the local Wrexham & District League, when he was offered a trial with Wrexham in the close season of 1926. Unfortunately, he failed to make an impression, and was quickly signed up by Denbigh United, with whom he spent the 1926/27 campaign. Wrexham returned for his signature in May 1927, but due to the fine form of 'The Robins' regular shot-stopper Ted Robson, he had to wait until the following February for his senior debut. This came in a 1-0 win at Rotherham when he was called upon to replace the injured Robson. He kept his place in the side for the next game, but a 5-0 defeat at Stockport County proved to be his last senior appearance for the 'Robins'. Arthur rejoined Denbigh United, where he was to earn international recognition by being capped by Wales in a Junior International with Ireland, before moving on to Bangor City after a year. He enjoyed his stay at Farrar Road before heading south to link up with Llanelli in August 1930.

Season	League		F.A.Cup		Welsh Cup		Total	
	apps	gls	apps	gls	apps	gls	apps	gls
1927/28	2	0	-	-	-	-	2	0
	2	**0**	**-**	**-**	**-**	**-**	**2**	**0**

EVANS, Arthur Victor

1935 - 1938

Position; *Right-Back*
D.O.B; *1918*
Birthplace; *Mold, Flintshire*
Height; *5ft 10in* ***Weight;*** *11st 10lbs*
Debut v. *Swansea Town (a) 18th March, 1935 (Welsh Cup)*
Total Appearances & Goals; *96 apps 0 gls*
Career; *WREXHAM (Am) Jul 1934, (Pro) 30th Aug 1934;*
Honours; *Welsh Schoolboy International;*

Vic Evans joined Wrexham as a sixteen year-old at the end of 1933/34 season after showing great promise as a schoolboy, culminating in representing Wales at that level. Vic's first season with Wrexham saw him step in for Mr.Consistency himself, Alf Jones, for a Welsh Cup match at Swansea, although he hardly had the best of starts as Wrexham lost 6-0!! He deputised for 'Our Alf' once more for his first Football League appearance at Crewe in April, and it was Evans who finally ousted Alf

Jones from the right back position he had held for almost thirteen consecutive seasons. He went on to make the position his own until Eddie Tunney replaced him during the 1937/38 season. Vic's most memorable game for Wrexham was the F.A.Cup Third Round match against Manchester City on the Racecourse, which 'The Robins' eventually lost 3-1. In addition to his defensive abilities he must also have been a reasonable goalkeeper because, in February 1938, it was reported that Wrexham were trying a very interesting experiment by attempting to convert him into a goalkeeper! Apparently he had played between the sticks as a youngster.

Season	League		F.A.Cup		Welsh Cup		N.S.C.		Total	
	apps	gls	apps	gls	apps	gls	apps	gls	apps	gls
1934/35	1	0	-	-	1	0	-	-	2	0
1935/36	24	0	-	-	1	0	2	0	27	0
1936/37	41	0	3	0	1	0	1	0	46	0
1937/38	18	0	1	0	1	0	1	0	21	0
	84	**0**	**4**	**0**	**4**	**0**	**4**	**0**	**96**	**0**

EVANS, Bernard

1954 - 1960

Position; *Centre-Forward*
D.O.B; *4th January, 1937*
Birthplace; *Chester, Cheshire*
Height; *6ft 1in* ***Weight;*** *13st 6lbs*
Debut v. *Bradford City (a) 15th September, 1954*
Total Appearances & Goals; *126 apps 56 gls*
Career; *Saltney Juniors; WREXHAM 13th Aug 1954; Queens Park Rangers 2nd Nov 1960 £2,000 77apps 34gls; Oxford United Dec 1962 £6,500 13apps 3gls; Tranmere Rovers Oct 1963 12apps 5gls; Crewe Alexandra Jul 1964 0apps; Guildford City Aug 1965; Hastings United Mar 1966; Rhyl 7th Sept 1966; Caernarvon Town 19th Nov 1966 to 11th Mar 1967;*
Honours; *Welsh Cup Winner 1960;*

Bernard Evans played his early football at the Wood Memorial School in Saltney, and then at Shotton Central School on Deeside, from where he was selected to play for Flintshire Schoolboys. He took up an apprenticeship as a chain-maker on leaving school, while continuing to play football for a local junior team, Saltney Juniors. It was then that he was recommended to Wrexham by the clubs Chief Scout, their former player Ted Regan, and joined the Racecourse club on amateur terms. Bernard quickly worked his way through Wrexham's junior and reserve teams to earn himself a first team place at Bradford City in September 1954 in place of Tommy Bannan. Seventeen year-old Bernard certainly made an impressive start when he scored for Wrexham after just twenty seven seconds of his debut in a 2-2 draw. However, he had to wait until midway through the following season before being given an extended run in the senior side, and not long after, in March 1957, he was called up for his National Service at Park Hall, Oswestry, with the Royal Artillery. This was to affect his availability for 'The Robins', and had to fight for his place with Peter Thompson, who was switched to centre-forward as his replacement. After completing his two years' National Service the big, strong striker returned to Wrexham to re-establish himself as a first team regular, and in 1960 he collected a Welsh Cup winners' medal against Cardiff City, having missed out on the 1957 and 1958 Finals. Evans had a very good goals per game ratio with Wrexham, and it was this ability that attracted an offer of £2,000 from Queens Park Rangers with the 1960/61 season just a few months old. He went straight into the Rangers side to make his debut at home against Shrewsbury Town in a 1-1 draw in November 1960. His next match saw Bernard score twice in a 9-2 home win over Tranmere Rovers, and remained with Q.P.R. until December 1962, when he was allowed to join Football League newcomers, Oxford United. Bernard failed to hit the net consistently at the Manor Ground, despite scoring regularly in the 'U's' reserve side in the Metropolitan League, and in first team friendly games, but struggled to find the net in the first team and therefore failed to hold on to a regular first team place. Unsurprisingly, he was soon on the move again, this time to Fourth Division Tranmere Rovers. He got off to a good start at Prenton Park, scoring on his debut in a 1-1 draw at Rochdale in October 1963, but a bad knee injury cost him his first team place, and he struggled to regain it when fit again. At the end of the 1963/64 season he joined Crewe Alexandra, but he still suffered with the knee injury and he failed to make the first XI in his one season at Gresty Road. Bernard then joined non-league side Guildford City in August 1965, followed by further spells in non-league football with Hastings United, Rhyl, and Caernarfon Town before finally ending his football career through injury. He eventually settled in his native city of Chester, where he set up an industrial cleaning business based at Shell Oil in Ellesmere Port, with which he has since been occupied for over thirty years.

Season	League		F.A.Cup		Welsh Cup		Total	
	apps	gls	apps	gls	apps	gls	apps	gls
1954/55	5	2	-	-	-	-	5	2
1955/56	29	11	-	-	1	0	30	11
1956/57	14	9	1	1	3	3	18	14
1957/58	20	7	-	-	-	-	20	7
1958/59	16	6	-	-	1	0	17	6
1959/60	26	10	-	-	5	5	31	15
1960/61	5	2	-	-	-	-	5	2
	115	**47**	**1**	**1**	**10**	**8**	**126**	**56**

EVANS, Dennis

1955 - 1958

Position; *Full-Back*
D.O.B; *23rd July, 1935*
Birthplace; *Chester, Cheshire*
Height; *5ft 9in* ***Weight;*** *11st 6lbs*
Debut v. *Grimsby Town (a) 14th April, 1956*
Total Appearances & Goals; *11 apps 0 gls*
Career; *Saltney Juniors; WREXHAM 16th Mar 1955; Tranmere Rovers 30th Jun 1958 3apps 0gls; Bangor City 10th Aug 1960; Colwyn Bay 23rd Jul 1962; Llandudno 16th Sept 1963; Nantlle Vale 21st Sept 1964;*

Dennis Evans had represented both Flintshire and North Wales schoolboys during his education, and upon leaving school he joined his local side, Saltney Juniors. He was then invited for trials by Wrexham and initially played as an amateur for the reserve team before asked to sign professional for the Racecourse club in March 1955. During his three years with the 'Robins', he was primarily a full-back with the reserve side in the Cheshire County League, though his Football League debut came at left-back in a 1-0 defeat at Grimsby Town in April 1956, when he stood in for centre-half Alan Fox, with Albert Parker playing in that position. Dennis went on to appear in a further nine League games over the next three seasons,being selected only when required as cover, before leaving the Racecourse in June 1958. He was then signed by Tranmere Rovers for 'a small fee', but only managed to make three League appearances at Prenton Park. His debut for the Birkenhead club came in March 1959, in a 1-0 home win over Hull City, playing in his usual position of left-back. Dennis then played in the following match, a 3-2 defeat at Chesterfield, making his final appearance for Tranmere in a 4-0 defeat at Colchester a year later. He was released by the Prenton Park club at the end of 1959/60, joining Bangor City in the summer of 1960. He later went on to play in non-league football in North Wales for Colwyn Bay, Llandudno and Nantlle Vale. After he ended his football professional career, Evans, had been employed by British Telecom until forced to retire in 1985 through ill-health. Dennis still lives in the Chester area.

Season	League		F.A.Cup		Welsh Cup		Total	
	apps	gls	apps	gls	apps	gls	apps	gls
1955/56	2	0	-	-	-	-	1	0
1956/57	3	0	-	-	1	0	4	0
1957/58	6	0	-	-	-	-	6	0
	11	**0**	**-**	**-**	**1**	**0**	**12**	**0**

EVANS, Elfed

1955 - 1956

Position; *Inside Forward*
D.O.B; *28th August, 1926*
Birthplace; *Ferndale, Glamorgan*
Died; *Burton-on-Trent, 13th May, 1988*
Height; *5ft 10in* ***Weight;*** *11st 11lbs*
Debut v. *York City (a) 20th August, 1955*
Total Appearances & Goals; *36 apps 19 gls*
Career; *Trelewis; Nelson; Treharris Athletic 1947; Cardiff City 12th May 1949 44apps 18gls; Torquay United 10th Mar 1951 (Loan) 12apps 6gls; West Bromwich Albion 13th Jun 1952 17apps 3gls; WREXHAM 17th Jun 1955; Southport 14th Dec 1956 £600 13apps 0gls; Caernarfon Town 27th Sept 1957; Burton Albion Aug 1958;*

Elfed Evans joined Cardiff City in May 1949 from Treharris Athletic after scoring 48 goals in one season in the Welsh League. He made his Football League debut for the 'Bluebirds' in a 1-1 draw at Sheffield Wednesday in August 1949 and, ended his first season as the club's leading marksman, notching eight League goals. Even so he was never really regarded as a regular in the side, and in March 1951 was loaned out to Torquay United. In June 1952, he joined First Division West Bromwich Albion where, in his first three matches, played in two victories over Cardiff City. He spent two further seasons at the Hawthorns, but failed to make another first team appearance during this period. In June 1955 Wrexham manager Cliff Lloyd stepped in to make a double signing, of both Elfed and Gren Jones. Evans was pitched into the first team at inside-forward for the first match of the 1955/56 season at York, and responded by scoring one of the goals in the 3-1 win. He remained in the side until October before being replaced by Jack Rowley. He then regained his first team place in January, and held on to it until the end of the season. The following campaign saw Elfed make just three League outings, stepping in for Ronnie Hewitt, and it was no real surprise when he was allowed to leave the Racecourse to join Southport in December. He made his debut for the 'Sandgrounders' in a 5-1 home defeat by Bradford City before finding another struggle to hold on to a regular first team place. His best performance for the Haig Avenue club was said to have come in a Lancashire Cup tie in January 1957, when he scored twice against Everton. Elfed was to leave Southport in the close season of 1957, after making just thirteen League appearances. He returned to Wales, joining Welsh League North side Caernarvon Town for a term before joining Birmingham & District League side Burton Albion. He ended his career with the Derbyshire side after sustaining a broken leg, and settled in the town of Burton, where he became employed with Bass Breweries as a Drayman. Elfed was later forced to give up work due to ill health. His home life disintegrated as he became beset by problems, mainly of his own making, and died in Burton in 1988, aged 61.

Season	League		F.A.Cup		Welsh Cup		Total	
	apps	gls	apps	gls	apps	gls	apps	gls
1955/56	31	14	-	-	2	3	33	17
1956/57	3	2	-	-	-	-	3	2
	34	**16**	**-**	**-**	**2**	**3**	**36**	**19**

EVANS, George Albert

1957 - 1963

Position; *Wing-Half*
D.O.B; *26th July, 1935*
Birthplace; *Rhostyllen, Denbighshire*
Height; *5ft 11in* ***Weight;*** *12st 6lbs*
Debut v. *Hartlepool United (h) 19th October, 1957*
Total Appearances & Goals; *208 apps 11 gls*
Career; *Bolton Wanderers; Blackpool; Oswestry Town; WREXHAM 23rd Jul 1957; Chester 11th Jun 1963 110/3apps 0gls; Bethesda 13th Aug 1969; Colwyn Bay 4th Sept 1970;*
Honours; *Welsh Cup Winner 1958; Welsh Cup runner-up 1962 & 1966;*

George Evans was employed as an apprentice fitter at Bersham Colliery, near Wrexham, when invited to join Bolton Wanderers on trial. He spent three months at Burnden Park, before joining Blackpool for a further eighteen months, though failing to make a first team appearance at either club. He returned home to continue working at Bersham Colliery, also playing football for Birmingham & District League side Oswestry Town. George remained at Victoria Road until Wrexham boss Cliff Lloyd signed him as a part-timer, enabling him to earn more money than he would have done had he become a full-time professional. Initially he found himself in the Cheshire County League with the Wrexham reserve side, and two seasons had passed before a first team opportunity arose. George made his Football League debut in October 1957, in a 3-1 home win over Hartlepool United, but it wasn't until the following season that he was to establish himself as a regular in the senior XI, although he did appear in the 1958 Welsh Cup Final win over Cardiff City. He remained in the half-back line at the Racecourse until the summer of 1963, during which time he helped the club to promotion in 1962 under Ken Barnes' leadership, and also took part in the club's great League Cup run in 1960/61 when they reached the quarter-finals. During his time at the Racecourse Evans was noted as a 'great hearted player, who never knows defeat,' and he was described as 'a very strongly built player, and a mighty useful man to have around when the going gets tough!' At the end of the 1962/63 season manager Ken Barnes exchanged both Stan Bennion and George for Chester's Billy Myerscough. George made his Sealand Road debut in the opening match of the 1963/64 season, a 2-0 home defeat by Oxford United, before going on to spend five seasons at with Chester. He clocked up 110 League appearances for the 'Seals', and played in the first two games of the 1966 Welsh Cup Final, unfortunately missing the replay which Swansea Town won 2-1. George finally left Chester in the close season of 1969, drifting into non-league football with Welsh League side Bethesda Athletic, where he played alongside another former Wrexham favourite, Don Weston. He later joined Colwyn Bay before finally retiring from football altogether. George Evans continued to work for the National Coal Board until he retired, and has since resided in the Hightown area of Wrexham.

Season	League		F.A.Cup		Welsh Cup		League Cup		Total	
	apps	gls	apps	gls	apps	gls	apps	gls	apps	gls
1957/58	13	1	1	0	4	0	-	-	18	1
1958/59	35	1	1	0	1	0	-	-	37	1
1959/60	34	3	3	0	4	1	-	-	41	4
1960/61	43	0	1	0	3	0	6	0	53	0
1961/62	33	3	3	0	3	1	1	0	40	4
1962/63	17	1	-	-	1	0	1	0	19	1
	175	**9**	**9**	**0**	**16**	**2**	**8**	**0**	**208**	**11**

EVANS, Jonathan 1921 - 1922

Position; *Inside-Left*
D.O.B; *1898*
Birthplace; *Denbighshire*
Height; *5ft 7in* **Weight;** *10st 7lbs*
Debut v. *Walsall (a) 27th December, 1921*
Total Appearances & Goals; *3 apps 1 gls*
Career; *Brymbo Green; WREXHAM Dec 1921; Brymbo Green Jan 1922; Rhos 11th Jul 1923;*
Honours; *Flintshire Charity Cup Winner 1923;*

Jonathan Evans, nicknamed 'Oxo', was playing for Brymbo Green during the 1921/22 season when both he and J.S.Williams were called upon by Wrexham to sign amateur forms in order help the club out of an injury crisis. This resulted in their replacing injured players Ernie Lloyd and Reg Leck for a League match at Walsall in December 1921. 'Oxo' was described as a 'strong attacker, who also assists the defence, and who can also use his head well.' He made a total of three League appearances for the 'Robins', and scored one goal in a 5-2 defeat at Barrow. After that match, Jonathan was allowed to leave the Racecourse and rejoin Brymbo Green, where he captained the club to success in the Flintshire Charity Cup in the following campaign. He left Brymbo in the close season of 1923 to join Welsh National League side Rhos Athletic.

Season	League		F.A.Cup		Welsh Cup		Total	
	apps	gls	apps	gls	apps	gls	apps	gls
1921/22	3	1	-	-	-	-	3	1
	3	**1**	-	-	-	-	**3**	**1**

EVANS, Medwyn John 1982 - 1984

Position; *Midfielder*
D.O.B; *8th November, 1964*
Birthplace; *Holyhead, Gwynedd*
Height; *5ft 10in* **Weight;** *10st 3lbs*
Debut v. *Sheffield United (a) 16th October, 1982*
Total Appearances & Goals; *13/4 apps 0 gls*
Career; *WREXHAM Aug 1983; Bangor City cs1984; Bethesda Athletic; Benllech; Moelfre; Bodeden; Glantraeth; Llanerchymedd; Gaerwen; Pentraeth; Bro Goronwy; Llanfairpwll;*
Honours; *Welsh Schoolboy international; Welsh Cup runner-up 1983;*

Medwyn Evans played his early football in his native Anglesey at the St.Thomas Jones Secondary School in Amlwch, representing the Island's Boys' team, as well as both Gwynedd and North Wales Schoolboys, before he was chosen for the Welsh Schoolboys team. Medwyn also appeared for Benllech's Junior teams during his school years. He signed for Wrexham after writing to the club requesting a trial during Arfon Griffiths' managership. He did well enough in trials to be offered the chance to join the groundstaff at the Racecourse upon leaving school in the summer of 1981. Medwyn was still an apprentice when he made his Football League debut, at Sheffield United in October 1982, coming on as a substitute for Gareth Davies in the 2-0 defeat. He remained in the side for two games before disaster struck in November, when he broke an ankle in a Youth Cup match, but recovered in time to add a further four full appearances that season. It was during this period that he was given trials by the Welsh Youth team, although not selected. Medwyn was given a professional contract by Wrexham in August 1983, making ten appearances through the campaign before released at the end of the season. He then signed for Northern Premier League side, Bangor City, going on to play for a number of teams in the North Wales area. He left Bangor for Bethesda Athletic, before enjoying spells at Benllech, Moelfre, Bodedern, Glantraeth, Llannerchymedd, Gaerwen, Pentraeth, Bro Goronwy and Llanfairpwll. Since leaving Wrexham and returning to Anglesey Medwyn has worked for Ellis Tyre Service on the island. He still lives on Ynys Mon, where he is involved running an under-11s team in Llanerchymedd, as well as assisting Osian Roberts, who is the Ynys Mon Youth Development Officer.

Season	League		F.A.Cup		Welsh Cup		League Cup		A.M.C.		Total	
	apps	gls	apps	gls	apps	gls	apps	gls	apps	gls	apps	gls
1982/83	6/1	0	-	-	1/1	0	-	-	-	-	7/2	0
1983/84	7/3	0	-	-	1/1	0	1	0	1	0	10/4	0
	13/4	**0**	-	-	**2/2**	**0**	**1**	**0**	**1**	**0**	**17/6**	**0**

EVANS, Michael Graham 1966 - 1979

Position; *Defender*
D.O.B; *4th June, 1947*
Birthplace; *Llanidloes, Powys*
Height; *5ft 10in* **Weight;** *11st 2lbs*
Debut v. *Exeter City (h) 20th August, 1966*
Total Appearances & Goals; *459/17 apps 26 gls*
Career; *Caersws; Wolves Jul 1964 0apps; WREXHAM 1st Jul 1966; Caersws Jul 1982 (manager);*
Honours; *Wales Schoolboy international; Four Welsh under-23 international caps; Welsh Cup Winner 1972, 1975 & 1978; Welsh Cup runner-up 1967 & 1971; Third Division Championship Winner 1978; Division Four runner-up 1970;*

Only four players have made more League appearances for Wrexham than loyal club man Mickey Evans, who joined 'The Robins' from Wolves in July 1966, following his release by the Black Country club. Mickey was spotted by Wolves playing for his local side, Caersws, having already been capped for the Wales Schoolboys' side. After two years with the Molineux club Mickey was signed by Wrexham as an inside-forward, but went on to play in nearly every position for the club, including that of emergency goalkeeper, standing in when David Gaskell was injured following a challenge with Aston Villa's Andy Lochhead in 1970. He went on to spend sixteen years with Wrexham, making his Football League debut in a scoreless home draw with Exeter City in the opening match of the 1966/67 season. The game also witnessed the Football Legaue debut of Dixie McNeil for the visitors. As for Mickey, he went on to collect three Welsh Cup Winners' medals, a Third Division championship medal in 1978, and four Welsh under-23 caps during his time at the Racecourse. He played in some of the club's greatest matches during that time, including a Football League Cup tie against Manchester United in 1969, when he marked George Best out of the game, and a European Cup-Winners' Cup quarter-final in 1976 when he did a similar job on Anderlecht's Robbie Rensenbrink. Mickey was granted a well-deserved testimonial by Wrexham in 1977 but, after being pipped at the post for promotion in the last game of the season, a disappointingly small crowd of just over 2,000 turned out to see Wrexham play a Wales XI. However, the following season Mickey finally helped Wrexham to realise the club's dream of playing Second Division football when they won the Third Division Championship in style. The following campaign was to be a personal disaster for Mickey, when he was stretchered off in only Wrexham's second match of the season at Fulham. That injury eventually forced him to retire from the game prematurely, on medical advice, but he continued to help out at the club in a coaching capacity, assisting manager and long-term friend Arfon Griffiths. Following Griffiths' departure towards the end of 1980/81 Mickey was appointed as assistant manager to Mel Sutton. By the end of the season with Wrexham relegated, both were informed that their contracts would not be renewed, whereupon Evans returned to Caersws, becoming manager of the local side, and leading them as founder members of the League of Wales in 1992. He is still in charge of the Caersws club, while also working as a sales manager for a Petroleum Company. His son Graham, who notched 13 goals for his father's club in 1997/98, has since joined Aston Villa on a two year contract following a month's trial. Mickey Evans will always be remembered with great affection by Wrexham's supporters, even though he was something of an 'unsung hero' during much of his time spent at the Racecourse

Season	League		F.A.Cup		Welsh Cup		League Cup		E.C.W.C.		Total	
	apps	gls	apps	gls	apps	gls	apps	gls	apps	gls	apps	gls
1966/67	36/2	9	2	0	2	3	1	1	-	-	41/2	13
1967/68	3/6	1	1	0	1	0	-	-	-	-	5/6	1
1968/69	13/1	2	-	-	1/2	0	-	-	-	-	14/3	2
1969/70	21	1	3	1	-	-	4	0	-	-	28	2
1970/71	29/4	0	-	-	4	0	-	-	-	-	33/4	0
1971/72	37	2	3	0	3	0	-	-	-	-	43	2
1972/73	42	1	3	0	1	0	2	0	4	0	52	1
1973/74	30	0	6	0	3	2	1	0	-	-	40	2
1974/75	46	0	1	0	5	0	1	0	-	-	53	0
1975/76	41	2	3	0	3	0	3	0	6	0	56	2
1976/77	43	0	4	0	3	0	5	0	-	-	55	0
1977/78	24	1	4	0	3	0	3	0	-	-	34	1
1978/79	3/2	0	-	-	-	-	2	0	-	-	5/2	0
	368/15	**19**	**30**	**1**	**29/2**	**5**	**22**	**1**	**10**	**0**	**459/17**	**26**

F

Steve Fox

FAIRBROTHER, Ian Andrew 1987 - 1987

Position; *Midfielder*
D.O.B; *2nd October, 1966*
Birthplace; *Bootle, Merseyside*
Height; *5ft 10in* **Weight;** *12st 0lbs*
Debut v. *Newport County (a) 24th October, 1987*
Total Appearances & Goals; *9 apps 0 gls*
Career; *Liverpool Jul 1984 0apps; 18th Bury Feb 1987 16/10apps 3gls; WREXHAM 23rd Oct 1987 (Loan);*
Honours; *Central League Championship Winner 1984 & 1986;*

Ian Fairbrother joined Liverpool straight from school in 1982. He then progressed through the ranks at Anfield, to sign a professional contract in July 1984. After almost three years in Liverpool's Central League side, during which he won two Central League Championship medals, he was informed of his release by Liverpool in 1987, but was quickly snapped up by Third Division Bury in February 1987. Fairbrother made his Football League debut for the 'Shakers' at Newport County in a 2-2 draw, in which he scored one of their goals. He was never able to establish himself as a regular with Bury and, in October 1987, Wrexham manager Dixie McNeil brought him to the Racecourse on loan. He made his debut in a 1-0 defeat again at Newport County, and after eight further League and Cup appearances for Wrexham was allowed to return to Gigg Lane without an offer for him being made. Ian was released by Bury at the end of the 1987/88 season, and drifted into non-league football.

Season	League		F.A.Cup		Welsh Cup		League Cup		S.V.T.		Total	
	apps	gls	apps	gls	apps	gls	apps	gls	apps	gls	apps	gls
1987/88	7	0	1	0	1	0	-	-	-	-	9	0
	7	**0**	**1**	**0**	**1**	**0**	**-**	**-**	**-**	**-**	**9**	**0**

FENTON, Alexandra Ewan 1959 - 1960

Position; *Wing-Half*
D.O.B; *17th November, 1929*
Birthplace; *Dundee, Tayside*
Height; *5ft 9'1/2in* **Weight;** *11st 4lbs*
Debut v. *Newport County (h) 22nd August, 1959;*
Total Appearances & Goals; *27 apps 0 gls*
Career; *Jeanfield Swifts; Blackpool Nov 1946 195apps 20gls; WREXHAM 20th May 1959 £3,000; Limerick (player/coach) 17th August 1960; Linfield (Manager) 15th May 1967;*
Honours; *F.A.Cup Winner 1953; Irish Cup Winner 1965;*

Ewan Fenton joined Blackpool shortly after the Second World War from his local Dundee club side, Jeanfield Swifts. He signed for the 'Seasiders' in November 1946, but had to wait nearly two years before figuring in the first team, his Football League debut coming in a home draw with Derby County in September 1948. A cultured right-half, Ewan was mainly an understudy to Hugh Kelly and Harry Johnston for the next few years, but his patience was rewarded when he appeared in the famous 1953 'Matthews' F.A.Cup final, as Blackpool beat Bolton Wanderers 4-3 at Wembley. Ewan eventually became a regular with the 'Tangerines', and in 1956 was appointed club captain. He was described as a 'shrewd passer of the ball and enjoyed joining the attack, scoring some crucial goals'. He did not achieve international honours with Scotland, the nearest he came to representative honours was playing for the British Army XI. When Jim Kelly replaced him in the side during the 1957/58 season Ewan had a transfer request turned down, but a year later was allowed to join Wrexham for a small fee, having made over 200 appearances for Blackpool. He was immediately appointed as club captain upon his arrival, but he was to spend just one season at the Racecourse eventually losing his place in the side to George Evans. It came as no surprise when released at the end of 1959/60, although he did apply for the vacant manager's post following the departure of John Love. The job was eventually handed to Billy Morris. Ewan then joined Irish League side Limerick during the summer of 1960, and later became player/manager. He experienced playing in the European Cup, and picked up a F.A.I. Cup Winners' medal in 1965. In May 1967 he was appointed manager of Linfield, inspiring them to the Irish League championship in 1969, the Irish F.A.Cup in 1970, the City Cup in 1968, the Gold Cup in 1968 & 1969 and the Ulster Cup in 1968. He also led them into Europe in each of the three seasons he held sway at Windsor Park -against Leipzig in 1967, Setubal in 1968, and Red Star Belgrade in 1969. Ewan left Linfield at the end of 1969/70, when he was succeeded by Billy Bingham. He returned to Limerick as manager, leading them to a F.A.I.Cup win in 1971, beating Drogheda 3-0 in the final replay, after a scoreless draw.

Season	League		F.A.Cup		Welsh Cup		Total	
	apps	gls	apps	gls	apps	gls	apps	gls
1959/60	24	0	1	0	2	0	27	0
	24	**0**	**1**	**0**	**2**	**0**	**27**	**0**

FERGUSON, Archibald 1948 - 1953

Position; *Goalkeeper*
D.O.B; *9th December, 1918*
Birthplace; *Glencraig, Fife*
Died; *Dunfermline, 19th March 1998.*
Height; *5ft 9'1/2in* **Weight;** *12st 0lbs*
Debut v. *Halifax Town (h) 21st August, 1948*
Total Appearances & Goals; *140 apps 0 gls*
Career; *St.Andrews United; Crossgates Primrose; Raith Rovers Jun 1938; Doncaster Rovers Dec 1941 61apps 0gls; WREXHAM 28th Jul 1948 (exchange for Jack Jones and cash); Dunfermline Athletic Mar 1953;*
Honours; *Third Division North Championship Winner 1947; Welsh Cup runner-up 1950;*

Archie Ferguson began playing football at Ballingry Public School in Lochore, Fife. As goalkeeper, he was selected for Crosshill Hearts, before appearing in Scottish Junior football for both St.Andrew's United and Crossgates Primrose. With them Archie was signed by Raith Rovers in June 1938 and remained with the Kirkcaldy club until the outbreak of World War Two, which seriously disrupted a promising football career. Archie served with the Royal Artillery, though he would play football whenever possible, and 'guested' for both Grimsby Town and Doncaster Rovers. He also featured in his regiment team, which included virtually the whole of the Bolton Wanderers side of the time. During WW2 he served in the Middle-East, Italy and North West Europe, and was evacuated from Dunkirk in 1941. When WW2 was over Archie resumed his career with Doncaster Rovers, making his Football League debut in the opening match of the 1946/47 season, a 2-1 home win over Rochdale. He went on to play in 61 League games for the Belle Vue club, winning a Third Division North championship medal in 1947 in a side that achieved two Football League national records which still stand today: 33 wins out of 42 games, and 72 out of 84 points. In July 1948 Archie was signed by Wrexham manager Tom Williams, in exchange for Jack Jones and a 'big fee'. He immediately took over the No.1 position for the new season from Geoff Atherton, and kept it until he lost his place to Dick Connor at the beginning of the 1951/52 season. Archie was given another chance to prove himself at the outset of the following term, but was again replaced by Connor by the end of September. He then earned a recall for Wrexham's biggest match since the end of the hostilities, an F.A.Cup Third Round match against First Division side Stoke City at the Victoria Ground. Unfortunately, two dreadful first-half mistakes by him cost Wrexham dear, and even a brilliant second-half performance by the rest of the team, deserving of at least a draw, could not make good the deficit. He was dropped for the following match, and never again appeared in a first team game for Wrexham. His only honour with the 'Robins' was a Welsh Cup runners-up medal from the 1950 final, against Swansea Town at Ninian Park, which Wrexham lost 4-1. Nevertheless, Archie Ferguson was a big favourite, both of the club's supporters and of his team-mates during his time at the Racecourse. He was a great character to have in the dressing room, always playing practical jokes. One story told recalls the time when he was driving his three-wheeler car in Wrexham town centre after training when he was stopped by a

Policeman for travelling the wrong way down a one-way street. The Officer explained to Archie the error of his ways, so he got out of the three-wheeler car, lifted up the front, and turned it around before driving off! A true character. Upon leaving Wrexham in March 1953 Ferguson returned to his native Scotland, and signed for Dunfermline Athletic. His time at East End Park was to be short as, by the close of the campaign, he had taken up work at the Naval Construction Research Establishment in Rosyth, where he was employed as a welder until retiring in the 1980s. He was awarded the I.S.M. following his retirement, in recognition of his work in development of metals to be used in Britain's nuclear submarines. Archie was a season ticket holder at his local side, Dunfermline Athletic, for a number of seasons, as well as being an active member of the Dunkirk Veterans' Association until 1990, when it was disbanded.

Season	League		F.A.Cup		Welsh Cup		Total	
	apps	gls	apps	gls	apps	gls	apps	gls
1948/49	35	0	-	-	2	0	37	0
1949/50	42	0	3	0	5	0	50	0
1950/51	32	0	2	0	1	0	35	0
1951/52	6	0	-	-	-	-	6	0
1952/53	11	0	1	0	-	-	12	0
	126	**0**	**6**	**0**	**8**	**0**	**140**	**0**

FERGUSON, Christopher

1931 - 1932

Position; *Inside-Right*
D.O.B;
Birthplace; *Kirkconnel, Dumfries & Galloway*
Height; *5ft 6in* ***Weight;*** *10st 12lbs*
Debut v. *Rochdale (h) 5th September, 1931*
Total Appearances & Goals; *18 apps 4 gls*
Career; *Chelsea Oct 1927 1app 0gls; Queens Park Rangers May 1930 15apps 1gls; WREXHAM 17th July 1931; Guildford City cs1932; Post Office Engineers' XI Aug 1934;*

Chris Ferguson first signed for Chelsea in October 1927, joining his older brother William Ferguson, who was already with the London club. Unlike Willie, who enjoyed 12 years with the 'Pensioners', Chris spent just three seasons at Stamford Bridge; making one appearance in a League match at Wolverhampton in April 1928, which Chelsea won 2-1. Ferguson replaced Albert Thain in the side for the above game, but it proved to be his one and only outing in a blue shirt. Another brother - Pearson Ferguson - also played League football, for Carlisle. Ferguson was allowed to leave Stamford Bridge in May 1930 and join Third Division South side Queens Park Rangers, for whom he made 15 League appearances during the 1930/31 season. In the summer of 1931 he was signed by Wrexham, making his League debut in place of the injured Jack Hughes in a 4-0 home win against Rochdale. Chris made seventeen further League appearances, scoring four goals. However, he found himself back in the reserve team when Hughes was fit again, and consequently left the Racecourse to return South, joining Southern League side Guildford City. Chris spent two seasons with Guildford before playing for his works team, the Post Office Engineers' F.C., who were based at Beddington in Surrey.

Season	League		F.A.Cup		Welsh Cup		Total	
	apps	gls	apps	gls	apps	gls	apps	gls
1931/32	18	4	-	-	-	-	18	4
	18	**4**	-	-	-	-	**1**	**4**

FERGUSON, Donald

1986

Position; *Goalkeeper*
D.O.B; *2nd January, 1963*
Birthplace; *Toronto, Canada*
Height; *ft in* ***Weight;*** *st lbs*
Debut v. *Crewe Alexandra (a) 11th January, 1986*
Total Appearances & Goals; *22 apps 0 gls*
Career; *Mississanga United; Toronto First Portugese; WREXHAM Jan 1986; Ottawa Capitals cs1986; Ottawa Pioneers 1987; Ottawa Intrepid 1988;*
Honours; *Four Canadian International Caps; Three Canadian 'B' International caps;*

Canadian born Don Ferguson made many friends during his stay with Wrexham. In 1985 he paid his own fare to come to Britain for trials with both Crystal Palace and Luton Town. With Wrexham in need of a goalkeeper following the departure of Mike Hooper to Liverpool, manager Dixie McNeil gave Don a trial at the Racecourse, signing him on a non-contract basis in January 1986. He made his Football League debut in a 3-2 defeat at Crewe in January 1986, replacing of Mike Keen, and went on to accumalate twenty two League and Cup appearances for the 'Robins' before returning to Canada in the summer to join up with the Canadian World Cup squad. He made a total of four full international appearances for Canada, playing in two Merlion Cup matches in Singapore that summer, as well as in friendlies against El Salvador and Mexico. Prior to joining Wrexham Ferguson had played for Canada in the 1982 World Student Games in Mexico, while the following year he played twice against Bermuda in Olympic qualifying matches, and a couple of times against the United States in the Pan-American games. In 1984 he played three games for Canada in the Great Wall of China Tournament. Don would have appeared in more matches for his country but for the fact that they had about five other very good goalkeepers at that time. Don played for a number of Canadian teams: Toronto & District League side Mississanga United; Toronto First Portugese, who played in the National Soccer League of Ontario; and Ottawa Pioneers (later Ottawa Intrepid, the club changing its name 1987) of the Canadian Soccer League.

Season	League		F.A.Cup		Welsh Cup		League Cup		F.R.T.		Total	
	apps	gls	apps	gls	apps	gls	apps	gls	apps	gls	apps	gls
1985/86	20	0	-	-	-	-	-	-	2	0	22	0
	20	**0**	-	-	-	-	-	-	**2**	**0**	**22**	**0**

FIDLER, Frank

1950 - 1951

Position; *Centre-Forward*
D.O.B; *16th August, 1924*
Birthplace; *Middleton, Lancashire*
Height; *6ft 1'1/2in* ***Weight;*** *12st 8lbs*
Debut v. *Mansfield Town (h) 19th August, 1950*
Total Appearances & Goals; *38 apps 17 gls*
Career; *Manchester United Aug 1941 (WW2) 1app 0gls; Aldershot (WW2) Sep 1944 1app 0gls; Witton Albion; WREXHAM 27th May 1950; Leeds United 27th Oct 1951 22apps 8gls; Bournemouth Dec 1952 61apps 32gls; Yeovil Town Jul 1955; Hereford United Jul 1957; Bridgewater Town;*
Honours; *Cheshire County League Championship Winner 1949 & 1950;*

Frank Fidler's promising football career was disrupted with the outbreak of WW2, during which time he served with the Irish Guards. He also managed to turn out for Manchester United, making his first team debut in a 3-3 draw at New Brighton in September 1941 at the age of 17. It proved to be his only first team appearance for United, as he was to leave Old Trafford at the end of the conflict and try his luck with Cheshire County League side Witton Albion. Here he was spotted by Wrexham, having scored a remarkable 122 goals in just three seasons for the Cheshire County League side, a club record that still stands. He also collected two League championship winners' medals, in 1949 and 1950 before signing for the Racecourse club in May 1950. He began the following season as the club's first choice centre-forward, making his Football League debut in the opening game of the season, a 2-2 home draw with Mansfield Town. Frank went on to score 15 goals in

31 League and Cup games that term, and this form soon began to attract the interest of other League clubs. At the commencment of the 1951/52 campaign Fidler again featured prominently on the score sheet, with two goals in seven games, which was enough to prompt Second Division side Leeds United to step in to sign him. He made his debut for the Yorkshire club in a 3-2 win at Blackburn Rovers in October 1951, scoring one of the goals. He went on to spend just over a season with Leeds, during which he notched eight goals in 22 appearances before moving south to Bournemouth. Frank continued to score goals regularly for the 'Cherries', averaging a goal every two games, but surprisingly was allowed to leave Dean Court in the summer of 1954. Still only 30 he drifted into non-league football, spending two seasons with Yeovil Town, and three years with Hereford United, finishing his career with Bridgewater Town. By this time Frank was employed by Westlands in Yeovil, and later worked for the Post Office. He settled in Farnborough, Hampshire, where he was residing at the time of writing.

Season	League		F.A.Cup		Welsh Cup		Total	
	apps	gls	apps	gls	apps	gls	apps	gls
1950/51	29	13	-	-	2	2	31	15
1951/52	7	2	-	-	-	-	7	2
	36	**15**	**-**	**-**	**2**	**2**	**38**	**17**

FILSON, Robert Martin — 1989 - 1989

Position; *Centre-Half*
D.O.B; *25th June, 1968*
Birthplace; *Manchester, Lancashire*
Height; *5ft 11in* ***Weight;*** *12st 0lbs*
Debut v. *Stockport County (a) 1st May, 1989*
Total Appearances & Goals; *0/2 apps 0 gls*
Career; *Preston North End; WREXHAM Feb 1989; Bath City 12th Sep 1989; Rhyl 1990; Stalybridge Celtic Aug 1992 34/1apps 2gls; Halifax Town Jul 1993 £3,500 13apps 1gls; Dagenham & Redbridge Jan 1994 5apps 0gls; Caernarfon Town Sept 1994; Leek Town Aug 1995; Boston United Nov 1997; Northwich Victoria Aug 1998; Bangor City Sept 1998 3apps 2gls; Stalybridge Celtic Nov 1998;*
Honours; *Unibond Premier League Championship Winner 1997;*

Martin Filson became a Wrexham player after successfully completing a trial period at the club in January 1989, following his release by Preston North End. He had been retained on non-contract terms at Deepdale, having previously attended trials with both Blackpool and Tranmere Rovers. Martin impressed for Wrexham in a reserve team match at Rhos Aelwyd, and was quickly signed on similar terms in February 1989. A lanky centre-half Filson made his Football League debut for Wrexham in May 1989, coming on as a substitute for Steve Buxton at Stockport County in a 2-2 draw. His only other senior game for the 'Robins' was, coincidentally, also at Stockport, when he again came on as a substitute for Graham Cooper in a 1-0 defeat in the following season. A week later Martin decided to quit Wrexham due to lack of first team opportunities and take up an offer to join Beazer Homes League side Bath City. He later returned to North Wales, where he played for Rhyl, before joining Stalybridge Celtic for their first season in the Conference League. After twelve months Martin was signed by fellow Conference League side Halifax Town, for a club record fee received of £3,000, in the summer of 1993. He failed to make any real impact at The Shay, and decided to turn semi-pro again in January 1994 when the offer of first team football came from another Conference League side, Dagenham & Redbridge. Filson joined Caernarfon Town in January 1994, playing in their final match in English league football, ironically in Scotland against Gretna! At the end of the 1994/95 season he signed for Leek Town of the Unibond Premier League, where he was a member of the championship winning side in 1996/97. He finished the season as the club's second highest scorer with nine goals, following his emergency switch to the forward line due to an injury crisis. Martin left Leek in November 1997, after making twelve appearances, to join another Unibond Premier League side, Boston United, where he remained for the rest of the campaign. He left the Lincolnshire club in the summer of 1998 to sign for Football Conference League side Northwich Victoria, in time for the beginning of 1998/99 season. However, his stay at the Drill Field was short, as in September 1998 he decided to return to North Wales and join League of Wales side Bangor City, for another short spell, signing for Stalybridge Celtic in November.

Season	League		F.A.Cup		Welsh Cup		League Cup		S.V.T.		Total	
	apps	gls	apps	gls	apps	gls	apps	gls	apps	gls	apps	gls
1988/89	0/1	0	-	-	-	-	-	-	-	-	0/1	0
1989/90	0/1	0	-	-	-	-	-	-	-	-	0/1	0
	0/2	**0**	**-**	**-**	**-**	**-**	**-**	**-**	**-**	**-**	**0/2**	**0**

FINDLAY, Alexander — 1932 - 1935

Position; *Right-Half*
D.O.B; *26th December, 1902*
Birthplace; *Wishaw, Strathclyde*
Died; *Bristol, October, 1985*
Height; *5ft 9in* ***Weight;*** *12st 0lbs*
Debut v. *Hull City (a) 29th August, 1932*
Total Appearances & Goals; *29 apps 6 gls*
Career; *Musselburgh Rose 1926; Musselburgh Brutonians 1929; Bristol Rovers 12th Feb 1930 £35 37apps 9gls; WREXHAM 23rd Jul 1932; Cheltenham Town Aug 1935; Gloucester City;*
Honours; *Birmingham and District League Championship Winner 1933;*

Alex Findlay joined Wrexham during the close season of 1932 from Third Division South side Bristol Rovers. He had previously signed for the West Country club for a £35 transfer fee in February 1930 from Musselburgh Brutonians, having also turned out for Musselburgh Rose. Alex went straight into the 'Pirates' first team for his Football League debut against Norwich City in a 1-0 home defeat, and went on to score nine goals in a total of 37 League appearances for Rovers in just over two years. After moving to North Wales Alex made his first team debut in the second match of the season, at Hull, which Wrexham lost 4-1. He was not to feature again until the following term, although he did collect a Birmingham and District League Championship medal as a member of the second XI. 1933/34 saw Findlay reappear in the first team mid-way through the season, when he stepped in for the injured George Frewin, and played in Wrexham's 11-1 win over New Brighton in a Third Division North Cup match in January 1934. However, he returned to the reserves when Frewin was fit again. The following year saw the Scot record just four more appearances before leaving the club during the summer of 1935 to join Cheltenham Town. Alex later played for Gloucester City, where he lived for many years. He died in Bristol in October 1985, aged 82.

Season	League		F.A.Cup		Welsh Cup		N.S.C.		Total	
	apps	gls	apps	gls	apps	gls	apps	gls	apps	gls
1932/33	1	0	-	-	-	-	-	-	1	0
1933/34	17	3	-	-	1	0	3	1	21	4
1934/35	4	1	1	1	1	0	1	0	7	2
	22	**4**	**1**	**1**	**2**	**0**	**4**	**1**	**29**	**6**

FINNEGAN, Richard Prytherch — 1922 - 1924 & 1929 - 1932

Position; *Goalkeeper*
D.O.B; *16th May, 1904*
Birthplace; *Wrexham, Denbighshire*
Died; *Halton, Cheshire, O/N/D 1979*
Height; *6ft 0in* ***Weight;*** *11st 4lbs*
Debut v. *Tranmere Rovers (h) 17th March, 1923*
Total Appearances & Goals; *118 apps 0 gls*
Career; *Oswestry Town; Holyhead Town; Connah's Quay & Shotton; WREXHAM 30th Aug 1922; Holyhead Town Sept 1924; Connah's Quay & Shotton 29th Aug 1925; Manchester City 4th May 1926 8apps 0gls; Accrington Stanley 23rd May 1927 42apps 0gls; Connah's Quay & Shotton 5th Sept 1928; WREXHAM 17th May 1929; Colwyn Bay United 27th Aug 1932; Chester 17th Feb 1933 13apps 0gls; Stockport County 17th Mar 1934 to June 1935 26apps 0gls; Winsford United Jun 1936; Bala Town 8th March 1939;*
Honours; *One Welsh international cap 1930; Welsh Cup Winner 1929 & 1931; Third Division North Challenge Cup runner-up 1934; North Wales Coast F.A.Challenge Cup Winner 1929; North Wales Coast F.A.Challenge Cup runner-up 1925;*

Dick Finnegan began his football career playing in the newly-formed Welsh National League and local competitions in and around North Wales with Oswestry Town, Holyhead Town, and Connah's Quay & Shotton before signing for Wrexham as an amateur in August 1922. He was recruited as

cover for first choice goalkeeper George Godding, and made his Football League debut for 'The Robins', deputising for Godding, in a 2-1 home win over Tranmere Rovers in March 1923. He went on to record two more League appearances during his two seasons at the Racecourse before returning to Holyhead and Connah's Quay & Shotton. In May 1926 Finnegan was signed by Manchester City, as cover for another Welsh custodian, Bert Gray. He spent one season at Maine Road, making eight first team appearances, before joining Accrington Stanley in the summer. Dick made 42 league appearances for the Peel Park club having his contract cancelled in September 1928, following a clash with a club director on a journey home from a game at Rotherham. He then rejoined Connah's Quay & Shotton, where he appeared in their 1929 Welsh Cup winning side as they defeated Cardiff City 3-0. He was on the move again in the summer of 1929, as he re-signed for Wrexham, and over the next two and a half seasons was the club's regular 'keeper until losing his place to both Wilf Burrows and Ted Adams. During that time, he collected another Welsh Cup winners' medal in 1931, when Wrexham beat Shrewsbury Town 7-0. It was said of him at the time 'His form could vary from brilliant to erratic', which probably shows why he never stayed at a club longer than three years! Even so, he did win his one and only Welsh international cap in February 1930, when selected to play against Ireland in Belfast, although on this occasion he was on the wrong end of a 7-0 hammering!! Finnegan was released by the Racecourse club during the summer of 1932, and signed for Colwyn Bay United, where he spent just over one season until signed by the Chester, and formerly Wrexham's manager Charlie Hewitt in February 1933. Chester were only into their second season as a Football League club, and Dick was signed mainly as cover, which restricted him to just thirteen League appearances in little over a year at Sealand Road. In March 1934 he joined Stockport County, making his debut in a 4-1 home win over Barrow. Before the season had ended he had also played in the final of the Third Division North Challenge Cup at Old Trafford against Darlington, which County lost 4-3 having led 3-2 with just two minutes remaining! Finnegan went on to make a total of 26 League appearances for Stockport before leaving Edgeley Park and the Football League in June 1935. He finally played for Winsford United and Bala Town. Dick died in Halton, Cheshire, in 1979.

Season	League		F.A.Cup		Welsh Cup		Total	
	apps	gls	apps	gls	apps	gls	apps	gls
1922/23	2	0	-	-	-	-	2	0
1923/24	1	0	-	-	-	-	1	0
1929/30	41	0	5	0	3	0	49	0
1930/31	40	0	3	0	4	0	47	0
1931/32	17	0	-	-	2	0	7	0
	101	**0**	**8**	**0**	**9**	**0**	**118**	**0**

***FISHER,* Peter McArthur** 1951 - 1954

Position; *Left-Back*
D.O.B; *17th February, 1920*
Birthplace; *Edinburgh, Lothian*
Height; *5ft 10in* ***Weight;*** *11st 0lbs*
Debut v. *Southport (h) 29th October, 1951*
Total Appearances & Goals; *97 apps 0 gls*
Career; *Northampton Town Sep 1947 8apps 0gls; Shrewsbury Town Aug 1950 39apps 0gls; WREXHAM 20th Oct 1951; Bedford Town Jul 1954;*

Like so many other professional footballers, Peter Fisher's football career was disrupted by the outbreak of the Second World War. He had been playing in his native Scotland when Third Division South side Northampton Town handed him the opportunity to play in the English Football League. He signed for the 'Cobblers' in September 1947, and made his Football League debut in a 1-1 draw at Watford in January 1948. Peter made a further seven appearances that season, but failed to claim a first team outing in the following year and, not surprisingly, was to move on in the summer. In August 1950 he was signed by Shrewsbury Town, who were strengthening their team for their first season in the Football League. Peter had the honour of playing at left back in Shrewsbury Town's inaugural Football League match against Scunthorpe United. He went on to make a total of 39 League appearances for the Gay Meadow club before he was signed by Wrexham manager Peter Jackson in October 1951 in a unique four way deal: Peter and Eric Hope left Shrewsbury Town to join Wrexham, and Eddie Beynon and Ray Williams moved in the opposite direction. Peter was immediately installed in the 'Robins' first team at left back, replacing Charlie Kelsall, for the visit of top of the table Southport, a match which Wrexham won 3-1. He remained 'The Robins' regular left-back until October 1953, when displaced by summer signing and fellow Scot, Aly McGowan. Peter had been a regular fixture in the Wrexham defence as the side finished third in the League in 1952/53, and played in the memorable F.A.Cup match against First Division Stoke City, which Wrexham were very unlucky to lose 2-1. Once out of favour at the Racecourse he continued in the reserve team until the end of 1953/54, when he was allowed to leave the club. Peter then returned south to play non-league football with Bedford Town. It is understood that he later took up scouting for Northampton Town in the late 1950s.

Season	League		F.A.Cup		Welsh Cup		Total	
	apps	gls	apps	gls	apps	gls	apps	gls
1951/52	30	0	3	0	4	0	37	0
1952/53	37	0	1	0	-	-	38	0
1953/54	18	0	3	0	1	0	22	0
	85	**0**	**7**	**0**	**5**	**0**	**97**	**0**

***FLEET,* Stephen** 1963 - 1966

Position; *Goalkeeper*
D.O.B; *2nd July, 1937*
Birthplace; *Salford, Lancashire*
Height; *6ft 1'1/2in* ***Weight;*** *13st 1lbs*
Debut v. *Bristol Rovers (h) 11th September, 1963*
Total Appearances & Goals; *96 apps 0 gls*
Career; *Manchester City Feb 1955 5apps 0gls; WREXHAM 24th Jun 1963; Stockport County 10th Jan 1966 36apps 0gls; Altrincham cs1969;*
Honours; *Division Four Championship Winner 1967; Welsh Cup runner-up 1965;*

Steve Fleet played at either centre-half or goalkeeper during his early school days at Ordsall School in his native Salford, but it was in the latter position that he represented both Salford and Lancashire Schoolboys. An all-round sportsman, Steve also represented his County at cricket at schoolboy level. At 15, he was signed by Bolton Wanderers as an amateur, playing in their junior sides before leaving Burnden Park to take up offer to join Manchester City, also on amateur forms. He was appearing for City in their Central League side at the age of 16, signing professional in February 1955. Steve's progress at that time was hindered by the presence of the great Bert Trautmann, but his career came to a halt in 1956 when he was called up for his National Service. Enlisting in the R.A.F. he was stationed at Bridgnorth, Shropshire, which enabled him to travel back most weekends to play for City. He also appeared in representative matches for the R.A.F., and while still serving made his Football League debut for City, replacing Bert Trautmann in a 4-3 defeat at Maine Road against Wolves in November 1957. Steve returned to Maine Road upon being demobilised, but his first team opportunities were limited and he was to make just four more League appearances in six years before allowed to leave in June 1963. The arrival of Harry Dowd had pushed Steve even further down the City 'pecking order'. Wrexham manager Ken Barnes, a former team mate, returned to Maine Road to sign him for £3,500 as a replacement for the departed Kevin Keelan, and went on to spend two and a half years at the Racecourse. During that time Steve was always fighting to retain his first team place, with a number of 'keepers competing for the position- Alan Jones, Ken Simpkins and Albert Dunlop. The club were relegated at the end of his first season, and Fleet had the unwanted distinction of being the Wrexham goalkeeper on the day that the club suffered their heaviest League defeat, still a record, as Brentford demolished them 9-0 in October 1963 at Griffin Park. He helped Wrexham to reach the Welsh Cup final in the following season, where they lost to Cardiff City after a replay. Midway through the 1965/66 season, with re-election problems looming, Ken Barnes left the club and Jack Rowley was appointed the new manager. Rowley's first job was to exchange Fleet for Stockport County's Graham Beighton, plus a small cash adjustment, in January 1966. Steve made his County debut in a 4-0 defeat at Rochdale in April 1966. The following season saw him vying for the 'keeper's shirt with Ken Mulhearn, as Stockport won the Fourth Division Championship. The new season brought competition with Alan Ogley, and in the summer of 1969 he left Edgeley Park, after 36 League games, to join Altrincham as player/coach. While at Moss Lane Steve qualified as an F.A.Coach, and later returned to Stockport, first as youth team manager, and then as chief coach. He spent three more years at Edgeley Park before invited back to Manchester City as youth team coach. He completed eight years in the position before moving abroad in 1981 to Iceland, managing Akranes for one season, and occupying a similar position with rivals I.B.Vestmann. Two years later he returned to Britain, and took up work at Birmingham City as goalkeeping coach. In 1986 he returned once more to Maine Road, sampling various jobs including those of Sports' Development Officer and goalkeeping coach prior to taking on his present job of Director of City's School of Excellence, a role that involves managing City's Platt Lane Training Complex.

Season	League		F.A.Cup		Welsh Cup		League Cup		Total	
	apps	gls	apps	gls	apps	gls	apps	gls	apps	gls
1963/64	14	0	-	-	1	0	4	0	29	0
1964/65	33	0	2	0	5	0	-	-	40	0
1965/66	22	0	2	0	1	0	2	0	27	0
	79	**0**	**4**	**0**	**7**	**0**	**6**	**0**	**96**	**0**

FLYNN, Brian 1988 - 1992

Position; *Midfielder*
D.O.B; *12th October, 1955*
Birthplace; *Port Talbot, Glamorgan*
Height; *5ft 4in* **Weight;** *12st 0lbs*
Debut v. *Torquay United (h) 20th February, 1988*
Total Appearances & Goals; *94/8 apps 5 gls*
Career; *Sandfields Comprehensive School; Neath Boys; Afan Lido; Burnley Oct 1972 115/5apps 8gls; Leeds United 4th Nov 1977 £175,000 152/2apps 11gls; Burnley 6th Mar 1982 (Loan) 2apps 0gls; Burnley 17th Nov 1982 £60,000 76/4apps 11gls; Cardiff City 8th Nov 1984 £15,000 32apps 0gls; Doncaster Rovers 20th Nov 1985 27apps 0gls; Bury 25th Jul 1986 19apps 0gls; Limerick 6th Jan 1987; Doncaster Rovers 11th Aug 1987 18/6apps 1gls; WREXHAM 12th Feb 1988;*
Honours; *66 Welsh International Caps; Two Welsh Under-23 caps; Welsh Youth International Caps; Welsh Schoolboy International Caps; Welsh Cup runner-up 1988;*

The longest serving manager in Wrexham Football Club's history, Brian Flynn began playing football with his School team, Sandfields Comprehensive, from where he represented Neath Boys. He then linked up with Afan Lido, as well as signing as a schoolboy for Cardiff. However, following an administrative oversight he joined Burnley on apprentice forms in 1970, making his way through the ranks at Turf Moor to sign professional in October 1972. Brian had to wait for his Football League debut, which came in a First Division match against Arsenal, at Highbury, in a 1-1 draw in February 1974. Although small in stature 'Flynnie' was full of commitment, always willing to battle it out with the burliest of midfielders, and his tenacity perfectly complemented his smooth constructive skills. He soon established himself as a regular member of the Burnley first team and, in the process earned international recognition, making his senior Welsh debut at just 19 in November 1974 as a substitute against Luxembourg. His first full match for Wales soon followed, when he was selected to play against Scotland at Ninian Park, and scored a memorable goal as he finished off an intricate five man move. He went on to earn 66 full Welsh caps. Burnley suffered the pain of relegation in 1976, though Flynn remained for their first season in the Second Division. In November 1977 he signed for Leeds United for £175,000, and went on to spend five years at Elland Road, in which time he made over 150 League appearances. He had a loan spell back at Turf Moor in March 1982, and by the November of the same year had re-signed for Burnley for £60,000. Another two years at Turf Moor were followed by joining up with a former Welsh team-mate - Alan Durban- at Cardiff City. After twelve months at Ninian Park, where he made 32 League appearances for the 'Bluebirds', he moved to Doncaster Rovers, making 27 league appearances until signing for Bury in the summer of 1986. After nineteen League games at Gigg Lane a former colleague, Billy Hamilton, persuaded Flynn to join him at Irish League side Limerick as his player/coach in February 1987. By August Brian had re-signed for Doncaster Rovers, but was aleardy looking to the future, and played part-time for the Belle Vue club whilst working for the 'Football in the Community' scheme. In February 1988 Wrexham manager Dixie McNeil signed 'Flynnie' to assist in the 'Robins' promotion bid. He made his debut in a 3-2 home defeat by Torquay United in February 1988, going on to play his part in taking Wrexham to the 1988 Welsh Cup final, scoring one of the goals in the two legged semi-final with Kidderminster Harriers. 1988/89 saw Brian and Wrexham reach the final of the Play-Offs, but they disappointingly lost to Leyton Orient in the final. They began the following season disastrously, winning just three of their opening fourteen games, before manager Dixie McNeil resigned. Brian was handed the job of caretaker manager, and despite the fact that Wrexham failed to win any of their League games under his temporary charge, was appointed as the new club manager in November 1989. He immediately appointed Kevin Reeves as his assistant, and Joey Jones as player/coach, and together they master minded Wrexham's bid to avoid relegation to the Conference League. At the same time the foundations were laid for a successful youth policy, producing talented youngsters such as Chris Armstrong, Lee Jones, Phil Hardy, Bryan Hughes, Gareth Owen, Steve Watkin and Neil Wainwright. It was a difficult start for him, especially with the club's desperate financial situation, but was helped by the agreement that there would be no relegation in either the 1990/91 or 1991/92 seasons. The club finished bottom of the Football League in 1991, as 'Flynnie' wisely used the breathing space to rebuild for the future. The turning point came when he led Wrexham to that famous 2-1 F.A.Cup Third Round victory over Arsenal in 1992, and the following season took the club to promotion in 1993. The Welsh Cup followed in 1995, and Wrexham marched on to the Quarter-Finals of the F.A.Cup in 1997. On the international front, Brian was appointed manager of the Welsh Under-21 team by Mike Smith, and held the job, with Joey Jones as his assistant, until unceremoniously dismissed when Bobby Gould was appointed the new Welsh manager, a job which Brian has stated he would eventually love to do. At the time of writing Flynn is still the current Wrexham manager, having virtually rebuilt the whole structure of the club, adding a new state of the art training ground at Colliers Park in 1997, with facilities that are the envy of many clubs, and which have been used and praised by the likes of Italy, Glasgow Rangers and Barcelona. This more than anything shows how far the club has progressed since the dark days of the 1980s. Brian is now the longest serving manager in Wrexham Football Club's history, having overtaken John Neal's record in the close season of 1998. Only two of the League's current 92 managers have bettered his long service record; Manchester United's Alex Ferguson and Crewe's Dario Gradi. One thing is for certain, Brian Flynn will always be remembered with affection and pride in the history of Wrexham Football Club.

Season	League		F.A.Cup		Welsh Cup		League Cup		F.R.T.		E.C.W.C.		Total	
	apps	gls	apps	gls	apps	gls	apps	gls	apps	gls	apps	gls	apps	gls
1987/88	17	1	-	-	3	1	-	-	-	-	-	-	20	2
1988/89	38/3	1	1	0	3	0	2	0	4	0	-	-	48/3	1
1989/90	19/4	2	1	0	2	0	1/1	0	-	-	-	-	23/5	2
1990/91	10/1	1	-	-	2	0	-	-	1	0	4	0	17/1	1
1991/92	6	0	-	-	-	-	-	-	2	0	-	-	8	0
	90/8	**5**	**2**	**0**	**10**	**1**	**3/1**	**0**	**7**	**0**	**4**	**0**	**116/9**	**6**

FOGG, David 1970 - 1976

Position; *Left-Back*
D.O.B; *28th May, 1951*
Birthplace; *Liverpool, Merseyside*
Height; *5ft 9in* ***Weight;*** *11st 4lbs*
Debut v. *Plymouth Argyle (a) 27th February, 1971*
Total Appearances & Goals; *159/2 apps 0 gls*
Career; *Belvedere Boys Club; WREXHAM May 1970, (Pro) 18th Feb 1971; Oxford United Jul 1976 £2,000 289/4apps 16gls;*
Honours; *Welsh Cup Winner 1972 & 1975; Northern Floodlit League Cup Winner 1970; Alves Cup Winner 1970;*

Dave Fogg began playing football at Dingle Vale Secondary School in his native Liverpool. Although he never enjoyed a particularly distinguished schoolboy career it was when playing for Belvedere Boys' Club on both Saturdays and Sundays that he was spotted by Wrexham scout Jack Daniels. By this time Dave had left school, and had begun working as a toolmaker with English Electric in Liverpool. Wrexham's coach John Neal invited him for a trial at the start of the 1968/69 season, following which he signed apprenticeship forms for the club. He was one of a number of players to come through the successful junior ranks at the time; others included Billy Ashcroft, Graham Whittle, Joey Jones Mickey Thomas, Dave Smallman, Bob Scott etc. Dave was given his first team debut in February 1971, replacing Steve Ingle at right-back in a Welsh Cup tie at the Racecourse against Merthyr Tydfil, which Wrexham won 1-0. He made his Football League debut the following Saturday ina 2-2 draw at Plymouth. Yet it was almost another twelve months before he was to feature in the first team again, as he took over the left back berth vacated by the unlucky Tommy Vansittart, who had broken his leg. He then became established as Wrexham's regular left-back, occasionally switching to right-back, over the next four seasons. Dave played in Wrexham's famous F.A.Cup run of 1973/74, as well as the club's European Cup-Winners' Cup matches against F.C.Zurich, Hadjuk Split, Djurgardens and Anderlecht, against whom Wrexham came so

close to beating the eventual winners of the competition. Dave picked up two Welsh Cup winners' medals with Wrexham, in 1972 and 1975, but in July 1976 was surprisingly allowed to leave the club and join Oxford United for a bargain £2,000 fee when Alan Dwyer began to show promise in his position. He soon became an automatic choice at Oxford, and though he was played in a number of positions proved to be a consistent performer, capable of slotting in anywhere in the back-four. He was a regular in the 'U's' side for seven seasons, joining the coaching staff at the Manor Ground in 1983, before going on to help the club to promotion in successive seasons in the eighties. Dave ended his Football League playing career in 1986, just after Oxford had won the Milk Cup, and although not featuring in the Wembley final enjoyed his testimonial year at the club. After retiring he continued on the coaching staff at the Manor Ground, later becoming assistant manager to Brian Horton in 1988. He left Oxford in 1991 and joined the coaching staff at Everton, where he was employed as youth team coach, a position he held until the summer of 1996. Dave was then invited to join Kevin Ratcliffe at Chester, working in a similar capacity, a job with which he is still currently involved.

Season	League		F.A.Cup		Welsh Cup		League Cup		E.C.W.C.		Total	
	apps	gls	apps	gls	apps	gls	apps	gls	apps	gls	apps	gls
1970/71	1	0	-	-	1	0	-	-	-	-	2	0
1971/72	14	0	-	-	4	0	-	-	-	-	18	0
1972/73	35/1	0	3	0	1	0	-	-	4	0	43/1	0
1973/74	46	0	7	0	2	1	2	0	-	-	57	1
1974/75	35	0	1	0	4	0	1	0	-	-	41	0
1975/76	28/1	0	2/1	0	3	0	1/1	0	3	0	37/3	0
	159/2	**0**	**13/1**	**0**	**15**	**1**	**4/1**	**0**	**7**	**0**	**198/4**	**1**

FOSTER, Bertram Ernest 1919 - 1921

Position; *Half-Back*
D.O.B; *O/N/D 1898*
Birthplace; *Wrexham, Denbighshire*
Died; *Wrexham, 10th September, 1922*
Height; *5ft 9in* ***Weight;*** *11st 0lbs*
Debut v. *West Bromwich Albion Res (a) 14th February, 1920*
Football League debut v. *Hartlepool United (h) 27th August, 1921*
Total Appearances & Goals; *58 apps 7 gls*
Career; *WREXHAM (Am) cs1919, (Pro) 19th Feb 1920;*
Honours; *Welsh Schoolboy international; Welsh Cup Winner 1921; Welsh Cup runner-up 1920;*

Bert Foster was a native of Wrexham and attended the town's National Schools, from where he was selected to play for the Welsh Schoolboys against England at Stockport. However, at the age of seventeen he was enlisted by H.M.Forces for the First World War. He saw 'considerable service' in France and had the honour of being the crack shot of his Regiment (13th Welsh), for which feat he was awarded the Bronze medal. Bert was demobbed from the Army in 1919, and took up working as a clerk for Messrs. F.W.Soames & Co in Wrexham, later becoming the company's travelling sales representative. It was at around this time that he took up playing football again, as he joined Wrexham during the club's first season since the end of WW1. Playing at half-back he completed two seasons in the Birmingham League side, as well as helping the club to win the Welsh Cup in 1921 when they beat Pontypridd in the final. Following their election to the Football League in the close season of 1921 Bert played in Wrexham's first ever Football League match against Hartlepool United on the Racecourse. He managed just one more appearance in the first team, due to the signing of Jack Moorwood. At the start of 1922/23 Foster was playing in the Wrexham reserve team in the Birmingham League. He had reported for training on the Tuesday (5th Sept) and afterwards went to a local dance. He complained of having a chill, and was later diagnosed as suffering from pneumonia. Bert Foster sadly passed away on Sunday 10th September 1922, at the Turf Hotel in Wrexham, where his father was the manager. He was only 23 years-old.

Season	League		F.A.Cup		Welsh Cup		Total	
	apps	gls	apps	gls	apps	gls	apps	gls
1919/20	13	1	-	-	1	0	14	1
1920/21	34	4	3	2	5	0	42	6
1921/22	2	0	-	-	-	-	2	0
	49	**5**	**3**	**2**	**6**	**0**	**58**	**7**
F/League	2	0	-	-	-	-	2	0

FOSTER, Robert 1933 - 1935

Position; *Goalkeeper*
D.O.B; *1911 (April quarter)*
Birthplace; *Dean, nr Bolton, Lancashire*
Height; *5ft 10in* ***Weight;*** *11st 7lbs*
Debut v. *Darlington (a) 30th September, 1933*
Total Appearances & Goals; *35 apps 0 gls*
Career; *Farnworth Standard; Accrington Stanley 6th Jan 1932 11apps 0gls; Southampton 24th June 1932 1app 0gls; WREXHAM 12th Jun 1933; Bury 23rd Aug 1935 7apps 0gls; Oldham Athletic 15th Sept 1936 10apps 0gls; Mossley Nov 1937; Tranmere Rovers (WW2 Guest) 1941/42 15apps 0gls; Bolton Wanderers (WW2 Guest) 1941/42 3apps 0gls;*

Bob Foster joined Accrington Stanley from local non-league club Farnworth Standard, after the 'Stanley' senior goalkeeper, Jack Bell, had been sent off in a previous match. When Bell joined Bradford in March 1932 Bob again came to the rescue and took over in goal for the remainder of the season, making his Football League debut in a 3-1 defeat at Doncaster on 16th January 1932. During the summer of 1932 he signed for Second Division side, Southampton. Bob was understudy to Bert Scriven at the Dell, being called upon to deputise only once, in a home match against Port Vale which Southampton drew 2-2. At the end of that season he was signed by Wrexham manager, Ernie Blackburn, who had first recruited him when he was manager at Accrington. Bob had the best spell of his career at the Racecourse, taking over from Ted Adams during the 1933/34 season, until Adams won his place back the following year. Bob failed to make a first team outing during 1934/35, and he signed for Bury in the close season. He remained with the 'Shakers' for just over a year, but by this time he had set up his own newsagents' business in the Bolton area. He later received a call from Third Division North side Oldham Athletic to attend a trial, with a view to acting as cover for first team 'keeper, Lewis Caunce. Following two weeks on trial, he was given a contract for the rest of the season. In fact, he ousted Caunce from his first team spot for a short spell. Bob left Boundary Park at the end of the season, and played non-league football for Mossley whilst continuing with his business. During the Second World War he appeared as a 'guest' player for both Tranmere Rovers and Bolton Wanderers. He was said to have been a 'cool, safe and skilful goalkeeper'.

Season	League		F.A.Cup		Welsh Cup		N.S.C.		Total	
	apps	gls	apps	gls	apps	gls	apps	gls	apps	gls
1933/34	29	0	1	0	1	0	4	0	35	0
	29	**0**	**1**	**0**	**1**	**0**	**4**	**0**	**35**	**0**

FOX, Alan 1954 - 1964

Position; *Centre-Half*
D.O.B; *10th July, 1936*
Birthplace; *Holywell, Flintshire*
Height; *5ft 11in* ***Weight;*** *11st 6lbs*
Debut; *v. Crewe Alexandra (a) 12th April, 1954*
Total Appearances & Goals; *414 apps 3 gls*
Career; *Carmel United; WREXHAM 14th April 1954; Hartlepool United 9th Jun 1964 58apps 0gls; Bradford City Oct 1965 33apps 0gls; Dundalk cs1966; Limerick cs1969; Sligo Rovers;*
Honours; *Welsh under-23 international; Six Welsh Youth international caps; Welsh Cup Winner 1957, 1958 & 1960; Welsh Cup runner-up 1962; League of Ireland Championship Winner 1967; League of Ireland Shield Winner 1967;*

Alan Fox showed early promise as a footballer at Holywell County Primary and Flint Secondary Modern Schools. Upon leaving school he took up work as a painter and decorator, continuing to play football at right half for his local team, Carmel United. It was at this time that ex-Wrexham player Gib Bellis recommended Alan to the Racecourse club. He was invited for a trial match, and signed amateur terms in May 1953. He made his way through the junior ranks at Wrexham, showing plenty of promise, which earned him his Football League debut at Crewe in April 1954 at the age of seventeen, replacing the injured Ronnie Wynn. Fox was soon signed on professional terms, having already been capped by Wales at youth level on six occasions, three as skipper. Shortly after signing professional Alan was switched to centre-half with great success. However, over the next two seasons he figured mainly in the reserves until February 1956, when again he was given a first team chance. From that game, he missed very few matches over the next eight seasons, and also earned further international recognition by being capped at Welsh under-23 level in 1959 against Scotland. In 1958 he was named in the initial squad of forty players for the World Cup squad to play in Sweden, although not included in the final party. Alan was called up for his National Service at the beginning of September 1957, but was lucky enough to be stationed at Chester, with the Cheshire Regiment, meaning that he missed only a handful of games over the next two years, and also representing the Western Command. In December 1958 Fox was the subject of a rumoured move to Arsenal for £17,500 but, after much newspaper talk, nothing came of it. Alan collected three Welsh Cup winners' medals with Wrexham and also played in the club's most famous match of the 1950s, against Manchester United and the 'Busby Babes', in front of the biggest crowd ever recorded on the Racecourse. In 1958, he helped the club to reach the newly formed Third Division, and also played a prominent part in the promotion-winning side of 1962. Following relegation in 1964 he was surprisingly released by manager Ken Barnes, and, despite offers to join Luton, Oldham and West Brom, decided to stick by an old friend, Alvan Williams, who was manager at Hartlepool United. He moved to the Victoria Ground on a free transfer in June 1964, and spent just over a season with the North-East club, unaware at the time that he would to later settle in the town. In October 1965 he joined Bradford City, after being transferred by the Chairman! Fox spent the rest of the season with Bradford, where he completed 33 League matches. He left Valley Parade at the end of the season, and, following a recommendation by the PFA secretary Cliff Lloyd, joined League of Ireland club Dundalk as player/coach. The manager resigned after just three matches, and Alan was reluctantly put in charge. He then led the Irish side to the greatest season in their history, as they won the League and the Shield. The following campaign saw Dundalk in the European Cup, and in 1968/69 they became the first Irish League side to win on foreign soil when they overcame FC Utrecht 2-1 in the Fairs' Cup. Fox left Dundalk at the end of that season to join Limerick for a short spell, before playing a couple of games for Sligo Rovers. He then returned to live in Hartlepool, due to his daughter's illness. He never played football again, despite offers to play in Australia and America. Instead, he took up working for a local brewery, where he was employed for over twenty years. He later joined a company who supply welding equipment for oil rigs. Alan's son, Andrew, showed signs of following in his father's footsteps as a footballer when he joined Sunderland. Unfortunately, after signing pro for the Roker Park club his ambitions were shattered following five cartilage operations in one season! Alan Fox still lives in the Hartlepool area, and only recently attended the Wrexham AFC Players' Grand re-union. He is arguably the best centre-half to have played for the club.

Season	League		F.A.Cup		Welsh Cup		League Cup		Total	
	apps	gls	apps	gls	apps	gls	apps	gls	apps	gls
1953/54	1	0	-	-	-	-	-	-	1	0
1954/55	4	0	-	-	-	-	-	-	4	0
1955/56	17	0	-	-	1	0	-	-	18	0
1956/57	40	0	7	0	4	0	-	-	51	0
1957/58	38	0	1	0	4	0	-	-	43	0
1958/59	46	0	1	0	3	0	-	-	50	0
1959/60	43	0	3	0	6	0	-	-	52	0
1960/61	46	0	1	0	3	0	6	0	56	0
1961/62	44	1	3	0	6	0	1	0	54	1
1962/63	44	1	4	0	1	0	1	0	50	1
1963/64	27	1	3	0	2	0	3	0	35	1
	350	**3**	**23**	**0**	**3**	**0**	**11**	**0**	**414**	**3**

FOX, Stephen Douglas 1978 - 1982

Position; *Midfielder*
D.O.B; *17th February, 1958*
Birthplace; *Tamworth, Staffordshire*
Height; *5ft 8in* ***Weight;*** *11st 2lbs*
Debut v. *Preston North End (a) 26th December, 1978*
Total Appearances & Goals; *173/8 apps 19 gls*
Career; *Tamworth; Birmingham City Feb 1976 26/3apps 1gls; WREXHAM 21st Dec 1978 £95,000; Port Vale 22nd Oct 1982 71/3apps 6gls; Chester Jul 1984 29/4apps 4gls; Rhyl; Llangollen; Tamworth;*
Honours; *Welsh Cup runner-up 1979 & 1981; Division Four P.F.A.XI 1983;*

Steve Fox was playing for Tamworth at 15, while also appearing in the town's Mercian School team, from where he represented Birmingham

County schoolboys. He also played for Aston Villa Boys, Gillway Boys and Wiggington Juniors before Birmingham City scout Don Dorman persuaded him to sign apprentice terms for Birmingham City at the age of 16 in 1974. Fox spent almost four years at St.Andrew's, mainly as understudy to Trevor Francis, making his Football League debut for the 'Blues' in February 1977 as a substitute for Kevan Broadhurst in a 2-1 defeat at West Bromwich Albion. Steve went on to make another 28 League appearances for Birmingham, scoring one goal in a 2-1 home defeat by Newcastle United in April 1977. In December 1978 Wrexham manager Arfon Griffiths splashed out a £95,000 fee to sign him, and he made his debut in a 2-1 defeat at Preston North End on Boxing Day 1978. At the Racecourse Steve Fox proved to be an exciting player to watch, becoming very popular with the fans, but despite his undoubted ability, his off-the-field exploits sometimes let him down. He won the Wrexham 'Player of the Season' award in 1981, and figured in the famous F.A.Cup wins over Nottingham Forest and holders West Ham United, as well as playing in Europe against the East German side 1.F.C.Magdeburg. He stayed with Wrexham until just after the start of the 1982/83 season, following the club's relegation to the Third Division. Due to the crippling financial situation Wrexham could no longer afford to pay his Second Division wages, and he was allowed to join Port Vale on a free transfer! This after turning down the chance of going to Newcastle United for a trial. He helped the 'Valiants' to promotion in 1982/83, and was voted by his fellow professionals into the P.F.A`s Division Four side. The following season turned sour, however, as Steve soon found himself out of favour with the club's new manager. At the end of 1983/84 he rejoined his previous manager at Vale, John McGrath, at Chester. It proved to be a big mistake: when McGrath left Sealand Road, Harry McNally took over, and he and Steve quickly fell out with each other. Fox became an outcast at the club, a situation which eventually led to him having his contract cancelled by Chester in October 1985. He then sampled non-league football with Rhyl, Llangollen and Tamworth before finally giving up playing altogether. Steve later returned to settle in the Tamworth area, working as a gardener. A brother-in-law to Nigel Edwards. This former Chester and Wales U23 full back.

Season	League		F.A.Cup		Welsh Cup		League Cup		E.C.W.C.		Total	
	apps	gls	apps	gls	apps	gls	apps	gls	apps	gls	apps	gls
1978/79	21/1	1	3	0	3	1	-	-	-	-	27/1	2
1979/80	36/2	2	4	0	2	0	2	0	2	1	46/2	3
1980/81	35/3	6	4/1	2	5	3	-	-	-	-	44/4	11
1981/82	38	1	4	0	3	2	3/1	0	-	-	48/1	3
1982/83	6	0	-	-	-	-	2	0	-	-	8	0
	136/6	**10**	**15/1**	**2**	**13**	**6**	**7/1**	**0**	**2**	**1**	**173/8**	**19**

FOYNE, John

1933 - 1934

Position; *Outside-Left*
D.O.B; *23rd November, 1914*
Birthplace; *Chorlton, Manchester*
Died; *Withenshawe, 19th July, 1984*
Height; *ft in* ***Weight;*** *st lbs*
Debut v. *Gateshead (h) 7th October, 1933*
Total Appearances & Goals; *1 app 0 gls*
Career; *WREXHAM Sept 1933; Colwyn Bay United Nov 1933; Winsford United Jan 1934;*

John Foyne joined Wrexham in September 1933, and made his Football League debut the following month, replacing Harry Waller at outside-left in a 3-2 home defeat against Gateshead. That game proved to be John's one and only first team appearance for Wrexham, as he was allowed to leave the Racecourse in November 1933. He then signed for Birmingham and District League side Colwyn Bay United, where he made his debut in the coast side's defeat at Burton on November 25th. John Foyne is later known to have played Cheshire County League football for Winsford United.

Season	League		F.A.Cup		Welsh Cup		N.S.C.		Total	
	apps	gls	apps	gls	apps	gls	apps	gls	apps	gls
1933/34	1	0	-	-	-	-	-	-	1	0
	1	**0**	-	-	-	-	-	-	**1**	**0**

FRASER, Nathan James

1937 - 1938

Position; *Inside-Right*
D.O.B; *16th April, 1913*
Birthplace; *Kelvin, Strathclyde*
Died; *East Dorset, October, 1997*
Height; *6ft 0in* ***Weight;*** *11st 4lbs*
Debut v. *Hull City (a) 28th August, 1937*
Total Appearances & Goals; *21 apps 3 gls*
Career; *Ashfield (Glasgow); Blackburn Rovers Oct 1935 0apps; WREXHAM 14th Jun 1937; Dumbarton cs1938; Tranmere Rovers Oct 1938 1app 0gls to Dec 1938; Sunderland (WW2 Guest) 1942/43 1app 0gls;*

Nathan Fraser was playing football in his native Glasgow for local side Ashfield when signed by Blackburn Rovers in October 1935. Nathan spent two seasons at Ewood Park, during which he failed to record a Football League outing, although making a first team appearance in a Third Round F.A.Cup tie in January 1937, against Accrington Stanley. Nathan did manage to get on to the score sheet that day, scoring Rovers' second goal in a disappointing 2-2 draw. He was released by Blackburn at the end of the season, but was then quickly snapped up by Wrexham manager Captain James Logan. His assistant at the time was Arthur Cowell, a former coach of Nathan's at Ewood Park, who had recommended the signing. Fraser spent just one season at the Racecourse, making his Football League debut in the opening match of 1937/38, a 3-2 defeat at Hull. He went on to make a further twenty appearances for Wrexham at inside-right, with his best game coming in a 6-3 home win over Hartlepool United in September 1937 when he notched two goals. He returned to Scotland in the close season of 1938, joining Dumbarton, but his stay was short-lived because in October 1938 he signed for Tranmere Rovers. He was with the Prenton Park club for just two months, making a solitary League appearance in a 2-0 home defeat by Sheffield United. During World War Two Nathan made one 'Guest' appearance for Sunderland, at Middlesbrough in a 1-0 defeat in March 1943.

Season	League		F.A.Cup		Welsh Cup		N.S.C.		Total	
	apps	gls	apps	gls	apps	gls	apps	gls	apps	gls
1937/38	18	2	2	1	-	-	1	0	21	3
	18	**2**	**2**	**1**	-	-	**1**	**0**	**21**	**3**

FREWIN, George William

1932 - 1936

Position; *Inside-Right*
D.O.B; *6th February, 1907*
Birthplace; *Fulham, London*
Died; *Portsmouth, August 1984*
Height; *5ft 7'1/2in* ***Weight;*** *11st 0lbs*
Debut v. *Barnsley (h) 27th August, 1932*
Total Appearances & Goals; *102 apps 33 gls*
Career; *Fulham May 1929 0apps; Belfast Celtic cs1930; WREXHAM 20th Aug 1932; Venner Sports (London) 27th Jul 1936;*
Honours; *Welsh Cup runner-up 1933; Irish League Representative XI;*

George Frewin signed for Wrexham during the close season of 1932, moving to the Racecourse from the now defunct Belfast Celtic club, where he had gained representative honours for the Irish League against the Scottish League. George had previously been on the books of his local club side, Fulham, but had failed to make a first team appearance during his time at Craven Cottage. He was named in the Wrexham side for the first game of the season at inside-right against Barnsley on the Racecourse, and responded by scoring one of the goals in a 3-0 win. He kept his place in the side for the rest of the season, helping Wrexham to the Welsh Cup Final where they lost 2-0 to local rivals Chester. He was described as 'noted for his constructive play', although George was to find himself in and out of the side over the next three seasons, due mainly to the form of Jack Fryer. During his four seasons at the Racecourse he was 'noted for his constructive play'. He parted company with Wrexham at the end of the 1935/36 season, and is believed to have returned to his native London, where he continued to play football with non-league Venner Sports.

Season	League		F.A.Cup		Welsh Cup		N.S.C.		Total	
	apps	gls	apps	gls	apps	gls	apps	gls	apps	gls
1932/33	36	19	3	2	6	1	-	-	45	22
1933/34	25	4	1	0	-	-	1	0	27	4
1934/35	16	6	1	0	1	0	-	-	18	6
1935/36	11	1	-	-	1	0	-	-	12	1
	88	**30**	**5**	**2**	**8**	**1**	**1**	**0**	**102**	**33**

FRYER, John Leavy 1933 - 1937

Position; *Inside-Right*
D.O.B; *23rd September, 1911*
Birthplace; *Widnes, Cheshire*
Height; *5ft 10in* **Weight;** *11st 7lbs*
Debut v. *Darlington (a) 30th September, 1933*
Total Appearances & Goals; *92 apps 29 gls*
Career; *Runcorn; Everton (Am) May 1930, (Pro) May 1931 0apps; WREXHAM 18th May 1933; Hull City May 1937 40apps 23gls; Nottingham Forest Jun 1938 22apps 8gls;*

Jack Fryer began his football career playing junior football in Runcorn, where he was spotted by Everton. He then progressed to play for Everton's Central League side, although never making the first team in the three years that he spent at Goodison Park. After scoring 14 goals in 21 Central League games for Everton's reserves he was snapped up by Wrexham in the close season of 1933. His first season at the Racecourse again found him playing mainly in the reserve side, although he did make two Football League appearances in place of George Snow. His debut came in a 2-1 defeat at Darlington in September 1933, but he capped it by scoring the Wrexham goal. It was not until the October of the following season that he finally began to establish himself in the first team, when he replaced George Frewin in the side. From then on Jack became a regular fixture in the first team, playing at either inside-right or at centre-forward. He was described as 'a well-built attacker, with progressive ideas, which included plenty of hard shooting.' However, he was to lose his place in the team in October 1936 to Alf White. Fryer never regained his place, and joined former Wrexham manager, Ernie Blackburn, at Hull City during the close season of 1937. Fryer got off to a great start with Hull City when he scored two goals on his debut, in a 3-2 win over.....Wrexham! He did well at Hull, scoring 23 goals in 40 League games, and soon attracted the attention of Second Division Nottingham Forest, who signed him in June 1938. Jack scored once again on his debut for his new side, in a 2-1 defeat at Burnley on 3rd September 1938. He made a further 21 appearances for Forest, scoring seven more goals before leaving the County Ground at the end of the 1938/39 season.

Season	League		F.A.Cup		Welsh Cup		N.S.C.		Total	
	apps	gls	apps	gls	apps	gls	apps	gls	apps	gls
1933/34	2	1	-	-	-	-	1	0	3	1
1934/35	29	7	1	2	2	0	2	1	34	10
1935/36	41	16	1	0	1	0	2	0	45	16
1936/37	10	2	-	-	-	-	-	-	10	2
	82	**26**	**2**	**2**	**3**	**0**	**5**	**1**	**92**	**29**

FUTCHER, Stephen Aaron 1995 - 1997

Position; *Midfield*
D.O.B; *24th October, 1976*
Birthplace; *Chester, Cheshire*
Height; *6ft 0in* **Weight;** *11st 7lbs*
Debut v. *Petrolul Ploiesti (h) 10th August, 1995 (E.C.W.C)*
Total Appearances & Goals; *2 apps 0 gls*
Career; WREXHAM Jul 1993, (Pro) 4th Jul 1995; Sligo Rovers 6th Dec 1996 (Loan); Gresley Rovers Feb 1997; Connah's Quay Nomads 4th Jul 1997 55/2apps 6gls; Cwmbran Town 31st Jul 1999;
Honours; *Three Welsh Youth International Caps; Welsh Cup runner-up 1998; Welsh Youth Cup Winner 1994; Welsh National Division Two Championship Winner 1994; Welsh Youth Cup runner-up 1995;*

Steve Futcher was born into a footballing family; his father Graham played League football for Chester during 1971/72, clocking up ten League appearances, and his more famous uncles- the Futcher twins, Ron and Paul - also played for Chester and Luton Town in the 1970s. Steve attended school at Christleton, where he progressed at football to play for Chester Schoolboys at under-15 and 16 levels. He later played for the Cheshire Schoolboys team, and it was at this time that several League clubs began to show an interest in him. Offers came from Liverpool, Aston Villa and Manchester City, but as a schoolboy he had been on the books of Crewe Alexandra. Steve later switched to Wrexham at 15, though upon leaving school was offered the chance of a YTS place with Manchester City. He turned it down to join 'The Robins', where he thought he would have a better opportunity to make the grade. His first term was spent playing for the Wrexham Colts team in the Welsh National League, and they won the championship. He also appeared in the club's Welsh Youth Cup winning side as they beat Swansea City 4-1 at Llanidloes. The following season Steve was selected for the Welsh Youth team for the European Championships in Italy, against the hosts and Lithuania, qualifying to play for Wales courtesy of his Welsh grandmother. Steve also played in the F.A.Youth Cup match at Old Trafford which Wrexham lost 4-1. He signed a professional contract at the end of the 1994/95 season, and the beginning of the new campaign brought an added bonus, through his Welsh qualification, of being eligible to play in both of the European Cup-Winners' Cup matches against the Romainian side, Petrolul Ploiesti. 'A good passer of the ball' Steve never really made an impression on the first XI after that, and in December 1996 he travelled to Southern Ireland to play for Irish League side Sligo Rovers. Upon returning to Wrexham he was informed that he would be released at the end of the season. However, he wanted to establish himself at a new club as soon as possible, and in February 1996 joined his uncle, Ron Futcher, who was manager of Gresley Rovers. Steve made a couple of appearances for Gresley, but left because of the travelling involved, and before he could see them claim the Dr.Marten's League Championship. He signed for League of Wales side Connah's Quay Nomads in the summer of 1997, where he was to help them reach the final of the Welsh Cup in his first season. The match against Bangor City had ended 1-1 after extra time, with Steve having the consolation of scoring the 'Nomads' goal. He eventually had to endure the pain of defeat when Bangor won on penalties. Steve joined Cwmbran Town in the close season of 1999, and played for them against Celtic in the U.E.F.A. Cup.

Season	League		F.A.Cup		Welsh Cup		A.G.T.		E.C.W.C.		Total	
	apps	gls	apps	gls	apps	gls	apps	gls	apps	gls	apps	gls
1995/96	-	-	-	-	-	-	-	-	2	0	2	0
	-	-	-	-	-	-	-	-	**2**	**0**	**2**	**0**

Arfon Griffiths

GARDINER, Archibald

1934 - 1936

Position; *Centre-Forward*
D.O.B; *17th March, 1913*
Birthplace; *Penicuik, Lothian*
Height; *5ft 9in* **Weight;** *11st 0lbs*
Debut v. *York City (a) 27th October, 1934*
Total Appearances & Goals; *51 apps 13 gls*
Career; *Burnbank Athletic; Penicuik Athletic; Clapton Orient (trial); Hearts May 1931 24apps 14gls; Leicester City Feb 1934 £1,000 18apps 11gls; WREXHAM 25th Oct 1934; Hamilton Academicals Aug 1936 £300 11apps 4gls; Lille Olympique; Brideville cs1937; Inverness Thistle Dec 1937;*

Archie Gardiner had played for Scottish Junior clubs Burnbank Athletic and Penicuik Athletic when deciding to try his luck South of the Border with a trial at Clapton Orient. Nothing came of it and he returned home to Scotland, joining Hearts in May 1931. Archie spent almost three seasons with the Edinburgh club as understudy to the Scottish international centre-forward, and goalscoring legend, 'Barney' Battles. He impressed enough at Tynecastle for Leicester City to pay out £1,000 for him in February 1934, and made a terrific start at Filbert Street, scoring four goals on his debut in a 5-3 away win at Portsmouth. This was followed two matches later with a hat-trick against the champions elect, Arsenal! All told, Archie scored 15 goals in 10 First Division matches for Leicester before the end of the season. He also appeared in Leicester's first ever F.A.Cup Semi-Final, when they lost 4-1 to Portsmouth. The following campaign Archie managed just three appearances before he was surprisingly allowed to leave 'The Foxes' and sign for Wrexham manager Ernie Blackburn in October 1934. He was brought in to replace the club's all-time record goalscorer, Tommy Bamford, who had just moved to Manchester United. Archie went straight into the first team for his debut at York City, in a scoreless draw, but on his home debut in the following match he scored a hat-trick in a 4-0 win over Darlington. He kept his first team place for the rest of the season, missing only the odd game, and scoring ten goals in 24 matches. He failed to live up to the fans' expectations following the loss of Bamford, however, and the 1935/36 season saw him eventually replaced in the side by Charles McCartney, although he returned to the first team in late September at inside-forward for a spell. Archie was to leave the Racecourse in the close season and return to his native Scotland, signing for Hamilton Academicals for a £300 transfer fee. His next move was to the continent signing for French side Lille Olympique. After a short spell he travelled to Ireland, to link up with Brideville, returning to Scotland in December 1937 to end his career with Inverness Thistle. In May 1938 Archie was jailed for four months for 'committing a felony and assaulting two Police Officers'. He had previously served a Borstal sentence before he joined Hearts. His father, Harry, also played professional football for both Bolton Wanderers and Rangers, and had the honour of selection for a Football League XI to play in the first ever match against the Scottish League in 1892.

Season	League		F.A.Cup		Welsh Cup		N.S.C.		Total	
	apps	gls	apps	gls	apps	gls	apps	gls	apps	gls
1934/35	24	10	2	0	-	-	1	0	27	10
1935/36	21	2	1	0	1	1	1	0	24	3
	45	**12**	**3**	**0**	**1**	**1**	**2**	**0**	**51**	**13**

GARDNER, David Scott

1997

Position; *Midfielder*
D.O.B; *17th September, 1976.*
Birthplace; *Salford, Lancashire*
Height; *5ft 9in* **Weight;** *11st 0lbs*
Debut v. *Crewe Alexandra (h) 28th January, 1997 (A.W.S.)*
Total Appearances & Goals; *0/1 app 0 gls*
Career; *Manchester United Jul 1993; Manchester City 1st Jul 1995; WREXHAM Dec 1996 (trial), 27th Jan 1997; Witton Albion Aug 1997; Stalybridge Celtic Aug 1998; Morecambe Oct 1998;*
Honours; *F.A.Youth Cup Winner 1995;*

David Gardner was first spotted by Manchester United as a schoolboy in his native Salford. He was playing for a local junior side, Barr Hill, at the age of ten, when Brian Kidd invited him to join United's School of Excellence, where he remained until he was 14. He was then signed by United as an Associate Schoolboy for the next two years eventually being offered a YTS place at Old Trafford when he turned 16. It was whilst playing for the youth team that David collected a F.A.Youth Cup winners' medal, as United beat Spurs in the final 4-3 on penalties. He appeared mostly for the two Lancashire League sides at United, although he did play in the occasional Pontin's League game. Unfortunately, he picked up a couple of injuries in the second year of his Y.T.S., which resulted in his release. He was contacted by Manchester City on the day after he left Old Trafford, and offered a one year professional deal by manager Brian Horton. His father, Geoff, had once been on the books of the Maine Road club. A change of manager saw Alan Ball clear out a number of players from Maine Road in the summer of 1996, and these included David. He then had a month's trial with Birmingham City, which came to nothing, followed by two weeks training with Nottingham Forest, which again proved fruitless. A conversation between Ryan Giggs (who is a great friend of Gardner's) and Wrexham manager Brian Flynn secured David a trial with 'The Robins' in December, and he signed non-contract terms the following month . It was that same month in which Gardner made his one and only first team appearance for Wrexham, coming off the substitute's bench to replace David Brammer in an Auto-Windscreens Shield match with Crewe Alexandra. David spent the last ten minutes trying to force the tie into extra-time, but Wrexham lost 1-0. He remained at the Racecourse until the end of the season without making a further first team appearance, following which he was released. He went on to spend a season with Unibond League Division One side Witton Albion which was followed by joining Stalybridge Celtic for the start of the 1998/99 campaign. His time with them was short as he re-joined Morecambe in October.

Season	League		F.A.Cup		League Cup		A.W.S.		Total	
	apps	gls	apps	gls	apps	gls	apps	gls	apps	gls
1996/97	-	-	-	-	-	-	0/1	0	0/1	0
	-	-	-	-	-	-	**0/1**	**0**	**0/1**	**0**

GARDNER, Thomas

1945 - 1947

Position; *Wing-Half*
D.O.B; *28th May, 1910*
Birthplace; *Huyton, Merseyside*
Died; *Chester, February, 1970*
Height; *5ft 9'1/2in* **Weight;** *11st 1lbs*
Debut v. *New Brighton (h) 31st August, 1946*
Total Appearances & Goals; *52 apps 6 gls*
Career; *Orrell 1926; Liverpool (Am) Aug 1928 (Pro) Apr 1929 5apps 0gls; Grimsby Town Jun 1931 13apps 0gls; Hull City May 1932 66apps 2gls; Aston Villa Feb 1934 £4,500 77apps 1gls; Burnley Apr 1938 39apps 3gls, WW2 218apps 46gls; Blackpool (WW2 Guest) Mar 1943 5apps 3gls; Manchester United (WW2 Guest) Apr 1944 1app 0gls; Preston North End (WW2 Guest) 1941/2 1app 0gls; Southport (WW2 Guest) 1943/44 2apps 0gls; Blackburn Rovers (WW2 Guest) May 1945 3apps 1gls; WREXHAM 18th Dec 1945; Wellington Town Aug 1947; Oswestry Town player/manager 1950; Saltney 31st Oct 1952;*
Honours; *Two England International Caps; Third Division North championship Winner 1933; Football League North Cup Winner 1943;*

Tommy Gardner began his football career with Orrell F.C. when he was just 16. He spent two years at the club before attracting interest from Liverpool, signing for them in 1928 an amateur before turning professional in April 1929. He made his Football League debut for Liverpool in January 1930 in a 1-0 victory against Manchester United at Anfield. Tom played four more first team games for the Anfield Club before joining Grimsby Town in the summer of 1931, where he made just thirteen League appearances. Twelve months later he moved on to Hull City, becoming a regular in 'The Tigers' first team and assisting them to the Third Division North championship in 1933. This brought him to the notice of Aston Villa, for whom he signed in February 1934. Gardner spent just over four years at Villa Park, during which time he won two full

England caps: against Czechoslovakia in 1934, and Holland in 1935. In April 1938 he was allowed to join Burnley, and remained with the 'Clarets' until signing for Wrexham in December 1945 for what was described as a 'record fee'. During WW2 Tom played regularly for Burnley, making over 200 appearances, as well as appearing as a 'Guest' for several other North-West clubs, including Blackpool, where he scored a crucial winning goal against Sheffield Wednesday in the 1943 League North War-time Cup final. Blackpool were a prominent side at this time, due to the large R.A.F. base nearby. Having signed for Wrexham at the end of the hostilities, he finished the season at the Racecourse before the Football League was re-introduced for 1946/47. Manager Tom Williams, decided to switch Tommy from his normal right-half position to that of outside-right, and continued in that role throughout the season, Wrexham ending it in a comfortable seventh position. He was allowed to leave the Racecourse in the summer, and joined Wellington Town. He spent almost three years at the 'Bucks Head' before becoming player/manager of Oswestry Town in 1950, followed by a spell as player/coach at the Shropshire club. He joined Saltney in October 1952, and was appointed as the assistant-trainer at Chester in July 1954, a position he held until the mid-1960s. In May 1967, he became steward of a Chester social club, later taking over an hotel in Wrexham. A keen billiards player, Tommy died in 1970 aged just 60. He was described during his career as 'an enthusiastic player, who was a long throw specialist, winning a Daily Mail competition in September 1932 with a throw of 32 yards, 2 inches' (remember, the ball was a lot heavier in those days!).

Season	League apps	gls	F.A.Cup apps	gls	League Cup apps	gls	A.W.S. apps	gls	Total apps	gls
1945/46	12	0	2	0	-	-	11	1	15	1
1946/47	33	4	3	1	1	0	-	-	37	5
	45	**4**	**5**	**1**	**1**	**0**	**11**	**1**	**52**	**6**
F/League	33	4	5	1	1	0	-	-	37	5

GASKELL, John David

1969 - 1972

Position; *Goalkeeper*
D.O.B; *5th October, 1940*
Birthplace; *Wigan, Lancashire*
Height; *5ft 11'1/2in* ***Weight;*** *10st 12lbs*
Debut v. *Exeter City (h) 9th August, 1969*
Total Appearances & Goals; *117 apps 1 gls*
Career; *Manchester United Oct 1957 137apps; Wigan Athletic Aug 1968 35apps 0gls; WREXHAM 11th Jun 1969 £2,500; South Africa 31st Jul 1973;*
Honours; *England Schoolboy international; England Youth international; F.A.Cup Winner 1963; F.A.Charity Shield Winner 1956; Welsh Cup runner-up 1971; Division Four runner-up 1970;*

David Gaskell joined his boyhood heroes Manchester United at the age of 15 after gaining England Schoolboy and Youth caps. Dave experienced a fairy-tale start at Old Trafford when, having finished his shift as an electrical engineer at Trafford Park, he went to watch United at Maine Road in the 1956 Charity Shield match against rivals Manchester City to be told on arrival that he was actually playing! Regular first team 'keeper Ray Wood had been injured in the pre-match warm up, so, at the age of 15, Dave made his United debut, keeping a clean sheet in a 1-0 win. Thereafter, he continued to learn his trade away from the limelight before making his First Division debut in November 1957 in a 4-3 home defeat against Tottenham Hotspur. Gaskell went on to make a total of 137 Football League appearances for United, collecting an F.A.Cup winners' medal in the 1963 final against Leicester City. He also enjoyed plenty of European action, as well as gaining England Youth team honours. However, between 1966 and 1968 David experienced difficulties with the Old Trafford management, and played Rugby Union for Orrell before returning to soccer with non-league side Wigan Athletic, after United had blocked several moves to other clubs. Gaskell made 35 Northern Premier League appearances for Wigan, as they finished runners-up in the League. In June 1969 Wrexham manager John Neal persuaded him to join the Racecourse staff for a £2,500 fee, with Dennis Reeves joining Wigan as part of the deal. Dave made his debut for Wrexham in the opening match of 1969/70 as Wrexham beat Exeter City 3-0. His first season saw him miss just one match as Wrexham gained promotion to the Third Division as runners-up. The following year was to see Dave pick up a Welsh Cup runners-up medal as Wrexham lost to Cardiff City in the Final, Gaskell having scored with a penalty in an earlier round against Porthmadog. The 1971/72 season turned out to be Gaskell's last in professional football, as he injured a knee in a collision with Aston Villa's Andy Lochhead in a League Cup tie at the beginning of the season. Although eventually making a short comeback he decided to retire from professional football. Dave then went on to play and coach in South Africa, before heading home to take a job as a salesman for a mineral water company. Following his retirement from football Gaskell kept up his involvment with other sports by playing rugby for Wrexham Rugby Club, and Cricket for both Wrexham and Marchwiel during the summer. In October 1982 he turned out in goal for a short time with Lex XI in the Welsh National League. Prior to this he had returned to football as coach of Kuwait Division One side Sulaibikhat Sporting Club, where he spent two seasons in the late 1970s. He returned to settle in Wrexham, finding work as a salesman for a concrete making firm, before becoming the North-West regional manager of a flooring company. The number of accumulated injuries from his playing days forced him to take early retirement in 1992. Since then, he has undergone a series of operations on his knee, just to enable him to walk. Although not fully recovered, he still enjoys playing bowls regularly on his local green in Wrexham.

Season	League apps	gls	F.A.Cup apps	gls	League Cup apps	gls	A.W.S. apps	gls	Total apps	gls
1969/70	45	0	4	0	2	0	4	0	55	0
1970/71	39	0	-	-	5	1	2	0	46	1
1971/72	11	0	1	0	2	0	2	0	16	0
	95	**0**	**5**	**0**	**9**	**1**	**8**	**0**	**117**	**1**

GIBSON, Robin John

1998 -

Position; *Outside-Right*
D.O.B; *15th November, 1979.*
Birthplace; *Crewe, Cheshire*
Height; *5ft 5in* ***Weight;*** *10st 0lbs*
Debut v. *Hull City (a) 5th January, 1999 (Auto Windscreen Shield)*
Total Appearances & Goals; *5/8 apps 1 gls*
Career; *WREXHAM 1st Jul 1996 (Y.T); 1st Jul 1998 (Pro);*

Robin Gibson attended the Victoria Community High School in Crewe from where he showed lot's of promise as a footballer, representing Crewe, South Cheshire and Cheshire Schoolboys sides. He also played for Wolverton Albion in Junior League football, and it was from playing for these sides that he was invited to become a member of Crewe Alexandra's School of Excellence. At the age of 14 he signed schoolboy forms for the Gresty Road club, but when he came to leave school he was

turned down for a Y.T.S. place as he was considered to be too small!! A number of clubs then showed an interest in taking him on with Rochdale, Manchester City, and Wrexham all offering him a position on Y.T.forms. Robin decided to accept Wrexham's offer, and he signed for the club in July 1996. He then progressed through the youth ranks at the Racecourse to sign professional terms in July 1998. Playing mainly as an outside-right, a position from which he enjoys to take defenders on, he continued to make rapid progress, and manager Brian Flynn gave him his first team debut for the 'Robins' in an Auto Windscreen Shield match against Hull City at Boothferry Park. An encouraging performance by Gibson prompted Wrexham's assistant manager Kevin Reeves to say after Wrexham's 2-1 win, "It was a very good debut for Robin, and he was probably our best player on the night." However a serious knee injury against Wigan Athletic in the A.W.S. Northern Final saw his season come to a premature end. Despite this setback his future lies very much in his own hands.

Season	League		F.A.Cup		W.P.C.		League Cup		A.W.S.		Total	
	apps	gls	apps	gls	apps	gls	apps	gls	apps	gls	apps	gls
1998/99	3/4	1	0/1	0	-	-	-	-	2/3	0	5/8	1
	3/4	**1**	**0/1**	**0**	**-**	**-**	**-**	**-**	**2/3**	**0**	**5/8**	**1**

GILES, David Charles

1978 - 1979

Position; *Midfielder*
D.O.B; *21st September, 1956*
Birthplace; *Cardiff, Glamorgan*
Height; *5ft 7in* ***Weight;*** *10st 5lbs*
Debut v. *Preston North End (a) 26th December, 1978*
Total Appearances & Goals; *38 apps 3 gls*
Career; *Cardiff City Sep 1974 51/8apps 3gls; WREXHAM 21st Dec 1978 £30,000; Swansea City 27th Nov 1979 £70,000 49/5apps 13gls; Leyton Orient Nov 1981 (Loan) 3apps 2gls; Crystal Palace Mar 1982 83/5apps 6gls; Birmingham City Aug 1984 0apps; Newport County 5th Oct 1984 (Loan), 6th Nov 1984 28/4apps 1gls; Cardiff City Sep 1985 50apps 0gls; Barry Town Feb 1987; Merthyr Tydfil Aug 1988; Newport County Nov 1988; Sully FC Mar 1989; AFC Cardiff cs1989; Abergavenny Thursdays Feb 1990; Stroud FC 1991; Barri cs1992; Inter Cardiff 1992/93 7/7apps 0gls; Ebbw Vale cs1993 26/6apps 1gls; Barry Town cs1995 0/1app 0gls;*
Honours; *12 Full Welsh international caps; 4 Welsh Under-21 caps; Welsh Schoolboy international; Welsh Cup Winner 1976; Welsh Cup runner-up 1975, 1977 & 1979;*

David Giles was spotted by Cardiff City as a 10 year-old and asked to train with their teenagers. He continued his already rapid progress, playing for the Welsh Schoolboys team, to sign apprentice terms with the 'Bluebirds', and made his senior debut in a Welsh Cup match with Oswestry Town. He signed professional terms in July 1974, and went on to gain further international recognition with the Welsh under-21 team. Despite this promising start to his career, Giles never really established himself as a regular at Ninian Park, but did play in some of the club's important matches, like the epic F.A.Cup Fourth Round tie with Wrexham in 1977, in which he scored City's opening goal, and in the club's European adventures. His younger brother, Paul, also played League football for Cardiff. In December 1978, David left Ninian Park and moved to the Racecourse for a fee of £30,000, and made his debut along with Steve Fox in a 2-1 home defeat by Preston North End on Boxing Day 1978. He remained in the first team throughout his time at the Racecourse, picking up a Welsh Cup runners'-up medal in his first season, and playing against 1.F.C.Magdeburg in the European Cup-Winners' Cup the following term. However, his time in North-East Wales was soured by the fact that he and Steve Fox occasionally found themselves making headlines for the wrong reasons. Even so, Giles was always a busy hard working midfield player on the field, and well liked by the club's fans, although it came as no real surprise when manager Arfon Griffiths allowed him to join Swansea City in November 1979 for a £70,000 fee. David went on to spend three years at the Vetch, during which time he won the first of his twelve full caps for Wales, against England. A £400,000 offer from Crystal Palace was turned down as he assisted the 'Swans' in their promotion drive to the First Division in 1981, though eventually leaving the Vetch to join Crystal Palace in March 1982, following a loan spell with Orient in November 1981. After just over two seasons at Selhurst Park Giles joined Birmingham City, but within a short time had completed a unique feat of playing League football for all four Welsh Football League clubs by joining Newport County. A season at Somerton Park was followed by another spell with his first club, Cardiff City. In 1987 Giles drifted into non-league football with Barry Town, followed by a spell with Conference League side Merthyr Tydfil between August and November 1988. He returned to Newport County in January 1989 for a £1,000 fee, before they were finally wound-up in March 1989. David then went on to play for a number of South Wales non-league teams that included Sully, AFC Cardiff, where he was player/manager, Abergavenny Thursdays and Stroud. He then appeared for the Welsh exiles, Barri, in the Beazer Homes League during 1992/93, and League of Wales side Ebbw Vale in 1993/94, taking over as their player/manager in the close season of 1994. A year later David was appointed the joint manager of Barry Town together with his brother Paul, and they led them to the League of Wales title and to the Welsh Cup Final. However, at the end of the term the Giles brothers were shocked when they were surprisingly relieved of their duties. David returned to Ebbw Vale, where he became the club's assistant manager to John Lewis, and the 1996/97 season saw them lead the Gwent club into Europe by qualifying for the Inter-Toto Cup. He later re-joined Lewis in a similar position at Merthyr Tydfil for the 98/99 season.

Season	League		F.A.Cup		Welsh Cup		League Cup		E.C.W.C.		Total	
	apps	gls	apps	gls	apps	gls	apps	gls	apps	gls	apps	gls
1978/79	23	1	3	0	4	1	-	-	-	-	30	2
1979/80	15	2	-	-	-	-	3	0	2	0	20	2
	38	**3**	**3**	**0**	**4**	**1**	**3**	**0**	**2**	**0**	**50**	**3**

GILLESPIE, Norman

1963 - 1964

Position; *Inside-Right*
D.O.B; *20th April, 1940*
Birthplace; *Edinburgh, Lothian*
Height; *ft in* ***Weight;*** *st lbs*
Debut v. *Southend United (a) 21st December, 1963*
Total Appearances & Goals; *3 apps 0 gls*
Career; *Falkirk; WREXHAM 18th Dec 1963 £2,500; Berwick Rangers Jul 1964;*

Norman Gillespie arrived at Wrexham from Falkirk, having enjoyed life as a prolific goalscorer with the Scottish League club. Only three days after he had joined the Racecourse club 'Norrie', as he was better known, made his Football League debut at Southend United in a 1-1 draw, playing at inside-right in place of the departed Mickey Metcalf. However, Wrexham also signed Sammy McMillan shortly afterwards, and Norman was relegated into the reserve team in the Cheshire County League. He was to make just two further League appearances that season, in a 4-1 defeat at Colchester United, and a 3-0 home defeat by Reading. Very few eyebrows were raised when he returned to his native Scotland at the end of the season, joining Berwick Rangers.

Season	League		F.A.Cup		Welsh Cup		League Cup		Total	
	apps	gls	apps	gls	apps	gls	apps	gls	apps	gls
1963/64	3	0	-	-	-	-	-	-	3	0
	3	**0**	**-**	**-**	**-**	**-**	**-**	**-**	**3**	**0**

GODDING, Earl George 1954 - 1959

Position; *Goalkeeper*
D.O.B; *6th January, 1934*
Birthplace; *Wrexham, Denbighshire*
Height; *5ft 10in* **Weight;** *9st 10lbs*
Debut v. *Bradford Park Avenue (h) 24th January, 1953*
Total Appearances & Goals; *24 apps 0 gls*
Career; *Caergwrle; WREXHAM 10th Nov 1952; Workington Aug 1959 10apps 0gls; Dolgellau & District 23rd Aug 1961; Colwyn Bay 11th Jan 1964;*

Earl Godding is the son of former Wrexham goalkeeper, George Godding, who was an established 'keeper with the 'Robins' in the 1920s. Earl followed in his father's footsteps as a custodian, and was keeping goal for Caergwrle at Bradley when he was spotted by a Wrexham scout. Godding junior was then asked to sign for Wrexham on amateur forms, and made his Football League debut for the club at the age of eighteen in a 3-0 defeat at Bradford Park Avenue in January 1953, in place of Bob Connor. With six or seven 'keepers already on the books, Earl had to wait almost two seasons for his next appearance in the senior side, by which time he had signed professional (in April 1954). During the 1954/55 season he took over from Derek Williams, and was doing well until called up for his National Service. On completion of his two years in the Army Earl returned to keep goal in four of the last five matches of 1956/57. He was deputy to both Roly Ugolini and Billy Waters during the following season, though he was recalled for the final four matches to help the team in their battle to secure qualification for the new Third Division by finishing in the top half the old Third Division North. Wrexham needed at least a draw in the last match of the season at Tranmere Rovers to make sure of qualifying, but Earl broke his thumb just before half-time, and Wrexham went on to lose 2-1. Nonetheless Wrexham did go on to qualify on goal difference, due to the results of the other teams around them. Earl featured in the first two matches of the 1958/59 season before Waters and Ugolini took over again. He was released in the summer, and went to West Bromwich Albion for talks before finally signing for Workington. He had one season with the Cumbrian club, making ten League appearances, before returning home to Caergwrle to help run the family garage because of his father's ill health. Earl continued to play football with Dolgellau & District and then Colwyn Bay, eventually hanging up his boots. He ran the family garage in Caergwrle, where he settled, until he retired. He still resides in Caergwrle, and attended the Players' Grand Gala Reunion Luncheon in Ewloe in September 1998.

Season	League		F.A.Cup		Welsh Cup		Total	
	apps	gls	apps	gls	apps	gls	apps	gls
1952/53	1	0	-	-	-	-	1	0
1954/55	10	0	3	0	-	-	13	0
1956/57	4	0	-	-	-	-	4	0
1957/58	4	0	-	-	-	-	4	0
1958/59	2	0	-	-	-	-	2	0
	21	**0**	**3**	**0**	**-**	**-**	**24**	**0**

GODDING, George Alfred 1919 - 1926

Position; *Goalkeeper*
D.O.B; *3rd May, 1896*
Birthplace; *Caergwrle, Denbighshire*
Died; *Caergwrle, 18th November, 1960*
Height; *5ft 10in* **Weight;** *11st 0lbs*
Debut v. *Witton Albion (a) 27th September, 1919*
Football League debut v. *Hartlepool United (h) 27th August, 1921*
Total Appearances & Goals; *188 apps 0 gls*
Career; *Caergwrle FC; Crichton Athletic; WREXHAM (Am) Apr 1920, (Pro) 22nd May, 1921; Llandudno 29th Jun 1926; Oak Alyn Rovers 25th Jan 1929;*
Honours; *Two Welsh International Caps; Welsh Cup Winner 1924 & 1925; North Wales Coast F.A.runner-up 1926;*

George Godding kept goal for his local side Caergwrle F.C., enjoying a successful trial with Cheshire County League side Crichton's Athletic in 1919. While attached to the latter he was invited to help out Wrexham in November of the same year by playing in two F.A.Cup matches, both against Witton Albion, as a replacement for Fred Boxley. The regular 'keeper was unavailable because of a rail strike, and was unable to reach Wrexham. George then continued with Crichton's until April 1921, when he finally signed for Wrexham who were building up a squad in preparation for their first season in the Football League. He did in fact, play in the club's opening Football League match against Hartlepool United on the Racecourse. He was to establish himself as the club's first choice goalkeeper for the next four seasons, becoming the first player to make one hundred Football League appearances for the club, and passing the milestone at New Brighton on the 9th February 1924. He was also the first goalkeeper to save a penalty for Wrexham in a Football League game, against Crewe Alexandra in April 1924. George picked up two Welsh Cup winners' medals in his time at the Racecourse, and was capped twice by Wales against Scotland and Ireland, both in 1923. George was described as 'having a safe pair of hands and good judgement', as well as being 'a good kicker with a fine understanding with his full-backs'. During the 1925/26 season, he lost his place in the side to Algernon Wilkinson, and at the end of that season parted company with the Club. George continued playing football for Llandudno Town in the Welsh National League, for two seasons. He later played for Oak Alyn Rovers, and in the 1930s was secretary to his first club, Caergwrle F.C., as well as earning a living as a lorry driver. He subsequently took over a garage and petrol filling station in his home village of Caergwrle, which was eventually passed on to his son, Earl, a former Wrexham goalkeeper in the 1950s (See previous entry). George Godding died on 18th November 1960, aged 64.

Season	League		F.A.Cup		Welsh Cup		Total	
	apps	gls	apps	gls	apps	gls	apps	gls
1919/20	-	-	2	0	-	-	2	0
1921/22	37	0	4	0	3	0	44	0
1922/23	36	0	3	0	3	0	42	0
1923/24	41	0	2	0	6	0	49	0
1924/25	39	0	1	0	4	0	44	0
1925/26	7	0	-	-	-	-	7	0
	160	**0**	**12**	**0**	**16**	**0**	**188**	**0**

GOODE, Bertram John 1910 - 1911, 1913 - 1922 & 1923 - 1926

Position; *Inside-Left*
D.O.B; *11th August, 1886*
Birthplace; *Chester, Cheshire*
Died; *Wrexham, 30th April, 1955*
Height; *5ft 6in* **Weight;** *11st 8lbs*
Debut v. *Halesowen (a) 3rd September, 1910*
Football League debut v. *Hartlepool United (h) 27th August, 1921*
Total Appearances & Goals; *276 apps 136 gls*
Career; *Old St.Mary's; Hoole; Saltney; Chester Dec 1907; Liverpool May 1908 7apps 1gls; WREXHAM 2nd Jun 1910; Aston Villa 27th Apr 1911 £250 7apps 3gls; Hull City May 1912 £300 28apps 10gls; WREXHAM 2nd May 1913 £225; Southampton (WW1 Guest) 1918/19 4apps 2gls; Rhos Athletic 25th Aug 1922; Chester 6th Sept1922; Wrexham 24th Aug 1923; Retired cs1926;*
Honours; *Welsh Cup Winner 1908, 1911, 1914, 1915, 1921 & 1925; Welsh Cup runner-up 1920; Birmingham & District League Championship Winner 1912;*

Bert Goode played inside-right for Old St.Mary's in Chester before joining Hoole, helping them to a West Cheshire Amateur Cup semi-final. Towards the end of the 1905/06 season he played for a Broughton Combination XI against Chester, following which he was invited for a trial with the Combination League side opponents. He was not offered terms and on this occasion, joined Saltney F.C. instead, although he continued to impress, and it wasn't long before he was given another opportunity with Chester in November 1907. He made his debut against Nantwich Town, and shortly afterwards was signed on professional terms by Chester. Bert went on to collect the first of his six Welsh Cup winners' medals as Chester defeated Connah's Quay in the 1908 final, and he scored two the goals in a 3-1 win. He notched an impressive 13 goals in 17 Combination

League games for Chester that season, and it came as no surprise when, during the summer of 1908, he was signed by Liverpool. Goode made his Football League debut at Bristol City in November 1908, but was to play in just six more League games, scoring one goal, before being allowed to join Wrexham in the summer of 1910. Goode made his debut for the Racecourse club in a 4-1 Birmingham & District League win at Halesowen in the opening game of the season, and capped it by scoring one of the Wrexham goals. He spent one season at the Racecourse, scoring 37 goals in 39 League and Cup games, and helping Wrexham to win the Welsh Cup by grabbing four goals in the 6-1 win over Connah's Quay. Bert joined Aston Villa for £250 before the last match of the 1910/11 season had been played. He spent one season at Villa Park, making seven League appearances and scoring three goals, but did win a Birmingham & District League Championship medal while playing for Villa's reserves, for whom he scored 46 goals. In May 1912, he moved on to Second Division side, Hull City, for £300, where he scored ten goals in 28 League appearances rejoining Wrexham a year later for a £225 fee. Bert picked up a further four Welsh Cup winners' medals, as well as scoring many important goals. In October 1920 he was awarded a benefit match against Liverpool, which Wrexham won 1-0, and in August 1921 played in the club's inaugural Football League match against Hartlepool United. He joined Rhos Athletic for a short spell in the close season of 1922, joining Cheshire County League side Chester a month later. He made just three appearances for Chester, scoring one goal in brief spell, returning to Wrexham in the summer of 1923. By this time he was combining playing with coaching duties at the Racecourse, and decided to end his playing career in 1926 in order to concentrate upon coaching. He then assumed the added responsibility of club groundsman. Bert averaged a goal every other game during his time with the 'Robins', and was certainly Wrexham's greatest goalscorer of that period. He was described as the 'possessor of plenty of craft, although in the latter part of his career he was more of a schemer than a goalscorer'. Bert later became Landlord of the King's Head Public House in Rhos, as well as a turnstile operator at the Racecourse. Sadly, he died in April 1950, while working as a night watchman at the Border Breweries bottling Works in the town. He was 68 years old. Once selected for Wales until the Welsh F.A. were informed that he was born in England by a certain R. E. Evans who actually played for Wales in a similar situation and later represented England!! A great character at the Racecourse, well liked by everyone. Often took a drink before a game and at half time although not to the excess recorded elsewhere.

Season	League		F.A.Cup		Welsh Cup		Total	
	apps	gls	apps	gls	apps	gls	apps	gls
1910/11	33	25	2	2	4	10	39	37
1913/14	33	16	4	2	8	7	45	25
1914/15	34	13	6	3	5	8	45	24
1919/20	32	13	5	3	5	0	42	16
1920/21	31	11	4	6	5	4	40	21
1921/22	32	5	4	0	3	0	39	5
1923/24	3	0	-	-	-	-	3	0
1924/25	17	4	-	-	4	3	21	7
1925/26	1	1	-	-	1	0	2	1
	216	**88**	**25**	**16**	**35**	**32**	**276**	**136**
F/League	53	10	4	0	8	3	65	13

GOSS, Frederick Charles 1938 - 1939

Position; *Outside-Right*
D.O.B; *25th May, 1914*
Birthplace; *Shardlow, Derbyshire*
Died; *Derby, A/M/J 1983*
Height; *5ft 9'1/2in* **Weight;** *11st 6lbs*
Debut v. *New Brighton (h) 1st October, 1938*
Total Appearances & Goals; *9 apps 1 gls*
Career; *Ilkeston St.Clare's; Ilkeston Town; Aston Villa Nov 1936 2apps 0gls; WREXHAM 1st Oct 1938; Aston Villa 6th Jan 1939;*

Fred Goss was playing non-league football for his local teams, Ilkeston St.Clares and Ilkeston Town, when Second Division Aston Villa showed an interest in the promising winger. Fred signed for Villa in November 1936, and he went on to spend almost two years at Villa Park. During this time he made just two Football League appearances, both during the 1936/37 season; his Football League debut came against Bury in a 4-0 home defeat, and was followed by the next home match against West Ham United, which Villa also lost, 2-0. It proved to be his last appearance for Villa before signing for Wrexham in September 1938. He was attracted to the Racecourse by Wrexham's caretaker manager, and former Villa player, Tommy Griffiths. Goss went straight into the first team at outside-right, at the expense of Cliff Lloyd but, after just nine games and one goal, he found himself out in the cold, having been replaced by new signing Jack Williams. His one goal for Wrexham came in an 8-3 defeat at Lincoln. In January 1939 Fred rejoined Aston Villa, but he failed to make any further impression at Villa Park, mainly because of the outbreak of World War Two.

Season	League		F.A.Cup		Welsh Cup		N.S.C.		Total	
	apps	gls	apps	gls	apps	gls	apps	gls	apps	gls
1938/39	9	1	-	-	-	-	-	-	9	1
	9	**1**	**-**	**-**	**-**	**-**	**-**	**-**	**9**	**1**

GRAHAM, John R. 1949 - 1953

Position; *Outside-Right*
D.O.B; *12th April, 1926*
Birthplace; *Leyland, Lancashire*
Height; *5ft 9'1/2in* **Weight;** *10st 9lbs*
Debut v. *Rotherham United (a) 20th August, 1949*
Total Appearances & Goals; *47 apps 7 gls*
Career; *Leyland Works; Aston Villa Nov 1946 10apps 3gls; WREXHAM 22nd Jun 1949 £2,000; Wigan Athletic Aug 1952 (loan) 11apps 1gls; Rochdale Feb 1953 10apps 1gls; Bradford City Jul 1953 18apps 1gls;*

John Graham joined First Division Aston Villa in November 1946 shortly after the Second World War. He had earlier been invited to Villa Park for trials from his local side, Leyland Works, and, while still on trial, created a sufficiently favourable impression to be handed his Football League debut in September 1946, at centre-forward in a 5-2 home win over Brentford, contributing one of the Villa goals. He registered a further six League appearances during that season, but despite this promising beginning he was to take part in just three more League outings for Villa over the next three seasons. John was then allowed to join Wrexham during the summer of 1949 for what was described as a 'four figure fee'. A Draughtsman by trade he made his debut for Wrexham in a 2-2 draw at Rotherham United in the opening match of the 1949/50 season, notching one of the goals on his debut. He remained in the 'Robins' first team until Christmas, but again found it difficult to hold down a regular first team place, which finally led to him leaving the Racecourse club of his own accord in the close season of 1952. He signed for Lancashire Combination League side Wigan Athletic, while Wrexham still retained his League registration. John made eleven appearances for Wigan, scoring one goal, as they went on to win the league Championship, but was to miss out on the celebrations as he had returned to the Football League in February 1953, joining Rochdale. He made his debut for Rochdale in a local 'derby' with Oldham Athletic at Spotland in front of the biggest home gate of the season, just over 15,000, who witnessed a 3-1 win for 'Dale'. His following game was at Wrexham, but it was to be a unhappy return to the Racecourse as the home side triumphed 3-0. He was allowed to leave the Lancashire club in the summer, signing for Bradford City. He made his debut in the opening match of the season, a 1-0 home win over Barnsley, the solitary goal being scored by Billy Tunnicliffe, a former Racecourse team mate. Graham spent just one season at Valley Parade, scoring one goal in 18 League appearances, before leaving the Football League scene altogether in 1954. A player who was described, "Promised so much, but never produced the goods".

Season	League		F.A.Cup		Welsh Cup		Total	
	apps	gls	apps	gls	apps	gls	apps	gls
1949/50	17	3	-	-	-	-	17	3
1950/51	21	4	1	0	1	0	23	4
1951/52	7	0	-	-	-	-	7	0
	45	**7**	**1**	**0**	**1**	**0**	**47**	**7**

GRAHAM, Robert Henry

1926 - 1930

Position; *Left-Half*
D.O.B; *12th October, 1900*
Birthplace; *Middlesbrough, Cleveland*
Died; *Middlesborough, J/A/S 1965*
Height; *5ft 8in* ***Weight;*** *11st 10lbs*
Debut v. *Chesterfield (h) 28th August, 1926*
Total Appearances & Goals; *144 apps 2 gls*
Career; *Middlesbrough (Am) Aug 1923, (Pro) Oct 1923 0apps; Darlington Aug 1924 4apps 0gls; WREXHAM 11th Aug 1926; Halifax Town Aug 1930 39apps 0gls; Workington cs1932;*

Bob Graham joined his home town team, Middlesbrough, as an amateur in August 1923, and went on to sign professional forms two months later. He remained at Ayresome Park for the rest of the season, but in the summer he found himself released without having made the first team. Despite this setback Bob was quickly snapped up by Third Division North side Darlington, for whom he made his Football League debut before going on to record a further four League appearances for the 'Quakers' in the two seasons that he spent at Feethams. He joined Wrexham in the close season of 1926, going straight into the first team at left-half for the opening game of the new season, a 3-1 win at home to Chesterfield. Graham went on to establish himself in the 'Robins' side as the season progressed, missing just five games. He remained at the Racecourse for three more seasons, during which he was a consistent performer, before losing his place to Teddy Read in February 1930. Bob was allowed to leave the Denbighshire club at the end of that season, and joined Halifax Town, with whom he spent three seasons and made 39 appearances. His time at the 'Shay' lasted until the close season of 1933, when he joined non-league Workington.

Season	League		F.A.Cup		Welsh Cup		Total	
	apps	gls	apps	gls	apps	gls	apps	gls
1926/27	37	1	4	1	1	0	42	1
1927/28	39	0	5	0	3	0	47	0
1928/29	28	1	1	0	-	-	29	1
1929/30	22	0	3	0	1	0	26	0
	126	**2**	**13**	**1**	**5**	**0**	**144**	**2**

GRAHAM, William

1924 - 1925

Position; *Outside-Left*
D.O.B; *14th October, 1893*
Birthplace; *Preston, Lancashire*
Height; *5ft 4in* ***Weight;*** *10st 10lbs*
Died; *Old Lenton, Nottingham, 29th April, 1984*
Debut v. *New Brighton (h) 6th September, 1924*
Total Appearances & Goals; *7 apps 2 gls*
Career; *Dick Kerr's XI; Lancaster Town Feb 1920; Northampton Town Feb 1922 45apps 10gls; WREXHAM 14th June 1924; Lancaster Town Jul 1925; Great Harwood Aug 1926; Burscough Rangers Aug 1927; Lytham cs1929;*
Honours; *Lancashire Combination League Championship Winner 1921;*

Bill Graham was appearing for Lancaster Town when he won a Lancashire Combination League Championship medal in 1921. He was then approached by Third Division South side Northampton Town, for whom he agreed to sign in February 1922. He went straight into the 'Cobblers' side at inside-left for the following home game against Portsmouth, which ended scoreless. Bill retained his place in the side for the rest of the season, although the following campaign would see him struggle to establish himself in the senior side. This prompted a transfer request, which resulted in him being signed up by Third Division North side Wrexham in June 1924. He made his debut for the 'Robins' at outside-left in the second match of the season, a scoreless home draw with New Brighton. He was to make just six further first team appearances for the club, his most memorable a 4-2 win over Nelson in April 1925, in which he scored two goals. Bill left the Racecourse at the end of the 1924/25 season. During his time at the club he was described as, 'short in stature, but a real opportunist'. After leaving the North Wales club he dropped back into the non-league circle, returning to Lancaster Town, followed by spells with Great Harwood, Burscough Rangers, and Lytham.

Season	League		F.A.Cup		Welsh Cup		Total	
	apps	gls	apps	gls	apps	gls	apps	gls
1924/25	6	2	-	-	1	0	7	2
	6	**2**	**-**	**-**	**1**	**0**	**7**	**2**

GRAINGER, Colin

1950 - 1953

Position; *Outside-Left*
D.O.B; *10th June, 1933*
Birthplace; *Ryehill, Wakefield, Yorkshire*
Height; *5ft 9in* ***Weight;*** *11st 2lbs*
Debut v. *Hartlepool United (h) 24th February, 1951.*
Total Appearances & Goals; *5 apps 0 gls*
Career; *South Elmsall; WREXHAM 20th Oct 1950; Sheffield United 26th Jun 1953 £3,000 88apps 26gls; Sunderland 6th Feb 1957 (£7,000 +S.Kemp in exchange) 120apps 14gls; Leeds United 26th Jul 1960 £15,000 33apps 5gls; Port Vale 20th Oct 1961 £6,000 39apps 6gls; Doncaster Rovers 6th Aug 1964 40apps 4gls; Macclesfield Town cs1966 to Oct 1966;*
Honours; *Seven Full England International caps; Three Football League representative caps;*

The 'Singing Winger'. That was Colin Grainger, a well known crooner on the Northern pub and club circuit, who also played for a number of football clubs on a Saturday afternoon. Colin first took up the game at Ryehill Junior and South Hindley Secondary Schools near his native Wakefield, where he supported Barnsley as a youngster. He also played for Ryehill and Haverscroft from the age of 14. Upon leaving school at 16 he began work as a car mechanic, followed by employment as an engineer. By this time he was appearing for local club side South Elmsall, and his ability prompted Colin's cousin (and Wrexham footballer), Dennis Grainger to recommend him to his manager, Les McDowall. After a trial, he was signed on the ground staff at the Racecourse in October 1950. Still only 17, he was called up earlier than expected for his Football League debut, in place of regular outside-left Billy Tunnicliffe against Hartlepool United on the Racecourse in February 1951, a match which Wrexham won 1-0. National Service was to interrupt Colin's football career, when he was enlisted with the R.A.F. It meant that Colin was not available for the 'Robins' first team for a further two years, and when his period of service had been completed played four matches towards the end of 1952/53. He was then snapped up by First Division Sheffield United for £3,000 in the close season. At Bramall Lane, Colin was described as 'A fast direct winger'; he went on to make a total of 88 League appearances, scoring 26 goals, and claimed the first of his seven England international caps. He also had the honour of selection for the Football League XI against the Irish League. Colin signed for Sunderland in February 1958, in a

player plus cash exchange deal, and was mentioned as a 'sprightly outside-left, mobile and aggressive'. He went on to spend three years at Roker Park, completing 120 League appearances, and scoring 14 goals, signing for Leeds United in July 1960 for a club record fee of £15,000. Colin was to spend just over a year at Elland Road, where he scored five goals in 33 League games, but a cartilage operation kept him out of action for a spell. In October 1961 he joined Port Vale, making 39 League appearances, scoring six goals, but suffered with a groin injury during his time at Vale Park and in August 1964 was allowed to join Doncaster Rovers on a free transfer. Colin spent two seasons at Belle Vue, scoring four goals in forty appearances moving on to Cheshire County League side Macclesfield Town in the close season of 1966. However, he was at Moss Roser only a brief time before beginning a new career.....singing! Colin sang around the clubs in the North, and even went on to produce a disc which did reasonably well in the charts entitled, 'Are you'. His singing career had in fact begun whilst with the England team in Finland during a dinner and cabaret night, and proved so successful that he was given a T.V. slot. Colin was later employed as a director of a wine and spirits company, Halewood Vintners, before retiring after 15 years in 1995. He is still involved with football as a scout for Huddersfield Town, with whom he has been associated with for around fifteen years, and has settled in the village of Skelmanthorpe, close to the town.

Season	League		F.A.Cup		Welsh Cup		Total	
	apps	gls	apps	gls	apps	gls	apps	gls
1950/51	1	0	-	-	-	-	1	0
1952/53	4	0	-	-	-	-	4	0
	5	**0**	**-**	**-**	**-**	**-**	**5**	**0**

***GRAINGER,* Dennis** 1947 - 1951

Position; *Outside-Right*
D.O.B; *5th March, 1920*
Birthplace; *Royston, Barnsley, Yorkshire*
Died; *Duckmanton, Nr. Chesterfield, 6th May, 1986.*
Height; *5ft 7in* ***Weight;*** *11st 0lbs*
Debut v. *Oldham Athletic (h) 6th December, 1947*
Total Appearances & Goals; *112 apps 14 gls*
Career; *South Kirby; Southport (Am) 5th Aug 1937, (Pro) 13th Oct 1938; Doncaster Rovers 1941/42 (WW2 Guest) 3apps 0gls; Millwall 1942/3 (WW2 Guest) 60apps 12gls; Walsall 1942/3 (WW2 Guest) 1app 0gls; Rotherham United (WW2 Guest) 1943/44 5apps 1gls; Lincoln City (WW2 Guest) 1944/45 3app 1gls; Sheffield United (WW2 Guest) 1944/45 1app 1gls; Leeds United 29th Sept 1945 £1,000 (WW2 35apps 9gls) 37apps 5gls; WREXHAM 29th Nov 1947; Oldham Athletic 18th Jun 1951 (Part-exchange for Bill Jessop) 3apps 0gls; Bangor City 6th Aug 1952; Flint Town 10th Aug 1953;*
Honours; *Welsh Cup runner-up 1950;*

Dennis Grainger's parents kept the Frickley Colliery Welfare Club at South Elmsall, where he was born. He left school at 14 to work in the pit, looking after Pit Ponies, while playing football for South Kirby and cricket for the Yorkshire Council. It was while playing for South Kirby that he was signed by Southport on amateur terms in August 1937, and his move to Haig Avenue saw him join older brother Jack on the club's books. He actually made his Football League debut for Southport in the opening game of the 1939/40 season at Darlington in a 1-0 defeat, but this match was to be scrubbed from the record books following the suspension of the season upon the outbreak of WW2. During the conflict Grainger joined the R.A.F. with whom he was to enhance his reputation as a footballer by playing in the Services' representative matches, as well as turning out as a 'guest' player for Doncaster Rovers, Rotherham United, Walsall, Sheffield United, Lincoln City and Millwall. In fact it was during this time that George Hardwick invited him to play a game for Chelsea, but the Commanding Officer of his RAF camp would only issue a pass for Millwall! He demonstrated sufficient ablity for Leeds United to pay a sizeable fee for him in September 1945, and

remained at Elland Road for two seasons, scoring five goals in 37 League matches. In December 1947 Dennis was allowed to leave Leeds to sign for Wrexham, and made an immediate impression at the Racecourse, described as 'fast and tricky, and possessing a powerful shot in either foot.' He went straight into the first team to make his debut against Oldham in a 2-1 home defeat. Despite that set back he went on to help the club to its highest position in the League since 1933, when the 'Robins' finished in third place. It was during his time at the Racecourse that he was to introduce his cousin, Colin Grainger, to the club, who went on to represent both Wrexham and England. Playing at outside-right Dennis was to form a formidable wing partnership with Billy Tunnicliffe, and this continued until the beginning of the 1950/51 season, when Peter Jackson became manager. Dennis made just eight appearances that season, and during the summer of 1951 was allowed to join Oldham Athletic in an exchange deal for Bill Jessop. At Boundary Park he was to find himself understudy to Bill Ormond, and only managed three further League appearances in that campaign. He was released by the 'Latics' at the end of 1951/52 and joined Bangor City, followed by a spell with Flint Town. At around the time of his playing for Oldham he had become the Landlord of both the Feather's Hotel in Chester Street, Wrexham, and the Cambrian Vaults Public House in the town. He later returned to Southport to work in the drilling and boring industry with 'Cementation', while his second wife, Eileen, became stewardess of the Birkdale Labour Club, where his brother, Jack, was chairman, and Harold Wilson was President. In 1960, Dennis was asked and accepted an offer to take over a company in Windy Arbour, near Wigan. He then joined Faircloughs in 1968, with whom he was to travel to Morrocco, Iran, Pakistan and Central America. In December 1970, he returned to the licencing trade by taking over the tenancy of the Double Top Inn in Inkersall near Chesterfield. He finally retired in 1982 due to ill health and sadly passed away in May 1986. Aged 66. His son Rob has become something of a 'Football Historian' researching his father's career and football in his area, also finding time to play the game locally.

Season	League		F.A.Cup		Welsh Cup		Total	
	apps	gls	apps	gls	apps	gls	apps	gls
1947/48	19	4	1	0	1	0	21	4
1948/49	42	5	1	0	2	1	45	6
1949/50	29	2	3	1	4	0	36	3
1950/51	8	1	2	0	-	-	10	1
	98	**12**	**7**	**1**	**7**	**1**	**112**	**14**

***GRANT,* David John** 1966 - 1967

Position; *Half-Back*
D.O.B; *18th December, 1947*
Birthplace; *Liverpool, Merseyside*
Height; *5ft 5in* ***Weight;*** *10st 3lbs*
Debut v. *Chester (a) 8th October, 1966*
Total Appearances & Goals; *8/6 apps 0 gls*
Career; *Everton Dec 1965; WREXHAM 21st Sept 1966; South Liverpool Jul 1967; Bangor City 17th Mar 1969; Rhyl 14th Mar 1972 to Aug 1973;*
Honours; *England Schoolboy international; F.A.Youth Cup Winner 1965; Cheshire County League Championship Winner 1972;*

David Grant first played football as an inside-forward for his school team in Liverpool. He was soon switched to wing-half, a position in which he became very effective and represented the Liverpool, Lancashire, and England Schoolboys. David played for England against Eire, in a 3-2 win on Leicester City's Filbert Street ground. He joined Everton as an apprentice on leaving school, making his way through the youth ranks, and helping the Goodison Park Youth team to an F.A.Youth Cup triumph in 1965, as they beat Arsenal 3-2 on aggregate in the final. By then, David had completed his apprenticeship and was also playing for Everton's reserve side in the Central League, and did well enough to earn a professional contract at the age of 18. Despite his early promise, Everton manager Harry Catterick decided to release him in September 1966 without having made a first team appearance at Goodison Park. David was then quickly snapped up by Wrexham manager Jack Rowley, and within a month had made his Football League debut coming on as a substitute for Albert Kinsey in a 3-1 derby win at Chester. He again appeared as a substitute in the next match, but did not figure in the first team again until March, also as a substitute. His full debut came in the following match, at home to Bradford City, replacing the injured Mickey Evans at inside-forward. He made a few more appearances before the end of the season, but manager Alvan Williams decided to release him. David then dropped into non-league football with South Liverpool, spending a couple of years until joining Bangor City in March 1969, where he enjoyed a three year stint. It was during his time at Farrar Road that the 'busy midfield player' became a member of the free-scoring City side of the late 1960s and early 1970s, in a side which also included ex-Robins Gareth Salisbury and Alec Lucas. He joined Cheshire County League side Rhyl in March 1972 in time to win a Cheshire County League championship medal and spent a further season at Belle Vue before leaving.

Season	League		F.A.Cup		Welsh Cup		League Cup		Total	
	apps	gls	apps	gls	apps	gls	apps	gls	apps	gls
1966/67	6/5	0	1	0	1/1	0	-	-	8/6	0
	6/5	**0**	**1**	**0**	**1/1**	**0**	**-**	**-**	**8/6**	**0**

GREATREX, George Kenneth W. 1928 - 1930

Position; *Goalkeeper*
Birthplace; *Liverpool, Merseyside*
Height; *5ft 9in* ***Weight;*** *11st 3lbs*
D.O.B; *16th May, 1904*
Died; *Wallasey, O/N/D 1981*
Debut v. *Chesterfield (h) 25th August, 1928*
Total Appearances & Goals; *17 apps 0 gls*
Career; *Orrell; Marine; WREXHAM 31st Aug 1928; New Brighton 29th Jul 1930 25apps 0gls; Crewe Alexandra (trial) 7th Sept 1933 0apps; Workington 20th Oct 1933 to Nov 1933; Runcorn; Stoneycroft St.Paul's FC Oct 1935; Manchester North End Jul 1936;*

George Greatrex had played football in the local leagues around Liverpool for Orrell and Marine before signing for Wrexham as a 20 year-old amateur in 1924. Four years had passed before he stepped up to the club's professional ranks, taking over 'between the sticks' from the departed Ted Robson. George made his Football League debut for the 'Robins' in the opening match of the 1928/29 season, a 4-3 home win over Chesterfield. He kept his place until November, when Wrexham signed the former England international goalkeeper Ted Taylor, who went straight into the senior side. George remained as understudy until Taylor left the Racecourse at the end of the campaign. However, the club then brought in another 'keeper, Dick Finnigan, and George again found himself second choice, making just one first team appearance in a 5-4 defeat at Rochdale in February 1930. It was no surprise when Greatrex left the Racecourse in the summer to join New Brighton. At Raker's Lane he again found himself facing keen competition for his first two seasons, but his patience was rewarded commencing the 1932/33 campaign as the club's first choice 'keeper. Yet again, he was to play second fiddle and his final League game for New Brighton was in the final match of 1932/33 against his former club, Wrexham! It was a vital match, as the 'Rakers' needed one point to ensure that they would not have to apply for re-election. Wrexham won a tense encounter 2-0, to leave New Brighton as re-election candidates. George left New Brighton at the end of the season, and had a brief trial with Crewe Alexandra without making a first team appearance before signing for Workington. He later had spells with non-league sides Runcorn, Stoneycroft St.Paul's FC, and Manchester North End. During his football career George also excelled in baseball, playing for New Brighton in Division One of the English Baseball Association.

Season	League		F.A.Cup		Welsh Cup		Total	
	apps	gls	apps	gls	apps	gls	apps	gls
1928/29	16	0	-	-	-	-	16	0
1929/30	1	0	-	-	-	-	1	0
	17	**0**	**-**	**-**	**-**	**-**	**17**	**0**

GREEN, Robert Colin 1971

Position; *Left-Back*
Birthplace; *Brynteg, Wrexham, Denbighshire*
Height; *5ft 8in* ***Weight;*** *10st 8lbs*
D.O.B; *10th February, 1942*
Debut v. *Barnsley (a) 23rd January, 1971*
Total Appearances & Goals; *3 apps 0 gls*
Career; *Everton Feb 1959 15apps 1gls; Birmingham City Dec 1962 £12,000 183apps 1gls; WREXHAM 18th Jan 1971 (Loan); Tamworth May 1971; Rhyl 3rd Sept 1973, to Dec 1973;*
Honours; *Fifteen Welsh International Caps; Seven Welsh under-23 caps; Football League Cup Winner 1963;*

Colin Green was playing for Wrexham & District Schoolboys when Wrexham manager Cliff Lloyd invited him to sign for Wrexham as a 17 year-old. However, Everton intervened and Colin agreed to sign amateur forms at Goodison Park in July 1957. He made his Football League debut at left-back a year later, at Blackpool, where he had the unenviable task of marking Stanley Matthews. Even so, Everton won 4-1, and Colin kept his place for the next match against Wolves. Tragedy then struck, as a knee injury limited him to just a 13 more League appearances, though he did manage to score one goal - against Gordon Banks! Colin joined Birmingham City in December 1962 for a £12,000 fee, and went on to spend almost ten years at St.Andrew's where he made over 200 appearances. He also gained international honours, representing Wales at under-23 and at full international levels. His biggest match for Wales, in front of a 160,00 crowd was against Brazil in Rio's Maracana Stadium. Green picked up a League Cup winners' tankard in his first season at St.Andrew's, when Birmingham beat Aston Villa 3-1 on aggregate. A 'cool, unflappable defender, with an ability to read difficult situations quickly', he was to make almost 200 league appearances for the 'Blues', although injuries were to prevent him from adding to this total. He broke his leg in 1966, and, during 1969/70 injury cost him his first team place again. Colin was loaned out to Wrexham in January of the following season, where he made three League appearances at left-back, at Barnsley and Chesterfield, and on the Racecourse in the return match with the Oakwell club. John Neal wanted to sign him permanently, but only on a free transfer, while Birmingham City wanted cash. At the end of the season he left the 'Blues' and signed for Southern League side, Tamworth..........on a free transfer!! Colin spent two seasons with Tamworth before joining Cheshire County League side Rhyl for a short spell, following which he retired from football in 1974 at the age of 32. He then went into a garage business, later becoming a rep with a veterinary company, and settling in his home town of Wrexham.

Season	League		F.A.Cup		Welsh Cup		League Cup		Total	
	apps	gls	apps	gls	apps	gls	apps	gls	apps	gls
1970/71	3	0	-	-	-	-	-	-	3	0
	3	**0**	**-**	**-**	**-**	**-**	**-**	**-**	**3**	**0**

GREEN, William Charles 1954 - 1957

Position; *Wing-Half*
D.O.B; *9th October, 1927*
Birthplace; *Hull, Humberside*
Height; *ft in* ***Weight;*** *st lbs*
Debut v. *Southport (a) 28th August, 1954*
Total Appearances & Goals; *70 apps 3 gls*
Career; *Wolves Sep 1945 0apps; Walsall 11th Oct 1949 182apps 8gls; WREXHAM 24th Jun 1954; Wellington Town 16th Jul 1956; Caernarvon Town 19th Jul 1958; Pwllheli & District 3rd Sept 1959 to May 1960;*

Bill Green signed for Wolves at the end of World War Two in September 1945. He went on to make his way through the junior ranks at Molyneux, where he was to spend four years, although failing to make a first team appearance during that time. In October 1949 he was allowed to join

neighbours Walsall for a 'modest fee', where he made his Football League debut in a 1-1 draw with fellow Third Division South side, Bristol Rovers. Bill accumulated over 200 appearances for the 'Saddlers', including a match against Southend United on Boxing Day 1951 when he played..........in goal! At the time Walsall had no cover for regular 'keeper Jack Lewis, so Bill was chosen as the best option! Despite his best efforts, Walsall lost 3-0. Bill was starved of excitement during his stay at Fellows Park as 1951/52 and 1952/53 saw the club finish bottom of the Third Division South, and had the dubious honour of being an ever present for both seasons. In spite of the club's plight Bill's experience and guile had already been noted by Wrexham manager Peter Jackson, and signed the experienced wing-half in June 1954. He made his 'Robins' debut in the third match of the season, replacing Dennis Griffiths in a 2-1 win at Southport. Bill spent three seasons at the Racecourse, proving to be very versatile as he appeared in most defensive positions for the club whilst covering for injuries. His most memorable game for the 'Robins', came in the F.A.Cup tie against Manchester United's 'Busby Babes' in January 1957, in front of the biggest ever crowd assembled on the Racecourse, 34,445. Bill left the Racecourse at the end of the season, joining Cheshire County League side, Wellington Town. He spent one season with the Buck's Head club before moving on to Welsh League North side, Caernarvon Town for 1958/59, followed by a season with Pwllheli & District.

Season	League		F.A.Cup		Welsh Cup		Total	
	apps	gls	apps	gls	apps	gls	apps	gls
1954/55	20	1	3	1	-	-	23	2
1955/56	25	1	-	-	2	0	27	1
1956/57	15	0	4	0	1	0	20	0
	60	**2**	**7**	**1**	**3**	**0**	**70**	**3**

GREGORY, David Harry

1982 - 1986

Position; *Forward*
D.O.B; *6th October, 1951*
Birthplace; *Peterborough, Cambridgeshire*
Height; *5ft 9in* ***Weight;*** *11st 6lbs*
Debut v. *Cardiff City (a) 28th August, 1982*
Total Appearances & Goals; *184/10 apps 45 gls*
Career; *Peterborough Rovers; Chatteris Town; Peterborough United Aug 1973 125/17apps 32gls; Stoke City Jun 1977 £55,000 22/1apps 3gls; Blackburn Rovers Jul 1978 (Loan) 5apps 3gls; Bury Sep 1978 £30,000 50/2apps 13gls; Portsmouth Dec 1979 £30,000 64/10apps 18gls; WREXHAM Aug 1982; Peterborough United Aug 1986 16/15apps 8gls; Kings Lynn Aug 1987; Holbeach United 1990; Watton United 1990/91; Spalding 1991; Holbeach United 1993/94;*
Honours; *Fourth Division Championship Winner 1974; Welsh Cup Winner 1986; Welsh Cup runner-up 1983 & 1984;*

David Gregory attended the Walton Secondary School in Peterborough, where he showed no signs of any potential to become a professional footballer as he was regarded as being too small! He took up employment as an apprentice mechanic upon leaving school, although playing football for his local side, Peterborough Rovers, with whom he had much early success. He was then signed by Chatteris Town, who competed in a higher grade League, where he impressed enough to be recommended to the Peterborough United manager, Noel Cantwell. After a few reserve team games during 1972/73 David was signed by 'The Posh' in August 1973 on a professional contract, although his first season at London Road saw him mostly on the sub's bench as the club stormed to the Fourth Division championship. Over the next three seasons Gregory became a virtual ever-present in the Peterborough team until Stoke City manager George Eastham paid a club record fee received of £55,000 for him in the summer of 1977. He spent just one season at the Victoria Ground, falling out with new manager Alan Durban over what was his best position. Blackburn Rovers stepped in to sign him on loan, where he scored four goals in six games, before Bury paid out £30,000 for him in September 1978. He remained at Gigg Lane for just over a year, following which he moved down to the south coast to join Portsmouth. David helped 'Pompey' to promotion in his first season at Fratton Park, although after two and a half years he was given a free transfer at the age of 31. New Wrexham manager Bobby Roberts, rebuilding a side following relegation the previous season, then persuaded him to join the North Wales club. They were hard times at Wrexham, and the club suffered relegation once again during his first season. He did, however, go on to enjoy some good times with Wrexham, including the club's European adventures against the likes of F.C.Porto and A.S.Roma, and winning a Welsh Cup medal in 1986 when Wrexham beat Kidderminster Harriers in the Final, to add to his two runners-up medals in the same competition. His most important goals for the 'Robins' came in the final match of 1983/84, a hat-trick in a 5-1 home win over Tranmere Rovers, which spared the club the indignity of having to apply for re-election. These were desperate times at the Racecourse, due to the crippling financial situation in which the club found itself, but even so, he was a big favourite among the 'Robins' fans, due to the way he could hold on to a ball and lay it off with precision, while also having a penchant for scoring spectacular goals. At the end of the 1985/86 season manager Dixie McNeil handed Dave a free transfer, although he remained in the professional ranks by rejoining Peterborough United for his final season in the Football League. After twelve months at London Road he joined Kings Lynn, in 1987, for three seasons, and prepared for the future by setting up his own business as a Ceramic tiler. Continuing to play football David later linked up with Holbeach United (twice), Watton United, and Spalding before ending his career in 1996. He was not to hang up his boots for long as he began playing Sunday football for his local pub side, The Crown. David, now settled in Holbeach, near Peterborough, is still a self-employed Ceramic tiler.

Season	League		F.A.Cup		Welsh Cup		League Cup		F.R.T.		E.C.W.C.		Total	
	apps	gls	apps	gls	apps	gls	apps	gls	apps	gls	apps	gls	apps	gls
1982/83	40/1	4	1	1	5/1	2	2	0	-	-	-	-	49/2	7
1983/84	43/1	19	1	0	8	4	2	0	3	1	-	-	57/1	24
1984/85	27/3	5	-	-	-	-	1	0	-	-	3/1	0	30/4	5
1985/86	36/2	3	3	1	3/1	2	4	3	1	0	-	-	47/3	9
	146/7	**31**	**6**	**2**	**16/2**	**8**	**9**	**3**	**4**	**1**	**3/1**	**0**	**184/10**	**45**

GRIEVE, Richard Maxwell

1950 - 1951

Position; *Inside-Left*
D.O.B; *29th June, 1924*
Birthplace; *Aberdeen, Grampian*
Height; *ft in* ***Weight;*** *st lbs*
Debut v. *Stockport County (a) 21st October, 1950*
Total Appearances & Goals; *1 app 0 gls*
Career; *Montrose; Rochdale May 1950 0apps; WREXHAM 25th Sep 1950; Dundee United Jan 1951 1app 0gls;*

Having left school during the Second World War any hopes Dick Grieve had harboured of making a career for himself in football were put on hold until the hostilities had ended. He was appearing in the Scottish League with Montrose when Third Division North side Rochdale tempted him south of the border in May 1950. Things never really worked out for him at Spotland, and he was allowed to leave the Lancashire club in the September of the same year, without having made a first team appearance. Dick then signed for fellow Third Division North side, Wrexham, together with Cyril Lawrence, and finally made his Football League debut for the North Wales club one month after signing. He was called into the side at inside-forward to replace Les Donaldson in a 2-1 defeat at Stockport County. It proved to be his one and only first team appearance for Wrexham, and in January 1951 returned to his native Scotland to join Dundee United, where he made just one Scottish League appearance.

Season	League		F.A.Cup		Welsh Cup		Total	
	apps	gls	apps	gls	apps	gls	apps	gls
1950/51	1	0	-	-	-	-	1	0
	1	**0**	**-**	**-**	**-**	**-**	**1**	**0**

***GRIFFITHS,* Arfon Trevor M.B.E.** 1959 - 1961 & 1962 - 1979

Position; *Midfielder*
D.O.B; *23rd August, 1941*
Birthplace; *Wrexham, Denbighshire*
Height; *5ft 6in* ***Weight;*** *10st 5lbs*
Debut v. *Darlington (h) 15th November, 1958 (F.A.Cup)*
Total Appearances & Goals; *713/8 apps 142 gls*
Career; *WREXHAM 15th May 1959; Arsenal 8th Feb 1961 £15,500 15apps 2gls; WREXHAM 19th Sept 1962 £8,000; Seattle Sounders May-Aug 1975 (Loan); May-Aug 1978 (Loan); Gresford Athletic Jan 1983;*
Honours; *17 Full Welsh International Caps; Three Welsh Under-23 caps; Welsh Cup Winner 1960, 1972, 1975 & 1978; Welsh Cup runner-up 1965, 1967 & 1971; Division Four runner-up 1970; Welsh Youth Cup Winner 1959; P.F.A.Third Division XI 1978;*

Arfon Griffiths was originally spotted in local junior football by former Wrexham player Frank Blew, who alerted the club's manager Cliff Lloyd. He initially signed Arfon on amateur forms in May 1957, as the youngster turned down offers of trials from both Liverpool and Sheffield Wednesday. In those days Arfon combined playing for Wrexham with his job in the wages department at Gresford Colliery. He made his first team debut at 17 in an F.A.Cup match against Darlington on the Racecourse in November 1958, stepping in to replace Brian Cripsey. That same season he was also a member of Wrexham's successful Welsh Youth Cup winning side. Arfon didn't feature in the first team again until the following November, against Reading, though he then kept his place for the rest of the season collecting a Welsh Cup winners' medal from a 1-0 win over Cardiff City. He became an established member of the side during 1960/61, and it was not long before the bigger clubs began to take an interest. In February 1961 Arsenal paid £15,500 to take the promising Welshman to Highbury, and he made his First Division debut against Wolves in April 1961. He went on to make a further 14 League appearances for the 'Gunners', before Billy Wright took charge and unwisely decided that Arfon was surplus to requirements. Hull City wanted his signature, but Wrexham manager Ken Barnes offered him the chance of a return to the Racecourse, which he accepted. This 'clever inside-forward/midfielder' thus began a nineteen-year link with the club that was to eventually lead to him becoming Club manager in 1977. Arfon was affectionately known to Wrexham fans as the 'Prince of Wales', and contributed massively to some of the best years in Wrexham Football Club's history: guiding the club to promotion in both 1963 and 1970; winning the Welsh Cup four times; playing in three European campaigns; helping 'The Robins' to reach the quarter-final stages of the European Cup-Winners' Cup in 1976, before losing out to the eventual winners Anderlecht, 2-1, on aggregate; being awarded a testimonial match in 1972 against Bill Shankly's Liverpool, which netted him £3,000 for his testimonial fund; making a club record 591 Football League appearances; and scoring the second highest total number of goals in the club's history, 120, most of which came from his 'probing and scheming, which so often resulted with him being on the end of a half-chance'. An impressive list, by anyone's standards. These successes also led him on to international recognition he gained 17 full Welsh caps, and crowned his contribution to his country by scoring the all important goal on the Racecourse against Austria in 1975, which enabled Wales to qualify for the 1976 European Championship finals. He was also selected for the 1971 Welsh F.A. tour to New Zealand, Australia, Tahiti and Malaysia. He actually played under eight managers at Wrexham, eventually taking charge himself in the summer of 1977 following the resignation of John Neal. Arfon had previously been his assistant manager for a year. Wrexham's directors had no hesitation in appointing him as Neal's replacement, and he kept faith with the same squad that had just missed out on promotion at the end of the previous season. He was soon to lose the services of Billy Ashcroft, however, who followed Neal to Middlesbrough. Griffiths then splashed out in the transfer market, spending £60,000 to bring in Dixie McNeil from Hereford as Ashcroft's replacement; £8,000 for Dai Davies from Everton; and £40,000 to Coventry for Les Cartwright. These three signings provided the right ingredients, and proved to be the missing pieces of the previous season's jigsaw, as Arfon went on to lead Wrexham to the Third Division championship, becoming the first manager in the club's history to win promotion to the then Second Division. The team was expected to do well in their new surroundings, but injuries affected the team's performances and struggled to come to terms with a higher grade of football. When the going got tough the crowds began to drop, and, in the summer of 1981, Arfon resigned on a matter of principle after an internal disagreement. Although he began to assist Bangor City with their training in an advisory capacity, he was to make a quick return to football management, when he was appointed manager of Crewe Alexandra on 3rd August 1981, spending just over a season at Gresty Road until relieved of his duties in October 1982. He did play for his local side, Gresford Athletic, in the Welsh National League, for a short while, before finishing

with football altogether to concentrate on his newsagents' shop in the village, where he can still be found at the time of writing. Arfon was awarded the M.B.E. in June 1976 for his services to Welsh soccer, a game with which he no longer has any connections. Golf is now his favourite pastime. Even so, his magnificent record speaks volumes for itself, and his place in Wrexham A.F.C.'s 'Hall of Fame' is assured.

Season	League		F.A.Cup		Welsh Cup		League Cup		E.C.W.C.		Total	
	apps	gls	apps	gls	apps	gls	apps	gls	apps	gls	apps	gls
1958/59	-	-	1	0	-	-	-	-	-	-	1	0
1959/60	22	5	2	0	5	2		-	-	-	29	7
1960/61	19	3	1	0	1	0	5	1	-	-	26	4
1962/63	38	7	4	1	2	1	-	-	-	-	44	9
1963/64	28	10	2	0	1		4	2	-	-	35	12
1964/65	43	10	2	0	6	1	1	0	-	-	52	11
1965/66	38	9	1	0	1	0	2	0		-	42	9
1966/67	43	4	2	0	6	0	1	0	-	-	52	4
1967/68	44	8	1	0	2	2	-	-	-	-	47	10
1968/69	26	9	2	2	4	1	-	-	-	-	32	12
1969/70	44	16	4	2	2	0	4	0	-	-	54	18
1970/71	32	12	1	0	3	0	2	1	-	-	38	13
1971/72	15	1	1	0	1	0	2	1	-	-	19	2
1972/73	21	5	2	0	-	-	-	-	1	0	24	5
1973/74	42	11	6		1	0	1	0	-	-	50	11
1974/75	40	2	1	0	3	2	1	0	-	-	45	4
1975/76	31	5	3	0	2	1	1	0	6	1	43	7
1976/77	41	2	6	0	3	0	5	0	-	-	55	2
1977/78	15/5	1	3	0	2	0	1/1	0	-	-	21/6	1
1978/79	3/1	0	-	1	1	-	0/1	0	-	-	3/2	1
	585/6	**120**	**45**	**5**	**46**	**11**	**30/1**	**5**	**7/1**	**1**	**713/8**	**142**

***GRIFFITHS,* Brian** 1952 - 1958

Position; *Inside-Forward*
D.O.B; *21st November, 1933*
Birthplace; *Penycae, Nr.Wrexham, Denbighshire*
Height; *5ft 8in* ***Weight;*** *10st 5lbs*
Debut v. *Chesterfield (a) 6th April, 1953*
Total Appearances & Goals; *23 apps 11 gls*
Career; *Ruabon Athletic; Blackpool 1950; WREXHAM (Am) May 1952, (Pro) 14th May 1953; Chester Jul 1958 2apps 1gls; Caernarfon Town 16th Jul 1959; Holywell Town 2nd Aug 1960;*
Honours; *Four Welsh Youth International caps; North Wales Coast F.A.Cup runner-up 1960;*

Brian Griffiths began playing football at Ruabon Grammar School, helping his school to win the Denbighshire Schools' Championship. He also

played for Ruabon Youth Club, followed by a spell with Ruabon Athletic, who competed in the First Division of the Welsh National League. It was during his time with the Youth club side that Brian, 16 at the time, was selected for various trials which eventually led to him representing Wales in five Boys' Club internationals. He was approached by scouts from a number of club's, which resulted in him signing amateur forms for First Division Blackpool. Brian played for the 3rd team at first, progressing to the Second XI by the beginning of 1951. At this time, manager Joe Smith insisted that he should sign professional forms, and move up to Blackpool to live. As he had secured employment with MANWEB in September 1951 he decided against turning professional at the time. By then Brian had also been selected to play for Wales at Youth level, making four appearances, the highlight coming in his first international against Ireland scoring a hat-trick in a 4-3 win. Wrexham began showing an interest towards the end of the year, but, as he was still at Bloomfield Road, no official approach could be made until the end of 1951/52. In February 1952, Griffiths was called up for his two years' National Service, enlisting with the Royal Air Force, and three months later joined the Racecourse staff on amateur terms. Brian served most of his time at R.A.F. Pershore, in Worcestershire, which enabled him to return to Wrexham to play on Saturdays. He also appeared for his Station XI during the week,going on to represent the Birmingham Wednesday League and R.A.F. Flying Command. He signed a part-time contract in May 1953, allowing him to continue with MANWEB when he finally completed his RAF service. Brian remained a part-time professional throughout his football career, although coming under pressure from the club's manager and Directors to turn full-time. They felt that his undoubted potential would not be realised by training twice a week, on Tuesday and Thursday evenings. He scored a hatful of goals for the reserves in the Cheshire County League, but, owing to the form of Ron Hewitt, Arthur Rowley and Johnny Anderson, found his first team chances limited. His Football League debut finally came in April 1953, replacing Hewitt in a 2-1 defeat at Chesterfield, and it proved to be his only first team game of that term. Over the next two seasons he added just six more first team appearances, although in 1955/56 he made the headlines in February when replacing Arthur Rowley at inside-forward, and in the remaining eleven matches scored seven goals. The following campaign would see both the most memorable and most disappointing moments of Brian's time at the Racecourse: he scored a hat-trick in a 5-0 victory over Darlington at the beginning of January, only to be left out of the following game at Barrow, which meant that he would miss the big F.A.Cup game with Manchester United the following week. He parted company with Wrexham in March 1958, when new manager John Love informed him that he wouldn't be retained at the end of the season. In July, Griffiths joined Chester, again as a part-time professional, allowing him to study three nights a week at Wrexham Tech for an Electrical Engineering degree, while training on the other two evenings. He was not to make his debut for Chester until January 1959, in a 3-3 draw at Gillingham, and he scored one of the goals. That same month he also made his final appearance for Chester in a 2-1 home defeat by Workington, before leaving Sealand Road in the summer. Griffiths then moved into Welsh League North circles with Caernarvon Town, picking up a North Wales Coast F.A runners-up medal in 1960, as they were beaten by Pwllheli in the final. He spent a season at the Oval before signing for Holywell Town in August 1960 for two years, helping them to the quarter-finals of the Welsh Cup, where they lost to Swansea Town. Shortly after, Brian decided to take a break from football in order to concentrate on his exams. After he had completed his studies he moved to Ludlow with the Midlands Electricity Board, and eventually took up playing again for Ludlow Town for a short while. In 1968 he gained further promotion and moved to Rhuddlan, where he has lived ever since. Brian retired from MANWEB in 1991, following 41 years in the industry. Today, he still keeps very active playing golf as a member of Rhuddlan Golf Club, and is also a Church Warden and treasurer of Rhuddlan Parish Church.

Season	League		F.A.Cup		Welsh Cup		Total	
	apps	gls	apps	gls	apps	gls	apps	gls
1952/53	1	0	-	-	-	-	1	0
1953/54	2	0	-	-	1	0	3	0
1954/55	3	0	-	-	-	-	3	0
1955/56	11	7	-	-	-	-	11	7
1956/57	3	3	-	-	-	-	3	3
1957/58	2	1	-	-	-	-	2	1
	22	**11**	**-**	**-**	**1**	**0**	**23**	**11**

GRIFFITHS, Carl Brian 1999

Position; *Forward*
D.O.B; *16th July, 1971.*
Birthplace; *Oswestry, Shropshire*
Height; *5ft 11in* ***Weight;*** *12st 6lbs*
Debut v. *Colchester United (a) 15th January, 1999.*
Total Appearances & Goals; *5apps 4gls*
Career; *Shrewsbury Town 26th Sept 1988 (Pro) 110/33apps 54gls; Manchester City 29th Oct 1993 £500,000 11/7apps 4gls; Portsmouth 17th Aug 1995 £200,000 2/12apps 2gls; Peterborough United 28th Mar 1996 £225,000 6/10apps 2gls; Leyton Orient 31st Oct 1996 (Loan) 5apps 3gls; Leyton Orient 7th Mar 1997 £100,000 60/5apps 29gls; WREXHAM 13th Jan 1999 (Loan); Port Vale 24th Mar 1999 £100,000 3apps 1gls;*
Honours; *One Welsh 'B' international cap; Two Welsh Under-21 international caps; Welsh Youth international;*

Carl Griffiths was a Wrexham supporter as a boy, as his dad came from the nearby village of Penycae. He later joined the club as a schoolboy when Dixie McNeil was manager, but got injured and drifted away. Living in the village of Forden, near Welshpool, it was local rivals Shrewsbury Town who signed the promising youngster when he left school in July 1987. He went on to progress at the Second Division club under a number of managers that included, Chic Bates, Ian McNeill, Asa Hartford, John Bond and finally Fred Davies. It was Ian McNeill who gave Carl his Football League debut for the 'Shrews' at the beginning of the 1988/89 season, when he came on as a substitute for Vic Kasule in a 4-1 defeat at Oxford. His first goal for Shrewsbury came in a 2-0 Welsh Cup win over Caernarfon Town a month later. Still only 17, Carl hit the headlines with two goals in the Gay Meadow club's 3-2 win at Leeds, which was followed in the next match by a further two goals at Manchester City in a 2-2 draw. Great things were expected of him at this stage, as he was soon being watched by a number of club's. He remained a valuable member of the first team squad for the rest of the campaign, the end of which, Shrewsbury, were to suffer the indignity of relegation. Over the next three seasons Griffiths only showed glimpses of his potential, and he found himself drifting in and out of first team contention. The 1992/93 season saw him regaining his confidence, and he finished the season as the club's top scorer with 27 League goals. The beginning of the following season saw Carl score five goals in nine games which was enough for Manchester City to step in and pay £500,000 for the talented forward, as Shrewsbury went on to win the Third Division championship. At Maine Road Carl made his debut as a substitute for Mike Sheron in a 3-1 defeat at West Ham, whilst scoring his first goal for City a month later in a 3-2 defeat at Leeds. He then held on to a first team place until March, but with the arrival of more seasoned strikers like Paul Walsh and Uwe Rosler, Griffiths was limited to just two substitute appearances for the 1994/95 season, despite scoring often for City's reserves'. At the end of that campaign he was allowed to leave Maine Road, turning down a move to Bristol Rovers, to join Portsmouth in a deal that involved Carl and Fitzroy Simpson in exchange for Kit Symons. He made his debut for 'Pompey' in a 1-0 League Cup defeat at Cardiff City in August 1995, but again he was to find his first team chances limited, spending much of his time at Fratton Park on the substitutes bench. Carl soon became unsettled, and Peterborough United manager Barry Fry stepped in to sign the 'classy striker' for a club record fee at the time of £225,000 before the season had ended in March 1996. He made an immediate impact with the 'Posh', scoring on his debut against Walsall, though ending up on the losing side in a 3-2 reserve. The following season saw him struggle to secure a first team place, spending much of the season on the sub's bench. He was allowed to join Leyton Orient on loan in November, and became an instant success when he scored the only goal in a 1-0 home win over Torquay United. He added two more goals in four further games for the 'O's' before returning to London Road when his month at Orient was up. Again he found a first team place with the 'Posh' hard to come by, although he did play and score against Wrexham in the F.A.Cup Fourth Round match at London Road. Just over a month later Leyton Orient manager Tommy Taylor returned to Peterborough to sign Carl for a knocked down fee of £100,000. He quickly repaid some of that fee by scoring twice on his debut in a 4-4 draw at Brighton, as he soon became a crowd favourite with the fans at Brisbane Road, acquiring a knack of scoring vital goals for them. He ended the 1997/98 season as the club's top scorer, by becoming the first Leyton Orient player to score over twenty goals in two decades, when he totalled 21 League and Cup goals, including a hat-trick in an 8-0 home win over Doncaster Rovers in December 1997, which equalled the 'O's' Football League record victory. Griffiths was described at the East London club as 'good with both feet, and head, and holds the ball up well while awaiting support from others'. Despite Carl's favouritism amongst the Orient fan's, this was not so with the management, and manager Tommy Taylor agreed for him to join Wrexham on loan in January 1999 with a view to a permanent move. He made his Wrexham debut against Colchester United, and scored the third goal in the 'Robins' 3-1 win at Layer Road with a superbly taken 15 yard angled drive. Carl went on to score three more goals in four games before his loan period ended. Despite the 'Robins' making an offer to Orient for his services, this was turned down by the 'O's' and Carl returned to Brisbane Road. However, before the transfer deadline in March, Port Vale paid out £100,000 to secure his services.

Season	League		F.A.Cup		W.P.C.		League Cup		A.W.S.		Total	
	apps	gls	apps	gls	apps	gls	apps	gls	apps	gls	apps	gls
1998/99	4	3	-	-	-	-	-	-	1	1	5	4
	4	**3**	**-**	**-**	**-**	**-**	**-**	**-**	**1**	**1**	**5**	**4**

GRIFFITHS, Dennis

1952 - 1958

Position; *Half-Back*
D.O.B; *12th August, 1935*
Birthplace; *Ruabon, Denbighshire*
Height; *5ft 8in* **Weight;** *10st 9lbs*
Debut v. *Tranmere Rovers (h) 1st March, 1952*
Total Appearances & Goals; *75 apps 3 gls*
Career; *WREXHAM 22nd Aug 1952; Bangor City 9th Aug 1958; Borough United 31st Dec 1960; Flint Town United 17th Aug 1961; Caernarvon Town 14th Oct 1961 to Jan 1962;*

Dennis Griffiths played football for his school team at Acrefair Secondary Modern, helping them capture the District Cup. It was whilst appearing for his school at outside-right that he came to the attention of Wrexham, and, following a trial in 1951 was invited to join the groundstaff by manager Peter Jackson. Dennis progressed steadily through the youth ranks until 1952, when as he was making his way to an 'A' team game at Pentre Broughton was told to return to the Racecourse. On arrival he found his name on the senior team sheet, as Len Wootton had missed his train connection! Griffiths was only sixteen when stepping out against Tranmere Rovers on St.David's Day 1952. However, there was to be no fairy-tale ending, as Wrexham lost 1-0. A local journal described him thus: - "what he lacks in inches, he makes up for in tremendous enthusiasm and effort." He returned to the junior ranks, but in August 1952 was signed on professional terms. His progress ground to a halt in the 1952/53 season, when breaking a leg in a Cheshire County League game for the reserves. After recovering from injury he was switched to wing-half, where he remained for the rest of his career. Dennis returned to first team football during 1953/54, appearing against Halifax Town just before Christmas 1953. By February he was playing regularly in the Wrexham first team, and over the next two seasons appeared quite frequently in the side, though mainly as cover for either Johnnie Tapscott, Brian Jarvis or Keith Bannister. The 1956/57 campaign saw Dennis involved in the opening three matches of the season until Gwyn Morgans took over, while the following season saw him make just one appearance, at home to Gateshead, in place of Gren Jones. It proved to be his last game for Wrexham as he left the Racecourse at the end of the season to join Bangor City, at the same time finding employment as a storeman for George Turner, a former Wrexham Football Club director. Dennis played in Bangor's Welsh Cup semi-final match with Cardiff City in 1960; the 'Bluebirds' had just won promotion to the First Division, and the Cheshire County League outfit battled to a creditable 1-1 draw before losing the replay. He continued at Farrar Road until December 1960, thereafter enjoying spells with a few Welsh League North clubs - Borough United, Flint Town United, and Caernarvon Town. Following his retirement from football in January 1962 Dennis found work in the fitters' shop at Shotton Steelworks until 1980, when he was made redundant following the closure of the plant. He then returned to the Racecourse, working as assistant to groundsman Johnny Edwards for about twelve months. County Council then engaged him in a similar capacity for their schools and colleges, before retiring in 1992. Today, Dennis still lives in the Wrexham area and can often be seen at the Racecourse, supporting the 'Robins'.

Season	League		F.A.Cup		Welsh Cup		Total	
	apps	gls	apps	gls	apps	gls	apps	gls
1951/52	1	0	-	-	-	-	1	0
1953/54	16	0	2	0	2	0	20	0
1954/55	19	1	-	-	4	0	23	1
1955/56	28	2	-	-	-	-	28	2
1956/57	3	0	-	-	-	-	3	0
1957/58	1	0	-	-	-	-	1	0
	67	**3**	**2**	**0**	**6**	**0**	**75**	**3**

GRIFFITHS, Estyn

1950 - 1952

Position; *Centre-Half*
D.O.B; *22nd July, 1927*
Birthplace; *Pontblyddyn, Nr.Mold, Flintshire*
Height; *ft in* **Weight;** *st lbs*
Debut v. *Shrewsbury Town (h) 30th August, 1950*
Total Appearances & Goals; *10 apps 0 gls*
Career; *Chester Oapps; Llay United; WREXHAM 4th Apr 1950; Chelmsford Jul 1952; Caernarfon Town 15th Aug 1956; Colwyn Bay 14th Nov 1956;*
Honours; *Two Welsh Amateur International caps; Welsh Amateur Cup Winner 1949;*

As a youngster Estyn Griffiths attended both Llay Primary and Grove Park Grammar Schools, although he spent his early football career on the books of Chester. Unfortunately, he failed to make the grade at Sealand Road and left without making a first team appearance. He then joined his local side, Llay United, where he collected a Welsh Amateur Cup winners' medal in 1949. Almost twelve months later, and following two Amateur international caps for Wales against England and Scotland, he was signed by Wrexham in April 1950. Estyn went on to make his Football League debut for the 'Robins' as a wing-half in a 1-0 home win over Shrewsbury Town, in place of Les Speed. He played another four matches

before returning to the reserve team. He made just one more appearance for Wrexham that season, at centre-half, in place of George Spruce. In 1951/52 Estyn recorded four more senior games before mid-September, but was not to feature in a 'Robins' first team shirt again, due primarily to an injury he had sustained. He was released in the summer, signing for Southern League side Chelmsford, where he became employed as a clerk for a local Engineering firm. Estyn returned to settle down in Wrexham in 1956, working as a Chief Clerk with Walton & Mason Bookmakers in the Town, and continued to play football for a short while for both Caernarvon Town and Colwyn Bay. He was also known to be a keen cricketer, and during the summer months played local League Cricket for Llay. It is understood that Estyn was one of the first players in Britain to wear contact lenses.

Season	League		F.A.Cup		Welsh Cup		Total	
	apps	gls	apps	gls	apps	gls	apps	gls
1950/51	6	0	-	-	-	-	6	0
1951/52	4	0	-	-	-	-	4	0
	10	**0**	**-**	**-**	**-**	**-**	**10**	**0**

GRIFFITHS, Ian James 1991 - 1992

Position; *Forward*
D.O.B; *17th April, 1960*
Birthplace; *Birkenhead, Merseyside*
Height; *5ft 6in* ***Weight;*** *11st 2lbs*
Debut v. *Cardiff City (h) 22nd March, 1991*
Total Appearances & Goals; *17 apps 0 gls*
Career; *Tranmere Rovers Feb 1979 110/6apps 5gls; Rochdale Aug 1983 40/2apps 5gls; Port Vale Sept 1984 9/3apps 0gls; Wigan Athletic Jul 1985 73/9apps 7gls; Mazda Hiroshima (Japan) cs1988; Wigan Athletic Aug 1990 6/5apps 0gls; WREXHAM 22nd Mar 1991; Rhyl cs1992;*
Honours; *Welsh Cup runner-up 1991 & 1993; Emperors Cup runner-up 1989;*

Ian Griffiths was brought up on the Wirral and played football for Shaftsbury Boys' Club as his own Rock Ferry High School was a rugby-only institution. Despite the lack of the round ball game at school it failed to hold Ian back, playing for Birkenhead Boys between the ages of 10 and 12, as well as selected for both Cheshire and Wirral Schoolboys through various stages. He was actually an all-round sportsman, representing his school at both rugby and cricket. At fourteen he was signed by Tranmere Rovers on schoolboy forms and, when leaving school, was faced with the choice of either joining Tranmere as an apprentice or of taking up a welding apprenticeship with British Nuclear Fuels at Capenhurst. He chose the latter, as he thought himself too small to succeed as a professional footballer. Nevertheless, he remained on Tranmere's books as a part-time professional. Despite competing with the club's full-time players Griffiths was given his Football League debut by manager John King towards the end of 1978/79, in a 2-1 home defeat by Mansfield Town. Having completed his apprenticeship as a welder Ian was offered professional terms by Tranmere, which he accepted. Shortly afterwards, King was replaced by Bryan Hamilton. Ian was playing for the reserves at this time, but was given his first team chance again by the new manager, and went on to miss just one more match during 1980/81. He became a regular in the Tranmere side over the next two seasons, before leaving Prenton Park in the close season of 1983 to join Rochdale. Griffiths made his debut for the Lancashire club in a 4-1 home win over Reading, and became a permanent in the side until the following season, when the club's manager Jimmy Greenhoff was replaced by Vic Halom. He played just one match under Halom, a 5-1 defeat at Mansfield, until he was allowed to leave. Ian then joined Port Vale, initially on trial, and scored on his full debut in a 4-1 F.A.Cup win over Scunthorpe United. He played regularly until February, when he trapped his finger in the toilet door of the team coach, and had to have a skin graft! The following month he damaged knee ligaments, and found himself released at the end of the season. Ian then teamed up again with Bryan Hamilton, by this time the manager at Wigan Athletic, and went on to help Wigan reach the Third Division play-offs in 1987 until injuries began to limit his first team outings. In 1988 he left Springfield Park to try Japanese football for two seasons, playing for Mazda Hiroshima, and collecting an Emperor Cup runners-up medal, which is the Japanese equivalent of the F.A.Cup. He returned to Wigan in August 1990, only to suffer with injuries, joining Wrexham in March 1991 in an exchange deal for Gary Worthington. Having made his debut the same month, in a 1-0 home win over Cardiff City, he remained in the team for the rest of the campaign, appearing in the Welsh Cup Final against Swansea City at the National Stadium in Cardiff, which Wrexham lost 2-0. During the summer he sustained an Achilles injury, forcing him to miss the start of the new season. He returned for three matches in September, but aggravated the injury, which eventually persuaded him to retire from professional football at the end of the season. He continued to play at non-league level, joining Cymru Alliance League side Rhyl for 1992/93, helping them finish runners-up in the League and thus gain promotion to the League of Wales, also reaching the Welsh Cup Final at the National Stadium, where they lost to Cardiff City.

Season	League		F.A.Cup		Welsh Cup		League Cup		L.D.C.		Total	
	apps	gls	apps	gls	apps	gls	apps	gls	apps	gls	apps	gls
1990/91	11	0	-	-	3	0	-	-	-	-	14	0
1991/92	3	0	-	-	-	-	-	-	-	-	3	0
	14	**0**	**-**	**-**	**3**	**0**	**-**	**-**	**-**	**-**	**17**	**0**

GRIFFITHS, Robert 1919 - 1922

Position; *Half-Back*
D.O.B; *27th March, 1889.*
Birthplace; *Brynteg, Nr Wrexham, Denbighshire*
Died; *Holyhead, 11th August, 1983*
Height; *5ft 8 1/2in* ***Weight;*** *11st 2lbs*
Debut v. *Willenhall Swifts (a) 30th August 1919*
Football League debut v. *Hartlepool United (h) 27th August 1921*
Total Appearances & Goals; *44 apps 1 gls*
Career; *Stansty Juniors; Brymbo Victoria; Summerhill Victoria; Bolton Wanderers Aug 1911 0apps; Chester Aug 1912; Garston Aug 1914; Tranmere Rovers Jan 1915; WREXHAM 29th Aug 1919; Shrewsbury Town cs1920 31apps 0gls; WREXHAM 14th May 1921; Holyhead Town 5th Sept 1922; Holyhead Railway Institute Aug 1923; Holyhead Railway Institute 21st Nov 1930;*
Honours; *Welsh Cup runner-up 1920;*

Bob Griffiths played his early football in the Wrexham area for Stansty Juniors, Brymbo Victoria, and Summerhill Victoria. He was signed by Bolton Wanderers in 1911, and did well enough to be offered terms at Burnden Park. However, he had his mother to support, and as Bolton would not allow any of their professionals to work, he returned home. He was quickly fixed up with another club when signing for Combination League side Chester in the close season of 1912, and went on to make 60 appearances, scoring four goals. He joined Liverpool non-league side Garston in August 1914. After a brief spell, Tranmere Rovers obtained his services in January 1915, shortly before he enlisted with the Welsh Guards in May 1915 for the First World War. He played football during this period when he could, representing the Brigade of Guards football team, the Guards Division while in France, and, in London, turned out for Crystal Palace. He was promoted to sergeant in January 1916, a position he held until the hostilities were over. Upon his demobilisation from the Army Bob signed for Wrexham, in time for the club's first season of Birmingham League football at the end of the Great War. He played the 1919/20

season for Wrexham at half-back, missing only one game in a campaign ending with him playing in the Welsh Cup Final against Cardiff City on the Racecourse, which Cardiff won 2-1. During the close season he surprisingly decided to leave the Racecourse to join fellow Birmingham & District League side Shrewsbury Town, making his debut in a 2-0 defeat against Birmingham's second XI. Bob missed just three matches for the 'Shrews' all season, returning to the Racecourse following Wrexham's election to the Football League. He appeared in the club's first ever match in the Football League in August 1921, which turned out to be his one and only Football League appearance spending the rest of his time at the club in the reserve team in the Birmingham & District competition. He was released in the summer. Griffiths then moved along the coast to Holyhead, where he obtained employment on the Railway, continuing to play football for both the successful Holyhead Railway Institute team, in railway cup competitions, and for Holyhead Town in the newly formed Welsh National League. During his time with the 'Harbourmen' he was chosen to represent the North Wales Coast F.A. against the Scottish Juniors in 1925. He was an influential member of the Town side for a number of years, at the same time continuing to turn out for the Holyhead Railway Institute. Bob settled in Holyhead, where he spent the rest of his working life on the 'Flat Ships' (Vessels which carried coal between Holyhead and Dun Laoghaire) until he retired. He became a well-known character in Holyhead with many yarns to tell, as well as the one time chairman of the Holyhead Town Supporters' Association, an organisation of which his father-in-law also occupied the top seat. Bob was a member of the Holyhead Railway Institute team who won the Railway Welfare Cup in 1928 v Carlisle after beating West Ham in the Semi-Finals.

Season	League		F.A.Cup		Welsh Cup		Total	
	apps	gls	apps	gls	apps	gls	apps	gls
1919/20	33	0	5	1	5	0	43	1
1921/22	1	0	-	-	-	-	1	0
	34	**0**	**5**	**1**	**5**	**0**	**44**	**1**
F/League	1	0	-	-	-	-	1	0

GRIFFITHS, Tom Percival 1922 -1926 & 1938 - 1939

Position; *Centre-Half*
D.O.B; *21st February, 1906*
Birthplace; *Moss, Wrexham, Denbighshire*
Died; *Denbigh, 25th December, 1981*
Height; *6ft 0in* ***Weight;*** *11st 10lbs*
Debut v. *Tranmere Rovers (a) 24th March, 1923*
Total Appearances & Goals; *51 apps 2 gls*
Career; *Wrexham Boys Club; Frith Valley; WREXHAM (Am) cs1922, (Pro) 10th Aug 1923; Everton 22nd Dec 1926 £3,000 76apps 9gls; Bolton Wanderers £7,000 Dec 1931 48apps 6gls; Middlesborough £6,500 March 1933 92apps 1gls; Aston Villa Nov 1935 £5,000 65apps 1gls; WREXHAM 22nd Aug 1938, WW2 1app 0gls; Retired during War;*
Honours; *21 Welsh international caps; Second Division Championship Winner 1931;One Welsh Junior international cap;*

Tommy Griffiths, or 'T.P.' as he was more popularly known, joined Wrexham as a 16 year-old in 1922. He had earlier impressed his relation, the Wales and Wrexham player Tommy Mathias in local junior football, playing for Ffrith Valley F.C. and Wrexham Boys' Club as a centre-forward. At that time he was working as a cabinet maker, but it was not long before he was playing football for a living. His chance in the 'Robins' senior side came sooner than he had expected, when he made his Football League debut at the age of 17, in a League game at Tranmere in March 1923, which Wrexham lost 4-0. He had been called into the team at inside-forward to replace Bill Cotton. Tom found himself back in the reserve team after the game, but was eventually given a chance at centre-half. He made such rapid progress in his new position that it resulted in him gaining inter-league and junior international caps. Tom went on to establish himself at the heart of the 'Robins' defence, turning in performances that soon attracted the attention of the bigger clubs, and in December 1926 Everton paid out £3,000 for him. Tom spent nearly five years at Goodison Park, making his Everton debut at Leicester in a 6-2 rout in February 1927, but he didn't record a further first team appearance until October 1928, thereby missing out on Everton's championship season of 1927/28. He later became a regular in the side, but couldn't stop the 'Toffees' slipping into the Second Division in 1930. Tom played a prominent part in the club's return to the Top Division as champions at the end of the following season, although missing most of the second half of the campaign through injury. By this time, he had become widely respected for his 'fine heading of the ball', and as a player who 'never messed around in clearing the ball out of defence, believing in the 'get rid' policy'. He won the first of his 21 Welsh caps, succeeding the immortal Fred Keenor as his country's regular centre-half, only to be replaced by Charlie Gee Everton's first choice number five in 1931/32. Tom then accepted an offer to sign for Bolton Wanderers in December 1931 in a £7,000 deal. He went straight into the 'Trotters' team, making his debut against..........Everton! Much to Tom's delight, Bolton won 2-1. He kept his place in the side for the rest of the season, but the following year found 'The Trotter' fighting to avoid relegation, and in March 1933 was to leave the then doomed Burnden Park club to join First Division Middlesbrough for £6,000. T.P. was a first team regular at Ayresome Park throughout the two and a half seasons that he spent at the club, where he was regarded as one of the best centre-halves ever to play for 'Boro. He was described as 'able to hang in the air longer than his opponent', while he 'rarely failed in a tackle'. In November 1935 he left the North-East and signed for fellow First Division side Aston Villa for £5,000. Villa's season had begun disastrously , and even Tom's signing couldn't help them avoid relegation - which meant that Griffith's had the unenviable record of experiencing the drop with three different clubs in five seasons! He disappointingly missed out on Villa's 1937/38 promotion season through illness, and at the end of the campaign was allowed to leave Villa Park and Tom returned to Wrexham in August 1938. By mid-September the Wrexham manager, Arthur Cowell, had resigned, and Tom was asked by the club's directors to become the caretaker-manager. He remained in the position until Tom Morgan was appointed as the new boss in April 1939. He did make one more appearance for The Racecourse Club during WW2 before finally retiring from playing. In 1949, he became a club director with Wrexham, though he gave up the position a season later when asked to take over from Charlie Leyfield as trainer/coach, to Peter Jackson. He remained at the Racecourse in the same capacity until May 1952. Tom later became the landlord of the Turf Hotel, followed by spells at the Hand Hotel in Wrexham and the Red Lion in Marchwiel before retiring from the trade in the late 1960s. By that time he had also become a well known cellist, performing in many local concerts in in the Wrexham and Rhos area. Tommy died on Christmas Day 1981. He was 75.

Season	League		F.A.Cup		Welsh Cup		Total	
	apps	gls	apps	gls	apps	gls	apps	gls
1922/23	1	0	-	-	-	-	1	0
1924/25	6	0	-	-	-	-	6	0
1925/26	9	1	-	-	2	0	11	1
1926/27	19	1	4	0	-	-	23	1
1938/39	10	0	-	-	-	-	10	0
1940/41	1*	0	-	-	-	-	1	0
	45*	**2**	**4**	**0**	**2**	**0**	**51**	**2**

* War-time games - not included in total.

GUNSON, Joseph Gordon 1926 - 1929 & 1935 - 1936

Position; *Outside-Left*
D.O.B; *1st July, 1904*
Birthplace; *Chester, Cheshire*
Died; *Broughton, Chester, 13th September, 1991*
Height; *5ft 9in* **Weight;** *11st 0lbs*
Debut v. *Chesterfield (h) 28th August, 1926.*
Total Appearances & Goals; *149 apps 45 gls*
Career; *Brickfields F.C.; Nelson cs1923 0apps; WREXHAM 18th Aug 1926; Sunderland 31st May 1929 £1,500 19apps 11gls; Liverpool 12th March 1930 81apps 24gls; Swindon Town Jun 1934 31apps 7gls; WREXHAM 22nd May 1935; Bangor City cs1936;*

Gordon Gunson began playing organised football with Chester junior side Brickfields. He was one of four members of the side who eventually progressed into professional football. Third Division North side Nelson first signed Gordon as an amateur in 1923, and he showed enough promise to be offered professional terms shortly afterwards. He failed to make a first team appearance with Nelson, however, and during the close season of 1926 moved closer to home when he signed for Wrexham. He went straight into the 'Robins' first team at outside-left for the opening match of the 1926/27 season, a 3-1 home win over Chesterfield, and held on to the position until leaving the Racecourse in the summer of 1929. Prior to that he had played for the 'Robins' in the 1928/29 side that came close to gaining promotion to the Second Division for the first time since their entry into the Football League in 1921, finishing third in the final League table. He also impressed in the club's first ever F.A.Cup match against First Division opposition, when Wrexham took on Birmingham in 1928. Gordon scored with a 30 yard goal in a 3-1 defeat, a score-line that did Wrexham scant justice. Soon after Gunson, much to his surprise, was selected to play for Wales. That was until he pointed out that he had been born in Chester!! During his time at the club Gordon was described as 'a fast, goalscoring winger, who liked to cut in and shoot'. At the end of the 1928/29 season Sunderland signed hm for what was then a large fee, £1,500. He made his debut for his new club in a 1-1 draw at Portsmouth in September 1929, and went on to score eleven goals in the next eighteen League games. This sort of form persuaded Liverpool to sign him in March 1930. He made his Liverpool debut at Bolton in a 2-0 win, and in the following match at Anfield scored in a 2-0 win over Aston Villa. Gordon remained in the side for the rest of the season, though he was to manage just eight appearances throughout 1930/31. He was an ever-present in 1931/32, but the next campaign saw him sustain a serious cartilage injury. He left Anfield in June 1934, and signed for Swindon Town in an attempt to resurrect his career, spending a season at the County Ground before rejoining Wrexham in May 1935. His return to the Racecourse was not a success, due mainly to the knee injury that he picked up at Liverpool, and it was to trouble him all season. He made just 15 League appearances until allowed to join Bangor City as player/manager in the summer of 1936, when his playing days were brought to an end during his stay at Farrar Road. Gordon later became trainer with Crewe Alexandra, before managing Flint Town until June 1960, when he resigned. He then took over as manager of Welshpool during the close season of 1960, where he remained for four years before taking charge at Welsh League North Dolgellau in 1964. He later scouted for a number of League clubs, including Coventry City. Gordon Gunson died in mid-September 1991 in a nursing home in Broughton, near Chester. He was aged 87.

Season	League		F.A.Cup		Welsh Cup		N.S.C.		Total	
	apps	gls	apps	gls	apps	gls	apps	gls	apps	gls
1926/27	37	3	4	1	4	1	-	-	45	5
1927/28	37	11	5	5	3	1	-	-	45	17
1928/29	42	17	1	0	1	1	-	-	44	18
1935/36	15	5	-	-	-	-	-	-	15	5
	131	**36**	**10**	**6**	**8**	**3**	**-**	**-**	**149**	**45**

GWATKIN, Phillip Arthur 1952 - 1956

Position; *Outside-Right*
D.O.B; *5th August, 1929*
Birthplace; *Harrow, London*
Height; *5ft 10'1/2in* **Weight;** *11st 5lbs*
Debut v. *Chesterfield (h) 26th August, 1953*
Total Appearances & Goals; *64 apps 12 gls*
Career; *WREXHAM 28th Oct 1952; Tranmere Rovers 26th Jun 1956 21apps 6gls; Northwich Victoria cs1957; New Brighton 1957; West Kirby 1959;*

Phil Gwatkin originated from Harrow, but he and his family moved up to Merseyside in the 1930s after his father was offered better employment. The outbreak of the Second World War saw Phil and his six brothers and sisters evacuated to Ynys Mon (Anglesey) to live on their Grandparents' farm, where they remained throughout the hostilities. He attended the Holyhead County School, who he represented at football, eventually leaving North Wales to take up work as an apprentice fitter at Liverpool Docks. He was then called up for his national service with the Army when until that time his football career had consisted of playing park football in his home town of Wallasey, although he had been invited for trials with Everton, which came to nothing. He joined the Army's R.E.M.E. Battalion, and underwent his basic training at Honiton in Devon. Phil then served at Malvern and in Germany before returning to his home base at the Dale Barracks in Chester. It was whilst playing for his Battalion team that he was spotted and invited to sign for Chester F.C. However, after four weeks and no further contact from the Sealand Road club he joined Wrexham! Phil had been recommended to the club by reserve team full-back Bob Hawkins, and was signed in October 1952 at the age of 23, remaining in the Army until he was demobbed. Gwatkin made his first appearance for the 'Robins' second XI in a Cheshire County League game against Macclesfield Town in August 1953, scoring four goals! The local press reported at the time, 'Gwatkin led the attack skilfully, distributed the ball cleverly and showed coolness and excellent judgment in the vicinity of goal.' After such a good start it was only a matter of time before Phil appeared in the first team, and his opportunity soon came against Chesterfield on the Racecourse the following week, when he replaced Glyn Hughes in a 2-1 defeat. Hughes returned for the following game, but Gwatkin was back in first team action in December and celebrated with two goals in a 5-0 win over Halifax Town. He was regarded at the time as one of the fastest wingers in the Third Division North, and as the team began to hit peak form played his part in Wrexham's run of seven wins from ten games, enabling the club to climb the table and finish in eighth place. The 1954/55 season was to see him contesting the outside-right position with Hughes but, by the end of the term, a change of manager had resulted in a new right winger being installed, Gren Jones. Phil was limited to just ten League games in 1955/56, and led to player and club parting company in the summer. He was described at Wrexham as 'often having to make way for new signings, but never failed to give a wholehearted display when called upon. A brilliant ball player who can easily be a match winner. However, he was by far a more prolific goalscorer with the Cheshire League team'. Phil moved on to Tranmere Rovers in June 1956, joining them as a part-timer and taking up work with BNFL at Capenhurst. He made his Rovers' debut in a 4-1 defeat at Hull in the opening game of the 1956/57 season, scoring the consolation goal. A further 20 League appearances followed, in which he notched five more goals before leaving Prenton Park at the end of the season after a disagreement over travel arrangements. Gwatkin then joined Cheshire County League side Northwich Victoria for a short spell, until linking up with Lancashire Combination League side New Brighton. Phil spent almost two seasons there, before joining West Kirby, coaching the second XI during his three year spell. He left Capenhurst in 1969 to work at Vauxhall, from where he retired in 1993 after completing 24 years with the company. He now lives in retirement in Wallasey.

Season	League		F.A.Cup		Welsh Cup		Total	
	apps	gls	apps	gls	apps	gls	apps	gls
1953/54	22	4	1	0	2	2	25	6
1954/55	24	4	1	0	3	2	28	6
1955/56	10	0	-	-	1	0	11	0
	56	**8**	**2**	**0**	**6**	**4**	**64**	**12**

RON HEWITT

HAIGH, Ian 1986 - 1987

Position; *Goalkeeper*
D.O.B; *26th February 1965*
Birthplace; *Liverpool, Merseyside*
Height; *ft in* **Weight;** *st lbs*
Debut v. *Tranmere Rovers (h) 25th November, 1986 (Freight Rover Trophy)*
Total Appearances & Goals; *1 app 0 gls*
Career; *Southport; South Liverpool; WREXHAM cs1986; Rhyl Mar 1987; Caernarfon Town 1987; Mossley; Rhyl Sept 1994 54/1apps 0gls; Bangor City Jan 1996 7apps 0gls; Knowsley United cs1996; Rhyl 1996/97 21apps 0gls; Knowsley United;*

Ian Haigh had played non-league football for both Southport and South Liverpool prior to joining Wrexham on trial during the close season of 1986. He was then signed on non-contract forms and played reserve team football until November, when called upon to play in a Freight Rover Trophy match against Tranmere Rovers, after regular 'keeper Chris Pearce was injured. Wrexham won the match 6-1, but Pearce returned to first team action for the following match, while Ian continued playing reserve team football at the Racecourse before leaving the club towards the end of the season. He then joined Multipart League side Caernarfon Town, with whom he spent seven seasons, including their period 'in exile' at Curzon Ashton. Following a trial with Tranmere Rovers he joined Mossley for a short spell, before returning to North Wales to sign for League of Wales side Rhyl, where he was described as being a 'brave and agile 'keeper'. Ian went on to spend one and a half seasons at Belle Vue, before leaving in January 1996 to sign for League of Wales Champions Bangor City. However, his stay at Farrar Road was brief, and he joined Knowsley United in the summer. Soon after joining the Northern Premier League side he was on the move again, returning to Rhyl where he stayed until 1997, when returning to Knowsley United.

Season	League		F.A.Cup		Welsh Cup		League Cup		F.R.T.		Total	
	apps	gls	apps	gls	apps	gls	apps	gls	apps	gls	apps	gls
1986/87	-	-	-	-	-	-	-	-	1	0	1	0
	-	**-**	**-**	**-**	**-**	**-**	**-**	**-**	**1**	**0**	**1**	**0**

HAMILTON, James Stevenson 1933 - 1938

Position; *Left-Back*
D.O.B; *16th August, 1906*
Birthplace; *New Cumnock, Strathclyde*
Height; *5ft 11in* **Weight;** *11st 7lbs*
Debut v. *Mansfield Town (h) 2nd September, 1933*
Total Appearances & Goals; *184apps 1 gls*
Career; *Girvan Juniors; Ayr United Sept 1928 1app 0gls; Rochdale 23rd Jun 1931 77apps 0gls; WREXHAM 24th Jun 1933; Carlisle United Jun 1938 28apps 0gls; Chester May 1939;*

Jimmy Hamilton had played football for Ayr Grammar School and was turning out for local club Girvan Juniors when signed by Scottish League club Ayr United in September 1928. Jim made just one League appearance in his only season at Somerset Park. In the summer of 1931 he was persuaded to move south of the border to join Third Division North side Rochdale. Jim made his Football League debut for the Lancashire club at Rotherham United, in the second game of the season, a 5-0 defeat. Even though this was not exactly the best of beginnings Hamilton became a regular with the Spotland club for the next two seasons, making 77 League appearances. By the summer of 1933 he had decided to try his luck elsewhere, and Wrexham beat off the challenge of a number of clubs to capture his signature. At the time Jim was quoted as saying, "North Wales suits me best". He didn't have to wait long before being plunged into Wrexham's first team; summoned to replace regular left-back, John Brown in the third game of 1933/34, Jim celebrated his debut with a 5-0 home win over Mansfield Town. He became a permanent fixture in the Wrexham side until the beginning of the 1937/38 season, playing in the opening match of the new season at Hull City. The game ended in a 3-2 defeat, and it proved to be his final match for the 'Robins'. He was then replaced by Bill Bellamy, who made the position his for the rest of the season. Jim was confined to reserve team football, and he left the club at the end of the season. During his time at the Racecourse Hamilton had been noted as a consistent full-back, missing only three games between his League debut and his final appearance against Hull. All told, he played in 184 games for the 'Robins'. Among them were the 11-1 victory over New Brighton in 1934, and also the club's biggest F.A.Cup match of the 1930s, when the 'Robins' lost 3-1 to First Division Manchester City after a spirited performance. Jim signed for Carlisle United in June 1938, where he had to wait until the end of September before making his debut, a disastrous 7-1 defeat at Southport.

Following this result he found himself out of favour again, though he was re-established in the team by December, and remained a regular in the side until the end of the season. After leaving the 'Cumbrians' in the summer he moved down to Chester but, due to the outbreak of WW2, he was never given the opportunity to impress.

Season	League		F.A.Cup		Welsh Cup		N.S.C.		Total	
	apps	gls	apps	gls	apps	gls	apps	gls	apps	gls
1933/34	37	0	1	0	1	0	4	0	43	0
1934/35	42	1	2	0	2	0	2	0	48	1
1935/36	41	0	-	-	2	0	2	0	45	0
1936/37	42	0	3	0	1	0	1	0	47	0
1937/38	1	0	-	-	-	-	-	-	1	0
	163	**1**	**6**	**0**	**6**	**0**	**9**	**0**	**184**	**1**

HANNIGAN, Brendan 1965 - 1966

Position; *Forward*
D.O.B; *3rd September, 1943*
Birthplace; *Dublin*
Height; *ft in* **Weight;** *st lbs*
Debut v. *Halifax Town (a) 10th December, 1965*
Total Appearances & Goals; *8 apps 2 gls*
Career; *East Wall Juniors; Shelbourne; WREXHAM 9th Dec 1965; Shelbourne Aug 1966; Dundalk 1966/67; Chelmsford City cs1967; Dundalk 1967/68; Shamrock Rovers cs1968; Sligo Rovers cs1969; St.Patricks Athletic cs1971; Shelbourne cs1972; Cork Celtic cs1973; Retired 1975;*
Honours; *League of Ireland Championship Winner 1962, 1967 & 1974; F.A.I.Cup 1963 & 1969; League of Ireland XI representative cap;*

Ben, as he was known, played football for East Wall School team in his native Dublin, without gaining any representative honours during the period. Upon leaving school he took up employment with a timber merchant in the City, where he stayed for three years before going on to work in the docks in the city. By this time Ben was turning out for local side East Wall Juniors, and it was there that he was spotted by League of Ireland club Shelbourne. They offered him a professional contract, which he gladly accepted. Hannigan won representative honours with Shelbourne, appearing for the League of Ireland against their Northern counterparts, as well as selection for a Dublin XI against Arsenal. In 1962, he helped Shelbourne to win the League of Ireland championship, and the following season he was involved in the club's European Cup games against Sporting Lisbon. Ben then assisted Shelbourne in lifting the Irish Cup, which brought them a European Cup-Winners' Cup tie in the Nou Camp, against Barcelona, and later achieved a UEFA Cup place at the end of the 1963/64 season. Ben figured in Shelbourne's 2-1 replay win over Portuguese club Beleneses, which took them forward to a meeting with Athletico Madrid, though they lost both legs 1-0. In December 1965 he took the plunge and left Dublin, to sign for Wrexham manager Billy Morris in a £3,000 deal. However, Ben never really settled in at the Racecourse, though his new Club's position, struggling at the foot of the Fourth Division, hardly helped. He was pitched straight into the first team at inside-forward for his League debut in a 4-0 defeat at Halifax Town, and although he scored in his next match, at home to Darlington, it ended in a 2-1 defeat. Ben played in the following two games before being replaced in the side. He appeared in three more League games towards the end of the season, but then decided to return to Ireland and rejoin Shelbourne in the summer. During his time with Wrexham he was described as 'an economist, in that he wastes no time in developing a move, and does not over play the ball.' He joined Dundalk during the 1966/67 season, and went on to win his second Irish League Championship medal with them. During the summer of 1967 Ben travelled back over to England to sign for Southern League side Chelmsford City, but within a couple of months had returned to Ireland to rejoin Dundalk. The close season of 1968 saw him link up with Shamrock Rovers for a season, where he collected his second F.A.I.Cup Winners' medal. It was not long before he was on the move again, this time signing for Sligo Rovers. Hannigan was by this time turning into a real 'journeyman' and after a couple of seasons with Sligo, his travels took him on to St.Patrick's Athletic, and then Shelbourne (again), before ending his playing career in style by gaining a third Irish League championship medal with Cork Celtic in 1974. Ben eventually hung up his boots in 1975, and he was last known to have been working at the docks in Dublin, where he had settled.

Season	League		F.A.Cup		Welsh Cup		League Cup		Total	
	apps	gls	apps	gls	apps	gls	apps	gls	apps	gls
1965/66	7	2	-	-	1	0	-	-	8	2
	7	**2**	**-**	**-**	**1**	**0**	**-**	**-**	**8**	**2**

HARBERTSON, Ronald 1960 - 1961

Position; *Inside-Forward*
D.O.B; *23rd December, 1929*
Birthplace; *Seghill, Northumberland*
Height; *5ft 10in* **Weight;** *11st 11lbs*
Debut v. *Barnsley (h) 9th March, 1960*
Total Appearances & Goals; *34 apps 14 gls*
Career; *East Chevington Juniors; North Shields; Newcastle United Jan 1949 £750 0apps; Bradford City Aug 1950 16apps 1gls; Brighton H.A. Oct 1951 0apps; Bradford City May 1952 13apps 3gls; Grimsby Town Jul 1954 (part-exchange for Fred Smith) 26apps 6gls; Ashington; Darlington Jan 1957 49apps 21gls; Lincoln City 15th Mar 1958 £2,500 57apps 22gls; WREXHAM 10th March 1960 £5,000; Darlington 18th Jan 1961 £1,500 14apps 2gls; Lincoln City Jul 1961 29apps 3gls; Grantham cs1962;*
Honours; *Welsh Cup Winner 1960;*

Ron Harbertson was playing for East Chevington Juniors when signed by North Shields, though he continued in his apprenticeship as a Marine Engineer at Swan Hunter on Tyneside. He soon impressed with North Shields, and was selected to play for Northumberland at amateur level where he was spotted by Newcastle United. Shortly after his 19th birthday, in December 1948, he was offered the chance to join the 'Magpies' as a professional. Ron failed to make a first team appearance in his eighteen months at St.James Park, and he was allowed to join Bradford City in August 1950. His Football League debut came in a 1-1 draw at Hartlepool United in September 1950, and he went on to spend just over a season at Valley Parade, making sixteen League appearances at outside-right, scoring one goal before being called-up for his National Service. Posted down south, he joined Brighton & Hove Albion on loan in October 1951, but was only used in the Club's reserve team games and, upon completing his two years for King and country, returned to Yorkshire. Ron made a further thirteen League appearances for the 'Bantams', this time at inside-right, scoring three goals. In July 1954 he joined Grimsby Town, and got off to a flying start by scoring in a 2-1 win, over Crewe Alexandra. He bagged six goals in 26 League appearances in one term with the 'Mariners' before leaving Blundell Park in the summer. He then drifted into non-league football with Northern League side Ashington, but was back in League football in January 1957, signing for Darlington. He spent just over twelve months with the Feethams club, making 49 League appearances and scoring 21 goals, following which he moved on to Lincoln City in March 1958. Ron spent two years at Sincil Bank, making a further 57 League appearances and scoring 22 goals, when signed by Wrexham caretaker-manager Cliff Lloyd for a then club record fee of £5,000 in March 1960. Ron went straight into the first team, making his League debut in the evening of the day that he had signed for the club, in a 1-0 victory against Barnsley on the Racecourse. He went on to finish the season in style, helping Wrexham lift the Welsh Cup with a 1-0 replay win over Cardiff City after the first game had ended 1-1, with Ron scoring the all important Wrexham goal. During the summer months, he excelled at Cricket, though football remained his principle sport. Ron began the following campaign at inside-forward, although he soon found himself out of favour, and this led to him rejoining Darlington in January 1961 for a fee described as 'less than £2,000' on the day that the two team's were due to play each other. However, the match had been postponed because of fog. It was not the best of returns for him (as is so often the case), as he made just 14 League appearances before rejoining Lincoln City in the summer. He finished his League career with the 'Red Imps', before moving to Midland League side Grantham in the close season of 1962, where he went on to spend six seasons eventually retiring from football to take up work as an engineer. He retained an involvement with football, though, acting in a scouting capacity for Ken Furphy when he was manager at both Watford and Blackburn Rovers. Ron joined the Prison Service at Lincoln Prison in 1971, where he remained until his retirement in 1986 and settled in the Lincoln area.

Season	League		F.A.Cup		Welsh Cup		League Cup		Total	
	apps	gls	apps	gls	apps	gls	apps	gls	apps	gls
1959/60	12	5	-	-	4	1	-	-	16	6
1960/61	16	8	1	0	-	-	1	0	18	8
	28	**13**	**1**	**0**	**4**	**1**	**1**	**0**	**34**	**14**

HARDING, David 1965 - 1966

Position; *Midfielder*
D.O.B; *14th August, 1946*
Birthplace; *Liverpool, Merseyside*
Height; *ft in* **Weight;** *st lbs*
Debut v. *Luton Town (h) 23rd August, 1965*
Total Appearances & Goals; *11/1 apps 0 gls*
Career; *WREXHAM (Am) 1964, (Pro) 13th Sept 1965; New Brighton Jul 1966; South Liverpool 1967; Hellenica (Australia) 1968;*
Honours; *Australian International caps;*

Dave Harding was educated at St.Matthew's Junior and St.Francis Xavier's Schools in his native Liverpool, where he gained four 'O' and two 'A' levels. At this time he was selected to play for a Mersey Grammar Schools XI against Cologne, before a 50,000 crowd. On completion of his schooldays he took up work as a clerk with the Merseyside and North Wales Electricity Board in October 1964, employed in the Sales and Service Department. On 29th July 1964 Dave had been signed on amateur forms for Wrexham, and, after playing in the 'B' team was quickly promoted to the Welsh League side, where he was an immediate success with his flair for goals. Towards the end of the 1964/65 season he stepped up to the reserves, and continued to score on a regular basis. At the beginning of the following campaign he was given his first team chance in the second match of the season, making his Football League debut in the home game against Luton Town, which Wrexham won 2-0. Harding added a further nine League appearances to his tally before the end of the season, one that had seen Wrexham finish 92nd in the Football League, forcing the club to seek re-election for the first time in its history. Dave was released by manager Jack Rowley, during the summer, and then drifted into non-league football with Cheshire League side New Brighton. He later joined South Liverpool before emigrating to Australia in 1968, where he continued to play football for Hellenica. It was whilst playing for them that he became a nationalised Australian, and a call up for the Australian national team followed shortly afterwards. He went on to help them to qualify for the 1974 World Cup finals in Munich.

Season	League		F.A.Cup		Welsh Cup		League Cup		Total	
	apps	gls	apps	gls	apps	gls	apps	gls	apps	gls
1965/66	9/1	0	1	0	-	-	1	1	11/1	1
	9/1	**0**	**1**	**0**	**-**	**-**	**1**	**1**	**11/1**	**1**

HARDY, Phillip 1990 -

Position; *Left-Back*
Birthplace; *Ellesmere Port, Cheshire*
Height; *5ft 8in* **Weight;** *11st 2lbs*
D.O.B; *9th April, 1973*
Debut v. *Hartlepool United (h) 5th May, 1990*
Total Appearances & Goals; *410/4 apps 0 gls*
Career; *WREXHAM 24th Nov 1990;*
Honours; *1 Republic of Ireland 'B' international cap; 9 Republic of Ireland Under-21 international caps; Football League Division Three runner-up 1993; Welsh Cup Winner 1995; Welsh Invitation Cup Winner 1998; Welsh Cup runner-up 1991;*

Phil Hardy was playing in his favoured left-back position for Ellesmere Port Town and Cheshire Schools when spotted by Wrexham Youth coach Cliff Sear. He had already attended training sessions with Everton, but it was Wrexham he chose upon leaving Whitby School in his native Ellesmere Port. Having first been signed on schoolboy forms Phil accepted YTS terms in 1988. His first season at the club found him in the 'A' team, as it reached the runners-up spot in the Welsh National League. He was also pitted against more senior professionals in the midweek Midland Senior League. Phil showed lots of promise, and his first team chance came much sooner than expected in the last match of the 1989/90 season against Hartlepool on the Racecourse. The following season saw him oust former England international Alan Kennedy from the senior left-back spot. He quickly became the club's regular left-back, and picked up a Welsh Cup runners'-up medal in May 1991. Phil played a big part in Wrexham's resurgence of the 1990s, impressing in the famous F.A.Cup win over Arsenal and then helping the club to promotion from the Third Division in 1993 as runners-up to Cardiff City. He was also nominated for the P.F.A.'s Fourth Division team of 1992, when he was still only eighteen. In 1995 he collected a Welsh Cup winners' medal as Wrexham beat Cardiff City 2-1 at the National Stadium in Cardiff. Primarily a defensive full-back Phil always appeared to enjoy his game more when Karl Connolly was playing on the left flank, due to their fine understanding. He was selected to play for the Eire Under-21 team in 1993, qualification coming courtesy of his grandfather, who had been born in Dundalk. Having made his debut against Germany Phil went on to total nine appearances for a side which he was eventually to captain. He did play a full international for the Republic of Ireland - against Hungary, in David O'Leary's testimonial at Lansdowne Road but, even though the Hungarians regarded the match as a full international, the Irish didn't award caps. The start of the 1996/97 season saw his left-back position wrested from him by Deryn Brace, whose blossoming form was quickly noted by the Welsh international manager. Phil, in the mean-time, fought hard to win back his place, but niggling injuries weren't helping his cause and in the close season of 1997 he turned down the offer of a new contract with Wrexham. However, he put that behind him when returning to the first team following an injury to Brace, and soon recaptured the kind of form that Wrexham's fans had come to expect. Phil even received a call-up for the Republic of Ireland 'B' team, but an ankle injury cost him his cap just hours before kick-off. That disappointment was soon forgotten, however, when he was called up to the full squad for the friendly with the Czech Republic in March 1998, even though he wasn't subsequently selected. Still only 25, he seems to have been around for years, and certainly lives up to his surname! In fact 'The Hardy Perennial' would be a very apt pseudonym for this most modest of characters.

Season	League		F.A.Cup		Welsh Cup		League Cup		L.D.C.		E.C.W.C.		Total	
	apps	gls	apps	gls	apps	gls	apps	gls	apps	gls	apps	gls	apps	gls
1989/90	1	0	-	-	-	-	-	-	-	-	-	-	1	0
1990/91	32	0	1	0	6	0	1	0	3	0	1	0	44	0
1991/92	42	0	5	0	3	0	2	0	5	0	-	-	57	0
1992/93	32	0	1	0	4	0	2	0	3	0	-	-	42	0
1993/94	25	0	2	0	2	0	4	0	3	0	-	-	36	0
1994/95	44	0	4	0	7	0	4	0	4	0	-	-	63	0
1995/96	41/1	0	4	0	-	-	2	0	3	0	2	0	52/1	0
1996/97	13	0	6	0	-	-	1	0	1	0	-	-	21	0
1997/98	34	0	4	0	9*	0*	-	-	1	0	-	-	48	0
1998/99	31/2	0	4	0	6/1*	0*	1	0	4	0	-	-	46/3	0
	295/3	**0**	**31**	**0**	**37/1**	**0**	**17**	**0**	**27**	**0**	**3**	**0**	**410/4**	**0**

*= Welsh Invitation/Premier Cup

HARRIS, William James

1927 - 1928

Position; *Inside-Forward*
D.O.B; *25th April, 1900*
Birthplace; *Crumlington, Northumberland*
Died; *Crumlington, A/M/J 1969.*
Height; *5ft 10in* ***Weight;*** *12st 0lbs*
Debut v. *Rotherham United (h) 15th October, 1927*
Total Appearances & Goals; *14 apps 2 gls*
Career; *Coventry City Aug 1923 0apps; South Shields Jul 1924 2apps 0gls; Walker Celtic; Colwyn Bay United; Ashington May 1926 21apps 11gls; Huddersfield Town Mar 1927 0apps; WREXHAM 14th Oct 1927; Ashington Aug 1928 19apps 2gls; to 1929;*

A native of the North-East Bill Harris won the Morpeth Sprint, and a £100 first prize, as a fine young athlete. He played football, too, and in August 1923 was signed by Coventry City, although he never actually made a first team appearance for the 'Sky Blues', and after a year he was allowed to return to his native North-East to join Third Division North side South Shields. He made his Football League debut for them, although it turned out to be one of just two appearances before leaving to join a local club side, Walker Celtic. He later enjoyed a short spell in North Wales for Colwyn Bay United until returning to the North-East to sign for another Third Division North side, Ashington, in May 1926. Bill made 21 League appearances, scoring 11 goals, and showed enough promise for First Division Huddersfield Town to chase his signature in March 1927. He failed to make a breakthrough into the 'Terriers' first team however, and in October 1927 he was allowed to join Wrexham. He made his debut on the Racecourse, against Rotherham in the same month, playing at inside-right in place of Jim Smith, and scored one of the 'Robins' goals in the 3-2 win. He remained in the side for the following match, and appeared on a further seven occasions in the League. Harris also figured in Wrexham's best-ever F.A.Cup run, during which the club played a First Division side in a competitive match for the first time in its history. Birmingham were the opposition in a Fourth Round tie at the Racecourse; Wrexham lost the game 3-1, but certainly didn't disgrace themselves. Bill left the Racecourse at the end of the season and re-signed for Ashington. He made a further 19 League appearances for them, scoring twice, in what was to be their final season in the Football League as they were not re-elected at the end of the following year.

Season	League		F.A.Cup		Welsh Cup		Total	
	apps	gls	apps	gls	apps	gls	apps	gls
1927/28	9	2	4	0	1	0	14	2
	9	**2**	**4**	**0**	**1**	**0**	**14**	**2**

HARRISON, William Ewart

1923 - 1924

Position; *Outside-Right*
D.O.B; *27th December, 1886*
Birthplace; *Wybunbury, Staffordshire*
Died; *Wolverhampton, August 1948.*
Height; *5ft 4in* ***Weight;*** *10st 10lbs*
Debut v. *Ashington (h) 25th August, 1923*
Total Appearances & Goals; *35 apps 0 gls*
Career; *Hough United; Crewe South End; Willaston White Star; Crewe Alex Dec 1904 53apps 11gls; Wolves May 1907 317apps 43gls; Stoke City (WW1 Guest) 99apps 17gls; Manchester United Oct 1920 44apps 5gls; Port Vale Sept 1922 21apps 2gls; WREXHAM 6th Jun 1923; Retired cs1924;*
Honours; *F.A.Cup Winner 1908; Welsh Cup Winner 1924; Two Football League XI representative caps;*

Billy Harrison began a long and distinguished career with Wolves, who had signed him for £400 from Birmingham and District League side Crewe Alexandra during the close season of 1907. Billy made his Football League debut in the opening match of the 1907/08 season, a local 'Derby' with rivals West Bromwich Albion, which Wolves lost 2-1. A regular in the outside-right position throughout the season Billy helped Wolves to the 1908 F.A.Cup final, where they met Newcastle United at Crystal Palace. He scored a brilliant individual goal in Wolves' 3-1 win. At Molineux he was described as a 'Master of the game, using great pace to get past a full-back, or tease the same defender with some mazy dribbling skills. He was only 5ft 4in tall, but was never afraid to go in with the burliest defenders'. Billy became a favourite with the Wolves crowd, and he stayed with the team in Old Gold until the close season of 1920, although he did have his career disrupted by the First World War. It was during the 1914-18 period that he played regularly for Stoke City, making 99 appearances and scoring 17 goals, one of which came in a 16-0 home win over Blackburn Rovers in November 1917. He was never capped at international level but did make two Football League representative XI appearances, both against the Scottish League, when he was at Molineux. In October 1920 Billy signed for Manchester United, where he was to replace the legendary Billy Meredith at outside-right. Harrison

spent two seasons at Old Trafford, leaving at the end of the 1921/22 season following United's relegation. He then signed for Second Division Port Vale and stayed with the Potteries club for a year, where he made a further 21 League appearances. He signed for Wrexham in the summer of 1923, which would prove to be his last season in the Football League before retiring. He went straight into the team for the opening game against Ashington, which Wrexham won convincingly, 4-0. He then added a further 28 League appearances before ending his professional career on a high note in Wrexham's 1-0 Welsh Cup Final win over Merthyr. Billy was 37, but he continued to play football in charity matches until well into his forties. He later became a landlord of the Rose and Crown public house in Tettenhall, near Wolverhampton, for many years, excelling on the bowling green.

Season	League		F.A.Cup		Welsh Cup		Total	
	apps	gls	apps	gls	apps	gls	apps	gls
1923/24	29	0	2	0	4	0	35	0
	29	**0**	**2**	**0**	**4**	**0**	**35**	**0**

HARVEY, James — 1987 - 1987

Position; *Midfielder*
D.O.B; *2nd May, 1958*
Birthplace; *Lurgan, Northern Ireland*
Height; *5ft 9in* ***Weight;*** *11st 4lbs*
Debut v. *Cardiff City (h) 12th September, 1987*
Total Appearances & Goals; *6 apps 0 gls*
Career; *Glenavon; Arsenal 6th Aug 1977 £20,000 2/1apps 0gls; Hereford United 14th March 1980 276/2apps 39gls; Bristol City 27th Mar 1987 £20,000 2/1apps 0gls; WREXHAM 11th Sep 1987 (Loan); Tranmere Rovers 8th Oct 1987 174/10apps 18gls; Crewe Alexandra Aug 1992 16/1apps 1gls;*
Honours; *One Northern Ireland under-23 cap; Fourth Division runner-up 1989; Leyland DAF Cup winner 1990; Leyland DAF Cup runner-up 1991;*

Jimmy Harvey was already being tipped as a future football star when he was just fourteen years old. He first took up playing senior football with Glenavon, where he won the vote as Ulster's 'Young Player of the Year' for 1976/77, and was also called up into the Northern Ireland senior squad, although not subsequently selected. The promising youngster was then offered the chance to join Arsenal in August 1977, and seized the opportunity with both feet! He played mainly in the Combination League team at Highbury, getting his first team chance in the final game of the 1977/78 season against Derby County, which Arsenal lost 3-0. He also played in the opening game of the following campaign, at home to Leeds United, in a 2-2 draw. Jimmy managed one further substitute appearance before returning to the reserve team. He was handed a chance of first team football at the beginning of 1980 - not at Highbury, but with Hereford United, who he joined on loan initially, and then permanently on a free transfer. He went on to make 278 League appearances for the 'Bulls', scoring 39 goals. In March 1987 Bristol City offered to pay £20,000 for him, a fee Hereford could not afford to turn down at the time. However, after just three League appearances at Ashton Gate he was loaned out to rejoin his former Hereford team-mate Dixie McNeil, then manager at Wrexham. Jimmy made his debut in a 3-0 home win over Cardiff City, in which he starred. He completed five more League appearances for the Racecourse club, making a big impression on both management and the fans with his skilful midfield displays, but although the club wanted to sign him on a permanent basis they could not afford the fee. Tranmere Rovers then stepped in to whisk the talented Irishman away to Prenton Park. A month later they were back to the Racecourse and popular striker Jim Steel went the same way!! Jimmy was to enjoy much success with the Wirral club, winning promotions from the Fourth to the Second Divisions, as well as capturing the Leyland DAF Cup in 1990. They were back at Wembley the following year, too, when they finished runners-up in the same competition. Harvey's successful time at Prenton Park came to a halt when he was allowed to join Crewe Alexandra in the close season of 1992. He spent one season at Gresty Road, in which he helped the club to reach the Third Division play-off final at Wembley. During the close season of 1993 he took his first steps on the game's managerial ladder, when Chester City's manager Graham Barrow appointed him as coach at the club. It was a position that he held until January 1994, when he took over as assistant manager of Northern Premier League side Morecambe before being appointed the club's manager in June. He guided the 'Shrimps' to the Conference League in his first season in charge, and still remains as manager of the Club at the time of writing.

Season	League		F.A.Cup		Welsh Cup		League Cup		S.V.T.		Total	
	apps	gls	apps	gls	apps	gls	apps	gls	apps	gls	apps	gls
1987/88	6	0	-	-	-	-	-	-	-	-	6	0
	6	**0**	-	-	-	-	-	-	-	-	**6**	**0**

HAYCOCK, Frederick Joseph — 1945 - 1947

Position; *Inside-Right*
D.O.B; *19th April, 1912*
Birthplace; *Liverpool, Merseyside*
Died; *Great Barr, 10th April, 1989*
Height; *5ft 8in* ***Weight;*** *10st 10lbs*
Debut v. *Barrow (h) 22nd December, 1945 (War-time North-West League)*
Football League Debut v. *New Brighton (h) 31st August, 1946*
Total Appearances & Goals; *24 apps 7 glsCareer; Bootle Boys Jun 1925; Waterford 1928; Blackburn Rovers 0apps; Prescot Cables 1932; Aston Villa Feb 1934 99apps 28gls (WW2) 84apps 24gls; Nottingham Forest (WW2 Guest) Dec 1939 1app 0gls; Northampton Town (WW2 Guest) 1940/1 26apps 3gls; Liverpool (WW2 Guest) Jan 1942 24apps 2gls; Walsall (WW2 Guest) Mar 1943 1app 0gls; Notts County (WW2 Guest) Feb 1944 1app 0gls; Wolves (WW2 Guest) Mar 1944 8apps 0gls; Leicester City (WW2 Guest) 13apps 3gls; Kidderminster Harriers; Plymouth Argyle (WW2 Guest) Dec 1945 1app 0gls; WREXHAM 22nd Dec 1945; Stourbridge Jul 1947;*
Honours; *Second Division Championship Winner 1938;*

Fred Haycock joined Wrexham towards the end of a footballing career that had begun with his local side, Bootle Boys, in 1925. Upon leaving school, where he had represented Liverpool and District Schoolboys, he took up work with his father's Butchery business. He spent the summer months in Ireland, and it was with Irish League side Waterford that his football career took off. Having signed for them he progressed enough to earn selection for an Irish League representative XI, despite being English. Fred later returned to England to play for Blackburn Rovers, but failed to make a first team appearance at Ewood Park and joined Prescot Cables in 1932, from where he was eventually signed by Aston Villa in February 1934. Haycock spent his first couple of seasons at Villa Park in the reserve team, but following Villa's relegation in 1936, was called upon at inside-forward for his Football League debut in December 1936, a 3-0 home win over Norwich City. He then became a regular in Villa's first team, helping them return to the First Division in 1938 as Second Division champions. At the time Fred was described as 'never happy unless he was in the thick of the action, heading the challenge on the

opposing goal from the inside-right position'. The Second World War was to put his career on hold. although he did manage to play some football during the hostilities, guesting for several clubs including Plymouth, Notts County, Wolves, Leicester City, Kidderminster, Walsall, Liverpool, Nottingham Forest and Northampton Town, as well as turning out for Villa when he could. In December 1945 he was signed by Wrexham manager Tom Williams, along with his Villa team mate Tom Gardner, in preparation for the resumption of the new Football League season in 1946. Haycock made his debut for 'The Robins' in the opening match of the season, a 3-2 home win over New Brighton, and scored one of the Wrexham goals. He then appeared in the next five League matches, but never played another first team game, joining Stourbridge at the end of the season. Fred, a dedicated dahlia grower, later managed Sutton Coldfield, and worked at I.C.I. in Witton, Birmingham for over thirty years. He died in 1989 in Great Barr, Birmingham, aged 76.

Season	League		F.A.Cup		Welsh Cup		War Cups		Total	
	apps	gls	apps	gls	apps	gls	apps	gls	apps	gls
1945/46	7	0	2	0	-	-	9	6	18	6
1946/47	6	1	-	-	-	-	-	-	6	1
	13	**1**	**2**	**0**	**-**	**-**	**9**	**6**	**24**	**7**
F/League	6	1	-	-	-	-	-	-	6	1

HAYES, William John 1950 - 1951

Position; *Goalkeeper*
D.O.B; *30th March, 1928*
Birthplace; *Ballyneety, County Limerick*
Height; *5ft 9in* ***Weight;*** *10st 7lbs*
Debut v. *Rotherham United (a) 26th August, 1950*
Total Appearances & Goals; *15 apps 0 gls*
Career; *Limerick 1944; WREXHAM 12th Jul 1950; Ellesmere Port Aug 1951; Torquay United Aug 1952 54apps 0gls; Portland cs1956; Bideford cs1958; St.Blazey cs1960;*
Honours; *One Republic of Ireland International Cap; One League of Ireland representative cap;*

Bill Hayes played in goal for the St.John's School team in his native Limerick, in Ireland, before leaving during World War Two. He began working for an agricultural firm in the town called, Boyd's, but continued to play football when he could for his local teams, Prospect and Star Rovers. Having assisted the latter to collect five trophies in one season he came to the attention of Limerick, and joined them at 16. Bill spent over five years at the Club, during which he became the first ever Limerick player to win a full international cap for the Republic of Ireland. He was called up to play against Belgium at Dublin's Dalymount Park in April 1949, the match ending in a 2-0 defeat. The following month he was selected for a League of Ireland XI in a representative match against a Football League XI, which the English League won 5-0! Bill was invited for a trial at Manchester City in March 1950, following a tip off from former City player Leo Ward. During his spell at Maine Road he was coached by Frank Swift, but at the end of the season was not offered a contract. Despite this setback Bill faced interest from a number of clubs, and joined Wrexham, signing for the club's caretaker manager Tommy Griffiths in the Queens Hotel in Piccadilly. Bill went straight into the first team for his Football League debut at Rotherham United in the third game of the season, but it was hardly the best of starts, as Wrexham lost 5-0! It didn't deter Bill, though, and he made a further thirteen League appearances despite spending most of 1950/51 vying for the 'keeper's position with Archie Ferguson. During the summer, which had seen a new manager appointed in Peter Jackson, Hayes found to his dismay he had been transfer-listed. However, he was soon fixed up with another club, joining Cheshire County League side Ellesmere Port Town. He stayed for one season, before returning to the Football League in August 1952 with Third Division South side, Torquay United. Bill had to wait patiently to make his debut for the 'Gulls', due to the form of regular first team 'keeper George Webber. Eventually, he got his chance in December at Coventry City, but once again it was not an auspicious start as Torquay lost 7-2! Despite that result Bill went on to spend four years with the Devon club, making 54 League appearances. During his time at Plainmoor, he broke his leg in a League match at Swindon in March 1954, following a collision with the home side's centre-forward. He struggled to regain his place in the team when fit again, and in the close season of 1956 joined Southern League side Portland. Bill spent two seasons with them before moving on to Bideford for a similar spell, whereupon he linked up with St.Blazey for a season in 1960. After retiring from professional football, Hayes took up work for a Torquay firm named Allams, and went on to spend over forty years working as their sales representative, selling crockery and cutlery to the main Hotels in the South West area. Bill still lives in Torquay at the time of writing, and attended Wrexham's 'Players Grand Gala Dinner Reunion' in September 1998.

Season	League		F.A.Cup		Welsh Cup		Total	
	apps	gls	apps	gls	apps	gls	apps	gls
1950/51	14	0	-	-	1	0	15	0
	14	**0**	**-**	**-**	**1**	**0**	**15**	**0**

HEATH, Seamus Martin Jayes Paul 1983 - 1984

Position; *Midfield*
D.O.B; *6th December, 1961*
Birthplace; *Belfast*
Height; *5ft 9in* ***Weight;*** *10st 5lbs*
Debut v. *Doncaster Rovers (a) 27th August, 1983*
Total Appearances & Goals; *41/3 apps 2 gls*
Career; *Cromac Albion; Luton Town Apr 1979 0apps; Lincoln City (Loan) Aug 1982 6/1apps 0gls; WREXHAM Aug 1983; Tranmere Rovers Aug 1984 6/11apps 0gls; BK-46 (Finland) Apr 1985; Northwich Victoria 1985/86; Ekenas IF (Finland) Apr 1986; Portadown Oct 1986 4apps 1gls; Oswestry Town Apr 1987; BK-46 (Finland) May 1987; Sychdyn cs1987; Rhyl Sept 1987; BK-46 (Finland) Apr 1988; Caernarvon Town Oct 1988; BK-46 (Finland) Apr 1989; Glentoran Oct 1989 10/1apps 0gls; BK-46 (Finland) Apr 1990; Glentoran Oct 1990 27/1apps 0gls; Distillery Jul 1992 (player/coach) 39/4apps 0gls; Derry City Aug 1994 9apps 0gls; Cliftonville Aug 1995 6/6apps 0gls;*
Honours; *Irish League Championship Winner 1992; Budweiser Floodlit Cup Winner 1990; Gold Cup Winner 1994;*

Belfast born, Seamus Heath was spotted by Luton Town playing local football for Cromac Albion. He was taken on as an apprentice at Kenilworth Road before turning professional in April 1979. Seamus failed to make the 'Hatters' first team, however, and in August 1982 was allowed to join Lincoln City on loan. His Football League debut came in the opening game of the season, a 2-1 home win over Wigan Athletic, at left-back as he slotted in to replace Phil Neale, who was still playing out the cricket season. Seamus made another half dozen League appearances for the 'Red Imps' before returning to reserve team football at Luton until the end of the 1982/83 season, when he was released. He joined Wrexham on a free transfer in August 1983, after being recommended to manager Bobby Roberts, by his Luton Town counterpart David Pleat. At that time the 'Robins' had just experienced two successive relegation's, and the club was struggling desperately to keep its head above water. Seamus was plunged straight into the first team for his debut at Doncaster Rovers in the first game of the season. He went on to make a further 31 League appearances for Wrexham in yet another dismal season, which saw them avoid having to apply for re-election by the skin of their teeth, beating Tranmere Rovers in the final match of the season. Seamus did not feature in this game, nor was he considered for

the Welsh Cup final against Shrewsbury Town, so it came as no surprise when he was released at the end of the season. He joined Tranmere Rovers in August 1984, and made his debut for the Prenton Park club in the opening match of the new campaign as a substitute for Andy Lee in a 1-0 defeat at Peterborough. After totting up 17 League appearances he was again released in the close season, whereupon he moved to Finland to play for BK-46 during the summer. He then returned home and joined Northwich Victoria for the 1985/86 season, but went back to Finland for the summer. It became a pattern that Seamus was to follow from the mid-80s, through to the early 90s: He would play in Finnish football during the summer, and return home in the winter months to play for a host of non-league clubs, including Oswestry Town, Rhyl and Caernarvon Town in the Northern Premier League, and Sychdyn in the Clwyd League. On returning home to Belfast he again divided his time between the Finnish and domestic league in Northern Ireland, where he played for a handful of clubs including Portadown and Glentoran, with whom he won a Irish League Championship medal in 1992 and a Budweiser Floodlit Cup Winners' medal in 1990. He also played for Distillery, where he won a Gold Cup Winners' medal in 1994, Derry City, and Cliftonville. By this time a part-time player with these clubs, Seamus combined playing football with working as a shopkeeper. Like his numerous christian names he also had a penchant for collecting football clubs!!

Season	League		F.A.Cup		Welsh Cup		League Cup		F.R.T.		Total
	apps	gls	apps	gls	apps	gls	apps	gls	apps	gls	apps gls
1983/84	32	1	1	0	5/1	1	2	0	1/2	0	41/3 2
	32	**1**	**1**	**0**	**5/1**	**1**	**2**	**0**	**1/2**	**0**	**41/3 2**

***HEGGIE,* William Campbell** 1952 - 1954

Position; *Forward*
D.O.B; *7th June, 1927*
Birthplace; *Scone, Tayside*
Height; *6ft 0in* ***Weight;*** *12st 8lbs*
Debut v. *Darlington (h) 18th October, 1952*
Total Appearances & Goals; *36 apps 15 gls*
Career; *Perth City Boy's Club; Earngrove FC; Jeanfield Swifts £75; New Brighton 9th Feb 1951 10apps 0gls; Leeds United 15th Jun 1951 (Joint transfer with J.Finlay for a combined fee of £6,000) 0apps; WREXHAM 1st Aug 1952; Winsford United 30th Nov 1954; Accrington Stanley 10th Feb 1955 £270 1app 0gls; New Brighton Aug 1955;*

Bill Heggie began playing football for a local Boys' Club in his home town of Perth. He progressed through to the Junior teams, Earngrove and Jeanfield Swifts, before signing for Football League side New Brighton in February 1951. Bill made his Football League debut for the 'Rakers' in a 2-0 defeat against York City at right-back, a position with which he was familiar and one where he had played most of his football career up to that point, but manager Walter Galbraith decided to switch him to centre-forward after two matches. It proved a great success, as Bill scored five goals in his next eight appearances for the 'Rakers', though he couldn't prevent them from finishing bottom of the Football League. During the summer New Brighton failed to gain re-election, and in June 1951, Heggie was transferred along with team mate Jack Finlay, to Leeds United for a combined fee of £6,000. He failed to break into the first team at Elland Road, and was signed by Wrexham manager Peter Jackson in the summer of 1952. Bill made his debut for Wrexham at inside-right replacing Ron Hewitt in a 4-2 home win over Darlington, and scored one of the goals.

Despite this early success he was unable to command a regular first team place, although proving to be an able deputy for both Tommy Bannan and Hewitt throughout his time at the Racecourse. He scored a total of 13 goals in 33 League matches during his two years with the 'Robins', a decent record by anyone's standards. Bill was allowed to leave Wrexham at the end of November 1954, and signed for Cheshire County League side Winsford United. However, he made a quick return to the Football League, when his former boss at New Brighton, Walter Galbraith, signed him for Accrington Stanley for a £270 fee in February 1955. Bill was to record just one appearance for the Peel Park outfit - against Wrexham, in a 3-1 defeat! He left them at the end of the season and rejoined New Brighton, by now performing in the Lancashire Combination. He featured in their wonderful F.A.Cup run of 1956/57, when they reached the fourth round, having accounted for three Football League clubs on the way: Stockport County (after a replay), Third Division North Champions Derby County, and Torquay United. On retiring from the game Bill took up work as a Coal Merchant.

Season	League		F.A.Cup		Welsh Cup		Total	
	apps	gls	apps	gls	apps	gls	apps	gls
1952/53	10	3	-	-	-	-	10	3
1953/54	18	9	2	0	1	2	21	11
1954/55	5	1	-	-	-	-	5	1
	33	**13**	**2**	**0**	**1**	**2**	**36**	**15**

***HENCHER,* Nicholas** 1977 - 1979 & 1985 - 1988

Position; *Midfielder*
D.O.B; *24th August, 1961*
Birthplace; *Wrexham, Denbighshire*
Height; *5ft 9in* ***Weight;*** *12st 0lbs*
Debut v. *Tranmere Rovers (h) 17th September, 1985*
Total Appearances & Goals; *35/8 apps 9 gls*
Career; *WREXHAM cs1977; Blaenau Ffestiniog cs1979; Caernarfon Town cs1980; Rhyl; Aberystwyth Town cs1981; Blaenau Ffestiniog 1981/82; Lex XI cs1982; Conwy United 1982/83; Lex XI; WREXHAM 8th Aug 1985; Oswestry Town Dec 1987; Lex XI cs1988;*
Honours; *Welsh Cup Winner 1986; Welsh Intermediate Cup Winner; Welsh Youth Cup Winner 1978; Welsh Schoolboy international caps;*

Nick Hencher played for both Alexandra Junior and Bromfield Secondary Schools in Wrexham, from where he represented the Wrexham Schools team at various age levels. From the age of 14 he was tied on schoolboy forms to Wrexham, and it was no surprise when the promising youngster was taken on by his home town club as an apprentice in 1977. In his first season he helped Wrexham to win the Welsh Youth Cup against Afan Lido, before being informed by manager Arfon Griffiths that he would not be offered a professional contract upon completion of his apprenticeship. He then drifted into Welsh non-league football with Blaenau Ffestiniog, picking up a Welsh Intermediate Cup winners' medal, scoring the winning goal in the final against Brymbo at Rhyl. Nick left Blaenau when he lost his job at Dunlop's Wrexham plant and found himself having to work on Saturday mornings for his new employers L.Rowland & Company. He eventually signed for Caernarfon Town, where he played in the 'Canaries' first ever game in an English League, a Lancashire Combination game against Chorley Reserves on the Oval, which they lost 2-1. He moved to Lex XI shortly afterwards and helped them reach the 5th round of the Welsh Cup in 1984/85 where they lost 6-0 at Third Division Newport County. When Dixie McNeil took charge at Wrexham he invited Nick to sign for the Club on non-contract terms as cover during an end of season injury crisis. He grabbed this second chance with both 'feet', capping a number of impressive performances in the reserves with a superb 25 yard equaliser on his League debut in a 1-1 home draw against Tranmere Rovers in September 1985. Nick went on to establish himself in the side, collecting a Welsh Cup Winners' medal in 1986 as the 'Robins' beat Kidderminster Harriers in a replayed Final, although he suffered a knee injury in the first game. 1986/87 saw him suffer a series of setbacks with the injury, and after the problem had persisted throughout the following season, was released once again by Wrexham. He moved back into non-league football, playing for Oswestry Town and Lex XI. Dixie McNeil once described Hencher as a 'determined player who never knows when he is beaten'. Since retiring from professional football he has worked for Rowlands Chemists in Wrexham, apart from two years - 1990 and 1991 - when he was employed by the musical entertainer, Joe Longthorne, and during this time Nick appeared on 'This is Your Life'! He still lives in the Wrexham area at the time of writing.

Season	League		F.A.Cup		Welsh Cup		League Cup		F.R.T.		Total	
	apps	gls	apps	gls	apps	gls	apps	gls	apps	gls	apps	gls
1985/86	22/3	4	2	1	3	2	2/1	0	1	0	30/4	7
1986/87	4	1	-	-	1	1	-	-	-	-	5	2
1987/88	0/3	0	-	-	-	-	-	-	0/1	0	0/4	0
	26/6	**5**	**2**	**1**	**4**	**3**	**2/1**	**0**	**1/1**	**0**	**35/8**	**9**

HEWITT, Leonard

1946 - 1947

Position; *Centre-Forward*
D.O.B; *20th March, 1920*
Birthplace; *Rhostyllen, Denbighshire*
Died; *Bersham Colliery, 24th May 1979*
Height; *5ft 10in* ***Weight;*** *12st 0lbs*
Debut v. *Crewe Alexandra (h) 11th November, 1944Football League debut v. Accrington Stanley (a) 21st September, 1946*
Total Appearances & Goals; *17 apps 9 gls*
Career; *WREXHAM May 1946; Altrincham Dec 1947; Oswestry Town cs1948; Blaenau Ffestiniog 18th Nov 1948; Rhos Rangers 17th Aug 1953;*

Born in Church Street at Rhostyllen near Wrexham, Len Hewitt attended the Bersham All Boys and Rhostyllen Senior Schools. He also worked for a local Coal Merchant at this time, before leaving school at the age of 14 to work at Bersham colliery. He continued to work in the pit throughout the Second World War, when he was also a member of the Home Guard. It was during this time that he played football when he could for Wrexham, making eleven War-time appearances for the 'Robins' from 1944, the first coming at left-back in a 4-2 home defeat by Crewe Alexandra in November 1944. It was said 'he would often turn out for the team covered in coal dust, having just finished a shift!' After WW2 had ended Len was signed by Wrexham manager Tom Williams on a permanent basis. He went on to make his Football League debut at centre-forward in a 1-0 win at Accrington in September 1946 while the following match, at home to Rochdale, saw him score the first of his two League goals in a 2-2 draw. Len then had to wait until December before being selected again for the first team, but after just four more matches he was returned to the reserves. He never made another senior appearance for Wrexham, and in December 1947 joined Cheshire County League side Altrincham. Len moved on to Oswestry Town for the beginning of the 1948/49 season, though he signed for Welsh League North side Blaenau Ffestiniog in November 1948, where he spent a number of seasons before joining Rhos Rangers in August 1953. During his time with them he was described by a team mate as a 'very physical player' and 'fearless'. After his playing days were over Len continued to work at Bersham Colliery. He also played cricket during the summer months for Bersham Cricket Club, and was a great racing pigeon enthusiast. Len died in May 1979, whilst working at Bersham Colliery. Today, the Hewitt football tradition is upheld by his family: his daughter and son-in-law help to run the Rhostyllen Villa Youth football team, a side which includes Len's grandson, and other members of the family turn out for a number of local teams.

Season	League		F.A.Cup		Welsh Cup		War Cups		Total	
	apps	gls	apps	gls	apps	gls	apps	gls	apps	gls
1944/45	1	0	-	-	-	-	-	-	1	0
1945/46	6	4	4	1	-	-	-	-	10	5
1946/47	5*	2*	-	-	1	2	-	-	6	4
	12	**6**	**4**	**1**	**1**	**2**	**-**	**-**	**17**	**9**

* = Football League record only

HEWITT, Ronald

1951 - 1957 & 1959 - 1960

Position; *Inside-Forward*
D.O.B; *21st June, 1928*
Birthplace; *Flint, Flintshire*
Height; *5ft 8in* ***Weight;*** *10st 3lbs*
Debut v. *Chester (a) 18th August, 1951*
Total Appearances & Goals; *267 apps 111 gls*
Career; *Oakenholt St.Davids; Wolves Jul 1948 0apps; Walsall Oct 1949 (loan) 8apps 2gls; Darlington Jun 1950 36apps 3gls; WREXHAM 21st Jul 1951; Cardiff City £4,500 1st Jun 1957 64apps 27gls; WREXHAM 11th Jul 1959 £2,000; Coventry City 4th Mar 1960 £4,500 59apps 23gls; Chester Mar 1962 29apps 6gls; Hereford United Aug 1963 £3,000; George Cross (Melbourne) Feb 1964; Northwich Victoria; Witton Albion 1965/66; Caernarfon Town 27th Aug 1966; Barmouth & Dyffryn United 9th Nov 1967; Bankstown (Sydney) 1970;*
Honours; *Five Full Welsh International Caps; Welsh Cup Winner 1957; Third Division North representative XI;*

Ron Hewitt first impressed in schoolboy football at Flint Central, from where he was selected to play for both Flintshire and North Wales Schoolboys. He also turned out for his local side, Oakenholt St.David's, who played in the Flintshire Youth League. Here Ron earned a Flintshire Junior Cup Winners' medal and soon after was approached by a Queensferry-based Wolves scout, who invited him for a trial at Molineux during his school holidays. He was eventually chosen, from about forty players, to sign on the ground staff at Molineux. Ron began to make a promising career in football, but it came to a stop, at eighteen, when called up for his National Service. He joined the Cheshire Regiment, and Catterick for his basic training before serving in Lisbon and Tel Aviv, although during this time he was to play football regularly for his Battalion. He resumed his football career with Wolves on completion of his two years' service, although he was to make his Football League debut with Walsall, for whom he had signed on loan in October 1949. He turned out at outside-right in their 5-1 win at Ipswich Town, and scored two of the goals! He went on to make a further seven League appearances with the 'Saddlers' before returning to Wolverhampton in January. His career with the Old Gold team never really took off, despite scoring regularly for the reserves. At the end of 1949/50 Ron took up the chance to play regular first team football when he joined Third Division North side Darlington. He became a virtual ever-present at Feethams throughout 1950/51, scoring three goals in 36 League games, though he was to leave at the end of the season to return nearer home, signing for Wrexham in July 1951. He made his debut for the North-East Wales club at outside-right in the opening game of the season at Chester, which ended in a 2-1 defeat. Ron Hewitt was to become a very popular player at the Racecourse, spending six seasons during which he came close to averaging a goal every other game. He was eventually switched to inside-right where he had considerable success, assisting the club to third position in 1952/53 as part of a formidable forward line of Ron, Glyn Hughes, Tommy Tilston, Billy Tunnicliffe and Tommy Bannan, notching seventy League goals between them. Wrexham were unlucky to lose to First Division Stoke City in a Third Round F.A.Cup tie that season, though Ron was to gain a Welsh Cup winners' medal in 1957, as Wrexham beat Swansea Town 2-0. In the same year he appeared in the famous F.A.Cup match against Manchester United's famous 'Busby Babes' on the Racecourse. By this time there was talk of his possible selection for Wales; he had already taken part in a representative match for the Third Division North team against their Southern counterparts, but surprisingly never got the call from his country. Second Division Cardiff City paid out £4,500 for Hewitt in June 1957, and only eight months after his arrival at Ninian Park made his full Welsh debut against Israel at Ninian Park. He went on to make four more appearances for his country, including three 1958 World Cup matches in Sweden: against the hosts, Hungary, and a quarter final match against Brazil. He had made his debut for the 'Bluebirds' in the first game of the season, in a goalless 'derby' against Swansea Town before a 45,000 Ninian Park crowd. He enjoyed two successful seasons in South Wales, scoring 27 goals in 64 League appearances before rejoining Wrexham in July 1959 for £2,000. Ron's second debut for Wrexham came against Brentford, a 3-2 home win in the fourth match of the 1959/60 season, claiming one of the goals from the penalty spot. He was now playing alongside another lethal striker, Don Weston, but by March 1960 was to move again when Third Division promotion hopefuls Coventry City paid out £4,500 to secure his services. Ron made his 'Sky Blues' debut in a 1-0 defeat at Barnsley, and his new side went on to end the campaign in fourth place. After two years at Highfield Road Ron left in March 1962, along with Billy Myerscough, following the arrival of Jimmy Hill as manager. They both signed for struggling Fourth Division side Chester, becoming new manager Bill Lambton's first recruits. Ron's debut saw no improvement in the 'Seals' predicament, as they lost 5-1 at York City, and went on to end the season in the League's basement, excused having to apply for re-election by Accrington Stanley's earlier resignation. Now coming to the end of his playing career Hewitt spent one more term at Sealand Road before dropping into non-league football with ambitious Southern League outfit Hereford United. He then took up an offer to move on to.........Australia! He signed for George Cross in Melbourne, but returned home on the conclusion of their season and joined Northwich Victoria. He went on to play non-league football for Witton Albion, Caernarvon Town, and Barmouth & Dyffryn United, returning 'Down Under' in 1970 to become player/manager of Bankstown, a suburb of Sydney. It was a part-time position, which necessitated Ron working during the week as a foreman for TNT Haulage company, and taking his players training two nights a week. He spent two years in Australia before returning home to Wrexham, taking up employment for BICC where he worked as a machine operator until retiring in 1995. Ron still resides in Wrexham, where he enjoys bowling and golf in the summer months. Ron's nephew, Andy Holden, also played for Wales and is currently on the coaching staff at Everton.

Season	League		F.A.Cup		Welsh Cup		Total	
	apps	gls	apps	gls	apps	gls	apps	gls
1951/52	38	16	3	0	3	0	44	16
1952/53	42	13	3	0	1	0	46	13
1953/54	36	15	5	1	1	0	42	16
1954/55	33	11	2	2	3	3	38	16
1955/56	24	6	1	0	1	1	26	7
1956/57	31	22	6	4	3	3	40	29
1959/60	27	11	3	2	1	1	31	14
	231	**94**	**23**	**9**	**13**	**8**	**267**	**111**

HEYES, Darren Lee 1987

Position; *Goalkeeper*
D.O.B; *11th January, 1967*
Birthplace; *Swansea, Glamorgan*
Height; *5ft 11in* ***Weight;*** *12st 9lbs*
Debut v. *Torquay United (h) 24th January, 1987*
Total Appearances & Goals; *2 apps 0 gls*
Career; *Nottingham Forest Jan 1984; WREXHAM 23rd Jan 1987 (Loan); Scunthorpe United Jul 1987 3apps 0gls; Shepshed Charterhouse Jul 1988; Matlock Town 1990/91; Shepshed Albion 1991/92; Tamworth 1991/92; Shepshed Albion 1992/93; Rocester cs1993; Halifax Town Sept 1993 63apps 0gls; VS Rugby 25th Oct 1997 (Loan) Jan 1997; Moor Green Feb 1998;*
Honours; *13 England Youth international caps; England Schoolboy international; England Student International; Northern Premier League Representative XI;*

Darren Heyes is the son of former Leicester, Swansea, Rochdale, Barrow, and Hereford goalkeeper George Heyes, and so it was no surprise when he followed in his father's footsteps. Darren joined Nottingham Forest straight from School on apprentice terms, and made his way through the junior ranks at Forest to earn a professional contract in January 1984. He played his early football for Blaby and Whetstone Boys' Club, the very same Junior side with whom Peter Shilton learned his trade. Darren went on to appear for the Beauchamp College in Oadby, where he earned selection for the Leicestershire County Schools team. This led to his involvement with England Schoolboys, following which a number of clubs showed an interest in him, and he chose Forest. Whilst at the City Ground Darren was chosen to play for the England Youth side, having qualified by his Father's birthplace since Heyes Junior was born in Swansea when his father was playing for the 'Swans'. Heyes made thirteen Youth international appearances, and they included the World championships in the USSR. He found it difficult to make a breakthrough into the Forest first team, however, and in January 1987 came to the rescue of Wrexham manager Dixie McNeil, who was searching for goalkeeping cover following an injury to regular 'keeper Chris Pearce. Darren played three matches for Wrexham: his League debut, a 2-1 home victory over Torquay was followed by two away matches, a 2-1 win at Scunthorpe in a Freight Rover Cup match, and a League game at Halifax which Wrexham lost 2-1. Darren then returned to Nottingham, only to be released in the summer of 1987. He joined Scunthorpe United at the beginning of 1987/88, but was to find his first team chances limited due to the form of Ron Green. He eventually made his debut for the 'Iron' in a 1-1 draw with Bolton Wanderers in September, and made two more League appearances that season as well as a Littlewoods Cup match with Leicester City. He was released by Scunthorpe at the end of the season, and drifted into non-league football with Shepshed Charterhouse. It was at this time that Heyes became a full-time student, gaining a H.N.C. in Business/Finance and a BSC (Hons) in Sports Science. Whilst at University he gained further international recognition, playing for England in the 1991 World Student Games in Sheffield. He earned a bronze medal as England played Iran, Japan, Holland, and USA before losing to Uruguay in the semi-finals. He moved from Shepshed to Tamworth, though he soon repeated the journey in the opposite direction, and followed this with a spell at Rocester during the close season of 1993. After only a couple of matches he was signed by Halifax Town in September 1993, who had just been relegated from the Football League. Darren played for the 'Shaymen' in the Conference League until November 1996, when joined VS Rugby initially on loan. The loan spell became permanent after three months, when appointed the club's player/coach. He remained at Rugby until February 1998 when moving on to fellow Midland League side Moor Green. Darren, who was still playing for Moor Green at the start of the 1998/99 season, combines playing football with working for Nottingham City Council as their Sports Development Officer.

Season	League		F.A.Cup		Welsh Cup		League Cup		F.R.T.		Total	
	apps	gls	apps	gls	apps	gls	apps	gls	apps	gls	apps	gls
1986/87	2	0	-	-	-	-	-	-	1	0	3	0
	2	**0**	**-**	**-**	**-**	**-**	**-**	**-**	**1**	**0**	**3**	**0**

HILL, Alan George 1973 - 1983

Position; *Right-Back*
D.O.B; *22nd June, 1955*
Birthplace; *Chester, Cheshire*
Height; *5ft 11in* ***Weight;*** *11st 4lbs*
Debut v. *Charlton Athletic (a) 4th January, 1975*
Total Appearances & Goals; *233/32 apps 8 gls*
Career; *WREXHAM Jul 1973; Oswestry Town Aug 1983;*
Honours; *Third Division Championship Winner 1978; Welsh Cup runner-up 1981 & 1983;*

Alan Hill was playing as a central defender for the Upton School team in Chester when chosen to play for Chester Schoolboys. It was then that he was spotted by the Wrexham secretary, Cliff Lloyd, and invited to the Racecourse for trials. Alan was signed on schoolboy forms in November 1969 and progressed through the Junior ranks, joining the groundstaff in 1971 to earn himself a professional contract in July 1973. He had to be patient before finally making his Football League debut in January 1975, replacing the injured Joey Jones at right-back in a Third Division match at Charlton Athletic, which Wrexham drew 1-1. That was to be the first of his 199 League matches for Wrexham, which he accumulated over ten years with the club. Throughout his time at the Racecourse Alan could always be relied upon to fill in wherever required, and was a major asset in the Wrexham senior squad due to his versatility. Whatever role he was asked to play, he always acquitted himself with credit. This ability was never more put to the test than during the 1979/80 season, when appearing in nine different first team shirts, including that of goalkeeper! He won a Third Division championship medal with Wrexham in 1978, two Welsh Cup runners-up medals in 1981 and 1983, and played in a number of important matches for the club. They included the F.A.Cup Quarter-Final match against Arsenal on the Racecourse in 1978, when he might have covered himself in glory and rewritten a chapter of the club's history. Vision and skill had combined to carry his solo run clear of the 'Gunners' off-side trap, before shooting narrowly wide with only the goalkeeper, Pat Jennings, to beat. Among other memorable games in which Alan participated were those against Newcastle United, West Ham United and Nottingham Forest in the F.A.Cup; Liverpool and Tottenham Hotspur in the League Cup; and the European challenges against Djurgardens, Stal Rzeszow, NK Rijeka and IF Magdeburg. Following the club's successive relegation's in 1982 and 1983, Hill found himself a victim of the sweeping changes that the club were forced to make at the time because of its dire financial situation. His final match for Wrexham was a 1-0 defeat at Reading in May 1983, a result which condemned the club to relegation for the second time in two seasons. He then joined Northern Premier League side Oswestry Town in the close season for a short spell, before taking up work at the local Tetra Pak factory on Wrexham's industrial estate. Alan has settled in the Wrexham area and can be occasionally found at the club's matches.

Season	League		F.A.Cup		Welsh Cup		League Cup		E.C.W.C.		Total	
	apps	gls	apps	gls	apps	gls	apps	gls	apps	gls	apps	gls
1974/75	14	0	-	-	1	0	-	-	-	-	15	0
1975/76	10	0	2	0	-	-	-	-	4	0	16	0
1976/77	9	0	2/1	0	1	0	1	0	-	-	13/1	0
1977/78	26/4	0	6	0	2/1	0	3	0	-	-	37/5	0
1978/79	15/2	3	1	0	1	0	1	0	2	0	20/2	3
1979/80	29/4	1	1/3	0	2	0	3	0	2	1	37/7	2
1980/81	26/7	1	5	0	4	0	2	0	-	-	37/7	1
1981/82	18/2	1	0/1	0	2	0	4	0	-	-	24/3	1
1982/83	26/7	1	-	-	6	0	2	0	-	-	34/7	1
	173/26	**7**	**17/5**	**0**	**19/1**	**0**	**16**	**0**	**8**	**1**	**233/32**	**8**

HILL, Albert Edward 1930 - 1931

Position; *Centre-Half*
D.O.B; *1906*
Birthplace; *Conisbrough, Yorkshire*
Height; *5ft 10'1/2in* ***Weight;*** *13st 2lbs*
Debut v. *Hull City (a) 22nd November, 1930*
Total Appearances & Goals; *4 apps 0 gls*
Career; *Mexborough; Tottenham Hotspur Mar 1928 (Am) 0apps; Denaby United cs1928; Huddersfield Town 1928/29; Wolves Dec 1929 2apps 0gls; WREXHAM 20th Sept 1930; Peterborough & Fletton United 1931; Bolton Albion; Conisbrough Welfare; Edlington Welfare; Motherwell (trial); York City (trial); Tunbridge Wells Rangers Jul 1932;*

Albert Hill was playing for Mexborough when invited to join Tottenham Hotspur on amateur terms in March 1928. Nothing came of his time at White Hart Lane, and he left to join non-league side Denaby United in the close season of 1928. It was here that Huddersfield Town became interested in the promising centre-half, and he signed for the 'Terriers' during the 1928/29 season. Albert again failed to make any breakthrough, and his next port of call was at Second Division Wolverhampton Wanderers, who he joined in December 1929. Albert finally made his Football League debut for the Molineux club, playing at centre-forward in a 4-0 win over Cardiff City in April 1930. He was selected for the following match, a 3-1 defeat at Barnsley, but was not to make any further outings for Wolves and was allowed to leave in September 1930. He then signed for Third Division North side Wrexham, playing initially for the reserve team in an 8-1 win over Llandudno, in which he was described as a 'well built pivot'. He made his first team debut for The Robins in November, when replacing Billie Rogers who was on international duty with Wales. He was named at half-back for a match at Hull City, which finished 3-2 in Wrexham's favour. Albert was described as 'justifying his inclusion by doing excellent work'. Hill returned to second XI football following Rogers' return, until earning a recall in January 1931 to replace Ralph Burkinshaw at centre-half for three consecutive games. In all four League matches that Albert played for Wrexham he never finished on the losing side! In July 1932, he signed for Tunbridge Wells Rangers.

Season	League		F.A.Cup		Welsh Cup		Total	
	apps	gls	apps	gls	apps	gls	apps	gls
1930/31	4	0	-	-	-	-	4	0
	4	**0**	-	-	-	-	**4**	**0**

HILTON, John 1950 - 1951

Position; *Centre-Forward*
D.O.B; *20th February, 1925*
Birthplace; *Rochdale, Lancashire*
Height; *ft in* ***Weight;*** *st lbs*
Debut v. *Chester (a), 6th September, 1950*
Total Appearances & Goals; *3 apps 0 gls*
Career; *Hyde United; WREXHAM 4th Jul 1950; Macclesfield Town 30th Jul 1951; Rossendale United; Northwich Victoria 1955/56;*

Jack Hilton signed for Wrexham from Cheshire County League side Hyde United in July 1950. He was called up for his Football League debut in September, replacing Frank Fidler at centre-forward for the local 'derby' against Chester at Sealand Road, a scoreless draw in front of a crowd of over 10,000. Jack played in the following match, a 3-0 defeat at York, again as a replacement for Fidler, but managed just one more appearance for the senior side as Wrexham drew 1-1 at Darlington in March 1951. Jack failed to score in each of his three first team games, and was released at the end of the season. He joined Cheshire County League side Macclesfield Town in the summer of 1951, and later appeared for Rossendale United and Northwich Victoria.

Season	League		F.A.Cup		Welsh Cup		Total	
	apps	gls	apps	gls	apps	gls	apps	gls
1950/51	3	0	-	-	-	-	3	0
	3	**0**	-	-	-	-	**3**	**0**

***HINNIGAN,* Joseph** 1987 - 1988

Position; *Centre-Half*
D.O.B; *3rd December, 1955*
Birthplace; *Liverpool, Merseyside*
Height; *6ft 0in* ***Weight;*** *12st 0lbs*
Debut v. *Torquay United (a) 15th August, 1987*
Total Appearances & Goals; *28/1 apps 1 gls*
Career; *South Liverpool; Wigan Athletic cs1975 £1,200 66apps 10gls; Sunderland 15th Feb 1980 £80,000 63apps 4gls; Preston North End 24th Dec 1982 £15,000 51/1apps 8gls; Gillingham Aug 1984 99/4apps 7gls; WREXHAM Jul 1987; Chester City 13th Aug 1988 52/2apps 2gls;*
Honours; Second Division runner-up 1980; Northern Premier League Shield Winner 1976; Lancashire Junior Cup Winner 1977 & 1978;

Joe Hinnigan hails from the Kirkby area of Liverpool, and was chosen to represent Kirkby Schoolboys, from where he joined Everton on schoolboy forms. However, he was to be disappointed when he was released by the Goodison Park club, but that was quickly forgotten when offered a chance with Aston Villa, though they too, allowed him to leave after six months. After leaving school Joe found employment with his father in Liverpool docks, working there for four years while continuing to play non-league football for South Liverpool. Impressing at centre-half, Joe soon began to attract the attention of the top North-West non-league sides at the time: Altrincham, Northwich Victoria and Wigan Athletic. It was Wigan who eventually signed him for a fee of £1,200 in the close season of 1975. He made his debut for the 'Latics' in September 1975, in a 1-0 Northern Premier League win at Worksop. He spent three seasons playing in N.P.L., collecting a N.P.L. Shield Winners' medal in 1976, and two Lancashire Junior Cup Winners medals in 1977 and 1978, making 119/1 N.P.L. appearances and scoring eight goals prior to Wigan's election into the Football League in 1978. Joe played in their first ever Football League match, a scoreless draw at Hereford United in August 1978, and he also has the distinction of scoring the 'Latics' first-ever Football League goal, the first of two strikes in a 3-2 home defeat by Newport County. He spent another two seasons at Springfield Park before being signed by Sunderland for £80,000 in February 1980. Joe enjoyed almost three years at Roker Park, during which he helped them to the First Division in 1980, but a change of manager found him out of favour, and was transferred to Preston North End in December 1982. What Hinnigan didn't realise at the time he joined the Deepdale club was that manager Gordon Lee had virtually broken the bank to sign him for £15,000, and his time at North End was to become a constant struggle against relegation. Joe remained at Deepdale until August 1984, when he moved south to join Gillingham, and so nearly helped them to promotion in each of his three seasons at Priestfield. He then returned north to sign for Wrexham manager Dixie McNeil in July 1987. His League debut for 'The Robins' is certainly one he doesn't need to be reminded about! Joe was one of four 'Robins' debutants at Torquay in August 1987. Everything seemed fine when fellow newcomer Mike Carter put Wrexham in front, but Torquay stepped up a gear and netted six goals without further reply from their despondent visitors. Despite this nightmare start he went on to become a regular in the side until February, after which he never played another senior match for the Club. During the close season of 1988 he joined English neighbours Chester City, making 54 League appearances for the 'Seals' while qualifying as their physiotherapist and coach. Joe worked under Graham Barrow at Chester, but they left after a dispute in the close season of 1994, despite having guided Chester to promotion to the Second Division. He then teamed up again with Barrow at Wigan Athletic, as coach, spending just over a season at Springfield Park before his partner was sacked in October 1995. Joe also left, and later rejoined Barrow at Rochdale in May 1996, again as coach/physio. He returned to Chester in June 1999 to take up the post of assistant manager/physio to Kevin Ratcliffe.

Season	League		F.A.Cup		Welsh Cup		League Cup		F.R.T.		Total	
	apps	gls	apps	gls	apps	gls	apps	gls	apps	gls	apps	gls
1987/88	28/1	1	2	1	3	1	1	0	2	0	36/1	3
	28/1	**1**	**2**	**1**	**3**	**1**	**1**	**0**	**2**	**0**	**36/1**	**3**

***HODGKINSON,* Robert** 1924 - 1925, 1926 - 1927

Position; *Centre-Forward*
D.O.B; *c1902*
Birthplace; *Burton-upon-Trent, Staffordshire*
Height; *5ft 11in* ***Weight;*** *11st 10lbs*
Debut v. *Doncaster Rovers (h) 18th October, 1924*
Total Appearances & Goals; *21 apps 6 gls*
Career; *Loughborough; Burton All Saints Nov 1923; WREXHAM 2nd Jul 1924 £200; Oswestry Town Jun 1925; Wrexham 20th Aug 1926; Whitchurch Sept 1927 (trial); Llandudno 15th Oct 1927 (trial); Middlewich 19th Nov 1927;*
Honours; *Welsh Cup Winner 1925;*

Bob Hodgkinson made his Wrexham debut during 1924/25, having signed for the club during the close season from Burton All Saints. He had been 'free scoring' in the Birmingham & District League after joining them from Loughborough in November 1923. Bob made his Football League debut for Wrexham against Doncaster Rovers on the Racecourse, and scored one of the goals in a 2-1 victory. He made just eight more appearances that season, one of which was the 1925 Welsh Cup Final, with Wrexham beating Flint Town 3-1. Although a centre-forward Bob was asked to play in the above match at centre-half, in place of the injured Bob Matthews. He moved in the close season, joining Birmingham & District League side Oswestry Town, but after a year with the Shropshire side made a surprising return to Wrexham. His second spell at the Racecourse would see him make nine League appearances for the Denbighshire club when replacing George Appleyard in the side for five matches but then had to wait until the New Year before he was called upon again. This was at centre-half, taking the place of the departed Tommy Griffiths, who had moved to Everton. Hodgkinson appeared twice more before Tommy Matthias took over. After one more senior game he was allowed to leave the Racecourse in the close season of 1927. He then joined Welsh League North side Llandudno in October 1927, until signing for Cheshire County League side Middlewich a month later.

Season	League		F.A.Cup		Welsh Cup		Total	
	apps	gls	apps	gls	apps	gls	apps	gls
1924/25	6	2	-	-	3	0	9	2
1926/27	9	2	-	-	3	2	12	4
	15	**4**	-	-	**6**	**2**	**21**	**6**

***HOLLAND,* Eric Reginald** 1960 - 1966

Position; *Left-Back*
D.O.B; *23rd January, 1940*
Birthplace; *Sutton-in-Ashfield, Nottinghamshire*
Height; *5ft 10in* ***Weight;*** *12st 1lbs*
Debut v. *Southend United (a) 5th March, 1960*
Total Appearances & Goals; *145 apps 0 gls*
Career; *Manchester United May 1957 0apps; WREXHAM 4th Mar 1960 £2,000; Chester 16th March 1966 5/1apps 0gls; Altrincham Jul 1966;*
Honours; *Four England Schoolboy international caps; Eight England Youth international caps; Welsh Cup Winner 1960; Welsh Cup runner-up 1962 & 1965; F.A.Youth Cup Winner 1956 & 1957;*

Reg Holland began his football career at Healdswood Secondary School, where he was selected for both Sutton-in-Ashfield and Nottinghamshire Schoolboys, and resulted in a call-up at centre-half for England Schools in 1955 at Wembley against Wales. Reg also played three more times for his country: against Wales (again), Eire, and Scotland. That same year he left School and joined the groundstaff at Manchester United, who beat off the likes of Aston Villa, Sheffield Wednesday, West Ham, and Notts County to acquire his services. As a United supporter there was no other choice for Reg! He was involved in two F.A.Youth finals at Old Trafford, and was twice on the winning side - against Chesterfield in 1956, and West Ham a year later - in a team that included Bobby Charlton, Johnny Giles, David Gaskell and Peter Jones, who was also subsequently to join Wrexham. These performances also earned Reg caps at Youth level for England, and actually captained the English Youth side in a tournament in Spain in 1957 against Greece. All this time he was playing at centre-half. In Easter 1957 he was signed on professional terms, and was soon given a place in the club's Central League side following his conversion to full-back, as Matt Busby was of the thinking that he was not big enough to

play at centre-half. He was also appointed captain of the reserves, remaining skipper until he left the club. Even so, Reg was never handed his chance to play in the first team at Old Trafford although coming close, as twelfth man for three matches against West Brom, Newcastle, and Burnley, and after five years at the club moved on, joining Wrexham in March 1960. In doing so, he became the second of three former 'Busby Babes' to join Wrexham in a period of three months, the first being Reg Hunter and the third Peter Jones. Holland quickly settled in at the Racecourse, and helped the 'Robins' to a Welsh Cup Final victory over Cardiff City, just two months after joining the club. He enjoyed another five seasons at the Racecourse, during which he played his part in helping the club gain promotion back to the Third Division in 1962. He picked up a Welsh Cup runners'-up medal the same year, when Wrexham lost to Bangor City in the Final. He also took part in the 1965 Welsh Cup Final, when Wrexham lost 3-0 to Cardiff City at neutral Shrewsbury. He experienced some bad times at the Racecourse, too, when the club was relegated in 1964, and 1965/66, when Wrexham completed their League programme in 92nd place. Reg, however, had left the club before the end of that nightmare campaign. Towards the end of his time with the 'Robins' Holland was described as 'a great club man, who always gave his best in either full-back position'. He joined Chester for a 'small fee' in March 1966, but clocked up just five League games for the Sealand Road club joining Cheshire County League side Altrincham in the close season of 1966. He spent just one season with 'Alty', leaving at the end of 1966/67 to begin a career with the Staffordshire Police Force. He continued to play football when available for Staffordshire England and British Police XIs. Reg spent almost 27 years with the Police Force before retiring in 1994, and settling in the Stafford area.

Season	League		F.A.Cup		Welsh Cup		League Cup		Total	
	apps	gls	apps	gls	apps	gls	apps	gls	apps	gls
1959/60	13	0	1	0	4	0	-	-	18	0
1960/61	10	0	-	-	-	-	-	-	10	0
1961/62	10	0	-	-	2	0	-	-	12	0
1962/63	11	0	-	-	1	0	-	-	12	0
1963/64	20	0	-	-	3	0	4	0	27	0
1964/65	35	0	2	0	7	0	-	-	44	0
1965/66	19	0	2	0	-	-	1	0	22	0
	118	**0**	**5**	**0**	**17**	**0**	**5**	**0**	**145**	**0**

HOLLAND, John

1925

Position; *Inside-Right*
D.O.B; *3rd April, 1901*
Birthplace; *Preston, Lancashire*
Height; *5ft 8'1/2in* **Weight;** *10st 7lbs*
Debut v. *Doncaster Rovers (a) 5th September, 1925*
Total Appearances & Goals; *9 apps 2 gls*
Career; *Preston North End (Am) Dec 1919, (Pro) Jun 1920 5apps 0gls; Swansea Town 14th June 1923 23apps 3gls; WREXHAM 5th May 1925; Crewe Alexandra 17th Dec 1925 23apps 3gls; Newport County 21st Jun 1926 10apps 2gls; Clapton Orient Oct 1927 19apps 4gls; Carlisle United Jul 1929 34apps 13gls; Barrow Jul 1930 8apps 0gls to Feb 1931;*
Honours; *Welsh League Representative XI;*

Preston born Jack Holland joined his home town club on amateur forms in 1919, having previously played junior football around the Preston area. He began in Preston's Central League side, signing professional terms in the summer of 1920. Jack made his Football League debut the following season in a First Division match. He managed just five senior appearances in four seasons with the Deepdale club before joining Swansea Town during the close season of 1923. He spent over two years at the Vetch Field, and was chosen to represent the Welsh League against the Irish League during 1924/25. Holland moved up to North Wales to join Wrexham in the summer of 1925, despite strong interest from both Orient and Portsmouth for his signature, but wanted to be nearer his Preston home. Jack made his League debut for the 'Robins' at inside-forward as a replacement for James Lyons in a match at Doncaster Rovers, which ended 1-1, and kept his place in the side for the following two matches until Lyons was reinstated. He returned to the side in October for six games, but during December was transferred to Crewe Alexandra. He made 23 appearances in the second half of 1926/27 for the Gresty Road outfit, his debut in a 3-1 home win over Rotherham United. He must have developed a liking for South Wales during his time at Swansea, as he moved south again to join Newport County in the close season of 1926, making his debut for them in the opening match of 1926/27 against Plymouth Argyle, and capped it with a goal in the 2-1 win. Jack made a further nine League appearances for the Monmouthshire club before joining Clapton Orient at the end of the season. He spent two years in East London, making 19 League appearances for the 'O's' until joining Carlisle United in the summer of 1929. His debut for the 'Cumbrians' came in a 2-0 home win over Crewe Alexandra in the opening match of 1929/30, going on to keep his place in the side throughout the season for the first time in his career. Even so, he was allowed to leave Brunton Park at the end of the season, and then spent almost a term with Barrow. During his career Holland was described as 'a forward of direct method with considerable power as a marksman'.

Season	League		F.A.Cup		Welsh Cup		Total	
	apps	gls	apps	gls	apps	gls	apps	gls
1925/26	9	2	-	-	-	-	9	2
	9	**2**	-	-	-	-	**9**	**2**

HOLLIS, Harold

1946 - 1947

Position; *Full-Back*
D.O.B; *12th December, 1913*
Birthplace; *Shotton, Flintshire*
Died; *18th August, 1982*
Height; *5ft 9in* **Weight;** *10st 7lbs*
Debut v. *Hartlepool United (h) 5th April, 1947*
Total Appearances & Goals; *1 app 0 gls*
Career; *Connah's Quay & Shotton; Flint Town 1929; Newry Town; Marine; Bangor City; Chester Mar 1940 23 apps 0gls; Stockport County (WW2 Guest) May 1940 1app 0gls; Brighton & Hove Albion (WW2 Guest) Mar 1944 1app 0gls; Bradford City (WW2 Guest) Oct 1944 3apps 0gls; Hull City (WW2 Guest) Dec 1944 8apps 0gls; Charlton Athletic (WW2 Guest) 1944/45 1app 0gls; Fulham (WW2 Guest) 1944/45 2apps 0gls; Falkirk (WW2 Guest) 1945; WREXHAM 6th Aug 1946; Bangor City 14th Jun 1947; Oswestry Town 1947/48; Holywell Town 20th Nov 1948; Colwyn Bay 17th Dec 1948; Llanfairfechan 15th Aug 1949; Llandudno Junction 26th Jun 1950; Penmaenmawr 6th Oct 1950; Pwllheli & District 20th Apr 1951; Llanrwst Town 14th Jul 1952; Holyhead Town 4th Oct 1952; Saltney 19th Aug 1953; Llanfairfechan 20th Aug 1954; Connah's Quay Albion 7th Mar 1955; Connah's Quay Nomads 12th Dec 1956;*

Harry began playing football at Shotton Council School, where he gained recognition as 'a youngster of merit'. He eventually signed for Connah's Quay & Shotton, who were then under the charge of former Wrexham manager Charlie Hewitt. During his time at the club they actually won the Welsh Senior Cup, in 1929, although too young to play in the Final. At the age of 16 Harry was offered trials with both Manchester United and Chester. He remained an amateur and not long after signed for Flint Town, with whom he spent six successful seasons winning the Flintshire Challenge Cup, Flintshire Charity Trophy (three times), as well as League honours. They joined the Welsh League North in 1933, and were crowned champions in their very first season, adding the League Shield, League Cup and Challenge Cup to their trophy cabinet. They actually retained the Challenge Cup for six successive seasons, and for their efforts each player received a miniature replica of the Cup. Harry was then selected to play representative football for the North Wales Coast F.A. in two matches against the Scottish Junior's, first at Wrexham and in Edinburgh the following year. In 1936 he left Flint to try his luck in Ireland, where he joined Newry Town. This was followed by spells with Liverpool Marine, and Bangor City, who were experiencing their first season in the Lancashire Combination League, finishing as runners-up, missing out on the Championship by a single point. Harry signed for Chester in 1939 as an amateur, but the outbreak of World War Two was to limit his appearances for them. He completed 23 WW2 League games, partnering his brother Ken at full-back, coming up against Stanley Matthews in his first match! Harry enlisted with the Royal Artillery during the War, and played in many first class matches during his time in the Forces, including the Combined Services XI versus the Czech Army XI. He also 'guested' for a number of other clubs: Stockport County, Brighton & Hove Albion, Hull City, Bradford City, Charlton Athletic, and Fulham, amongst others. From Craven Cottage he moved up to Scotland, 'guesting' for Falkirk, and also represented the Scottish Command against the Royal Navy. After playing - with and against - many famous stars of the football world Hollis was demobilised from the Army in 1946 and looked to restart his football career, not at Chester, but with neighbours Wrexham. He was signed by Wrexham manager Tom Williams in August 1946, mainly as cover for his full-backs. He was described as 'an excellent right-back, who was a cultured player, and who knew the game inside out'. At the age of 33 he finally made his Football League debut for 'The Robins' in a home match against Hartlepool United in April 1947, replacing the injured Eddie Tunney at right-back. This proved to be Harry's one and only Football League appearance, as he was released at the end of the 1946/47 season. He then joined Bangor

City and Oswestry Town for a season, from where he went on something of a tour of North Wales, appearing for a number of clubs up and down the coast!

Season	League		F.A.Cup		Welsh Cup		Total	
	apps	gls	apps	gls	apps	gls	apps	gls
1946/47	1	0	-	-	-	-	1	0
	1	**0**	**-**	**-**	**-**	**-**	**1**	**0**

HOLMES, George William — 1922 - 1923

Position; *Left-Back*
D.O.B; *J/A/S 1892*
Birthplace; *Golden Hill, Staffordshire*
Height; *5ft 7'1/2in* ***Weight;*** *12st 0lbs*
Debut v. *Barrow (h) 16th September, 1922*
Total Appearances & Goals; *39 apps 0 gls*
Career; *Goldenhill Wanderers; Leek Alexandra; Port Vale Aug 1916; Merthyr Town Oct 1920 17apps 0gls; Sheffield Wednesday Jun 1921 20apps 0gls; WREXHAM 9th Sept 1922;*

George Holmes was playing for local side Leek Alexandra when joining Port Vale in August 1916. He made his debut for Vale in a 5-1 defeat at Liverpool in a Lancashire Regional Section match in December 1916, and became a regular in the Burslem side a year later until released at the end of 1918/19. He joined Third Division South side Merthyr Town in October 1920, and during his time in South Wales made his Football League debut. George went on to complete 17 appearances for the Welsh side that season before signing for Second Division side Sheffield Wednesday in August 1921. He made his debut for 'The Owls' in the following month, a scoreless draw at Hillsborough against Notts County, and clocked up a total of twenty League appearances for Wednesday that season in either of the full-back berths. In the close season of 1922, Holmes was signed by Third Division North side Wrexham, as a replacement for veteran right-back Billy Cope, and he made his bow in only the fourth game of the season, a scoreless home draw against Barrow. George kept his place in the side for the rest of the season, missing only the final game at Chesterfield. At the end of the season, however, he was deemed surplus to requirements and left the club.

Season	League		F.A.Cup		Welsh Cup		Total	
	apps	gls	apps	gls	apps	gls	apps	gls
1922/23	34	0	3	0	2	0	39	0
	34	**0**	**3**	**0**	**2**	**0**	**39**	**0**

HOOPER, Michael Dudley — 1985

Position; *Goalkeeper*
D.O.B; *10th February, 1964*
Birthplace; *Bristol, Avon*
Height; *6ft 2in* ***Weight;*** *13st 0lbs*
Debut v. *Exeter City (a) 13th February, 1985*
Total Appearances & Goals; *38 apps 0 gls*
Career; *Mangotsfield; Bristol City 8th Nov 1983 1app; WREXHAM 8th Feb 1985 £4,000; Liverpool 25th Oct 1985 £40,000 50/1apps; Leicester City 21st Sept 1990 (Loan), to 17th Dec 1990 14 apps; Newcastle United 23rd Sept 1993 £550,000 23/2apps 0gls;*
Honours; *England Schoolboy international; Charity Shield Winner 1986; Super Sport Screen Cup Winner 1986;*

Mike Hooper had an impressive start as a goalkeeper; not only did he represent his school teams in Bristol, but also gained international honours for England Schoolboys at both under-15 and under-18 levels. He also featured in the British Universities side for the World Student Games. Even though he was more interested in continuing with his studies Mike was persuaded to sign for Bristol City from local club side Mangotsfield in January 1984, where he had been able to combine playing football with studying at Swansea University for a degree in English Literature. Mike was to make just one Football League appearance at Ashton Gate, his debut coming in December 1984 in a home match against Lincoln City, replacing John Shaw in a 2-1 win. Meanwhile, in North Wales Wrexham manager Bobby Roberts was faced with serious goalkeeping problems following an injury to Stuart Parker, and signed Mike on loan in February 1985. He made his debut in a 2-0 defeat at Exeter, and continued as the club's keeper until the end of the season, missing only two games. He then returned to Bristol City, having made a big impact during his loan spell, though he was soon back at the Racecourse on a permanent basis when the 'Robins' new manager, Dixie McNeil, successfully bid £4,000 for the flame-haired custodian. The bigger clubs were quickly alerted to his potential following some outstanding displays at the start of 1985/86 and, not surprisingly, he made his last appearance for Wrexham in October 1985 at Aldershot, where he conceded six goals! Liverpool paid out £40,000 for him, with further payments dependant upon appearances. Mike had been brought to Anfield as cover for Bruce Grobbelaar, and made his first appearance for Liverpool in the 1986 Charity Shield as a substitute for the extrovert Zimbabwean. In his eight years with the Anfield club Hooper made just 51 League appearances, although he did play in many important Cup matches. Overall though, he found it difficult to oust the consistent Grobbelaar and in September 1990 went out on loan to Leicester City, in a rare loan-exchange deal that saw Carl Muggleton join Liverpool. Mike made 14 League appearances for the Filbert Street club before returning to Anfield in December. A permanent transfer materialised in September 1993, when Newcastle United manager Kevin Keegan splashed out £500,000 for him. He was pitched straight into the first team at St.James' Park for his debut, replacing Tommy Wright in a 2-0 home win over West Ham United. Following a total of nineteen consecutive League games he was injured, and replaced by Pavel Srnicek for the rest of the season. Over the next two seasons Hooper was to suffer both illness and injuries, which restricted his appearances, and was not helped by the subsequent arrival of Shaka Hislop. Mike then surprised the football world by announcing his retirement from the game at the end of 1995/96 due to a persistent back injury, claiming that he wished to do something more fulfilling. He had been the victim of a vicious hate campaign by a lunatic fringe following Newcastle's F.A.Cup exit at Luton, and a Premeirship defeat at Wimbledon, and played a part in his decision to retire from the game prematurely. Despite offers to join other Clubs Mike settled in Northumberland, becoming a school teacher.

Season	League		F.A.Cup		Welsh Cup		League Cup		F.R.T.		Total	
	apps	gls	apps	gls	apps	gls	apps	gls	apps	gls	apps	gls
1984/85	20	0	-	-	-	-	-	-	-	-	20	0
1985/86	14	0	-	-	-	-	4	0	-	-	18	0
	34	**0**	**-**	**-**	**-**	**-**	**4**	**0**	**-**	**-**	**38**	**0**

HOPE, Eric — 1951 - 1954

Position; *Inside-Forward*
D.O.B; *2nd December, 1927*
Birthplace; *Oakengates, Shropshire*
Height; *5ft 6'1/2in* ***Weight;*** *10st 13lbs*
Debut v. *Southport (h) 20th October, 1951*
Total Appearances & Goals; *45 apps 13 gls*
Career; *Oakengates YC; Manchester City Jan 1946 0apps; Shrewsbury Town Aug 1950 27apps 3gls; WREXHAM 19th Oct 1951; GKN Sankeys Aug 1954 (Loan), 18th Mar 1955;*

Eric Hope began playing football for his school team, Wrockwardine Wood in Telford, from where he was chosen to play for Shropshire Schoolboys. Upon leaving school at fourteen Eric continued to play the game for Oakengates Youth Club until was signed by Swansea Town two years later on Associate schoolboy forms. He struggled at the Vetch Field, and quickly returned home, though not long after was spotted by a Manchester City scout, and signed for the Maine Road club in January 1946. Even so, National Service was again to interrupt a promising football career, when Eric was posted to the Far East with the R.A.F. He kept himself fit as he was detailed as a Physical Education instructor, reaching the position of sergeant. After his two years conscription Eric returned to Manchester City, playing regularly in City's Central League

side before suffering a knee ligament injury that almost brought his football career to a premature end. Manchester City had virtually written him off when he was offered the chance of a fresh start with Shrewsbury Town, then newly promoted to the Football League. The 'Shrews' physio Sam Powell worked wonders on Eric in getting him fit for the new season, and played in their first ever Football League match at Scunthorpe United. He went on to make a further 26 League appearances for the Gay Meadow club before surprisingly allowed to join Wrexham. It was an exchange deal which saw Eric and Peter Fisher join Wrexham, with Eddie Beynon and Ray Williams moving in the opposite direction. Hope went straight into the 'Robins' first team for his debut in an impressive 3-0 home win over table toppers Southport. He remained a part of the Wrexham forward line until sustaining a torn cartilage in a Welsh Cup match at Chester in February 1952, and managed just three more League games during 1952/53 due to the extent of the injury. Eric returned to the first team for the following season but, despite his efforts, was to leave the Racecourse at the end of the campaign following a dispute with the manager Peter Jackson. GKN Sankey in Wellington was his next port of call, where he also began working as a Production Foreman. Wrexham were to retain his Football League registration until March 1955. He later managed the Sankey's football team, and led them into the Cheshire County League, continuing to play football up until he was 38. Eric settled in the Hadley area of Telford, and later coached a number of junior teams in the locality. At the beginning of the 1998/99 season, he was one of over 100 players to attend a 'Players Grand Gala Reunion' at Ewloe.

Season	League apps	League gls	F.A.Cup apps	F.A.Cup gls	Welsh Cup apps	Welsh Cup gls	Total apps	Total gls
1951/52	19	6	3	2	3	2	25	10
1952/53	3	0	-	-	-	-	3	0
1953/54	15	3	1	0	1	0	17	3
	37	**9**	**4**	**2**	**4**	**2**	**45**	**13**

HORNE, Barry

1984 - 1987

Position; *Midfield*
D.O.B; *18th May, 1962*
Birthplace; *St.Asaph, Flintshire*
Height; *5ft 10in* ***Weight;*** *11st 6lbs*
Debut v. *Swindon Town (a) 25 August, 1984*
Total Appearances & Goals; *184 apps 29 gls*
Career; *Greenfield; Rhyl 1983; WREXHAM 26th Jun 1984; Portsmouth 27th Jul 1987 66/4apps 7gls £70.000; Southampton 22nd Mar 1989 £700,000 111/1apps 6gls; Everton 29th July 1992 £675,000 118/5apps 3gls; Birmingham City 5th June 1996 £250,000 33apps 0gls; Huddersfield Town 14th Oct 1997 49/1apps 1gls;*
Honours; *59 Welsh International Caps; F.A.Cup Winner 1995; Welsh Cup Winner 1986; Zenith Data Systems runner-up 1992;*

Barry Horne enjoyed considerable success in football during his school days, winning a number of trophies and representing district teams. On leaving school he received a number of offers from League clubs but decided to continue his Education, studying Chemistry for three years at Liverpool University. Barry continued playing football, representing the University team, winning the National University Trophy. He also played for Greenfields during this time, later joining Northern Premier League side Rhyl. Barry played for the Belle Vue club in a Welsh Cup match at Wrexham, which the 'Seasiders' lost 3-1 after a replay. Wrexham manager Bobby Roberts had been impressed with Horne's contribution in those games, and invited him for trials with the 'Robins'. With his University studies completed, and a BSC and a Master's Degree in Engineering attained, Barry took up the offer and in June 1984 signed professional for Wrexham. He went straight into the first team for the opening match of the new season at Swindon, missing just two League games in the three years that he spent at the Racecourse. During that time Barry collected a Welsh Cup winners' medal in 1986, when Wrexham beat Kidderminster in the final. He also played in two European campaigns for the 'Robins', including the famous victory over F.C.Porto in 1984 when he scored one of the most important away goals in the history of the club. He was selected for the full Welsh squad in 1985, but it was after he left Wrexham that Horne was to gain the first of his 59 caps. He captained his country on 33 occasions, a record bettered only by Terry Yorath and Kevin Ratcliffe. Barry moved on from Wrexham in May 1987, when Portsmouth manager Alan Ball signed the popular Welshman for £70,000. 'Pompey' had just won promotion but he immediately won a place in the side, contributing some impressive performances earning his first Welsh cap as a substitute against Denmark in September 1987. Barry went on to make 70 League appearances for 'Pompey' before neighbours Southampton splashed out £700,000 for him in March 1989, thereby becoming the first player to move from Fratton Park to the Dell since 1946. He featured in 112 League games for the 'Saints', and picked up a Zenith Data Systems Cup runners'-up medal in 1992. Horne was slow to settle in at first, but his 'combative style, determined tackling and steady work-rate' eventually made him a firm favourite with the 'Saints' supporters. In July 1992 Horne moved nearer home, signing for Everton in a £675,000 deal. He went on to make 123 League appearances for the 'Toffeemen', collecting an F.A.Cup winners' medal in 1995, when Everton beat Manchester United, and a winners' medal from the 1995 Charity Shield following a 1-0 win over Blackburn Rovers. He has a penchant for scoring spectacular long distance goals, and it was one of these scored from 25 yards which helped keep Everton in the Premier Division in the last match of the 1993/94 season against Wimbledon, when they avoided relegation by coming from 2-0 down to win 3-2. In July 1996 he quit Goodison Park to sign for Birmingham City for £250,000. At St.Andrew's he played against Wrexham for the first time since leaving the Racecourse, when Wrexham met the 'Blues' in an F.A.Cup game at St.Andrew's, with Wrexham running out 3-1 winners to reach the quarter-finals of the F.A.Cup. In September 1997 Barry was installed as the P.F.A.'s new chairman in succession to Pat Nevin, beating off the challenge of Brian McClair, Iain Dowie and Gary Mabbutt for the post. However, he was soon on the move again, leaving Birmingham to join up with his former Welsh international team manager Terry Yorath at First Division Huddersfield Town. He played a major part in helping the 'Terriers' to escape the very realistic threat of relegation in 1997/98, and was still at the Sir Alfred McAlpine Stadium at the beginning of the 1998/99 campaign. Barry's brother Darren is also well known in local football regularly appeared for North Wales clubs.

Season	League apps	League gls	F.A.Cup apps	F.A.Cup gls	Welsh Cup apps	Welsh Cup gls	League Cup apps	League Cup gls	F.R.T. apps	F.R.T. gls	E.C.W.C. apps	E.C.W.C. gls	Total apps	Total gls
1984/85	44	5	1	0	3	1	2	0	2	0	4	1	56	7
1985/86	46	3	3	1	7	4	4	1	2	0	-	-	62	9
1986/87	46	8	3	2	5	1	4	0	4	1	4	1	66	13
	136	**16**	**7**	**3**	**15**	**6**	**10**	**1**	**8**	**1**	**8**	**2**	**184**	**29**

HOUGHTON, Peter

1984

Position; *Forward*
D.O.B; *30th November, 1954*
Birthplace; *Liverpool, Merseyside*
Height; *5ft 11in* ***Weight;*** *12st 7lbs*
Debut v. *Southend United (h) 24th November, 1984*
Total Appearances & Goals; *5 apps 2 gls*
Career; *South Liverpool; Wigan Athletic Jan 1978 169/16apps 62gls; Preston North End Oct 1983 52/4apps 16gls; WREXHAM 22nd Nov 1984 (Loan); Chester City Aug 1985 78/7apps 13gls; Northwich Victoria Runcorn cs1988 0/14apps 0gls; General Chemicals 1989;*
Honours; *Northern Premier League runner-up 1978; Lancashire Junior Cup Winner 1978;*

Peter Houghton was a member of the Liverpool Schools F.A. squad that won the English Schools Trophy. After leaving school he took up work at Ford's Hailwood factory on Merseyside, while continuing to turn out for local non-league side South Liverpool. He would often finish a night shift to go and play football. Even though he was part of a struggling team Peter was scoring plenty of goals, and that was incentive enough for progressive non-League side Wigan Athletic to sign him for £500 in January 1978. He assisted the 'Latics' to achieve Football League status by the end of the season, and appeared in their first ever Football League match alongside another former Wrexham player, Joe Hinnigan, in a scoreless draw at Hereford United in August 1978. Houghton endeared himself to the Wigan fans with his 'powerful running and several memorable goals'. He was the club's leading scorer with fourteen goals in their initial season in the League, and in 1981/82, he formed a lethal partnership with Les Bradd as the 'Latics' won promotion to the Third Division. In just over five seasons of League football at Springfield Park Peter made over 200 League and Cup appearances, and only recently (1997/98) saw his record of Wigan Athletic's Football League aggregate goals of 62 beaten by David Lowe. In October 1983 he left Springfield Park to join Preston North End, where he made 56 League appearances and scored 16 goals. During his time at Deepdale Peter joined Wrexham on loan in November 1984, making his debut in a 2-1 home defeat by Southend United. He made a further four League appearances for the 'Robins', scoring two goals, creating a favourable impression during his short spell at the Racecourse. However, the desperate state of the club's finances once again prevented manager Bobby Roberts from making the signing permanent. He returned to Preston, where he remained until the end of the season, when he was signed by Chester City. He made his debut for the 'Seals' in a 3-0 defeat at Peterborough United in the second match of the season, and went on to make 85 League appearances and score 13 goals before his release in 1987. Peter then had a spell with Northwich Victoria, followed by a short time with Runcorn, before playing for West Cheshire League side General Chemicals.

Season	League		F.A.Cup		Welsh Cup		League Cup		F.R.T.		Total	
	apps	gls	apps	gls	apps	gls	apps	gls	apps	gls	apps	gls
1984/85	5	2	-	-	-	-	-	-	-	-	5	2
	5	**2**	-	-	-	-	-	-	-	-	**5**	**2**

***HOUSTON,* William M.** 1923 - 1924

Position; *Inside-Right*
D.O.B;
Birthplace; *Stirling, Central*
Height; *5ft 7in* ***Weight;*** *10st 0lbs*
Debut v. *Lincoln City (a) 22nd December, 1923*
Total Appearances & Goals; *3 apps 1 gls*
Career; *St.Ninians Thistle; Crewe Alex Apr 1921 9apps 2gls; Macclesfield Town Aug 1922; WREXHAM 19th Jun 1923; Nantwich cs1924; Llandudno 4th Oct 1924; Crewe Alex Oct 1925 4apps 1gls; Runcorn; Stafford Rangers cs1928;*

Billy Houston was playing for St.Ninian's Thistle in his native Scotland when signed by Third Division North side Crewe Alexandra in April 1921. Billy made his Football League debut for the Gresty Road club in a 2-1 home defeat by Chesterfield in October, and scored the Crewe goal. He went on to record a total of nine League appearances for the 'Railwaymen' until released at the end of the 1921/22 season. He joined Cheshire County League side Macclesfield Town, for a year before returning to the Football League with Wrexham during the close season of 1923. He played for Wrexham's reserve team at inside-forward initially, and eventually winning his first team chance in December, when replacing Bill Cotton at inside-right in a 4-2 defeat at Lincoln City. Following that game Billy returned to reserve team action, where he remained there until April 1925 when again turning out at inside-right in a home game against Accrington Stanley. 'The Robins' won 1-0, with Billy scoring the only goal, and remained in the team for the following match at his former club, Crewe. Wrexham drew 1-1, but that game proved to be Houston's 'Swan' Song for 'The Robins' as he was to leave the Racecourse during the close season of 1924. He is then believed to have joined Nantwich, although by October had signed for Welsh League side Llandudno. Almost twelve months later he was re-signed by Crewe Alexandra, and Billy made four more Football League appearances with the 'Railwaymen' eventually returning to non-league football with Runcorn and Stafford Rangers. He was believed to have been a joiner by trade.

Season	League		F.A.Cup		Welsh Cup		Total	
	apps	gls	apps	gls	apps	gls	apps	gls
1923/24	3	1	-	-	-	-	3	1
	3	**1**	-	-	-	-	**3**	**1**

***HOWARD,* Frederick** 1924 - 1925

Position; *Centre-Forward*
D.O.B; *1893*
Birthplace; *Walkden, Tyne & Wear*
Height; *5ft 10in* ***Weight;*** *11st 9lbs*
Debut v. *Lincoln City (h) 1st October, 1924*
Total Appearances & Goals; *1 app 0 gls*
Career; *Walkden Wednesday; Manchester City (Am)18th Sept 1912, (Pro) Oct 1912 79apps 40gls; Mid Rhondda 25th Aug 1920; Pontypridd; Gillingham Nov 1921 11apps 3gls; Dundee Hibernian (trial); Ayr United Oct 1922 (trial); Clyde Nov 1922 (trial); Port Vale 3rd July 1923 12apps 2gls; New Brighton 13th Feb 1924 10apps 4gls; WREXHAM 30th Sept 1924; Welshpool 15th Oct 1925; Holyhead Town 28th Jan 1926;*

Fred Howard made one appearance for Wrexham against Lincoln City on the Racecourse in a 1-0 defeat in October 1924. His professional career had begun in sensational style with First Division Manchester City, who he had joined when just seventeen. Fred made his Football League debut for City against Liverpool, at City's Hyde Road ground, on 18th January 1913. Within the first 13 minutes of the game he had recorded a hat-trick! and twenty minutes into the second half added City's fourth goal in the 4-1 win. He went on to make another 78 League appearances for City, with an impressive return of a goal every other game. However, the First World War interrupted his footballing career, and made just one further appearance for City before released in the summer of 1920. After the hostilities of the Great War were over he went on to play for Welsh League sides Mid-Rhondda and Pontypridd. He then signed for Gillingham in November 1921, and made his debut in the following month at Millwall in a 1-0 defeat. He went on to score three goals in eleven games for the 'Gills,' moving on at the end of 1921/22 to try his luck in the Scottish League, first with Dundee Hibernians, and then both Ayr United and Clyde. He returned south in July 1923 and signed for Port Vale, where he spent just under a year, making his debut in a 2-1 win at Crystal Palace in August, becoming a regular in the side until November. However, difficulties arose because he was having to travel to the 'Potteries' from his home in Liverpool, which eventually led to him joining New Brighton in February 1924. Fred found himself playing between the posts for the 'Rakers' at Rochdale when 'keeper Bert Mehaffy was injured. Naturally, he was far better at putting the ball into the net than he was at keeping it out as he let in five out of the six goals put past his side at Spotland that day! He then signed for Wrexham manager, Charlie Hewitt, in October 1924, but managed just the appearance against Lincoln City. He later played for both Welshpool and Holyhead Town.

Season	League		F.A.Cup		Welsh Cup		Total	
	apps	gls	apps	gls	apps	gls	apps	gls
1924/25	1	0	-	-	-	-	1	0
	1	**0**	-	-	-	-	**1**	**0**

***HUDSON,* Robert Sanford** 1928 - 1930

Position; *Outside-Right*
D.O.B; *Apr qtr, 1902*
Birthplace; *Liverpool, Merseyside*
Died; *North Liverpool, 18th September, 1965*
Height; *5ft 7in* ***Weight;*** *10st 8lbs*
Debut v. *Tranmere Rovers (a) 27th August, 1928*
Total Appearances & Goals; *40 apps 13 gls*
Career; *Marine; Earle; Wallasey United Nov 1923; Earle; Mold Town 22nd Oct 1927; WREXHAM 27th Jul 1928; Runcorn Sept 1930; Crewe Alex Sept 1931 0apps;*
Honours; *North Wales Coast F.A.Challenge Cup runner-up 1927;*

Bob Hudson was signed by Wrexham from Mold Town during the close season of 1928, having previously been on the books of Merseyside clubs Marine, Wallasey United, and Earle. He had played for Mold in the 1927 Final of the North Wales Coast Challenge Cup, where they were beaten 3-2 by Bangor City. Bob made his Football League debut for Wrexham in the second match of the 1928/29 season at Tranmere Rovers, and scored his side's only goal in a 1-1 draw. He remained in the inside-right position for a further 21 League matches, helping the 'Robins' to achieve their highest position, (third), since joining the Third Division North in 1921. Hudson spent most of the following season playing for the reserve team, though called upon on fourteen occasions to cover at either inside-right or outside-right when required. He was released by Wrexham at the end of 1929/30 and drifted back into non-league football with Runcorn. He was later to sign for Crewe Alexandra in

September 1931, although he never made a first team appearance for the 'Railwaymen'.

Season	League		F.A.Cup		Welsh Cup		Total	
	apps	gls	apps	gls	apps	gls	apps	gls
1928/29	22	9	1	0	1	0	24	9
1929/30	14	3	1	0	1	1	16	4
	36	**12**	**2**	**0**	**2**	**1**	**40**	**13**

HUGHES, Arthur Robert 1924 - 1926

Position; *Centre-Forward*
D.O.B;
Birthplace; *Abermorddu, Denbighshire*
Height; *5ft 6in* ***Weight;*** *10st 7lbs*
Debut v. *New Brighton (a) 9th February, 1924*
Total Appearances & Goals; *18 apps 5 gls*
Career; *Oak Alyn Rovers; WREXHAM (Am) 7th Feb 1924, (Pro) Jun 1924; Oak Alyn Rovers Apr 1924; WREXHAM (Pro) 1st May, 1925; Llandudno Jul 1926; Oak Alyn 1928;*

Arthur Hughes joined Wrexham as an amateur in February 1924 from Oak Alyn Rovers. He made his Football League debut, at short notice along with R.D.Williams, at New Brighton in February 1924 in a scoreless draw, deputising at centre-forward for Ralph Lenney. The selections of both Arthur and Williams caused a rumpus at the time, and the local press commented; "These selections were a mistake. Apparently the result of the Club's desperation following the poor game on 2nd February, and the difficulties in the Wrexham Club filling the centre-forward, and right-wing positions. It was a big jump from Division Two of the Welsh League to the Third Division- too long a leap, and even good recruits like Arthur Hughes and R.D.Williams can hardly be expected to step up so fast and succeed at once. Both players promised well, and did their best. It should be remembered that both players were only chosen 48 hours before the match and had no previous trials in the reserves." It was stated in the report of the match that Arthur 'made a fairly successful debut, and made a commendable effort in the first half, which deserved a better fate'. Despite the reporter's comments he did keep his place in the side for the next match, at home to Grimsby Town, and enjoyed some success by scoring Wrexham's only goal in a 1-1 draw. He played in the subsequent game, which was the return at Grimsby, ending in a scoreless draw. He was then replaced in the side by Horace Jackson, and spent a time in the reserves before returning to Oak Alyn at the beginning of April. However, he rejoined Wrexham at the end of the season, and signed professional for the club on 1st May. Hughes spent the following couple of years in and out of the first team, recording a further fifteen appearances, and scoring four goals, during which he was described as 'an opportunist'. His final game for Wrexham came in a 1-0 home defeat against Walsall in April 1926, and he left the Racecourse at the end of the season. Arthur then moved into local football with Welsh National League side Llandudno, followed by another spell with his former club, Oak Alyn.

Season	League		F.A.Cup		Welsh Cup		Total	
	apps	gls	apps	gls	apps	gls	apps	gls
1923/24	3	1	-	-	-	-	3	1
1924/25	12	4	-	-	-	-	12	4
1925/26	3	0	-	-	-	-	3	0
	18	**5**	**-**	**-**	**-**	**-**	**18**	**5**

HUGHES, Bryan 1994 - 1997

Position; *Midfield*
D.O.B; *19th June, 1976*
Birthplace; *Liverpool, Merseyside*
Height; *5ft 10in* ***Weight;*** *11st 2lbs*
Debut v. *Cambridge United (a) 22nd January, 1994*
Total Appearances & goals; *73/23 apps 12 gls*
Career; *WREXHAM 7th July 1994 (Pro); Birmingham City 11th Mar 1997 £800,000 63/15apps 8gls;*
Honours; *Welsh Cup Winner 1995; Football League representative XI 1997; Welsh Youth Cup Winner 1994; Welsh Youth Cup runner-up 1993;*

Bryan Hughes was a promising footballer at St.Brigit's School on Scotland Road in his native Liverpool. When it closed down he switched to the Archbishop Beck School in Walton. Despite playing regularly for his school teams he did not play representative football as a youngster. At fourteen 'Yosser', as he was affectionately nicknamed at Wrexham joined the Liverpool School of Excellence, although staying just eight months as he was not happy. Despite offers from other clubs, including Manchester City, Bryan continued to play for his school and Sunday League teams until joining Wrexham on schoolboy forms, having been recommended by the then physio, Steve Wade. Upon leaving school he signed on YTS forms, and made rapid progress up to his Football League debut at

Cambridge in January 1994 as a substitute for Wayne Phillips. He was still only seventeen at the time. He made a handful of appearances before the end of the season as Wrexham worked to establish themselves in the Second Division following their promotion the previous season. The 1994/95 season turned out to be a successful campaign as he helped Wrexham lift the Welsh Cup with a 2-1 victory over Cardiff City at the National Stadium in Cardiff. To cap the occasion Bryan was named as the club's 'Young Player of the Season'. However, disaster was to strike during the summer as a mini-bus ran over his foot when on a player's holiday in Spain! He had recovered in time for the start of the new season, but then suffered a loss of form. The signing of the experienced Peter Ward saw him faced with further competition for a first team place, and 1995/96 turned out to be frustrating year for the promising youngster. His career blossomed in the following season, however, as he stepped in to win a regular first team place following an early injury to Wayne Phillips. He was soon back to his best in central midfield, where he was a major influence in Wrexham's memorable F.A.Cup run to the quarter-finals, and from where he scored a number of important Cup and League goals. He so impressed Birmingham City manager Trevor Francis when Wrexham beat the 'Blues' in the Fifth Round of the F.A.Cup that he returned to make a successful bid as soon as Wrexham's Cup run had come to a end at Chesterfield. Hughes then became Wrexham's first ever one million pound deal, including knock-on clauses. In February, prior to signing for the St.Andrew's club Bryan had been named in the Football League representative XI to play against their Italian counterparts in Genoa. He was the only Second Division player in the side. During his time at Wrexham he was said to possess a 'good first touch, keen awareness as well as a good passer of the ball with an eye for goal, attributes which are just part of this promising youngster's make-up'. Bryan was pitched straight into the Birmingham first team following his transfer, making his debut as a substitute in a local 'derby' against West Brom at the Hawthorns. He then became a regular in the side until the end of the season. His contribution throughout the following season helped the 'Blues' to the verge of a play-off place, only to miss out at the death, though he had more than his fair share of injury problems with which to contend. The following season saw Bryan help Birmingham reach the play-off's only to disappointingly lose on penalties to Watford.

Season	League		F.A.Cup		Welsh Cup		League Cup		A.G.T.		E.C.W.C.		Total	
	apps	gls	apps	gls	apps	gls	apps	gls	apps	gls	apps	gls	apps	gls
1993/94	3/8	0	-	-	-	-	-	-	-	-	-	-	3/8	0
1994/95	37/1	9	4	1	8	1	1	0	4	0	-	-	54/1	11
1995/96	11/11	0	0/3	0	-	-	1	0	2	1	-	-	14/14	1
1996/97	20/3	3	9	6	-	-	-	-	0/1	0	-	-	29/4	9
	71/23	**12**	**13/3**	**7**	**8**	**1**	**2**	**0**	**6/1**	**1**	**-**	**-**	**100/27**	**21**

HUGHES, **Charles James** 1958 - 1961

Position; *Goalkeeper*
D.O.B; *7th September, 1939*
Birthplace; *Blackpool, Lancashire*
Height; *5ft 10'1/2in* ***Weight;*** *10st 5lbs*
Debut v. *Swindon Town (a) 23rd September, 1959*
Total Appearances & Goals; *44 apps 0 gls*
Career; *WREXHAM 9th Oct 1958; Rhyl 25th Jul 1961; Oswestry Town Aug 1963; Blaenau Ffestiniog 2nd Oct 1967; Oswestry Town 10th Nov 1967; Prestatyn 12th Jan 1968; Caernarvon Town 16th Aug 1971; Pwllheli & District 5th Sept 1973; New Broughton cs1974; Llay Welfare; Coedpoeth;*
Honours; *Welsh Cup Winner 1960;*

Although born in Blackpool Charlie Hughes was brought up on Merseyside. He attended the Warbreck Secondary Modern School, where he made a big impression when playing for the Liverpool Schools team as a goalkeeper. He was recommended to Wrexham by his school teacher, who was from the town. He also had the chance to join Everton, but as they couldn't guarantee him a game every week signed for the 'Robins' when leaving school in 1954. He progressed through the 'A' and 'B' teams at the Racecourse signing as a part-time professional in October 1958, combining football with his job as a railway fireman. Despite signing semi-pro Charlie had to wait a further year before making his Football League debut at Swindon Town in September 1959. He replaced Billy Waters and kept his place for the next two matches, including the home match against Swindon Town when the floodlights were used for the very first time for a Football League game on the Racecourse. After that match Charlie was replaced by Roly Ugolini, though he wrested the place back from him later in the season in time to play against Cardiff City in the Welsh Cup Final, which Wrexham won 1-0. The following season began with new signing Arthur Johnson being preferred in goal, though Charlie replaced him in September for five matches, and again in November a further nine. However, he was released by Wrexham at the end of the 1960/61 season, but was quickly fixed up with another club when Cheshire County League side Rhyl signed him. Charlie spent almost two seasons at Belle Vue, moving on to Oswestry Town in August 1963, where he spent over four years before joining Welsh League North side Blaenau Ffestiniog for a month. He then returned to Oswestry Town for a short spell followed by a time at Prestatyn in January 1968, where he spent over three seasons. He signed for Caernarvon Town during the summer of 1971 and went on to spend two terms with the 'Canaries' before joining Pwllheli & District for 1973/74. He later played in the Welsh National League (Wrexham area) for New Broughton, winning a championship medal, followed by spells with both Llay Welfare and Coedpoeth. Hughes finally ended his football career at the age of 47 with Wrexham Sunday League side Four Dogs. On leaving the Racecourse Charlie found work with British Celanese, with whom he spent 24 years before becoming a market trader having settled in the Wrexham area.

Season	League		F.A.Cup		Welsh Cup		League Cup		Total	
	apps	gls	apps	gls	apps	gls	apps	gls	apps	gls
1959/60	21	0	1	0	4	0	-	-	26	0
1960/61	14	0	-	-	1	0	3	0	18	0
	35	**0**	**1**	**0**	**5**	**0**	**3**	**0**	**44**	**0**

HUGHES, **David John** 1970 - 1971

Position; *Outside-Right*
D.O.B; *23rd September, 1951*
Birthplace; *Liverpool, Merseyside*
Height; *5ft 4in* ***Weight;*** *10st 11lbs*
Debut v. *Gillingham (h) 1st March, 1971*
Total Appearances & Goals; *1 app 0 gls*
Career; *Everton 1966; WREXHAM (Amateur) 1968, (Pro) May 1970; South Liverpool 1972; Paran Slavia (Australia) 1974; South Liverpool 1975; Marine 1977;*
Honours; *Northern Floodlit League Championship Winner 1971; Northern Floodlit League Challenge Cup Winner 1970 & 1971; Alves Cup Winner 1969 & 1970; Northern Premier League Representative XI; Northern Premier League Challenge Cup runner-up 1981; Lancashire Senior Cup Winner 1980 & 1981; Lancashire FA Junior Cup Winner 1979; Cheshire County League Championship Winner 1978;*

David Hughes was playing football at Gilmore and Heath Road Schools in his native Liverpool, where he lived in the same street as Billy Ashcroft. It was as a result of the promise that he had shown at school that he was approached by a scout from Everton, who then signed him on schoolboy terms for the Goodison Park club. He went on to sign for 'The Toffee's' when he left school in 1966, though released at the end of his apprenticeship. Wrexham then stepped in, and he signed for the North Wales club as an amateur in 1968. He then went on to enjoy considerable success with the reserve team, winning the Northern Floodlit League Championship, the Northern Floodlit League Challenge Cup and the Alves Cup. David was to spend most of the 1970/71 season playing reserve team football for 'The Robins', though he finally made his Football League debut in March 1971, when called into the first team to deputise for Bobby Park in an exciting home game against Gillingham, which ended in a 4-3 defeat. That match proved to be David's one and only first team appearance for Wrexham, although he went on to spend another season at the Racecourse before being released. He then joined Northern Premier League side South Liverpool, where he was to play against his boyhood heroes, Tommy Lawrence, Ian St.John and Ron Yeats in a F.A.Cup First Round match with Tranmere Rovers, which the Prenton Park club won 2-0. Hughes went on to spend almost two seasons with South Liverpool before going to Australia, where he played football for Paran Slavia in the Victoria State League. He returned home in 1975, rejoining South Liverpool, for a further two seasons, before going on to play for Marine in both the Cheshire County and Northern Premier Leagues. David was to have much success with the Liverpool non-League side, winning the Cheshire County League Championship in 1977 in addition to a number of Cups, and twice gaining selection for the Northern Premier League's Representative XI. He finally left Marine in 1983. In 1976, David Hughes took up employment as a financial adviser for an insurance company, a job that he has been doing ever since. He still resides in the Liverpool area.

Season	League		F.A.Cup		Welsh Cup		League Cup		Total	
	apps	gls	apps	gls	apps	gls	apps	gls	apps	gls
1970/71	1	0	-	-	-	-	-	-	1	0
	1	**0**	**-**	**-**	**-**	**-**	**-**	**-**	**1**	**0**

HUGHES, **Derek** 1961 - 1962

Position; *Outside-right*
D.O.B; *22nd November, 1940*
Birthplace; *Wrexham, Denbighshire*
Height; *5ft 8in* ***Weight;*** *11st 7lbs*
Debut v. *Barrow (h) 13th January, 1962*
Total Appearances & Goals; *1 app 0 gls*
Career; *Victoria YC; Rhostyllen Villa; Johnstown United; Druids United; Bolton Wanderers (trial); Connah's Quay Nomads Dec 1957; Blackpool (Trial); Cardiff City (trial); Manchester United (trial); WREXHAM (Am) Jul 1960, (Pro) 12th May 1961; Bangor City cs1962; Oswestry Town; Pwllheli; Ellesmere Town; Llay Welfare; Overton FC; Buckley Wanderers; Courtaulds FC;*
Honours; *Three Welsh Boys Clubs caps; Welsh Youth Cup Winner 1957;*

Derek Hughes attended the Victoria School in Wrexham, from where he moved on to the Denbighshire Technical College. At this time he joined the Victoria Youth Club in the town, also playing football and progressing to earn selection to play for the Welsh Boys' Club side - against England at both Wolves and Eastbourne, plus Scotland at Llanelli. He was still at school when first playing for Rhostyllen Villa in the Welsh National League, and later joined Johnstown United followed by a spell with Druids United. Derek took up work as an apprentice with the National Coal Board after leaving school, initially at Gresford, then at both Llay Main and Hafod Collieries. He was a member of the Druids youth side that reached the 1958 Welsh Youth Cup Final against Swansea, which they won 2-1 at Llanidloes. It proved to be the launch-pad for his football career as he was invited for trials at a number of clubs including, Bolton Wanderers, Blackpool, Cardiff City, and then Manchester United. It was after being turned away from Old Trafford that he was signed by Cliff Lloyd at Wrexham. He then played under Billy Morris and Ken Barnes, who eventually gave Derek his first team debut. The cousin of another former Wrexham player, Glyn Hughes, Derek was due to play for the reserves when called into the side for his Football League debut against Barrow in January 1962, playing at outside-right in place of Ron Barnes. The match ended 1-1, but found himself back in the reserves for the following match, and the game proved to be his only first team appearance as he was allowed to leave the Racecourse at the end of season. Hughes joined Cheshire County League side Bangor City, followed by spells at Oswestry Town in the same League and Pwllheli in the Welsh League North. He moved around the local football scene, turning out for Ellesmere Town in the Shropshire League, Llay Welfare, Overton, Buckley Town, and Courtaulds FC. It was when playing for Overton in the Welsh National League that he scored four hat-tricks in consecutive League games. As for work, he left the pits to take up employment with Fullwood & Bland in Ellesmere as an installation fitter. He was later employed as a fitter at Hawker Siddley in Broughton, Fullwood & Bland (again), Vauxhall Motors in Ellesmere Port and Courtaulds. More recently he has been working at the Nightingale House Hospice in Wrexham as a handyman and driver, having settled in his home town. A great character, Derek, by error, had been ommitted from all player records and will no doubt be delighted to resurface. Has also won many trophies at darts and snooker.

Season	League		F.A.Cup		Welsh Cup		League Cup		Total	
	apps	gls	apps	gls	apps	gls	apps	gls	apps	gls
1961/62	1	0	-	-	-	-	-	-	1	0
	1	**0**	-	-	-	-	-	-	**1**	**0**

HUGHES, Glyn

1952 - 1955

Position; *Outside-Right*
D.O.B; *29th November, 1931*
Birthplace; *Coedpoeth, Denbighshire*
Died; *Wrexham, 19th August, 1995*
Height; *5ft 8in* ***Weight;*** *11st 0lbs*
Debut v. *Grimsby Town (a) 23rd August, 1952*
Total Appearances & Goals; *106 apps 25 gls*
Career; *Connah's Quay Juniors; Llay Welfare 1947; Sheffield Wednesday Jan 1951 0apps; WREXHAM 2nd Aug 1952; Newport County 2nd Aug 1955 4apps 0gls; Caernarvon Town 30th Jul 1956; Pwllheli 12th Aug 1959; Holywell Town 25th Aug 1960;*
Honours; *N.W.C.F.A. Cup Winner 1957; Cookson Cup Winner 1957; Alves Cup Winner1957 & 1958;*

Although a native of Llay Glyn Hughes played his early football for the Deeside-based Connah's Quay Juniors, who were coached at the time by former Welsh international Tommy (T.G.) Jones. He continued playing for the side until he was 16, when leaving school. Glyn then took up working at Llay Colliery as a trainee machinist, affiliated to Llay Welfare football team. He had only been with Llay for around six months when he was invited for a trial by local Sheffield Wednesday scout, Jack Love, following which he was offered terms on the groundstaff by 'The Owls', shortly after his 17th birthday. He obtained employment at the Nunnery Colliery in Sheffield at the same time. Glyn made his way through Wednesday's youth ranks, signing part-time professional forms, and winning Yorkshire League and Cup winners' medals with the reserves. As a tradesman Glyn was exempt from National Service, which enabled him to progress with his football. However, at the end of the 1951/52 season he was given an ultimatum by the 'Owls' to turn professional, which he turned down. Despite offers from both Chesterfield and Halifax Town, which would have enabled him to continue working in Sheffield, Hughes found the lure of home too much and joined Wrexham, leaving Hillsborough without having made a first team appearance. At the Racecourse Glyn became an immediate success at outside-right, part of a formidable forward line which also included Tommy Bannan, Ron Hewitt, Tommy Tilston and Billy Tunnicliffe. In his first season the side failed to gain promotion by just three points, finishing third behind champions Oldham Athletic. His fine wing play soon began to attract the scouts of the bigger clubs, but failed to live up to his early promise due largely to the fact that he kept picking up niggling injuries. Although still involved in first team affairs he was released by the club at the end of the 1954/55 season. Glyn joined Newport County in July 1955, but failed to settle at Somerton Park, finding that he was restricted mostly to reserve team appearances. He managed just four senior appearances for County before returning to North Wales to join Welsh League (North) club Caernarvon Town in July 1956. Glyn played against Wrexham for the 'Canaries' in the Welsh Cup during the 1956/57 season at the Oval, a game which the 'Robins' won 4-0. With the 'Cofies' Glyn collected both a North Wales Challenge Cup and a Cookson Cup winners' medal in 1957, in addition to two Welsh League North Alves Cup winners trophies. He again appeared against Wrexham in a Welsh Cup semi-final for Caernarvon in 1958, which Wrexham won 4-1. In 1959 Glyn joined Pwllheli for a season, followed by a year with Holywell Town, having been persuaded to join them by former Wrexham team mate Les Speed. After finally hanging up his boots Hughes took up coaching with Llay United, which prompted an invitation from Ken Barnes to coach the youngsters at the Racecourse, later working under Billy Morris. Glyn Hughes remained a part-timer throughout his football career, and after retiring from football he continued to work for the N.C.B., later finding employment at both Brymbo Steelworks and B.I.C.C. A first cousin to another former Wrexham player, Derek Hughes, Glyn was a keen Wrexham supporter in his later years. He sadly passed away when on his way to a cricket match at Brymbo in August 1995, aged just 63.

Season	League		F.A.Cup		Welsh Cup		Total	
	apps	gls	apps	gls	apps	gls	apps	gls
1952/53	43	13	3	2	1	0	47	15
1953/54	22	4	5	1	-	-	27	5
1954/55	27	3	2	0	3	2	32	5
	92	**20**	**10**	**3**	**4**	**2**	**106**	**25**

HUGHES, John Henry 1930 - 1933

Position; *Outside-Right*
D.O.B; *25th September, 1911*
Birthplace; *Chester, Cheshire*
Died; *Wrexham, June 1991*
Height; *5ft 7in* ***Weight;*** *11st 5lbs*
Debut v. *Cardiff City (h) 23rd April, 1930 (Welsh Cup)*
Total Appearances & Goals; *145 apps 25 gls*
Career; *Llangollen; WREXHAM (Am) Dec 1929, (Pro) 6th May 1930; Bolton Wanderers 10th May 1933 9apps 3gls; Chester Dec 1934 82apps 22gls; Chesterfield Jun 1936 102apps 17gls; Bradford Park Avenue May 1939 3apps; Wrexham (WW2) Oct 1939 43apps 6gls; Chester (WW2 Guest) May 1940 3apps 0gls; Oswestry Town; Tywyn;*
Honours; *Welsh Cup Winner 1931; Welsh Cup runner-up 1932, 1933 & 1935;*

Season	League		F.A.Cup		Welsh Cup		Total	
	apps	gls	apps	gls	apps	gls	apps	gls
1929/30	1	0	-	-	1	0	2	0
1930/31	19	1	2	0	3	2	24	3
1931/32	19	2	1	0	6	2	26	4
1932/33	40	12	3	0	6	0	49	12
1939/40	24	1	-	-	1	0	25	1
1940/41	3	0	-	-	-	-	3	0
1943/44	6	3	-	-	-	-	6	3
1944/45	8	2	-	-	-	-	8	2
1945/46	2	0	-	-	-	-	2	0
	122	**21**	**6**	**0**	**17**	**4**	**145**	**25**
F/League	79	15	6	0	16	4	101	19

Although christened John Hughes he was best known to Wrexham fans as 'Jackie'. Joined Wrexham from Llangollen as an amateur in December 1929, signing professional forms a couple of days after making his Football League debut for the 'Robins' in the final match of 1929/30, a 5-1 home win over Nelson. Jackie did not feature in the first team again until the November of the following season, coming into the side for the injured Les Williams. By February, he had become a regular in the side as Wrexham went on to finish the season in fourth place. To cap a fine season Jackie collected a Welsh Cup winners' medal as Wrexham thrashed Shrewsbury 7-0, in the Final, and scored one of the goals. He missed much of the early part of 1931/32 through injury, though back in the side by February, enabling him to play in the Welsh Cup Final against Swansea Town, Wrexham losing 2-0 after a replay. The 1932/33 season was to be Wrexham's best since joining the Football League in 1921, and Jackie was to miss only the opening two matches before playing a major part in helping the 'Robins' finish runners-up to Hull City in the Third Division North. He picked up another Welsh Cup runners'-up medal, as Wrexham lost 2-0 to Chester in the Final. His form had made other clubs take notice, and in May 1933 was signed by Bolton Wanderers, where his arrival was hailed as follows: 'Bolton Wanderers' new player Hughes from Wrexham will certainly improve the attack'. Jackie made his debut for the 'Trotters' in the opening game of the 1933/34 season, and scored in a 4-2 defeat at West Ham United. He was also on the score sheet in the following match, his home debut, a 2-0 win over Plymouth Argyle. This early success was not to last, however, and Jackie made just seven more League appearances before being allowed to join Chester in December 1934. He enjoyed a mixed debut for the 'Cestrians' as he scored the two goals in a 3-2 defeat at York. Jackie became a regular at Sealand Road over the next eighteen months, appearing in the 1935 Welsh Cup Final, where Chester lost 1-0 at home to Tranmere Rovers. In the summer of 1936 he signed for Chesterfield, and was a fixture in the side for the next three years, making 102 League appearances and scoring 17 goals. He joined Bradford Park Avenue in the summer of 1939, playing in the opening three matches of the 1939/40 season before his career came to an abrupt halt with the outbreak of World War Two. Hughes served in the Royal Navy during the conflict, though he managed to make 41 appearances for Wrexham, and turning out for Chester on three occasions as a 'Guest' towards the end of 1939/40. After WW2 Jackie Hughes continued playing football for Oswestry Town for three years, completing his playing career as player-coach with the Cambrian Coast League side Tywyn.

HUGHES, Kenneth David 1991 - 1992

Position; *Goalkeeper*
D.O.B; *9th January, 1966*
Birthplace; *Barmouth, Gwynedd*
Height; *6ft 0in* ***Weight;*** *11st 6lbs*
Debut v. *Rochdale (h) 22nd August, 1992*
Total Appearances & Goals; *10 apps 0 gls*
Career; *Everton 1982; Wrexham cs1984; Porthmadog 1984; Charlton Athletic (Trial) 1984/85; Crystal Palace Aug 1985 0apps; Shrewsbury Town Jul 1986 74apps; WREXHAM 8th June 1992; Telford United cs1993 43apps 0gls;*
Honours; *Welsh Schoolboy international; F.A.Youth Cup runner-up 1983;*

Ken Hughes first played football in goal at his school in Harlech, North Wales. It was there that he was spotted by an Everton scout and invited for trials with the Goodison Park club. From those trials he was signed on schoolboys forms, and throughout his school years played representative football for a number of teams which led to selection for Wales at Schoolboy level. During his school holidays Ken would train with Everton, which eventually led to him signing apprentice terms for the 'Toffeemen'. During his apprenticeship he played in an F.A.Youth Cup Final where Everton lost to Norwich City. Ken was released in the close season of 1984 and joined Wrexham on trial, but was not offered a contract and returned home. He then joined Porthmadog, taking up a two year catering course at the same time, but continuing to look for another chance in football and, after writing to a few Football League clubs, was invited by Charlton Athletic for a trial. He played a few reserve team matches but was not offered a contract, although they did recommend him to Crystal Palace. He did enough at Selhurst Park to sign for the 'Eagles' in August 1985. It was with Palace that Hughes enjoyed his first taste of senior football, a Full Members' Cup match against Brighton & Hove Albion at Selhurst Park in October 1985, which ended in a 3-1 defeat. That proved to be his only first team match for Palace as he was released in the close season of 1986. Ken then joined Second Division Shrewsbury Town, where he was recruited as understudy to Steve Perks. He made his Football League debut for the 'Shrews' in a 2-1 home defeat against Huddersfield Town in February 1987. Ken spent a total of six years at the Gay Meadow, making just thirteen League appearances in his first four seasons. 1990/91 saw Ken finally establish himself in the senior side, and played in one of Shrewsbury's best ever F.A.Cup runs when they eventually lost to Arsenal in the Fifth Round. Hughes was released by 'Shrews' manager John Bond at the end of 1991/92 season, but was quickly snapped up by Wrexham manager Brian Flynn. He made a promising start with his new club in the Isle of Man pre-season tournament, but by October was ousted by Mark Morris following some rather indifferent performances in the Wrexham goal. Hughes was unable to maintain the early promise he had shown, as Wrexham went on to clinch promotion to the Second Division. He was released at the end of the season, signing for Conference League side Telford United, where he spent three seasons, accumulating 43 appearances for the Bucks Head club. His availability

during that time had been limited by his training with the Fire Brigade who he had joined in the summer of 1994. Ken still work's as a fireman with the Leicestershire Fire Brigade at the time of publication.

Season	League		F.A.Cup		League Cup		Welsh Cup		A.G.T.		Total	
	apps	gls	apps	gls	apps	gls	apps	gls	apps	gls	apps	gls
1992/93	8	0	-	-	2	0	-	-	-	-	10	0
	8	**0**	**-**	**-**	**2**	**0**	**-**	**-**	**-**	**-**	**10**	**0**

HUGHES, Robert Ian

1966 - 1967

Position; *Outside-Right*
D.O.B; *17th March, 1946*
Birthplace; *Cefn Mawr, Denbighshire*
Height; *5ft 7in* ***Weight;*** *10st 9lbs*
Debut v. *Hartlepool United (a) 5th February, 1966*
Total Appearances & Goals; *9 apps 3 gls*
Career; *Manchester United Jul 1962; Druids United 1963; Oswestry Town Dec 1963; WREXHAM 4th Feb 1966 £1,250; Bradford Park Avenue Jul 1967 13apps 0gls; Rhyl 16th Jul 1968; Oswestry Town 6th Feb 1969; Rhos Aelwyd 21st Aug 1973;*
Honours; *Welsh Youth International cap; Welsh schoolboy international cap; Welsh Amateur international cap; North Wales Coast F.A.representative cap; Cheshire County League Cup Winner 1972;*

Ian Hughes began playing football at Ruabon Grammar School and was chosen to represent both Wrexham & District and Denbighshire Schoolboys. This was followed by selection for Wales Schoolboys, which included at Wembley against England. Upon leaving school he was signed by Manchester United as a junior in July 1962, following trials. He was described at the time as 'one of the best youngsters the Wrexham area has produced in years.' Ian progressed still further by winning a Welsh Youth cap. However, his early promise wasn't fulfilled and was released at the end of his first season at Old Trafford. He then played amateur football for Druids before signing for Cheshire County League side Oswestry Town in December 1963. In September 1964 Ian enrolled as a full-time student at Swansea University, and during his time in South Wales was selected for the Welsh Amateur side against England, a game that Wales lost 7-0 at Shrewsbury's Gay Meadow ground. He continued to impress whilst playing for Oswestry, and in February 1966 was signed by Wrexham for a £1,250 fee. He made his Football League debut for the 'Robins' the day after signing at Hartlepool, in a 4-2 defeat, scoring Wrexham's second goal. Two games later he made his home debut against Doncaster Rovers, and scored twice in a 4-3 win. Although great things were once again predicted, Ian failed to make a senior appearance throughout the following season, although playing for the North Wales Coast F.A. against the Scottish Junior XI at Llandudno, and scored the only goal of the game. He was allowed to leave the Racecourse at the end of the 1966/67 season, but was soon recruited by his former manager at Wrexham, Jack Rowley, who was then managing Bradford Park Avenue. He went on to make thirteen League appearances for the West Yorkshire club, until released in the summer. He returned home to North Wales and joined Cheshire County League side Rhyl, eventually moving back to Oswestry Town in February 1969. Ian went on to collect a Cheshire County League Cup Winners' medal with the Shropshire club in 1972. He announced his retirement in January 1973, after consulting a specialist over 'repeated and severe migraine attacks'. However, he did turn out for Rhos Aelwyd for a short time after that. Ian became qualified as a teacher after leaving Bradford, and settled in the Cefn Mawr area.

Season	League		F.A.Cup		Welsh Cup		League Cup		Total	
	apps	gls	apps	gls	apps	gls	apps	gls	apps	gls
1965/66	9	3	-	-	-	-	-	-	9	3
	9	**3**	**-**	**-**	**-**	**-**	**-**	**-**	**9**	**3**

HUMES, Anthony

1992 -

Position; *Centre-Half*
D.O.B; *19th March, 1966*
Birthplace; *Blyth, Northumberland*
Height; *5ft 11in* ***Weight;*** *11st 0lbs*
Debut v. *Chesterfield (a) 28th March, 1992*
Total Appearances & Goals; *247/8 apps 10 gls*
Career; *Ipswich Town 26th May 1983 107/13apps 10gls; WREXHAM 27th March 1992 £40,000;*
Honours; *Third Division Championship runner-up 1993; Welsh Invitation Cup Winner 1998; Welsh Premier Cup runner-up 1999;*

Although born in the heart of Geordie-land Tony Humes slipped through the North-East net and signed apprentice forms with Suffolk club Ipswich Town. He had been playing for his local team Cramington Juniors from the age of twelve, alongside Andy Sinton. Tony played in both County and Area representative sides, where he came to the notice of a number of League clubs. He had trials with Everton, Middlesbrough, West Brom, and Ipswich, to where he would travel down for training during the summer holidays on a coach with other trialists from the North East. After leaving school Humes was offered an apprenticeship (despite having suffered a broken leg) by Ipswich manager Bobby Robson before he left to take over as England manager. He then went on to make steady progress through the ranks, signing professional in May 1983. Tony made his Football League debut at the age of twenty, as a substitute against Blackburn Rovers at Ewood Park, in November 1986. He retained his place in the side, missing just four matches before the end of the season, helping the Portman Road club to finish in sixth position and earn a play-off Final place against Charlton Athletic, which they lost. Humes made a total of 120 League appearances for the Portman Road club, despite a long list of injuries. He was appearing for the second XI when Wrexham manager Brian Flynn offered him the chance of a regular first team place in March 1992. 'The Robins' were in the Fourth Division at that time, and it was a big step down, but after talks was persuaded to sign for a £40,000 transfer fee. Tony ended the 1991/92 season settling himself into the team, but the following campaign he was made club captain and enjoyed helping Wrexham to finish Third Division runners-up. Life in the Second Division was frustrating for Humes as he was continually plagued by injuries and suspension, but overcame these to become a prominent figure in the Wrexham defence over the next five seasons. He led the club to Welsh Cup success in 1995, although missing the Final through injury, and he skippered the side as Wrexham reached the Quarter-Finals of the F.A.Cup in 1997. Tony is regarded as one of manager Brian Flynn's best buys - epitomising the word 'Battler'. He is strong and aggressive, but fair. A fine example to younger players in how to give 100% for their clubs. He has also played in midfield as a ball winner. Injuries seem to be part and parcel of his game, but he always has the ability to bounce back. A manager's dream, and a loyal club man of Wrexham Football Club. He still remains Club captain at the time of writing.

Season	League		F.A.Cup		Welsh Cup		League Cup		F.R.T.		E.C.W.C.		Total	
	apps	gls	apps	gls	apps	gls	apps	gls	apps	gls	apps	gls	apps	gls
1991/92	8	0	-	-	-	-	-	-	-	-	-	-	8	0
1992/93	38	0	1	0	5	0	2	0	2	0	-	-	48	0
1993/94	25/2	1	2	0	1	0	2	0	2	0	-	-	32/2	1
1994/95	28/1	0	3	0	4	0	3	0	2	0	-	-	40/1	0
1995/96	26/1	3	4	0	-	-	-	-	3	0	-	-	33/1	3
1996/97	34	4	8	1	-	-	-	-	-	-	-	-	42	5
1997/98	22/2	0	1	0	7*	1*	-	-	-	-	-	-	30/2	1
1998/99	10/2	0	-	-	3*	0*	1	0	-	-	-	-	14/2	0
	191/8	**8**	**19**	**1**	**19**	**1**	**8**	**0**	**9**	**0**	**-**	**-**	**247/8**	**10**

*= Welsh Invitation/Premier Cup games

HUMPHRIES, Stephen Rodney 1982

Position; *Goalkeeper*
D.O.B; *29th May, 1961*
Birthplace; *Hull, Humberside*
Height; *5ft 11'1/2in* ***Weight;*** *12st 9lbs*
Debut v. *Preston North End (a) 28th September, 1982*
Total Appearances & Goals; *2 apps 0 gls*
Career; *Goole Town; Leicester City Sept 1978 0apps; Vancouver Whitecaps; Doncaster Rovers 9th Jun 1981 13apps 0gls; Cardiff City Aug 1982 1app 0gls; WREXHAM 24th Sept 1982 (Loan); Oldham Athletic 9th Oct 1982 0apps; Leicester City Jan 1983 0apps; Kettering Town cs1983; Barnet cs1984 £4,000; Welling United 1990/91; Bangor City; Telford United £4,000; Kettering Town Oct 1992; Solihull Borough 1992/93 (Loan); Stafford Rangers cs1993;*
Honours; *England Semi-Professional International cap; Bob Lord Challenge Trophy Winner 1986;*

Although born in Hull Steve Humphries was signed by Leicester City upon leaving school in 1977. He went on to sign professional terms with the Filbert Street club in September 1977, but was never actually called upon to make a first team appearance during the following three years, due mainly to the consistent form of Mark Wallington in the Leicester goal. Steve left the Midlands club in the summer of 1981, and joined Fourth Division Doncaster Rovers. Here he finally made his Football League debut, stepping in to replace Billy Boyd in a 4-2 home victory against Bristol Rovers in October 1981. Steve went on to make twelve more League appearances for the Yorkshire club until leaving to join Cardiff City in August 1982 on non-contract terms. He made just one League appearance for the 'Bluebirds', a 2-1 defeat at the Racecourse in the first game of 1982/83. Wrexham manager Bobby Roberts' must have been impressed, however, because the following month he signed him on loan due to a goalkeeping crisis, as regular first choice 'keeper Eddie Niedzwiecki was suspended. Steve made his 'Robins' debut in a 3-0 defeat at Preston in which he was said to have 'starred, despite the score line, with his handling superb in treacherous conditions'. He played in the following game, a 1-0 win over Bournemouth on the Racecourse, before Niedzwiecki returned to take over from him. He was then allowed to leave Wrexham, joining Oldham Athletic on loan to help with their goalkeeping cover. He failed to make a first team appearance at Boundary Park, and in January 1983 he was re-signed by Leicester City. Once again he left Filbert Street without having seen any senior action and drifted into non-league football with Kettering Town, before trying his luck in Canada with Vancouver Whitecaps. He eventually returned home to play non-league football again for Kettering, and then for Barnet, where he was capped by England at Semi-Professional level. He later played for Welling United, Bangor City, Telford United, Kettering Town (again), Solihull Borough and Stafford Rangers, where he became assistant manager to Brendan Phillips during the 1993/94 season. Steve was last known to have been appointed goalkeeping coach with Nuneaton Borough in April 1998.

Season	League		F.A.Cup		Welsh Cup		League Cup		Total	
	apps	gls	apps	gls	apps	gls	apps	gls	apps	gls
1982/83	2	0	-	-	-	-	-	-	2	0
	2	**0**	**-**	**-**	**-**	**-**	**-**	**-**	**2**	**0**

HUNT, Simon 1981 - 1984

Position; *Midfield*
D.O.B; *17th November, 1962*
Birthplace; *Chester, Cheshire*
Height; *5ft 6in* ***Weight;*** *10st 1lbs*
Debut v. *Leicester City (a) 5th September, 1981*
Total Appearances & Goals; *133/9 apps 23 gls*
Career; *WREXHAM 1979, (Pro) Aug 1981; IF Elfsborg cs1984; IK Braga;*
Honours; *Welsh Cup runner-up 1983 & 1984; Welsh Youth Cup runner-up 1980;*

Simon Hunt began playing football for Saltney Ferry Primary School, moving on to St.David's Secondary School in Saltney, where he won almost every honour with his school team. He appeared in representative matches for both Clwyd and North Wales Schoolboys, and it was during a trial match for the Clwyd Youth side that he was spotted by Wrexham's North Wales scout at the time, Wyn Jones. An approach led to trials with Wrexham, and it was quickly followed by the acceptance of an apprenticeship, even though Simon was a Chester fan at the time! His father, Robert, had also been on Wrexham's books in the 1950s, although he didn't record a senior appearance. Simon worked his way through the club's junior ranks to sign professional in August 1981, and a month later made his Football League debut in a Second Division match at Leicester City, as a substitute for Steve Buxton in a 1-0 defeat. He then enjoyed an unbroken run in the first team until February, but missed the final stages of a season that ended in relegation. Simon became established in the Wrexham midfield during the following season, but it proved to be a frustrating time as the club's crippling debts led to the departure of a number of experienced players, and inevitably the club suffered relegation for a second successive year. Even so, Hunt did pick up a Welsh Cup runners-up medal, when the 'Robins' lost to Swansea City in the Final. The 1983/84 season was another year of struggle, with Simon one of few players to shine as Wrexham again reached the Welsh Cup Final, only to lose to Shrewsbury Town. With the prospect of European football poised to lighten the gloom of the past couple of years, Simon shocked the club by announcing his decision to move to Sweden with his Swedish wife, where

once settled, took up playing football again with Second Division side IF Elfsborg. He later switched to First Division side IK Braga, where he spent a number of seasons. Simon is still living in Sweden, where he has retained an involvement with football by acting as a co-presenter of televised matches.

Season	League		F.A.Cup		Welsh Cup		League Cup		A.M.C.		Total	
	apps	gls	apps	gls	apps	gls	apps	gls	apps	gls	apps	gls
1981/82	15/4	2	1	0	2/1	0	3/1	0	-	-	21/6	2
1982/83	45	7	2	1	7	2	1/1	1	-	-	55/1	11
1983/84	42/2	9	1	0	9	1	2	0	3	0	57/2	10
	102/6	**18**	**4**	**1**	**18/1**	**3**	**6/2**	**1**	**3**	**0**	**133/9**	**23**

HUNTER, Barry Victor 1993 - 1996

Position; *Centre-Half*
D.O.B; *18th November, 1968*
Birthplace; *Coleraine, Northern Ireland*
Height; *6ft 3in* ***Weight;*** *12st 0lbs*
Debut v. *Crewe Alexandra (h) 24th August, 1993 (Coca-Cola Cup)*
Total Appearances & Goals; *118/4 apps 6 gls*
Career; *Coleraine; Newcastle United Jul 1986; Coleraine 1988; Crusaders Jul 1988 75apps 3gls; WREXHAM 19th August 1993 £50,000; Reading 8th July 1996 £400,000 26/1apps 2gls; Southend United Mar 1999 (loan) 5apps 2gls;*
Honours; 12 Northern Ireland Full International caps; Two Northern Ireland 'B' International caps; Welsh Cup Winner 1995; Irish League Championship runner-up 1993;

Barry Hunter grew up on the north coast of Ireland in his native Coleraine, attending the local rugby-playing Grammar School. Playing at full-back he represented his country at rugby, but football was his first love and joined Coleraine at 15, appearing for their reserve side in an adult league. Offers from English League clubs came to nothing until close relative Willie McFaul at Newcastle gave him his chance, and it culminated in a two year YTS contract. Barry progressed through the ranks at St. James' Park and became a regular member of the Central League side. However, after the completion of his two year stint, the 'Magpies' decided to release the 'Big Man'. Despite offers to join other English League clubs Barry moved back to Northern Ireland. Initially he returned to Coleraine, but before playing a first team match joined Crusaders, with Glentoran and Linfield also showing an interest. He suffered a bad start with 'Crues', as he broke the same leg twice. After recovering he helped Crusaders to runners'-up spot in the League championship of 1993, losing out on goal difference to Linfield. His football career was to be re-launched during the summer at the Isle of Man international Football tournament, where he caught the eye of Wrexham manager Brian Flynn, who invited Barry to play for Wrexham in a friendly against Linfield in Belfast the following week. He must have impressed, as just over a week later Wrexham paid out £60,000 for the towering centre-half, who is the son of Northern Ireland international goalkeeper Vic Hunter and nephew

of former Ipswich Town and Northern Ireland international, Allan Hunter. Barry made his first team debut for the 'Robins' against Crewe Alexandra in a Coca Cola Cup match, quickly becoming a regular in the Wrexham defence. He went on to contribute some impressive performances, and it was no surprise to anyone at the club when he became the first ever Wrexham player to win a full international cap for Northern Ireland against Latvia in 1995. He was described at the Racecourse as 'tall, slim and angular - holds the defence well and has fine distribution for a tall player, good awareness, outstanding in the air and a sound tackler are strong features of his play'. He picked up a Welsh Cup winner's medal with the 'Robins' in 1995, and played in Europe at the start of the following season against Romanian side Petrolul Ploiesti. He also took part in Wrexham's big Cup matches against Manchester United, Ipswich Town, Coventry City and Nottingham Forest, while adding a further five caps to his Northern Ireland tally. In the close season of 1996 he was sold to First Division Reading, who were managed by his Irish team-mate, Jimmy Quinn, for a club record fee received by Wrexham of £400,000. In his first season at Elm Park Barry was quickly installed as the club's captain, but his appearances were limited due to injuries. He was then to suffer a serious injury which kept him out of action for all of Reading's 1997/98 relegation season and most of 1998/99. He recovered in the new year enough to go on loan to Southend United before returning to the 'Royals' for the end of the season.

Season	League		F.A.Cup		Welsh Cup		League Cup		A.G.T.		E.C.W.C.		Total	
	apps	gls	apps	gls	apps	gls	apps	gls	apps	gls	apps	gls	apps	gls
1993/94	23	1	2	0	2	1	1	0	2	0	-	-	30	1
1994/95	35/2	0	3	0	7	1	3	0	4	0	-	-	52/2	1
1995/96	30/1	3	2/1	1	-	-	2	0	-	-	2	0	36/2	4
	88/3	**4**	**7/1**	**1**	**9**	**2**	**6**	**0**	**6**	**0**	**2**	**0**	**118/4**	**6**

HUNTER, Geoffrey — 1987 - 1991

Position; *Midfield*
D.O.B; *27th October, 1959*
Birthplace; *Hull, Humberside*
Height; *5ft 10in* ***Weight;*** *10st 12lbs*
Debut v. *Torquay United (a) 15th August, 1987*
Total Appearances & Goals; *141/11 apps 16 gls*
Career; *Manchester United Nov 1976 0apps; Crewe Alexandra Aug 1979 86/1apps 8gls; Port Vale Aug 1981 £15,000 218/3apps 15gls; WREXHAM Aug 1987; Left club May 1991;*
Honours; *Welsh Cup runner-up 1988; P.F.A. Division Four team 1983;*

Geoff Hunter's football career took off when he signed as an apprentice for Manchester United during Tommy Docherty's managership of the club. He made his way through the Old Trafford ranks and was appearing regularly for United's Central League side when offered a professional contract in November 1976. However, Geoff failed to break into the first team and in the summer of 1979 was allowed to join Crewe Alexandra on a free transfer. He made his first team debut for the 'Railwaymen' in a Football League Cup first round match at Huddersfield Town, which ended in a 2-1 defeat. He went on to become a first team regular over the next two seasons, making a total of 87 League appearances for the Gresty Road club, before a £15,000 move to near neighbours Port Vale during the summer of 1981, following the completion of his contract. He then helped Vale to promotion from the Fourth Division, only for them to be relegated the following year. Vale and Geoff won promotion again in 1986, but he found his first team chances limited during the following season and, when his contract had expired in the summer of 1987, began to look for another club. Wrexham manager Dixie McNeil stepped in with an offer, which Geoff accepted. He made his debut in a disastrous 6-1 defeat at Torquay, but went on to assist the 'Robins' in reaching the Welsh Cup Final, only to lose 2-0 to Cardiff City at Swansea's Vetch Field. The following season he was fully involved in Wrexham's play-off bid, which ended in disappointment as Leyton Orient edged the two-legged Final 2-1. The next two years were frustrating for Geoff, as he suffered with niggling injuries, which led to him missing the 1990 Welsh Cup Final. Despite this he enjoyed European experience the following season, against Lyngby of Denmark and his former club, Manchester United. At the end of a disappointing 1990/91 season he was released by Wrexham, and is believed to have left football altogether, taking up work as a sales representative back in his home town of Hull.

Season	League		F.A.Cup		Welsh Cup		League Cup		F.R.T.		E.C.W.C.		Total	
	apps	gls	apps	gls	apps	gls	apps	gls	apps	gls	apps	gls	apps	gls
1987/88	36/2	5	1	0	4	0	2	0	2	0	-	-	45/2	5
1988/89	36/2	4	2	0	0/1	0	0/2	0	4	0	-	-	42/5	4
1989/90	21	3	1	0	1	0	-	-	1	0	-	-	24	3
1990/91	22/2	3	1	0	3	1	-	-	3	0	1/2	0	30/4	4
	115/6	**15**	**5**	**0**	**8/1**	**1**	**2/2**	**0**	**10**	**0**	**1/2**	**0**	**141/11**	**16**

HUNTER, John Reginald — 1960 - 1962

Position; *Forward/Winger*
D.O.B; *25th October, 1938*
Birthplace; *Mochdre, Flintshire*
Height; *5ft 9in* ***Weight;*** *10st 10lbs*
Debut v. *Norwich City (a) 6th February, 1960*
Total Appearances & Goals; *40 apps 4 gls*
Career; *Colwyn Bay; Manchester United Nov 1956 1app 0gls; WREXHAM 4th Feb 1960 £3,000; Bangor City 9th Feb 1962; Colwyn Bay United 24th Oct 1963; Borough United 31st Jan 1964; Llandudno 1st Oct 1966; Prestatyn 16th Oct 1967; Caernarfon Town 27th Jun 1968 to Jan 1969;*
Honours; *Welsh Cup Winner 1960 & 1962; F.A.Youth Cup Winner 1957;*

Reg Hunter first impressed as a footballer at Colwyn Bay Grammar School. He played for the various school teams and also for Denbighshire Schoolboys. Upon leaving school a number of clubs showed interest and he joined Arsenal for a weeks' trial. Nothing developed and he continued to play for his local side, Colwyn Bay United. Some impressive displays saw him signed up by Manchester United, doing enough in the Junior teams at Old Trafford to be offered a professional contract in November 1956. 1956/57 was to see Reg involved in all ten of United's matches in the F.A.Youth Cup, which finished with Hunter and United lifting the trophy, defeating West Ham United in the Final. Reg scored in both legs of the Final, in a United team that included Bobby Charlton, Johnny Giles, Reg Holland and Dave Gaskell. He spent six years at Old Trafford, playing most of the time in the Central League side, although serving his National Service with the Royal Air Ordinance Corps - with fellow team mate Peter Jones - when the Munich Air disaster occurred. As he had lost so many friends in the disaster Reg was given three weeks' compassionate leave from the Army, and during this time was called upon to make his Football League debut on 27th December 1958 against Aston Villa, at Villa Park, which United won 2-0. This proved to be Reg's only Football League appearance for the crest fallen club although he was to remain at Old

Trafford until February 1960 when he was given the opportunity to join Wrexham. 'The Robins' paid out £3,000 for his services, and Reg was pitched straight into the first team for a League match at Norwich City in place of Stan Bennion at outside-left. He remained in the side for the rest of the season, but couldn't prevent the club avoiding relegation. He did, however, collect a Welsh Cup winners' medal as Wrexham beat Cardiff City 1-0 in the Final. The 1960/61 season would see Reg start the season at outside-left, only to be replaced by Ron Roberts after five matches. In January 1961 he asked for a transfer, after failing to regain a regular first team place. During his time with Wrexham, Reg Hunter was described as a 'Strong, direct type of player, who is very useful in any team.' He was allowed to leave the Racecourse in early February 1962, joining Bangor City. Wrexham were soon to regret that decision, as Reg played in the 1962 Welsh Cup Final against them, and the Cheshire County League club caused a major upset as they lifted the trophy and earned themselves a place in the European Cup-Winners' Cup competition the following season. Bangor were drawn against Italian giants Napoli and, after forcing a replay, eventually lost 2-1 in a play-off match at Highbury. Reg played in all three games as part of a Bangor side that did Welsh football proud. During his time at Farrar Road, Reg took up work in the Wrexham offices of Border Breweries, while continuing to train with the 'Robins'. He joined Colwyn Bay United in October 1963, followed by a spell with Borough United in January 1964. Reg then enjoyed short spells with Llandudno, where his father Harold Hunter had a long spell as an outstanding full-back

Season	League		F.A.Cup		Welsh Cup		League Cup		Total	
	apps	gls	apps	gls	apps	gls	apps	gls	apps	gls
1959/60	16	2	-	-	5	1	-	-	21	3
1960/61	13	0	-	-	-	-	-	-	13	0
1961/62	5	1	1	0	-	-	-	-	6	1
	34	**3**	**1**	**0**	**5**	**1**	**-**	**-**	**40**	**4**

INCE, Clayton

1997 & 1998

Position; *Goalkeeper,*
D.O.B; *13th July, 1972*
Birthplace; *Arime, Trinidad*
Height; *6ft 4ins* ***Weight;*** *14st 0lbs*
Debut; v. *Newtown (h) 16th December 1997 (Welsh Invitation Cup)*
Total Appearances & Goals; *1 app 0 gls*
Career; *Trinidad & Tobago Defence Force; WREXHAM Nov 1997 & 11th Mar 1998; Sunderland (trial) 1998; Millwall (trial) 1998;*
Honours; *Trinidad & Tobago Full International caps; Trinidad & Tobago League Championship Winner 1995, 1996 & 1997.*

Clayton Ince first came to Wrexham in November 1997 for "a period of training and development", during which - because of the Department of Employment regulations - the club were prevented from signing him on loan or on trial, or from playing him in a first team game. However, the regulations didn't prohibit him from turning out in the Welsh Invitation Cup match against Newtown in December, which Wrexham won 1-0 and the towering 'keeper turned in a very impressive performance. He was described by manager Brian Flynn as having 'hands the size of buckets' and 'commands his box well, and is a good talker'. After his month at the Racecourse he returned to Trinidad with an invitation to return in March 1998. Clayton worked as a pay clerk for the Trinidad & Tobago Army, and played in goal for his regimental side, Defence Force, with whom he had already won three League Championship medals in 1995, 1996 and 1997. His return to Wrexham in March 1998 came after he had played for his country in the Gold Cup Tournament in Los Angeles, but he again had to be released because of those DoE regulations. His Tobago side won the Caribbean Cup that same season, beating World Cup finalists Jamaica en route to the Final. He was to return to the UK in the summer of 1998, where he was to have brief trials with both Sunderland and Millwall, but failed to earn a contract with either. However, with the departure of Andy Marriott from the Racecourse in September 1998 the situation changed, and at the end of that month manager Brian Flynn, applied to the DoE for a work permit for Clayton, who by then had accepted personal terms with the Racecourse club. However, the application was turned down, and again at appeal much to the club's and Clayton's disapointment.

Season	League		F.A.Cup		League Cup		A.W.S.		W.I.C.		Total	
	apps	gls	apps	gls	apps	gls	apps	gls	apps	gls	apps	gls
1997/98	-	-	-	-	-	-	-	-	1	0	1	0
	-	**-**	**-**	**-**	**-**	**-**	**-**	**-**	**1**	**0**	**1**	**0**

INGLE, Stephen Paul

1967 - 1972

Position; *Right-Back*
D.O.B; *22nd October, 1946*
Birthplace; *Bradford, Yorkshire*
Height; *5ft 11'1/2ins* ***Weight;*** *12st 7lbs*
Debut v. *Luton Town (h) 19th August, 1967*
Total Appearances & Goals; *172/6 apps 8 gls*
Career; *Bradford City 1st Aug 1964 89/1apps 15gls; Southend United 20th Jan 1967 £5,000 14/1apps 3gls; WREXHAM 4th Jul 1967 £2,000; Stockport County Jul 1972 29apps 0gls; Southport 12th Jul 1973 2apps 0gls; Darlington Oct 1973 8apps 0gls; Arcadia Shepherds (Pretoria, South Africa) 1974;*
Honours; *Welsh Cup runner-up 1971; Division Four runner-up 1970;*

Steve Ingle was a promising all-rounder at his Green Lane Junior and Frizinghall Secondary Schools, representing Bradford Schoolboys at football and Yorkshire Schoolboys at cricket. Upon leaving school he had to seek a career outside sport commencing an apprenticeship as a master plumber, before Bradford City stepped in to sign him as an apprentice professional. Steve made his way through the Northern Intermediate and Northern Regional League sides before signing full-time professional for the Valley Parade club at seventeen. He made his Football League debut shortly afterwards, against Lincoln City in September 1964, which was no mean feat as he had previously broken his leg twice when only 15! He scored in the following match, a 3-3 draw with local rivals Bradford Park Avenue, and it was around this time that he was invited for trials with the England Youth team. He was switched to centre-forward by the 'Bantams', but never really settled in his new role, and in January 1967 joined Southend United, where he reverted to his old right-back position. He hastily left Roots Hall in July of the same year, after just 15 League games, joining up with former 'Shrimpers' manager Alvan Williams at Wrexham for £2,000. Steve soon settled in at the Racecourse, becoming a big crowd favourite through his fierce tackling and aggressive runs at opposing defenders. His aggression often got the better of him, and it spelt trouble with the Welsh F.A., as they came down heavily upon him. Steve spent five years with Wrexham, helping them to win promotion to the Third Division in 1970 in a season when he played at both Anfield and Old Trafford for the 'Robins' in Cup competitions, and added a Welsh Cup runners'-up medal the following season. Steve left the Racecourse in July 1972, joining Stockport County. He spent a year at Edgeley Park before beginning a three month trial with Southport, playing in the 'Sandgrounders' first two games back in the Third Division. He concluded his Football League career with Darlington, making eight League appearances before emigrating to South Africa early in 1974. Ingle then played for Arcadia Shepherds in Pretoria, along with Peter Withe, and in 1980 he appeared for Bobby Charlton's XI. In 1983 he was still playing for Arcadia reserves at the age of 37. On retiring from professional football he remained in South Africa, taking up work as a Lift Engineer. It was while he was working as a Lift Inspection Engineer in 1995 that he suffered serious damage to his ribs and legs, after plunging four floors down a lift shaft. Steve is understood to be still residing in South Africa.

Season	League		F.A.Cup		Welsh Cup		League Cup		Total	
	apps	gls	apps	gls	apps	gls	apps	gls	apps	gls
1967/68	29/1	0	1	0	1	0	1	0	32/1	0
1968/69	31	2	2	0	4	0	2	1	39	3
1969/70	39/1	2	3	1	2	0	2	0	46/1	3
1970/71	31	1	1	0	1/1	1	2	0	35/1	2
1971/72	15/2	0	1/1	0	1	0	3	0	20/3	0
	145/4	**5**	**8/1**	**1**	**9/1**	**1**	**10**	**1**	**172/6**	**8**

IRELAND, Simon Piers
1992

Position; *Forward*
D.O.B; *23rd November, 1971*
Birthplace; *Barnstaple, Devon*
Height; *5ft 11in* ***Weight;*** *11st 12lbs*
Debut v. *Barnet (a) 14th March, 1992*
Total Appearances & Goals; *2/3 apps 0 gls*
Career; *Huddersfield Town 1st Jul 1990 10/9apps 0gls; WREXHAM 11th Mar 1992 (Loan); Blackburn Rovers 3rd Nov 1992 £200,000 0/1app 0gls; Mansfield Town 8th Mar 1994 (Loan) 8/1apps 1gls; Mansfield Town 12th Aug 1994 £60,000 81/4apps 10gls; Doncaster Rovers 18th Oct 1996 (Loan), 28th Jan 1997 £50,000 61apps 2gls; Boreham Wood Mar 1998;*
Honours; *England Schoolboy International;*

Simon Ireland signed for Huddersfield Town straight from school, having already represented England at Schoolboy level. He made his way through the youth ranks at Leeds Road to sign professional in July 1990. A year later, in March 1991, he made his Football League debut, substituting Gary Haylock against Crewe Alexandra in a 3-1 home win. Throughout his time with the 'Terriers' he could not command a regular first team place, and in March 1992 was allowed out on loan to Wrexham, after the 'Robins' had just lost the services of Lee Jones to Liverpool. Simon made his debut at Barnet but was to make just four further appearances, three of which were as a substitute, before returning to Leeds Road. He never really shone during his time in North Wales, so it came as quite a surprise to Wrexham's fans when he was signed by big spending Blackburn Rovers manager Kenny Dalglish for a £200,000 fee in November 1992, following an impressive League Cup Second Round match for Huddersfield at Ewood Park. Ireland made his League debut for 'Rovers' as a substitute at Manchester City in January 1993, coming on for Kevin Moran in a 3-2 defeat. His hopes of progressing at Blackburn were dashed when he broke his leg in a reserve team game at Bolton Wanderers. As he recovered the first team squad was strengthened even more and, when fit again, found himself playing reserve team football until March 1994 when he joined Mansfield Town on loan for the rest of the season. He made his debut for the 'Stags', again as a substitute, in a 3-0 home win over Wycombe Wanderers, and the Field Mill club made the move permanent in the summer when they splashed out £60,000 to secure his signature. Simon was quick to repay some of that fee by scoring the only goal in a two-legged Coca-Cola Cup battle upset against shocked Premier League side Leeds United. He remained a regular in the 'Stags' midfield for two seasons until he was loaned to Doncaster Rovers in October 1996. That move became permanent in January 1997, when Rovers paid out £50,000 to sign him. However, the 1997/98 season saw Simon playing in a struggling side that eventually finished 92nd, and suffered relegation from the Football League. By that time he had already left Belle Vue to join Ryman Football League side Boreham Wood, who were managed by Doncaster's former boss, Kerry Dixon.

Season	League		F.A.Cup		Welsh Cup		League Cup		Auto Glass		Total	
	apps	gls	apps	gls	apps	gls	apps	gls	apps	gls	apps	gls
1991/92	2/3	0	-	-	-	-	-	-	-	-	2/3	0
	2/3	**0**	-	-	-	-	-	-	-	-	**2/3**	**0**

ISLIP, Ernest
1928 - 1929

Position; *Inside-Left*
D.O.B; *31st October, 1892.*
Birthplace; *Parkwood Springs, Sheffield, Yorkshire*
Died; *Huddersfield, 22nd February, 1941*
Height; *5ft 9in* ***Weight;*** *12st 0lbs*
Debut v. *Accrington Stanley (a) 17th November, 1928.*
Total Appearances & Goals; *15 apps 1 gls*
Career; *Douglas F.C (Sheffield) 1910; Huddersfield Town Jun 1911 152apps 44gls; (WW1 guest for Sheff Wed Feb 1916-May 1916 14apps 3gls; Rotherham County; West Ham Utd Dec 1917-Feb 1918 4apps 0gls;) Birmingham Nov 1923 £1,500 83apps 23gls; Bradford City May 1927 £400 6apps 1gls; Kidderminster Harriers Aug 1928; Ashton National Gas Sept 1928; WREXHAM (trial) Oct 1928, (Pro) 10th Nov 1928; Retired February 1929;*
Honours; *F.A.Cup Winner 1922; F.A.Cup runner-up 1920*

Ernie Islip was playing for his local side in Sheffield, Douglas F.C., when signed by Huddersfield Town in June 1911. He had to wait until November 1913 before making his Football League debut, in a Second Division match at Bristol City. A little over a month later Ernie had established himself in the 'Terriers' first team, where he remained until the outbreak of World War One. He then played as a 'guest' for Sheffield Wednesday, before enlisting in the Army, with whom he saw service in Egypt. Following the end of the Great War Islip rejoined Huddersfield, where he went on to become a 'determined and dangerous forward'. 1919/20, however, found him struggle to retain his place in the side, and made just three League appearances in a season that saw the Leeds Road club gain promotion and reach the F.A.Cup Final, where they lost 1-0 to Aston Villa. Ernie played in the Final as Billy Smith was suspended. He re-established himself in the side in the following season, as he helped the West Yorkshire club to reach Wembley once again in the 1922 F.A.Cup Final where they met Preston North End. This time Ernie and the 'Terriers' were victorious with a 1-0 win. He joined Birmingham for around £1,500 in November 1923, and got off to a great start by scoring on his debut against West Ham United. He kept his place in the 'Blues' line-up until replaced by George Briggs in November 1925, whereupon he played mainly reserve team football, occasionally stepping into the first team as cover. Ernie joined Bradford City in June 1927, in a double deal which saw Aubrey Scriven and himself move to Valley Parade for £400. He made just six League appearances for Bradford in his one season in Yorkshire before being released in the summer. Birmingham & District League side Kidderminster Harriers was his next port of call, in August 1928, but after only a month left to join Ashton National Gas. He was back in the Football League by November, when Third Division North side Wrexham stepped in to sign the veteran forward. Ernie made his debut at Accrington Stanley in a 4-3 defeat, scoring one of the goals. He added a further thirteen League appearances before being replaced by Bob Hudson, and at the end of the season brought the curtain down on an impressive football career when he retired from football altogether. Ernie returned to the Huddersfield area where he took over a public house in Lindley. He died in February 1941, aged just 48. At his peak, he had been described as 'having speed, balance, good close control and a strong right-foot shot', while another source remarked that he was 'a determined and dangerous forward'.

Season	League		F.A.Cup		Welsh Cup		Total	
	apps	gls	apps	gls	apps	gls	apps	gls
1928/29	14	1	-	-	1	0	15	1
	14	**1**	-	-	**1**	**0**	**15**	**1**

J

Joey Jones

JACKSON, David

1954 - 1955

Position; *Inside-Forward*
D.O.B; *23rd January, 1937*
Birthplace; *Stoke-on-Trent*
Height; *5ft 11in* **Weight;** *12st 0lbs*
Debut v. *Carlisle United (h) 2nd October, 1954*
Total Appearances & Goals; *7 apps 1 gls*
Career; *WREXHAM Jul 1954; Marine Feb 1955; Bradford City Mar 1955 250apps 61gls; Tranmere Rovers 24th Jul 1961 38apps 5gls; Halifax Town Jul 1963 66apps 2gls; Frickley Athletic cs1965; Altrincham; Hyde United;*
Honours; *England Youth international;*

David Jackson is the twin brother of Peter Jackson, and they both played for Wrexham where their father, Peter Jackson senior, was manager between 1950 and 1955. The twins represented Grove Park and Wrexham and District Schoolboy sides before they were signed by their father on amateur forms in July 1954. In October of the same year both David and Peter made their Football League debuts on the Racecourse in a 1-1 draw against Carlisle United, becoming the first set of twins to play in a Football League match for the 'Robins', a feat that has not since been repeated. David, like his brother, made a further six League appearances for Wrexham, with his only goal for the club coming in a 3-1 win at Grimsby Town a week after his debut. In February 1955 his father resigned as manager of the club, and both twins also left at the same time. They joined Liverpool non-league side Marine, and were chosen to play for the Liverpool County F.A. XI, followed by selection for a North versus South amateur international trial match, and then for the English F.A. against the Combined Services at Sandhurst. All this culminated in trials for the England youth team, following which David was named in the England squad to play in the World Youth tournament in Italy during Easter 1955, and he appeared in all three matches. They both remained at Marine until dad was appointed manager of Bradford City, joining him at Valley Parade in March 1955. David was the first to make his debut for the 'Bantams', in the home match against Grimsby Town, and scored in the 4-0 win. He spent a little over six years at Bradford, making a total of 250 League appearances and only missing 18 games in that time. In July 1961 both David and Peter left Valley Parade to sign for Tranmere Rovers, a year after they had been awarded a joint benefit match by Bradford City. David made 38 League appearances for the Prenton Park club, his most memorable game being a 5-1 home win over Mansfield Town in April 1963 when he scored the only Football League hat-trick of his career. In July 1963 he joined Halifax Town, clocking up 66 League appearances in two seasons. He left the Shay in the summer of 1965 to rejoin Peter at Frickley Athletic, before the pair of them went on to play for both Altrincham and Hyde United. David retired from football in 1968 to concentrate on his career in architecture, something for which he had been preparing since 1957, when he became a part-time pro with Bradford City. He became an associate partner with the firm John Brunton, before leaving in 1993. Having settled in the Bradford area he was at the time of writing working for another firm of architects, with golf taking up most of his spare time. He attended the 'Players' Grand Gala Reunion' in September 1998. By an amazing coincidence (or is it!) As well as being inseparable as twins, both David and Peter had identical records for Wrexham in League and Cup!!

Season	League		F.A.Cup		Welsh Cup		Total	
	apps	gls	apps	gls	apps	gls	apps	gls
1954/55	7	1	3	0	-	-	10	1
	7	**1**	**3**	**0**	**-**	**-**	**10**	**1**

JACKSON, Horace

1929 - 1931

Position; *Left-Back*
D.O.B; *O/N/D 1905*
Birthplace; *Wrexham, Denbighshire*
Height; *ft in* **Weight;** *st lbs*
Debut v. *New Brighton (a) 25th October, 1930*
Total Appearances & Goals; *1 app 0 gls*
Career; *New Broughton; Chester cs1928 10apps 0gls; Middlewich 1928/29; Rhyl Aug 1929 (trial); WREXHAM Sept 1929; Gwersyllt Aug 1933;*

Horace Jackson was playing for New Broughton when signed by Chester prior to their Football League days in the close season of 1928. He made his debut at Sealand Road in a Cheshire County League fixture against Port Vale Reserves on the opening day of the season which they lost, 2-0. He played in the next six matches before finding himself in the reserves. Horace made three more appearances for Chester that season before he joined another Cheshire League side, Middlewich. It wasn't long before he began the 1929/30 season on trial with Rhyl signing for Wrexham as an amateur in September 1929. Playing at left-back, Horace was to appear regularly for the reserves throughout the rest of that term. The following season, 1930/31, saw him finally make his Football League debut for the club at New Brighton in October 1930, when he stepped in to replace Wynne Crompton, who was required for international duty with Wales on the same day. However, it didn't prove to be a very successful occasion for Horace, as he had to 'retire from taking any further part in the game, owing to an injury to his right knee early in the second-half'. Wrexham did manage to hold on to earn a 1-1 draw with ten men, as there were no substitutes in those days. However, that game proved to be Horace's only first team appearance for Wrexham, and he later played for local side, Gwersyllt, signing for them in August 1933.

Season	League		F.A.Cup		Welsh Cup		Total	
	apps	gls	apps	gls	apps	gls	apps	gls
1930/31	1	0	-	-	-	-	1	0
	1	**0**	**-**	**-**	**-**	**-**	**1**	**0**

JACKSON Peter

1954 - 1955

Position; *Outside-Left*
D.O.B; *23rd January, 1937*
Birthplace; *Stoke-on-Trent, Staffordshire*
Died; *Bradford, September, 1991.*
Height; *5ft 11in* **Weight;** *12st 0lbs*
Debut v. *Carlisle United (h) 2nd October, 1954*
Total Appearances & Goals; *10 apps 1 gls*
Career; *WREXHAM Jul 1954; Marine Feb 1955; Bradford City Mar 1955 199apps 15gls; Tranmere Rovers 24th Jul 1961 81apps 3gls; Frickley Athletic cs1965; Altrincham; Hyde United; Macclesfield Town; Guiseley;*

Peter Jackson is the twin brother of the afore mentioned David, and the son of the former Wrexham manager Peter Jackson, with Peter Junior ten minutes older than his twin brother. They both joined Wrexham as amateurs, having played for Grove Park school and the Wrexham and District schoolboy side that reached the Welsh Schools Shield final. This led to them both being given trials for the Welsh Schoolboys side, with Peter selected as a reserve for the team that played England at St.Andrew's, Birmingham. With Wrexham, they both played in the F.A.Youth Cup match against Manchester United in 1953, a game which saw a number of the future 'Busby Babes' in the United side. The twins made their Football League debuts for Wrexham in the home match against Carlisle United in October 1954, in place of Les Samuals and Eli Tapscott. The game ended in a 1-1 draw. The twins played a further six League matches for Wrexham, with Peter scoring his solitary goal for the club in a 2-1 defeat at Rochdale. Their father, Peter Jackson senior, resigned as the Wrexham manager in February 1955, and the twins soon followed him out of the Racecourse, as they both joined Marine. However, this was only a temporary step; two weeks after leaving Wrexham Peter's father was appointed as the manager of Bradford City. He quickly recruited his two sons, and Peter made his debut for Bradford in a 4-1 win at Grimsby Town in March 1955. Jackson went on to make a total of 199 League appearances for Bradford City, before he and his brother joined Fourth Division side Tranmere Rovers for a combined £3,000 fee in July 1961. Peter made his debut for Tranmere in August 1961, in a 2-1 home defeat by Aldershot, going on to become a key figure in the Rovers side, remaining with them to the end of his Football League career in 1965. In the close season of 1965, Peter rejoined brother, David, at non-league Frickley Athletic, before they both went on to play together again at Altrincham and Hyde United. Peter also played for Macclesfield Town, and Guiseley before finally calling it a day. Both twins were also good cricketers and golfers, and retained their involvement in those sports after they finished playing football. Peter became a partner with a firm of chartered accountants, and was also treasurer of the City/Park Avenue ex-Players' Association, of which his brother is also an active member. Peter died in September 1991, aged only 54.

Season	League		F.A.Cup		Welsh Cup		Total	
	apps	gls	apps	gls	apps	gls	apps	gls
1954/55	7	1	3	0	-	-	10	1
	7	**1**	**3**	**0**	**-**	**-**	**10**	**1**

JACKSON, Ronald 1945 - 1949

Position; *Left-Back*
D.O.B; *15th October, 1919*
Birthplace; *Crook, Durham*
Died; *Althorpe, Lincs, 28th February, 1980*
Height; *5ft 8in* ***Weight;*** *11st 7lbs*
Debut v. *New Brighton (h) 31st August, 1946*
Total Appearances & Goals; *154 apps 1 gls*
Career; *WREXHAM 1st Oct 1945; Leicester City 23rd Dec 1949 £9,000 161apps 0gls; Kettering Town; Rugby Town;*
Honours; *Second Division Championship Winner 1954;*

Ron Jackson signed for Wrexham having been discovered during the War-time period. He was recommended to Wrexham manager Tom Williams by England international Sam Weaver, who had been playing for Wrexham, as a 'guest' from Chelsea. After he was demobbed from the A.P.T.C. Ron was given a trial at the Racecourse, following which he was signed on a part-time basis, combining playing football with his role as a science teacher at the Victoria Junior School in Wrexham. This popular, hard-tackling left back made his debut for the Club during War-time football in a 3-2 defeat at Rochdale in the second match of the 1945/46 season. He was later described as a 'cool, clean kicker, with excellent positional sense.' Ron made his Football League debut in the opening match of the 1946/47 season following the resumption of League football. He remained a regular fixture in the Wrexham side for most of that season, helping them to finish in 7th place, but this was bettered the following year as the Club reached third, their highest position since 1933. Ron remained in the left-back position for the next two seasons, and soon caught the attention of the bigger League clubs, agreeing to sign for Leicester City for a 'four-figure' fee in December 1949. During his time with Wrexham Ron scored just one goal, a penalty in a 3-1 defeat, in a Third Division North Cup match at Southport in February 1946. At Leicester Jackson went on to make 161 League appearances, winning a Second Division championship medal in 1954. He finally left Filbert Street in July 1955, and later played non-league football for Kettering Town and Rugby Town. As at Wrexham, Ron continued to teach throughout his time at Leicester, where he was a games master. He later taught at a school in Althorpe in Lincolnshire, where he passed away in February 1980 aged 60. Ron's son Roy, was the commercial manager of Leicester Tigers.

Season	League		F.A.Cup		Welsh Cup		War Cup		Total	
	apps	gls	apps	gls	apps	gls	apps	gls	apps	gls
1945/46	18	0	6	0	-	-	10	1	34	1
1946/47	31	0	4	0	1	0	-	-	36	0
1947/48	15	0	-	-	1	0	-	-	16	0
1948/49	42	0	1	0	2	0	-	-	45	0
1949/50	20	0	3	0	-	-	-	-	23	0
	108*	**0**	**14**	**0**	**4**	**0**	**10**	**1**	**154**	**1**

* Does not include 18 War league matches.

JACKSON, William Kennedy 1922 - 1924

Position; *Centre-Forward*
D.O.B; *24th December, 1899*
Birthplace; *Jamestown, Highland*
Died; *Aberdeen, 9th February, 1986*
Height; *5ft 8in* ***Weight;*** *11st 7lbs*
Debut v. *Accrington Stanley (h) 28th October, 1922*
Total Appearances & Goals; *65 apps 17 gls*
Career; *Vale of Leven Juniors; Duntocher Hibernian Jul 1921; Everton Mar 1922 £400 0apps; WREXHAM 26th Oct 1922; Vale of Leven cs1924; Aberdeen March 1925 to 1932 183apps 7gls;*
Honours; Welsh Cup Winner 1924;

Billy Jackson had played early football in his native Scotland for Vale of Leven Juniors and Duntocher Hibernian before he was signed by Everton in March 1922 for a £400 fee. However, he failed to make an impression at Goodison Park, and in the October of the same year was allowed to join Third Division North side, Wrexham. With the North Wales club Bill made his Football League debut against Accrington Stanley on the Racecourse, and got his Wrexham career off to a flying start, scoring two goals in as many minutes in a 2-0 win. He was described on his debut as a 'strong, never ceasing type of player.' Billy went on to spend two seasons with Wrexham as a first team regular before leaving in the close season of 1924 to return to his native Scotland. Prior to leaving he scored in the Welsh Cup final of 1924 against Merthyr Tydfil in a 2-2 draw, Wrexham eventually winning the replay 1-0. Billy rejoined Scottish Football League side Vale of Leven, where he was made club captain. However, he had done enough to impress the watching scouts, before the end of his first season with them, and Jackson signed for Aberdeen in March 1925, eventually enjoying seven years playing for the 'Dons'. During his time with Aberdeen he was described as a 'kind and considerate player, in the father-figure mould, who would nurture the young ones along.' Although he played centre-forward with Wrexham Bill was more versatile with the 'Dons', appearing in both full-back positions as well as inside left. The nearest he came to honours with Aberdeen was the semi-final of the Scottish Cup in 1925/26, where they lost 2-1 to Celtic. In later life, Billy was a successful newsagent in Aberdeen, where he had remained after ending his football career.

Season	League		F.A.Cup		Welsh Cup		Total	
	apps	gls	apps	gls	apps	gls	apps	gls
1922/23	25	8	3	3	3	1	31	12
1923/24	27	2	2	1	5	2	34	5
	52	**10**	**5**	**4**	**8**	**3**	**65**	**17**

JARVIS, John Brian 1951 - 1959

Position; *Wing-Half*
D.O.B; *26th August, 1933*
Birthplace; *Bangor-on Dee, Denbighshire*
Height; *5ft 8'1/2in* ***Weight;*** *11st 2lbs*
Debut v. *Accrington Stanley (h) 16th January, 1954*
Total Appearances & Goals; *71 apps 4 gls*
Career; *WREXHAM (Am) May 1951, (Pro) 9th Jul 1952; Oldham Athletic 23rd Jul 1959 88apps 2gls; Bankstown (Sydney) March 1963; Altrincham 7th Sep 1963; Witton Albion; Colwyn Bay 20th Aug 1966; Borough United 17th Sept 1966 to May 1967;*
Honours; *Welsh Youth international;*

Brian Jarvis represented the Welsh Boys Club side as a half-back, and was soon snapped up by Wrexham on amateur forms straight from school. Brian remained as an amateur with Wrexham until the close season of 1956, when he became a full-time professional, following completion of his National Service with the R.A.F. He had already made his Football League debut by that time, in a 4-2 home win over Accrington Stanley in January 1954 . During his time at the Racecourse Jarvis had

to battle for his place in the side with the likes of Dennis Griffiths, Johnnie Tapscott, Gwyn Morgans and finally Fred Davis. But despite the stiff opposition for places in the side Brian did make 64 League appearances before he left Wrexham to join Oldham Athletic in July 1959. During his time at the Racecourse Jarvis was described as a 'whole-hearted player who showed tremendous grit and perseverance, even though he was only of average build. His fearless approach was allied to his speed and the ability to play constructive football'. Brian was plunged straight into the Oldham first team for his debut in the opening match of the 1959/60 season, a 2-0 home win over Bradford Park Avenue. He went on to spend almost four seasons at Boundary Park, which included fourteen League appearances in Oldham's promotion-winning campaign of 1962/63. However, in March 1963 Brian was allowed to leave the 'Latics', to take up an offer of travelling to Australia to play for Sydney club Bankstown, where he spent the summer period. He returned home in September 1963, signing for Cheshire League side Altrincham, and within a few months was playing on the Racecourse once again, against Wrexham this time, in an F.A.Cup match, which the Robins won 3-0 after a replay in November 1963. Brian later played football for Witton Albion, Colwyn Bay and Borough United. After retiring from football he took up work in insurance, settling in the village of Bayston Hill, near Shrewsbury, where he was working as a driver for the W.R.V.S. at the time of writing, helping the handicapped.

Season	League		F.A.Cup		Welsh Cup		Total	
	apps	gls	apps	gls	apps	gls	apps	gls
1953/54	7	0	-	-	-	-	7	0
1954/55	10	0	1	0	-	-	11	0
1955/56	2	0	-	-	-	-	2	0
1956/57	13	2	1	0	2	0	16	2
1957/58	22	1	-	-	1	1	23	2
1958/59	10	0	-	-	2	0	12	0
	64	**3**	**2**	**0**	**5**	**1**	**71**	**4**

***JEAVONS,* William Henry** 1935

Position; *Outside-Right*
D.O.B; *9th February, 1912*
Birthplace; *Woodhouse Mill, Sheffield, Yorkshire*
Died; *Burnley, 2nd April, 1992.*
Height; *5ft 6'1/2ins* ***Weight*** *10st 11lbs*
Debut v. *Hartlepool United (h) 18th September, 1935*
Total Appearances & Goals; *2 apps 0 gls*
Career; *Woodhouse WM; Woodhouse Brunswick; Huddersfield Town 4th Oct 1930 (trial); Scarborough Apr 1931 (trial); Chesterfield (Am) 28th Aug 1931, (Pro) 2nd Dec 1931 4apps 0gls; Burnley 24th Jun 1932 1app 0gls; Accrington Stanley 24th Jun 1933 17apps 7gls; Oldham Athletic 24th Feb 1934 3apps 1gls; Southport 19th Jul 1934 16apps 1gls; WREXHAM 29th Jul 1935; Shrewsbury Town 18th Dec 1935 18apps 7gls; Burton Town Aug 1936; Worcester City Jan 1938 30apps 9gls; Burnley (WW2 Guest) Oct 1940 1app 0gls;*

Bill Jeavons went to school in Rotherham and turned out for his local clubs, Woodhouse Working Men's' Club and Woodhouse Brunswick, where he began to attract the attention of Football League clubs. He first went to Huddersfield Town for a trial in October 1930, before signing amateur forms for Second Division Chesterfield almost a year later. It was whilst still an amateur that Bill made his Football League debut for Chesterfield at outside-right, in a 2-2 home draw with Bradford City in November 1931. He then played in two more games, and had obviously done enough to earn a professional contract with the Saltergate club the following month. However, he was to make just one further appearance for the 'Spireites', a 4-0 defeat at Plymouth in the last match of the 1931/32 season. In June 1932 Billy was signed by Burnley, but after only one League appearance, a 4-1 defeat at Millwall in November, he was allowed to join Accrington Stanley at the end of the season. Bill didn't break into the 'Stanley' first team until early November 1933 but, as he had scored in almost every reserve game up until then, his elevation into the first team was not unexpected. 'Stanley' had not won for over a month when he made his debut, but he scored within 15 minutes of the kick-off and added a second in the second-half as they won 3-0 at New Brighton. He went on to make 17 League appearances and scored seven goals as, not surprisingly, other clubs began to take an interest. Oldham Athletic signed him in February 1934, but he failed to show his best form at Boundary Park, and was released at the end of the season. Jeavons then joined Southport during the summer, and made his debut in the opening match of the 1934/35 season, a 6-1 defeat at Stockport. Although he was never a regular choice for Southport, Bill did make sixteen League appearances, playing on either flank. At the end of the 1934/35 season, he left Southport and signed for Wrexham manager, Ernie Blackburn. During his time at the Racecourse he was only called upon to play two games, in both cases as a replacement for Jack Mustard. His debut came in a 1-0 home win over Hartlepool, and his second appearance was made in a 1-0 home defeat to Rochdale. Bill was described as 'not of a very big build, but is said to have been a hard and plucky forward.' He played mostly reserve team football at Wrexham, and it was no surprise when allowed to join non-league Shrewsbury Town in December 1935. He later played for Burton Town and Worcester City, where he was one of only two players to play in both their final Birmingham & District League match and their initial game in the Southern League. He was released by Worcester in May 1939, but did make one more appearance for a League club during the Second World War when he played for Burnley as a 'guest' player. During his playing career Bill was described as being 'of frail physique, but his speed and footwork could take him through the most compact of defences.' He settled in Burnley, where he lived for almost 60 years, working as an engineer with Joseph Lucas, before retiring in 1974. He later suffered from angina, eventually dying of a heart attack in hospital in Burnley a few weeks after his 80th birthday in 1992.

Season	League		F.A.Cup		Welsh Cup		N.S.C.		Total	
	apps	gls	apps	gls	apps	gls	apps	gls	apps	gls
1935/36	2	0	-	-	-	-	-	-	2	0
	2	**0**	**-**	**-**	**-**	**-**	**-**	**-**	**2**	**0**

***JESSOP,* William** 1951 - 1952

Position; *Inside-Forward*
D.O.B; *2nd April, 1922*
Birthplace; *Preston, Lancashire*
Died; *May 1994.*
Height; *5ft 7'1/2in* ***Weight;*** *10st 12lbs*
Debut v. *Chester (a) 18th August, 1951*
Total Appearances & Goals; *14 apps 2 gls*
Career; *Preston North End 6th Sept 1940 4apps 0gls; Accrington Stanley (WW2 Guest) Oct 1944 1app 0gls; Walsall (WW2 Guest) Oct 1944 1app 0gls; Fulham (WW2 Guest) Nov 1945 1app 1gls; Stockport County 24th May 1947 17apps 4gls; Oldham Athletic 19th Feb 1948 £1,250 94apps 16gls; WREXHAM 19th Jun 1951 (Part-exchange for Dennis Grainger); Bloxwich Strollers July 1952; Nuneaton Borough Jul 1953; Rugby Town Jul 1958; Hinckley Athletic Dec 1958;*

Billy Jessop was a junior star who joined the Preston North End groundstaff straight from school. He was described as 'a direct raider whether at outside-left or centre-forward, his game featured excellent ball control and the ability to beat opponents by sheer artistry.' However, his career was interrupted by the Second World War, during which time he played as a 'guest' for Accrington Stanley, Walsall and Fulham, scoring for the latter in his only game for them, a 5-2 home win over Arsenal in November 1945. After WW2 was over Billy made his Football League debut for Preston, although he managed just three more League appearances for the 'Lilywhites' before allowed to leave Deepdale and join Stockport County in May 1947. He got off to a good start at Edgeley Park, as he scored on his debut in the opening match of the 1947/48 season, a 4-0 win at Southport. However, with just two more goals to his credit in a further fifteen League games he was allowed to leave in February 1948, when Oldham Athletic paid out a sizeable fee of £1,250 for him. He again got off to an impressive start with Oldham, scoring twice on his debut in a 5-3 win at Gateshead. Billy remained at Boundary Park for just over three years, making 94 League appearances for the Lancashire club and scoring sixteen goals in what were three rather mediocre seasons for Oldham. During the close season of 1951 Jessop was involved in a player-exchange deal, which saw Dennis Grainger leave Wrexham and Billy join the North Wales club. He made his debut for the 'Robins' in the opening match of the 1951/52 season, a local 'derby' with Chester at Sealand Road which was lost 2-1. He made just fourteen League appearances for the Racecourse Club, scoring two goals, before being released at the end of the season. Billy then went into non-league football, playing for a number of Midlands clubs that included Bloxwich Strollers; Nuneaton Borough; Rugby Town; and Hinckley Athletic.

Season	League		F.A.Cup		Welsh Cup		Total	
	apps	gls	apps	gls	apps	gls	apps	gls
1951/52	14	2	1	0	1	1	16	3
	14	**2**	**1**	**0**	**1**	**1**	**16**	**3**

JOHNSON, Arthur 1960 - 1963

Position; *Goalkeeper*
D.O.B; *23rd January, 1933*
Birthplace; *Liverpool, Merseyside*
Height; *6ft 1'1/2in* ***Weight;*** *13st 0lbs*
Debut v. *Peterborough United (a) 20th August, 1960*
Total Appearances & Goals; *61 apps 0 gls*
Career; *Blackburn Rovers Jan 1950 1app 0gls; Halifax Town Mar 1955 216apps 0gls; WREXHAM 30th May 1960; Chester (trial) Aug 1962 3apps 0gls; WREXHAM 22nd Dec 1962; New Brighton May 1963; Rhyl 8th Jul 1963; Holyhead Town 29th Feb 1964;*

Although born in Liverpool it was Blackburn Rovers who signed Arthur Johnson as an apprentice in 1949. He had first come to prominence whilst playing for his School team, Alsop Grammar School, from where he was chosen to play for Southport and District schoolboys. Arthur went on to sign professional forms for Blackburn in January 1950, and made his Football League debut against Doncaster Rovers at Ewood Park in August 1951 in a 3-3 draw. He five years at Ewood Park, although two of these were taken up by his National Service in the R.A.F., when he was stationed mainly in South Wales, near Cardiff. Upon being demobbed from the R.A.F. Arthur was allowed to leave Blackburn, joining Halifax Town in March 1955, where he made 216 League appearances. At Halifax, he was described as a 'safe and reliable goalkeeper, though some feel he takes risks advancing from his goal.' In May 1960 Arthur left The Shay, signing for Wrexham for a 'substantial fee' after being awarded a joint benefit match at Halifax with Stan Lonsdale at the end of the 1959/60 season. Arthur joined Wrexham as a part-time professional, combining football with the role of a cost accountant at the Metal Box factory in Aintree, Liverpool, where he continued to live. Arthur made his debut for Wrexham in the opening game of the 1960/61 season, a 3-0 defeat at Peterborough United, which was their first ever game in the Football League. Despite opposition from Charlie Hughes, Arthur remained Wrexham's first choice 'keeper until December 1961, when manager Ken Barnes signed Kevin Keelan from Kidderminster Harriers. Following his arrival, Johnson never played another first team match for Wrexham, and in August 1962 was allowed to join Chester on loan. He made his 'Seals' debut in a scoreless home draw with York City, making two further League appearances before returning to Wrexham in December 1962 as the Club were in desperate need of goalkeeping cover for the injured Kevin Keelan and Ken Simpkins. However, he wasn't called upon, remaining in the reserves until the end of the season when he was released. Arthur then joined Cheshire League side New Brighton for a short spell, before going on to play for Rhyl and Holyhead Town on the North Wales coast.

Season	League		F.A.Cup		Welsh Cup		League Cup		Total	
	apps	gls	apps	gls	apps	gls	apps	gls	apps	gls
1960/61	32	0	1	0	1	0	3	0	37	0
1961/62	20	0	3	0	-	-	1	0	24	0
	52	**0**	**4**	**0**	**1**	**0**	**4**	**0**	**61**	**0**

JOHNSON, Brian Arthur Bentley 1950 - 1952

Position; *Outside-Right*
D.O.B; *28th May, 1930*
Birthplace; *Northwich, Cheshire*
Height; *5ft 7in* ***Weight;*** *11st 2lbs*
Debut v. *Rotherham United (a) 26th August, 1950*
Total Appearances & Goals; *14 apps 2 gls*
Career; *WREXHAM 12th Apr 1950; Released 1952; Witton Albion; Rhyl 18th Sept 1956; Borough United 8th Apr 1960;*

Brian Johnson signed for Wrexham in April 1950, but it wasn't until the following season that he made his Football League debut for the Club when stepping in to replace the injured regular outside-right, Dennis Grainger, in the third match of the 1950/51 season at Rotherham in a 5-0 defeat. Despite the result Brian remained in the side until November, during which time he played in a 2-0 home win over Chester before Dennis Grainger returned to fitness. Johnson then reverted to reserve team football, where he stayed until the end of the season, when called up for his National Service. He continued to play for Wrexham's second string when he could, and on New Year's Day 1952 was included in the first team while on home leave. He made what proved to be his last first team appearance for the Club in a 1-0 defeat at Hartlepool United as a replacement for George Jones. At the end of the 1951/52 season Brian was released by Wrexham and he then drifted into non-league football, playing for Cheshire League sides Witton Albion and Rhyl, where he finished the 1958/59 season as the club's top scorer. He left Rhyl towards the end of 1959/60, when joining Welsh League side, Borough United.

Season	League		F.A.Cup		Welsh Cup		Total	
	apps	gls	apps	gls	apps	gls	apps	gls
1950/51	13	2	-	-	-	-	13	2
1951/52	1	0	-	-	-	-	1	0
	14	**2**	**-**	**-**	**-**	**-**	**14**	**2**

JOHNSON, Eric 1963 - 1966

Position; *Wing-Half*
D.O.B; *16th December, 1944*
Birthplace; *Birkenhead, Merseyside*
Height; *5ft 8in* ***Weight;*** *11st 0lbs*
Debut v. *Southend United (a) 21st December, 1963*
Total Appearances & Goals; *33 apps 0 gls*
Career; *Everton (amateur); Stork Aug 1961; WREXHAM (Am) Feb 1962, (Pro) 14th Jun 1963; Rhyl 16th Jun 1966; Shaftsbury Old Boys Aug 1967;*
Honours; *Welsh Cup runner-up 1965;*

Eric Johnson began playing football at Woodlands Primary and Hamilton Secondary Schools in Birkenhead, captaining both School teams from his inside-forward position. Immediately upon leaving school Eric was signed on amateur forms by Everton, while he also commenced work in the packing department at the Stork Company. For two seasons he played regularly for the Goodison Park 'A' team, but at the start of the 1961/62 season he decided that, out of courtesy, he should sign for the Stork works team who played in the West Cheshire League. During that season he was honoured by selections for both the Wirral Youth XI and the Cheshire F.A.Youth XI. Mid-way through the season, Eric was spotted by Wrexham scout Bob Bennett, and was signed on amateur forms by the Racecourse club in February 1962. He played in the Cheshire League side before the end of the season, becoming a regular the following term, although still an amateur. In June 1963, Johnson signed professional forms with Wrexham, making his Football League debut for the Club at Southend United in December 1963 in a 1-1 draw. Eric went on to make

a further 16 League appearances that season, and also played in the 1965 Welsh Cup final which Wrexham lost to Cardiff City. Over the next two seasons he was to play in only a further eleven League games, and at the end of 1965/66, was released. He then joined up with the former Wrexham goalkeeper, Albert Dunlop, who was managing Cheshire League side Rhyl, for the duration of 1966/67 season. At the end of the campaign, Eric decided to join his local club, Shaftesbury Old Boys, who performed in the West Cheshire League a partnership which lasted over twenty years, mostly as manager. After he had finished playing professional football, Eric became employed at Cammell Laird in his native Birkenhead, working the ship-repair yard, and later on the production side which eventually closed in 1992. Since then, he has worked for Wirral Borough Council as a caretaker in a handicapped school on the Wirral, where he still lives.

Season	League apps	gls	F.A.Cup apps	gls	Welsh Cup apps	gls	League Cup apps	gls	Total apps	gls
1963/64	17	0	-	-	1	0	-	-	18	0
1964/65	10	0	-	-	3	0	1	0	14	0
1965/66	1	0	-	-	-	-	-	-	1	0
	28	**0**	**-**	**-**	**4**	**0**	**1**	**0**	**33**	**0**

JONES, Alan 1964 - 1966

Position; *Outside-Right*
D.O.B.; *13th January, 1944*
Birthplace; *Abermorddu, Denbighshire*
Height; *5ft 4 1/2in* ***Weight;*** *9st 7lbs*
Debut; v. *Doncaster Rovers (a) 8th September, 1964*
Total Appearances & Goals; *2 apps 0 gls*
Career; *WREXHAM 1961; Preston North End (Trial) 1963; Blackburn Rovers (Trial) 1963; Swindon Town (Trial) 1963; Johnstown 1963/64; WREXHAM 20th July 1964; Witton Albion cs1965; Nantwich Town; Ellesmere Port Town; Oswestry Town; Colwyn Bay 20th Aug 1966; Portmadoc 22nd Oct 1966; Caernarvon Town 9th Dec 1967; Pwllheli & District 7th Jun 1968; Caernarvon Town 1st Feb 1969; Pwllheli & District 18th Sept 1969; Barmouth & Dyffryn United 22nd Jul 1970;*
Honours; *Welsh Youth Cup Winner 1962 & 1963; Three Welsh Youth International caps; Welsh League North Championship Winner 1967;*

Alan Jones was educated at Abermorddu Primary, and Buckley Elfed Secondary Schools, and played football at inside-forward for the latter, when they won the Flintshire County Cup. Alan left school at Christmas 1959 and started work at Brymbo Steelworks, but not long after that he signed for Wrexham on amateur forms in 1960. He then took up work with a local Building and Contracting firm operated by Mr.Iorwerth Evans, who was a Wrexham director at that time. Alan played in both the 1962 and 1963 Welsh Youth Cup winning sides for Wrexham, along with Ken Simpkins and David Powell. He also won three Welsh Youth caps, but in August 1963 left the North to try his luck elsewhere. Jones then went for trials with Preston North End, Blackburn Rovers and Swindon Town. With the latter he was admitted into hospital for an appendicitis operation, and had to return home to Wrexham. Once fit he played for Johnstown in the Welsh National League, but very shortly afterwards returned to the Racecourse and became a regular in the Cheshire League side. In July 1964 he was signed on professional forms by Wrexham, and fairly soon was to make his Football League debut at Doncaster Rovers in a 1-1 draw, when he replaced an injured Arfon Griffiths. Jones also played in the next game at Crewe, in a 1-0 defeat, which proved to be his last first team game for the club as Griffiths returned to the side. In May 1965 Jones was released. He moved into non-league football, following his former manager at the Racecourse, Ken Barnes, to Cheshire League side Witton Albion and went on to have short spells with Nantwich and Ellesmere Port Town. Alan later returned to North Wales, where he played for a number of Welsh League sides including, Colwyn Bay, Portmadoc, with whom he won a Welsh League North championship medal in his first season, Caernarvon Town (twice), Pwllheli & District (twice) and Barmouth & Dyffryn United. After retiring from playing he went into management, with the very successful 'Grapes' Welsh National League side of the 1980s, followed by a spell managing Gresford Athletic, who he is still involved with. Alan was employed as an insurance agent for 23 years, but was recently working for Wrexham County Borough Council as a housing assistant.

Season	League apps	gls	F.A.Cup apps	gls	Welsh Cup apps	gls	League Cup apps	gls	Total apps	gls
1964/65	2	0	-	-	-	-	-	-	2	0
	2	**0**	**-**	**-**	**-**	**-**	**-**	**-**	**2**	**0**

JONES, Alfred 1923 - 1936

Position; *Right-Back*
D.O.B; *10th January, 1900*
Birthplace; *Chester, Cheshire*
Died; *Wrexham, March 1959*
Height; *5ft 7in* ***Weight;*** *10st 7lbs*
Debut v. *Ashington (h) 25th August, 1923*
Total Appearances & Goals; *581 apps 6 gls*
Career; *Brookhirst; Chester cs1919 51apps 0gls; Brickfields; Saltney Athletic; WREXHAM 16th May 1923; Winsford United Jul 1936;*
Honours; *Welsh Cup Winner 1924, 1925 & 1931; Welsh Cup runner-up 1932 & 1933;*

Alf Jones was born and brought up in the Hoole area of Chester. He first began playing football for the All Saints' School team, and subsequently Brookhirst on leaving school, with whom he was also employed. Upon the outbreak of World War One Alf served with the Royal Flying Corps when he was old enough to enlist. After WW1 he signed for Chester who, at that time, played in the Cheshire County League. Alf spent two seasons with them, making his debut in September 1919 in a 5-2 home win over Mossley. He made a further fifty Cheshire League appearances, without scoring, before leaving the club in the close season of 1921. He later played for local teams Brickfields and Saltney Athletic. Four members of that Brickfields side went on to play League football including Gordon Gunson who also later played for Wrexham. Alf, though, first signed for Saltney Athletic before moving to the Racecourse in the summer of 1923. So began a thirteen year association with Wrexham Football Club that was to endure until the close season of 1936. He made his Football League debut against Ashington, in the opening game of the 1923/24 season, and didn't miss a game all season. Alf displayed remarkable consistency, and his appearance record of 503 League games for Wrexham has only ever been surpassed by Arfon Griffiths. It probably constitutes an all-time record for the old Third Division North. He was affectionately known to

Wrexham fans as 'Our Alf' and the 'Pride of Wrexham'. During his time at the club he won three Welsh Cup winners' and two runners-up medals in the same competition, and was also honoured as the only Wrexham player to have been awarded two Benefit matches, the first against Everton in October 1928. Alf was said to have been 'a hard tackling full back, who had great distribution.' His Football League career came to an end after the 1935/36 season. He then joined Cheshire League side Winsford United, teaming up with two other former Wrexham team-mates of his, Dick Finnigan and Albert Lumberg. After hanging up his boots Alf became a caretaker at Acton School in Wrexham, up until his sudden death at the War Memorial Hospital in March 1959, aged 59. He was one of the most popular players ever to have graced the Racecourse.

Season	League		F.A.Cup		Welsh Cup		N.S.C.		Total	
	apps	gls	apps	gls	apps	gls	apps	gls	apps	gls
1923/24	42	1	2	0	6	0	-	-	50	1
1924/25	40	0	1	0	4	0	-	-	45	0
1925/26	39	0	1	0	3	0	-	-	43	0
1926/27	42	2	4	0	4	1	-	-	50	3
1927/28	42	1	5	0	3	0	-	-	50	1
1928/29	40	0	1	0	-	-	-	-	41	0
1929/30	32	1	5	0	3	0	-	-	40	1
1930/31	42	0	3	0	4	0	-	-	49	0
1931/32	40	0	1	0	6	0	-	-	47	0
1932/33	42	0	3	0	6	0	-	-	51	0
1933/34	42	0	1	0	1	0	4	0	48	0
1934/35	41	0	2	0	1	0	2	0	46	0
1935/36	19	0	1	0	1	0	-	-	21	0
	503	**5**	**30**	**0**	**42**	**1**	**6**	**0**	**581**	**6**

JONES, Arthur

1931 - 1932

Position; *Outside-Right*
D.O.B; *22nd August, 1912*
Birthplace; *Gwersyllt, Denbighshire*
Height; *5ft 7in* ***Weight;*** *10st 7lbs*
Debut v. *Lincoln City (h) 19th December, 1931*
Total Appearances & Goals; *6 apps 1 gls*
Career; *Cross Street FC; Holyhead; WREXHAM (Am) 1931, (Pro) 4th May 1932; Hyde United Sept 1932; Oldham Athletic 2nd July 1935 98apps 30gls; to cs1939; Bradley Rangers 11th Jan 1940; Bath City (WW2 Guest); Chester (WW2 Guest); Tranmere Rovers (WW2 Guest);*
Honours; *Welsh Cup runner-up 1932; Welsh Junior International 1932/33; Birmingham & District League championship Winner 1933; Chums League Championship Winner;*

Arthur Jones attended his local school, Gwersyllt Chruch School, from where he began playing football for Cross Street Church FC, who played in the local Wrexham area, 'Chums League', winning a championship medal. He was later invited to join his friend, Albert Baker, playing for Holyhead in the Welsh League, and while playing against Wrexham's reserves was spotted and signed on amateur terms by the Wrexham manager of that time, Mr.Jack Baynes. Jones was still an amateur when he was called upon for his Football League debut against Lincoln City on the Racecourse in December 1931, replacing Billie Rogers in the 3-1 defeat. He played in the next two matches, both against Accrington Stanley, before returning to reserve team football. Arthur made his final League appearance for the Club in May 1932 when he replaced Tommy Lewis in a 5-0 defeat at Hull. He again replaced Lewis to play in the 1932 Welsh Cup final against Swansea Town, scoring the goal in the 1-1 draw on the Racecourse. However, Arthur ended up on the losing side, as Wrexham crashed to a 2-0 defeat in the replay at Swansea. He was signed on professional terms at the end of the season, but shortly into the new campaign was allowed to leave the Racecourse and join Cheshire League side Hyde United, because of a dispute over wages and cutbacks in the playing staff. He spent almost three years with Hyde, winning a Cheshire League Cup winners medal in 1934 and two Ashton Challenge Cup winners' medals 1933 and 1934. He was an ever-present throughout 1934/35, impressing Oldham Athletic sufficiently for them to sign him in the close season. 'Taffy' Jones as he became affectionately known at Boundary Park, made his debut for the 'Latics' in a 3-2 home defeat by Lincoln City in September 1935. That was to be his only first team appearance until December, following which he became a regular at outside-right. Arthur enjoyed four seasons at Oldham, making over 100 appearances. He was described as having 'neat footwork, and the ability to centre the ball accurately, which were important features of his play. His goalscoring average was excellent for a winger', and ironically his best game for Oldham came when made captain for the day against his old club, Wrexham, in January 1936, and responded by scoring four goals in a 5-2 win. He left them at the end of the 1938/39 season. World War Two then broke out and Jones became a Physical Training Instructor in the Army, which enabled him to play as a 'Guest' for Bath City, Tranmere Rovers and Chester before badly breaking his ankle, which was to end his playing career. After WW2, Arthur took up work at Hooton, and was later employed with Rubery Owens in Wrexham, where he became trainer of the factory football team in the Welsh National League. He eventually moved to Llay Main Colliery, in the workshop until his retirement in 1977. Arthur has since lived in the Wrexham area.

Season	League		F.A.Cup		Welsh Cup		Total	
	apps	gls	apps	gls	apps	gls	apps	gls
1931/32	4	0	-	-	2	1	6	1
	4	**0**	**-**	**-**	**2**	**1**	**6**	**1**

JONES, Barry

1992 - 1998

Position; *Right-Back*
D.O.B; *30th June, 1970*
Birthplace; *Prescot, Merseyside*
Height; *5ft 11in* ***Weight;*** *11st 3lbs*
Debut v. *Rochdale (h) 22nd August, 1992*
Total Appearances & Goals; *237/15 apps 6 gls*
Career; *Prescot Cables 1986; Liverpool 0apps 19th Jan 1989; WREXHAM 25th May 1992; York City 17th Dec 1997 (Loan), 19th Jan 1998 £40,000 67/1apps 4gls;*
Honours; *Third Division Championship runner-up 1993; Welsh Cup Winner 1995; Central League Championship Winner 1992; Isle Of Man Steam Packet International tournament Cup Winner 1993 & 1997;*

Barry Jones was brought up in Prescot, and educated at the local comprehensive school. He represented his school team from the under-11s to 16s. He also played for a local junior side, All Saints, who competed in the St.Helens and District Junior League. At School Barry was chosen to play for both Liverpool and Merseyside Boys. When he was 15 Jones was one of a group of lads who formed their own Sunday League side, called Napoli, for whom Karl Connolly also later played. After leaving school Barry became an apprentice painter and decorator, and was soon invited to play for Prescot Cables FC in the North West Counties League. After just one

game with their reserve team Barry was asked to attend training sessions at the Liverpool School of Excellence, following a recommendation from the Prescot manager. His progress with Liverpool was rapid: after just one week with the 'B' team he was promoted to the 'A' side, and soon after that stepped up to the Central League XI as a part-timer. Around Christmas 1988 Barry was given the chance to join Liverpool full-time for a trial period, and after a month he signed professional forms. Over the next four years Jones played mainly for the Central League side, which he captained to the 1992 Championship. By the time his contract was due for renewal, during the summer of 1992, Barry wanted first team football. His only appearance in the Liverpool senior eleven had been in a UEFA Cup match in Finland against Lathi. Despite offers from Huddersfield, Stockport, Preston, and Crewe, Barry chose to sign for Wrexham where he was to replace right back Andy Thackeray, who had left the club for Rochdale. In his first season he was an ever present, playing in all the Club's League and Cup games. In doing so, he helped the club to gain promotion to the Second Division. Over the next three seasons, Jones remained a regular fixture in the Wrexham defence, winning a Welsh Cup Winners' medal in 1995, playing in F.A.Cup games against Manchester United, and in Europe against Petrolul Ploesti of Romania. With the emergence of youngster, Mark McGregor at right-back, Barry was switched to his old position in the centre of defence, where he played during his time at Liverpool. Initially he lined up alongside either Tony Humes or Northern Ireland international, Barry Hunter, prior to his move to Reading, which saw Brian Carey's arrival. He then found that Humes and Carey were the preferred partnership, and had to be content with waiting for either of them being injured or suspended before he could get a game. Eventually, Jones was given the opportunity of first team football at York City, whom he initially joined on loan in December 1997, before the move was made permanent the following month, with York paying £40,000 for his services. He still remains a first team regular at Bootham Crescent, although the 'Minstermen' suffered relegation to the third division at the end of 1998/99.

Season	League		F.A.Cup		Welsh Cup		League Cup		A.G.T.		E.C.W.C.		Total	
	apps	gls	apps	gls	apps	gls	apps	gls	apps	gls	apps	gls	apps	gls
1992/93	42	2	1	0	5	0	2	0	3	0	-	-	53	2
1993/94	33	2	-	-	-	-	4	0	1	0	-	-	38	2
1994/95	44	0	4	0	8	0	4	1	4	0	-	-	64	1
1995/96	39/1	0	4	0	-	-	2	0	3	0	2	0	50/1	0
1996/97	14/8	0	1/1	0	-	-	0/1	0	0/1	0	-	-	15/11	0
1997/98	12/2	1	1/1	0	-	-	2	0	-	-	-	-	17/3*	1*
	184/11	**5**	**11/2**	**0**	**13**	**0**	**14/1**	**1**	**11/1**	**0**	**-**	**-**	**237/15**	**6**

* = Includes 2apps 0gls in the Welsh Invitation Cup.

JONES, Charles Wilson

1932 - 1934

Position; *Centre-Forward*
D.O.B; *29th April, 1914*
Birthplace; *Pentre Broughton, Denbighshire*
Died; *Birmingham, 9th January, 1985*
Height; *5ft 10in* ***Weight;*** *10st 10lbs*
Debut v. *Hartlepool United (a) 3rd September, 1932*
Total Appearances & Goals; *11 apps 6 gls*
Career; *Brymbo Green 1930; Oswestry Town; Blackburn Rovers (trial); Bolton Wanderers (trial); WREXHAM 27th May 1932; Birmingham Sept 1934 £1,500 135apps 63gls; (WW2) 1939-1943 38apps 20gls; Wrexham (WW2 Guest) Jan 1940-1943 4apps 2gls; Blackpool (WW2 Guest) Mar 1941-1943 39apps 40gls; Manchester City (WW2 Guest) Oct1942 8apps 3gls; Mansfield Town (WW2 Guest) 1942-44; West Bromwich Albion (WW2 Guest) May 1942 1app 0gls; Nottingham Forest Sept 1947 7apps 5gls; Redditch United; Kidderminster Harriers cs1948; Retired 1950;*
Honours; *Two Welsh International Caps; Birmingham & District League Championship Winner 1932 & 1933;*

Charlie Wilson-Jones a red haired centre forward was playing for Brymbo Green when he was signed by Wrexham in August 1932, having previously attended both Blackburn Rovers and Bolton Wanderers. He had earlier played football at the same school as former Wrexham and Welsh international defender Tommy Griffiths. Charlie's opportunities with Wrexham were to be limited because of the form of the club's goalscoring sensation at that time, Tommy Bamford. However, he shone in the reserve team, becoming a prolific scorer whose goals helped Wrexham clinch two Birmingham and District League championships. He made his Football League debut at Hartlepool at the beginning of the 1932/33 season, replacing Bamford in a 3-1 defeat. Over the next couple of seasons Charles was to make just seven more appearances, scoring four goals. During his time with Wrexham Wilson Jones would cycle many miles to the ground each day, and then train with the rest of the team! At the beginning of the 1933/34 season Birmingham must have seen something in him as they splashed out £1,500 to obtain his signature. Within a month of arriving at St.Andrews he was in the first

team, leading the First Division club's attack. Six months later he was back at Wrexham, playing for Wales against Ireland, and celebrating with a goal in the 3-1 win. He won a second cap in 1939, against France in Paris, before WW2 was to interrupt his football career. He continued to play for Birmingham during WW2 when available, making sixty appearances and scoring forty goals during this period. He also played as a 'guest' for a number of other clubs that included Blackpool, Manchester City, West Brom, Nottingham Forest and also Wrexham, on three occasions, scoring twice in one match against Liverpool in 1941 in a 5-3 win for the Welshmen. After WW2 was over Charles resumed his career with Birmingham, until September 1947 when he signed for Nottingham Forest. He had spent a total of 13 years with the St.Andrews club. Wilson Jones stayed just one season with Forest before dropping into non-league football with Redditch United. He later played for Kidderminster Harriers, finally retiring from playing in 1950. He then went into the licensing trade in the Birmingham area, where he remained until his retirement in 1978. Charlie died seven years later, in January 1985, in Birmingham.

Season	League		F.A.Cup		Welsh Cup		N.S.C.		Total	
	apps	gls	apps	gls	apps	gls	apps	gls	apps	gls
1932/33	4	1	-	-	1	1	-	-	5	2
1933/34	2	2	-	-	-	-	-	-	2	2
1934/35	1	0	-	-	-	-	-	-	1	0
1941/42	2	2	-	-	-	-	-	-	2	2
1942/43	1	0	-	-	-	-	-	-	1	0
	10	**5**	**-**	**-**	**1**	**1**	**-**	**-**	**11**	**6**

JONES, Cyril

1941 - 1947

Position; *Full-Back*
D.O.B; *17th July, 1920*
Birthplace; *Ponciau, Denbighshire*
Died; *Johnstown, Nr.Wrexham 21st Nov, 1995*
Height; *5ft 8in;* ***Weight;*** *10st 7lbs*
Debut v. *New Brighton (h) 31st August, 1946*
Total Appearances & Goals; *199 apps 4 gls*
Career; *Ponciau; Penycae; Johnstown; WREXHAM (Am) 1939, (Pro) 3rd Feb 1941; Blackburn Rovers (WW2 Guest) Apr 1942 2apps 0gls; Blaenau Ffestiniog 16th Aug 1948; Portmadoc 2nd Jan 1951; Rhos Rangers 17th Aug 1953;*

Cyril Jones had played football during his school days in the Rhos area, progressing to play for local sides Ponciau Dragons, Penycae and Johnstown. It was whilst playing at right-back for Johnstown that Cyril was spotted by Wrexham, and he was persuaded to sign amateur forms by their manager Tom Morgan, in 1939. Cyril would combine playing for Wrexham's reserve side with working at Hafod Colliery as an electricians mate, but WW2 was soon to interrupt his playing career. His first taste of senior action came in 1941 in a Football League North regional match against Manchester City at Maine Road, which Wrexham lost 2-0. Cyril went on to record more appearances for Wrexham during the War-time period than any other player, as well as making two 'Guest' appearances for Blackburn Rovers in April 1942. It was during WW2 that Jones was to play alongside, and against, some of the top players in football at that time, and on some of the biggest Football League grounds in the North-West. - e.g. Anfield, Old Trafford, Maine Road and Goodison Park. Cyril would combine playing football with working at the Colliery, and this would often mean joining the team coach immediately upon completion of his shift. One of the highlights of Cyril's career was his selection for a Wales XI against the Combined Services in May 1942. He was a very versatile player, and would play in any position that he was asked. He even played in goal for Wrexham against Wolves at Molineux in February 1945, when Dave Whitelaw got injured. After WW2 Cyril was re-signed by Wrexham for the new Football League season by manager Tom Williams. He then made his Football League debut for Wrexham on the Racecourse against New Brighton in a 3-2 win, almost seven years after signing for the club! He went on to make 28 League appearances for Wrexham, but after suffering a knee and ankle injury in the 7-1 win over Darlington in November 1946 he struggled to maintain his form, and at the end of the 1946/47 season he was to leave the Racecourse. However, Jones continued to play football at non-league level, and went on to serve Blaenau Ffestiniog and Portmadoc in the Welsh League, before retiring from football altogether after a short spell with Rhos Rangers. Cyril continued to work at the Hafod Colliery, where he spent a total of 35 years working for the N.C.B. before retiring. After his retirement, Cyril, kept himself busy at the family bakery in Johnstown right up until when he died in November 1995, aged 75. Cyril a devout Christian, was a gentleman both on and off the field, and he and his fine wife Mair were kindness personified

Season	League		F.A.Cup		Welsh Cup		War Cup		Total	
	apps	gls	apps	gls	apps	gls	apps	gls	apps	gls
1941/42	21	2	-	-	-	-	-	-	21	2
1942/43	35	0	-	-	-	-	-	-	35	0
1943/44	36	0	-	-	-	-	-	-	36	0
1944/45	40	0	-	-	-	-	-	-	40	0
1945/46	21	1	6	1	-	-	10	0	37	2
1946/47*	29	0	-	-	1	0	-	-	30	0
	182	**3**	**6**	**1**	**1**	**0**	**10**	**0**	**199**	**4**

*1946/47 season is the only Football League season.

JONES, David 1992

Position; *Forward*
D.O.B; *6th May, 1971*
Birthplace; *Wrexham, Denbighshire*
Height; *5ft 9in* ***Weight;*** *11st 4lbs*
Debut v. *Colwyn Bay (h) 11th February, 1992 (Welsh Cup)*
Total Appearances & Goals; *1/1 apps 0 gls*
Career; *Aston Villa Jun 1989 0apps; WREXHAM Jan 1992; Caernarfon Town Aug 1992; Brymbo cs1993;*
Honours; *Welsh Schoolboy International;*

A pupil at the Groves School in Wrexham Dave Jones played for his School team; Wrexham Schoolboys; North Schoolboys; and eight times for the Welsh International Schoolboy XI. The promise shown by David at that level saw him quickly snapped up by Aston Villa straight from school in July 1987, going on to sign professional in June 1989. In the following three years as a professional played mostly reserve team football at Villa Park, failing to make a first team appearance. He was eventually released by Villa in January 1992, and joined his home town team soon afterwards. Jones was given his first team opportunity in a Welsh Cup match against Colwyn Bay in February 1992, which Wrexham lost 3-1. He then made his Football League debut for the Club as a substitute replacing Karl Connolly at Barnet in March 1992 in a 2-0 defeat. He failed to impress sufficiently to earn an extended contract, and was released at the end of the season. He joined Northern Premier League side Caernarfon Town for a short spell, where he scored six goals in 33 matches, before signing for Cymru Alliance League side Brymbo, with whom he has been ever since. They are now known as Brymbo Broughton, following the amalgamation of the Brymbo Steelworks and New Broughton FC clubs in 1996. David still resides in the Wrexham area.

Season	League		F.A.Cup		Welsh Cup		League Cup		A.G.T.		Total	
	apps	gls	apps	gls	apps	gls	apps	gls	apps	gls	apps	gls
1991/92	0/1	0	-	-	1	0	-	-	-	-	1/1	0
	0/1	**0**	**-**	**-**	**1**	**0**	**-**	**-**	**-**	**-**	**1/1**	**0**

JONES, David Edward 1955 - 1959

Position; *Forward*
D.O.B; *5th March, 1936*
Birthplace; *Whitefriars, Chester, Cheshire*
Height; *5ft 8in* ***Weight;*** *9st 12lbs*
Debut v. *Chester (h) 18th August, 1956*
Total Appearances & Goals; *88 apps 13 gls*
Career; *Saltney; WREXHAM 18th Apr 1955; Crewe Alex Jul 1959 1app 1gls; Bangor City 6th Jul 1960; Rochester (USA); Holyhead Town 2nd Nov 1963; Dolgellau & District 9th Sept 1964; Nantlle Vale 31st Oct 1964; Oswestry Town 25th Feb 1965; Colwyn Bay 22nd Jan 1966;*
Honours; *Welsh Cup Winner 1958;*

David Jones was born on the English side of Saltney, near Chester, and while playing for his local side was spotted by Wrexham. He signed for the 'Robins' in April 1954, and just a year later stepped up to the professional ranks. Dave spent his first full season in the reserve side in the Cheshire League, before he got his first team chance at the beginning of the 1956/57 season. He was called up following an injury to Gordon Richards, and played in the 'derby' match with Chester on the Racecourse in the opening game of the new season. David made an instant impression by scoring in the 2-2 draw, and kept his place in the side for most of that season, including the famous F.A.Cup match against Manchester United in January 1957. Jones showed tremendous promise at this time and many thought that he was a better prospect than former Wrexham outside-left Colin Grainger, who had gone on to play for England. He missed the 1957 Welsh Cup Final victory over Swansea, but made up for it the following season when playing in the 2-1 Welsh Cup Final win over local rivals Chester. However, David's early promise was not maintained, and he lost his place in the Wrexham first team to Brian Cripsey during the 1958/59 season. At the end of the latter Jones left Wrexham on a free transfer and joined Crewe Alexandra. He was to make just one League appearance for the Gresty Road club, a 2-0 home win over Workington in March 1960, scoring one of the goals, before he was released at the end of the season. He joined Bangor City in the close season of 1960 until moving to play football in the U.S.A. with Rochester. David returned home in 1963, joining Welsh League (North) side, Holyhead Town in the November, followed by spells with Dolgellau & District, Nantlle Vale, Oswestry Town, and Colwyn Bay.

Season	League		F.A.Cup		Welsh Cup		Total	
	apps	gls	apps	gls	apps	gls	apps	gls
1956/57	36	5	7	1	3	0	46	6
1957/58	25	4	1	0	2	0	28	4
1958/59	10	2	-	-	4	1	14	3
	71	**11**	**8**	**1**	**9**	**1**	**88**	**13**

JONES, David Oswald Edwards 1929 & 1932 - 1933

Position; *Forward*
D.O.B; *15th July, 1909*
Birthplace; *Ruabon, Denbighshire*
Height; *5ft 9ins* ***Weight:*** *11st 4lbs*
Debut v. *New Brighton (a) 7th September, 1929*
Total Appearances & Goals; *3 apps 0 gls*
Career; *Afongoch Chums; WREXHAM (Amateur) 8th May 1929; Aberystwyth Town 1929; Llanerch Celts; Gywlfia; Connah's Quay & Shotton FC 1930; Nottingham Forest Oct 1931 0apps; WREXHAM 7th Jul 1932; Oswestry Town cs1933; Macclesfield Town Jul 1934; Tranmere Rovers May 1936 £1,000 54apps 14gls; Watford May 1938 2apps 0gls; Southport 21st Nov 1938 7apps 2gls; Crewe Alexandra 19th May1939; Rochdale (WW2 Guest) 1941/42 1app 0gls; Monsanto (Works team) 1946;*
Honours; *Third Division Championship Winner 1937; Birmingham & District League Championship Winner 1933;*

Season	League		F.A.Cup		Welsh Cup		Total	
	apps	gls	apps	gls	apps	gls	apps	gls
1928/29	1	0	-	-	-	-	1	0
1932/33	2	0	-	-	-	-	2	0
	3	**0**	**-**	**-**	**-**	**-**	**3**	**0**

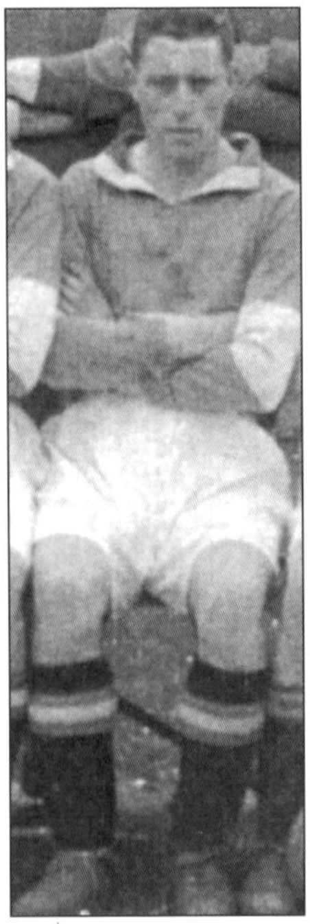

'Os' Jones played football for Johnstown Council School before leaving at the tender age of 14 to take up employment as an assistant store-man at the Vauxhall Colliery, which was situated between the villages of Johnstown and Ruabon. During that time he played football for another village side, Afongoch, in the local Chums League, winning a League runners-up medal. 'Os' eventually left Afongoch to play in a higher standard of non-league football with Aberystwyth Town in the mid-Wales League, followed by spells with Llanerch Celts in Rhos, and Connah's Quay. With Afongoch 'Os' had been given the opportunity to play for Wrexham's reserves, and after one game was asked to travel with the first team to New Brighton in September 1929. The unexpected happened when inside forward Johnny Neal failed to turn up; (it was later found out that his train had not run to time, and that he was stranded at Liverpool Station). Manager Jack Baynes had no option but to give Jones his Football League debut for Wrexham. There was to be no fairy-tale ending though, as Wrexham lost the match 2-1. He was not offered a contract following his debut, although he did continue to play for the Club's 'A' and reserve teams when required. 'Os' was playing for Connah's Quay during the 1930/31 season, where he was spotted by a scout from Nottingham Forest. During the close season of 1931, he signed professional for Forest, where he was to spend a season, but was released at the end of it after he had failed to break through into the first team at the City Ground. He was then invited to sign for Wrexham, which he did, but again found himself playing reserve team football in the Birmingham and District League. With 'Os' in the side, Wrexham were Champions for the 1932/33 season, although he did make two first team appearances, both at centre-forward in place of George Frewin, in a 1-1 home draw with Tranmere Rovers and a 2-0 win at Rotherham United. However, at the end of the season Jones was released by Wrexham and along with team-mate Tommy Molloy joined Oswestry Town in the close season of 1933. In his first season with the Shropshire club 'Os' finished leading marksman, and in the close season was signed by Cheshire County League side Macclesfield Town. He again impressed, finishing top scorer in both of the two season's that he spent at Moss Rose. That led to a return to the Football League, Tranmere Rovers paying out £1,000 for him in the close season of 1936. He got off to a great start with the Prenton Park club, scoring twice on his debut in the opening match of the season, a 5-1 home win over Carlisle United. He enjoyed two seasons with 'The Pentonians', winning a Third Division Championship medal in 1938, before leaving Prenton Park to join Watford. 'Os' had a couple of unsettled months with the 'Hornets', making just two League appearances moving on to Southport in November 1938. His first game for the 'Sandgrounders', was a reserve match against Horwich RMI, in which he got off to a great start by scoring a hat-trick. Overall however, he had few first team opportunities at Haig Avenue, and joined Crewe Alex on a free transfer in the close season of 1939. World War Two signalled the end of his playing career, as he returned to his home near Wrexham and enlisted in the Royal Artillery. During WW2 he served in Sicily, Egypt, and Palestine. As for football, he played for his regiment team when he could, and also 'guested' for Rochdale. After the hostilities he settled in his native Ruabon, working for Monsanto Chemicals and turning out for the works team until back trouble necessitated an operation. Jones later worked for MANWEB, which spanned 33 years before retiring. At the time of writing 'Os' was living in sheltered accommodation, just across the road from his old house in Ruabon.

JONES, Ernest Peter 1960 - 1966

Position; *Right-Back*
D.O.B; *30th November, 1937*
Birthplace; *Salford, Lancashire*
Height; *5ft 11in* ***Weight;*** *12st 0lbs*
Debut v. *Halifax Town (a) 30th April, 1960*
Total Appearances & Goals; *271/1 apps 8 gls*
Career; *Wolves 1953 0apps; Manchester United Apr 1954 1app 0gls; WREXHAM 16th Mar 1960; Stockport County Jul 1966 51/3apps 1gls; Altrincham Jul 1968; Chorley cs1970; Radcliffe Borough cs1972;*
Honours; *Two England Youth international caps; Fourth Division Championship Winner 1967; Welsh Cup runner-up 1962 & 1965;*

The son of a Salford Rugby League player Peter Jones attended Wellington Street School in his native Salford. He represented both Salford Schoolboys and Lancashire Schools, becoming a trainee miner at Newtown Colliery in Swinton upon leaving school at 15. At this time he also signed amateur forms for Manchester United, but within twelve months had signed apprentice forms for Wolves. Peter's stay at Molineux was to last just one season, becoming home sick and rejoining Manchester United as an amateur, while also taking up work at Simpson's Steelworks. In 1955 Peter signed part-time professional forms for United, by which time he was working as a cabinet maker as well as capped by England at Youth level against Denmark at Plymouth in October 1955, and Holland at Norwich in November 1955. He had been playing in United's Central League side, and it was not long before he made his Football League debut for United against Portsmouth in a 3-0 home defeat in November 1957, replacing Roger Byrne at left-back. A few months later, in February 1958, Byrne perished in the Munich Air Disaster. Jones, was extremely fortunate not to have been on the aeroplane, Geoff Bent was injured, and Peter was called up to take his place - but Bent recovered, so Jones stood down. Sadly, Geoff Bent was another who perished in the tragedy. Shortly afterwards Peter was called up for his National Service, joining the Royal Army Ordinance Corp, initially in 1958 at Bordon Barracks, and then at Chidwell in Nottingham. He played regularly for the British Army side during his two years' service, as well as continuing to play for United at weekends, though after he was demobbed in March 1960 was allowed to leave Old Trafford, when they sold him to Wrexham for what was described as a 'four

figure fee'. He joined Wrexham weighing thirteen stone, but after just a few months at the Racecourse had lost over two stones. Peter certainly had his ups and downs during his time with Wrexham: he made his debut in a 2-0 defeat at Halifax Town in April 1960, but over the next six seasons remained a regular in the side at right-back. He also covered at wing-half when required. Jones went on to help Wrexham win promotion in 1962, gaining Welsh Cup runners-up medals in both 1962 and 1965, and suffered relegation back to Division Four in 1964. Worse was to come in 1966, when he was a member of the side that finished 92nd in the Football League, forcing the Club to seek re-election for the first and only time in the its history. Peter was to leave Wrexham in the close season following a wage dispute, and was transferred to Stockport County where he spent two seasons, winning a Fourth Division Championship medal in 1967 before drifting into non-league football with Altrincham in 1968, for two years. He then enjoyed a further two years with Chorley until joining Radcliffe Borough for a season, finally hanging up his boots in 1973. Since then Peter has tried his hand at window cleaning and running a fish and chip shop in Salford, joining Carrington Vijella, a textile company, in the mid 70s. He was employed by Magnesium Electron, a chemical company, in 1977, where he was still employed at the time of writing. Today Peter still lives in the Manchester area in Swinton, where he retains an involvement with football by managing a local football team, Norweb Villa, who play in the famous Manchester Accountants League! He is also a member of the 'Former Manchester United Players Association', which helps raise funds for Charity. He also keeps very active by playing Golf and caravanning.

Season	League		F.A.Cup		Welsh Cup		League Cup		Total	
	apps	gls	apps	gls	apps	gls	apps	gls	apps	gls
1959/60	1	0	-	-	-	-	-	-	1	0
1960/61	36	0	1	0	3	0	6	0	46	0
1961/62	42	2	3	0	6	0	1	0	52	2
1962/63	46	0	4	0	2	0	1	0	53	0
1963/64	34	2	1	0	3	0	3	0	41	2
1964/65	39	3	2	0	5	0	1	0	47	3
1965/66	27/1	0	2	1	-	-	2	0	31/1	1
	225/1	**7**	**13**	**1**	**19**	**0**	**14**	**0**	**271/1**	**8**

JONES, Frank

1924 - 1927

Position; *Outside-Left*
D.O.B;
Birthplace; *Chester, Cheshire*
Height; *5ft 6in* ***Weight;*** *10st 0lbs*
Debut v. *Durham City (a) 25th October, 1924*
Total Appearances & Goals; *40 apps 10 gls*
Career; *Brickfield Athletic; WREXHAM (Am) Jul 1924, (Pro) 24th Oct 1924; Wellington Town 1927; Chester July 1927; Caernarvon Athletic 28th Aug 1928; Connah's Quay & Shotton 30th Aug 1929; Flint Town 12th Oct 1929; Runcorn Oct 1929; L.M.S.Sheds (Chester) Nov 1933;*
Honours; *Welsh Cup Winner 1925; North Wales Coast F.A.Challenge Cup runner-up 1926;*

Frank Jones was signed by Wrexham from Chester side Brickfields Athletic in the close season of 1924. He was signed as a professional prior to making his Football League debut at Durham in October 1924 at outside-left in place of Billy Toms. He then went on to make a further 15 League appearances that season, as well as playing in Wrexham's Welsh Cup win over Flint in the final after scoring a goal against Swansea Town in the 3-1 semi-final win. The following term Frank made a further 15 League appearances at inside-right, but was to find himself totally out of favour in 1926/27 because of the form of Jack Smith. Jones was to only make four more League appearances before leaving the Racecourse and joining Birmingham & District League side Wellington Town. He spent a short time at the Bucks Head before signing for non-league Chester, who were appearing in the Cheshire County League at the time. Frank was to find his first team opportunities limited at Chester, making just six appearances, scoring three goals, as they finished the season in fifth place. At the end of the campaign he joined Welsh League side Caernarvon Athletic, starting the new campaign in spectacular fashion, scoring four goals in the 'Canaries' 8-1 win over Holyhead. Caernarvon had to settle for a runners-up spot behind Connah's Quay & Shotton, who during the close season of 1929 persuaded Frank to join them. After just a couple of months he left to join neighbours Flint Town, later playing for L.M.S. Sheds in Chester before bringing down the curtain on his football playing days. He then became a football Referee and, in 1957, was known to have been the trainer of Holt Nomads.

Season	League		F.A.Cup		Welsh Cup		Total	
	apps	gls	apps	gls	apps	gls	apps	gls
1924/25	16	5	-	-	4	1	20	6
1925/26	15	3	-	-	1	0	16	3
1926/27	4	1	-	-	-	-	4	1
	35	**9**	**-**	**-**	**5**	**1**	**40**	**10**

Jones, Frank

1979 - 1981 & 1985 - 1987

Position; *Central Defender*
D.O.B; *3rd October, 1960*
Birthplace; *Llandudno, Gwynedd*
Height; *5ft 11in* ***Weight;*** *11st 0lbs*
Debut v. *Luton Town (h) 7th May, 1979*
Total Appearances & Goals; *38/1 apps 0 gls*
Career; *WREXHAM 11th Jun 1979; Chelsea Jul 1981 (trial); Oswestry Town Aug 1981; Bangor City Aug 1982; IK Kraft (Finland) Apr 1983; Conwy United Aug 1983; WREXHAM Sept 1984 (non-contract) 0apps; Conwy United 1984; WREXHAM Apr 1985; Rhyl Feb 1987; Conwy United Oct 1989; Llandudno 1991;*
Honours; *One Welsh Under-21 International cap; Two Welsh Youth International caps; Welsh Cup Winner 1986; Welsh Youth Cup Winner 1978; Welsh Alliance League Championship Winner 1985;*

Frank Jones is the brother of Wrexham's famous son, Joey Jones. He attended the same schools in Llandudno as Joey, Lorecco Primary and John Bright Secondary schools, progressing to play for both Aberconwy & District and North Wales schoolboys, although he failed to make the Welsh schoolboys side despite trials. It was also around this time that Frank signed schoolboy forms for Wrexham at 14, and impressed enough to sign apprentice terms when he left school in 1977. As an trainee he helped Wrexham to win the Welsh Youth Cup in 1978, overcoming Afan Lido in the final. The following season Frank was capped for Wales at Youth level, playing in both legs of a UEFA tournament defeat by Norway. Towards the end of the 1978/79 season, Jones, who was still an apprentice, was given his first team chance in place of John Roberts, in a Football League game against Luton Town, playing alongside 'big' brother, in the 2-0 home win. He played one more game that season, at home to Bristol Rovers, but added just seven more first team outings over the following two seasons. In September 1980, he did gain further international recognition, when he played for the Welsh under-21 side against Holland in Dordrecht, Wales winning 2-0, a side that included Ian Rush and Kevin Ratcliffe. However, that season was to end on a sour note for Frankie, as he was given a free transfer. He took up an offer from Chelsea manager John Neal of a trial with the London club, but nothing came of his two weeks in the capital and returned home to join Northern Premier League side, Oswestry Town. One season with the Victoria Road club saw him move on in the summer of 1983 to join fellow Northern Premier League side, Bangor City, whilst taking up employment as a fork lift truck driver at the Hotpoint factory near Llandudno. Jones spent almost a season here before taking up an offer to go to Finland and play for IK Kraft, with whom he played most of their season in midfield. He returned home for the start of the 1983/84 season and joined Welsh League side, Conwy United. However, in September 1984, he was invited back to the Racecourse by Bobby Roberts to help out as cover, but soon returned to Conwy, as no more first team opportunities beckoned. He won a Welsh Alliance Championship medal with Conwy, but before the season had ended, received another call to return to Wrexham in April 1985 from Dixie McNeil, who had replaced Roberts as manager, and wanted him to help the club out during an injury crisis. Frank played two first team matches towards the end of the season, a 3-2 win at Bury and a 1-0 home win over Aldershot, which helped him to earn a two year contract. The first year of his contract saw him hold down a regular place alongside Jackie Keay, and helped Wrexham to lift the Welsh Cup, with a 2-1 win over Kidderminster Harriers, after a 1-1 draw. Despite this success, the following season saw McNeil sign Joe Cooke, and Frank found his first team chances limited to just three games. Before his contract had ended he decided to leave the Racecourse and join Northern Premier League side, Rhyl, whilst returning to work at Hotpoint. He remained with Rhyl until October 1989, when he rejoined Conwy United. He spent almost two years with them, before he signed for Llandudno where he finished his playing career. Today, Frank still lives in his native Llandudno, where he works in the local hospital as a porter.

Season	League		F.A.Cup		Welsh Cup		League Cup		F.R.T.		E.C.W.C.		Total	
	apps	gls	apps	gls	apps	gls	apps	gls	apps	gls	apps	gls	apps	gls
1978/79	2	0	-	-	-	-	-	-	-	-	-	-	2	0
1979/80	2	0	-	-	-	-	-	-	-	-	-	-	2	0
1980/81	4	0	-	-	-	-	1	0	-	-	-	-	4	0
1984/85	2	0	-	-	-	-	-	-	-	-	-	-	2	0
1985/86	27/1	0	3	0	6	0	1	0	2	0	-	-	37/1	0
1986/87	1	0	1	0	-	-	1	0	1	0	0/1	0	4/10	
	38/1	**0**	**4**	**0**	**6**	**0**	**3**	**0**	**3**	**0**	**0/1**	**0**	**54/2**	**0**

JONES, George

1950 - 1954

Position; *Half-Back*
D.O.B; *19th July, 1930*
Birthplace; *Wrexham, Denbighshire*
Height; *5ft 8in* ***Weight;*** *10st 7lbs*
Debut v. *Gateshead (h) 14th October, 1950*
Total Appearances & Goals; *127 apps 7 gls*
Career; *Bersham R.B.L; WREXHAM 3rd Aug 1950; Oswestry Town cs1955; Winsford United Aug 1956; Oswestry Town cs1957; Holywell Town 11th Jul 1963; Barmouth & Dyffryn United 28th Sept 1966;*

George Jones began playing football at the Victoria School in Wrexham. He left at the tender age of 14 to take up work in a grocer's shop, while continuing to play football for Bersham Royal British Legion. He helped them reach the semi-finals of the Welsh Amateur Cup, and his form soon began to attract other clubs' interest, particularly after his selection for the Welsh Youth squad. Although travelling with the team to Stoke's Victoria Ground, he never played, but did receive a cap from the Welsh F.A! George was then called up for his two years National Service, serving with the Royal Engineers. He completed his initial training in Farnborough, Hampshire, before serving with the British Army on the Rhine in Germany. He played representative football for the Army, and it was from playing in one of those games that George was recommended to Tottenham Hotspur by a watching Army Captain. He was checked out by a scout from the London club, and offered the chance to sign. However, in the mean-time Wrexham caretaker manager, Tommy Griffiths, had stepped in to offer George the chance to join his home town club, and he accepted. Jones joined Wrexham upon his demobilisation from the Army in 1950. Playing at half back he was quickly promoted to the first team for his Football League debut in a scoreless draw with Gateshead in October 1950. It wasn't until January 1951 that he finally made the position his own, going on to play in the memorable F.A.Cup matches of the early 1950s against Stoke City, Brighton & Hove Albion, and Leyton Orient. Jones was a regular member of the Wrexham team until Christmas 1953, when he received a serious knee injury, falling awkwardly in a match against Barrow on the Racecourse and damaging both his knee ligaments and cartilage. He had two operations to repair the damage, but broke down each time he attempted a comeback. Although working hard to regain his fitness it was not to be, and, at the end of the 1954/55 season, was allowed to leave the Racecourse. He was a popular figure at Wrexham but the injury bogey put him out of action for a long time and when returning seemed to have lost his confidence. He continued to play football at a lower level by signing for Alan Ball Senior, who was the manager of Oswestry Town at the time. George spent one season with the Cheshire League side, helping them to the semi-finals of the Welsh Cup where they lost to Cardiff City. He then joined fellow Cheshire League side Winsford United for the 1956/57 season. It was with them that he returned to play at the Racecourse against Wrexham's reserves, when he was described as being a "terrier of a wing half who hails from Rhosddu'. He regained his confidence at Winsford and was the fearless tackler that Wrexham fans knew so well." George rejoined Oswestry after a season in Cheshire, and later played for Holywell Town and Barmouth & Dyffryn United. After he had finished playing professional football George settled in Rhostyllen, where he worked for British Rail for 36 years, retiring in 1993.

Season	League		F.A.Cup		Welsh Cup		Total	
	apps	gls	apps	gls	apps	gls	apps	gls
1950/51	24	0	-	-	2	0	26	0
1951/52	26	1	3	0	2	2	31	3
1952/53	39	4	3	0	1	0	43	4
1953/54	24	0	3	0	-	-	27	0
	113	**5**	**9**	**0**	**5**	**2**	**127**	**7**

JONES, Gordon

1921 - 1922

Position; *Centre-Forward*
D.O.B; *1st February, 1889*
Birthplace; *Birkenhead, Merseyside*
Height; *5ft 10in* ***Weight;*** *11st 8lbs*
Debut v. *Nelson (h) 26th November, 1921*
Total Appearances & Goals; *1 app 1 gls*
Career; *Bebington St.Andrews; Melrose Sept 1905; Birkenhead Aug 1907; Bolton Wanderers 22nd Sept 1909 22apps 6gls; Tottenham Hotspur 1st Jun 1912 8apps 0gls; Chester cs1913; South Liverpool Sept 1914; Hurst Feb 1915; Tranmere Rovers Jan 1916; Gresford; Chester cs1919; Crichtons Athletic; WREXHAM 11th Aug 1921; Connah's Quay 23rd Sept 1922; Hurst Feb 1924; Flint Town 13th Dec 1924;*

Gordon Jones played local football in the Birkenhead area for Bebington St.Andrews, Melrose, and Birkenhead when spotted by Bolton Wanderers, for whom he signed in 1909. Gordon made his Football League debut for the Trotters at centre-forward in a 4-3 home defeat against Notts County. Despite the result, the game was a personal triumph for Gordon as he scored two of the goals. He made another 16 League appearances that season, playing mainly at inside-right and adding five more goals to his tally. However, it wasn't enough to keep Bolton in the First Division as they were relegated. Gordon was to find his first team chances limited over the next two seasons, making just five first team appearances, failing to score in any of them and was released in May 1912. He was quickly snapped up by Tottenham Hotspur, where he made his debut in the second match of the season, at home to Sheffield Wednesday. He was switched to defence, playing at half-back, as Spurs lost 4-2. Despite that result Jones was to keep his place in the side for seven more League games before banished to the reserves until the end of the season, when he was again released. Gordon then returned closer to home and joined Lancashire Combination League side Chester, where he made nine appearances at right-back before being suspended by the club for failing to appear for a Boxing Day home game with Nelson. He went on to have spells with South Liverpool, Hurst, and Tranmere Rovers during World War One. Following the Great War, Gordon was playing local football for Gresford, before he re-signed for Chester in the close season of 1919. His second spell with the 'Seals' resulted in him playing their first three Cheshire County League games of the season, before he signed for Crichtons Athletic, also of the Cheshire County League. It was from Crichtons that Gordon Jones moved to Wrexham in August 1921, in time for the beginning of the club's first season in the Football League. Gordon was to make only one Football League appearance for his new Club, against Nelson on the Racecourse in November 1921, when he replaced Ted Regan in the side scoring once in the 4-2 win. Surprisingly, he never played another match for Wrexham. Jones was described in his only match as "played a hard game, but did not help to solve the problem of leadership". He did much better at inside-right, where he played throughout the second-half and scored Wrexham's third goal by simply ploughing his way through the Nelson defence!! In September 1922

Gordon was signed by Welsh League side Connah's Quay, and two years later, at the age of 35, he joined Flint Town.

Season	League		F.A.Cup		Welsh Cup		Total	
	apps	gls	apps	gls	apps	gls	apps	gls
1921/22	1	1	-	-	-	-	1	1
	1	**1**	**-**	**-**	**-**	**-**	**1**	**1**

JONES, Graham Osborne 1967 - 1968

Position; *Centre-Half*
D.O.B; *16th September, 1949*
Birthplace; *Wrexham, Denbighshire*
Height; *6ft 1in* ***Weight;*** *12st 0lbs*
Debut v. *Bethesda Athletic (h) 24th January, 1968 (Welsh Cup)*
Total Appearances & Goals; *3 apps 0 gls*
Career; *WREXHAM Oct 1967; Port Vale cs1968; Bradford Park Avenue 196?; Rhyl 9th Nov 1968; Blaenau Ffestiniog 1st Mar 1969; Bethesda Athletic 31st Oct 1970; Oswestry Town; Nantlle Vale 13th Sept 1974; Blaenau Ffestiniog 1979; Welshpool cs1982; Tywyn Bryncrug cs1984; Lex XI cs1986; Oswestry Town cs1987; Chirk AAA cs1988; Lex XI 1989/90;*
Honours; *One Welsh Youth International cap; Welsh Schoolboy International cap; Welsh League North Championship Winner; Alves Cup Winner; Welsh Intermediate Cup Winner;*

Graham Jones - or 'Ossie', as he is more popularly known - played football for his school team, St.Davids, in his native Wrexham. From there he was chosen to play representative football for both Wrexham & District Schoolboys and the Welsh Schoolboy side. Graham received offers from a number of clubs including trials with Shrewsbury Town, Burnley, and Manchester United, before he was signed by Wrexham on schoolboy forms. However, when he came to leave school, the club released him! Graham then began working at the John Summers Steelworks in Shotton as an apprentice, and upon completion of his six month apprenticeship was invited back to rejoin the groundstaff at Wrexham. 'Ossie' then progressed enough to sign professional forms in October 1967, as well as representing the Welsh Youth team against Ireland. In January 1968 He was given his first team chance, replacing Graham Turner in a Welsh Cup match against Bethesda Athletic on the Racecourse, which Wrexham won 1-0. He had to wait until the following March for his next senior call-up, when both 'Ossie' and Gareth Davies stepped into the side, to form one of the youngest ever central defensive pairings to have played for the Club. They featured together for three consecutive matches; the first, and Graham's Football League debut, was at Darlington in a 1-1 draw, while the following two League matches were both away, a 2-2 draw at Barnsley and a 3-1 defeat at Chesterfield. They were to be Graham's only League games for Wrexham, as he was released at the end of the season. Jones was then invited to join Port Vale on trial, who were managed by Stanley Matthews at the time. He spent most of the season with Vale, but following a change of manager to Gordon Lee was allowed to leave Vale Park without making a first team appearance. Despite this setback Graham was quickly snapped up by Bradford Park Avenue, who were managed by former Wrexham manager, Jack Rowley. His assistant, Ken Roberts, had also been on the coaching staff at the Racecourse. Graham remained with the Bradford club until the end of the season returning home to Wrexham without having played a first team game. He then had offers from a number of non-league clubs in the North Wales area, and opted for Welsh League (North) side Blaenau Ffestiniog, playing against Wrexham in a Welsh Cup match on the Racecourse in January 1970 in a 1-0 defeat. Jones enjoyed considerable success in North Wales football with Cheshire County League side Rhyl, Bethesda Athletic, Nantlle Vale, Blaenau Ffestiniog again, Welshpool, Tywyn, Lex XI, and Oswestry Town for their final season in the Northern Premier League, 1987/88. Graham then managed both Chirk AAA and Lex XI, followed by an appointment as assistant manager to Dixie McNeil at League of Wales side Flint Town United from November 1993 to 1995. Upon finishing with professional football Graham worked for Dunlop on the Wrexham Industrial Estate for over ten years. He has held his present position as a sales representative with Pearl Assurance for over fifteen years, whilst still living in the Wrexham area.

Season	League		F.A.Cup		Welsh Cup		League Cup		Total	
	apps	gls	apps	gls	apps	gls	apps	gls	apps	gls
1967/68	3	0	-	-	1	0	-	-	4	0
	3	**0**	**-**	**-**	**1**	**0**	**-**	**-**	**4**	**0**

JONES, Grenville Arthur 1955 - 1960

Position; *Outside-Right*
D.O.B; *23rd November, 1932*
Birthplace; *Nuneaton, Warwickshire*
Died; *15th October, 1991.*
Height; *5ft 11½in* ***Weight;*** *11st 6lbs*
Debut v. *York City (a) 20th August, 1955*
Total Appearances & Goals; *281 apps 43 gls*
Career; *Erdington; W.B.A. Dec 1949 2apps 0gls; WREXHAM 17th Jun 1955; Prague (Australia) Jul 1961; Sydney FC to 1967:*
Honours; *Welsh Cup Winner 1957, 1958 & 1960; England Schoolboy and Youth international;*

Gren Jones began his football career with West Bromwich Albion in June 1947 when he signed for the Hawthorns club straight from school. He had also played for his local junior side, Erdington. By that time Gren had already been capped for England schoolboys, and with West Bromwich he was capped at Youth level. In December 1949 Jones signed professional forms for Albion, but had to wait until the end of the 1953/54 season before making his Football League debut in a 2-1 defeat at Sunderland. He was to make just one further League appearance with West Brom, a 3-0 defeat at the end of the 1953/54 season at Portsmouth. Gren remained in Albion's reserve side until June 1955, when he joined Wrexham in a double signing, along with Elfed Evans. Their new manager, Cliff Lloyd, put both players straight into the first team, with Gren making his debut at outside right, a position that he was to make his own over the next six years. During that time Jones, whose 'deceptive shuffles could tie opponents in knots, but was sometimes reluctant to shoot at goal', won three Welsh Cup winners' medals with Wrexham. He was also chosen for the Third Division North representative side against their Southern counterparts in April 1957, although he was unable to play in the game because of injury. He also figured in Wrexham's F.A.Cup match of 1957, against the famous 'Busby Babes', in front of the Racecourse's biggest-ever crowd. He also took part in the Club's fine League Cup run of the 1960/61 season, when they beat the previous year's F.A.Cup finalists, Blackburn Rovers, after a replay. At the end of that season Gren decided to leave Wrexham and take up an offer in Australia in July 1961. 'Down under' he played for New South Wales club Prague, and later signed for Sydney FC, whilst working as a foreman in a clothing factory. In all he spent six years in Australia returning to the Wrexham area in 1967 to take up the running of a nursery school with his wife, later taking over a general store. Gren had also been a very good cricketer, and during the summers he played for both Brymbo and Pontblyddyn Cricket Clubs, where he was described as 'a cricketer of no mean ability.' Gren Jones died in 1991, aged only 58.

Season	League		F.A.Cup		Welsh Cup		League Cup		Total	
	apps	gls	apps	gls	apps	gls	apps	gls	apps	gls
1955/56	34	5	1	0	2	0	-	-	37	5
1956/57	44	6	7	1	5	2	-	-	56	9
1957/58	43	9	-	-	5	1	-	-	48	10
1958/59	44	6	1	0	3	0	-	-	48	6
1959/60	37	5	3	0	6	2	-	-	46	7
1960/61	39	5	1	0	2	0	4	1	46	6
	241	**36**	**13**	**1**	**23**	**5**	**4**	**1**	**281**	**43**

JONES, Harvey Cunningham 1959 - 1960

Position; *Half-Back*
D.O.B; *16th August, 1935*
Birthplace; *Rhosllanerchrugog, Denbighshire*
Height; *5ft 11in* **Weight;** *11st 8lbs*
Debut v. *Reading (h) 28th November, 1959*
Total Appearances & Goals; *17 apps 0 gls*
Career; *Puglia FC (Toronto) 1951; Olympia FC (Toronto) 1952; Plymouth Argyle cs1955; Italia FC (Toronto) 1956; Sparta FC (Toronto) 1957; WREXHAM 10th Nov 1959; Chester Aug 1960 19apps 0gls; Ellesmere Port Town Jul 1961; Caernarvon Town 15th Nov 1966; Colwyn Bay 17th Sept 1968;*
Honours; *Two Canadian National League Championship Winner; Three Cheshire League Championship Winner; National Soccer League Representative XI; Canadian Continental Soccer All Star Representative XI;*

Harvey Jones was born in the North Wales village of Rhosllanerchrugog. He resided in the Wrexham area, attending Grove Park School until his parents decided to emigrate to Canada in 1946 when he was eleven. In Canada, he didn't take up playing soccer until he was 15, when his older brother, Dennis, invited him along to play for a local church team. It was through this involvement that he signed for an Italian ethnic team in Toronto named Puglia, who played in the Continental League. He later switched to play for a German ethnic side Olympia, who played in the National League, winning a championship medal. During this time Harvey had qualified as a chartered secretary, which is the equivalent of a public accountant in the UK, and gained valuable work experience with a company called Fairbanks Soap in Toronto. Not long after qualifying he took up an offer to join English Third Division South side Plymouth Argyle, having previously been approached by a number of clubs. At this time Plymouth were managed by Jack Rowley, who later became boss at Wrexham, and after receiving a letter from the Devon club's secretary in 1955 decided to leave Canada. Jones spent twelve months at Home Park returning to Canada after refusing to sign professional terms. He continued to play football for another Italian ethnic side, Italia FC, followed by two seasons with a Czech ethnic XI, Sparta FC, winning another championship medal. During his time in Canadian football he was chosen to represent Canada against UK and Russian club sides, as well as representing the National Soccer League Representative XI against Lima of Peru, Palermo of Sicily, the Mexican National team, and four games in Bermuda as guests of the Bermudan FA. He also appeared for a Canadian Continental All Star XI against Guiliana F.C. in the Giants' Stadium in New York. In the summer of 1959 Harvey and his brother Dennis decided to travel to Europe, taking up an offer of a trial in Munich. However, upon their arrival they found that the rules had been changed regarding the number of foreign players allowed to play. The two brothers then travelled to the U.K., visiting relatives in Wrexham. During their stay in North Wales they were allowed to train with Wrexham by Cliff Lloyd and, following a Tuesday night practice match, were both asked to play in the Cheshire County League side. After one game Harvey was promoted to the senior side for his Football League debut at wing-half against Reading in a 2-1 win on the Racecourse in November 1959. He went on to remain with the 'Robins' for the rest of the 1959/60 season, being described as a 'strong fearless tackler, possessing intelligent distribution.' His most memorable game was the F.A.Cup third round match with Leicester City, which Wrexham unluckily lost 2-1. Just before that game Harvey had learned of his call-up to represent Wales in an Amateur international against Ireland in Belfast, but as the match was on the same day as the Leicester cup-tie, he was unable to play. He left Wrexham at the end of 1959/60 returning to Canada, but before the new season had commenced returned to the UK to join Chester, after turning down an offer from Chesterfield. At Sealand Road, he went on to make his debut in the opening game of the season, a 2-2 home draw with Gillingham, before going on to make a further eighteen League appearances. He was to leave Chester in the close season, joining Cheshire County League side Ellesmere Port Town, for five and a half seasons. During that time he helped them win the League title three times, and reach the first round proper of the F.A.Cup on three occasions. Harvey, who was a qualified FA coach, took up an appointment as player/manager of Welsh League (North) side Caernarfon Town in November 1966. He remained with the 'Canaries' until September 1968, when he joined Colwyn Bay for a short spell before deciding to hang up his boots. Harvey had worked as a commercial manager for British Celanese since 1962, eventually leaving to take up a similar position with Lego UK in Wrexham, later becoming General Sales Manager in 1980. He held that position until his retirement in 1995, which involved extensive travel to Europe. He visited Germany, France and Denmark, with occasional trips to the U.S., as well as spending six months as General Manager for Lego Australia. Today, Harvey still resides in the Wrexham area, where he is now retired. As for his brother Dennis, he returned to Canada after his short spell with Wrexham, and played for a number of Canadian teams in the National League before finishing playing at the age of 36. He later worked for the Sheraton Hotel group, and he now resides in San Francisco. In many ways one could call Harvey Jones 'The Gulliver' of the Football World due to his extensive travelling and interesting life!

Season	League		F.A.Cup		Welsh Cup		Total	
	apps	gls	apps	gls	apps	gls	apps	gls
1959/60	13	0	2	0	2	0	17	0
	13	**0**	**2**	**0**	**2**	**0**	**17**	**0**

JONES, Haydn 1964 - 1966

Position; *Right-Back*
D.O.B; *8th May, 1946*
Birthplace; *Caernarfon, Gwynedd*
Height; *5ft 9in* **Weight;** *11st 2lbs*
Debut v. *York City (h) 20th March, 1965*
Total Appearances & Goals; *18/1 apps 1 gls*
Career; *Menai Bridge Tigers; Caernarfon Town; WREXHAM 12th Jun 1964; Rhyl 16th Jun 1966; Watford 1966/67 (Non-contract); Portmadoc 2nd Sept 1967; Bethesda Athletic 13th Aug 1969; Portmadoc 27th Jun 1970; Pwllheli & District 5th Jul 1972; Caernarfon Town 17th Aug 1974; Porthmadog Dec 1975; Caernarfon Town cs1977; Pwllheli Nov 1980;*
Honours; *Welsh Cup runner-up 1965; One Welsh Youth international cap; Alves Cup Winner 1975 & 1978; Welsh Intermediate Cup Winner 1978; Welsh League (North) Division One Championship Winner 1978 & 1979; Cookson Cup Winner 1978; North Wales Intermediate Cup Winner 1978; North Wales Youth Cup Winner 1961; North Wales Coast F.A.representative cap;*

Haydn Jones played centre forward for the same school team as Wyn Davies -Sir Huw Owen Secondary Modern School- in his home Town of Caernarvon. Haydn was selected for -and captained- the Caernarvonshire Schoolboys team, and was also chosen for Wales Boys' Clubs against England at Bath. It was also at around this time that Haydn was playing for a Junior team Menai Bridge Tigers winning a North Wales Youth Cup Winners' medal when they beat Wrexham in the 1961 final. On leaving school in July 1962 Jones commenced work at a local brick-works as a fitter's mate, while also signing amateur forms for Caernarvon Town. Almost immediately he was recommended to Wrexham by the then Canaries manager, Billy Russell. Haydn was invited to join the club's groundstaff, and the following season was selected to play for the Welsh Youth team. He was injured in the third minute of the match against Scotland, which forced him to miss the rest of the season following a cartilage operation.

Once recovered he was signed on professional terms by Wrexham, in the summer period of 1964. However, he had to wait until March 1965 before making his Football League debut, at right-back in a 2-0 home win over York City. He then kept his place in the side for the following five League games, as well as the Welsh Cup final against Cardiff City, which Wrexham eventually lost after three matches. The start of the 1965/66 season saw Haydn add a further seven matches to his tally. He followed these with an appearance as a substitute, replacing Sammy McMillan in a game against Southport, in which he scored his only goal for Wrexham, with a rasping thirty yard drive, in a 2-2 draw. It was a personal highlight in a disastrous season, as Wrexham ended it 92nd in the Football League, and Jones was then released. He joined Cheshire County League side Rhyl, before going on to have considerable success in North Wales football with Portmadoc, Bethesda Athletic, Pwllheli & District, and Caernarvon Town, where he was appointed player/manager in March 1975. He later returned to play for Pwllheli, visiting the Racecourse in November 1980 for a Welsh Cup match which they lost 6-0. Haydn won every honour possible in North Wales football, as well as representing the North Wales Coast F.A. against the Scottish Junior League on six occasions. He still lives in his native Caernarfon, where he works in the construction trade.

Season	League		F.A.Cup		Welsh Cup		League Cup		Total	
	apps	gls	apps	gls	apps	gls	apps	gls	apps	gls
1964/65	6	0	-	-	3	0	-	-	9	0
1965/66	7/1	1	-	-	-	-	2	0	9/1	1
	13/1	**1**	**-**	**-**	**3**	**0**	**2**	**0**	**18/1**	**1**

JONES, Herbert — 1935 - 1937

Position; *Goalkeeper*
D.O.B; *5th October, 1910*
Birthplace; *Mostyn, Flintshire*
Died; *Wollongong, Australia 11th September, 1990*
Height; *6ft 0in* ***Weight;*** *12st 0lbs*
Debut v. *Mansfield Town (a) 11th September, 1935*
Total Appearances & Goals; *20 apps 0 gls*
Career; Rhyl Athletic; Bolton Wanderers (Trial); WREXHAM 14th May 1935; Rhyl 6th July 1937;

Bert Jones was born on the Lord Mostyn Estate in Mostyn, Flintshire, the son of the Estate's Gamekeeper. It was while playing in goal for Rhyl Athletic that Herbert was recommended to Wrexham by his eventual Father-in-law, Tommy Matthias, the ex-Wrexham and Wales half back who was scouting for Wrexham at the time. Bert was signed by the Wrexham manager Ernie Blackburn in the close season of 1935, as cover for regular first team 'keeper, Pat McMahon. Jones however was to make his Football League debut sooner than expected, when called into the side to play at Mansfield in September 1935, in a 3-2 defeat. He went on to make a further eleven League appearances that season, adding a further six League appearances in 1936/37 before his release in the summer. Jones then returned to his former club, Rhyl, where he was capped twice by the North Wales Coast F.A. against the Scottish Juniors at Greenock in 1937/38, and at Llandudno in 1938/39. Following the outbreak of World War Two Bert, who was employed by P.M.Jones, Builders at the time, worked on the building of the Barrack huts at Kinmel Park before moving to the War factory in Wrexham. At the end of WW2 he found work at Shotton Steelworks, before deciding to emigrate to Australia in 1956 with his wife and seven children. They travelled to their new life on the S.S.Strathaird and, once in Australia, Bert took up work for a firm called B.H.P. He also kept involved with football by coaching his local side, Fairy Meadow. Herbert's son, Alan, was later selected for the Australian Olympic Basketball team, but he was unable to play because of problems with his nationality papers -which happened, not once, but twice! Bert died in Australia in September 1990. His widow Betty who is also the daughter of Tommy Matthias still resides Down Under, always thinking of North Wales!!

Season	League		F.A.Cup		Welsh Cup		N.S.C.		Total	
	apps	gls	apps	gls	apps	gls	apps	gls	apps	gls
1935/36	12	0	-	-	1	0	1	0	14	0
1936/37	6	0	-	-	-	-	-	-	6	0
	18	**0**	**-**	**-**	**1**	**0**	**1**	**0**	**20**	0

JONES, Herbert Neville — 1951 - 1952

Position; *Inside-Forward*
D.O.B; *20th January, 1929*
Birthplace; *Mold, Flintshire*
Height; *5ft 9in* ***Weight;*** *11st 3lbs*
Debut v. *Southport (a) 8th March, 1952*
Total Appearances & Goals; *1 app 0 gls*
Career; *Bolton Wanderers (Trial) Aug 1945; Rhyl 1946; Mold Alexandra Mar 1949; Colwyn Bay Feb 1950, (Pro) 30th Oct 1950; WREXHAM 31st Jul 1951; Llandudno 22nd Jul 1952; Borough United 17th Dec 1954; Buckley Rovers 26th Mar 1955; Colwyn Bay 14th Aug 1956; Penmaenmawr 13th Oct 1956; Holywell Town 25th Jun 1957;*

Neville Jones attended Mold Alun Grammar School, where he played football at inside-right and at the age of 16 was invited for trials with Bolton Wanderers. Despite scoring four goals nothing came of this trial period, and he returned home, where he was invited to play for Rhyl's Welsh League side. He was then called up for his National Service with the Army, serving in Egypt, playing for the G.H.Q.Middle-East Land Forces. Unfortunately, he sustained a serious knee injury whilst in the Army, which meant spending many months in hospital and remedial centres. Upon his demobilisation in March 1949 he assisted the Rustproof Metal Co and Mold Alex, before signing for Colwyn Bay in February 1950, managed at the time by former Wrexham player, Gib Bellis. His debut was a game of very mixed fortunes: he scored twice against Portmadoc, but unfortunately, also sustained a serious knee injury and was unable to turn out again for the rest of the season. The 1950/51 season saw Neville become a regular with Colwyn Bay, and signed professional forms in October. His form throughout that season persuaded Wrexham to sign him in July 1951, although playing mainly Cheshire League football for the reserve side. He finally made his Football League debut for the Club in March 1952, at Southport, in place of Ron Hewitt. Wrexham lost 2-1, although Jones did hit the upright with just a few minutes remaining. After that game, he returned to the reserve team, remaining until the end of the season, when released by the club. Neville then joined Welsh League side Llandudno, for just under three seasons, before signing for Borough United. He went on to play for a number of North Wales teams, including Buckley Rovers, another spell with Colwyn Bay, Penmaenmawr, and Holywell Town, meeting up again with ex-Wrexham players Les Speed, Ron Wynn, Charlie Kelsall, and Albert Parker. Neville finished playing football in 1958, after his firm insisted that he did so. He worked as an Insurance Inspector until 1973, when branching out on his own as an Insurance broker. Neville now lives in retirement in Hawarden, Flintshire.

Season	League		F.A.Cup		Welsh Cup		Total	
	apps	gls	apps	gls	apps	gls	apps	gls
1951/52	1	0	-	-	-	-	1	0
	1	**0**	**-**	**-**	**-**	**-**	**1**	**0**

JONES, James — 1924 - 1926

Position; *Centre-Forward*
D.O.B; *1901*
Birthplace; *Treorchy, Glamorgan*
Died; *Pontypool c1977*
Height; *5ft 10in* ***Weight;*** *11st 7lbs*
Debut v. *Tranmere Rovers (a) 22nd November, 1924*
Total Appearances & Goals; *45 apps 27 gls*
Career; *Ton Pentre 6th Oct 1919; Cardiff City 10th May 1922 £1,000 11apps 2gls; WREXHAM 14th Nov 1924; Aberdare Athletic 22nd Sept 1926 31apps 19gls; Torquay United Jun 1927 20apps 6gls; Worcester City Jan 1929 (trial);*
Honours; *One Welsh international cap; Welsh Cup Winner 1925; Welsh Cup runner-up 1922;*

Jimmy Jones joined Wrexham from Cardiff City in November 1924. He had previously played for Ton Pentre since 1919, where he had impressed in the 1922 Welsh Cup final against Cardiff City, and they wasted no time in signing him up. Jimmy made his Football League debut for the

'Bluebirds' on New Year's Day 1924 at Middlesbrough, in a 1-0 win. He went on to make a further ten League appearances that season, scoring twice. However, the following season he found himself out of favour, and by November was allowed to move North and sign for the new Wrexham manager Charlie Hewitt, along with his Cardiff team mate, Jack Nock. Jimmy went straight into the first team at Tranmere, but failed to score in Wrexham's 2-0 defeat. He did score in the following match though, a 2-2 draw at Barrow, and his goalscoring record for Wrexham became very impressive. As a result Jones was chosen to play for Wales against Ireland in a full international in April 1925. The game was played on the Racecourse, and ended in a 0-0 draw. It proved to be his only cap for Wales, but, a few days later, won a Welsh Cup winners' medal when he scored two goals in Wrexham's 3-1 win over Flint Town. He continued to score goals throughout the following season, but was surprisingly allowed to leave the Racecourse at the end of it, returning to South Wales where he joined Football League Division Three South side Aberdare Athletic. During his time with Wrexham Jimmy was described as a 'centre forward with great shooting and heading powers'. He scored 19 goals in 31 League games for Aberdare, but not enough to save them from going out of the Football League at the end of the season. Jayes was then transferred to their replacement in the Football League, Torquay United, and played in their first ever Football League game on 27th August, 1927, which ended in a 1-1 draw with local rivals Exeter City. Jimmy stayed with the 'Gulls' for a season before later joining Worcester City in January 1929 for a trial. However, he made just one appearance for Worcester, in a friendly against Bristol Rovers, but was not offered a contract, as Worcester signed former England international Jimmy Moore instead. After retiring from football he became a steward of Tonypandy Businessmen's Club, and was later reported to be working as a baker in Cardiff. He is believed to have died in 1977, in the Pontypool area.

Season	League		F.A.Cup		Welsh Cup		Total	
	apps	gls	apps	gls	apps	gls	apps	gls
1924/25	23	11	1	0	4	4	28	15
1925/26	17	12	-	-	-	-	17	12
	40	**23**	**1**	**0**	**4**	**4**	**45**	**27**

JONES, John 1947 - 1948

Position; *Outside-Right*
D.O.B; *9th April, 1921*
Birthplace; *Gwersyllt, Denbighshire*
Height; *5ft 8in* ***Weight;*** *11st 4lbs*
Debut v. *York City (a) 27th May, 1947*
Total Appearances & Goals; *24 apps 5 gls*
Career; *Army; WREXHAM Sept 1946, (Pro) 20th Jun 1947; Doncaster Rovers 28th Jul 1948 (Part-exchange) 6apps 0gls; New Brighton 4th Aug 1949 77apps 11gls; Ellesmere Port Town cs1951; Llandudno 18th Aug 1952;*

Jack Jones joined Wrexham after the end of World War Two in September 1946, following his demobilisation from the Army. He initially played for the reserve side in the Cheshire League, mainly to gain match fitness, before making his senior bow towards the end of the 1946/47 season. His Football League debut came at centre forward in place of Jack Boothway, in a 2-2 draw at York City, and he kept his place for the remaining three matches of the season. Jack Then began the following season at outside right, before he was displaced by Dennis Grainger, though Jones was to win the tussle for the shirt again for a short spell later in the season. He was allowed to join Doncaster Rovers in the summer of 1948 in an exchange deal which saw goalkeeper Archie Ferguson move in the opposite direction. A 'big fee' was also paid to 'Rovers' as part of the deal. Jack made his 'Rovers' debut in the opening match of the season, a 2-2 draw at Mansfield Town. He played in the next five League games, but received a leg injury and was unable to regain his place in the side. In July 1949, he joined New Brighton, and placed straight into their first team for his debut in a 1-0 home win over Darlington in the opening game of the 1949/50 season. Jones became a regular in the New Brighton side for the next two seasons at inside-right, rarely missing a match. During his time with 'The Rakers', he was described as having 'one of the neatest body feints in the division, and it was a joy to see him sending the defence the wrong way before slipping the ball through to the wing man.' However, Jack's Football League career came to an unexpected end in the summer of 1951. He played in the final match of the season against Shrewsbury Town which saw New Brighton lose 4-2 to finish bottom of the Third Division North. Less than a month later New Brighton failed to gain re-admission to the Football League. Jack then went into non-league football with Ellesmere Port Town, where he spent one season before returning to North Wales to join Llandudno in August 1952.

Season	League		F.A.Cup		Welsh Cup		Total	
	apps	gls	apps	gls	apps	gls	apps	gls
1946/47	4	0	-	-	-	-	4	0
1947/48	16	1	1	1	3	3	20	5
	20	**1**	**1**	**1**	**3**	**3**	**24**	**5**

JONES, John Allan 1963 - 1965

Position; *Goalkeeper*
D.O.B; *12th September, 1939*
Birthplace; *Cefn Mawr, Denbighshire*
Height; *6ft 1in* ***Weight;*** *12st 7lbs*
Debut v. *Southend United (h) 31st August, 1963*
Total Appearances & Goals; *23 apps 0 gls*
Career; *Druids United; Cardiff City Jun 1957 (am) 9th May 1958 (pro) 1app 0gls; Exeter City 14th Jul 1959 90apps 0gls; Norwich City 25th July 1962 9apps 0gls; WREXHAM 29th Aug 1963 (Exchange for Ron Barnes and small fee); Worcester City Jul 1964; Sydney FC (Australia) 1965; Witton Albion; Ellesmere Port Town; Sydney FC (Australia);*
Honours; *Welsh Youth International; Welsh Youth Cup Winner 1957;*

Allan Jones showed a great deal of early promise as a goalkeeper, having attended Ruabon Grammar School, where he had represented Denbighshire Schoolboys. Upon leaving school he joined local side, Druids United, with whom he won a Welsh Youth Cup Winners' medal, following their 4-2 victory over Swansea Town in the 1957 final. Not long after this he gained international recognition when he won a Welsh Youth cap, playing for Wales in a 0-0 draw against Scotland in Edinburgh. Not surprisingly, he soon attracted the attention of the Football League clubs, although it wasn't his local side who signed him, but Cardiff City, who tempted him away from Druids at the age of seventeen. However, Allan had to wait patiently for his first team debut, which didn't come until April 1958 when he made his Football League baptism in a 3-1 defeat at Rotherham United. It was following that match that Jones was signed on professional terms, but remained in Cardiff's reserve side throughout the whole of following season and, at the end of it was released. Allan then joined Exeter City for three years, making his debut in a 2-0 home win over Chester in September 1959. He established himself in the Exeter team until July 1962, when he was signed by Norwich City. Allan made nine League appearances for the 'Canaries' before returning to North Wales in the close season of 1963 in a part-exchange deal that saw him (and a small fee) join Wrexham in exchange for Ron Barnes. At the Racecourse, Jones made his debut in a 3-1 home defeat by Southend in August 1963. He was to spend the season contesting the 'keeper's shirt with Steve Fleet, before finding himself released in the summer. He then joined Worcester City, before trying his luck in Australia and playing for Sydney FC. On his return he continued playing football for Cheshire County League side Witton Albion, and then Ellesmere Port Town eventually moving permanently to Australia. He kept playing football once again for Sydney, while also becoming a Policeman, and later set up his own haulage business. He is still residing Down Under.

Season	League		F.A.Cup		Welsh Cup		League Cup		Total	
	apps	gls	apps	gls	apps	gls	apps	gls	apps	gls
1963/64	18	0	3	0	2	0	-	-	23	0
	18	**0**	**3**	**0**	**2**	**0**	**-**	**-**	**23**	**0**

JONES, John R. 1922 - 1924

Position; *Inside-Left*
D.O.B;
Birthplace; *Hawarden, Flintshire*
Height; *5ft 6in* ***Weight;*** *10st 6lbs*
Debut v. *Grimsby Town (a) 26th August, 1922*
Total Appearances & Goals; *64 apps 15 gls*
Career; *Whitchurch; WREXHAM 26th Jun 1922; Crewe Alexandra cs1924 8apps 1gls; Sandbach Ramblers 1926;*

Jack Jones had signed for Wrexham from Whitchurch during the close season of 1922. He was plunged straight into the first team at inside left for his Football League debut, in the initial game of the 1922/23 season at Grimsby, where Wrexham suffered the indignity of losing 4-0. Despite the result, Jack went on to miss just four League games that season, scoring his first goal on his home debut in the return match with Grimsby in a 1-1 draw. He scored a total of eleven League goals that season, but the following campaign eventually lost his place to Billy Toms, a new signing from Stockport County in October. Jones made a further ten League appearances, but was transferred to Crewe Alexandra at the end of the season. He made his debut for the 'Railwaymen' in the opening match of the 1924/25 season, a 2-0 home defeat by Tranmere Rovers. However, in the two years that he spent with the Gresty Road club he was to make just seven more League appearances, scoring one goal in a 2-1 home win over Hartlepool United in December 1925. He is later believed to have joined Sandbach Ramblers.

Season	League		F.A.Cup		Welsh Cup		Total	
	apps	gls	apps	gls	apps	gls	apps	gls
1922/23	34	11	3	0	3	1	40	12
1923/24	21	2	1	0	2	1	24	3
	55	**13**	**4**	**0**	**5**	**2**	**64**	**15**

JONES, Joseph Patrick 1973 - 1975, 1978 - 1982 & 1987-1992

Position; *Defender*
D.O.B; *4th March, 1955*
Birthplace; *Bangor, Gwynedd*
Height; *5ft 10in* ***Weight;*** *11st 1lbs*
Debut v. *Chester (a) 13th January, 1973 (Welsh Cup)*
Total Appearances & Goals; *472/3 apps 22 glsCareer; WREXHAM Jan 1973; Liverpool 15th July 1975 £110,000 72apps 3gls; WREXHAM 19th Oct 1978 £210,000 (Record transfer fee paid by Wrexham); Chelsea 25th Oct 1982 £40,000 76/2apps 2gls; Huddersfield Town 16th Aug 1985 £30,000 67/1apps 3gls; WREXHAM 12th Aug 1987 £7,000;*
Honours; *72 Welsh International caps; 4 Welsh under-21 International caps; Welsh Youth International cap; European Cup Winner 1977; Football League Championship Winner 1977; Second Division Championship Winner 1984; European Super Cup Winner 1977; F.A.Cup runner-up 1977; Welsh Cup Winner 1975; Welsh Cup runner-up 1981, 1988 & 1991; F.A.Charity Shield Winner 1976 & 1977; Central League Championship Winner 1976; Welsh Youth Cup Winner 1971;*

Joey Jones is a Wrexham legend, and will forever retain a prominent part in the Club's history. His affinity with the Club began when he left school in 1971 to become one of manager John Neal's crop of promising youngsters. Joey progressed quickly, and was called up for his first team debut at the age of just 17 in a local 'derby' against Chester in a Welsh Cup tie, which Wrexham lost 1-0. Shrugging off that disappointment Joey went on to make his Football League debut in the following match, a 1-1 draw at Rotherham. He immediately established himself in the first team at right-back, going on to become a member of the Wrexham team that reached the quarter-finals of the F.A.Cup for the first time in the club's history during the 1973/74 season, beating Second Division sides, Crystal Palace and Middlesbrough, and First Division Southampton before going out to First Division Burnley. Joey won his first domestic honour in 1975 when Wrexham beat Cardiff City in the Welsh Cup final, but before he could make his debut in European football, was sold to Liverpool, the Club that he had supported as a boy, for a club record fee received by Wrexham of £110,000. Joey went straight into the first team for his debut, a 2-0 defeat at Queens Park Rangers. He made twelve more League appearances that season before replaced initially by Alec Lindsay and then by Tommy Smith as Liverpool went on to win the League Championship. Meanwhile Joey helped the reserve side to the Central League Championship. The following season saw him re-establish himself in the first team, as he missed just three League games, Liverpool winning yet another title as well as lifting the European Cup, the first English side to do so since Manchester United in 1968. Co-incidentally it was United who had beaten Liverpool in the F.A.Cup final four days prior to that European Cup win over Borussia Monchengladbach. That season saw Joey become the idol of the Anfield 'Kop', with the clenched fist salute that became his hallmark throughout his playing career. He also scored his first goal for Liverpool against Leicester City. It came at the Anfield Road end of the ground, and he ran the full length of the pitch to take the applause of the 'Kop'. At Liverpool, he won the first of his 72 Welsh caps, a record finally beaten by Peter Nicholas in 1991, when he selected for the 1-0 European Championship win over Austria on his beloved Racecourse Ground. In October 1978 Joey rejoined the now Second Division Wrexham, for £210,000, which still stands as a record fee paid by the Club. During this second spell at the Racecourse, he added only a Welsh Cup runners-up medal to his trophy cabinet, although it did give him the opportunity to play alongside his brother Frank in a League match. In October 1982, after Wrexham had been relegated to the Third Division, Joey joined his former manager John Neal at Chelsea, teaming up again with his close friends and former Wrexham players Eddie Niedzwiecki and Mickey Thomas. All three helped Chelsea to win the Second Division Championship in 1984, despite Joey commuting from his Wrexham home throughout his time at Stamford Bridge! The 1984/85 season saw Jones appearances for Chelsea limited as Doug Rougvie was preferred at left back, and in August 1985 he returned North to join Huddersfield Town for £30,000. He stayed at Leeds Road for two seasons before rejoining Wrexham for his third spell in August 1987. In his first season back at the Racecourse he helped the club to reach the Fourth Division play-off final against Leyton Orient, where Wrexham disappointingly lost 2-1 on aggregate. Then in December 1989, he was appointed player/coach to the new manager Brian Flynn, adding two more Welsh Cup runners'-up medals to his honours tally in 1988 and 1991. On his 37th birthday, in March 1992, Joey announced his retirement from playing first team football to concentrate on his coaching, although continuing to turn out for the reserves on a regular basis. He was even called upon to play for the first team against the Isle of Man in 1997, at the age of 42! Joey is, and always will be, remembered for his 100% effort given on the football field. He is one of the most likeable characters in football; never stops thinking of others, and has done so much work for charity. Joey Jones still remains on the coaching staff at Wrexham.

Season	League		F.A.Cup		Welsh Cup		League Cup		F.R.T.		E.C.W.C.		Total	
	apps	gls	apps	gls	apps	gls	apps	gls	apps	gls	apps	gls	apps	gls
1972/73	17	0	-	-	1	0	-	-	-	-	-	-	18	0
1973/74	41	0	7	0	3	0	2	0	-	-	-	-	53	0
1974/75	40	2	1	0	5	0	1	0	-	-	-	-	47	2
1978/79	30	2	1	0	3	0	-	-	-	-	-	-	34	2
1979/80	36	3	4	1	2	0	4	0	-	-	2	0	48	4
1980/81	37	1	5	0	4	0	2	0	-	-	-	-	48	1
1981/82	35	0	4	0	2	0	5	0	-	-	-	-	46	0
1982/83	7	0	-	-	-	-	2	0	-	-	-	-	9	0
1987/88	35	0	-	-	4	0	2	0	2	1	-	-	43	1
1988/89	41	8	2	0	3	0	2	0	4	1	-	-	52	9
1989/90	23/1	1	1	0	4	0	2	0	1	0	-	-	31/1	1
1990/91	21	2	1	0	4	0	-	-	0/1	0	0/1	0	26/2	2
1991/92	11	0	1	0	1	0	2	0	2	0	-	-	17	0
	374/1	**19**	**27**	**1**	**36**	**0**	**24**	**0**	**9/1**	**2**	**2/1**	**0**	**472/3**	**22**

JONES, Kenneth Boothroyd 1954 - 1960

Position; *Left-Back*
D.O.B; *11th May, 1937*
Birthplace; *Rhosllanerchrugog, Denbighshire*
Height; *5ft 10in* **Weight;** *11st 3lbs*
Debut v. *Carlisle United (h) 2nd November, 1957*
Total Appearances & Goals; *36 apps 0 gls*
Career; *WREXHAM 14th May 1954; Crystal Palace 28th May 1960 4apps 0gls; Swindon Town 6th Mar 1961 35apps 0gls; Colwyn Bay 15th Aug 1962; Stafford Rangers 1966; Oswestry Town Jan 1967; Staffordshire Police;*
Honours; *Three Welsh Youth International Caps; Three Welsh Schoolboy international caps;*

Ken Jones played for his school team, Ysgol Grango, in his native Rhos from an early age. He also represented Wrexham and District Schoolboys, playing in the final of the Welsh Schools' Shield. He was also selected to play for the Welsh Schoolboys side, making three appearances, which eventually led to trials with Wrexham. He was then taken on to the groundstaff at the Racecourse upon leaving school, and quickly made his way through the junior ranks at the club. Jones played for the Welsh National League side at first, before moving up to the reserve team in the Cheshire League. His progress was also monitored by the Welsh selectors, who called him up for the Welsh Youth side, with whom he also made three appearances. Ken's hopes of pushing for a first team place were knocked back in 1955 when called up for his National Service. He joined the Royal Welch Fusiliers, together with Roy Vernon, who went on to play for Everton and Wales. Ken was fortunate to be stationed at the barracks in Hightown, Wrexham, which meant he could continue playing for Wrexham. However, it wasn't until his demobilisation that he was to finally able to make his first team debut, replacing Aly McGowan for a Football League match at Carlisle United in November 1957 which Wrexham won 1-0. Ken also played in the following match against Southport, which Wrexham also won, 3-1. His next game was a Welsh Cup tie against Flint Town United, this time deputising for Albert Parker in a 7-0 win. That same season Jones was invited for a trial with the Welsh under-23 squad, though he never actually won a cap at that level. The consistency of both Parker and McGowan, the regular full-backs at this time, meant Jones found it difficult to secure a regular first team place in the side, but the 1958/59 season saw him have a decent run in the first team in the newly formed Third Division. It was back to mostly reserve team football the following season, and he asked for a transfer in January 1960. In May, Ken was allowed to leave the Racecourse to join Crystal Palace for a 'small fee'. He had earlier turned down an offer from Southampton. Making his Palace League debut in a 2-2 draw at Hartlepool United, Ken once again found his first team chances limited. He made just three more League appearances before moving to Swindon Town on the transfer deadline day in March 1961. With Swindon fighting relegation Ken made an immediate impact as they beat Hull City 3-0 on his debut, going on to avoid the drop. The following season he was appointed captain, and went on to make a total of 35 League appearances before the end of 1961/62. Jones left Swindon following a dispute with manager Bert Head over a move to Leicester City. He decided to return to North Wales, to join the Denbighshire Constabulary as a Police Constable in May 1962. However, Ken did continue to play non-league football for Colwyn Bay, as well as the Denbighshire Police team. He spent three seasons with Colwyn Bay, also playing against Wrexham in a Welsh Cup match. He joined the Staffordshire Police Force in 1966, and in doing so, also signed for Stafford Rangers. Ken was with Stafford for a couple of seasons before he joined Oswestry Town where he once again played against Wrexham in a Welsh Cup match. During his time with the Police Ken also represented both the Welsh and British Police XIs, appearing in three European Police tournaments, each time finishing runners-up to West Germany. After leaving Oswestry in 1972 he continued to play football for the Police side in the Midlands League. As for his career, he worked his way up the ranks from constable right through to Chief Superintendent, in which position he retired in 1993. Ken then took up work with Staffordshire County Council as Emergency planning officer, which involved co-ordinating all the emergency services in the event of a local disaster. During the 1996/97 season Ken took up an offer to coach Eastern Albanian side, Sopoti, which he did until their mid-season break, although he had a hasty return home following the outbreak of Civil War when he was involved in a dramatic escape! He has since been involved with coaching youngsters at Stafford Rangers.

Season	League		F.A.Cup		Welsh Cup		Total	
	apps	gls	apps	gls	apps	gls	apps	gls
1957/58	3	0	-	-	1	-	4	0
1958/59	22	0	-	-	4	0	26	0
1959/60	6	0	-	-	-	-	6	0
	31	**0**	**-**	**-**	**5**	**0**	**36**	**0**

JONES, Kevin Richard 1990 - 1994

Position; *Right-Back*
D.O.B; *16th February, 1974*
Birthplace; *Wrexham, Denbighshire*
Height; *5ft 10in* **Weight;** *11st 0lbs*
Debut v. *Manchester United (h) 7th November, 1990 (European Cup Winners Cup)*
Total Appearances & Goals; *5/2 apps 0 gls*
Career; *WREXHAM Jul 1990; Bangor City Jul 1994 89/17apps 3gls; Holywell Town Mar 1997 9/3apps 0gls; Flint Town United Aug 1997 34/2apps 1gls;*
Honours; *Welsh Youth international; Two Welsh Youth Cup Winner 1991 & 1992; Welsh National League Championship Winner 1992; League of Wales Championship Winner 1995; Welsh Semi-professional International cap;*

Kevin Jones played his schoolboy football for Pen-y-ffordd Primary, and Castell Alun Secondary School teams. He also represented Deeside Primary Schools, Flintshire Schoolboys, North Wales Schoolboys, and had trials for the Welsh Schoolboy team. Later, he appeared for Pen-y-ffordd in the local Junior League, during which time he was a prolific goalscorer leading him to trials with both Crewe Alexandra and Everton. Upon leaving school in July 1990 he signed for Wrexham on Y.T.S. forms, and what a dream start he had! He had been on the club's books only a few months when, due to UEFA's foreign player ruling at that time, he was selected to travel to Denmark as a substitute in a European Cup-Winners' Cup match against Lyngby. After Wrexham achieved a 1-0 aggregate win they were drawn against the team Kevin supported, Manchester United. He was again on the substitutes bench for the match at Old Trafford, as he was for the return match on the Racecourse. This proved to be the highlight of his career, when he replaced Chris Armstrong in the second half, as a very spirited Wrexham side, battled to restrict United to a 2-0 victory. Kevin went on to represent Wales at Youth level, and also picked up a Welsh National League Championship medal with the reserve side in a season when he scored many goals. However, youth coach Cliff Sear was to convert Kevin from a forward into a promising right back, a

position where he did sufficiently well to earn himself a professional contract. He made his Football League debut in March 1992, at home to Lincoln City, when he came on as substitute for an injured Brian Flynn, before going on to make a further five appearances over the next two seasons. Kevin remained as understudy to the club's regular right back, Barry Jones, throughout this time and, at the end of the 1993/94 season, was released. Despite the setback, he soon found another club when joining League of Wales Champions, Bangor City. Kevin played in both their UEFA Cup matches against the Icelandic side, IA Akranes, which they lost 4-1 on aggregate. That same season, Jones went on to help Bangor win the League of Wales championship for the second successive year, as well as earning selection for the Welsh semi-pro team against England. He remained at Farrar Road until March 1997, when signed by Holywell Town to boost their relegation battle. However, they failed to pull clear of the drop zone and the Halkyn Road club were relegated to the Cymru Alliance League. Kevin continued in the League of Wales when he signed for Flint Town United in August 1997 and is still at Cae-y-Castell at the time of writing.

Season	League		F.A.Cup		Welsh Cup		League Cup		F.R.T.		E.C.W.C.		Total	
	apps	gls	apps	gls	apps	gls	apps	gls	apps	gls	apps	gls	apps	gls
1990/91	-	-	-	-	-	-	-	-	-	-	0/1	0	0/1	0
1991/92	0/1	0	-	-	-	-	-	-	-	-	-	-	0/1	0
1992/93	3	0	-	-	-	-	-	-	-	-	-	-	3	0
1993/94	2	0	-	-	-	-	-	-	-	-	-	-	2	0
	5/1	**0**	**-**	**-**	**-**	**-**	**-**	**-**	**-**	**-**	**0/1**	**0**	**5/2**	**0**

JONES, Philip Lee — 1991 - 1992, 1996 & 1997

Position; *Forward*
D.O.B; *29th May, 1973*
Birthplace; *Wrexham, Denbighshire*
Height; *5ft 9in* ***Weight;*** *10st 5lbs*
Debut v. *Manchester United (h) 7th November, 1990 (ECWC)*
Total Appearances & Goals; *56/24 apps 24 gls*
Career; *Lex XI; WREXHAM (YTS) Jun 1990 (Pro) 5th Jul 1991; Liverpool 12th March 1992 £300,000; Crewe Alexandra 3rd Sept 1993 4/4apps 1gls (Loan); WREXHAM 26th Jan 1996 (Loan); WREXHAM 30th Jan 1997 (Loan); Tranmere Rovers 27th Mar 1997 (Loan) 8apps 5gls; Tranmere Rovers 3rd Jun 1997 £100,000 46/16apps 11gls;*
Honours; *Two Welsh International caps; Twelve Welsh Under-21 international caps;*

Wrexham-born, Lee Jones attended Rhosddu and Groves Schools in the town. His progress through schoolboy football was steady, but unspectacular with his only representative honours gained with the district team at 12 years-old. He played for Druids at under-12 and 14 levels before switching to play for Garden Village at under-16s, and also turning out for Lex XI. After leaving school Lee went to Yale College to re-sit a number of GCSEs. However, his life took a dramatic turn around while playing for the college team against Lex XI, when spotted by Wrexham coach, Idris Pryce. He was offered a YTS place after a trial, but Lee was to finish his exams before joining the other Wrexham players for pre-season training in 1990, and didn't have long to wait for his first team debut. It came in sensational style, when he played in the second round second leg match of a European Cup-Winners' Cup match against Manchester United on the Racecourse, which Wrexham eventually lost 2-0 on the night. Lee was soon playing first team football; most of his early appearances were as a substitute, including a dramatic intorduction against West Ham United in an F.A.Cup Fourth Round tie in 1992, when he scored the equalising goal in a 2-2 draw at Upton Park. Not long after that match, Liverpool manager Graeme Souness, splashed out a equal record fee received by Wrexham at the time, of £300,000 for Lee, including the possibility of raising the fee a further £300,000 depending on appearances made for the Anfield club. Jones spent most of his time at Liverpool playing in the Central League side, and just when a first team spot beckoned he was struck by an injury jinx, which also saw him suffer a broken leg, meaning a certain Robbie Fowler stepping ahead of him in the pecking order for a first team place. The rest is history, as they say. As for Lee, once recovered from his set back, he was loaned out to Crewe Alexandra in September 1993, where he made eight League appearances, scoring one goal. He then had two further loan spells back at the Racecourse, in January 1996 to the end of that season and in January 1997 for just over a month. In between, he had made three Premier League substitute appearances for Liverpool, before he finally turned down an offer from Wrexham manager, Brian Flynn to return on a permanent basis, deciding instead to join First Division Tranmere Rovers on loan in March 1997. He had a successful spell at Prenton Park, scoring five goals in just eight League appearances, which saw a petition from Rovers' fans to sign him, which manager, John Aldridge eventually did for £100,000, just weeks after he had made his full international debut for Wales, as a substitute against Scotland in a 1-0 win in June 1997. He won his second cap, also as a substitute, in a World Cup match in Turkey in August 1997, helping Tranmere to a finish in a mid-table position the following season. His forte is 'pace' and is used as a wide right winger to get around opposing defences at Prenton Park, but has been unfortunate with injuries.

Season	League		F.A.Cup		Welsh Cup		League Cup		F.R.T.		E.C.W.C.		Total	
	apps	gls	apps	gls	apps	gls	apps	gls	apps	gls	apps	gls	apps	gls
1990/91	13/5	5	-	-	2/1	1	-	-	-	-	1	0	16/6	6
1991/92	11/10	4	1/2	1	1/2	2	2	0	3	2	-	-	18/14	9
1995/96	20	9	-	-	-	-	-	-	-	-	-	-	20	9
1996/97	2/4	0	-	-	-	-	-	-	-	-	-	-	2/4	0
	46/19	**18**	**1/2**	**1**	**3/3**	**3**	**2**	**0**	**3**	**2**	**1**	**0**	**56/24**	**24**

JONES, Mark Anthony — 1981 - 1982

Position; *Full-Back*
D.O.B; *27th May, 1963*
Birthplace; *Colwyn Bay, Flintshire*
Height; *5ft 6in* ***Weight;*** *11st 3lbs*
Debut v. *Cardiff City (a) 9th February, 1982 (Welsh Cup)*
Total Appearances & Goals; *1 app 0 gls*
Career; *WREXHAM cs1981; Conwy United cs1982; IK Kraft (Finland) 1983; Conwy United 1983/84; IK Kraft (Finland) 1984; Conwy United 1984/85; Bethesda Athletic cs1986; Rhyl cs1987; Caernarfon Town Feb 1988; Conwy United cs1990 33/20apps 2gls; Llandudno Aug 1994; Holywell Town Oct 1994 59/3apps 6gls; Flint Town United Sept 1996 10apps 0gls; Llandudno Jul 1997;*
Honours; *Welsh Youth Cup Winner 1981; Welsh Youth Cup runner-up 1980; N.W.C.F.A. Representative matches; Welsh Alliance League Championship Winner 1985, 1986 & 1987;*

Mark Jones played his early football for Deganwy Primary and Aberconwy Secondary Schools on the North Wales coast. He was also selected for his District School team, and for the North Wales Coast under-18s side in their Cymro Cup games at Bangor and in South Wales. It was at the age of 14 that Mark came to the attention of Wrexham's North Wales Coast scout, the late Mr.Evan Williams from Llandudno, who had previously discovered the likes of Joey Jones and Mickey Thomas. Mark was playing for Conwy United at the time, in the old Welsh League, and he was persuaded to sign schoolboy forms for Wrexham. Mark progressed through the Wrexham schoolboy teams and signed apprentice forms for the Club upon leaving school at the age of 16 in 1979. He went on to spend two years as an apprentice, during which time he played for the Wrexham Youth side that beat Liverpool 1-0 at Anfield, in an English F.A.Youth Cup first round tie. He also appeared in the semi-finals of a youth tournament held at PSV Eindhoven in Holland. Mark played in the 1980 Welsh Youth Cup final for Wrexham, where they were beaten 2-1 by Cardiff City at Rhayader. However, he improved upon that the following season, helping them to lift the trophy with a 6-1 win over South Wales side Afan Lido at Llanidloes. He was still an apprentice when making his first team debut, against Cardiff City in a Welsh Cup quarter-final match at Ninian Park, which Wrexham lost 4-1 with Jones playing at left-back in place of Phil Bater. Mark was signed on professional terms, upon finishing his apprenticeship in 1981, but with a new manager in Mel Sutton, and the club fighting against relegation, it was not the time to give youth a chance. Because of this situation Mark was never actually given another opportunity to play for the first team, and was released at the end of the 1981/82 season, after three years at the club. He then returned to Conwy United, at the same time taking up a job offer of working in the building trade as a labourer and painter. After six months with Conwy, he accepted a chance of playing in Finland with Second Division side, I.F.Kraft in May 1983. He then returned to Conwy for the following season, moving back to Finland at the end of the 1983/84 season, again playing for I.F.Kraft. On resuming with Conwy United once again, he picked up two Welsh Alliance League Championship trophies in 1985 and 1986, as well as a Barritt Cup winners' medal. He joined Bethesda Athletic for the 1986/87 season, winning another Welsh Alliance League Championship medal, before playing for Rhyl in the Northern Premier League for around a season and a half. Mark followed his spell at Belle Vue by joining fellow Northern Premier League side Caernarfon Town, but his season was over by Christmas when having to go into hospital for a hernia operation. Once fit, Jones left the Oval to rejoin Conwy United, and soon was appointed as the Club's player/manager in the close season of 1990. Mark went on to lead Conwy into the newly formed League of Wales in 1992 and played in and

managed The Morfa club for the opening game in the Welsh flagship League, at Briton Ferry Athletic, in August 1992. Mark led Conwy to finish in a very respectable seventh position in that inaugural season, and followed this by ending their second season in 13th place. However, Mark was disappointingly relieved of his duties in May 1994. He signed for Cymru Alliance League side, Llandudno in August, but soon returned to the League of Wales when Holywell Town manager Glyn Griffiths snapped up the popular left back, and spent the rest of the season at Halkyn Road. However, the 1995/96 season was only a few months old when Griffiths resigned as the manager and, in December 1995, Mark was given his second chance in management. He went on to remain in that position until the start of the 1996/97 season, when he was dismissed. Mark was quickly signed by Flint Town United, where he spent the rest of that season. 1997/98 saw Jones playing for Cymru Alliance League side Llandudno, combining playing with working as a self-employed electrician. His father, Ron Jones, was a Football League referee, and had been a F.I.F.A. linesman at many big matches involving the likes of Manchester United, Liverpool, Barcelona etc. However, following his return from refereeing a match between Hereford United and Swindon Town in September 1975, Ron was involved in a car crash in which he died. He had just qualified as a F.I.F.A referee and was due to take control of Ireland v. Belgium the following week.

Season	League		F.A.Cup		Welsh Cup		League Cup		Total	
	apps	gls	apps	gls	apps	gls	apps	gls	apps	gls
1981/82	-	-	-	-	1	0	-	-	1	0
	-	-	-	-	1	0	-	-	1	0

JONES, Norman Glyn

1941 - 1947

Position; *Goalkeeper*
D.O.B; *15th November, 1923*
Birthplace; *Rhostyllen, Denbighshire*
Height; *6ft 0in* **Weight;** *12st 7lbs*
Debut v. *Doncaster Rovers (h) 26th December, 1946*
Total Appearances & Goals; *16 apps 0 gls*
Career; *WREXHAM (Am) Mar 1941, (Pro) 15th Sept 1941; Crewe Alexandra (WW2 Guest) 1app 0gls; Runcorn Jun 1947; Worcester City Jul 1949; Runcorn cs1951; Holywell Town Jan 1952; Tonbridge Jul 1952;*
Honours; *Cheshire County League representative XI;*

As a youngster Norman Jones would stand behind the goal where older fellows would be playing football and 'fielded the goals and misses by stopping as many as possible'. And so a goalkeeper was born! He became a big Wrexham fan in the 1930's when he was attending the Victoria School in Poyser Street, which later became known as the Central School. He played in goal for the school team, and impressed sufficiently to earn a call-up to the Wrexham & District Schools side that reached the quarter-finals of the Welsh Schools Shield in 1936/37. He ended up on the losing side following a 3-0 defeat to a Swansea Boys team that included Trevor Ford, in front of a Vetch Field crowd of 7,000. He was later capped by the Welsh Boys team, playing three times, against England at Ninian Park, Scotland at Hamilton's Douglas Park, and Ireland at Distillery's ground in Belfast. Norman finally left school in 1937, when he was only 14, becoming a trainee salesman with John Leach (Furnishers) in the Town. He would do everything from window cleaning and deliveries to a little selling, but by then he had also become associated with Wrexham Football Club. There was no 'A' team in those days, so manager Tom Morgan arranged for Norman to play for Cross Street in the Wrexham Amateur League. In those days Wrexham's reserve side were operating in the Midlands Mid-Week League, and for the very last game of the 1938/39 season he had progressed enough to be selected against Leicester City at Filbert Street. He was later told that his chance of first team football would come during the following season, but World War Two broke out after just two weeks of the new season and all football was suspended. Norman was still only 15 at that time, too young to be called up for the Army, so he continued working at Leach's while remaining on the books of Wrexham Football Club. He eventually made his first team debut against Liverpool in a Football Regional League North Division match at Anfield in March 1941, but Wrexham lost 7-2! He continued playing for Wrexham until he was called up for the Army, joining the Royal Engineers based at Aldershot, from where he was to later see service in Egypt and Palestine. He was also involved in the 'D' Day landings, which he once reckoned was "more frightening than goalkeeping!" Norman's football opportunities at this time were confined to the occasional game for Wrexham when home on leave, and in total made just thirteen further War-time appearances. He did play one game for Reading against Brentford as a 'Guest', as well as turning out for both the Royal Engineers' Depot in Aldershot, and the South Eastern Command. He also represented the British Army against the Belgian Army at the Command Central Ground, and the Palestine United Services against the Wanderers touring side. With WW2 at an end Jones wasn't demobilised until December 1946, by which time the new Football League season was already well under way. Even so, Norman's Football League debut for Wrexham came sooner than he had expected. He had left Cairo on a troopship in December 1946, only for it to break down in Malta. From there he made his way in another 'tub' to the South of France, where he spent a further two and a half days on a stop start train before finally arriving in Wrexham for Christmas Day. The following day saw Wrexham manager Tom Williams arrive on his doorstep to tell him that he was playing against the top of the League side, Doncaster Rovers.........that afternoon! Despite a 2-0 defeat, Norman was blameless for either of the goals, but his next match also proved to be his last. He played in an 8-1 Welsh Senior Cup tie win at Caernarvon, but could only follow that with a few reserve team games before being given a free transfer at the end of the season. He then joined Cheshire County League side Runcorn along with another Wrexham player, Albert Malam. During his time here he was chosen to represent the Cheshire County League XI against the Southern League XI at Wrexham in October 1948. He spent two seasons with Runcorn before being transferred to Birmingham & District League side Worcester City in July 1949. He returned to Runcorn a couple of years later after Worcester had run into dire financial problems. He spent one season with them before taking up an offer of employment with his brother's business in Ruthin. However, this fell through and he began playing football once again for Welsh League side Holywell Town. At the end of that season he received a letter from Tonbridge manager Harry Curtis, who had previously managed Brentford, offering him a good wage playing for the Kent club, and a job as an accounts clerk for Standard Telephone and Cables. He accepted, going on to spend a further three seasons in the South, before deciding to call it a day at the end of the 1954/55 season. A knee injury had helped him to make the decision to retire. He then moved to the Brewing firm, John Courage, at Tower Bridge in London, working in their accounts department. He later joined a firm of City Solicitors, initially as an assistant Admin Manager, before retiring in November 1989 as office manager. Norman, who settled in Orpington in Kent, seldom misses any Wrexham games that are played in the London area.

Season	League		F.A.Cup		Welsh Cup		Total	
	apps	gls	apps	gls	apps	gls	apps	gls
1940/41	4	0	-	-	-	-	4	0
1941/42	5	0	-	-	-	-	5	0
1942/43	3	0	-	-	-	-	3	0
1943/44	2	0	-	-	-	-	2	0
1946/47	1	0	-	-	1	0	2	0
	15	**0**	**-**	**-**	**1**	**0**	**16**	**0**
F/League	1	0	-	-	1	0	2	0

JONES, Paul Anthony 1989

Position; *Midfield*
D.O.B; *6th September, 1965*
Birthplace; *Walsall, West Midlands*
Height; *5ft 9in* ***Weight;*** *10st 4lbs*
Debut v. *Burnley (h) 27th March, 1989*
Total Appearances & Goals; *5 apps 0 gls*
Career; *Walsall Sept 1983 125/18apps 15gls; WREXHAM 23rd March 1989 (Loan); Wolves 9th Nov 1989 £15,000 7/7apps 0gls; Kettering Town cs1991 15/3apps 0gls; Stafford Rangers Mar 1992 43/2apps 2gls; Moor Green Aug 1993; Bilston Town Jul 1996; Moor Green Aug 1997;*

Paul Jones was signed straight from school on apprentice forms by Walsall, where he made his way through their Junior ranks to earn a professional contract on his eighteenth birthday in September 1983. By that time he had already made his Football League debut, a scoreless home draw with Gillingham in February 1983, as a substitute for Craig Shakespeare. Paul went on to record a total of 143 League appearances for the 'Saddlers', missing just three League games during their promotion season of 1987/88, when the 'Saddlers' were elevated to the old Second Division via the play-offs. Paul missed those play-off games because of an injury sustained against Notts County at the end of the season. Once recovered, he couldn't regain his place in the Walsall first team and was loaned out to Wrexham in March 1989. At the Racecourse, Paul replaced Brian Flynn in the side, making his debut in a 4-2 home win over Burnley. He failed to make a lasting impression, however, as Wrexham failed to win any of their next four League games, and he was allowed to return to Walsall at the end of his loan spell. Wrexham went on to reach the final of the Fourth Division play-offs. As for Paul, he found himself still very much out of favour at Walsall the following season, and in November 1989 joined Wolves for £15,000. He made his debut as a substitute in a 3-1 defeat at Watford, before going on to make a further twelve League appearances that season. The 1990/91 season saw Jones make just one further substitute appearance, as he spent most of the season in the Wolves reserve team, and not surprisingly was allowed to leave Molineux at the end of the season. He drifted into non-league football when he signed for GM Conference League side, Kettering Town, during the close season of 1991. By March 1992 he was on the move again signing for Stafford Rangers, for whom he made 45 GM Conference League appearances, while also employed as a van driver. However, he left Marston Road at the end of the 1992/93 season, and joined Dr.Martens Midland League side, Moor Green. Paul spent three seasons here before he joined fellow Midlands League side Bilston Town in the close season of 1996. After one season with Bilston he returned to Moor Green, in the summer of 1997, where he still remains playing at the time of writing.

Season	League		F.A.Cup		Welsh Cup		League Cup		F.R.T.		Total	
	apps	gls	apps	gls	apps	gls	apps	gls	apps	gls	apps	gls
1988/89	5	0	-	-	-	-	-	-	-	-	5	0
	5	**0**	**-**	**-**	**-**	**-**	**-**	**-**	**-**	**-**	**5**	**0**

JONES, Paul Phillip 1993 - 1997

Position; *Left-Back*
D.O.B; *2nd October, 1976*
Birthplace; *Wirral, Merseyside*
Height; *5ft 11in* ***Weight;*** *11st 8lbs*
Debut v. *Millwall (h) 28th March, 1997*
Total Appearances & Goals; *6 apps 0 gls*
Career; *WREXHAM 4th Jul 1995; Bangor City Jul 1997 1/4apps 0gls; Connah's Quay Nomads Sept 1997 45/2apps 5gls;*
Honours; *Welsh Youth Cup Winner 1994;*

Paul Jones grew up as a schoolboy on the Wirral. He played for his local junior side, Heswall, from the age of 11, but by then had already been signed as a schoolboy by Tranmere Rovers. He remained with Tranmere until he was 15 years old, by which time he had represented Wirral Schools, playing as a left-winger. It was around this time that Wrexham began to take an interest in him, though he had to turn them down due to his signing for Tranmere. Following his release from Prenton Park he played a few schoolboy matches for the club, before signing YTS forms for Wrexham in the summer of 1993. Within six months of being at the Racecourse Paul was switched to left-back, but disaster was to strike when he broke his leg towards the end of his apprenticeship with the club but was given a professional contract. Once he had recovered Paul began playing for the reserve side in the Pontin's League, and made a first team appearance in the summer of 1996 in Cliff Sear's testimonial match against Manchester City, when he played the second half. His Football League debut came the following Easter, when injuries to both the senior left-backs, Phil Hardy and Deryn Brace, coupled with the refusal of Manchester United's John O'Kane to join the club on loan, saw the youngster given his opportunity against Millwall on Good Friday. He played well in the 3-3 draw, despite getting booked, prompting manager Brian Flynn to say, "Sometimes you throw people in at the deep end and they come out swimming. That is what Paul did". He kept his place in the side for the next five League games when he was injured at Bristol City. Despite Paul's progress his Wrexham career came to a sudden halt at the end of the season, when he was told the disappointing news that he would not be retained. During the close season he signed for Graeme Sharp, manager of League of Wales side Bangor City, but things didn't go well for him at Farrar Road and left to join Connah's Quay Nomads towards the end of September 1997. He went on to help them reach the final of the 1998 Welsh Cup, only to disappointingly miss the game himself through suspension.

Season	League		F.A.Cup		League Cup		A.W.S.		Total	
	apps	gls	apps	gls	apps	gls	apps	gls	apps	gls
1996/97	6	0	-	-	-	-	-	-	6	0
	6	**0**	**-**	**-**	**-**	**-**	**-**	**-**	**6**	**0**

JONES, Percival 1922 - 1923

Position; *Centre-Forward*
D.O.B;
Birthplace; *Acrefair, Denbighshire*
Height; *5ft 2in* ***Weight;*** *11st 0lbs*
Debut v. *Southport (a) 6th January, 1923*
Total Appearances & Goals; *1 app 0 gls*
Career; *Acrefair United; WREXHAM (Am) Jan 1923; Acrefair United Mar 1923; Colwyn Bay Utd Aug 1923 (trial), 30th Oct 1923; Druids United 26th Aug 1927; Buckley Dec 1927;*

When Percy Jones signed for Wrexham he was described by the local newspapers as: 'Hails from Acrefair and signed from Welsh National League side Acrefair United in January 1923 as an amateur'. Percy was recruited by Wrexham at short notice to replace the injured Bill Cotton, making his Football League debut at centre forward at Southport. Despite Percy's presence Wrexham lost the match 1-0, and he found himself out of the side for the following match when Cotton returned. The Southport game proved to be Percy's one and only first team appearance for Wrexham, although he did play a few reserve team matches before March, when he returned to play for Acrefair United. Percy Jones later signed for Colwyn Bay United, in October 1923, and then went on to play local football for Druids United and Buckley.

Season	League		F.A.Cup		Welsh Cup		Total	
	apps	gls	apps	gls	apps	gls	apps	gls
1922/23	1	0	-	-	-	-	1	0
	1	**0**	-	-	-	-	**1**	**0**

JONES, Phillip Eric — 1967

Position; *Inside-Forward*
D.O.B; *30th March, 1948*
Birthplace; *Ellesmere Port, Cheshire*
Height; *5ft 8in* ***Weight;*** *10st 8lbs*
Debut v. *Halifax Town (a) 16th May, 1967*
Total Appearances & Goals; *1 app 0 gls*
Career; *Blackpool 1964, (Pro) Jan 1966; Blackburn Rovers (trial); WREXHAM 6th May 1967;*

Phil Jones had served his apprenticeship with Blackpool before he signed professional terms with the 'Tangerines' in January 1966. However, he was allowed to leave Bloomfield Road at the end of the season. Phil then joined Blackburn Rovers on trial some time during the 1966/67 season, prompting the new Wrexham manager, Alvan Williams, to take him on loan, in May 1967 until the end of the season. He made his debut for the Club in the last match of 1966/67 in a 3-1 defeat at Halifax Town, proving to be his one and only Football League appearance. Phil then returned to Ewood Park.

Season	League		F.A.Cup		Welsh Cup		League Cup		Total	
	apps	gls	apps	gls	apps	gls	apps	gls	apps	gls
1966/67	1	0	-	-	-	-	-	-	1	0
	1	**0**	-	-	-	-	-	-	**1**	**0**

JONES, Price — 1926 - 1927

Position; *Forward*
D.O.B; *21st May, 1903*
Birthplace; *Brymbo, Denbighshire*
Height; *5 ft 9in* ***Weight;*** *10st 7lbs*
Died; *Wrexham, 1983.*
Debut v. *Ashington (h) 22nd January, 1927*
Total Appearances & Goals; *1 app 0 gls*
Career; *Brymbo Juniors FC 1919; Brymbo Green FC Aug 1923; Llandudno Aug 1924; Buckley Town 16th Dec 1925; WREXHAM (Am) cs1926, (Pro) 20th Nov 1926; Rhos 7th Jul 1927; Buckley United 8th Dec 1927; Mold 8th Aug 1928; Holywell United Jan 1929; Brymbo Green Utd;*
Honours; *Flintshire League Championship Winner 1924;*

Price Jones began playing football when he was sixteen years-old for Brymbo Juniors FC in the Frith & District League in 1919. At centre forward, he scored plenty of goals in the three seasons that he spent with them. He then moved on to Brymbo Green FC, becoming the fourth brother to have played for the club. Brymbo Green later amalgamated with Brymbo Institute, becoming Brymbo and Green United, and when Price joined them they appeared in the Welsh National League. Although there are no records for this period it was well known that Price was again among the leading goalscorers. Due to the high costs of travelling, Brymbo left the W.N.L. in 1923 and joined the Flintshire League, winning the championship at the first attempt. Despite this success, it had come against weaker opposition and support for the club fell, which eventually led to them having to be disbanded. Price then joined Llandudno for a short spell, before he signed for W.N.L. side Buckley Town, where he spent a couple of seasons. He again scored frequently, finishing with 38 goals in his first season with Buckley. Wrexham began to take an interest, and they signed him on amateur forms during the close season of 1926. He played mainly for the reserve team during his one season at the club, but did make one senior appearance, when replacing Billie Rogers at inside forward in a 1-1 draw at Ashington, in January 1927. Price was to leave Wrexham at the end of the season, whereupon he joined Rhos FC for a short period before leaving the Brymbo area to go and work in Mold, playing for both Buckley and Mold. The Brymbo Steelworks re-opened in 1936, and Price returned to the village, taking over the captaincy of the works cricket team. He went on to play for them for 46 years, holding the offices at one time or another of captain, committee man, secretary and vice-president. Some months after the Second World War had broken out Price, together with his friend, Bill Hallam, formed the present day Brymbo Steelworks Football Club, operating in the Victory League. In 1945, after WW2 was over, Price was elected to the committee of the newly-formed Welsh National League (Wrexham area), later becoming an executive council member of the North East Wales F.A. In August 1950, he was to return to the Racecourse when appointed coach to the Wrexham 'A' team that played in the Welsh National League. He was later to become Secretary of Brymbo Steelworks Football & Cricket Clubs, and the Brymbo Male Voice choir, all at the same time. A keen sportsman, he also won many trophies at Billiards, Snooker and Crown Green Bowls.

Season	League		F.A.Cup		Welsh Cup		Total	
	apps	gls	apps	gls	apps	gls	apps	gls
1926/27	1	0	-	-	-	-	1	0
	1	**0**	-	-	-	-	**1**	**0**

JONES, Robert Stuart — 1990 - 1991

Position; *Midfield*
D.O.B; *12th November, 1971*
Birthplace; *Liverpool, Merseyside*
Height; *ft in* ***Weight;*** *st lbs*
Debut v. *Halifax Town (a) 26th January, 1990*
Total Appearances & Goals; *5/2 apps 1 gls*
Career; *WREXHAM Jul 1990; Rhyl cs1991; Brymbo cs1994;*
Honours; *Welsh Cup runner-up 1993;*

Rob Jones joined Wrexham straight from school, and moved on through the junior ranks to sign professional for the club in July 1990. He had already made his Football League debut in January 1990, as a substitute at Halifax Town in a 4-2 defeat when he replaced Geoff Hunter. The following season Rob made a further six League appearances for Wrexham before he was released at the end of the season. During the summer of 1991 he signed for Rhyl of the Cymru Alliance League, going on to help them reach the 1993 Welsh Cup final against Cardiff City, which Rhyl lost 5-0 in a match played at the National Stadium, in Cardiff. An incident during the following season saw Rob leave Belle Vue under a cloud. He had an altercation with a Rhyl supporter, whilst playing for the Lilywhites at Welshpool in March 1994, and was immediately released by the club. Rob then signed for Cymru Alliance side Brymbo during the close season of 1994, becoming one of many former Wrexham players to sign for the club at that time.

Season	League		F.A.Cup		Welsh Cup		League Cup		F.R.T.		Total	
	apps	gls	apps	gls	apps	gls	apps	gls	apps	gls	apps	gls
1989/90	0/1	0	-	-	-	-	-	-	-	-	0/1	0
1990/91	5/1	1	-	-	-	-	-	-	-	-	5/1	1
	5/2	**1**	-	-	-	-	-	-	-	-	**5/2**	**1**

JONES, Robert Trevor 1927 - 1928

Position; *Inside-Right*
D.O.B;
Birthplace; *Bethesda, Gwynedd*
Died; *St.Helens, January 1930*
Height; *5ft 6in* ***Weight;*** *10st 4lbs*
Debut v. *Rochdale (h) 18th February, 1928*
Total Appearances & Goals; *2 apps 2 gls*
Career; *Holyhead; WREXHAM (Am) Jul 1927; Holyhead 31st Aug 1928; Bethesda Vic 25th Sept 1930;*
Honours; *Wales schoolboy international; Welsh Amateur international;*

Bob Jones signed for Wrexham from Holyhead during the close season of 1927. However, he had to wait for his debut until February 1928, after he had impressed in Wrexham's Welsh League team. He made his long awaited senior bow in a home match against Rochdale, a 2-1 win for Wrexham, with Bob scoring one of the two goals. His next match was a Welsh Cup game on the Racecourse against Lovells Athletic, when he again found himself on the score sheet with the only goal of the game. Despite his 100% goalscoring record in the first team, Bob surprisingly never played another match for the club, rejoining Holyhead in the close season of 1928. A few months later he broke his leg, after colliding with the Connah's Quay 'keeper in a Welsh National League match. He joined his local side, Bethesda Athletic, in September 1930.

Season	League		F.A.Cup		Welsh Cup		Total	
	apps	gls	apps	gls	apps	gls	apps	gls
1927/28	1	1	-	-	1	1	2	2
	1	**1**	**-**	**-**	**1**	**1**	**2**	**2**

JONES, Ronald 1935 - 1938

Position; *Outside-Right*
D.O.B;
Birthplace; *Mold, Flintshire*
Height; *5ft 8in* ***Weight;*** *11st 4lbs*
Debut v. *Barrow (a) 30th November, 1935 (F.A.Cup)*
Total Appearances & Goals; *89 apps 24 gls*
Career; *Mold Alexandra; WREXHAM (Am) Aug 1935, (Pro) 7th Nov 1935; Liverpool 10th Mar 1938 5apps 1gls; Wrexham (WW2 Guest) 2apps 1gls; Crewe Alex (WW2 Guest);*

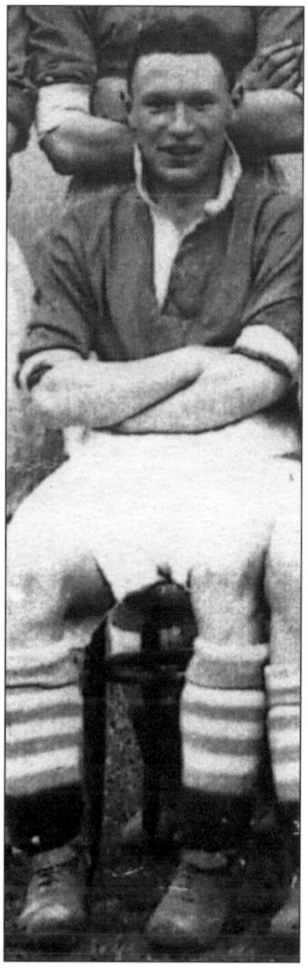

Ron Jones signed for Wrexham in August 1935 from his local side, Mold Alexandra. He arrived at the Racecourse as an amateur, but soon impressed manager Ernie Blackburn in the second string, who then signed him as a professional in November 1935. He made his Football League debut the following month, replacing Jack Mustard at outside-right against Crewe Alexandra on the Racecourse in a match which Wrexham lost 1-0. Ron made a couple more appearances before he established himself in the side for the rest of the season. Jones was again a regular in the side in 1936/37, and played against Manchester City in the F.A.Cup Third Round on the Racecourse in a 3-1 defeat. He was a virtual ever-present in the side the following season, and his consistent form soon began attracting the scouts to the Racecourse. First Division Liverpool were the first club to make an acceptable offer for his services, and he signed for them in March 1938. He made his League debut at Anfield a couple of weeks after signing, a 2-0 win against Manchester City, in which he scored Liverpool's second goal. Ron kept his place for the following match, but then had to wait until the following season before next selected for the Liverpool first team, although he only made three more League appearances that season. The Second World War gave him the opportunity to play for Wrexham again as a 'guest' player, but was also to see him die prematurely when he was killed in action.

Season	League		F.A.Cup		Welsh Cup		N.S.C		Total	
	apps	gls	apps	gls	apps	gls	apps	gls	apps	gls
1935/36	17	4	1	0	1	0	-	-	19	4
1936/37	33	7	3	2	-	-	-	-	36	9
1937/38	28	10	2	0	1	0	1	0	32	10
1944/45	1	1	-	-	-	-	-	-	1	1
1945/46	1	0	-	-	-	-	-	-	1	0
	80	**22**	**6**	**2**	**2**	**0**	**1**	**0**	**89**	**24**
F/League	78	21	6	2	2	0	1	0	87	23

JONES, Stephen Anthony 1981 - 1982

Position; *Forward*
D.O.B; *28th November, 1962*
Birthplace; *Wrexham, Denbighshire*
Height; *5ft 11in* ***Weight;*** *12st 0lbs*
Debut v. *Luton Town (h) 31st March, 1981*
Total Appearances & Goals; *4/4 apps 0 gls*
Career; *WREXHAM Aug 1981; Crewe Alex Aug 1982 6/4apps 1gls; Dunedin City (New Zealand) Aug 1983; Rhyl Aug 1983; IK Kraft (Finland) May 1984; Rhyl Oct 1984; Penycae Aug 1987;*
Honours; *Four Wales Youth International caps; Wales Schoolboy International cap; Welsh Youth Cup Winner 1981; Welsh Youth Cup runner-up 1980;*

Steve Jones proved to be a promising young footballer during his time at St.David's Comprehensive School in Wrexham, and played for a number of representative teams that included Wrexham & District, Clwyd, North Wales, and Wales Schoolboys. He was signed by Wrexham on schoolboy forms at 14, having been spotted playing for the Queens Park Youth team. Steve was still at school when he was first called into the Welsh Youth squad, though he had to withdraw due to an ankle injury, and signed apprentice terms with the 'Robins' shortly afterwards. It was a dream come true for the youngster, who had supported the club from the Crispin Lane 'Kop'. He finally won his first Welsh Youth cap against the Republic of Ireland in a European Championship qualifier, and made three further appearances against West Germany, Belgium, and Greece. He continued to make swift progress at the Racecourse, his Football League debut coming in March 1981 when replacing Les Cartwright in a scoreless home draw with Luton Town. However, he picked up a niggling ankle injury after only ten minutes of the match eventually forcing him to be substituted by Peter Williams in the second half. More seriously, it put him out of action for the remainder of the season. Despite his injury Steve signed professional forms for the club during the summer, and the following season made a further five League appearances. He was also called up into the Welsh under-21 squad for the match against Holland on the Racecourse in March 1982, although not subsequently selected. He was released by Wrexham at the end of that season, whereupon his former manager Arfon Griffiths, signed him for Crewe Alexandra in August 1982. Jones made his debut for the Cheshire club at Gresty Road in a 1-1 League Cup First Round tie against Tranmere Rovers. He went on to record ten League appearances for the 'Railwaymen', scoring one goal in a 1-0 win at Bury, but was again released at the end of the 1982/83 season. He then headed for New Zealand, where he played football for Dunedin City whilst working part-time as a Sales Representative for Rothmans. He remained with the Kiwi side for almost twelve months before returning home, during which time he helped them reach their equivalent of the F.A.Cup Final. On his return Steve signed for Northern Premier League side Rhyl, although he left Belle Vue after just three months to spend a season in Finland with IK Kraft. Jones then returned home to rejoin Rhyl, where he spent almost two years eventually taking a break from football because of work commitments and a long suffering ankle injury. Two years later he took up playing football again for Welsh National League side Penycae, where he won a League Championship medal and promotion to the Cymru Alliance. He continued playing for Penycae for a number of seasons, although work commitments often forced him to miss games. He decided to retire from playing following his appointment as joint-manager of Penycae in July 1997, but relinquished the position during the 1997/98 season. Steve, who still lives in the Wrexham area, has worked for Dalgetty Agriculture on the Wrexham Industrial Estate for over ten years as a Supervisor.

Season	League		F.A.Cup		Welsh Cup		League Cup		Total	
	apps	gls	apps	gls	apps	gls	apps	gls	apps	gls
1980/81	1	0	-	-	-	-	-	-	1	0
1981/82	2/3	0	0/1	0	1	0	-	-	3/4	0
	3/3	**0**	**0/1**	**0**	**1**	**0**	**-**	**-**	**4/4**	**0**

JONES, Steven Wyn 1983 - 1984

Position; *Full-Back*
D.O.B; *23rd October, 1964*
Birthplace; *Wrexham, Denbighshire*
Height; *5ft 10in* ***Weight;*** *11st 7lbs*
Debut v. *Bradford City (h) 2nd April, 1983*
Total Appearances & Goals; *9/2 apps 1 gls*
Career; *WREXHAM 8th Aug 1983; Runcorn Jul 1984; Rhyl Nov 1984; Bangor City Nov 1984; Towyn Mar 1985; Brymbo Aug 1985; British Aerospace Aug 1989;*
Honours; *Welsh Cup runner-up 1984*

Steve Jones initially began playing football while attending the Victoria Primary and Bryn Offa Secondary Schools in his home Town of Wrexham. It was whilst he was at Bryn Offa that 'Wynnie', as he is more popularly known, was selected to play for both the Wrexham & District schoolboys side, and North Wales schoolboys. He did have trials for the Welsh schoolboys side, but was never actually chosen to play. It was while he was playing for the Wrexham & District schoolboys team that he was spotted by Wrexham A.F.C. scout, Wyn Jones, and not long afterwards, signed schoolboy forms at the age of 14. Steve then went on to do enough to be taken on the ground staff, joining the club straight from school. During his apprenticeship he was picked for the Welsh Youth squad, but again never actually played. He was still an apprentice in April 1983, when he made his Football League debut for Wrexham, deputising for the injured Jack Keay in a 4-0 home defeat by Bradford City. 'Wynnie' made a further five League appearances for the Club before the end of that season, which was followed in the summer by signing professional terms. The following campaign he was to make just four League appearances, in October, at left-back in place of the injured Shaun Cunnington, which also saw him score his only goal for Wrexham in a 2-2 home draw with Torquay United. Steve's last appearance for Wrexham surprisingly earned him a medal, when he came on as a substitute for Cunnington in the 1984 Welsh Cup Final second leg match on the Racecourse, which Wrexham drew 0-0 with Shrewsbury Town, but lost 2-1 on aggregate. Despite playing in that game, he was released by Wrexham manager, Bobby Roberts at the end of that season. He then received a couple of offers to go abroad, including one from South Africa, but turned them down to join Gola League side, Runcorn. Despite this decision he left the 'Linnets' in November, taking up an offer to join Rhyl, although he never actually made an appearance for the Belle Vue club. He was then signed by Bangor City the same month, and remained at Farrar Road until the following March when joining Mid-Wales side, Towyn. This lasted until the end of the season, before signing for Welsh National League side, Brymbo Steelworks, in the summer of 1985. He spent almost three seasons with the 'Steelmen' before a knee cartilage injury and a dislocated shoulder saw his career come to a temporary halt. It was at this time that he began to follow Liverpool, which saw him on the Leppings Lane terrace on the day of the Hillsborough disaster. Although lucky to escape unscathed, it is still a memory that he will never forget. Steve took up playing again for the 1989/90 season, appearing for British Aerospace in the Welsh National League, for two years before ending his career because of cartilage and ligament injuries to both knees. For the last nine years, Steve, who still lives in the Wrexham area, has been self-employed, working as a Civil Engineer with his father.

Season	League		F.A.Cup		Welsh Cup		League Cup		Total	
	apps	gls	apps	gls	apps	gls	apps	gls	apps	gls
1982/83	5/1	0	-	-	-	-	-	-	5/1	0
1983/84	4	1	-	-	0/1	0	-	-	4/1	1
	9/1	**1**	**-**	**-**	**0/1**	**0**	**-**	**-**	**9/2**	**1**

JONES, Tecwyn 1953 - 1954

Position; *Left-Back*
D.O.B; *3rd January, 1930*
Birthplace; *Holywell, Flintshire*
Height; *5ft 9in* ***Weight;*** *11st 4lbs*
Debut v. *Hartlepool United (h) 7th November, 1953*
Total Appearances & Goals; *5 apps 0 gls*
Career; *Brentford Mar 1950 5apps 0gls; WREXHAM 2nd Jul 1953; Dartford; Chelmsford; Clacton Town Jul 1956;*

Tecwyn Jones had been an outstanding prospect in North Wales junior football, but it was Brentford who signed him in March 1950 at the age of twenty. They did so on the recommendation of Irish International Bill Gorman, who had seen Jones in action during his National Service. Tecwyn spent over three years with the London club, but only managed five Football League appearances. He made his 'Bees' debut at left back in October 1951 in a 4-0 home win over Bury, though his only appearance that season. He made four more League appearances for the Griffin Park club before allowed to return to North Wales with Wrexham in July 1953. He had to wait until November to make his League debut for Wrexham, when he replaced Aly McGowan in the side at right-back for three matches. His next chance came at York at the end of February when he deputised for Brian Jarvis at wing-half in a 5-2 defeat. That proved to be Tecwyn's last match for Wrexham, as he was released in the close season of 1954. He then returned South playing in non-league football for Dartford, Chelmsford and Clacton Town, signing for the latter in July 1956.

Season	League		F.A.Cup		Welsh Cup		Total	
	apps	gls	apps	gls	apps	gls	apps	gls
1953/54	4	0	1	0	-	-	5	0
	4	**0**	**1**	**0**	**-**	**-**	**5**	**0**

JONES, Tecwyn Lloyd 1959 - 1964

Position; *Wing-Half*
D.O.B; *27th January, 1941*
Birthplace; *Ruabon, Denbighshire*
Height; *5ft 10'1/2in* ***Weight;*** *10st 6lbs*
Debut v. *Doncaster Rovers (a) 10th October, 1961*
Total Appearances & Goals; *72 apps 3 gls*
Career; *Brymbo Steelworks; WREXHAM (Am) 22nd Nov 1956, (Pro) 12th May 1959; Colchester United 1st Oct 1964 (exchange for Martyn King and £3,000) 28apps 0gls; Crewe Alexandra Oct 1965 8apps 0gls; Porthmadog 3rd Aug 1966; Oswestry Town 1967/68; Vauxhall Motors FC 22nd Jul 1968;*
Honours; *Welsh under-23 international; Welsh Youth Cup Winner 1959;*

Tecwyn Lloyd Jones attended Gwersyllt Council School, from where he was chosen to play for Wrexham and District Schoolboys. He also played around this time for Gwersyllt Youth Club, alongside the famous snooker referee, John Williams. After leaving school Tecwyn went to work at Brymbo Steelworks as an apprentice fitter, appearing for the works team in the Welsh National League. At this time he was spotted by a local Wrexham scout, Gwilym Edwards, who invited Jones for a trial. He signed junior forms for Wrexham in November 1956, progressing through the ranks at the Racecourse, and helping the Club to win the Welsh Youth Cup in 1959. At the end of the season, he accepted part-time professional terms at the Racecourse. Tecwyn played for the reserves in the Cheshire County League for a couple of seasons, before Billy Morris became manager and invited Jones to become a full-time professional. He accepted, and gave up his job at Brymbo Steelworks. However, it wasn't until the beginning of the 1961/62 season, when Ken Barnes had taken charge, that the talented wing-half finally broke into the first team, making his Football League debut in a 2-0 win at Doncaster Rovers in October 1961, deputising for player/manager Ken Barnes. Tecwyn then made a further nine League appearances that season, as Wrexham won promotion to the Third Division. He was also recognised at international level, when earning himself a Welsh under-23 cap against Scotland. The

following season saw him make 28 League appearances, as well as playing in the F.A.Cup third round match against Liverpool on the Racecourse, which Wrexham lost 3-0. The 1963/64 season proved to be a frustrating one, as he found himself in and out of the side, making only eighteen League appearances. He managed just one League outing the following season before Ken Barnes set up a part exchange deal which saw Martyn King and £3,000 come from Colchester United to the Racecourse in exchange for himself. Colchester had a number of experienced players in the side, as Tecwyn made his debut in a 1-1 draw at Bristol City. He spent around twelve months at Layer Road, during which time they suffered relegation to the Fourth Division. Jones found himself out of favour at the start of 1965/66, and made just three appearances before signing for Crewe Alexandra in October 1965. He went straight into the Crewe side for his debut in a 3-0 defeat at Chester but, overall, found his chances limited at Gresty Road, making seven more League appearances before released in the summer of 1966. Disillusioned with professional football Tecwyn took up employment at Shotton Steelworks, but continued playing for Welsh League side Porthmadog, where he spent almost two seasons before joining Oswestry Town for a short while during 1967/68. By this time Jones had gone to work for Vauxhall Motors in Ellesmere Port, playing in the West Cheshire League before taking over as player/manager for a short while, prior to finally hanging up his boots. Tecwyn then took up 'the whistle', officiating in the Wrexham area for around five years, until forced to retire from active sport when a knee injury finally caught up with him. In 1974, he returned to work at Brymbo Steelworks in the security department until the works closed. Afterwards, Tecwyn found employment as a taxi driver, and then with the Ambulance Service. He still lives in the Wrexham area.

Season	League		F.A.Cup		Welsh Cup		League Cup		Total	
	apps	gls	apps	gls	apps	gls	apps	gls	apps	gls
1961/62	10	0	-	-	2	0	-	-	12	0
1962/63	28	2	4	0	2	0	1	0	35	2
1963/64	18	0	2	1	-	-	4	0	24	1
1964/65	1	0	-	-	-	-	-	-	1	0
	57	**2**	**6**	**1**	**4**	**0**	**5**	**0**	**72**	**3**

JONES, Thomas George

1934 - 1936

Position; *Centre-Half*
D.O.B; *12th October, 1917*
Birthplace; *Connah's Quay, Flintshire*
Height; *6ft 0in* ***Weight;*** *12st 6lbs*
Debut v. *Rotherham United (h) 28th December, 1935*
Total Appearances & Goals; *16 apps 0 gls*
Career; *Primrose Hill Athletic; Llanerch Celts; WREXHAM (Am) May 1934, (Pro) 31st Oct 1934; Everton 13th Mar 1936 £3,000 165apps 4gls, WW2 139apps 31gls; Swansea Town (WW2 Guest) 1942/3 3apps 3gls; Stockport County (WW2 Guest) Apr 1945 2apps 0gls; Pwllheli & District (player/manager) Apr 1950; Bangor City (manager) cs1956; Rhyl (manager) cs1967; Retired cs1968;*
Honours; *17 Welsh international caps; 10 War-time Welsh international caps; Football League Championship Winner 1939; Welsh Schoolboy international;*

Tommy, or 'T.G', Jones was recommended to Wrexham at the age of just 15 by his school teacher, and by this time had already represented both Flintshire and Wales schoolboys. After signing for Wrexham as an amateur in May 1934, he began playing for Wrexham reserves in the Birmingham and District League, but showed sufficient promise to be offered professional terms in October. Even so, he had to wait until the following year for his first team debut, when he was called into the side at centre-half for Jack Lewis in a 2-0 home win over Rotherham. Tommy made a further five League appearances that season, and did well enough to attract the attention of Everton. The Goodison Park club then paid out £3,000 for the promising youngster in March 1936. Tommy was bought for the future, but he made his debut in the October of the following season in a 3-0 defeat at Leeds. He went on to make over 300 appearances for Everton in fourteen years, including the Second World War period, during which time he also returned to play for Wrexham making seven 'guest' appearances as well as playing as a 'guest' for Tranmere Rovers. Prior to WW2, Tommy won the first of his seventeen caps for Wales against Ireland in a 1-0 defeat in Belfast, and also featured in ten War-Time internationals for Wales. The famous Everton player Dixie Dean once said of him, "Tommy was the best all round player I've seen. He had everything. No coach could ever coach him or teach him anything. He was neater than John Charles, for instance, and could get himself out of trouble just by running towards the ball and letting it through his legs, knowing a team mate would be in a position to take it." It came something of a surprise when he turned his back on professional football in 1950, and took over the Tower Hotel in Pwllheli, becoming player/manager of the local football team. At Pwllheli he created a team that everyone in the Welsh League wanted to beat at that time known as the Invincibles, before leaving in 1956 to become the manager of Cheshire County League side Bangor City. After several near misses he steered them to a Welsh Cup win over his former club Wrexham in 1962, and thereby qualify for Europe. He was still Bangor's manager when they played the Italian giants of Napoli, losing narrowly in a play-off match at Highbury. In 1967, Tommy took over the manager's job at Rhyl for a season before becoming a soccer journalist with the Daily Post. He later took over a newsagent's business close to Bangor Pier, but now lives in retirement in the renovated shop.

Season	League		F.A.Cup		Welsh Cup		Total	
	apps	gls	apps	gls	apps	gls	apps	gls
1935/36*	6	0	-	-	1	0	7	0
1941/42	5	0	-	-	-	-	5	0
1942/43	2	0	-	-	-	-	2	0
1945/46	2	0	-	-	-	-	2	0
	15	**0**	**-**	**-**	**1**	**0**	**16**	**0**

* = Only Football League season.

JONES, William Lot

1922

Position; *Inside-Right*
D.O.B; *April, 1882*
Birthplace; *Chirk, Denbighshire*
Died; *Chirk 13th July, 1941*
Height; *5ft 6in* ***Weight;*** *10st 2lbs*
Debut v. *Halifax Town (h) 18th March, 1922*
Total Appearances & Goals; *7 apps 2 gls*
Career; *Chirk 1901; Druids 1902; Manchester City Jan 1903 281apps 69gls; Southend United Aug 1919 35apps 7gls; Aberdare Athletic 10th May 1920 (Player/manager) 18apps 0gls; WREXHAM 11th Mar 1922; Oswestry Town Sept 1922; Chirk Jul 1923; Retired 1926; Re-registered for Chirk 11th Mar 1926. still playing 1927/28;*
Honours; *20 Welsh International caps; Two Welsh WW1 Victory International caps; Second Division Championship Winner 1910;*

Lot Jones was the nephew of Bolton and Manchester City full back Dai Jones, but it was his schoolmaster, Mr.T.E.Thomas, to whom he owed much of his skill, because of the extra tuition he provided instruction out of school hours. Lot had attended Chirk Boys' and Bronygarth Schools, and after leaving the latter in 1901, took up work as a Collier while playing football for his local club, Chirk. A season year or so later he joined local rivals Druids, in 1902, and it was during his time with them that he began to attract the attention of League clubs. He had a trial with

Bolton Wanderers, where he was rejected for being too small, before signing for Manchester City in January 1903. Lot then had to wait patiently before he made his debut for the club in a 1-0 home win over Stoke in January 1905. Two months later he won the first of his twenty international cap's for Wales against England at Liverpool. With City, he went on to make over 300 League and Cup appearances, where he was described as being "Clever in control of the ball, his awareness, bigness of heart, making one oblivious to the smallness of his stature". Jones was an extremely gifted footballer, often described as "the brainiest forward in the league". He was also a grafter, prepared to do his share of defensive work: "He had an uncanny skill in drawing the defence before delivering a pass". In 1908, he was awarded a benefit match when City played Middlesbrough, with a sum of £835 being raised. After World War One, when he served in France with the 'Sportsman's Battalion', Jones left Manchester City in August 1919 and signed for Southern League side Southend United. He became the only Welshman to be capped while on their books, a record that still stands to this day. Lot returned to his native Wales in the close season of 1920, to take up an appointment as the player/manager of Aberdare Athletic, helping them to gain election to the Football League in 1921, though he was to resign early in 1922 following a disappointing run. He then signed for Wrexham as a player, in March 1922 and at 39, became the oldest player ever to appear in a Football League match for the 'Robins', another record that also stands to this day. He made his debut in a 5-1 home win over Halifax Town, scoring twice. His final appearance came in a 3-1 home defeat by Tranmere Rovers at the end of April 1922. He was released at the end of the season, and joined Birmingham & District League side Oswestry Town as their player/manager in September 1922. He stayed at the Victoria Road ground for one season before returning to play out his career with his first club, Chirk. Lot then retired in 1926, although he did make the odd appearance after this. It was also at around this time that he began running a Greengrocer's business in the Chirk and Oswestry areas, which he continued to do up until his death in July 1941, aged 59.

Season	League		F.A.Cup		Welsh Cup		Total	
	apps	gls	apps	gls	apps	gls	apps	gls
1921/22	7	2	-	-	-	-	7	2
	7	**2**	**-**	**-**	**-**	**-**	**7**	**2**

Albert Kinsey

KEARNS, Oliver Anthony 1987 - 1990

Position; *Centre-Forward*
D.O.B; *12th June, 1956*
Birthplace; *Banbury, Oxfordshire*
Height; *6ft 0in* **Weight;** *12st 0lbs*
Debut; v. *Stockport County (a) 26th December, 1987*
Total Appearances & Goals; *50/10 apps 23 gls*
Career; *Banbury United; Reading Mar 1977 75/11apps 40gls; Oxford United Aug 1981 9/9apps 4gls; Walsall Aug 1982 31/7apps 11gls; Hereford United Jun 1983 166/4apps 58gls; WREXHAM 24th Dec 1987 £6,000; Kettering Town cs1990 1app 0gls; Rushden & Diamonds 1991 £3,000; Racing Club Warwick cs1993;*

Ollie Kearns is the youngest of five brothers. The eldest, Mick, was a goalkeeper who played for five League clubs, and also represented the Republic of Ireland on 18 occasions. Ollie's own career began with his local side, Banbury United, in the Southern League, where he formed a formidable partnership with Tony Jacques. His finishing power began to attract the attention of Football League clubs, and he was signed by Reading in March 1977. He made his Football League debut as a substitute on 30th April, and kept his place in the side for the last four games of the season, scoring twice. However, Ollie was not to appear in the Reading senior side again until the following November, though he still managed to finish the season as the Royals top scorer in the League, with 16 goals from 27 games. He continued to score on a regular basis over the next couple of years, until the talents of Kerry Dixon began to emerge. His progress led to Ollie being granted a free transfer in the summer of 1981. Oxford United saw his potential, and signed him, but he never really hit it off at the Manor Ground as he competed for a first team place with Keith Cassells and Trevor Hebberd. He was one of a number of players freed in a clear out at the end of 1981/82, but soon found another Club when he signed for Walsall. Ollie spent one season with the 'Saddlers', making 38 League appearances and scoring 11 goals, before joining Hereford United at the end of that season. Kearns went on to spend just over four years at Edgar Street, scoring his 100th League goal during that time before signing for his former team-mate, Dixie McNeil, at Wrexham in December 1987. A £6,000 fee had secured his services as a replacement for Jim Steel. However, he didn't have the best of starts, as he failed to score in his first six games, though finding the perfect moment to open his Wrexham account, with both goals in a 2-0 win against his former Club, Hereford. Ollie scored a further six goals in his next ten league games up to the end of the term. His 1988/89 season was disrupted with injuries, though he did regain his fitness in time to help the club reach the Fourth Division play-off final against Leyton Orient, after scoring twice against Scunthorpe United in the semi-final. Ollie began the following season at centre-forward, but by December he was out of the side through injury. Although he overcame these latest setbacks, Kearns never played another match for Wrexham, and was released at the end of season. He then joined GM Conference side Kettering Town for a short time, linking up with Beazer Homes League side Rushden and Diamonds until the close season of 1993. 1993/94, found him at Beazer Homes Midlands League side Racing Club Warwick, but had to retire from playing during that season because of a persistent knee problem. Ollie then concentrated on his business interests in his native Banbury, a delicatessen and a property development company.

Season	League		F.A.Cup		Welsh Cup		League Cup		S.V.T.		Play/Off		Total	
	apps	gls	apps	gls	apps	gls	apps	gls	apps	gls	apps	gls	apps	gls
1987/88	16/1	8	-	-	2	0	-	-	-	-	-	-	18/1	8
1988/89	10/7	4	2	2	2	4	-	-	1	1	4	2	19/7	13
1989/90	10/2	2	-	-	-	-	1	0	2	0	-	-	13/2	2
	36/10	**16**	**2**	**2**	**4**	**4**	**1**	**0**	**3**	**1**	**4**	**2**	**50/10**	**23**

KEAY, John Paul 1982 - 1986

Position; *Central Defender*
D.O.B; *14th June, 1960*
Birthplace; *Glasgow, Strathclyde*
Height; *6ft 0in* **Weight;** *12st 6lbs*
Debut; v. *Lincoln City (h) 7th September, 1982*
Total Appearances & Goals; *199 apps 11 gls*
Career; *Glasgow Celtic; Shrewsbury Town Jul 1977 152/3apps 20gls; WREXHAM 3rd Sept 1982 £17,500; Derry City Jul 1986; Finn Harps 1991/92 16/1apps 0gls;*
Honours; *Third Division Championship Winner 1979; Welsh Cup Winner 1979; Welsh Cup runner-up 1980, 1983 & 1984; Irish League Championship Winner 1989; Irish League Division Two Championship Winner 1987; F.A.I.Cup Winner 1989; Irish League Cup Winner 1989;*

Jack Keay first played football whilst at St.Brendan's Catholic school in Linwood, Paisley, in his native Scotland. He was also called up to the Scottish schoolboys squad at under 15 level, although never actually selected. By this time he was already turning out for St.Mirren Boys club, going on to the Celtic Boys Club, from where he was offered an apprenticeship with Glasgow Celtic upon leaving school. He spent one season at Parkhead before given the news that he was to be released. Still only seventeen years-old Jack was given the chance to continue in professional football when accepting an offer to move south and join Shrewsbury Town on trial during the close season of 1977. Keay was awarded a contract after just one week, and went straight into the Shrewsbury Town first team squad for his Football League debut, coming on for Steve Cross at Chesterfield in September 1977 in a 3-1 defeat. He quickly established himself as a regular in the 'Shrews' defence, and the 1978/79 season saw him pick up Third Division Championship and Welsh Cup winners' medals with the Gay Meadow Club, as well as helping them to reach the sixth round of the F.A.Cup for the first time in their history. Jack remained with Shrewsbury until September 1982, when he joined Wrexham for £17,500 just after the Racecourse Club had been relegated to the Third Division. The stylish Scottish defender soon established himself in the side, though Wrexham suffered a second successive relegation in his first season at the club. However, The Glaswegion did enjoy some good times at Wrexham, especially in Europe, when he played in that famous victory over F.C.Porto, on away goals. Jack also picked up Welsh Cup runners'-up medals in 1983 and 1984, he missed the 1986 final win over Kidderminster Harriers. Keay was allowed to leave Wrexham on a free transfer during the close season of 1986, much to the annoyance of the supporters who thought that he was worth a fee, but it was mainly down to the club's financial situation that forced him to move on. He then joined League of Ireland side Derry City who he helped to promotion in his first season, and then went on to win an Irish League and Cup treble two years later, as well as experiencing more European football with the Brandywell club against the likes of Benfica, Vitesse Arnhem and Cardiff City. However, a burst hamstring forced him to hang up his boots in 1990, although retained by Derry who appointed him as their player/coach. He left Derry at the start of the 1991/92 season, and enjoyed a short spell with Finn Harps, before finishing playing altogether. Jack was then invited back to Derry in 1993 to take up a coaching position, which he is still involved in on a part-time basis, while also working as an insurance broker from his Derry home.

Season	League		F.A.Cup		Welsh Cup		League Cup		F.R.T.		E.C.W.C		Total	
	apps	gls	apps	gls	apps	gls	apps	gls	apps	gls	apps	gls	apps	gls
1982/83	37	2	2	1	7	0	1	0	-	-	-	-	47	3
1983/84	38	3	-	-	7	0	2	0	1	0	-	-	48	3
1984/85	41	4	-	-	2	0	2	0	2	0	3	0	50	4
1985/86	40	0	3	1	5	0	4	0	2	0	-	-	54	1
	156	**9**	**5**	**2**	**21**	**0**	**9**	**0**	**5**	**0**	**3**	**0**	**199**	**11**

***KEELAN,* Kevin Damien M.B.E.** 1961 - 1963

Position; *Goalkeeper*
D.O.B; *5th January, 1941*
Birthplace; *Calcutta, India*
Height; *5ft 11in* ***Weight;*** *12st 10lbs*
Debut; v. *Colchester United (a) 9th December, 1961*
Total Appearances & Goals; *80 apps 0 gls*
Career; *Carpet Traders FC; Kidderminster Harriers; Aston Villa 5th Jul 1958 5apps 0gls; Stockport County 4th Apr 1961 (Loan) 3apps 0gls; Kidderminster Harriers cs1961; WREXHAM 3rd Nov 1961; Norwich City 26th Jul 1963 to Feb 1980 £6,500; New England Teamen (USA) Apr 1978 to Aug 1980 (Summers only); Tampa Bay Rowdies (USA) May 1981 to Sept 1981;*
Honours; *M.B.E; Second Division Championship Winner 1972; Football League runner-up 1973 & 1975; Welsh Cup runner-up 1962;*

Kevin Keelan, the second eldest of six children, was born in Calcutta, the son of an Anglo-Irishman who was serving in India as a British Warrant Officer. Kevin's mother was of Indian and Portuguese extraction. He lived with his family in Delhi until 1948, when they moved to England, and it was then that he began playing football for his school team, St.Ambrose R.C.School in Kidderminster, as a left winger. He was soon to make the switch to playing between the posts, a position in which he represented Worcestershire schoolboys. Kevin began an apprenticeship in a steelworks after leaving school, continuing to play football for his local side, Carpet Traders F.C., but his life changed one day when he went to watch Kidderminster Harriers. Their 'keeper had failed to turn up, and Keelan was offered the chance to take his place. Shortly after, he was signed by Aston Villa as a junior in 1957, and made his way through the youth ranks at Villa Park, to sign professional forms in July 1958. He made his Football League debut for Villa at Middlesbrough in March 1960 in a 1-0 win. He made two more appearances as Villa went on to win the Second Division Championship, and clocked up another two the following season before joining Stockport County on loan. Kevin made three League appearances for Stockport before returning to Villa to be told that he was being released. He then returned to Kidderminster Harriers in the close season of 1961, but by November was back in the Football League when he signed for Wrexham manager, Ken Barnes. The deal had been struck following a recommendation by Barnes' assistant, Ken Roberts', who had been with Keelan at Villa. Kevin proved to be an instant success at Wrexham, replacing Arthur Johnson for his debut in a 4-2 win at Colchester United. He kept his place in the side for the rest of the season, as Wrexham went on to clinch promotion back to the Third Division. They also reached the 1962 Welsh Cup final, though they disappointingly lost to Bangor City after a replay, thus missing out on their first opportunity of European football. Keelan enjoyed playing cricket during the summer, and actually represented Denbighshire in 1962/63. Keelan soon begin to attract the attention of bigger clubs with some fine performances, as he became a firm favourite with the Wrexham fans. He was described at the time as a 'fearless goalkeeper and wonderfully built.' At the end of the season it came as no surprise when he left the Racecourse to join Second Division Norwich City for a 'bargain' £6,500 fee. Ron Ashman was later quoted as saying that he was the 'bargain of the century'. Kevin made his debut for the 'Canaries' in a 3-1 defeat at Cardiff in the opening game of the 1963/64 season; he went on to spend 17 years at Carrow Road, clocking up a total of 571 League appearances, just 22 short of the club's record held by Ron Ashman himself. He helped Norwich win promotion to the First Division twice, played in two Football League Cup finals, and was an ever-present over five consecutive seasons, as well as twice winning the club's player of the season award. He was described as an 'extrovert' character who overcame early hot-headedness and rashness, but was daring and had agility and dedication'. He once had to deal with the goal frame falling on him in a League game. His loyalty to Norwich was rewarded when honoured with the M.B.E. in February 1980. Kevin finally left Norwich to go to America, where he had already spent two summers with the New England Teamen. This time however, he joined Tampa Bay Rowdies, before finally settling down in Florida where he has a number of business interests in the leisure and holiday fields. He became employed as a salesman with a contact lens company, travelling over 45,000 miles a year, as well as keeping involved with football by coaching students three evenings a week at the nearby University in Tampa. In 1996, he was appointed as the goalkeeping coach of the Major League Soccer (MSL) team, Tampa Bay Mutiny, and still holds that position.

Season	League		F.A.Cup		Welsh Cup		League Cup		Total	
	apps	gls	apps	gls	apps	gls	apps	gls	apps	gls
1961/62	24	0	-	-	6	0	-	-	30	0
1962/63	44	0	3	0	2	0	1	0	50	0
	68	**0**	**3**	**0**	**8**	**0**	**1**	**0**	**80**	**0**

***KEEN*, Michael Andrew Charles** 1985 - 1986

Position; *Goalkeeper*
D.O.B; *12th February, 1963*
Birthplace; *Wrexham, Denbighshire*
Height; *5ft 9in* ***Weight;*** *11st 0lbs*
Debut; v. *Bolton Wanderers (h) 16th November, 1985 (F.A.Cup)*
Total Appearances & Goals; *8 apps 0 gls*
Career; *Lex XI 1983; WREXHAM Nov 1985; LEX XI Jan 1986; Penley;*
Honours; *Welsh schoolboy international;*

Mike Keen showed his promise as a goalkeeper while attending St.David's Secondary school in his native Wrexham. It was there that Mike was selected to play for Wrexham & District schoolboys, North Wales schoolboys and finally for Wales at Schoolboy international level. Upon leaving school he was snapped up by Chester, for six months before injury dashed his chances of playing full time football, and was released. Mike then began playing local football around the Wrexham area, and joined Lex XI in 1983, as they progressed through the local Leagues. During the 1984/85 season Keen had the enviable record of not conceding a goal between October and March, which did not go unnoticed by Wrexham manager, Dixie McNeil. He called upon Mike to play in the Duke of Westminster Cup Charity game with Chester in May 1985, in aid of the Bradford Fire Disaster Appeal, and did his chances of a contract no harm at all when he saved a penalty. Keen then played against Altrincham in a pre-season friendly, and signed non-contract forms for the Club in the November of the following season. His first team chance came sooner than he had expected when following Mike Hooper's departure to Liverpool and John Vaughan's return to West Ham after a loan spell, he was called up to make his first team debut in a F.A.Cup first round tie against Bolton Wanderers on the Racecourse, which Wrexham won 3-1. He made his Football League debut a week later at Torquay, again in a 3-1 win, and went on to make a further six appearances in the Wrexham first team before Canadian trialist Don Ferguson took over. He never played for the senior team again, and was allowed to return to Lex XI before the season had ended. Mike later became a Police Officer with the West Mercia Police Force, stationed in Whitchurch. He continued to play football when he could, turning out for Welsh National League side Penley.

Season	League		F.A.Cup		Welsh Cup		League Cup		F.R.T.		Total	
	apps	gls	apps	gls	apps	gls	apps	gls	apps	gls	apps	gls
1985/86	5	0	3	0	-	-	-	-	-	-	8	0
	5	**0**	**3**	**0**	**-**	**-**	**-**	**-**	**-**	**-**	**8**	**0**

***KEEP,* Vernon** 1984 - 1985

Position; *Midfield*
D.O.B; *23rd May, 1963*
Birthplace; *Chester, Cheshire*
Height; *ft in* ***Weight;*** *st lbs*
League Debut; v. *Hartlepool United (a) 23rd February, 1985*
Total Appearances & Goals; *0/3 apps 1 gls*
Career; *Hawarden Rangers; Connah's Quay Nomads 1981; WREXHAM Oct 1984; Connah's Quay Nomads; Mold Alex 1989; Flint Town United 1990/91; Conwy United 1993/94 53/6apps 6gls; Porthmadog Mar 1995 6apps 0gls; Connah's Quay Nomads Aug 1995 64/21apps 16gls; Holywell Town Jul 1998 12/8apps 2gls;*
Honours; *Welsh Cup runner-up 1998; League of Wales League Cup Winner 1996;*

Vernon Keep joined Wrexham on trial in September 1984, after impressing for Connah's Quay Nomads in a Clwyd League game against their reserves. Vernon made three appearances for Wrexham, all as a substitute; his first team debut came at the Racecourse in a Welsh Cup match against Chirk AAA in November 1984, when he replaced Jim Steel in the 4-1 win. His second opportunity didn't arrive until January 1985, a Freight Rover Trophy match at home to Wigan Athletic, when Kevin Rogers

made way for him to score the equaliser with his first touch of the game in the 2-2 draw. Vernon's last appearance for Wrexham was his Football League debut, when he again came on as substitute for Kevin Rogers at Hartlepool United in a 2-0 defeat. He was not retained at the end of the season, and returned to Connah's Quay Nomads in the close season of 1985. He later played for Mold Alexandra, Flint Town United, and Conwy United, before leaving in March 1995 to join up with new manager and former Wrexham player Mickey Thomas at Porthmadog. However, his stay at 'Yr Traeth' was brief, as he returned to play for Connah's Quay Nomads in the close season of 1995, where he was to be described as 'an excellent signing, can play in midfield or up front, and would give his all on the field, he hates to get beat'. Vernon went on to pick up a League of Wales League Cup winners' medal with the 'Nomads' against Ebbw Vale at the end of the 1995/96 season, while in 1998, helped Connah's Quay reach the Welsh Cup Final, where he played in the 1-1 draw with Bangor City, before they disappointingly lost 4-2 in a penalty shoot-out. During that season, Vernon, a 'tenacious midfielder', also assisted Holywell Town, who went on to win promotion to the League of Wales, and the 1998/99 season saw him begin the season with the Halkyn Road club. During his time with Connah's Quay, he was described as a 'nightmare for referees!' In January 1999 he was appointed manager of Holywell Town following a spell in the 'caretaker' role.

Season	League		F.A.Cup		Welsh Cup		League Cup		F.R.T.		E.C.W.C		Total	
	apps	gls	apps	gls	apps	gls	apps	gls	apps	gls	apps	gls	apps	gls
1984/85	0/1	0	-	-	0/1	0	-	-	0/1	1	-	-	0/3	1
	0/1	0	-	-	0/1	0	-	-	0/1	0	-	-	0/1	1

KEETLEY, Joseph Frederick 1925 - 1926

Position; *Inside-Left*
D.O.B; *28th June, 1897*
Birthplace; *Derby, Derbyshire*
Died; *Allerton, 30th March, 1958*
Height; *5ft 9in* ***Weight;*** *12st 0lbs*
Debut; v. *Chesterfield (h) 5th December, 1925*
Total Appearances & Goals; *7 apps 3 gls*
Career; *Victoria Ironworks (Derby); Bolton Wanderers (Am) 17th Aug 1920, (Pro) May 1921 1app 0gls; Accrington Stanley 12th Jun 1923 13apps 8gls; Liverpool 9th Nov 1923 £1,200 9apps 3gls; Wolves 26th May 1925 10apps 5gls; WREXHAM 21st Nov 1925; Doncaster Rovers 29th Jan 1926 2apps 0gls; Horwich RMI Mar 1926; Lancaster Town; Ribble Motors (Preston) Aug 1932;*

Joe Keetley was the eldest of five brothers, all of whom went on to play League football: Charles for Leeds, Bradford City and Reading; Frank for Derby, Doncaster, Bradford City and Lincoln; Harold for Doncaster; and Thomas for Bradford Park Avenue, Doncaster, Notts County and Lincoln. Joe began his football career with his local club, Victoria Ironworks, in Derby, who at one time had Joe and six of his brothers playing in the same team. There were, altogether, eleven boys and one girl in his family. From the Ironworks club, Joe was signed by Bolton Wanderers as an amateur in August 1920, before signing professional in May 1921. The following season would see him make his Football League debut for Bolton, playing at left-back against Manchester United on 8th April 1922 in a 1-0 win. That proved to be his one and only first team appearance for the 'Trotters', and in June 1923 signed for Accrington Stanley on a free transfer. He made his debut for 'Stanley' in a 2-1 defeat at Darlington in the opening game of the season in which he scored his side's only goal. Joe went on to score seven goals in twelve games before he was signed by Liverpool for a four-figure fee in November 1923. Whilst at Accrington he was described as 'A player of the artistic type, clever in ball control and artful in beating an opponent'. Joe spent nearly two seasons at Anfield, where he scored three goals in nine League appearances, before moving to Second Division Wolves in the close season of 1925. Joe was only at Molineux for a short time but scored five goals in just ten League games, which included a goal on his debut, a 3-0 home win over Preston. However, he was allowed to leave Wolves in November 1925, when he joined Wrexham. At the Racecourse, he stepped straight into the side at inside left for the League game at home to Chesterfield, in place of Frank Jones. Keetley scored the only Wrexham goal in that match, a neat header, in a 1-1 draw. He made a further six appearances for Wrexham, scoring two goals, before losing his place in the side, and by the end of January had joined Doncaster Rovers, teaming up with two of his brothers, Tom and Harold. Joe made just two League appearances for Doncaster, both alongside his brothers. However, he was released at the end of the season. In the summer he joined non-league side Horwich RMI, later turning out for Lancaster Town and Ribble Motors of Preston in a local League.

Season	League		F.A.Cup		Welsh Cup		Total	
	apps	gls	apps	gls	apps	gls	apps	gls
1925/26	7	3	-	-	-	-	7	3
	7	**3**	-	-	-	-	**7**	**3**

KELLY, James 1975

Position; *Forward*
D.O.B; *6th February, 1954*
Birthplace; *Aldergrove, Northern Ireland*
Height; *5ft 6in* ***Weight;*** *10st 2lbs*
Debut; v. *Rotherham United (a) 20th September, 1975*
Total Appearances & Goals; *4 apps 0 gls*
Career; *Cliftonville; Wolves Dec 1971 20/2apps 0gls; Portland Timbers (USA) May 1975 (Loan); WREXHAM 17th Sept 1975 (Loan); Walsall 10th Aug 1978 19/7apps 3gls; Portland Timbers (USA) Apr 1981; Kidderminster Harriers;*

Jimmy Kelly was highly rated at Wolves after signing for the Molineux club in December 1971 from Irish League side Cliftonville, whom he had joined straight from School. At Molineux Jimmy waited patiently for his first team opportunity which came in February 1974, when his Football League debut in place of Dave Wagstaffe against Sheffield United in a First Division match, which Wolves lost 1-0. Jimmy's lack of senior appearances at Molineux was mainly due to the consistent form of the Wolves left-winger, Dave Wagstaffe, and he didn't figure in the first team again that season. In the summer of 1975 Kelly went to America to play for Portland Timbers, whom he helped reach the knock-out final where they lost 2-1 to Miami. Jimmy returned to Britain on the 26th August, and shortly afterwards was allowed to join Wrexham for a two months' loan spell in September 1975, which was to end sooner than he or Wrexham had expected. Jimmy made his Wrexham debut at Rotherham, but it ended prematurely, when limping off after fifty minutes of the 2-1 defeat. He then made three more League appearances before returning to Wolves because of injury. Jimmy clocked up a further 21 League appearances for Wolves, over the next three seasons, before being allowed to join Walsall in August 1978. Jimmy made his debut for the 'Saddlers' in the opening game of the 1978/79 season, a 4-2 home defeat by Watford. The rest of the season saw him in and out of the side though he began 1979/80 in style with one of the goals in a 2-1 home win over Stockport County. That however, proved to be his last League appearance for Walsall as he left Fellows Park at the end of the season, having made a total of just 26 League appearances, scoring three goals. It is not certain where Jimmy went after this, but he did have a second spell back with Portland Timbers in America in 1981, and later with Kidderminster Harriers, before returning to Northern Ireland.

Season	League		F.A.Cup		Welsh Cup		League Cup		Total	
	apps	gls	apps	gls	apps	gls	apps	gls	apps	gls
1975/76	4	0	-	-	-	-	-	-	4	0
	4	0	-	-	-	-	-	-	4	0

***KELLY,* James** 1990 - 1992 & 1994

Position; *Midfield*
D.O.B; *14th February 1973*
Birthplace; *Liverpool, Merseyside*
Height; *5ft 7in* **Weight;** *11st 10lbs*
Debut; v. *Scunthorpe United (h) 24th November, 1990*
Total Appearances & Goals; *27/13 apps 0 gls*
Career; *WREXHAM Jul 1991; Wolves Feb 1992 (Exchange for John Paskin) 4/3apps 0gls; Walsall (loan) Mar 1993 7/3apps 2gls; WREXHAM 11th Mar 1994 (Loan); Hednesford Town Aug 1998 22/6apps 1gls;*
Honours; *Welsh Youth Cup Winner 1991;*

James Kelly joined Wrexham straight from school on a two year Youth Training Scheme (YTS). He made rapid progress, under Brian Flynn, as the clubs perilous financial state had forced the manager to blood young players in the senior side. James was one of these, and made his Football League debut in a 1-0 home win against Scunthorpe United in November 1990 as a substitute for Geoff Hunter. Most of his other appearances that season were also as a substitute, but he rounded off an encouraging years work with a Welsh Youth Cup winners' medal, after a victory over Swansea City in the Final. James made further progress in the following season, and was selected in the starting line-ups on sixteen occasions. He was regarded as a 'tough tackling midfielder, who can always be relied upon to give 100%'. In February 1992 Kelly was to leave Wrexham, and join Wolves in an exchange deal that saw John Paskin move to the Racecourse. No cash was involved, but a performance-related sum was agreed, payment of which was dependent upon the number of first team games that James would play. He played mainly for Wolves Central League side at first, but did make three substitute appearances before the season was over, his debut coming in a 6-2 home win over Newcastle United when he substituted Kevin Ashley. He spent the following season in the reserves, failing to make a first team appearance, and in March 1993 was loaned out to Walsall, where he helped them to reach the Third Division play-off's before going out to Crewe Alexandra at the semi-final stage. James then returned to Wolves, but in March 1994 Wrexham manager Brian Flynn was successful in a bid to bring him back to the Racecourse for a month on loan. He added nine more League appearances for Wrexham before returning to Wolves at the end of the season, where former England manager, Graham Taylor, had just been appointed the new manager following Graham Turner's shock resignation. However, James' football career was in tatters in August 1994, when he was arrested and remanded in custody on a murder charge, along with his brother and a friend, following a night out in his home city of Liverpool. Jamie was later sentenced to five years' imprisonment for manslaughter, which saw his contract with Wolves come to an end. Having served his sentence he was released in the summer of 1998, and after training with Wrexham during the summer, he signed for Conference League side Hednesford Town for the start of the 1998/99 season.

Season	League		F.A.Cup		Welsh Cup		League Cup		F.R.T.		Total	
	apps	gls	apps	gls	apps	gls	apps	gls	apps	gls	apps	gls
1990/91	2/10	0	-	-	0/1	0	-	-	0/2	0	2/13	0
1991/92	9	0	2	0	3	0	-	-	2	0	16	0
1993/94	9	0	-	-	-	-	-	-	-	-	9	0
	20/10	**0**	**2**	**0**	**3/1**	**0**	**-**	**-**	**2/2**	**0**	**27/13**	**0**

***KELLY,* Raymond** 1997 & 1998

Position; *Forward*
D.O.B; *29th December, 1976*
Birthplace; *Athlone, Republic of Ireland*
Height; *5ft 11in* **Weight;** *12st 0lbs*
Debut v. *Bristol Rovers (a) 4th October, 1997*
Total Appearances & Goals; *7/1 apps 1 gls*
Career; *Athlone Town; Manchester City 1st Aug 1994 £30,000 1app 0gls; WREXHAM 30th Sept 1997 (Loan) & 25th Mar 1998 (Loan);*
Honours; *8 Republic of Ireland Under-21 international caps;*

Ray Kelly began playing football in his native Ireland for his school team. It was while at school that he played for a local junior team named Willow Park coming under the influence of Padrig Nicholson, who was also Chief Scout for the Irish schoolboy team. Ray at this time also played for the Irish schoolboys side, as well as his team doing well in the All-Ireland schools Cup. He later teamed up again with Nicholson, who was working for Athlone Town as youth team coach, and Kelly signed, to play for their Dublin League side. In his first season with the Athlone youth XI, Kelly scored 76 goals, which soon brought him to the attention of English League clubs. He received a number of offers, but it was Manchester City with whom he was impressed and eventually signed for in 1994, when still only seventeen, with City paying out £30,000 to get their man, who had not even played for Athlone's senior XI. He remained in Ireland until sitting his 'A' levels, before travelling over to Manchester. Ray had a good first season with City's reserve side, but with a succession of managerial changes his form began to dip, and with new players being brought in, he was pushed further and further down the pecking order. Despite his problems with City, Ray was chosen to play for both the Irish youth and under-21 teams during this period. Without having made the first team at Maine Road, Kelly was given a chance of first team football by Wrexham manager Brian Flynn, towards the end of September 1997, when signed on loan following Steve Watkin's transfer to Swansea, and because of a number of injuries to the club's other forwards. Ray made his Football League debut for Wrexham at Bristol Rovers in a 1-0 defeat, and went on to make a further seven League and Cup appearances, scoring one goal in a 3-1 home win over Southend United in an enjoyable spell, but after Flynn had agreed another month on loan, Kelly was suddenly recalled by Manchester City, and finally made his first team debut for City in the following match at Port Vale as a substitute. He was then chosen to start the next match against Huddersfield Town, which proved to be Ray's last match for City, finding himself back playing reserve team football, following Joe Royle's appointment. He was on the verge of signing for Norwegian League side, Stavanger on loan in March, but due to the weather, he remained training with City, before first St.Johnstone and then Wrexham again offered him the chance of another loan spell. He decided to join Wrexham, but his second spell was not so impressive as his first stint, and only made four substitute appearances. With his contract out at the end of the season Ray was released by the Maine Road club.

Season	League		F.A.Cup		League Cup		A.W.S		W.I.C.		Total	
	apps	gls	apps	gls	apps	gls	apps	gls	apps	gls	apps	gls
1997/98	5/5	1	-	-	-	-	-	-	2	0	7/5	1
	5/5	**1**	**-**	**-**	**-**	**-**	**-**	**-**	**2**	**0**	**7/5**	**1**

KELSALL, Charles 1939 - 1952

Position; *Full-Back*
D.O.B; *15th April, 1921*
Birthplace; *Buckley, Flintshire*
Height; *5ft 8in* **Weight;** *10st 10lbs*
Debut; v. *Stockport County (a) 4th April, 1947*
Total Appearances & Goals; *42 apps 0 gls*
Career; *Mynydd Isa Wanderers cs1937; Buckley cs1938; WREXHAM 4th Aug 1939; New Brighton (WW2 Guest) 1940/41 1app 0gls; Holywell Town 3rd Jul 1952; Buckley Rovers 20th Aug 1954;*
Honours; *Flintshire League Championship Winner 1938; Welsh League Division One Championship Winner 1953; Alves Cup runner-up 1953; Flintshire League Challenge Cup runner-up 1938;*

Charlie Kelsall began playing football at St.Matthew's School in Buckley, and Hawarden County School, where he was selected at all age levels. Upon leaving school he obtained work at a Buckley brickworks and continued playing football for local side, Mynydd Isa Wanderers, winning a Flintshire League Championship and a runners-up medal in the Flintshire League's Challenge Cup in 1938. Charlie played for Buckley Town the following season, where he was spotted by a Wrexham scout. After a visit to his Buckley home by the Wrexham director George Turner in the close season of 1939, Kelsall signed for the Racecourse club on a part-time basis. He was playing in Wrexham's Cheshire League side when the Second World War broke out, but continued to combine semi-professional football with work at the brickworks, because of his age. He made his first team debut for Wrexham in a Football Regional League West Division match against Chester in March 1940, making two further appearances before the end of the campaign. He became a regular in the Wrexham team the following season, but was called up to the Army in the close season. Charlie joined the 2nd Survey Regiment, with whom he served in Burma. After WW2 was over Charlie re-signed for Wrexham on a part-time basis, and returned to work at the brickworks. He went on to give loyal service to The Robins, spending a further six seasons at the Racecourse, though he was never regarded as a first team regular. He played mainly in the Cheshire League side, but could always be relied upon to cover at full-back in the first team when required. Charlie finally left the Racecourse in May 1952, when he joined Welsh League side Holywell Town, who were managed by former Wrexham player Gordon Gunson. In his first season Charlie featured in their Welsh League Division One Championship winning side, and also collected a Welsh League Alves Cup runners'-up medal. He spent one more season with Holywell before joining his local side, Buckley Rovers, turning out for a season until knee trouble forced his retirement. Charlie continued working at the brickworks in Buckley, later becoming a manager eventually working for British Aerospace, from where he retired. Charlie can still be found in the Buckley area, where he has spent most of his life.

Season	League		F.A.Cup		Welsh Cup		Total	
	apps	gls	apps	gls	apps	gls	apps	gls
1939/40	3	0	-	-	-	-	3	0
1940/41	20	1	-	-	-	-	20	1
1946/47	3	0	-	-	-	-	3	0
1947/48	1	0	-	-	-	-	1	0
1948/49	3	0	-	-	-	-	3	0
1949/50	8	0	-	-	1	0	9	0
1950/51	18	0	2	0	-	-	20	0
1951/52	6	0	-	-	-	-	6	0
	62	**1**	**2**	**0**	**1**	**0**	**65**	**1**
F/League	39	0	2	0	1	0	42	0

KENNEDY, Alan Phillip 1990

Position; *Left-Back*
D.O.B; *31st August, 1954*
Birthplace; *Sunderland, Tyne & Wear*
Height; *5ft 9in* **Weight;** *10st 7lbs*
Debut; v. *Barry Town (a) 21st March, 1990 (Welsh Cup)*
Total Appearances & Goals; *20/2 apps 0 gls*
Career; *Newcastle United Aug 1972 155/3apps 9gls; Liverpool 14th Aug 1978 £330,000 249/2apps 15gls; Sunderland 21st Sept 1985 £100,000 54apps 2gls; Hartlepool United Oct 1987 4/1apps 0gls; Beerschot (Belguim) Nov 1987; Wigan Athletic Dec 1987 22apps 0gls; Grantham; Northwich Victoria; Enfield; Colne Dynamoes; WREXHAM Mar 1990-Dec 1990; Morecambe 1990/91; Netherfield 1991/92; Radcliffe Borough 1992/93; Barrow;*
Honours; *Two England International caps; England 'B' International cap; Six England Under-23 cap; European Cup Winner 1981 & 1984; European Cup runner-up 1985; Football League Championship Winner 1979, 1980, 1982, 1983 & 1984; F.A.Cup runner-up 1974; Football League Cup Winner 1981, 1982, 1983 & 1984; Football League Cup runner-up 1976; Welsh Cup runner-up 1990;*

Alan Kennedy was signed as an apprentice with Newcastle United in July 1971, straight from his school in Sunderland. He made his Football League debut in April 1972 in a 1-0 defeat at Nottingham Forest in place of Frank Clark, before signing a professional contract in August 1972. He was still only nineteen years' old when he played in the 1974 F.A.Cup final for Newcastle against his future club, Liverpool. Alan made a total of 158 League appearances at St.James Park, as well as playing at Wembley again in the 1976 Football League Cup final, which Newcastle lost 2-1 to Manchester City, before leaving the 'Magpies' following relegation in 1978. He was signed by Liverpool for £330,000 in August, and soon became their regular left-back after taking over the position from a certain Joey Jones. Alan went on to win many top honours in the game at Anfield, including European Cup, League Cup winners' and runners'-up medals'. He also won his two England international caps with Liverpool in 1984, against Northern Ireland and Wales. The famous 'Kop' fans affectionately nicknamed him 'Barney Rubble', as he was a 'powerful left-back, fierce in the tackle, and had good positional sense, mixing his defensive duties with attacks down the left wing'. One of these produced a highlight in a dazzling career when he scored the winning goal in the 1981 European Cup final against Real Madrid, a left wing run that was finished off with a powerful left-foot shot. Kennedy was allowed to leave Anfield in September 1985, when he joined Second Division Sunderland for £100,000, but it wasn't a good time for either Alan or 'The Rokerites' as the club flirted with relegation. He left Roker Park at the end of the 1986/87 season, and played in Sweden over the summer months before returning to join Hartlepool United in October 1987 on non-contract terms. After just five League games he moved to Belgian side, Beerschot, a month later, for a short time before returning to England and linking up Grantham. He was soon back in the Football League, however, as Wigan Athletic recruited him in December 1987. Alan made 22 League appearances for the Springfield Park club before his release at the end of the season. He then played for several non-league clubs, including Northwich Victoria and Enfield, before joining Wrexham on non-contract terms from Colne Dynamoes in March 1990. Alan had been signed by Brian Flynn to bring experience to a young side that was fighting off the prospect of relegation to the Conference League at the time. With survival eventually assured he was given a six month contract, and started the new season as the club's regular left-back until he was injured at Gillingham in October 1990. That proved to be Kennedy's last match for Wrexham, as his place was then filled by a promising young prospect, Phil Hardy, who went on to make the place his own for a number of seasons. Alan was released by Wrexham in December, following the completion of his short-term contract. He then returned to non-league football, playing for Morecambe, Netherfield, (where he had a brief spell as player/manager), Radcliffe Borough, and Barrow. Alan has recently been running soccer schools for boys and girls between the ages of six and sixteen.

Season	League		F.A.Cup		Welsh Cup		League Cup		F.R.T.		Total	
	apps	gls	apps	gls	apps	gls	apps	gls	apps	gls	apps	gls
1989/90	6/1	0	-	-	2/1	0	-	-	-	-	8/2	0
1990/91	9	0	-	-	-	-	3	0	-	-	12	0
	15/1	**0**	**-**	**-**	**2/1**	**0**	**3**	**0**	**-**	**-**	**20/2**	**0**

KENWORTHY, Steven

1977 - 1981

Position; *Left-Back*
D.O.B; *6th November, 1959*
Birthplace; *Wrexham, Denbighshire*
Height; *6ft 1in* ***Weight;*** *12st 0lbs*
Debut; v. *Sheffield Wednesday (a) 3rd May, 1978*
Total Appearances & Goals; *26/1 apps 1 gls*
Career; *WREXHAM 7th Nov 1977; Bury Aug 1981 14apps 0gls; Bangor City cs1983; Brymbo Steelworks cs1985; Gresford Athletic Mar 1990; Llay R.B.L. cs1990; New Broughton cs1994; Chirk AAA cs1996; Borras Park Albion Aug 1998.*
Honours; *Welsh Youth international; Welsh Schoolboy international; Welsh Youth Cup runner-up;*

Steve Kenworthy first came to prominence while playing for Bryn Offa School in Wrexham. It was during his time there that he represented both Wrexham & District and North East Wales Schoolboys, as well as appearing for Wales at that level against Scotland, England and Northern Ireland. Steve joined Wrexham as a schoolboy at the age of 15, and earned himself a place on the ground staff upon leaving school in 1977. He made rapid progress at the Racecourse, representing Wales again at youth level in Iceland and at home to Holland in Newport, which culminated in his Football League debut in the last match of the 1978 Third Division Championship winning season at Hillsborough, against Sheffield Wednesday. During the subsequent close season Steve was taken on tour with the first team squad, to Sweden where he played in two of the five matches. The 1978/79 season was only a few weeks' old when Alan Dwyer dislocated his shoulder, and Kenworthy got his chance again for two matches. However, he wasn't to appear in the first team again until the following season, after chipping a bone in his knee during a reserve match in February. Steve trained throughout the summer to get himself fit for the new season, though he had to wait until December when Dwyer was again injured. Steve made ten League appearances, and also played against Everton in an F.A.Cup match at Goodison Park, while returning to the reserves when Dwyer was fit again. His next chance came in December 1980, when he made the side on seven occasions. But these turned out to be his final first team games for the Club and was released at the end of the season. Kenworthy then joined Bury, staying with the Shakers for a couple of years, but only managed to make fourteen League appearances, due to a broken leg sustained in a match with Colchester United at Gigg Lane. Not long after he had recovered from the injury Steve was told that he was to be released at the end of the 1982/83 season! He then drifted into non-league football, with Alliance League side Bangor City, for two seasons. Next stop was a move closer to home, when he joined Brymbo Steelworks, for five seasons and winning a

Welsh National League Championship medal. A short spell with Gresford Athletic in the Cymru Alliance League followed, and it was then on to Llay Royal British Legion in the Welsh National League. Steve was to spend four years with Llay, helping them reach the Fourth round of the Welsh Cup in 1992 losing to the eventual finalists, Hednesford Town, after a replay. Steve left Llay in the close season of 1996, when he joined Chirk AAA, where he spent two years before joining Borras Park Albion in the summer of 1998. He still lives in the Wrexham area, working for D.H.D.Engineering in Llay.

Season	League		F.A.Cup		Welsh Cup		League Cup		E.C.W.C.		Total	
	apps	gls	apps	gls	apps	gls	apps	gls	apps	gls	apps	gls
1977/78	1	0	-	-	-	-	-	-	-	-	1	0
1978/79	2	0	-	-	-	-	-	-	-	-	2	0
1979/80	9/1	0	4	0	-	-	-	-	-	-	13/1	0
1980/81	7	0	1	0	2	1	-	-	-	-	10	1
	19/1	**0**	**5**	**0**	**2**	**1**	**-**	**-**	**-**	**-**	**26/1**	**1**

KING, John

1982 - 1985

Position; *Defender*
D.O.B; *29th January, 1955*
Birthplace; *Glasgow, Strathclyde*
Height; *5ft 10in* ***Weight;*** *11st 0lbs*
Debut; v. *Portsmouth (a) 11th September, 1982*
Total Appearances & Goals; *91/1 apps 5 gls*
Career; *Shrewsbury Town Jan 1973 304/2apps 20gls; WREXHAM 28th Jul 1982; Cardiff City 23rd Nov 1984 30apps 0gls; Limerick City; Derry City; Newtown 1992/93 1/5apps 0gls;*
Honours; *Third Division Championship Winner 1979; Welsh Cup Winner 1977 & 1979; Welsh Cup runner-up 1980, 1983 & 1984;*

Jake King was brought up in the Drumchapel area of Glasgow where he played football for his school team, Kingsridge School, as well as turning out for Drumchapel Amateurs in the Glasgow Junior League. It was whilst playing for them that he was spotted by a Shrewsbury Town scout, and joined the Shropshire club as an apprentice straight from school at the age of 15. Jake went on to sign professional terms in January 1973, and made his Football League debut two months later in a 1-0 defeat at Rochdale, replacing regular right-back Paul Bevan. He went on to make a total of 306 League appearances in his ten years at the Gay Meadow, scoring twenty goals, collecting a Third Division Championship medal in 1979 and three Welsh Cup medals' - two winners and one runners-up. He also helped the 'Shrews' to reach the Quarter-Finals of the F.A.Cup on two occasions, in 1979 and 1982. Even though he was a regular in their Second Division side and the club captain, Jake was surprisingly released in the close season of 1982. He had offers from Wrexham and two other clubs, and chose Wrexham even though they had just been relegated from the Second Division. 'The Robins' had just appointed fellow Scot Bobby Roberts as their new manager. King missed the beginning of the season because of a hamstring injury, eventually making his debut in a 3-0 defeat at Portsmouth in September. It was the start of more injury problems for him as he pulled a thigh muscle. Once fit he went on to make the right-back position his own. However, his first season at the Racecourse saw Wrexham relegated once again , and a Welsh Cup Final defeat against Swansea City didn't help. The following season found Jake in his second successive Welsh Cup Final for the club, this time against his former employers Shrewsbury Town. Another disappointing defeat was eased by Wrexham's qualification for European competition, by virtue of the fact that their opponents were an English club in a Welsh competition. In the first round the 'Robins' played the Portuguese Cup winners, F.C.Porto, and they shocked the football world by winning the home leg 1-0, before going to Porto and progressing to the second round on the away goals rule. At one stage they were 3-0 down, but staged a remarkable comeback with Jake scoring two of Wrexham's three goals in the 4-3 defeat. He played against A.S.Roma in the next round before being allowed to join Cardiff City for £30,000 due to Wrexham's crippling financial situation. King made 30 League appearances in the two seasons that he spent at Ninian Park, retiring prematurely from League football due to a knee injury. He later had short spells with both Limerick and Derry in Ireland returning to settle in Shrewsbury, concentrating on the Wine Bar business that he had opened in the Town. Jake was later invited to join League of Wales side Newtown, before having to finish playing altogether because of his knee problem. He was then appointed assistant manager at Newtown, to his former Shrewsbury team-mate Brian Coyne. The pair then led the Latham Park outfit to the runners-up spot in the League of Wales in 1995/96, and the following season took the club into Europe in the UEFA Cup against Riga of Latvia. King left Latham Park in November 1996 to take over as manager of Conference League side Telford United, where he ended what had been a disappointing season in ninth place. However, with Fred Davies' departure from Shrewsbury Town Jake was appointed as the Gay Meadow club's new manager on 20th May 1997, a job he is still involved in at the time of going to print.

Season	League		F.A.Cup		Welsh Cup		League Cup		F.R.T.		E.C.W.C		Total	
	apps	gls	apps	gls	apps	gls	apps	gls	apps	gls	apps	gls	apps	gls
1982/83	33/1	1	2	0	7	1	-	-	-	-	-	-	42/1	2
1983/84	44	4	1	0	8	0	2	1	3	0	-	-	58	5
1984/85	14	0	1	0	-	-	2	0	-	-	4	2	21	2
	91/1	**5**	**4**	**0**	**15**	**1**	**4**	**1**	**3**	**0**	**4**	**2**	**121/1**	**9**

KING, Martyn Noel Geoffrey 1964 - 1966

Position; *Centre-Forward*
D.O.B; *23rd August, 1937*
Birthplace; *Birmingham, West Midlands*
Height; *5ft 9in* ***Weight;*** *10st 12lbs*
Debut; v. *Rochdale (h) 3rd October, 1964*
Total Appearances & Goals; *56 apps 26 gls*
Career; *Colchester United May 1957 211apps 132gls; WREXHAM 1st Oct 1964 (Exchange deal for Tecwyn. Jones & £3,000); Porthmadog 2nd Aug 1966 to May 1968;*
Honours; *Fourth Division runner-up 1962; Welsh Cup runner-up 1965; Welsh League (North) Championship Winner 1967;*

Although born in Birmingham Martyn King was evacuated to Yorkshire at the outbreak of the Second World War, where he stayed until 1946 when his family moved to the Colchester area. He was educated at the Lexden Primary and Earls Colne Grammar Schools, and at the latter represented Essex Grammar Schools for three seasons. He was also selected to play for the England Public and Grammar Schools side against Scotland in April 1956. By this time, Martyn had already signed amateur forms for Colchester United (in December 1955), and in the August of the following season made his Football League debut against Crystal Palace in a 3-3 home draw. In the mean-time he continued with his studies by entering University - St.Edmund's Hall, Oxford - where he remained for twelve months. He decided to leave and devote more time to football, though not before selected for the Varsity match at Wembley in December 1957. In October 1957 King became a management trainee with Courtaulds before serving three years' National Service with the R.A.F. Martyn was the regular centre-forward in the R.A.F's representative matches, and it was during his time in the forces that he eventually signed professional forms for Colchester United in September 1958. Martyn then helped the club to gain promotion as Fourth Division runners'-up in 1962, when he scored 31 League goals. In October 1964 he was allowed to leave Layer Road where he still remains as the 'The U's' all-time Football League record goalscorer with 132 goals. He joined Wrexham in an exchange deal that saw Tecwyn Lloyd Jones and £3,000 move in the opposite direction. Martyn went straight into the 'Robins' first team in a 3-2 defeat against Rochdale, but remained in the side until March when Ernie Phythian was to win his place back. King did return to play in the Welsh Cup final against Cardiff City, which Wrexham eventually lost after a replay. The following season saw him begin the season as the club's regular centre-forward but found himself out of favour following a change of manager in January. An on-the-field altercation with team mate Ben Hannigan didn't exactly help matters either, and he was allowed to leave the Racecourse in the close season of 1966. He joined progressive Welsh League North side Porthmadog, who he helped win the League championship in 1967, finishing the season as the club's leading goalscorer, playing alongside a number of former Football League players including Mel Charles and Colin Webster. A knee ligament injury at the start of the 1967/68 season curtailed his appearances, and an operation in December 1967 was not completely successful, which brought an earlier retirement from the game than he had envisaged. Martyn then began a three year Teachers Training course at Cartrefle College in Wrexham, qualifying in June 1970. He returned to the Essex area where he became a Maths and Games teacher at his old school, Earls Colne Grammar School and later at the Ramsey School in Halstead, Essex. In August 1988 Martyn moved to the Derby area where he has worked as a supply and part-time teacher, which he is still presently doing. His interests now centre around vintage and classic cars, which he restores.

Season	League		F.A.Cup		Welsh Cup		League Cup		Total	
	apps	gls	apps	gls	apps	gls	apps	gls	apps	gls
1964/65	27	13	2	1	5	4	-	-	34	18
1965/66	18	2	2	3	-	-	2	3	22	8
	45	**15**	**4**	**4**	**5**	**4**	**2**	**3**	**56**	**26**

KINSELLA, Patrick Gerard 1967 - 1968

Position; *Forward*
D.O.B; *8th November, 1943*
Birthplace; *Liverpool, Merseyside*
Height; *5ft in* ***Weight;*** *18st 6lbs*
Debut; v. *Tranmere Rovers (a) 23rd August 1967 (League Cup).*
Total Appearances & Goals; *1 app 0 gls*
Career; *Liverpool Nov 1960; Wigan Athletic cs1962; Bangor City 29th Jul 1963; Tranmere Rovers Aug 1966 1app 0gls; WREXHAM 26th Jul 1967; Rhyl 21st Sept 1967; New Brighton cs1968; Stockport County Oct 1968 12/1apps 0gls; Holyhead Town 28th Aug 1969; Oswestry Town Sept 1969; released cs1970;*
Honours; *Welsh Cup runner-up 1964; Liverpool non-league Senior Cup Winner 1962; Inter-League Cup runner-up 1962;*

Pat Kinsella began his football career by signing for Liverpool as an apprentice straight from school. He progressed to a professional contract in November 1960, but never made the first team in his three years at Anfield. Following his release in 1962 he linked up with Cheshire County League side Wigan Athletic, for whom he made 32 appearances and scored 12 goals. The club won the Liverpool non-league Senior Cup, and Pat scored the all-important goal in the 1-0 win over South Liverpool. He left Springfield Park in July 1963 to join Bangor City, and went on to enjoy three years at Farrar Road, during which he helped the club to reach the 1964 Welsh Cup eventually losing to Second Division Cardiff City after a replay. King was then signed by Tranmere Rovers in August 1966, and made his Football League debut in a 1-0 home win over Halifax Town in September. He kept his place for the next game, a 2-0 League Cup defeat at Carlisle, though they proved to be his only senior appearances for the Prenton Park club. Pat was then offered a trial by Wrexham manager Alvan Williams during the build-up to the start of the 1967/68 season, and went on to make his first team debut for the 'Robins' at inside-right in a League Cup match against his former club, Tranmere Rovers. It wasn't to be a happy return to Prenton Park however, as Wrexham lost 2-1, and that game proved to be his one and only first team game for the Welsh club, as he was released in September. He then signed for Cheshire County League side Rhyl, making his debut at Hyde United on 23rd September 1967, and going on to become an ever-present in the Rhyl side until he signed for New Brighton in the close season of 1968. However, in October 1968 Pat was back with a Football League club when he joined Stockport County, making his debut in a 1-0 win at Torquay in November. He recorded twelve more League appearances that season, without scoring, before his release in the summer. He joined Welsh League side Holyhead Town for the start of the 1969/70 season, but by September had moved on to Oswestry Town, where he remained until the end of the campaign.

Season	League		F.A.Cup		Welsh Cup		League Cup		Total	
	apps	gls	apps	gls	apps	gls	apps	gls	apps	gls
1967/68	-	-	-	-	-	-	1	0	1	0
	-	**-**	**-**	**-**	**-**	**-**	**1**	**0**	**1**	**0**

***KINSEY,* Albert John** 1966 - 1973

Position; *Inside-Forward*
D.O.B; *19th September, 1945*
Birthplace; *Liverpool, Merseyside*
Height; *5ft 11in* ***Weight;*** *12st 0lbs*
Debut; v. *Torquay United (h) 5th March, 1966*
Total Appearances & Goals; *293/8 apps 100 gls*
Career; *Manchester United Oct 1962 0apps; WREXHAM 2nd Mar 1966; Crewe Alex 3rd Mar 1973 30/2apps 1gls; Wigan Athletic Dec 1973 (Loan) 5apps 1gls; Australia 1974;*
Honours; *Division Four runner-up 1970; Welsh Cup Winner 1972; Welsh Cup runner-up 1967 & 1971; England Schoolboy international; F.A.Youth Cup Winner 1964;*

The popular Albert Kinsey was a promising young footballer when he was at school in Liverpool. He represented the Liverpool Schoolboys team that reached the final of the English Schools' Trophy, only to be beaten by Barnsley at the last hurdle. It was as a left-winger that he sparkled in those days, to such good effect that he represented Lancashire Schoolboys which was followed by being selected for the England Schoolboys, firstly against Wales at Wembley in front of a 90,000 crowd, and then against Scotland. When he left school at fifteen he was missed by both Merseyside giants, Liverpool and Everton, and instead joined Manchester United as an apprentice. Albert then made his way through the Junior teams at Old Trafford, playing at either centre-forward or inside-forward, before chosen for the Central League side when he was 17 years-old. He won an F.A.Youth Cup winners' medal during the 1963/64 season, as United beat Swindon Town in the two-legged final. Despite rapid progress he had to wait for his first team debut, which finally came in an F.A.Cup Cup match at home to Chester when he replaced an injured Denis Law. Despite scoring the winning goal in the 2-1 win, it proved to be Albert's one and only first team appearance for United, and after tiring of reserve team football he asked for a transfer in 1966. Former Manchester United player, and new Wrexham manager, Jack Rowley then quickly stepped in to secure Albert's signature in February 1966. Kinsey went into the first team in March for his debut in a 2-0 home defeat by Torquay United. He kept his place until the end of the season, but it wasn't a good time for either Albert or Wrexham as the club finished bottom of the Fourth Division and had to seek re-election for the first and only time in the Club's history. The following season saw a vast improvement, with Wrexham finishing seventh, and Albert collecting a Welsh Cup runners'-up medal after losing to Cardiff City. He had scored for Wrexham in both legs of the Final. By this time Kinsey was the regular inside-left, and in the 1969/70 season under John Neal he topped the Fourth Division goalscoring charts with 27 League goals - a major contribution as Wrexham finished runners'-up in the League to Chesterfield. The following season he picked up a Welsh Cup runners'-up medal following another Final defeat at the hands of Cardiff City. However, 1971/72 finally saw Wrexham triumph over the 'Bluebirds' in the Final with Albert scoring Wrexham's goal in the second leg at Ninian Park to finally lay the jinx to rest. 'The Robins' were then to represent Wales in Europe for the first time, with by now 'Racecourse Hero' Kinsey scoring Wrexham's first ever goal in European competition, a 1-1 draw in Switzerland against F.C.Zurich. However, the excitement of playing in Europe coincided with the emergence of youngsters like Billy Ashcroft, David Smallman, Mike McBurney and Roger Mostyn, and Albert was eventually allowed to leave the Racecourse in March 1973 and join Crewe Alexandra as player/coach to Jimmy Melia. He made his debut for the 'Railwaymen' in a 2-0 home win over Hartlepool United, and went on to make a total of thirty League appearances for the Gresty Road club before joining Northern Premier League side Wigan Athletic on loan in December 1973, where he scored one goal in five N.P.L. appearances. Before the season was over, Albert had decided to emigrate to Australia, where he has lived ever since. At the Racecourse he was part of a fine attacking partnership with centre forward Ray Smith, where his enthusiastic displays always posed problems for defences. He is still regarded with great affection in Wrexham, especially by those who were fortunate enough to see him play.

Season	League		F.A.Cup		Welsh Cup		League Cup		E.C.W.C		Total	
	apps	gls	apps	gls	apps	gls	apps	gls	apps	gls	apps	gls
1965/66	14	2	-	-	-	-	-	-	-	-	14	2
1966/67	36	11	1	0	5	4	-	-	-	-	42	15
1967/68	37	13	-	-	1	0	-	-	-	-	38	13
1968/69	37/4	5	2	1	2	2	3	0	-	-	44/4	8
1969/70	46	27	4	1	2	0	4	1	-	-	56	29
1970/71	32	17	1	0	5	0	2	1	-	-	40	18
1971/72	32/3	8	3	1	3	2	3	0	-	-	41/3	11
1972/73	11/1	1	-	-	1	0	2	1	3	1	17/1	3
	248/8	**84**	**11**	**3**	**19**	**8**	**14**	**3**	**3**	**1**	**293/8**	**100**

***KIRKBY,* John** 1951 - 1953

Position; *Right-Back*
D.O.B; *29th November, 1929*
Birthplace; *U.S.A.*
Died; *Wrexham, 4th April, 1953*
Height; *5ft 11in* ***Weight;*** *12st 0lbs*
Debut; v. *Chester (a) 18th August, 1951*
Total Appearances & Goals; *5 apps 0 gls*
Career; *Banks o'Dee; Stoke City Dec 1946 1app 0gls; WREXHAM 3rd Aug 1951;*

John Kirkby was born in the United States, but he moved with his family to Aberdeen at an early age. He came to the notice of the professional clubs when he played for a Junior team called Banks o'Dee during the Second World War, and it was First Division Stoke City who brought him south of the border in December 1946. 'Jock', as he was soon christened at Stoke for obvious reasons, then worked his way through the junior ranks at the Potteries club before making his football League debut at left-back towards the end of the 1948/49 season in a 1-1 draw at Middlesbrough. However, this proved to be Kirby's one and only senior appearance for the 'Potters', as he then returned to the reserve side where he remained until he joined Third North side Wrexham in August 1951. Jock made his 'Robins' debut at right-back in the opening match of the 1951/52 season, a 2-1 defeat in a 'derby' at Chester. He then missed a game before being selected at left-back for the next match at home to Chesterfield, which Wrexham again lost, 3-0. John Kirkby spent the rest of the season in the reserve team before coming back into the side for the first three matches of the 1952/53 campaign. He was then replaced by Albert Parker, and returned to reserve team football. On 4th April 1953 he was taking part in a Cheshire County League reserve match against Crewe Alexandra on the Racecourse when, after 65 minutes of the match having been played and with no-one else around him, Jock suddenly collapsed. Despite frantic efforts to revive him he was found to have died upon arrival at the hospital. He was just 23 years-old, and it was subsequently established that he died from 'natural causes'.

Season	League		F.A.Cup		Welsh Cup		Total	
	apps	gls	apps	gls	apps	gls	apps	gls
1951/52	2	0	-	-	-	-	2	0
1952/53	3	0	-	-	-	-	3	0
	5	**0**	**-**	**-**	**-**	**-**	**5**	**0**

KNIGHT, Craig 1990 - 1994

Position; *Centre-Half*
D.O.B; *24th October, 1973*
Birthplace; *Wrexham, Denbighshire*
Height; *6ft 1in* **Weight;** *12st 0lbs*
Debut; v. *Rotherham United (h) 28th April, 1992*
Total Appearances & Goals; *1 app 0 gls*
Career; *WREXHAM Jul 1990; Crusaders Jan 1994 (Loan); Bangor City Jul 1994; Flint Town United Aug 1994 2/2apps 0gls; Holywell Town Aug 1995 5apps 0gls; Buckley United 1996; Lex XI Oct 1997; Halkyn United 1997/98; Flint Town United Jan 1998;*
Honours; *Welsh Youth Cup Winner 1991 & 1992; Welsh National League Championship Winner 1992;*

Craig Knight signed for his home town club straight from school on Youth Training Scheme (YTS) forms. During his two year course Craig picked up two Welsh Youth Cup winners' medals in 1991 and 1992, as well as a Welsh National League Championship medal with the reserve team. It was towards the end of the 1991/92 season that Craig, who had been inspirational in the Second XI side, was called up into the senior squad to replace the injured Tony Humes at centre-half for the final home match of the season against Rotherham United. Wrexham lost the match 3-0 to a strong South Yorkshire side who had already gained promotion, with Craig doing well in his first appearance. However, disaster was just around the corner for the promising youngster; during the summer months he was struck down with Glandular fever, and this was to affect his football over the next twelve months. Then, just as he was getting back to full fitness, he suffered torn cartilage's in his knee. When he was fully recovered Craig found it hard to recapture the kind of form that he had shown prior to his illness and when the opportunity arose, took up an offer to go to Northern Ireland in January 1994 and join Crusaders on loan. He made five appearances for 'Crues' before returning to the Racecourse, though he was released at the end of the season. Knight then moved on to League of Wales side Bangor City, along with two other players who had also been released by Wrexham in the summer - Kevin Jones and Phil Myddleton. However, Craig decided to leave Farrar Road before the season had begun and to join another League of Wales side Flint Town United. He spent a year with Flint, during which he failed to establish himself as a regular first team player, and he linked up with Holywell Town in the summer of 1995. Knight later went on to play for Welsh National League side Buckley United, Cymru Alliance League side Lex XI and Halkyn United before rejoining Flint Town United in January 1998.

Season	League		F.A.Cup		Welsh Cup		League Cup		A.G.T.		Total	
	apps	gls	apps	gls	apps	gls	apps	gls	apps	gls	apps	gls
1991/92	1	0	-	-	-	-	-	-	-	-	1	0
	1	**0**	**-**	**-**	**-**	**-**	**-**	**-**	**-**	**-**	**1**	**0**

Gordon Livsey

LAKE, Michael Charles

1992 - 1995

Position; *Midfield*
D.O.B; *15th November 1966*
Birthplace; *Denton, Lancashire*
Height; *6ft 1in* **Weight;** *12st 11lbs*
Debut; v. *Walsall (a) 28th November, 1992*
Total Appearances & Goals; *71/2 apps 6 gls*
Career; *Denton Youth; Curzon Ashton; Macclesfield Town 1984; Sheffield United 11th Oct 1989 £60,000 19/16apps 4gls; WREXHAM 26th Nov 1992 (Loan); WREXHAM 3rd Mar 1993 £60,000; Released 11th May 1995*
Honours; *Third Division runner-up 1993; F.A.Trophy runner-up 1989; Northern Premier League Championship Winner 1987; England Semi-professional International;*

Mike Lake was one of three footballing brothers who all played the game at a high standard. Paul starred for Manchester City before a knee injury curtailed his career, and David acquitted himself in semi-pro football for Cheadle Town. Mike played for several local junior sides when at school, and it was from the Denton Youth team that he was signed by Curzon Ashton, working his way up through their junior sides to the first team in the North-West Counties League. He was still only 17 years old when invited to sign for Northern Premier League side Macclesfield Town. Mike became firmly established in the 'Silkmen's' midfield and helped them to win the N.P.L. championship in 1987, thereby gaining promotion to the Conference League. Following a number of good Cup runs Lake helped them reach Wembley in the F.A.Trophy final in 1989, where they lost to Telford United 1-0 after extra-time. By this time he had been attracting the attention of a number of Football League clubs, and in October 1989 was signed by Sheffield United for a £60,000 fee. He was now faced with the prospect of becoming a full-time footballer, having combined working for British Rail and then British Telecom with the responsibilities at Moss Rose, but had no hesitation in signing for the Bramall Lane club. He went on to make his Football League debut in a Division Two game at Newcastle United on 25th November 1989, which the 'Blades' lost 2-0. He was to make just three more appearances when disaster struck. He broke his leg at Ipswich in January 1990, forcing him out of action for the rest of the season. Following his return to fitness he struggled with a series of niggling injuries, and they included a lengthy spell on the sidelines with a thigh problem. Mike found it hard to establish a regular first team place when he finally put his problems behind him, but just when he seemed to be overcoming them by playing in the opening five matches of the 1992/93 season was called into the manager's office and told that he was being transfer-listed!! That led to him taking up an offer of a loan move to Wrexham in November 1992. His arrival at the Racecourse coincided with the club's rise from 13th place in the League to a promotion spot by February. Mike was then recalled by Sheffield United, and he played for the 'Blades' in a 3-2 defeat at Southampton. The following week, however, Wrexham manager Brian Flynn tabled a firm offer of £60,000 for Mike which manager David Bassett accepted. He returned to the Racecourse, where he went on to play a major part in helping the 'Robins' secure promotion to the Second Division. The following season Wrexham consolidated their position at the higher level, with Mike again leading the midfield with style, enjoying a starring role in the memorable Coca-Cola Cup game with Nottingham Forest on the Racecourse that finished 3-3. However, more bad luck was just around the corner when suffering a recurrence of a knee injury in a League game at Shrewsbury Town at the beginning of the 1994/95 season. Sadly, it proved to be his last game in the Football League, despite strenuous efforts to regain his fitness. He left Wrexham on 11th May 1995, forced to quit the game because of the injury, still only 28 years old. Mike then took up work for the Royal Mail in his home town of Denton.

Season	League		F.A.Cup		Welsh Cup		League Cup		A.G.T.		Total	
	apps	gls	apps	gls	apps	gls	apps	gls	apps	gls	apps	gls
1992/93	25/1	5	-	-	3	0	-	-	3	0	31/1	5
1993/94	29/1	1	1	0	2	0	2	0	3	0	37/1	1
1994/95	2	0	-	-	-	-	1	0	-	-	3	0
	56/2	**6**	**1**	**0**	**5**	**0**	**3**	**0**	**6**	**0**	**71/2**	**6**

LAMBERT, David

1963 - 1964

Position; *Left-Back*
D.O.B; *7th July, 1939*
Birthplace; *Ruabon, Denbighshire*
Height; *5ft 9in* **Weight;** *10st 10lbs*
Debut; v. *Bristol Rovers (h) 11th September, 1963*
Total Appearances & Goals; *5 apps 0 gls*
Career; *Druids United; Cardiff City (Pro) 28th Mar 1959 0apps; WREXHAM 3rd Jul 1963; Oswestry Town Aug 1964; Witton Albion cs1966; Oswestry Town 14th Sept 1970; Weston Rhyn cs1973;*
Honours; *Welsh Youth International; Welsh Youth Cup Winner 1957;*

Although born in Ruabon, near Wrexham, and attending Acrefair Central School, playing for the School XI, it was Cardiff City who gave David Lambert his chance of a professional career in League football after he had turned down an offer from Wrexham. He had to complete an extra 6 months of National Service due to the building of the Berlin Wall. David had been spotted by Cardiff while playing for Druids, where he had earned a Welsh Youth Cup Winners' medal following a 4-2 victory over Swansea Town in the 1957 Final. This was followed by being capped for the Welsh Youth team. Lambert won two Welsh Youth Caps - one v. England who included a certain Jimmy Greaves. He went on to spend four years with the Ninian Park club, without making a first team appearance during that time, and he was released at the end of the 1962/63 season. Wrexham then stepped in to bring him home and give him a chance to resurrect his career. He spent the early part of the new campaign playing reserve team football, although finally called into first team action for the home game with Bristol Rovers in September 1963, deputising at left-back in place of Terry Morrall. David then played in the following two games before losing his place to Reg Holland. He was to play just two more games for the 'Robins' before becoming a victim of the club's end-of-season clear out, following relegation to the Fourth Division. Lambert had been rather unfortunate throughout his time at the Racecourse, as he was dogged by injury for much of the time. He then joined Cheshire County League side Oswestry Town while as a part-timer also worked at Wilsons/National Tyre Co. for 11 years at Wrexham, later playing for Witton Albion in the same League, rejoining former Wrexham Manager Ken Barnes, where he spent over four seasons. David returned to Oswestry in September 1970, and played against Wrexham in the Welsh Cup. On leaving the Shropshire club in the summer of 1973, he played for Weston Rhyn in the Shropshire County League. He is a keen golfer at Clay Farm Golf Club, Wrexham and also a cousin to Ken Roberts another 'Racecourse Robin'. Dave, who retired at the age of 38, still lives in the Wrexham area working at the B.I.C.C. Factory on the town's Industrial Estate for the past 19 years.

Season	League		F.A.Cup		Welsh Cup		League Cup		Total	
	apps	gls	apps	gls	apps	gls	apps	gls	apps	gls
1963/64	5	0	-	-	-	-	-	-	5	0
	5	**0**	-	-	-	-	-	-	**5**	**0**

LAMBOURNE, Dennis James

1964 - 1966

Position; *Forward*
D.O.B; *7th October, 1945*
Birthplace; *Swansea, Glamorgan*
Height; *5ft 11in* ***Weight;*** *11st 2lbs*
Debut; v. *Newport County (h) 5th September, 1964*
Total Appearances & Goals; *15 apps 4 gls*
Career; *Swansea Town (Pro) 17th Aug 1961; Llanelli 26th Oct 1963; WREXHAM 8th Jul 1964; Bangor City 5th Feb 1966; Merthyr Tydfil 7th Sept 1966; Ammanford Town 4th Aug 1967; Llanelli 11th Nov 1967;*
Honours; *Wales Schoolboy International;*

Dennis Lambourne began playing football as a centre-half during his schooldays in Swansea later switching to centre-forward. It was the latter position that he was selected to play for Swansea Schools in 1958. He later represented Wales Schoolboys against England at Wembley in March 1961, as well as excelling in Athletics at school, where he was a South Wales Athletics champion for four years. After leaving school in December 1961, Dennis joined his home town club, Swansea Town, as an apprentice. He soon became a regular for their reserve side, though allowed to leave the Vetch after two years, whereupon he joined Welsh League side Llanelli in November 1963. Dennis went on to score a club record 30 goals by the end of the season for Llanelli, but it was his performance in a Welsh Cup tie against Wrexham on the Racecourse in February 1964 that brought him to the attention of Wrexham manager Ken Barnes. He was then invited to join the North Wales club at the end of the season, and Dennis went on to sign for the 'Robins' in July 1964. He was to make his Football League debut at centre-forward in the fourth game of the season, a 4-2 home win over Newport County, although he failed to put his name on the score sheet. Lambourne struggled to repeat the goalscoring prowess that he had shown at Llanelli, and spent most of his time at the Racecourse playing reserve team football. Although primarily a centre-forward he made the odd appearance anywhere along the front-line as the occasion demanded. Dennis was allowed to leave Wrexham in February 1966 when he signed for Bangor City. He remained at Farrar Road until the end of the season, when he returned home to South Wales to sign for Merthyr Tydfil. He later played for Ammanford Town before returning to Llanelli.

Season	League		F.A.Cup		Welsh Cup		League Cup		Total	
	apps	gls	apps	gls	apps	gls	apps	gls	apps	gls
1964/65	5	0	-	-	-	-	-	-	5	0
1965/66	10	4	-	-	-	-	-	-	10	4
	15	**4**	-	-	-	-	-	-	**15**	**4**

LANE, Martin John

1988

Position; *Defender*
D.O.B; *12th April, 1961*
Birthplace; *Altrincham, Lancashire*
Height; *5ft 9in* ***Weight;*** *11st 4lbs*
Debut; v. *Crewe Alexandra (h) 8th October, 1988*
Total Appearances & Goals; *6 apps 0 gls*
Career; *Manchester United May 1979 0apps; Chester Aug 1982 175apps 3gls; Coventry City Jan 1987 £27,500 0/3apps 0gls; WREXHAM 6th Oct 1988 (Loan); Chester City 13th Jan 1989 97/2apps 0gls; Walsall Aug 1991 6/4apps 0gls; Shepshed Albion cs1992; Worcester City Feb 1993; Hinckley Town Feb 1993;*
Honours; *F.A.Charity Shield runner-up 1988; F.A. Youth Cup Winner 1980; Division Four runner-up 1986;*

Martin Lane joined Manchester United as an apprentice in 1977, and went on to progress through their junior ranks to sign professional forms in May 1979. He spent a further three years playing reserve team football without having recorded a single senior appearance, before allowed to leave Old Trafford to join Fourth Division Chester City in August 1982. Martin made his Football League debut for Chester in the opening match of the 1982/83 season, a 1-0 home win over Cheshire rivals Crewe Alexandra. He went on to establish himself in the Chester defence where he helped the 'Cestrians' to promotion, to the Third Division in 1986 as runners'-up to Swindon Town - only the second time in the club's history that they had achieved promotion. Martin's consistent performances for Chester soon began to attract the attentions of the bigger clubs, and in January 1987 was signed by Coventry City manager John Sillet for a £27,500 fee. However, his senior opportunities at Highfield Road were seriously restricted by the consistency of Greg Downs, the club's regular left-back. Indeed, in the two years that he spent with the 'Sky Blues' Martin made just three substitute appearances, his debut coming in the final match of the 1986/87 season, a 1-1 home draw with Southampton, replacing Nick Pickering. He was eventually given the chance of first team football in October 1988 when loaned out to Fourth Division Wrexham, replacing the out of favour Nigel Beaumont in the centre of defence for his debut in a scoreless draw with Crewe Alexandra. Lane made five more League appearances for the 'Robins' before returning to Coventry, while Wrexham continued to progress, reaching the play-off final, where they lost to Leyton Orient. Lane eventually left Highfield Road in January 1988 to rejoin Chester on a free transfer, where he made a further 99 League appearances before being released in the close season of 1991. He then joined Walsall, but he failed to make a big impression with the 'Saddlers' and, after just ten League appearances, left the club at the end of the season. Martin then drifted into non-league football, where he had spells with Shepshed Albion, Worcester City, and Hinckley Town, while working in the security business.

Season	League		F.A.Cup		Welsh Cup		League Cup		F.R.T.		Total	
	apps	gls	apps	gls	apps	gls	apps	gls	apps	gls	apps	gls
1988/89	6	0	-	-	-	-	-	-	-	-	6	0
	6	**0**	-	-	-	-	-	-	-	-	**6**	**0**

LANYON, William James

1932 - 1933

Position; *Outside-Right*
D.O.B; *April qtr, 1906*
Birthplace; *Abercwmboi, Glamorgan*
Died; *Walsall, 20th September, 1962*
Height; *5ft 8'1/2in* ***Weight;*** *10st 8lbs*
Debut; v. *Barnsley (h) 27th August, 1932*
Total Appearances & Goals; *2 apps 0 gls*
Career; *Aberdare Athletic Nov 1926 7apps 0gls; Portsmouth Oct 1928 0apps; Walsall May1929 20apps 3gls; Peterborough & Fletton United 1931; WREXHAM 14th Jun 1932 £500;*
Honours; *Wales Schoolboy International;*

Bill Lanyon had represented Wales as a Schoolboy International before tasting Football League action with Aberdare Athletic. He made seven Football League appearances for the South Wales side prior to joining Portsmouth in October 1928. However, Bill didn't record a first team appearance for 'Pompey', and was allowed to join Third Division South side Walsall in the close season of 1929. He made his debut for the 'Saddlers' in their first game of the 1929/30 season at outside-right in a 2-1 defeat at Gillingham. Bill spent two years with Walsall, making twenty League appearances, though most of his second term was spent playing reserve team football. It came as no real surprise therefore, when he was released at the end of the season. Bill then moved across to Midland League side Peterborough & Fletton United, but the club folded due to heavy debts at the end of his first season with them. It was then that Wrexham manager Ernie Blackburn stepped in, and paid £500 for Bill to resurrect his career. He went straight into the first team at outside-right for the first game of the season at home to Barnsley, which Wrexham won 3-0. In his second match for the 'Robins', at Hull, disaster struck as Bill suffered a broken leg. He had rushed in to meet a centre from Tommy

Lewis, and as he turned around to shoot at goal, fell awkwardly. He was rushed to the Hull Royal Infirmary, and even though only 23 years old the injury was so severe that it ended his professional football career. Wrexham were later given credit for their treatment of Bill: one national sports paper reported, 'Wrexham's sportsman-like treatment of Lanyon merits mention. Compensated by the League, the player had no further call on the club, but they provided him nevertheless with the services of a masseur, in addition to the use of a motor car to convey him to and from the hospital.' Bill later settled in the Walsall area.

Season	League		F.A.Cup		Welsh Cup		Total	
	apps	gls	apps	gls	apps	gls	apps	gls
1932/33	2	0	-	-	-	-	2	0
	2	**0**	**-**	**-**	**-**	**-**	**2**	**0**

LAPHAM, Edgar Harold

1936 - 1939

Position; *Inside-Right*
D.O.B; *3rd September, 1909*
Birthplace; *Liverpool, Merseyside*
Height; *5ft 9'1/2in* **Weight;** *11st 9lbs*
Debut; v. *Lincoln City (a) 10th October, 1936*
Total Appearances & Goals; *76 apps 42 gls*
Career; *Peter Lunt Athletic Club; Netherton FC; Everton (trial) Mar 1933; Netherton FC; Marine; Blackburn Rovers Nov 1934 (amateur) 25th Jun 1935 (pro) 2apps 0gls; Accrington Stanley 13th Feb 1936 7apps 2gls; WREXHAM 25th Jul 1936; Barrow 16th Aug 1939;*

Harold Lapham began playing football at the Beaufort Street Council School in Liverpool. He then turned out for the Peter Lunt Athletic Club before later joining Netherton. It was whilst he was with Netherton that Harold was invited to Everton for a trial, though nothing came of it, and he returned to Netherton. However, he was soon approached by Blackburn Rovers, and signed for them as an amateur in November 1934. After scoring 10 goals in 17 Central League matches Harold was given a professional contract at the end of the season. The following season saw him again playing in the reserves, but in December 1935 was given his Football League debut at centre-forward in a 3-2 home win home over Sheffield Wednesday. He then played in the following match at Portsmouth, but a 3-1 defeat proved to be Lapham's last first team game for 'Rovers'. In February 1936 he was allowed to join Accrington Stanley, where he got off to a great start by scoring twice in his first three matches. His goalscoring touch soon deserted him, and at the end of the season moved on to join Wrexham. Although he had to wait patiently before making his first team debut it came in October 1936, when replacing Charles McCartney at centre-forward in a 6-2 defeat at Lincoln. Harold consoled himself by collecting one of the Wrexham goals. He then scored five times in the next three games, and became a big success at

the Racecourse. He established himself as the club's regular centre-forward over the next two seasons, scoring some important goals and ending each of the campaigns as the club's leading marksman. Harold was described as a 'Bustler, with a strong shot in either foot.' However, with the arrival of George Burditt from Millwall his position was put under threat. The club tried to accommodate both players at first, but the 1938/39 season saw Burditt given preference, and Lapham made only seven League appearances. He was to leave Wrexham at the end of the season, signing for Barrow. However, with the campaign just three matches old, the Second World War began, and put an end to the Football League for the next seven years. Harold made a total of 15 WW2 appearances for Barrow before returning home to Liverpool. He later worked for Ribble Motor Services as a PSV driver, completing thirty years service before retiring although continuing to play for the Ribble works team in Bootle until he was 45 years old, captaining the side for most of his time at the Company. After his retirement Harold settled at Blundell Sands, near Crosby, on Merseyside, where he was still residing at the time of writing.

Season	League		F.A.Cup		Welsh Cup		N.S.C.		Total	
	apps	gls	apps	gls	apps	gls	apps	gls	apps	gls
1936/37	30	22	3	1	1	1	1	0	35	24
1937/38	32	16	-	-	-	-	1	0	33	16
1938/39	7	2	1	0	-	-	-	-	8	2
	69	**40**	**4**	**1**	**1**	**1**	**2**	**0**	**76**	**42**

LARGE, Herbert

1924 - 1925

Position; *Inside-Forward*
D.O.B; *18th July 1901*
Birthplace; *Brymbo, Denbighshire*
Died; *Wrexham, 20th June 1968*
Height; *5ft 7in* **Weight;** *11st 0lbs*
Debut; v. *Grimsby Town (h) 17th January, 1925*
Total Appearances & Goals; *1 app 0 gls*
Career; *Brymbo Green; Druids Jul 1923; Brymbo Green Dec 1923; Llandudno Feb 1924; WREXHAM 16th Aug 1924; Llandudno 12th Feb 1925; Connah's Quay & Shotton 29th Jan 1926; Denbigh Utd 4th Aug 1926; Rhos 19th Feb 1927; Mold 16th Sept 1927; Blaenau Ffestiniog 29th Nov 1927; Bangor City 27th Sept 1930;*

A native of Brymbo, Herb, or 'Herbie' as he was known, played for his local side Brymbo Green United when they reached the Quarter-Finals of the Welsh Cup in 1922, losing to Pontypridd. He was offered a trial with South Wales Football League side Aberdare Athletic in the following season, though nothing came of it, and in the Summer of 1923 joined Druids, However, he soon returned to his roots at Brymbo. In February 1924, Herb signed for Llandudno, where he stayed until the end of the season. Wrexham organised a pre-season trial for local Junior amateurs during the summer of 1924. Large was one of those who had requested a chance, and following the trial match in August he was signed immediately after the match had ended. He then played in Wrexham's reserve team in the Birmingham & District League before given his Football League debut in January 1925, replacing Jimmy Jones at inside-right in a 2-1 defeat against Grimsby Town at the Racecourse. Large was allowed to leave Wrexham shortly after that match, and joined Welsh National League (North) side Llandudno in February 1925. At the time he was described as having 'scored freely for Wrexham reserves.' 'Herb' later played for several other North Wales clubs, including Connah's Quay & Shotton, Denbigh United, Rhos, Druids, Mold, Blaenau Ffestiniog, and Bangor City. During this period, he worked as a storekeeper at Brymbo Steelworks, a job he held until his retirement in 1966. Large, who lived in Coedpoeth at that time, sadly passed away two years later at Wrexham's War Memorial Hospital, aged 68.

Season	League		F.A.Cup		Welsh Cup		Total	
	apps	gls	apps	gls	apps	gls	apps	gls
1924/25	1	0	-	-	-	-	1	0
	1	**0**	-	-	-	-	**1**	**0**

LAWRENCE, Cyril

1950 - 1952

Position; *Outside-Right*
D.O.B; *12th June, 1920*
Birthplace; *Salford, Lancashire*
Height; *5ft 8'1/2in* ***Weight;*** *11st 7lbs*
Debut; v. *Gateshead (h) 14th October, 1950*
Total Appearances & Goals; *58 apps 12 gls*
Career; *Blackpool Feb 1946 0apps; Rochdale Apr 1947 44apps 5gls; WREXHAM 25th Sept 1950 - May 1952;*

Cyril Lawrence was spotted as a junior by First Division side Blackpool, in 1939. The outbreak of the Second World War threatened to put paid to any thoughts he might have had of a career in football. Fortunately, he was able to return to Blackpool after the conflict had ended, signing professional forms in February 1946. He failed to make a first team appearance at Bloomfield Road, and left the 'Seasiders' in April 1947 to join Third Division North side Rochdale. It was here that Cyril was to make his Football League debut in the second match of the 1947/48 season, playing at centre-forward in a scoreless draw at Hull in front of a crowd of over 25,000. Later that season Cyril switched positions to outside-right, and spent the remainder of his time at Spotland on the right wing. Lawrence left Rochdale in September 1950, when he joined fellow Third Division North side Wrexham, along with his Rochdale team-mate, Dick Grieve. He went straight into the Wrexham side, making his debut on the Racecourse in a scoreless draw against Gateshead in his old centre-forward position in place of Frank Fidler. He led the attack for the following nine games, during which he scored three goals. He was then switched back to play at outside-right in place of Dennis Grainger, as he went on to make a total of fifty League appearances for Wrexham, before leaving the club at the end of the 1951/52 season. Cyril, who was then 32 years old, drifted into non-league football.

Season	League		F.A.Cup		Welsh Cup		Total	
	apps	gls	apps	gls	apps	gls	apps	gls
1950/51	25	5	2	1	2	0	29	6
1951/52	25	4	1	1	3	1	29	6
	50	**9**	**3**	**2**	**5**	**1**	**58**	**12**

LAWRENCE, Edward

1925 - 1928

Position; *Left-Half*
D.O.B; *24th August, 1907*
Birthplace; *Cefn Mawr, Denbighshire*
Died; *Nottingham, 20th July, 1989.*
Height; *5ft 7in* ***Weight;*** *11st 6lbs*
Debut; v. *Durham City (h) 24th April, 1926*
Total Appearances & Goals; *23 apps 0 gls*
Career; *Druids; WREXHAM (Am) Feb 1926, (Pro) 25th Feb 927; Clapton Orient Aug 1928 100apps 2gls; Notts County May 1931 £275 138apps 4gls; Bournemouth Aug 1936 39apps 1gls; Clapton Orient May 1937 21apps 0gls; to cs1938; Notts County 1939*
Honours; *Two Welsh International caps; One Welsh Junior International cap; Welsh F.A. Canada Tour 1929;*

Eddie Lawrence was first signed as an amateur by Wrexham from local non-league side Druids in February 1926. He was soon involved in first team action when stepping in to replace Alf Beevor for the last three matches of the season, his Football League debut coming in a 3-0 win over Durham City. Eddie had completed another three League appearances by the end of February of the following season, when he was signed as a professional. He then established himself as the club's regular left-half until the end of the term. However, 1927/28 again saw Eddie playing mainly reserve team football and managed just seven senior outings all season. It came as no surprise, therefore, when he was allowed to leave the Racecourse in the summer of 1928 to sign for Second Division Clapton Orient. At first Eddie again found himself in the reserves at his new club, before his debut finally came in November, a 3-0 home win over Middlesbrough. He must have impressed his manager as he kept his place in the side for the rest of the season, although it was hardly a cause for celebration as the 'O's' finished bottom of the League and were relegated to the Third Division South. By the close season of 1929 Eddie had done enough to be selected for the Welsh F.A.'s tour of Canada. He returned to Orient for the new season, where he was to become a regular in the 'O's' side for the next couple of years. In 1930 he won his first full cap for Wales in a 7-0 defeat by Ireland in Belfast and, in the close season of 1931 his football career really took off when he signed for newly promoted Second Division side Notts County for a £275 transfer fee. He was described as a "Scientific wing-half, never content to kick the ball and hope for the best, he always tried to be constructive" during his time at Meadow Lane, where he was also complimented: "A strong point of Eddie's play is his headwork, this is especially useful in defence where he seems able to rise to seemingly impossible heights. His side pass though, is soundest of all". All this led to him being described in 1934, as "one of the best wing-half backs Notts County have had for years". Eddie had made his debut for County in a 2-0 win at Bradford City, and went on to become the club's regular left-half over the next four seasons, winning a further Welsh cap in a 5-2 victory over Scotland in 1932. However, he had lost his place in his club side by March 1935, as the 'Magpies' struggled against relegation, which became reality at the end of the season. Eddie remained with the oldest League Club, however, although making only a further ten League appearances throughout 1935/36 until a change of club policy during the close season would see him become a casualty of a wholesale clear out of players. He then joined Bournemouth for a season, where he made 39 League appearances, before rejoining Clapton Orient in May 1937 for a second spell. Eddie went straight into the 'O's' senior side for the first game of the 1937/38 season, a 1-1 draw with Cardiff City, which was also their first ever Football League game at Brisbane Road. He went on to make a further twenty League appearances for Orient that season before leaving in the summer of 1938, to return to Notts County, though never actually making a first team appearance for them before the outbreak of World War Two. By that time Eddie was working for the John Player cigarette company. He joined the R.A.F. in 1940, spending three years of WW2 in North Africa. Lawrence returned to live in Nottingham after the conflict, where he scouted for Notts County until the late 1970s. Eddie remained active in his later life enjoying walks around the Nottingham area. He died at St.Francis Hospital in his adopted city in 1989, aged 81.

Season	League		F.A.Cup		Welsh Cup		Total	
	apps	gls	apps	gls	apps	gls	apps	gls
1925/26	3	0	-	-	-	-	3	0
1926/27	11	0	-	-	2	0	13	0
1927/28	7	0	-	-	-	-	7	0
	21	**0**	-	-	**2**	**0**	**23**	**0**

LAWRENCE, Matthew

1930 - 1937

Position; *Right-Half*
D.O.B; *3rd April, 1909*
Birthplace; *Cefn-Y-Bedd, Denbighshire*
Height; *5ft 7in* ***Weight;*** *11st 3lbs*
Debut; v. *Chesterfield (h) 26th December, 1930*
Total Appearances & Goals; *147 apps 4 gls*
Career; *Cross Street Church; WREXHAM (Am) Nov 1930, (Pro) 9th Jan 1931; Hull City 4th Sept 1937 25apps 1gls;Honours; Welsh Cup runner-up 1932 & 1933;*

Matt Lawrence was working at Llay Hall Colliery when he won a Chum's League Championship medal with Cross Street Church FC. On the back of this he was invited to sign for Wrexham as an amateur in November 1930 by manager Jack Baynes. He was to make his Football League debut for the 'Robins' in December against Chesterfield on the Racecourse, replacing Jack Hughes at inside-forward. Soon after this game, in January 1931, Matt signed professional, whereupon he gave up his job at the Colliery to combine playing football with working at the Racecourse, where he would tackle odd jobs under the guidance of former Wrexham player Bert Goode. The one appearance against Chesterfield proved to be Matt's only first team outing for the 1930/31 season, though he had established himself in his more formidable right-half position by the end of the following term, a position in which he would play regularly for Wrexham over the next six seasons, completing 132 League appearances. Matt, the cousin of former Wrexham and Wales player Wynne Crompton, was described as 'a sturdy wing-half, who was compactly built, while his long-throw was always a threat to opposing defences'. He collected two Welsh Cup runners'-up medals with the 'Robins' in 1932 and 1933, and was also a vital member of the 1932/33 team, arguably the best inter-war Wrexham side, who finished runners'-up in the Third Division North. However, he was to leave Wrexham after just one match of the 1937/38 season, joining their opponents in that opening game, Hull City, who were managed by the former Wrexham manager Ernie Blackburn. Matt had to wait until December before making his debut for the 'Tigers', which came in a 3-1 defeat at Tranmere, and went on to make a further 24 League appearances for the Humberside club in just under two seasons. He left Boothferry Park following the outbreak of World War Two, as playing activities were suspended. He returned home to the Wrexham area where, after trying his hand at different types of work, finally settled in the village of Tan-Y-Fron and obtained employment at the nearby Brymbo Steelworks. He went on to complete 33 years service at Brymbo until retiring in 1974. Matt was still living in Tan-Y-Fron at the time of writing.

Season	League		F.A.Cup		Welsh Cup		Total	
	apps	gls	apps	gls	apps	gls	apps	gls
1930/31	1	0	-	-	-	-	1	0
1931/32	13	0	-	-	5	0	18	0
1932/33	33	0	3	0	5	0	41	0
1933/34	34	2	-	-	1	0	35	2
1934/35	12	0	1	0	-	-	13	0
1935/36	22	1	1	0	1	0	24	1
1936/37	16	1	-	-	-	-	16	1
1937/38	1	0	-	-	-	-	1	0
	132	**4**	**5**	**0**	**12**	**0**	**147**	**4**

LECK, Reginald 1921 - 1922

Position; *Inside-Left*
D.O.B; *29th January, 1890*
Birthplace; *Aigburth, Liverpool, Merseyside*
Died; *North Liverpool, 18th April, 1966*
Height; *5ft 9in* ***Weight;*** *11st 5lbs*
Debut; v. *Hartlepool United (a) 8th September, 1921*
Total Appearances & Goals; *17 apps 6 gls*
Career; *St.Michael's 1904; Aigburth Vale 1907; Zalkyrie FC 1911; Tranmere Rovers May 1912; WREXHAM 15th June 1921 to cs1922;Honours; Lancashire Combination League Championship Winner 1914;*

Reg Leck was a promising footballer in his School team at Aigburth Vale, where he began to play for a local side, St.Michael's, in 1904. He then linked up with two more local sides, Aigburth Vale, and Zalkyrie, from where he signed for Lancashire Combination League side Tranmere Rovers in May 1912. Leck spent nine years on Tranmere's books, although that period was disrupted by the First World War, winning a championship medal in 1914. In the close season of 1921 he signed for Wrexham, who were preparing at the time for the club's inaugural season in the Football League. Although Reg didn't figure in the club's first ever Football League match, at home to Hartlepool, he did appear in the return match - coincidentally also against Hartlepool - a week later, when he wrote his name into the record books by scoring Wrexham's first ever goal in the Football League in the 1-0 win. Reg made a further twelve League appearances for Wrexham in his inside-forward position before allowed to leave the club at the end of the season. During his time in football he was nicknamed 'Ragtime', apparently because of his 'musical prowess in being able to entertain musically in off the field activities'.

Season	League		F.A.Cup		Welsh Cup		Total	
	apps	gls	apps	gls	apps	gls	apps	gls
1921/22	13	3	4	3	-	-	17	6
	13	**3**	**4**	**3**	**-**	**-**	**17**	**6**

LEE, Anthony 1986 - 1990

Position; *Forward*
D.O.B; *2nd March, 1970*
Birthplace; *Wirral, Merseyside*
Height; *5ft 7in* ***Weight;*** *10st 7lbs*
Debut v. *Bury (a) 9th December, 1989 (Leyland DAF Cup)*
Total Appearances & Goals; *0/1 app 0 gls*
Career; *WREXHAM Jul 1986, (Pro) Jul 1988; Chester cs1990 0apps; Runcorn; Winsford United; Manurewa (New Zealand); Bangor City; Rhyl 1991 52/9apps 5gls; Flint Town United Aug 1997 20/3apps 2gls;*
Honours; *Welsh Cup runner-up 1993;*

Tony Lee's association with Wrexham began as a 14 year old when he attended an open-age trial at the Racecourse. Despite the presence of much bigger and stronger adults, he did enough to be asked back, and after training twice a week for two years was offered an apprenticeship with the Racecourse club upon leaving school in 1986. He became a prolific goalscorer throughout his two years as an apprentice, averaging almost a goal a game, before signing professional forms during the close season of 1988. However, he couldn't maintain the early promise and his only first team appearance came in December 1989 at Gigg Lane, Bury in a Leyland DAF Cup match that the 'Shakers' won 4-1. Tony experienced just eleven minutes of first team action when he came on as substitute for Roger Preece, before being released at the end of the season. He then joined Chester where he was to spend almost a season before released without making a first team appearance. Lee then drifted into non-league football with short spells at both Runcorn and Winsford United before going to New Zealand to play for Manurewa where he remained until he broke his ankle and returned home. He then had a short spell with Bangor City joining Cymru Alliance League outfit Rhyl in 1991, but was again to suffer with injury when he cracked a rib which punctured a lung shortly afterwards. Having overcome these set-backs, Lee went on to enjoy considerable success with the Belle Vue club, though not before switching from playing as a striker to that of right-back. He went on to help Rhyl gain promotion to the League of Wales, and reach the 1993 Welsh Cup Final where they eventually lost to Cardiff City

at the National Stadium in Cardiff. Tony spent a number of seasons with the Lilywhites, although his appearances became limited. He played against the Welsh National side in a warm-up game at Belle Vue prior to the World Cup Qualifier against Holland in October 1996. He finally left Rhyl at the end of the season to sign for fellow League of Wales side Flint Town United where he spent the 1997/98 season.

Season	League		F.A.Cup		Welsh Cup		League Cup		L.D. Cup		Total	
	apps	gls	apps	gls	apps	gls	apps	gls	apps	gls	apps	gls
1989/90	-	-	-	-	-	-	-	-	0/1	0	0/1	0
	-	**-**	**-**	**-**	**-**	**-**	**-**	**-**	**0/1**	**0**	**0/1**	**0**

LEE, Frederick Stuart — 1975 - 1978

Position; *Forward*
D.O.B; *11th February, 1953*
Birthplace; *Manchester, Lancashire*
Height; *5ft 7in* ***Weight;*** *8st 11lbs*
Debut; v. *Halifax Town (h) 29th November, 1975*
Total Appearances & Goals; *57/12 apps 19 gls*
Career; *Bolton Wanderers Oct 1971 85apps 20gls; WREXHAM 26th Nov 1975 £15,000; Stockport County Aug 1978 49apps 21gls; Manchester City Sept 1979 £80,000 7apps 2gls; Portland Timbers Apr 1980-1982; Los Angeles Lazers; St.Louis Steamboats; Tampa Bay Rowdies May 1984;*

Stuart Lee had an impressive schoolboy career, and was quickly snapped up by Bolton Wanderers in 1969. He went on to sign professional terms with the 'Trotters' in October 1971, and made his Football League debut for the Club on New Years Day 1972 when he came on as sub for Paul Hallows in a scoreless draw with York City. Stuart then went on to make a further 84 League appearances for Bolton, scoring twenty goals, before leaving Burnden Park in November 1975. He was signed by Wrexham manager John Neal, who was searching for a striker to partner Billy Ashcroft. Neal matched the club record fee of £15,000 to bring Stuart to the Racecourse, after his interest in Portsmouth's Ray Hiron had been rebuffed. Stuart made an impressive start to his Wrexham career, scoring a penalty on his debut against Halifax in a 1-1 draw before going on to miss just three games throughout the remainder of the season. By joining the club in November he had missed the first two rounds of that seasons Cup-Winners' Cup competition, but played in both of the Quarter-Final matches against Anderlecht in March, and scored the Wrexham goal in the home leg which ended 1-1. Stuart spent much of the 1976/77 season on the substitute's bench, due mainly to Graham Whittle's outstanding form, and managed just a handful of appearances in 1977/78 as the club won promotion to the Second Division for the first time in its history. Lee then left Wrexham in the summer on a free transfer, and joined Stockport County. It proved to be a successful move for him, as he forged a deadly partnership with Les Bradd, and ended his first season at Edgeley Park as leading scorer with twenty league goals. His form soon attracted the attention of other clubs, and in September 1979 he was transferred to Manchester City for a £80,000 fee. However, he never really hit it off at Maine Road under Malcolm Allison, making just seven League appearances and scoring twice, not once was he on the winning side. He left City before the season was over to go to the U.S.A., where he played in the N.A.S.L. for Portland Timbers. This was followed by spells with Los Angeles Lazers, St.Louis Steamboats, and Tampa Bay Rowdies. Stuart was last known to be living back in the Manchester area.

Season	League		F.A.Cup		Welsh Cup		League Cup		E.C.W.C.		Total	
	apps	gls	apps	gls	apps	gls	apps	gls	apps	gls	apps	gls
1975/76	27	8	-	-	3	4	-	-	2	1	32	13
1976/77	14/7	4	1	1	1/3	1	3	0	-	-	19/10	6
1977/78	5/1	0	-	-	-	-	1/1	0	-	-	6/2	0
	46/8	**12**	**1**	**1**	**4/3**	**5**	**4/1**	**0**	**2**	**1**	**57/12**	**19**

LEEMING, William Brian — 1929 - 1930

Position; *Half-Back*
D.O.B; *A/M/J 1909*
Birthplace; *Blean, Nr.Canterbury, Kent*
Died; *Hillingdon, August 1997*
Height; *5ft 8in* ***Weight;*** *11st 7lbs*
Debut; v. *Rotherham United (a) 26th April, 1930*
Total Appearances & Goals; *1 app 0 gls*
Career; *Farnborough Town; Wolves; WREXHAM (Am) Aug 1929, (Pro) 7th Sept 1929; Bradford City (Trial) Jul 1930 0apps; Oswestry Town Oct 1930; Aldershot (Trial) Sept 1932; Camberley & Yorktown Dec 1932;*

Bill Leeming was signed by Wrexham as an amateur in August 1929 from Wolves, where he had failed to make a first team appearance. When he joined Wrexham it was claimed that he also played for Farnborough Town. He made sufficient progress at the Racecourse and signed professional forms in September, but spent most of the season playing for the 'Robins' reserve side in the Birmingham & District League. His Football League debut came in the penultimate match of the 1929/30 campaign in a 3-1 win at Rotherham, when he replaced Albert Lumberg at left-back, but was then released in the summer. However, he was soon invited to join Bradford City for a two month trial period in July 1930. He failed to make a first team appearance for the Yorkshire Club, and after his trial period was completed was released. Bill then signed for Birmingham & District League side Oswestry Town in October, where he is believed to have spent two seasons until accepting the offer of a trial period with Aldershot in September 1932, following their election to the Football League. Bill's stay at the Recreation Ground was short-lived, and he left without making any impression. He is then believed to have joined Camberley & Yorktown.

Season	League		F.A.Cup		Welsh Cup		Total	
	apps	gls	apps	gls	apps	gls	apps	gls
1929/30	1	0	-	-	-	-	1	0
	1	**0**	**-**	**-**	**-**	**-**	**1**	**0**

LEMAN, Dennis — 1982

Position; *Midfield*
D.O.B; *1st December, 1954*
Birthplace; *Newcastle-upon-Tyne, Tyne & Wear*
Height; *5ft 5in* ***Weight;*** *10st 9lbs*
Debut; v. *Charlton Athletic (a) 20th February, 1982*
Total Appearances & Goals; *17 apps 1 gls*
Career; *Manchester City Jul 1970, (Pro) 1st Dec 1971 10/7apps 1gls; Sheffield Wednesday 1st Dec (Loan), 5th Jan 1977 £10,000 89/12apps 9gls; WREXHAM 18th Feb 1982 (Loan); Scunthorpe United Aug 1982 38apps 3gls; Burton Albion Jan 1984; Cardiff City March 1984 (Non Contract) 0apps;*
Honours; *England Schoolboy International;*

Dennis Leman played football from an early age, and his talents saw him represent his school team at Heaton Grammar School as well as being chosen for both Newcastle and Northumberland Boys. His promising displays brought him to the attention of several large clubs and also earned him international recognition with England Schoolboys, for whom he played nine times against West Germany (3 times), Scotland (twice), Holland, Wales, Northern Ireland, and Eire. At sixteen Dennis had Manchester United, Burnley, Stoke City, Everton, and his native Newcastle all clamouring for his signature, but chose Manchester City, progressing well enough to sign professional forms on his seventeenth birthday. He had to wait almost two years before making his Football League debut for City, which came in a 1-1 home draw with Southampton in October 1973. However, he never really established himself as a regular at Maine Road, although he did play in both legs of the League Cup semi-finals in 1974, before missing out on a Final appearance. In December 1976 he left Maine Road to join Third Division Sheffield Wednesday on loan. Dennis scored on his League debut for Wednesday at home to Tranmere Rovers in a 3-1 win, and a month later was signed permanently by the 'Owls' for £10,000. He became a regular in midfield, helping them to promotion in 1980. However, the 1981/82 season saw him fall from favour at Hillsborough, and in February was allowed to join Wrexham, initially on a month's loan. Dennis made his debut for the 'Robins' in a 1-0 defeat at Charlton, and his loan period was later extended until the end of the season. When he joined Wrexham the club were fighting to steer clear of the relegation zone, but despite Dennis' best efforts they couldn't prevent themselves from falling through the trapdoor. Relegation saw manager Mel Sutton leave the club, and the consequent need for economies to be made meant there was no prospect of Dennis signing on a permanent basis. He returned to Sheffield, only to find that he had been released by the 'Owls'. He then received an offer to play in Sweden, but decided to stay at home and sign for Scunthorpe United on a free transfer in August 1982. Making his

debut in a scoreless draw at Hartlepool Dennis went on to help the 'Iron' win promotion to the Third Division. Before the following season had begun he had sustained a knee injury, and this restricted him to just two appearances before Christmas. Shortly afterwards, a disagreement with manager Allan Clarke saw Dennis' contract being settled early. He was then invited to join Burton Albion in January 1984, by their up-and-coming manager Neil Warnock, and played a few games for Burton before being given the opportunity to return to League football by Cardiff City manager Jimmy Mullen. Nothing came of this, and Dennis left Ninian Park at the end of the season without having made a first team appearance for the 'Bluebirds'. He then began working for a Double Glazing company, before returning to college to pursue a career in recreation and leisure. On completion of his studies Dennis took up work with the Professional Footballers' Association, as a Football in the Community Officer. He is still employed by the P.F.A. in Manchester as part of their administration unit, supporting ninety projects, as well as playing the odd match for Manchester City Veterans. Dennis is also a fully qualified coach and physiotherapist.

Season	League		F.A.Cup		Welsh Cup		League Cup		Total	
	apps	gls	apps	gls	apps	gls	apps	gls	apps	gls
1981/82	17	1	-	-	-	-	-	-	17	1
	17	**1**	-	-	-	-	-	-	**17**	**1**

LENNEY, Ralph Curry

1923 - 1924

Position; *Outside-Left*
D.O.B; *11th January, 1895*
Birthplace; *South Shields, Tyne & Wear*
Died; *Cleadon, County Durham, 10th November 1971*
Height; *5ft 9in* ***Weight;*** *11st 0lbs*
Debut; v. *Ashington (h) 25th August 1923*
Total Appearances & Goals; *15 apps 1 gls*
Career; *South Shields; West Bromwich Albion Feb 1922 0apps; WREXHAM 23rd Jun 1923; Carlisle United Aug 1924;*

Ralph Lenney was playing for Football League side South Shields when signed by First Division West Bromwich Albion in February 1922. However, he failed to make a first team appearance at the Hawthorns in his sixteen months with the club, playing regularly for Albion's reserve side, before joining Wrexham in the close season of 1923. Ralph was plunged straight into the 'Robins' first team for his debut in the first match of the 1923/24 season, playing at outside-left in a 4-0 win over Ashington on the Racecourse. He remained a regular in the side until he lost his place to youngster Jesse Williams in October, and then had to wait until January for his next opportunity, at centre-forward in place of Billy Jackson at Tranmere Rovers. Ralph was allowed to leave the Racecourse at the end of the season, and joined North-Eastern League side Carlisle United in the summer.

Season	League		F.A.Cup		Welsh Cup		Total	
	apps	gls	apps	gls	apps	gls	apps	gls
1923/24	15	1	-	-	1	0	16	1
	15	**1**	-	-	**1**	**0**	**16**	**1**

LEWIS, Dudley Keith

1992

Position; *Central Defender*
D.O.B; *17th November, 1962*
Birthplace; *Swansea, Glamorgan*
Height; *5ft 10in* ***Weight;*** *10st 9lbs*
Debut; v. *Crewe Alexandra (h) 21st March, 1992*
Total Appearances & Goals; *8/1 apps 0 gls*
Career; *Swansea City Nov 1979 228/2apps 2gls; Huddersfield Town Jul 1989 £50,000 32/2apps 0gls; Halifax Town Oct 1991 (loan) 11apps 0gls; WREXHAM March 1992; Halifax Town Aug 1992 10/3apps 0gls; Torquay United Dec 1992 9apps 0gls; Weymouth Feb 1993; Merthyr Tydfil Aug 1993 34apps 0gls; Carmarthen Town Jul 1994; Llanelli Nov 1996; Bridgend Town;*
Honours; *One Welsh International cap; Nine Welsh Under-21 caps; Welsh Youth International; Welsh Schoolboy International; Welsh Cup Winner 1981, 1983 & 1989;*

Dudley Lewis was an outstanding performer at schoolboy level. He played for both Waun Wen and Pentre Hafod Schools in Swansea and represented Swansea Schoolboys. Dudley was also capped by Wales Schoolboys before he signed apprentice forms for Swansea City. He made his debut for Swansea six months before turning professional with the club, coming on as a substitute against Notts County in February 1981, while the following week made his debut for Wales at Youth level. Dudley's first team place at the Vetch was not assured until the 1982/83 season, Swansea's last in the First Division, which led to him being called up into the full Welsh International squad. By that time he had already been capped at Under-21 level for Wales. In June 1983 he made his one and only full international appearance for Wales when he played against Brazil. Dudley was 'a very defensive minded player', later forming a vital rearguard partnership with another Welsh international, Andy Melville. Cartilage trouble in March 1987 dealt him a heavy blow, but he recovered, and in July 1989 signed for Huddersfield Town for a £50,000 fee. His first match for the 'Terriers' was ironically against Swansea, in the opening game of the season in which the Yorkshire side won 1-0 at Leeds Road. Dudley recorded 34 League appearances in his two years at Leeds Road, before being loaned out to Halifax Town in October 1991. He made eleven League appearances for the 'Shaymen' before returning to Huddersfield, and in March 1992 Wrexham manager Brian Flynn, who was rebuilding, signed him on non-contract terms until the end of the season. He made his debut for the 'Robins' in a 1-0 home win over Crewe Alexandra, adding eight more League appearances for the North Wales club until told that he would not be offered a contract at the end of the season. Lewis commenced 1992/93 with Halifax Town, but after making just thirteen League appearances he moved south and signed for Torquay United in the December. He made nine League appearances for the 'Gulls' before leaving Plainmoor in February to join Southern League side Weymouth, where he completed the 1992/93 season. During the close season Dudley returned to Wales, where he signed for Conference League side Merthyr Tydfil. However, following the 'Martyrs' relegation that season, he joined League of Wales side Carmarthen Town, before later signing for Llanelli and was recently on the Board of Welsh League Bridgend Town.

Season	League		F.A.Cup		Welsh Cup		League Cup		F.R.T.		Total	
	apps	gls	apps	gls	apps	gls	apps	gls	apps	gls	apps	gls
1991/92	8/1	0	-	-	-	-	-	-	-	-	8/1	0
	8/1	**0**	-	-	-	-	-	-	-	-	**8/1**	**0**

LEWIS, John

1933 - 1938

Position; *Centre-Half*
D.O.B;
Birthplace; *Gwersyllt, Denbighshire*
Height; *6ft 0in* ***Weight;*** *13st 0lbs*
Debut; v. *York City (h) 23rd December, 1933*
Total Appearances & Goals; *111 apps 2 gls*
Career; *Gwersyllt; WREXHAM (Am) Apr 1932, (Pro) 23rd Aug 1932; Luton Town 14th February, 1938 2apps 0gls; Crewe Alexandra May 1939; Barmouth & Dyffryn United 1949/50;*

Jack Lewis joined Wrexham from local village side Gwersyllt in April 1932. Although having to wait until December 1933 before making his Football League debut, he had done enough to earn himself a professional contract by August 1932. Jack finally made the breakthrough into the senior side when he stepped in at half-back for Harry Beck in a 3-2 defeat against York City. That was his one and only first team appearance that season, but he returned to the side the following October for the injured Jim Bulling, and went on to make a further eleven League appearances before the summer break. 1935/36 finally would see Jack establish

himself in the first team, and over the following three seasons he became the pivot of the Wrexham defence, described as 'of the third back type, he gave little away in defence, and his big kicking was an asset.' His most memorable match for Wrexham came against Manchester City in an F.A.Cup Third Round tie which they lost 3-1 on the Racecourse. In February 1938 he was signed by Second Division Luton Town, and went straight into the side at centre-half in a scoreless draw with West Ham United at Upton Park. He then played in the following game, a 3-1 home defeat by Southampton. However, they proved to be his only appearances for the 'Hatters' in his one and a half seasons at the club, which led to him leaving Kenilworth Road in the close season of 1939. Jack then signed for Crewe Alexandra, but after making just two League appearances for the 'Railwaymen', his football career came to an abrupt stop with the outbreak of the Second World War. He is known to have played for Barmouth & Dyffryn United after WW2 had come to a conclusion.

Season	League		F.A.Cup		Welsh Cup		N.S.C.		Total	
	apps	gls	apps	gls	apps	gls	apps	gls	apps	gls
1933/34	1	0	-	-	-	-	-	-	1	0
1934/35	12	0	2	0	-	-	1	0	15	0
1935/36	19	0	1	0	1	0	1	0	22	0
1936/37	37	0	3	0	1	0	1	0	42	0
1937/38	27	2	2	0	1	0	1	0	31	2
	96	**2**	**8**	**0**	**3**	**0**	**4**	**0**	**111**	**2**

LEWIS, Thomas Hewitt

1930 - 1933

Position; *Inside/Outside-Left*
D.O.B; *11th October, 1909*
Birthplace; *Ellesmere Port, Cheshire*
Height; *5ft 9in* ***Weight;*** *13st 6lbs*
Debut; v. *Southport (a) 30th August 1930*
Total Appearances & Goals; *122 apps 48 gls*
Career; *Everton (Am) Mar 1927, (Pro) Apr 1927 1app 0gls; WREXHAM 26th June 1930; Bradford Park Avenue June 1933 193apps 7gls; Blackpool Dec 1938 12apps 3gls, WW2 7apps 2gls; Wrexham (WW2 Guest) Sept 1942 3apps 1gls; Crewe Alexandra (WW2 Guest) 1942/43 4apps 0gls;*
Honours; *Welsh Cup Winner 1931; Welsh Cup runner-up 1933;*

Tommy Lewis joined Everton in 1926 and progressed through the junior ranks to make his one and only Football League appearance for the Toffee's in the final match of the 1928/29 season, a 2-0 defeat at Newcastle. He was allowed to leave Goodison Park and join Third Division North side Wrexham in June 1930. At the Racecourse he made his debut in the opening game of the new campaign, a 1-1 draw at Southport, playing at outside-left. Tommy went on to be a regular in the Wrexham side for the next three seasons, making 105 League appearances, and scoring forty goals during which time he won a Welsh Cup winners' medal in 1931, scoring twice in the 'Robins' 7-0 win over Shrewsbury Town. Two years later he added a runners'-up medal in the same competition to his trophy cabinet, and that same season helped Wrexham to their highest inter-war League position as they finished runners-up in the Third Division North to Champions, Hull City. However, Tommy was allowed to leave the Racecourse at the end of that season, and moved on to Bradford Park Avenue. He spent over five seasons with the West Yorkshire side, making over 200 appearances before he was signed by First Division Blackpool in December 1938. Tommy went straight into the 'Tangerines' side at outside-left for his debut, a 2-1 home win over Birmingham. He made a further eleven League appearances, scoring three goals, before ill health forced him to retire from playing - although he did recover enough to make the odd appearance during World War Two for both Wrexham and Crewe Alexandra. Tommy's son, Kevin, also played League football for both Sheffield United and Liverpool in the 1950s and 1960s.

Season	League		F.A.Cup		Welsh Cup		Total	
	apps	gls	apps	gls	apps	gls	apps	gls
1930/31	39	15	3	1	4	2	46	18
1931/32	37	8	1	1	4	4	42	13
1932/33	29	17	3	0	2	0	34	17
1942/43	3	0	-	-	-	-	3	0
	108	**40**	**7**	**2**	**10**	**6**	**125**	**48**
F/League	105	40	7	2	10	6	122	48

LEYFIELD, John George

1946 - 1950

Position; *Wing-Half*
D.O.B; *5th August, 1923*
Birthplace; *Handbridge, Chester, Cheshire*
Height; *6ft 0in* ***Weight;*** *12st 2lb*
Debut; v. *Doncaster Rovers (a) 25th December, 1946*
Total Appearances & Goals; *38 apps 1 gls*
Career; *Chester (Am) 15th Jun 1940 3apps 0gls; WREXHAM 21st Jun 1946; Southport 7th Aug 1950 26apps 0gls; Winsford United cs1951; Ellesmere Port Town cs1952; Macclesfield Town Jun 1956;*

Jack Leyfield, brother of the Wrexham trainer Charlie Leyfield, was denied the opportunity to take up a career in football by the outbreak of the Second World War. He had played for Chester College, and represented Chester Schoolboys before leaving school at the age of fourteen to become a business trainee. This put an end to his playing of competitive football until he was approached by Chester manager Frank Brown, who was also a neighbour of his, and invited for an assessment and training at Sealand Road. He was signed as an amateur shortly afterwards in June 1940 but then the Second World War intervened, and 18 years-old Jack was enlisted in the Royal Tank Regiment, switching after training to the Scots Guards. He then saw active service as a Tank commander in North West Europe, passing through France, Belgium, Holland, Denmark, and finally Germany. His tank was, in fact, one of the first to arrive at the Belsen Concentration Camp following its Liberation. Jack played football during WW2 whenever possible, turning out for Chester when he could, as well as for the British Army on the Rhine (BAOR) team as they staged morale-boosting friendlies for the troops. Jack remained in Germany after the War had ended, where he played in a Cup Final in the Berlin Olympic Stadium in front of a 90,000 crowd. It was when he was on home leave that Jack was invited to sign for Wrexham by manager Tom Williams, which he did in June 1946, but it wasn't until the following March that he was finally demobbed from the Army. In the meantime, however, Leyfield had made his Football League debut for the 'Robins' in a 5-0 defeat at Doncaster Rovers on Christmas Day 1946, replacing Walter Roberts. He remained with Wrexham for the next four years, but in all that time never really established himself as a regular in the first team. Although recognised as a wing-half he played in almost every position for Wrexham, and in so doing gained the reputation of being 'regarded as a reliable utility player'. In 1948 Jack returned to Germany on a tour of the Rhine with the Wrexham team, and they played three friendlies against the British Forces' teams still stationed there. Jack left the Racecourse in the summer of 1950 to join Southport, making his debut for the 'Sandgrounders' in a 1-0 home defeat against Tranmere Rovers. By January he had become their sixth captain of the campaign in a match at Gateshead, but even so was still allowed to leave Haig Avenue at the end of the season, when he moved on to Cheshire County League side Winsford United. He spent one season with them before joining Ellesmere Port Town, who played in the same League, and where he spent four seasons eventually joining another Cheshire County League side Macclesfield Town, in June 1956 for a short spell. After ending his career with 'Macc' Jack helped out briefly with managing and coaching the Ellesmere Port reserve team, before becoming a scout for Joe Mercer when he managed both Aston Villa and Sheffield United. After the end of his professional football career he took up working for Shell in Ellesmere Port as a Control and Purchasing manager until his retirement in 1981. Jack then settled to live in retirement in the Chester area.

Season	League		F.A.Cup		Welsh Cup		Total	
	apps	gls	apps	gls	apps	gls	apps	gls
1946/47	7	0	-	-	-	-	7	0
1947/48	4	1	-	-	-	-	4	1
1948/49	19	0	1	0	-	-	20	0
1949/50	4	0	2	0	1	0	7	0
	34	**1**	**3**	**0**	**1**	**0**	**38**	**1**

LITTLEHALES, Henry 1924 - 1926

Position; *Left-Half*
D.O.B; *26th August, 1901*
Birthplace; *Burslem, Stoke-on-Trent, Staffordshire*
Died; *Wrexham Maelor Hospital, 24th May 1989*
Height; *5ft 7'1/2in* ***Weight;*** *11st 0lbs*
League Debut; v. *Hartlepool United (a) 3rd September 1932*
Total Appearances & Goals; *5 apps 0 gls*
Career; *Goldenhill Wanderers; Rudyard FC; Port Vale 0apps; Reading Aug 1922 6apps 1gls; Tranmere Rovers Aug 1923 163apps 49gls; WREXHAM 12th May 1932 to cs1933;*
Honours; *Birmingham & District League Championship Winner 1933;*

The second eldest of nine children 'Harry' Littlehales had to wear leg braces until he was ten years-old, but overcame this disability and started playing football for his Sunday School team, later representing both Goldenhill Wanderers and Rudyard F.C. He then joined his local side, Port Vale, as a left-winger, but left Vale Park in the close season of 1922 without having made a first team appearance. Third Division South side, Reading, was his next port of call, where he made his Football League debut. Harry went on to record five more League appearances for the 'Royals', scoring one goal, leaving after just one season to join Tranmere Rovers. He made his debut for the Wirral club a month after signing in a 3-0 home win over Barrow. Harry went on to spend nine happy years at Prenton Park completing 163 League appearances and scoring 49 goals for Tranmere. He became affectionately known as 'Handsome Harry', and struck up a friendship with the legendary Dixie Dean, which lasted for many years. At the end of the 1931/32 season Harry was signed by Wrexham, and made his debut for the club at Hartlepool in the third match of the season, a 3-1 defeat. Harry made four more appearances in the senior side before he was replaced by Matt Lawrence. He never figured in a first team match after that, although he spent the rest of the season playing for the reserves in the Birmingham & District League as they won the Championship for the second season in succession. Harry was released by Wrexham in the summer, whereupon he settled in the Wrexham, taking up employment at Monsanto Chemicals in Acrefair, where he remained until he retired at the age of 65 in 1966. During his time with the Company he played hockey, cricket, and billiards for the works teams. He had also coached at Druids United for a while. His grandson is a regular at the Racecourse and a member of the Kop Choir!!

Season	League		F.A.Cup		Welsh Cup		Total	
	apps	gls	apps	gls	apps	gls	apps	gls
1932/33	5	0	-	-	-	-	5	0
	5	**0**	-	-	-	-	**5**	**0**

LITTLER, Eric Joseph 1955

Position; *Centre-Forward*
D.O.B; *14th April, 1929*
Birthplace; *St.Helens, Merseyside*
Height; *5ft 11in* ***Weight;*** *11st 0lbs*
Debut; v. *York City (a) 20th August, 1955*
Total Appearances & Goals; *12 apps 1 gls*
Career; *St.Helens Town 1946; Stubshaw Cross 1950; Leicester City May 1951 5apps 2gls; Lincoln City Dec 1954 £5,000 6apps 2gls; WREXHAM 21st Jun 1955; Crewe Alexandra 30th Dec 1955 10apps 2gls; Chorley cs1956; Fleetwood cs1960; Prescot Cables 1960; Sutton Parish 1961;*

Eric Littler played his early football at Kirk Sandall Junior and St.Helens Catholic Grammar Schools. He also represented his schools at Rugby Union, but football was his first love, and he signed for St.Helens Town during the 1946/47 season. Eric remained with them until 1950, when he joined Stubshaw Cross of the Lancashire Combination League. Here he came to the attention of the Accrington Stanley manager Jimmy Porter; but, before he was given the chance to join Accrington Porter had resigned, although appointed chief scout at Leicester City shortly afterwards. It was to his new club that he then invited Eric for a trial, and he eventually signed for the Filbert Street club in May 1951. Eric spent most of his first season playing reserve team football before being handed his first team opportunity in April 1952, when he made his Football League debut against Notts County, and scored the Leicester goal in a 1-1 draw. Despite this success Eric was to make just four more League appearances over the next two years at Filbert Street, scoring one more goal, as he was the understudy to the consistent Derek Hines. In December 1954 Littler took the opportunity of signing for Lincoln City in a record deal, as he and £30,000 headed for Sincil Bank and Andy Graver moved in the opposite direction. Eric was valued at £5,000 in the deal. However, things didn't work out as he would have hoped: he made just six League appearances, scoring twice before falling out with the manager Bill Anderson. He was then involved in another exchange deal, as he and £1,000 went to Wrexham in exchange for Tommy Bannan in the close season of 1955. Eric began the season at centre-forward, marking an impressive debut by scoring one of the goals in a 3-1 win at York City. After nine more League games failing to find the net he found himself replaced and consigned to reserve team football. Littler made a return to the side at Christmas for two matches against Workington, but the following match on the Racecourse, against Crewe Alexandra on New Year's Eve, saw Eric playing - not for Wrexham but for........Crewe! He had signed for the 'Railwaymen' on the day before the game, but after ten appearances and two goals he again found himself playing reserve team football until the end of the season when he was released from Gresty Road. Eric then returned home to St.Helens, where he took up working for Triplex Safety Glass in the town, his employers prior to his move to Leicester. He continued to play football for Chorley, where he spent four seasons, later playing for Fleetwood and Prescot Cables, his final semi-pro team. Eric continued to play football, in the local leagues around St.Helens for Sutton Parish, until he was 42 years old. After finally hanging up his boots, he became involved with St.Helens Town, where he sat on their committee, and worked with the club's Junior teams. He later worked as a self-employed taxi driver in the town.

Season	League		F.A.Cup		Welsh Cup		Total	
	apps	gls	apps	gls	apps	gls	apps	gls
1955/56	12	1	-	-	-	-	12	1
	12	**1**	**-**	**-**	**-**	**-**	**12**	**1**

LIVSEY, Gordon William 1967 - 1971

Position; *Goalkeeper*
D.O.B; *24th January, 1947*
Birthplace; *Keighley, Yorkshire*
Height; *5ft 10 1/2in* ***Weight;*** *10st 12lbs*
Debut; v. *Barnsley (h) 9th September, 1967*
Total Appearances & Goals; *90 apps 0 gls*
Career; *Kettering Town 1962; WREXHAM 4th Jan 1967 (Trial), 12th Oct 1967 (Pro); Chester 6th Aug 1971 £2,500 44apps 0gls; Kettering Town Jul 1972; Workington Jul 1977 (Player/Manager); Hartlepool United Dec 1977 6apps 0gls; Weymouth Aug 1978; Nuneaton Borough Feb 1979 (Loan); Scarborough cs1979; Corby Town cs1980 (Player/Manager); AP Leamington Jan 1981; Kidderminster Harriers (Asst manager) 1983; Hamlet Stuart & Lloyd's (Manager) 1985;*
Honours; *Southern League Cup Winner; Northern Floodlit League Cup Winner 1970; Alves Cup Winner 1970;*

Although born in Yorkshire Gordon Livsey lived most of his early life in the Kettering area, after his family uprooted and moved south. He first played football as a centre-forward for Park Road Junior School in Kettering, but he was moved into goal following an injury, a position in which he was to excel for the rest of his footballing career. He played for both the Central and Grammar Schools in Kettering, from where he represented Kettering & District and the Northamptonshire Youth teams. It was not only football at which Gordon excelled, however, as he also represented Northamptonshire Schools at cricket as well as having trials for the England Schools' side. He was still at school when he began playing in goal for Kettering Town in the Southern League at the age of 15! It was this early exposure that led him to be recommended to Wrexham by the Club's former goalkeeper, Pat Egglestone. He was first taken on trial in January 1967, but tragedy struck after just ten minutes of his first match for the reserve side in a Cheshire County League fixture against Hyde United, when he broke his leg. He worked hard to get his fitness back, and returned to Wrexham in the summer of 1967 for a further trial, by which time there had been a change of manager with Alvan Williams replacing the departed Jack Rowley. Gordon played in a few friendly and reserve team games, and his trial period was extended for a further month before he was signed on professional terms in September 1967. His first team opportunity was to follow, but only after he let in eight goals against Tranmere Rovers reserves! Gordon's Football League debut came against Barnsley on the Racecourse, in place of John Schofield in September, Wrexham won 2-0, and Livsey remained in the side for the next three games. He was then to face competition for the 'keeper's jersey from Dennis Reeves, but went on to claim the number one spot for the next two seasons. During his time at the Racecourse Gordon was an active member of the local Salvation Army, playing the cornet in their band. He also became well known through the 'Football League Review' a supplement included in the club's match programme, as it ran a series where fans could vote for the country's best looking player. Gordon was always in the top ten, along with the likes of George Best! Wrexham signed another goalkeeper in the summer of 1969, Dave Gaskell, and Gordon found himself demoted to the reserve team for two seasons. He was to make only nine League and Cup appearances during this time, all of them as cover for Gaskell. In August 1971 he decided to leave Wrexham, as he wanted regular first team football, and signed for

Chester for £2,500. He made his debut in the opening game of the new season, a 1-1 home draw with Cambridge, and went on to miss just two matches all season. However, he was injured on the eve of the 1972/73 season, and once fit found John Taylor installed as the first choice 'keeper. Gordon left Sealand Road in the summer and returned to Kettering, who were managed at the time by Ron Atkinson. He remained at Kettering until 1977, helping them to twice lift the Southern League Cup. Gordon then applied for the player/manager's job at Workington in the 1977 close season, following their relegation from the Football League. He played what he regarded as the best football of his career at Borough Park, and in December 1977 was back in the Football League with Hartlepool United. He made six League appearances at the Victoria Ground until leaving at the end of the season. He then joined Weymouth, managed by Graham Carr, following him to Nuneaton Borough in February and where he remained until the end of the season. Gordon was then approached by Colin Appleton at Scarborough, who competed in the Northern Premier League at the time. He spent a season here moving nearer home to join Corby Town as player/manager in the close season of 1980. He was soon on the move again, however, accepting an invitation to join Graham Allner as his assistant at AP Leamington, who were then in the Alliance Premier, now the Conference. Gordon later joined up with Allner again as his assistant at Kidderminster Harriers, playing one more game. The travelling eventually became too much, and quit some time in 1984. A year later he returned to football for a short spell as manager of United Counties League side Hamlet S & L of Corby. He was forced to resign because of work commitments, although he later set up a school of excellence in Northamptonshire for Ron Atkinson when he was at Aston Villa. Gordon, who is now settled in the Kettering area, has worked as a self-employed salesman for a number of years.

Season	League		F.A.Cup		Welsh Cup		League Cup		Total	
	apps	gls	apps	gls	apps	gls	apps	gls	apps	gls
1967/68	33	0	-	-	1	0	-	-	34	0
1968/69	38	0	2	0	4	0	3	0	47	0
1969/70	1	0	-	-	-	-	-	-	1	0
1970/71	7	0	1	0	-	-	-	-	8	0
	79	**0**	**3**	**0**	**5**	**0**	**3**	**0**	**90**	**0**

LLOYD, Brian William 1971 - 1977

Position; *Goalkeeper*
D.O.B; *18th March, 1948*
Birthplace; *St.Asaph, Flintshire*
Height; *6ft 2in* ***Weight;*** *12st 7lbs*
Debut; v. *Blackburn Rovers (a) 28th August, 1971*
Total Appearances & Goals; *333 apps 0 gls*
Career; *Rhyl Mar 1966; Stockport County Mar 1967 £1,000 32apps 0gls; Southend United Sept 1969 £10,000 46apps 0gls; WREXHAM 4th Aug 1971; Chester 29th Sept 1977 £6,000 94apps 0gls; Port Vale Feb 1981 (loan) 16apps 0gls Stockport County Aug 1981 91apps 1gls; Bangor City Aug 1984; Colwyn Bay Aug 1985; Lex XI 1988/89; Brymbo Apr 1996;*
Honours; *Three Welsh international caps; Two Welsh under-23 caps; Welsh Cup Winner 1972 & 1975; Welsh Cup runner-up 1985;*

At Glyndwr School in Rhyl Brian Lloyd had played mainly as an outside-right, and appeared in Welsh Youth team trials in that position. However, he later decided that he was better at stopping goals than making them, and it was as a Custodian that he signed for Cheshire County League side, Rhyl, where he was taken under the guidance and watchful eye of former Everton and Wrexham keeper Albert Dunlop. Brian actually signed professional for Rhyl at the age of 18, in March 1966. He was keeping goal when Stockport County approached the Belle Vue club and offered £1,000 for his services, which was accepted. Brian made his Football League debut for Stockport a year later, when he replaced ex-Wrexham 'keeper Steve Fleet in a 1-1 draw at Colchester United in April 1967. He then kept his place until the end of the season, going on to make a further 24 appearances during 1968/69, until Southend United signed him for £10,000 in September 1969. Lloyd spent just under two seasons with the Essex club, making 46 League appearances, before wanting a move nearer home. Wrexham manager, and former Southend coach, John Neal returned to his old club to sign him in August 1971, after he had been on tour to the Far East and New Zealand with a Wales XI. It was Wrexham's 'keeper of that time, Dave Gaskell, who had recommended him to Neal, and it was he who Brian later replaced in the team! Lloyd went on to clock up a record number of consecutive League appearances for the 'Robins', 248, at the time a Football League record. The run began on 4th March 1972, at Rochdale, and ended on 20th August 1977 at Shrewsbury. During his time with Wrexham he collected two Welsh Cup Winners' medals and helped the club to the Quarter-Finals of both the F.A.Cup and the European Cup-Winners' Cup. He was capped by Wales three times: in 1976, against Austria, England and Scotland. His debut, against Austria, came in a vital European Championship match following an injury to Dai Davies, the 'keeper who was eventually to replace him at

Wrexham. In addition to playing in that Austrian match Brian also designed the front cover of the match programme for the game. Following the 1977 match against Shrewsbury Brian was surprisingly dropped by manager Arfon Griffiths for a young, and inexperienced, Eddie Niedzwiecki. Later that month Dai Davies was signed from Everton to replace Brian, who then left the Racecourse to join neighbours Chester for £6,000. He spent four seasons at Sealand Road, being loaned out to Port Vale in February 1981 until the end of the season. At the end of the 1980/81 season he was released by Chester, and rejoined Stockport County. He made a further 91 League appearances for Stockport, where he joined a select band of 'keepers by scoring directly from a kick out against Bradford City in March 1982. While at Stockport Lloyd gained a HND in building design, a career he was to follow on leaving the professional game. He was released by Stockport at the end of the 1983/84 season, and joined Bangor City, with whom he picked up a Welsh Cup runners'-up medal in 1985. The following season Brian played for Colwyn Bay in the North-West Counties League, and later helped out at local side Lex XI, as well as at a number of Sunday League sides in the Wrexham area. In April 1996 Brian stepped out of retirement, at the age of 48, to play for Cymru Alliance League side Brymbo. He still lives in the Wrexham area, where he works as a design consultant on housing projects and can often be seen attending matches at the Racecourse.

Season	League		F.A.Cup		Welsh Cup		League Cup		E.C.W.C.		Total	
	apps	gls	apps	gls	apps	gls	apps	gls	apps	gls	apps	gls
1971/72	35	0	2	0	3	0	1	0	-	-	41	0
1972/73	46	0	3	0	1	0	2	0	4	0	56	0
1973/74	46	0	7	0	3	0	2	0	-	-	58	0
1974/75	46	0	1	0	5	0	1	0	-	-	53	0
1975/76	46	0	3	0	3	0	3	0	6	0	61	0
1976/77	46	0	6	0	4	0	5	0	-	-	61	0
1977/78	1	0	-	-	-	-	2	0	-	-	3	0
	266	**0**	**22**	**0**	**19**	**0**	**16**	**0**	**10**	**0**	**333**	**0**

LLOYD, Clifford

1937 - 1939

Position; *Outside-Right*
D.O.B; *14th November, 1916*
Birthplace; *Brymbo, Denbighshire*
Died; *Brymbo, 3rd June, 1973*
Height; *5ft 7in* ***Weight;*** *10st 8lbs*
Debut; v. *Rochdale (h) 5th March, 1938*
Total Appearances & Goals; *12 apps 2 gls*
Career; *Lodge; Oswestry Town cs1932; Brymbo; WREXHAM 6th Nov 1936; Bangor City 25th Aug 1939;*

Cliff Lloyd will always be remembered in the history of Wrexham Football Club. He served the club in nearly every capacity possible - as supporter, player, secretary, caretaker manager and manager. Cliff played his early football for Lodge (Brymbo), Oswestry Town, and Brymbo, before he had a trial with Liverpool in 1935. In November 1936 he signed for Wrexham as a part-time professional, though it was not until March 1938 that he finally made his League debut on the Racecourse in a 2-1 win over Rochdale. He played eleven more League matches for the 'Robins' before signing for Bangor City during the close season of 1939, but with the outbreak of the Second World War returned to Wrexham, where he played when he could. After WW2 had ended Cliff resumed his football career with Bangor City in the Lancashire Combination League for a season, before returning to Wrexham as the assistant secretary to secretary/manager Tom Williams. He remained in that position until Les McDowall was appointed Boss in May 1949. McDowall was Wrexham's first ever player/manager, and Cliff was given responsibility for all of the club's secretarial duties. However, McDowall left Wrexham after just one season to take charge at Manchester City and Cliff was appointed as caretaker/manager, a position he held until Peter Jackson took over the hot seat in November 1950. Cliff then returned to his secretarial duties, though he was forced to pull on his boots again in January 1953, when an acute player shortage led him to turn out for the reserves in a Cheshire County League match at Mossley! In February 1955 Cliff was appointed Wrexham's new manager following Peter Jackson's resignation. The club were languishing near the foot of the Third Division North League table at that time, but he succeeded in improving matters so much that the team finished in 18th place. Towards the end of 1956/57 Cliff also resigned, but agreed to stay in charge until a new man was found. This eventually proved to be John Love, who took over in October 1957, with Cliff reverting to his secretarial duties once again. He was to be called upon to take charge of team affairs on a caretaker basis on a further three occasions; in October 1959, after Love's resignation, remaining in charge until the end of the 1959/60 season, when Billy Morris was appointed; in October 1965, he again stepped in when Morris left, continuing in the post until Jack Rowley was instated in January 1966; and his final spell in the Managerial seat, in April 1967, came when Rowley resigned, and was asked to take over for the few days before Alvan Williams was appointed. He then resumed his secretarial duties until 1973, when succeeded by Norman Wilson. Sadly, after so many years of loyal service, Cliff was to be denied a long and well deserved retirement. On 3rd June 1973 he collapsed and died at the age of 56 whilst batting for his beloved Brymbo Cricket Club. Cliff had been a keen cricket player ever since his schooldays, captaining Brymbo since 1947, with the exception of the 1957 and 1958 seasons. He had also played for Denbighshire CCC for 26 years, one of the youngest cricketers to have represented the county following his debut at the age of 17. Cliff's brother Jackie also played League football for Wrexham, while one of his three sons, John, played for Wrexham twice before becoming a Football League and FIFA referee. To a man, all the players we made contact with regarding this book held a very high regard for Cliff, both as a person and Manager.

Season	League		F.A.Cup		Welsh Cup		N.S.C.		Total	
	apps	gls	apps	gls	apps	gls	apps	gls	apps	gls
1937/38	6	1	-	-	-	-	-	-	6	1
1938/39	6	1	-	-	-	-	-	-	6	1
	12	**2**	-	-	-	-	-	-	**12**	**2**

LLOYD, Ernest

1921 - 1922

Position; *Outside-Left*
D.O.B; *12th February, 1894*
Birthplace; *Chester, Cheshire*
Died; *Chester, 2nd December 1979*
Height; *5ft 10ins* ***Weight;*** *11st 10lbs*
Debut; v. *Hartlepool United (h) 27th August, 1921*
Total Appearances & Goals; *37 apps 2 gls*
Career; *Chester 1912/13; Stockport County May 1914; Winsford c1919; WREXHAM 14th May 1921; Ellesmere Port Cement Works FC Aug 1922; Rhyl Athletic 21st June 1923; Chester cs1924; Rhos 8th Sept 1925; Flint Town 24th Sept 1926;*
Honours; *Cheshire County League Championship Winner 1921;*

A young Ernie Lloyd was playing in the reserve side of his local club, Chester, when called up for his senior debut in a 1-1 draw at Heywood United in February 1913. Ernie made another 24 Lancashire Combination League appearances for the 'Cestrians', scoring four goals, before he was signed by Football League Second Division side Stockport County in

the close season of 1914. However, it wasn't until Boxing Day 1914 that he finally made his Football League debut, playing at outside-left in a 1-0 defeat at Fulham. Ernie completed a further nine League appearances before returning to the reserves until the end of the season, when the Football League was suspended following the outbreak of World War One. At the end of the conflict Ernie took up playing football again, this time with Winsford, where he won a Cheshire County League Championship medal in 1921. At the end of that season he became one of the first players to be signed by Wrexham following the club's elevation to the Football League. He went on to play in Wrexham's first ever Football League match against Hartlepool United, occupying his usual outside-left position, and missed just seven League games in that historic season, all of which were down to injuries. Despite his consistency he was allowed to leave the Racecourse at the end of the season, when he joined the Ellesmere Port Cement Works team. This was followed by a season with Rhyl Athletic, before he linked up again with Chester for the 1924/25 campaign. Ernie's second spell at Sealand Road was spent playing mainly reserve team football, although he did make six Cheshire County League (first team) appearances until leaving at the end of the season. He then returned over the border to sign for Welsh League side Rhos, which was followed by a spell with Flint Town for the 1926/27 season as his football career was drawing to a close.

Season	League		F.A.Cup		Welsh Cup		Total	
	apps	gls	apps	gls	apps	gls	apps	gls
1921/22	31	2	3	0	3	0	37	2
	31	**2**	**3**	**0**	**3**	**0**	**37**	**2**

LLOYD, John Henry 1938 - 1939

Position; *Outside-Right*
D.O.B; *20th June, 1916*
Birthplace; *Lodge, Brymbo, Denbighshire*
Died; *Wrexham, 4th May 1999*
Height; *5ft 4ins* ***Weight;*** *9st 0lbs*
Debut; v. *Rochdale (h) 17th September, 1938*
Total Appearances & Goals; *1 app 0 gls*
Career; *Lodge; Brymbo; Llanerch Celts; Chester (Am) Jun 1937 1app 0gls; WREXHAM Sept 1938; Bangor City; Wrexham (WW2) Dec 1940 14apps 3gls; Bangor City 1946; Oswestry Town Aug 1949; Played for Connahs Quay Nomads for a spell in 1957;*
Honours; *Welsh Amateur International; North Wales Coast F.A.representative cap; Welsh Amateur Cup Winner 1938; North Wales Coast F.A.Challenge Cup runner-up 1951; Also turned out for a North Wales XI v. Queens Park (Glasgow) in 1946/47.*

Jackie Lloyd was the brother of former Wrexham manager Cliff Lloyd, and the uncle of John Lloyd, the former Football League and FIFA referee. Like his brother Jackie was born in Brymbo, and played football and cricket for the village side. However, he never actually played football for his school team, although after leaving school turned out for his local village side, Lodge. That was followed by a spell in the Brymbo Steelworks team before he joined Llanerch Celts, collecting a Welsh Amateur Cup winners' medal in 1938. During his time with the Rhosllanerchrugog Club he joined Chester as an amateur in June 1937, and with the Sealand Road outfit Jackie made his Football League debut, in a 3-2 home defeat by Rotherham United on Christmas Day 1937. It proved to be his only senior appearance for Chester, though continuing to turn out for the Llanerch Celts[1] (Rhos). In September 1938 Lloyd was signed by Wrexham, and he made his one and only League appearance for the 'Robins' in the same month, replacing his brother in a 1-0 win against Rochdale on the Racecourse. In that match Jackie was said to have 'played pluckily'. He then joined Bangor City before the outbreak of the Second World War, though he was to make fourteen appearances for Wrexham during the conflict, scoring three goals. Jackie continued his association with Bangor at the end of the War, going on to become coach at the club. In July 1951 he took up a similar coaching appointment at the Racecourse, with responsibility for the Welsh League side, and also played a number of games in the side. At the end of the season Lloyd returned to play for Bangor City at the age of 35, a club where he spent a total of eleven years as a player, having appeared in almost every position at Farrar Road, although he did have a short spell with Oswestry Town during that time. At the age of 42 he was still playing football for Brymbo Steelworks. Throughout Jackie's football career he had also played cricket during the summer months for Brymbo since he was 16 years-old, winning many trophies. He finally finished playing around 1976, the same time that he retired as groundsman at the Brymbo Steelworks sports complex, where he had worked for 28 years. Jackie finally settled in the Wrexham area at Caego. He died in Wrexham Maelor Hospital during early May 1999. Described as a friend to everyone just like his brother Cliff.

Season	League		F.A.Cup		Welsh Cup		N.S.C.		Total	
	apps	gls	apps	gls	apps	gls	apps	gls	apps	gls
1938/39	1	0	-	-	-	-	-	-	1	0
	1	**0**	**-**	**-**	**-**	**-**	**-**	**-**	**1**	**0**

LLOYD, John Walter 1965 - 1967

Position; *Outside-Right*
D.O.B; *12th February, 1948*
Birthplace; *Rossett, Denbighshire*
Height; *5ft in* ***Weight;*** *1st lbs*
Debut; v. *Barnsley (h) 8th January, 1966*
Total Appearances & Goals; *2 apps 0 gls*
Career; *WREXHAM Aug 1965; Witton Albion cs1968; Rhyl 29th Jul 1969; Porthmadog 17th Oct 1969; Rhos Aelwyd 15th Aug 1973;*
Honours; *Welsh Youth International;*

John Lloyd is the son of the former Wrexham manager Cliff Lloyd, while his uncle Jackie also played for the club. John played his early football at Rhosddu Junior School in the town, continuing to progress at the town's Grove Grammar School. And where he represented Wrexham & District Schoolboys. However, upon leaving his education he took up employment with MANWEB as a trainee accountant, though signing as an amateur for Wrexham at the same time. He quickly progressed through the Junior ranks at the Racecourse, and his first team chance came when Jack Rowley replaced Billy Morris as the club's manager in January 1966. In his first game in charge he named John at outside-right, and he didn't disappoint as Wrexham went on to beat Barnsley 6-3 on the Racecourse. John was then selected for the Welsh Youth side, winning a cap in February 1966 against

Ireland in Coleraine. It was also at around this time that he played for the Wrexham Youth side as they beat Everton 1-0 in an F.A.Youth Cup match. The match against Barnsley proved to be his one and only first team game for Wrexham that season, as Rowley failed to stop the club's slide to 92nd in the Football League for the first time in the Club's history. His next appearance in the first team came under another new manager, Alvan Williams, in April 1967. He again played at outside-right at Aldershot, but Wrexham lost 2-0 and, at the end of the season, was disappointingly released. He joined Witton Albion in the close season, where he spent a season playing in the Cheshire County League. He then moved on to another Cheshire County League side, Rhyl, in July 1969, but spent only a short time there as he signed for Welsh League (North) side Porthmadog in October 1969. He stayed at Y Traeth for over three years, and returned to the Racecourse to play against Wrexham in a Welsh Cup match in January 1971. He joined Welsh National League side Rhos Aelwyd in August 1973, but shortly afterwards quit playing to take up refereeing, initially taking charge of Welsh National League matches. He progressed to the Northern Premier League, and on to the Gola League. In 1981 he was selected as a linesman for the Football League, and within four years was appointed as a Football League Referee, quickly followed by being named as a F.I.F.A. official. John went on to referee at the top level until the end of the 1995/96 season, when he had to retire because of the age limit for referees at that level. John's other sporting love is cricket, and he played for both Wrexham and Brymbo Cricket Clubs for a number of years, as well as representing both Denbighshire CCC and North Wales. Lloyd still lives in the Wrexham area where he is employed as an accountant by Wrexham Maelor Borough Council. As well as playing Golf, John also compere's and is a competent guest speaker on the after dinner circuit. He still attends the Racecourse on matchdays where he plays host to the match officials.

Season	League		F.A.Cup		Welsh Cup		League Cup		Total	
	apps	gls	apps	gls	apps	gls	apps	gls	apps	gls
1965/66	1	0	-	-	-	-	-	-	1	0
1966/67	1	0	-	-	-	-	-	-	1	0
	2	**0**	-	-	-	-	-	-	**2**	**0**

LLOYD, Joseph Millington

1946 - 1947

Position; *Left-Half*
D.O.B; *30th September, 1910*
Birthplace; *Shotton, Flintshire*
Died; *Shotton, Flintshire, 1st April, 1996.*
Height; *5ft 10in* ***Weight;*** *11st 10lbs*
Debut; v. *New Brighton (h) 31st August, 1946*
Total Appearances & Goals; *24 apps 0 gls*
Career; *Connah's Quay & Shotton FC; Everton Feb 1931 0apps; Swansea Town 27th Aug 1932 212apps 0gls; WREXHAM 10th Jul 1946;*
Honours; *Welsh Cup runner-up 1938;*

Joe Lloyd played for Shotton Council School and Flintshire Schoolboys as a youngster and was playing for his local side, Connah's Quay & Shotton FC, when coming to the attention of Everton, who he signed for as an amateur in February 1931. He stayed at Goodison Park for eighteen months, turning out mostly for the 'A' team without managing to break into the senior side. Second Division Swansea Town made an offer for him in August 1932 which he accepted. He went on to make 212 Football League appearances for the Vetch Field club, collecting a Welsh Cup' runners-up medal from the 1938 Final as the 'Swans' lost 2-1 to Shrewsbury Town after a replay. Described as a stylish strong left-half, who was a fine athlete and excellent cricketer for Connah's Quay, he remained with Swansea until his career was interrupted by the outbreak of the Second World War, when he served with the Royal Air Force. In July 1946, after the conflict had ended, he signed for Wrexham as a part-time professional, although by now he was 35. Joe made his League debut for the 'Robins' in the first game of the 1946/47 season against New Brighton, playing at wing-half in the 3-2 win. He then went on to make a further nineteen League appearances that season before being released in the summer. A cousin to ex-Robin Billy Tudor and Geoff Thelwell of Connah's Quay, during his time at the Racecourse he was described as a 'ball playing left-half, and a good passer of the ball.' After his football career had ended Joe worked as a Joiner, where his skills promoted him to Charge-Hand/Foreman for the Contractors, having settled in the Shotton area, where he died in April 1996, aged 85.

Season	League		F.A.Cup		Welsh Cup		Total	
	apps	gls	apps	gls	apps	gls	apps	gls
1946/47	20	0	4	0	-	-	24	0
	20	**0**	**4**	**0**	-	-	**24**	**0**

LLOYD, Robert Geoffrey

1966 - 1967

Position; *Forward*
D.O.B; *10th August, 1942.*
Birthplace; *Rhosymedre, Denbighshire*
Height; *5ft 8in* ***Weight;*** *10st 12lbs*
Debut; *v. Chester (a) 8th October, 1966*
Total Appearances & Goals; *14/2 apps 6 gls*
Career; *Rhosymedre Boys 1959; Llangollen 1960; Druids 1963; Llangollen 1964; WREXHAM 25th October 1966; Bradford Park Avenue Jul 1967 32apps 10gls; Rhyl 16th Jul 1968; Oswestry Town 4th Apr 1969; Llangollen 20th Feb 1974;*
Honours; *Three Welsh Amateur international caps; Cheshire County League Cup Winner 1972;*

Geoff Lloyd's early football was played at Acrefair Secondary School between 1954 and 1957. However, any thoughts of progressing with a football career came to an abrupt halt upon leaving school, as he did not play competitive football for almost two years, his job as a butcher's boy keeping him fully occupied on Saturdays. Geoff began playing football again, when he was almost eighteen for Rhosymedre Boys under-18s in the Oswestry League. As soon as he became too old to continue in that League he signed for Welsh National League side Llangollen, where he spent a total of six seasons, interrupted by a year at Druids. His consistent marksmanship and promising ability soon attracted the Welsh selectors, and was chosen for the Welsh Amateur International squad to play Scotland. However, disaster was to strike just two days before the team was announced as Geoff broke his leg playing in a League game against Rhos. This set back did not deter him though, and he regained his fitness for the following season when he was selected once more to play for Wales as an amateur international. His first game for his country came in a 2-1 defeat by England at Aberystwyth. His second, in January 1966, saw a scoreless draw with Ireland at Portadown, while his final match at this level was against Eire during the 1966/67 season. Geoff's appearances for Wales did not go unnoticed, and in October 1966 he was signed by Wrexham as an amateur. He was soon called upon for the 'Robins' first team, stepping into the side at inside-forward for Sammy McMillan, who had switched position to cover for the injured David Powell. It was a dream debut for Geoff, as he scored two goals in a 3-1 'Derby' victory against Chester at Sealand Road. Lloyd signed professional forms two days after that match, giving up his job as a long distance lorry driver. However, his career didn't continue as well has it had begun; he found himself in and out of the side for the rest of the season, as the club had a number of quality forwards on the books at the time, players like Sammy McMillan, Don Weston, and Albert Kinsey. At the end of the season he was disappointingly given a free transfer by new manager Alvan Williams, who had replaced the departed Jack Rowley. He had joined Bradford Park Avenue as manager in April 1967, and he soon returned to Wrexham to sign Geoff for his new club, where he was to have what he regarded as a pretty good season, finishing as the Club's top goalscorer with ten League goals. Even so, Geoff was given a free transfer once again and he returned to North Wales, turning down offers to stay in professional football from Halifax Town, Aldershot and the top non-league side of that time, Wigan Athletic. He decided to remain nearer home, and signed for Cheshire County League side Rhyl. However, after a fairly good start to the season, he sustained a bad knee injury in January 1969, and was out of action for about six weeks. When he returned to fitness he fell out with the Rhyl Chairman and decided to leave. Geoff then signed for Oswestry Town manager Freddie Morris, in April 1969, where he went on to stay over two seasons, helping the Shropshire club to win the Cheshire County League Cup. At Victoria Road, Lloyd was described as a 'strong and volatile player, who hates losing.' He played for Oswestry against Wrexham in the 1971 Welsh Cup semi-final, and again in the same competition during the following season in a fifth round tie on the Racecourse. He ended his playing days at Oswestry Town in 1972, though he did later make a brief comeback with Llangollen. Since he finished playing professional football Geoff has settled in the Wrexham area where he was employed for 17 years as a HGV driver for Dobson & Crowther in Llangollen, from where he moved on to work for Flexsys Rubber Chemicals as a Warehouse Worker.

Season	League		F.A.Cup		Welsh Cup		League Cup		Total	
	apps	gls	apps	gls	apps	gls	apps	gls	apps	gls
1966/67	13/1	5	1/1	1	-	-	-	-	14/2	6
	13/1	**5**	**1/1**	**1**	**-**	**-**	**-**	**-**	**14/2**	**6**

LONGMUIR, Archibald McDonald — 1924 - 1930

Position; *Outside-Right*
D.O.B; *17th April, 1897*
Birthplace; *Saltcoats, Strathclyde*
Height; *5ft 9in* ***Weight;*** *11st 2lbs*
Debut; v. *Halifax Town (a) 30th August, 1924*
Total Appearances & goals; *254 apps 39 gls*
Career; *Gordon Highlanders; Ardrossan Winton Rovers; Aberdeen WW1 (Guest); Glasgow Celtic 11th May 1920 10apps 6gls; Blackburn Rovers 25th Nov 1921 £1,000 24apps 2gls; Oldham Athletic 6th Aug 1923 £500 22apps 4gls; WREXHAM 11th Jun 1924 £400; Cowdenbeath Jul 1925 (Loan); Retired May 1930;*
Honours; *Welsh Cup Winner 1925;*

Archie Longmuir played for his local club side, Ardrossan Winton Rovers, having 'guested' for Aberdeen during the First World War. At the end of the 1919/20 season he was signed by Glasgow Celtic, where he had to wait patiently before making his debut in a Scottish League match against Raith Rovers. Celtic recorded a 5-0 home win, with Archie scoring two of their goals. He made one further appearance for the 'Bhoys' before the season was over, and during the close season of 1921 went with the club on tour to France, playing in both Lille and Paris. Although Archie never actually played in a match on tour, it did give him the opportunity to re-visit the Battlefields where he had served in the Great War. The 1921/22 season saw Longmuir make a further eight appearances, as well as scoring another four goals, before he was signed by Blackburn Rovers in November 1921 for a £1,000 transfer fee. He was pitched straight into the first team at centre-forward in a 1-0 defeat at Birmingham, and played in the following match in the same position before being replaced. Archie then returned to the side in January 1922, playing at outside-right, and keeping his place until the end of the season. However, the following season he managed just seven League appearances, scoring his first League goals, before he was signed by Oldham Athletic for £500 in the summer. Archie went straight into the Oldham first team at centre-forward for the opening match of the 1923/24 season at Blackpool, where he scored in a 2-2 draw. By November, he was out of favour, and it was March before he returned to the first team, this time at inside-right. During the close season of 1924 Longmuire was allowed to sign for Wrexham for a £400 fee. He was to play at outside-right at the Racecourse, becoming a firm favourite with the Wrexham fans over the next six seasons. He only ever missed games through injury, and was described as 'speedy and clever on the ball, causing many problems for opposing full-backs'. Archie collected a Welsh Cup winners' medal with the 'Robins' in 1925, beating Flint in the Final, after which he was allowed to return temporarily to Scotland to join Cowdenbeath on loan, enabling him to play in a summer tournament in the Isle of Man for them. He then returned to Wrexham in time for the start of the new season, and went on to star in the club's first ever F.A.Cup match against First Division opposition, when Birmingham visited the Racecourse in 1928. He also played in the side that narrowly missed out on promotion as they finished third in 1929, the highest League position the club had then achieved. Archie finally lost his place in the side towards the end of 1929/30, when he was replaced by Les Williams, and at the end of that season, announced his retirement from football. He remained in the Wrexham area, setting himself up in business, and in December 1935 he won a 'fortune' of £16,982 11s 4d on the football pools!

Season	League		F.A.Cup		Welsh Cup		Total	
	apps	gls	apps	gls	apps	gls	apps	gls
1924/25	40	2	1	0	4	1	45	3
1925/26	40	6	1	0	3	1	44	7
1926/27	35	3	4	2	4	0	43	5
1927/28	38	8	5	1	2	0	45	9
1928/29	41	12	1	0	1	0	43	12
1929/30	29	3	3	0	2	0	34	3
	223	**34**	**15**	**3**	**16**	**2**	**254**	**39**

LOUGHLAN, John — 1972

Position; *Left-Back*
D.O.B; *12th June, 1943*
Birthplace; *Coatbridge, Strathclyde*
Height; *5ft 9in* ***Weight;*** *11st 0lbs*
Debut; v. *Torquay United (h) 11th March, 1972*
Total Appearances & Goals; *6 apps 0 gls*
Career; *Leicester City Aug 1961 0apps; Morton; Crystal Palace 26th Sept 1968 £15,000 58/2apps 0gls; WREXHAM 8th Mar 1972 (Loan); Wimbledon; Kettering Town; Corby Town (Manager);*
Honours; *Second Division runner-up 1969;*

Although born in Scotland John Loughlan joined Leicester City as a junior before signing professional forms for the Filbert Street club in August 1961. In the East Midlands he failed to make a first team appearance during his time with Leicester, and was eventually released. He then returned home to Scotland, playing for Scottish League Club Morton before heading south of the border once again to sign for Crystal Palace in September 1968 for £15,000. Noted as 'a strong tackling full-back', with fine control, John made his Football League debut at Selhurst Park, in a 1-1 draw against Sheffield United in October 1968, replacing Jack Bannister at left-back. He then kept his place in the Palace team for

the rest of the season as they finished runners-up in the Second Division. Loughlan established himself in the side throughout 1969/70, although Palace only just avoided relegation. The following season would see him lose his place in the side to new signing Peter Wall, who had previously played for Wrexham. He managed just three League outings that season, though worse was to come in 1971/72, as he made just two substitute appearances. He was allowed to join Wrexham on a month's loan in March 1972, turning out in five League games for the 'Robins' at left-back, and also fitted in a Welsh Cup semi-final appearance against Newport County. John returned to Palace at the end of his loan period, and was released by the London club in the summer. He signed for Wimbledon, then of the Southern League, before moving on to play for Kettering Town, and then taking over as manager of Corby Town. John, who returned to live in the Leicester area, was once 'mine host' at the 'Turnstile', which is the closest public house to Filbert Street. His son, Tony, was an apprentice striker with Leicester between 1986 and 1988, before going on to play League football for both Nottingham Forest and Lincoln City.

Season	League		F.A.Cup		Welsh Cup		League Cup		Total	
	apps	gls	apps	gls	apps	gls	apps	gls	apps	gls
1971/72	5	0	-	-	1	0	-	-	6	0
	5	**0**	**-**	**-**	**1**	**0**	**-**	**-**	**6**	**0**

LOVATT, Harold Albert 1926 - 1927

Position; *Centre-Forward*
D.O.B; *18th August, 1905*
Birthplace; *Audley, Staffordshire*
Died; *Stafford, O/N/D 1971*
Height; *5ft 9in* ***Weight;*** *11st 7lbs*
Debut; v. *Barrow (a) 4th December, 1926.*
Total Appearances & Goals; *13 apps 5 gls*
Career; *Wood Lane United; Red Street St.Chads; Audley FC 1923; Sunderland (Trial); Stoke City (Trial); Port Vale March 1924 (Trial) 0apps; Preston North End July 1924 (Trial) 0apps; Crewe Alexandra Sept 1925 27apps 14gls; Bradford City Mar 1926 £500 13apps 3gls; WREXHAM 25th Nov 1926 £300; Scarborough Aug 1927; Leicester City May 1928 10apps 9gls; Notts County Dec 1930 9apps 3gls; Northampton Town 12th Oct 1931 14apps 7gls; Macclesfield Town Jul 1932; Stafford Rangers 22nd Nov 1934; Winsford United Jul 1936;*
Honours; *Third Division South Championship Winner 1931;*

Harry Lovatt played local football in Staffordshire attending trials with Sunderland, Stoke City, Port Vale and Preston North End. He spent three months at Deepdale before being released without having made a first team appearance. He was signed by Crewe Alexandra in June 1925, and it was with 'The Railwaymen that he made his Football League debut. Harry went on to play around ten matches at outside-right before switched to play at centre-forward, where he scored 14 goals in 16 games for the Gresty Road club. This kind of form soon attracted other clubs, and it was no surprise when Second Division Bradford City stepped in to sign him for £500 in March 1926. Harry was plunged straight into the City team in his favourite centre-forward position in a 2-1 defeat at home to Wolves, although he had the consolation of scoring the Bradford goal. He kept his place until the end of the season, but after playing in four of the opening five matches of 1926/27, and failing to score in any of them, was eventually replaced. Not content with reserve team football, Lovatt was allowed to sign for Wrexham in November 1926 for a £300 fee. He made his debut on the Racecourse in a 5-0 win over Barrow, scoring one of the goals, and went on to play in another ten League games, scoring another four goals including a hat-trick in a 3-1 win at Chesterfield. By March he had lost his place in the team, and was allowed to leave at the end of the season. He then joined Midland League side Scarborough, and his scoring record soon began attracting the attention of the League clubs once again. Leicester City stepped in and signed Harry in May 1928 following a trial period. However, he had to wait until the following February before making his first team debut a 2-0 home win against Cardiff City in which he scored. He had returned an impressive 33 goals from 19 reserve team matches for the 'Foxes' prior to his senior debut, but was to make just nine more League appearances for the club in which he scored an impressive eight goals, including two hat-tricks - both against Bolton Wanderers. He couldn't establish a regular place at centre-forward due to the consistent form of Arthur Chandler, Leicester's all-time record goalscorer, and in December 1930 left Filbert Street to join Third Division South side Notts County. He once again scored on his debut in a 4-1 home win over Coventry City, but made just six more League appearances that season, as Notts County ran away with the Championship. The following season saw him add just two more League appearances before he was again allowed to move on, this time to Northampton Town in October 1931. Inevitably, he scored in his first game for the 'Cobblers', a 3-2 defeat at Queens Park Rangers, and went on to make another thirteen League appearances and score six goals for the club before leaving in the close season of 1932. Harry then joined Macclesfield Town, for two seasons before moving on to Stafford Rangers in November 1934. He then had a year out of the game due to illness joining Winsford United in the summer of 1936.

Season	League		F.A.Cup		Welsh Cup		Total	
	apps	gls	apps	gls	apps	gls	apps	gls
1926/27	11	5	1	0	1	0	13	5
	11	**5**	**1**	**0**	**1**	**0**	**13**	**5**

LOVELADY, Edward Richard 1924 - 1925

Position; *Outside-Right*
D.O.B; *24th June, 1898*
Birthplace; *Liverpool, Merseyside*
Died; *Liverpool, June 1983*
Height; *5ft 9in* ***Weight;*** *st lbs*
Debut; v. *Halifax Town (a) 30th August, 1924*
Total Appearances & Goals; *10 apps 0 gls*
Career; *Bangor City; WREXHAM (AM) Aug 1924, (Pro) 10th Sept 1924; Bangor City 31st Jan 1925; Marine Jul 1925; Bangor City 1925/26; Winsford United Aug 1927;*
Honours; *North Wales Coast F.A. representative cap; North Wales Coast F.A.Challenge Cup runner-up 1924;*

Eddie Lovelady joined Wrexham from Bangor City as an amateur in the close season of 1924 . He was still registered as an amateur when making his Football League debut for Wrexham in the opening match of the 1924/25 season at Halifax Town. Eddie occupied his usual outside-right slot in the 3-1 defeat, and did enough to persuade the club to sign him on professional terms in September. He went on to make a further eight League appearances before being replaced in the side by Jesse Bird. He then managed just one more first team appearance that season for the 'Robins' in a 1-1 home draw with Walsall in November. At the end of January 1925 he was allowed to leave the Racecourse and rejoin his former club, Bangor City. However, he only remained at Farrar Road until the end of that season when he signed for Liverpool non-league side, Marine, but was to return to North Wales and rejoin Bangor some time during the 1925/26 season, which he capped by selection for the North Wales Coast F.A.Representative XI against the Scottish Junior F.A. in May 1926. Eddie again left Bangor in the summer of 1927 to join Cheshire County League side, Winsford United.

Season	League		F.A.Cup		Welsh Cup		Total	
	apps	gls	apps	gls	apps	gls	apps	gls
1924/25	10	0	-	-	-	-	10	0
	10	**0**	**-**	**-**	**-**	**-**	**10**	**0**

LOVETT, Percy Reginald 1947

Position; *Goalkeeper*
D.O.B; *1st August, 1921*
Birthplace; *Bayston Hill, Shrewsbury, Shropshire*
Died; *1982*
Height; *5ft 11'1/2in* ***Weight;*** *12st 0lbs*
Debut; v. *Oldham Athletic (a) 15th February, 1947*
Total Appearances & Goals; *14 apps 0 gls*
Career; *Bomere Heath Aug 1936; Shrewsbury Town 1936/37; Leighton Comrades 1937/38; Kenwood Juniors; Everton Mar 1938 0apps (WW2 18apps 0gls); Wrexham (WW2 Guest) Mar 1942 4apps 0gls; Tranmere Rovers (WW2 Guest) 1941/42 16apps 0gls; WREXHAM 14th Feb 1947; Hereford Town Sept 1947;*

Upon leaving school in Shrewsbury, Percy Lovett began playing for Bomere Heath in the Shrewsbury Works League at the start of the 1936/37 Season. However, after just a few games he was chosen to play for Shrewsbury Town's Reserve side. Shortly afterwards, the sale of first team keeper Walter Rigby to Aston Villa saw Percy called up to make his debut for the Birmingham and District League side against Wrexham Reserves in October 1936. The Robins' second string winning 4-2. It was said of Percy, "He made one mistake for the second goal, but he has the making of a good goalkeeper". He was replaced by former Wrexham keeper Wilf Burrows for the next game. The 1937/38 Season saw him turning out for Leighton Comrades in the Shrewsbury and District League, as well as Kenwood Juniors in the Junior League. He was spotted and signed by Everton in March 1938, still only sixteen years old. At that time Kenwood Juniors were enjoying considerable success, and other League clubs were watching a number of their players. Keen to keep the side together until the end of the season, the Kenwood secretary persuaded Everton to sign seven of their players on amateur forms to keep other club's at bay, while Percy signed on professional terms for the 'Toffeemen'. The Second World War disrupted Percy's career, but despite playing regularly for Everton's reserve side in the Central League, he was to make eighteen appearances during this period for the first team. He also appeared as a 'Guest' player for both Tranmere Rovers and Wrexham, making his first appearance for the 'Robins' in a 3-0 win at Bury in March 1942. He returned to Everton after the conflict had ended, and continued playing in the Central League side without making a single first team appearance for the Goodison Park club before leaving in February 1947, having accepted an offer to join Third Division North side Wrexham. Percy made his Football League debut for the 'Robins' at Oldham, replacing Frank Williams in a 5-1 win, and he remained in the team until May, when Frank Williams won his place back after thirteen League games. Percy was to leave at the beginning of the 1947/48 season to join Southern League side, Hereford Town.

Season	League		F.A.Cup		Welsh Cup		Total	
	apps	gls	apps	gls	apps	gls	apps	gls
1941/42	1	0	-	-	-	-	1	0
1942/43	2	0	-	-	-	-	2	0
1943/44	1	0	-	-	-	-	1	0
1946/47	13*	0	-	-	1	0	14	0
	17	**0**	**-**	**-**	**1**	**0**	**18**	**0**

* = Football League season only.

LUCAS, Arthur

1928 - 1929

Position; *Goalkeeper*
D.O.B; *28th February, 1904*
Birthplace; *Gwersyllt, nr.Wrexham, Denbighshire*
Died; *Wrexham, 14th November 1949.*
Height; *5ft 8in* ***Weight;*** *11st 4lbs*
Debut; v. *New Brighton (a) 7th March, 1928*
Total Appearances & Goals; *4 apps 0 gls*
Career; *Conway; Runcorn; WREXHAM (Am) March 1928, (Pro) 12th Mar 1928; Caernarvon Athletic 6th Jul 1929; Burton Town Jun 1930; Aston Villa (Trial) Aug 1931; Runcorn 9th Oct 1931;*
Honours; *One Welsh Junior International Cap; Welsh National League Division One Championship medal 1929;*

Arthur Lucas had played in goal for both Conway and Runcorn, when Wrexham signed him as an amateur in March 1928. He accepted professional terms within a week of joining the club, by which time he had already been plunged straight into first team action for his Football League debut at New Brighton, replacing the injured Ted Robson. Arthur got off to a good start by keeping a clean sheet on his debut, a scoreless draw. However, two subsequent 2-1 defeats, at home to Darlington and away to Ashington, saw Ted Robson resume his first team place with Lucas playing for the reserves in the Birmingham & District League until the end of the season. Arthur remained in the Second XI during the following term despite the summer departure of Ted Robson, as new signing George Greatrex was preferred in goal. He made just one more first team appearance for Wrexham, in a 2-2 draw with Halifax Town, in October 1928 before allowed to leave the club at the end of the 1928/29 season. Arthur then signed for Caernarvon Athletic, where he spent a very successful season, helping them reach the F.A.Cup Second Round proper, winning a Welsh National League Division One Championship medal, and selection for a Welsh Junior International against Ireland in 1930. In the summer of 1930 Arthur Lucas became the third Caernarvon player to have been transferred to Burton Town, who were one of the teams that the Canaries had beaten during their F.A.Cup run, in a match where Arthur had saved two penalties. Lucas's performances for Burton attracted the attention of Aston Villa, and they invited him for trials at the beginning of the 1931/32 season. However, nothing permanent came from this and in October he rejoined one of his former clubs, Cheshire County League side Runcorn. After his professional football career had ended, Arthur worked at Gresford Colliery as a Fireman until his premature death in November 1949 at the age of only 45. Arthur is the father of Malcolm Lucas who played for Wales at full international level, and Alec who played for Wrexham. *(see next entry).*

Season	League		F.A.Cup		Welsh Cup		Total	
	apps	gls	apps	gls	apps	gls	apps	gls
1927/28	3	0	-	-	-	-	3	0
1928/29	1	0	-	-	-	-	1	0
	4	**0**	**-**	**-**	**-**	**-**	**4**	**0**

LUCAS, Alec

1965 - 1967

Position; *Full-Back*
D.O.B; *1st December, 1945*
Birthplace; *Bradley, Nr.Wrexham, Denbighshire*
Height; *5ft 7in* ***Weight;*** *11st 4lbs*
Debut; v. *Barrow (a) 21st August, 1965*
Total Appearances & Goals; *59/4apps 0gls*
Career; *Q.P.R 1961; WREXHAM 1962; Oswestry Town 1963/64; Bexley United 1964; WREXHAM Aug 1965; Bangor City 3rd Jul 1967; Oswestry Town 6th March 1972; Connah's Quay Nomads 16th Aug 1973; Nantle Vale 2nd Feb 1974; Lex XI;*
Honours; *Welsh Under-23 International; Welsh Youth International; Welsh Cup runner-up 1967; Welsh Youth Cup Winner 1962; Northern Premier Cup Winner 1969; Cheshire League Cup Winner 1972;*

Alec Lucas is the son of former Wrexham goalkeeper Arthur Lucas. He initially took up playing football while at Gwersyllt Junior and Bryn Alyn Schools where he went on to represent the Wrexham & District Schoolboys side. He first joined Wrexham on schoolboy forms when Ken Barnes was the club's manager. However, his brother Malcolm, a professional footballer with Orient at that time and a future Welsh international, persuaded him to go to London and take his apprenticeship with Third Division Queens Park Rangers. He returned home after just six months and rejoined Wrexham, where he went on to complete his apprenticeship with the Racecourse club. During that time Alec was capped by Wales at Youth level, and with that side toured Holland, while with Wrexham he picked up a Welsh Youth Cup winners' medal in 1962. He was released by Wrexham following the completion of his two year apprenticeship, whereupon he joined Oswestry Town. Alec had only made one appearance for the Shropshire club when his brother once again stepped in to introduce him to Kent non-league side Bexley United. He played for them at centre-forward, but soon became home-sick and returned to Wrexham to take up work at Brymbo Steelworks. During the close season of 1965 Alec, still only 20, asked manager Billy Morris for another chance, and was offered terms after a month's trial. He made his Football League debut for Wrexham at Barrow in the opening match of the 1965/66 season at left-back, a position that he filled for most of that season, one which Wrexham ended 92nd in the Football League. The following season saw new signing Steve Stacey preferred at left-back, but Alec got another first team chance following the double transfer to Liverpool of Peter Wall and Stuart Mason, and played in the Welsh Cup Final second leg at Cardiff, which Wrexham lost 2-1. During the close season new manager Alvan Williams released Alec, who then joined Bangor City. He made a quick return to the Racecourse with his new club for a Welsh Cup fifth round replay in January 1969, which they lost narrowly 4-3. Bangor became founder members of the Northern Premier League in 1968, and Alec helped them win the Northern Premier Cup in the first season. At Farrar Road Lucas played some of the finest football of his career with his strong defensive play. A feature of the Clubs success was forming a fine full-back partnership with John Edwardson, Holyhead, C. Palace, Crewe Alex., Caernarfon and Bethesda and Denny Jones, Caernarfon. He joined Oswestry Town in March 1972, where he collected a Cheshire County League Cup winners' medal, and then represented a number of Welsh League (North) sides that included Connah's Quay Nomads and Nantlle Vale, before finally hanging up his boots in the 1980s whilst playing for Lex XI. He later managed the Wrexham area side. Alec settled in the Wrexham area where he has worked in the building trade as a bricklayer.

Season	League		F.A.Cup		Welsh Cup		League Cup		Total	
	apps	gls	apps	gls	apps	gls	apps	gls	apps	gls
1965/66	33/1	0	1	0	1	0	2	0	37/1	0
1966/67	18/3	0	1	0	3	0	-	-	22/3	0
	51/4	**0**	**2**	**0**	**4**	**0**	**2**	**0**	**59/4**	**0**

LUMBERG, Albert Arthur

1924 - 1930

Position; *Left-Back*
D.O.B; *20th May, 1901*
Birthplace; *Connahs Quay, Flintshire*
Died; *Wrexham, 16th February, 1986*
Height; *5ft 8'1/2in* ***Weight;*** *11st 8lbs*
Debut; v. *Chesterfield (a) 1st January, 1925*
Total Appearances & Goals; *191 apps 0 gls*
Career; *Flint Town 29th Aug 1923; Connah's Quay & Shotton FC 26th Sept 1923; Liverpool (Trial) cs1924; Mold Town Aug 1924; WREXHAM 20th Nov 1924; Wolves 19th May 1930 £650 20 apps 0gls; Brighton & Hove Albion 16th Jun 1933 £250 21apps 0gls; Stockport County 31st May 1934 2apps 0gls; Clapton Orient 1st Feb 1935 0apps; Lytham (Player/Manager) Aug 1935; New Brighton 13th Nov 1935 2apps 0gls; Winsford United Jun 1936; Newry Town Nov 1937 (Player/Manager); Rhyl 15th Sept 1938; Newry Town (Player/Manager) Jan 1939; Mold Alex 31st Oct 1946;*
Honours; *Four Full Welsh International Caps; Welsh Cup Winner 1925;*

Albert Lumberg spent his formative football years with Welsh National League sides Flint Town and Connah's Quay & Shotton FC, from where he was invited for a trial with Liverpool in 1924. He was then offered 'generous terms to change his status from amateur to professional, but declined to give up his work'. Albert began the new 1924/25 season with Mold Town, joining Wrexham in November 1924 in the face of stiff competition from Hull City. The move was due mainly to Wrexham's new manager Charlie Hewitt, who had encountered Albert at both Mold and Connah's Quay. At the Racecourse Lumberg formed a great full-back partnership with the long serving Alf Jones, where he was described as 'a 'resolute defender, who was equally at home in either full-back slot and never gave less than 100 per cent'. He collected a Welsh Cup Winners' medal with Wrexham in 1925, as well as three of his four Welsh International caps. He was also selected for the Welsh F.A. party to tour Canada in 1929, during which he made thirteen appearances on the month long tour. Albert was spotted by Wolves while playing for the 'Robins' reserves in a Birmingham & District League match during the following season, and they paid out £650 for him in May 1930. Wolves were intent on building a promotion-winning side, and had been impressed by Albert's positional play, and 'out of the ordinary' defensive work. However, he couldn't establish himself in a regular first team place at Molineux, and after twenty League games he was sold to Brighton & Hove Albion for £250 in June 1933. He stayed at the Goldstone Ground for a year, during which he made 21 League appearances until returning North to join Stockport County, where his stay was to be even shorter. He made just two League appearances for the Edgeley Park club returning South to join Clapton Orient, though he failed to record a first team appearance for the 'O's', and drifted into non-league football with Lytham in the close season of 1935. However, by November he had signed for New Brighton as they struggled to cope with an injury crisis, and he made his debut for them against his old club, Wrexham, on 16th November 1936. Wrexham won 4-0. Albert was to make just one more League appearance for the 'Rakers' before moving back into non-league football with Winsford United in the close season of 1936. He later became the player/manager of Irish League side Newry Town, before signing for Rhyl at the beginning of the 1938/39 season. He had committed himself to the Belle Vue club for 1939/40 season, when World War Two put a stop to football. He did play for Mold Alex after WW2 before appointed as Wrexham's 'A' team trainer in 1950, acting as coach to the Wrexham Old Boys. After his playing days were over Albert had worked for a firm of furniture removers. He died in February 1986 aged 84.

Season	League		F.A.Cup		Welsh Cup		Total	
	apps	gls	apps	gls	apps	gls	apps	gls
1924/25	10	0	-	-	3	0	13	0
1925/26	22	0	1	0	-	-	23	0
1926/27	30	0	-	-	4	0	34	0
1927/28	30	0	2	0	3	0	35	0
1928/29	41	0	1	0	1	0	43	0
1929/30	37	0	4	0	2	0	43	0
	170	**0**	**8**	**0**	**13**	**0**	**191**	**0**

LUNT, Robert John

1990 - 1992

Position; *Forward*
D.O.B; *11th December, 1973*
Birthplace; *Widnes, Cheshire*
Height; *5ft 7in* ***Weight;*** *10st 10lbs*
Debut; v. *Halifax Town (h) 12th March, 1991*
Total Appearances & Goals; *1/8 apps 0 gls*
Career; *WREXHAM Jul 1990; Released May 1992;*
Honours; *Welsh Youth Cup Winner 1991 & 1992; Welsh National League Championship Winner 1992;*

Robbie Lunt first took up football at Southgate Primary School in his home town of Widnes. He then played for his school team at Norton Priory as well as turning out for Halton Lodge in the Runcorn Junior Sunday League. He was also selected to represent Cheshire Schoolboys, and it was when playing for his County that he came to the attention of Wrexham youth coach Mike Buxton, who then signed him on schoolboy forms. Upon leaving school Robbie continued his association with Wrexham by signing for the Club on Youth Training Scheme forms. He progressed to the extent that, not long after his seventeenth birthday he was selected for the first team squad following some impressive performances in the reserves. Robbie went on to make his Football League debut in March 1991 against Halifax Town as a substitute for Dave O'Gorman in a 2-1 home defeat. He made a further six substitute appearances before the end of the 1990/91 season, his full debut coming in a 2-1 win against Torquay United on the Racecourse in April, when he replaced the injured Ian Griffiths. Robbie capped the season by gaining a Welsh Youth Cup winners' medal after beating Swansea City in the final. After this encouraging beginning the following season was a disappointment for Rob, as he was to make just one appearance as a substitute for Karl Connolly in a 1-1 draw at Northampton Town. It proved to be Lunt's last match for Wrexham, as his early promise was not maintained and was released in May 1992. Robbie was later known to have been playing West Cheshire League football.

Season	League		F.A.Cup		Welsh Cup		League Cup		F.R.T.		E.C.W.C.		Total	
	apps	gls	apps	gls	apps	gls	apps	gls	apps	gls	apps	gls	apps	gls
1990/91	1/7	0	-	-	-	-	-	-	-	-	-	-	1/7	0
1991/92	0/1	0	-	-	-	-	-	-	-	-	-	-	0/1	0
	1/8	**0**	**-**	**-**	**-**	**-**	**-**	**-**	**-**	**-**	**-**	**-**	**1/8**	**0**

LYONS, James

1925 - 1926

Position; *Inside-Right*
D.O.B; *27th September, 1897*
Birthplace; *Hednesford, Staffordshire*
Died; *Lichfield, J/A/S, 1970*
Height; *5ft 11in* ***Weight;*** *12st 3lbs*
Debut; v. *Southport (h) 29th August, 1925*
Total Appearances & Goals; *37 apps 14 gls*
Career; *Hednesford Vics; Hednesford Colliery (Trial); Hednesford Town; Derby County Jan 1920 £1,000 80apps 31gls; WREXHAM 11th Jul 1925; Hednesford Town Jul 1926; Stourbridge Sept 1927; Cannock Town Aug 1930;*
Honours; *North Wales Coast F.A.Challenge Cup runner-up 1926;*

As a youngster Jimmy Lyons had represented Walsall Boys before going on to play for Hednesford Vics. He was then given a trial by the Hednesford Colliery team, later snapped up by his home town team Hednesford Town, who played in the Birmingham & District League. With them he was spotted by First Division Derby County and, in January 1920, signed for the 'Rams' for £1,000 then a record fee for a Birmingham and District League player. James was plunged straight into their first team at inside-right for his League debut at Sunderland on 17th January 1920, and scored Derby's only goal in a 2-1 defeat. He kept his place in the side for the rest of the season, and was described as a 'thrusting player, with a splendid shot'. Jimmy made just thirteen League appearances in the following season as Derby suffered relegation, and it was stated around this time that he 'could do with some speed'. 1921/22 saw him out of favour until Christmas Eve, when he played at home against West Ham. He remained in the side for the rest of the season, and scored all four goals in Derby's 4-0 win over Rotherham County in April 1922. The following season again saw Lyons established as a regular at inside-left until April 1923. However, he spent the next couple of years in Derby's reserve team, before signed by Third Division North side Wrexham in July 1925. He made his League debut for the 'Robins' in the first match of the 1925/26 season, a 3-2 home win against Southport. Jimmy became a regular in the Wrexham side throughout the season, scoring thirteen goals in 34 League games including a hat-trick in a home game against Nelson in February 1926. He also played for the 'Robins' reserve side in the Final of the North Wales Coast F.A.Challenge Cup, where Wrexham were to lose 2-0 to Llandudno. Surprisingly, he was allowed to leave the Racecourse at the end of the season, when he returned to play for Hednesford Town. Jimmy later played for fellow Birmingham & District League sides Stourbridge and Cannock Town.

Season	League		F.A.Cup		Welsh Cup		Total	
	apps	gls	apps	gls	apps	gls	apps	gls
1925/26	34	13	1	0	2	1	37	14
	34	**13**	**1**	**0**	**2**	**1**	**37**	**14**

LYONS, John Patrick

1975 - 1979

Position; *Forward*
D.O.B; *8th November, 1956*
Birthplace; *Buckley, Flintshire*
Died; *Colchester, 11th November 1982*
Height; *5ft 11in* ***Weight;*** *11st 12lbs*
Debut; v. *Peterborough United (h) 22nd March, 1975*
Total Appearances & Goals; *85/29 apps 33 gls*
Career; *WREXHAM Jun 1975; Bangor City (Loan) 26th Sept 1977; Millwall 24th Jul 1979 £50,000 55apps 20gls; Cambridge United 3rd Oct 1980 £90,000 21apps 6gls; Colchester United Feb 1982 £35,000 33apps 9gls;*
Honours; *Third Division Championship Winner 1978; Welsh Cup Winner 1975 & 1978; Welsh Cup runner-up 1979; Welsh Youth Cup Winner 1975;*

Wrexham fan John Lyons joined his favourite club straight from school in 1973. He worked his way through the Junior teams at the Racecourse to make his Football League debut for the Club at the age of 18, against Peterborough United in March 1975. He scored the Wrexham goal in the 2-1 home defeat, after replacing the departed David Smallman in the side. John played in the home tie of the Welsh Cup Final at the end of the season against Cardiff City, and scored again in Wrexham's 2-1 win. He began the following season in the first team, but the arrival of Stuart Lee found him spending much of his time either in the reserves or on the substitute's bench. He was to make his European Cup-Winners' Cup debut as a substitute for Dave Fogg in the first leg, first round match, against Djurgardens of Sweden, but 1976/77 was much the same as the previous season, the pattern continued until March 1978, when John stepped in for the injured Dixie McNeil and remained in the side until the end of the season, one which saw Wrexham gain promotion to the Second Division for the first time in the Club's history. To cap a delightful season, Lyons then went on to score Wrexham's goal in the 1-0 second leg win over Bangor City in the Welsh Cup Final. The first season in the Second Division saw John establish himself in the side on a regular basis. He did in fact score Wrexham's first ever Second Division goal, in the 1-0 away win at Fulham. He also scored the 'Robin's' first ever Second Division goal on the Racecourse, in a 2-1 defeat by Cardiff City, almost a month later! and registered the first hat-trick by a Wrexham player in the Second Division when he scored three goals in the 4-3 memorable home win over West Ham United. For good measure he added two goals in a 3-3 F.A.Cup draw at White Hart Lane against Spurs. He ended the season as the Club's top scorer with 15 League and Cup goals. He also gained a Welsh runners'-up medal, when Wrexham lost 2-1 on aggregate to Shrewsbury Town. During the summer of 1979 Millwall manager George Petchey offered £50,000 for John, which was accepted by Wrexham. Ironically, he had scored in his last League match for Wrexham, against Millwall in a 2-2 draw. Lyons proved to be a consistent performer at the Den, missing only one League match during his time at the club, and scoring twenty goals in 55 League games before being sold to Cambridge United for £90,000 in October 1980. He didn't enjoy too much success at the Abbey Stadium, and in February 1982 he moved to Colchester United for £35,000. John made 33 League appearances, scoring nine goals, for the 'U's' before he tragically took his own life on 11th November 1982 at his Layer-de-la-Haye home, two days after he had played in a 1-0 home win over Chester. He was only 26 years-old. John was buried in his home Town of Buckley, with many personalities from the soccer world attending to pay their last respects. The church was packed to the rafters as he was a popular lad. John's brother Mike, was also an accomplished sportsman, as he played Rugby Union for London Welsh.

Season	League		F.A.Cup		Welsh Cup		League Cup		E.C.W.C.		Total	
	apps	gls	apps	gls	apps	gls	apps	gls	apps	gls	apps	gls
1974/75	3/1	3	-	-	1	1	-	-	-	-	4/1	4
1975/76	15/4	3	-	-	1	0	3	1	0/1	0	19/5	4
1976/77	3/4	1	-	-	0/1	0	-	-	-	-	3/5	1
1977/78	14/7	6	0/3	0	3	1	3	2	-	-	20/10	9
1978/79	28/7	10	3	3	4	2	3	0	1/1	0	39/8	15
	63/23	**23**	**3/3**	**3**	**9/1**	**3**	**9**	**3**	**1/2**	**0**	**85/29**	**33**

M

Dixie McNeil

McADAM, David Frederick
1950 - 1951

Position; *Left-Back/Half-Back*
D.O.B; *3rd April, 1923.*
Birthplace; *Hereford*
Height; *5ft 9 1/2in* **Weight;** *10st 4lbs*
Debut v. *Rotherham United (a) 26th August, 1950.*
Total Appearances & Goals; *10 apps 0 gls*
Career; *Branston M.o.D. 1946/47; Stapenhill FC Jul 1947; Leeds United May 1948 24apps 0gls; Burton Albion Aug 1951; Matlock Town cs1960; Stapenhill FC cs1964;*
Honours; *Birmingham & District League Cup Winner 1954; Bass Charity Vase Winner 1954;*

David McAdam first attended Abingdon Council School, near Oxford, leaving at the age of 14 to work at the Radley Steam Bakery. He spent about a year there before moving to Radley College as a messenger boy. He had no opportunity to play football during this period, and any thoughts of a career in the game were put out of his mind by the outbreak of World War Two in 1939. It was shortly after this that his father, who worked for the Ministry of Defence at Didcot, was transferred to Burton-on-Trent. David also took up employment with the M.o.D., at the Branston Ordnance Depot, until he was called up for the Army in April 1941 at the age of eighteen. At first he served with the 70th Battalion Royal Warwickshire Regiment, remaining until 1943, when the Regiment was broken up. David and most of his comrades stayed together, joining the Gloucestershire Regiment, with whom they served in Egypt. This was followed by being shipped to India and the Deolali Transit Camp, where they transferred to the 1st Battalion Wiltshire Regiment and went straight into Burma. McAdam spent nine months in Burma before going to Rawlpinde for a six month break, moving on to the North-West Frontier for one more year before being demobbed in September 1946. Following the end of WW2 David began playing organised football, captaining the Wiltshire Regiment football team for over two years. Upon leaving the Army he resumed his old job with the M.o.D. at the Branston Ordnance Depot, and began playing football for the works team during 1946/47 in the local Burton & District League. The following season saw a change of Club, as he signed for Stapenhill FC. They had only just been founded, with his father a founder member, and persuaded David to join them for their initial season. He was soon spotted by a local Leeds United scout, and in May 1948 accepted an offer from the Leeds manager, Major Frank Buckley. Within months of signing David was playing in first team football, when he made his Football League debut in September 1948 at the age of 25 in a Second Division match at Tottenham Hotspur, which ended in a 2-2 draw. He went on to play a total of 24 League games for the Yorkshire club over the next two years, and it was during this period that he played alongside the legendary John Charles, with whom he became a good friend. However, McAdam was allowed to leave Elland Road in May 1950 when signing for Wrexham in the Post Office in Burton, after Tommy Griffiths and Cliff Lloyd had seen him playing on the previous Saturday for Leeds reserves. He made his first team debut for the 'Robins', in place of Stuart McCallum at half-back, at Rotherham United in a 5-0 defeat. He went on to make nine more appearances, playing at either left-back or half-back, but left the Racecourse at the end of the 1950/51 season after he was asked to take a cut in wages. McAdam then decided to return home and sign for Burton Albion, where he spent nine seasons, playing in the 1954 Burton side that finished runners-up in the Birmingham & District League, and won both the Birmingham & District League Cup and the Bass Charity Vase. In 1960 David left Burton to join Cheshire County League side Matlock Town as reserve team coach, although he did play the odd first team game. He became a Civil Servant which lasted for 35 years until his retirement in 1987. Has recently had two unsuccessul hip operations but still able to hobble to the pub though!!

Season	League		F.A.Cup		Welsh Cup		Total	
	apps	gls	apps	gls	apps	gls	apps	gls
1950/51	10	0	-	-	-	-	10	0
	10	**0**	**-**	**-**	**-**	**-**	**10**	**0**

McALEER, Joseph
1937 - 1938

Position; *Inside-Right*
D.O.B; *8th March, 1910*
Birthplace; *Blythswood, Glasgow, Strathclyde*
Height; *5ft 8 1/2in* **Weight;** *11st 7lbs*
Debut; v. *Southport (h) 19th March, 1938*
Total Appearances & Goals; *7 apps 1 gls*
Career; *Glenboig St.Josephs; Bridgeton Waverley; Arbroath; Rochdale Jul 1931 35apps 8gls; Glenavon Jul 1933; Northampton Town Aug 1933 8apps 6gls; Lincoln City Jul 1934 6apps 5gls; Clapton Orient Jul 1935 18apps 4gls; Gillingham Aug 1936 9apps 3gls; Brideville Jul 1937; Partick Thistle (trial) Aug 1937; WREXHAM 29th Oct 1937;*

Joe McAleer played in his native Scotland for Bridgetown Waverley before signing for Scottish League side Arbroath. From here he moved south of the border in July 1931 to sign for Third Division North side Rochdale. McAlleer made his Football League debut for 'Dale' at centre-forward in a 1-1 home draw with Darlington at the end of September, and scored the Rochdale goal. Joe spent two years at Spotland before moving to Ireland in the summer of 1933 to play for Glenavon. However, before the new season had begun he had a change of heart, and joined Third Division South side Northampton Town, making his debut at outside-left in a 1-1 draw at Aldershot in the second match of the 1933/34 season. He made just seven more League appearances for the 'Cobblers' that season, and despite scoring six goals he was allowed to leave at the end of the season. Joe then signed for Lincoln City, but found himself playing mostly reserve team football at Sincil Bank. McAleer was given six first team outings at outside-left, although he did score five goals, including a hat-trick in a 6-0 home win over Barrow on Good Friday 1935. Joe left Lincoln in the season, and signed for Clapton Orient, where he made eighteen League appearances, again at outside-left, scoring four goals. After twelve months with Orient he was on the move again, joining fellow Third Division South side Gillingham. McAleer made his debut for the 'Gills' in the opening match of the 1936/37 season, and scored the only goal in a 1-0 home win over Brighton, yet by mid-September found himself out of favour. Again he was unable to hold down a regular first team place, and was released at the end of the season. This time Joe returned to Ireland, where he joined Brideville before returning to Scotland for a trial with Partick Thistle. October 1937 saw him return to the Football League when he signed for Third Division North side Wrexham. However, he had to wait patiently until March before making his first team debut for the 'Robins', due to the consistency of Archie Burgon and Ron Jones. In fact it was the latter's move to Liverpool which led to Joe's first team debut, in a 4-1 home win against Southport. McAleer made six further League appearances for the North-East Wales club, scoring one goal in a 1-1 draw with York City on the Racecourse, but was released at the end of the season.

Season	League		F.A.Cup		Welsh Cup		N.S.C.		Total	
	apps	gls	apps	gls	apps	gls	apps	gls	apps	gls
1937/38	7	1	-	-	-	-	-	-	7	1
	7	**1**	**-**	**-**	**-**	**-**	**-**	**-**	**7**	**1**

McBURNEY, Michael Leslie
1971 - 1973

Position; *Forward*
D.O.B; *12th September, 1953*
Birthplace; *Wrexham, Denbighshire*
Height; *5ft 11in* **Weight;** *10st 9lbs*
Debut; v. *Plymouth Argyle (a) 27th February, 1971*
Total Appearances & Goals; *23/4 apps 7 gls*
Career; *WREXHAM 1st Jul 1971; Bolton Wanderers 24th May 1973 1app 0gls; Hartlepool United 28th Nov 1974 5/1apps 1gls (Loan); Tranmere Rovers 5th Mar 1975 4/1apps 0gls (Loan); Blaenau Ffestiniog; Welshpool; Caernarfon Town Oct 1980; Blaenau Ffestiniog cs1981; Lex XI Oct 1982; Caernarfon Town Jan 1983;*
Honours; *Welsh Youth International; Welsh Schoolboy International; Welsh Youth Cup Winner 1971; Lancashire Combination Cup Winner 1981;*

Mike McBurney began playing football as a goalkeeper for St.Giles Primary School in Wrexham. As he moved on to the Bryn Offa Secondary School in the Town he switched to playing at full-back, eventually settling into the forward line. It was there that he found his best position, earning selection for Wrexham & District Schoolboys, and representing Wales Schoolboys on six occasions. A host of clubs began to take an interest, with Wolves apparently the favourites for his signature. Following a leg injury he attended the Racecourse for treatment, and it was during this time that Wrexham manager John Neal persuaded him to sign for the Club. Mike progressed through the ranks at the Racecourse, earning himself a call-up for the Welsh Youth side against Ireland, and travelled to Iceland and Czechoslovakia to take part in a European Youth tournament. Mike was still an apprentice when he made his Football

League debut for the 'Robins', in a 2-2 draw at Plymouth Argyle in February 1971, after illness had ravaged the Wrexham side. Only 72 hours earlier he had been presented with the 1970 BBC Wales Junior Sportsman of the Year Trophy. He made five more League appearances that season, and capped it with a Welsh Youth Cup winners' medal from a 4-3 victory over Cardiff City in the Final, scoring a last minute winner. The following two seasons saw him pushing for a first team place, but with competition from the likes of Albert Kinsey, David Smallman, Billy Ashcroft and Roger Mostyn, found it difficult to establish himself in the senior side, and was released at the end of the 1972/73 season. He soon found another League Club, signing for Bolton Wanderers, but though he spent two seasons at Burnden Park, made just one League appearance for the trotters. He did have two loan spells, with Hartlepool United and Tranmere Rovers, before being released by Bolton at the end of 1974/75. McBurney then returned to live in the Wrexham area where he went on to play for several Welsh non-league sides, including Blaenau Ffestiniog, Welshpool and Caernarfon Town, where he picked up a Lancashire Combination Cup winners' medal in 1981 following a 3-1 aggregate victory over Bacup Borough in the Final. Mike later played for Lex XI, and had another spell with Caernarfon Town. He still lives in the Wrexham area, having worked at Bicc on the town's industrial estate for over twenty years. Appointed coaching officer for North East Wales F.A. in October 1990 – organising courses for junior and intermediate badges etc.

Season	League		F.A.Cup		Welsh Cup		League Cup		E.C.W.C.		Total	
	apps	gls	apps	gls	apps	gls	apps	gls	apps	gls	apps	gls
1970/71	6	1	-	-	1	2	-	-	-	-	7	4
1971/72	11	3	1	1	-	-	-	-	-	-	12	3
1972/73	3/4	0	1	0	-	-	-	-	-	-	4/4	0
	20/4	**4**	**2**	**1**	**1**	**2**	**-**	**-**	**-**	**-**	**23/4**	**7**

McCABE, Thomas Bernard 1933 - 1934

Position; *Forward*
D.O.B; *15th January, 1903*
Birthplace; *Middle St.George, Durham*
Died; *Worcester, 7th December, 1963*
Height; *5ft 7'1/2in* ***Weight;*** *11st 4lbs*
Debut; v. *Barnsley (a) 26th August, 1933*
Total Appearances & Goals; *5 apps 0 gls*
Career; *Teesdale United; Middleton Athletic; Darlington Aug 1928 1app 0gls; Ferryhill Athletic; Newcastle United (trial) Mar 1930 0apps; Spennymoor United Nov 1930; York City Feb 1931 21apps 10gls; Wigan Athletic Aug 1932; WREXHAM 9th May 1933; Burton Town Aug 1934; Worcester City Jun 1935; Stourbridge Jan 1937; Heevans FC Aug 1938;*

'Barney' McCabe began his career with Teesdale United and Middleton Athletic before he was signed by Third Division North side, Darlington. It was for 'The Quakers' that he made his Football League debut, though that proved to be his only game before returning to non-league football with Ferryhill Athletic. Barney was then signed by Newcastle United in March 1930, but was allowed to move to Spennymoor United without having made a senior appearance for the 'Magpies'. In February 1931 he joined York City, where he made 21 League appearances at centre-forward, scoring ten goals - including one on his debut in a 4-2 home win over Doncaster Rovers. Barney started the 1931/32 season as York's centre-forward, but by October he had been replaced by Reg Baines. He then found himself playing reserve team football for the rest of the season before joining the reformed Wigan club, 'Athletic', in August 1932. Playing in the Cheshire County League, Barney featured in his new club's first ever match against Port Vale Reserves at Springfield Park. At Wigan he was said to have earned between £3.00 and £4.00 per week, and repaid that with 43 goals in his first season. This type of form soon attracted attention of the Football League clubs, and at the end of the season was signed by Wrexham. However, he never really hit it off at the Racecourse, making his debut alongside Tommy Bamford in a 3-0 defeat against Barnsley in the first match of the 1933/34 season. McCabe kept his place for the next two matches, but failed to get on the score sheet and was then replaced. He made two further League appearances for Wrexham before leaving the club at the end of the season. He then returned to non-league football, joining Birmingham and District League side Burton, a year before joining Worcester City in June 1935. He again became a scoring sensation, scoring 29 goals in 38 League games in his first season. However, he eventually fell out of favour once again, and in January 1937 joined Stourbridge. In August 1938 Barney joined his local amateur side, Heevans FC. Following his retirement from the game, Barney remained in the Worcester area, where he settled. He died in December 1963 aged 60.

Season	League		F.A.Cup		Welsh Cup		League Cup		Total	
	apps	gls	apps	gls	apps	gls	apps	gls	apps	gls
1933/34	5	0	-	-	-	-	-	-	5	0
	5	**0**	**-**	**-**	**-**	**-**	**-**	**-**	**5**	**0**

McCALLUM, Stewart 1950 - 1953

Position; *Half-Back*
D.O.B; *9th May, 1927*
Birthplace; *Bearsden, Glasgow, Strathclyde*
Height; *5ft 8'1/2in* ***Weight;*** *10st 12lbs*
Debut; v. *Mansfield Town (h) 19th August, 1950*
Total Appearances & Goals; *76 apps 0 gls*
Career; *Clydebank Athletic; Glencairn 1943; Hearts c1944; Renfrew; Newall Old Boys (Argentina) Aug 1948; Rhyl 4th Mar 1949; WREXHAM 2nd Jun 1950; Arsenal Sept 1953 (Trial); Kettering Town Oct 1953 Workington 18th May 1954 10apps 1gls; Coventry City Feb 1956 0apps; Rhyl 27th Mar 1956; Hartlepool United 11th Jul 1956 2apps 0gls; Southport 13th Aug 1957 9apps 0gls; Holyhead Town 8th Nov 1957; Bedford cs1959;*
Honours: *Welsh League (North) Championship Winner 1958; North Wales Coast F.A.Challenge Cup runner-up 1958 & 1959; North Wales Coast F.A. Challenge Cup Winner with Rhyl 1950 v Bangor City.*

Stewart McCallum left school during the Second World War, and played football for his local side, Clydebank Athletic, in the Secondary Juvenile League, followed by a spell with Glencairn. At the age of 16 he signed for Hearts, and played in their reserve team, along with former Wrexham player, Les Donaldson. After the conflict had ended Stewart linked up with another Junior side, Renfrew, but his football career really took off when he went on tour to Argentina, during which he accepted an invitation to sign for Newalls Old Boys of Rosario. In his first match for them he played in front of a 90,00 crowd, supplying the cross for the first goal in a 3-0 win against a River Plate side that included a young Alfredo Di Stefano. Stewart spent seven months in Argentina before returning home due to contractual difficulties, when ALL players in the country were banned from playing! On his return he played in a practice game for Plymouth Argyle whilst awaiting clearance from Argentina, but nothing came of it and joined Cheshire County League side Rhyl in March 1949. At Belle Vue Stewart was a member of the very successful Rhyl outfit of the time managed by the inspirational Billy Russell, which no doubt prompted his move to the Racecouse. Just over twelve months later, in June 1950, Stewart was signed by Third Division North side Wrexham, along with Donaldson, for £2,500 and the promise of a Rhyl v. Wrexham match. Stewart made his Football League debut for 'The Robins' in the opening match of the new season, a 2-2 home draw with Mansfield Town. He went on to establish himself at half-back in the Wrexham side for two seasons, but 1952/53 saw him struggle to hold down a first team place due to the form of George Jones and Johnny Tapscott. At the end of the campaign, he was placed on the transfer list, but turned down a move to Accrington Stanley and instead joined Arsenal for a month's trial. He played in Arsenal's Combination League side for a couple of matches, before returning to Wrexham at the end of the month. McCallum then joined Kettering Town, where he stayed until the end of the 1953/54 season before making a return to League football with Workington, who were managed by Bill Shankly at the time. He made ten League appearances for Workington, following which he was invited to Coventry City in February 1956 for a trial. That came to nothing, and he rejoined Rhyl towards the end of the season. Stewart signed for Hartlepool United in the summer, where he spent a year, but managed just two League appearances. In the close season of 1957 he moved on to Southport, making nine League appearances before joining Holyhead Town as player/coach in November 1957, leading to the Welsh League (North) championship in his first season with the 'Harbourmen', and runners-up in the North Wales Coast F.A.Challenge Cup in 1958 and 1959. He was then signed by Bedford in the close season of 1959, where the ex-Arsenal centre-forward Ronnie Rooke was the manager, who he had earmarked McCallum to become his midfield link man. However, a serious cheekbone injury during a match in November 1959 cost Stewart his sight in one eye, and forced his retirement from football. He then returned to Rhyl where he settled, later becoming vice-chairman of the seaside club when they played in the Northern Premier League. Stewart continued to play five-a-side football until well into his sixties, and still occasionally visits the Racecourse. A fine probing type of wing half always encouraging his forwards.

Season	League		F.A.Cup		Welsh Cup		Total	
	apps	gls	apps	gls	apps	gls	apps	gls
1950/51	32	0	2	0	2	0	36	0
1951/52	31	0	3	0	2	0	36	0
1952/53	4	0	-	-	-	-	4	0
	67	**0**	**5**	**0**	**4**	**0**	**76**	**0**

MacCARTNEY, Charles William 1932 - 1937

Position; *Centre-Forward*
D.O.B; *4th February, 1910*
Birthplace; *Stamford, Lincolnshire*
Died; *Peterborough 1982*
Height; *5ft 9in* ***Weight;*** *11st 7lbs*
Debut; v. *Rotherham United (a) 31st August, 1935*
Total Appearances & Goals; *53 apps 28 gls*
Career; *Stamford Town; Notts County Jun 1932 50apps 19gls; WREXHAM 6th Jun 1935; Carlisle United Jul 1937 4apps 0gls; York City Nov 1937 1app 0gls; Darlington Mar 1938 2apps 0gls; Peterborough United Aug 1938; Grantham Town 1946;*

Charlie MacCartney attended St.Martin's School in his native Stamford where, from an early age, he showed much ability in most sports. After leaving school he played for his local team, Stamford Town, signing for Second Division Notts County in the close season of 1932. He made his Football League debut for the 'Magpies' in a 2-0 home win over Bradford City in September 1932. Charlie went on to score nineteen goals in fifty League games in his three years at Meadow Lane, before he signed for Third Division North side Wrexham. In 1984 one football scribe mentioned that he "shows promise but required steadying influence, enthusiastic and a good shot". MacCartney got off to a good start with the 'Robins' by scoring on his debut, in a 2-1 win at Rotherham, and made on to make a big impression as a free scoring centre-forward. He ended 1935/36 as the club's leading marksman, but lost his place in the side to new signing Harold Lapham after he had scored just two goals in the opening nine matches of 1936/37. Charlie joined Carlisle United in the summer of 1937, making his debut for the 'Cumbrians' in a 1-0 home defeat against Lincoln City in September. He was to make just three more League appearances, before leaving Brunton Park to sign for York City in November 1937. At York, he went straight into the first team for his debut against his former club, Wrexham, which York won 2-1. However, that proved to be his only first team match for the 'Minstermen', and he is believed to have returned to Grantham Town before the season was over, although he did sign for Midland League side Peterborough United in the close season of 1938. MacCartney finished 1938/39 as the 'Posh's' top goalscorer, with 38 goals in 47 League and Cup matches. They included five goals in Peterborough's record 12-0 home win over Boston United in December 1938. The Second World War then brought Charlie's football career to a halt, continuing to appear for Peterborough when he could until November 1945, when he played his last match for them. Charlie then began a long association with Grantham Town in 1946, where he carried out a number of roles, including that of the club's manager.

Season	League		F.A.Cup		Welsh Cup		N.S.C.		Total	
	apps	gls	apps	gls	apps	gls	apps	gls	apps	gls
1935/36	36	24	1	1	2	1	1	0	40	26
1936/37	12	2	-	-	1	0	-	-	13	2
	48	**26**	**1**	**1**	**3**	**1**	**1**	**0**	**53**	**28**

McCLELLAND, Joseph 1964 - 1965

Position; *Left-Back*
D.O.B; *12th October, 1935*
Birthplace; *Edinburgh, Lothian*
Died; *Edinburgh, April 1999*
Height; *5ft 11in* ***Weight;*** *11st 7lbs*
Debut; v. *Notts County (h) 22nd August, 1964*
Total Appearances & Goals; *38 apps 0 gls*
Career; *Edinburgh Thistle; Armadale Juniors; Hibernian 1952; WREXHAM 15th Jun 1964; Rhyl 29th Jul 1965; Barmouth & Dyffryn United 28th Sept 1966 to May 1967;*
Honours; *Scottish Youth International; Scottish Schoolboy International; Scottish F.A.Cup runner-up 1958;*

Joe McClelland showed lots of promise as a schoolboy, and it was at this level that he went on to represent Scotland. At the age of 14 he was signed on schoolboy forms by his local club, Hibernian and on leaving school turned out for Edinburgh Thistle, who were a nursery side for Hibs. Joe later signed for Armadale Juniors, and it was at around this time that he was capped by Scotland once again, this time at Youth level. In 1954 he finally earned a professional contract with the Edinburgh club, only to be called up for his National Service two years later. McClelland then played representative football for the British Army XI, until he was demobbed two years later. He rejoined the Easter Road club, where he went on to make 178 Scottish League appearances. He also appeared in Europe in the notorious Inter-Cities Fairs Cup tie against Barcelona in 1960, before going out to the eventual winners, Roma, in the semi-finals after a replay staged in Belgrade! Joe also figured in the 1958 Scottish Cup Final, having beaten Rangers in the semi-final. However, he was to suffer bitter disappointment when Hibs lost 2-1 to Clyde. He stayed at Easter Road until June 1964, when his wonderful record of consistency came to an end. He was given the opportunity to move into the Football League when signed by Wrexham manager Ken Barnes in the close season of 1964. MacCelland made his Football League debut for Wrexham at left-back in the opening match of the season, a 4-0 home win over Notts County, and became a consistent performer in the Wrexham defence until March 1965. Even so, he was released by Wrexham at the end of the season, but remained in North Wales when signing for Cheshire County League side Rhyl. Joe spent just over a year at Belle Vue before he joined his last known Club, Welsh League (North) side, Barmouth & Dyffryn United, in September 1966, remaining until the end of the season. In a 'Scotsman' Obituary, Joe was described "His tigerish tackling and powerful running made him an ideal counterpoise to the more refined playing styles of the men he partnered at full back. "Few wearers of the Hibs Green and White have been more wholehearted or exhibited such a never-say-die spirit on the the field of play".

Season	League		F.A.Cup		Welsh Cup		League Cup		Total	
	apps	gls	apps	gls	apps	gls	apps	gls	apps	gls
1964/65	32	0	2	0	3	0	1	0	38	0
	32	**0**	**2**	**0**	**3**	**0**	**1**	**0**	**38**	**0**

McCREADIE, William Harvey 1960 - 1961

Position; *Centre-Forward*
D.O.B; *1st October, 1942*
Birthplace; *Glenluce, Dumfries & Galloway*
Height; *5ft 9'1/2in* **Weight;** *11st 3lbs*
Debut; v. *Bradford Park Avenue (a) 12th November, 1960*
Total Appearances & Goals; *14 apps 2 gls*
Career; *Girvan Amateurs; Stranraer; Accrington Stanley 31st Jan 1958; 6th Oct 1959 (Pro) 28apps 10gls; Luton Town 29th Jan 1960 £6,500 1app 0gls; WREXHAM 8th Nov 1960 £1,000; Northwich Victoria Aug 1961; Mossley Oct 1961; Hibernian Sept 1962 £1,100;*

Harvey McCreadie joined Accrington Stanley straight from his School in Scotland, having been an amateur player with Stranraer. He became the Peel Park club's youngest ever player to appear in a Football League match, at 16 years and 143 days. He showed a lot of early promise, too, as he was described as 'able to use the ball intelligently both in the air and on the ground'. These skills were to soon attract the attention of several higher grade clubs, and it was First Division Luton Town who won the race for his signature in January 1960. Harvey was to make just one League appearance for the 'Hatters' against Wolves at Molineux in a 3-2 defeat a month after signing, as they tumbled towards relegation. During his time at Kenilworth Road McCreadie was described as a 'free spirit', who did not take kindly to discipline, after various club fines for failure to report for training and going absent without leave. The final straw came when he was arrested following an altercation at the California Ballroom in Dunstable. Luton's new manager, Sam Bartram, decided that player and club should part company, and, after a few tentative enquiries from Queens Park Rangers and Oxford United had come to nothing, Wrexham took the plunge and signed him in November 1960. McCreadie went straight into the 'Robins' first team for his home debut against Northampton Town, and promptly repaid manager Billy Morris's faith in him by scoring both goals in Wrexham's 2-2 draw. However, they turned out to be his only goals in the fourteen League and Cup matches that he played in for the Club, and was released at the end of the season. Harvey then signed for Cheshire County League side Northwich Victoria, though he swiftly moved on to join fellow Cheshire County League side Mossley just two months later. Almost twelve months later he returned to his native Scotland and joined Hibernian.

Season	League		F.A.Cup		Welsh Cup		League Cup		Total	
	apps	gls	apps	gls	apps	gls	apps	gls	apps	gls
1960/61	10	2	-	-	2	0	2	0	14	2
	10	**2**	**-**	**-**	**2**	**0**	**2**	**0**	**14**	**2**

McDOWALL, Leslie John 1949 - 1950

Position; *Wing-Half*
D.O.B; *25th October, 1912*
Birthplace; *India*
Height; *5ft 10in* **Weight;** *11st 4lbs*
Died; *Tarporley, 18th August 1991*
Debut; v. *Gateshead (a) 5th November, 1949*
Total Appearances & Goals; *4 apps 0 gls*
Career; *Glentyre Thistle; Sunderland Dec 1932 13apps 0gls; Manchester City 8th Mar 1938 £8,000 120apps 8gls; (WW2 116apps 8gls); Glasgow Rangers (WW2 Guest); WREXHAM May 1949, (Registered as a player 3rd Nov, 1949);*
Honours; *Second Division Championship Winner 1947;*

The son of a Scottish missionary Les McDowall was working as a shipyard draughtsman when he became a victim of the 1930s 'slump'. It was whilst playing for Glentyre Thistle, a team of unemployed men that he was spotted by a Sunderland scout, and went on to sign for the Roker Park club in December 1932. He spent almost six years in the North-East, making his Football League debut in November 1934 in a 1-0 home defeat by West Bromwich Albion. He managed just twelve more League appearances before his transfer to relegation-threatened First Division side Manchester City in March 1938 for an £8,000 fee. Les made his debut for City in the first match after signing against West Brom in a 1-1 draw, but couldn't stop their fall from grace. Within twelve months of his arrival at Maine Road McDowall was appointed club captain, but the Second World War was to interrupt his playing career. He resumed his trade of draughtsman, working in a local aeroplane factory near Manchester, and this enabled him to continue to play War-time football for City. When League football was resumed Les returned to trying to lead City back into the top flight. The first season after the War saw success, as City won the Second Division Championship and Les continued playing in the First Division for the next two years. In May 1949 he was invited to become the new manager of Wrexham, and accepted in time to take charge of the club's final match of the 1948/49 season. However, City were not happy at losing him, and withheld his playing registration until November - before finally agreeing to give him a free transfer! Two days after the registration he made his debut for the 'Robins' at Gateshead, becoming the club's first ever player/manager. Despite his efforts the side struggled throughout the campaign and ended the season third from bottom of the Third Division North. At the end of the season his former club, Manchester City, who had just suffered another relegation, turned to him in hope that he would be their new messiah whereupon McDowall asked the Wrexham directors to release him from his contract. He became an instant success at Maine Road leading them back into the top flight at his first attempt, and in 1955 he took them to their first F.A.Cup Final since 1934, where they lost 3-1 to Newcastle United. They were back at Wembley again the following year, but this time returned home with the Cup after beating Birmingham City 3-1. As a manager with City Les proved to be very innovative, and was responsible for the famous 'Revie plan' of the 1950s, which involved the use of a deep-lying centre forward in a fashion similar to that employed to such good effect by Hungary against England in 1953. He also signed some fine players, and paid a British record fee of £55,000 to Huddersfield Town for Denis Law. However, in 1963 City were relegated and in May of that year his thirteen-year reign as manager at Maine Road was finally over. Not surprisingly, he was back in football management within a month with Oldham Athletic, who had just been promoted to the Third Division. In his first season at Boundary Park he consolidated their position with a respectable ninth place. However, the following season saw Oldham fall to the edge of the relegation zone by Easter and, without an away win in 1965, Les was relieved of his duties as manager.

Season	League		F.A.Cup		Welsh Cup		Total	
	apps	gls	apps	gls	apps	gls	apps	gls
1949/50	3	0	1	0	-	-	4	0
	3	**0**	**1**	**0**	**-**	**-**	**4**	**0**

McGILL, James Hopkins 1963 - 1964

Position; *Left-Back*
D.O.B; *2nd October, 1939*
Birthplace; *Belshill, Strathclyde*
Height; *5ft 11in* **Weight;** *11st 0lbs*
Debut; v. *Bournemouth (a) 30th October, 1963*
Total Appearances & Goals; *20 apps 0 gls*
Career; *Larkhall Thistle; Partick Thistle 1956; Oldham Athletic 8th May 1959 38apps 2gls; Crewe Alexandra 19th August 1960 81apps 2gls; Chester 29th Oct 1962 32apps 0gls; WREXHAM 30th Oct 1963; Macclesfield Town May 1964; Bournemouth 17th Oct 1964 0apps; Macclesfield Town 13th Nov 1964; Bangor City July 1965; Porthmadog;*

Jimmy McGill began playing football at Union Street Primary and Larkhall Academy Schools in his native Glasgow. It was there that he was chosen to play County football for Lanarkshire, appearing in the same team as Joe Baker and Sammy Reid. He was chosen to represent Scotland at this level, but missed out when laid up with tonsillitis. At this time he was playing for local Scottish Junior side Larkhall Thistle, and at fifteen years-old was invited to join Partick Thistle having played in a reserve team game against Dunfermline Athletic. Upon leaving School he took up an apprenticeship as a joiner, combining his job with Partick's Second XI team, helping them win three reserve League titles. He remained at Firhill Park until May 1959, without making a breakthrough into the first team, so when an offer to join Oldham Athletic came along, he accepted the move south of the border. McGill made his Football League debut at Boundary Park in the opening match of the 1959/60 season, a 2-0 win against Bradford Park Avenue. He went on to miss just eight League games all season, but asked for a transfer following the departure of manager Norman Dodgin, by 'mutual consent', in the wake of subsequently unfounded allegations of match rigging. He then joined

Crewe Alexandra for the start of the 1960/61 season, having to wait until the middle of September for his senior debut, a 3-0 home win against Hartlepools United. He spent over two seasons with the 'Railwaymen', playing in the most memorable game of his career, a 2-1 F.A.Cup win over Chelsea at Stamford Bridge, against a Pensioner side that contained Jimmy Greaves, Bobby Tambling, Frank Blunstone and many other internationals. Having made 81 League appearances for Crewe, he finally left Gresty Road in October 1962 to sign for Chester. He made his debut for the 'Cestrians' in a 2-0 home win against Bradford City at half-back, a position he occupied for most of the twelve months spent with the Sealand Road club, and where he recorded 32 League appearances. He joined Wrexham in October 1963, as cover for the injured Aly McGowan, and made his debut in a 2-0 defeat at Bournemouth. After six matches in the first team Jimmy was replaced by Reg Holland, finally winning his place back in March, remaining at left-back until the end of the season. It was during this spell that Bournemouth offered Wrexham £4,000 for his service, which was accepted, only for Jim to turn down the move because he was playing regular first team football. However, he was to later regret that decision as manager Ken Barnes was sacked, and Jimmy found himself released at the end of the season. He then joined Cheshire County League side Macclesfield Town, but by October he was back in League football with.........Bournemouth! He joined them on trial, but was to return to Macclesfield after a month without having made an impression with the 'Cherries'. However, a recurrence of a knee injury that he had received when with Crewe, saw him fail to make a further appearance for the Moss Rose club. In the summer of 1965 he signed for Bangor City for one season later joining Welsh League (North) side Porthmadog for a short spell before finally hanging up his boots. Jim returned to working as a joiner, starting up his own builders business, until 1991 when he was forced to retire because of severe arthritis. Jimmy, who had also become a greyhound owner and trainer since finishing with football, settled in the Chester area where he still resides.

Season	League		F.A.Cup		Welsh Cup		League Cup		Total	
	apps	gls	apps	gls	apps	gls	apps	gls	apps	gls
1963/64	17	0	3	0	-	-	-	-	20	0
	17	**0**	**3**	**0**	**-**	**-**	**-**	**-**	**20**	**0**

McGINN, Francis

1947 - 1948

Position; *Outside-Right*
D.O.B; *2nd March, 1919.*
Birthplace; *Cambuslang, Strathclyde*
Died; *Bramalea, Toronto, December 1995*
Height; *ft in* ***Weight;*** *st lbs*
Debut; v. *Darlington (a) 7th June, 1947*
Total Appearances & Goals; *2 apps 0 gls*
Career; *Petershill; Bradford City Dec 1943 6apps 0gls; Lincoln City (WW2 Guest) Apr 1944 1app 0gls; Glen Cairn; Forth Wanderers 1946/47; WREXHAM 14th Apr 1947; Ipswich Town Aug 1948 8apps 2gls;*

Frank McGinn began playing football in his native Scotland at Bushy Hill School in Cambuslang. After leaving school at 16 he played for a local side, Petershill, where he became their youngest player to win a Gold Badge. Upon the outbreak of the Second World War Frank enlisted in the Army, serving with the Camerons. In 1944 he was wounded in action during the 'D-Day' landings, and was mentioned in despatches for helping a wounded colleague after he had sustained a piece of shrapnel in a head wound which later needed a metal plate inserted. For this, Frank received a Laurel Reef in recognition of his bravery. It was during the War period that he 'guested' for both Bradford City and Lincoln City in the 1943/44 season. He made six appearances for Bradford City, and one outing for Lincoln City in the final game of the season, a 3-2 defeat by........Bradford City! Frank was demobbed from the Army in 1947 and returned home to Scotland, where he again took up playing football. Glen Cairn of the Scottish Junior League, was his first port of call, followed by Forth Wanderers, where his performances soon began to attract the attention of League clubs south of the border. It was then that Frank decided to sign for Third Division North side Wrexham in April 1947, where he played in the final two League games of the 1946/47 season, both at outside-Right in place of Ambrose Brown. His debut was at Darlington and the next game at home to Tranmere Rovers, both matches ending with honours even. McGinn must have impressed in those games because, in the summer, he was signed by Ipswich Town. He spent a year at Portman Road, making eight League appearances, and scoring two goals. Shortly after leaving Suffolk Frank emigrated to Canada, where he ended his football career, living in the Toronto area until he died of a heart attack in Bramalea, Toronto, in December 1995 at the age of 75. Frank had worked in a Men's outfitters' shop for a number of years, and at one time had done some modelling for the shop's catalogue!

Season	League		F.A.Cup		Welsh Cup		Total	
	apps	gls	apps	gls	apps	gls	apps	gls
1946/47	2	0	-	-	-	-	2	0
	2	**0**	**-**	**-**	**-**	**-**	**2**	**0**

McGOWAN, Aloysius

1953 - 1965

Position; *Full-Back*
D.O.B; *22nd January, 1930*
Birthplace; *Whiterigg, Strathclyde*
Height; *5ft 5'3/4in* ***Weight;*** *10st 10lbs*
Debut; v. *Crewe Alexandra (h) 15th August, 1953*
Total Appearances & Goals; *478 apps 2 gls*
Career; *Fauldhouse United; St.Johnstone 1950 52apps 0gls; WREXHAM 25th May 1953; Bethesda Athletic 23rd Nov 1965 to Feb 1966;*
Honours; *One Scottish 'B' International cap; One Scottish League Representative cap; Welsh Cup Winner 1957, 1958 & 1960; Welsh Cup runner-up 1962;*

Aly McGowan hails from a large Lanarkshire mining family, and attended the same school in Scotland as another former Wrexham player, Tommy Bannan. After leaving school, he played in the local leagues around Airdrie for Fauldhouse United, who competed in the Scottish Junior Leagues, which proved to be a vast nursery for the Scottish League teams at that time. It was whilst playing for Fauldhouse that he was spotted by Jimmy Crapnell, the manager of St.Johnstone, and he signed Aly on professional forms for The Muriton Park Club at the age of 19. Aly made his Scottish League debut for the 'Saints' in a 2-0 win at Stenhousmuir in March 1951, and went on to make a total of 52 Scottish League appearances for the Perth club, as well as being capped for Scotland 'B' against Ireland at Windsor Park. A change of manager then saw 25 of the club's 27 players given free transfers. By this time Tommy Bannan was at Wrexham, and he mentioned about McGowan's availability to his manager Peter Jackson, who then invited him to join his old school mate at Wrexham. Aly, who was working down the mines at the time, agreed to sign in May 1953, despite Raith Rovers being keen on keeping him in Scotland. He made his Football League debut for Wrexham against Crewe Alexandra on the Racecourse in the opening match of the 1953/54 season, and went on to become a regular in the Wrexham side for the next eleven seasons, completing a total of 408 League games - a record only bettered by three other players. During his time at the Racecourse McGowan played in the famous F.A.Cup matches against Manchester United in 1957, and against Liverpool in 1963, as well as helping the Club reach the Quarter-Finals of the League Cup, beating First Division Blackburn Rovers on the way before going out to Aston Villa, the eventual winners' of the competition. He helped the club to promotion in 1962, and collected three Welsh Cup winners' - and one runners-up - medals. He was respected as a 'hard tackling defender, who never knew when he was beaten', and was described as 'on the small side for a defender, but his lack of inches was discounted by the fact that he never knew when he was beaten'. His career came to an unexpected end in September 1963, when he broke his leg at the Racecourse against Watford, and though attempting a come-back Aly soon realised that he would never be quite the same player. During his time at the Racecourse he was awarded two testimonial matches: the first against Falkirk was a joint affair, along with Billy Waters, Gren Jones and Fred Davis: and the second came in 1966 against Chester, after he had finished playing to take charge of the Club's 'A' team following a spell with Welsh League (North) side Bethesda Athletic. Aly later became groundsman at the Racecourse, combining those duties with running the club's Northern Floodlit League side. It was once said of him, "His whole hearted endeavour made him a great favourite with the supporters. He was a tenacious tackler, with a very keen sense of anticipation." He later became steward at the Centenary Club, beneath the Yale Stand at the Racecourse, for a short while, and was also the steward at the St.Mary's Catholic Club in the Town. This great servant to Wrexham Football Club is still living in the Wrexham area.

Season	League		F.A.Cup		Welsh Cup		League Cup		Total	
	apps	gls	apps	gls	apps	gls	apps	gls	apps	gls
1953/54	38	0	4	0	1	0	-	-	43	0
1954/55	44	0	1	0	4	0	-	-	49	0
1955/56	35	1	1	0	2	0	-	-	38	1
1956/57	43	0	7	0	5	0	-	-	55	0
1957/58	43	0	1	0	5	0	-	-	49	0
1958/59	38	0	1	0	4	0	-	-	43	0
1959/60	46	1	3	0	5	0	-	-	54	1
1960/61	43	0	1	0	3	0	6	0	53	0
1961/62	42	0	3	0	6	0	1	0	52	0
1962/63	35	0	4	0	1	0	1	0	41	0
1964/65	1	0	-	-	-	-	-	-	1	0
	408	**2**	**26**	**0**	**36**	**0**	**8**	**0**	**478**	**2**

McGREGOR, Mark Dale Thomas — 1994 -

Position; *Centre-Half*
D.O.B; *16th February, 1977*
Birthplace; *Chester, Cheshire*
Height; *5ft 11in* ***Weight;*** *11st 5lbs*
Debut; v. *Cambridge United (h) 6th May, 1995.*
Total Appearances & Goals; *196/8 apps 4 gls*
Career; *WREXHAM 4th Jul 1995;*
Honours; *Welsh Invitation Cup Winner 1998; Welsh Premier Cup runner-up 1999; Welsh Youth Cup Winner 1994 & 1995; Welsh Youth Cup runner-up 1996;*

Mark McGregor played his early football just over the Welsh border, for Blacon Youth Club in his native Chester. He turned out in the Clwyd Youth League, from under-12 to under-16 levels, and his early promise didn't go unnoticed as he was signed by Crewe Alexandra at the age of twelve. Mark trained with the Gresty Road club for around eighteen months. He was then playing in a under-14 youth final for Blacon against Mochdre, when he came to the attention of Wrexham, after being recommended to Cliff Sear. Mark was then invited for trials, that led to him signing schoolboy forms for the club at 15. It was around this time that he was selected to play for the Cheshire Schoolboys under-19s team! becoming their youngest ever player. Mark signed YTS forms for Wrexham after leaving school, and enjoyed considerable success in his first season at the Racecourse, helping the Colts' team to win the Clwyd Under-18 League and Cup, as well as lifting the Welsh Youth Cup with a 4-1 Final win over Swansea City at Llanidloes. McGregor also captained the youth side that enjoyed successful English F.A.Youth Cup run in 1994, which culminated in playing Manchester United at Old Trafford, though a 4-1 defeat ended the club's interest in the competition. He continued to make rapid progress, playing regular reserve team football, and his senior debut came in the final home match of the season with Cambridge United, replacing the injured Tony Humes at centre-half in a 1-0 home defeat. During the close season he signed professional forms for the club, and the following campaign began to stake a claim for a regular first team place, initially playing at centre-half, he later switched to play most of the season at right-back, a position that he was still appearing in at the start of the 1998/99 season. The 1996/97 season saw Mark play a major part in helping the club reach the quarter-finals of the F.A.Cup before losing to Chesterfield, and collecting a winners' medal in the first ever Final of the Welsh Invitation Cup. He has also been voted by the Club's supporters as 'Young Player of Season' for both the 1995/96 and 1996/97 seasons. An assured stylish right-back, who looks as comfortable going forward to help with attacks down the flank, as he does at stopping his opponents. Much is still expected of Mark, who can also fill in more than adequately at the heart of the defence.

Season	League		F.A.Cup		W.I.C.		League Cup		Auto Tro.		E.C.W.C.		Total	
	apps	gls	apps	gls	apps	gls	apps	gls	apps	gls	apps	gls	apps	gls
1994/95	1	0	-	-	-	-	-	-	-	-	-	-	1	0
1995/96	27/5	1	2/1	0	-	-	-	-	3	0	-	-	32/6	1
1996/97	37/1	1	8	0	-	-	1	0	-	-	-	-	46/1	1
1997/98	41/1	2	3	0	6	0	2	0	1	0	-	-	53/1	2
1998/99	43	1	5	0	8	1	2	0	6	0	-	-	64	2
	149/7	**5**	**18/1**	**0**	**14**	**1**	**5**	**0**	**10**	**0**	**-**	**-**	**196/8**	**6**

McILVENNY, Edward Joseph — 1947 - 1948

Position; *Outside-Right*
D.O.B; *21st October, 1924*
Birthplace; *Greenock, Strathclyde*
Died; *Eastbourne, Sussex 18th May, 1989.*
Height; *5ft 9in* ***Weight;*** *10st 10lbs*
Debut; v. *Carlisle United (a) 10th May, 1947*
Total Appearances & Goals; *8 apps 1 gls*
Career; *Klondyke Athletic; WREXHAM 13th Mar 1947; Philadelphia Nationals (USA) cs1948; Manchester United Aug 1950; Headington United 1951; Waterford Jun 1953;*
Honours; *U.S.A. International caps; Scottish Youth International cap;*

As a youngster Eddie McIlvenny played for St.Mungo's R.C.School in Greenock, where he earned himself a Scottish Youth cap. He combined working in the dockyards with playing for local Scottish Junior club, Klondyke Athletic when he was signed by Wrexham in March 1947. Playing at outside-right Eddie replaced former England international Tom Gardner for his Football League debut, a 1-1 draw at Carlisle United in May 1947, going on to add another three League appearances before the end of the season. Eddie found life a little harder south of the border the following year, as he only mustered three more football league outings for the 'Robins' before being released in the summer of 1948. After a trial period with Oldham Athletic Eddie, disillusioned that he had failed to make the grade in the Football League, crossed the Atlantic to join his sister in Philadelphia U.S.A. He landed in New York on 7th March 1949, and by the fall of 1949 was playing for the Philadelphia Nationals in the American Soccer League. Eddie took up American citizenship during this time, and was quickly appointed captain of the U.S.A. national side for the 1950 World Cup Finals in Brazil. It was then that he made a name for himself, when he was instrumental in the U.S.A's goal that secured a famous 1-0 victory over England at Belo Horizonte. His was the throw-in that led to the solitary goal. Eddie's performances for the American side so impressed Manchester United, that they brought him back over to the U.K. in August 1950. Unfortunately, he managed just two League appearances during his stay at Old Trafford: which were the first two League games of the 1950/51 season, his United debut coming at Old Trafford against Fulham in a 1-0 win, and his second and final game for United, a 2-1 defeat against Liverpool at Anfield. He then signed for Southern League side Headington United in 1951, but almost two years later travelled overseas again, when joining Irish League side Waterford, in June 1953, in time for the club's tour of Iceland. In August he was appointed as the club's player/manager on the recommendation of Manchester United player Johnny Carey. It is not known exactly how long Eddie spent with Waterford, but he did make three representative appearances for the League of Ireland between March and May 1955. The first, against the Irish League at Dalymount Park, Dublin, while the other two came against the Hessen League, in Frankfurt and Kassel. He later returned to England and continued with coaching in Sussex. He died in May 1989.

Season	League		F.A.Cup		Welsh Cup		Total	
	apps	gls	apps	gls	apps	gls	apps	gls
1946/47	4	0	-	-	1	0	5	0
1947/48	3	1	-	-	-	-	3	1
	7	**1**	**-**	**-**	**1**	**0**	**8**	**1**

McKENNA, Francis Charles 1932 - 1933

Position; *Inside-Left*
D.O.B; *9th December, 1902*
Birthplace; *Wallsend, Tyne & Wear*
Height; *5ft 6in* ***Weight;*** *10st 7lbs*
Debut; *v. Barnsley (h) 27th August, 1932*
Total Appearances & Goals; *10 apps 5 gls*
Career; *Swan Hunter (Tyneside); Spennymoor United; Wallsend FC; Grimsby Town 17th May 1922 114apps 31gls; Fulham 9th May 1927 25apps 10gls; Norwich City 11th Jul 1928 £250 41apps 18gls; Newport County 23rd Aug 1929 24apps 3gls; Walker Celtic Aug 1930; WREXHAM 21st Jun 1932; Walker Celtic Jun 1933;*
Honours; *Third Division North Championship Winner 1926*

Frank McKenna began playing football in the North-East for the Shipbuilders works' side, Swan Hunter. He later joined Spennymoor United, followed by a spell with Wallsend, before signing for Grimsby Town in May 1922. Frank made his Football League debut for Grimsby in a 1-0 defeat at Walsall in November 1922, and just a month later scored his first goals in a 7-1 home win over Accrington Stanley on Christmas Day. He collected a Third Division North championship medal at the end of the 1925/26 season, having missed just two matches, and scoring 14 goals from his formidable inside-left position. During his time at Blundell Park Frank was described as 'slightly built, yet a plucky performer displaying adroit footwork and a fair turn of speed.' He was to leave Grimsby in the summer of 1927, after just one season in the higher division. He moved south to join fellow Second Division side Fulham, along with Grimsby team-mate Charlie Devan. Frank made 25 League appearances for the Craven Cottage club, scoring 10 goals, including one on his home debut against Chelsea in a 1-1 draw in front of a 40,000 crowd. He left Fulham at the end of 1927/28, after they had been relegated. Although placing a £250 fee on his head, Fulham eventually reduced it to just £100, which appealed to Third Division South side Norwich City, who then signed him. Frank missed just one game at Carrow Road, during the 1928/29 season, again finding the net on his home debut when he scored two of Norwich's goals in a 3-0 win over Bournemouth. He ended the season as the 'Canaries' top scorer, with 18 League goals. However, he was on the move again in the summer after Norwich signed Jimmy Thompson. McKenna then joined fellow Third Division South side Newport County, where he was to spend one season scoring three goals in 24 League games, before dropping into non-league football with a return to the North-East to join Walker Celtic and spent two years here before returning to the Football League with Wrexham in the summer of 1932. He made his debut for the 'Robins' in the opening game of the 1932/33 season, against Barnsley on the Racecourse, scoring one of the goals in the 3-1 win, and followed that by hitting the target in each of the following two games. Despite this good start he could manage just seven further League and Cup appearances throughout the season, due to the form of his team mates, Tommy Bamford, Jack Hughes and George Frewin. Wrexham finished the term in their highest League position since joining the Football League, runners-up to Hull City in the Third Division North, but Frank was to collect a Birmingham & District League Championship medal for the club's reserves, who had clinched their first title success in that competition. Despite Frank's record with Wrexham he was allowed to leave the club at the end of the season, whereupon he returned to the North-East to rejoin his former club, Walker Celtic.

Season	League		F.A.Cup		Welsh Cup		Total	
	apps	gls	apps	gls	apps	gls	apps	gls
1932/33	7	4	-	-	3	1	10	5
	7	**4**	**-**	**-**	**3**	**1**	**10**	**5**

McLARTY, Jesse Jones 1945 - 1948

Position; *Inside-Forward*
D.O.B; *3rd March, 1920*
Birthplace; *Waterside, Strathclyde*
Height; *ft in* ***Weight;*** *st lbs*
Debut; v. *Rotherham United (h) 11th September, 1946*
Total Appearances & Goals; *38 apps 16 gls*
Career; *Chester; WREXHAM 7th Sept 1945; South Liverpool 20th Dec 1947; Llandudno 6th Sept 1951; Colwyn Bay 24th Dec 1951; Holywell Town 8th Jul 1954; Colwyn Bay 23rd Sept 1955;*

Jesse McLarty was serving in the R.A.F. when he was signed by Wrexham from neighbours Chester in September 1945, following the end of World War Two. He made his first team debut for Wrexham in the second match of the final season of War League football, a 3-1 defeat at Rochdale, in which he scored the 'Robins' goal. He went on to register a further eight appearances for the North-East Wales club that season, scoring three more goals, before re-signing for the Club for the first season of League football after WW2. It was then that Jesse finally made his Football League debut, when he played on the Racecourse against Rotherham United in a 1-1 draw in September 1946. A cousin of the great Joe Mercer, Jesse went on to make a total of 23 League appearances at inside-forward for Wrexham that season, scoring nine goals. However, the 1947/48 season saw Eddie Beynon and Norman Sharp fill the inside forward positions, following which Mclarty was to manage just one more appearance for the club, against Accrington Stanley in a 1-1 draw. He left Wrexham in December 1947 to join South Liverpool, scoring on his debut against Chester reserves, in a game played on the same day that he had signed for the club. He later moved on to Welsh League (North) side Llandudno in September 1951, but within a couple of months had joined Colwyn Bay. Jesse spent almost three seasons with the Welsh League (North) club, which included a home game against Wrexham in a Welsh Cup match in January 1952, Colwyn Bay losing 7-2. He left the seaside club in the close season of 1954 and signed for Holywell Town, returning to Colwyn Bay just over a season later.

Season	League		F.A.Cup		Welsh Cup		War League		Total	
	apps	gls	apps	gls	apps	gls	apps	gls	apps	gls
1945/46	-	-	1	1	-	-	8	3	9	4
1946/47	23	9	4	1	1	2	-	-	28	12
1947/48	1	0	-	-	-	-	-	-	1	0
	24	**9**	**5**	**2**	**1**	**2**	**8**	**3**	**38**	**16**

McLAUGHLIN, John Thomas 1977

Position; *Midfielder*
D.O.B; *25th February, 1952*
Birthplace; *Liverpool*
Height; *5ft 8in* ***Weight;*** *10st 3lbs*
Debut; v. *Shrewsbury Town (a) 26th April, 1977 (Welsh Cup)*
Total Appearances & Goals; *1 app 0 gls*
Career; *Liverpool Feb 1969 38/2apps 2gls; Philadelphia Atoms Apr to Aug 1975; Portsmouth Oct 1975 (Loan) 5apps 0gls; Dallas Tornados Apr 1976; Barrow cs1976; WREXHAM (trial) Feb 1977, (Pro) 8th Mar 1977 to Jun 1977;*

John McLaughlin was brought up in his native Liverpool, and while at school represented Kirkby Schoolboys. Upon leaving his education in 1967 he was snapped up by Liverpool on apprentice terms, and progressed through the youth ranks at Anfield to finally make his first

team debut in place of Emlyn Hughes in the final League match of the 1969/70 season, a 2-1 defeat at Chelsea. The following campaign John established himself in a Liverpool side that contained the likes of Alun Evans, Tommy Smith, Ian Callaghan, Peter Thompson, Larry Lloyd etc. He made 33 appearances that season, scoring two goals as Liverpool reached the F.A.Cup Final against Arsenal. However, John was to miss out on a Wembley appearance as Alun Evans was preferred. Over the next four years he was to find a first team place difficult to obtain, and during that time made just six further appearances. In October 1975 he joined struggling Second Division side Portsmouth, on a month's loan. 'Pompey' had won just one of their opening eight games when Mclaughlin made his debut in a scoreless home draw with Sunderland. He made four more appearances for the Fratton Park club, failing to help 'Pompey' return to winning ways. He returned to Anfield until April 1976 when his contract was cancelled. He then travelled to America in the North American Soccer League (NASL) for Dallas before returning home at the end of the season to join Barrow on non-contract terms. He was to join Third Division Wrexham on trial in the New Year, before signing on a permanent basis in March 1977. Wrexham at this time were making an assault on promotion, but he struggled to make an impression on the first team, although chosen for his 'Robins' debut in a 4-1 Welsh Cup semi-final defeat against Shrewsbury Town at the Gay Meadow, with John being substituted by John Lyons after 72 minutes, the local press stating that 'he did not look match fit'. He failed to make a further appearance for the Racecourse club, and at the end of the season was allowed to leave.

Season	League		F.A.Cup		Welsh Cup		War League		Total	
	apps	gls	apps	gls	apps	gls	apps	gls	apps	gls
1976/77	-	-	-	-	1	0	-	-	1	0
	-	**-**	**-**	**-**	**1**	**0**	**-**	**-**	**1**	**0**

McLAUGHLIN, Robert 1950

Position; *Wing-Half*
D.O.B; *6th December, 1925*
Birthplace; *Belfast*
Height; *5ft 6in* ***Weight;*** *10st 8lbs*
Debut; v. *Tranmere Rovers (h) 21st January, 1950*
Total Appearances & Goals; *21 apps 0 gls*
Career; *St.Martins Belfast; Distillery; WREXHAM 20th Jan 1950 £3,000; Cardiff City 9th May 1950 £10,000 48apps 3gls; Southampton 22nd Oct 1953 169apps 5gls; Yeovil Town Jul 1959; Salisbury Jun 1963;*
Honours; *Irish League representative cap; Second Division runner-up 1952; Welsh Cup runner-up 1951;*

Bobby McLaughlin played for St.Martin's Belfast, and Irish League side Distillery, resulting in selection for an Irish League representative appearance against the Football League in 1947, in Belfast. Bobby joined Wrexham in January 1950 for a Club record fee paid of £3,000. He quickly impressed at the Racecourse, making his Football League debut at home to Tranmere Rovers in a scoreless draw. After just 17 League games for the 'Robins', he was signed by Second Division Cardiff City in May 1950 for a £10,000 transfer fee, and went straight into the 'Bluebirds' side for the opening match of the 1950/51 season, at Grimsby Town. He went on to make a further 22 League appearances for Cardiff that season, and picked up a Welsh Cup runners'-up medal at the end of it, when they surprisingly lost to Merthyr Tydfil in the Final. The following season Bobby earned a Second Division Championship runners'-up medal as Cardiff returned to the First Division. 1952/53 proved to be a disaster as he made only three League appearances, due mainly to injury problems. After regaining his fitness at the beginning of the 1953/54 season, he was unable to win back his first team place, and in October was involved in an exchange deal with Southampton's Frank Dudley, with McLaughlin going to the Dell. Small, but tenacious, Bobby became very popular with the fans at Southampton, and served the 'Saints' admirably over a six year period. In the close season of 1959, he left the South Coast to drop down into non-league football with Yeovil Town, where he had a four year stay until moving to Salisbury. After finishing his playing career Bobby returned to Southampton, to take up work with Union Castle in the City's Docks. He settled in Southampton, where he was only too happy to help out coaching youngsters. He now lives in retirement in the city.

Season	League		F.A.Cup		Welsh Cup		Total	
	apps	gls	apps	gls	apps	gls	apps	gls
1949/50	17	0	-	-	4	0	21	0
	17	**0**	**-**	**-**	**4**	**0**	**21**	**0**

McLOUGHLIN, Anthony Joseph 1966 - 1967

Position; *Forward*
D.O.B; *24th September, 1946*
Birthplace; *Liverpool, Merseyside*
Height; *6ft 1in* ***Weight;*** *12st 10lbs*
Debut; v. *Exeter City (h) 20th August, 1966*
Total Appearances & Goals; *32/2 apps 13 gls*
Career; *Everton Feb 1964 0apps; WREXHAM 5th Jul 1966; Chester 7th Oct 1967 2/2apps 0gls; Wigan Athletic Jul 1968 51/1apps 34gls; Sutherland Shire FC (Australia);*
Honours; *Welsh Cup runner-up 1967;*

Tony McLoughlin joined Everton straight from school as a junior. He went on to spend three years at Goodison Park without realising his potential, and failing to make a first team appearance. In July 1966 he joined Wrexham, and went straight into the side for the opening match of the 1966/67 season, a scoreless home draw with Exeter City. Tony got on the score sheet in the next match, at Hartlepools United, although Wrexham lost 2-1. He kept his place in the side until late December, before Dave Carrick took over. McLoughlin, then managed a further six League games before the end of the season, though he did play in the second leg of the 1967 Welsh Cup Final against Cardiff City at Ninian Park, which Wrexham lost 2-1, and 4-3 on aggregate. In October 1967 Tony, and £1,500, were exchanged for Chester's goalkeeper, Dennis Reeves, having impressed Chester when he scored two goals against them for the 'Robins' in the previous season's Welsh Cup semi-final. However, he failed to make an impression at Sealand Road, and after goalless draws with Doncaster Rovers and Bradford Park Avenue was dropped. He made two more substitute appearances for Chester before being released at the end of the season. He then drifted into non-league football with Wigan Athletic, for their first season in the newly-formed Northern Premier League. Tony who was quite a character spent two years at Springfield Park, ending both seasons as the club's top goalscorer. During 1969/70 he was suspended for three months having been caught playing Sunday League football. Following his suspension McLaughlin broke Wigan's single match goal-scoring record when scoring 7 out a 11-1 Lancashire flood-lit cup match win over Darwen. He later had a spell in Australian football, playing for Sutherland Shire FC in New South Wales, before returning home in 1973.

Season	League		F.A.Cup		Welsh Cup		War League		Total	
	apps	gls	apps	gls	apps	gls	apps	gls	apps	gls
1966/67	26/2	9	1	0	3	4	1	0	31/2	13
1967/68	1	0	-	-	-	-	-	-	1	0
	27/2	**9**	**1**	**0**	**3**	**4**	**1**	**0**	**32/2**	**13**

McMAHON, Hugh

1932 - 1936

Position; *Centre-Half*
D.O.B; *7th July, 1906*
Birthplace; *Saltcoats, Strathclyde*
Died; *Saltcoats, 22nd December, 1997.*
Height; *5ft 10in* ***Weight;*** *12st 0lbs*
Debut; v. *Stockport County (h) 15th October, 1932*
Total Appearances & Goals; *165 apps 7 gls*
Career; *Saltcoat Vics; Cowdenbeath Mar 1928 53apps 0gls; Blackpool May 1930 26apps 0gls; Stoke City Jul 1931 £500 8apps 1gls; WREXHAM 7th Oct 1932; Doncaster Rovers Aug 1936 5apps 0gls; Albion Rovers Dec 1936 7apps 1gls;*
Honours; *Welsh Cup runner-up 1933;*

Upon leaving school Hugh McMahon took up work as a joiner, and played football for his local side Saltcoats Vics. It was during his time with the Scottish Junior club that he came to the notice of Scottish League side Cowdenbeath. He signed for the 'Blue Brazilians' in 1927, and went on to play in 53 Scottish League games, turning in some impressive performances. They soon attracted the attention of clubs from south of the border. Blackpool manager Harry Evans, was first in the race for Hugh's signature in May 1930, with Blackpool having just won the Second Division Championship. Hugh made his Football League debut for the 'Seasiders' in their first ever match in the First Division at home to Arsenal in August 1930, in front of nearly 29,000 fans. However, it wasn't exactly a dream start for either Hugh or Blackpool, as Arsenal won 4-1. Hugh quickly established himself in the first team, though he lost his place in February 1931, and didn't win it back before the end of the season, and he left Bloomfield Road in the summer to join Stoke City for a £500 fee. Hughie made an immediate impact with Stoke, when he scored on his debut in a 2-1 home win over Chesterfield. However, he encountered similar problems to those he had experienced at Blackpool, as he was unable to command a regular first team place, making just eight League appearances before being transferred to Third Division North side Wrexham in October 1932. He went straight into the first team replacing Harry Beck at centre-half for his debut in a 2-0 home win over Stockport County. McMahon soon established himself as the club's regular centre-half, although sometimes switched to right-half, but wherever he was asked to play was described as a 'prodigious worker, who never knew when he was beaten', and during his four seasons with Wrexham missed just fifteen matches following on from his debut. Hugh played in many memorable matches for Wrexham during that time, especially during the 1932/33 season, which saw the club finish in their highest position since they joined the Football League in 1921, as runners-up to Hull City. That same season saw the 'Robins' inflict a number of crushing defeats upon their opponents; they included an 8-1 hammering of Hartlepool's, a 7-0 home win over Crewe, and a 6-0 home thrashing of Southport. Wrexham's side that season was a formidable one: it included the famous Tommy Bamford, with Hugh commanding his defence alongside Jim Bulling, Alf Jones, and John Brown, while the forward line was led by none other than Tommy Bamford who was ably assisted by the likes of Jack Hughes, Tommy Lewis, and Harry Waller. He played in the 1933 Welsh Cup Final, which the 'Robins' lost 2-0 to rivals Chester, and the following season appeared in the 11-1 win over New Brighton in the Northern Section Cup. 1934/35 saw the popular Scot appointed as the club captain, a position he held for two seasons before his move to Doncaster Rovers in August 1936. With Doncaster Hugh had the experience of playing in their first ever overseas match against the Dutch National XI in Rotterdam. The Dutch were preparing for a match against Austria, and had invited Doncaster over to play as part of their build-up to the game. Hugh spent four months in Yorkshire before returning to Scotland in December to join Albion Rovers, for a short time before announcing his retirement. He later settled in his home town of Saltcoats, where he returned to work as a joiner. Hugh died on 22nd December 1997, he was aged 91. His son - Hugh junior - is a Member of the European Parliament for Strathclyde West at the time of writing.

Season	League		F.A.Cup		Welsh Cup		N.S.C.		Total	
	apps	gls	apps	gls	apps	gls	apps	gls	apps	gls
1932/33	32	2	3	0	4	0	-	-	39	2
1933/34	40	2	1	0	1	0	3	0	45	2
1934/35	38	2	1	0	2	0	1	0	42	2
1935/36	34	1	1	0	2	0	2	0	41	1
	144	**7**	**6**	**0**	**9**	**0**	**6**	**0**	**165**	**7**

McMAHON, Patrick

1935 - 1939

Position; *Goalkeeper*
D.O.B; *26th October, 1908*
Birthplace; *Glasgow, Strathclyde*
Died; *Wrexham, 28th January, 1992*
Height; *5ft 10in* ***Weight;*** *11st 0lbs*
Debut; v. *Chesterfield (h) 22nd April, 1935*
Total Appearances & Goals; *126 apps 0 gls*
Career; *Pollockshaw Hibernians; St.Anthony's; West Ham United Oct 1932 16apps 0gls; St.Mirren cs1934 25apps 0gls; WREXHAM 13th April 1935; Stoke City May 1939, WW2 3apps 0gls; Wrexham (WW2 Guest) Nov 1939 1app 0gls;*

Pat McMahon played in goal for Pollockshaw Hibernians after leaving school in his native Glasgow, and later joined the famous 'star-finders' team of St.Anthony's. It was during this time that he was signed by English First Division side West Ham United in October 1932. Pat made a sensational first team debut for the 'Hammers' in an F.A.Cup Sixth Round match against Birmingham at Upton Park in March 1933, stepping into the side for regular 'keeper George Watson, who had been injured in a car crash. Pat was to make some crucial saves before the 'Hammers' went on to a comfortable 4-0 win. He clocked up a total of fifteen League appearances for the East London club before leaving in the close season of 1934 to join St.Mirren, where he made 25 Scottish League appearances prior to being signed by Wrexham manager Ernie Blackburn in April 1935. Pat replaced Ted Adams in goal to make his debut for the 'Robins' in a 2-1 home win over Chesterfield, and completed one more outing that season before Adams left the club in the summer. The start of the 1935/36 season saw McMahon established as the first choice 'keeper, and made the position his own until 1938/39, when the club signed Welsh international George Poland. Pat's three seasons as the club's regular 'keeper turned out to be rather mediocre, as they finished 18th, 8th and 10th, with the only bright spots coming in the cup competitions when Wrexham reached the Third Round of the F.A.Cup in the 1936/37 season, losing 3-1 to Manchester City. Following George Poland's arrival in the summer of 1938, McMahon was confined mainly to the reserve team, although injuries didn't help his battle to regain his first team place. It was no real surprise when he was allowed to leave the Racecourse at the end of the 1938/39 season, but a few eyebrows were raised when he joined First Division Stoke City! Pat played in Stoke's opening three matches 1939/40 but with the outbreak of the Second World War, his career came to a standstill, just when it had began to take off again. He returned to his Wrexham home, making one WW2 appearance for Wrexham as a 'guest' player. After the conflict had ended, he hung up his boots, and took up work in the construction industry where he remained until his retirement, whereupon he settled in the Wrexham area. Pat resided in his Rhosnesni home until January 1992, when he passed away at the age of 83. His son 'Roy Mack' is a musical entertainer who has won awards in the trade.

Season	League		F.A.Cup		Welsh Cup		N.S.C.		Total	
	apps	gls	apps	gls	apps	gls	apps	gls	apps	gls
1934/35	2	0	-	-	-	-	-	-	2	0
1935/36	30	0	1	0	1	0	1	0	33	0
1936/37	36	0	3	0	1	0	1	0	41	0
1937/38	42	0	2	0	1	0	1	0	46	0
1938/39	3	0	1	0	-	-	-	-	4	0
	113	**0**	**7**	**0**	**3**	**0**	**3**	**0**	**126**	**0**

McMILLAN, George Sneddon 1952 - 1953

Position; *Forward*
D.O.B; *15th March, 1930*
Birthplace; *Motherwell, Strathclyde*
Height; *ft in* ***Weight;*** *10st 6lbs*
Debut; v. *Gateshead (a) 25th October, 1952*
Total Appearances & Goals; *1 app 0 gls*
Career; *Aberdeen 1app 0gls; WREXHAM 27th May 1952; Newport County 26th Jun 1956 to 18th Mar 1957;*

George McMillan joined Wrexham from Aberdeen in May 1952, where he had made just one Scottish League appearance in January 1951, in a 1-1 home draw with St.Mirren. He signed for Wrexham during the close season of 1952, but had to wait until October before making his Football League debut at Gateshead, in a 1-0 defeat. That proved to be George's only first team appearance for Wrexham, and he left the Racecourse in the close season of 1953. It is not known what became of George after this, but he did return to Wales in the close season of 1956, when he joined Newport County. He failed to impress at Somerton Park and left the club in March 1957 without having made a first team appearance.

Season	League		F.A.Cup		Welsh Cup		Total	
	apps	gls	apps	gls	apps	gls	apps	gls
1952/53	1	0	-	-	-	-	1	0
	1	**0**	**-**	**-**	**-**	**-**	**1**	**0**

McMILLAN, Sammy 1963 - 1967

Position; *Inside-Forward*
D.O.B; *29th September, 1941*
Birthplace; *Belfast*
Height; *5ft 8in* ***Weight;*** *12st 3lbs*
Debut; v. *Shrewsbury Town (h) 26th December, 1963*
Total Appearances & Goals; *172 apps 62 gls*
Career; *Ards 1955; Linfield 1957; Boyland B.C; Manchester United Nov 1959 15apps 6gls; WREXHAM 24th Dec 1963 £8,000; Southend United 26th Sept 1967 £6,000 76/1apps 5gls; Chester 17th Dec 1969 £2,000 16/2apps 0gls; Stockport County Jul 1970 74apps 29gls; Oswestry Town 6th Jun 1972; Lex XI 1973;*
Honours; *Two Northern Ireland International caps; One Northern Ireland Under-23 International cap; Northern Ireland Schoolboy International; Welsh Cup runner-up 1965, 1967 & 1970;*

Sammy McMillan was educated at the Mersey Street Primary and Ashfield Secondary Schools in his native Belfast, but it was only when he arrived at the latter that he began to show his football ability. His school team won all four Northern Ireland schools' trophies for three consecutive seasons, and Sammy was chosen to represent County Down Schoolboys before playing for Northern Ireland at that level. It was around this time that he was signed by Irish League side Ards on schoolboy forms. He left school at 15 to become an apprentice fitter, while continuing to play for Ards. He later joined Linfield, at the age of 16, before quitting the game due to his father's untimely death. Sammy eventually began playing again with Boyland Boys' Club, and it was whilst he was turning out for them in a summer League that he was spotted by Manchester United scout Bob Bishop, the man who discovered George Best. After a successful trial period Sammy was signed on to the United groundstaff in July 1958. He then progressed through the ranks at Old Trafford to the Central League side, where he found fierce competition for a first team place. Even so, Sammy was selected for his Football League debut in November 1961, at Hillsborough against Sheffield Wednesday, playing at outside-right in a 3-1 defeat. He went on to make a further fourteen League appearances for United, scoring six goals, as well as capped by Northern Ireland at full international level in 1962 against both Scotland and England, as a replacement for Derek Dougan. He spent almost five seasons with the Old Trafford club before allowed to sign for Wrexham on Christmas Eve 1963 for an £8,000 transfer fee. McMillan went straight into the 'Robins' first team for his debut on Boxing Day, a 3-2 defeat against Shrewsbury Town on the Racecourse. The return match at Gay Meadow the next day saw Sammy score the winner in a 2-1 win. He then went on to establish himself in the Wrexham side for the next four years, when the 'tough tackling inside-forward' gained further international recognition with an Under-23 cap. Sammy was to experience many ups and downs during his time at the Racecourse; he saw the club relegated in 1964, and finish bottom of the entire Football League in 1966, though he became the Club's leading goalscorer in 1967, a season after establishing a formidable goalscoring partnership with Keith Webber. He also helped the club to reach two Welsh Cup Finals, in 1965 and 1967, although they lost them both to Second Division Cardiff City. In September 1967 he was surprisingly allowed to leave the Racecourse, and join Southend United for a £6,000 fee. He spent just over two seasons at Roots Hall, where he played mainly as a wing-half, scoring twelve goals in 77 League appearances for the Essex club. In December 1969 Sammy left the 'Shrimpers' to join Chester, going on to play in another Welsh Cup Final, Cardiff City again preventing him from gaining a winners' medal. McMillan made just eighteen League appearances for the Sealand Road club before being allowed to sign for Stockport County in the close season of 1970. He was one of a number of players to leave Chester at the time because of the club's financial problems. Sammy was immediately appointed captain at Edgeley Park, and finished the season as the Club's leading goalscorer with eighteen goals, as well as being voted the fans' 'Player of the Season'. The following season saw him again finish as leading scorer, with 13 goals, but at the end of the term was forced to quit the professional game because of a persistent back injury. However, he did manage to continue playing for a short time with Cheshire County League side Oswestry Town, where he spent the 1972/73 season. He ended his playing days with local Wrexham side, Lex XI, becoming their coach until 1986. Sammy Mac as he was affectionately known at the Racecourse settled in the Wrexham area and found work as a self-employed builder at the end of his professional football career. The popular Ulsterman still resides locally.

Season	League		F.A.Cup		Welsh Cup		War League		Total	
	apps	gls	apps	gls	apps	gls	apps	gls	apps	gls
1963/64	20	7	-	-	3	2	-	-	23	9
1964/65	38	10	1	2	3	0	1	0	43	12
1965/66	40	16	2	0	1	1	2	1	45	18
1966/67	45	18	2	1	6	3	1	0	54	22
1967/68	6	1	-	-	-	-	1	0	7	1
	149	**52**	**5**	**3**	**13**	**6**	**5**	**1**	**172**	**62**

McNAB, Thomas Copeland 1957 - 1959

Position; *Right-Half*
D.O.B; *15th July, 1933*
Birthplace; *Glasgow, Strathclyde*
Height; *5ft 10 1/2in* ***Weight;*** *11st 3lbs*
Debut; v. *Tranmere Rovers (h) 16th March, 1957*
Total Appearances & Goals; *47 apps 6 gls*
Career; *Gordon Park CofS 1948; Balliston Juniors 1950; Partick Thistle 1951; Nottingham Forest Mar 1954 0apps; Partick Thistle; WREXHAM 16th Mar 1957 £2,500; Barrow 21st Mar 1959 £1,500 44apps 4gls; East Stirlingshire cs1960; Eastern Suburbs (New Zealand) 1964;*
Honours; *Welsh Cup Winner 1957; Scottish Second Division runner-up 1963; New Zealand International Cap;*

Tom McNab began playing football at Hamilton Crescent Secondary School, where he learned the game on the same pitch as the very first Scotland v. England match was played back in 1872. He gained representative honours with Glasgow Schoolboys, but, upon leaving school at 15 took up work as a painter and decorator while continuing to play football for a local side, Gordon Park Church of Scotland. Tom had a couple of years with them between 1948 and 1950, before moving on to Scottish Junior side Balliston Juniors, where he spent twelve months before joining Partick Thistle. Tommy went on to make over twenty Scottish League appearances for the 'Jags' before he was called up for his National Service in 1953. He enlisted in the R.A.F., later being posted

close to Nottingham. In March 1954 whilst he was serving there, he signed amateur forms with Nottingham Forest, and played a few reserve team games for the club. Upon being demobbed Tom returned to Scotland and rejoined Partick Thistle in time for their triumphant run to the League Cup Final in 1956. There was to be no place for Tom in the team, however, as he was having to contest his position with Scottish international centre-half, J.A.Davidson. Tommy left Firhill in March 1957, after being recommended to Wrexham by Aly McGowan's brother, Jimmy, who was playing for Partick at the time. Wrexham paid £2,500 for McNab, and he went straight into the team at centre-half for his Football League debut in a 1-0 home win against Tranmere Rovers. He was given his chance straight away because of an injury to Alan Fox. Following Fox's return Tom was switched to half-back, where he played in the 1957 Welsh Cup Final against Swansea Town, and collected a winners' medal in a 2-1 success. The following season saw Tom playing regularly until February, when he lost his place to Ken Murray. He struggled to establish himself back in the first team after that, and in March 1959 was transferred to Barrow for a £1,500 fee. He spent eighteen months with the Cumbrian team, scoring four goals in 44 League appearances, before returning to Scotland in the close season of 1960 to join Second Division side East Stirlingshire. He went on to become a regular in the 'Shire' team for the next four seasons, helping them to promotion to the First Division in 1963, when they finished runners'-up to St.Johnstone. Tom played right-back in a team that included a very young Eddie McCreadie, who later went on to play for - and manage - Chelsea. With his career coming to an end, McNab decided to emigrate to New Zealand, where he became player/coach of Eastern Suburbs. He led them to the National Cup Final three times in five years, and also won the League title. In 1967 Tom captained New Zealand against a Manchester United team that included George Best, Bobby Charlton, and Denis Law; He toured South East Asia with the 'Kiwis', and later coached the National side when they played a Welsh XI touring party in 1971. In New Zealand he set up his own painting and decorating business which he continued to do until disaster struck in 1978 when he suffered an accident at work. He was working on a school roof when he fell, the injuries left him a paraplegic. Undeterred, he continued to coach a First Division side from his wheelchair. Tom was later given a testimonial in which a number of the All Blacks Rugby Union side turned out to play with the round ball. Tom still remains in New Zealand, living in Pakuranga, Auckland, where he is secretary of the New Zealand branch of the Glasgow Rangers Supporters' Club.

Season	League		F.A.Cup		Welsh Cup		Total	
	apps	gls	apps	gls	apps	gls	apps	gls
1956/57	11	0	-	-	1	1	12	1
1957/58	27	5	-	-	1	0	28	5
1958/59	5	0	-	-	2	0	7	0
	43	**5**	**-**	**-**	**4**	**1**	**47**	**6**

McNEE, Terence Allan 1946 - 1947

Position; *Goalkeeper*
D.O.B; *5th June, 1925*
Birthplace; *Birkenhead, Merseyside*
Height; *5ft 10in* ***Weight;*** *12st 2lbs*
Debut; v. *Barrow (h) 28th September, 1946*
Total Appearances & Goals; *15 apps 0 gls*
Career; *Port Sunlight Boys Brigade; Bromborough Port; Park Villa; WREXHAM (Am) Sept 1946, (Pro) 19th Dec 1946; Rhyl 20th Aug, 1947; Ellesmere Port Town;*
Honours; *Cheshire County League Championship Winner 1948;*

Terry McNee first began playing football at school in his native Birkenhead. He was selected for both the Woodlands Junior and Alpha Drive Senior Schools, from where he was also chosen to represent Birkenhead Schoolboys. However, any thoughts of a career in football had to be put to the back of his mind because of the Second World War, Terry, who was just 15 at the time, took up employment at Cammell Laird & Co. instead, where he worked on the building of ships. He found time to play some football, however, and appeared in goal for the 1st Port Sunlight Boys Brigade side, followed by a spell with Bromborough Port in the Bebington League. He was later invited to join Park Villa, who played in the much stronger Birkenhead League, where he came up against the likes of R.A.F.Hooton and R.A.F.West Kirby, both of whom had many ex-professionals playing for them at the time. After the War was over Terry continued to play football for Park Villa, but Football League clubs were then scouring the local League's for new players in readiness for the re-start of the 1946/47 Football League season. McNee got his opportunity to play in the Football League, when a local scout asked him and three other players from Park Villa to attend a trial at Chester, following which he was asked to sign amateur forms. However, a month or so later his registration with Chester was cancelled, and he signed for Wrexham as an amateur in September 1946. He soon made his Football League debut, when called into the side to replace Frank Williams in goal, in a 1-1 home draw with Barrow. Terry kept his jersey for fifteen consecutive League and Cup games, before he lost his place in the side at Christmas through illness. Travelling home on the train from a game against Doncaster Rovers, who were top of the League at that time, he collapsed, and his problem was later diagnosed as pneumonia. Frank Williams then re-established himself in the first team to the extent that Terry did not play in the first team again, and was released at the end of the season. Throughout his time with Wrexham Terry had continued to work at Cammell Laird, and trained with Eddie Tunney and John Mortimer at Tranmere Rovers, as they all lived in the Birkenhead area. McNee's most memorable match for Wrexham, was the F.A.Cup Second Round, second replay at Manchester City's, Maine Road ground against Lincoln City, which was played on a pitch so treacherous that the markings were barely visible. Wrexham lost 2-1 after conceding a hotly disputed goal, as the referee ruled that the ball had crossed the line having rebounded off the inside of the post and run across the goal line before Terry dived on the ball to save it. Following his release by Wrexham, McNee joined Cheshire County League side Rhyl, where he enjoyed considerable success. He was the only ever-present in Rhyl's championship winning side of 1947/48, and also played against Swansea Town in the semi-final of the Welsh Cup on the Racecourse. This was to have no fairy tale ending, however, as Rhyl lost 3-0, in a game which saw Terry stretchered off ten minutes from time with a back injury sustained after he had crashed into a goal post. He had played in the home game against Wrexham, in a previous round of the competition, which Rhyl won 1-0. Terry remained at Belle Vue until the end of November 1949, when he signed for Ellesmere Port Town, and stayed with them until the end of the 1951/52 season. He then injured his right knee in a match ironically against Wrexham reserves, following a collision with the 'Robins' centre-forward Frank Fidler. It led to the eventual removal of both his cartilage's (at different times), and the damage to his knee was so severe that he had to end his football career. Which resulted in him having a right knee replacement in 1995. Terry McNee retired in 1990 as a Foreman Shipbuilder after 51 years at Cammel Laird.

Season	League		F.A.Cup		Welsh Cup		Total	
	apps	gls	apps	gls	apps	gls	apps	gls
1950/51	11	0	4	0	-	-	15	0
	11	**0**	**4**	**0**	**-**	**-**	**15**	**0**

McNEIL, Richard 1977 - 1982

Position; *Centre-Forward*
D.O.B; *16th January, 1947*
Birthplace; *Melton Mowbray, Leicestershire*
Height; *5ft 10in* ***Weight;*** *11st 12lbs*
Debut; v. *Swindon Town (h) 24th September, 1977*
Total Appearances & Goals; *210/2 apps 88 gls*
Career; *Holwell Works; Leicester City Nov 1964 0apps; Exeter City Jun 1966 31apps 11gls; Corby Town cs1967; Northampton Town May 1969 £5,000 85/1apps 33gls; Lincoln City Jan 1972 £10,000 96/1apps 53gls; Hereford United Aug 1974 £15,000 128/1apps 85gls; WREXHAM 21st Sept 1977 £60,000; Hereford United 16th Oct 1982 12apps 3gls;*
Honours; *Third Division Championship Winner 1976 & 1978; Welsh Cup runner-up 1976 & 1979; PFA Division Three XI 1976 & 1978;*

Upon leaving school Dixie McNeil took up work for Brush, a local company in Loughborough, as an apprentice electrical technician. He had been chosen to represent his County at football, and it was whilst he was playing for Leicestershire against Lincolnshire that he was spotted and invited to play for Leicester City's 'A' team on the following weekend. After just two appearances for the 'A' team he was signed on full-time terms in November 1964. Dixie progressed through the junior teams at Filbert

Street, but was handed a free transfer at the end of the 1965/66 season. He was quickly snapped up by Fourth Division Exeter City in the close season, and made his Football League debut in the opening match of the new season, a scoreless draw against Wrexham on the Racecourse. After a season with the St.James' Park club, one in which he topped the club's scoring chart with eleven goals - he was released! He then joined non-league Corby Town, taking up work as an industrial painter at Corby Steelworks at the same time. His consistent goalscoring continued with the Southern League side, and he was soon back in the Football League when Northampton Town manager Dave Bowen paid £5,000 for him in May 1969. Dixie went on to spend three years with the 'Cobblers', during which he played in their famous F.A.Cup match against Manchester United, as George Best grabbed six goals, with Dixie scoring for the 'Cobblers' in the 8-2 defeat. He left the County Ground in January 1972 to join Lincoln City for £10,000, where he was to spend two years. At Sincil Bank he played alongside the former England manager Graham Taylor, and he averaged better than a goal every other game. In January 1974 he was signed by Football League newcomers Hereford United for £15,000, where he recorded the club's first ever Football League hat-trick in a 5-0 win over Chesterfield. At the end of his first full season at Edgar Street, his new employers had to pay a further £5,000 to Lincoln as part of the transfer agreement if Dixie scored over twenty goals. He scored 31!, and - with Peter Eastoe - was joint top scorer of the entire Football League. He won a Third Division Championship medal in 1976, in a season that saw him score 35 goals, but Hereford were relegated after just one year in the Second Division. At the beginning of 1977/78 Dixie signed for fellow Third Division side Wrexham, after turning down an offer from Preston North End. He became an instant success at the Racecourse, scoring on his debut in a 2-1 win over Swindon Town, and notching many key goals in the great Cup matches of that season against the likes of Newcastle, Bristol City, and Arsenal. He became a remarkably consistent performer, and his scoring exploits in the Club's League matches were a major contribution as Wrexham stormed to the Third Division Championship. McNeil continued to hit the back of the net on a regular basis throughout the next four seasons in the Second Division for Wrexham before they were relegated in 1982. The 1982/83 season saw Wrexham and Dixie begin the new season in the Third Division, but by October he had left the Racecourse to rejoin his former club Hereford United on a free transfer. By then, Dixie was approaching his 37th birthday, and decided to bring down the curtain on his playing career in January 1983. He returned to the Wrexham area where he was to settle, and continued with the stone-cladding business that he had begun during his days at the Racecourse. He continued to play football in the Welsh National League for Chirk AAA, with whom he won a Championship medal in 1984, and the Fairfield Tavern in the Sunday League. During his time with Chirk, he returned to the Racecourse to play against Wrexham in a Welsh Cup tie, which they lost 4-1. Before that 1984/85 season had ended Dixie was back at the Racecourse on a more permanent basis, when he was appointed the Club's new manager in succession to Bobby Roberts. In his first full season in charge he led Wrexham to Welsh Cup success, beating Kidderminster Harriers in the 1986 Final after a replay. That season also saw him turn out in Wrexham's colours once again, as a substitute in a replayed F.A.Cup tie at home to Notts County. He led the 'Robins' into Europe in the following season against FC Zurrieq of Malta and Real Zaragoza of Spain, to whom they lost on the away goals rule. 1988/89 ended with the Club in the Fourth Division play-off final, losing narrowly to Leyton Orient, and though the new season began with much optimism the Club struggled, winning just three of their opening thirteen matches. It prompted Dixie's resignation in October, but he wasn't out of the game long, as a couple of months later, he was invited to join his former boss at Hereford, John Sillett, as first team coach at Coventry City. He spent a little over a year at Highfield Road, until Terry Butcher took over from Sillett in November 1990. The new man brought in his own coaching staff, rendering Dixie surplus to requirements. He then began working for Marston's Brewery as a sales representative, as well as reporting on Wrexham's games for local radio. In November 1993 he returned to football management as manager of League of Wales side Flint Town United, and immediately turned around the fortunes of the Cae-Y-Castell side, leading them from near relegation certainties to finish the season in a very respectable fourth position. However, he resigned as Flint manager on 20th March 1995 following an internal disagreement. By that time he had been awarded a testimonial by Wrexham, against Kevin Keegan's Premier League side, Newcastle United. They were the ideal opposition for such an occasion, for the 'Magpies' were the side against whom Dixie loved to score during his glory days at the Racecourse. He played for part of the first half, in a 4-3 win for Wrexham. Dixie's two sons, Richard and Jamie, have both been on the Racecourse club's books as apprentices, and still play in local football. McNeil who has settled in the Wrexham area, is now employed as a salesman for a book company, also as a summariser for B.B.C. Radio Wales 'Sportstime' programme during the football season often on Wrexham encounters.

Season	League		F.A.Cup		Welsh Cup		League Cup		E.C.W.C.		Total	
	apps	gls	apps	gls	apps	gls	apps	gls	apps	gls	apps	gls
1977/78	23	13	9	11	1	1	-	-	-	-	33	25
1978/79	30/1	4	3	3	3	1	1	1	2	1	39/1	10
1979/80	38	14	3	4	2	1	4	1	2	1	49	21
1980/81	35	13	5	2	5	5	2	0	-	-	47	20
1981/82	33	9	4	2	2	0	5	0	-	-	44	11
1982/83	7	1	-	-	-	-	1	0	-	-	8	1
1985/86	-	-	0/1	0	-	-	-	-	-	-	0/1	0
	166/1	**54**	**24/1**	**22**	**13**	**8**	**12**	**2**	**4**	**2**	**210/2**	**88**

McTURK, John

1957 - 1958

Position; *Left-Back*
D.O.B; *11th July, 1936*
Birthplace; *Lugar, Strathclyde*
Height; *5ft 10in* ***Weight;*** *11st 0lbs*
Debut; v. *Darlington (a) 24th August, 1957*
Total Appearances & Goals; *2 apps 0 gls*
Career; *Lugar; Auchinleck Thistle; Auchinleck Talbot; St.Mirren 1954; WREXHAM 29th Jul 1957; St.Mirren 20th Nov 1957; Queen of the South cs1961; Morton cs1963; Stirling Albion cs1964; Albion Rovers cs1965; Lugar cs1967; Cumnock 1967;*
Honours; *Scottish Second Division Championship Winner 1964 & 1965; Scottish Second Division runner-up 1962;*

John McTurk first played organised football for his local Junior school in Lugar, a small town near Cumnock in Ayrshire. He continued to progress when he went to Cumnock Academy at the age of 12, and it was whilst there that he represented both East Ayrshire and Ayrshire Schoolboys. He was also invited for Scottish Schoolboys' trials held in Glasgow. John took up employment as an apprentice joiner on leaving school, but continued to play football for Lugar before he went to work in nearby Auchinleck. He then joined up with a local Juvenile team, Auchinleck Thistle, playing just a few games for them before being invited to play for Auchinleck Talbot, a Scottish Junior League side. It was from there that McTurk signed for St.Mirren, having just turned seventeen. He made his debut in the opening match of the 1953/54 season against Hibernian, and was handed the job of marking Gordon Smith, one of the 'Famous Five'. John continued playing regularly for St.Mirren, earning a call-up to the Scottish under-23 squad, although never actually selected to play. He collected a Renfrewshire Cup Winners' medal with the Paisley club, before being called up for his National Service in 1957. John enlisted with the Royal Engineers, and after six weeks' training at Malvern was posted to Fleet, near Aldershot. Shortly after he had joined the Army Wrexham's Scottish scout, Jimmy McGowan, recommended him to the Racecourse club along with Willie Dallas of Stirling Albion. They both signed for the 'Robins' on the same day in July 1957, though John's was a type of loan transfer arrangement. He made his Football League debut at left-back in the opening match of the 1957/58 season in a 2-1 defeat at Darlington. He had been on duty at his Army camp in Farnborough until 4pm on the Friday, and didn't arrive at the team hotel in Darlington until 2am the following morning! Despite his lack of sleep and a tiring journey it was stated in the press, 'It didn't stop him from playing extremely well, once he had recovered from a shaky start'. John's second appearance for Wrexham, again at left-back, came towards the end of September in a 3-1 defeat at Bradford City, and it proved to be his last match for the Club. His contract was cancelled on the 20th November 1957 after St.Mirren had requested his return even though he was still in the Army. During his time in the Forces John had captained the British Army side, where he played with - and against - a number of top class players. He left the Army in 1959 and returned home, where he continued his career with St.Mirren. He stayed at Love St. until 1961, when joining Scottish Second Division side Queen of the South. In his first season with the Dumfries club he helped them to promotion, finishing runners-up to Clyde. He spent a further year here, before signing for Morton in 1963, where he featured in their Scottish Second Division Championship side in his one and only season at Cappielow Park. In the summer of 1964 McTurk signed for Stirling Albion, and enjoyed instant success again as they won the Scottish Second Division Championship. In 1965 John signed for another Second Division club, Albion Rovers, two seasons before leaving to play for his local side, Lugar. He followed this with a short spell with Cumnock, later playing in the Churches League. John continued to play in a number of charity games, lining up in a team of ex-professional players until he was 59 years-old. Throughout his time in football McTurk was employed by the National Coal Board as a joiner, first working for the N.C.B. Housing Department in Lugar, then at the Barony Colliery in Auchinleck. He also spent some time at the High House Colliery in the same town before returning to work at the Barony Colliery until it closed around 1987, when he was made redundant. John is now in retirement in Cumnock, where he still retains an interest in football by following the fortunes of his beloved St.Mirren.

Season	League		F.A.Cup		Welsh Cup		Total	
	apps	gls	apps	gls	apps	gls	apps	gls
1957/58	2	0	-	-	-	-	2	0
	2	**0**	**-**	**-**	**-**	**-**	**2**	**0**

***McWHINNIE,* Archibald** 1951 - 1952

Position; *Wing-Half*
D.O.B; *17th July, 1926*
Birthplace; *Glasgow, Strathclyde*
Height; *5ft 9in* ***Weight;*** *11st 0lbs*
Debut; v. *Bradford Park Avenue (a) 1st September, 1951*
Total Appearances & Goals; *2 apps 0 gls*
Career; *Rutherglen Glencairn; WREXHAM 4th July 1951;*

Archie McWhinnie was playing for Scottish Junior side Rutherglen Glencairn when he was spotted by Wrexham's North of the Border scout, Bobby Archibald. He then signed for Wrexham in May 1951, and made his Football League debut at half-back at Bradford Park Avenue in a 5-0 defeat in September 1951. He stepped into the side as a replacement for another Scot, Stewart McCallum, and lined up alongside Ken Roberts, who was making Club and Football League history by equalling the record set by Albert Geldard in 1929, as the youngest ever player to compete at that level. Archie kept his place in the side for the following match at Workington, this time at centre-half in place of Ronnie Wynn, which Wrexham also lost, 2-0. He then lost his place in the side to Estyn Griffiths, and was unable to make a further breakthrough into the senior side. Archie left the Racecourse club at the end of the 1951/52 season.

Season	League		F.A.Cup		Welsh Cup		Total	
	apps	gls	apps	gls	apps	gls	apps	gls
1951/52	2	0	-	-	-	-	2	0
	2	**0**	**-**	**-**	**-**	**-**	**2**	**0**

***MACKRETH,* Stephen Francis** 1967 - 1969

Position; *Left-Back*
D.O.B; *1st July, 1950*
Birthplace; *Rossett, Denbighshire*
Height; *5ft 8in* ***Weight;*** *10st 7lbs*
Debut; v. *Notts County (a) 5th April, 1969*
Total Appearances & Goals; *1/1 apps 0 gls*
Career; *WREXHAM 20th Oct 1967; Oswestry Town 7th Sept 1970; Weston Rhyn cs1972; Llangollen 1975; Druids 1978; Overton 1981 (Player/manager);*
Honours; *Northern Floodlit League Cup Winner 1970; Alves Cup Winner 1970; N.W.C.F.A. Representative XI 1970; Shropshire County League Division One Championship Winner 1975;*

Steve Mackreth came from a non-footballing family, and never took the game seriously until he was about 14, when he was invited to play for his school team at Bryn Offa. This led to him appearing for the Wrexham & District Schoolboys team, who reached the semi-finals of the Welsh Schools Shield in 1965, as well as representing the Welsh Boys Club team. He was described at that time as 'fearless in the tackle and good in distribution'. He joined Wrexham as a junior in June 1966, having already played for the reserve team as a schoolboy at the age of 15 after he had asked for a trial. At full-back, he was highly rated at the time by his coaches, and made sufficient progress enough to be offered professional terms at the Racecourse in October 1967. However, he found his first team opportunities limited, as manager John Neal prepared a team for promotion. Steve finally made his Football League debut for the 'Robins' at Notts County towards the end of the 1968/69 season, when he replaced Alan Bermingham at right-back, but it ended disappointingly, as Wrexham lost 5-0. His next appearance proved also to be his last, when he came on as a substitute for Brian Tinnion in a 2-2 home draw with Exeter City in April 1969. During his time at the club Steve was selected to play for the North Wales Coast F.A. in their annual representative match with the Scottish Junior F.A. in Aberdeen, scoring from his full-back position in the 4-3 win. The 1969/70 season would see him captain the reserve side that won both the Northern Floodlit League Cup and the Alves Cup. However, he was released at the end of that season, and was on the verge of travelling to Australia to play for Sydney FC, when he decided to remain at home and join Oswestry Town in September 1970. That same season he appeared for the Border club against Wrexham in the 1971 Welsh Cup semi-final at the Victoria Road, and a year later returned to the Racecourse with the Shropshire club for a fifth round match in the same competition, which Wrexham again won 2-0. Steve was to leave Oswestry in the close season of 1972 to join Weston Rhyn as their first ever professional. They played in the Shropshire County League Division One, and he led them to the League title in the 1974/75 season, when they also lifted the West Midland Tyre Cup. Mackreth then went on to join Llangollen in 1975, which was followed by spells with both Druids and Overton, with whom he was manager for a short time. Having settled in Wrexham, Steve is employed as a printer at the Continental Can factory on the Wrexham Industrial Estate, and a keen supporter of his home town team. He was accepted on to Wrexham Football Club's Board of Directors on 2nd February 1990, and still remains in that capacity at the present time.

Season	League		F.A.Cup		Welsh Cup		League Cup		Total	
	apps	gls	apps	gls	apps	gls	apps	gls	apps	gls
1968/69	1/1	0	-	-	-	-	-	-	1/1	0
	1/1	**0**	**-**	**-**	**-**	**-**	**-**	**-**	**1/1**	**0**

MADDEN, Craig Anthony 1990

Position; *Forward*
D.O.B; *29th May, 1958*
Birthplace; *Manchester, Lancashire*
Height; *5ft 8in* **Weight;** *10st 2lbs*
Debut; v. *Peterborough United (h) 6th January, 1990*
Total Appearances & Goals; *6/2 apps 0 gls*
Career; *Northern Nomads; Bury Mar 1978 278/19apps 129gls; West Bromwich Albion 21st Mar 1986 £50,000 10/2apps 3gls; Blackpool Feb 1987 £50,000 73/18apps 24gls; WREXHAM 3rd Jan 1990 (Loan); York City 3rd Mar 1990 3/1apps 0gls; Fleetwood Town cs1990;*

Craig Madden represented Stockport and East Cheshire youth teams before he was signed by Third Division Bury from non-league side Northern Nomads in March 1978. He went on to spend eight years at Gigg Lane, during which he re-wrote the record books of the Lancashire club by scoring a total of 129 League goals in 296 appearances. He also broke their record of the most goals in a season, with 35 during 1981/82. At five foot eight inches Craig was somewhat small for a striker, but he had marvellous control and was deceptively quick, especially around the penalty area. Craig helped the 'Shakers' to promotion to the Third Division in 1985, but the following season his goalscoring prowess, which hadn't gone unnoticed, saw him sign for First Division side West Bromwich Albion in March 1986, as part of their bid to starve off relegation. He made his debut for the 'Baggies' in a 1-0 defeat at Ipswich, but couldn't prevent the Hawthorns club from sliding into the Second Division. The following season Craig made only a handful of appearances, and by February was on his way back to Lancashire when he signed for Third Division Blackpool for £50,000. He made an immediate impact with the 'Seasiders' by scoring on his debut, albeit in a 4-1 defeat at Wigan! Craig became a regular for the 'Tangerines' over the next three seasons, but niggling injuries gradually began to take their toll, and in January 1990 he was allowed to join Wrexham on loan in a bid to boost the club's lack of firepower. Madden spent two months on loan at the Racecourse, but scored just one goal in ten outings, and that came in a 2-0 Welsh Cup win at Rhyl. Sadly, he failed to recapture his old goalscoring prowess during the eight weeks that he spent in North Wales, and he was allowed to return to Bloomfield Road. Craig then joined York City on loan for a month, but again failed to impress and so returned to Blackpool, from where he was released at the end of the season. Craig then went into non-league football with Fleetwood Town, before becoming the Football in the Community Officer at Blackpool.

Season	League		F.A.Cup		Welsh Cup		League Cup		F.R.T.		Total	
	apps	gls	apps	gls	apps	gls	apps	gls	apps	gls	apps	gls
1989/90	6/2	0	-	-	1/1	1	-	-	-	-	7/3	1
	6/2	**0**	**-**	**-**	**1/1**	**1**	**-**	**-**	**-**	**-**	**7/3**	**1**

MALAM, Albert 1946 - 1947

Position; *Inside-Forward*
D.O.B; *20th January, 1913*
Birthplace; *Liverpool, Merseyside*
Died; *February, 1992*
Height; *5ft 6 1/2in* **Weight;** *10st 8lbs*
Debut; v. *New Brighton (h) 31st August, 1946*
Total Appearances & Goals; *40 apps 15 gls*
Career; *Colwyn Bay 31st Mar 1932; Everton (trial) 1932; Chesterfield 4th Nov 1932 58apps 26gls; Huddersfield Town 15th Sept 1934 21apps 11gls; Doncaster Rovers 25th Sept 1936 96apps 22gls; New Brighton Nov 1939 81apps 37gls; Tranmere Rovers (WW2 Guest) 1939/40 1app 1gls; Manchester City (WW2 Guest) Aug 1942 12 apps 7gls; Crewe Alexandra (WW2 Guest) Nov 1942 33apps 13gls; WREXHAM Nov 1943; Southport (WW2 Guest) 1944 27apps 9gls; Rochdale (WW2 Guest) 1944/45 2apps 0gls; WREXHAM 16th Feb 1946; Runcorn Jan 1947;*
Honours; *North Wales Coast F.A.Challenge Cup runner-up 1931;*

Albert Malam was playing for Colwyn Bay in the Birmingham & District League when he was signed by Third Division North side Chesterfield in November 1932. He made his Football League debut for the 'Sprirites' in a 2-1 home defeat by Grimsby Town, in which he scored his side's only goal. Albert went on to make a total of 58 League appearances, scoring 26 goals, as an inside-forward with the Saltergate club before signing for First Division side Huddersfield Town in September 1934. He scored eleven goals in 21 League games for the 'Terriers', all during the 1934/35 season, including a hat-trick against Liverpool in an 8-0 win, which no doubt pleased him as he was a Scouser! He didn't play a first team game for Huddersfield during the 1935/36 season, and in September 1936 joined Second Division side Doncaster Rovers for a Club record fee. Albert made his Rovers' debut in front of 23,000 at Belle Vue, in a 1-0 win over Aston Villa. However, Doncaster were to win just five more matches before the end of that season, and so suffered relegation. Albert stayed at Belle Vue until the start of the Second World War, during which he figured in the first Doncaster team to play overseas - alongside another former Wrexham player, Hugh McMahon, as they played a Dutch National XI in Rotterdam. They were preparing for a match against Austria, and Doncaster lost 7-2! He returned to live in his native Liverpool during WW2, when he 'guested' for a number of clubs in the North-West. He first played for New Brighton, for whom he became an ever-present from his debut in November 1939 until their final WW2 match in April 1942, and also 'guested' for Tranmere Rovers around the same time. His debut for New Brighton against Stockport County, provided the 'Rakers' with their first regional League win. Following the suspension of New Brighton in 1942 Albert joined Manchester City for 1942/43, and played in their first twelve matches, scoring seven goals, including a hat-trick in a 5-1 win over Wrexham in September. He moved on to Crewe Alexandra in November 1942, scoring 13 goals in 33 appearances. 1943/44 saw Albert make one appearance for Doncaster Rovers, as well as turning out for Crewe Alexandra, before he joined Wrexham in November 1943. He scored on his War-time debut for The North-East Wales Club in a 4-1 win over Stockport County, and remained with the 'Robins' until the end of the 1943/44 campaign. The following season Albert began with Southport, although he also made two appearances for Rochdale. 1945/46 was the final Malam season before the resumption of the Football League, which saw Albert sign permanently for Wrexham in February 1946, at the age of 33. He made his League debut for the 'Robins' in the first League game of the new season, against New Brighton in a 3-2 win. The following match at Rochdale Albert scored his one and only League goal for Wrexham in a 1-0 victory. He completed five more League games before being released in January 1947 to allow him to become player/ manager of Runcorn. Not much is known about what he did after his football career came to an end, except that sadly, he died in late February 1992, aged 79. His son, Colin, is a sportswriter for the Daily Telegraph.

Season	League		F.A.Cup		Welsh Cup		War League		Total	
	apps	gls	apps	gls	apps	gls	apps	gls	apps	gls
1943/44	-	-	-	-	-	-	27	12	27	12
1945/46	-	-	-	-	-	-	6	2	6	2
1946/47*	6	1	1	0	-	-	-	-	7	1
	6	**1**	**1**	**0**	**-**	**-**	**33**	**14**	**40**	**15**

* = Football League Record

MANUEL, Percival Edward 1934 - 1935

Position; *Outside-Left*
D.O.B; *A/M/J, 1909*
Birthplace; *Wantage, Oxfordshire*
Height; *5ft 8'1/2ins* **Weight;** *11st 0lbs*
Debut; v. *Stockport County (h) 6th April, 1935*
Appearances; *2 apps 0 gls*
Career; *Marlborough; Oxford City; Swindon Town (Am) Jan 1934 0apps; Stourbridge; WREXHAM 30th Mar 1935; Montreal FC (Canada) May 1935;*

Percy Manuel was believed to have signed for Swindon Town as an amateur in January 1934 from Oxford City, having previously played for Marlborough. He failed to make a Football League appearance, but did record one first team appearance in a Division Three South Section Cup match at Newport County in January 1934, which they lost 7-2. After leaving the County Ground, Percy played for Birmingham and District League side Stourbridge for a short time before joining Third Division North side Wrexham in March 1935. His first appearance for the North Wales club came in a 5-0 win over Bangor, in a Birmingham & District League match, with his performance being described in the local press as, 'His shooting was above average of the other forwards, and his ball control and centring were good.' Percy went on to make his Football League debut for Wrexham, in the following April, a 2-1 victory at home to Stockport County, when he stepped in for Bob Weale at outside-left. He kept his place for the following match at Crewe, but it ended in disappointment as Wrexham lost 2-0, and it proved to be his last match for the club. Percy was to leave both Wrexham and Britain at the end of the season, when it is believed he moved to Canada to join the professional staff of Montreal FC in July 1935.

Season	League		F.A.Cup		Welsh Cup		N.S.C.		Total	
	apps	gls	apps	gls	apps	gls	apps	gls	apps	gls
1934/35	2	0	-	-	-	-	-	-	2	0
	2	**0**	-	-	-	-	-	-	**2**	**0**

MARRIOTT, Andrew

1993 - 1998

Position; *Goalkeeper*
D.O.B; *11th October, 1970*
Birthplace; *Sutton-in-Ashfield, Nottinghamshire*
Height; *6ft 0in* ***Weight;*** *12st 6lbs*
Debut; v. *Cambridge United (h) 9th October, 1993*
Total Appearances & Goals; *261 apps 0 gls*
Career; *Arsenal 22nd Oct 1988 0apps; Nottingham Forest 20th June 1989 £50,000 11apps 0gls; W.B.A. 6th Sept 1989 3apps 0gls (Loan); Blackburn Rovers 29th Dec 1989 2apps 0gls (Loan); Colchester United 21st Mar 1990 10apps 0gls (Loan); Burnley 29th Aug 1991 15apps 0gls (Loan); WREXHAM 8th Oct 1993 (Loan), 1st Dec 1993 £200,000; Sunderland 17th Aug 1998 (Loan), 21st Sept £275,000 1app 0gls;*
Honours; *Five Welsh International caps; Welsh Cup Winner 1995; Third Division Championship 1992; Zenith Data Systems Cup Winner 1992; Football League Cup runner-up 1992; One England Under-21 International cap; Two England Youth International caps; England Schoolboy International; Pontins Premier League Championship Winner 1999;*

Although schooled in Nottingham it was Arsenal who first spotted Andy Marriott as a youngster playing in a local Nottingham Schools' side. He was invited to Highbury for trials as a 12 year-old, eventually signing for the North London club on schoolboy forms. He then gained a place at the F.A.School of Excellence at Lilleshall in Shropshire, and after graduating from there he joined Arsenal as a full-time apprentice. Andy signed professional forms with the 'Gunners' in October 1988 but, having become home-sick, he returned to sign for Nottingham Forest for a £50,000 fee in June 1989. He had not made a first team appearance for Arsenal by that time, and it was much the same story at Forest, where he remained in their reserve side until September 1989. He was then given the opportunity to join West Bromwich Albion on loan because of an injury to regular 'keeper, Paul Bradshaw, and made his Football League debut in a 3-1 win at Leicester City. He completed two further League appearances for Albion before returning to Forest at the end of his loan period. He eventually took up an offer of a further loan spell, this time with Blackburn Rovers, in December 1989, making two League appearances for the Lancashire club before returning to the City Ground. However, in March 1990 he was on his travels again, joining Colchester United on loan for whom he made his debut against Wrexham in a very emotional relegation battle. Wrexham won the match 3-2, and went on to preserve their League status. For Colchester, however, the defeat sent them into a downward spiral, and though Andy made nine more appearances for the U's, they were relegated to the Conference at the end of the season. Having returned to Nottingham, 1990/91 saw Marriott languishing in the shadow of Mark Crossley, but another loan spell at Burnley in August 1991 saw him clock up an impressive 15 League appearances in a three month spell at Turf Moor. During that time he conceded just thirteen goals, and played in the 6-2 victory at...........Wrexham! The result equalled Wrexham's worst ever home defeat in the Football League. Andy was to receive a Third Division championship medal for his part in helping Burnley to win the championship that season. He finally made his senior debut for Forest in a 1-0 home win over Manchester United, and kept his place for the following five League games. He also played in the Zenith Data Systems Cup Final at Wembley where he helped Forest to beat Southampton 3-2. Two weeks later, he was back at Wembley when Forest took on Manchester United in the Rumbelows Cup Final, although they lost 1-0. His England under-21 debut followed at the end of the season, when he was selected to play against Mexico in a tournament in Toulon. However, 1992/93 found Andy again acting as understudy to Crossley, though he did make five League appearances towards the end of a season that was to see Forest relegated. They signed Tommy Wright at the beginning of the new season so, when the opportunity came to join Wrexham on loan, he accepted. Andy made his debut in a 1-1 home draw with Cambridge, and went on to impress everyone at the club with some fine goalkeeping that eventually led Brian Flynn to spend £200,000 - almost equalling the club record - for him. He repaid Flynn with some superb displays that carried Wrexham through a number of memorable cup games, including the run to the Quarter-Finals of the F.A.Cup in 1997, and the 1995 Welsh Cup Final victory over Cardiff City in the National Stadium. In April 1996 Marriott received international recognition, when he made his Welsh international debut against Switzerland in Lugano, this despite having played for the England Under-21, Youth, and Schoolboy teams. Qualification for Wales came through his Welsh grandparents, and he was able to play against Switzerland because all the previous games for England were classed as competitive. Andy was voted Wrexham's 'Player of the Season' for 1996/97, and he capped it by playing for Wales again, against Scotland in Kilmarnock, in a 1-0 win. He requested a transfer in the summer in order to progress with his career, although no offers were forthcoming so remained with the 'Robins', and the following season was awarded two more caps: a European Championship match in Belgium, and a mid-season friendly in Brazil. He also played his part in helping Wrexham reach the Second Division play-offs, only to miss out on goals scored. The close season of 1998 saw a disagreement with manager Brian Flynn, which led to Andy being demoted to second choice 'keeper to Mark Cartwright. A week into the new season he took up an option to join First Division Sunderland on a month's loan, which eventually led him to sign for the Wearside club for a fee of £275,000. However, Andy spent most of the season as understudy to Thomas Sorensen, making just one league appearance in a 2-0 win at Grimsby as Sunderland ran away with the First Division Championship. Andy Marriott is a fine shot stopper and at the Racecourse he was described as one of the better keepers in the second division although lacking a little in organisational skills around his area.

Season	League		F.A.Cup		Welsh Cup		League Cup		A.G.T.		E.C.W.C.		Total	
	apps	gls	apps	gls	apps	gls	apps	gls	apps	gls	apps	gls	apps	gls
1993/94	36	0	2	0	2	0	-	-	2	0	-	-	42	0
1994/95	46	0	4	0	8	0	4	0	4	0	-	-	66	0
1995/96	46	0	4	0	-	-	2	0	3	0	2	0	57	0
1996/97	43	0	10	0	-	-	2	0	1	0	-	-	56	0
1997/98	42	0	4	0	1*	0*	2	0	1	0	-	-	50	0
	213	**0**	**24**	**0**	**11**	**0**	**10**	**0**	**11**	**0**	**2**	**0**	**261**	**0**

* = Welsh Invitation Cup.

MARSHALL, Colin

1991

Position; *Forward*
D.O.B; *1st November, 1969*
Birthplace; *Glasgow, Strathclyde*
Height; *5ft 5in* ***Weight;*** *9st 5lbs*
Debut; v. *Scunthorpe United (h) 28th September, 1991*
Total Appearances & Goals; *3 apps 0 gls*
Career; *Barnsley Apr 1988 0/4apps 0gls; WREXHAM 26th Sept 1991 (Loan); Scarborough Mar 1992 4apps 1gls;*

Colin Marshall did not play football at his school, Royston Hill: instead, he turned out for Possil Y.M., a youth team that boasted Kenny Dalglish among its former players. A number of Clubs showed an interest in signing Colin, but it was Barnsley who made him the first firm offer, and he signed for the Yorkshire club as a Y.T.S. Trainee in the summer of 1986. A professional contract followed the completion of his two year training period in April 1988. He made his Football League debut five months later, coming on as a substitute for Steve Lowndes in a 2-1 defeat against Manchester City. Colin found his first team chances limited at the Oakwell Ground, and in September 1991 joined Wrexham on a month's loan. He made his 'Robins' debut in a 4-0 win against Scunthorpe United on the Racecourse, but after just two more League appearances - a 5-0 defeat at Cardiff City, and a record-equalling 6-2 home defeat by Burnley - he was allowed to return to Barnsley. Before the end of the season he signed for Scarborough, in March 1992, where he made four League appearances scoring one goal. He was released by Scarborough in the close season of 1992.

Season	League		F.A.Cup		Welsh Cup		League Cup		F.R.T.		Total	
	apps	gls	apps	gls	apps	gls	apps	gls	apps	gls	apps	gls
1991/92	3	0	-	-	-	-	-	-	-	-	3	0
	3	**0**	-	-	-	-	-	-	-	-	**3**	**0**

MASON, Stuart James 1964 - 1966 & 1968 - 1973

Position; *Full-Back*
D.O.B; *2nd June, 1948*
Birthplace; *Whitchurch, Shropshire*
Height; *5ft 8 1/2in* ***Weight;*** *10st 9lbs*
Debut; v. *Lincoln City (a) 1st January, 1966*
Total Appearances & Goals; *200/17 apps 3 gls*
Career; *Whitchurch Alport; WREXHAM 23rd Nov 1964; Liverpool 7th Oct 1966 0apps; Doncaster Rovers Nov 1967 1app 0gls (Loan); WREXHAM 24th Jun 1968; Chester Jun 1973 132/5apps 7gls; Rochdale Dec 1976 2apps 0gls (Loan); Crewe Alexandra 28th Oct 1977 4apps 1gls (Loan); Bangor City 8th Dec 1977; Oswestry Town 1984/85;*
Honours; *Three England Youth caps; Fourth Division runner-up 1970; Welsh Cup Winner 1972; Welsh Cup runner-up 1971 & 1978; Division Four runner-up 1970; Northern Floodlit League Cup Winner 1970; Alves Cup Winner 1970;*

Stuart Mason attended the Grammar School in his home town of Whitchurch, where 'soccer' was a forbidden word. Rugby was the game at this school, so he signed for Shropshire County League side Whitchurch Alport, where he quickly made his mark. Stuart was spotted by a Wrexham scout, and the club's assistant manager Ken Roberts, was quick to sign him up, even though he was about to go to Teacher Training College in Birmingham. He spent a very short time in the Racecourse Club's junior teams and, on New Year's Day 1966, made his Football League debut at right-back in place of Reg Holland in a 2-0 win at Lincoln City. Stuart's progress was remarkable and was capped three times by England at Youth level as he became a regular in the 'Robins' first team line-up. He continued this form into the 1966/67 season, and in October 1966 Liverpool manager Bill Shankly swooped to sign both Stuart and fellow full-back Peter Wall in a joint deal reported to be in the region of £30,000. Stuart played regularly for Liverpool's Central League side, but found severe competition for a first team place, and in November 1967 was loaned out to Doncaster Rovers. He made just one League appearance for the Belle Vue club, in a 2-0 defeat at Rochdale in February 1968. Wrexham's interest in Stuart was then rekindled, and he returned to the Racecourse at the end of the 1967/68 season. His second spell with the Club saw him figure in the 1970 promotion side, and he collected a Welsh Cup Winners' medal in 1972. He played in Wrexham's inaugural match in Europe against F.C.Zurich, and also added a Welsh Cup runners'-up medal in 1971. Mason left the Racecourse in June 1973 after five seasons, when he signed for Chester. He helped them to promotion in 1975 for the first time in their history, and also played a part in their run to the Football League Cup semi-finals in that same season, where they lost to Aston Villa 5-4 on aggregate. Stuart then had loan spells with both Rochdale and Crewe Alexandra before joining Bangor City in December 1977. He played for the Farrar Road club in the 1978 Welsh Cup Final against Wrexham, before finally finishing his playing days with Oswestry Town, where he became manager for the 1984/85 season, leaving in March 1985. He later managed Coedpoeth in the Welsh National League, before working as the assistant commercial manager at the Racecourse. He eventually set himself up in business, opening up a sports shop in Wrexham, which he still runs at the time of writing. Also a very talented cricketer winning many honours in local cricket and on the minor counties scene.

Season	League		F.A.Cup		Welsh Cup		League Cup		E.C.W.C.		Total	
	apps	gls	apps	gls	apps	gls	apps	gls	apps	gls	apps	gls
1965/66	19	0	-	-	1	0	-	-	-	-	20	0
1966/67	9	0	-	-	-	-	1	0	-	-	10	0
1968/69	19/2	0	-	-	-	-	-	-	-	-	19/2	0
1969/70	32/7	1	2/2	0	2	0	2/1	0	-	-	38/10	1
1970/71	26/4	0	1	0	2/1	0	2	0	-	-	31/5	0
1971/72	39	2	3	0	4	0	-	-	-	-	46	2
1972/73	28	0	2	0	-	-	2	0	4	0	36	0
	172/13	**3**	**8/2**	**0**	**9/1**	**0**	**7/1**	**0**	**4**	**0**	**200/17**	**3**

MASSEY, Stephen 1986 - 1988

Position; *Forward*
D.O.B; *28th March, 1958*
Birthplace; *Denton, Lancashire*
Height; *5ft 11in Weight; 11st 5lbs*
Debut; v. *Hereford United (a) 23rd August, 1986*
Total Appearances & Goals; *55/9 apps 18 gls*
Career; *Stockport County Jul 1975 87/14apps 20gls; Bournemouth Jul 1978 £5,000 85/12apps 19gls; Peterborough United Aug 1981 13/5apps 2gls; Northampton Town Feb 1982 60apps 26gls; Hull City Jul 1983 £20,000 34/8apps 9gls; Cambridge United Aug 1985 28/3apps 11gls; WREXHAM Jul 1986; Truro City 1988;*
Honours; *Welsh Cup runner-up 1988;*

Steve Massey began playing football at Aspinall Primary and Wright Robinsons Schools in his native Manchester, and represented Manchester Schoolboys at all levels before signing schoolboy forms with Stockport County. He was offered a two year apprenticeship at Edgeley Park in 1974, and it was during this time that he made his Football League debut at the age of 16 in February 1975. Steve came on as a substitute for Norman Lloyd in a 2-1 home win over Darlington, and underlined his early promise by scoring the winning goal. He remained at Edgeley Park until July 1978, playing three games alongside the legendary George Best, when he signed for Bournemouth in a £5,000 move. He teamed up with Ted MacDougall at Dean Court, and scored on his debut in a 3-1 win over Newport County. Steve spent three happy years with Bournemouth, under manager Alec Stock. He was released by the 'Cherries' in the summer of 1981, whereupon he joined Peterborough United, although things didn't work out for him at London Road as he was deployed as a wide player. He was on the move again before the season had ended, signing for Northampton Town in February 1982. The goals began to flow with the 'Cobblers', and he scored his first League hat-trick for them, in a 5-1 win over Swindon Town in May 1983. It was the kind of form that persuaded Hull City to pay out £20,000 for him during the close season of 1983. Once again he scored on his debut; in fact, he scored twice in a 4-1 win over Burnley on the opening day of the season. Massey went on to help the 'Tigers' to promotion from the Third Division in 1985, but during the summer he decided to move on when manager Brian Horton told him that he couldn't guarantee a first team place for the new season. Steve then stepped down to the Fourth Division with Cambridge United. He spent just one season at the Abbey Stadium before being released along with five other players. It was then that Wrexham manager Dixie McNeil approached him at a time when he was also considering an offer from his first club, Stockport County. He was persuaded to sign for Wrexham following a conversation with McNeil in the Racecourse car park, when a bird flew over and did what it does naturally....all over Dixie's head! Steve thought "that man's lucky", and promptly signed for him! He got off to a good start when he scored five times in pre-season friendlies, but his first League goal didn't come until the seventh match of the season, in a 2-1 defeat at Colchester. He played in all four European matches that season, against FC Zurrieq and Real Zaragoza, and scored four goals - making him the Club's all-time leading goalscorer in European matches. However, disaster was to Strike at the beginning of the following season when Steve received an ankle injury, which put him out of first team action for six months. He did manage another ten appearances before being released in the summer of 1988. Massey then moved to Cornwall, where he took up running a Caravan Park. He also continued his football career with Truro City, as the club's player/manager, leading them to League and Cup success in 1993. Steve still lives in Cornwall, where he is still running his own Caravan Parks.

Season	League		F.A.Cup		Welsh Cup		League Cup		F.R.T.		E.C.W.C.		Total	
	apps	gls	apps	gls	apps	gls	apps	gls	apps	gls	apps	gls	apps	gls
1986/87	30/3	9	2	2	4/1	0	4	0	1/2	2	4	4	45/6	17
1987/88	8/2	1	-	-	2/1	0	-	-	-	-	-	-	10/3	1
	38/5	**10**	**2**	**2**	**6/2**	**0**	**4**	**0**	**1/2**	**2**	**4**	**4**	**55/9**	**18**

MATHIAS, James Thomas 1937 - 1940

Position; *Centre-Half*
D.O.B; *J/F/M 1914*
Birthplace; *Cemey Moss, Nr.Wrexham, Denbighshire*
Height; *5ft 9in* ***Weight;*** *11st 6lbs*
Debut; v. *Darlington (h) 5th February, 1938*
Total Appearances & Goals; *31 apps 0 gls*
Career; *Flint Town; WREXHAM 1937 (Am) Aug 1937, (Pro) 30th Dec 1937;*

James Mathias was signed by Wrexham manager Captain James Logan from Flint Town, firstly as an amateur in August 1937 and then on professional terms at the end of December. However, it wasn't until February 1938 that he was to make his Football League debut for the 'Robins' in a 4-0 home win over Darlington, when he replaced Vic Evans at full-back. At the end of February James took over from the club's regular centre-half, Tommy Lewis, who had been transferred to Luton Town, and kept his place for the rest of the season. 1938/39 saw him used mostly as first team cover, as Jim Smith and Tommy Griffiths were preferred in the centre-half position throughout that campaign, and he managed just twelve League appearances. The 1939/40 season saw Jimmy re-established in the first team for the first three matches of the new term, but his career was to come to an abrupt halt with the outbreak of the Second World War, when the Football League was suspended. Those three games were to be Mathias's last for Wrexham, as he didn't play for the club during the conflict. It is not known what happened to him after this.

Season	League		F.A.Cup		Welsh Cup		N.S.C.		Total	
	apps	gls	apps	gls	apps	gls	apps	gls	apps	gls
1937/38	15	0	-	-	-	-	-	-	15	0
1938/39	12	0	1	0	-	-	3	0	16	0
	27	**0**	**1**	**0**	**-**	**-**	**3**	**0**	**31**	**0**

MATTHEWS, John Keith 1952 - 1955

Position; *Forward*
D.O.B; *7th March, 1934*
Birthplace; *Llay, Denbighshire*
Height; *5ft 9in* ***Weight;*** *10st 7lbs*
Debut; v. *Tranmere Rovers (h) 21st January, 1953*
Total Appearances & Goals; *9 apps 0 gls*
Career; *Llay United; WREXHAM 4th Dec 1952; Witton Albion 2nd Jul 1957; Runcorn 1957; Colwyn Bay 15th Apr 1960; Blaenau Ffestiniog 9th Aug 1960; Holyhead Town 24th Jul 1962;*
Honours; *Welsh League (North) Championship Winner 1961; North Wales Coast F.A.Challenge Cup runner-up 1962;*

Keith Matthews completed his education at the Llay Central School and the Wrexham Technical College, gaining representative honours with both Wrexham & District and Denbighshire Schoolboys, as well as playing for the Great Britain Youth Clubs' side. Keith was playing for Llay United in the Welsh National League and working as an apprentice wood machinist at Thomas' timber yard near the General station, when he was handed the opportunity to sign for Wrexham in December 1952. He made his Football League debut for the 'Robins' the following month at home to Tranmere Rovers, stepping into the side at outside-right after Billy Tunnicliffe had left the Racecourse to join Bradford Park Avenue. Wrexham won 1-0, and Keith kept his place for the following match, a 4-2 defeat at Oldham. However, he then found his first team chances limited, with the form of Glyn Hughes, and later Phil Gwatkin. In March 1955 he was called up for his National Service with the Royal Air Force and played his last match for the reserves in a Cheshire County League game at Stockport County on 12th March 1955. He spent most of his two years serving as an electrician at RAF Cosford in Shropshire, which meant he could play football for Wrexham most weekends. Upon his return from serving his country in 1957 Keith found that he was to be released at the end of the season. During the summer he joined Cheshire County League side Witton Albion, where he spent a short spell before signing for fellow Cheshire County League side, Runcorn. In April 1960 Matthews moved on to Welsh League (North) side Colwyn Bay for a short spell before joining Blaenau Ffestiniog in the summer with whom he picked up a Championship and Cup winners' medal. He signed for Holyhead Town in July 1962, where he ended his playing career. After hanging up his boots Keith was employed by the Britannic Insurance company. He later took over a newsagents in Poyser Street, Wrexham and later ran similar ventures in both Llay and Bradley before retiring in November 1997. Keith and his family have since settled in the village of Summerhill near Wrexham.

Season	League		F.A.Cup		Welsh Cup		Total	
	apps	gls	apps	gls	apps	gls	apps	gls
1952/53	2	0	-	-	-	-	2	0
1953/54	1	0	-	-	-	-	1	0
1954/55	6	0	-	-	-	-	6	0
	9	**0**	**-**	**-**	**-**	**-**	**9**	**0**

MATTHEWS, Robert William 1923 - 1925

Position; *Centre-Half*
D.O.B; *14th April, 1897*
Birthplace; *Plas Benion, Ruabon, Denbighshire*
Died; *Wrexham, 18th December, 1987*
Height; *6ft 2in* ***Weight;*** *13st 0lbs*
Debut; v. *Southport (a) 3rd November, 1923*
Total Appearances & Goals; *71 apps 2 gls*
Career; *Colwyn Bay; Liverpool 1916 9apps 4gls; Bristol City 2nd Mar 1922 £750 42apps 1gls; WREXHAM 5th November 1923 £350; Northwich Victoria May 1925; Barrow 13th Nov 1925 9apps 0gls; Bradford Park Avenue 31st Jan 1926 £600 112apps 5gls; Stockport County 9th May 1930 5apps 0gls; New Brighton 11th Oct 1930 (exchange for Joseph Taylor) 41apps 1gls; Chester 8th Jan 1932; Oswestry Town Jun 1932; Witton Albion Sept 1932; Sandbach Ramblers Nov 1932; Colwyn Bay 3rd Mar 1933; Rossendale United Aug 1933;*
Honours; *Three Full Welsh International caps; Third Division South Championship Winner 1923; Third Division North Championship Winner 1928; Welsh Cup Winner 1924; Two Victory International appearances 1919;*

Billy Matthews was playing for Colwyn Bay during the First World War when he signed for Liverpool. After the Great War - during which he fought in the Battle of the Somme - he went on to make nine League appearances at centre-forward for Liverpool, scoring four goals, although he had made his Football League debut for them at centre-half in a 3-0 home win over Derby County in April 1920. Billy was allowed to leave Anfield in March 1922 for a £750 fee to join Third Division South side Bristol City, where he was switched to centre-half. The move was a resounding success, as he went on to win a Third Division South championship medal with City during the 1922/23 season. He became a 'tall cultured defender who believed in positional play, ball control and intelligent distribution'. However, by the end of the season Billy was keen to move nearer to his Ruabon home, and in November 1923 was allowed to join Wrexham for a cut-price fee of £350. During his time at the Racecourse opinions about

him were divided: some reckoned he was the most constructive centre-half in the League; whilst others criticised his inconsistency and lack of sharpness in the tackle. In 1924 Billy collected a Welsh Cup winners' medal with the 'Robins' when they beat Merthyr 1-0 in the Final. It was his lack of consistency that persuaded Wrexham to allow him to join Northwich Victoria at the end of the 1924/25 season. However, he soon returned to League football when Barrow snapped him up in November 1925. He made just nine League appearances for the Holker Street club before Bradford Park Avenue signed him in January 1926. Billy confounded all his critics at Park Avenue as he went on to make 112 League appearances, earning a Third Division North Championship medal in 1928, and adding a third Welsh cap against Ireland in 1926. He finally left Yorkshire in May 1930 to join Stockport County, but after just five League appearances joined New Brighton in October 1930. There, he was described as 'big, burly and boisterous, and was prominent in most things that New Brighton did.' Matthews made 41 League appearances for the 'Rakers' before joining Chester in January 1932. He didn't figure in Chester's first team, and then drifted into non-league football with Oswestry Town, followed by spells at Witton Albion, Sandbach Ramblers, Colwyn Bay United, and Rossendale United before taking over as manager of Llangollen in July 1947. He also carried out scouting duties for Nottingham Forest. In 1937 Billy was mentioned as a potential candidate for the vacant manager's job at Wrexham, before Captain James Logan was appointed. He later scouted for Blackpool, and was responsible for discovering Glyn James. He was a fitness fanatic throughout his life, and a keen cyclist until he was almost 80 years old. He became known locally as 'Billy White Hat', because of the distinctive headgear he wore while cycling along country lanes where his white hat could be seen above the hedgerows. Billy died in Wrexham on 18th December 1987, aged 90.

Season	League		F.A.Cup		Welsh Cup		Total	
	apps	gls	apps	gls	apps	gls	apps	gls
1923/24	27	1	2	0	5	0	34	1
1924/25	35	1	1	0	1	0	37	1
	62	**2**	**3**	**0**	**6**	**0**	**71**	**2**

MATTHEWS, William Downes 1921 - 1922

Position; *Centre-Forward*
D.O.B; *O/N/D 1896*
Birthplace; *Wrexham, Denbighshire*
Died; *Lewes, 24th February, 1964*
Height; *ft in* **Weight;** *st lbs*
Debut; *v. Barrow (a) 31st December, 1921*
Total Appearances & Goals; *3 apps 1 gls*
Career; *WREXHAM Dec 1921;*

Billy Matthews was the brother of Herbert Matthews, who was also on Wrexham's books at the same time as his brother. Herbert had played for Wrexham in the Birmingham & District League during the 1920/21 season, and Billy was signed by the club as an amateur in December 1921, following a trial. His first appearance came in a reserve team game against Oswestry Town on the Racecourse - and what a start he made, scoring four goals in a 7-2 win. Four days later he made his Football League debut at Barrow in a 5-2 defeat, when he stepped into the side to replace Ted Regan at centre-forward. He then played in the following match at Nelson, which Wrexham lost 4-0. His last first team appearance for Wrexham, against Durham City on the Racecourse, saw him score one of the goals in a 3-1 win. Nothing is known about Billy's football career after this game, although he is believed to have died in Lewes in February 1964, when he was described as being 'a clerk in Holy orders'.

Season	League		F.A.Cup		Welsh Cup		Total	
	apps	gls	apps	gls	apps	gls	apps	gls
1921/22	3	1	-	-	-	-	3	1
	3	**1**	**-**	**-**	**-**	**-**	**3**	**1**

MATTHIAS, Albert 1924 - 1925

Position; *Centre-Half*
D.O.B; *J/A/S 1902*
Birthplace; *Wrexham, Denbighshire*
Height; *ft ins* **Weight;** *st lbs*
Debut; v. *Accrington Stanley (a) 2nd May 1925*
Total Appearances & Goals; *1 app 0 gls*
Career; *Brymbo Green United; WREXHAM Oct 1924;*

Not much is known about Albert Mathias except that he began the 1924/25 season playing football for Brymbo & Green United in the Flintshire League. However, by October he was invited to sign for Wrexham as an amateur. Having played for the 'Robins' reserve side, he was not to make his Football League debut until the final match of that season. Albert was then asked to step into the side to replace his namesake, Tommy Mathias in a 1-0 defeat at Accrington Stanley.

Season	League		F.A.Cup		Welsh Cup		Total	
	apps	gls	apps	gls	apps	gls	apps	gls
1924/25	1	0	-	-	-	-	1	0
	1	**0**	**-**	**-**	**-**	**-**	**1**	**0**

MATTHIAS, Thomas James 1912 - 1928

Position; *Wing-Half*
D.O.B; *7th November, 1890*
Birthplace; *Brynteg, Nr.Wrexham, Denbighshire*
Died; *Towradgi, New South Wales, Australia*
Height; *5ft 6in* **Weight;** *10st 8lbs*
Debut; v. *Wolves Reserves (h) 7th September, 1912 (Birmingham League) 27th June, 1965*
Football League Debut; v. *Hartlepool's United (h) 27th August, 1921*
Total Appearances & Goals; *390 apps 28 gls*
Career; *Pentre Broughton; Mold Town; Saltney; Summerhill; Shrewsbury Town cs1910; Chester cs1911; WREXHAM 1st Jun 1912; Whitchurch Sept 1928; Oak Alyn 25th Jan 1929;*
Honours; *12 Welsh International caps; Welsh Cup Winner 1914, 1915, 1921 & 1925; Welsh Cup runner-up 1920;*

Tommy Matthias played his early football for local side Pentre Broughton before moving on to Mold, Saltney, and Summerhill. He was then signed by Birmingham and District League side Shrewsbury Town in the summer of 1910. He spent a season with the Shropshire club before joining Chester of the Lancashire Combination League in 1911. He then helped them to reach the semi-finals of the Welsh Cup, where they lost to Cardiff City on the Racecourse. After one season with the 'Cestrians', in which he made 26 League appearances and scored two goals, Tommy joined Wrexham to begin a 16 year association with the club. He made his debut for the 'Robins' in a Birmingham & District League match, a 3-0 home win over Wolves Reserves, and went on to become a very consistent performer, rarely missing a match. He collected four Welsh Cup winners' medals, and one runners-up medal with Wrexham, as well as being capped by Wales on twelve occasions. In August 1921 he played in Wrexham's inaugural Football League match against Hartlepool United, which ended in a 2-0 home defeat. That same year he became landlord of the Old Swan public house in Abbott Street, Wrexham, which he continued to run for several years after his playing days were over. It was also at around this time that Tommy was described as a 'wholehearted and tenacious player of skill and certainty'. Although rejected by the Welsh Amateur team because of his size he was strong in the air, and could out jump most forwards. Towards the end of his career with Wrexham Tommy stepped down to the reserves, where his experience and encouragement were invaluable to the club's younger players. He joined Whitchurch in September 1928, and then Oak Alyn in January 1929, before retiring from playing in 1930. Throughout most of his career he had combined playing football with working as a coal miner, often seen underground keeping fit by skipping. After ending his playing career he also took up scouting for Wrexham. He was later employed as an office caretaker before emigrating to Australia in January 1964 at the age of 73. Tommy died in Towradgi, New South Wales, in June 1965. His daughter Betty still resides in Australia and is the widow of another Racecourse Robin, Bert Jones.

Season	League		F.A.Cup		Welsh Cup		Total	
	apps	gls	apps	gls	apps	gls	apps	gls
1912/13	34	2	5	0	1	0	40	2
1913/14	33	0	4	0	8	0	45	0
1914/15	33	3	5	0	5	1	43	4
1919/20	30	5	5	2	5	1	40	8
1920/21	31	4	4	0	5	1	40	5
1921/22	37	4	4	1	3	0	44	5
1922/23	37	0	3	1	3	0	43	1
1923/24	14	0	1	0	2	0	17	0
1924/25	21	1	1	0	4	0	26	1
1925/26	13	0	1	0	1	0	15	0
1926/27	28	2	4	0	4	0	36	2
1927/28	-	-	-	-	1	0	1	0
	311	**21**	**37**	**4**	**42**	**3**	**390**	**28**

MAWSON, Ronald — 1948 - 1949

Position; *Goalkeeper*
D.O.B; *16th September, 1914*
Birthplace; *Bishop Auckland, Durham*
Died; *Coventry, 1981*
Height; *6ft 1in* **Weight;** *13st 0lbs*
Debut; v. *Accrington Stanley (a) 25th September, 1948*
Total Appearances & Goals; *6 apps 0 gls*
Career; *RAF Tern Hill; Crewe Alex Jun 1945 23apps 0gls; WREXHAM 25th Sept 1948;*

The seeds of Ron Mawson's football career were sown during the conflict of World War Two. He was stationed at R.A.F. Tern Hill when invited to play in goal as a 'guest' for Port Vale in a Football League North, Second Championship game against Tranmere Rovers at Vale Park, on 28th April, 1945. The 'Potteries' club lost 1-0, and proved to be his only game for them, although he was later signed by Crewe Alexandra in June 1945. Mawson went on to spend three seasons at Gresty Road, where he made 23 League appearances, before joining Wrexham at the relatively advanced age of 33 in 1948. Ron was signed as cover for regular first team 'keeper Archie Ferguson, and his Football League debut came in a 1-0 victory at Accrington Stanley shortly after his arrival at the Racecourse. He went on to make a further six League and Cup appearances for the club that season, before leaving in the summer of 1949. Any information following this period has proved elusive.

Season	League		F.A.Cup		Welsh Cup		Total	
	apps	gls	apps	gls	apps	gls	apps	gls
1948/49	6	0	1	0	-	-	7	0
	6	**0**	**1**	**0**	**-**	**-**	**7**	**0**

MAY, Edwin Charles — 1968 - 1976

Position; *Centre-Half*
D.O.B; *19th May, 1943*
Birthplace; *Epping, Essex*
Height; *6ft 1'1/2in* **Weight;** *13st 4lbs*
Debut; v. *Aldershot (a) 10th August, 1968*
Total Appearances & Goals; *406/4 apps 44 gls*
Career; *Dagenham; Southend United Jan 1965 107/4apps 3gls; WREXHAM 1st Jun 1968 £5,000; Chicago May 1975 (Loan); Swansea City Aug 1976 90apps 8gls;*
Honours; *Welsh Cup Winner 1972; Welsh Cup runner-up 1971; Division Four runner-up 1970;*

Eddie May played football for both his Primary and Secondary School teams in West Ham, but didn't quite make the West Ham Boys team. At the age of 15 he followed in his father's footsteps by working at London's famous meat emporium, Smithfield Market. Handling huge carcasses of meat was no job for a weakling, and Eddie's tall, lean frame soon filled out. Work took precedence over football for a while, but he soon got back into the game he loved when joining Athenian League side Dagenham. His consistent performances soon caught the eye of Southend United manager Ted Fenton, particularly so during a London

Challenge Cup match. Eddie was signed by Southend as a full-back in January 1965, quickly progressing to his Football League debut two months later in a 3-1 defeat at Colchester. However, injury then struck, and he remained in the shadows for a while. A change of manager, with Alvan Williams taking over, saw Eddie switched to centre-half. He went on to make 111 League appearances for Southend before Williams, who had joined Wrexham as manager, returned to his old club and signed him for a £5,000 fee in the summer of 1968. May soon became very popular with the Racecourse regulars, the towering pivot being best described as 'Strong and commanding at the heart of the Wrexham defence. A great danger at set pieces'. He went on to spend eight seasons with Wrexham, helping them to promotion in 1970, and lifting the Welsh Cup in 1972 to ensure entry into European competition for the first time in the Club's history. He also played a vital part in helping the 'Robins' to reach the Quarter Finals of both the F.A.Cup in 1974, and the European Cup-Winners' Cup in 1976. At the end of the 1975/76 season he was surprisingly allowed to leave the Racecourse, when he joined Swansea City on a free transfer. 'Big Eddie' finished his playing career with Swansea, helping them to promotion to the Third Division in 1978. He then moved into coaching with Leicester City in 1978, and was on the Filbert Street coaching staff when the club won the Second Division championship in 1981. Eddie joined Charlton Athletic in 1983 as assistant manager to Lennie Lawrence, and spent three years with 'The Addicks' before moving to Saudi Arabia as coach with Al Hahda. He later coached in both Kenya and Qatar, before taking the manager's job with KS in Iceland in May 1988. After just six games in charge Eddie returned home to take charge of Conference League side Newport County on 7th July 1988. They had just been relegated from the Football League, and were in desperate financial trouble. One of Eddie's few acts at Somerton Park was to sell Andy Thackeray to Wrexham, before he resigned within a month of taking charge following an internal dispute. He was then appointed as assistant-manager at Lincoln City, before going to Norway as coach at IFK Ravdeberg in 1989. In July 1991 he was handed the manager's job at Cardiff City, where he went on to win both the Third Division championship and the Welsh Cup in 1993. May was then replaced at Ninian Park, by Terry Yorath, who was leading a consortium to take over the club. However, on the 30th March 1995, he was re-appointed as the 'Bluebirds' boss after Yorath had resigned following the collapse of the take-over deal. Eddie had in the meantime been managing League of Wales side Barry Town. Cardiff were deep in the relegation zone when he took over and, in spite of his best efforts, they were relegated at the end of the season. However, he did lead them to the 1995 Welsh Cup Final against his former club, Wrexham, in a match where the North Wales club triumphed 2-1. Shortly after that match Eddie resigned, due to the uncertainty over his - and the Club's future - as rumours abounded of yet another consortium take-over at Ninian Park. He was soon back in football, however, as he rejoined Barry Town in May 1995 following an announcement that they were becoming the first League of Wales side to turn professional. On 15th September 1995, with the season only a couple of weeks old, Eddie was surprisingly sacked by Barry, though he quickly found employment as manager of

Torquay United in December. Life was far from easy at Plainmoor: the club were in a deep financial crisis, and they finished the season bottom of the Football League - escaping relegation to the Conference League because Champions Stevenage Borough's ground was not considered up to Football League standard. Eddie resigned as Torquay's manager after their final match of the season in May 1996. He was appointed the new manager of Brentford on the eve of the 1997/98 season with Clive Walker as his assistant, replacing Dave Webb, who had become a director of the club. However, it was to be another brief stay as, with the team failing to live up to the expectations of the previous season, he and Walker were relieved of their duties at the beginning of November 1997. Even so, he returned into management towards the end of that season, taking charge of League of Wales side Haverfordwest. However, before the 1998/99 season had even started, he was given a temporary release by the West Wales club to answer an S.O.S. call to coach struggling Helsinki side FinnPa, in August 1998. He remained in charge of the Finnish side until the end of their season, before returning to South Wales to take charge of Merthyr Tydfil for a brief spell.

Season	League		F.A.Cup		Welsh Cup		League Cup		E.C.W.C.		Total	
	apps	gls	apps	gls	apps	gls	apps	gls	apps	gls	apps	gls
1968/69	45	5	2	0	4	0	3	0	-	-	54	5
1969/70	41	7	4	1	2	0	4	0	-	-	51	8
1970/71	44/1	5	1	0	5	0	2	2	-	-	52/1	7
1971/72	46	6	3	1	4	2	3	2	-	-	56	11
1972/73	43	6	3	0	1	0	2	1	3	0	52	7
1973/74	43	1	7	0	3	0	2	0	-	-	55	1
1974/75	22/3	0	1	0	2	0	-	-	-	-	25/3	0
1975/76	46	5	3	0	3	0	3	0	6	0	61	5
	330/4	**35**	**24**	**2**	**24**	**2**	**19**	**5**	**9**	**0**	**406/4**	**44**

MAYERS, Derek

1963 - 1964

Position; *Outside-Right*
Birthplace; *Liverpool, Merseyside*
Height; *5ft 8in* ***Weight;*** *10st 6lbs*
D.O.B; *24th January, 1935*
Debut; v. *Notts County (a) 26th October, 1963*
Total Appearances & Goals; *27 apps 3 gls*
Career; *Everton Aug 1952 18apps 7gls; Preston North End 24th May 1957 118apps 25gls; Leeds United 10th Jun 1961 20apps 5gls; Bury 17th Jul 1962 32apps 6gls; WREXHAM 25th Oct 1963; South Coast United (Australia) 1964; Rhyl 9th Feb 1966;*
Honours; *Football League Championship runner-up 1958;*

Derek Mayers joined Everton from local schoolboy football in his native Liverpool. He went on to sign professional forms with the 'Toffeemen' in August 1952 and in April 1953, was chosen to make his Football League debut, replacing Ted Buckle at outside-right in a 3-0 Second Division win over Bury. It was a dream debut for Derek, as he scored two of Everton's goals. He made one further appearance that season, a 3-0 defeat at Lincoln City, but managed just one more during Everton's promotion-winning campaign of 1953/54. Over the next three years he made a further fifteen appearances, at a time when his opportunities were restricted by his period of National Service. In May 1957 Mayers was signed by First Division Preston North End along with Alex Farrall, for a combined £4,000 fee. A speedy and skilful outside-right he was bought to provide the crosses for Tom Finney, who was by then playing mostly at centre-forward. Derek went on to make 118 League appearances for the Deepdale club, playing the best football of his career as he helped them to finish as Football League runners-up in his first season. However, the 1960/61 season saw Preston relegated, and Mayers left Deepdale in the close season of 1961 when Don Revie signed him for Leeds United. The Yorkshire club were also in Division Two at that time, and Derek spent just one season at Elland Road, making twenty League appearances and scoring five goals before joining another Second Division club, Bury, in July 1962. He remained at Gigg Lane for a little over a year before joining Wrexham in October 1963. He went straight into the 'Robins' first team at Notts County, but was disappointed when they lost 3-0. He made a further 26 League and Cup appearances for the Racecourse club that season until leaving in the summer of 1964. He then took up an offer to travel over to Australia, where he played for South Coast United until returning to Britain in February 1966, when he joined Cheshire County League side Rhyl. Derek stayed at Belle Vue until the end of the season.

Season	League		F.A.Cup		Welsh Cup		League Cup		Total	
	apps	gls	apps	gls	apps	gls	apps	gls	apps	gls
1963/64	21	2	3	0	3	1	-	-	27	3
	21	**2**	**3**	**0**	**3**	**1**	**-**	**-**	**27**	**3**

MAYS, Albert William

1928 - 1930

Position; *Centre-Forward*
D.O.B; *18th July, 1902*
Birthplace; *Ynyshir, Nr. Merthyr, Glamorgan*
Died; *Derby, 3rd November, 1959*
Height; *5ft 9in* ***Weight;*** *11st 4lbs*
Debut; v. *Chesterfield (h) 25th August, 1928*
Total Appearances & Goals; *60 apps 46 gls*
Career; *Ynyshir Swallows; Porth; Wattstown; Bristol City Sept 1923 19apps 4gls; Plymouth Argyle Jun 1926 0gls; Merthyr Town 21st Jun 1927 34apps 14gls; WREXHAM Aug 1928; Notts County 7th Mar 1930 £650 8apps 4gls; Burnley May 1930 2apps 0gls; Walsall Jan 1931 17apps 11gls; Halifax Town Jun 1931 25apps 8gls; Margate Jul 1932; Gresley Rovers Sept 1934; Shardlow St.James Jul 1936;*
Honours; *One Welsh International cap;*

Albert Mays began playing football for his local side in South Wales, Ynyshir Swallows, where he scored 154 goals in two seasons! He then had spells with both Porth and Wattstown before quitting his work in the pits to join Bristol City in September 1923. Albert made his Football League debut for the Ashton Gate club in a scoreless home draw with Crystal Palace on Christmas Day 1923, and stayed with them for almost three years, making a total of 19 League appearances, and scoring four goals. In June 1926 he joined Plymouth Argyle, but failed to make a first team appearance at Home Park, and a year later was allowed to join Football League side, Merthyr Town. Albert scored 14 goals in 34 League matches for the South Wales outfit, before moving on at the end of the season. He signed for Wrexham in August 1928, after having impressed the directors of the North Wales club with a hat-trick against them in a Welsh Cup tie played the previous season. Installed at centre-forward Albert got off to a flying start when he scored four goals on his League debut in a 4-3 home win over Chesterfield - and he didn't stop there, as he became the first player to score thirty Football League goals or more in a season for Wrexham with 32 goals in just 34 matches in 1928/29. It earned him the nickname 'The Amazing Mays', and his contribution saw Wrexham finish in their highest position since joining the Football League, when they reached third place. Albert's goalscoring ability was soon recognised by the Welsh selectors and he was capped for Wales against Ireland in February 1929. The match which was played on the Racecourse, ended in a 2-2 draw, and Albert celebrated his international debut by scoring one of the Welsh goals. Strangely, it proved to be his only appearance for his country. The following season Albert formed a formidable striking partnership with Tommy Bamford, but in March 1930, Notts County paid out £650 to sign him to help in their bid to avoid relegation. Even though Mays scored four goals in eight appearances for County they couldn't avoid the drop, and at the end of the season he was transferred to Burnley. The move to Turf Moor proved to be a disappointing one for Albert, as he made only two League appearances before being transferred to Walsall in January 1931. He remained with the 'Saddlers' until the end of the season, notching eleven goals in just seventeen League games. In the summer of 1931 he joined Halifax Town, for one season before moving south to play for Margate Town in July 1932. He later settled in Derby, working in the local NAAFI offices, and then on the maintenance staff at Derby Police Station. His son, also Albert, played for Derby at wing-half between 1949 and 1959. Albert senior passed away in Derby in 1959. He was 57.

Season	League		F.A.Cup		Welsh Cup		Total	
	apps	gls	apps	gls	apps	gls	apps	gls
1928/29	34	32	1	0	1	1	36	33
1929/30	20	9	4	4	-	-	24	13
	54	**41**	**5**	**4**	**1**	**1**	**60**	**46**

MEIGH, Thomas 1923 - 1924

Position; *Inside-Right*
Birthplace; *Stoke-on-Trent, Staffordshire*
Height; *5ft 6in* ***Weight;*** *10st 8lbs*
D.O.B; *6th June, 1899*
Died; *Stoke-on-Trent, A/M/J 1972*
Debut; v. *Rochdale (h) 20th October 1923*
Total Appearances & Goals; *3 apps 0 gls*
Career; *Stoke c1916; Shelton United 1917/18; Stoke United 1919; Ravenscliffe Mission; Hanley Town; WREXHAM (trial) Aug 1923, (pro) 5th Sept 1923; Port Vale cs1924 0apps; Blyth Bridge; Fenton Town Dec 1930;*

Tom Meigh joined Stoke during World War One at the age of seventeen. However, he was to leave them and join local 'Potteries' side Shelton United for the 1917/18 season. This was followed by spells with Stoke United, Ravenscliffe Mission, and Hanley Town from where he was signed by Third Division North side Wrexham. Tom was initially signed on trial in August 1923, but was to impress enough to sign on a permanent basis the following month. He finally made his Football League debut in October against Rochdale in a 1-1 draw on the Racecourse, playing at inside-right in place of Jack Jones. Meigh was described after the match as 'a lively little forward, with plenty of dash and a fund of skill.' He kept his place in the side for the following two games, both away: the return match at Rochdale, which ended scoreless, and at Southport in a 1-0 defeat. It proved to be Tom's last senior appearance for Wrexham, because in the close season of 1924 he was to leave the Racecourse. He returned to the 'Potteries' where he joined Port Vale, failing to record a first team appearance at Vale Park, before allowed to leave, whereupon, he drifted into non-league football with Blyth Bridge and Fenton Town.

Season	League		F.A.Cup		Welsh Cup		Total	
	apps	gls	apps	gls	apps	gls	apps	gls
1923/24	3	0	-	-	-	-	3	0
	3	**0**	**-**	**-**	**-**	**-**	**3**	**0**

METCALF, Michael 1956 - 1963

Position; *Inside-Left*
D.O.B; *24th May, 1939*
Birthplace; *Liverpool, Merseyside*
Height; *5ft 8'1/2in* ***Weight;*** *10st 9lbs*
Debut; v. *Hartlepool United (h) 19th October, 1957*
Total Appearances & Goals; *145 apps 73 gls*
Career; *Everton; WREXHAM (Am) May 1956, (Pro) 10th May, 1957; Chester 20th Dec 1963 £3,000 221apps 68gls; Altrincham Dec 1968; Bangor City 23rd Aug 1969; Connah's Quay Nomads 6th Mar 1971; Bethesda Athletic 2nd Aug 1971; Witton Albion 1972; Hawarden 23rd Oct 1972; Cheshire NALGO;*
Honours; *Welsh Cup runner-up 1962 & 1966; North Wales Coast F.A. representative cap;*

Although born in Liverpool Mike Metcalf spent much of his early life on Deeside, North Wales. However, upon leaving school he joined Everton as a junior. It was following Wrexham manager Cliff Lloyd's visit to watch the Everton Youth side that he enquired about the possibility of signing Mike, and to his surprise Everton agreed to release him. That was in May 1956, and Metcalf went on to make steady progress in the Wrexham reserve side in the Cheshire County League. He was given his first team opportunity in October 1957, when he made his Football League debut at home to Hartlepool United in a 3-1 win. He also played in the following match at Bradford, which Wrexham lost 2-0, but had to wait almost two years before he played in the senior side again. His chance came in a 3-2 home defeat by Chesterfield in October 1959, and scored both Wrexham goals. Mike played in the next three matches before being replaced, but the 1960/61 season saw him make the inside-left position his own, as he helped Wrexham reach the Quarter-Finals of the newly-formed Football League Cup competition, scoring a hat-trick against First Division Blackburn Rovers on the way. His goals helped the 'Robins' to gain promotion in the following season, though he missed out on a Welsh Cup winners' medal as Wrexham crashed to Bangor City in the Final. 'A Clever ball player', Mike's impressive record for Wrexham averaged a goal every other game, yet he was surprisingly allowed to leave the Racecourse in December 1963 to join rivals Chester. Mike went on to make over 250 appearances for the 'Cestrians', scoring 86 goals in League and Cup competitions, collecting another Welsh Cup runners'-up medal in 1966, and playing at Old Trafford in a F.A.Cup Third Round match that saw Chester come close to a shock in their 2-1 defeat. Following the signing of Derek Draper Mike decided to leave Sealand Road and join Cheshire County League side Altrincham, where he remained until the end of the 1968/69 season. He then signed for Bangor City, where he spent a little under two years before being appointed player/manager of his local side, Connah's Quay Nomads, in March 1971. However, he was on the move again at the end of the season joining Welsh League side, Bethesda Athletic. Mike took up another managerial appointment in 1972 as player/manager of Cheshire County League side, Witton Albion. But by October 1972 had joined Hawarden, which was followed by appearing for a number of local sides in the Chester district until well into his fifties. After retiring from professional football Mike became a qualified chemist, later running his own highly successful laboratory supplies firm based in Deeside, where he also resides.

Season	League		F.A.Cup		Welsh Cup		League Cup		Total	
	apps	gls	apps	gls	apps	gls	apps	gls	apps	gls
1957/58	2	0	-	-	-	-	-	-	2	0
1959/60	4	2	1	0	-	-	-	-	5	2
1960/61	40	16	1	0	3	0	5	6	49	22
1961/62	28	17	3	3	1	0	1	0	33	20
1962/63	29	13	-	-	1	0	1	0	31	13
1963/64	18	10	3	2	-	-	4	4	25	16
	121	**58**	**8**	**5**	**5**	**0**	**11**	**10**	**145**	**73**

MIELCZAREK, Raymond 1962 - 1967

Position; *Centre-Half*
D.O.B; *10th February, 1946.*
Birthplace; *Caernarvon, Gwynedd*
Height; *5ft 11 1/2in* ***Weight;*** *11st 7lbs*
Debut v. *Aldershot (a) 19th October, 1964*
Total Appearances & Goals; *91 apps 0 gls*
Career; *Caernarvon Town 1962; WREXHAM 11th Sept 1962 £500, (Pro) 1st May 1964; Huddersfield Town 29th Sept 1967 £20,000 25/1apps 1gls; Rotherham United Jan 1971 £10,000 114/1apps 7gls; Druids United cs1975; Llay R.B.L. 1978;*
Honours; *One Welsh International cap; Two Welsh Under-23 International caps; Welsh Youth international; Welsh Cup runner-up 1965 & 1967; Welsh Youth Cup Winner 1963;*

Although Welsh speaking Ray has a Polish Grandfather, an Irish Grandmother and a father who hails from Luxembourg he was born in Caernarfon, where he attended both the St.Helen's R.C. and Caernarfon Grammar Schools. It was during this period that he represented - and captained - the Caernarvon Schoolboys team. Upon completion of his Education he left school to work on a timber ship, though this lasted only two weeks before he joined his father in the wholesale and toy business. He continued to play football throughout this time, having joined Caernarvon Town straight from school as an amateur before being plunged into the first team at the Oval at the age of 16 for his debut against the Wrexham 'A' team. He must have made an impression, because Wrexham manager Ken Barnes and his assistant Ken Roberts arrived on his door step within a week and asked him to sign for Wrexham! Ray joined the Racecourse Club in September 1962, and went on to progress through the 'Robins' junior teams, picking up a Welsh Youth Cup winners' medal in 1963, as well as international honours for Wales at youth level against Holland. In May 1964 Ray was signed on professional terms by Wrexham, and in October of the following season made his Football League debut at centre-half, in place of the injured Terry Morrall, at Aldershot in a 5-0 defeat. Despite the result, Ray soon established himself as the Club's first choice centre-half. Only injuries restricted his appearances over the next three seasons, during which time he twice helped the club reach the Welsh Cup Final in 1965 and 1967, only to be defeated on both occasions by Cardiff City. The 1967/68 season was barely a month old when Ray left the Racecourse, as Second Division Huddersfield Town paid out £20,000 for him much to the dismay of the Racecourse faithful. It was the kind of money that Wrexham couldn't refuse at the time. Ray stepped straight into the 'Terriers' side for his debut, replacing Roy Ellam in a 2-1 home defeat by Blackburn Rovers, and went on to make a further 17 League and Cup appearances that season. He also made his Wales under-23 debut against England, before disaster was to strike in the second game of the 1968/69 season. He suffered a bad knee injury in a match against Crystal Palace. It was later found that he had ruptured a cruciate ligament in his right knee, which was an even more serious injury in those days. Even so, Ray battled his way back, but made just five more appearances for Huddersfield before being sold to Rotherham United for £10,000 in January 1971. Ray's career took off again at Millmoor as, four months after signing, he was awarded his first full Welsh international cap against Finland in Helsinki in May 1971. He was also selected for a summer tour of the Pacific with a Welsh select XI that same year. Mielczarek went on to make 115 League appearances in his four seasons at Millmoor before he was forced to retire from professional football at the age of 28 because of his troublesome knee injury. Wrexham manager John Neal did attempt to sign Ray, but he couldn't give any assurances that his knee would stand up to the vigour of League football. He then returned to settle in the Wrexham area, where he took up a job as a Van salesman for Lyons Cakes, but the lure of football soon returned and he had short spells in local football with both Druids United and Llay R.B.L. before hanging up his boots for good. Ray later worked at the Plas Madoc Leisure Centre and then at Brymbo Steelworks in their security department, where he worked for 16 years until the factory was closed down. Ray has since worked as a driving instructor, as well as running a market stall, having settled in Wrexham.

Season	League		F.A.Cup		Welsh Cup		League Cup		Total	
	apps	gls	apps	gls	apps	gls	apps	gls	apps	gls
1964/65	24	0	-	-	6	0	-	-	30	0
1965/66	22	0	1	0	-	-	2	0	25	0
1966/67	22	0	-	-	4	0	1	0	27	0
1967/68	8	0	-	-	-	-	1	0	9	0
	76	**0**	**1**	**0**	**10**	**0**	**4**	**0**	**91**	**0**

MILES, Robert
1924 - 1925

Position; *Outside-Left*
D.O.B; *26th December, 1898*
Birthplace; *Ponciau, Denbighshire*
Died; *Hafod, Wrexham 19th March, 1940*
Height; *5ft 5in* **Weight;** *10st 7lbs*
Debut; v. *Durham City (h) 13th December, 1924*
Total Appearances & Goals; *4 apps 0 gls*
Career; *Ponciau; Rhos Athletic; Denbigh United Jun 1922; WREXHAM 17th Dec 1924; Rhyl Athletic 4th Jul 1925; Denbigh United 17th Aug 1926;*
Honours; *Welsh Junior International; Welsh Amateur Cup Winner 1924; North Wales Coast Amateur Cup Winner 1924; Welsh National League Championship Winner 1926;*

Bob Miles played football for his school teams at Ponciau Infants and Ysgol Y Grango in Rhos. On completion of his education he joined local side, Ponciau F.C., and took up work at Hafod Colliery. He later played for Rhos Athletic and Denbigh United, where he was a member of the side that won both the Welsh Amateur Cup and North Wales Coast Amateur Cup in 1924. Denbigh thus became the first side to win both of these prestigious competitions in the same season. Bob was then approached by Wrexham, and made his Football League debut for the 'Robins' in December 1924 in a 3-1 home win over Durham City. He was described as having made a 'very creditable debut, he is a young winger, who knows how to give a smart inside pass, and he is fearless - A great asset in Third Division football.' In spite of this early promise, Bob managed just three more League appearances for the Racecourse club before being released in the summer. He then joined Welsh National League side Rhyl, where he won a championship medal in his season. He also helped them to reach the Welsh Cup semi-finals, where they eventually went out to Swansea Town. Miles re-signed for Denbigh United for the following season, but sustained a bad knee injury which was to bring his playing career to a premature end. He did however, recover sufficiently to turn out for Hafod Colliery's football side when he could be persuaded. Tragically, Bob was about to have an operation on his knee when he was killed in a mining accident at the Hafod Colliery on 19th March 1940. He was 41. His son was headmaster of a local school in the Wrexham area and a leading figure with the world famous Rhos male voice choir.

Season	League		F.A.Cup		Welsh Cup		Total	
	apps	gls	apps	gls	apps	gls	apps	gls
1924/25	4	0	-	-	-	-	4	0
	4	**0**	**-**	**-**	**-**	**-**	**4**	**0**

MILES, Uriah
1926 - 1927

Position; *Outside-Right*
D.O.B; *4th January, 1907*
Birthplace; *Newcastle-under-Lyme, Staffordshire*
Died; *Littleborough, Lancashire, J/F/M 1970*
Height; *5ft 6in* **Weight;** *10st 0lbs*
Debut; v. *New Brighton (h) 11th September, 1926*
Total Appearances & Goals; *13 apps 1 gls*
Career; *Connah's Quay & Shotton FC 27th Oct 1925; WREXHAM 15th May 1926; Rochdale Aug 1927 10apps 2gls; Witton Albion 1929; Bacup Borough Jun 1931;*

Wrexham manager Charlie Hewitt was the man responsible for bringing Uriah Miles to the Racecourse, having secured his transfer from Connah's Quay and Shotton during the close season of 1926. Uriah spent just one year at the Racecourse, clocking up twelve League appearances. He made his debut in September 1926, when he replaced Archie Longmuir in the side in a 2-2 draw at home to New Brighton, but found himself back in the reserves by November, having completed another eleven games. Even though he spent the rest of the season playing for the second XI he was offered a new contract in the summer, but turned it down, and signed instead for fellow Third Division North side Rochdale in August 1927. Uriah had to wait until March 1928 before making a long awaited debut for his new side, in a 3-1 defeat at Lincoln. He went on to record a further nine League appearances, before leaving Spotland to sign for Witton Albion some time in 1929. Whilst with Rochdale he was described as 'one of the smallest players in the League, but he is amazingly fast and centres well.'

Season	League		F.A.Cup		Welsh Cup		Total	
	apps	gls	apps	gls	apps	gls	apps	gls
1926/27	12	0	1	1	-	-	13	1
	12	**0**	**1**	**1**	**-**	**-**	**13**	**1**

MILLINGTON, Grenville
1983 - 1984

Position; *Goalkeeper*
D.O.B; *10th December, 1951*
Birthplace; *Queensferry, Flintshire*
Height; *5ft 10in* **Weight;** *11st 6lbs*
Debut; v. *Darlington (h) 31st December, 1983*
Total Appearances & Goals; *14 apps 0 gls*
Career; *Queensferry Wanderers YFC; Chester Jul 1968 1app 0gls; Rhyl cs1970; Witton Albion cs1972; Brighton & Hove Albion Jul 1973; Chester Sept 1973 289apps 0gls; Holywell Town Jul 1983; Oswestry Town Sept 1983; WREXHAM Dec 1983; Buckley Town cs1984;*
Honours; *Welsh under-23 International; Nine Welsh Amateur International caps; Debenhams Cup Winner 1977; Cheshire County League Championship Winner 1972; Cheshire League Cup Winner 1971; N.W.C.F.A. representative cap;*

The brother of Welsh international goalkeeper Tony Millington, Grenville was raised on Deeside and impressed as a goalkeeper at a very early age. He played for both Queensferry Primary and Deeside High Schools, and did well enough to earn selection for Flintshire Schoolboys. His performances didn't go unnoticed, as he had trials at a number of clubs that included Liverpool, Everton, Spurs, Arsenal, and Crewe. However, he left school with no firm offers received, and began playing for his local side Queensferry Wanderers Youths. It was with them that he was invited to join Chester on amateur terms in July 1968, as first team cover for Terry Carling. Grenville finally made his Football League debut in April 1969, when he stepped in to play in a 2-0 home win over Lincoln City.

However, that proved to be his one and only senior appearance for Chester as he was released at the end of the 1969/70 season. He then joined Cheshire County League side Rhyl, with whom he accumulated nine Welsh Amateur international caps, also representing the British Olympic side in their qualification rounds for the 1970 Olympic Games. Grenville spent two seasons with 'The Lilywhites', during which he represented the North Wales Coast F.A. against the Scottish Junior League at Rhyl, and collected both Cheshire League Cup and Cheshire County League championship medals. He joined another Cheshire County League side, Witton Albion, in the summer of 1972, where he spent a year under former Wrexham player Mike Metcalf. Gren toured Japan with the Middlesex Wanderers representative side the following close season, enjoying six weeks playing exhibition matches. Upon his return home he was invited for trials with Brighton and Hove Albion, where he spent twelve weeks. However, in September 1973 he was asked to re-join Chester, and agreed because they were near to his home. He went on to serve the 'Cestrians' for nine seasons, during which he played in many memorable matches. The club's 1974/75 League Cup run saw Grenville keeping out the likes of Newcastle and Leeds United, before finally being overcome by Aston Villa in the semi-finals, and also played in Chester's first ever promotion winning side, when they were promoted to the Third Division in 1975. In 1977, he collected a Debenhams Cup winners' medal, which they qualified for by reaching the F.A.Cup Fifth Round for the first time in their history that same season, before losing to Wolves. Gren went on to make a total of 290 Football League appearances until leaving Chester at the end of the 1982/83 season, when he 'officially' retired. His decision had been prompted by the arrival of new manager, John Sainty, who was not keen on part-time players, and Millington was running his own sports business by that time. However, it was far from the end of his football career, as he soon joined Holywell Town for a short spell before signing for Northern Premier League side Oswestry Town. Gren was playing for Oswestry when he got a call from Chester, where his former team-mate, Trevor Storton, had become caretaker manager. However, Chester couldn't offer him a contract, and Wrexham manager Bobby Roberts then stepped in to ease his goalkeeping problems. He signed Gren on a non-contract basis until the end of the season, and made his 'Robins' debut in a 1-1 home draw with Darlington on New Year's Eve 1983. He went on to add 13 League and Cup appearances, but missed out on Wrexham's run to the Welsh Cup Final as he was ineligible, having played in an earlier round for Oswestry Town. He was later replaced in the first team by loan signing Ron Sinclair, and was released at the end of the season. There followed short spells with both Connah's Quay Nomads and Buckley, before becoming involved helping out with the disabled supporters section at the Racecourse, which is run by his brother Tony. Gren followed this by coaching the up and coming goalkeepers at the Racecourse, which he is still involved with at the time of writing.

Season	League		F.A.Cup		Welsh Cup		League Cup		A.M.C.		Total	
	apps	gls	apps	gls	apps	gls	apps	gls	apps	gls	apps	gls
1983/84	13	0	-	-	-	-	-	-	1	0	14	0
	13	**0**	-	-	-	-	-	-	**1**	**0**	**14**	**0**

***MILLINGTON,* Thomas** 1924 - 1925

Position; *Outside-Right*
D.O.B; *12th January, 1906*
Birthplace; *Wrexham, Denbighshire*
Died; *Oswestry, 5th April, 1968*
Height; *5ft 8'1/2in* ***Weight;*** *11st 10lbs*
Debut; v. *Brymbo Green (h) 14th February, 1923 (Welsh Cup)*
Total Appearances & Goals; *4 apps 0 gls*
Career; *Oswestry Town; WREXHAM 20th Jan 1923; Oswestry Town Aug 1924; Everton Mar 1925 £400 13apps 0gls; Gillingham Mar 1928 38apps 2gls; Oswestry Town Jun 1929; Crewe Alexandra Jul 1930 38apps 6gls; Yeovil & Petters United May 1931; Tottenham Hotspur (trial); Oswestry Town Jul 1933; Brierley Hill Alliance; Treffach Nov 1935;*

Tommy Millington signed for Wrexham from Oswestry Town in January 1923, and he made his first team debut for the club the following month in a Welsh Cup tie with Brymbo Green, which the 'Robins' comfortably won 5-0. He was to make just three more first team appearances for the Welsh club during the following eighteen months, when he played against New Brighton in February 1924, in a scoreless home draw, which was followed with a 1-0 Welsh Cup win at Wellington Town the same month. A 1-0 home win over Crewe Alexandra in April 1924 completed his senior appearances at the Racecourse. Despite being retained by the club at the end of that season, he was allowed to return to Oswestry, and it was during this second spell with the Shropshire side that he came to the notice of First Division Everton, who signed him in March 1925 for £400, with £300 going to Oswestry and £100 to Wrexham - as they still held his Football League registration! Tommy spent three years at Goodison Park, making his debut in September 1926 in a 1-0 defeat at Birmingham. He went on to make a further thirteen League and Cup appearances for the 'Toffeemen' that season, all of them in his usual outside-right position, from where he provided the crosses for the great 'Dixie' Dean. In March 1928 he was allowed to leave Merseyside along with Arthur Dominy, both signing for Third Division South side Gillingham. Millington spent just over a year at Priestfield, scoring twice in 38 League games, leaving at the end of the 1928/29 season. He then returned home to play for Oswestry Town in the Birmingham and District League, before joining Crewe Alexandra in the close season of 1930. Tom made 38 League appearances for the 'Railwaymen', scoring six goals before being signed by the progressive Southern League side, Yeovil & Petters United, in May 1931. It is believed Tom spent two seasons with Yeovil, during which he was signed on trial by First Division Tottenham Hotspur, though this subsequently came to nothing. He rejoined Oswestry Town in the close season of 1933, where brought his career to a close.

Season	League		F.A.Cup		Welsh Cup		Total	
	apps	gls	apps	gls	apps	gls	apps	gls
1922/23	-	-	-	-	1	0	1	0
1923/24	2	0	-	-	1	0	3	0
	2	**0**		-	**2**	**0**	**4**	**0**

***MITCHELL,* Adam Edmond** 1936 - 1937

Position; *Wing-Half*
D.O.B; *14th December, 1908*
Birthplace; *Prestonpans, Lothian*
Died; *Morecambe, 23rd April, 1989*
Height; *5ft 9in* ***Weight;*** *11st 3lbs*
Debut; v. *Chester (a) 29th August, 1936*
Total Appearances & Goals; *42 apps 2 gls*
Career; *Penicuik; Hearts; Cowdenbeath; Bo'Ness; Bradford City Dec 1928 143apps 15gls; WREXHAM 29th May 1936; Doncaster Rovers 9th Sept 1937 53apps 1gls;*

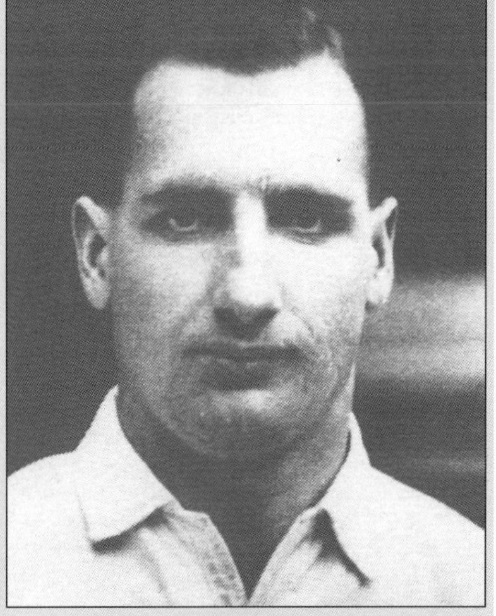

Adam Mitchell was playing for non-league side Penicuik when he had trials with Hearts, Cowdenbeath, and Bo'Ness before signing for Bradford City in December 1928. He made his Football League debut that same month in a 1-1 draw at South Shields. Adam added a further eight League appearances that season, in a side that contained another former Wrexham player - Ralph Burkinshaw - as 'The Bantams' won the Third Division North championship. He was never regarded as a regular first teamer at Valley Parade, apart from the 1934/35 season when he never missed a match, despite some consistently powerful displays at wing-half. In August 1935 Adam was rewarded for his loyalty to the club by being granted a benefit match against Blackpool, though by the end of the season, having again lost his place in the side, he decided to leave the Yorkshire club. Mitchell was then signed by Wrexham in May 1936, and made his debut in a 4-1 defeat at Chester in the opening game of the 1936/37 season. However, he went on to keep his place in the side for the rest of the season, missing only five games. He also played in the F.A.Cup Third Round match against Manchester

City, which the 'Sugarbags', as Wrexham were also known at that time because of their blue shirt with white chest band, were unlucky to lose 3-1. 1937/38 found him out of favour as Alex Smith and Walter Odell were preferred, and in September Adam was allowed to leave the Racecourse when he joined Doncaster Rovers. He remained at Belle Vue until his retirement during the Second World War, after having made 53 League appearances for Doncaster. After WW2, he worked as a telephone engineer in Southport, where he became a keen golfer.

Season	League		F.A.Cup		Welsh Cup		N.S.C.		Total	
	apps	gls	apps	gls	apps	gls	apps	gls	apps	gls
1936/37	37	2	3	0	1	0	1	0	42	2
	37	**2**	**3**	**0**	**1**	**0**	**1**	**0**	**42**	**2**

MOFFAT, Andrew Naysmith 1922 - 1923

Position; *Centre-Forward*
D.O.B; *5th September, 1900*
Birthplace; *Rosewell, nr. Bonnyrigg, Midlothian*
Died; *Dunfermline, 27th January 1990.*
Height; *5ft 8ins* ***Weight;*** *11st 0lbs*
Debut; v. *Darlington (h) 4th November, 1922*
Total Appearances & Goals; *10 apps 0 gls*
Career; *Glencraig Rovers 1916; Kinglassie United 1916/17; Glencraig Celtic cs1917; Lochgelly United 1919; East Fife Aug 1920; Everton Jan 1921 £750 1app 0gls; WREXHAM 4th Nov 1922; East Fife cs1923 2apps 0gls; Lochgelly United; Dunfermline Athletic;*
Honours; *Scottish Qualifying Cup Winner 1920;*

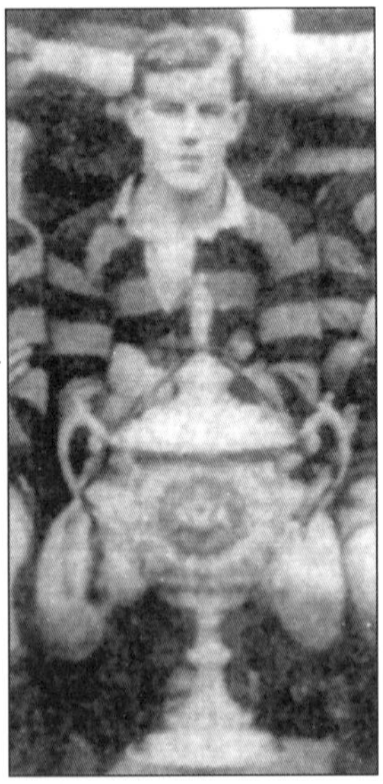

Andy Moffat was born in the mining village of Rosewell, near Bonnyrigg, before his family moved to Glencraig when he was five. A promising schoolboy footballer, he won County caps at the age of 13 playing at right-half. He left Lochgelly East School a year later to commence work in Glencraig Pit working on the bogies. In 1916 he signed for the Fife Juvenile team Glencraig Rovers, later joining another juvenile XI Kinglassie United. He was to only play two games for them, a Semi-Final and Final of the Fife Juvenile Cup before signing for Junior League side Glencraig Celtic in 1917. He eventually turned senior two years later with Lochgelly United, who played in the Eastern League, and for whom Andrew played at centre forward earning 10 shillings a week. With Lochgelly he became a prolific goalscorer during the 1919/20 season, which saw East Fife manager Dave McLean duly sign the promising player for the Scottish Second Division side in August 1920. He began the new season once again scoring goals, and helped his club to the Final of the Scottish Qualifying Cup in December 1920, where they beat Bo'Ness United 3-1 in front of a 20,000 crowd at Cowdenbeath's Central Park ground, with Andrew scoring East Fife's third goal a minute from time. He had earlier claimed their second goal in a 2-0 home win over Queen of the South in the Semi-Final of the same competition. This kind of form soon attracted the attention of English League clubs, and First Division Everton stepped in to sign the promising youngster for £750 in January 1921. Andrew made his Football League Division One debut in April 1921 in a 1-0 win at Oldham Athletic. However, this proved to be his only first team appearance for the 'Toffeemen', as he suffered with a knee injury which was to eventually end his football career at an early age. However, in November 1922 he was allowed to leave Goodison Park and sign for Third Division North side Wrexham. He made his debut for the 'Robins' at centre-forward, at the expense of Alf Rowlands, in a scoreless draw with Darlington on the Racecourse. He added a further nine League and Cup appearances for Wrexham, but failed to score in any of them, and left the North-East Wales club at the end of the season. He then returned to Scotland, where he took up employment back in the mining industry at Glencraig. He continued to play football with short spells at East Fife, Lochgelly United, and Dunfermline Athletic until the knee injury received at Everton saw him finally hang up his boots in 1927. Andrew went on to raise a family of 6 boys and 4 girls, before finally retiring from the Glencraig pit in 1963. He then became a keen participant of bowls.

Season	League		F.A.Cup		Welsh Cup		Total	
	apps	gls	apps	gls	apps	gls	apps	gls
1922/23	8	0	1	0	1	0	10	0
	8	**0**	**1**	**0**	**1**	**0**	**10**	**0**

MOIR, Ian 1968 - 1972 & 1973 - 1975

Position; *Winger*
D.O.B; *30th April, 1943*
Birthplace; *Aberdeen, Grampian*
Height; *5ft 10 3/4in* ***Weight;*** *11st 5lbs*
Debut; v. *Swansea Town (h) 20th January, 1968*
Total Appearances & Goals; *189/10 apps 24 gls*
Career; *Manchester United Jul 1960 45apps 5gls; Blackpool 12th Feb 1965 £27,500 61apps 12gls; Chester 19th May 1967 £10,000 25apps 3gls; WREXHAM 12th Jan 1968 £8,000 (plus Graham Turner); Shrewsbury Town 9th Mar 1972 £10,000 22/3apps 2gls; WREXHAM 5th Jul 1973; South Africa 19th Jun 1975; Oswestry Town 28th Oct 1975; Colwyn Bay 2nd Feb 1976;*
Honours; *First Division runner-up 1964; Division Four runner-up 1970; Welsh Cup runner-up 1971;*

This popular Scot was spotted playing schoolboy football around his native city of Aberdeen by Manchester United's Scottish scout Andy Beattie, the man who had launched the career of Denis Law. Of his latest discovery, Beattie said, "When I first saw young Moir, I was convinced I'd found the greatest of them all." By this time Ian had represented Aberdeen Schoolboys, as well as Scotland at Junior level. He joined the Old Trafford club at the age of 15, and after two years on schoolboy forms he was signed on professional terms by Matt Busby. Ian progressed quickly, and nearly won an England Youth cap! However, he was rumbled as a 'foreigner' as he was about to board the train for Sunderland! Ian made his senior debut for United in October 1961, in a 1-1 draw at West Bromwich Albion alongside the likes of Bobby Charlton, Johnny Giles, Billy Foulkes, Nobby Stiles, and Dave Gaskell. He spent a total of six years with United, during which he made 46 League appearances, scoring five goals, and earned a First Division Championship runners'-up medal in 1964. However, with the emergence of a young player by the name of George Best, Moir was allowed to leave Old Trafford in February 1965 when he was signed by First Division Blackpool for £25,000. He went straight into their team for his debut at home to Leicester City in a 1-1 draw, and kept his place for the rest of the season. Ian then went on a world tour with the 'Seasiders' to New Zealand, Honolulu, Hong Kong and Canada. He recorded a total 61 League appearances for Blackpool, scoring 12 goals, before he was allowed to leave Bloomfield Road at the end of the 1966/67 season to join Chester for £10,000, a record transfer fee paid by the Fourth Division side. However, with Chester struggling in the bottom four of the Football League Moir, who had been the 'shining light in the team, but lacked support up front, thus reducing his effectiveness', was to leave Sealand Road in January 1968, and join neighbours Wrexham. He had made 25 League appearances for Chester, scoring three goals, with two of them coming in what proved to be his final game for the club - a 6-0 thrashing of fellow strugglers Lincoln City. Wrexham paid £8,000 to secure his services, with Graham Turner also moving across to Sealand Road as part of the deal. Ian went straight into the 'Robins' side for his debut, a 2-1 home win over Swansea Town, and went on to become a real asset to the club, and a big favourite with the fans, through his dazzling wing play. He was described as being a 'brilliant ball player, who could be devastating on his day.' 1968/69 saw him at his best, and helped Wrexham to gain promotion to the Third Division at the end of the following season, a campaign which also saw him return to Old Trafford for a League Cup match, which Wrexham unfortunately lost 2-0. Ian played in the 1971 Welsh Cup Final against Cardiff City, which Wrexham lost 4-1 on aggregate. In March 1972 he was allowed to leave the Racecourse, when he was sold to Third Division Shrewsbury Town for £10,000, where he made his debut as a substitute in a 1-1 home draw with Aston Villa. After just 25 League games for the 'Shrews' Ian returned to the Racecourse on a free transfer a little over a year later, in the summer of 1973. However, he found it difficult to establish a regular first team place in his second spell with the Club because of either injury or loss of form. He spent two seasons with Wrexham before leaving the Racecourse to travel to South Africa, where he played football over the summer period of 1975. When Ian returned home he signed for Cheshire County League side Oswestry Town, but left after only a couple of months. He then joined Colwyn Bay until the end of the season, before hanging up his boots. Having settled in Chester, he had a spell managing Tarvin in 1986, having taken up employment at BNFL Capenhurst, where he was still working at the time of writing. A great character who could no doubt have earned a living as an entertainer (which he did!) but in this case off the field!

Season	League		F.A.Cup		Welsh Cup		League Cup		Total	
	apps	gls	apps	gls	apps	gls	apps	gls	apps	gls
1967/68	21	6	-	-	1	0	-	-	22	6
1968/69	41	6	2	1	4	0	3	0	50	7
1969/70	27/1	1	4	0	2	0	2	0	35/1	1
1970/71	29/5	2	-	-	4	0	2	0	35/5	2
1971/72	26	5	3	2	2	0	3	1	34	8
1973/74	5/3	0	-	-	1	0	1	0	7/3	0
1974/75	6/1	0	-	-	-	-	-	-	6/1	0
	155/10	**20**	**9**	**3**	**14**	**0**	**11**	**1**	**189/10**	**24**

MOLLOY, John Thomas 1932 - 1933

Position; *Centre-Half*
D.O.B; *A/M/J 1907*
Birthplace; *Middlewich, Cheshire*
Height; *5ft 9'1/2in* ***Weight;*** *12st 2lbs*
Debut; v. *Tranmere Rovers (h) 17th September, 1932*
Total Appearances & Goals; *1 app 0 gls*
Career; *Sandbach Ramblers; Arsenal (Trial); Witton Albion; Nantwich Town; WREXHAM 10th May 1932; Oswestry Town Aug 1933; Witton Albion; Winsford United Jul 1935; Mossley; Halifax Town May 1936 6apps 0gls; Macclesfield Town May 1937; Rhyl 6th Aug 1938;*
Honours; Birmingham & District League Championship Winner 1933;

John Molloy was playing for his local side, Sandbach Ramblers, when taken on trial by Arsenal. Nothing came of this, and he went on to play for Witton Albion and Nantwich Town before coming to the attention of Wrexham, who he joined in the close season of 1932. John was to make just one League appearance for the 'Robins' that season, against Tranmere Rovers on the Racecourse in September 1932, when he played at centre-half in place of Harry Beck in a 1-1 draw. He then returned to the reserve side, and helped them to win the Birmingham & District League Championship for the first time. It was whilst playing for the reserves that he was described as being 'finely built, and a shrewd general.' However, he was released by Wrexham at the end of the season, only to be snapped up by another Birmingham and District League side, Oswestry Town. Molloy later went on to play for Witton Albion, Winsford United, and Mossley before returning to League football with Halifax Town in May 1936. He made six League appearances for the 'Shaymen' without scoring, before being allowed to join Macclesfield Town at the end of the season. After one season with 'The Silkmen' John joined Rhyl in August 1938.

Season	League		F.A.Cup		Welsh Cup		Total	
	apps	gls	apps	gls	apps	gls	apps	gls
1932/33	1	0	-	-	-	-	1	0
	1	**0**	**-**	**-**	**-**	**-**	**1**	**0**

MOONEY, Brian John 1985 - 1986

Position; *Midfield*
D.O.B; *2nd February, 1966*
Birthplace; *Dublin*
Height; *5ft 11in* ***Weight;*** *11st 2lbs*
Debut; *v. Stockport County (a) 13th December, 1985*
Total Appearances & Goals; *11 apps 4 gls*
Career; *Home Farm; Liverpool Aug 1983 £20,000 0apps; WREXHAM 6th Dec 1985 (Loan); Preston North End 9th Oct 1987 125/3apps 20gls; Sheffield Wednesday Jul 1990 (Loan) 0apps; Sunderland 7th Feb 1991 £225,000 21/6apps 1gls; Burnley 11th Sept 1992 (loan) 6apps 0gls;*
Honours; *Republic of Ireland Youth International cap;*

Brian Mooney was spotted playing in the League of Ireland for Home Farm by Liverpool, and they signed the promising seventeen year-old midfield player for £20,000 in August 1983. He became a regular in the club's Central League side, and whilst at Anfield he was capped at youth level by the Republic of Ireland. In December 1985 Brian enjoyed his first taste of League football, when he was loaned to Wrexham for two months. He made his Football League debut in a 2-0 defeat at Stockport County, and went on to add a further ten League and Cup appearances for Wrexham before returning to Liverpool. He then resumed reserve team football at Anfield, though eventually he made his senior debut for Liverpool in October 1986 at Fulham, when he replaced Jim Beglin as a substitute in a Football League Cup match. Liverpool won the game 3-2, and the tie with an aggregate score of 13-2! A year after that match, in October 1987, Brian was allowed to leave Anfield when he signed for Third Division side Preston North End. He made his debut for his new club in a 3-2 home win over Port Vale, and went on to record well over 100 League appearances in the three and a half years that he spent at Deepdale. Mooney had a loan period with Sheffield Wednesday in July 1990, with a view to a permanent transfer, but was allowed to return to Preston without making a first team appearance for the 'Owls'. Back at Deepdale, Brian continued to play the best football of his career, and by February 1991 had done enough to impress a higher division club, as Sunderland paid out a fee of £225,000 for his services. The Dubliner made his debut for the 'Rokerites' in a 1-0 home win over Nottingham Forest, though his career never really took off at Roker Park, remaining on the fringe of first team action. He missed out on Sunderland's 1992 F.A.Cup Final, where they were beaten 2-0 by his former Club, Liverpool. In September 1992 he was allowed to go on a month's loan to Burnley, and recorded six League appearances for the Turf Moor club. He then returned to Sunderland, where he forced his way back into the first team reckoning, only to be released in May 1993. He had made just thirty League appearances during his time at Roker Park.

Season	League		F.A.Cup		Welsh Cup		League Cup		F.R.T.		Total	
	apps	gls	apps	gls	apps	gls	apps	gls	apps	gls	apps	gls
1985/86	8	2	-	-	1	2	-	-	2	0	11	4
	8	**2**	**-**	**-**	**1**	**2**	**-**	**-**	**2**	**0**	**11**	**4**

MOORWOOD, John Edwin 1921 - 1924

Position; *Centre-Half*
D.O.B; *J/A/S 1896*
Birthplace; *Sheffield, Yorkshire*
Height; *5ft 7in* ***Weight;*** *11st 2lbs*
Debut; v. *Hartlepool United (a) 8th September, 1921*
Total Appearances & Goals; *77 apps 2 gls*
Career; *Alfreton Town; Stoke (Am) Feb 1920, (Pro) Mar 1920 9apps 0gls; WREXHAM 15th Aug 1921; Bangor City 17th Dec 1923; Gleadless cs1926; Sheffield Forge Aug 1927; Woodhouse W.M.C. Sept 1929;*

Jack Moorwood was signed by Second Division Stoke as an amateur from Alfreton Town for a fee of £300 in February 1920. After a month he accepted professional terms, though having to wait almost twelve months before making his Football League debut in February 1921, at centre-half in a 1-0 away win at Cardiff. Jack added a further eight League appearances that season, helping Stoke to avoid relegation. Despite his efforts he was allowed to leave the Victoria Ground at the end of the season, though he was soon fixed up with another club when he signed for Wrexham, who had just been accepted for the newly formed Football League Third Division North. Moorwood missed the opening match with Hartlepools United, but he was selected for the following game, also against Hartlepools, which Wrexham won 1-0. He then established himself in the side, and became an ever-present until the end of the season. He kept his place at centre-half for the start of the new campaign, but then had to switch to half-back following the signing of George Savage. 1923/24 saw Jack playing mostly reserve team football as Savage, Teddy Regan, and Billy Matthews formed the heart of the Wrexham defence. By December he had taken up the opportunity to leave the Racecourse, when he joined Bangor City. Jack spent almost three seasons at Farrar Road before returning to his native Sheffield, where he played for Gleadless during 1926/27, followed by two years with Sheffield Forge and then Woodhouse Working Men's Club.

Season	League		F.A.Cup		Welsh Cup		Total	
	apps	gls	apps	gls	apps	gls	apps	gls
1921/22	37	2	4	0	3	0	44	2
1922/23	25	0	3	0	2	0	30	0
1923/24	3	0	-	-	-	-	3	0
	65	**2**	**7**	**0**	**5**	**0**	**77**	**2**

MORGAN, Stephen James 1990

Position; *Forward*
D.O.B; *28th December, 1970*
Birthplace; *Wrexham, Denbighshire*
Height; *5ft 9in* **Weight;** *11st 5lbs*
Debut; v. *Aldershot (a) 27th March, 1990*
Total Appearances & Goals; *8 apps 1 gls*
Career; *Oldham Athletic 13th July 1987 1/1apps 0gls; WREXHAM 22nd Mar 1990 (loan); Rochdale 28th Mar 1991 12/11apps 3gls; Stalybridge Celtic cs1992 13/4apps 2gls; Colwyn Bay cs1993;*
Honours; *Welsh Youth International cap; Welsh Schoolboy international cap; Welsh Cup runner-up 1990; Lancashire League Second Division Championship Winner 1988;*

Steve Morgan was signed by Oldham Athletic after being spotted playing schoolboy football in the Wrexham area. He worked his way through the junior ranks at Boundary Park, winning a Lancashire League Second Division championship medal in 1988 with the club's 'B' team. He made his Football League debut in a 1-1 home draw with Leeds United in October 1987, when he came on as a substitute for Gary Williams at the age of 16, thus becoming one of Oldham's youngest ever debutants. However, Steve did not fulfil his early promise, and in March 1990 was loaned out to his home town club, Wrexham. Steve made his debut in a 1-0 defeat at Aldershot, before adding a further six League appearances for the 'Robins', with whom he remained until the end of the season. He was also selected to play against Hereford United in the first ever Welsh Cup Final to be staged at the National Stadium in Cardiff. Wrexham lost 2-1 and it proved to be Morgan's last match for the club as he then returned to Oldham. He remained at Boundary Park until March 1991, when he was given a free transfer. Steve then joined Rochdale, getting off to a flying start by scoring twice on his Football League debut in a 2-0 home win over York City. He stayed at Spotland until the end of the 1991/92 season, making a total of 23 League appearances, almost half of them as a substitute. Steve was released at the end of that season, and joined Conference League side Stalybridge Celtic. He spent one season with them before returning to North Wales, when he joined Unibond Premier League side Colwyn Bay in the close season of 1993.

Season	League		F.A.Cup		Welsh Cup		League Cup		F.R.T.		Total	
	apps	gls	apps	gls	apps	gls	apps	gls	apps	gls	apps	gls
1989/90	7	1	-	-	1	0	-	-	-	-	8	1
	7	**1**	**-**	**-**	**1**	**0**	**-**	**-**	**-**	**-**	**8**	**1**

MORGANS, Morgan Gwyn 1956 - 1958

Position; *Half-Back*
D.O.B; *20th April, 1932*
Birthplace; *Blaenau Ffestiniog, Gwynedd*
Height; *5ft 10in* **Weight;** *12st 6lbs*
Debut; v. *Hartlepool United (a) 27th August, 1956*
Total Appearances & Goals; *28 apps 2 gls*
Career; *Blaenau Ffestiniog 1947; Llanberis 1949; Blaenau Ffestiniog 1951; Northampton Town Aug 1955 0apps; WREXHAM 2nd Jul 1956; Southport 16th Jul 1958 14apps 0gls; Blaenau Ffestiniog 20th Aug 1959; New Brighton Sept 1959; Colwyn Bay 18th Aug 1960; Blaenau Ffestiniog Oct 1962;*
Honours; *Welsh Amateur International cap;*

Gwyn Morgans was a relatively late starter in football. Brought up in his native Blaenau Ffestiniog, he was not regarded as being good enough to represent his school team. After leaving school he obtained work at the Oakley Quarry in his home town as a slate dresser. It was at this time that Gwyn began to take an interest in football, following the fortunes of Blaenau Ffestiniog in the Welsh League (North), and it was when watching their reserve side one day that his football career took off, when asked to play because the team were one short. From that day on, and for the next two seasons, Gwyn became a regular in the reserve team before joining Llanberis, where he spent a couple of years until returning to play for Blaenau Ffestiniog's first team. Following some impressive performances, the Football League clubs began to take notice, with both Cardiff City and Bolton Wanderers showing an interest. Wrexham manager Cliff Lloyd visited Gwyn's house and wanted him to go to the Racecourse on trial, but when Northampton Town made him a firm offer he joined them as an amateur in 1954, before signing professional in August 1955. That same year Morgans had represented Wales at Amateur level against Scotland in a 5-0 defeat at Bangor. Gwyn failed to record a first team appearance for the 'Cobblers', and after just one season he returned to North Wales to join Wrexham in July 1956. It was there that he finally made his Football League debut, at the advanced age of 24. Gwyn played at half-back, in place of Dennis Griffiths, in a 2-1 defeat at Hartlepools. However, in the following match, which was also his home debut, Gwyn scored in a 2-0 win. He then went on to establish himself in the first team, until he suffered strained stomach muscles against Reading in an F.A.Cup match. That injury was to force him to miss Wrexham's most glamorous F.A.Cup match against Manchester United and the 'Busby's Babes'. It also resulted in him missing the rest of the season, and the Welsh Cup Final against Swansea Town. He managed just seven first team appearances in the following year, before he was allowed to leave the Racecourse in the summer of 1958. Morgans then joined Southport, where he played in the opening eleven games of the season at left-half before losing his place. He was later tried at centre-forward, but failed to impress, and was eventually released. He then returned home and played in the opening games of the 1959/60 season for Blaenau Ffestiniog, before joining former Football League side, New Brighton, in September, who were playing in the Lancashire Combination League at that time. He turned out for 'The Rakers' until the end of the season before joining Colwyn Bay in the summer of 1960. Despite being based in Ormskirk, where he lived for nine years, Gwyn would travel to North Wales to play for both Colwyn Bay and Blaenau Ffestiniog, where he later finished his football career. After hanging up his boots Morgans had taken up work as a fitter's mate, then as a mechanical fitter, before becoming a painter and decorator for the fifteen years prior to his retirement. Gwyn eventually settled in Llandudno, where he was resided since 1972.

Season	League		F.A.Cup		Welsh Cup		Total	
	apps	gls	apps	gls	apps	gls	apps	gls
1956/57	21	2	3	0	-	-	24	2
1957/58	7	0	1	0	1	0	9	0
	28	**2**	**4**	**0**	**1**	**0**	**33**	**2**

MORRALL, Terence Stephen 1963 - 1965

Position; *Centre-Half*
D.O.B; *24th November, 1938*
Birthplace; *Smethwick, West Midlands*
Height; *5ft 11in* ***Weight;*** *11st 7lbs*
Debut; v. *Peterborough United (a) 24th August, 1963*
Total Appearances & Goals; *48 apps 0 gls*
Career; *Church Rovers; Aston Villa 24th Nov 1955 8apps 0gls; Shrewsbury Town 29th Apr 1961 31apps 0gls WREXHAM 4th Jul 1963; Southport 3rd Jul 1965 1app 0gls; Stourbridge Nov 1965;*

Terry Morrall came from a prominent Midlands football family, his uncle - George Morrall - having played in the 1931 F.A.Cup Final for Birmingham. Terry played his early football at the Holly Lodge Grammar School for Boys, from where he was selected to represent Smethwick Boys, Staffordshire Boys and Birmingham & District Schoolboys. It was no surprise, therefore, that a host of clubs began to take an interest in the promising centre-half; included Bolton, West Brom, Wolves, and Walsall, but it was Aston Villa who won the race for his signature on his seventeenth birthday. However, his football career with Villa received a set-back when he was called up for his two years' National Service. He served with the 26th Field Royal Artillery as a Physical Training Instructor, based mostly at either Rhyl or Folkestone, although spending a period in the Middle-East in Lebanon. Terry managed to turn out for Villa's reserve side on most Saturdays during this period, and it was whilst he was still in the Army that he made his Football League debut. Still only nineteen, Morrall was called into the side for the opening game of the 1959/60 season at Brighton. Playing at centre-half, he went on to help Villa to a 2-1 win, and added two more League appearances before the summer as Villa won the Second Division Championship. He managed five First Division appearances the following season before allowed to leave the club in April 1961, when he was transferred to Shrewsbury Town. His first game for the Shropshire side was a memorable one for Terry, as playing at Bradford City, not only did he see Arthur Rowley break the all-time goals record for a Football League player, but also suffered damaged knee ligaments. He had to be carried off at half-time, and the injury was so serious that it put him out of the game for almost six months. Upon regaining his fitness Terry recorded a further 30 League appearances for the Gay Meadow club before he was allowed to join Wrexham in the close season of 1963. He made his debut for the 'Robins' at left back in the opening game of the new season at Peterborough United, which Wrexham lost 5-2! Terry struggled to command a regular first team place that season due to the consistency of Alan Fox at centre-half, although he did play in almost half of the games, albeit in any of the back four positions. The following season saw him begin the campaign as the club's regular centre-half following Fox's departure, but by December he found that up and coming youngster Ray Mielczarek was preferred, and was released at the end of the season. Terry then moved on to Southport, but was to make just one League appearance in the opening match of the 1965/66 season, a 3-1 defeat at Hartlepools. He then found himself playing reserve team football at Haig Avenue, and it was in one of these games that he established a club record by scoring seven goals, as a make shift centre-forward, against Leyland Motors. However, a month later, Morrall's contract with Southport was cancelled by mutual consent, and he returned to his roots, joining West Midlands League side Stourbridge. He later became their player/manager, until 1968, when he was appointed manager of another West Midlands League side, Warley. Terry later coached junior sides, and did some scouting for Brian Clough during his time at Nottingham Forest. He later settled in Gainsborough, where he was working as a sales manager for a frozen foods company. He was to also play Table Tennis for both Grimsby and Lincolnshire.

Season	League		F.A.Cup		Welsh Cup		League Cup		Total	
	apps	gls	apps	gls	apps	gls	apps	gls	apps	gls
1963/64	22	0	-	-	-	-	2	0	24	0
1964/65	20	0	2	0	1	0	1	0	24	0
	42	**0**	**2**	**0**	**1**	**0**	**3**	**0**	**48**	**0**

MORRELL, Andrew Jonathan 1998 -

Position; *Forward*
D.O.B; *28th September, 1974.*
Birthplace; *Doncaster, Yorkshire*
Height; *5ft 10in* ***Weight;*** *11st 7lbs*
Debut v. *Hull City (a) 5th January, 1999 (Auto Windscreen Shield)*
Total Appearances & Goals; *4/6 apps 1 gls*
Career; *Northumbria University; Newcastle Blue Star Aug 1996; WREXHAM Dec 1998;*

Andy Morrell attended the Twycross House Public School in Twycross, Warwickshire from the age of 6 until he left at 18. During that time he showed promise as a footballer by representing Nuneaton Schoolboys, but it was his studying that came first and on leaving school was accepted for a place at the Northumbria University in Newcastle. He continued to play football, representing his University team in a League comprising of other University's in the North-East. He also helped the side to reach the semi-finals of the National competition, where they disappointingly lost 3-2 to Crewe. The start of the 1996/97 season saw Andy sign for Newcastle Blue Star in the Northern League, and in his first season finished as leading scorer. His second campaign with Blue Star saw him finish not only as the club's top scorer with 36 goals, but also the League's joint top marksman, but despite his goalscoring prowess did not receive any invitation to join a Football League side during this time. Having completed his studies with a degree in sports science, Morrell took up employment as assistant-manager and fitness instructor at a Fitness/Leisure club in Leeds. It was whilst working here that he got talking to Sky T.V. reporter, Rob McCaffrey, who in turn contacted Wrexham's coach Joey Jones. He was then given a short trial in February 1998, and invited to return to the club in May, and then again in August. However, an injury in training saw him return home before coming back to the Racecourse in October. He made some impressive performances in the club's reserve team, and stayed for a second month before signing a contract in December until the end of the 1998/99 season. He was then to make his first debut for the 'Robins' in January 1999, when coming on as a substitute for Kevin Russell with five minutes remaining in an Auto Windscreen Shield game at Hull City, and helped Wrexham to maintain their 2-1 lead. Andy went on to earn himself a further contract with the club and scored the goal which helped the 'Robins' reach the F.A.W. Premier Cup Final which is sponsored by B.B.C. Wales.

Season	League		F.A.Cup		W.P.C		League Cup		A.W.S.		Total	
	apps	gls	apps	gls	apps	gls	apps	gls	apps	gls	apps	gls
1998/99	4/3	0	-	-	0/2	1	-	-	0/1	0	4/6	1
	4/3	**0**	**-**	**-**	**0/2**	**1**	**-**	**-**	**0/1**	**0**	**4/6**	**1**

MORRIS, Elfed 1960 - 1962

Position; *Outside-Left*
D.O.B; *9th June, 1942*
Birthplace; *Colwyn Bay, Flintshire*
Height; *5ft 11in* **Weight;** *11st 4lbs*
Debut; v. *Aston Villa (a) 22nd February, 1961 (League Cup)*
Total Appearances & Goals; *13 apps 8 gls*
Career; *Colwyn Bay 1958; Crystal Palace 1959 (trial); WREXHAM 13th May 1960; Chester 26th Jun 1962 £750 164/3apps 69gls; Halifax Town 16th Mar 1968 9apps 2gls; Caernarvon Town 28th Nov 1968; Bethesda Athletic 13th Aug 1969; Llandudno Borough 25th Oct 1969; Colwyn Bay 25th Mar 1970; Bethesda Athletic 5th Jun 1972; Colwyn Bay 20th Dec 1972;*
Honours; *Welsh Cup runner-up 1966;*

The nephew of former Wrexham manager Billy Morris, Elfed Morris first played football for Abergele Grammar School, as well as representing the North Wales Youth side. He joined Colwyn Bay upon leaving school, but it wasn't long before he began to attract the attention of Football League clubs. Crystal Palace were one, and he attended Selhurst Park for a three month trial period, but failed to win a contract. It was then that Cliff Lloyd invited him to the Racecourse, and he scored four goals in his first reserve team match. Not surprisingly, he was offered professional terms immediately afterwards. Elfed duly signed in May 1960, just a month after his 18th birthday. He quickly established himself in the reserve side in the Cheshire County League, and in February 1961 was selected to make his first team debut in a Football League Cup match against Aston Villa, following an injury to the regular outside-right, Gren Jones, although Wrexham lost the match 5-0! His Football League debut came the following month, in a 2-0 defeat at Millwall, but went on to finish the season in style, scoring in the last three matches of the season: a 3-1 home win, over Aldershot. 2-0 at Oldham, and a 2-1 home success against Workington. The club appointed a new manager in the summer, Ken Barnes, and Elfed found himself back in the reserves for the start of the 1961/62 campaign, one which saw him make just eight more senior appearances before he was transferred to Chester for £750 in the summer of 1962. He again found himself playing second team football at Sealand Road, and it wasn't until April 1963 that he finally made his first team debut for Chester in a 1-0 home win over Rochdale. He went on to become a regular in the Chester side for the next five seasons, making almost 200 appearances, and scoring 84 goals. He was the club's top scorer in 1965/66, the same season that he collected a Welsh Cup runners'-up medal as Chester lost to Swansea Town in the Final. He also received a call-up to the Welsh Under-23 squad, but failed to win a cap. Morris left Chester in March 1968, and joined Halifax Town for an undisclosed fee. He made just nine League appearances for the 'Shaymen' before moving on at the end of the season. He returned to North Wales and joined Caernarvon Town where, on 22nd November 1968, was appointed player/manager. He left the club at the end of the season, after reported differences between himself and the executive committee. Elfed later played for Bethesda Athletic and Llandudno Borough eventually joining his home town team, Colwyn Bay, in March 1970. He spent two years before returning to Bethesda in the summer of 1972, though back at Colwyn bay yet again in December of the same year following his appointment as the club's player/manager. He remained in that position until 1974, whereupon he helped to run five junior teams. On giving up professional football he began working as a milkman, later becoming an insurance agent. He eventually opened his own entertainment agency, a business with which he was still occupied at the time of writing, having settled in Colwyn Bay where he is a keen supporter of the Colwyn Bay team.

Season	League		F.A.Cup		Welsh Cup		League Cup		Total	
	apps	gls	apps	gls	apps	gls	apps	gls	apps	gls
1960/61	4	4	-	-	-	-	1	0	5	4
1961/62	5	2	-	-	3	2	-	-	8	4
	9	**6**	**-**	**-**	**3**	**2**	**1**	**0**	**13**	**8**

MORRIS, Mark 1985 - 1994

Position; *Goalkeeper*
D.O.B; *1st August, 1968*
Birthplace; *Chester, Cheshire*
Height; *5ft 11in* **Weight;** *12st 0lbs*
Debut; v. *Exeter City (a) 25th January, 1986*
Total Appearances & Goals; *137 apps 0 gls*
Career; *WREXHAM Aug 1987; Runcorn Jul 1994 40apps 0gls;*
Honours; *Third Division Championship runner-up 1993; Welsh Cup runner-up 1991;*

Between the ages of eight and sixteen Mark Morris played football for his local junior side, Broughton Super Saints, and at 14 played for Wales under-15s against Glamorgan Schoolboys. He was about to join Wrexham when Burnley stepped in at the last minute, and signed him on schoolboy forms. However, when they wanted him to sign on apprentice terms Mark decided to join Wrexham instead, as he had enrolled on a one-year City & Guilds' PE course. Mark then signed YTS forms for the Racecourse club, but in January 1986 received an early call to first team football, following an injury to Don Ferguson. Morris made his Football League debut at Exeter City in a 1-0 win for Wrexham. He stayed in the side for the following two games before Ferguson returned from injury. Mark then injured himself in a training accident with Paul Comstive, and it was serious enough to put him out of action for six months. His YTS agreement came to an end during that time, but was given a further four month contract, and actually went on to spend a further seven years at the Racecourse, showing great loyalty to the Club. In his first five years he learned his trade playing mostly in the reserve team, making only eighteen League appearances as understudy to a number of 'keepers that included Mike Hooper, Don Ferguson, Chris Pearce, Mike Salmon and Vince O'Keefe. The opportunity for which he had been waiting came at the beginning of the 1990/91 season, when the 'four foreigners' rule in European competition enabled him to play in goal, instead of Vince O'Keefe, against Danish side Lyngby. His performance in Denmark was good enough to earn him a run in the senior side, and he kept his place for the rest of the season. At the end of it Mark picked up a Welsh Cup runners-up medal when the 'Robins' lost 2-0 to Swansea City in the first ever Final to be played at the National Stadium in Cardiff. The following season saw Vince O'Keefe regain the 'keepers jersey, although Mark did make eight appearances before he asked for a transfer in the summer. Ken Hughes was then signed from Shrewsbury Town to replace O'Keefe, who had retired, and he began the new campaign as the club's first choice 'keeper. However, some indifferent performances soon cost Hughes his place, and Mark resumed in goal, going on to help Wrexham to promotion as Third Division runners-up. Rule changes at the start of 1993/94 brought new pressure to bear upon Mark, as a substitute goalkeeper was allowed for the first time, and manager Brian Flynn also paid out £200,000 for England under-21 international Andy Marriott from Nottingham Forest. He then became the first choice 'keeper. Mark was released at the end of the season, after almost ten years' loyal service to Wrexham. He was soon fixed up with another club when he joined Conference League side Runcorn in July 1994. He combined playing for the 'Linnets'

with employment in his father-in-law's gardening business, and he has remained with Runcorn until having his contract terminated by mutual consent in July 1999 in order to take up employment with the Probation Service. Mark has now settled in Pen-Y-Ffordd, near Chester.

Season	League		F.A.Cup		Welsh Cup		League Cup		A.G.T.		E.C.W.C.		Total	
	apps	gls	apps	gls	apps	gls	apps	gls	apps	gls	apps	gls	apps	gls
1985/86	3	0	-	-	-	-	-	-	-	-	-	-	3	0
1987/88	6	0	-	-	1	0	-	-	-	-	-	-	7	0
1988/89	3	0	-	-	1	0	-	-	-	-	-	-	4	0
1989/90	3	0	1	0	-	-	-	-	-	-	-	-	4	0
1990/91	40	0	1	0	6	0	1	0	3	0	4	0	55	0
1991/92	8	0	1	0	1	0	-	-	2	0	-	-	12	0
1992/93	34	0	1	0	5	0	-	-	3	0	-	-	43	0
1993/94	4	0	-	-	-	-	4	0	1	0	-	-	9	0
	101	**0**	**4**	**0**	**14**	**0**	**5**	**0**	**9**	**0**	**4**	**0**	**137**	**0**

***MORRIS,* Stephen** 1994 - 1997

Position; *Forward*
D.O.B; *13th May 1976*
Birthplace; *Liverpool, Merseyside*
Height; *5ft 9in* ***Weight;*** *10st 7lbs*
Debut; v. *Stockport County (a) 26th December, 1994*
Total Appearances & Goals; *35/21 apps 11 gls*
Career; *Liverpool Jul 1992; WREXHAM 5th Sept 1994; Rotherham United Jul 1997 (Trial) 0apps; Rochdale 18th Aug 1997 (Loan) 0apps; Torquay United Nov 1997 (Trial) 0apps; Southport Feb 1998 5/5apps 1gls;*
Honours; *Welsh Cup Winner 1995;*

Steve Morris was playing for the Liverpool Primary Schools side, when spotted by Liverpool manager, Kenny Dalglish. From the age of ten he was associated with the Anfield club, and when fourteen years old he signed schoolboy forms with Liverpool. As a forward Steve went on to earn further representative honours whilst at the Bluecoats School, when he played for both Liverpool and Merseyside Schoolboys. He also had trials for the England Schoolboy team, spending a week with the squad at Nottingham. Upon leaving school, Steve signed Y.T.S. forms with Liverpool, and began playing in their Lancashire League XI, before progressing to the Central League side in his second year. In over two years at Anfield Morris scored over sixty goals in all matches, so it came as a big disappointment, when he was informed of his release at the end of 1993/94. A few clubs took an interest in the promising eighteen year-old, including Bolton, Bury, and Dundee, but after a trial period with Wrexham he signed a professional contract with the Welsh club in August 1994. Steve had to wait until Christmas 1994 for his chance in the first team, making his Football League debut in place of Steve Watkin at Stockport County in a 1-1 draw. He played in the following match, a 3-3 home draw with Peterborough United, and scored his first goal. Over the next two and a half years, Steve regularly found himself in and out of the side. His inability to establish himself was due to a failure to repeat in the first team his free scoring form in the reserves, as well as the consistent form of the regular strike duo of Steve Watkin and Gary Bennett. In the close season of 1997, Steve, who was out of contract, decided to leave the Racecourse. He attended trials with Rotherham United, before joining Rochdale on a months loan. However, an ankle injury meant he never made a first team appearance at Spotland, and returned to Wrexham on a weekly contract. Having recovered from that injury he joined Torquay United for another trial in November 1997, but again nothing came of it, and eventually joined Conference League side Southport in February 1998. At Haig Avenue Morris assisted the 'Sandgrounders' to reach the F.A.Trophy Final, scoring a vital away goal against Slough in the semi-finals. However, Morris missed out on a Wembley appearance when the unemployed youngster had a job interview in Southend days before the big game, which saw manager Paul Futcher omit him from the squad because of his missing the preparations for the Wembley showpiece. Steve left Haig Avenue in the summer of 1998, and is now believed to be training to become a Police Officer.

Season	League		F.A.Cup		Welsh Cup		League Cup		A.W.S.		E.C.W.C.		Total	
	apps	gls	apps	gls	apps	gls	apps	gls	apps	gls	apps	gls	apps	gls
1994/95	10/2	2	-	-	3	1	-	-	0/1	0	-	-	13/3	3
1995/96	4/9	2	1	0	-	-	1/1	0	0/1	0	-	-	6/11	2
1996/97	10/7	4	5	2	-	-	-	-	1	0	-	-	16/7	6
	24/18	**8**	**6**	**2**	**3**	**1**	**1/1**	**0**	**1/2**	**0**	**-**	**-**	**35/21**	**11**

***MORTIMER,* John McCormick** 1946 - 1949

Position; *Left-Back*
D.O.B; *5th December, 1923*
Birthplace; *Birkenhead, Merseyside*
Height; *5ft 9'1/2in* ***Weight;*** *10st 9lbs*
Debut; v. *Southport (h) 21st December, 1946*
Total Appearances & Goals; *27 apps 0 gls*
Career; *Prenton Villa; Park Villa; WREXHAM (Am) 17th Dec 1946, (Pro) 20th Jun 1947; New Brighton 15th Oct 1949 5apps 0gls; Ellesmere Port Town 1951/52; Northwich Victoria 1954/55; Rhyl 29th Sept 1956; Caernarvon Town Dec 1957; Pwllheli & District 19th Aug 1958;*
Honours; *Cheshire County League Representative cap;*

John Mortimer played football for both Temple Road and Claughton High Grade Schools in his native Birkenhead. He was still only 15 years old when World War Two broke out, and any notions of a career in football were quickly forgotten. Instead, when he left school, he took up work for the Birkenhead to Liverpool Ferry Company, before moving on to Cammell Laird Ship Builders in his home town. John played football when he could for local side Prenton Villa, followed by a spell with Park Villa, from where he was given a trial by Chester after WW2 had ended. He was later recommended to Wrexham manager Tom Williams, who signed him on amateur forms to enable him to play in the F.A.Cup during the 1945/46 season. His first team debut came against Crewe Alexandra on the Racecourse in November 1945, as Wrexham won 3-0, and 4-2 on aggregate, in the only season that the F.A.Cup was contested on a home and away basis. He played both two games against Shrewsbury Town in the next round, which Wrexham won 2-1 on aggregate. However, it wasn't until the following season that Mortimer made his next senior appearance, this time in a Football League match, when he replaced Billy Tudor at wing-half in a 1-1 draw against Southport on the Racecourse. He went on to play in a further six League games that season before he was signed as a professional in the close season. With Ron Jackson established as the club's regular left-back John's appearances were always going to be limited, but he did play in a further nineteen League and Cup games during 1947/48. The summer of 1948 saw John go on tour to Germany with the Wrexham team, where they played three matches against British Army teams stationed on the Rhine. The following season saw him playing mainly reserve team football, but he was honoured when selected for the Cheshire County League XI against the Southern League in a match staged on the Racecourse in October 1948. Even so, he was released by Wrexham at the end of the season. John joined New Brighton on trial, but had an unfortunate start when he broke a leg in a reserve match at Fleetwood, which put him out of action for three months. Given the precarious financial position in which New Brighton found themselves at the time, it was a sporting gesture by the Club's directors to give him a contract until the end of the season. However, once fit, he found his first team chances limited, as he made just four League appearances during 1949/50, and managed to add just one more during the following season before being released on

5th May 1951. A month later, the 'Rakers' application for re-election failed, and they lost their place in the Football League. John then signed for Cheshire County League side Ellesmere Port Town, where he spent three seasons before moving on to Northwich Victoria for the 1954/55 campaign. He remained at Drill Field for just over a season, following which he returned to North Wales to join Rhyl in September 1956. After a little over a year at Belle Vue, Mortimer signed for Welsh League (North) side Caernarvon Town, around Christmas of 1957, and played for the 'Canaries' against Wrexham in their 4-1 Welsh Cup semi-final defeat in March 1958 His last match for the Oval outfit was against Borough United in May 1958, when Caernarvon won 15-4! He then signed for Pwllheli & District in August 1958, where he ended his football career. John had worked at Cammell Laird throughout this time, but later switched to the Unilever Soap Company in Port Sunlight. Another move took him to Shell in Ellesmere Port, where he spent many years working as a quality control inspector with Vauxhall's. John retired in 1988, and settled in the Birkenhead area.

Season	League		F.A.Cup		Welsh Cup		Total	
	apps	gls	apps	gls	apps	gls	apps	gls
1946/47	7	0	-	-	-	-	7	0
1947/48	15	0	2	0	2	0	19	0
1948/49	1	0	-	-	-	-	1	0
	23	**0**	**2**	**0**	**2**	**0**	**27**	**0**

MOSTYN, Roger 1971 - 1974

Position; *Forward*
D.O.B; *31st August, 1953*
Birthplace; *Wrexham, Denbighshire*
Height; *5ft 9in* **Weight;** *10st 10lbs*
Debut; v. *Brighton & Hove Albion (h) 5th February, 1972*
Total Appearances & Goals; *18/4 apps 7 gls*
Career; *WREXHAM 5th Nov 1971; Bath City 11th Jan 1974 (Loan) to 7th Mar 1974; Australia Mar 1974; Bangor City 19th Nov 1974; Oswestry Town Aug 1975 to Dec 1975; Rhyl 1976/77;*
Honours; *Welsh Youth International; Welsh Youth Cup Winner 1971;*

Roger Mostyn was educated in Wrexham at Gwenfro Primary and Grove Park Secondary Schools. He first began playing football as a goalkeeper, but his innate ball sense and strong physique saw him switch to play in midfield. He then became an automatic choice in the Wrexham Schoolboys team, as well as the North Wales Triple Jump champion, where he represented Wales in an international A.A.A. meeting at Hartford, Cheshire. It was at around this time that Roger replied to an advert in the local newspaper inviting young amateur players to the Racecourse for trials. He went along, and was offered amateur terms with the Club by manager John Neal. Upon leaving school Roger's ambition to teach P.E. was put to one side as he was signed on apprentice terms by the Racecourse club. Mostyn was then switched to playing in the forward line, where he quickly became a success, scoring 58 goals during the 1970/71 season with the reserves and youth sides. He picked up a Welsh Youth Cup Winners' medal at the end of that season as Wrexham beat Cardiff City 4-3 in the Final, after he had been capped by Wales Youth against Ireland in February 1971. Roger later toured Czechoslovakia with the Welsh Youth team, but it wasn't until the following season that he was to make his Football League debut for the 'Robins' in a 2-1 home defeat by Brighton & Hove Albion in February 1972. He did well enough to keep his place in the side, adding a further 13 first team appearances that season, although he did miss out on the Welsh Cup Final. 1972/73 saw Roger play in Wrexham's first European match on the Racecourse, the second leg of the European Cup-Winners' Cup tie against F.C.Zurich, when he came on as substitute for Albert Kinsey in a thrilling 2-1 victory. He remained on the sub's bench for the second round matches with Hajduk Split, but was to manage just seven more senior appearances for the club, as he found his opportunities limited by the emerging talents of both Dave Smallman and Billy Ashcroft. In January 1974 Mostyn was loaned out to Southern League side Bath City, where he spent two months before being released at the end of the season. He then went to Australia to play during the summer, and upon his return joined Oswestry Town part-time, having turned down an offer from Southport manager Jimmy Melia. It was at that time that Roger took up employment with the Royal Mail in Wrexham, a job that he still holds today. Even though a Wrexham lad he is, sadly, a big Stoke City supporter!

Season	League		F.A.Cup		Welsh Cup		League Cup		E.C.W.C.		Total	
	apps	gls	apps	gls	apps	gls	apps	gls	apps	gls	apps	gls
1971/72	11/1	3	-	-	2	3	-	-	-	-	13/1	6
1972/73	4/2	1	-	-	-	-	-	-	0/1	0	4/3	1
1973/74	1	0	-	-	-	-	-	-	-	-	1	0
	16/3	**4**	**-**	**-**	**2**	**3**	**-**	**-**	**0/1**	**0**	**18/4**	**7**

MULDOON, John Patrick Joseph 1982 - 1986

Position; *Forward/Midfield*
D.O.B; *21st November, 1964*
Birthplace; *Clatterbridge, Merseyside*
Height; *5ft 8in* **Weight;** *10st 5lbs*
Debut; v. *Preston North End (a) 28th September, 1982*
Total Appearances & Goals; *91/27 apps 16 gls*
Career; *WREXHAM Dec 1982; HIK Helsinki (Finland) Apr 1986; Oswestry Town Nov 1986; Morecambe Aug 1987; Oswestry Town Oct 1987; Colne Dynamos; Newtown; Llansantffraid 1992/93 1/4apps 0gls; Llandudno 1993/94; Gresford Athletic 1994/95;*
Honours; *Cymru Alliance Championship Winner 1993;*

John Muldoon was playing schoolboy football around his home area when manager Arfon Griffiths offered him a trial with Wrexham, having seen him playing Sunday League football for Excelsior. John, who was still only 16 years old, had just begun work as a Warehouse assistant, and needed no second invitation to sign apprentice forms with the Racecourse club. It was during his apprenticeship that he was given his first team chance, though this was due mainly to the club's crippling financial situation at the time. His debut came in a Third Division match at Preston in which he replaced David Gregory in a 3-0 defeat. His home debut came in the following match, against Bournemouth, when he substituted Jack Keay and broke the deadlock with the only goal of the game. At the end of the following month he was named as the Wales and West area's, 'Young Player of the Month', and by December 1982 had been signed on professional terms. John's career with Wrexham was to be interrupted by a series of niggling injuries, and the club's inability to cope with mounting financial problems saw the 1982/83 season end in a second successive relegation. He did collect a Welsh Cup runners-up tankard at the end of the following year, however, as Wrexham lost to Shrewsbury in the Final. The fact that their opponents were located to the east of Offa's Dyke meant that Wrexham - and John - would be involved in the 1984/85 season's European Cup-Winners' Cup competition, and they went on to cross swords with some of the World's best players in their games against F.C.Porto of Portugal and A.S.Roma of Italy. John played a major part in the magnificent away-goals victory over Porto, providing pinpoint crosses for Jim Steel's decisive header in the 1-0 win at the Racecourse, and then for Barry Horne to claim the all-important third goal in Portugal. He managed just ten League

appearances during the following season, before being released in the summer. Muldoon then signed for Northern Premier League club Morecambe, and later had spells with Colne Dynamos, Oswestry Town, and Newtown until joining Llansantffraid as player/coach. He helped the 'Saints' clinch the Cymru Alliance championship in 1993, which also meant promotion for the Montgomeryshire village side to the League of Wales. The 1993/94 season would see John struggle to regain a first team place after injury, and eventually moved on to Cymru Alliance League side, Llandudno. He again failed to establish a regular first team spot, and joined Gresford Athletic of the same League. John, who was employed with British Telecom, later opened his own business in Gwersyllt, near Wrexham, running a fast food takeaway called 'J.J.'s'.

Season	League		F.A.Cup		Welsh Cup		League Cup		F.R.T.		E.C.W.C.		Total	
	apps	gls	apps	gls	apps	gls	apps	gls	apps	gls	apps	gls	apps	gls
1982/83	23/2	4	2	1	6	1	-	-	-	-	-	-	31/2	6
1983/84	25/7	4	1	0	7/2	1	2	0	1/1	0	-	-	36/10	5
1984/85	10/5	3	1	0	1	2	2	0	-	-	1/3	0	15/8	5
1985/86	6/4	0	1/1	0	0/1	0	2/1	0	-	-	-	-	9/7	0
	64/18	**11**	**5/1**	**1**	**14/3**	**4**	**6/1**	**0**	**1/1**	**0**	**1/3**	**0**	**91/27**	**16**

MURPHY, Leslie A. 1920 - 1922

Position; *Goalkeeper*
D.O.B;
Birthplace; *Dunamana, County Tyrone*
Height; *5ft 11'1/2in* ***Weight;*** *12st 5lbs*
Debut; v. *Coventry City Reserves (a) 28th August, 1920 Football League Debut; v. Halifax Town (h) 18th March, 1922*
Total Appearances & Goals; *42 apps 0 gls*
Career; *Belfast Celtic 1911; Leeds City May 1911 18apps 0gls; Glentoran cs1912; Linfield; WREXHAM 18th Aug 1920; Bristol Rovers Aug 1922 0apps; Reading cs1923 0apps;*
Honours; *Two Irish League representative apps;*

Leslie Murphy was playing in goal for Belfast Celtic when he was signed by English Second Division side Leeds City. Les made eighteen Football League appearances for the Yorkshire club during the 1911/12 season, his Football League debut coming in a 2-1 defeat at Nottingham Forest in the opening match of the season. However, he returned to Ireland at the end of that season and signed for Glentoran, where he won two Irish League Representative caps - the matches against the Football League in Belfast on 23rd October 1912, and against the Scottish League two weeks later. Murphy then joined Linfield, from where Wrexham signed him in August 1920. The Racecourse club were playing in the Birmingham & District League at the time, and Les made his debut in the opening match of the new season in a 3-1 win at Coventry City Reserves. He went on to miss just one game that season, as the 'Robins' finished in a very creditable third place, and were then elected to play in the newly formed Football League Division Three North. However, disaster was to strike during the summer when Les returned to his native Ireland to visit family and friends. He contracted Rheumatic Fever, and was detained at Downpatrick Infirmary for many weeks. His recovery was slow, and he didn't return to Wrexham until January 1922, by which time Wrexham had signed a promising goalkeeper in George Godding. Les then had to be content with reserve team football until he was called up to make his Football League debut in March 1922, appearing in a 5-1 home win over Halifax Town. However, it proved to be his final senior outing for the North Wales club, as he was signed by Third Division South side Bristol Rovers in the summer. Les failed to record a League appearance during his time with the 'Pirates', and at the end of the 1922/23 season he joined Reading, where he again spent a season without making a League breakthrough.

Season	League		F.A.Cup		Welsh Cup		Total	
	apps	gls	apps	gls	apps	gls	apps	gls
1920/21	3	0	3	0	5	0	41	0
1921/22	1	0	-	-	-	-	1	0*
	34	**0**	**3**	**0**	**5**	**0**	**42**	**0**

* = Football League Season

MURRAY, Joseph Ernest 1991

Position; *Midfield*
D.O.B; *5th November, 1971*
Birthplace; *Liverpool, Merseyside*
Height; *5ft 8in* ***Weight;*** *10st 11lbs*
Debut; v. *Hereford United (a) 30th March, 1991*
Total Appearances & Goals; *14 apps 0 gls*
Career; *Liverpool 1987; Marine 1990; WREXHAM Mar 1991 to Aug 1991; Marine 1991;*
Honours; *Welsh Cup runner-up 1991;*

England Schoolboy International;Joey Murray was a promising schoolboy footballer, playing for his school team in his native Liverpool, De La Salle, and also representing Liverpool Schoolboys. He was eventually selected to play for England Schoolboy under-15s, making trips to Italy and Belgium. He earned a total of nine caps at that level, scoring four goals, and it was no surprise when he signed schoolboy forms for Liverpool in 1985, going on to earn himself a two year YTS contract upon leaving school. Joey played for Liverpool's 'A' and 'B' teams in the Lancashire League, and made just one appearance for the reserve team in a pre-season game at Aberystwyth before he was released at the end of his Youth Training Scheme. Murray then completed trials with Burnley, Bolton Wanderers, and Chester, none of which resulted in any firm offers. In the summer of 1990 he went on an F.A. preliminary coaching course at Everton's training ground, and was then linked to take part in the Goodison Park club's pre-season training. This arrangement was eventually extended to playing in the Lancashire League side. Shortly afterwards he went to Tranmere Rovers for a trial, but left after a few reserve team games. He then joined Northern Premier League side Marine, and shortly afterwards was invited for trials with Wrexham. After a few reserve team outings he was signed on non-contract terms by the club, in March, until the end of the 1990/91 season. It was towards the end of March that he made his Football League debut, at Hereford United in a 1-0 defeat. He completed a further thirteen first team appearances, including the 1991 Welsh Cup Final at the National Stadium in Cardiff, which Wrexham lost 2-0 to Swansea City. Following that game Joey was given a further three months contract with Wrexham. He played in a number of pre-season friendlies prior to the start of the 1991/92 season, but failed to progress and was released just before the season had begun. Joey then returned to play for Marine for a short spell.

Season	League		F.A.Cup		Welsh Cup		League Cup		A.G.T.		E.C.W.C.		Total	
	apps	gls	apps	gls	apps	gls	apps	gls	apps	gls	apps	gls	apps	gls
1990/91	11	0	-	-	3	0	-	-	-	-	-	-	14	0
	11	**0**	**-**	**-**	**3**	**0**	**-**	**-**	**-**	**-**	**-**	**-**	**14**	**0**

MURRAY, Kenneth 1958 - 1959

Position; *Inside-Forward*
D.O.B; *2nd April, 1928*
Birthplace; *Darlington, Durham*
Died; *Newcastle-on-Tyne, 8th January, 1993.*
Height; *5ft 11in* ***Weight;*** *12st 0lbs*
Debut; v. *Barrow (h) 22nd February, 1958*
Total Appearances & Goals; *32 apps 10 gls*
Career; *Bishop Auckland (Am); Darlington 27th Jul 1950 70apps 19gls; Mansfield Town 18th Jul 1953 140apps 60gls; Oldham Athletic 9th March 1957 £1,500 35apps 14gls; WREXHAM 22nd Feb 1958; Yeovil & Petters United 23rd Jul 1959; Gateshead 1st Aug 1959 to cs1960 18apps 7gls;*
Honours; *Welsh Cup Winner 1958;*

Ken Murray began his football career in his native North-East with leading amateur side Bishop Auckland. He combined playing with working in the shipyards, and after some impressive displays was signed by Football League club Darlington in July 1950. Ken went on to spend three years with the Feethams club, making 70 League appearances for the 'Quakers' before joining Mansfield Town in July 1953. Playing at inside-

forward he made his debut in the opening match of the season, a 4-0 defeat by Derby County, but scored twice in the next match, a 3-2 win over Scunthorpe United, his home debut. Ken went on to become virtually an ever-present in almost four years with the 'Stags', finishing top scorer in his first two seasons at Field Mill with 21 and 13 goals respectively. He left Mansfield in March 1957 to join Oldham Athletic for a fee of around £1,500, making his debut in a 3-2 home win over Darlington. The following season Ken was made captain at Oldham, but by the following February was allowed to leave the 'Latics' and join fellow Third Division North side Wrexham. It proved to be a good move for him, because by the end of the season he had helped Wrexham gain a place in the newly-formed Third Division, and he added a Welsh Cup winners' medal, as he scored in a 2-1 Final victory over Chester. However, Murray found that he couldn't hold down a regular senior place the following season, and he was released in the summer. He then headed south, linking up with Southern League side Yeovil & Petters United, but just over a week later he returned to the North-East to join Gateshead where he spent one season, scoring two goals on his debut in a 5-4 defeat at Gillingham. Gateshead failed to regain re-election to the Football League at the end of that season, and Ken's professional career was at an end. He then returned to the Shipyards, continuing to work there until he was made redundant in the 1980s. He was a keen golfer a racing pigeon enthusiast, maintaining an active interest in both until he passed away in January 1993, aged 64.

Season	League		F.A.Cup		Welsh Cup		Total	
	apps	gls	apps	gls	apps	gls	apps	gls
1957/58	15	4	-	-	3	3	8	7
1958/59	17	6	1	1	2	2	20	9
	32	**10**	**1**	**1**	**5**	**5**	**38**	**16**

MUSTARD, John

1930 - 1932 & 1935 - 1936

Position; *Outside-Right*
Birthplace; *Boldon, Tyne & Wear*
Height; *5ft 7in* **Weight;** *10st 10lbs*
D.O.B; *J/F/M 1905*
Debut; v. *Southport (a) 30th August, 1930*
Total Appearances & Goals; *101 apps 21 gls*
Career; *Boldon Colliery FC; Crawcrook Albion; Queens Park Rangers 13th Nov 1926 37apps 4gls; South Shields 21st Sept 1929 31apps 5gls; WREXHAM 4th June 1930; Preston North End 11th May 1932 15apps 5gls; Burnley 16th March 1933 15apps 4gls; Southend United 27th Dec 1933 20apps 3gls; Crewe Alexandra 26th Jul 1934 38apps 17gls; WREXHAM 13th May 1935; New Brighton 22nd July 1936 78apps 11gls;*
Honours; *Welsh Cup Winner 1931; Welsh Cup runner-up 1932;*

Jack Mustard was a much travelled right winger who first played football for local side, Boldon Colliery, before moving to another club in the area, Crawcrook Albion. It was there that he came to the attention of Queens Park Rangers, and they signed him in November 1926. Jack made his Football League debut for the London club in a 2-0 defeat at Plymouth in December 1926, and went on to make a further 36 League appearances in almost three years before returning to his native North-East in September 1929 to join Third Division North side, South Shields (Gateshead). He stayed with them for one season before moving on to join Wrexham in the close season of 1930, though he had almost signed for another Southern club who had endeavoured to secure his services. Ironically, he signed for Wrexham in London and Jack collected a Welsh Cup winners' medal in his first season with the Racecourse club, when the 'Robins' beat non-league side Shrewsbury Town 7-0 in the Final. The following season he added a runners'-up medal in the same competition, as they lost 2-0 to Swansea. Whilst at Wrexham Jack was regarded as 'a very fast winger indeed, and was a sprinter of some repute'. He left at the end of the 1931/32 season, when he joined Second Division side Preston North End, though he spent less than a year at Deepdale before moving on to fellow Second Division side Burnley in March 1933. At Turf Moor he scored four goals in 15 League appearances before moving South to join Southend United in December 1933. Jack then scored three goals in 20 League appearances for the 'Shrimpers' joining Crewe Alexandra during the close season of 1934. He enjoyed a successful season with the Cheshire club, scoring 17 goals in 38 League games, though he was on the move again in the summer. This time, he returned to Wrexham for a second spell, and began the season as the club's regular outside-right, making his second debut for the club in a 2-1 win at Rotherham in the opening match of the 1935/36 season. After sixteen League games, however, he lost his place to the promising youngster, Ron Jones. During his spells with Wrexham Mustard was described as 'handily versatile. A strong raiding winger, who carries a good shot, and often uses it, as well as crossing centres very accurately.' He joined New Brighton in the summer, and was immediately appointed club captain, though he relinquished that position shortly afterwards, stating that outside-right 'was not a suitable position to supervise players.' Jack spent his first two seasons with the 'Rakers' playing regularly on either flank, but at the start of the 1938/39 season lost his place in the side to new signing, Jimmy Stein, and in December 1938 he was to leave the club.

Season	League		F.A.Cup		Welsh Cup		Total	
	apps	gls	apps	gls	apps	gls	apps	gls
1930/31	41	14	3	1	4	2	48	17
1931/32	29	3	1	0	6	0	36	3
1935/36	16	1	-	-	1	0	17	1
	86	**18**	**4**	**1**	**11**	**2**	**101**	**21**

MYERSCOUGH, William

1963 - 1964

Position; *Inside-Forward*
D.O.B; *22nd June, 1930*
Birthplace; *Bolton, Lancashire*
Died; *Glossop, 16th March 1977*
Height; *5ft 9in* **Weight;** *11st 6lbs*
Debut; v. *Peterborough United (a) 24th August, 1963*
Total Appearances & Goals; *43 apps 7 gls*
Career; *Manchester City; Ashfield; Walsall Jun 1954 26apps 6gls; Aston Villa 23rd Jul 1955 64apps 15gls; Rotherham United 29th Jul 1959 39apps 11gls; Coventry City 8th Jul 1960 £6,000 58apps 16gls; Chester 3rd Mar 1962 36apps 11gls; WREXHAM 6th Jun 1963; Macclesfield Town cs1964;*
Honours; *F.A.Cup Winner 1957;*

Billy Myerscough was on Manchester City's books as a youngster, but failed to make an impression and was later released. He dropped down into non-league football with Ashfield, from where he was signed by Walsall in June 1954 at the relatively late age of 24. Billy, who was then playing at inside-forward, made his Football League debut for Walsall in the opening match of the 1954/55 season, a 2-2 draw at Reading. He had completed fourteen matches before finding the net for the first time, when he scored in a 6-1 home win over Bournemouth. Although Walsall finished the season in 23rd position in the Third Division South Billy must have done enough to impress, as Aston Villa signed him during the summer of 1955. However, he had to wait almost 18 months before making his first team debut for Villa, replacing Jackie Sewell at inside-left in a 2-0 win at Charlton Athletic in December 1956. By the end of the season he was playing regularly at centre-forward, and scored three goals in thirteen matches, as well as notching the goal that helped Villa reach the 1957 F.A.Cup Final, when they beat West Bromwich Albion 1-0 in the semi-finals. He was selected to play in the Final against Manchester United, and Villa won 2-1. Over the next two years, Myerscough, who was described as a 'brilliant ball player, who was hard to knock off the ball', played in over fifty games for Villa, but at the end of the 1958/59 season was allowed to join Second Division side Rotherham United. He spent one season at Millmoor, scoring on his debut in a 3-3 home draw with Charlton Athletic, and also helped 'The Millermen beat Arsenal in the F.A.Cup. At the end of the season he joined Third Division Coventry City for a £6,000 fee, and was a regular in the side at Highfield Road until he became a victim of new manager Jimmy Hill's new regime. Billy was to leave Coventry, together with Ron Hewitt, and they both joined Chester in March 1962. He made his debut in a 5-1 defeat at York City alongside Hewitt, who was nearing the end of his career. The pair couldn't prevent Chester from finishing bottom of the Football League, although they were saved from applying for re-election by the resignation of Accrington Stanley. Myerscough spent one more season at Sealand Road before he was signed by Wrexham in July 1963, in a part-exchange deal that saw George Evans move to Chester. Billy, then 33 years old, made his debut for the 'Robins' in a 5-2 defeat at Peterborough United, and scored one of his sides goals. He spent a year at the Racecourse, one which saw the club relegated to Division Four, before being released in the summer of 1964. He then joined Macclesfield Town in the Cheshire County League, and played against Wrexham in an F.A.Cup First Round match that season, a tie that the Welsh club won 2-1. Billy passed away in 1977, aged only 47.

Season	League		F.A.Cup		Welsh Cup		League Cup		Total	
	apps	gls	apps	gls	apps	gls	apps	gls	apps	gls
1963/64	35	5	1	0	3	1	4	1	43	7
	35	**5**	**1**	**0**	**3**	**1**	**4**	**1**	**43**	**7**

Gareth Owen

NEAL, John Edward — 1929 - 1930

Position; *Inside-Left*
D.O.B; *29th November, 1898*
Birthplace; *Llandudno, Gwynedd*
D.O.B; *29th November, 1898*
Height; *5ft 6'1/2in* **Weight;** *11st 8lbs*
Died; *Rhos-on-Sea, 14th January, 1965*
Debut; v. *Bradford City (a) 23rd March, 1929*
Total Appearances & Goals; *17 apps 3 gls*
Career; *UCNW Bangor 1919; Llandudno 25th Jan 1922; Derby County Jun 1923 (trial); Colwyn Bay United 1st Jan 1924; WREXHAM 18th Mar 1929 £100; Colwyn Bay United 7th Dec 1929 to 1931;*
Honours; *Two Full Welsh International caps; Three Welsh Junior International caps; Five North Wales Coast F.A. Representative caps; Welsh National League Representative cap;*

John Neal was born the son of a Butcher and cattle dealer in Llandudno, and following the end of the First World War, attended University College of North Wales (UCNW) in Bangor. The duration was for 3 years, but left before completing his degree course. He played football regularly for the College team, where he showed much promise, and in 1920 he was selected for the Welsh Amateur XI as a reserve. After leaving University John took up playing for Llandudno, and in his two years with the club became a free-scoring forward, while in October 1922 he scored 13 goals in just eight games. This kind of form prompted Sheffield United to make a bid of £750 for his services, but he turned down the move. The following year he was selected to play in the first of five representative matches for the North Wales Coast F.A., their annual fixture against the Scottish Junior F.A. In January 1924 John signed for neighbours Colwyn Bay United, of the Welsh National League. He spent five seasons with the Bay, which included a spell as player/manager. The 1928/29 season saw him at his best, notching 42 goals, 22 of which came in seven matches between December 1928 and January 1929. A number of clubs began to take notice and Wrexham were first in the race for his signature, acquiring his services for £100 in March 1929. Unfortunately his League debut was an occasion that he preferred to forget, as Wrexham lost 5-0 at Bradford City. Despite the result, he kept his place in the side for the rest of the campaign, scoring three goals in nine League games, and during the summer was selected for a month long tour of Canada with a Welsh F.A. XI. He appeared in twelve of the sixteen matches on the tour, scoring eleven goals, including two hat-tricks against Calgary and Saskatoon. Back at the Racecourse Neal began the new season in his familiar inside-left position, but problems arose when he failed to turn up for an away game at New Brighton, having found himself stranded on Liverpool Station. By late October he was out of favour, having failed to find the net in eight League games, and in January 1930 decided to leave the Racecourse and re-join Colwyn Bay United. It was following his return to Colwyn Bay that John was to win his first cap for Wales, playing against Scotland in October 1930 in a Welsh team that was to become famous as 'The Great Unknowns'. This was a Welsh side assembled from mostly lesser League and non-league players. They had been written off by the press, but surprised everyone as they secured a 1-1 draw in Glasgow. The following month he was awarded a second cap, against England, and the game ended in a 4-0 defeat. Shortly after this John decided to retire from football becoming the entertainment and publicity manager for Colwyn Bay Corporation, a job that he enjoyed for many years. It was in this capacity that he had much to do with the development of the town's Eirias Park. He later became Chairman of the football team, as well as a keen cricketer, golfer, and crown green bowler to county standard.

Season	League		F.A.Cup		Welsh Cup		Total	
	apps	gls	apps	gls	apps	gls	apps	gls
1928/29	9	3	-	-	-	-	9	3
1929/30	8	0	-	-	-	-	8	0
	17	**3**	-	-	-	-	**17**	**3**

NELSON, Albert Oswin — 1938 - 1939

Position; *Inside-Right*
D.O.B; *7th March, 1917*
Birthplace; *Aberaman, Glamorgan*
Died; *Sutton, Surrey, December, 1997*
Height; *5ft 10in* **Weight;** *10st 12lbs*
Debut; v. *New Brighton (h) 1st October, 1938*
Total Appearances & Goals; *32 apps 13 gls*
Career; *Aberaman Athletic; Wolves (Am) Mar 1938, (Pro) Apr 1938 0apps; WREXHAM (Am) Jul 1938, (Pro) 30th Sept 1938;*

Albert Nelson was signed by Wolves on a month's trial from Aberaman Athletic in March 1938. He successfully completed his trial and accepted professional terms with the Molineux club in April, only to be released at the end of the season without having made a first team appearance. In the summer he was given another chance in the Football League by Third Division North side, Wrexham, and did enough to be handed a professional contract by the 'Robins' at the end of September 1938. Playing at inside-forward he made his Football League debut for the club against New Brighton in a 2-1 home defeat, and Albert marked the occasion by scoring the 'Robins' goal. He began to fulfil his potential during 1938/39, but his career at the Racecourse came to an abrupt halt with the outbreak of the Second World War. He had played in the opening two games of the 1939/40 season, scoring in the first match, a 2-0 home win over New Brighton. However, he left Wrexham immediately following the start of the conflict, and returned home to his native South Wales.

Season	League		F.A.Cup		Welsh Cup		N.S.C.		Total	
	apps	gls	apps	gls	apps	gls	apps	gls	apps	gls
1938/39	29	11	1	0	1	0	1	2	32	13
1939/40	2	1	-	-	-	-	-	-	2	1*
	29	**11**	**1**	**0**	**1**	**0**	**1**	**2**	**32**	**13**

* Deleted from the records.

NICOLL, Paul — 1984 - 1985

Position; *Midfield*
D.O.B; *10th November, 1966*
Birthplace; *Chester, Cheshire*
Height; *ft in* **Weight;** *st lbs*
Debut; v. *Port Vale (h) 1st September, 1984*
Total Appearances & Goals; *1/1 apps 0 gls*
Career; *WREXHAM Jul 1984; Porthmadog Aug 1985;*

Paul Nicoll was a promising apprentice who had signed for Wrexham from Schools football in the Ellesmere Port area in 1983. He was only half way through his apprenticeship when he was called upon to make his Football League debut for the club in September 1984, coming on as a substitute for Dave Gregory in a 1-1 home draw with Port Vale. Three days later Paul was to start his first senior game, in the second leg of a Milk Cup First Round tie at Wigan Athletic, which Wrexham lost 2-0. It proved to be Paul's last senior appearance for the Racecourse club because he was released at the end of the 1984/85 season, whereupon he joined Porthmadog in August 1985.

Season	League		F.A.Cup		Welsh Cup		League Cup		F.R.T.		E.C.W.C.		Total	
	apps	gls	apps	gls	apps	gls	apps	gls	apps	gls	apps	gls	apps	gls
1984/85	0/1	0	-	-	-	-	1	0	-	-	-	-	1/1	0
	0/1	**0**	-	-	-	-	**1**	**0**	-	-	-	-	**1/1**	**0**

NIEDZWIECKI, Andzej Edward — 1976 - 1983

Position; *Goalkeeper*
D.O.B; *3rd May, 1959*
Birthplace; *Bangor, Gwynedd*
Height; *6ft 0ins* **Weight;** *11st 0lbs*
Debut; v. *Oxford United (h) 22nd August, 1977*
Total Appearances & Goals; *141 apps 0 gls*
Career; *WREXHAM Jul 1976; Chelsea 25th Jun 1983 £45,000 136apps 0gls;*
Honours; *Two Full Welsh International caps; Six Welsh Youth International caps; Three Welsh Schoolboy Caps; Second Division Championship Winner 1984; Third Division Championship Winner 1978; Welsh Cup runner-up 1979 & 1983;*

With a name like Niedzwiecki you could be forgiven for thinking that Eddie came from some far-flung Eastern European country. This popular Welshman actually hails from Bangor in Gwynedd, although his father originated from Poland. Eddie began playing football at the Stella Marie Primary School in Llandudno, appearing in the unfamiliar position of centre-half. He was selected for the same Llandudno Primary Schools team as Neville Southall, later going on to Aberconwy Secondary School - by which time he had reverted to his more accustomed goalkeeping position - and from where he was chosen for the Welsh Schoolboys side. A host of Football League clubs began to track the progress of the

promising 'keeper, but it was Wrexham who signed him as a 14 year-old schoolboy. He completed apprentice forms upon leaving school in July 1975, and not long after that won the first of his six Welsh Youth caps. A year later, in July 1976, Eddie signed professional forms for the Racecourse club and made his Football League debut in August 1977, replacing the out of favour Brian Lloyd in a 2-2 home draw with Oxford United. He was involved in the following five League games before manager Arfon Griffiths signed another Welsh international goalkeeper from Everton, Dai Davies. When Dai suffered a broken finger Eddie took over again in March for a number of matches, including the F.A.Cup Quarter-Final with Arsenal. He played his part in helping Wrexham to win the Third Division championship, which meant Second Division football at the Racecourse for the first time in the Club's history. Over the next three seasons life proved frustrating for Eddie, as Dai Davies' consistent form limited him to just twelve more outings. In the summer of 1981 Davies joined Swansea, and his patience was finally rewarded as he took over the green jersey and become a regular in the side for the next two years. He was in sparkling form during this period, and was 'noted for his courage, clean handling and massive goal-kicks', but unable to prevent the Club's slide from the Second to the Fourth Division in successive years. At the end of the 1982/83 season former Wrexham manager John Neal paid out a bargain £45,000 to take Eddie to Chelsea. He went straight into the first team, replacing Steve Francis, and remained an ever-present in a side that also included two of his best mates from the North Wales Coast, Joey Jones and Mickey Thomas. Chelsea won the Second Division Championship in his first season at Stamford Bridge, and he remained a fixture in the side for the next two season's, gaining international recognition earning caps twice for Wales, against Norway and Denmark. Throughout this period he received coaching from former England international Peter Bonetti. However, tragedy was just around the corner, as he sustained a knee injury against Q.P.R. in March 1986 that was ultimately to end his playing career in May 1988, following a two year fight to regain his fitness as he underwent five operations on his knee. During this time he was kept involved in the game by coaching the youth and reserve teams at Stamford Bridge. He finally lost his battle against the injury, but was then appointed youth team coach at Chelsea. In 1990 he left London to join Reading as assistant to his former Chelsea manager, Ian Porterfield. He was appointed caretaker-manager at Elm Park in April 1991, following Porterfield's dismissal, despite the fact that he had also been shown the door at the same time! However, he worked out his notice, and was then given the opportunity to return to Chelsea as reserve team and specialist goalkeeping coach. He worked under both Glenn Hoddle and Ruud Gullit at Stamford Bridge, and still remains on the coaching staff under Gianluca Vialli. Since his playing days have ended he has become a very accomplished media summariser of the game. Commenting on BBC Wales TV and radio at Welsh international matches, his views are widely respected as both intelligent and authoritative. Often Eddie has appeared on B.B.C. Wales in english while at the same match his mentor Dai Davies has been employed in a similar capacity in Welsh on S.4.C. The Welsh Media is in safe hands!!

Season	League		F.A.Cup		Welsh Cup		League Cup		E.C.W.C.		Total	
	apps	gls	apps	gls	apps	gls	apps	gls	apps	gls	apps	gls
1977/78	15	0	1	0	1	0	1	0	-	-	18	0
1978/79	6	0	-	-	2	0	-	-	-	-	8	0
1979/80	6	0	-	-	-	-	2	0	-	-	8	0
1980/8	-	-	-	-	1	0	-	-	-	-	1	0
1981/82	42	0	4	0	3	0	5	0	-	-	54	0
1982/83	42	0	2	0	6	0	2	0	-	-	52	0
	111	**0**	**7**	**0**	**13**	**0**	**10**	**0**	**0**	**0**	**141**	**0**

NOCK, Jack

1924 - 1926

Position; *Inside-Left*
D.O.B; *c1900*
Birthplace; *Halesowen, West Midlands*
Height; *5ft 9'1/2in* ***Weight;*** *11st 7lbs*
League Debut; v. *Walsall (h) 15th November, 1924*
Total Appearances & Goals; *73 apps 25 gls*
Career; *Stourbridge; Millwall Oct 1915; Leicester Fosse 1919; Merthyr Town 27th May 1919; Nuneaton Town; Tamworth Castle; Cradley Heath; Cardiff City 31st Mar 1922 2apps 0gls; WREXHAM 14th Nov 1924; Flint Town United 21st Jan 1927; Oswestry Town 11th Apr 1928;*
Honours; *Welsh Cup Winner 1924;*

Jack Nock was signed by Millwall from Stourbridge during the Great War, in October 1915. He spent three seasons with the Lions during the conflict, making 54 appearances and scoring 25 goals, but he joined Leicester Fosse after the cease-fire, appearing in their last eleven regional matches. He had the distinction of scoring the last ever goal for 'Fosse', in a 1-1 friendly draw against a BEF (France) XI, before they became known as Leicester City. Even so, Jack failed to gain a contract with Leicester and signed for Merthyr Town during the summer of 1919. He eventually moved on to spend some time at Nuneaton Town, Tamworth Castle, and Cradley Heath, before joining First Division Cardiff City in March 1922. He made his debut the following month in a 1-1 home draw with Sheffield United, and went on to spend eighteen months with the 'Bluebirds', making just three League and Cup appearances and scoring one goal in a 7-0 Welsh Cup win over Rhymney. In November 1924 Nock and his fellow reserve forward, Jimmy Jones, both accepted a transfer to Third Division North side Wrexham. They were signed by Charlie Hewitt who had just been appointed as the 'Robins' first ever team manager. Jack made his debut in a 1-1 home draw with Walsall, playing in his usual inside-left position. His first goals for the 'Robins' came in the following home game against Durham City, scoring twice in a 3-1 win. He continued in the position until the end of the season, by which time he had notched a total of ten league goals. He also collected a Welsh Cup winners' medal following a 3-1 victory against Flint Town in the Final. Nock established himself as a regular in the senior side throughout the following campaign, and contributed a further twelve League goals. He left the Racecourse at the end of 1925/26 following manager Charlie Hewitt's departure. In January 1927 Jack signed for Flint Town, who were then managed by Hewitt. He remained a little over a season before signing for Oswestry Town in April 1928.

Season	League		F.A.Cup		Welsh Cup		Total	
	apps	gls	apps	gls	apps	gls	apps	gls
1924/25	25	10	1	0	3	1	29	11
1925/26	40	12	1	0	3	2	44	14
	65	**22**	**2**	**0**	**6**	**3**	**73**	**25**

NORTHAM, Cyril George

1920 - 1922

Position; *Outside-Right/Centre-Forward*
D.O.B; *O/N/D 1894*
Birthplace; *Hendon, North London*
Height; *ft in* ***Weight;*** *st lbs*
Debut; v. *Durham City (h) 7th January, 1921*
Total Appearances & Goals; *16 apps 4 gls*
Career; *Dulwich Hamlet; WREXHAM (Am) Jul 1920; Connah's Quay & Shotton FC; Dulwich Hamlet; WREXHAM (Am) Aug 1921, (Pro) 18th Jan 1922; Connah's Quay & Shotton FC cs1923; Whitchurch Oct 1924;*

Cyril Northam was a 'sprightly winger' who first signed for Birmingham & District League Wrexham from Dulwich Hamlet in July 1920. He failed to make an impression, and joined Cheshire County League side Connah's Quay & Shotton FC. On rejoining Wrexham in January 1922 he went straight into the first team for his Football League debut, a 3-1 home win over Durham City, and celebrated by scoring with what was described in the local press as a 'brilliant goal'. It was also stated at the time that he 'had inspired with his skill, speed and great intelligence, and was instrumental in the 3-1 win'. Cyril kept his place in the side until the end of the season, when he was disappointingly released. He then re-joined Connah's Quay & Shotton FC, later moving on to Shropshire side Whitchurch. In the summer of 1939 Cyril was President of Connah's Quay Albion Football Club, when described as a player formerly with 'Buckley United, Connah's Quay and Wrexham'.

Season	League		F.A.Cup		Welsh Cup		Total	
	apps	gls	apps	gls	apps	gls	apps	gls
1921/22	16	4	-	-	-	-	16	4
	16	**4**	**-**	**-**	**-**	**-**	**16**	**4**

O'GORMAN, David John 1990 - 1991

Position; *Forward*
D.O.B; *20th June, 1972*
Birthplace; *Chester, Cheshire*
Height; *5ft 8in* **Weight;** *11st 12lbs*
Debut; v. *Northampton Town (a) 9th November, 1990*
Total Appearances & Goals; *8/9 apps 0 gls*
Career; *WREXHAM Jul 1990; Northwich Victoria (Loan) 4th Dec 1990 3apps 2gls, Jul 1991 7/1apps 2gls; Hyde United cs1992; Connah's Quay Nomads Oct 1992 78/2apps 51gls; Barry Town Jun 1995 36/35apps 18gls; Swansea City 8th Aug 1997 £30,000 13/26apps 5gls; Connah's Quay Feb 1999 8apps 4gls; Hellenic (South Africa) Jun 1999;*
Honours; *League Of Wales Championship Winner 1996 & 1997; Welsh Cup Winner 1997; Welsh Cup runner-up 1996; Welsh Youth Cup runner-up 1989; North Wales Coast F.A. representative XI;*

Dave O'Gorman joined Wrexham as a junior, and progressed through Brian Flynn's revitalised youth policy to sign professional forms for the club in July 1990. He made his Football League debut soon after he had agreed terms, in November 1990, appearing as a substitute for Andy Preece in a 1-0 defeat at Northampton. Dave managed a further 22 first team appearances before the end of 1990/91, half of which were as substitute. Playing as a striker, he found the target just once that season, in a 5-0 victory at Ammanford in the Welsh Cup. In December 1990 he took up an offer of a loan move to Conference League side Northwich Victoria, where he scored twice in three games before returning to the Racecourse. Following that loan spell he was to feature more regularly in the 'Robins' first team, but even so he was still released at the end of the season. He rejoined Northwich Victoria on a permanent basis, accumulating just eight appearances and scoring two before leaving the Drill Field at the end of the campaign. He then joined Hyde United for a short spell, returning to North Wales in October 1992 to link up with League of Wales side Connah's Quay Nomads. Dave became a prolific goalscorer with the 'Quaymen' , assisting them into the semi-finals of the Welsh Cup in 1993, where they lost to Rhyl over two legs. Described at the Halfway Ground as 'small in stature, with tremendous pace, and a lethal shot' he earned representative honours in the summer of 1994, turning out for the North Wales Coast F.A. against the Scottish Juniors XI at Holywell in their centenary year. He returned to the Racecourse with the 'Quaymen' in December 1994 for a Welsh Cup match, which Wrexham won 4-0. Before the end of the season 'The Deesiders' had turned down a five figure bid for his services from Bangor City, although he eventually left the 'Nomads' when former Wrexham player, Eddie May, obtained his signature for Barry Town, who had just announced they would become the first League of Wales side to turn full-time professional. O'Gorman enjoyed considerable success at Jenner Park, twice winning the League of Wales Championship in 1996 and 1997. Although conceding the 1996 Welsh Cup Final to Llansantffraid on penalties, they were back at the National Stadium a year later and this time lifted the trophy following a victory over Cwmbran Town. That same season had seen Dave play for Barry in their impressive UEFA Cup run that was to end following a defeat at the hands of Scottish Premier League side, Aberdeen, after a great fight. 1997/98 again saw European participation, when the South Wales club played Dinamo Kiev in a preliminary round game. However, the day before the League season was to begin Barry accepted a joint bid of £25.000 from Third Division Swansea City for O'Gorman and Tony Bird. Dave made his Football League debut for the 'Swans' the following day in a 1-0 win over Brighton & Hove Albion, but he was to spend most of the season on the substitute's bench. O'Gorman became less involved with the Vetch Field set up the following season and Manager John Hollins released him from his Contract in February 1999 when he rejoined former club Connahs Quay Nomads, who beat off competition from Bangor City and Southport among others. Dave decided to try his luck in South Africa during the close season of 99 and joined Hellenic F.C.

Season	League		F.A.Cup		Welsh Cup		League Cup		A.G.T.		E.C.W.C.		Total	
	apps	gls	apps	gls	apps	gls	apps	gls	apps	gls	apps	gls	apps	gls
1990/91	8/9	0	1	0	1/3	1	-	-	1	0	-	-	11/12	1
	8/9	**0**	**1**	**0**	**1/3**	**1**	**-**	**-**	**1**	**0**	**-**	**-**	**11/12**	**1**

O'KEEFE, James Vincent 1989 - 1992

Position; *Goalkeeper*
D.O.B; *2nd April, 1957*
Birthplace; *Coleshill, Warwickshire*
Height; *6ft 2in* **Weight;** *13st 0lbs*
Debut; v. *Scarborough (a) 19th August, 1989*
Total Appearances & Goals; *108 apps 0 gls*
Career; *Paget Rangers; Birmingham City Jul 1975 0apps; Peterborough United 11th Mar 1976 (Loan) 0apps; Walsall Jul 1976 0apps; AP Leamington 1977; Exeter City Jun 1978 £3,000 53apps 0gls; Torquay United 29th Feb 1980 £25,000 108apps 0gls; Blackburn Rovers Aug 1982 £30,000 68apps 0gls; Bury Oct 1983 2apps 0gls (Loan); Blackpool Dec 1986 1app 0gls (Loan); Blackpool 17th Feb 1989 6apps 0gls (Loan); WREXHAM Jul 1989; Exeter City Aug 1992 2apps 0gls; Chorley 1992/93;*
Honours; *Full Members' Cup Winner 1987; Welsh Cup runner-up 1990; England Semi-Professional International cap;*

Vince O'Keefe began playing competitive football at Perry Common School in Erdington, Birmingham. With Pat Jennings his boyhood idol he naturally wanted to become a goalkeeper himself, and earned selection for his school as well as for teams Erdington & Saltley District, Birmingham, and Warwickshire Boys. He attended trials for the England under-19s when only sixteen, though by this time had already appeared for Paget Rangers in the Midland Combination League at 14! He was still playing for them when he left school, doing enough to impress West Bromwich Albion, who were on the verge of signing him when he picked up an injury to his knee that resulted in a cartilage operation. Once fit, Birmingham City began to show an interest in the promising young 'keeper, and he signed professional terms in July 1975 at the age of 17. Vince was to encounter stiff opposition for a first team place over the next two seasons, as the 'Blues' had six keepers on their books, and in March 1976 he accepted a loan deal with Peterborough United until the end of the season. He failed to make a senior appearance whilst at London Road, and, following his release from St.Andrew's in the summer, joined Walsall, as understudy to Mick Kearns - the brother of former Wrexham player, Ollie Kearns. Vince had to be content with reserve team football once again failing to make a single first team appearance, and left Fellows Park in 1977 totally disillusioned. He then obtained employment at the Rover factory, making car parts, while continuing to play football for Southern League side AP Leamington. His performances soon began to attract the attention of a number of Football League Clubs, and was called up into the England semi-pro team. This sort of form earned him the AP Leamington fans 'Player of the Season' award in 1977/78. It also convinced Exeter City boss, Bobby Saxton, who obtained his signature in June 1978 for a £3,000 fee. Vince finally made his Football League debut in the opening match of 1978/79 season, a scoreless draw with Mansfield Town at St.James' Park, but disaster was to strike in December when he broke a finger in four places. Having recovered he struggled to win back his first team place, and in February 1980 accepted a move to Torquay United for a Club record fee of £25,000. At Plainmoor he became a firm favourite with the 'Gulls' fans, twice winning the 'Player of the Season' award, and, after some impressive performances, his former manager Bobby Saxton returned to sign him for Second Division Blackburn Rovers for a £30,000 fee in August 1982. At Ewood Park, he vied for the first team 'keeper's shirt with Terry Gennoe. Although never enjoying the same popularity as Gennoe he was involved in the 1987 Full Members' Cup Final at Wembley, where a splendid performance earned him the 'Man of the Match' award in a 1-0 win over Charlton Athletic. The 1987/88 season saw Vince become the regular 'keeper at Blackburn, and was on the verge of international honours with the Republic of Ireland, qualification coming through his Irish-born parents, when disaster struck again as he broke his leg in a fifty-fifty challenge with Jason Dozzell of Ipswich Town. 1988/89 saw him make just two League appearances for Blackburn, and in February 1989 he moved to Blackpool for a second loan period; the first, in December 1986 had seen him make just one appearance for the 'Seasiders'; while this latest spell saw him play in six League games. With his contract up at the end of the season he decided to look elsewhere for first team football, despite an offer of an extended contract

with Blackburn. He received offers from Bury, Blackpool, Peterborough United, and Wrexham, who at that time had just lost the services of Mike Salmon to Charlton. Vince was more than happy to sign for the North Wales club. It took him a while to win over the fans at the Racecourse, with the Club struggling after having just missed out on promotion at the end of the previous season via the play-offs. He did however, help the Club to reach the first Welsh Cup Final to be played at the National Stadium in Cardiff, although finishing on the losing side. Despite the 2-1 defeat, the 'Robins' did qualify for Europe, as winners Hereford were an English club. This ultimately proved to be Vince's undoing as though he began the following season as the Club's regular 'keeper, Mark Morris stepped in for the European games to comply with the 'Four Foreigners' rule, and then did well enough to keep his place in the side. The 1991/92 season saw O'Keefe reinstated as the club's first choice 'keeper, and enjoyed considerable success in the F.A.Cup as Wrexham beat the Football League Champions Arsenal, 2-1, on the Racecourse, and took West Ham United to a replay. He decided to leave Wrexham at the end of the season, and to take up a job with the P.F.A. as a Financial Executive. He had acquired the necessary qualifications during his spare time with Wrexham. He remains on the payroll of the P.F.A. to this day, combining his role as a sponsors host at Blackburn Rovers on match days. After he left Wrexham Vince did help out at Exeter City for a couple of games during the 1992/93 season, and also played a few games for Chorley that same season. He plays for Blackburn Rovers Veterans XI and appeared in the Final of the Umbro Professional Cup against Inter-Wales (Cardiff) in May 97.

Season	League		F.A.Cup		Welsh Cup		League Cup		F.RT.		E.C.W.C.		Total	
	apps	gls	apps	gls	apps	gls	apps	gls	apps	gls	apps	gls	apps	gls
1989/90	43	0	-	-	7	0	2	0	2	0	-	-	54	0
1990/91	6	0	-	-	-	-	3	0	-	-	-	-	9	0
1991/92	34	0	4	0	2	0	2	0	3	0	-	-	45	0
	83	**0**	**4**	**0**	**9**	**0**	**7**	**0**	**5**	**0**	**-**	**-**	**108**	**0**

ODELL, Walter Reginald 1937 - 1939

Position; *Left-Half*
D.O.B; *19th March, 1912*
Birthplace; *Biggleswade, Bedfordshire*
Died; *Bedford, 27th July, 1971*
Height; *5ft 8in* ***Weight;*** *11st 7lbs*
Debut; v. *Lincoln City (h) 1st September, 1937*
Total Appearances & Goals; *68 apps 0gls*
Career; *Sandy Albion 1927; Biggleswade 1929; Hitchin Town 1931; Tottenham Hotspur Jun 1935 0apps; WREXHAM 26th Jun 1937; Darlington Jul 1939; Tottenham Hotspur (WW2 Guest) 1940; Clapton Orient (WW2) 1941 70apps 14gls;*
Honours; *Spartan League Premier Division Championship Winner 1935; Southern Counties Amateur Cup Winner 1935;*

As a Schoolboy Walter Odell began playing football in Caldecote, appearing as a centre-forward and captaining his school team. At the age of 15 he played for Sandy Albion in the Bedford League as an inside-forward, until joining Biggleswade in 1929 which lasted two seasons, switching to Hitchin Town in 1931. He played mostly for their reserve XI until fate intervened to launch his career during 1932/33. He was involved in an F.A. Amateur Cup match at Slough, when an injury to a team mate forced a switch to left-half. He impressed in his new role, and never looked back, soon becoming a regular member of the side. Before the end of the season he was selected for the Hertfordshire County side, while the 1934/35 campaign was a memorable one when capped by Hertfordshire winning the Southern Counties Amateur Championship, beating Somerset 5-0 in the Final at Hitchin. He collected a Spartan League Premier Division Championship with Hitchin Town, and enjoyed several cup successes in the Hertfordshire Senior Cup. Tottenham Hotspur soon took an interest, and signed him on professional forms, with a condition that he could remain with the non-league side until the end of the season. In June 1935 he moved to North London, but his first season at Tottenham was spent playing for Northfleet, a Spurs nursery club at the time. The following year he was based at White Hart Lane, turning out for Spurs' second string. Wally failed to make an impression at Tottenham, however, and in June 1937 was transferred to Third Division North side Wrexham. He was one of five Football League debutants for the 'Robins' in their 1-0 home win over Lincoln City in the second game of the 1937/38 season. Odell went on to enjoy two years with the Racecourse club, missing only a couple of matches in his first term, while his second year saw him lose his place in the side mid-way through the season following Robert Savage's arrival from Manchester United. George Snow was preferred at left-half, with Savage alongside him at right-half. At the end of the season Wally was transferred to Darlington, making three League appearances before football was suspended upon the outbreak of the Second World War. He returned home to the Biggleswade area, turning out for Spurs reserves during the War, and as a 'guest' for Clapton Orient during 1941/42. Upon his retirement from League football he became trainer-coach to Letchworth Town, for three seasons. The club were not particularly successful during this period, but they did have their longest run in the F.A.Amateur Cup. Owing to the increasing pressure of his work, as manager of the Ye Olde George Inn at Ickleford, Wally resigned from his position with Letchworth. The love of the game soon lured him back however and in the close season of 1951, became part/time trainer/coach of Hitchin Town.

Season	League		F.A.Cup		Welsh Cup		N.S.C.		Total	
	apps	gls	apps	gls	apps	gls	apps	gls	apps	gls
1937/38	40	0	2	0	1	0	1	0	44	0
1938/39	21	0	1	0	1	0	1	0	24	0
	61	**0**	**3**	**0**	**2**	**0**	**2**	**0**	**68**	**0**

OGHANI, George William 1987

Position; *Forward*
D.O.B; *2nd September, 1960*
Birthplace; *Manchester, Lancashire*
Height; *5ft 11in* ***Weight;*** *12st 1lbs*
Debut; v. *Orient (h) 14th March, 1987*
Appearances; *6/1 apps 0 gls*
Career; *Sheffield United 0apps; Bury Feb 1978 0apps; Hyde United; Bolton Wanderers Oct 1983 £5,000 86/13apps 27gls; WREXHAM 12th Mar 1987 (Loan); Burnley 24th June 1987 73/1apps 21gls; Stockport County June 1989 5/3apps 2gls; Hereford United Oct 1989 7/1apps 2gls; Hyde United Dec 1989; Scarborough Feb 1990 43/7apps 18gls; Evagoras (Cyprus) 1991; Carlisle United Aug 1992 45/8apps 15gls; Northwich Victoria May 1994 31/29apps 13gls; Guiseley 1996/97 (Loan);*
Honours; *Freight Rover Trophy runner-up 1986; Sherpa Van Trophy runner-up 1988; Cheshire County League Championship Winner 1982; Cheshire County League Cup Winner 1982;*

George Oghani was signed by Sheffield United as a junior, only to be released upon completion of his apprenticeship. He joined Bury in February 1978, but was discarded before the end of the season without making a first team appearance. George then dropped into non-league football with Cheshire County League side Hyde United, where they won the League and Cup double in 1982. He was also selected to play for the Cheshire County League Representative XI. By this time George had impressed a number of Football League sides, but it was Bolton Wanderers who were the first to sign him in October 1983 at the age of 21. He made his Football League debut for the 'Trotters' in January 1984, as a substitute for Wayne Foster in a 4-0 defeat at Wimbledon, and went on to make over 100 League and Cup appearances in his four years with the Burnden Park club. He also appeared at Wembley in the 1986 Freight Rover Trophy Final, as Bolton lost 3-0 to Bristol City. In March 1987 he joined Wrexham on loan, making his debut in a 1-1 home draw with Orient. Oghani played in the following six matches, before returning to Bolton, who suffered relegation to Division Four at the end of the season. He was subsequently released by the Lancashire club, joining Burnley in the summer of 1987. He spent two seasons at Turf Moor, finishing top scorer with 14 goals in his first season, and appearing at Wembley once again in the 1988 Sherpa Van Trophy Final, where the 'Clarets' lost 2-0 to Wolves. The following term George established himself as a regular in the Burnley side, but was released following a training ground incident in April 1989. In June he joined up with Stockport County, but by October was on the move again, this time joining Hereford United. After another short spell he re-joined Hyde United in December, but soon returned to the Football League in February 1990 with

Scarborough. He went on to make 50 League appearances for the North Yorkshire side, until going abroad in 1991 to play for Cypriot side Evagoras. He returned to join Carlisle United in the close season of 1992, and spent two years with the Cumbrians, entering the record books - along with Walsall's Rod McDonald - when they each scored for both teams in a Football League match! Upon leaving Brunton Park at the end of 1993/94 George joined Conference League side Northwich Victoria, but missed out on a third Wembley appearance in the 1996 F.A.Trophy Cup Final. He spent a period on loan with Guiseley during the following season before being released by the 'Vic's' in the summer of 1997.

Season	League		F.A.Cup		Welsh Cup		League Cup		F.R.T.		Total	
	apps	gls	apps	gls	apps	gls	apps	gls	apps	gls	apps	gls
1986/87	6/1	0	-	-	-	-	-	-	-	-	6/1	0
	6/1	**0**	**-**	**-**	**-**	**-**	**-**	**-**	**-**	**-**	**6/1**	**0**

OLDFIELD, Terence James 1966 - 1967

Position; *Wing-Half*
D.O.B; *1st April, 1939*
Birthplace; *Bristol, Avon*
Height; *5ft 10in* ***Weight;*** *11st 2lbs*
Debut; v. *Exeter City (h) 20th August, 1966*
Total Appearances & Goals; *47/1 apps 7 gls*
Career; *Bristol Boys; Bristol City; Clifton St.Vincents; Bristol Rovers Feb 1958 131/1apps 11gls; WREXHAM 5th Jul 1966; Bradford Park Avenue Aug 1967 (Trainer);*
Honours; *Welsh Cup runner-up 1967;*

Terry Oldfield showed plenty of promise as a youngster. He was selected to represent Bristol Boys, and it came as no surprise when signed by Bristol City upon leaving school. However, on completion of his apprenticeship at Ashton Gate he was released, whereupon he joined local amateur side Clifton St.Vincents. Terry was playing as a forward at the time, and eventually captured the attention of City's neighbours, Bristol Rovers, who signed him on amateur terms in February 1958. He signed professional forms a year later becoming a permanent fixture in the senior side throughout his eight years at Eastville. He made his Football League debut as a centre-forward in November 1960, a 2-0 defeat at Sunderland, but in the New Year of 1963 was switched to play at right-half, where he formed a formidable partnership with Ray Mabbutt (Gary's father). This was the season that a 'Bribery Scandal' erupted involving the Rovers 'keeper, Esmond Million and centre-forward Keith Williams, when the story was featured prominently in the national press. In fact, it was Terry and team-mate Alfie Biggs who had brought it to the attention of the Avon club's management, when they discovered that a bet had been placed on Bradford Park Avenue to beat Rovers in an end-of-season relegation match.

Terry went on to complete almost 150 League and Cup appearances for the 'Pirates', including an F.A.Cup tie at Old Trafford against Manchester United in January 1964, which Rovers lost 4-1. He was allowed to join Fourth Division side Wrexham in the summer of 1966, where manager Jack Rowley immediately installed him as Club captain. He made his debut in the opening match of the 1966/67 season, a scoreless home draw with Exeter City, and became a regular member of the Wrexham defence, impressing with 'determination and skilful performances'. Jack Rowley and assistant Ken Roberts, both left the club in April 1967, and Oldfield was appointed as temporary assistant-manager to Cliff Lloyd. Unfortunately, tragedy was not far away, as he received an horrific knee injury in the second leg of the Welsh Cup Final against Cardiff City at Ninian Park, and was so serious that it put an end to his playing career. His former manager, Jack Rowley, then invited Terry to join him at Bradford Park Avenue as first team trainer in September 1967, and he accepted. He eventually returned to settle in his native Bristol, becoming a scout for Bristol Rovers, as well as working as an estate agent and auctioneer in Keynsham. Oldfield also managed his former amateur club Clifton St.Vincents for a spell, later running the Red Lion Public House at Odd Down, Bath, and in recent years has been working as a taxi driver in the Bedminster Down area of Bristol. Throughout his football career Terry always enjoyed a game of cricket during the summer recess, and this continued after his playing days were over, as he represented Brislington for many years. He was also a keen member of Saltford Golf Club.

Season	League		F.A.Cup		Welsh Cup		League Cup		Total	
	apps	gls	apps	gls	apps	gls	apps	gls	apps	gls
1966/67	39/1	6	2	1	5	0	1	0	47/1	7
	39/1	**6**	**2**	**1**	**5**	**0**	**1**	**0**	**47/1**	**7**

OUCHTERLONIE, William Wood Mitchell 1937 - 1938

Position; *Centre-Forward*
D.O.B; *29th November, 1912*
Birthplace; *Dundee, Tayside*
Height; *5ft 8in* ***Weight;*** *11st 7lbs*
Debut; v. *Lincoln City (h) 1st September, 1937*
Total Appearances & Goals; *3 apps 0 gls*
Career; *Dundee Osborne FC; Raith Rovers (Trial) Mar 1932; Dundee United Sept 1932 51apps 40gls; Raith Rovers cs1934; Reds United (Dublin) cs1935; Barrow Aug 1936 32apps 22gls; WREXHAM 23rd Jun 1937;*

Willie Ouchterlonie was playing for his local side Dundee Osborne when taken on trial by Raith Rovers in March 1932. Although nothing came of it, the Kirkcaldy side's loss became Dundee United's gain as they took him on in September 1932, and repaid their faith in him by scoring fifteen goals in 22 League games during his first season. He continued to find the net on a regular basis throughout the following campaign, scoring 25 goals in 29 League games, including 'going nap' in a 9-3 win over Edinburgh City in November 1933. Despite his prolific goalscoring record for the 'Tangerines' Willie was transferred to Raith Rovers in the summer of 1934. He spent a year at Stark's Park before moving on to Dublin side Reds United, where he returned a twenty goal haul during 1935/36. His goalscoring prowess soon attracted the attention of Football League sides, and Third Division North side Barrow obtained his signature in August 1936. In his time at Holker Street he hit the target 22 times in just 32 League games, but was allowed to leave in the summer of 1937 when he was persuaded to join Wrexham's former Raith manager Captain James Logan. Willie found it difficult to hold down a regular first team place at the Racecourse, with Harold Lapham playing consistently well at centre-forward. He made his bow for the 'Robins', along with four other debutants, in the first home game of the new campaign, a 1-0 home win over Lincoln City. However, he was to make just two more League appearances that season. It is believed that he then returned to Scotland, where he played for Scottish Junior side Lochee Harp. During his time with them he was selected to represent the Scottish Junior League XI against the North Wales Coast F.A. at Llandudno in March 1939.

Season	League		F.A.Cup		Welsh Cup		N.S.C.		Total	
	apps	gls	apps	gls	apps	gls	apps	gls	apps	gls
1937/38	3	0	-	-	-	-	-	-	3	0
	3	**0**	**-**	**-**	**-**	**-**	**-**	**-**	**3**	**0**

OWEN, Aled Watkin 1963 - 1964

Position; *Outside-Left*
D.O.B; *7th January, 1934*
Birthplace; *Caeysegamen, Ynys Mon*
Height; *5ft 7in* ***Weight;*** *10st 11lbs*
Debut; v. *Southend United (h) 31st August, 1963*
Total Appearances & Goals; *3 apps 0 gls*
Career; *Bangor City 1951; Tottenham Hotspur Sept 1953 1app 0gls; Ipswich Town Jul 1958 30apps 3gls; WREXHAM 29th Jun 1963 £3,000; Holyhead Town 19th Aug 1964; Bethesda Athletic 14th Jul 1965; Penmaenmawr 3rd Sept 1966;*

Born and bred on the island of Anglesey (Ynys Mon) Aled Owen played for his school teams at Tynygongl and Llangefni, from where he was chosen to represent Anglesey Schoolboys. After completing his education he took

up work as an apprentice fitter with 'Saunders Roe' in Beaumaris, where he was spotted playing football during his lunch breaks. He was then invited to join Bangor City, who were a Cheshire County League outfit at that time. He spent almost three years at Farrar Road, before a Tottenham Hotspur scout - Maldwyn Roberts of Caernarfon - recommended him for trials. Aled impressed sufficiently to be signed by the London Club in September 1953, making his 'Spurs' debut a few days later in an annual friendly with Scottish League side Hibernian at Easter Road. It was not until the following May before he made his Football League debut, against Preston North End, and they beat 'Spurs' 6-2! It proved to be Aled's one and only League match for Tottenham, as he was then called up for his two years' National Service, which no doubt interrupted his progress. Owen left White Hart Lane in July 1958 after almost five years of reserve team football, to join his former Tottenham team mate, Alf Ramsey, who was by then manager at Ipswich Town. A fee of £2,000 was paid for his services and he enjoyed a lengthy stay at Portman Road, making thirty League appearances in five years. Although never a regular with the Suffolk club he was still a valuable member of the first team squad, and toured both Germany and Denmark as well as sampling European Cup action against Floriana of Malta. He made one appearance in Ipswich's Championship season of 1962, but was allowed to leave Portman Road in July 1963. Both Lincoln City and Wrexham showed an interest, but chose Wrexham so that he could move nearer to his home. He joined the 'Robins' for a fee of around £2,000, and made his League debut in a disappointing 3-1 home defeat by Southend United in August 1963. Further disappointment in the following match against Watford saw Aled fall out of favour. He found it hard to adapt to Third Division football, and left the Racecourse in May 1964, by 'mutual agreement' to help with the running of his family business back in Anglesey. Aled did play briefly for Welsh League sides Holyhead Town, Bethesda Athletic, and Penmaenmawr before finally hanging up his boots. He then concentrated on the haulage business that he still runs today on the island. He is also a keen chorister, and during his football career he would often entertain his fellow team-mates with his singing before and after matches. Aled, who is the brother-in-law of the current Welsh under-21 management team of Ernie and Tom Walley, is a member of the 'Cor-Y-Traeth' and 'Colin Jones Cantorian Singers' who have often entertained abroad as well as all over Britain.

Season	League		F.A.Cup		Welsh Cup		League Cup		Total	
	apps	gls	apps	gls	apps	gls	apps	gls	apps	gls
1963/64	3	0	-	-	1	0	-	-	4	0
	3	**0**	**-**	**-**	**1**	**0**	**-**	**-**	**4**	**0**

OWEN, Gareth

1988 -

Position; *Midfielder*
D.O.B; *21st October, 1971*
Birthplace; *Chester, Cheshire*
Height; *5ft 9in* **Weight;** *11st 4lbs*
Debut; v. *Porthmadog (h) 25th October, 1989 (Welsh Cup)*
Total Appearances & Goals; *334/57 apps 36 gls*
Career; *WREXHAM Jul 1988, (Pro) 6th July 1990;*
Honours; *1 Wales 'B' international cap; 8 Wales under-21 International caps; Third Division Championship runner-up 1993; P.F.A. Third Division team 1993; Welsh Cup Winner 1995; Welsh Invitation Cup Winner 1998; Welsh Cup runner-up 1991; Welsh Youth Cup runner-up 1989; Welsh Premier Cup runner-up 1999;*

Gareth's father, Don Owen, had earned a Welsh Cup winners' medal with Flint Town United in their 1954 Final victory over Chester, and Owen Junior showed enough promise as a youngster to suggest that he would follow in his father's footsteps. He gained representative honours with Deeside Primary Schools, and was there spotted by Chester's Youth team coach, Cliff Sear. Gareth had played his early junior football for Buckley Hawarden Rangers, and in the Eastham League also representing both Flintshire and Clwyd Schoolboys. He had been at Sealand Road for almost four years as a schoolboy when former Welsh international Sear joined Wrexham as youth team coach, and invited Owen along with him. He was then offered YTS terms by the Racecourse club, as well as trials with Aston Villa, Everton, and West Brom, but it was his affinity to Sear that was to prove decisive, signing for Wrexham in the close season of 1988. It was the beginning of a long association with the Club that still exists to date. Gareth showed plenty of early promise, and manager Dixie McNeil gave him his first team opportunity in a Welsh Cup match at Porthmadog, coming on as substitute for Andy Thackeray in a 4-1 win. His next appearance came under the new managership of Brian Flynn, who brought Gareth in for his first game in charge, a Leyland DAF Cup match with Blackpool at the Racecourse. He was a revelation in the middle of the park, assisting Wrexham to a 1-0 win at a time that the side were really struggling. An injury in an F.A.Youth Cup tie against Manchester City sidelined him until March, but once re-established he confirmed his potential by being chosen as the March 'Barclays Young Eagle of the Month' for the Wales and West. At the start of the following season Gareth took something of a back seat, and didn't really feature in the side until the European Cup-Winners' Cup matches with Lyngby and Manchester United, when he played in all four games. This was followed by a call-up into the Welsh Under-21 squad, with whom he made his debut as a substitute against England in December 1990. It was to be the first of eight caps at this level. He then became a regular in the 'Robins' midfield until the end of that season, playing in the Welsh Cup Final defeat by Swansea as a substitute for Andy Thackeray. The 1991/92 season saw him thrown into the limelight once again, with tremendous performances in the Wrexham midfield against Arsenal in that famous 2-1 F.A.Cup victory, and especially in the following round against West Ham United. 1992/93 saw him play a major part in Wrexham's rise up the League, finishing runners-up, and his efforts were rewarded by selection for the P.F.A.'s Third Division team. The North Wales club's first season in Division Two would see Owen miss the start of the programme through injury, and it was much the same over the following two years as he was continually plagued by niggling injuries which also affected his form. Even so, he kept bouncing back, helping Wrexham beat Ipswich Town in the F.A.Cup to line up another meeting with his favourite 'other' team, Premier League Champions Manchester United, at Old Trafford. In May 1995 he collected a Welsh Cup winners' medal from a 2-1 victory over Cardiff City at the National Stadium in Cardiff. The next two seasons again saw him suffering with both injuries and loss of form, although called up to the full Welsh squad in October 1996 for a World Cup qualifying game with Holland. The preparations saw him playing for the National side in a warm up game at Rhyl. 1997/98 was to be Gareth's best ever, as he at last showed the consistency to go with his abundance of potential. The long passing game is just one of his forte's, while strong foraging in midfield is also a prominent feature of his play. He almost helped Wrexham to reach the play-offs just missing out on goals scored, and it was a campaign that saw him complete his most unusual game for the 'Robins'. An injury to goalkeeper Mark Cartwright at Burnley in February 1998, with the score at 1-1, saw Gareth pull on the gloves. All five feet nine of him! For over an hour he kept Burnley at bay, and so helped Wrexham to an important 2-1 win! He followed this by playing a major part in helping Wrexham to beat Cardiff City in the first ever final of the Welsh Invitation Cup. Gareth still remains an important member of the Wrexham team, and was rewarded for his loyalty to the 'Robins' with a testimonial which will extend into the year 2000. Wrexham F.C.'s Mr Millenium! Father Don was a prominent player in the haleyon days of the Welsh League North in the 50's and 60's and was a player very similar in style to his son with Connahs Quay Nomads and Flint T.U. Don Owen was also twice capped for the North Wales Coast F.A. against the Scottish Juniors.

Season	League		F.A.Cup		Welsh Cup		League Cup		A.G.T.		E.C.W.C.		Total	
	apps	gls	apps	gls	apps	gls	apps	gls	apps	gls	apps	gls	apps	gls
1989/90	8/5	0	0/1	0	1/1	1	-	-	1	0	-	-	0/7	1
1990/91	24/3	2	1	0	2/2	1	0/1	0	2	0	4	0	33/6	3
1991/92	33/3	7	5	0	2	0	1	0	5	0	-	-	46/3	7
1992/93	38/3	3	0/1	0	5	1	2	0	3	0	-	-	48/4	4
1993/94	24/3	3	2	0	1/1	0	-	-	1	0	-	-	27/4	3
1994/95	24/4	3	4	0	6	0	2	0	4	1	-	-	40/4	4
1995/96	11/8	2	-	-	-	-	1	0	0/1	0	2	0	14/9	2
1996/97	12/11	1	4/2	0	-	-	1	0	1	0	-	-	18/13	1
1997/98	36/3	7	4	0	5/2*	2*	-	-	1	0	-	-	46/5	9
1998/99	35	3	2/1	0	7*	0*	2	0	5/1	1	-	-	53/2	2
	245/43	**31**	**22/5**	**0**	**29/6**	**5**	**9/1**	**0**	**24/2**	**2**	**6**	**0**	**334/57**	**36**

* = Welsh Invitation/Premier Cup.

Bobby Park

PALMER, David Philip 1977 - 1979

Position; *Left-Back/Midfield*
D.O.B; *18th March 1962*
Birthplace; *New Cross, London*
Height; *5ft 8in* ***Weight;*** *10st 0lbs*
Debut; v. *Porthmadog (h) 18th December 1978 (Welsh Cup)*
Total Appearances & Goals; *0/1 apps 0 gls*
Career; *WREXHAM 1st Aug 1980; Bourne Town Mar 1981; Grantham Town Aug 1984; Three Bridges Aug 1986;*
Honours; *Welsh Youth Cup runner-up 1980;*

David Palmer joined the Wrexham groundstaff from Bourne in Lincolnshire upon leaving school in the summer of 1978. He was brought to the Racecourse by the club's Youth Development Officer at the time, Terry Bates, and progressed quickly enough to be considered as a substitute for a Welsh Cup match at Porthmadog in December 1978. Wrexham won the game 4-1, and the seventeen year-old made his first team debut when he replaced Joey Jones. That game proved to be his only first team appearance for the 'Robins', although in April 1980 played in the Welsh Youth Cup Final against Cardiff City, which Wrexham lost 2-1, with David scoring the Wrexham goal. He signed professional terms in the summer of 1980, but failed to make any further impression on the first team squad, and he was released by the Racecourse club in March 1981. Returning home to Lincolnshire, David joined Bourne Town, who were then managed by Terry Bates, the same man who had brought him to North Wales. He went on to spend over three seasons with Bourne, whilst taking up employment in Recreation and Leisure at a local Sports Centre. Palmer joined another Lincolnshire side, Grantham Town, in the close season of 1984, and spent a further two seasons with them before he was accepted as the Football Development Officer with Crawley Borough Council in 1986. He continued to play football for a short while for Sussex County League side Three Bridges, but he spent just one season with them before hanging up his boots to concentrate on his work. In 1991 David was taken on as the Regional Director for the P.F.A. for London and the south-east, which involves being the link between the P.F.A. and football clubs in that area. It's a job that he is still involved with at the time of writing, while he is now residing back in Bourne.

Season	League		F.A.Cup		Welsh Cup		League Cup		E.C.W.C.		Total	
	apps	gls	apps	gls	apps	gls	apps	gls	apps	gls	apps	gls
1978/79	-	-	-	-	0/1	0	-	-	-	-	0/1	0
	-	**-**	**-**	**-**	**0/1**	**0**	**-**	**-**	**-**	**-**	**0/1**	**0**

PARDEN, Bernard 1930 - 1932

Position; *Centre-Forward*
D.O.B; *14th April, 1907*
Birthplace; *Jump, Nr. Barnsley, Yorkshire*
Height; *5ft 8'1/2in* ***Weight;*** *11st 4lbs*
Debut; v. *Carlisle United (h) 11th October, 1930*
Total Appearances & Goals; *13 apps 9 gls*
Career; *Worksop; WREXHAM 11th May 1930; Rhyl 7th Jun 1932; Denaby United Sept 1934;*
Honours; *North Wales Coast F.A.Challenge Cup Winner 1933 & 1934;*

Bernard Parden scored 47 goals in 40 matches for Midland League side Worksop during the 1929/30 season. This kind of form soon attracted Football League clubs, with Wrexham being first to his signature in May 1930. Due to the prolific form of the club's regular centre-forward, Tommy Bamford, Bernard was forced to wait for his Football League debut until October, when he replaced Bamford in a 2-1 win against Carlisle United on the Racecourse. The game also saw him register his first goal for the club. Despite this early promise Parden remained as understudy to the great Bamford, making seven further appearances that season and notching four more goals. The following campaign was to see him complete just four League appearances, all in January, including a hat-trick in a 4-2 away win at Rochdale. He then returned to reserve team football in the Birmingham & District League when Bamford was fit again. However, he was allowed to leave the Racecourse club at the end of the season, and in July 1932 joined Rhyl for their inaugural season in the Birmingham & District League. Bernard went on to collect two North Wales Coast F.A.Challenge Cup winners' medals over the next two seasons at Belle Vue, before joining South Yorkshire non-league side Denaby United in September 1934.

Season	League		F.A.Cup		Welsh Cup		Total	
	apps	gls	apps	gls	apps	gls	apps	gls
1930/31	8	5	1	0	-	-	9	5
1931/32	4	4	-	-	-	-	4	4
	12	**9**	**1**	**0**	**-**	**-**	**13**	**9**

PARK, Robert Clydesdale 1969 - 1972

Position; *Midfielder*
D.O.B; *3rd July, 1946*
Birthplace; *Edinburgh, Lothian*
Height; *5ft 8in* ***Weight;*** *9st 8lbs*
Debut; v. *Exeter City (h) 9th August, 1969*
Total Appearances & Goals; *121/4 apps 8 gls*
Career; *Aston Villa Jul 1963 60/14apps 7gls; WREXHAM 5th May 1969; Peterborough United 6th Jun 1972 15/3apps 1gls; Northampton Town Feb 1973 21/3apps 0gls; Hartlepool United Jul 1974 14/3apps 0gls; Easington C.W.;*
Honours; *Division Four runner-up 1970; Welsh Cup runner-up 1971;*

Although born in Edinburgh Bobby Park's family moved to Peterlee in County Durham when he was still a young child. He went on to impress at schoolboy football, earning selection at 14 for East Durham Schoolboys in the English Schools Trophy, and appearing in the same side as Colin Bell, who later played for Manchester City and England. Around this time he signed schoolboy forms for Middlesbrough, but his football career stalled upon leaving school as the Ayresome Park club decided against offering him an apprenticeship. He took up work at Darlington wool firm, Paton & Baldwins, continuing to play for the works side in the local league. It was when playing for them that an employee of the company, who had connections at Villa Park, recommended him to Aston Villa, and he was subsequently invited for a two-week trial. At the end of the trial Park left the North-East and signed as an apprentice professional with Villa, making rapid progress before earning a Football League debut in September 1964 against Sheffield Wednesday in a 2-0 home win. A few days later he scored the only goal in a 1-0 League Cup victory over Luton Town. Bobby ended the season on a high note, scoring the winner in a 2-1 home win over Manchester United. Although never a regular with the 'Villains' he did make over eighty appearances, including the relegation season of 1966/67. Tommy Docherty's arrival as manager during 1968/69 saw the end of his Villa career and he was released in the summer. He was then recommended to Wrexham manager John Neal by former team-mate, Jimmy Dugdale, and went straight into the 'Robins' team for the opening match of the new season against Exeter City. In May of the following year he was celebrating the Club's successful promotion winning campaign as runners-up in Division Four. During this period he was involved in the Club's memorable cup matches against Manchester

United at Old Trafford, and Liverpool at Anfield. The following season he played in Wrexham's Welsh Cup Final defeat by Cardiff City, as the North Wales club consolidated their position in the Third Division. Mid-way through 1971/72, however, Bobby found himself out of favour, and was allowed to join Peterborough United on a free transfer in June. He couldn't settle at London Road, and within eight months was on the move again, joining Northampton Town. He stayed with the 'Cobblers' until the end of 1973/74, when returning to the North-East to join Hartlepool United for a season. He became player/manager of Easington C.W. in 1975, serving them for five years before accepting a position as assistant-manager at Peterlee Newtown, where he remained for ten years. After he had retired from professional football in 1975 he began working in the credit business, firstly as a traveller, before gaining promotion to area manager of a National company. Bobby, who is now settled in the North-East at Peterlee Newtown, left that job in 1993 to become General Manager of a family credit company in Sunderland.

Season	League		F.A.Cup		Welsh Cup		League Cup		Total	
	apps	gls	apps	gls	apps	gls	apps	gls	apps	gls
1969/70	37	3	4	0	2	0	4	0	47	3
1970/71	37/2	3	1	0	5	0	2	0	45/2	3
1971/72	24/2	2	2	0	-	-	3	0	29/2	2
	98/4	**8**	**7**	**0**	**7**	**0**	**9**	**0**	**121/4**	**8**

PARKER, Albert Edward 1951 - 1959

Position; *Full-Back*
D.O.B; *13th September 1927*
Birthplace; *Liverpool, Merseyside*
Height; *5ft 10'1/2in* ***Weight;*** *11st 12lbs*
Debut; v. *Darlington (a) 10th November, 1951*
Total Appearances & Goals; *248 apps 1 gls*
Career; *Everton; South Liverpool; Crewe Alexandra Dec 1948 111apps 0gls; WREXHAM 7th Nov 1951; Holywell Town 24th Jul 1959;*
Honours; *Welsh Cup Winner 1957 & 1958;*

Albert Parker is one of twelve children, eight girls and four boys. One of his brothers, David, was with Wolves prior to the Second World War. Albert attended Lander Road and Central Schools in Litherland, Liverpool, and it was here that he began to make a name for himself playing football for Litherland Youth Club. He was spotted by Everton, and eventually signed schoolboy forms for them. The outbreak of WW2 saw Albert's football career disrupted, like so many others, although he was too young to take part in the conflict himself. He did make some appearances for Everton's Schoolboy and Youth teams until the end of the hostilities. He had left school during WW2, taking up work as a Painter and Decorator for the Sanitary Paint Company in Liverpool. He was eventually released by Everton and began playing for South Liverpool, where he established himself as a 'tough tackling no-nonsense full-back'. His above average performances soon attracted the attention of a number of Football League clubs, and Third Division North side Crewe Alexandra were first to his signature in December 1948. Albert made his Football League debut for the Gresty Road club on 15th January 1949, in a 3-0 home win over Carlisle United, and went on to play in over a hundred League games for the 'Railwaymen'. He left the Cheshire club in November 1951, after three years at Gresty Road, following a disagreement with the club Chairman, and despite interest from both Chester and Reading he joined Wrexham. Parker was slotted straight into the side at right-back, in place of Les Speed, in a 2-1 defeat at Darlington. He managed another seven League outings that season before establishing himself in the side the following year. He then became installed as a regular for the next seven years, clocking up almost 250 appearances for the Denbighshire club, and scoring one goal! And what a memorable goal that was! Wrexham were playing Workington on the Racecourse on 1st October, 1952 when Albert received the ball in his right-back position. He noticed that the Workington goalkeeper was off his line, so he hit this shot from about seventy yards, and the ball skidded past the bemused 'keeper. 'The Robins' won the game 3-0. He earned two Welsh Cup winners' medals with Wrexham, beating Swansea Town in the 1957 Final, and Chester in the following year. Just before the game against Swansea Albert had played in his most memorable game for Wrexham against Manchester United, and the great 'Busby Babes', in an F.A.Cup tie on the Racecourse. It drew the biggest ever crowd assembled on the Ground, as the game ended in a 5-0 win for United. In 1957 Albert, along with Ron Hewitt, were awarded a benefit match against Coventry City. He remained with the 'Robins' until the end of 1958/59, when told that he was no longer required by manager John Love. He then joined Welsh League (North) side Holywell Town for just over a season. In December 1960 Parker returned to the Racecourse upon his appointment as the Club's new groundsman, spending four years working on the pitch before taking up employment with the council. Albert later stood as a candidate in the 1968 local elections for the Wat's Dyke ward. Having retired from playing he took up refereeing, and progressed through the Welsh Leagues, eventually becoming listed as a linesman with F.I.F.A. In 1970 he ran the line at the Inter-Cities Fairs Cup match between Athletico Bilbao and Sparta Prague in Spain. In 1977 Albert, a fine character, returned to the Racecourse to work as a turnstile operator, a job he enjoyed until the early 1990s, when he retired having settled in Wrexham.

Season	League		F.A.Cup		Welsh Cup		Total	
	apps	gls	apps	gls	apps	gls	apps	gls
1951/52	8	0	3	0	1	0	12	0
1952/53	34	1	2	0	1	0	37	1
1953/54	18	0	-	-	1	0	19	0
1954/55	23	0	2	0	4	0	29	0
1955/56	31	0	1	0	-	-	32	0
1956/57	40	0	7	0	5	0	52	0
1957/58	38	0	1	0	4	0	43	0
1958/59	24	0	-	-	-	-	24	0
	216	**1**	**16**	**0**	**16**	**0**	**248**	**1**

PARKER, Stuart Kevin 1981 - 1985

Position; *Goalkeeper*
D.O.B; *13th April, 1963*
Birthplace; *Nantwich, Cheshire*
Height; *6ft 1in* ***Weight;*** *12st 9lbs*
Debut; v. *Oswestry Town (a) 1st December, 1982 (Welsh Cup)*
Total Appearances & Goals; *51 apps 0 gls*
Career; *WREXHAM Aug 1981; Oswestry Town cs1985; Mold Alex 1986; Oswestry Town 1986/87; Brymbo Feb 1987; Lex XI; Brymbo cs1993;*
Honours; *Welsh Youth Cup Winner 1981; Welsh Youth Cup runner-up 1980;*

Stuart Parker played for Mid-Cheshire Schoolboys while attending school in Winsford, from where he wrote to Wrexham manager Arfon Griffiths asking for a trial. He was invited to join a Sunday morning practice game, and two years' later, in the summer of 1979, signed apprentice forms with the North Wales club. He progressed through the ranks at the Racecourse, collecting a Welsh Youth Cup winners' medal in 1981, having lost in the Final the previous year. He signed professional terms with the Racecourse club in August 1981, and went on to spend almost two years as understudy to first choice 'keeper, Eddie Niedzwiecki. He finally made his first team debut in December 1982 in a Welsh Cup tie against Oswestry

Town on the Racecourse, the home side running out 4-0 winners. His Football League debut came in the worst possible circumstances! It was the final match of the 1982/83 season at Reading, with Wrexham needing a victory to avoid relegation for the second successive season. Stuart was called into the side as Eddie Niedzwiecki was suspended but, despite his brave efforts, the 'Robins' lost 1-0. The close season saw Niedzwiecki join Chelsea, but manager Bobby Roberts was forced to bring in the experienced Bob Wardle on loan after Stuart was plagued with a mystery knee injury following the opening game of the 1983/84 season, a 3-0 defeat at Doncaster. The injury was to trouble him throughout the season, restricting him to just nine League games, and it meant that Roberts then had to recruit the experienced ex-Chester 'keeper Grenville Millington on non-contract terms before signing Ron Sinclair on loan from Nottingham Forest. 1984/85 was Stuart's most memorable season; he began it as the Club's first choice 'keeper, and appeared in the biggest games of his career - four fascinating European Cup-Winners' Cup games against FC Porto and AS Roma. However, by February he had been replaced by Mike Hooper, signed on loan from Bristol City, a move which was later made permanent. It saw Stuart released by Wrexham in the summer of 1985, and following an unsuccessful trial with Rochdale he began the new season with Oswestry Town in the Northern Premier League. After almost a season with the Shropshire club he moved around the local football scene with Mold Alexandra, Brymbo Steelworks, Lex XI, and Brymbo again. In October 1995 Stuart was appointed manager at Brymbo following the resignation of his former Wrexham team mate, Neil Salathiel, though he, too, resigned in March 1996. Having settled in the Wrexham area, Stuart took up work as a fork lift truck driver for Jamont UK Ltd.

Season	League		F.A.Cup		Welsh Cup		League Cup		F.R.T.		E.C.W.C.		Total	
	apps	gls	apps	gls	apps	gls	apps	gls	apps	gls	apps	gls	apps	gls
1982/83	1	0	-	-	1	0	-	-	-	-	-	-	2	0
1983/84	9	0	1	0	4	0	1	0	1	0	-	-	16	0
1984/85	21	0	1	0	3	0	2	0	2	0	4	0	33	0
	31	**0**	**2**	**0**	**8**	**0**	**3**	**0**	**3**	**0**	**4**	**0**	**51**	**0**

***PARKER,* Thomas Blood** 1925 - 1926

Position; *Centre-Half*
D.O.B; *A/M/J 1893*
Birthplace; *Fenton, Stoke-on-Trent, Staffordshire*
Height; *5ft 9in* ***Weight;*** *12st 0lbs*
Debut; v. *Southport (h) 29th August, 1925*
Total Appearances & Goals; *36 apps 1 gls*
Career; *Carr Vale FC; Sheffield Wednesday Apr 1914 0apps; Bolsover Colliery; Luton Town Aug 1919 36apps 0gls; Portsmouth 1st Mar 1923 43apps 1gls; WREXHAM 19th May 1925;*
Honours; *Third Division South Championship Winner 1924; North Wales Coast F.A.Challenge Cup runner-up 1926;*

Tom Parker was playing local football with Sheffield Junior side Carr Vale FC when he was spotted by Sheffield Wednesday, and signed for the 'Owls' in April 1914. He failed to record a single senior appearance at Hillsborough, as the First World War disrupted his playing career. Following the end of the hostilities Tom signed for Southern League side Luton Town in August 1919. He made forty appearances for the 'Hatters' in his first season, before they were accepted into the Football League Third Division South in 1920. Tom made his Football League debut for Luton in the opening game of the 1920/21 season, the Kenilworth Road club's first game in the League since 1900, when they had failed to gain re-election. However, it turned out to be a disastrous return, as Luton lost 9-1 at Swindon! Despite that defeat Tom went on to remain a regular in the 'Hatters' side before his transfer to Third Division South side Portsmouth in March 1923. He made his debut for 'Pompey' at centre-half in a 4-3 home defeat by Exeter City, and remained an ever-present in the side until the end of the season. 1923/24 saw him become a prominent member of 'Pompey's' Third Division South Championship winning side. However, he was limited to a single game in the club's initial season in the Second Division, and so moved back up North in the summer, to join Wrexham in May 1925. He made his League debut for the 'Robins' at centre-half in the first match of the 1925/26 season, a 3-2 home win over Southport, and became a regular in the side throughout the campaign, scoring his only goal in a 5-1 defeat at Nelson. Tom was to leave the Racecourse at the end of that season.

Season	League		F.A.Cup		Welsh Cup		Total	
	apps	gls	apps	gls	apps	gls	apps	gls
1925/26	34	1	1	0	1	0	36	1
	34	**1**	**1**	**0**	**1**	**0**	**36**	**1**

***PARRISH,* Donald Arthur** 1963 - 1966

Position; *Outside-Left*
D.O.B; *22nd November, 1944*
Birthplace; *Bilston, West Midlands*
Height; *5ft 11in* ***Weight;*** *11st 0lbs*
Debut; v. *Watford (h) 13th April, 1963*
Total Appearances & Goals; *5 apps 0 gls*
Career; *Rhos Aelwyd; Johnstown; Preston North End (Trial); Crystal Palace 1961; WREXHAM Sept 1961, (Pro) 15th Jun 1963; Ellesmere Port Town Oct 1963 (loan); Rhyl 4th Jul 1966; Winsford United cs1968; Fibreglass cs1970;*
Honours; *Wales Schoolboy International; Welsh F.A.Youth Cup Winner 1962 and 1963;*

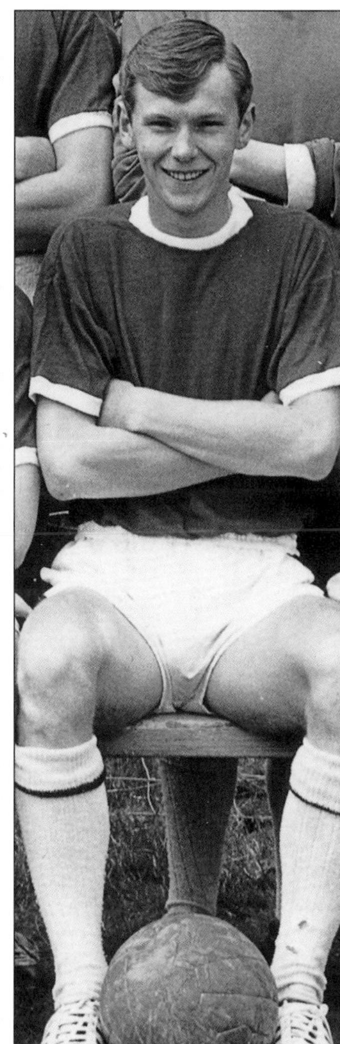

The Welsh parents of Don Parrish moved to the Wrexham area a year after his birth in 1945. They settled in the village of Johnstown, where he attended Johnstown Primary and Ruabon Boys Grammar School. He was chosen to play football for Rhos & District under-14s and Wrexham & District Schoolboys, as well as representing his school at both athletics and cricket. He also appeared for Ruabon Boys Youth Club around this time, which resulted in him representing the North Wales Youth Clubs, and turning out for Rhos Aelwyd in the Welsh National League, again while still at school. However, his father Wilf Parrish himself a former prominent Non League player was heavily involved with Johnstown FC, and persuaded the promising youngster to sign for them, though his football career really took off when invited for trials with the Welsh Youth team at Llandudno in 1960. On arrival he was turned down on a technicality, as he had been born in England. Despite this rejection Don was then invited to Preston North End by manager Cliff Britton, following the recommendation of a North Wales scout who had been present at the Welsh F.A. trials. He returned to Preston during school holidays, but managerial changes at Deepdale saw his contract cancelled. Parrish was soon approached by a scout from Crystal Palace, who then recommended him to manager Arthur Rowe, and was invited to join the ground staff of the London club in 1961. Having signed for the Selhurst Park club Don soon became home-sick, and during a telephone call home, he decided to pack his bags. After a discussion with Wrexham manager Ken Barnes in September 1961, he was offered a place on the ground staff at the Racecourse, where he progressed via the Welsh League, and also tasted success in both the Welsh and North Wales Youth Cups in successive years, 1962 and 1963. He eventually stepped up to the reserves in the Cheshire County League, before making his Football League debut in April

1963, when he replaced Clive Colbridge in an unfamiliar outside-left role in a scoreless draw with Watford on the Racecourse. His next match saw him make a return to Crystal Palace, and in front of almost 20,000 it was a personal disappointment as the North Wales club lost 5-0! Don signed professional forms for the 'Robins' at the end of the season, though he joined Ellesmere Port Town on loan shortly afterwards, a move which saw him become part-time, and take up a job as a Process worker at the Dunlop factory in Ellesmere Port. He was recalled to the Racecourse for the start of the 1964/65 season, enabling him to continue as a part-time player. An unfortunate ankle injury around Christmas put him out of action for three months, recovering in time to play in the final game of the season, a 3-2 home defeat by Torquay United. His final game for Wrexham was at Tranmere Rovers in a 6-3 defeat in October 1965, before he was released by manager Jack Rowley in the summer of 1966. Don then joined Cheshire County League side Rhyl in July, who were then managed by the former Wrexham goalkeeper Albert Dunlop. He returned to the Racecourse in January 1967 for a Welsh Cup fifth round tie, which Rhyl lost 5-0. After two years with the Belle Vue club Don signed for Winsford United, who were also members of the Cheshire County League. He remained with the Cheshire club until 1970, when family and work commitments took priority. He did play for the Fibreglass works team for a short while, where he was employed, but ended his playing career after breaking an ankle. Don, who settled in the Wrexham area, was employed as a Plant Supervisor at 'Owens Corning' from 1971 until 1998. He still enjoys five a side games to keep himself fit!, becoming something of a 'Super Sleuth' when helping us find the whereabouts of Derek Hughes, whose Football League Records we were able to resurrect for the Racecourse Robins!!

Season	League		F.A.Cup		Welsh Cup		League Cup		Total	
	apps	gls	apps	gls	apps	gls	apps	gls	apps	gls
1962/63	2	0	-	-	1	0	-	-	3	0
1964/65	1	0	-	-	-	-	-	-	1	0
1965/66	1	0	-	-	-	-	-	-	1	0
	4	**0**	**-**	**-**	**1**	**0**	**-**	**-**	**5**	**0**

PASKIN, **John William** 1992 - 1994

Position; *Forward*
D.O.B; *1st February, 1962*
Birthplace; *Cape Town, South Africa*
Height; *5ft 10in* ***Weight;*** *11st 10lbs*
Debut; v. *Maidstone United (a) 22nd February, 1992*
Total Appearances & Goals; *28/23 apps 11 gls*
Career; *Hellenic (South Africa) Jul 1980; Crystal Palace (Trial); Toronto Blizzard (Canada) May 1984; South China (Hong Kong) Aug 1984; Seiko (Hong Kong) Aug 1985; Dundee United (Trial) Jul 1987; K.V.Kortijik (Belguim) 1987; West Bromwich Albion 27th Aug 1988 14/11apps 5gls; Wolves 26th Jun 1989 £75,000 21/13apps 2gls; Stockport County 11th Sept 1991 (loan) 3/2apps 1gls; Birmingham City 21st Nov 1991 (loan) 8/2apps 3gls; Shrewsbury Town 13th Feb 1992 (loan) 1app 0gls; WREXHAM 21st Feb 1992 (Exchange for James Kelly); Bury 22nd Jul 1994 15/23apps 8gls; Hellsinbourg, Hellenic (South Africa) 1996;*
Honours; *Third Division Championship runner-up 1993; N.A.S.L. Championship runner-up 1994;*

Born in South Africa globetrotter John Paskin attended a rugby playing school, learning his football with a local junior club. By the age of 16 he had been spotted by former West Ham United player Johnny Byrne, then boss of top South African side, Hellenic. Byrne arranged for John to travel to London for a trial with Crystal Palace, but problems in obtaining a work permit proved an obstacle and he returned home. He then enlisted for his National Service in South Africa, and once completed moved to Canada, playing for Toronto Blizzard. He travelled to Hong Kong in August 1985 to appear for South China, followed by a spell with Seiko. He then moved to Portugal for a training stint with Benfica, followed by a trial with Dundee United in the close season of 1987, finally settling down with K.V.Kortijik in the Belgian First Division. A year later he met his English-born wife, and through contacts of the former England international Tony Morley, who had been a team mate in Hong Kong, he underwent trials with West Bromwich Albion. John signed a contract with Albion in August 1988, and made his Football League debut in the opening game of the season, a 1-1 draw at Leicester City, and scored the 'Baggies' goal. He totted up twenty five League games, scoring five goals, before leaving the Hawthorns to join Wolves in the summer of 1989. He found his first team chances limited at Molyneux, and in two and a half years managed just 34 League matches, scoring two goals. During his time with the Midlands club he was loaned out to Stockport County, Birmingham City, and Shrewsbury Town, and it was after he had made just one appearance for the Gay Meadow club that Wrexham manager Brian Flynn stepped in to sign him in a part-exchange deal that saw James Kelly move in the opposite direction. He went straight into the 'Robins' first team alongside Lee Jones, to bring some experience to a young Wrexham side. John quickly showed his ability to hold the ball up well and bring his team

mates into the game, and it paid off handsomely as Wrexham won 4-2 at Maidstone on his debut, the club's first away win in the League for eighteen months! He remained in the first team until the end of that season, as manager Brian Flynn continued to rebuild the side. 1992/93 saw Wrexham gain promotion to the Second Division, with John playing his part in scoring some important goals, although most of them were registered when he came off the substitutes bench when the team had to adopt different tactics as stalemate had ocurred. It was a record that saw him dubbed 'Super Sub' by the Racecourse faithful. John's appearances were restricted by the prolific partnership of Gary Bennett and Steve Watkin, and they also kept Paskin out of the side for most of the following season, although he was hardly helped by some niggling injuries that he picked up. At the beginning of April manager Brian Flynn announced that the South African would be released at the end of the season. He immediately joined Bury on trial, doing enough to earn a contract with the Lancashire club in June 1994. His first season at Gigg Lane was spent in helping the 'Shakers' to reach the Play-off Final at Wembley, although they lost 2-0 to Chesterfield. He left Bury at the end of the 1995/96 season, and returned to South Africa, where he has been regularly turning out in front of 30,000 crowds.

Season	League		F.A.Cup		Welsh Cup		League Cup		A.G.T.		Total	
	apps	gls	apps	gls	apps	gls	apps	gls	apps	gls	apps	gls
1991/92	14/3	3	-	-	-	-	-	-	2	1	16/3	4
1992/93	10/9	8	-	-	0/1	0	1	0	0/1	0	11/11	8
1993/94	4/11	0	-	-	-	-	0/3	2	1/1	1	5/15	3
	28/23	**11**	**-**	**-**	**0/1**	**0**	**1/3**	**2**	**3/2**	**2**	**32/29**	**15**

PEARCE, **Christopher Leslie** 1986 - 1987

Position; *Goalkeeper*
D.O.B; *7th August, 1961*
Birthplace; *Newport, Gwent*
Height; *6ft 0in* ***Weight;*** *11st 4lbs*
Debut; v. *Hereford United (a) 23rd August, 1986*
Total Appearances & Goals; *41 apps 0 gls*
Career; *Wolves 1977 0apps; Barry Town 1978; Blackburn Rovers Oct 1979 0apps; Rochdale Aug 1980 (Loan) 5apps 0gls; Barnsley 0apps; Rochdale Aug 1982 36apps 0gls; Port Vale Jun 1983 48apps 0gls; WREXHAM Jul 1986; Burnley 14th Jul 1987 £4,000 181apps 0gls; Bradford City Aug 1992 9apps 0gls; Accrington Stanley; Fleetwood; Rossendale; Chorley;*
Honours; *Fourth Division Championship Winner 1992; Welsh Schoolboy International; Sherpa Van Trophy runner-up 1988;*

The brother of professional boxer David Pearce, Chris was also a keen sportsman, playing rugby at Milton Junior and Hartridge High Schools in his home town of Newport, Gwent. Switching to football he soon began to impress, representing Newport and Gwent Boys, and finally Wales Schoolboys. At 14 he joined Cardiff City as a Schoolboy, although when he left school he was not offered an apprenticeship at Ninian Park. Following trials with Aston Villa, West Ham United and Wolves, he was invited to Molyneux for further examination before being accepted as a trainee. He made his way through the 'A' team to the reserves, breaking an arm in the process, and spending months wondering whether he would play again as the specialist had given him only a 50/50 chance of recovery. Released by Wolves Chris returned home to South Wales, where the fracture mended well, and a second assault on a football career began with Barry Town. After just one game for them he was invited to Blackburn Rovers for a week's trial, after which he signed a contract in

October 1979. Pearce spent three years at Ewood Park, but failed to make a first team appearance in that time. He made his Football League debut during a loan spell with Rochdale in August 1980, playing in a 2-2 draw at Stockport County in the opening match of the season. He completed five League outings for the 'Hornets', which was followed by another loan spell with Barnsley, although he never played in their first team. In August 1982 he left Ewood Park to join Rochdale permanently making 36 League appearances before signing for Port Vale in June 1983. They had just been promoted to the Third Division, and Chris marked his debut by saving a penalty in a 3-0 defeat at Orient. That season was spent as understudy to Barry Siddall; it was the first of three years at Vale Park, over which he made 48 League appearances. He missed just ten League games in his second season, while 1985/86 saw him as understudy to Jim Arnold. He then returned to his native Wales in the summer joining Fourth Division Wrexham on a free transfer. His signing was seen as the solution to the club's long standing goalkeeping problem, and things progressed nicely for the first half of the season, with Chris playing in the four European Cup-Winners' Cup matches against FC Zurrieq of Malta and Real Zaragoza of Spain. However, a freak injury was to sideline him in February, and David Powell was signed on loan from West Brom, followed by another loan signing, Mike Salmon from Bolton. Significantly, it was Salmon's arrival that signalled the end of Chris' time at Wrexham as, once fit, he failed to regain his first team place. Disillusioned, and unable to command a regular first team place, Chris took advantage of his freedom from contract to sign for Burnley in July 1987. He had been a very popular character with the Wrexham fans, and a similar rapport was soon established at Turf Moor, where he became installed as the 'Clarets' regular 'keeper for over four seasons. He helped the Lancashire club reach the Sherpa Van Trophy Final at Wembley in 1988, where they lost 2-0 to Wolves, and earned a Fourth Division championship medal in what proved to be his final season with the Turf Moor club. During the summer of 1992 he was contacted by the Bradford City manager Frank Stapleton, who invited him to join the Valley Parade club on the understanding that he would be understudy to Paul Tomlinson. He subsequently appeared in nine League games over the season, during which he underwent an operation to have discs removed from his back. It forced his premature retirement from the game at the end of the season. Even so, it didn't prevent him from 'helping friends out' at Accrington Stanley, Fleetwood, Rossendale and Chorley! He later played for the Burnley veterans' side, while taking up employment with a firm who supply machinery for the paper industry in the Blackburn area, where he has settled.

Season	League		F.A.Cup		Welsh Cup		League Cup		F.R.T.		E.C.W.C.		Total	
	apps	gls	apps	gls	apps	gls	apps	gls	apps	gls	apps	gls	apps	gls
1986/87	25	0	3	0	2	0	4	0	3	0	4	0	41	0
	25	**0**	**3**	**0**	**2**	**0**	**4**	**0**	**3**	**0**	**4**	**0**	**41**	**0**

PEJIC, Melvyn

1992 - 1995

Position; *Defender*
D.O.B; *27th April, 1959*
Birthplace; *Newcastle-under-Lyme, Staffordshire*
Height; *5ft 9in* ***Weight;*** *10st 13lbs*
Debut; v. *Maidstone United (h) 11th January, 1992*
Total Appearances & Goals; *127/3 apps 5 gls*
Career; *Stoke City Jul 1975 1app 0gls; Hereford United Jun 1980 404/8apps 14gls; WREXHAM 9th Jan 1992 £7,000;*
Honours; *Third Division Championship runner-up 1993; Welsh Cup Winner 1990;*

Mel Pejic joined his home town club, Stoke City, straight from school - following in the footsteps of his brother, Mike, who played for Stoke City, Everton, Aston Villa, and England. After completing his apprenticeship Mel was signed on professional terms in July 1977, but he found his first team opportunities were very limited, and made just one Football League appearance for the club, a 1-0 home defeat by Ipswich Town in January 1980. Mel was allowed to leave at the end of that season, and joined Hereford United in June 1980 to begin a near twelve year association with the Edgar Street club. Throughout his time with Hereford he never ventured out of the Fourth Division, making a total of 520 League and Cup appearances, and scoring 23 goals. He holds the club record of having appeared in the most Football League games for the Edgar Street club with 412, while his only major honour was a winners' medal from the 1990 Welsh Cup Final when the 'Bulls' beat Wrexham 2-1 in the first ever Final to be played at the National Stadium in Cardiff. Appearing either in the centre of defence, or at right-back, he was appointed Club captain in 1986, having been voted Hereford's 'Player of the Season' for three successive years between 1983-5. Towards the end of his time at Edgar Street Mel became involved with coaching the club's YTS players, but following the appointment of Greg Downs as the new manager in the summer of 1991, he found that he didn't fit in to the new regime. In January 1992 he was allowed to leave Hereford and join Wrexham for a bargain £7,000, at a time when the 'Robins' were just beginning to see a welcome turn of fortune. He was ineligible to play in the memorable F.A.Cup match with Arsenal, but helped to stabilise the League results for the rest of the 1991/92 season. The following campaign saw him form a solid defensive partnership with Tony Humes, although a 6-1 F.A.Cup defeat at Crewe in November had to be endured before he and the club progressed to gain promotion to the Second Division as runners-up to Cardiff City. The new season was to see the arrival of Barry Hunter to strengthen the defence. However, with injuries to both Humes and Hunter, the Staffordshire- born defender missed just six League games all season, playing consistently well as Wrexham consolidated their position in the new division. Described as a 'strong tackling, rugged defender, who made sure his opponents knew they were in a game', Mel picked up some niggling injuries during the following season, and with Barry Hunter's emergence he managed just 26 outings. In the summer he was given a new contract, which included more responsibility with coaching duties. However, before the season had begun he was called upon to take over the job of Physiotherapist at the Club, following the sudden departure of Mark Taylor. He had trained for this opportunity since arriving at Wrexham, and it virtually signalled the end of his playing career, although he did play a few reserve games. He has since settled down to become a first class physio, and remains an important part of the Racecourse back room staff.

Season	League		F.A.Cup		Welsh Cup		League Cup		A.G.T.		Total	
	apps	gls	apps	gls	apps	gls	apps	gls	apps	gls	apps	gls
1991/92	6/1	1	-	-	-	-	-	-	-	-	6/1	1
1992/93	39	2	-	-	4	0	2	1	3	0	48	3
1993/94	40	0	2	0	2	0	3	1	2	0	49	1
1994/95	18/2	1	1	0	2	0	2	0	1	0	24/2	1
	103/3	**4**	**3**	**0**	**8**	**0**	**7**	**2**	**6**	**0**	**127/3**	**5**

PHILLIPS, David Samuel 1936 - 1939

Position; *Inside-Left*
D.O.B; *27th March, 1916*
Birthplace; *Bala, Gwynedd*
Died; *Germany, 2nd March 1945.*
Height; *5ft 5ins* **Weight;** *10st 2lbs*
Debut; v. *Tranmere Rovers (h) 3rd April, 1937*
Total Appearances & goals; *16 apps 1gls*
Career; *Bala Town; Blaenau Ffestiniog; Blackburn Rovers (Am) Aug 1935; WREXHAM (Am) Oct 1936, (Pro) 6th Nov 1936; Bangor City 12th Nov 1938;*
Honours; *Lancashire Combination League runner-up 1939; Cambrian Coast F.A.Cup Winner;*

At Bala Grammar School Dai Phillips was regarded as a 'fine all round athlete, winning the 'Victor Ludorum' at school sports, as well as becoming a prolific goalscorer for the school football team. He was a member of Bala Urdd FC before signing for Bala Town, who played in the Cambrian Coast League, and who he assisted to victory in the Final of the Cambrian Coast Cup against Aberystwyth Town. He later moved on to Blaenau Ffestiniog, who played in the same League. Better known as 'Dei Sam', he was invited to join Blackburn Rovers as an amateur in August 1935. He had been noted at the time as the 'finest inside-forward in Merioneth football circles and interested many Football League clubs, and also figured in a Welsh Amateur trial match'. Nothing came of his time at Ewood Park, but Wrexham seized on the opportunity to sign him on amateur terms in October 1936. The 'Robins' manager, Captain James Logan, described his signing as 'Alex James II', - and was perfectly placed to make this judgement since he had discovered the Arsenal legend during his time as manager of Raith Rovers. He added, 'Watch him this season, and you will see why I call him the second Alex James, five feet nothing, but oh my has he got a football brain, as soon as I saw him playing he reminded me of James.' A month after signing as an amateur he completed professional terms, but his first team debut did not materialise until April 1937, when he replaced Ambrose Brown at inside-forward in a 2-0 home win over Tranmere Rovers. Dai kept his place and played in the last five matches of the season, scoring in a 2-1 win at Halifax, which proved to be his only goal for Wrexham. He made nine first team appearances the following season, but the inside-forward position was held by George Snow for most of that time. 1938/39 saw Phillips enjoy just one League outing, a 1-0 defeat at York, and it proved to be his final match for Wrexham, as he was transferred to Bangor City in November 1938, having not quite lived up to his early promise. He joined Bangor for their first season in the Lancashire Combination League, and assisted them to finish as runners-up. 'Dei Sam' remained at Farrar Road until the outbreak of the Second World War, when he was called up to the Army in September 1939. He served in the Royal Welsh Fusiliers, later rising to the rank of Platoon Sergeant in the King's Own Scottish Borderers, and it was whilst serving with them on the Western Front in Germany that he was tragically 'killed in action' on 2nd March 1945, just two months before the Germans surrendered.

Season	League		F.A.Cup		Welsh Cup		N.S.C.		Total	
	apps	gls	apps	gls	apps	gls	apps	gls	apps	gls
1936/37	6	1	-	-	-	-	-	-	6	1
1937/38	7	0	-	-	1	0	1	0	9	0
1938/39	1	0	-	-	-	-	-	-	1	0
	14	**1**	**-**	**-**	**1**	**0**	**1**	**0**	**16**	**1**

PHILLIPS, Stewart Gavin 1991

Position; *Forward*
D.O.B; *30th December, 1961*
Birthplace; *Halifax, Yorkshire*
Height; *5ft 11'1/2in* **Weight;** *11st 7lbs*
Debut; v. *Mansfield Town (a) 3rd September, 1991*
Total Appearances & Goals; *1/1 apps 1 gls*
Career; *Hereford United Nov 1979 285/8apps 83gls; West Bromwich Albion 4th Mar 1988 £25,000 15apps 4gls; Swansea City 6th Jan 1989 £25,000 10/10apps 1gls; Hereford United Aug 1990 £10,000 31/6apps 10gls; WREXHAM Aug 1991 (non contract); Aldershot Oct 1991 5apps 0gls; Sudbury Town Dec 1991; Worcester City; AFC Newport 1993;*
Honours; *P.F.A. Fourth Division XI 1984;*

Stewart Phillips joined Hereford United straight from Haywood High School in Hereford, where he had represented Herefordshire Schoolboys at both under 14s and 16s. He served a two year apprenticeship at Edgar Street before signing professional forms in November 1979. His Football League debut in a 1-0 defeat at Swindon arrived in April 1978, when he became the youngest-ever player to have represented the 'Bull's' in the Football League at the age of just 16 years and 112 days. His father, Archie, was a director and later the chairman of Hereford United during his time at the club. Stewart went on to make almost 300 League appearances at Edgar Street, at one time forming a lethal strike partnership with another former Wrexham player, Ollie Kearns, and it was not long before Second Division West Bromwich Albion shelled out £25,000 for him, in March 1988. Stewart topped Hereford's goal scoring charts for four consecutive seasons between 1981 and 1985, and he still holds the Club record of scoring their most goals in the Football League with 93. This figure also includes his second spell at Edgar Street. He made his debut for the 'Baggies' in a scoreless home draw with Middlesbrough, and went on to miss just one game before the end of that season as he successfully assisted Albion in their quest to avoid relegation. He managed just five League appearances for Albion in 1988/89, scoring twice, before being allowed to leave the Midlands in January 1989 to join Third Division Swansea City. It was to be a disappointing time for Stewart in South Wales, as he was to suffer with injury and illness in the eighteen months that he spent at the Vetch Field. He eventually re-joined Hereford United for a £10,000 fee in August 1990, making his debut in a 2-0 home win over York City, when he came on as a substitute and scored. He went on to notch ten goals in 37 outings before being released at the end of the season. It was then that Wrexham manager Brian Flynn signed Stewart on non-contract terms, making his League debut for the 'Robins' in September 1991, coming on as a substitute for Lee Jones in a 3-0 defeat at Mansfield Town. He started the next match at Doncaster Rovers, and scored the Wrexham consolation goal in a 3-1 reverse. Though he was offered a contract by Wrexham he decided to take up an offer to play in Hong Kong. On his return he joined Fourth Division Aldershot in October 1991, with whom he made five League appearances before he was released. However, those appearances have been scratched from the record books as the 'Shots' failed to complete the season, going into liquidation. As for Stewart he drifted into non-league football, first with Sudbury Town and followed by spells with Worcester City, where he was their top scorer in 1992/93, before moving on to AFC Newport as a non-contract player in 1993. It was then that he began studying for Diploma's in F.A.Management of injuries, Fitness & Nutrition, Sports Therapy and Sport Psychology. Having settled in Hereford, he is now employed by local G.P's as an 'Exercise Prescription', in which he has to assess clients with various problems with diet etc., and he has since opened up his own Sports Injury Clinic in Hereford.

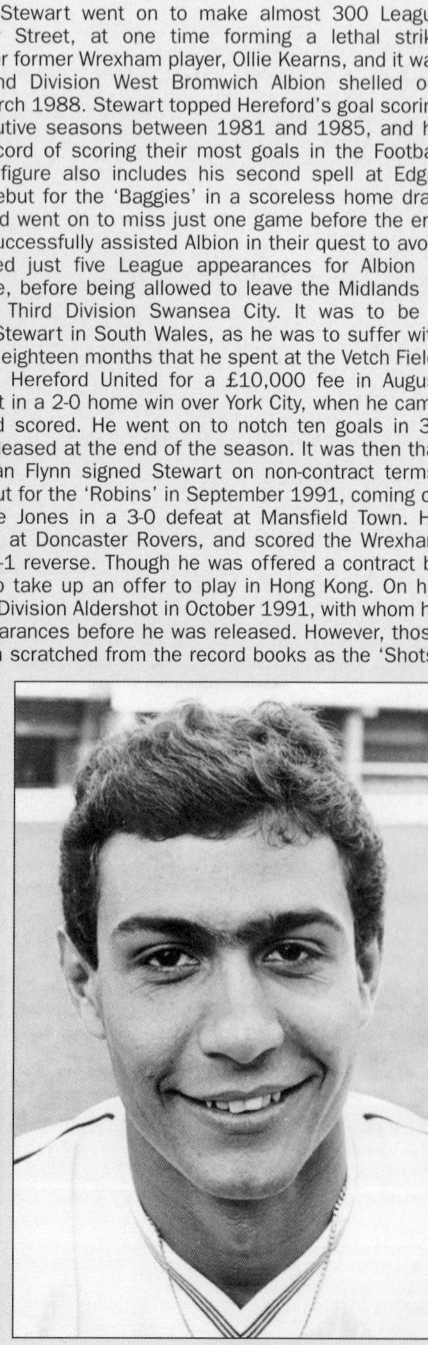

Season	League		F.A.Cup		Welsh Cup		League Cup		F.R.T.		Total	
	apps	gls	apps	gls	apps	gls	apps	gls	apps	gls	apps	gls
1991/92	1/1	1	-	-	-	-	-	-	-	-	1/1	1
	1/1	**1**	**-**	**-**	**-**	**-**	**-**	**-**	**-**	**-**	**1/1**	**1**

PHILLIPS, Wayne 1989 - 1998

Position; *Midfield*
D.O.B; *15th December 1970*
Birthplace; *Bangor, Gwynedd*
Height; *5ft 10in* ***Weight;*** *11st 2lbs*
Debut; v. *Rhyl (h) 6th February 1990 (Welsh Cup)*
Total Appearances & Goals; *248/32 apps 20 gls*
Career; *Caernarvon United; Caernarvon Town 1986; Llanrug 1987; WREXHAM 23rd Aug 1989; Stockport County 13th Feb 1998 £200,000 13/9apps 0gls; Wrexham 8th July 1999 £50,000;*
Honours; *Welsh Cup Winner 1995; Welsh Cup runner-up 1990 & 1991;*

Welsh speaking Wayne showed plenty of promise as a schoolboy when he represented Sir Hugh Owen School, and gained representative honours with Caernarvon, Gwynedd and North Wales Schoolboys. He played junior football for Caernarvon United from under-11 level until he was 15, when joining Caernarfon Town. Wayne played for their reserves in the Welsh Alliance League but, with no first team place forthcoming, joined Gwynedd League side Llanrug at the age of 17, during the 1987/88 season. He was then invited to attend a three week trial with Wrexham, extended by a further week before eventually offered a YTS place with the Racecourse club in the summer of 1988. Professional terms were agreed in August 1989, and Wayne was given his first team opportunity when replacing Joey Jones in defence for a Welsh Cup tie with Rhyl in February 1990, in which he capped his debut with a stunning 25 yard goal. By the end of the season he had made a further four league appearances, and was also picked to play in the 1990 Welsh Cup Final against Hereford United, the first to be held at the National Stadium in Cardiff. Although Wrexham lost 2-1, they had qualified for Europe by virtue of the fact that Hereford were an English club. The following season saw him play in all four European Cup-Winners' Cup games against both Lyngby of Denmark and Manchester United. Performing consistently over the season he once again featured in a Welsh Cup Final, this time against Swansea City, but was again on the losing side in a 2-0 defeat. 1991/92 saw Wayne participate in his most memorable match for the club, as Wrexham beat the Football League Champions, Arsenal, 2-1 in one of the greatest ever F.A.Cup shocks. He also starred in the next round against West Ham United, scoring one of the goals to earn Wrexham a 2-2 draw, before unluckily losing the replay on the Racecourse. The following season he was installed as a regular member of the club's midfield, though eventually squeezed out by Mike Lake's arrival on loan from Sheffield United. He then had to content himself with a place on the substitute's bench, but was denied even that following an injury in a reserve game that put him out of action for the rest of the season. It was a particular cruel blow as he missed out on an involvement in the club's successful bid for promotion to the Second Division. Wayne began the first season at the higher level as a regular in the senior side, until another injury forced on to the sidelines, and was to limit his appearances for that season. Injuries dogged him again throughout the following year, but he at last collected a Welsh Cup winners' medal when the 'Robins' beat Cardiff City 2-1 in the Final. He was also able to participate in the F.A.Cup match against Manchester United at Old Trafford as a substitute. 1995/96 found Wayne revitalised, and he showed tremendous consistency throughout the season, missing just two League games. His impressive form in central midfield continued, and he was rewarded with a call-up to the Welsh international squad - and a place on the sub's bench - for a friendly international in Switzerland in April 1996. He capped the season by deservedly carrying off the club's 'Player of the Season' trophy. 1996/97 began much as the previous season had ended, with Phillip's called up into the Welsh squad for the World Cup games. A substitute's place in Turkey was the best that he achieved, before an injury at Wycombe in October put him out of action until the following March. He had recovered some of his best form by February 1998, which didn't go unnoticed, as Stockport County manager Gary Megson paid out £200,000 for him. Wayne made his debut for the First Division side, as a substitute for Chris Byrne, in a 1-0 home win over Stoke City and remained in the side for the rest of the season as the 'Hatters' finished in a very creditable eighth place although struggling to be involved with the first team in 98/99. With Wrexham, he had been described as 'a workmanlike type of performer, who can also adapt to a defensive position when asked. His up and down the park play always a feature, he is quite liable to have a crack at goal - while his enthusiastic approach is an example to many young players. Always likes to be in the thick of the action'. His ability to speak Welsh has often resulted in him appearing on Radio Cymru and S4C as a summariser'. Wayne was a very popular figure during his days at the Racecourse, and is warmly welcomed whenever he turns up at the ground. His brother has also played in North Wales Non League Football. As if to 'epitomise' the latter comments he returned to Wrexham in July 1999 signing a three year contract. The prodical son returns to the Racecourse!!

Season	League		F.A.Cup		Welsh Cup		League Cup		F.R.T.		E.C.W.C.		Total	
	apps	gls	apps	gls	apps	gls	apps	gls	apps	gls	apps	gls	apps	gls
1989/90	2/3	0	-	-	3	1	-	-	-	-	-	-	5/3	1
1990/91	24/4	0	1	0	5	0	4	0	1	0	4	0	39/4	0
1991/92	28/2	3	3	1	2	0	-	-	5	1	-	-	38/2	5
1992/93	14/1	0	1	0	2	0	2	0	0/1	0	-	-	19/2	0
1993/94	20/1	2	-	-	1	0	4	0	1	0	-	-	26/1	2
1994/95	13/6	1	1/2	0	2/2	0	2	0	0/1	0	-	-	18/11	1
1995/96	43/1	5	4	0	-	-	1/1	0	3	0	2	0	53/2	5
1996/97	26	5	-	-	-	-	2	0	-	-	-	-	28	5
1997/98	14/6	1	2	0	4*	0*	2	0	0/1	0	-	-	22/7	1
	184/24	**17**	**12/2**	**1**	**15/2**	**1**	**17/1**	**0**	**10/3**	**1**	**6**	**0**	**248/32**	**20**

* = Welsh Invitation Cup.

PHYTHIAN, Ernest Rixon 1962 - 1965

Position; *Centre-Forward*
D.O.B; *16th July, 1942*
Birthplace; *Farnworth, Lancashire*
Height; *5ft 8'1/2in* ***Weight;*** *11st 6lbs*
Debut; v. *Darlington (a) 10th March, 1962*
Total Appearances & Goals; *161 apps 48 gls*
Career; *Bolton Wanderers 17th July 1959 10apps 3gls; WREXHAM 9th Mar 1962 £20,000 and Ernie in part exchange for Wyn Davies; Hartlepool United 10th Jun 1965 £3,500 124apps 50gls; Southern Suburbs Johannesburg, South Africa, June 1968 £4,000;*
Honours; *Seven England Youth International caps; Welsh Cup runner-up 1962 & 1965;*

Ernie Phythian is related to ex-Bolton player Jimmy Seddon (375 apps 1914-1932), while his cousin, Ken Seddon, was a Football League referee. Ernie began playing football at the Queen Street and George Tomlinson Schools in Bolton, where he was to captain Farnworth Schoolboys, and also represented Lancashire Schoolboys. Upon leaving school at the age of 15 he signed amateur forms with Bolton Wanderers, while also taking up work for engineering firm 'Silcons' as an apprentice toolmaker. He could easily have become a first class cricketer with Lancashire, appearing in two minor games as a wicket-keeper and representing England at Schoolboy level. However, it was at football that Ernie wished to excel, and he continued to impress at Burnden Park until his seventeenth birthday, when signing professional terms for the club. At this time he was capped by England at Youth level, and was included in the squad that toured Bulgaria. Ernie went on to make his Bolton Football League debut at Hillsborough in February 1960, when he was still only seventeen. The 'Trotters' lost 1-0, although they did finish the match with just nine players! He made a total of ten League appearances for Bolton before joining Fourth Division Wrexham in March 1962 in a part-exchange deal which involved Wyn Davies moving to Bolton and Ernie - valued at £10,000 - travelling in the opposite direction, along with a £20,000 fee. He was plunged straight into the void left by Davies at Darlington, as the 'Robins' were in a promising position for promotion. They gathered just one point from his first three games, all away, but on his home debut he scored twice in a 4-2 win over Chesterfield as the 'Robins' went on to clinch promotion to the Third Division. Ernie was a regular in the Wrexham side over the next three seasons, missing only the odd game, and was described as a 'small, stocky number nine who always had to be watched because of his quickness, worrying play and whole heartiness'. He picked up two Welsh Cup runners'-up medals in 1962 and 1965, and was handed the opportunity to try out his prowess as a goalkeeper in an F.A.Cup match with Altrincham, when Albert Dunlop was injured! Ernie left the Racecourse in June 1965 when he joined Hartlepool United for £3,500, amassing 124 League appearances in his three seasons at the Victoria Ground. In June 1968 he took up an opportunity to move to South Africa, when agreeing to a transfer to Southern Suburbs in Johannesburg for a £4,000 fee. Ernie Phythian eventually settled in South Africa, where he became employed as a car salesman.

Season	League		F.A.Cup		Welsh Cup		League Cup		Total	
	apps	gls	apps	gls	apps	gls	apps	gls	apps	gls
1961/62	13	3	-	-	3	1	-	-	16	4
1962/63	35	11	4	0	2	0	1	0	42	11
1963/64	45	20	2	0	2	0	3	0	52	20
1964/65	41	10	2	0	7	3	1	0	51	13
	134	**44**	**8**	**0**	**14**	**4**	**5**	**0**	**161**	**48**

PITT, Howard Vincent 1924 - 1925

Position; *Outside-Left*
D.O.B; *J/F/M 1907*
Birthplace; *Wrexham, Denbighshire*
Died; *Grays, Essex 17th April 1963.*
Height; *5ft 8'1/2ins* ***Weight;*** *11st 0lbs*
Debut; v. *Southport (h) 26th December, 1924*
Total Appearances & Goals; *7 apps 0 gls*
Career; *WREXHAM Nov 1924; Northern Nomads;*
Honours; *Welsh Amateur International cap; North Wales Coast F.A. Challenge Cup runner-up 1926;*

Howard Pitt joined Wrexham during the close season of 1924 and made his debut on Boxing Day of that year, replacing Bob Miles at outside-left for the home game with Southport, which ended in a 3-2 defeat. He made a total of four League appearances that season, without scoring, adding just three more throughout the following year. At the end of the campaign he played for the 'Robins' reserve team against Llandudno in the North Wales Coast F.A. Challenge Cup Final, where they lost 2-0. Howard was then released by the Racecourse club in the summer of 1926. He is known to have subsequently played for Northern Nomads, and also won a Welsh Amateur International cap against Scotland in 1930. At the end of his playing career Howard moved to Essex, where he was employed as a teacher at the Aedale School in North Stifford. He passed away in April 1963, aged 56.

Season	League		F.A.Cup		Welsh Cup		Total	
	apps	gls	apps	gls	apps	gls	apps	gls
1924/25	4	0	-	-	-	-	4	0
1925/26	3	0	-	-	-	-	3	0
	7	**0**	**-**	**-**	**-**	**-**	**7**	**0**

POLAND, George 1938 - 1939

Position; *Goalkeeper*
D.O.B; *21st September, 1913*
Birthplace; *Penarth, Glamorgan*
Died; *Penarth, 6th October, 1988*
Height; *5ft 11in* ***Weight;*** *12st 4lbs*
Debut; v. *Southport (a) 27th August, 1938*
Total Appearances & Goals; *44 apps 0 gls*
Career; *Cogan FC (Cardiff); Penarth Mission FC; Swindon Town (amateur) Jul 1934 0apps; Cardiff City (Am) Apr 1935, (Pro) 18th Dec 1936 24apps 0gls; WREXHAM 14th Jul 1938; Liverpool 29th Jun 1939 £3,000; Cardiff City (WW2 Guest) Dec 1939 2apps 0gls; Brentford (WW2 Guest) 1940 21apps 0gls; Crystal Palace (WW2 Guest) Sept 1942 9apps 0gls; Leeds United (WW2 Guest) Sept 1943 10apps 0gls; Cardiff City 29th Aug 1946 2apps 0gls; Lovells Athletic 12th Aug 1947; Penarth Albion 26th Sept 1950;*
Honours; *Two Welsh International caps;*

George Poland first played football as an outfield player, and was a goalscoring centre-forward with Penarth Mission when Ted Vizard invited him for trials with Swindon Town. There, he was tried out at outside-right, having earlier been rejected by Cardiff City. Nothing materialised with the Wiltshire club, and he returned to play for the Mission. He then began to fancy his chances as a goalkeeper, and following his change of role was given a second opportunity with Cardiff City, rejoining them as a 'keeper on amateur terms in April 1935. George was still unpaid when making his Football League debut in January 1936, in a 2-1 defeat at Torquay. In the last game prior to his debut, a reserve fixture, he had conceded seven goals! He made six more senior appearances that season, but did not turn professional until December 1936. George went on to make a total of 24 League appearances for Cardiff before they signed Bob Jones from Bolton Wanderers, and his arrival forced Poland to take a back seat for most of the 1937/38 season. He decided to leave Ninian Park in the summer of 1938 and move North to join Wrexham. His career really began to take off with the North-East Wales club, going straight into the first team at the expense of Pat McMahon for the opening game of 1938/39, a 3-1 defeat at Southport. Despite the result, he missed just three games that season, impressing enough to earn international recognition with Wales in 1939 - against Ireland in March and France in May. Following his caps for Wales he attracted scouts from the bigger clubs, and at the end of the season was signed by Liverpool for £3,000. The outbreak of the Second World War at the start of the following season put paid to his chances of success at Anfield, however, and George enlisted in the Welsh Guards. He made four War-time international appearances for Wales, and while serving at Esher he appeared as a 'guest' for Brentford in the Regional War Leagues. Poland also played as a 'guest' for Cardiff City, Crystal Palace, and Leeds United - where he broke an arm. The injury troubled him, and didn't play again until the hostilities were over. He then rejoined Cardiff City, but enjoyed only two first team outings before leaving at the end of the season to join Lovells Athletic. He later played for his local side Penarth Albion before retiring. Following the end of his professional football career, George became employed as a postman in the Cardiff area. At his peak he was described as 'a confident goalkeeper who was agile and safe, commanding his area well'.

Season	League		F.A.Cup		Welsh Cup		N.S.C.		Total	
	apps	gls	apps	gls	apps	gls	apps	gls	apps	gls
1938/39	39	0	-	-	2	0	3	0	44	0
	39	**0**	**-**	**-**	**2**	**0**	**3**	**0**	**44**	**0**

PORTER, George 1959 - 1960

Position; *Outside-Left*
D.O.B; *5th February, 1935*
Birthplace; *Chirk, Denbighshire*
Height; *6ft 0in* ***Weight;*** *12st 7lbs*
Debut; v. *Chesterfield (a) 7th September, 1959*
Total Appearances & Goals; *1 app 0 gls*
Career; *Chirk A.A.A; Peritus 1955; Chirk A.A.A; WREXHAM May 1959; Chirk A.A.A; Colwyn Bay; Oswestry Town;*
Honours; *Welsh Amateur Cup Winner 1959, 1960 & 1963; Welsh Amateur Cup runner-up 1955 & 1956;*

George Porter played football at Llangollen Secondary School, and after progressing to the University College of North Wales in Bangor (UCNW) he continued to play the game, as skipper of the college side, and also Peritus, a combined colleges' team. George was to qualify as a Chemistry teacher, and he taught at the Maelor Secondary College in Penley for many years until his retirement. During his football career, he played in five Welsh Amateur Cup Finals, the first of which came in 1955, when he played for his local side Chirk A.A.A. against Newtown, although they lost 4-2. He was at college the following year, where he was appearing for the combined college side Peritus. They reached the Final where he was again on the losing side, this time by 5-2 to Portmadoc at Bangor. Upon completing his University Degree George returned to play for Chirk A.A.A., and then collected his first winners' medal as the Border club beat

Shropshire side Whitchurch Alport 2-0 in the Final on the Racecourse after a 2-2 draw. His performance in this game impressed the watching Wrexham manager, John Love, who then signed George on amateur terms in May 1959 at the age of 24. Porter was soon to make his first team debut for the Racecourse club, stepping in to replace Idris Pryce at outside-left in September 1959 at Chesterfield. He hadn't even played a reserve team game for the Club before his senior call-up! Wrexham lost the game 5-1, but George was described in the local reports as having 'Done his best, and showed some neat touches, but was bewildered by the pace!" He remained at the Racecourse for a little while longer before returning to join Chirk A.A.A., where he went on to add a second Welsh Amateur Cup Winners' medal with a 3-2 victory over Caerau Athletic in the 1960 Final at Newtown. Three years later Porter collected his third winners' medal, when his club beat Caersws Amateurs 2-0 at Wrexham. He spent a total of almost twenty years playing for Chirk A.A.A., where he was also a notable cricketer for Chirk over the same period, going on to play for Colwyn Bay, mostly in Cup games, and also for Oswestry Town. George, who is now retired and settled in Chirk, is a very modest and likeable man who plays down most of his achievements, but the authors of the book - like most Wrexham fans reading this - would have given up everything to have made just one appearance in a Wrexham A.F.C. shirt like he did!

Season	League		F.A.Cup		Welsh Cup		Total	
	apps	gls	apps	gls	apps	gls	apps	gls
1959/60	1	0	-	-	-	-	1	0
	1	**0**	-	-	-	-	**1**	**0**

POSTIN, Eli

1935 - 1936

Position; *Outside-Right*
D.O.B; *3rd June, 1908*
Birthplace; *Dudley, West Midlands*
Died; *Dudley, August, 1991*
Height; *5ft 10in* ***Weight;*** *11st 7lbs*
Debut; v. *Chesterfield (h) 23rd November, 1935*
Total Appearances & Goals; *12 apps 2 gls*
Career; *Halesowen 1928; Cradley Heath May 1929; West Bromwich Albion Apr 1931 0apps; Dudley Town; Cardiff City 5th Jul 1933 33apps 13gls; Bristol Rovers 27th Jul 1934 4apps 1gls; WREXHAM 22nd Nov 1935;* Brierley Hill Alliance Jul 1936;
Honours; England Junior International;

Eli Postin joined West Bromwich Albion from Cradley Heath as a Junior, having previously played for Halesowen. At the Hawthorns he took part in the Junior internationals (of that time) for the Birmingham F.A. against Scotland, although he failed to make Albion's first team and eventually left to join Birmingham and District League side Dudley Town. Cardiff City signed him in the summer of 1933, and he went on to become their leading scorer in 1933/34, with thirteen goals in 33 League games, although his contribution was not enough to prevent the 'Bluebirds' from finishing at the basement of the Third Division South, and having to seek re-election. There followed a clear out of players from Ninian Park which was to include Eli, and in May 1934 he joined fellow Third Division South side Bristol Rovers. Postin found first team appearances hard to come by with the Bristol club, and managed just four games in eighteen months. Most of his time was spent playing for the reserves, for whom he scored freely. In November 1935 he was transferred to Wrexham, making his debut in a 1-0 home defeat by Chesterfield. He was selected at outside-right in place of Jack Mustard, who had switched to centre-forward as cover for Charles McCartney. Eli made just ten League appearances for the 'Robins', scoring twice before leaving the Racecourse in the summer of 1936. He then joined Birmingham and District League side Brierley Hill Alliance.

Season	League		F.A.Cup		Welsh Cup		N.S.C.		Total	
	apps	gls	apps	gls	apps	gls	apps	gls	apps	gls
1935/36	10	2	-	-	-	-	2	0	12	2
	10	**2**	-	-	-	-	**2**	**0**	**12**	**2**

POWELL, David

1963 - 1968

Position; *Central Defender*
D.O.B; *15th October, 1944*
Birthplace; *Dolgarrog, Gwynedd*
Height; *5ft 10in* ***Weight;*** *11st 0lbs*
Debut; v. *Bristol Rovers (a) 11th May, 1963*
Total Appearances & Goals; *152/2 apps 5 gls*
Career; *Gwydyr Rovers; WREXHAM 11th January 1962, (Pro) 14th May 1963; Sheffield United 12th Sept 1968 £28,500 89apps 2gls; Cardiff City 22nd Sept 1972 36apps 1gls;*
Honours; *11 Welsh international caps; 4 Welsh under-23 caps; Welsh Youth International; Second Division runner-up 1971; Welsh Cup Winner 1973; Welsh Cup runner-up 1965; Welsh Youth Cup Winner 1962 & 1963;*

Dave Powell attended Dolgarrog Secondary Modern and Llanrwst Grammar Schools. During his schooldays he played football for local junior team Gwydyr Rovers, from where he was chosen to play for Wales at Youth level. He was then recommended to Wrexham, and joined the groundstaff in January 1962. At the Racecourse he quickly graduated from the Colts to the reserve XI in the Cheshire County League, before making his Football League debut in May 1963 in a 1-1 draw at Bristol Rovers. Three days later, he signed professional forms for the 'Robins'. At around this time he was described as a 'slim, stylish defender with speed, tenacious tackling and accurate distribution'. Over the next three seasons David Powell stood out in a struggling Wrexham side that suffered relegation to the Fourth Division in 1964, finally reaching rock bottom of the Football League in 1966, and losing in the 1965 Welsh Cup Final to Cardiff City. 1966/67 saw a vast improvement in the club's League position, and it began to progress under the guidance of Alvan Williams. David's career also blossomed, as he won the first of four Welsh under-23 international caps. His form was eventually to see him become the first Wrexham player since 1939 to win a full international cap for Wales when he was selected to play against West Germany in May 1968 at Cardiff, in a 1-1 draw. This major honour for both David and Wrexham soon began to attract the attention of the bigger clubs, and in September 1968 the Wrexham board of directors accepted a £28,500 bid from Second Division Sheffield United - much to the annoyance of manager Alvan Williams, who resigned shortly afterwards. David spent four years at Bramall Lane, making 89 League appearances, and helping the 'Blades' to gain promotion to the First Division in 1971, although he missed the run-in to the end of the season through injury. He had fallen awkwardly and damaged knee ligaments in a game at Q.P.R. in March 1971. He made a number of attempted come backs, but each time he broke down with a recurrence of the injury, missing most of 1971/72. The following year found him playing reserve team football before Cardiff City came in for him in September, and he left Bramall Lane, along with Gil Reece, in an exchange deal that saw Alan Warboys join the 'Blades'. During his time with Sheffield United David had gained a further ten caps for Wales. One of which was awarded for a game against Italy, when Powell was handed the task of marking Juventus' £440,000 forward, Pietro Anastasi. So thoroughly did he do his job that the Italian, unhappy with the close attention that he was being given, failed to appear for the second half! He made his debut for Cardiff, along with Reece, in a disastrous 3-1 home defeat by Bristol City, as they fought to stave off relegation. The summer found Cardiff and David still in the Second Division, with a Welsh Cup winners' medal following a 5-1 aggregate victory over Bangor City. His knee problem flared up again, and it began to affect his game. After just 36 League games for the 'Bluebirds'. Powell was forced to retire at the end of the 1973/74 season, aged only 29. He then joined the South Wales Police, where he managed the Police football team also going on to train recruits at Bridgend. David retired from the Force in 1993, and has settled in the Cardiff area.

Season	League		F.A.Cup		Welsh Cup		League Cup		Total	
	apps	gls	apps	gls	apps	gls	apps	gls	apps	gls
1962/63	4	0	-	-	-	-	-	-	4	0
1963/64	14	0	3	0	1	0	-	-	18	0
1964/65	25	1	-	-	5	0	1	0	31	1
1965/66	32/1	1	2	0	1	0	1	0	36/1	1
1966/67	26	1	-	-	3	1	1	0	30	2
1967/68	27/1	1	-	-	1	0	-	-	28/1	1
1968/69	4	0	-	-	-	-	1	0	5	0
	132/2	**4**	**5**	**0**	**11**	**1**	**4**	**0**	**152/2**	**5**

POWELL, David Robert — 1987

Position; *Goalkeeper*
D.O.B; *24th September, 1967*
Birthplace; *Hednesford, Staffordshire*
Height; *6ft 1in* **Weight;** *12st 4lbs*
Debut; v. *Rochdale (h) 28th February, 1987*
Total Appearances & Goals; *2 apps 0 gls*
Career; *Cherry Valley 1983; West Bromwich Albion Apr 1986 2apps 0gls; WREXHAM 28th Feb 1987 (Loan); Stoke City 16th Mar 1988 (Loan) 0apps;*

David Powell first played football at Brockmoor Middle and Buckpool Senior Schools in his home town of Hednesford, before being spotted playing in local football for Cherry Valley by West Bromwich Albion. He agreed YTS terms with Albion in 1984, and progressed to sign professional forms in April 1986. However, it was with Wrexham that he was to make his Football League debut, having joined the 'Robins' on loan after the club's regular first team goalkeeper, Chris Pearce, had been injured. Manager Dixie McNeil had asked his West Brom counterpart, Ron Saunders, for the services of David, and he had agreed to the loan spell in February 1987. David made his Football League debut for the 'Robins' in a 2-2 home draw with Rochdale, and got off to what was hardly an auspicious start by conceding a goal after just one minute! The following game against Scunthorpe United on the Racecourse, ended 1-1, but it proved to be his final game for the club. He was then recalled by West Bromwich Albion as cover, following the bizarre injury to their reserve 'keeper. He had severed an artery and tendon in his hand when attempting to open a window in the dressing room after a reserve team game at Preston! David went on to make just two League appearances for the 'Baggies', a 2-0 defeat at Swindon in January 1988, and a 1-0 home win over Plymouth Argyle in the following match, both in place of Stuart Naylor. He later had a loan spell with Stoke City in March 1988, but failed to record a first team appearance. He was described as 'a confident keeper who was not short of ability, but he decided to retire from football in June 1988.

Season	League		F.A.Cup		Welsh Cup		League Cup		F.R.T.		Total	
	apps	gls	apps	gls	apps	gls	apps	gls	apps	gls	apps	gls
1986/87	2	0	-	-	-	-	-	-	-	-	2	0
	2	**0**	**-**	**-**	**-**	**-**	**-**	**-**	**-**	**-**	**2**	**0**

PREECE, Andrew Paul — 1990 - 1991

Position; *Forward*
D.O.B; *27th March, 1967*
Birthplace; *Evesham, Worcestershire*
Height; *6ft 1in* **Weight;** *12st 0lbs*
Debut; v. *Cambridge United (a) 30th March, 1990*
Total Appearances & Goals; *60/9 apps 13 gls*
Career; *Worcester City; Evesham United; Northampton Town 31st Aug 1988 0/1apps 0gls; Weymouth 1988/89(Loan); Aylesbury 1988/89(Loan); Bedworth United 1988/89 (Loan); Worcester City 1st Aug 1989; WREXHAM 20th Mar 1990 £4,000; Stockport County 18th Dec 1991 £10,000 89/8apps 42gls; Crystal Palace 23rd June 1994 £350,000 17/3apps 4gls; Blackpool 5th July 1995 £200,000 114/12apps 35gls; Bury 2nd Jul 1998 19/20apps 3gls;*
Honours; *Welsh Cup runner-up 1991; Autoglass Trophy runner-up 1993;*

Andy Preece joined Worcester City's youth scheme while still at school, and made such rapid progress that he was promoted to the senior side at the age of just sixteen. He was a great all-rounder as a schoolboy, earning selection for Hereford and Worcester at under-18 level at both football and cricket. He also represented Worcestershire under-19s at cricket, and was picked to tour Australia with the Worcester second XI, spending six months near Perth. He was then given the opportunity of playing football for Worcester City by manager Bobby Shinton, the ex-Wrexham striker. However, glandular fever sidelined him for a number of months, and upon returning to fitness he found that a new manager had been appointed who had brought in a large number of players. He then joined his home-town club, Evesham United, also playing Sunday football for Sundat. His connection with Sundat landed him a trial with Northampton Town, as the manager was a friend of Cliff Carr, the man in charge at the County Ground. He arranged for Andy to attend trials prior to the start of the 1988/89 season, the outcome of which was that he then signed professional terms for the 'Cobblers'. He made his first team debut within weeks as a substitute against Charlton Athletic in a 2-1 Littlewoods Cup defeat. Just one more sub appearance followed, a 2-1 home defeat by Gillingham, before he was allowed on loan to Weymouth, Aylesbury and Bedworth United, until his release at the end of 1988/89. He then took up employment for Nexday, a parcel delivery firm, and turned out for their Sunday League side as they reached the Semi-finals of the F.A. Sunday Cup. By this time he had been contacted by Worcester City, and he then re-signed for them. His second spell included a game against Wrexham in a Welsh Cup tie in January 1990, and this resulted in an invitation to the Racecourse for a three month trial. After a few outings with the club's reserves he made his senior debut at Cambridge United as a substitute for his namesake, Roger Preece, in a 1-1 draw. He made a further six appearances that season before being rewarded with a two year contract in the summer. Andy was playing in a struggling side at this time, but it was also a very inexperienced squad, as Brian Flynn was forced to give youth its chance because of the financial constraints at the time. Even so, he collected a Welsh Cup runners'-up medal at the end of the 1990/91 campaign, when Wrexham lost 2-0 to Swansea City in the Final at the National Stadium in Cardiff. He struggled to secure a regular first team place throughout the first half of the following season, and when Stockport County offered £10,000 for him in December 1991, both Wrexham and Andy accepted gratefully. He made his County debut at Preston on Boxing Day as a substitute, and went on to become a great success at Edgeley Park, forming a prolific strike partnership with Kevin Francis. Andy scored 42 goals in just 96 League games for Stockport before newly-promoted Premier League side Crystal Palace paid out £350,000 for him with a percentage of the fee going to Wrexham. He had made three Wembley appearances for the Cheshire club: the Play-Off Finals of 1992, 1993 and 1994, although on each occasion he was on the losing side. On joining Palace he teamed up once again with his former Wrexham striking partner, and great friend, Chris Armstrong, and in his first season at Selhurst Park they led the 'Eagles' to the semi-finals of both the Coca Cola and F.A.Cup's. Despite this success in the Cup competitions Palace were relegated, and during the summer of 1995 he left Palace to join Second Division Blackpool for a £200,000 fee. In his first season with the 'Tangerines' he helped them reach the play-offs where they lost to Bradford City in the semi-finals. He spent two further campaigns with the 'Seasiders' joining First Division Bury in the summer of 1998 as a free agent. However, he couldn't prevent the 'Shakers' from relegation the following season, and in the summer of 1999 he was released.

Season	League		F.A.Cup		Welsh Cup		League Cup		F.R.T.		E.C.W.C.		Total	
	apps	gls	apps	gls	apps	gls	apps	gls	apps	gls	apps	gls	apps	gls
1989/90	4/3	1	-	-	-	-	-	-	-	-	-	-	4/3	1
1990/91	31/3	4	1	2	4	1	4	1	2	0	1	0	43/3	8
1991/92	9/1	2	-	-	1/1	1	1/1	0	2	1	-	-	13/3	4
	44/7	**7**	**1**	**2**	**5/1**	**2**	**5/1**	**1**	**4**	**1**	**1**	**0**	**60/9**	**13**

PREECE, Roger 1986 - 1990

Position; *Right-Back/Midfield*
D.O.B; *9th June, 1969*
Birthplace; *Much Wenlock, Shropshire*
Height; *5ft 9in* **Weight;** *10st 4lbs*
Debut; v. *Exeter City (a) 21st February, 1987*
Total Appearances & Goals; *116/26 apps 15 gls*
Career; *Wolves; Leicester City; Coventry City 1985; WREXHAM 15th Aug 1986; Chester 14th Aug 1990 165/5apps 4gls; Southport 18th Oct 1996 9apps 0gls; Telford United Feb 1997 8apps 1gls; Shrewsbury Town 26th Jun 1997 (Player/coach) 41/6apps 3gls;*
Honours; *Welsh Cup runner-up 1988;*

Third Division Runner-up 1994;Roger Preece was signed on apprentice forms with Wolves straight from school in Much Wenlock. At the time the Midlands club were in considerable financial disarray and he was soon to find himself part of the cost cutting exercise. He then joined Leicester City for a two month trial before Frank Upton, Coventry City's youth team coach invited him to Highfield Road. Roger spent most of that season playing regularly in the 'Sky Blues' Central League side, only to be released in the summer. He was then recommended to Wrexham manager Dixie McNeil, who invited him to the Racecourse for a trial period in July, and he signed a contract the following month. He went on to enjoy four seasons with the North Wales club, making his first team debut as a substitute for Barry Horne in a European Cup-Winners' Cup match in Malta, in a 3-0 win against FC Zurrieq. He had to wait until the end of February for his Football League debut, again as a sub, this time for Paul Emson in a 4-2 defeat at Exeter. Over the next three seasons Roger became a regular in the 'Robins' side, appearing either at right-back or on the right side of midfield. He played in the 1988 Welsh Cup Final against Cardiff City at the Vetch Field, where Wrexham lost 2-0. The following term saw him play his part in taking Wrexham to the Division Four Play-Off Final, although he missed the final games because of injury. 1989/90 proved to be his last season with Wrexham, as he was surprisingly released. At the Racecourse, he was described as a 'hard working, strong tackling midfielder, always in the thick of the action! He showed a lot of promise, was competitive, but his fiery temper often let him down, which resulted in him receiving his marching orders on a number of occasions. Following his release he was all set to join Conference League side Telford United when Chester City stepped in to sign him in June 1990. He made his debut for the 'Cestrians' in a 2-1 defeat at Bury in the opening game of the season. Despite relegation in 1992/93 he went on to help them gain promotion to the Second Division in 1994, when they ended the season as runners'-up to Shrewsbury Town. However, they were relegated at the end of the following year, although Roger was voted the club's 'Player of the Year'. In the opening game of the 1995/96 season he suffered a serious knee injury in a clattering tackle by Hartlepool's Mick Tait. That proved to be his final appearance for Chester, although he worked hard to regain his fitness. Roger was released in October 1996 and joined Conference League side Southport, where he made nine appearances before moving back to his native Shropshire in February 1997 to join fellow Conference League side Telford United. He made eight appearances, scoring one goal, when invited to rejoin his former manager at Telford, Jake King, as player/coach with Shrewsbury Town. Preece was given responsibilities as youth team coach, although he continued to play first team football, making his debut in a 2-1 defeat at Hartlepool in September 1997. He still remains in that capacity at Gay Meadow at the time of writing.

Season	League		F.A.Cup		Welsh Cup		League Cup		F.R.T.		E.C.W.C.		Total	
	apps	gls	apps	gls	apps	gls	apps	gls	apps	gls	apps	gls	apps	gls
1986/87	6/1	2	-	-	0/1	0	-	-	1	0	0/1	0	7/3	2
1987/88	33/7	4	2	0	4/2	1	2	0	2	0	-	-	43/9	5
1988/89	23/8	5	2	0	2	1	-	-	3	1	-	-	30/8	7
1989/90	27/5	1	1	0	6	0	0/1	0	2	0	-	-	36/6	1
	89/21	**12**	**5**	**0**	**12/3**	**2**	**2/1**	**0**	**8**	**1**	**0/1**	**0**	**116/26**	**15**

PRICE, Brian 1968 - 1970

Position; *Midfield*
D.O.B; *31st December, 1947.*
Birthplace; *Deganwy, Gwynedd*
Height; *5ft 9in* **Weight;** *11st 0lbs*
Debut; v. *Blaenau Ffestiniog (h) 12th January, 1970 (Welsh Cup)*
Total Appearances & Goals; *1 app 0 gls*
Career; *Llandudno; WREXHAM 1969; Porthmadog cs1970; Bangor City 1972; Conwy United Aug 1976; Porthmadog 16th Aug 1980;*
Honours; *Five Welsh Amateur International caps; Northern Floodlit League Cup Winner 1970; Alves Cup Winner 1970; North Wales Coast F.A.Representative cap;*

Brian Price was brought up on the North Wales coast at Deganwy, where he attended the local Primary school before going on to Ysgol John Bright in Llandudno. Upon completion of his education he went into the family building business, though he continued to play football for Llandudno. He progressed in the amateur game at that time, and impressed enough to be awarded five caps for Wales at Amateur level. It was whilst appearing in one of these games on the Racecourse that Brian was spotted by Wrexham manager John Neal, and eventually persuaded the promising midfielder to sign amateur terms for the 'Robins' after he had declined the offer to turn professional. His first team debut for Wrexham came in January 1970, when he stepped into the side for a Welsh Cup fifth round match with Blaenau Ffestiniog on the Racecourse, which the 'Robins' won 1-0. Brian played in midfield in place of Gareth Davies, but that game proved to be his only senior outing for the club, although he did continue to turn out for the reserves until the end of the season. He captained the side to the Northern Floodlit League Cup Final, where they beat Tranmere Rovers over the two legs. The summer of 1970 saw Brian leave the Racecourse, reluctantly, because of the travelling involved, and he then signed for Welsh League (North) side, Portmadoc. A couple of years at Yr Traeth were followed by a spell at Bangor City, who played in the Northern Premier League at the time. He was appointed club captain of the Farrar Road club, and remained with them until 1976 when he joined the newly founded Conwy United, becoming their first ever captain. Price later returned to Porthmadog for a while before finally hanging his boots up. He continued to run his family business throughout this time, as he does at present, having settled in the Deganwy area. Brian is brother-in-law to Dai Davies, the former 'Robin' and Welsh International custodian.

Season	League		F.A.Cup		Welsh Cup		League Cup		Total	
	apps	gls	apps	gls	apps	gls	apps	gls	apps	gls
1969/70	-	-	-	-	1	0	-	-	1	0
	-	**-**	**-**	**-**	**1**	**0**	**-**	**-**	**1**	**0**

PRICE, Cyril 1931 - 1932

Position; *Inside-Forward*
D.O.B; *10th March, 1908*
Birthplace; *South Elmsall, Yorkshire*
Died; *Pontefract J/A/S 1998*
Height; *5ft 7'1/2in* **Weight;** *10st 7lbs*
Debut; v. *Rochdale (a) 16th January, 1932*
Total Appearances & Goals; *2 apps 1 gls*
Career; *South Kirkby Colliery; Doncaster Rovers Aug 1928 24apps 5gls; WREXHAM 11th Jul 1931; Scunthorpe & Lindsey United Sept 1932; Frickley Colliery Oct 1934;*

Cyril Price was signed by Doncaster Rovers in August 1928 from local side South Kirkby Colliery, but he had to wait until February 1929 for his Football League debut, playing in their 2-1 home win over South Shields. Cyril couldn't quite command a regular first team place while at Belle Vue, but did make a further 23 League appearances for the club, scoring five goals. He left the South Yorkshire club in July 1931 after refusing the terms offered to him, and took up an invitation to join fellow Third Division North side Wrexham. His time at the Racecourse was to be even shorter, as he made just two League outings. Cyril's debut for the 'Robins' was delayed until January, because of the consistent form of Chris Ferguson at inside-forward. It came at Rochdale, where the 'Robins' recorded a 4-2 win. The following game turned out to be against his former club, Doncaster Rovers, on the Racecourse. Cyril was delighted to have been selected for this match, and he celebrated the occasion in the best possible way by scoring one of the side's goals in a 2-1 win. Despite these successes, it proved to be his last appearance in a blue & white Wrexham shirt (the club's colours at that time), and was released at the end of the season. In September 1932 Cyril joined Midland League side Scunthorpe & Lindsey United, for whom he scored 24 goals during the 1932/33 season.

Season	League		F.A.Cup		Welsh Cup		Total	
	apps	gls	apps	gls	apps	gls	apps	gls
1931/32	2	1	-	-	-	-	2	1
	2	**1**	**-**	**-**	**-**	**-**	**2**	**1**

PRINCE, John — 1931

Position; *Goalkeeper*
D.O.B; *6th June, 1906*
Birthplace; *Crewe, Cheshire*
Died; *Crewe, 13th October, 1971*
Height; *5ft 11in* ***Weight;*** *12st 10lbs*
Debut; v. *Walsall (a) 14th November, 1931*
Total Appearances & Goals; *4 apps 0 gls*
Career; *Northwich Victoria; Oldham Athletic 7th Nov 1927 1app 0gls; Port Vale 17th May 1928 43apps 0gls; Rochdale 1st August 1930 15apps 0gls; WREXHAM 13th Nov 1931 Shrewsbury Town Dec 1931; Derby County cs1932 0apps; Northwich Victoria Aug 1933; Crewe Alexandra 14th July 1937 0apps;*
Honours; *Third Division North Championship Winner 1930;*

'Jack' Prince joined Oldham Athletic from Northwich Victoria in November 1927. He was mainly the understudy to Jack Hacking at Boundary Park, though he made his Football League debut at home to Leeds United in a 1-0 defeat in March 1928. It proved to be his only senior game for the 'Latics' as he joined Port Vale at the end of the season, making his debut in a 'Potteries' derby match with Stoke City in September 1928, which ended in a 2-1 defeat. Jack made a total of 31 League appearances that season, which was to end in relegation for the Vale Park club. 1929/30 saw him record twelve League appearances, as the Staffordshire club went on to win the Third Division Championship at their first attempt. Despite this success Prince was transferred to Rochdale in the summer where he was to spend just over a year, making his debut in a 5-4 home win over Nelson in the opening match of the season. He then became established as the Lancashire club's regular 'keeper until he sustained an injury in a 5-3 home defeat by Doncaster Rovers in November 1930, which necessitated surgery and rest. It meant that he missed most of the remaining matches, and even though he fought his way back to full fitness, was released by Rochdale at the end of the season. He then began training with Crewe Alexandra, though in November 1931 was signed by Wrexham's caretaker manager Ralph Burkinshaw for a trial period, after the North Wales club's regular first team 'keeper - Wilf Burrows - had broken his arm. Jack made his debut for the 'Robins' at Walsall in a 2-0 defeat. He completed three more appearances until released following the signing of Ted Adams from Barrow. Jack then joined Midland League side Shrewsbury Town, saving a penalty on his debut, and going on to make a total of 21 Midland League appearances for the Shropshire club before being transferred to Derby County in the summer of 1932. However, he failed to break through into the 'Rams' senior side, and the following summer signed for Northwich Victoria. He spent a number of seasons at the Drill Field before returning to League football with Crewe Alexandra in July 1937, as first team cover for Tom Poskett. Prince made just one first team appearance for the 'Railwaymen', an F.A.Cup Second Round match against New Brighton, which ended 2-2. In his final season at Northwich, prior to signing for Crewe, Jack was reputed to have saved 11 out of 12 penalty kicks awarded against his side.

Season	League		F.A.Cup		Welsh Cup		Total	
	apps	gls	apps	gls	apps	gls	apps	gls
1931/32	3	0		0	-	-	4	0
	3	**0**	**1**	**0**	**-**	**-**	**4**	**0**

PRITCHARD, Arthur Vincent — 1946 - 1950

Position; *Inside-Forward*
D.O.B; *31st August, 1920*
Birthplace; *Chester, Cheshire*
Died; *Chester, 9th May 1995*
Height; *5ft 6 1/2in* ***Weight;*** *11st 0lbs*
Debut; v. *New Brighton (h) 31st August, 1946*
Total Appearances & Goals; *40 apps 8 gls*
Career; *Dumbarton; WREXHAM 30th Aug 1946; Macclesfield Town 19th Oct 1949; Pwllheli & District 9th Sept 1951; Flint Town United 20th Aug 1955; Oswestry Town Jul 1957 to Feb 1958;*
Honours; *Welsh League (North) Championship Winner 1952, 1956 & 1957; North Wales Coast F.A. representive cap;*

Vince Pritchard joined Wrexham in time for the recommencement of Post War football. He had previously spent four seasons with Dumbarton before linking up with the Racecourse club in August 1946, and made his Wrexham - and Football League - debut on his 26th birthday, in a 3-2 home win over New Brighton on the opening day of 1946/47. He appeared at centre-forward, and celebrated the occasion by scoring one of the 'Robins' goals. Vince went on to make a further twenty League appearances that season, hitting the target on seven occasions, although his first team opportunities soon faded with the arrival of Jack Boothway. Nevertheless, Vince remained at the Racecourse for another three years, although he played mostly reserve team football during this period, when called upon to deputise following injuries to the club's senior forwards. Pritchard moved on in the close season of 1950, joining Cheshire County League side Macclesfield Town, where he was to spend just under twelve months before returning to North Wales in September 1951 to play for Pwllheli & District. They were managed by the former Welsh international Tommy G.Jones, and Vince became a member of the side that became known as the 'Invincibles' as they remained unbeaten during the 1951/52 season. They averaged four goals a game - a remarkable record in what were the halcyon days of North Wales Coast football, which was of a very high standard at that time. During his time with Pwllheli he collected a Welsh League (North) Championship medal as well as winners' medal's in both the Cookson and Alves Cups, and also represented the North Wales Coast F.A. against the Scottish Junior League in a 2-2 draw at Flint's Holywell Road ground in April 1952. It was Flint Town United who became Vince's next port of call, in the summer of 1955 another most impressing side of that period where he spent two seasons as they lifted the Welsh League (North) championship trophy on both occasions. He joined Oswestry Town for 1957/58, although only staying with the Shropshire club until the February. He was later appointed trainer with Chester, also performing coaching duties throughout his time at Sealand Road. Vince, who owned a cycle shop in Chester for many years, passed away in May 1995 at the age of 74.

Season	League		F.A.Cup		Welsh Cup		Total	
	apps	gls	apps	gls	apps	gls	apps	gls
1946/47	21	7	-	-	2	0	23	7
1947/48	8	0	-	-	1	0	9	0
1948/49	5	1	-	-	1	0	6	1
1949/50	2	0	-	-	-	-	2	0
	36	**8**	**-**	**-**	**4**	**0**	**40**	**8**

PROCTOR, David — 1959 - 1960

Position; *Wing-half*
D.O.B; *10th October, 1929*
Birthplace; *Belfast,*
Height; *6ft 0ins* ***Weight;*** *12st 2lbs*
Debut; v. *Port Vale (h) 31st October 1959*
Total Appearances & Goals; *2 app 0 gls*
Career; *Portadown; Grimsby Town 11th Jan 1949 0apps; Blackpool 6th Aug 1949 0apps; Norwich City 19th Jan 1953 17apps 0gls; Northwich Victoria cs1954; Barrow 16th Oct 1954 160apps 2gls; WREXHAM (Trial) 25th Aug 1959, (Pro) 19th Sept 1959 to May 1960;*

David Proctor joined Grimsby Town from Northern Irish League side Portadown in January 1949. He failed to make a first team appearance for the 'Mariners' and was released at the end of the season. David then joined First Division Blackpool, spending over three years with the Tangerines again without recording a senior appearance. He was signed by Third Division South side Norwich City in January 1949, where he was to make his Football League debut in a 1-1 home draw with Coventry City, playing at right-back. He completed a further nine League appearances that season, and appeared in the opening two games of the 1953/54 campaign before being dropped from the side. David played a further five times until allowed to leave Carrow Road at the end of the season. He moved on to Cheshire County League side Northwich Victoria in the summer of 1954, but by October was back in the Football League with Barrow, of the Third Division North. Proctor enjoyed almost five years at Holker Street, during which time he made 160 League appearances, scoring just two goals before he was released at the end of 1958/59. He was given a chance to continue in the Football League by Wrexham manager John Love, undergoing a month's trial before signing professional terms in September 1959. He made his debut for the 'Robins' the following month, replacing Fred Davis in a 1-0 home win over Port Vale. After the game he was described as, 'essentially a wing-half, while he is a capable centre-half, but lacked speed on his debut'. His next match came at Bury in a 3-2 defeat, but it also proved to be his last first team game for the club, and in the Football League. He continued in the Cheshire County League side, passing on his experience to the youngsters in the side until the end of the campaign when he decided to quit. David is then believed to have returned to his native Northern Ireland.

Season	League		F.A.Cup		Welsh Cup		Total	
	apps	gls	apps	gls	apps	gls	apps	gls
1959/60	2	0	-	-	-	-	2	0
	2	**0**	**-**	**-**	**-**	**-**	**2**	**0**

PROVAN, Andrew McKelvie Hughes 1970 - 1972

Position; *Forward*
D.O.B; *1st January, 1944*
Birthplace; *Greenock, Strathclyde*
Height; *5ft 5ins* ***Weight;*** *10st 0lbs*
Debut; v. *Bury (h) 15th August, 1970*
Total Appearances & Goals; *63/2 apps 14 gls*
Career; *Port Glasgow Rangers; St.Mirren 1960 8apps; Barnsley 30th May 1963 3apps 0gls; York City Aug 1964 159/1apps 49gls; Chester Aug 1968 77/3apps 19gls; WREXHAM 22nd Apr 1970 £7,500; Southport 18th Jul 1972 82/1apps 28 gls; Philadelphia Atoms 1973 & 1974; Torquay United Aug 1974 83/8apps 14gls; Bath City 1977; Totnes Birdwatchers 1979; Windsor United 1980; WBB 1982-1990;*
Honours; *Scottish Youth international cap; Fourth Division Championship Winner 1973; Welsh Cup runner-up 1971; North American Soccer League Championship Winner 1973; Southern League Championship Winner 1978;*

Andy Provan was spotted in local football with Port Glasgow Rangers by Scottish League side St.Mirren. He then signed for the Paisley club as an amateur in 1960, turning professional in 1961. Andy made eight first team appearances for the 'Buddies' before he was given a free transfer at the end of the 1962/63 season. St.Mirren then had a change of heart and offered him a new contract, but by then it was too late as he had already taken up an offer to join Barnsley in May 1963. He made his Football League debut for the 'Tykes' in the opening match of the season, a 4-1 defeat at Colchester United. The man from Greenock was replaced for the next game, making just two more League appearances for the Oakwell club before his release in the summer of 1964. He was taken on a month's trial by York City, who signed him permanently in August. His career really took off with the 'Minstermen', as he became an ever-present in his first season at Bootham Crescent, helping York to promotion to the Third Division. The following campaign was nowhere near as successful, however, as York were relegated. Andy continued at Bootham Crescent until the beginning of the 1968/69 season, when Chester stepped in to sign him. He spent almost two years at Sealand Road, helping them reach the Welsh Cup Final in 1970, where they lost to Cardiff City, though by the time the game had been played he had left the Cheshire club to move over the border and join Wrexham for a £7,500 fee. The 'Robins' had just won promotion to the Third Division, and Andy had been brought in to strengthen the first team squad for the new season. He was an exciting winger on his day, but couldn't show enough consistency to command a regular first team place in his two seasons at the Racecourse, although he collected a Welsh Cup runners'-up medal in 1971. Due to the emergence of promising youngster Graham Whittle, Andy was allowed to join Southport in July 1972, where he formed a prolific goalscoring partnership with Jim Fryatt. Their goals helped Southport to win the Fourth Division Championship in 1973, Andy topping the Haig Avenue's goalscoring charts with 21 League goals. During the summer of 1973 both Andy and Jim Fryatt travelled to America to play for Philadelphia Atoms. They were nicknamed 'Batman and Robin' by the American fans, as the Atoms won the North American Soccer League. Both returned to Southport for the start of 1973/74, which turned out to be a disaster for the 'Sandgrounders' as they were relegated. Provan returned to the States the next summer, rejoining the Philadelphia side. Upon his return again in August 1974, he linked up with Torquay United, where he was to spend three years. However, he found the goals harder to come by, scoring just 14 times in 91 League games for the Devon club. He eventually left Plainmoor, and the Football League scene, in 1977, joining Southern League side Bath City, where he won a championship medal in his first season. Having settled in the Torquay area he continued to appear in local football in Devon, playing for the quaintly named Totnes Birdwatchers, Windsor United, and W.B.B. until 1990, when well into his forties. Following the end of his professional career Andy became qualified as a psychiatric nurse, a job which he was still doing at the time of writing.

Season	League		F.A.Cup		Welsh Cup		League Cup		Total	
	apps	gls	apps	gls	apps	gls	apps	gls	apps	gls
1970/71	30/2	7	-	-	5	2	2	1	37/2	10
1971/72	19	3	2	1	2	0	3	0	26	4
	49/2	**10**	**2**	**1**	**7**	**2**	**5**	**1**	**63/2**	**14**

PRYCE, Idris 1959 - 1960

Position; *Outside-Left*
D.O.B; *24th February, 1941.*
Birthplace; *Rossett, Denbighshire*
Height; *5ft 8in* ***Weight;*** *11st 2lbs*
Debut; v. *Accrington Stanley (a) 29th August 1959*
Total Appearances & Goals; *3 apps 0 gls*
Career; *Holt Nomads; WREXHAM 17th Sept 1959; Rhyl 18th Jul 1960; Colwyn Bay 17th Jul 1962; Oswestry Town; Pwllheli & District 1st Jul 1965; Stafford Rangers 29th Oct 1965; Colwyn Bay 11th Mar 1966; Llandudno 30th Aug 1966; Pwllheli & District 24th Sept 1966; Colwyn Bay 8th Oct 1966; Blaenau Ffestiniog 2nd Dec 1966; Llandudno 11th Sept 1967; Oswestry Town 14th Oct 1967; Barmouth & Dyffryn United 9th Nov 1967; Berriew 23rd Aug 1973; Nantlle Vale 3rd Jan 1974; Oswestry Town 1976/77;*
Honours; *Welsh Youth Cup Winner 1959; North Wales Coast F.A.Challenge Cup Winner 1969 & 1971;*

Idris Pryce joined the ground staff at Wrexham as an amateur in 1958 upon leaving school, having played local football for Holt Nomads. He earned a professional contract with the 'Robins' in September 1959, making his Football League debut in a 2-2 draw at Accrington Stanley in the third match of the 1959/60 season as a replacement for Brian Cripsey at outside-left. Reports from the game stated that 'he laid on the pass for the last minute equaliser by Aly McGowan - a 100% trier'. The speedy winger played in the following two home games against Brentford (3-2) and Bournemouth (1-2), but then made way for George Porter followed by Peter Brown. The Bournemouth game proved to be his last senior outing for Wrexham, as he spent the remainder of the season playing for the reserves in the Cheshire County League. It was a campaign that was to end with the club's relegation to the Fourth Division, and Idris was a victim of the consequent clear-out in the summer. He was soon fixed up with another club, however, when he joined Cheshire County League side Rhyl, and he spent two seasons at Belle Vue before signing for Colwyn Bay in the summer of 1962. He later went on to play for a number of clubs, amongst which were Stafford Rangers and several North Wales Coast sides, including Pwllheli &

District, Llandudno, Blaenau Ffestiniog, Berriew, Nantlle Vale and Barmouth & Dyffryn United - where he collected two North Wales Coast F.A.Challenge Cup winners' medals, proving his liking for the sea air! He was later appointed manager of Barmouth, and also had spells in charge at Newtown, Nantlle Vale and Oswestry Town, enjoying much success. Following the appointment of Dixie McNeil as manager at Wrexham Idris was put in charge of the club's reserve side, along with Brian Prandle. With Cliff Sear he coached many of the youngsters who broke into the first team under Brian Flynn's management, players like Gareth Owen, Wayne Phillips, Steve Watkin, Chris Armstrong, Phil Hardy, and Lee Jones, to name but a few. However, Idris was to leave the Racecourse in 1993 following an internal dispute, though he soon returned to the game following his appointment as manager of the reformed Oswestry Town team, entrusted with the task of putting a team together for the start of the 1993/94 season in the Welsh National League. He suddenly resigned from the job in December 1993, because of 'family and work commitments'. Idris still resides in the Oswestry area, where he has been employed with ATS Tyres in the town for over twenty years.

Season	League		F.A.Cup		Welsh Cup		Total	
	apps	gls	apps	gls	apps	gls	apps	gls
1959/60	3	0	-	-	-	-	3	0
	3	**0**	**-**	**-**	**-**	**-**	**3**	**0**

PUGH, Gary

1984 - 1985 & 1986 - 1988

Position; *Centre-Half*
D.O.B; *10th January, 1967*
Birthplace; *Wrexham, Denbighshire*
Height; *6ft 1in* **Weight;** *11st 8lbs*
Debut; v. *Wigan Athletic (a) 4th September 1984 (League Cup)*
Total Appearances & Goals; *2 apps 0 gls*
Career; *Coedpoeth; WREXHAM Jul 1984; Porthmadog cs1985; Rhyl Sept 1985; Tywyn; WREXHAM Jul 1986; Lex XI cs1988; Brymbo Steelworks; Lex XI;*
Honours; *Welsh Youth international cap;*

Gary Pugh began playing football at Bryn Offa School in Wrexham, gaining selection for both his school and District teams. He also appeared for the Coedpoeth Junior teams at the same time, and remained with them until he was 14, when signed on Schoolboy forms by Wrexham in 1981. On leaving school Gary was enrolled on a Youth Training Scheme by the Racecourse club, and after only twelve months was called into the first team because of injuries. His senior debut came in September 1984, the 'Robins' losing 2-0 in a League Cup tie at Wigan Athletic. His Football League debut followed within a month in a 1-0 defeat at Mansfield Town. It was at this time that the Racecourse club were paired against F.C.Porto and Real Zaragoza in the European Cup-Winners' Cup, with Gary on the substitutes' bench for all four games. Later that season he was called up for Welsh Youth team trials at Cardiff and, deemed good enough to win a place in the squad, making his Wales Youth team bow against Holland at Rhyl. At the end of the 1984/85 season Pugh was disappointingly released by Wrexham. He then joined Porthmadog, but after just a few outings signed for Northern Premier League side Rhyl, later followed by a spell with Tywyn. Gary was invited back to the Racecourse club in the summer of 1986 on non-contract terms, where he was involved with the reserve side for two seasons. He did not figure in the senior XI during that spell, and at the end of 1987/88 he joined Lex XI, returning to the Racecourse in November 1988 for a Welsh Cup tie, which the non-league side lost 8-0! He has remained at Lex XI for much of the time since that defeat, apart from a short spell with Brymbo Steelworks, and was still turning out for them in the Cymru Alliance League at the start of the 1998/99 season, alongside former 'Racecourse Robins' Nigel Beaumont and Steve Scott. Gary still resides in the Wrexham area and is currently employed by 'Jarvis', a franchise of Rail Track, as a track man. He has been connected with the firm for over ten years, since leaving Wrexham F.C. in 1988.

Season	League		F.A.Cup		Welsh Cup		League Cup		F.R.T.		E.C.W.C.		Total	
	apps	gls	apps	gls	apps	gls	apps	gls	apps	gls	apps	gls	apps	gls
1984/85	1	0	-	-	-	-	1	0	-	-	-	-	2	0
	1	**0**	**-**	**-**	**-**	**-**	**1**	**0**	**-**	**-**	**-**	**-**	**2**	**0**

PUGH, James William

1923 - 1925

Position; *Left-Back*
D.O.B; *J/A/S, 1891*
Birthplace; *Hereford, Herefordshire*
Height; *5ft 8ins* **Weight;** *11st 6lbs*
Debut; v. *Ashington (h) 25th August, 1923*
Total Appearances & Goals; *40 apps 0 gls*
Career; *Clapton Orient (WW1 Guest); Coventry City (WW1 Guest); Luton Town (WW1 Guest); Brighton & Hove Albion cs1919 22apps 0gls; Hereford 1920/21; Bridgend Town Apr 1921; Abertillery 3rd Jun 1921; Manchester United 6th Apr 1922 2apps 0gls £250; WREXHAM 16th Jul 1923 £150; Rhos 6th Aug 1925; Bangor City 26th Nov 1926; Buckley United 22nd Jan 1927; Holywell Town 28th Jul 1927; Denbigh United 1st Oct 1927;*

Jimmy Pugh played as a 'guest' for Clapton Orient, Coventry City, and Luton Town during the First World War before joining Southern League side Brighton & Hove Albion in the close season of 1919. He made 23 Southern League and Cup appearances for the 'Seagulls' leaving the Goldstone Ground in the summer of 1920. He is believed to have then joined Hereford, from where he moved on to Bridgend Town towards the end of the 1920/21 season. He switched to Abertillery in the summer of 1921, where he impressed enough to be signed by Manchester United in April 1922 for a £250 fee. Jimmy made his Football League debut for United in the same month, at left-back in a 1-1 draw against Cardiff City. By that time United can already been consigned to relegation from the First Division. Jimmy was to make just one more League appearance in October 1922, in another 1-1 home draw - this time against Fulham. At the end of that season he was allowed to leave Old Trafford, joining Third Division North side Wrexham for a £150 fee. He made his debut for the 'Robins' in the opening match of 1923/24, a 4-0 home win over Ashington, and kept his place in the side until November when he was replaced by Noel Edwards. Pugh managed another two League games that season, while he clocked up 22 senior outings in 1924/25 before Albert Lumberg began to show promise in the left-back position. The emergence of the new man led to Jimmy's release in the summer. He remained in North Wales as he moved around Rhos, Bangor City, Buckley United, Holywell Town, and finally Denbigh United, who he joined in October 1927.

Season	League		F.A.Cup		Welsh Cup		Total	
	apps	gls	apps	gls	apps	gls	apps	gls
1923/24	18	0	-	-	-	-	18	0
1924/25	22	0	-	-	1	0	23	0
	40	**0**	**-**	**-**	**1**	**0**	**41**	**0**

***PUGH,* Stephen** 1992 - 1995

Position; *Forward*
D.O.B; *27th November, 1973*
Birthplace; *Bangor, Gwynedd*
Height; *5ft 10in* ***Weight;*** *11st 0lbs*
Debut; v. *Hereford United (a) 3rd October, 1992*
Total Appearances & Goals; *3/8 apps 0 gls*
Career; *Watford Jul 1990; WREXHAM Feb 1992 (trial), 3rd Jul 1992; Runcorn 3rd Oct 1994 4/3apps 1gls (Loan); USA May 1995; Bangor City 18th Sept 1995 4/1apps 1gls; USA May 1996; Porthmadog Aug 1996 55/6apps 15gls;*
Honours; *Two Wales Under-21 International caps; Welsh Youth International; Welsh Schoolboy international; Welsh F.A.Youth Cup Winner 1992;*

Brought up in Pwllheli, North Wales, Steve Pugh was sufficiently talented to be chosen to represent his country at various Schoolboy levels, and this led him to sign Schoolboy forms for Crewe Alexandra at the age of 12, where he would spend his holidays. Eventually, he took up an offer to join Watford on Schoolboy forms, again spending his holidays with them! On completing his Education he secured a Y.T.S. placement with the 'Hornets' in July 1990. As he progressed through the ranks at Vicarage Road he gained further international recognition for his country at Youth level, although told that he would be released before his training scheme had ended, as the club felt that they had too many strikers on their books. Wrexham manager Brian Flynn agreed to allow him to complete his YTS course at the Racecourse, and he impressed sufficiently after his arrival in February 1992 to be offered a professional contract at the end of that season. He was soon handed his senior debut, coming on as substitute for Mark Taylor in a 1-1 draw at Hereford in October 1992. Steve went on to make four more first team appearances that season, as he continued to progress, and two Welsh under-21 appearances, both against Belgium, came in the following year. He also added a further seven League appearances, though his first team opportunities were restricted by a series of niggling injuries, and by the form of first team strikers Gary Bennett and Steve Watkin. He was best described at the Racecourse as 'a very pacy player who lays the ball off well, but injuries hampered his progress'. 1994/95 was to see little sign of a breakthrough, so when offered the chance to join Conference League side Runcorn on loan in October to give him more experience, he accepted. He spent two months with the Canal Street club, during which he made seven Conference League appearances, scoring one goal. On his return to North Wales Pugh made an appearance as substitute in a 3-3 home draw with Peterborough United in December 1994, but it proved to be his final game for the 'Robins' as he was released on 11th May 1995. He then took up an offer to travel to America, playing for a local League side during the summer before returning to North Wales in September 1995 to join Bangor City. At the end of that season he returned once again to the States before joining League of Wales side, Porthmadog for the start of the 1996/97 season. Steve is still currently playing at Ytraeth at the time of writing, despite having been relegated into the Cymru Alliance League in 1998.

Season	League		F.A.Cup		Welsh Cup		League Cup		A.G.T.		Total	
	apps	gls	apps	gls	apps	gls	apps	gls	apps	gls	apps	gls
1992/93	1/2	0	-	-	1/1	0	-	-	-	-	2/3	0
1993/94	2/5	0	0/2	0	0/1	0	-	-	1	0	3/8	0
1994/95	0/1	0	-	-	-	-	-	-	-	-	0/1	0
	3/8	**0**	**0/2**	**0**	**1/2**	**0**	**-**	**-**	**1**	**0**	**5/12**	**0**

***PURDIE,* Bernard Charles** 1967 - 1971

Position; *Forward*
D.O.B; *20th April, 1949*
Birthplace; *Pentre Broughton, Denbighshire*
Height; *5ft 9in* ***Weight;*** *11st 0lbs*
Debut; v. *Colchester United (a) 2nd November, 1968*
Total Appearances & Goals; *10/3 apps 3 gls*
Career; *WREXHAM 17th Oct 1967; Chester 15th Jul 1971 54/9apps 14gls; Crewe Alexandra Jul 1973 203/10apps; Huddersfield Town 5th Oct 1979 37/9apps 1gls; Crewe Alexandra Aug 1982 14/2apps 0gls; Bangor City cs1983; Oswestry Town cs1984;*
Honours; *Welsh Youth International cap; Northern Floodlit League Cup Winner 1970; Alves Cup Winner 1970;*

Bernard Purdie began his schoolboy football with Pentre Broughton when invited to Wrexham for trials by Ken Roberts and Jack Rowley. He signed schoolboy forms, followed by an apprenticeship with the Racecourse club on leaving school in 1965, and progressed to the professional ranks in October 1967. Although he may appear to have spent a fairly brief spell at the Racecourse he was on the verge of the first team for almost four years having made his Football League debut in November 1968 in a 2-1 defeat at Colchester United, where he replaced former England centre-forward Ray Charnley. However, he had to cope with intense competition for a first team place in his position from Charnley, Ray Smith, Brian Tinnion and Albert Kinsey. At the end of the 1970/71 season, with Bernard having managed just ten first team appearances for the 'Robins', he accepted an offer to join Chester, along with 'keeper Gordon Livsey. He made a promising start at Sealand Road, scoring on his full debut in a 1-1 draw against Tranmere Rovers in the League Cup. Bernard spent two seasons with the 'Cestrians', clocking up over sixty appearances before joining Crewe Alexandra in July 1973. Again, he made an immediate impact by scoring the only goal in a 1-0 home win over Gillingham in the opening game of the season, lining up alongside his ex-Wrexham team mate Albert Kinsey. Bernard enjoyed his most successful years with the 'Railwaymen', making over 200 League appearances, and adapting to whatever position he was required to play - a real 'utility player'. With this versatility in mind Huddersfield Town manager Mick Buxton was persuaded to sign him in October 1979. Bernard made his debut in October 1979, as a substitute in a 2-2 home draw with York City. He was deployed mainly in defence at Leeds Road, and in almost three seasons with the 'Terriers' played in over fifty League and Cup games until rejoining Crewe Alexandra in the summer of 1982. His second spell at Gresty Road was much shorter, making his debut in a Cheshire 'derby' at Chester in the opening game of the 1982/83 season, which Crewe lost 1-0. He made just fifteen more League appearances for the 'Railwaymen' as they had to gain re-election at the end of the season. In the summer of 1983 Purdie moved into non-league football with Alliance Premier League side Bangor City, before going on to have a spell with Oswestry Town. After his professional football career had ended Bernard settled in the Wrexham area where he took up employment with the Royal Mail.

Season	League		F.A.Cup		Welsh Cup		League Cup		Total	
	apps	gls	apps	gls	apps	gls	apps	gls	apps	gls
1968/69	3	1	-	-	1	0	-	-	4	1
1969/70	4/3	2	-	-	-	-	2	0	6/3	2
	7/3	**3**	**-**	**-**	**1**	**0**	**2**	**0**	**10/3**	**3**

QUIGLEY, Michael Anthony 1995

Position; *Midfield*
D.O.B; *2nd October, 1970*
Birthplace; *Manchester, Lancashire*
Height; *5ft 7in* ***Weight;*** *11st 4lbs*
Debut; v. *Leyton Orient (a) 18th February, 1995*
Total Appearances & Goals; *4 apps 0 gls*
Career; *Manchester City 1st Jul 1989 3/9apps 0gls; WREXHAM 17th Feb 1995 (Loan); Hull City 5th Jul 1995 36/15apps 3gls;*
Honours; *F.A.Youth Cup runner-up 1989;*

Mike was actually born in the Old Trafford area of Manchester, where he was quite naturally brought up as a United fan. As a schoolboy he was linked with Oldham Athletic, but upon leaving school in July 1987 was offered an apprenticeship by Manchester City, which he gladly accepted. He enjoyed a successful apprenticeship with City, playing in the 1989 F.A.Youth Cup Final in a 2-1 aggregate defeat against Watford. He then accepted professional terms at Maine Road, but had to wait over two years before making his first team debut in October 1991, a Zenith Data Systems Cup match against Sheffield Wednesday at Hillsborough, which City lost 3-2. Over the next four years Mike's career with City was constantly interrupted by a series of niggling injuries, which saw him complete just twelve League games in that time, mostly as a substitute. In February 1995 he was given the opportunity of first team football signing or Second Division Wrexham on a month's loan. He was signed in a bid to strengthen the midfield while an outside chance of a play-off place was still possible, and made a bright start on his debut at Leyton Orient. He then played reasonably well in a 3-1 home win over Plymouth Argyle, before the 'Robins' came unstuck at Birmingham City with a 5-2 defeat. Following a 1-0 home defeat by Blackpool he was allowed to return to Maine Road before his loan spell had expired. Mike remained with City until the end of the season when he found that he was to be released. He then accepted an offer to join Hull City on a free transfer, but made a disastrous start to his 'Tigers' career when he broke his leg in only the second match of the 1995/96 campaign at Rotherham United. He returned to full fitness by the end of February, in what was a disappointing season for Hull as they finished bottom of Division Two. The 1996/97 season saw him again hit by his injury jinx, when he was laid low with a mystery stomach virus, and then suffered calf and thigh injuries! Described as a 'pocket battleship' at Boothferry Park, he was released by the 'Tigers' in the summer of 1998.

Season	League		F.A.Cup		Welsh Cup		League Cup		A.W.S.		Total	
	apps	gls	apps	gls	apps	gls	apps	gls	apps	gls	apps	gls
1994/95	4	0	-	-	-	-	-	-	-	-	4	0
	4	**0**	**-**	**-**	**-**	**-**	**-**	**-**	**-**	**-**	**4**	**0**

John Roberts

R

RAVEN, James 1937 - 1939

Position; *Right-Half*
D.O.B; *29th March, 1908*
Birthplace; *Nottingham, Nottinghamshire*
Died; *Nottingham, 2nd January, 1965*
Height; *5ft 11in* **Weight;** *11st 6lbs*
Debut; v. *Hull City (a) 28th August, 1937*
Total Appearances & Goals; *55 apps 1 gls*
Career; *Notts County (Am) Aug 1931, (Pro) Nov 1931 0apps; Folkestone cs1933; Brentford Apr 1934 1app 0gls; Bristol Rovers 22nd Apr 1936 7apps 0gls; WREXHAM 6th Aug 1937; Nottingham Corinthians; East End Nottingham Co-operative Dairy;*
Honours; *Western League Championship Winner 1937;*

James Raven joined Notts County in August 1931 as an amateur, and signed professional terms in November. He failed to make a breakthrough into the first team during his two years at Meadow Lane, and in the summer of 1933 moved south to join Southern League side Folkestone. Jim spent one season with the south coast club moving on to Brentford in April 1934. He remained an amateur at Griffin Park and settled for a place in the 'Bees' reserve side before finally making his Football League debut against Nottingham Forest on 28th February 1935, in a scoreless draw at the City Ground. Brentford went on to win the Second Division Championship, but in May 1936 Jim was transferred to Bristol Rovers, along with fellow team mates Bert Watson and Leslie Sullivan for a combined fee of £975.00. He spent just over twelve months with 'Rovers', completing a total of nine League and Cup appearances. He played in the Gloucestershire Cup Final for the 'Pirates' before making his debut against Northampton Town in September 1936. That same season he also helped the Eastville club's reserve's side retain the Western League championship. In the summer of 1937 Raven left 'Rovers' to join Wrexham, who were then managed by Captain James Logan. He immediately went into the first team in his favourite right-half position for the opening game of the 1937/38 season, a 3-2 defeat at Hull. He was not selected for the next six matches, but returned at the end of September to keep his place for the rest of the campaign. During the summer of 1938 he almost signed for Colchester United, after the Essex club had sent him the rail fare for the journey to Layer Road, but for some unknown reason failed to turn up! James began the new term as a first team regular at the Racecourse, but by November had lost his place in the side to Robert Savage. He was then restricted to the odd appearance, as cover for the central defensive positions, before the Second World War intervened to put paid to his football career. He did turn out again for the 'Robins' during 1945/46, when he made two appearances on the Racecourse, a 2-0 win over Tranmere in September, and a 1-1 draw with Oldham the following month. With his professional football career over he returned to settle in his native city of Nottingham, where he continued to play amateur football for local non-league sides Nottingham Corinthians and East End, as well as Nottingham Co-operative Dairy, where he was employed for over 20 years.

Season	League		F.A.Cup		Welsh Cup		N.S.C.		Total	
	apps	gls	apps	gls	apps	gls	apps	gls	apps	gls
1937/38	36	1	2	0	1	0	-	-	39	1
1938/39	19	0	-	-	1	0	2	0	22	0
1945/46	2*	0*	-	-	-	-	-	-	2*	0*
	55	**1**	**2**	**0**	**2**	**0**	**2**	**0**	**61**	**1**

* = War period appearances, not included in total

RAWLINS, David 1965 - 1966

Position; *Outside-Left*
D.O.B; *12th December 1943*
Birthplace; *Llay, Denbighshire*
Height; *5ft 9in* **Weight;** *10st 11lbs*
Debut; v. *South Liverpool (h) 13th November, 1965 (F.A.Cup)*
Total Appearances & Goals; *1 app 0 gls*
Career; *Rhos Aelwyd 1958; WREXHAM Nov 1965; Rhos Aelwyd cs1966; Caernarvon Town Nov 1966; Pwllheli cs1967; Barmouth & Dyffryn United cs1968;*
Honours; *Welsh Youth Cup Winner 1959, 1960 & 1962; North Wales Coast F.A.Challenge Cup Winner 1969 & 1971;*

David Rawlins began playing football seriously at Llay Junior and Llay Senior Schools, where he was to represent Wrexham & District Schoolboys. He left school at 15 to take up employment as an apprentice joiner. It was also around this period that he attended trials with both Liverpool and Wrexham, eventually signing amateur forms for the latter in 1958/59. David had been turning out for Rhos Aelwyd in the Welsh National League at the time, where he collected a League Cup winners' medal. At the Racecourse he progressed through the ranks, playing for the club's teams in the Welsh National League, Welsh League (North) and eventually for the reserves in the Cheshire County League. Rawlins had considerable success during this period with the 'Robins' youth team, collecting three Welsh Youth Cup winners' medals: the first in 1959, a 4-2 win at Llanidloes; a 2-1 win over Newtown in 1960 at Welshpool, after a 2-2 draw; and finally in 1962, following a 1-0 success over Cardiff City at Aberystwyth. He continued to progress, finishing as the club's leading scorer for the reserves in 1963/64, and eventually made a break through into the first team in November 1965. Called up as a replacement for Dave Campbell his debut came in an F.A.Cup First Round match with South Liverpool on the Racecourse, as Wrexham convincingly won 4-1. His Football League debut followed a week later in a home match with Bradford City, which ended in a 1-1 draw. It turned out to be a disastrous game for Dave as he suffered a broken leg, which sidelined him for five months and, once fit, found that he was to be released. He returned to Rhos Aelwyd, hoping to regain strength and fitness, before moving up the coast to join Caernarvon Town, where he spent the remainder of the 1966/67 season. A year with Pwllheli was followed by a move to Barmouth & Dyffryn United, where he enjoyed a successful period. There, he collected three League championship and two North Wales Coast F.A.Challenge Cup winners' medals - one of which came in the 1969 Final. Rawlins had scored one of the Barmouth goals in a 3-3 draw with Holyhead, lifting the trophy after their opponents failed to fulfil the replay fixture. The following season he played at Ninian Park against Cardiff City in the Welsh Cup, but was forced to give up playing football a year later because of damage to his knee. David, who settled in Llay, is employed by the Health Authority as a joiner at the time of writing, where he has worked since 1967. His son, Richard, was at one time on Wrexham's books as an apprentice, and is a Welsh Youth international. He currently helps out with the club's 'A' team as physio.

Season	League		F.A.Cup		Welsh Cup		League Cup		Total	
	apps	gls	apps	gls	apps	gls	apps	gls	apps	gls
1965/66	1	0	1	0	-	-	-	-	2	0
	1	**0**	**1**	**0**	**-**	**-**	**-**	**-**	**2**	**0**

RAYNOR, Paul James

1988

Position; *Forward*
D.O.B; *29th April, 1966*
Birthplace; *Nottingham, Nottinghamshire*
Height; *6ft 0in* ***Weight;*** *11st 4lbs*
Debut; v. *Tranmere Rovers (h) 22nd October, 1988*
Total Appearances & Goals; *6 apps 0 gls*
Career; *Nottingham Forest 2nd Apr 1984 3apps 0 gls; Bristol Rovers 28th Mar 1985 (Loan) 7/1apps 0gls; Huddersfield Town 15th Aug 1985 38/12apps 9gls; Swansea City 27th Mar 1987 170/21apps 27gls; WREXHAM 17th Oct 1988 (Loan); Cambridge United 10th Mar 1992 46/3apps 2gls; Preston North End 23rd Jul 1993 £36,000 70/7apps 9gls; Cambridge United 12th Sept 1995 78/1apps 7gls (Exchange deal for Dean Barrick); Guang Deong Wen Yuan (China) Jun 1997 £20,000; Leyton Orient Feb 1998 5/5apps 0gls; Stevenage Borough Aug 1998 (trial); Kettering Town Sept 1998;*
Honours; *Welsh Cup Winner 1989 & 1991;*

Paul Raynor began his Football career with home town club Nottingham Forest, signing as an apprentice on leaving school in 1982. He progressed to the club's professional ranks, making his Football League debut in November 1984 at Southampton, replacing Trevor Christie at centre-forward in a 1-0 defeat. He played in the next two matches, at Coventry and at home to Spurs, but they were to be his only games for Forest, although joining Bristol Rovers on loan in March 1985, where he made eight League appearances. Paul left the City Ground in the summer, and signed for Huddersfield Town on a free transfer. In his two seasons at Leeds Road he made fifty League appearances, scoring nine goals. Another free transfer move, this time to Swansea City, followed in March 1987, and he went on to spend five years at the Vetch. During this period he helped the 'Swans' win the Welsh Cup in both 1989 and 1991. That success gave him the opportunity to sample some European action, making the most of the opportunity by scoring a memorable goal in Athens against Panathinaikos in September 1989. In October 1988 he was loaned out to Wrexham, where he made his debut for the 'Robins' in a 3-3 home draw with Tranmere Rovers, replacing Steve Buxton. His spell at the Racecourse proved to be uneventful, turning out on a further five occasions without scoring before returning to the Vetch upon completion of his stay. After clocking up almost 200 League games with Swansea Raynor joined Cambridge United in March 1992, where he recorded 49 League appearances, and scored two goals. A £36,000 transfer to Preston North End followed in July 1993, where he teamed up again with John Beck, his former boss at Cambridge. He then helped the 'Lilywhites' reach the 1994 Play-Off Final, having scored against Torquay United in the semi-final to earn Preston a trip to Wembley and a meeting with Wycombe Wanderers. Sadly for Paul, Wycombe won 4-2. The Lancashire club qualified for the Play-Off's again at the end of the following season, but fell at the semi-final hurdle to Bury. During his time at Deepdale Paul was described as 'undoubtedly the most skilful ball player with either foot on the Preston staff'.

Despite missing just nine games during 1994/95 he was allowed to return to Cambridge United in the close season in an exchange deal that saw Dean Barrick join Preston. Paul spent a further two seasons at the Abbey Stadium, remaining a regular in the side until the summer of 1997. He accepted an offer to join the superbly named Chinese side, Guang Deong Wen Yuan (Canton), in July 1997, who paid £20,000 for his services. He returned to England in February 1998 to join Third Division Leyton Orient, where he stayed until the end of the campaign. In the summer of 1998 he linked up with Stevenage Borough for a trial period, before agreeing a permanent move to fellow Conference League side Kettering Town in September 1998.

Season	League apps	League gls	F.A.Cup apps	F.A.Cup gls	Welsh Cup apps	Welsh Cup gls	League Cup apps	League Cup gls	A.W.S. apps	A.W.S. gls	Total apps	Total gls
1988/89	6	0	-	-	-	-	-	-	-	-	6	0
	6	**0**	-	-	-	-	-	-	-	-	**6**	**0**

READ, Edward

1926 - 1930

Position; *Centre-Half*
D.O.B; *16th June, 1903*
Birthplace; *Rhosllanerchrugog, Denbighshire*
Died; *Wrexham, 10th April, 1997*
Height; *5ft 9in* ***Weight;*** *11st 4lbs*
Debut; v. *New Brighton (h) 7th April, 1928*
Total Appearances & Goals; *43 apps 0 gls*
Career; *Bersham Reserves; Rhos Athletic; Penycae; WREXHAM (Am) Sept 1927, (Pro) Oct, 1927; Macclesfield Town Aug 1930; Halifax Town Aug 1931; Rochdale (Trial) 1934; Bellfield St.Annes;*
Honours; *Welsh Junior International cap;*

Having attended school in the Rhos area Teddy Read began his working life at the Hafod Colliery, near Johnstown. He would combine work with playing football, initially for Bersham Reserves followed by Rhos Athletic and then Penycae. It was while Teddy was playing for Rhos that a friend, Sammy Davies, suggested that he joined Wrexham's reserve side, and he accepted an invitation to play in a Welsh League match at Flint. Teddy was asked back for the following match against Druids after which Wrexham director Sam Clutton offered him £2.00 a week to sign semi-professional terms. He accepted, and continued to work at Hafod Colliery. A month later, throughout which he had shown some impressive form, he was asked to sign full-time. His new terms were £5.00 per week when appearing in the first team, and £4.00 when not involved. For the first two years Teddy played mostly reserve team football in the Birmingham and District League. His first team debut came towards the end of the 1927/28 season, a 2-0 home defeat by New Brighton in April. Over the next two seasons he had regular spells in the first team, when described as 'possessing strong tackling qualities and the ability to drive the ball out to the wings. He takes half the sting out of the attack by subduing the opposing centre-forward.' Teddy remained with the Racecourse club until the end of 1929/30, during which he had been unable to secure a regular first place because of the form of Billie Rogers, George Bellis and Bob Graham. At the end of the season he was told that he was to be placed on the transfer list with a fee of £500 required. He joined Cheshire County League side Macclesfield Town during the summer on a 'temporary' transfer, which meant Wrexham could still receive a fee for him. Read spent the 1930/31 season with the 'Silkmen', playing alongside another ex-Wrexham player - and Rhos man - Jonathan Davies, and although they wanted to retain him at the end of the season, Halifax Town were also keen on his signature. He went to the 'Shay' for a month's trial, and the Yorkshire club agreed a 12 month contract after two matches. Read became a regular in the Halifax side for three years, before suffering knee cartilage problems, and resulted in him having to end his professional career at the end of the season, with £250 being paid in compensation. During this time he was living in Rochdale, and not long after leaving the Shay was approached by the town's Mayor, Mr.Dutton, who was also a director of the local football club. He invited Teddy along to Spotland for a month's trial. When Rochdale tried to pursue their interest in him the F.A. stated that he would have to pay back his compensation; as he was 31 at the time, Teddy decided against a return to the professional game. He then took up employment with the Royal Liver, where he remained until his retirement in 1967. He continued to play football for Bellfield St.Annes, in the Rochdale and District Sunday Schools League until he was 57! On finally hanging up his boots he joined the club's committee. His second love, cricket, kept him active even longer, until he was 63 years-old! It was a game that he had played in the summer months throughout his football career, turning out for Rhos when he was with

Wrexham. He was a very good wicket-keeper, and won the McAlpine Cup with Rhos in the first year of this prestigious Wrexham area competition. In 1967 Teddy returned to settle in Penycae, near Wrexham, where he became a well loved personality in the Rhos and Penycae District, walking many miles a day. He died in April 1997, aged 91.

Season	League		F.A.Cup		Welsh Cup		Total	
	apps	gls	apps	gls	apps	gls	apps	gls
1927/28	2	0	-	-	-	-	2	0
1928/29	17	0	-	-	1	0	18	0
1929/30	20	0	2	0	1	0	23	0
	39	**0**	**2**	**0**	**2**	**0**	**43**	**0**

READETT, Harold 1936 - 1937

Position; *Right-Back*
D.O.B; *15th October, 1910*
Birthplace; *Darwen, Lancashire*
Died; *Blackburn, April 1990.*
Height; *5ft 10'1/2in* ***Weight;*** *12st 0lbs*
Debut; v. *Oldham Athletic (a) 26th September, 1936*
Total Appearances & Goals; *1 app 0 gls*
Career; *Blackburn Corinthians; Blackburn Rovers (Am) 1928 0apps; Manchester Central Jun 1931; Horwich RMI; Hurst cs1933; Burnley (Am) May 1934 3apps 0gls; WREXHAM 15th May 1936; Stalybridge Celtic Jun 1937; Hurst FC Dec 1937; Rossendale United Jun 1938; Oldham Athletic (WW2 Guest) 1940/41 8apps 0gls; Burnley (WW2 Guest) 1941/42 4apps 0gls; Lincoln City (WW2 Guest) 1943/44 1app 0gls; Luton Town (WW2 Guest) 1app 0gls; Southport (WW2 Guest) 1942/43 1app 0gls;*

Harold Readett represented Blackburn Schoolboys as a youngster, and while playing for the Lancashire town's Corinthians he was signed by the local Football League side as an amateur in 1928. Harold couldn't force his way into the senior side at Ewood Park, however, and in June 1931 joined non-league outfit Manchester Central. He went on to spend some time with both Horwich RMI and Hurst F.C. before joining Second Division side Burnley as an amateur in May 1934. Harold made three League appearances for the Turf Moor club, all at right-back, in October 1934. His Football League debut came in a 2-0 defeat at Swansea, followed by a 1-0 defeat at Blackpool and a 3-3 home draw with Bury, but after another two years of reserve team football for the 'Clarets' he was allowed to move on. In May 1936 Readett was transferred to Third Division North side Wrexham, spending the majority of his one year stay at the Racecourse in the club's second string in the Birmingham and District League. He made his one and only first team appearance for the 'Robins' in September 1936, when replacing the regular right-back Vic Evans in a 2-2 draw at Oldham. Harold was released by Wrexham at the end of the season, and in June he joined Stalybridge Celtic. A spell with Rossendale United followed, and during World War Two appeared as a 'guest' player for a number of Football League clubs, including Oldham Athletic, Burnley, Lincoln City, Luton Town, and Southport.

Season	League		F.A.Cup		Welsh Cup		N.S.C.		Total	
	apps	gls	apps	gls	apps	gls	apps	gls	apps	gls
1936/37	1	0	-	-	-	-	-	-	1	0
	1	**0**	**-**	**-**	**-**	**-**	**-**	**-**	**1**	**0**

RECK, Sean Mark 1989 - 1991

Position; *Midfield*
D.O.B; *5th May, 1967*
Birthplace; *Oxford, Oxon*
Height; *5ft 10in* ***Weight;*** *12st 7lbs*
Debut; v. *Scarborough (a) 19th August, 1989*
Total Appearances & Goals; *54/4 apps 3 gls*
Career; *Oxford United Apr 1985 11/3apps 0gls; Newport County 30th Aug 1985 15apps 0gls (Loan); Reading 28th Mar 1986 1app 0gls (Loan); WREXHAM 18th Jul 1989 £25,000; Cheltenham Town Aug 1991 9/3apps 0gls; Oxford City 93/94;*
Honours; *Welsh Cup runner-up 1990;*

Sean Reck was spotted playing for Oxford Schoolboys by Oxford United, who invited him along for training at 14. He made steady progress through the junior ranks, and at only 15 was chosen to play for the Manor Ground outfit's reserve team in a Combination League match. In fact he had to obtain permission for a day off school to play! Upon completing his education in 1984 Coventry City offered him an apprenticeship, after he had undergone trials with the 'Sky Blues'. However, they wanted him to play at right-back, so when Oxford offered him the same terms a couple of weeks later in his preferred midfield role he was happy to sign. Sean progressed at the Manor Ground to sign professional terms for the 'U's' a month before his eighteenth birthday, having already established himself in the reserve team with some fine performances in the Combination League side. In August 1985 he was loaned out to Newport County to enhance his experience, and it was for the South Wales club that he made his Football League debut in a 1-0 win at Bournemouth, before going on to complete 15 League appearances during his stay at Somerton Park. Although Newport rated him highly they could not afford to sign him, and so he returned to the Manor Ground following his three month loan spell. Before he had made a breakthrough at Oxford he was again allowed out on loan, this time to Reading, although he was limited to just one League appearance for the 'Royals', in a 3-0 defeat at Gillingham, before returning to Oxford. The following season eventually saw Sean make his Oxford debut in October 1986, when he substituted David Leworthy in a 6-1 defeat at First Division Sheffield Wednesday. He spent a further two years at the Manor Ground, adding just twelve more League appearances before leaving in July 1989. Wrexham manager Dixie McNeil paid out £25,000 for the 'tough tackling midfielder', but his time at the Racecourse was to be hindered by injury. Sean made his League debut for the 'Robins' in a 2-1 defeat at Scarborough in the opening match of the 1989/90 season. He became a regular in the midfield throughout that season, signing off with an appearance in the first ever Welsh Cup Final to be staged at the National Stadium in Cardiff, although a 2-1 defeat by Hereford United resigned him to a runners'-up medal. He began the following term in the first team, and played in the European Cup-Winners' Cup match with Manchester United at Old Trafford. However, niggling injuries forced him to miss the rest of the season from November, and at the end of the campaign he was given a three month contract to prove his fitness. He was released in August and joined Cheltenham Town in the Conference League, before going on to play for both Oxford City and St.Albans City, having settled back in the Oxford area.

Season	League		F.A.Cup		Welsh Cup		League Cup		F.R.T.		E.C.W.C.		Total	
	apps	gls	apps	gls	apps	gls	apps	gls	apps	gls	apps	gls	apps	gls
1989/90	28/4	1	-	-	6	1	1	0	1	0	-	-	36/4	2
1990/91	13	1	-	-	-	-	4	0	-	-	1	0	18	1
	41/4	**2**	**-**	**-**	**6**	**1**	**5**	**0**	**1**	**0**	**1**	**0**	**54/4**	**3**

REEVES, Dennis John 1967 - 1969

Position; *Goalkeeper*
D.O.B; *1st December, 1944*
Birthplace; *Lochmaben, Dumfries & Galloway*
Height; *5ft 11in* ***Weight;*** *11st 7lbs*
Debut; v. *Swansea Town (h) 20th January, 1967*
Total Appearances & Goals; *17 apps 0 gls*
Career; *Prestatyn; Chester Sept 1963 139apps 0gls; WREXHAM 5th Oct 1967; Wigan Athletic cs1969;*
Honours; *Welsh Cup runner-up 1966; F.A.Trophy runner-up 1973; Northern Premier League Championship Winner 1971 & 1975; Northern Premier League Cup Winner 1972 & runner-up 1973;*

Although born in Dumfries Dennis Reeves' family moved to Malpas when he was about two years old. They later moved to Wrexham, where Dennis attended St.David's School, becoming a keen follower of Wrexham F.C. He also played the game himself as a left winger, later converting to goalkeeper, a position he occupied for North Wales Youth Clubs. On leaving school he took up work for the Denbighshire Education Authority as an apprentice painter and decorator, and began playing football for Garden Villa, a local Wrexham junior side where former Wrexham and Wales player Ron Hewitt set up a trial for him at Chester in 1961. He began training regularly with the Sealand Road club, although competition for places was fierce, and he was asked to eventually turn out for Prestatyn in the North Wales League. They operated as something of a nursery club to Chester at that time. However, his display for Chester in the F.A.Youth Cup against Bradford City earned him an opportunity with the club's 'A' team in the West Cheshire League. At this time he was playing part-time, as he continued to work as a painter and decorator. Regular reserve team football followed in 1962/63, and he eventually made his Football League debut in October 1963, replacing the injured Frank Adams in a 2-0 victory against Rochdale. Over the next four years Dennis became a regular fixture in Chester's first team, missing only a few games during 1964/65 after fracturing a cheekbone. In 1966 he picked up a Welsh Cup runners'-up medal when Chester lost to Swansea Town in the Final. During the following season Dennis was displaced in the side by Terry Carling, and after briefly regaining the No.1 spot returned to the reserves, whereupon he requested a transfer. In October 1967 Reeves agreed to sign for close rivals Wrexham in exchange for £1,500 and Tony McLoughlin - who moved to Sealand Road. Gordon Livsey was the 'Robins' regular 'keeper at the time, and Dennis was unable to oust him from the first team spot. He spent most of his time at the Racecourse in the reserves, although making seven League appearances in mid-season. He continued in the second XI, and agreed to sample non-league football with Wigan Athletic following his release in the summer of 1969. Dennis then reverted to part-time professional status, and started his own decorating business. He spent six years at Springfield Park, playing some of the best football of his career with consistency and confidence. In his first season he was voted 'Player of the Season', and throughout his time at Wigan the club were never out of the top three in the Northern Premier League. He won two championship medals, the Northern Premier League Cup twice, and a runners'-up medal for good measure. In 1973 he made a Wembley appearance for Wigan in the F.A.Trophy Final, where they lost 2-1 to Scarborough after extra time. He also helped the Springfield Park club reach the F.A.Cup First Round proper in all six of those seasons, with their best run coming in 1970/71. They then lost 3-1 to Manchester City in the Third Round, with Dennis pulling off some tremendous saves. However, misfortune befell him when he split a boot as he was taking a goal-kick. The misdirected ball then fell at the feet of a City player, who promptly set up Colin Bell for what proved to be the decisive strike! He decided to quit the game completely in the summer of 1975 to concentrate on his painting and decorating business, which he was still running recently, having settled in the Chester area. He has assisted with the running of the Christleton youth football team, as well as playing cricket in the summer months for Christleton. In a recent publication on Wigan Athletic F.C. Dennis was described as 'one of the most efficient 'keepers to wear the Wigan Athletic colours. He was a firm favourite with the Latics fans, who admired his solid dependable performances'.

Season	League		F.A.Cup		Welsh Cup		League Cup		Total	
	apps	gls	apps	gls	apps	gls	apps	gls	apps	gls
1967/68	7	0	1	0	1	0	-	-	9	0
1968/69	8	0	-	-	-	-	-	-	8	0
	15	**0**	**1**	**0**	**1**	**0**	**-**	**-**	**17**	**0**

REGAN, Edward Gerald Patrick
1921 - 1928

Position; *Half-Back*
D.O.B; *27th December, 1900*
Birthplace; *Chester, Cheshire*
Died; *Runcorn, O/N/D 1973.*
Height; *5ft 7'1/2in* ***Weight;*** *11st 8lbs*
Debut; v. *Accrington Stanley (h) 29th October, 1921*
Total Appearances & Goals; *216 apps 14 gls*
Career; *Crichton Athletic; WREXHAM 22nd May 1921; Manchester Central Jun 1928; Fulham Jun 1929 1app 0gls; Derry City (Trial) Jun 1930; Belfast Celtic Jul 1930; Connah's Quay Mar 1931; Colwyn Bay United Nov 1932; Milford Haven 17th Sept 1935; Buckley Town 23rd Jan 1937;*
Honours; *Welsh Cup Winner 1924; North Wales Coast F.A.Challenge Cup runner-up 1926;*

Ted Regan joined Wrexham in May 1921 as the club were about to begin a new life in the Football League Third Division North. He was signed from junior side Crichton Athletic to act as cover for the wing-halves, but after just nine matches of the inaugural season he was called upon to play at centre-forward following an injury to Bill Cotton. He got off to a great start, scoring twice on his debut in a 2-1 win over Accrington, and in the following match registered the club's first ever Football League hat-trick in the 6-1 win over Chesterfield. Even so, Ted had to wait until the following season before establishing himself in a regular first team place, this in his original half-back position. He became a prominent performer for the 'Robins' over the next six seasons, during which time he picked up a Welsh Cup winners' medal in the 1924 Final, beating Merthyr Town 1-0 after a replay. He was surprisingly allowed to leave the Racecourse in the close season of 1928 to join Manchester Central, who at that time were a progressive non-league club looking to attain Football League status. Regan spent one season with the now defunct club before moving south to join Fulham in the summer of 1929. He managed just one match for the Craven Cottage club, in a 1-0 home win over Northampton Town in September 1929. He was released by the London club at the end of 1929/30, and travelled to Ireland for a trial with Derry City before signing for Belfast Celtic a month later. Regan spent two seasons with them, following which he returned to North Wales to join Colwyn Bay United. After three years with the Bay he moved down to South Wales side Milford Haven, returning North in January 1937 to play for Buckley Town. On hanging up his boots Ted became a scout for Wrexham in the Chester area, discovering many notable players for the club who went on to make a name for themselves in League football including George Spruce, Bernard Evans etc. Ted became chief scout for Wrexham F.C in July 1960.

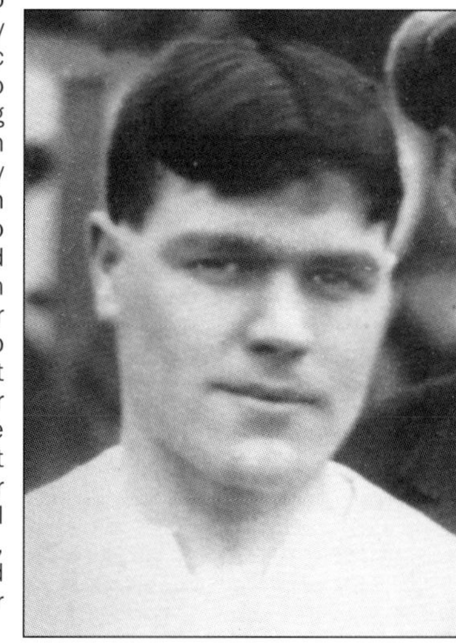

Season	League		F.A.Cup		Welsh Cup		Total	
	apps	gls	apps	gls	apps	gls	apps	gls
1921/22	9	5	1	0	1	0	11	5
1922/23	23	0	-	-	3	0	26	0
1923/24	34	0	-	-	6	0	40	0
1924/25	29	3	1	0	-	-	30	3
1925/26	22	1	1	0	2	0	25	1
1926/27	33	5	4	0	4	0	41	5
1927/28	38	0	4	0	1	0	43	0
	188	**14**	**11**	**0**	**17**	**0**	**216**	**14**

REILLY, David John
1983 - 1985

Position; *Midfield*
D.O.B; *24th November, 1966*
Birthplace; *Chester, Cheshire*
Height; *ft in* ***Weight;*** *st lbs*
Debut; v. *Wigan Athletic (a) 4th September, 1984 (League Cup)*
Total Appearances & Goals; *0/2 apps 0 gls*
Career; *WREXHAM 20th Jul 1984; Rhyl cs1985;*

David Reilly made his first team debut for Wrexham as an apprentice, when just 17 years and 284 days old. He replaced Paul Nicoll as substitute in a Football League Cup match at Wigan Athletic in September 1984. David had to wait until the following May before figuring in the first team again, making his Football League debut against Aldershot on the Racecourse as a substitute for Kevin Rogers in a 1-0 win. At the end of the season he was released by manager Bobby Roberts. David then joined Northern Premier League side Rhyl during the summer of 1985.

Season	League		F.A.Cup		Welsh Cup		League Cup		E.C.W.C.		Total	
	apps	gls	apps	gls	apps	gls	apps	gls	apps	gls	apps	gls
1984/85	0/1	0	-	-	-	-	0/1	0	-	-	0/2	0
	0/1	**0**	**-**	**-**	**-**	**-**	**0/1**	**0**	**-**	**-**	**0/2**	**0**

RICE, James
1934 - 1935

Position; *Centre-Forward*
D.O.B;
Birthplace;
Height; *ft in* **Weight;** *st lbs*
Debut; v. *Hartlepool United (a) 1st January 1935*
Total Appearances & Goals; *7 apps 7 gls*
Career; *Holytown United; Manchester United (Trial) Oct 1934 0apps; WREXHAM 25th Oct 1934; Albion Rovers May 1935; Alloa Athletic Jul 1938;*

Jimmy Rice was signed by Wrexham from Manchester United's reserve side in October 1934 (at the same time Tommy Bamford moved the other way) without having made a first team appearance at Old Trafford during his month's trial. He had a brief, but successful stay at the Racecourse, scoring seven goals in as many League and Cup matches. Jim made his Football League debut in a 4-3 defeat at Hartlepool on New Year's Day 1935, scoring one of the Wrexham goals. He then scored twice in the following match, a 4-2 home win over Carlisle, but despite this prolific form couldn't secure a regular first team place at the North Wales Club, and in the summer he was allowed to join Albion Rovers. Jim then scored the first goal of the new season for the Scottish First Division side in a 3-1 defeat at Dunfermline Athletic on 10th August 1935. After eleven games he had scored twelve goals, while his team-mates were criticised for 'not keeping pace' with him! That same season he figured in the Albion team that faced Rangers in a Scottish Cup Second Round match in February 1936. The tie attracted a record crowd of 27,381, which remains a record to this day for Albion's Cliftonhill Stadium. Despite losing 3-1 Jimmy did score 'The Wee Rovers' consolation goal. He joined Alloa Athletic in the close season of 1938 and was a member of the 'Wasps' team who won promotion to the Scottish First Division in 1938/39. In the suspended 1939/40 campaign he scored twice against Motherwell which were the clubs final goals before Hitlers intervention!! The Alloa Athletic Commemorative Handbook states that he was also ex Falkirk.

Season	League		F.A.Cup		Welsh Cup		N.S.C.		Total	
	apps	gls	apps	gls	apps	gls	apps	gls	apps	gls
1934/35	5	5	-	-	1	2	1	0	7	7
	5	**5**	**-**	**-**	**1**	**2**	**1**	**0**	**7**	**7**

RICHARDS, David
1933 - 1936

Position; *Left-Half*
D.O.B;
Birthplace; *Pentrebach, Merthyr Tydfil, Glamorgan*
Height; *5ft 9in* **Weight;** *11st 0lbs*
Debut; v. *Darlington (a) 16th April, 1934 (Football League Northern Section Cup)*
Total Appearances & Goals; *56 apps 0 gls*
Career; *Pentrebach, Merthyr Town 9th Dec 1927 11apps 0gls; Middlesborough 31st Jan 1929 0apps; Merthyr Town 9th Aug 1930 0apps; Bolton Wanderers 1st May 1931 0apps; WREXHAM 21st Jun 1933; Newport County 4th Jul 1936 1app 0gls; Burton Town Jul 1937;*

David Richards was signed by Third Division South side Merthyr Town from his village club, Pentrebach (Little Village) in December 1927. He had combined playing with working in the local pit. Dai, a promising wing-half, was to make his Football League debut with Merthyr Town, but after just eleven Football League appearances promotion-chasing Second Division side Middlesbrough snapped him up in January 1929. 'Boro' went on to clinch promotion to the First Division that season, but Dai was unable to make the break-through into the first team at Ayresome Park, and in August 1930 returned to Merthyr without having made a first team appearance for the North-East club. The 'Martyrs' had, by this time, dropped out of the League. A year later Dai joined First Division Bolton Wanderers, although again a first team appearance was to prove elusive. In July 1933 he joined Third Division North side Wrexham, and his first season at the Racecourse was a case of 'deja vue' as he again had to content himself with reserve team football. He did make one senior appearance, however, in a Football League Northern Section Cup Semi-final match at Darlington, when he replaced Matt Lawrence at wing-half in a 3-1 defeat. It was not until the following season that Dai finally broke into first team football at the Racecourse on a regular basis, and he had clocked up fifty League appearances by the end of the 1935/36 season. At the time he was described as a 'half-back, who is a good tackler, and a useful attacker.' At the end of that campaign Richards returned to South Wales joining Third Division South side Newport County, although he only managed one first team appearance. He then joined Birmingham & District League side Burton Town in the close season of 1937.

Season	League		F.A.Cup		Welsh Cup		League Cup		N.S.C.		Total	
	apps	gls	apps	gls	apps	gls	apps	gls	apps	gls	apps	gls
1933/34	-	-	-	-	-	-	-	-	1	0	1	0
1934/35	31	0	1	0	2	0	2	0	2	0	36	0
1935/36	19	0	-	-	-	-	-	-	-	-	19	0
	50	**0**	**1**	**0**	**2**	**0**	**3**	**0**	**3**	**0**	**56**	**0**

RICHARDS, Gordon
1952 - 1958

Position; *Outside-Left*
D.O.B; *23rd October, 1933*
Birthplace; *Rhos, Nr.Wrexham, Denbighshire*
Died; *Johnstown, 17th November, 1993*
Height; *5ft 8in* **Weight;** *10st 7lbs*
Debut; v. *Mansfield Town (a) 27th September, 1952*
Total Appearances & Goals; *106 apps 28 gls*
Career; *WREXHAM 6th May 1952; Chester 31st Jan 1958 £750 74apps 16gls; GKN Sankeys (Wellington) 1961;*
Honours; *Three Welsh Youth International caps;*

Gordon Richards signed for Wrexham's junior side after being spotted playing for Ruabon. He completed amateur forms for the Racecourse club in May 1950, while still working at a local colliery, and scored in his first match for Wrexham reserves in the Cheshire County League against Stalybridge Celtic. Gordon was awarded three Welsh Youth International caps for Wales: against Scotland and Ireland - scoring twice in each match; and against England. He progressed enough to sign professional forms for Wrexham in May 1952, making the breakthrough into the first team the following season in a Football League match with Mansfield Town, which the 'Robins' won 2-0. By the end of 1952/53 he had established himself in the first XI, but niggling injuries then forced him to miss a number of games early into the new season. He recovered in time to star in the F.A.Cup tie with Brighton & Hove Albion, however, following two draws, a second replay was necessary at Selhurst Park, where Gordon scored with a terrific diving header which rendered him unconscious! The following year was to be a personal disaster for him, as he missed most of the campaign due to a perforated appendix, but he returned to dazzle in his outside left position throughout 1955/56. Injury problems then returned to haunt him, forcing him to miss most of the 1956/57 programme, including the club's biggest match of the 50s against the 'Busby Babes' of Manchester United in an F.A.Cup Fourth Round tie. The following season began with Richards installed as the club's regular outside-left, but he had lost his place by October, and was eventually allowed to join Chester in January for a fee of around £750. Gordon, who had so often been the torment of the Chester defence found himself scoring on his debut for the 'Cestrians' in a 4-2 win against Southport. He missed the Welsh Cup Final against Wrexham, as he had made one appearance for the 'Robins' earlier in the competition. Gordon spent almost three years at Sealand Road, making 74 League appearances and scoring 16 goals before a knee injury forced him to quit League football. He later turned out for GKN Sankeys of Wellington in the Cheshire County League, but after only four months was forced to hang up his boots. He later began working for United Gravel, followed by employment with Bond Delivery, where he spent over twenty years before taking early retirement in 1989. Gordon died in November 1993, aged 60.

Season	League		F.A.Cup		Welsh Cup		Total	
	apps	gls	apps	gls	apps	gls	apps	gls
1952/53	14	4	-	-	1	0	15	4
1953/54	25	6	4	2	1	0	30	8
1954/55	8	1	-	-	-	-	8	1
1955/56	35	9	1	1	1	1	37	11
1956/57	5	1	-	-	1	0	6	1
1957/58	9	3	-	-	1	0	10	3
	96	**24**	**5**	**3**	**5**	**1**	**106**	**28**

RICHARDS, Iorwerth 1929 - 1930

Position; *Inside-Right/Outside-Right*
D.O.B;
Birthplace; *Rhosllanerchrugog, Denbighshire*
Debut; v. *York City (h) 11th September, 1929*
Height; *5ft 6'1/2in* ***Weight;*** *11st 0lbs*
Total Appearances & Goals; *2 apps 0 gls*
Career; *Rhos Church F.C. 1923; Johnstown; WREXHAM 28th Aug 1929; Oswestry Town Aug 1930; Llanerch Celts 7th Nov 1931; Blaenau Ffestiniog 3rd Nov 1933;*
Honours; *Chums League Shield Winners;*

Iorwerth Richards was playing for nearby Rhos and District Local teams in the early twenties, and following some impressive form for Johnstown, Wrexham took an interest in him. He signed for the 'Robins' after he had taken part in a pre-season trial match on the Racecourse. Iorwerth played for the Possibles against the Probables, and was described at the time as a 'youngster from Rhos, who was a shining light in a team that was full of talent and distinct promise.' He went on to make his Football League debut in September 1929, at inside-right in a 1-1 home draw against York City. Iorwerth was accompanied by fellow debutant George Wynne, and both were described at the time as 'too small against a physical opposition.' Nevertheless, Ior played in the following match against Port Vale, this time at centre-forward, in a 2-0 home defeat. He found himself back in reserve team football for the rest of the season, in the Birmingham & District League, and he was not given a further opportunity in the senior side. Iorwerth was released in the summer, whereupon he signed for Birmingham & District League side Oswestry Town. He later played for both Llanerch Celts and Blaenau Ffestiniog, and after ending his professional football career he became the publican of the Bull's Head Public House in Rhos, known to locals as Y Dafarn Geiniog. As one might expect from Rhosllanerchrugog he and brothers Tommy, Billy and Wilfred all had fine singing voices with Tommy particularly gifted.

Season	League		F.A.Cup		Welsh Cup		Total	
	apps	gls	apps	gls	apps	gls	apps	gls
1929/30	2	0	-	-	-	-	2	0
	2	**0**	-	-	-	-	**2**	**0**

RICHARDS, John William 1929 - 1930

Position; *Right-Half*
D.O.B; *16th May, 1909*
Birthplace; *Rhosllanerchrugog, Denbighshire*
Died; *Johnstown, Nr.Wrexham, 12th June, 1965*
Height; *5ft 11in* ***Weight;*** *11st 8lbs*
Debut; v. *York City (a) 4th September, 1929*
Total Appearances & Goals; *4 apps 0 gls*
Career; *Denbigh United; WREXHAM 28th Aug 1929; Blackburn Rovers Aug 1930 2apps 0gls; Chester Jun 1932 0apps; Colwyn Bay United 9th Aug 1933; Accrington Stanley (trial) Aug 1934; Darwen Sept 1934; Rochdale (trial);*

Originating from the Pentre Dwr area of Rhos Jack Richards attended the Rhos National Primary and Grango Schools. Jack and his brother Cyril would often take a tennis ball down to the Cae Dwr Ground (Home of Rhos Athletic F.C. in those days) and sharpen their soccer skills. After leaving school Jonathan Davies, a teacher and 'Racecourse Robin' was instrumental in securing employment for Jack as an orderly in Denbigh Hospital, where he also turned out for the local club, Denbigh United. He was eventually spotted and signed by Wrexham during the close season of 1929, and was to make his Football League debut in a scoreless draw with York City in the following September, playing at right-half. Jack played in the next three matches before returning to the 'Robins' reserve side in the Birmingham and District League. He left the Racecourse at the end of the season and joined First Division side Blackburn Rovers, where he played mostly for their reserve side in the Central League. He did appear twice in the first team for the Ewood Park club, his debut coming in a 1-1 draw at Blackpool in January 1931. Described as a 'solid type of wing-half' his next match for Rovers was, co-incidentally, also at Blackpool at the start of the following season, which ended in a 2-1 defeat. That proved to be his last appearance for Rovers as he was released in the summer of 1932, although he did have a trial with Manchester United during that time which came to nothing. Jack was then signed by Third Division North side Chester, but he failed to make a first team appearance in his one year at Sealand Road, and joined Colwyn Bay United in August 1933. He later tried to resurrect his Football League career when he joined Accrington Stanley on trial for the start of the 1934/35 season, but was released after a month and joined Lancashire League side Darwen. He also had a short spell with Rochdale, but returned to his native Rhos without having made a first team appearance for the Spotland club. During his playing days Jack was described as a 'red haired fiery character, who would always give you 100% on the football field'.

Back on home soil he began a garage and haulage enterprise which eventually became very successful. He had started from scratch by purchasing a lorry, and despite the pressures of establishing a new business he kept involved with football by scouting for Chester and becoming coach/manager of Rhos Rangers. His brother Cyril a prolific goalscorer played for Rhos, Penycae, Druids, and Caergwrle, and also spent two seasons with Wrexham as an amateur. He was on the verge of signing professional forms with the Racecourse club when a clash of heads with an Army XI opponent resulted in him lying unconscious in hospital for 13 days! He never played the game again.

Season	League		F.A.Cup		Welsh Cup		Total	
	apps	gls	apps	gls	apps	gls	apps	gls
1929/30	4	0	-	-	-	-	4	0
	4	**0**	-	-	-	-	**4**	**0**

RICHARDSON, Nicholas John 1994

Position; *Midfield*
D.O.B; *11th April, 1967*
Birthplace; *Halifax, Yorkshire*
Height; *6ft 1in* ***Weight;*** *12st 6lbs*
Debut; v. *Oxford United (h) 22nd October, 1994*
Total Appearances & Goals; *4 apps 2 gls*
Career; *Leicester City; Emley; Halifax Town 15th Nov 1988 89/12apps 17gls; Cardiff City 13th Aug 1992 £35,000 106/5apps 13gls; WREXHAM 21st Oct 1994 (Loan); Chester City 16th Dec 1994 (Loan) 6apps 1gls; Bury 8th Aug 1995 £22,500 3/2apps 0gls; Chester City 7th Sept 1995 £40,000 127/6apps 9gls;*
Honours; *England Youth International; Third Division Championship Winner 1993; Welsh Cup Winner 1993; Welsh Cup runner-up 1994 & 1995;*

Nick Richardson joined Leicester City straight from school as an apprentice, and at Filbert Street was selected for the England Youth side. He failed to make the 'Foxes' first team, however, and was released following the completion of his apprenticeship. Nick then returned home, and took up non-league football with Emley in the Northern Premier League. He was persuaded to join his home town club, Halifax Town, in November 1988, where he made his Football League debut as a 21 year-old in January 1989, a substitute in a 2-0 win against Torquay United. His brother Lee also played for Halifax, as well as Watford, Blackburn, Aberdeen and Oldham. Life with the 'Shaymen' was a constant struggle, and in the close season of 1992 he joined Cardiff City for a £35,000 fee. In his first season at Ninian Park he became a major influence in the 'Bluebirds' midfield, as they won both the Third Division Championship and the Welsh Cup, but missed out on playing in Europe. He made up for that disappointment in the following season, however, when he played against Standard Liege, though also having to endure Cardiff's shock Welsh Cup Final defeat at the hands of Barry Town. The summer of 1994 saw him linked with a move nearer to his native Halifax, with Wrexham showing more than a passing interest. Nick joined the Racecourse club in October - initially on loan, with a view to a permanent signing. His League debut for the 'Robins' came at home to the Second Division front-runners, Oxford United, and he got off to a dream start by scoring twice

in the 3-2 win. He appeared in three more League games before deciding not to play in the F.A.Cup match with Stockport County, which would have seen him cup-tied. After failing to agree terms he returned to South Wales, where he turned out in a few more games for the 'Bluebirds' before joining Chester City on loan. Richardson made six appearances, scoring one goal for Chester in that spell, although not once on the winning side. He returned to Ninian Park, remaining a part of the Cardiff first team, although he couldn't prevent the 'Bluebirds' from suffering relegation. Trying to put a disappointing season behind him he turned out for Cardiff in the Welsh Cup Final against Wrexham, where the 'Robins' inflicted more agony following a 2-1 victory. In the summer of 1995 Nick finally got a move nearer to his Yorkshire home, when he joined Bury for a £22,500 fee. He made just five appearances at Gigg Lane before he was transferred a month later to Chester for a £40,000 fee. Nick made his debut in a 2-1 win at Colchester, and became a regular in the Cheshire club's midfield until disaster struck in October 1996: he suffered an horrendous knee injury in a match at Hartlepool which required major surgery to repair two knee ligaments, which sidelined him for the rest of the season. He returned to fitness for the beginning of 1997/98, and is still with Chester at present.

Season	League		F.A.Cup		Welsh Cup		League Cup		A.W.S.		Total	
	apps	gls	apps	gls	apps	gls	apps	gls	apps	gls	apps	gls
1994/95	4	2	-	-	-	-	-	-	-	-	4	2
	4	**2**	-	-	-	-	-	-	-	-	**4**	**2**

RIDLER, David George

1996 -

Position; *Centre-Half*
D.O.B; *12th March, 1976*
Birthplace; *Liverpool*
Height; *6ft 1in* ***Weight;*** *12st 2lbs*
Debut; v. *Crewe Alexandra (h) 28th January, 1997 (A.W.S.)*
Total Appearances & Goals; *88/9 apps 2 gls*
Career; *Prescot Cables 1992; Rockys; WREXHAM 3rd Jul 1996;*
Honours;

David Ridler was a late starter to the professional game. He was playing Merseyside Sunday League football for Rocky's, who were managed by Wrexham striker Karl Connolly, who alerted Wrexham boss Brian Flynn. A midfield player at that time Dave was later converted to the centre of defence, where he went on to have considerable success with Wrexham. Living in Huyton, Liverpool, Dave went to school in Prescot. He played for his school team, and was selected for the Kirkby and Knowsley Schoolboys' sides as well as for his County. He also had a spell with a junior side, Whiston Juniors, who played in the Rainhill Junior League, and it was with them that he took part in a tournament in Holland, which they won at under-16s level. Upon leaving school he began playing for the reserve side at his local club, Prescot Cables, and soon made the step up to the first team in the North-West Counties League First Division. He was still only sixteen at that time, and went to college to complete a catering course, gaining an NVQ certificate, which led to a job in a bakery. In 1994 Dave played in a tournament in USA, the Dallas Cup, for a Knowsley XI which reached the Quarter-Finals. Around this time he also turned out for Nicosia, a team in the Liverpool Business House Sunday League, and was with them for two years before joining Karl Connolly's Sunday side. Ridler was then invited to play in a Welsh National League game for the 'Robins', and was later called back and asked to sign non-contract terms for the Club in the summer of 1995. He progressed to make his first team debut in January 1997, facing Crewe Alexandra in an Auto Windscreen Shield match on the Racecourse which ended in a 1-0 defeat. His development continued at such a pace that manager Brian Flynn was able to allow Barry Jones to join York City. At the time of writing Dave is firmly established as a key member of the 'Robins' senior squad. The qualified Chef and Baker who hopes to continue to 'Cook up' selection problems for manager Brian Flynn, can also fill well in the full back role and has been known to score the odd goal.

Season	League		F.A.Cup		League Cup		A.W.S.		W.I.C.		Total	
	apps	gls	apps	gls	apps	gls	apps	gls	apps	gls	apps	gls
1996/97	7/4	0	-	-	-	-	1	0	-	-	8/4	0
1997/98	18/2	0	4	0	-	-	1	0	4/1	0	27/3	0
1998/99	35/1	1	4	0	1	0	5/1	1	8	0	53/2	2
	60/7	**1**	**8**	**0**	**1**	**0**	**7/1**	**1**	**12/1**	**0**	**88/9**	**2**

RIGBY, Norman

1930 - 1931

Position; *Goalkeeper*
D.O.B;
Birthplace;
Height; *ft in* ***Weight;*** *st lbs*
Debut; v. *Accrington Stanley (a) 3rd January 1931*
Total Appearances & Goals; *2 apps 0 gls*
Career; *Atherton Town; WREXHAM (Am) Jul 1930, (Pro) Aug 1930; Wigan Borough (Am) Aug 1931;*

Norman Rigby joined Wrexham as a goalkeeper on amateur terms from Atherton Town in July 1930, and quickly signed professional forms the following month. He then played in goal for the club's reserve team in the Birmingham & District League, until the opportunity arose to step in between the posts for regular first team 'keeper, Dick Finnegan in a 3-1 win at Accrington Stanley in January 1931. His next appearance for the 'Robins' came at the end of the same month, a 3-2 home win against Halifax Town, Finnegan's consistency provided him with too great a challenge, however, and he was released at the end of the season. Rigby then signed for Wigan Borough on amateur terms, but they then went out of business in October 1931. Ironically, their last ever game in the Football League was at the Racecourse, when Wrexham beat them 5-0! on 24th October, though Norman was not selected on that occasion. Because of Wigan's demise the result was deleted from the record books.

Season	League		F.A.Cup		Welsh Cup		Total	
	apps	gls	apps	gls	apps	gls	apps	gls
1930/31	2	0	-	-	-	-	2	0
	2	**0**	-	-	-	-	**2**	**0**

RISHWORTH, Stephen Peter

1998

Position; *Midfield*
D.O.B; *8th June 1979*
Birthplace; *Chester*
Height; *5ft 11'1/2in* ***Weight;*** *12st 0lbs*
Debut v. *Gillingham (a) 1st September, 1998.*
Total Appearances & Goals; *0/4 apps 0 gls*
Career; *Manchester City Jul 1996; WREXHAM Jun 1998;*
Honours; *One Welsh Youth International cap; Welsh Schoolboy International; Welsh Youth Cup runner-up 1997;*

Steve Rishworth hit the tabloid newspaper headlines at the beginning of the 1998/99 season when he decided to defer a career in football to begin a four year degree course in Engineering Science at Oxford University. He had attended the same school as a certain Wales and

Wrexham player, Ian Rush - the Richard Gwyn Secondary School in Flint, having already played in the same Deeside Primary Schools team as the England international striker, Michael Owen. Apart from playing football for his school XI he was also chosen to represent Flintshire Schoolboys for a number of years along with Owen. Rishworth had joined the Liverpool School of Excellence, and progressed to earn selection for the Welsh Schoolboys side at under-15 level. After leaving school in 1996 he joined Manchester City on YTS forms, where he gained further international recognition by playing for the Welsh Youth team in a friendly against Northern Ireland. However, after fifteen months as a trainee with City he left Maine Road at his own request, to concentrate on completing his 'A' levels. His reward was three straight A grades. With his exams completed Steve turned to Wrexham manager Brian Flynn to enquire about the possibility of training with the club before taking up his University place at Oxford. 'Prof', as he was quickly nicknamed by his team mates at the Racecourse, had already spent some time with the 'Robins' after he left City, turning out for the Lancashire League side during the 1997/98 season. He would play for the club when time allowed away from his studies, during holidays and weekends, as he wanted to retain an involvement in a good standard of football. Steve progressed rapidly with the 'Robins', and he was eventually called upon for his Football League debut in September 1998 at Gillingham, when he came on as a substitute for Gareth Owen. However, it was not to be a fairy tale debut for Rishworth as Wrexham, who were already 3-0 down when he took to the field, eventually lost 4-0. Steve continued to be a part of the first team squad until he left the club at the beginning of October to take up his place at Balliol College in Oxford, although manager Brian Flynn still holds his playing registration.

Season	League		F.A.Cup		W.I.C.		League Cup		A.W.S.		Total	
	apps	gls	apps	gls	apps	gls	apps	gls	apps	gls	apps	gls
1998/99	0/4	0	-	-	-	-	-	-	-	-	0/4	0
	0/4	**0**	-	-	-	-	-	-	-	-	**0/4**	**0**

***ROBERTS,* Cledwyn** 1965 - 1966

Position; *Wing-Half*
D.O.B; *12th August, 1947*
Birthplace; *Colwyn Bay, Flintshire*
Height; *ft in* ***Weight;*** *st lbs*
Debut; v. *Barrow (a) 21st August, 1965*
Total Appearances & Goals; *1 app 0 gls*
Career; *Glan Conwy; WREXHAM Aug 1965; Penmaenmawr 22nd Aug 1966; Colwyn Bay 6th Aug 1968; Pwllheli & District 28th Sept 1968;*

After representing the Welsh Grammar Schools XI Cledwyn Roberts joined Wrexham as a junior upon completion of his education, having also played for local side Glan Conwy. He went on to sign professional terms with the Racecourse club in August 1965, and made his Football League debut in the same month, a 4-2 defeat at Barrow on the opening day of the 1965/66 season. It proved to be Cledwyn's one and only first team game for the 'Robins', as he was released at the end of the season. He then signed for Penmaenmawr, where he enjoyed two years before joining Colwyn Bay in August 1968. He was soon on the move again, however, after just a month he joined fellow Welsh (North) League side Pwllheli & District. He is believed to have joined the Metropolitan Police in London some time during the early 1970s.

Season	League		F.A.Cup		Welsh Cup		League Cup		Total	
	apps	gls	apps	gls	apps	gls	apps	gls	apps	gls
1965/66	1	0	-	-	-	-	-	-	1	0
	1	**0**	-	-	-	-	-	-	**1**	**0**

***ROBERTS,* Edward Daniel** 1919 - 1923

Position; *Right-Half*
D.O.B; *20th February, 1891*
Birthplace; *Rhos*
Died; *Wrexham, 28th December, 1970*
Height; *5ft 8in* ***Weight;*** *10st 7lbs*
Debut; v. *Willenhall Swifts (a) 30th August, 1919*
Football League Debut; v. *Hartlepool United (a) 8th September, 1921*
Total Appearances & Goals; *125 apps 9 gls*
Career; *Chirk; Druids; Rhos; Southport Vulcan 1918; Bristol City Jun 1919 0apps; WREXHAM 27th Jun 1919; Rhos Jul 1923; Druids 1924/25;*
Honours; *Welsh Cup Winner 1921; Welsh Cup runner-up 1920;*

Edward Daniel Roberts had played local football for Chirk, Druids, and Rhos before joining Southport Vulcan in 1918, who were a non-league club at that time. In June 1919 'E.D.', as he was known, joined Second Division Bristol City, but made little impact and quickly returned to North Wales to join Birmingham and District League side Wrexham. He had failed to register a first team appearance at Ashton Gate. Edward who was said to be hard of hearing even in his playing days then made his 'Robins' debut in a 3-0 defeat at Willenhall in the opening match of the 1919/20 season. He became a regular in the Denbighshire club's side at right-half for the next two years, during which he collected a Welsh Cup runners'-up medal in 1920, after losing 2-1 to Cardiff City in the Final. The following season saw him go one better, when the Racecourse club lifted the Welsh Cup with a 3-1 replay win over Pontypridd after a 1-1 draw. 'E.D.' remained with Wrexham following their acceptance into the Football League in 1921, but was to miss the club's inaugural match against Hartlepools on the Racecourse. He did, however, feature in the return match in the North-East a week later, which saw the 'Robins' gain revenge for their earlier defeat with a 1-0 win. Roberts went on to miss just four matches that season, but began to find his first team chances limited, which resulted in him leaving the Racecourse in the summer of 1923. During his time at the club he was described as a 'thrustful hard working wing-half'. He then returned to play for Rhos, where he also worked in his trade as a joiner and undertaker. After his playing days were over 'E.D.', who lived in Ponciau, supported Wrexham A.F.C. on a regular basis until he passed away at Wrexham Maelor Hospital in 1970, aged 79.

Season	League		F.A.Cup		Welsh Cup		Total	
	apps	gls	apps	gls	apps	gls	apps	gls
1919/20	33	6	5	0	5	1	43	7
1920/21	30	2	4	0	5	0	39	2
1921/22	34	0	4	0	1	0	39	0
1922/23	8	0	-	-	-	-	8	0
	101	**8**	**13**	**0**	**11**	**1**	**125**	**9**
F/League	42	0	4	0	1	0	47	0

***ROBERTS,* Frank** 1925 - 1926

Position; *Centre-Forward*
D.O.B;
Birthplace; *Llangollen, Denbighshire*
Height; *5ft 7in* ***Weight;*** *10st 6lbs*
Debut; v. *Rotherham United (a) 23rd January, 1926*
Total Appearances & Goals; *8 apps 4 gls*
Career; *Chester; WREXHAM 28th Aug 1925; Shell Mex 1926;*
Honours; *North Wales Coast F.A.Challenge Cup runner-up 1926;*

Frank Roberts joined Wrexham in August 1925 from Cheshire County League side Chester following a trial. Described as 'on the small side, but looks a sturdy youngster' he had to wait until January 1926 to make his Football League debut, when playing at inside-forward in a 6-2 defeat at Rotherham, although he did score one of the Wrexham goals. Roberts went on to feature in seven more League and Cup games that season, scoring another three goals. He played for the 'Robins' Second XI in the

Final of the North Wales Coast F.A.Challenge Cup in April 1926, where they suffered a 2-0 defeat at the hands of Llandudno, and in the summer he found himself released. Frank then apparently joined Chester and District League side, Shell Mex.

Season	League		F.A.Cup		Welsh Cup		Total	
	apps	gls	apps	gls	apps	gls	apps	gls
1925/26	7	3	-	-	1	1	8	4
	7	**3**	**-**	**-**	**1**	**1**	**8**	**4**

ROBERTS, Ian Mark 1979 - 1980

Position; *Forward*
D.O.B; *28th February, 1961*
Birthplace; *Colwyn Bay, Flintshire*
Height; *5ft 6in* **Weight;** *10st 6lbs*
Debut; v. *Luton Town (h) 7th May, 1979*
Total Appearances & Goals; *2/5 apps 0 gls*
Career; *Hotpoint Juniors; WREXHAM Jul 1979; Bangor City 20th Aug 1980; Conwy United Dec 1980; Llandudno cs1992;*
Honours; *Welsh Youth Winner 1978; Welsh Intermediate Cup Winner 1982; Welsh Alliance League Championship Winner 1985 & 1986; Barritt Cup Winner 1985; North Wales Coast Challenge Cup Winner 1995;*

'Eli' Roberts, as he was 'commonly' known at Wrexham, began playing football at Maelgwyn Junior and Aberconwy Secondary Schools in Conwy. He also turned out for Hotpoint Juniors in Llandudno Junction at the time, representing Conwy Borough at under-16 level as well as North Wales Schoolboys. It was upon leaving school in 1997 that Eli was to sign for Wrexham as an apprentice, along with Frank Jones and Bruce Urquhart, who were also from the Llandudno area. In his first season on the ground staff he helped Wrexham lift the Welsh Youth Cup, beating Afan Lido in the Final. With the 'Robins' youth side he travelled to Eindhoven, Holland, to take part in a club tournament, where they beat Fortuna Dussledorf into third place. 'Eli' progressed to sign professional forms in July 1979, having already made his Football League debut two months earlier in a Second Division match against Luton Town, when he substituted Mel Sutton in the 2-0 home win. During his time at the Racecourse 'Eli' was described as 'a small, but very energetic player, full of enthusiasm for the game'. The following season he made his full League debut in a 3-0 home win against Watford. However, by the end of the campaign he had been informed of his release by the club. He then joined Alliance Premier League side Bangor City in the summer of 1980, but before Christmas he was to move on to Cymru Alliance League club Conwy United where he enjoyed considerable success. He pocketed two League championship medals' in 1985 and 1986, and helped to lift the Barritt Cup in 1985 to add to the Welsh Intermediate Cup he had already won in 1982. Ian left Conwy in 1992 to join Llandudno where he added a North Wales Coast F.A.Challenge Cup winners medal to his collection in 1995. In 1993 he was appointed assistant-manager at Llandudno, while continuing to play, and in July 1997 he was installed as the manager, replacing Dean Martin. However, things did not turn out well in his first managerial spell, and he left the club at the end of October 1997, following which he severed all connections with the game. On leaving the full-time professional game Roberts became employed as a bank clerk. In 1992 he took up a course at the John Moore University in Liverpool studying construction management, and this culminated in employment as a training adviser with the Construction Industry Training Board (CITB). 'Eli' has settled in the Llandudno area.

Season	League		F.A.Cup		Welsh Cup		League Cup		E.C.W.C.		Total	
	apps	gls	apps	gls	apps	gls	apps	gls	apps	gls	apps	gls
1978/79	0/1	0	-	-	-	-	-	-	-	-	0/1	0
1979/80	2/3	0	-	-	-	-	0/1	0	-	-	2/4	0
	2/4	**0**	**-**	**-**	**-**	**-**	**0/1**	**0**	**-**	**-**	**2/5**	**0**

ROBERTS, James 1922 - 1923

Position; *Outside-Left*
D.O.B; *7th January, 1891*
Birthplace; *Mold, Flintshire*
Height; *5ft 8in* **Weight;** *11st 2lbs*
Debut v. *Stourbridge (a) 6th March, 1911*
Football League Debut; v. *Rochdale (a) 23rd September, 1922*
Total Appearances & Goals; *73 apps 8 gls*
Career; *Mold Villa 1905; Mold Town 1907; WREXHAM 4th Jul 1910; Crewe Alexandra May 1913 31apps 3gls; Everton Apr 1914 1app 0gls; Tranmere Rovers 1920 32apps 1gls; Crewe Alexandra Jun 1922 0apps; WREXHAM 21st Sept 1922; Mold Town 18th Oct 1924;*
Honours; *Two Full Welsh International caps; Welsh Amateur International;*

Jas Roberts was turning out for Mold Villa at the tender age of 14! Two years later he joined Mold Town, finishing as the club's top scorer in their Chester League Championship winning season of 1907/08. He was described as a 'spirited player' and a 'very effective forward', but was criticised for holding on to the ball for too long. In 1910 James joined Wrexham, along with brother Jack. Although not a regular, he crowned his first season at the Racecourse with a Welsh Amateur cap. The first of his two full Welsh international caps followed two years later, when he replaced Lot Jones for the game against Ireland in January 1913. James scored the only goal in that match, which was played in Belfast, before appearing on the Racecourse in a scoreless draw with Scotland. In May 1913 he was recruited by Central League side Crewe Alexandra, along with the Irish International forward Cunningham. One newspaper commented approvingly about Roberts' displays at Gresty Road by stating 'his clever manipulation of the ball, coupled with his shooting makes him a thorn in the side of his opponents.' His good form at Crewe quickly brought him to the attention of a number of League clubs, and in April 1914 he signed for Everton. He was to make just one League appearance for the 'Toffees', a 5-1 win at Aston Villa in February 1915, before football was suspended due to the First World War. After the conflict had ended he joined Tranmere Rovers in 1920, where he clocked up 32 League appearances, scoring one goal before returning to Crewe Alexandra in the close season of 1922, who by this time had been accepted into the Football League. However, he was soon on the move again, as he linked up with Wrexham for a second spell in September 1922. James' Football League debut for the 'Robins' came in a disappointing 5-0 defeat at Rochdale, replacing Matt Burton. He started off well, but lost his place when Burton was reinstated, although remaining at the Racecourse until the summer of 1923, playing mostly reserve team football. On his release from the Denbighshire club he rejoined yet another of his former sides, Mold Town, turning out for one season before hanging up his boots.

Season	League		F.A.Cup		Welsh Cup		Total	
	apps	gls	apps	gls	apps	gls	apps	gls
1910/11	3	0	-	-	-	-	3	0
1911/12	32	3	2	0	2	0	36	3
1912/13	26	5	-	-	1	0	27	5
1922/23*	7	0	-	-	-	-	7	0
	68	**8**	**2**	**0**	**3**	**0**	**73**	**8**

* Football League season only.

ROBERTS, John Dilwyn 1951

Position; *Outside-Right*
D.O.B; *22nd July, 1928*
Birthplace; *Pentre Broughton, Denbighshire*
Height; *5ft 7'1/2in* **Weight;** *11st 2lbs*
Debut; v. *Rochdale (a) 30th April, 1951*
Total Appearances & Goals; *1 apps 0 gls*
Career; *Brymbo Steelworks 1944; WREXHAM Jul 1949; Llay Welfare cs1951; Marine; Oswestry Town; Barmouth; Colwyn Bay;*
Honours; *One Welsh Amateur International Cap; Welsh Amateur Cup Winner 1967; Welsh National League Division One Championship Winner 1970;*

Dilwyn Roberts attended the Black Lane School in Pentre Broughton until 1939, then qualifying for Grove Park Grammar school, which was a Rugby orientated establishment until the round ball game was introduced in 1941. He represented the school team at football, as well as turning out for a local youth side, Brynmally Rovers. On completion of his education in 1944 he took up employment at Brymbo Steelworks, where he began as an apprentice fitter in the Locomotive and Steam Maintenance Department, although he was subsequently to progress to Project Engineer, Engineering Shops Manager and finally Billet and Bar Mill Manager. Throughout his time at Brymbo he played football for the works XI, turning out for them until 1977, when he finally hung up his boots at the age of 49! During his football career Dilwyn made one Football League appearance for Wrexham, having signed for the club on amateur terms in July 1949. His debut did not follow until almost two years later, against Rochdale at Spotland in a match which Wrexham lost 2-0, with Dilwyn playing at outside-right in place of Cyril Lawrence. In the summer of 1951 he left the Racecourse to join Llay Welfare, before having short spells in non-league football with Marine, Oswestry Town, Barmouth, and Colwyn Bay. In 1959 he gained a Welsh Amateur Cap when he represented his country against England at the Gay Meadow, Shrewsbury. Roberts spent well over twenty years playing for Brymbo Steelworks, collecting a Welsh Amateur Cup winners' medal in 1967 when they beat the City of Cardiff College of Education 3-2 at Llanidloes. The Cardiff side included a young Dai Davies. During the summer months Dilwyn excelled as a member of Brymbo Cricket Club, playing for many years and attaining numerous honours in North Wales cricket. He represented Denbighshire on many occasions, his first appearance coming in 1948, and his final game in 1983, although he continued to turn out for Brymbo until 1993, when he retired at the age of 65! He was Chairman of Brymbo Cricket Club from 1971 to 1996, a span of 25 years, though he continued to serve as a committee member after standing down. Dilwyn, who is related through marriage to another 'Racecourse Robin', Jackie Lloyd, retired from the steelworks in 1986 at the age of 58, having settled in the Wrexham area. In November 1998 he was honoured for his services to Denbighshire Cricket which spanned four decades when elected Honorary Life Vice-President of the County.

Season	League apps	gls	F.A.Cup apps	gls	Welsh Cup apps	gls	Total apps	gls
1950/51	1	0	-	-	-	-	1	0
	1	**0**	-	-	-	-	**1**	**0**

ROBERTS, John Griffith

1976 - 1980

Position; *Centre-Half*
D.O.B; *11th September, 1946*
Birthplace; *Abercynon, Glamorgan*
Height; *6ft 0in* ***Weight;*** *12st 2lbs*
Debut; v. *Portsmouth (h) 21st August, 1976*
Total Appearances & Goals; *189/2 apps 6 gls*
Career; *Abercynon Athletic; Swansea Town 29th Jul 1964 36/1apps 16gls; Northampton Town 24th Nov 1967 £15,000 62apps 11gls; Arsenal 1st May 1969 £45,000 56/3apps 4gls; Birmingham City 13th Oct 1972 £140,000 61/5apps 1gls; WREXHAM 5th Aug 1976 £30,000; Hull City 6th Aug 1980 £17,500 26apps 1gls; Oswestry Town cs1982;*
Honours; *22 Full Welsh International caps; 5 Welsh Under-23 caps; One Welsh Under-21 cap; First Division Championship Winner 1971; Third Division Championship Winner 1978; Welsh Cup Winner 1978; Welsh Cup runner-up 1979;*

John Roberts was playing at centre-forward for Abercynon Athletic in his native South Wales, while also working as a locomotive fireman for British Railways, when Swansea Town took an interest in him. He joined the Vetch Field club on amateur terms at first, turning professional in July 1964. He stayed with Swansea for three years, scoring 16 goals in 37 League appearances before a £15,000 transfer took him to Northampton Town in November 1967. John made his debut for the 'Cobblers' as a centre-forward, and scored in a 1-0 home win over Bournemouth. He completed 62 League games for Northampton, scoring 11 goals, though the majority of these came after a switch to defence. It was in his new role that Arsenal saw his potential in May 1969, and they paid £45,000 for him. His debut for the 'Gunners' came in a 1-0 home defeat by Coventry City in October. He managed only ten more League games that season, but earned both Football Combination Championship and London F.A.Challenge Cup winners' medals for the Highbury club's second string. The following season, 1970/71, saw John installed alongside Frank McClintock in the centre of defence for the opening 17 matches of the campaign before Peter Simpson took over. He made one further appearance that season, but by now he was a vital cog in the Arsenal machine, assisting the club to the Football League Championship and Cup double. It was also a year that saw John collect the first of his 22 Welsh Caps, when he made his international debut against Scotland. He remained an important member of the 'Gunners' squad throughout the following season, making 23 League appearances, as well as playing in the European Cup against Stromgodset, Grasshoppers Zurich, and the eventual winners Ajax. In 1972/73 Roberts added another seven League appearances before signing for Birmingham City in October for a £140,000 fee. He went straight into the first team at St.Andrew's alongside Roger Hynd, and became a first team regular over the next two seasons until a serious injury forced him out of action. Joe Gallagher deputised for John during his lengthy absence, and he then established himself. John's appearances became sporadic over the next two years, and in August 1976 he signed for Wrexham manager John Neal for what later proved to be a bargain £30,000, as a ready-made replacement for the departed Eddie May. He made his 'Robins' debut in a 2-0 home win over Portsmouth, and soon became an inspiration in the heart of the defence, alongside Gareth Davies. His form led to a Welsh under-21 cap as an over-age player in 1977. He formed the back bone of arguably the greatest ever Wrexham team, as they went on to win the Third Division Championship in 1978, and also lifted the Welsh Cup in the same season. He played in two European campaigns for the 'Robins', against Rijeka of Yugoslavia and Magdeburg of East Germany. John was described at the Racecourse as a 'wholehearted performer, who was powerful in the air'. He left Wrexham in August 1980 for Hull City, joining up with his former Welsh team manager Mike Smith for £15,000. Roberts spent two seasons at Boothferry Park, making 26 League appearances before having to retire in June 1982 through injury. He returned West to settle in the Chester area, where he became a salesman for a North Wales Stationery firm and continued to play football for a short while with Oswestry Town. He later ran his own driving school in Chester, but today he and his wife own three designer wear shops in Chester and Nantwich. John nicknamed 'Garth' due to his physique, turns out for the Veterans over 50's Chester Nomads XI and appeared in the Final of the over 50's Umbro/William Hill Cup in May 1997 against Corinthian Casuals.

Season	League apps	gls	F.A.Cup apps	gls	Welsh Cup apps	gls	League Cup apps	gls	E.C.W.C. apps	gls	Total apps	gls
1976/77	44	1	6	0	3	1	5	0	-	-	58	2
1977/78	41	4	8	0	4	0	6	0	-	-	59	4
1978/79	40	0	3	0	4	0	2	0	1	0	50	0
1979/80	20	0	-	-	-	-	0/2	0	2	0	22/2	0
	145	**5**	**17**	**0**	**11**	**1**	**13/2**	**0**	**3**	**0**	**189/2**	**6**

ROBERTS, Kenneth Owen 1951 - 1953

Position; *Outside-Right*
D.O.B; *27th March, 1936*
Birthplace; *Cefn Mawr, Denbighshire*
Height; *5ft 7in* **Weight;** *10st 5lbs*
Debut; v. *Bradford Park Avenue (a) 1st September, 1951*
Total Appearances & Goals; *1 app 0 gls*
Career; *Maelor Y.C; WREXHAM May 1951; Aston Villa 8th May 1953 38apps 3gls; Oswestry Town cs1958;*
Honours; *Welsh Youth International;*

Ken Roberts attended Acrefair Central School from where he was selected to represent Wrexham Schoolboys. He also played for the Maelor Youth Club around this time, and it was there that he came to the notice of Wrexham A.F.C. He joined the club straight from school in the summer of 1951, but his first team chance was to come much sooner than even he had expected. On Wrexham's arrival at Bradford Park Avenue for a League fixture in September 1951 it was found that Len Wootton had missed his train connection, and manager Peter Jackson had no alternative, than to turn to Ken who had only made the journey to broaden his experience. He then made his Football League debut, to equal Albert Geldard's record of the youngest ever player to feature in a Football League match, at the age of 15 years and 158 days - one that still stands to this day. As for the match, Wrexham lost 5-0! Ken was back in the reserve team by the following week, where he remained until he was signed by Aston Villa in May 1953. Peter Jackson had broken the news that he was not being retained on the day before his nineteenth birthday. However, his disappointment soon turned to joy, as he played for the Welsh youth side against Scotland on the day following his birthday, and on arriving home on the Sunday following the game found that he had six clubs chasing his signature! He chose Aston Villa, mainly due to the influence of Wrexham trainer, Tommy Griffiths, former Welsh international who had also played for Villa. Roberts had to wait until January 1954 before making his debut at outside-right in a 3-2 defeat at Blackpool. He found himself in and out of the Villa first team over the next four seasons, before a seemingly innocuous ankle injury against Manchester United at Villa Park in December 1956 eventually led to the end of his playing career. He was told to rest the ankle for a few days, but tried it out in a reserve team match at Notts County, during which he sustained damage to his cruciate ligaments. It cost him a trip to Wembley for the 1957 F.A.Cup Final, and also a place on the Welsh party to tour South Africa. He worked hard to regain his fitness, but managed just two more first team appearances before having to admit defeat. Ken then returned home to Cefn Mawr, and took up work at Aston's furnishers in Wrexham. He attempted to play football again, with Oswestry Town in the Cheshire County League, but had to quit after a couple of matches due to the knee problems. In May 1961 he was asked by Ken Barnes to become first team coach at Wrexham, and stayed in that position until all the coaching staff were dismissed in February 1965. Ken returned to work at Aston's until January 1966, when Jack Rowley invited him to return to the Racecourse as coach and Chief Scout. He held the position until Rowley left for Bradford Park Avenue in April 1967, when he, too, headed for Yorkshire, though not before he had been offered - and refused - the managerial seat at the Racecourse. Another twelve months was spent at Bradford, and within a month of his departure from Park Avenue was offered the manager's job at Chester, which he accepted. Ken led the club to the Welsh Cup Final in 1970, and then to promotion in 1975 for the first time in the club's history. He also masterminded an exciting run in the League Cup that saw the 'Seals' reach the competition's semi-finals. In 1976 Ken was made General Manager with Alan Oakes becoming manager, although he was to serve for only three years in this capacity before leaving. Roberts had spent a total of twelve years at Sealand Road, and had been responsible for some of the best times known at the club. He was soon back in football when Arfon Griffiths offered him a three year contract as Chief Scout and Youth Development Officer at the Racecourse. He stayed at the club until his contract expired in 1982, when he was allowed to leave. He then opened a sports shop in Cefn, before becoming the manager at the Tennis Centre in Wrexham, although he retained an involvement in football by managing Cymru Alliance League side Cefn Druids. In 1995 he returned to Chester City, taking up an offer from Kevin Ratcliffe to become the club's Youth Development Officer, as well as continuing to run the Tennis Centre in Wrexham which he is still doing at the time of writing, having left the Deva Stadium Club.

Season	League		F.A.Cup		Welsh Cup		Total	
	apps	gls	apps	gls	apps	gls	apps	gls
1950/51	1	0	-	-	-	-	1	0
	1	**0**	**-**	**-**	**-**	**-**	**1**	**0**

ROBERTS, Neil Wyn 1996 -

Position; *Forward*
D.O.B; *7th April, 1978*
Birthplace; *Wrexham, Denbighshire*
Height; *5ft 10in* **Weight;** *11st 1lbs*
Debut; v. *Chesterfield (h) 27th September, 1997*
Total Appearances & Goals; *58/22 apps 18 gls*
Career; *WREXHAM (YTS) Jul 1994, (Pro) 3rd July 1996;*
Honours; *One Welsh Under-21 cap; Welsh Invitation Cup Winner 1998; Welsh Youth International cap; Welsh Youth Cup Winner 1996; Welsh Youth Cup runner-up 1995; Welsh National League Championship Winner 1996;*

Neil Roberts showed plenty of promise as a footballer at an early age. He attended Acton Junior School, and also played football for Garden Village under-10s. It was whilst he was playing for them that he was spotted by a Wrexham scout and invited to the Racecourse, where he would turn up regularly for training sessions. He continued playing for Garden Village, progressing through the different age levels as he moved on to St.David's School in the town, from where he was selected to represent North Wales Schoolboys. On leaving education he was offered a Y.T.S. place with Wrexham, and signed for the club in the summer of 1994. Neil progressed through the youth ranks at the Racecourse, and it was during this time that he was called up to play for the Welsh Youth side. He also picked up two Welsh Youth Cup winners' medals in 1995 and 1996. At the end of the 1995/96 season he was signed on professional terms by the club, but then had to wait until the end of September 1997 before making his Football League debut in a scoreless home draw with Chesterfield, when he came on as a substitute for Karl Connolly. Neil had just eight minutes to make his mark, and only a lightning reaction save by Billy Mercer denied him a debut goal. He played in the club's Welsh Invitation fixture at Cardiff in October, and starred in the 1-1 draw. It proved to be the game that launched his career. His full League debut followed in the next match, as he replaced Dean Spink for the trip to Carlisle, and celebrated in style by scoring both goals in the 2-2 draw. Neil went on to establish himself as a first team regular for the rest of that season, earning international recognition with the Welsh under-21 team for a friendly match in Italy, although he had to pull out of the squad because of injury. His goals and commitment took Wrexham to within a whisker of the Second Division play-offs, only for them to miss out on goals scored. However, he did help 'The Robins' to win the Welsh Invitation Cup in its inaugural season, beating Cardiff City 2-1 in the Final. The beginning of the 1998/99 season saw Neil once again called up for the Welsh under-21 squad to face Italy on the Racecourse, and he made his first appearance at that level when he came on as a substitute in the 2-1 defeat. Showed immense promise in first full season in the Football League. Workrate is first class while his chasing of lost causes is appreciated by the fans. A notable aspect of his play is an ability to use the body to lay the ball off, often with his chest. Neil missed the run in to the end 1998/99 season due to niggling injuries but remains one for the future.

Season	League		F.A.Cup		League Cup		A.W.S.		W.I.C.		Total	
	apps	gls	apps	gls	apps	gls	apps	gls	apps	gls	apps	gls
1997/98	29/5	8	3/1	1	-	-	0/1	0	6/3	1	38/10	10
1998/99	11/11	3	3	1	1	1	2/1	2	3	1	20/12	8
	40/16	**11**	**6/1**	**2**	**1**	**1**	**2/2**	**2**	**9/3**	**2**	**58/22**	**18**

ROBERTS, Paul 1996 - 1998

Position; *Forward*
D.O.B; *29th July, 1977*
Birthplace; *Bangor, Gwynedd*
Height; *5ft 11in* ***Weight;*** *11st 9lbs*
Debut; v. *Stockport County (h) 26th December, 1996*
Total Appearances & Goals; *0/2 apps 0 gls*
Career; *Llanystymdwy; Porthmadog 1995 12/22apps 14gls; WREXHAM 20th Dec 1996 £10,000; Bangor City Jul 1998; Porthmadog Sept 1998;*
Honours; *One Welsh Under-21 International cap;*

Paul Roberts began his football career with Caernarfon & District League side Llanystymdwy (the home of David Lloyd George). He progressed sufficiently to be chosen for the North Wales Coast F.A. Representative XI to meet the Scottish Junior League XI, before catching the eye of League of Wales side Porthmadog with his goalscoring prowess. He became an instant success in the League of Wales, as he continued to find the net on a regular basis, prompting the Welsh management team to select him for the under-21 squad to play Holland in October 1996. A 'pacy player with an eye for goal' Paul had begun a Leisure and Tourism course at Bangor College, but his goalscoring feats in the League of Wales soon started to attract the scouts to Yr Traeth. It was Wrexham manager Brian Flynn who made the first significant move, and he brought Paul to the Racecourse club in December 1996 for a £10,000 fee. He was described as 'one for the future', and he took his time to settle into the role of a professional footballer. However, he didn't have to wait long before he was given his first team chance as a substitute for Gareth Owen in a 3-2 home defeat against Stockport County in 1996 on a Boxing Day League encounter. His second appearance came against Premier League side West Ham United, again on the Racecourse, in an F.A.Cup Third Round tie played on a snow covered pitch. Paul again came on as a sub this time for Steve Morris, but there was to be no fairy-tale match winning goal for the youngster. Wrexham did take the 'Hammers' to a replay, however, which they then won 1-0 at Upton Park. The cup-tie at the Racecourse proved to be Paul's final first team appearance in a Wrexham shirt, as he returned to reserve team football to await another first team chance, which was not to come. He was offered a three month contract at the end of the 1997/98 season to push for a senior place in 1998/99, but turned it down in favour of a return to the semi-pro game with League of Wales side Bangor City. However, he had only been at Farrar Road for a couple of months before he accepted an offer from his old club, Porthmadog, to return as player/coach while running the club's Football in the Community scheme.

Season	League		F.A.Cup		League Cup		A.W.S.		Total	
	apps	gls	apps	gls	apps	gls	apps	gls	apps	gls
1996/97	0/1	0	0/1	0	-	-	-	-	0/2	0
	0/1	**0**	**0/1**	**0**	-	-	-	-	**0/2**	**0**

ROBERTS, Robert 1982 - 1985

Position; *Goalkeeper (Wing-Half)*
D.O.B; *2nd September, 1940*
Birthplace; *Edinburgh, Lothian*
Height; *5ft 9'1/2in* ***Weight;*** *11st 4lbs*
Debut; v. *Worcester City (h) 29th November, 1983 (Welsh Cup).*
Total Appearances & Goals; *1 app 0 gls*
Career; *Edinburgh Norton; Motherwell 1958; Leicester City Sept 1963 £41,000 224/5apps 26gls; Mansfield Town 23rd Sept 1970 76/4apps 4gls; Coventry City (coach) cs1972; Colchester United Jul 1973 0/2apps 0gls (Player/Coach, followed by manager 1975); WREXHAM Jun 1982 (Manager);*
Honours; *Football League Cup Winner 1964; F.A.Cup runner-up 1969; One Scottish under-23 international cap; One Scottish Football League representative appearance;*

Bobby Roberts had an illustrious Football career, playing for Motherwell in the Scottish League, where he won Scottish under-23 and Scottish Football League representative caps, followed by a move south of the border in September 1963 to join Leicester City for £41,000. He struggled at first to fulfil the Filbert Street fans high expectations of him. Bobby missed out on the 1964 Football League Cup win over Stoke City, having scored in both legs of the semi-finals, but finally won over the Leicester faithful with his '100% effort and skilful prompting'. He played at Wembley in the 1969 F.A.Cup Final, although the 'Foxes' lost to Manchester City. Bobby spent one more season with Leicester following which he moved on to Mansfield Town in September 1970, where he remained for a little under two years before moving into coaching with Coventry City. A season at Highfield Road under the managership of Gordon Milne ended with a move to Colchester United in July 1973 as coach to Jim Smith. He came out of retirement to make two substitute appearances for the Essex club, eventually becoming manager in June 1975. Bobby remained in that position until April 1982, when he was sacked after refusing to resign! In June of that year he was given the opportunity to make a swift return to football management at Wrexham. In taking the job he accepted that he would have to work in very difficult circumstances, at a club who were in dire financial straits. Despite the hardship Bobby coped well on a shoestring budget, and brought some glory to the club during his time as manager. He guided the 'Robins' to the 1984 Welsh Cup Final, where they were defeated by Shrewsbury Town, and so clinched a place in the following season's European competition by virtue of the Shropshire club's position to the east of Offa's Dyke. This opened up new opportunities for Roberts, and he responded superbly to the challenge by plotting the destruction of Portuguese giants F.C.Porto, before going out to the Italian aces of A.S.Roma. Few would begrudge the genial Scot his moment of glory following the away goals victory in Portugal, especially as he had laid his reputation on the line a little under a year previously. Because of critical injury problems prior to the club's Welsh Cup tie against Worcester City the 41 year old manager was forced to dust off his boots and turn out - not at wing-half, but in goal! Regular first choice keeper Stuart Parker was injured, and so limited were the club's resources at the time that they had no suitable stand-by available. He did have some previous experience between the posts, when he took over from an injured Peter Shilton in goal against Manchester United at Old Trafford in 1967. Despite his lack of expertise! he helped the 'Robins' hold out for a 1-1 draw, and go on to qualify for Europe. In March 1985 Bobby Roberts was sacked by Wrexham, having done his level best in extremely difficult circumstances. He then helped out with coaching duties at Stoke City before going to Kuwait to coach with Al-Shabab for two years. He returned home in 1987 to become manager of Grimsby Town, a position he held for a season, again beset with financial problems, when he left after the 'Mariners' had been relegated. This signalled a return to Filbert Street in a coaching capacity in June 1988, where he spent three and a half years. He went back to his old club in Kuwait for a short while until becoming Chief Scout at Derby County in 1995, where he still remains at the time of writing.

Season	League		F.A.Cup		Welsh Cup		League Cup		A.M.C.		Total	
	apps	gls	apps	gls	apps	gls	apps	gls	apps	gls	apps	gls
1983/84	-	-	-	-	1	0	-	-	-	-	1	0
	-	-	-	-	**1**	**0**	-	-	-	-	**1**	**0**

ROBERTS, Ronald 1960 - 1963

Position; *Outside-Left*
D.O.B; *14th September, 1942*
Birthplace; *Llay, Denbighshire*
Height; *5ft 8in* **Weight;** *10st 10lbs*
Debut; v. *Llandudno (h) 27th January, 1960 (Welsh Cup)*
Total Appearances & Goals; *83 apps 4 gls*
Career; *WREXHAM (Am) Jan 1958, (Pro) 22nd Apr 1960; Tranmere Rovers 22nd Mar 1963 56apps 2gls; Oswestry Town Jul 1964; Stafford Rangers Dec 1964; GKN Sankeys; Pwllheli 20th Aug 1965; Barmouth & Dyffryn United 21st Aug 1970;*
Honours; *Two Welsh Under-23 International caps; Three Welsh Youth International caps; Welsh Youth Cup Winner 1959 & 1960;*

Ron Roberts first played football at Llay Secondary Modern School, later representing Wrexham & District Schoolboys. Following fine displays he was invited for trials with Wolves in August 1957, but it was local Football League side Wrexham who signed the promising winger on to the ground staff as a 15 year-old in January 1958. He progressed through the 'B' and 'A' teams at the Racecourse to play regularly in the reserve side. During that time he made one appearance for the Welsh Boys' Club team, and won three caps with the Welsh Youth side, as well as collecting two Welsh Youth Cup winners' medals in 1959 and 1960. Ron made his first team debut for the 'Robins' in a 4-0 Welsh Cup victory against Llandudno in January 1960. His Football League debut followed three months later, replacing Reg Hunter at outside-left in a 3-1 home win over York City, and then agreed professional terms with the club. The 1960/61 season saw Ron secure a regular first team place at outside-left, and he played a part in the demolition of First Division Blackburn Rovers in the Football League Cup. Further international recognition came his way, with two Welsh under-23 caps against Scotland and Northern Ireland in 1962. Ron was to lose his place to new signing Clive Colbridge towards the end of the 1961/62 season, as the 'Robins' clinched promotion to the Third Division. The following campaign again saw Colbridge preferred, with Roberts resigned to reserve team football until March 1963 when he was offered a fresh start with Tranmere Rovers. He made his debut for the 'Prentonians' in a scoreless draw at Chester, and became virtually an ever-present in the Rovers team for the rest of that and the 1963/64 seasons, making 56 League appearances and scoring two goals. However, he then found that he was surplus to requirements and was released in the summer of 1964. He was offered the chance to remain in the Football League with Barrow, but was not prepared to uproot his young family, and so he signed for Cheshire County League side Oswestry Town on a part-time basis, combining football with employment at the Firestone Tyre factory in Wrexham. Ron continued in non-league football, having spells with Stafford Rangers, GKN Sankey's of Wellington, Pwllheli & District, and, finally, Barmouth & Dyffryn United. Ron Roberts still lives in the Wrexham area in Gresford, while working as a manager at the Sharp Manufacturing factory in nearby Llay.

Season	League		F.A.Cup		Welsh Cup		League Cup		Total	
	apps	gls	apps	gls	apps	gls	apps	gls	apps	gls
1959/60	1	0	-	-	1	0	-	-	2	0
1960/61	36	4	1	0	3	0	6	0	46	4
1961/62	9	0	1	0	3	0	1	0	34	0
1962/63	1	0	-	-	-	-	-	-	1	0
	67	**4**	**2**	**0**	**7**	**0**	**7**	**0**	**83**	**4**

ROBERTS, Stanley 1946 - 1948

Position; *Forward*
D.O.B; *10th April, 1921*
Birthplace; *Wrexham, Denbighshire*
Died; *Wrexham, 3rd April, 1995*
Height; *5ft 8in* **Weight;** *11st 0lbs*
Debut; v. *Doncaster Rovers (a) 25th December, 1946*
Total Appearances & Goals; *29 apps 11 gls*
Career; *Hightown Athletic; Cross Street FC; WREXHAM (Amateur) 1939/40, re-registered 28th Sept 1946; Crewe Alexandra (WW2 Guest) 1942/43 2apps 0gls; Rochdale (WW2 Guest) 1944/45 3apps 0gls; New Brighton 22nd Jan 1947 103apps 25gls; Ellesmere Port Town cs1951;*

Stan Roberts played football for Rhosddu School as a lad, and scored one of the goals that secured victory in the Denbighshire and District Schools Cup Final. On leaving school he played for Hightown Athletic in his native Wrexham, before turning out for Cross Street in the local Wrexham area Chum's League. He notched 78 goals, and his prolific goalscoring prowess soon came to the attention of Wrexham, who signed him as an amateur at the beginning of the 1939/40 season. Unfortunately, the Second World War interrupted the progress of his playing career, and he enlisted in the Royal Air Force, serving in both India and Singapore. During the conflict Stan continued to play football when he could for his station team, and also appeared as a 'guest' for both Crewe Alexandra and Rochdale. After WW2 was over he re-signed for Wrexham as an amateur in September 1946, and soon progressed to make his Football League debut against Doncaster Rovers on Christmas Day 1946. He was signed on professional terms the following month, and soon established himself as a regular member of the 'Robins' team, taking over Jesse McLarty's position at inside-forward. Stan stepped in at centre-forward for Jack Boothway at the beginning of the following season, but by January 1947 was allowed to leave the Racecourse. He joined New Brighton, where he went on to spend four years. At the 'Tower Ground' he was described as 'retaining his place on the strength of his midfield creativity, which effectively kept the attack on the move.' He made over 100 appearances for the 'Rakers' before they failed in their bid for re-election to the Football League in the summer of 1951, having finishing bottom of the Third Division North the previous season. Stan then left the Wirral club and joined Cheshire County League side Ellesmere Port Town. He later worked at Courtaulds and Betts Plastics in Wrexham before finding employment at the town's Cambrian Leather Works, where he remained until his retirement in 1987. Stan passed away at the Wrexham Maelor Hospital in April 1995, aged 73.

Season	League		F.A.Cup		Welsh Cup		Total	
	apps	gls	apps	gls	apps	gls	apps	gls
1946/47	18	7	-	-	1	1	19	8
1947/48	9	3	-	-	1	0	10	3
	27	**10**	**-**	**-**	**2**	**1**	**29**	**11**

ROBERTS, Stephen Wyn 1998 -

Position; Central-Defender
D.O.B; 24th February, 1980
Birthplace; Wrexham, Denbighshire
Height; 6ft 1in **Weight;** 12st 7lbs
Debut; v. Swansea City (h) 27th October, 1998 (FAW Premier Cup)
Total Appearances & Goals; 1/1 apps 0 gls
Career; WREXHAM 7th Jan 1998;
Honours; Welsh Youth International cap;

Steve Roberts is the younger brother - by two years - of Neil. They both played for their school teams at Acton Primary and St.David's Schools in Wrexham, and like his brother, Steve also represented Wrexham & District, Clwyd, and North Wales Schoolboys at different age levels Unlike Neil, who is a striker, Steve plays in the centre of defence. He was signed by Wrexham at the age of 12 having been spotted in the same Garden Village Youth Club team that had been responsible for launching his brother's career. He turned out for them through to under-16 level, and although also playing for Wrexham at the different age levels he spent two years training with Liverpool. On completing his education in the summer of 1996 Steve signed on the 'Robins' Youth Training Scheme. He progressed rapidly, playing for Wales in the UEFA under-16s championship against the Faroe Islands and Spain, as well as earning caps for the Welsh Youth team. He also collected a Welsh Youth Cup winners' medal. Little wonder, then, that he was signed on professional forms six months before the completion of his YTS contract. The beginning of the 1998/99 season saw him called up into the first team squad, before he made his senior bow at the age of 18 in a F.A.W. Premier Cup match against Swansea City in October 1998. Steve teamed up with his brother in the 2-0 home defeat, becoming only the eighth pair of brothers to have played for the club since joining the Football League in 1921. Manager Brian Flynn said of Steve, "losing the Swansea game overshadows his performance because he played very well". Much is expected of Steve in the future. By the way, there is another brother, Danny also waiting in the wings!

Season	League		F.A.Cup		League Cup		A.W.S.		W.P.C.		Total	
	apps	gls	apps	gls	apps	gls	apps	gls	apps	gls	apps	gls
1998/99	-	-	-	-	-	-	0/1	0	1	0	1/1	0
	-	**-**	**-**	**-**	**-**	**-**	**0/1**	**0**	**1**	**0**	**1/1**	**0**

ROBERTS, Walter 1938 - 1948

Position; *Right-Half*
D.O.B; *23rd November, 1917*
Birthplace; *Wrexham*
Height; *5ft 8'1/2in* ***Weight;*** *11st 4lbs*
Debut; v. *Doncaster Rovers (a) 31st December, 1938*
Total Appearances & Goals; *69 apps 1 gls*
Career; *WREXHAM 29th Aug 1938, WW2 19apps 4gls; Bournemouth 4th Aug 1948 14apps 0gls; Ellesmere Port cs1949; Winsford United cs1950; Blaenau Ffestiniog 23rd Jul 1951;*

Walter Roberts first played football at the Victoria and Alexandra Schools in Wrexham. He began his working life as a shop assistant, and continued to play park football for fun with his friends. He was invited to take part in a few representative matches for Wrexham Police, and it was following one of these games that he was recommended to Wrexham by the Chief Constable of Wrexham Police. Walter was then invited to the Racecourse for trials, and after a few reserve team games he signed for the club in August 1938. He played mostly reserve team football in his first season, but was given his first team chance on New Year's Eve 1938, replacing the injured Archie Burgon at outside-left in a scoreless draw against Doncaster Rovers. Walter made one more first team appearance that season, against New Brighton in a Northern Section Cup match, before the Second World War brought everything to a sudden halt. When he had been playing for Wrexham Walter had joined the Territorial Army, serving in the Royal Artillery, so he was one of the first to be called up when the conflict began. He was posted to France, and was one of many to be plucked to safety from Dunkirk in June 1940, serving later in the Middle-East. Walter made nineteen appearances for Wrexham in the War-time Regional Leagues when home on leave, and after the hostilities had ended he re-signed for the club, missing only five matches in 1946/47. He was an ever-present in the side in the early part of the following season, until he picked up an injury against Mansfield Town on Boxing Day 1947.Once fit he couldn't regain his place in the side, though offered new terms in the summer. However, because manager Tom Williams couldn't guarantee him a first team place Roberts asked to be transfer-listed. Third Division South side Bournemouth showed an interest, and manager Harry Lowe arranged a meeting with Walter while visiting his wife's family near Hartlepools. They agreed terms, with Fred Rowell moving in the opposite direction in the part-exchange deal. Walter continued to reside in Wrexham throughout his stay at Dean Court, travelling down by train to each match! He made twelve League appearances for the South Coast Club, but decided to leave at the end of the season as Bournemouth were unable to offer him suitable accommodation. He then joined Cheshire County League side Ellesmere Port Town, followed by a spell with Welsh League (North) side Blaenau Ffestiniog. He was then invited back to Wrexham to serve as reserve team coach under manager Peter Jackson. Walter worked in that position for a year before returning to his old job as a shop assistant in Wrexham, remaining in that occupation until his retirement. He was given another opportunity to coach at the Racecourse by Jack Rowley in the 1960s, but turned it down. Walter settled in Wrexham, and was one of many former players to attend the club's 'Players Grand Gala Reunion Luncheon' at the St.David's Hotel in Ewloe in September 1998.

Season	League		F.A.Cup		Welsh Cup		N.S.C.		Total	
	apps	gls	apps	gls	apps	gls	apps	gls	apps	gls
1938/39	1	0	-	-	-	-	1	0	2	0
1946/47	37	1	4	0	2	0	-	-	43	1
1947/48	22	0	2	0	-	-	-	-	24	0
	60	**1**	**6**	**0**	**2**	**0**	**1**	**0**	**69**	**1**

ROBERTSON, Edward Harold Yeoman 1963 - 1964

Position; *Right-Back*
D.O.B; *19th December, 1935*
Birthplace; *Edinburgh, Lothian*
Died; *December, 1981*
Height; *5ft 8in* ***Weight;*** *11st 12lbs*
Debut; v. *Notts County (a) 26th October, 1963*
Total Appearances & Goals; *24 apps 0 gls*
Career; *Linlithgow Rose Juniors; Leeds United 0apps; Preston North End 0apps; Bury Jul 1954 196apps 5gls; WREXHAM 26th Oct 1963 £3,000; Tranmere Rovers 1st Jul 1964 143/4apps 1gls; Ellesmere Port Town cs1969;*
Honours; *Two Third Division North representative XI appearances;*

It was as a forward that Eddie Robertson first made an impression, with Scottish Junior League side Linlithgow Rose Juniors. He was first spotted by Leeds United, and invited for trials, but was later allowed to leave Elland Road without making any impact. He then joined Preston North End, where he again failed to make an impression. It was the Bury manager David Russell who first saw Eddie's potential as a defender, and signed him in July 1954, whereupon the Scot was switched to a full back position. With his speed and quick anticipation Eddie quickly took the eye and was twice selected for the Third Division North Representative side against their counterparts from the Third Division South. Eddie returned to Gigg Lane in the summer of 1956 after completing his National Service and quickly established himself in the side, going on to make over 200 League and Cup appearances for the Lancashire club. In October 1963 Wrexham manager Ken Barnes paid out £3,000 to bring Robertson to the Racecourse, to help strengthen a weakening defence. He made his debut at Notts County, replacing Peter Jones in a 3-0 defeat, and went on to make a further 23 League appearances in a season which would eventually end in relegation. At the end of the campaign Eddie was a victim of a big clear out by Ken Barnes, and was allowed to join Tranmere Rovers in July 1964 on a free transfer. He made his debut for the Prenton Park club in a 2-1 defeat at Darlington in September, and went on to complete over 150 League and Cup appearances for Tranmere, helping them to promotion to the Third Division in 1967. He finally left the Birkenhead club in the close season of 1969, but continued to play football for Cheshire County League side Ellesmere Port Town. In 1975 he returned to Prenton Park as assistant-manager and coach under John King. Eddie remained with Tranmere until his tragic death in December 1981, aged just 46. He was with the players out training when he collapsed and died.

Season	League		F.A.Cup		Welsh Cup		League Cup		Total	
	apps	gls	apps	gls	apps	gls	apps	gls	apps	gls
1963/64	24	0	3	0	2	0	-	-	29	0
	24	**0**	**3**	**0**	**2**	**0**	**-**	**-**	**29**	**0**

ROBERTSON, Hugh 1937 - 1938

Position; *Right-Half*
D.O.B;
Birthplace; *Perth, Tayside*
Height; *5ft 9in* ***Weight;*** *12st 0lbs*
Debut; v. *Mansfield Town (h) 17th April, 1937*
Total Appearances & Goals; *6 apps 0 gls*
Career; *St.Johnstone YMCA; WREXHAM 1st Apr 1937; St.Johnstone 1938/39 1app 0gls;*
Honours; *Scottish Junior International;*

Hugh Robertson was signed by Wrexham in April 1937 from Scottish Junior League side St.Johnstone YMCA, with whom he had won a Scottish Junior International cap. He made his Football League debut shortly after joining the club in a 3-2 home defeat by Mansfield Town, when he replaced Matt Lawrence at right-half. He made five more League appearances for the 'Robins' the following season, playing at either half-back or at right-back, before he was released at the end of 1937/38. Hugh later signed for Scottish League side, St.Johnstone, where he is known to have made one Scottish League appearance during 1938/39.

Season	League		F.A.Cup		Welsh Cup		N.S.C.		Total	
	apps	gls	apps	gls	apps	gls	apps	gls	apps	gls
1936/37	1	0	-	-	-	-	-	-	1	0
1937/38	5	0	-	-	-	-	-	-	5	0
	6	**0**	**-**	**-**	**-**	**-**	**-**	**-**	**6**	**0**

ROBINSON, William
1923 - 1924

Position; *Half-Back*
D.O.B; *1900*
Birthplace; *Birkenhead*
Height; *5ft 6in* **Weight;** *11st 0lbs*
Debut; v. *New Brighton (a) 9th February, 1924*
Total Appearances & Goals; *1 app 0 gls*
Career; *Tranmere Rovers WW1; Everton 1917 WW1 58apps 0gls, 7apps 0gls; Saltney Ath 1920; Chester cs1921 68apps 0gls; WREXHAM 27th Jun 1923; Mold Town 16th Jul 1924;*
Honours; *Cheshire County League Championship Winner 1922; North Wales Coast F.A. Challenge Cup Winner 1925;*

Billy Robinson is believed to have played for Tranmere Rovers during the First World War before joining Everton in the close season of 1917. He made 58 War-time appearances for Everton in either full-back position, occasionally filling in at half-back. He made his Football League debut for the 'Toffeemen' after the conflict had ended, in a 3-2 home defeat by Chelsea on the opening day of the 1919/20 season. Billy made six further Football League appearances for Everton, but by January had fallen out of favour. He then moved on to Saltney Athletic before making the short journey to Chester in the summer of 1921, and in his first season with the 'Cestrians' helped them to the Cheshire County League championship, missing just four games. He remained at Sealand Road for the following season, but in the summer of 1923 he returned to the Football League by signing for Third Division North side Wrexham. However, he was to play mostly reserve team football at the Racecourse, though he did manage a single Football League appearance for the 'Robins' when replacing Billy Matthews in a scoreless draw at New Brighton in February 1924. At the end of that season Billy joined Mold Town, where he collected a North Wales Coast F.A. Challenge Cup winners' medal as they beat Bangor City 2-0 in the Final. The following year he helped Mold reach the fourth qualifying round of the F.A.Cup, beating his former club Chester 5-0 on the way.

Season	League		F.A.Cup		Welsh Cup		Total	
	apps	gls	apps	gls	apps	gls	apps	gls
1923/24	1	0	-	-	-	-	1	0
	1	**0**	-	-	-	-	**1**	**0**

ROBSON, Edward Riddell
1926 - 1928

Position; *Goalkeeper*
D.O.B; *21st August, 1890*
Birthplace; *Hexham, Northumberland*
Died; *Hexham area, J/F/M 1977*
Height; *6ft 0in* **Weight;** *12st 0lbs*
Debut; v. *Chesterfield (h) 28th August, 1926.*
Total Appearances & Goals; *83 apps 0 gls*
Career; *Gateshead; Watford Jun 1914 4apps 0gls; Sunderland (WW1 Guest); Portsmouth Jul 1919 75apps 0gls; Sunderland 29th May 1922 38apps 0gls; Swansea Town 20th May 1924 £250 29apps 0gls; WREXHAM 12th Jun 1926; Grimsby Town Jul 1928 0apps; Rochdale Mar 1929 12apps 0gls;*
Honours; *Third Division South Championship Winner 1925; Welsh Cup runner-up 1926; Southern League Championship Winner 1920;*

Ted Robson played in goal for Gateshead in his native North-East before moving south to join Watford in the summer of 1914. The 1914/15 season saw Watford win the Southern League Championship, though Ted had made just four appearances for the 'Hornets' in that campaign. With World War One already underway Robson's football career - like so many others - was put on hold. Following the end of the conflict he resumed with another Southern League side, Portsmouth, winning a championship medal in his first season. The following campaign saw him take his place in goal for 'Pompey's' first ever Football League match, a 3-0 home win over Swansea Town. He remained the Fratton Park club's regular 'keeper until April 1922, when he was displaced by Tom Newton, and in the summer of 1922 left Portsmouth to join First Division side Sunderland. In his first season at Roker Park Ted helped them finish as runners-up to Liverpool, but the following term he lost his place in the side to Albert McInroy. At the completion of 1923/24 he joined Swansea Town as a 'guest' on their summer tour to Denmark, with a view to a permanent signing. Following his return from the tour he signed for the 'Swans' for a £250 fee, and earned a Third Division South championship medal in his first season at the Vetch Field. Robson was to spend one more season with the 'Swans', although not as a regular, but did collect a Welsh Cup runners'-up medal when Swansea lost 3-2 to Ebbw Vale in the 1926 Final. He moved to North Wales in the summer of 1926 to join Wrexham, making his League debut in the opening match of the 1926/27 season, a 3-1 home win over Chesterfield. Ted was a regular between the posts at the Racecourse for two years, although not a lucky talisman this time around. During his stay with Wrexham he opened his own business in

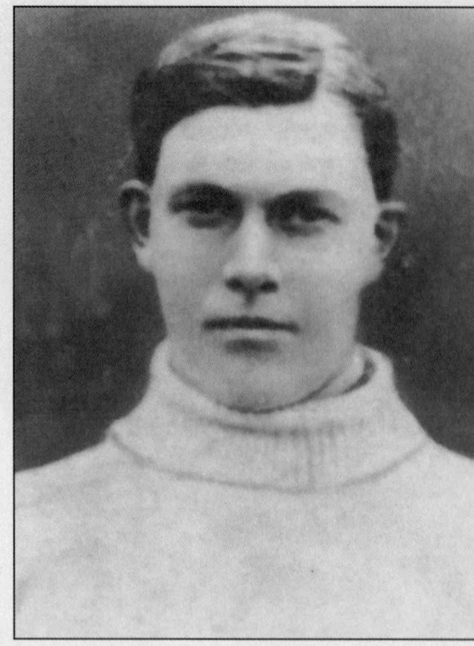

Chester Street, which continued after he had left the Racecourse in the close season of 1928 to join Grimsby Town. It was hardly a successful move as he failed to make a first team appearance at Blundell Park, playing reserve team football as understudy to Tommy Read. Ted left the Cleethorpes club in March 1929 to join Rochdale, where he went straight into the first team for his debut, replacing Jackie Mittell in a 2-1 home win over Crewe Alexandra. He remained in the Spotland senior side for the rest of the season, making a further eleven League appearances. Ted Robson is known to have passed away in his native Hexham in 1977. He was 86.

Season	League		F.A.Cup		Welsh Cup		Total	
	apps	gls	apps	gls	apps	gls	apps	gls
1926/27	35	0	4	0	4	0	43	0
1927/28	34	0	3	0	3	0	40	0
	69	**0**	**7**	**0**	**7**	**0**	**83**	**0**

ROGERS, Ehud
1934 - 1935 & 1945 - 1947

Position; *Outside-Right*
D.O.B; *15th October, 1909*
Birthplace; *Wrexham*
Died; *Chirk, 25th January, 1996*
Height; *5ft 7in* **Weight;** *10st 6lbs*
Debut; v. *York City (a) 27th October, 1934*
Total Appearances & Goals; *97 apps 34 gls*
Career; *Weston Rhyn; Llanerch Celts; Chirk; Oswestry Town 1933; WREXHAM 23rd May 1934; Arsenal 14th Jan 1935 £2,600 16apps 5gls; Newcastle United Jun 1936 £2,500 56apps 10gls; Swansea Town 15th May 1939 £700; Everton (WW2 Guest) Apr 1944 1app 0gls; WREXHAM (WW2 Guest) Oct 1939 62 apps 34gls; WREXHAM 11th Dec 1945; Oswestry Town Feb 1947;*
Honours; *Welsh Amateur International; London F.A.Challenge Cup Winner 1936;*

Although born in Chirk Ehud - or 'Tim', as he was later known - moved to Normanton, Yorkshire, when he was just three years old, due to his father's job as a miner. He returned to Chirk in 1926, and played his early football with Weston Rhyn, followed by spells with Llanerch Celts, Chirk, and Oswestry Town. After leaving school Ehud began working as a chauffeur for a local businessman, as well as distributing newspapers around Chirk. He had the chance to join Wrexham in 1932, when he was invited to play for the reserve side in a Birmingham and District League match against Hednesford Town, but he declined the offer, preferring to stay with Chirk. He later played for Oswestry Town in the Birmingham & District League where he was awarded a Welsh Amateur cap against Scotland, before finally giving in to Wrexham's persistent approaches. He finally signed for the Racecourse club on the boot of director George Turner's car outside his house in Chirk. Ehud made his Football League debut for the 'Robins' on the right wing in October 1934 at York City, replacing the departed Bill Bryant who had signed for Manchester United. He kept his place in the side until January, when Arsenal manager George Allison stepped in and signed the promising winger for a fee in the region of £2,600. It was Ehud's speed that had attracted the 'Gunners', as he could cover 100 yards in 10.2 seconds at the time. It was at Highbury that he earned the nickname 'Tim', because some of the players had difficulty in pronouncing his proper name! Ehud didn't have long to wait for his First Division debut, as it came in April at home to Middlesbrough. And what a start it was, as the 'Gunners' won 8-0 with Ehud scoring twice. He remained in the side for the following four matches, which were to see Arsenal clinch the First Division Championship for the third year running. His League appearances were limited to eleven in the following season, but did play in the famous match at Villa Park when Ted Drake scored a record seven goals in Arsenal's 7-1 win. In May 1935 he played in the King George's Jubilee match for a combined Wales/Ireland XI against a combined Scotland/England team. He also added a London F.A.Challenge Cup winners' medal in that same season as Arsenal beat Brentford 4-2 in the Final, but he missed out on the 1936 F.A.Cup Final. Although he was named in the 14-man squad for the Wembley showpiece he had only just recovered from injury, and so was not selected for the final eleven. In June 1936 'Tim' was to leave Highbury to move on to St.James' Park, when Newcastle United paid out £2,500 for him. He went straight into the first team for the new 1936/37 season, and made his debut in front of a crowd of 35,000 against Barnsley. Newcastle lost 1-0, but Ehud missed just four matches in the League that season. Despite his early success he struggled to establish himself in a regular first team place over the next couple of seasons, as his appearances were limited by a series of injuries. During his time at Newcastle he was described as 'on the small side, though this does not handicap this thrustfulness of purpose' and that he 'has played in almost every position in the forward line and thrives on it'. In the summer of 1939 Ehud asked for a move nearer home, and returned to Wales, joining Swansea Town in May 1939 for a £700 fee. He played in the first three League matches for the 'Swans' before the outbreak of the Second World War. Ehud then returned to Chirk, and turned out as a 'guest' for Wrexham, missing just one match throughout the 1939/40 season. He continued to appear for the 'Robins' until 1941 when he enlisted in the R.A.F. as an aircraft fitter. He was based at St.Athan near Cardiff, which meant that he could play for Swansea. During that time he also 'guested' for Aberaman and Lovells Athletic. Rogers was posted to Egypt in 1944, by which time he had already played in two War-time internationals for Wales against England, and was soon appointed captain of the R.A.F. side. Following the end of the War he was given the chance to move back North to Wrexham, but Swansea refused to release him at first, eventually, however, they relented and he returned to the Racecourse in December 1945. Ehud made his debut for the 'Robins' in a 1-1 home draw with Barrow, but this proved to be his only match because, in January 1947, he decided to leave the club to concentrate on his family newspaper business in Chirk. Ehud did continue to play football for a short while with Oswestry Town, and after retiring he took over coaching duties at Chirk. Throughout his football career Ehud was a keen cricketer, as well as a golfing enthusiast. He passed away in Chirk on 25th January 1996, at the grand age of 87. Until recently, his family newspaper business had continued under the control of his son, Peter. Ehud's brother Joe played for Manchester City and Shrewsbury Town.

Season	League		F.A.Cup		Welsh Cup		N.S.C.		War-Cup		Total	
	apps	gls	apps	gls	apps	gls	apps	gls	apps	gls	apps	gls
1934/35	11	2	2	1	-	-	1	0	-	-	14	3
1939/40	24	15	-	-	-	-	-	-	-	-	24	15
1940/41	18	5	-	-	-	-	-	-	2	1	19	6
1941/42	6	1	-	-	-	-	-	-	-	-	6	1
1942/43	3	0	-	-	-	-	-	-	-	-	3	0
1943/44	11	4	-	-	-	-	-	-	-	-	11	4
1944/45	2	1	-	-	-	-	-	-	-	-	2	1
1945/46	6	1	1	0	-	-	-	-	10	3	17	4
1946/47	1	0	-	-	-	-	-	-	-	-	1	0
	82	**29**	**3**	**1**	**-**	**-**	**1**	**0**	**12**	**4**	**97**	**34**
F/League	12	2	3	1	-	-	1	0	-	-	15	3

ROGERS, Kevin Penry 1984 - 1985

Position; *Forward*
D.O.B; *23rd September, 1963*
Birthplace; *Merthyr Tydfil, Glamorgan*
Height; *5ft 9in* ***Weight;*** *11st 3lbs*
Debut; v. *Swindon Town (a) 25th August, 1984*
Total Appearances & Goals; *42/4 apps 4 gls*
Career; *Aston Villa Sept 1981 0apps; Birmingham City Apr 1983 8/1apps 1gls; WREXHAM Jul 1984; Rhyl Aug 1985 Merthyr Tydfil Oct 1986; AFC Newport Aug 1995; Afan Lido Dec 1995 26/1apps 2gls; Cwmbran Town cs1996 11/10apps 1gls; Ton Pentre 1996/97 15apps 3gls; Hoover Sports Aug 1997;*
Honours; *Welsh Cup Winner 1987; Welsh Youth International; Welsh Schoolboy International; Welsh Semi-Professional International cap; Southern League Premier Division Championship Winner 1989;*

Kevin Rogers represented Wales as a schoolboy at various age levels. He also played local junior football for Georgetown Boys' Club in his native Merthyr, signing for Aston Villa as an apprentice on leaving school. Kevin remained with them for his two year apprenticeship, gaining Welsh honours against Holland, but towards the end of his time at Villa Park he was informed of his release, without having made a first team break-through. This prompted a move across the city in April 1983 to rejoin his former manager Ron Saunders at neighbours Birmingham City. Kevin made his Football League debut for the 'Blues' as a substitute for Mick Harford in a 2-1 home defeat against Coventry City. He managed eight more League appearances in a season that ended with relegation for the St.Andrew's club. He had failed to feature once in a winning side during his nine matches for the 'Blues'! Not surprisingly, he was released at the end of the season, but was soon fixed up when Wrexham manager Bobby Roberts signed the young forward on a free transfer in July 1984. Kevin made his debut for the 'Robins' in the opening game of the 1984/85 season, a 2-1 defeat at Swindon. In the following League game, at home to Port Vale, he registered his first goal for the club in a 1-1 draw. He went on to play in club's four European Cup-Winners' Cup matches, enjoying the memorable victory over F.C.Porto before bowing out to the Italian giants of A.S.Roma. Kevin was a regular in the side throughout that campaign, but he was to be disappointed with news of his release at its conclusion. He then joined Northern Premier League side Rhyl, almost two seasons before returning to his home town club, Merthyr Tydfil, in October 1986. He helped them gain promotion to the Southern League Premier Division, and then the Conference League in 1989/90. Two years earlier he had been a member of the 'Martyrs' Welsh Cup winning side, and was able to experience more European action against another Italian team, Atlanta. At Merthyr Kevin was selected to play for the Welsh semi-professional team on several occasions, before leaving Penydarren Park in 1995, following relegation from the Conference League. He had made over 200 appearances for the South Walians. He joined forces with AFC Newport in the close season, but by December he had moved on to League of Wales side Afan Lido. He continued playing in the League of Wales for both Cwmbran Town and Ton Pentre.

Season	League		F.A.Cup		Welsh Cup		League Cup		F.RT		E.C.W.C.		Total	
	apps	gls	apps	gls	apps	gls	apps	gls	apps	gls	apps	gls	apps	gls
1984/85	30/5	3	1	0	3	1	2	0	2	0	4	0	42/5	4
	30/5	**3**	**1**	**0**	**3**	**1**	**2**	**0**	**2**	**0**	**4**	**0**	**42/5**	**4**

ROGERS, William 1926 - 1932

Position; *Inside-Right*
D.O.B; *O/N/D 1905*
Birthplace; *Summerhill, Nr Wrexham*
Died; *Pen-Y-Ffordd, 14th January, 1936*
Height; *5ft 6in* **Weight;** *10st 6lbs*
Debut; v. *Chesterfield (h) 28th August, 1926*
Total Appearances & Goals; *200 apps 29 gls*
Career; *Summerhill; Oak Alyn Rovers; Flint Town; Tranmere Rovers (Trial) 1925; Bury (Amateur Aug 1925; Flint Town 1925/26; WREXHAM 23rd Jul 1926; Newport County 10th Aug 1932 22apps 3gls; Bristol Rovers Aug 1933 0apps; Clapton Orient Nov 1933 3apps 0gls; Bangor City 21st Sept 1934;*
Honours; *Two Welsh International Caps; Welsh Cup runner-up 1932;*

Billie Rogers began playing football for his local side Summerhill, after leaving school. He later stepped up to the Welsh National League with Oak Alyn Rovers, eventually moving on to Flint Town in the same League. During the close season of 1926 he was signed by Third Division North side Wrexham, making his Football League debut in the opening match of the following season at home to Chesterfield, where he collected a debut goal in the 3-1 win. He went on to become a regular in the 'Robins' line-up over the next six years, playing in practically every position apart from goalkeeper, although his most effective role was at either right-half or inside-right. His versatility and consistently wholehearted displays endeared him to the Wrexham crowd, and the Chairman of the time described him as a 'wholehearted player, who can play anywhere. His love is in the game and he fears nothing. All he knows when he is on the field is that he is playing for Wrexham'. In 1929 Billie was selected to tour Canada with a Wales F.A.XI, when he made six appearances, and this eventually led to him winning his first full Welsh cap in 1931. He had been called up to face Scotland, as a member of the Welsh team that became famous as the 'Great Unknowns'. Billie won another cap for Wales against England on the Racecourse that same year. He also collected a Welsh Cup runners'-up medal from the 1932 Final as Wrexham lost 2-0 to Swansea, though he had missed out on the previous year's Welsh Cup win through injury. Billie was awarded a benefit match against Everton during his final season with Wrexham, 1931/32, when 1,500 turned up to support him. Tommy Griffiths appeared too: the Wales and Aston Villa centre-half guested in the Wrexham side that day, in a match that ended 1-1. In August 1932 Billie left the Racecourse to join Third Division South side Newport County. Although injured early in the season he managed to make 21 League appearances for the Monmouthshire club before allowed to join Bristol Rovers in August 1933. However, he left Eastville after just three months, without having made a first team appearance, to join Clapton Orient. His debut for the East London club came on Christmas Day 1933 in a 2-0 defeat at Queens Park Rangers, and he then played in the next two games, although they proved to be his last for the 'O's' before his release in May 1934. He returned home to North Wales, joining Birmingham and District League side Bangor City, where he enjoyed one more season before retiring. Billie had opened a Billiards Hall in Gwersyllt, near Wrexham by that time. However, he then fell ill with tuberculosis, and after a long illness he passed away in January 1936 at the Meadowslea Hospital, Pen-y-Ffordd, leaving his wife and a two month old child. He was just thirty years old. A poignant feature of Billie's death was that his father-in-law died within a couple of days of him.

Season	League		F.A.Cup		Welsh Cup		Total	
	apps	gls	apps	gls	apps	gls	apps	gls
1926/27	33	9	2	0	4	5	39	14
1927/28	25	6	4	0	3	0	32	6
1928/29	42	2	1	0	1	0	44	2
1929/30	21	5	3	0	3	1	27	6
1930/31	23	1	3	0	-	-	26	1
1931/32	27	0	-	-	5	0	32	0
	171	**23**	**13**	**0**	**16**	**6**	**200**	**29**

RONSON, William 1981 - 1982

Position; *Midfield*
D.O.B; *22nd January, 1957*
Birthplace; *Fleetwood, Lancashire*
Height; *5ft 6in* **Weight;** *9st 9lbs*
Debut; v. *Chelsea (a) 10th October, 1981*
Total Appearances & Goals; *38/1 apps 3 gls*
Career; *Blackpool Feb 1974 124/4apps 12gls; Cardiff City 10th Jul 1979 £130,000 90apps 4gls; WREXHAM Oct 1981 £90,000; Barnsley 12th Aug 1982 £50,000 111/2apps 3gls; Birmingham City 8th Nov 1985 (Loan) 2apps 0gls; Blackpool Jan 1986 3apps 0gls;*

Billy Ronson joined Second Division Blackpool as an apprentice, signing professional for the 'Seasiders' in February 1974 and making his Football League debut in March 1975, as a replacement for Alan Ainscow in a scoreless home draw with Nottingham Forest. He went on to complete 128 League appearances for Blackpool in the five years that he was a professional with them. 1978/79 proved to be his final season at Bloomfield Road, as the club were then relegated to the Third Division. In July 1979 Billy joined Second Division Cardiff City for what was a record fee paid out by the South Wales club at the time, £130,000. He made his 'Bluebirds' debut in the opening match of the season, a 4-1 defeat at Notts County, but he soon settled, and missed just one League game all season, which was to see him run away with the Cardiff supporters' 'Player of the Season' award. He was an ever-present throughout the 1980/81 League campaign, and was also installed as club captain. He crowned an excellent year's work by winning the 'Player of the Season' award for a second time. Billy began the 1981/82 season with the 'Bluebirds', but soon became unsettled, and by October he had signed for Second Division Wrexham for a £90,000 fee. He made his first team debut for the 'Robins' at Chelsea replacing Steve Fox as substitute in a 2-0 defeat. He missed just three games in a season that saw the 'Robins' relegated, and manager Mel Sutton sacked, although the midfield dynamo had helped Wrexham to a shock F.A.Cup win over Brian Clough's Nottingham Forest. A busy, hard running midfield player, he soon became unhappy at the thought of playing Third Division football, and left the Racecourse in the summer of 1982 to join Second Division Barnsley. Billy made his debut for the Oakwell club in the opening game of the season, a 1-1 draw at Crystal Palace, and remained a regular member of the senior side throughout the following three years. However, he fell out of favour in 1985/86 and, having made 113 League appearances for the Yorkshire club, was allowed to join Birmingham City on loan in November 1985. He made two League appearances for the 'Blues' before joining Blackpool on non-contract terms in January 1986. Three more appearances for the 'Tangerines' were added before he was released.

Season	League		F.A.Cup		Welsh Cup		League Cup		Total	
	apps	gls	apps	gls	apps	gls	apps	gls	apps	gls
1981/82	31/1	1	4	0	3	2	-	-	8/1	3
	31/1	**1**	**4**	**0**	**3**	**2**	**-**	**-**	**38/1**	**3**

ROONEY, Walter Francis 1929 - 1930

Position; *Left-Half*
D.O.B; *31st March, 1902*
Birthplace; *Liverpool, Merseyside*
Died; *Liverpool, 27th January, 1963*
Height; *5ft 8in* **Weight;** *11st 7lbs*
Debut; v. *Chesterfield (h) 23rd November, 1929*
Total Appearances & Goals; *13 apps 0 gls*
Career; *Everton Dec 1922 14apps 0gls; WREXHAM 22nd Nov 1929; Runcorn Sept 1930; Northwich Victoria Sept 1932;*

Walter Rooney joined First Division Everton in December 1922. After playing reserve team football for over two years he finally made the breakthrough into the first team, his Football League debut coming in February 1925 at wing-half in a 3-1 home win over Nottingham Forest. He kept his place for the following three games, but then had to wait until the 1926/27 season for his next appearance in an Everton shirt, when he was involved in three F.A.Cup matches. Walter remained at Goodison Park as Everton won the Football League championship, although he managed just three Football League appearances during that 1927/28 campaign. His final match for the 'Toffee's' came in September 1929, a 1-1 draw against Burnley at Turf Moor. Two months later he was allowed to leave Merseyside and transfer to Third Division North side Wrexham, where he made his League debut for the club in a 1-1 home draw with Chesterfield, replacing Bob Ross at left-half. Walter went on to make eleven further League appearances for the 'Robins' that season before being allowed to join Cheshire County League side Runcorn in the summer of 1930. He later turned out for Northwich Victoria.

Season	League		F.A.Cup		Welsh Cup		Total	
	apps	gls	apps	gls	apps	gls	apps	gls
1929/30	12	0	-	-	1	0	13	0
	12	**0**	**-**	**-**	**1**	**0**	**13**	**0**

***ROSS,* Robert** 1929 - 1930

Position; *Centre-Half*
D.O.B; *27th December, 1898*
Birthplace; *Stenhousmuir, Central Scotland*
Height; *6ft 0in* ***Weight;*** *12st 7lbs*
Debut; v. *Stockport County (h) 31st August, 1929*
Total Appearances & Goals; *34 apps 1 gls*
Career; *Camelon Juniors F.C; Falkirk cs1919; Stenhousmuir cs1920; Plymouth Argyle cs1923 2apps 0gls; Coventry City May 1924 20apps 0gls; Workington Jun 1925; Carlisle United Jun 1927 22apps 2gls; WREXHAM 24th Jun 1929; Scunthorpe & Lindsey United Oct 1930; Boston Town Sept 1931; Hyde United;*

Bob Ross had played Scottish League football for Falkirk and Stenhousmuir before making the long journey south to join Third Division South side Plymouth Argyle during the close season of 1923. His Football League debut was held back until the following year, when he appeared in a 2-0 win at Luton, followed by a 2-1 home win over Reading, before returning to reserve team football. Bob did not make another first team appearance for the 'Pilgrims', and at the end of the season was transferred to Second Division Coventry City. He made his debut for the 'Sky Blues' in the third match of the new season, a 4-2 home win over Stockport County. It was said of Bob, 'Despite being a big man -standing six feet tall -he had neat footwork to complement his decisive tackling'. Ross made twenty League appearances for the 'Sky Blues', but was axed following a bad run of results. When matters did not improve he returned to the first team, but his final match for Coventry ended in a 5-0 defeat at Oldham. They were relegated at the end of the season, and Ross was released. He joined non-league side Workington, for two seasons captaining the side from centre-half. A journal of the time remarked: - 'recognised as one of the best pivots in the North-Eastern League'. He was equally cool in defence or attack, and in the summer of 1927 accepted a move to neighbours Carlisle United, who were also members of the North-Eastern League at the time. In his first season with the 'Cumbrians' Bob helped them to attain Football League status, when they were elected to replace Durham City at the end of the 1927/28 season. He then went on to feature in Carlisle United's first ever match in the Football League, a 3-2 win at Accrington Stanley. He also played in the 'Cumbrians' F.A.Cup win over Wrexham that season, before leaving Brunton Park and joining the North Wales club in June 1929. Bob made his debut for the 'Robins' in the first match of the 1929/30 season, a 1-1 draw at home to Stockport County. Playing at Centre-half he went on to complete 29 League appearances, scoring one goal for Wrexham in a 1-1 draw at Gateshead. He also helped the 'Robins' to their most successful F.A.Cup run of that time, as they reached the Fourth Round, where they lost to Bradford City after a replay. During his time at the Racecourse Bob was described as an 'aggressive pivot, always plying his forwards and often having a pop at goal himself'. He moved back into non-league football in October 1930, when he joined Scunthorpe and Lindsey United, later followed by a switch to fellow Midland League side Boston Town in September 1931. He subsequently appeared for Hyde United.

Season	League		F.A.Cup		Welsh Cup		Total	
	apps	gls	apps	gls	apps	gls	apps	gls
1929/30	29	1	3	0	2	0	34	1
	29	**1**	**3**	**0**	**2**	**0**	**34**	**1**

***ROWLAND,* Leonard Charles** 1949 - 1950

Position; Full-Back
D.O.B; *23rd June, 1925*
Birthplace; *Manchester, Lancashire*
Height; *6ft 1in* ***Weight;*** *12st 7lbs*
Debut; v. *Bradford City (a) 14th September, 1949*
Total Appearances & Goals; *18 apps 0 gls*
Career; *Mansfield Town; Workington; WREXHAM May 1949; Ashton United 1951; Stockport County Dec 1952 61apps 0gls; Winsford United 1958/59;*
Honours; *Welsh Cup runner-up 1950; England Amateur International cap;*

Len Rowland joined Wrexham as an amateur in May 1949 from North-Eastern League side Workington to become new manager Les McDowall's first signing for the club. After he had moved to the Racecourse in the summer of 1949 Len toured Italy, France, and Switzerland with the England Amateur XI, returning home to make his Football League debut in a 1-0 defeat at Bradford City in September. Although he spent most of that season in the reserve side Len still managed fifteen League appearances - fourteen of them coming at left-back in place of Ron Jackson. He was capped again for the England Amateur team in 1950, when he toured Scandinavia. Rowland figured in the opening three League games of the 1950/51 season, but left shortly the Racecourse shortly afterwards to join non-league side Ashton United. He was soon back in League football however, when he signed for Stockport County in December 1952 as a professional. Len went on to make his debut for Stockport in January 1953 against......Wrexham! in a 3-1 win for County. He remained in the first team for the rest of the season, while the following year he added another thirty League games. Len was never regarded as a regular first-teamer at Edgeley Park, but throughout his five seasons with the 'Hatters' he was a useful member of the first team pool (in those days!), making a total of 61 League appearances, without scoring. He later turned out for Cheshire County League side Winsford United.

Season	League		F.A.Cup		Welsh Cup		Total	
	apps	gls	apps	gls	apps	gls	apps	gls
1949/50	15	0	-	-	4	0	19	0
1950/51	3	0	-	-	-	-	3	0
	18	**0**	**-**	**-**	**4**	**0**	**22**	**0**

***ROWLANDS,* Alfred Stanley** 1912 - 1913 & 1922 - 1923

Position; *Centre-Forward*
D.O.B; *12th November, 1889*
Birthplace; *Coedway, Nr Welshpool, Powys*
Died; *Barnstaple, Devon 7th October, 1974*
Height; *6ft 0in* ***Weight;*** *11st 4lbs*
Debut; v. *Brierley Hill Alliance (h) 24th September 1910.*
Football League Debut; v. *Grimsby Town (a) 26th August, 1922*
Total Appearances & Goals; *46 apps 20 gls*
Career; *Snailbeach WS 1905; Abbey Juniors, Welshpool; Wellington Town cs1909; Birkenhead North End 1909; WREXHAM Sept 1910 1app 1gls; Liverpool Dec 1910 0apps; Nottingham Forest Feb-April 1911 1app 0gls; South Liverpool cs1911; WREXHAM 23rd May 1912 30apps 18gls; Tranmere Rovers Jul 1913; Reading May 1914; Crewe Alexandra 1918 23apps 10gls & 60apps 37gls (Central League); WREXHAM 30th Jun 1922; Oswestry Town Aug 1923; South Molton Sept 1924-1926;*
Honours; *One Welsh International cap; Lancashire Combination League Championship Winner 1914; Welsh National League Championship winner 1924;*

Stan Rowlands began playing football as a 16 year-old with Shropshire & District League side Snailbeach White Stars, which he followed with spells at both Abbey Juniors in Welshpool and Birmingham & District League side Wellington Town. In 1909 he moved to Birkenhead to take up work, and it was at this time that he signed for Birkenhead North End. He scored 38 goals in six months with them, and in September 1910 he was invited to take part in a trial match for Wrexham against Brierley Hill Alliance on the Racecourse. Even though he scored in the 2-1 win nothing

materialised with the Welsh club, and in December 1910 Liverpool took him on trial. Stan then sustained a knee injury, which put him out of action for a long spell, after which Liverpool dismissed him as 'unsound' and released him. He signed for South Liverpool, and again impressed enough to earn a second opportunity of League football when he was invited to spend a few weeks with Nottingham Forest in February 1911. It was with Forest that he made his Football League debut in April 1911, a 1-0 home defeat against Sheffield Wednesday, but after the match he refused the Second Division club's terms and returned to South Liverpool! In June 1912 Rowlands signed for Birmingham & District League side Wrexham, and scored 18 goals in 30 League games in his one season at the Racecourse. He left the Denbighshire club in the summer of 1913 to join Lancashire Combination League club Tranmere Rovers, where he was awarded his one and only Welsh international cap in March 1914, a 2-0 defeat against England at Ninian Park. He became a prolific goalscorer at Tranmere, hitting the target 32 times as they swept to the League title. However, he moved on at the end of the season to join Reading, though he was at Elm Park for only a short time before football was suspended due to the outbreak of World War One. Stan spent the War years serving in the Army, mostly in France. After WW1 was over he resumed his football career with Crewe Alexandra, who were playing in the Central League at that time. He was still with the 'Railwaymen' when they rejoined the Football League in 1921, and he made 23 League appearances, scoring ten goals, in their first season back in the fold. He left Gresty Road in the summer of 1922 and returned to the Racecourse, as the 'Robins' had also joined the Football League by this time. However, his opportunities were limited and he made just nine League appearances for the 'Robins' during the 1922/23 season before his release in the summer. He then joined Oswestry Town, winning a Welsh National League championship medal before ending his football career as player/coach to South Molton. During his playing days Stan was described as a 'robust leader who was a continual worry to defenders. He had an excellent shot, made good use of his head and lost few opportunities to open out the game, giving the wing men plenty to do.' After his playing career was over, Stan continued in the tailoring profession.

Season	League		F.A.Cup		Welsh Cup		Total	
	apps	gls	apps	gls	apps	gls	apps	gls
1910/11	1	0	-	-	-	-	1	0
1912/13	30	18	5	2	1	0	36	20
1922/23*	9	0	-	-	-	-	9	0
	40	**18**	**5**	**2**	**1**	**0**	**46**	**20**

* = Only season in Football League

ROWELL, John Frederick

1948 - 1950

Position; *Forward*
D.O.B; *31st December, 1918*
Birthplace; *Dawdon,*
Died; *9th March 1988*
Height; *5ft 11'3/4in* ***Weight;*** *11st 10lbs*
Debut; v. *Halifax Town (h) 21st August, 1948*
Total Appearances & Goals; *41 apps 4 gls*
Career; *Bournemouth Sept 1941 31apps 11gls; WREXHAM 22nd Jul 1948; Aldershot Aug 1950 5apps 0gls; Weymouth Jun 1951; Portland United Jun 1953; Bournemouth Gasworks (Trainer);*
Honours; *Welsh Cup runner-up 1950;*

Fred Rowell joined Bournemouth during the Second World War in September 1941, making twelve appearances and scoring 5 goals for the Dean Court club during the 1941/42 season. This was to be his only war-time experience with Bournemouth, as they were one of the club's who would suspend matches until after the conflict had ceased. Once peace had been restored, and the Football League restarted for the 1946/47 season, Fred continued his playing career with the 'Cherries', and over the next two seasons scored eleven League goals in 31 appearances. In the close season of 1948 Fred was to leave Dean Court to sign for Third Division North side Wrexham, in a part-exchange deal that saw Walter Roberts, and a small fee going to the south coast in return. At the Racecourse Rowell made his League debut at inside-forward, in a 2-1 home win over Halifax Town in the opening match of the 1948/49 season. His first goal came in a 1-1 draw at Barrow, in September, but his promising start came to an abrupt end when injured in October. He remained out of action until the following April, and the next campaign Norman Sharp was preferred until Fred returned to the first team in January. He remained in the side until the end of the season, missing just an odd game, but helping the 'Robins' to reach their first Welsh Cup Final since 1933. However, it was to end in disappointment as Swansea Town won 4-1. In the summer of 1950 Fred was released by Wrexham, and joined Third Division South side Aldershot. He made his League debut for the 'Shots' in a disastrous 7-0 defeat at Newport County in September, and made just four more League appearances before allowed to leave the Recreation Ground at the end of the season. He then joined Southern League side Weymouth, where he spent two years before joining rivals Portland United. He later joined the Bournemouth Gasworks team as trainer. Fred is later believed to have settled in the North-East where his son, Gary, was born, and who went on to follow in his father's footsteps by playing League football for Sunderland, Norwich City, Middlesbrough, Brighton, Carlisle and Burnley, as well as representing England at under-21 level.

Season	League		F.A.Cup		Welsh Cup		Total	
	apps	gls	apps	gls	apps	gls	apps	gls
1948/49	19	5	-	-	-	-	19	5
1949/50	22	0	1	0	5	1	28	1
	41	**5**	**1**	**0**	**5**	**1**	**47**	**6**

ROWLEY, Arthur

1954 - 1957

Position; *Inside-Forward*
D.O.B; *9th May, 1933*
Birthplace; *Fazakerley, Liverpool, Merseyside*
Height; *5ft 6'1/2 in* ***Weight;*** *10st 7lbs*
Debut; v. *Chesterfield (a) 4th December, 1954*
Total Appearances & Goals; *54 apps 8 gls*
Career; *Florence Melley Boys' Club; Liverpool May 1951 13apps 1gls; WREXHAM 27th Nov 1954; Crewe Alexandra 11th Feb 1957 £500 34apps 7gls; Tranmere Rovers Sept 1958 0apps; Burscough Rangers Aug 1959; Chorley 1961/62;*
Honours; *Lancashire Combination League Championship Winner 1964; Lancashire Combination League Cup Winner 1963; Lancashire Junior Cup Winner 1964 & 1965;*

Arthur Rowley first played football at the Florence Melley School in his native Liverpool, from where he went on to represent both Liverpool and Lancashire Schoolboys. He played for Liverpool Boys in the Final of the English Schools Trophy which they shared with Stockport after a 1-1 draw at Anfield in front of over 40,000. Arthur scored his side's equaliser in the last minute of the game. He also represented the Liverpool Boys' Club, with whom he toured the France, Belgium, and Germany. Following his return home from that tour he played against a Liverpool representative side, and this led to approaches after the game from both Everton and Liverpool. Having already obtained employment with Pickfords in their Transport

Office in Liverpool he subsequently signed for Liverpool in May 1951. Arthur progressed to make his Football League debut for the 'Reds' in the opening match of the 1952/53 season at inside-left, in a 1-1 draw at Preston North End, a game that saw both Billy Liddell and Preston's Tom Finney miss penalties! He completed a further twelve League appearances for Liverpool, scoring just one goal in his penultimate game for the club in April 1954, a 4-1 home win over Middlesbrough. As he was struggling to establish a first team place at Anfield Arthur accepted an offer to join Third Division North side Wrexham in November 1954. He went straight into the first team at inside-left, replacing David Jackson in a 3-1 defeat at Chesterfield, before scoring twice on his home debut in a 3-3 draw at York. At the Racecourse he was described as a 'skilful little forward', remaining an ever-present in the side until the end of the season. The following campaign saw him make 27 League appearances, scoring two goals. 1956/57 was to see him out of favour as he was to add just two League appearances before being allowed to move on to Crewe Alexandra in February. Arthur made his debut for the 'Railwaymen' in a 1-1 draw at Rochdale and spent just over a season at Gresty Road, completing 34 League appearances, and claiming seven goals. He left the Cheshire club to sign for Tranmere Rovers in September 1958, but failed to make a first team appearance at Prenton Park, and at the end of the season accepted an offer to join Lancashire Combination League side Burscough Rangers. He then helped the Victoria Park club to reach the First Round proper of the F.A.Cup for the first time in their history, where they lost 3-1 to his former club Crewe Alexandra. After a little over two years with Burscough he joined fellow Lancashire Combination League side Chorley, where he won a championship medal in 1964, adding a number of other trophies during his four years with them. His most memorable game came when Burscough beat Cheshire County League champions Wigan Athletic in the Final of the Lancashire Junior Cup at Preston's Deepdale ground. Having finished playing professional football Arthur became a self-employed builder until he retired, following a hip replacement operation. He still resides in the Aintree area of Liverpool, where he can regularly be found playing on the local bowling greens during the summer months.

Season	League		F.A.Cup		Welsh Cup		Total	
	apps	gls	apps	gls	apps	gls	apps	gls
1954/55	25	6	1	0	4	1	30	7
1955/56	27	2	1	0	2	0	30	2
1956/57	2	0	-	-	-	-	2	0
	54	**8**	**2**	**0**	**6**	**1**	**62**	**9**

RUSH, Ian James M.B.E. 1998 - 1999

Position; *Centre-forward*
D.O.B; *20th October, 1961*
Birthplace; *St.Asaph, Denbighshire*
Height; *6ft 0in* ***Weight;*** *12st 6lbs*
Debut; v. *Reading (h) 8th August, 1998*
Total Appearances & Goals; *20/7 apps 0 gls*
Career; *Chester (Pro) 25th Sept 1979 33/1apps 14gls; Liverpool 1st May 1980 £300,000 182apps 109gls; Juventus 1st Jul 1986 £3,200,000 29apps 7gls; Liverpool 1st Jul 1986 (Loan) 42apps 30gls; Liverpool 23rd Aug 1988 £2,800,000 223/22apps 90gls; Leeds United 24th May 1996 34/2apps 3gls; Newcastle United 15th Aug 1998 6/4apps 0gls; Sheffield United 23rd Feb 1998 (Loan) 4apps 0gls; WREXHAM 5th Aug 1998;*
Honours; *73 Welsh international caps (28gls -record scorer); 2 Welsh under-21 international caps; Welsh schoolboy international; European Cup Winner 1984; European Cup runner-up 1985; First Division Championship Winner 1982, 1983, 1984, 1986 & 1990; F.A.Cup Winner 1986, 1989 & 1992; Football League Cup Winner 1981, 1982, 1983, 1984 & 1995; Screen Sport Super Cup Winner 1986; European Super Cup runner-up 1985; F.A.Cup runner-up 1996; Football League Cup runner-up 1987; Welsh Premier Cup runner-up 1999;*

Regarded as one of the biggest ever signings in the history of Wrexham Association Football Club Ian Rush arrived at the Racecourse in the twilight of his football career at the age of 36. He had joined the 'Robins' as player/coach, combining his playing role with that of assisting Joey Jones as reserve team coach, a first step towards a new career in football management. His association with the club might have begun twenty years earlier, when he was still a schoolboy, but he wasn't offered a cup of tea following a trial! so he turned to Chester! The son of a Shotton steelworker, and one of ten children, seven of which were boys, the Rush family are well known for their football tradition throughout the Flint area where he grew up. As well as playing for his school team in Flint he also represented Deeside Schoolboys, for whom he set a sensational goalscoring record, one which has only recently been overtaken by a certain youngster named, Michael Owen. He then went on to earn selection for Flintshire, North Wales and the Welsh Schoolboys teams. At around this time he also played for Hawarden Rangers, before joining Chester on schoolboy forms where he was to be nurtured by the current

Wrexham youth team coach Cliff Sear, who was then employed in a similar capacity at Sealand Road club. It was Wrexham who inadvertently gave Ian his big breakthrough into League football, when the 'Robins' manager Arfon Griffiths stepped in to sign the 'Seals' Welsh international striker Ian Edwards. It led to the youngster being given his chance at centre-forward, having occupied a midfield role until that time. His goalscoring abilities at Sealand Road were soon noted by both Liverpool and Manchester City, and they both made attempts to sign the prolific marksman. However, there was only ever going to be one winner of this particular race, and Ian agreed to join the Anfield club as they splashed out what proved to be a bargain £300,000 for him in May 1980. He made his debut in the following December replacing Kenny Dalglish in a 1-1 draw at Ipswich, though it wasn't until the following season that he was to able to establish himself as a first team regular. He had failed to hit the net in his first nine games for Liverpool, but he certainly made up for lost time after that! Ian went on to form a lethal strike partnership with Kenny Dalglish as he finished leading goalscorer in the championship season of 1982, when he also scored in the Milk Cup Final success over Tottenham. He established himself as one of the most dangerous strikers in European football, as well as a 'Kop' idol. In 1984 he added a European Cup winners' medal, when he scored one of the goals in the penalty shoot-out win over A.S.Roma. It was with Liverpool that Rush won the first of his 73 Welsh caps, as a substitute for Ian Walsh against Scotland in Glasgow in May 1980. He went on to have considerable success in a Welsh shirt, eventually beating Trevor Ford's all-time scoring record with 28 goals, but this was counterbalanced with the disappointment of not reaching the finals of a major tournament with Wales. In July 1986 he joined the Italian giants Juventus for a British record of £3.2 million, but he was immediately loaned back to Liverpool for the 1986/87 season. At the peak of his career Ian was said to have possessed, 'good control, lightning speed, good positional awareness with a remarkable finishing ability which made him into a formidable striker'. He was to add even more strength to his game when he eventually linked up with the Italian club in the close season of 1987, and although his time in Turin was not an unqualified success it did see him, in his own words, 'grow up'. The highlight of this chapter of his career story was in scoring four goals against Pescara in a cup-tie. Generally, however, he struggled to win over the cynical Italian press; he was relieved to return to Anfield in the summer of 1988, and he was not slow to pick up where he had left off..........scoring goals. Ian went on to fall 16 goals short of Roger Hunt's all-time goalscoring record for the Anfield club, having collected 229 goals from 469 League games, as well as claiming the most F.A.Cup goals in post-war competition. He was awarded a testimonial game against Glasgow Celtic before leaving Merseyside in the summer of 1996 to join fellow Premier League side Leeds United on a free transfer. However, he was to hit the worst goalscoring drought of his career at Elland Road, as he failed to score in fifteen games, although asked to play on the right-side of midfield in some by new manager George Graham. Looking as fit as ever his commitment and endeavour never waned in a Leeds side that lacked creativity. He decided to leave Elland Road after just one season when he was offered the chance to rejoin his former Anfield strike partner, Kenny Dalglish, who was then managing Newcastle United. His signing, along with another former Anfield favourite, John Barnes, was seen as a bid to strengthen the 'Magpies' squad for their first tilt at the Champions' League, but most of his time at St.James' Park was spent on the substitutes' bench, and this eventually saw him take up a month's loan with Sheffield United in February 1998. He made four appearances for the 'Blades' without scoring. Ian became a free agent at the end of the 1997/98 season, and despite lucrative offers from Switzerland, America, and Japan, he decided to end his playing career in his native North Wales with Second Division

Wrexham, for whom he made his debut in the opening match of the 1998/99 season against Reading in a 3-0 win. However, his season with the club was one of frustration as he disappointingly failed to find the net and with injuries limiting his appearances. In July 1999 Ian decided against accepting a new 12 month Player-Coach Contract at the Racecourse.

Season	League		F.A.Cup		League Cup		A.W.S.		W.P.C.		Total	
	apps	gls	apps	gls	apps	gls	apps	gls	apps	gls	apps	gls
1998/99	12/5	0	4	0	2	0	0/1	0	2/1	0	20/7	0
	12/5	**0**	**4**	**0**	**2**	**0**	**0/1**	**0**	**2/1**	**0**	**20/7**	**0**

RUSSELL, Kevin John

1987 - 1989 & 1995 -

Position; *Forward*
Birthplace; *Portsmouth, Hampshire*
Height; *5ft 8in* ***Weight;*** *10st 12lbs*
D.O.B; *6th October, 1966*
Debut; v. *Torquay United (a) 15th August, 1987*
Total Appearances & Goals; *256/24 apps 70 gls*
Career; *Brighton & Hove Albion; Portsmouth 9th Oct 1984 3/1apps 1gls; WREXHAM 17th Jul 1987 £10,000; Leicester City 20th Jun 1989 £175,000 24/19apps 10gls; Peterborough United 6th Sept 1990 7apps 3gls (Loan); Cardiff City 17th Jan 1991 3apps 0gls (Loan); Hereford United 7th Nov 1991 3apps 1gls (Loan); Stoke City 2nd Jan 1992 5apps 1gls (Loan); Stoke City 16th Jul 1992 £95,000 30/10apps 5gls; Burnley 28th Jun 1993 £140,000 26/2apps 6gls; Bournemouth 3rd Mar 1994 £125,000 30apps 1gls; Notts County 23rd Feb 1995 £60,000 9/2apps 0gls WREXHAM 13th Jul 1995 £60,000;*
Honours; *Six England Youth international caps; Second Division Championship Winner 1993; Welsh Cup runner-up 1988; Welsh Premier Cup runner-up 1999;*

'Rooster', as he had been nicknamed at school in his native Portsmouth, was given his first chance in football by Brighton and Hove Albion manager Alan Mullery, who signed him on apprentice terms following a trial period in 1983. Kevin spent one season with the Sussex Club until he was deemed surplus to requirements. He then joined Portsmouth, the club he had supported as a boy, and he progressed to represent England at Youth level on six occasions, including an international tournament in Yugoslavia. A professional contract followed on his eighteenth birthday, though he failed to make the first team that season. The breakthrough came in the following campaign, as he made his first team debut in a 4-1 Full Members Cup victory against Charlton Athletic, though having to wait until the end of the 1985/86 season to make his Football League debut, when he substituted Nicky Morgan in 'Pompey's 4-0 home win over Bradford City in May 1986. Kevin spent the following season in reserve team football, although he did play against Wrexham in a Littlewoods Cup match. In the summer of 1987 'Robins' boss Dixie McNeil splashed out £10,000 to sign him, and he quickly won over the club's fans, despite a disastrous debut as Wrexham lost 6-1 at Torquay United! Kevin went on to become a big hero at Wrexham, averaging a goal every other game in the two seasons that he spent at the Racecourse. It was his non-stop running and eye for goal that played a big part in helping the 'Robins' reach the Third Division play-off finals in 1989, where they lost the two-legged Final 2-1 on aggregate to Leyton Orient. Well before those games his goalscoring exploits had attracted the attention of a number of other clubs, and he eventually signed for Leicester City for £175,000. However, he struggled to make an impression in the first team at Filbert Street, as he was plagued with fitness problems, and they resulted in him being loaned out to a number of clubs, including Cardiff, Peterborough, Hereford, and Stoke. It was during his loan spell with the 'Posh' that Kevin was involved in a car crash, in which he suffered a stress fracture. Eventually, he was brought out of the wilderness at Leicester by Gordon Lee, as the club battled to avoid relegation in 1991, and his impact in the last thirteen games proved crucial in their last gasp escape. With Brian Little taking over he again found himself dropping out of the picture, but a late season return provided another substantial fillip as he helped Leicester to the 1992 Play-Off Final by scoring in both legs of their semi-final against Cambridge United. They eventually lost to Blackburn Rovers in the Wembley Final. Out of contract during the close season Russell took up an offer to join Stoke City, where he became a regular member of their Second Division Championship winning side, missing just six League games all season. He was surprisingly allowed to join Burnley during the close season of 1993, for a fee of £150,000, and enjoyed an excellent rapport with the Burnley fans, even though he struggled to rediscover the kind of form that had brought him much success with his previous clubs. In February 1994 he was allowed to join Bournemouth for £125,000. 'Rooster' spent almost twelve months with the 'Cherries', making thirty League appearances for them before signing for the newly-appointed Notts County manager, Howard Kendall, for £60,000 in February 1995. However, things didn't turn out well for Kevin at the County Ground, as Kendall was dismissed before the season was over, and the 'Magpies' suffered relegation. During the summer of 1995 Wrexham manager Brian Flynn stepped in to sign him for a £60,000 fee. A real 'jokey' character in the dressing room, he had returned to the Racecourse a different type of player: the willingness to chase and to run at defenders was still evident, but injury problems had robbed him of some of the blistering pace that he had displayed in the early part of his career, although he had become a more accomplished player with a keenness to make himself available. Kevin went on to enjoy some good times in his second spell with Wrexham, his most memorable moments coming in the club's run to the Quarter-Finals of the F.A.Cup during 1996/97, when he scored a last minute replay winner against Premier League side West Ham United, followed by two goals in the next round against Peterborough United. 1997/98 saw him suffer with injury problems, and he missed out on the Welsh Invitation Cup Final victory over Cardiff City. Having fully recovered, he is still an important member of the club's first team squad at the time of writing. As if to epitomise his humerous side, Kevin has managed to score two goals at the Racecourse from the 'front' and 'back' of the lower part of his anatomy!!

Season	League		F.A.Cup		Welsh Cup		League Cup		L.D.C.		Play-Off's		Total	
	apps	gls	apps	gls	apps	gls	apps	gls	apps	gls	apps	gls	apps	gls
1987/88	38	21	2	0	6	3	2	1	-	-	-	-	48	25
1988/89	46	22	2	0	2	2	2	0	4	1	4	2	60	27
1995/96	37/3	7	3	0	-	-	2	1	2	0	-	-	44/3	8
1996/97	37/4	0	6/2	3	-	-	1	0	1	0	-	-	45/6	3
1997/98	11/5	0	2	0	-		-	16/6	2					
1998/99	25/6	2	4/1	1	7/1*	2*	1/1	0	6	0	-	-	43/9	5
	194/18	**52**	**19/3**	**4**	**17/2***	**9***	**9/1**	**2**	**13**	**1**	**4**	**2**	**256/24**	**70**

* = Includes Welsh Invitation/Premier Cup.

S

David Smallman

***SALATHIEL,* Neil David** 1979 - 1981 & 1983 - 1990

Position; *Right-Back*
D.O.B; *19th November, 1962*
Birthplace; *Wrexham, Denbighshire*
Height; *5ft 7in* ***Weight;*** *12st 0lbs*
Debut; v. *Queens Park Rangers (a) 25th October, 1980*
Total Appearances & Goals; *324/1 apps 3 gls*
Career; *WREXHAM May 1980; Crewe Alexandra Jun 1981; Arcadia Shepherds (South Africa) May 1983; WREXHAM Dec 1983; Telford United cs1990 15apps 1gls; Northwich Victoria 1991 14/1apps 0gls; Newtown cs1991; Bangor City 1992 19/2apps 0gls; Mold Alexandra 1992/93 5apps 0gls; Brymbo Steelworks cs1993; Flint Town United Dec 1995 33/1apps 1gls; Oswestry Town 31st Jan 1997; Holywell Town Aug 1997;*
Honours; *Welsh Youth international; Welsh Schoolboy international; Welsh Cup winner 1986; Welsh Cup runner-up 1984, 1988 & 1990; Welsh Youth Cup Winner 1981; Welsh Youth Cup runner-up 1980; Cymru Alliance League Cup Winner 1998;*

At first Neil Salathiel decided against joining Wrexham, his home town club, on schoolboy forms, and opted instead for a similar arrangement with Sheffield Wednesday. He had already played for his school teams at Victoria Road, New Broughton and Grove Park, and was eventually chosen for the Welsh Schoolboys side. Following his disappointment at not being retained by the 'Owls' he accepted an apprenticeship with Wrexham, going on to play in two Welsh Youth Cup Finals, successful in one. In between those two finals he was to make his first team debut at the age of 17, in October 1980. He had travelled to London with the first team squad not knowing that he would be replacing Alan Hill at right-back for the League match at Queens Park Rangers until manager Arfon Griffiths informed him on the coach on the way down. It proved to be a successful baptism, as the 'Robins' won the match 1-0. He made four more first team appearances before being released at the end of the season, following which he was quickly snapped up by Crewe manager Tony Waddington. He made his debut for the 'Railwaymen' in the opening game of the 1981/82 season, a 2-0 defeat at Bournemouth. It turned out to be a nightmare season for the 'Alex' as they finished bottom of the Football League. The following campaign was much the same, as Crewe struggled again, and Neil found himself out of favour by the New Year. Unhappy with reserve team football he decided to leave Gresty Road, having made 65 League appearances, and take up an offer in South Africa with Arcadia Shepherds. Upon his return home Salathiel accepted an invitation from manager Bobby Roberts to rejoin Wrexham on a non-contract basis in a bid to prove his fitness. Two months later he accepted a contract offer, and went on to become the 'Robins' regular right-back until the summer of 1990. During that time he picked up a Welsh Cup winners' medal against Kidderminster Harriers in 1986, and three runners'-up medals in the same competition in 1984, 1988 and in 1990, when Wrexham played in the first ever Welsh Cup Final at the National Stadium in Cardiff. He also played a part in helping the club to reach the Final of the Third Division play-offs in 1989, before eventually losing to Leyton Orient 2-1 on aggregate. He was involved in two European Cup-Winners' Cup campaigns, in 1984 and 1987, the first of which included a famous victory over Portuguese Cup holders, F.C.Porto. The November of the 1989/90 season saw him appointed club captain, and led the team to a 'great escape' as they avoided relegation to the Conference League. He was surprisingly released at the end of the season, but was soon fixed up with another club when joining Conference League side Telford United. However, before the end of that campaign he had joined fellow Conference side Northwich Victoria on loan. In the summer of 1991 he was released by the Bucks Head club, and joined Newtown, then of the HFS Loans League First Division. He later moved on to League of Wales side Bangor City during 1992/93, and was followed by a short spell with another League of Wales outfit, Mold Alexandra. The 1993/94 season saw Neil turn out for Brymbo in the Cymru Alliance League, where he later became player/manager before resigning in October 1995. He returned to the League of Wales with Flint Town United in December 1995, until joining Oswestry Town in January 1997. He then linked up with Holywell Town in the summer of 1997, helping them regain their League of Wales status at the end of the season as they finished runners-up to Rhydymwyn, as well as winning the League Cup. Neil still lives in the Wrexham area, where he has been employed with Jamont UK as a production operator. He has been playing for both Holywell in the League of Wales and Flint Town United in the Cymru Alliance during the 1998/99 season.

Season	League		F.A.Cup		Welsh Cup		League Cup		F.R.T.		E.C.W.C.		Total	
	apps	gls	apps	gls	apps	gls	apps	gls	apps	gls	apps	gls	apps	gls
1980/81	4	0	-	-	1	0	-	-	-	-	-	-	5	0
1983/84	29	0	-	-	7	0	-	-	3	0	-	-	39	0
1984/85	36	0	1	0	2	0	1	0	-	-	4	0	44	0
1985/86	42	1	2	0	7	0	3	0	2	0	-	-	56	1
1986/87	45	2	3	0	5	0	4	0	4	0	4	0	65	2
1987/88	24	0	-	-	3	0	-	-	-	-	-	-	27	0
1988/89	34/1	0	2	0	3	0	2	0	4	0	4*	0*	49/1*	0*
1989/90	29	0	1	0	5	0	2	0	2	0	-	-	39	0
	243/1	**3**	**9**	**0**	**33**	**0**	**12**	**0**	**15**	**0**	**8**	**0**	**324/1***	

* = Play off matches included

***SALISBURY,* Gareth** 1959 - 1962

Position; *Forward*
D.O.B; *11th March, 1941*
Birthplace; *Caernarfon, Gwynedd*
Height; *5ft 9in* ***Weight;*** *11st 7lbs*
Debut; v. *Grimsby Town (a) 13th February, 1960*
Total Appearances & Goals; *18 apps 0 gls*
Career; *WREXHAM 8th May 1959; Norwich City Jul 1962 0apps; Luton Town Jul 1963 12apps 2gls; Colchester United Jul 1964 15apps 2gls; Chesterfield Jul 1965 34apps 9gls; Kidderminster Harriers 1966/67; Bangor City 29th Jul 1967; Juventus (Australia) 13th May 1969; Bethesda Athletic 3rd Mar 1972;*
Honours; *Welsh Cup Winner 1960; Northern Premier League Cup runner-up 1969; Welsh Youth Cup winner 1958; Welsh Youth international cap;*

Gareth Salisbury began playing football while attending Beaumaris Grammar School on the Isle of Anglesey. During this time he underwent trials with the Welsh Schoolboys side, and was also invited for trials with a number of Football League sides, including Everton, Blackpool, and Wrexham. His mother preferred him to continue with his studies, but they came to a compromise as he signed for Wrexham, having been recommended to the 'Robins' after he was spotted playing for Menai Bridge. Gareth joined the ground staff at the Racecourse, and helped the club win the Welsh Youth Cup for the first time in its history in 1958, beating Llanidloes 4-2 in the Final. International honours for his country followed, with caps at Youth level against both Ireland and Scotland. Gareth turned professional in May 1959, and finally made his Football League debut for Wrexham in February 1960, replacing Ron Hewitt at inside-forward in a 3-1 defeat against Grimsby Town. He made two more League appearances that season, and played in two Welsh Cup games. They included the Final against Cardiff City at Ninian Park, which was drawn 1-1. The following season saw him make seven League and Cup appearances, including the League Cup Fourth Round match against Aston Villa. 1961/62 brought a major change at the Racecourse, with Ken Barnes taking over as player/manager. Gareth's fortunes were not to change for the better, and he was restricted to just a handful of outings before his transfer to Norwich City in the summer, as one of manager George Swindin's first signings. Described as a 'strongly built inside-forward, constantly probing for openings' he spent a season at Carrow Road, although he could not break into the first team. In July 1963 he joined Luton Town, where he quickly established himself, making twelve League appearances and scoring two goals before an Achilles tendon injury put him out of action for two months. After recovering he was unable to regain his first team place, and in the summer of 1964 was allowed to join Colchester United on a free transfer. Salisbury made his debut for 'U's' at inside-forward in a 1-0 home defeat against Carlisle United in the opening match of the season, and went on to make a further sixteen League and Cup appearances for the Layer Road club, scoring three goals, before breaking his collar bone. Again he struggled to regain his place following recovery, and after the Essex club had been relegated at the end of the season was allowed to join Chesterfield. Salisbury made his debut for the 'Spireites' in a 2-1 home defeat by Newport County in the opening game of the season, as he went on to enjoy a two year spell at Saltergate, making 34 League appearances, and scoring nine goals. Towards the end of 1966/67 he joined Kidderminster Harriers, playing just a few games before returning to North Wales and Bangor City for the start of the 1967/68 season. At Farrar Road he was installed as the midfield 'playmaker' of the Bangor team, who were founder members of the newly-formed Northern Premier League in 1968/69, and became one of the most exciting teams in non-league football during that period providing the ammunition for the prolific goalscorers Jimmy Conde and George Morton. He made a return trip to the Racecourse with Bangor for a Welsh Cup tie, and was also chosen to play for the North Wales Coast F.A.representative side against the Scottish Junior League. In May 1969 Gareth left Wales to join Juventus........of Victoria, Australia!! He spent three years 'down under', and in his second year was voted 'Player of the Year' for the state of Victoria. He made several representative appearances for the state team, against the likes of Manchester City, Dynamo Kiev, Dynamo Moscow, Presario of Brazil, and a Japanese National XI. Salisbury eventually returned home to North Wales in 1972, where he played for Bethesda Athletic for a short while, and took up work in the computer industry for the local Health Authority, before having to take early retirement because of chronic asthma. Gareth has since settled on Ynys Mon (Anglesey).

Season	League		F.A.Cup		Welsh Cup		League Cup		Total	
	apps	gls	apps	gls	apps	gls	apps	gls	apps	gls
1959/60	3	0	-	-	2	0	-	-	5	0
1960/61	5	0	-	-	1	0	1	0	7	0
1961/62	3	0	1	0	1	0	1	0	6	0
	11	**0**	**1**	**0**	**4**	**0**	**2**	**0**	**18**	**0**

SALMON, Michael Bernard 1987 - 1989

Position; *Goalkeeper*
D.O.B; *14th July, 1964*
Birthplace; *Leyland, Lancashire*
Height; *6ft 2in* ***Weight;*** *13st 0lbs*
Debut; v. *Cambridge United (a) 7th March, 1987*
Total Appearances & Goals; *126 apps 0 gls*
Career; *Blackburn Rovers 16th Oct 1981 1app 0gls; Leeds United Aug 1982 0apps (Loan); Chester 18th Oct 1982 16apps 0gls (Loan); Stockport County 3rd Aug 1983 118apps 0gls; Bolton Wanderers 31st Jul 1986 £18,000 26apps 0gls; WREXHAM 7th Mar 1987 (Loan), 28th Jul 1987 £18,000; Charlton Athletic 6th Jul 1989 £100,000 148apps 0gls; Oxford United 10th Dec 1998 (Loan) 1app 0gls; Ipswich Town 8th Jul 1999;*
Honours; *Welsh Cup runner-up 1988;*

Mike Salmon played at centre-forward throughout most of his schooldays at Farrington Junior School, but it was as goalkeeper that he impressed Blackburn Rovers who signed him on apprentice terms in 1980 after he had left Wellfield High School. He progressed to sign professional terms with the Ewood Park club in October 1981, but had to wait until May 1982 for his senior outing, replacing Terry Gennoe for the visit of Chelsea in the last game of the season which ended in a 1-1 draw. The beginning of the following campaign saw him accept a loan move to Leeds United as first team cover, but he only managed seven reserve team appearances before returning to Blackburn. He then took up the offer of a loan spell at Chester in October 1982, where he turned out in sixteen League games. His impressive form at Sealand Road had been noted by a number of other clubs, and in the summer of 1983 joined Stockport County. There he replaced another former 'Robin', Brian Lloyd, making his debut in the opening game of the season, a 2-0 home defeat by York City. He went on to become an ever-present in the 'Hatters' side until January 1986, amassing 118 League appearances, before losing his place to Gary Walker. Mike then had to content himself with reserve team football for the remainder of the season, though he secured an £18,000 move to Bolton Wanderers in the summer. He was immediately thrust into the first team at Burnden Park, replacing youngster Simon Farnworth, but the 'Trotters' struggled, and by the turn of the year he found himself the scapegoat. He was then replaced by new signing, Welsh international David Felgate, and by March he had accepted an offer of a loan deal from Wrexham manager Dixie McNeil. Salmon made an immediate impact at the Racecourse as the club lost just four of the seventeen games in which he played, before returning to Bolton at the end of the season. However, a few weeks later Wrexham managed to raise enough money to sign him permanently for the £18,000 required, and he went on to help the 'Robins' reach the Welsh Cup Final in the following season, which they lost 2-0 to Cardiff City. During his time at the Racecourse Mike was noted as a 'fine shot stopper, but a little suspect on crosses'. 1988/89 saw him assist the club to the Play-Off Final, although Wrexham eventually lost 2-1 on aggregate to Leyton Orient. Those two games proved to be his last for Wrexham, as he was signed by Charlton Athletic for £100,000 in the summer. Mike made his debut for the 'Addicks' in January 1990, a 1-0 F.A.Cup defeat at West Bromwich Albion. However, overall he found himself acting as cover for Bob Bolder during his first four season's at the Valley, but by February 1993 he had begun a spell in the first team which eventually saw him established as first team 'keeper. A run

of injuries during the 1994/95 season then limited his appearances, but he won his place back, and remained first choice until December 1996, when injured in a home game with Wolves. Andy Patterson took over from him until the end of the season. He was understudy to Patterson at the start of the 1997/98 promotion season but regained his place in early December, playing in eleven consecutive games until injured at Manchester City, which kept him out of action for the rest of the season. The 1998/99 season saw Mike join crisis club Oxford United on loan in December, but his debut was not one that he is likely to forget in a hurry, as Oxford lost 7-1 to Birmingham City. He immediately returned to the Valley following that game claiming that he was not match fit! Mike left Charlton in the summer of 1999 to join Ipswich Town.

Season	League		F.A.Cup		Welsh Cup		League Cup		F.R.T.		Play-off		Total	
	apps	gls	apps	gls	apps	gls	apps	gls	apps	gls	apps	gls	apps	gls
1986/87	17	0	-	-	2	0	-	-	-	-	-	-	19	0
1987/88	40	0	2	0	5	0	2	0	2	0	-	-	51	0
1988/89	43	0	2	0	2	0	2	0	3	0	4	0	56	0
	100	**0**	**4**	**0**	**9**	**0**	**4**	**0**	**5**	**0**	**4**	**0**	**126**	**0**

SAMUELS, Leslie 1954

Position; *Inside-Forward*
D.O.B; *8th December, 1928*
Birthplace; *Oldham*
Died; *Burnley, 3rd May 1998.*
Height; *5ft 9in* ***Weight;*** *11st 7lbs*
Debut; v. *Scunthorpe United (h) 6th March, 1954*
Total Appearances & Goals; *26 apps 11 gls*
Career; *Burnley Dec 1949 2apps 0gls; Exeter City Jul 1953 £500 12apps 1gls; WREXHAM 4th Mar 1954; Crewe Alexandra 13th Nov 1954 42apps 13gls; Bradford City Dec 1955 84apps 38gls; Stockport County Mar 1958 25apps 5gls; Buxton; Stalybridge Celtic Pwllheli & District 30th Jun 1960; Bacup Borough 1962;*
Honours; *Welsh League (North) Championship Winner 1961; Derbyshire Senior Cup Winner;*

The youngest of four brothers, Leslie Samuels served in the Royal Navy following the end of World War Two. He played football during this time, and was spotted in a representative match for the Navy by a scout of Tottenham Hotspur. Les was invited for trials, playing in the Spurs 'A' team alongside Tommy Harmer, later to become a Spurs 'great'. Remaining in the Navy Les, unimpressed by the London scene, contacted Burnley, and they invited him to become a part-time professional in 1948. He began work as a sheet metal worker before turning fill-time professional with the 'Clarets' in December 1949. A senior debut followed in September 1950, a 1-1 home draw against Portsmouth, for which Samuels was selected at inside-forward in place of Billy Morris, who was to later manage Wrexham. He was to make just one more League appearance for the Turf Moor club, a 2-0 home defeat against Fulham in April 1951, before his transfer to Exeter City in July 1953. He made his debut for the 'Grecians' in the opening match of the new season, a 2-1 home win over Leyton Orient. By March 1954 he was on the move again, after scoring twice in fourteen League and Cup games. He headed back north, signing for Third Division North side Wrexham, for whom he made his debut in a 3-1 home win over Scunthorpe United, and scored one of the goals. Les kept his place in the side for the rest of the season, hitting the target eight times in just thirteen games. The following season began with Les notching three goals in thirteen games, but by November 1954 he had left the Racecourse to join Crewe Alexandra. His debut for the 'Railwaymen' came in a 4-0 defeat at Oldham, and he went on to score thirteen goals in 42 League games before joining Bradford City in December 1955. Samuels made his debut for Bradford in a scoreless home draw with Oldham, and became a regular in the side for over two years, during which he scored 38 goals in 84 League games. Nineteen League goals in 1956/57 were good enough to make him top scorer, but he was to lose his pace in the side in the New Year of 1958. By March he had been transferred to Stockport County, where he made his debut in a 2-2 home draw with Chester, and figured in four more games that season, scoring once in a 2-1 away defeat at Chesterfield. The following year saw him playing in a number of positions, in both defence and attack, as he added another twenty League appearances, scoring four goals. He left Edgeley Park in the summer and dropped into the Cheshire County League with Stalybridge Celtic. This was followed by a spell with Buxton, where he picked up a Derbyshire Senior Cup winners' medal before joining Freddie Pye's Pwllheli & District side in the summer of 1960. He was a member of the side that played against Wrexham in a Welsh Cup tie in February 1961, and collected a Welsh League (North) Championship medal the same season. In 1962 he became player/manager of Bacup Borough, but broke his leg shortly after his appointment and retired from the game, although he did turn out occasionally for Lucas Aerospace, where he had returned to work as a sheet metal worker. Having settled in the town of Burnley he became one of Burnley Golf Club's most competitive players, with his handicap in single figures. He also represented East Lancashire Golf Club for many years, before later taking to Crown Green bowling. Les passed away in May 1998. He was 69.

Season	League		F.A.Cup		Welsh Cup		LTotal	
	apps	gls	apps	gls	apps	gls	apps	gls
1953/54	13	8	-	-	-	-	13	8
1954/55	13	3	-	-	-	-	13	3
	26	**11**	-	-	-	-	**26**	**11**

SANDER, Christopher Andrew 1984

Position; *Goalkeeper*
D.O.B; *11th November, 1962*
Birthplace; *Swansea, Glamorgan*
Height; *6ft 0in* ***Weight;*** *11st 5lbs*
Debut; v. *Crewe Alexandra (a) 22nd September, 1984*
Total Appearances & Goals; *5 apps 0 gls*
Career; *Swansea City 20th Nov 1979 20apps 0gls; WREXHAM 19th Sept 1984 (Loan); Cardiff City Aug 1985 8apps 0gls; Haverfordwest Dec 1985; Cardiff City Mar 1986 5apps 0gls; Barry Town Aug 1986; Aberystwyth Town Oct 1989;*
Honours; *Welsh Cup Winner 1983; Welsh Youth International; Welsh Schoolboy international; Welsh League Championship Winner 1989;*

Chris Sander joined Swansea City straight from school, having played for the Welsh Schoolboys side. He progressed to sign professional terms for his home town club in November 1979, and gained further international recognition at Youth level making his Football League debut in a 3-0 defeat against Aston Villa in May 1982, replacing former 'Racecourse Robin', Dai Davies. The following season saw him experience European Cup-Winners' Cup action in Malta, as the 'Swans' romped to a 5-0 victory against Sliema Wanderers. He kept goal twelve times for the Vetch field club in a campaign that ended in relegation, although he did collect a winners' medal from the1983 Welsh Cup Final victory over Wrexham. By September 1984 he had been loaned out to the North Wales club as cover for the injured Stuart Parker, making his debut in a 3-0 defeat at Crewe Alexandra. He went on to play in the following match, a 4-3 home defeat by Stockport County, before Parker was fit to resume. In the five games that he played in goal for the 'Robins' Chris had the unenviable record of never appearing on the winning side! However, his best game was in a 1-1 draw at Hereford when he saved a penalty. He returned to South Wales in November, where he went on to complete a total of twenty League games for the Vetch Field club - playing in all four divisions! He eventually signed for Cardiff City on non-contract terms in the close season of 1985, and made his debut in the opening game of the season, a 4-1 win at Notts County, but by December had been told that he was surplus to requirements. He then joined Welsh League side Haverfordwest, but Chris was to return to Ninian Park in March following a goalkeeping crisis. However, he couldn't prevent the 'Bluebirds' relegation to the Fourth Division, although during his second spell with Cardiff, he became the first goalkeeper in the club's history to save two penalties in the same match against Walsall at Ninian Park in April 1986. He was again released in the summer, joining Barry Town, where he collected an Abacus League championship medal in 1989, as the side completed their League programme without losing a single game. In October 1989 he joined fellow Abacus League side, Aberystwyth Town.

Season	League		F.A.Cup		Welsh Cup		League Cup		F.R.T.		E.C.W.C.		Total	
	apps	gls	apps	gls	apps	gls	apps	gls	apps	gls	apps	gls	apps	gls
1984/85	5	0	-	-	-	-	-	-	-	-	-	-	5	0
	5	**0**	-	-	-	-	-	-	-	-	-	-	**5**	**0**

SAVAGE, George 1922 - 1925

Position; *Left-Half*
D.O.B; *J/F/M 1896*
Birthplace; *Aston, Birmingham, West Midlands*
Died; *Birmingham, J/A/S 1968*
Height; *5ft 10in* ***Weight;*** *11st 6lbs*
Debut; v. *Grimsby Town (a) 26th August, 1922*
Total Appearances & Goals; *127 apps 2 gls*
Career; *Willenhall Swifts; West Bromwich Albion May 1921 2apps 0gls; WREXHAM 1st June 1922; Shrewsbury Town Aug 1925; Alfreton Town cs1927; Cradley Heath Jan 1928;*
Honours; *Welsh Cup Winner 1924 & 1925;*

George Savage turned professional when he joined West Bromwich Albion from Willenhall Swifts in May 1921. He had begun playing football at Aston Cross and Rocky Lane Schools, followed by turning out for Farm Street Unity in Hockley. At the Hawthorns he had to wait until November before making his Football League debut at inside-left, playing for Albion in a 1-0 home defeat against Bolton Wanderers. He kept his place for the following match, also against the Burnden Park club, though it subsequently proved to be his last match for the 'Throstles'. He was allowed to leave the Hawthorns during the summer of 1922, and to join Third Division North side Wrexham. His 'Robins' debut came at centre-forward in the opening game of the season, a 4-0 defeat at Grimsby. He remained in this strikers role for a few more games before resuming his best position of half-back. Once installed in this role George became an established member of the side for almost three years, helping Wrexham win the Welsh Cup in both 1924 and 1925. Even so, at the end of the 1924/25 season he was surprisingly allowed to leave the Racecourse, and join Birmingham & District League side Shrewsbury Town for a trial in the close season of 1925. He again played up front, and scored five goals in a second trial match, which convinced the Gay Meadow club to secure his services. George became a regular with Shrewsbury over the next two seasons, although he was eventually to resume his favoured half-back position. During his time with the Shropshire club he was described as a 'half-back who could fill in adequately at inside or outside-left'. A spate of leg injuries were later to ruin a promising career, although he is known to have later turned out for both Alfreton Town and Cradley Heath before finally having to retire from the game through injury. After occupying a number of coaching positions he returned to West Bromwich Albion in 1948, where he joined the coaching staff. He gave up his job as a sports master in Derbyshire, one which he had been employed in since 1928.

Season	League		F.A.Cup		Welsh Cup		Total	
	apps	gls	apps	gls	apps	gls	apps	gls
1922/23	30	0	3	0	1	1	34	1
1923/24	40	1	2	0	5	0	47	1
1924/25	41	0	1	0	4	0	46	0
	111	**1**	**6**	**0**	**10**	**1**	**127**	**2**

***SAVAGE,* Robert Edward** 1938 - 1939

Position; *Right-Half*
D.O.B; *J/F/M, 1912*
Birthplace; *Louth, Lincolnshire*
Died; *Wallasey, 30th January 1964*
Height; *6ft 0in* ***Weight;*** *12st 9lbs*
Debut; v. *Barnsley (h) 3rd December, 1938*
Total Appearances & Goals; *47 apps 0 gls*
Career; *Louth Grammar School; Stewton (Lincs); Lincoln City Oct 1928 96apps 3gls; Liverpool May 1931 100apps 2gls; Manchester United Dec 1938 4apps 0gls; WREXHAM 22nd Nov 1938; Carlisle United (WW2 Guest) 1939/40 1app 0gls; West Ham United (WW2 Guest) Oct-Dec 1940 7apps 0gls; Chelsea (WW2 Guest) Mar 1943 1app 0gls; Fulham (WW2 Guest) 1942/43 1app 0gls; Millwall (WW2 Guest) Feb 1944 1app 0gls; Southport (WW2 Guest) 1943/44 2apps 0gls; York City (WW2 Guest) 1943/44 2apps 0gls;*

Ted Savage was signed by Lincoln City from his local side, Stewton, following a promising schoolboy career at Louth Grammar School. He forced his way into the first team at Sincil Bank when he was still only 17, making his debut in a 3-1 defeat at Carlisle United on New Year's Day 1929. Ted had completed almost 100 Third Division North appearances by the time that he joined First Division Liverpool in May 1931. During his time at Lincoln he was described as 'fast, resourceful and a good judge in defence or attack', and regarded as one of the 'Red Imps' best discoveries of the inter-war period. At Anfield Savage made his League debut towards the end of September in a 4-0 home win over Grimsby Town, when he contributed two of the goals. He added a further six League appearances that season, and over the next six years found himself in and out of the side on a regular basis, clocking up a total of 100 League appearances before he was allowed to join Second Division Manchester United in December 1937. Ted made just four League appearances for the Old Trafford club, his debut coming on New Year's Day in a 2-2 draw at Newcastle. He played in the next three games before losing his place in the side, as United went on to gain promotion from the Second Division as runners-up. He was not considered for the United first team after this, and at the end of November 1938 he was allowed to join Third Division North side Wrexham. Ted went straight into the 'Robins' first team in December, replacing Walter Odell for the 1-1 home League fixture against Barnsley. He kept his place for the rest of the season, making 26 League appearances, before football was disrupted by the outbreak of World War Two in September 1939. It was then decreed that football was 'good for morale', so the regional Leagues were formed. Ted continued to play football when he could, making sixteen appearances for Wrexham during the conflict, as well as turning out as a 'guest' player for Carlisle United, Fulham, Chelsea, Millwall, West Ham United, Southport, and York City. Towards the end of WW2 Ted retired from football, and went into the licensing trade as a publican at the Primrose Hotel in Wallasey. As well as excelling at football he was also a distinguished swimmer, and a noted runner with the Grimsby Harriers A.C. Ted passed away in January 1964. He was only 51.

Season	League		F.A.Cup		Welsh Cup		N.S.C.		Total	
	apps	gls	apps	gls	apps	gls	apps	gls	apps	gls
1938/39*	26	0	-	-	2	0	3	0	31	0
1939/40	3	0	-	-	-	-	-	-	3	0
1943/44	13	0	-	-	-	-	-	-	13	0
	42	**0**	**-**	**-**	**2**	**0**	**3**	**0**	**47**	**0**

* = Football League record only.

***SAVAGE,* Robert James** 1982 - 1983

Position; *Midfielder*
D.O.B; *8th January, 1960*
Birthplace; *Liverpool, Merseyside*
Height; *5ft 7in* ***Weight;*** *11st 1lbs*
Debut; v. *Oxford United (h) 23rd October, 1982*
Total Appearances & Goals; *34 apps 13 gls*
Career; *Liverpool Jan 1978 0apps; WREXHAM Oct 1982 (Loan); Liverpool May 1983 0apps; Stoke City 26th Jul 1983 £10,000 5/2apps 0gls; Bournemouth Dec 1983 £15,000 80/2apps 18gls; Bradford City 11th Dec 1986 11apps 0gls; Bolton Wanderers 10th Sept 1987 £35,000 83/4apps 11gls;*
Honours; *Welsh Cup runner-up 1983; Sherpa Van Trophy Winner 1989;*

A life-long Liverpool supporter, Robbie Savage attended the Sir John Hamilton School close to the Anfield Road ground. As well as playing for his school team Robbie also represented Liverpool Schoolboys, and was signed by Liverpool as an Associate Schoolboy at the age of 15. A year later his boyhood dreams came true when he was offered apprentice terms, and he progressed to sign a professional contract on his eighteenth birthday. Playing for Liverpool's reserves Robbie continued to develop at Anfield, and it was with his future in mind that he was allowed to join Wrexham on loan in October 1982 to broaden his experience. He arrived at the Racecourse at a time when the club were under a great deal of financial pressure and were forced to sell their best players. He made his 'Robins' debut in a 1-1 home draw with Oxford United, and made an immediate impact by scoring the Wrexham goal. Robbie's loan spell was eventually extended until the end of the season as, playing in midfield, he shone in a struggling Wrexham side as the club battled to avoid relegation to Division Four. However, just when the side most needed the popular Scouser - for the final match of the season at Reading, which they needed to win to avoid relegation - he missed the team coach! He did manage to reach Elm Park, but it was 15 minutes after the team sheets had been handed in, and so had to watch the match from the stands. Even so, Robbie was still voted the club's 'Player of the Season' despite being on loan! That summer Wrexham had the chance to sign Savage for £10,000, but they couldn't afford the fee, and so Liverpool allowed him to join First Division Stoke City. He made his debut at left-back in the opening match of the season, a 1-0 defeat at Everton. Just four more full League appearances followed, plus another two as substitute, including one against his former club Liverpool in a 1-0 defeat at Anfield. That proved to be his last game for the Victoria Ground club, as he was allowed to join Bournemouth in December 1983 for a £15,000 fee. Robbie went on to make 82 League appearances for the 'Cherries', scoring 18 goals in the three years that he spent at Dean Court. In December 1986 he moved on to Second Division Bradford City, and went straight into the first team at left-back for a 3-1 defeat by West Bromwich Albion. The match was played at the Odsal Stadium in Bradford, due to the fire disaster at Valley Parade the previous year. Robbie was to make just seven more League appearances for the 'Bantams' that season, and three more at the outset of 1987/88 before joining Bolton Wanderers in September 1987 for £35,000. Robbie added 87 League appearances for the 'Trotters', scoring eleven goals before having to retire from the game in 1990 due to complications arising from a broken leg that he had sustained at Rotherham in September 1989. During his time with the Burnden Park club he helped them to gain promotion to the Third Division in 1988, and also appeared at Wembley in the 1989 Sherpa Van Trophy Final, where Bolton beat Torquay United 4-1. Robbie later managed Knowsley United during the 1994/95 season and has since returned to the club.

Season	League		F.A.Cup		Welsh Cup		League Cup		Total	
	apps	gls	apps	gls	apps	gls	apps	gls	apps	gls
1982/83	27	10	2	1	5	2	-	-	34	13
	27	**10**	**2**	**1**	**5**	**2**	**-**	**-**	**34**	**13**

SCHOFIELD, John Reginald — 1966 - 1968

Position; *Goalkeeper*
D.O.B; *8th February, 1931*
Birthplace; *Atherstone, Warwickshire*
Height; *6ft 1'1/2in* **Weight;** *12st 12lbs*
Debut v. *Exeter City (h) 20th April, 1966.*
Total Appearances & Goals; *62 apps 0 gls*
Career; *Atherstone; Grendon United; Nuneaton Borough; Birmingham City Feb 1950 212apps 0gls; WREXHAM 8th Jul 1966; Cork City 12th Oct 1968; Bromsgrove Rovers 1969; Tamworth 1969;*
Honours; *Second Division Championship Winner 1955; Football League Cup Winner 1963; Welsh Cup runner-up 1967;*

Johnny Schofield first began playing football in his home town of Atherstone, appearing for Ansley Hall Colliery. He then had a spell with Grendon United before signing amateur forms for Nuneaton Borough. It was while turning out for Nuneaton's reserve side that he was spotted by Birmingham City, and they invited him for trials. A part-time contract followed a week later in February 1950, as he continued to work in the pits. Johnny progressed at St.Andrew's, becoming understudy to Gil Merrick before he eventually made his Football League debut in October 1952 in a Second Division match at Bury, which ended in a 3-0 defeat for the visitors. Over the following five seasons Johnny continued to deputise for Merrick as and when required, as well as working in his local colliery. During the 1954/55 season he was described as having 'performed brilliantly' as Merrick's replacement in the run-in to the Second Division title, which earned him a championship medal. Two years later, in November 1957, Johnny - who was then employed at the Baddesley Colliery, near Tamworth - was involved in a pit accident that left him in hospital for three weeks. In his own words he counted himself "Bloody lucky to be alive!" After the explosion Johnny, not surprisingly, decided to leave mining altogether, and to sign as a full-time professional with the 'Blues'. In 1959 he finally became the first choice 'keeper at St.Andrew's, remaining in the side until November 1960, when he fractured his skull in a First Division match with Manchester United. He had dived at the feet of the oncoming Alex Dawson, who failed to avoid a collision with the 'keeper, resulting in the injury. Johnny, described as 'big-handed, big-hearted and a dedicated professional', bounced back to play against Blackpool towards the end of 1960/61. He went on to appear in the 1963 Football League Cup Final against arch-enemies, Aston Villa, which the 'Blues' won 3-1 after a replay. Two years later Birmingham were relegated, and the following season Schofield decided to retire from football to open up an off-licence business in Atherstone. However, Wrexham manager Jack Rowley and his assistant Ken Roberts paid him a visit, attempting to persuade him to come out of retirement and play for Wrexham. He agreed, signing for the North Wales club in July 1966. It was a time of rebuilding at the Racecourse, and Johnny made his debut in the opening game of the season, a scoreless home draw with Exeter City. He went on to play in every League and Cup match that season, including the 1967 Welsh Cup Final against Cardiff City, which Wrexham lost 4-3 on aggregate. He was considered by many fans of the period to be one of the best goalkeepers to have graced the Racecourse with his all-round ability, 'a goalkeeper full of heart and bravery'. The following season he was still number one for the opening six League games, but was then replaced by Gordon Livsey. He was allowed to go to Ireland shortly afterwards, playing a couple of games for Cork City before having his Wrexham contract terminated. He then returned to Atherstone, where he helped out an old friend, Gil Merrick, by appearing in a couple of games for Bromsgrove Rovers, followed by a further six games for Tamworth. He continued to run his off-licence in Atherstone throughout this time, as well as coaching the local side for a spell. Johnny has now retired, having settled in the town.

Season	League		F.A.Cup		Welsh Cup		League Cup		Total	
	apps	gls	apps	gls	apps	gls	apps	gls	apps	gls
1966/67	46	0	2	0	6	0	1	0	55	0
1967/68	6	0	-	-	-	-	1	0	7	0
	52	**0**	**2**	**0**	**6**	**0**	**2**	**0**	**62**	**0**

SCOTT, Robert — 1959

Position; *Inside-Forward*
D.O.B; *20th May, 1930*
Birthplace; *Belshill, Strathclyde*
Height; *5ft 9in* **Weight;** *10st 10lbs*
Debut; v. *Brentford (a) 25th August, 1959*
Total Appearances & Goals; *2 apps 0 gls*
Career; *Stonehouse Violet 1947; Burnbank Athletic 1948; Dunfermline Athletic 1951; Alloa Athletic 1953/54; Accrington Stanley 6th Sept 1954 149apps 32gls; WREXHAM 14th July 1959; Oldham Athletic 3rd October 1959 9apps 1gls; Nelson Jun 1960; Bacup Borough;*

Bert Scott played his early football in Glasgow with both Stonehouse Violet and Burnbank Athletic. In 1951 he joined Dunfermline Athletic, only for his career to be interrupted when he was called up for National Service. Upon completion of his two years Bert linked up with Scottish 'B' Division side Alloa Athletic during the 1953/54 season, at the end of which he was invited to join Accrington Stanley on trial. He eventually joined them and made his Football League debut on 4th September 1954 in a 2-0 home win over Workington. Bert signed a professional contract on the following Monday. Playing mainly at outside-left, although sometimes switched to the right, he went on to establish himself in the Accrington side over the next five years, eventually moving to an inside-forward position. During his time at Peel Park he was described as 'Fast, strong and two-footed, an adaptable forward whose impressive approach work on either flank made many openings for his team mates.' His creative skills shone no better than when he played in the Accrington side that twice finished as runners-up in the Third Division North, missing out on promotion as only the champions went up. During the close season of 1959 he was allowed to leave Accrington, signing for Third Division Wrexham. Bert made his debut for the Racecourse club in the second game of the season at Brentford, a 3-1 defeat. He played in the following match, a 2-2 draw against his old club Accrington, again failing to score. That match proved to be his last for the 'Robins', as he was transferred to Oldham Athletic at the beginning of October, having spent just three months at the Racecourse. He made his 'Latics' debut in a 3-1 defeat at Notts County, but again made little impact at Boundary Park, and at the end of the season he was allowed to leave having accumulated just nine League appearances. In the close season of 1960 he moved into non-league football, initially with Nelson, and followed by a spell with Bacup Borough. After retiring from football Bert ran his own window cleaning business.

Season	League		F.A.Cup		Welsh Cup		Total	
	apps	gls	apps	gls	apps	gls	apps	gls
1959/60	2	0	-	-	-	-	2	0
	2	**0**	**-**	**-**	**-**	**-**	**2**	**0**

SCOTT, Robert William — 1971 - 1976 & 1986

Position; *Centre-Half*
D.O.B; *22nd February, 1953*
Birthplace; *Liverpool, Merseyside*
Height; *6ft 2'1/2in* **Weight;** *13st 4lbs*
Debut; v. *Brighton & H.A. (h) 7th May, 1971*
Total Appearances & goals; *19/5 apps 0 gls*
Career; *WREXHAM (Pro) 1st Jul 1971; Reading 9th Jan 1975 5apps 0gls (Loan); Hartlepool United Jul 1976 37apps 0gls; Rochdale Jul 1977 71apps 0gls; Crewe Alexandra Aug 1979 238/1apps 15gls; Northwich Victoria 1985 14apps 1gls; WREXHAM Jan 1986;*
Honours; *Welsh Cup Winner 1975; Welsh Youth Cup Winner 1970; North Wales Coast F.A. XI.*

Bob Scott joined Wrexham in 1969, one of many players from the Liverpool area who signed apprentice forms for the club during this period. It was a time when the youth policy at the Racecourse was turning out many excellent players, and Bob was one of these, picking up a Welsh Youth Cup winners' medal in 1970. He went on to make his Football

League debut in the final game of the 1970/71 season, replacing Eddie May at centre-half in a home fixture against Brighton & Hove Albion. He stepped up to the club's professional ranks in the summer, but a full year had passed before he came back into the first team reckoning, and by that time had represented the North Wales Coast F.A. against the Scottish Juniors in March 1972, in a 3-2 defeat at the home of Kirkintilloch Rob Roy F.C.. The Coast side also included fellow 'Robins', Billy Ashcroft and Joey Duncan. Bob was to find his first team chances limited throughout his time at the Racecourse, due to the consistent performances of both Gareth Davies and Eddie May. In January 1975 he was loaned out to Reading to gain first team experience, where he made five League appearances before returning to the Racecourse. However, at the end of that season Bob was allowed to leave the North Wales club permanently, though he was soon fixed up when he signed for Hartlepool United. He spent a year with the North-East club, making 37 League appearances, and in the summer of 1977 he joined Fourth Division Rochdale. His debut for the Spotland club came in the opening match of the season, a 4-0 defeat at Barnsley, and he went on to miss just six games in a season that ended with Rochdale at the bottom of the Football League. Bob spent another term at Spotland, making 31 League appearances, before being transferred to Crewe Alexandra in the summer of 1979. He made his debut for Crewe in a League Cup game at Huddersfield, and went on to make well over 200 appearances in the six years that he spent at Gresty Road, eventually becoming assistant-manager to Dario Gradi. He later took over the post of commercial manager at the club. Scott then joined Gola League side Northwich Victoria for a short spell, until returning to Wrexham in January 1986 to help out manager Dixie McNeil at a time of financial crisis at the club. He made three League appearances, following which he continued in his job with a finance company in Chester. At around this time he had also begun promoting after dinner speakers, but in 1988/89 he became assistant-manager of Northern Premier League First Division club Newtown. Today, Bob still lives in the Wrexham area running his own popular night-club in the town, appropriately called 'Scott's'.

Season	League apps	gls	F.A.Cup apps	gls	Welsh Cup apps	gls	League Cup apps	gls	E.C.W.C. apps	gls	Total apps	gls
1970/71	1	0	-	-	-	-	-	-	-	-	1	0
1972/73	5/1	0	-	-	-	-	-	-	-	-	5/1	0
1973/74	3/1	0	-	-	-	-	-	-	-	-	3/1	0
1974/75	5	0	-	-	2	0	-	-	-	-	7	0
1975/76	1/2	0	-	-	-	-	-	-	-	-	1/2	0
1985/86	2/1	0	-	-	-	-	-	-	-	-	2/1	0
	17/5	**0**	**-**	**-**	**2**	**0**	**-**	**-**	**-**	**-**	**19/5**	**0**

SCOTT, Stephen Richard 1986 - 1988

Position; *Full-Back*
D.O.B; *5th November, 1966*
Birthplace; *Johnstown, Denbighshire*
Height; *5ft 8in* ***Weight;*** *11st 5lbs*
Debut; v. *Tranmere Rovers (a) 6th November, 1987*
Total Appearances & Goals; *0/4 apps 0 gls*
Career; *WREXHAM Jul 1983; Oswestry Town Aug 1985; WREXHAM Mar 1986; Oswestry Town Mar 1988; Lex XI Jul 1988; Bridgnorth Town Jun 1993; Brymbo Steelworks Dec 1993; Shifnal Town Feb 1994; Lex XI Jul 1994;*
Honours; *Welsh National League Championship Winner 1989; North-East Wales Cup Winner; Cymru Alliance League Cup Winner;*

Steve Scott played football from an early age. He was selected for the St.Joseph's Roman Catholic Secondary School in Wrexham, from where he represented Wrexham & District, Clwyd, and North Wales Schoolboys. He was called up to the Welsh Schoolboys squad, though he was not subsequently capped. It was whilst he was turning out for his local youth side, Borras Park Albion, that he was approached by Wrexham, and he signed schoolboy forms at the age of 14. An apprenticeship followed in the summer of 1983, when Bobby Roberts was manager, and he progressed through the youth ranks to reserve team football. Steve's most memorable moment during this time came as a substitute for the European Cup-Winners' Cup matches against F.C.Porto of Portugal and A.S.Roma of Italy. However, he was disappointingly released at the end of the 1984/85 season without having made a first team appearance at the Racecourse. He then signed for Northern Premier League side Oswestry Town, where he spent the 1985/86 season, also taking up Business Studies at the North-East Wales Institute. A second opportunity of League Football was handed to him towards the end of that season when Dixie McNeil invited him to rejoin Wrexham for a trial period in March 1986. He played a few reserve team games before securing a short term contract in the summer of 1986. Steve was selected for the sub's bench on a number of occasions before eventually making his Football League debut at Tranmere Rovers in November 1987, replacing Ian Fairbrother with just two minutes remaining. His next match saw him again come off the bench in a F.A.Cup tie at Rochdale, replacing Paul Emson in the 2-0 win. He made two more substitute appearances for the 'Robins' before released by the club in March, whereupon he rejoined Oswestry Town until the end of the season. He then made the wise decision of attending Liverpool Polytechnic for four years, training to become a P.E.teacher, during which time he played for the British Polytechnics team in both the 1991 and 1992 British Student Games, winning a Gold and a Silver medal. Steve continued playing football, joining local Wrexham side Lex XI, with whom he won a Welsh National League championship medal in his first season, 1988/89. Over the next four years he played for Lex in the Cymru Alliance League, adding two North-East Wales Cup, and two Cymru Alliance League Cup winners' medals. In the close season of 1993 Scott moved on to Bridgnorth Town, until a change of manager at the Crown Meadow saw him join Cymru Alliance League side Brymbo Steelworks in December 1993. He signed for Shifnal Town in the New Year, and remained with them until the end of that season, when he rejoined Lex XI where he is still playing at the present. During his time with Lex XI Steve became a qualified P.E.teacher and football coach. Currently based at the Abraham Darby School in Telford, where he is head of the P.E. department, he is also the recruitment officer for a soccer coaching school in Philadelphia, America, with whom he has been associated since 1994 as a Camp Director. Steve now lives in the Shrewsbury area, and was one of over 100 ex-Racecourse Robins who attended the Grand Gala Players Reunion at the St.David's Hotel in Ewloe in September 1998.

Season	League apps	gls	F.A.Cup apps	gls	Welsh Cup apps	gls	League Cup apps	gls	F.R.T. apps	gls	Total apps	gls
1987/88	0/2	0	0/1	0	0/1	0	-	-	-	-	0/4	0
	0/2	**0**	**0/1**	**0**	**0/1**	**0**	**-**	**-**	**-**	**-**	**0/4**	**0**

SERTORI, Mark Anthony 1990 - 1994

Position; *Centre-Half*
D.O.B; *1st September, 1967*
Birthplace; *Manchester, Lancashire*
Height; *6ft 2in* ***Weight;*** *12st 0lbs*
Debut; v. *Hereford United (h) 10th February, 1990*
Total Appearances & Goals; *140/7 apps 2 gls*
Career; *East Manchester FC; Stockport County 7th Feb 1987 3/1apps 0gls; Lincoln City Aug 1987 43/7apps 9gls; WREXHAM 9th Feb 1990 £30,000; Preston North End 9th Mar 1994 0apps (Loan); Bury 22nd Jul 1994 0/2apps 0gls; Witton Albion 1st Mar 1996 (Loan); Scunthorpe United 22nd Jul 1996 82/1apps 2gls; Halifax Town Jun 1998 39/1apps 0gls;*
Honours; *Welsh Cup runner-up 1990 & 1991; GM Conference League Championship Winner 1988;*

While at School Mark Sertori represented both Manchester and Lancashire Schoolboys, but embarked upon a career in the family catering business upon completing his education. Shortly after he was persuaded to try his luck with Stockport County, having been spotted playing for East Manchester F.C. in the Manchester Premier League. After a trial period with Stockport's reserve side he was offered a full-time contract by manager Colin Murphy in February 1987. Mark made his Football League debut at Northampton Town the following month, in a 2-1 defeat, before appearing in the final two games of the season. He made a substitute appearance in the opening match of the 1987/88 season, a 2-0 home defeat by Swansea, but only a few days after that game he was transferred to Conference League side Lincoln City, linking up with his former manager at Stockport, Colin Murphy. In his first year at Sincil Bank Mark, playing at centre-forward, helped the club regain Football League status, and played in their first match back in the Fourth Division. He made a total of fifty League appearances for the 'Red Imps', scoring nine goals. However, following the arrival of new signing Tony Lormor Mark found his first team chances limited, and eventually accepted a transfer to Wrexham in February 1990 for £30,000. At the time the 'Robins' were fighting desperately to avoid relegation to the Conference League themselves, and Mark's presence and commitment in attack gave them extra options, and renewed determination. He played a major part in helping to guide the Club to safety. During the summer of 1990 Wrexham manager Brian Flynn decided to experiment with Mark in a central defensive role, and the switch proved so successful that he remained in that position throughout the rest of his time at the Racecourse, playing his part in Wrexham's continuing resurgence. With no relegation from the Football League in 1991 Brian Flynn used the time wisely, bringing a number of his promising young players through to the first team, and

Sertori's strength and experience were invaluable in helping them to cope with the rigours of League football. He was to experience European football that season, playing in the two legged European Cup-Winners' Cup victory over Danish side Lyngby, but was disappointed to miss the Second Round games against Manchester United. However, he did take part in the Club's greatest ever Cup match in the following season, when the 'Robins' defeated the reigning Football League champions Arsenal, 2-1, on the Racecourse in an F.A.Cup Third Round tie. Mel Pejic's and Tony Humes' solid defensive partnership forced Mark into the shadows during 1992/93, as the Racecourse club secured promotion to the Second Division. That partnership continued into the following season, and with the signing of Barry Hunter during the summer of 1993, Mark found a first team place even more difficult to secure. In March 1994 he accepted a loan move to Preston North End, but returned to Wrexham before the month had ended as he had only played in reserve team games. He was released at the end of the season, having been a loyal servant during some of Wrexham Football Club's darkest days. Mark was soon fixed up with another club, joining Bury, but was again to find his first team opportunities limited, making just two sub appearances in his first year with the 'Shakers'. The next season was much the same, as Bury won promotion to the Second Division, although Mark found himself joining Witton Albion on loan towards the end of that season. In July 1996 he took up an offer to join Scunthorpe United, where he was a virtual ever-present in the first team, playing against Wrexham in two F.A.Cup matches in December 1997. He left Glanford Park in the summer of 1998 to join newly promoted Halifax Town for their first season back in the Football League, and made another return to the Racecourse for a Worthington Cup First Round tie.

Season	League		F.A.Cup		Welsh Cup		League Cup		F.R.T.		E.C.W.C.		Total	
	apps	gls	apps	gls	apps	gls	apps	gls	apps	gls	apps	gls	apps	gls
1989/90	18	2	-	-	3	0	-	-	-	-	-	-	21	2
1990/91	27/2	0	-	-	4	0	3	0	2	0	2	0	38/2	0
1991/92	36	0	5	0	3	0	2	0	3/1	0	-	-	49/1	0
1992/93	10/2	0	1	0	1/1	0	0/1	0	1	0	-	-	13/4	0
1993/94	15	0	-	-	-	-	3	0	1	0	-	-	19	0
	106/4	**2**	**6**	**0**	**11/1**	**0**	**8/1**	**0**	**7/1**	**0**	**2**	**0**	**140/7**	**2**

SETTLE, John Arthur Frederick 1921 - 1923

Position; *Left-Back*
D.O.B; *A/M/J, 1895*
Birthplace; *Chester, Cheshire*
Died; *St.Asaph, 6th December, 1955*
Height; *5ft 9'1/2in* ***Weight;*** *12st 2lbs*
Debut; v. *Darlington (a) 15th October, 1921*
Total Appearances & Goals; *28 apps 0 gls*
Career; *Chester 1919 50apps 15gls; WREXHAM 28th May 1921; Bangor City 8th Aug 1923; Chester 18th Sept 1924 3apps 0gls; Holyhead 1924/25; Caernarfon Athletic 31st Jul 1926; Rhyl 3rd Sept 1927;*
Honours; *North Wales Coast F.A. Challenge Cup Winner 1928; North Wales Coast F.A. Challenge Cup runner-up 1924 & 1925;*

John Settle joined Wrexham from Cheshire County League side Chester in May 1921, where he had been a first team regular for the previous two seasons. He arrived at the Racecourse at a time when the club was preparing a new squad for their first ever season in the Football League, though he did not make his Football League debut for the 'Robins' until October, replacing Jack Ellis at right-back in a 1-1 draw at Darlington. Playing in either full-back position John went on to add a further 23 League appearances that season, as the 'Robins' ended the campaign in a respectable 12th place in the Third Division North. The following year he made just two more League appearances before leaving the Racecourse at the end of the season. He joined Bangor City in the summer of 1923, helping them to reach the Final of the North Wales Coast F.A.Challenge Cup where they lost 2-1 to Mold. He began the new campaign at Farrar Road, but after just one month was transferred to Chester, who were still playing in the Cheshire County League. His stay at Sealand Road was brief, and he managed just three appearances before moving up the North Wales coast to sign for Holyhead Town. There, he played in the Final of the North Wales Coast F.A.Challenge Cup, alongside two former 'Racecourse Robins' Dick Finnegan and Bob Griffiths, although he finished on the losing side once again following a 2-0 defeat at the hands of Mold. He left the 'Harbourmen' in the summer of 1926 to join Caernarfon Athletic, where he spent another year before joining Rhyl. He again reached the North Wales Coast Challenge Cup Final, and this time succeeded in picking up a winners' medal following a 2-0 success against Bangor. John remained with the Belle Vue club until 1930.

Season	League		F.A.Cup		Welsh Cup		Total	
	apps	gls	apps	gls	apps	gls	apps	gls
1921/22	22	0	1	0	3	0	26	0
1922/23	2	0	-	-	-	-	2	0
	24	**0**	**1**	**0**	**3**	**0**	**28**	**0**

***SHARP,* Norman Winslow** 1946 - 1950

Position; *Inside-Left*
D.O.B; *26th November, 1919*
Birthplace; *Anfield, Liverpool, Merseyside*
Died; *Leeds, 9th May, 1977.*
Height; *5ft 7'1/2in* ***Weight;*** *10st 6lbs*
Debut; v. *Chester (a) 18th September, 1946*
Total Appearances & Goals; *133 apps 20 gls*
Career; *Everton Nov 1938 0apps; Chester (WW2 Guest) Dec 1941 27apps 10gls; Leeds United (WW2 Guest) Nov 1943 1app 0gls; WREXHAM 17th Sept 1946;*

Norman Sharp showed plenty of promise as a schoolboy footballer in his native Liverpool. He was selected to represent Liverpool Schoolboys, captaining the side, and upon completion of his education was signed by Everton, although he combined playing football with working for the Liverpool Evening Express. He turned out for the Central League side at Goodison Park, but failed to make a first team appearance before the outbreak of World War Two. During the hostilities Norman enlisted with the Army in 1940, serving with the Royal Corps of Signals. He spent some time stationed at Prestatyn, as well as later serving in India with Lord Woolton's squadron. Despite the conflict he still managed to play football when he could, and it was during this time that he broke into the first team at Everton, when he played in a 3-1 home win over Manchester City in November 1939. Over two years passed before his next game for the 'Toffeemen' in May 1942, a 5-1 home defeat by West Bromwich Albion, which was followed by a 4-2 home defeat by Tranmere Rovers on Christmas Day 1944. He made four more appearances that season, the last coming in a 2-0 home defeat by Accrington Stanley. He also turned out as a 'guest' player during this period for Chester, where he scored ten goals in 27 games, as well as making one appearance for Leeds United in November 1943 in a 6-1 defeat at Bradford Park Avenue. After WW2 had ended Norman remained in the Army for a short while before his discharge in 1946. He then took up work at the Goodlass Paint factory, near Speke as a sales representative, though he was to continue playing football when he was signed by Wrexham manager Mr.Tom Williams in September 1946. By that time Norman was working in Northern Ireland, and in his earlier days with the club he would fly over from Ireland to play, and return after the game. Norman's Football League debut came in a local derby with Chester in September 1946, although the 'Robins' lost 2-0. Playing at inside-forward he will always be remembered for his fine left-sided partnership with winger Billy Tunnicliffe. He made thirty League appearances in his first season at the Racecourse, but it was the 1947/48 season that provided the highlight of his time at the club as they reached third place, their best position since finishing runners-up in 1933. Sharp was an established member of the Wrexham side until February 1950, when he announced that he was taking up a business appointment in Scotland, and would only occasionally be available for matches. He never played a first team match for Wrexham again, and was released at the end of the season. He later moved to Bangor in Northern Ireland, where he remained for a number of years before returning to the Liverpool area. He then uprooted to Leeds where he eventually settled, working as a sales manager for the Central Electricity Generating Board until his untimely death at the age of 57 in May 1977.

Season	League		F.A.Cup		Welsh Cup		Total	
	apps	gls	apps	gls	apps	gls	apps	gls
1946/47	30	5	4	1	-	-	34	6
1947/48	41	9	2	0	1	0	44	9
1948/49	34	2	1	0	1	1	36	3
1949/50	17	1	2	1	-	-	19	2
	122	**17**	**9**	**2**	**2**	**1**	**133**	**20**

***SHARPE,* Frederick Arthur** 1948 - 1949

Position; *Inside-Right*
D.O.B; *26th January 1924*
Birthplace; *Norwich, Norfolk*
Height; *ft in* ***Weight;*** *st lbs*
Debut; v. *Chester (a) 4th December 1948*
Total Appearances & Goals; *1 app 0 gls*
Career; *B.A.O.R; WREXHAM May 1948;*

Fred Sharpe was signed by Wrexham as the club were touring Germany in May 1948. Sergeant Sharpe was serving with the British Army on the Rhine at the time, and he played against the Denbighshire side in all three of the games staged on tour, against the B.A.O.R and Combined Services teams, with Fred scoring one of the Army's six goals. Despite signing for Wrexham at that time he had to wait until his demobilisation before joining up with his new team-mates, which was not until the following season. He finally made his Football League debut for the club in December 1948, in a local derby with Chester at Sealand Road. Playing at inside-right in place of Eddie Beynon, Fred couldn't prevent the 'Robins' from being on the wrong end of a 2-0 scoreline. That game proved to be Fred's one and only match for Wrexham.

Season	League		F.A.Cup		Welsh Cup		Total	
	apps	gls	apps	gls	apps	gls	apps	gls
1948/49	1	0	-	-	-	-	1	0
	1	**0**	**-**	**-**	**-**	**-**	**1**	**0**

***SHELDON,* Alfred** 1922 - 1923

Position; *Outside-Right*
D.O.B; *O/N/D 1886*
Birthplace; *Smethwick, West Midlands*
Height; *5ft 6in* ***Weight;*** *11st 4lbs*
Debut; v. *Grimsby Town (a) 26th August, 1922*
Total Appearances & Goals; *40 apps 5 gls*
Career; *Good Shepherd FC cs1903; Portway Villa cs1905; Rowley United cs1906; Coombs Wood cs1908; Worcester City Oct 1908; Dudley 1911; Oldbury Town; Birmingham City WW1 1917 4apps 0gls; Coventry City May 1919 12apps 1gls; Wellington Town cs1920; WREXHAM 17th May 1922; Wellington Town Jul 1923; Redditch cs1924 to 1926;*

Alf Sheldon began playing football seriously in 1903 by appearing at left-back for the Good Shepherd, Church Bridge, Oldbury, in the Tipton & District League. He spent a couple of years with them and during that time, they finished as runners-up and also champions. In the summer of 1905 he signed for Portway Villa, who competed in the Dudley & District League. He stayed here for one season, but it was long enough to pick up a League Championship medal and five cups. In the close season of 1906 Alf joined Rowley United for two years before turning out for Coombs Wood in 1908, where he switched from left-back to left-half. After just six matches in his new position he was signed by Birmingham & District League side Worcester City in October. They converted him to an outside-left, a position in which he was to excel by finishing top scorer for the next two seasons, until his promising career was halted when he broke his leg in a match against Stoke. Alf was in hospital for four weeks, at the end of which it was found that the leg needed to be re-set. Once recovered he made a comeback during the 1910/11 season before joining another Birmingham League side, Dudley, in 1911. There he went on to play in almost every position including a spell between the posts - before World War One interrupted his career. During the Great War Sheldon made four appearances for Birmingham, followed by a spell with Oldbury Town towards the end of the conflict. In May 1919 he joined Football League Division Two side Coventry City, making his Football League debut for the 'Sky Blues' against Leeds City in a 3-0 defeat, as cover for Fred Gibson. Alf went on to make another thirteen League and Cup appearances until leaving Highfield Road at the end of the season to join Birmingham and District League side Wellington Town. He spent two seasons with the Buck's Head club eventually returning to the Football League with Third Division North side Wrexham in May 1922. Alf made his debut for the Racecourse outfit in a 4-0 defeat at Grimsby on the opening day of the season, and went on to establish himself at outside-left for the rest of the season, making 36 League appearances and scoring five goals. However, he was allowed to return to Wellington Town at the end of the season, and later spent a couple of years with Redditch.

Season	League		F.A.Cup		Welsh Cup		Total	
	apps	gls	apps	gls	apps	gls	apps	gls
1922/23	36	5	3	0	1	0	40	5
	36	**5**	**3**	**0**	**1**	**0**	**40**	**5**

SHINTON, Robert Thomas 1976 - 1979

Position; *Forward*
D.O.B; *6th January, 1952*
Birthplace; *West Bromwich, West Midlands*
Height; *5ft 11in* ***Weight;*** *11st 0lbs*
Debut; v. *Portsmouth (h) 21st August, 1976*
Total Appearances & Goals; *175 apps 56 gls*
Career; *Lye Town; Walsall Mar 1972 78/1apps 20gls; Cambridge United 14th Mar 1974 £22,000 99apps 25gls; WREXHAM 10th Jul 1976 £15,000; Manchester City 11th Jul 1979 £300,000 5apps 0gls; Millwall 11th Feb 1980 5apps 3gls (Loan); Newcastle United 7th Mar 1980 £175,000 41/1apps 10gls; Millwall Feb 1982 29/5apps 4gls; Worcester City; Weymouth Mar 1985; Malvern Town 1986;*
Honours; *Third Division Championship Winner 1978; Welsh Cup Winner 1978; Welsh Cup runner-up 1979; P.F.A.Third Division XI 1978;*

Bobby Shinton was appearing for West Midlands non-league side Lye Town and working as a glazier when he was signed by Third Division Walsall in March 1972, at the relatively advanced age of 20. He went straight into the 'Saddlers' team for his Football League debut in a 4-0 home win over Swansea City, scoring one of the goals. He kept his place in the side, and quickly established himself as a regular for the next two seasons until March 1974, when he was bought by Cambridge United manager Ron Atkinson for £22,000. At the Abbey Stadium Bobby again impressed with his skilful wing play, spending just over two years with the club before signing for Wrexham manager John Neal in what proved to be a bargain £15,000 deal in the summer of 1976. He made his 'Robins' debut in a 2-0 home win over Portsmouth in the opening game of the 1976/77 season, and scored both his new sides goals. His initial season at the Racecourse was to see the 'Robins' in fifth place in the League, missing out on promotion despite having been in what had seemed an unassailable position with five matches remaining. This period in the club's history saw Wrexham - and Bobby - achieve many giant-killing cup feats, registering wins over a number of First Division opponents like Sunderland, Leicester City and Spurs. The sadness of missing out on promotion was soon forgotten as Wrexham powered their way to the Third Division Championship a year later, also winning the Welsh Cup. Bobby played a major role forming a superb understanding with midfield maestro Mel Sutton, as he mesmerised opposing defences with his silky skills and spectacular goals. He was described as 'a good honest grafter, whose curling banana shot beat many a keeper'. The Welsh team manager Mike Smith said of him, "He has lovely control and pace on the ball. He can do special things a lot of players can't do". 1977/78 also saw the 'Robins' achieve further giant-killing feats, accounting for First Division Bristol City (twice), and Newcastle United to reach the Quarter-Finals of both the F.A.Cup and League Cup. The following campaign found Bobby playing Second Division football, and he took part in European football for the first time against Rijeka of Yugoslavia, but at the end of the season he turned down a new contract at the Racecourse and accepted a move to First Division Manchester City. The move equalled the record fee received by the club of £300,000. However, he spent only a short time at Maine Road, during which he was

not used to his full potential, making his League debut in a scoreless draw at Arsenal... at left-back! He went on to add just four more League appearances for City before being loaned out to Millwall in February 1979, where he proved to be a hit during his month's stay, scoring on his debut in a 2-1 home defeat by Southend, and then twice more in four appearances. He was then snapped up by Second Division Newcastle United for a cut-price £175,000, and went straight into the first team in a scoreless draw at Cambridge. He turned out in the remaining nine matches of the season, scoring one goal, and continued at St.James' Park until February 1982 during what was a difficult period for the 'Magpies', but once again failed to produce the sort of form that had brought him stardom at the Racecourse. He was then signed by Millwall, and stayed at the Den until the end of the 1982/83 season, when he returned to live in Worcester and start his own double-glazing business. Bobby continued to play football for Worcester City, returning to the Racecourse to take part in a Welsh Cup tie against Wrexham in November 1983, on a night when Wrexham manager Bobby Roberts was forced to name himself in goal. He was later appointed player/manager at Worcester, before having short spells with both Weymouth and Malvern Town. In 1987 he scored the winning goal for Lodge Cottrill in the final of the FA Sunday Cup at St.Andrew's, Birmingham. He was appointed coach of Newmarket Town in September 1997, and in their opening League game he came on as sub and laid on the winning goal at the age of 45! Bobby still lives in the Worcester area, where he still runs his own Double Glazing business.

Season	League		F.A.Cup		Welsh Cup		League Cup		E.C.W.C.		Total	
	apps	gls	apps	gls	apps	gls	apps	gls	apps	gls	apps	gls
1976/77	46	15	6	4	4	3	4	0	-	-	60	22
1977/78	46	16	9	4	5	2	6	2	-	-	66	24
1978/79	36	6	3	2	5	1	3	1	2	0	49	10
	128	**37**	**18**	**10**	**14**	**6**	**13**	**3**	**2**	**0**	**175**	**56**

SHONAKAN, Joseph Francis 1933 - 1934

Position; *Outside-Right*
D.O.B; *29th November, 1913*
Birthplace; *Bolton, Lancashire*
Died; *Bolton, 24th November, 1973*
Height; *5ft 6in* ***Weight;*** *10st 7lbs*
Debut; v. *Hartlepool United (a) 9th September, 1933*
Total Appearances & Goals; *4 apps 0 gls*
Career; *Bolton Wanderers (Am) 22nd Aug 1930, (Pro) 29th Oct 1931 0apps; Rochdale 13th Oct 1932 27apps 2gls; WREXHAM 5th Jul 1933; Horwich RMI cs1934; Southport 20th Dec 1934 1app 0gls; Northwich Victoria (trial) Aug 1935; Chorley Jan 1935; CW Norris (Bolton) 10th Nov 1936;*

John Shonakan was a promising schoolboy footballer in his native Bolton, playing for Bolton Boys' Federation. He also captained the town's Schoolboy team at the age of 13. It was therefore no major surprise when he joined the Bolton Wanderers' staff as an amateur in August 1930, after appearing in the Boys' Realm Under-19 League. The following year John signed professional terms with the 'Trotters', in October, but then became troubled with a knee injury. This later required an operation,

which was performed on a kitchen table without any anaesthetic! He was to leave Burnden Park in October 1932 without having made a first team appearance. He then signed for Third Division North side Rochdale, where he made his Football League debut against Accrington Stanley in a 2-0 home win. At Spotland, Shonakan quickly established himself as a regular in the Rochdale team, making a further 26 League appearances and scoring two goals. However, at the end of the season he was allowed to sign for Wrexham, where he had to bide his time before making his 'Robins' debut. He became the fourth outside-right to be tried by the club in that position, when he played in a 4-1 defeat at Hartlepool in September 1933. Two more appearances followed before he found himself playing reserve team football. John was recalled to the first team in December, for a 3-2 home defeat by York City, but it was hardly a cause for celebration as he broke his leg! He was released by Wrexham at the end of 1933/34, and joined Lancashire Combination League side Horwich RMI in the summer. In December he was invited for a month's trial with Third Division North side Southport, where he made one first team appearance, ironically at home against Wrexham, in a 2-1 win for the Haig Avenue club. John was released at the end of his trial period, and joined Chorley, later playing for a works team in Bolton, CW Norris. He became employed as a lorry driver for a timber merchant, and later worked at a paper mill before passing away in 1973, five days before his 60th birthday, after having contracted bronchitis and pneumonia. Apparently, John's unusual name was a misinterpretation of 'Shanahan' by an immigration official when his father originally arrived from Ireland!.

Season	League		F.A.Cup		Welsh Cup		Total	
	apps	gls	apps	gls	apps	gls	apps	gls
1933/34	4	0	-	-	-	-	4	0
	4	**0**	**-**	**-**	**-**	**-**	**4**	**0**

SHOWELL, George William 1966 - 1968

Position; *Full-Back*
D.O.B; *9th February, 1934*
Birthplace; *Bilston, West Midlands*
Height; *5ft 11'1/2in* ***Weight;*** *12st 7lbs*
Debut; v. *Stockport County (a) 2nd December, 1966*
Total Appearances & Goals; *54 apps 1 gls*
Career; *Wolves Aug 1951 200apps 3gls; Bristol City May 1965 9/2apps 0gls; WREXHAM 12th Nov 1966;*
Honours; *F.A.Cup Winner 1960; Welsh Cup runner-up 1967;*

George Showell played schoolboy football and represented South East Staffordshire Schoolboys before signing for his favourite team, Wolves, on amateur forms as a 15 year-old in July 1949. He took up work as a fitter at a local engineering factory at this time, before signing professional terms in August 1951. George had to wait four years before he actually made his first team debut for the Molyneux club, a 1-1 home draw with Preston North End in March 1955, and played well enough to retain his place in the side for the final seven matches of the season. During his time with the team in 'Old Gold' George enjoyed tours of South Africa, Russia, USA, Spain, and the West Indies, though he was mainly understudy to Eddie Stuart, and it was not until around the 1959/60 period that he began to command a regular first team spot. At the end of that season he played in the F.A.Cup Final against Blackburn Rovers, which Wolves won 3-0. George also competed in Europe with Wolves against Vorwaerts of East Germany, Red Star Belgrade, Barcelona, F.K.Austria and Rangers. Injuries took their toll in the early 60s, but it was a change of manager that signalled the end of his playing career at Molyneux. He made his final appearance in a 2-0 defeat at Fulham in October 1964, having played in over 200 games for the club that he had supported as a boy. He had been a loyal servant throughout his time at Molyneux and also proved to be a versatile performer by playing in either full-back position, centre-half and also at centre-forward. In the summer of 1965 he was given a free transfer in recognition of his service to the club, and joined Bristol City, where he got off to a frustrating start as he was injured in a pre-season friendly. By the time that he had regained his fitness he struggled to win a place in the side, though he wrote himself into Bristol City's record books when he did finally make his debut. It came at Manchester City, and Showell became the club's first ever substitute in a Football League match, replacing John Atyeo. He managed just ten more League appearances that season, while 1966/67 began with another struggle to establish himself. When the opportunity came to join Wrexham in November 1966 he jumped at it, though his debut was delayed by a thigh strain. He eventually got his chance at Stockport County in December, playing at left-back in a 1-0 defeat. He clocked up a further fifteen league appearances that season, adding 32 in the next term. During his time as a player at the Racecourse he was described as a 'shrewd reader of the game which is a great asset, as also is his one hundred per cent loyalty to the club. A tower in defence.' At the end of the 1967/68 season George decided to end his playing career due to his persistent knee problem. Manager Alvan Williams invited him on to the coaching staff, though by September Williams had left the club and John Neal was appointed as the new manager. George was then appointed trainer, and played a big part in helping the 'Robins' to win promotion in 1970. As well as coaching he later took over the physio's role, and his time with Wrexham coincided with the club's greatest era in the 1970s. He went on to spend almost 25 years at the Racecourse, including managing the club on a caretaker basis between the departure of Bobby Roberts and the arrival of Dixie McNeil. However, he was forced to leave the club in 1990 under the Football League's new mandate for physiotherapists, as he did not have the adequate qualifications! He then took up work at the local Maelor Hospital as a porter, and also joined Wrexham Rugby Club as their match day physio. In 1991 he was awarded a testimonial by Wrexham, and they played his beloved former club Wolves, in which George turned out for part of the game. He is now very much settled in the Wrexham area.

Season	League		F.A.Cup		Welsh Cup		League Cup		Total	
	apps	gls	apps	gls	apps	gls	apps	gls	apps	gls
1966/67	16	0	1	0	3	0	-	-	20	0
1967/68	32	1	-	-	1	0	1	0	34	1
	48	**1**	**1**	**0**	**4**	**0**	**1**	**0**	**54**	**1**

SIMPKINS, Kenneth 1962 - 1964

Position; *Goalkeeper*
D.O.B; *21st December, 1943*
Birthplace; *Wrexham*
Height; *5ft 11in* ***Weight;*** *14st 6lbs*
Debut; v. *Port Vale (a) 15th December, 1962*
Total Appearances & Goals; *5 apps 0 gls*
Career; *WREXHAM 12th May 1962; Runcorn Apr 1962 (Loan); Hartlepool United 4th March 1964 121apps 1gls; Boston United cs1968;*
Honours; *One Welsh Under-23 International cap; Welsh Youth Cup Winner 1960 & 1962;*

A native of Wrexham Ken Simpkins attended the Victoria School in the town, from where he was chosen to represent Wrexham Schoolboys for three successive years as a centre-forward. It was after playing for them that he was invited to join the Racecourse staff as a junior in 1958. Soon after his arrival at the club Ken's football career took a sudden change in direction, in a first XI against second XI match. Regular goalkeeper Roly Ugolini broke his collar bone, and Ken took over in goal, remaining in the custodian position for the rest of his playing days. He picked up two Welsh Youth Cup winners' medals from the 1960 and 1962 Finals, before accepting a month on loan with Cheshire County League side Runcorn in April 1962. On his return to Wrexham in May he signed professional forms. The following season saw Ken become understudy to Kevin

Keelan, and his first team chance came in December at Port Vale, in a 2-2 draw. He played in the following match at Shrewsbury, a 4-2 defeat, and then returned to the reserves as Keelan regained his fitness. Ken's biggest moment of his time with the 'Robins' came a few weeks later, when he again stepped in for Keelan to play in an F.A.Cup Third Round match on the Racecourse against Liverpool, in front of a crowd of 30,826, which Wrexham lost 3-0. The start of the 1963/64 season saw Keelan transferred to Norwich, and Ken played in the opening two matches, at Peterborough and Bristol Rovers, but proved to be his last games for the club as Alan Jones then took over following his arrival from Norwich as part of the Keelan deal. Both Steve Fleet and Albert Dunlop later dominated the 'keepers position, and in March 1964 Simpkins, who was then playing regularly in the reserve side in the Cheshire County League, decided to take up an opportunity to join Hartlepool United for a 'small' fee. He went on to make 121 League appearances at the Victoria Ground,scoring one goal! That came about after he had been asked to step down for a reserve team game to allow a trialist to play in goal. Ken was named as a substitute, and when an outfield player was injured he went on and scored two goals! He played a few more reserve games at centre-forward, and not long after was selected to play for the first team, when he scored! In fact, he made five appearances for Hartlepool as an outfield player. Most of his matches with Hartlepool were played under Brian Clough, who had just started out on his managerial career. During this time Ken was selected for the Welsh under-23 side in 1966 against Scotland at Wrexham. After helping the North-East club to promotion in 1968 Simpkins was given a free transfer. He left League football and joined non-league side Boston United, playing part-time until his career was to end prematurely due to a bad knee injury. With his professional football career at an end Ken took up employment at a nuclear power station, before working as a factory supervisor. He still resides in his adopted Hartlepool, and attended Wrexham Football Club's 'Grand Gala Players Reunion' at the St.David's Hotel in Ewloe in September 1998, travelling down from the North-East with former 'Racecourse Robins' Alan Fox and Peter Thompson.

Season	League apps	League gls	F.A.Cup apps	F.A.Cup gls	Welsh Cup apps	Welsh Cup gls	League Cup apps	League Cup gls	Total apps	Total gls
1962/63	2	0	1	0	-	-	-	-	3	0
1963/64	2	0	-	-	-	-	-	-	2	0
	4	**0**	**1**	**0**	-	-	-	-	**5**	**0**

SIMPSON, Robert Henry 1919 - 1922

Position; *Right-Back*
D.O.B; *A/M/J, 1889*
Birthplace; *Redcar, Cleveland*
Height*; 5ft 6'1/2in* ***Weight;*** *11st 4lbs*
Debut v. *Stoke City Reserves (a) 1st November, 1919*
League Debut; v. *Hartlepool United (h) 27th August, 1921*
Total Appearances & Goals; *104 apps 0 gls*
Career; *Redcar Juniors; Old Corinthians; Teeside Amateurs; South Bank; Grangetown Athletics' Club; Blackburn Rovers (Trial); Bradford City (Trial); Everton Aug 1912 21apps 0gls; WREXHAM 23rd Oct 1919; Chester cs1922 to cs1924;*
Honours; *Welsh Cup Winner 1921; Welsh Cup runner-up 1920;*

Bobby Simpson had played football as a schoolboy on Teeside for Coatham Grammar School, going on to appear for local sides, Redcar Juniors, Old Corinthians, Teeside Amateurs, South Bank, and Grangetown Athletics' Club. It was during his time with these clubs that he was invited for trials with both Blackburn Rovers and Bradford City, before joining Everton in August 1912. He made his Football League debut for the Goodison Park club in October 1912, turning out at right-back in a 6-0 home defeat by Newcastle United. Bobby went on to make a further twenty League appearances for the 'Toffees', playing in either full-back berth before World War One was to suspend all Football League fixtures in 1915. He ended his final Football League season with Everton on a high note, as they completed 1914/15 as Football League Champions, with Bobby figuring in nine games that season. A description at this time had him as a 'one-time schoolmaster'. During WW1 he made sixteen appearances for Everton in the Lancashire Section Principal Tournament games. However, following the end of the Great War Bobby was to leave the Goodison Park club in October 1919 to join Birmingham & District League side Wrexham. The 'fearless full-back' made his debut in a 2-1 win at Stoke Reserves in November 1919, and went on to collect a Welsh Cup runners'-up medal at the end of the season, as Wrexham lost 2-1 to Cardiff City in the Final. The following season would see Bobby and Wrexham go one better, beating Pontypridd in the Final after a replay, by which time the 'Robins' had been selected as founder members of the Football League Division Three North. The 1921/22 season saw Bobby turn out against Hartlepools United in the club's inaugural Football League match on the Racecourse. He then earned the unwanted 'distinction' of becoming the first ever Wrexham player to be sent-off in a Football League match against Southport. Known to many fans as the 'Little Bull' because of his tenacious play, he played a total 24 League games that season before leaving the club in the summer of 1922. He joined Cheshire County League side Chester for two seasons making 63 League appearances before leaving Sealand Road in the summer of 1924. Bobby later held an important position on the staff of the Cunard Ship Company in Liverpool.

Season	League apps	League gls	F.A.Cup apps	F.A.Cup gls	Welsh Cup apps	Welsh Cup gls	Total apps	Total gls
1919/20	28	0	2	0	5	0	35	0
1920/21	32	0	4	0	5	0	41	0
1921/22*	24	0	3	0	1	0	28	0
	84	**0**	**9**	**0**	**11**	**0**	**104**	**0**

* Full Football League Record only.

SINCLAIR, Ronald McDonald 1984

Position; *Goalkeeper*
D.O.B; *19th November, 1964*
Birthplace; *Stirling, Central Scotland.*
Height; *5ft 10in* ***Weight;*** *11st 9lbs*
Debut; v. *Hereford United (a) 21st March, 1984 (Welsh Cup)*
Total Appearances & Goals; *16 apps 0 gls*
Career; *Nottingham Forest 30th Oct 1982 0apps; WREXHAM 1st Mar 1984 (Loan); Derby County 10th Nov 1984 (Loan) 0apps; Sheffield United 28th August 1985 0apps (Loan); Leeds United 29th March 1996 (Loan), 27th Jun 1986 £10,000 8apps 0gls; Halifax Town 1st Mar 1987 4apps 0gls (Loan); Halifax Town 23rd Dec 1988 10apps 0gls (Loan); Bristol City 1st Sept 1989 44apps 0gls; Walsall 5th Sept 1991 10apps 0gls (Loan); Stoke City 21st Nov 1991 £25,000 78apps 0gls; Bradford City 26th Aug 1994 0apps (Loan); Chester City 12th Aug 1996 70apps 0gls;*
Honours; *Second Division Championship Winner 1993; Scottish Youth International cap; Scottish Schoolboy cap;*

Ron Sinclair initially joined Wrexham on a month's loan from Nottingham Forest, an arrangement which was later extended until the end of the 1983/84 season. He made his debut in a Welsh Cup semi-final second leg match against Hereford United on the Racecourse, which the 'Robins' won 1-0 (losing 3-1 on aggregate). His Football League debut for North Wales club came on the following Saturday, in a 2-1 home defeat against Stockport County. He remained in the Wrexham team for the rest of the season, playing in the club's final match of the campaign against Tranmere Rovers, the 'Robins' winning 5-1 on the Racecourse and avoiding re-election. Only five feet ten inches, Ron compensated for his lack of height with his excellent positional play. He returned to Nottingham Forest after that match where he continued to play reserve team football, failing to make a first team breakthrough, although he did enjoy further loan spells with both Sheffield United and Derby County before joining Second Division Leeds United in June 1986. A Scottish Schoolboy and Youth international Ron spent three years at Elland Road, during which he recorded just eight League appearances. He had two more loan spells, both with Halifax Town, before joining Bristol City in September 1989. In just over two seasons at Ashton Gate Ron completed 44 League appearances before accepting a loan move to Walsall in September 1991. His debut for the 'Saddlers' came in a 3-0 home win over Halifax Town, and he remained with them for the maximum three months, during which he made ten League appearances. In November 1991 Stoke City stepped in to sign him for £25,000, and he took over from Jason Kearton at the Victoria Ground. Sinclair made his League debut in a 3-0 home win over Torquay United, and went on to miss just four League games throughout the remainder of that season, helping Stoke to reach the play-offs where they lost to Stockport County. Disappointingly, he missed out on Potteries club's trip to Wembley in the Autoglass Trophy because he was cup-tied. Ron made 29 League appearances in 1992/93 before being injured at Bournemouth. It was to prove to be a setback that would keep him out of action for over twelve months, and was forced to watch from the sidelines as Stoke went on to clinch the Second Division championship in 1993. Ron missed all of the 1993/94 season because of his serious knee injury, but the start of 1994/95 saw him loaned out to Bradford City. He left the 'Bantams' without making a first team appearance and returned to Stoke. He regained his first team place in December 1994, and kept it until the following season when he was replaced by Carl Muggleton, and then Mark Prudhoe. In the summer of 1996 Sinclair took up an offer of first team football with Chester City, and he made his debut in a 2-1 defeat at Brighton in the opening game of the season. He was established in the first team at the Deva Stadium until an injury forced him to miss most of the 1997/98 campaign. Ron was released by Chester in the close season of 1998, and accepted an invitation to join the coaching staff at Stoke City as goalkeeping coach.

Season	League		F.A.Cup		Welsh Cup		League Cup		A.M.C.		Total	
	apps	gls	apps	gls	apps	gls	apps	gls	apps	gls	apps	gls
1983/84	11	0	-	-	4	0	-	-	1	0	16	0
	11	**0**	**-**	**-**	**4**	**0**	**-**	**-**	**1**	**0**	**16**	**0**

***SKINNER,* Craig Richard** 1995 - 1999

Position; *Right-Winger/Midfield*
D.O.B; *21st October, 1970*
Birthplace; *Heywood, Lancashire*
Height; *5ft 9in* ***Weight;*** *11st 6lbs*
Debut; v. *Notts County (h) 12th August 1995*
Total Appearances & Goals; *88/25 apps 11 gls*
Career; *Blackburn Rovers 13th Jun 1989 11/5apps 0gls; Plymouth Argyle 21st Aug 1992 (exchange deal) 42/11apps 3gls; WREXHAM 10th Jul 1995 £50,000; York City 25th Mar 1999 £20,000 3/2apps 0gls*

Mancunian Craig Skinner was sufficiently talented as a youngster to earn selection for Greater Manchester Schoolboys, and after one match appearing for his County at Under-14 level he was approached by Blackburn Rovers scout Ted Taylor. He was invited for a trial at Ewood Park, whereupon he quickly completed schoolboy forms. After leaving school at 16 Craig was offered an apprenticeship with the Ewood Park club, and progressed to earn a professional contract in June 1989. It was a year before he made his Football League debut, when he substituted Jason Wilcox in a 1-0 home defeat against Bristol City. Regular first team football came when manager Don Mackay departed, and Tony Parkes was put in temporary charge, but following Kenny Dalglish's appointment as the new manager Craig suffered an injury. At the end of the 1991/92 season he was offered a new contract, but the lure of first team football persuaded him to leave. Blackburn arranged a swap deal with Plymouth Argyle, with Nicky Marker joining the Ewood Park club, and Craig and Keith Hill moving in the opposite direction. However, Craig found it difficult to settle in Devon, spending most of his first year on the sidelines with an ankle injury. His second year at Home Park ended with Argyle narrowly missing out on promotion, as they were beaten in the play-off's. The

'Pilgrims' began 1994/95 as Championship favourites, but they surprisingly struggled and eventually suffered the indignity of relegation. In March 1995 Wrexham manager Brian Flynn attempted to sign Craig on loan, and though Plymouth declined that approach, he did finally make the move in the summer for a £50,000 fee. Skinner hardly got off to the best of starts with the 'Robins', as he suffered with glandular fever whilst on a pre-season tour in the Isle of Man, but recovered in time to make his debut in the opening match of the season at home to Notts County. He struggled at first to reproduce the kind of form that had persuaded Flynn to sign him, but by the end of October he was fast improving and soon began to win over the Wrexham crowd with some dazzling runs down the right flank. However, this kind of form was not sustained, and over the next two years he struggled to command a regular first team place, hampered by niggling injuries and inconsistent form. He was at his best running at defenders, although he was always keen to help out with defensive duties. Craig has been described as 'similar in style to former 'Robins' favourite Brian Tinnion although not as quick, an industrious wide midfield player who drops back to help out with defensive cover with a penchant to go on mazy runs'. In March 1999 he signed for York City in a £20,000 deal, but he couldn't prevent the 'Minstermen' from avoiding the drop to the third division.

Season	League		F.A.Cup		League Cup		A.G.T.		W.I.C.		Total	
	apps	gls	apps	gls	apps	gls	apps	gls	apps	gls	apps	gls
1995/96	21/2	3	3	0	1	0	3	0	-	-	28/2	3
1996/97	21/6	4	3/1	0	0/1	1	-	-	-	-	25/8	5
1997/98	16/9	1	2	0	2	0	0/1	0	1/2	0	21/1	1
1998/99	12	2	-	-	0/2	0	-	-	2/1	0	14/3	2
	70/17	**9**	**8/1**	**0**	**3/3**	**1**	**3/1**	**0**	**3/3**	**0**	**88/25**	**11**

***SKIPPER,* Peter Dennis** 1991

Position; *Central Defender*
D.O.B; *11th April, 1958*
Birthplace; *Hull, Humberside*
Height; *5ft 11in* ***Weight;*** *12st 5lbs*
Debut; v. *Mansfield Town (a) 3rd September, 1991*
Total Appearances & Goals; *2 apps 0 gls*
Career; *Schultz Y.C; Hull City Feb 1978 22/1apps 2gls; Scunthorpe United 1st Feb 1980 0/1apps 0gls (Loan); Darlington May 1980 91apps 4gls; Hull City Aug 1982 £10,000 264/1apps 17gls; Oldham Athletic 14th Oct 1988 £35,000 27apps 1gls; Walsall 10th Jul 1989 £35,000 81apps 2gls; WREXHAM 30th Aug 1991; Wigan Athletic 30th Oct 1991 15/3apps 0gls; Stafford Rangers cs1992 5apps 0gls; Wigan Athletic Oct 1992 73apps 4gls;*
Honours; *Fourth Division runner-up 1983;*

Peter Skipper began playing football at school in his home town of Hull, where he also represented Hull Schoolboys. It was whilst playing for Schultz Youth Club that he came to Hull City's attention, and was offered a trial in September 1978 which led to him accepting professional terms with the 'Tigers' in February 1979 at the age of 20. He made his Football League debut for Hull in March 1979, a 5-3 away defeat at Swansea City. Peter went on to complete a further seventeen League matches before the end of that season, scoring two goals. However, he struggled to command a regular first team place the following season, and in February 1980 joined Scunthorpe United on a month's loan, though he only made one substitute appearance at the Old Show Ground. He was eventually allowed to leave Boothferry Park and join Darlington, where he spent just over two years - missing just one league game. In August 1982 Skipper rejoined Hull for a £10,000 fee, which was funded partly by Hull's supporters. He was to repay that many times over in his second spell with the 'Tigers', as his consistent form was a major factor in their rise from the Fourth to the Second Division, and entirely appropriate that this great-hearted defender's header at Walsall in May 1985 should prove to be the goal that clinched promotion to the Second Division. Peter enjoyed a run of 149 consecutive League appearances for Hull, becoming an indispensable part of the 'Tigers' rearguard before losing his place at the beginning of the 1988/89 season to new signing Steve Terry. In October 1988 he was sold to Oldham Athletic, making 27 League appearances in a short spell at Boundary Park, ending in July 1989 with a move to Walsall. His first season with the 'Saddlers' saw them suffer relegation to the Fourth Division, though he was described as a 'strong defender, who enjoyed a battle. He was always totally committed and ever reliable' during his time at Fellows Park. At the end of 1990/91 Peter was released by Walsall at the age of 34. He accepted Wrexham's offer of non-contract terms in September 1991, with a view to a full-time contract. He made his 'Robins' debut at Mansfield Town in a 3-0 defeat, which was followed by an away match at Doncaster, also ending in defeat, 3-1. Skipper received a knee injury in that game and was substituted by Karl Connolly. That proved to be his final game for the club, and the following month joined Wigan Athletic. He had to wait until February to make his debut for Wigan, when he came on as a substitute in a 1-0 home win over Stoke City, and went on to make a further seventeen League appearances for the Springfield Park club before being released in the summer. He joined Conference League side Stafford Rangers for 1992/93, but returned to Springfield Park after five games, thereafter, missing just one League game until the end of the 1993/94 season. He also helped the club to reach the Northern area Final of the Autoglass Trophy, where they were beaten by Stockport County. Peter left Wigan at the end of that campaign.

Season	League		F.A.Cup		Welsh Cup		League Cup		F.R.T.		Total	
	apps	gls	apps	gls	apps	gls	apps	gls	apps	gls	apps	gls
1991/92	2	0	-	-	-	-	-	-	-	-	2	0
	2	**0**	-	-	-	-	-	-	-	-	**2**	**0**

SLATER, James Jonathan

1987 - 1988

Position; *Forward*
D.O.B; *27th October, 1968*
Birthplace; *Wrexham, Denbighshire*
Height; *5ft 10in* **Weight;** *11st 5lbs*
Debut; v. *Leyton Orient (h) 3rd October, 1987*
Total Appearances & Goals; *1/6 apps 1 gls*
Career; *WREXHAM Jun 1987; Lex XI cs1988; Cefn Druids Mar 1998;*
Honours; *Welsh Youth International; Welsh Schoolboy International; Cymru Alliance League Championship Winner 1999; North East Wales Cup Winner 1999;*

It was no surprise that Jamie Slater signed for Wrexham. His father, Reg Slater, was the Club's Commercial Manager, having worked for the club in that capacity for a number of years. Jamie did have an offer to join Everton, but signed for the Racecourse club straight from St.David's School, having been on schoolboy forms with the club since October 1983. During this time he had earned selection for Wrexham & District, Clwyd and North Wales Schoolboys, as well as an international call-up for Wales at this level. He quickly made a name for himself at the Racecourse as a striker, progressing to sign professional forms in June 1987, having earned further international honours for Wales at Youth level. However, Jamie was to struggle to break into the senior side at the Racecourse because of the consistent form of Kevin Russell, and the experienced Steve Massey and Ollie Kearns were also ahead of him in the queue. He finally made his Football League debut in a home game against Leyton Orient in October 1987, when he substituted Russell in a 2-2 draw. Only one of Jamie's seven first team appearances for the 'Robins' was as a starter. It came in a 3-2 defeat against Cardiff City in a Sherpa Van Trophy match. Jamie recorded just one goal in his seven appearances, in a 3-0 Welsh Cup home win over Ruthin Town. At the end of 1987/88 he was released by the club, and dropped into local football in the Wrexham area with Lex XI. He spent a number of seasons with them before turning out for Cefn Druids with whom he helped to clinch the Cymru Alliance league championship in 1998/99 and earn the club a place in the League of Wales. Jamie still lives in the Wrexham area, where he is employed as a computer analyst at the Glan Clwyd Hospital.

Season	League		F.A.Cup		Welsh Cup		League Cup		S.V.T.		Total	
	apps	gls	apps	gls	apps	gls	apps	gls	apps	gls	apps	gls
1987/88	0/3	0	0/2	0	0/1	1	-	-	1	0	1/6	1
	0/3	**0**	**0/2**	**0**	**0/1**	**1**	-	-	**1**	**0**	**1/6**	**1**

SMALLMAN, David Paul

1971 - 1975

Position; *Forward*
D.O.B; *22nd March, 1953*
Birthplace; *Connah's Quay, Flintshire*
Height; *5ft 8in* **Weight;** *10st 4lbs*
Debut; v. *Middlesborough (a) 5th September, 1972 (League Cup)*
Total Appearances & Goals; *122/3 apps 51 gls*
Career; *Shotton Westminster; WREXHAM May 1971; Everton 12th Mar 1975 £75,000 19/2apps 5gls; WREXHAM 1st Aug 1980 0apps; Oswestry Town Jan 1981; Bangor City Aug 1981; Green Gully Ajax (Australia) 1982-1988; Newtown Sept 1988; Colwyn Bay; Hawarden Rangers Nov 1988;*
Honours; *7 Welsh International caps; 5 Welsh Under-23 International caps; 1 Welsh Youth International cap; Welsh Youth Cup Winner 1971;*

David Smallman had represented Deeside Schools as a boy and was playing for his local youth side, Shotton Westminster, when spotted by Wrexham. Commencing his apprenticeship at the Racecourse in 1969 he progressed to gain international recognition with the Welsh Youth side, and earned a Welsh Youth Cup winners' medal with the 'Robins' as they beat Cardiff City 4-3 in the 1971 Final at Knighton. In May of the same year Dave signed professional terms with Wrexham, although he had to wait until September 1972 before making his first team debut, as a substitute for Billy Ashcroft in a League Cup match at Middlesbrough. Just over a month later Dave was appearing in European football for

Wrexham, when he played and scored in the 3-1 Second Round first leg home win over Hajduk Split. He then went on to establish himself in the first team forward line, playing alongside either Billy Ashcroft or Geoff Davies. He was a skilful forward, with a good eye for a scoring opportunity, and this showed in his most memorable season for the 'Robins' - 1973/74 - when his goals helped Wrexham to reach the Quarter-Finals of the F.A.Cup for the first time in the Club's history. His winning goals against Crystal Palace, Middlesbrough, and Southampton, will forever be remembered by the Wrexham fans who witnessed them, but they also led to interest from the bigger clubs, who began to track this emerging talent. His full international debut for Wales came in May 1974, when he took the Ninian Park field as a substitute against England. 1974/75 ended with Smallman as the Racecourse clubs top scorer; he bagged a total of 17 goals, all of them coming before March, when he was to play his last match for the Racecourse club in a 4-0 home win over Aldershot. He signed off in style with a hat-trick! Everton then stepped in to pay a record fee received by Wrexham at that time of £75,000. A debut for the 'Toffee's' quickly followed in April in a 2-1 defeat at Luton Town, but his move to Goodison was to prove to be a nightmare. In his five years on Merseyside Dave managed just 21 League appearances, as he had the misfortune of twice breaking his leg. Those injuries were to ruin a promising career, as he was just beginning to establish himself in the Welsh international squad, having made seven appearances for his country. In September 1980 he tried to resurrect his playing career with Wrexham, playing in a number of reserve team games, but couldn't recapture the kind of form that everyone knew he could produce. In January 1981 he joined Oswestry Town until the end of the season, moving to Bangor City in the summer for a year. In 1982 Dave and his family emigrated to Australia where they were to live for six years, during which time he continued to play football for Green Gully Ajax, as well as obtaining employment at a chemical plant in Melbourne. Upon his return to the UK in 1988 he joined Newtown, and later played for both Colwyn Bay and Hawarden Rangers, later taking up coaching around his Deeside home. Today, Dave has settled in the Wrexham area, keeping active during the summer period playing cricket for his beloved Shotton XI.

Season	League		F.A.Cup		Welsh Cup		League Cup		E.C.W.C.		Total	
	apps	gls	apps	gls	apps	gls	apps	gls	apps	gls	apps	gls
1972/73	32/1	11	3	3	1	0	0/1	0	1/1	1	37/3	15
1973/74	35	10	7	4	3	1	2	1	-	-	47	16
1974/75	33	17	1	0	3	2	1	1	-	-	38	20
	100/1	**38**	**11**	**7**	**7**	**3**	**3/1**	**2**	**1/1**	**1**	**122/3**	**51**

SMALLWOOD, Fred

1933 - 1934

Position; *Outside-Left*
D.O.B; *16th September, 1910*
Birthplace; *Brynteg, Nr Wrexham, Denbighshire*
Height; *5ft 6in* ***Weight;*** *10st 3lbs*
Debut; v. *New Brighton (h) 14th April, 1934*
Total Appearances & Goals; *8 apps 1 gls*
Career; *Llanerch Celts; WREXHAM (Am) Sept 1933; Chester (Am) Sept 1934, (Pro) Oct 1934 1app 0gls; Macclesfield Town Jun 1935; Southampton Jun 1936 48apps 10gls; Reading Jun 1938 £500; Wrexham (WW2 Guest) Mar 1940 7apps 1gls; Newcastle United (WW2 Guest) Mar 1943 2apps 0gls; Sunderland (WW2 Guest) Jan 1942 18apps 8gls; Hartlepool United (WW2 Guest) 1943/44 12apps 4gls;*
Honours; *Welsh Amateur International;*

Fred Smallwood was a coal miner at Gresford Colliery, near Wrexham, and was playing amateur football for Llanerch Celts when he was signed by Wrexham as an amateur in September 1933. His first match for the Racecourse club came in a reserve team game, a 5-0 Welsh League win over Colwyn Bay. He gained international recognition during 1933/34 season, when he was capped at amateur level for Wales against Scotland. Even so, his first team debut for the 'Robins' didn't materialise until April 1934, when he played in a 5-4 victory over New Brighton on the Racecourse, and celebrated by scoring one of the goals. This proved to be his one and only Football League outing for Wrexham, as he was allowed to leave the Racecourse and join Chester when still an amateur in September 1934. Fred accepted professional terms at Sealand Road a month later, making his debut for the Cheshire club on New Year's Day 1935 in a 1-1 home draw with Tranmere Rovers. Once again, that game proved to be his one and only first team appearance, as he was to join Macclesfield Town at the end of 1934/35. It was his goalscoring exploits with the 'Silkmen' that soon attracted the attention of Football League clubs, and Third Division South side Southampton who eventually signed him in July 1936. Smallwood was plunged straight into the 'Saints' first team at outside-left for the opening match of the season, a 3-2 home win over Chesterfield in which he scored. He missed only two matches that season, scoring ten goals. However, during a pre-season practice match he sustained a bad injury, despite the fact that he always carried a rabbit's foot in his shorts for luck! When fit again he was unable to win back his first team place, although he did add a further eight League appearances for the 'Saints' before leaving the Dell to join Reading for a £500 transfer fee in June 1938. Fred spent one season with the 'Royals' before the Second World War began. During the conflict he made 36 appearances, and scored 13 goals for the Berkshire club, which continued until 1942/43. During this period he also appeared as a 'guest' for a number of other clubs that included Wrexham, Newcastle United, Sunderland, and Hartlepool. Fred Smallwood retired from playing professional football during WW2. He was regarded as a joker by reputation, and also a good musician, playing in a small dance band in the Sunderland area where he had settled after the War. Noted as a small but sprightly flanker who had pace to get behind opponents.

Season	League		F.A.Cup		Welsh Cup		N.S.C.		Total	
	apps	gls	apps	gls	apps	gls	apps	gls	apps	gls
1933/34*	1	1	-	-	-	-	-	-	1	1
1939/40	2	0	-	-	-	-	-	-	2	0
1940/41	4	0	-	-	-	-	-	-	4	0
1941/42	1	0	-	-	-	-	-	-	1	0
	8	**1**	**-**	**-**	**-**	**-**	**-**	**-**	**8**	**1**

* = Football League record only.

SMITH, Alexander Mason Oran

1937 - 1938

Position; *Right-Half*
D.O.B; *1915*
Birthplace; *Forfar*
Height; *5ft 8'1/2in* ***Weight;*** *11st 7lbs*
Debut; v. *Lincoln City (h) 1st September, 1937*
Total Appearances & Goals; *7 apps 0 gls*
Career; *Hall's Russell FC; Forfar Athletic; Forfar East End; WREXHAM 5th Jun 1937; Forfar Athletic Jul 1938;*

Alex 'Zander' Smith played his early football in Scotland for Hall's Russell FC, from where he signed for Forfar Athletic, followed by a spell with neighbours Forfar East End. It was whilst he was playing for them that he was recommended to Wrexham manager Captain James Logan, who had previously managed Raith Rovers and had plenty of contacts in Scotland. 'Zander', as he was popularly known, signed for the 'Sugarbags', a name given to Wrexham at the time because of their blue shirts with a white hoop around the chest area, in June 1937. He made his Football League debut at right-half in the second match of 1937/38, a 1-0 home win over Lincoln City. 'Zander' was one of five changes from the opening game line-up. He kept his place for the following five League games and a Northern Section Cup match at New Brighton, though this proved to be his swan song in the first team as he was replaced in the side by James Raven. He then played reserve team football for the 'Robins' until the end of the season, when he left the North Wales club and returned to his native Scotland to join Forfar Athletic in July 1938. Alex remained with them until the outbreak of World War Two.

Season	League		F.A.Cup		Welsh Cup		N.S.C.		Total	
	apps	gls	apps	gls	apps	gls	apps	gls	apps	gls
1937/38	6	0	-	-	-	-	1	0	7	0
	6	**0**	**-**	**-**	**-**	**-**	**1**	**0**	**7**	**0**

SMITH, Arthur Harold

1927 - 1928

Position; *Goalkeeper*
D.O.B;
Birthplace; *Marchwiel, Denbighshire*
Height; *ft in* ***Weight;*** *st lbs*
Debut; v. *Southport (h) 27th December 1927*
Total Appearances & Goals; *5 apps 0 gls*
Career; *WREXHAM (Am) Aug 1927, (Pro) Nov 1927;*

Arthur Smith was the brother of Wrexham centre-forward Cecil Smith, who was already on the staff at the Racecourse when Arthur joined the 'Robins' on amateur forms in August 1927. He accepted professional terms in November 1927, and, almost immediately, made his Football League debut in place of regular `keeper Ted Robson in a 3-0 home win over Southport. Brother Cecil, made it a family occasion by scoring one of the goals. Smith also played in the following match on the Racecourse, a 2-1 defeat against Chesterfield, but missed the next game at Bradford due to Robson's return. However, he was back in goal again for a 2-1 F.A.Cup Third Round home win over Swansea Town. He also appeared in a 2-0 victory over Tranmere Rovers on the Racecourse, before making his final appearance for the 'Robins' in what was regarded as the 'biggest' match in the club's history at that time, an F.A.Cup Fourth Round tie against First Division Birmingham, which Wrexham unfortunately lost 3-1. Arthur was to leave the Racecourse club at the end of the season.

Season	League		F.A.Cup		Welsh Cup		Total	
	apps	gls	apps	gls	apps	gls	apps	gls
1927/28	3	0	2	0	-	-	5	0
	3	**0**	**2**	**0**	**-**	**-**	**5**	**0**

SMITH, Frederick Cecil

1926 - 1928

Position; *Centre-Forward*
D.O.B; *30th October, 1904*
Birthplace; *Marchwiel, Denbighshire*
Died; *Burnley, J/F/M 1977*
Height; *5ft 10in* ***Weight;*** *12st 5lbs*
Debut; v. *Doncaster Rovers (a) 19th February, 1927*
Total Appearances & Goals; *51 apps 29 gls*
Career; *Marchwiel FC; Oswestry Town cs1924; Welshpool; WREXHAM (Am) Oct 1925, (Pro) Feb 1927; Wigan Borough Jul 1928 38apps 22gls; Bournemouth 1929 2apps 0gls; Notts County Mar 1930 0apps; Macclesfield Town Aug 1930; Stalybridge Celtic Jul 1931; Burnley Jun 1932 106apps 49gls; Cardiff City 1st May 1936 16apps 7gls; Stalybridge Celtic Jun 1937; Rhyl 4th Feb 1938; Bangor City cs1939;*

Cecil Smith first played football for local side Marchwiel. He signed for Oswestry Town in the summer of 1924 before joining Welshpool, where he worked as a railway booking clerk. It was from Welshpool that Cecil joined Wrexham, initially on trial, and was still a trialist when making his Football League debut for the 'Robins' at Doncaster in February 1927, scoring in a 2-2 draw. He subsequently signed professional forms for the Racecourse club and kept his place in the side until the end of the season, scoring a remarkable thirteen goals in fifteen matches. Cecil continued to score goals throughout the following term, but was surprisingly allowed to join fellow Third Division North side Wigan Borough in the summer of 1928. He spent just over a year with the Lancashire club before moving on to Third Division South side, Bournemouth. Two League appearances, without scoring followed for the 'Cherries' until a switch to Notts County in March 1930. However, he failed to make a first team appearance for the 'Magpies' in his short spell, and joined Macclesfield Town in the summer of 1930. Cecil scored 66 goals for the 'Silkmen' during 1930/31, before joining fellow Cheshire County League side Stalybridge Celtic for the following campaign. He continued his phenomenal goalscoring record with the 'Celtic' during 1931/32, netting 77 goals. That kind of form hardly went unnoticed, and in June 1932 he was signed by Second Division Burnley. Cecil made his debut for the Turf Moor club in a 1-1 home draw with Chesterfield, and went on to score 14 goals in 27 League matches that term. During his four seasons with the 'Clarets' he was the club's top scorer in the 33/34 and 34/35 campaigns before losing his place in the Burnley team to a 17 year-old youngster named Tommy Lawton. Cecil was affectionately known as 'Tiger' by the Burnley faithful, and was a real favourite with the crowd due to 'his fearless leadership of the line, bringing goals for himself and his colleagues. He was feared by goalkeepers as he would shoulder charge in the six yard box at every opportunity. His game was built around aggression, but only during matches - off the field he was a perfect gent'. At the end of the 35/36 season Smith was allowed to leave Turf Moor, whereupon he returned to his native Wales to join Third Division South side, Cardiff City. He made his debut in a 1-0 defeat at Walsall, and scored on his home debut in the following match, a 2-1 win over Clapton Orient. He made a total of 16 League appearances for Cardiff, scoring seven goals before leaving them in the summer of 1937 to rejoin Stalybridge Celtic. However, he couldn't match the goalscoring form seen in his first spell at club, and was allowed to join fellow Cheshire County League side Rhyl, in February 1938. Smith spent over twelve months at Belle Vue before moving to Lancashire Combination League side Bangor City in the summer of 1939. The Second World War put an end to his football career, throughout which he had been described as a 'bustling player, and very speedy off the mark'. At the end of his playing days he returned to live in Burnley, working for the local hospital service, later being employed by an engineering firm in the town until he retired. Cecil passed away in Burnley in 1977 at the age of 72.

Season	League		F.A.Cup		Welsh Cup		Total	
	apps	gls	apps	gls	apps	gls	apps	gls
1926/27	15	13	-	-	-	-	15	13
1927/28	31	13	3	1	2	2	36	16
	46	**26**	**3**	**1**	**2**	**2**	**51**	**29**

SMITH, James 1926 - 1928

Position; *Inside-Left*
D.O.B; *21st October, 1902*
Birthplace; *Dundee, Tayside*
Height; *5ft 7in* **Weight;** *10st 4lbs*
Debut; v. *Chesterfield (h) 28th August, 1926*
Total Appearances & Goals; *72 apps 24 gls*
Career; *Pembroke Dock; WREXHAM 5th Aug 1926 to cs1928;*

Despite being of Scottish descent James Smith joined Wrexham in the close season of 1926 from South Wales side Pembroke Dock. He went straight into the first team for his Football League debut in the opening match of the 1926/27 season, a 3-1 win over Chesterfield, and scored one of the 'Robins' goals. James missed just one match that season, notching a total of 16 goals, and ending the campaign as the club's leading goalscorer. However, 27/28 season saw him fail to produce the kind of prolific form that had made him the leading marksman a year earlier and with the emergence of Billie Rogers, he was allowed to leave the Racecourse in the summer of 1928.

Season	League		F.A.Cup		Welsh Cup		Total	
	apps	gls	apps	gls	apps	gls	apps	gls
1926/27	41	16	4	2	4	1	49	19
1927/28	23	5	-	-	-	-	23	5
	64	**21**	**4**	**2**	**4**	**1**	**72**	**24**

SMITH, James A. 1938 - 1939

Position; *Centre-Half*
D.O.B;
Birthplace; *Worcester, Worcestershire*
Height; *5ft 10'1/2in* **Weight;** *12st 10lbs*
Debut; v. *Southport (a) 27th August, 1938*
Total Appearances & Goals; *22 apps 0 gls*
Career; *Cardiff City 1936 15apps 0gls; WREXHAM 18th Jul 1938; Bangor City cs1939; Worcester City 1939;*
Honours; *Southern League Cup Winner 1940;*

Jim Smith had joined Third Division South side Cardiff City in 1936, making his Football League debut for the 'Bluebirds' in December as centre-half in a 2-0 home win over Torquay United. He added six more appearances that season, while the following year he turned out a further seven times as a full-back before allowed to leave Ninian Park in the close season of 1938. Jim was quickly snapped up by Wrexham's new manager Arthur Cowell, who gave him his first team chance at centre-half in the opening match of the season, a 3-1 defeat at Southport. Despite that result he kept his place in the first team until just before Christmas, when James Raven took over at centre-half. Jim only made another one League appearance that season, before leaving the Racecourse in the summer. He apparently signed for Bangor City before the outbreak of World War Two, but with football suspended he returned to his native Worcester. When organised football was re-introduced to boost morale, Smith began playing for his local side, Worcester City, picking up a Southern League Cup Winners' medal during the 1939/40 season. He continued to turn out for Worcester when available until April 1942, when the club ceased playing. During this time he had been stationed near the city as a Physical Training Instructor with the Army. Following Worcester's demise Jim concentrated upon Army football, continuing to play even when he was stationed in China.

Season	League		F.A.Cup		Welsh Cup		N.S.C.		Total	
	apps	gls	apps	gls	apps	gls	apps	gls	apps	gls
1938/39	22	0	1	0	1	0	-	-	24	0
	22	**0**	**1**	**0**	**1**	**0**	**-**	**-**	**24**	**0**

SMITH, John 1963 - 1966

Position; *Half-Back*
D.O.B; *13th September, 1944*
Birthplace; *Johnstown, Denbighshire*
Height; *5ft 9in* **Weight;** *11st 0lbs*
Debut; v. *Southport (a) 19th April, 1965*
Total Appearances & Goals; *25/1 apps 0 gls*
Career; *Rhos Aelwyd; Oswestry Town; Burnley; WREXHAM 29th May 1963; Caernarvon Town 29th Jun 1967; Runcorn 27th May 1969; Rhos Aelwyd 21st Aug 1973;*
Honours; *Welsh Youth International; Welsh Schoolboy International;*

John Smith lived in Johnstown, near Wrexham, and attended both Johnstown Primary School and Grango Secondary Modern School in Rhos before moving on to Yale Grammar School when he was thirteen years-old. During this period John represented Wrexham Schoolboys, as well as the Welsh Schoolboys XI on three occasions. At 14, Smith had started playing football for Rhos Aelwyd in the Welsh National League, stepping up to the Cheshire County League a year later with Oswestry Town. Upon leaving school John took up employment at the local Rubery Owen factory in the town at Whitegate as an apprentice Engineer. However, his performances with Oswestry soon attracted the interests of First Division Burnley, and they signed him as an amateur. He spent two years at Turf Moor, during which time he represented Wales six times in Youth international matches, and had the additional honour of captaining the side. He also played in the 'Clarets' reserve side alongside players like Ralph Coates and Willie Morgan. At the end of the 1962/63 season Smith was allowed to leave Turf Moor, and finally signed as an amateur for Wrexham in May 1963. He continued to play part-time at the Racecourse while completing his engineering apprenticeship, and soon after joining the 'Robins' he was selected as a reserve for the Rest of Great Britain Youth side to play England at Wembley in September 1963. The following season saw John finally break into the 'Robins' first team on Easter Monday 1965 when he played at right-back in place of Peter Jones in a 2-0 win at Southport. He appeared in two more matches before the end of the season, and although 1965/66 saw him making 21 League appearances it proved to be a disastrous year for the Club, as they finished bottom of the Football League for the first time in their history, forcing them to seek re-election. John was released in the summer and went on to play in non-league football for number of clubs, including Caernarvon Town, Runcorn, and Rhos Aelwyd, to name but a few. He was later employed at the Continental Can factory on the Wrexham Industrial Estate, playing in the local Sunday League before managing the side and leading them to two successive promotions. John, who has settled in Penycae, near Wrexham, has been actively involved in the training of Greyhounds for a number of years. He has raced his dogs on many of the local greyhound stadia, including Ellesmere Port and Stoke, and has enjoyed considerable success - training a number of winners and collecting an impressive array of trophies.

Season	League		F.A.Cup		Welsh Cup		League Cup		Total	
	apps	gls	apps	gls	apps	gls	apps	gls	apps	gls
1964/65	3	0	-	-	-	-	-	-	3	0
1965/66	20/1	0	1	0	1	0	-	-	22/1	0
	23/1	**0**	**1**	**0**	**1**	**0**	**-**	**-**	**25/1**	**0**

SMITH, John Joseph 1937

Position; *Inside-Right*
D.O.B; *1910*
Birthplace; *Clydebank, Strathclyde*
Height; *5ft 10in* **Weight;** *12st 8lbs*
Debut; v. *Rochdale (h) 20th February, 1937*
Total Appearances & Goals; *12 apps 1 gls*
Career; *Clydebank Juniors; Hearts Jun 1931; Hibernian Jan 1934 72apps 15gls; WREXHAM 19th Feb 1937; Bray Unknowns; Babock & Wilcox;*

John Smith began his football career with home town club, Clydebank Juniors, and it was when playing for them that he was spotted by Hearts, joining the Tynecastle club in June 1931. He remained with the 'Jam Tarts' until joining Edinburgh rivals Hibernian in January 1934. At the time John was described as 'a major acquisition who was noted for his ball work and creating of goals rather than actually scoring them'. He went on to make 72 Scottish League appearances for Hibs in just over three years, scoring fifteen goals, leaving Easter Road in February 1937 to move south of the border to join Third Division North side Wrexham, who were managed by the former Raith Rovers boss, Captain James Logan. John stepped straight into the 'Robins' side to make his Football League debut replacing Alf White at inside-right in a 1-0 home defeat by Rochdale. However, in the following match he scored his first goal for the 'Robins' in a 1-1 draw at Barrow. John went on to make ten more League appearances for the Racecourse club, before being allowed to leave at the end of the season. He is then believed to have travelled over to Ireland, where he played for Bray Unknowns, and is later known to have appeared for a works team, Babock and Wilcox.

Season	League		F.A.Cup		Welsh Cup		N.S.C.		Total	
	apps	gls	apps	gls	apps	gls	apps	gls	apps	gls
1936/37	12	1	-	-	-	-	-	-	12	1
	12	**1**	**-**	**-**	**-**	**-**	**-**	**-**	**12**	**1**

SMITH, John Richard

1929 - 1930

Position; *Outside-Right*
D.O.B; *1905*
Birthplace; *Bristol, Avon*
Height; *5ft 9in* ***Weight;*** *12st 4lbs*
Debut; v. *Doncaster Rovers (h) 22nd March, 1930*
Total Appearances & Goals; *6 apps 2 gls*
Career; *Victoria Albion (Bristol); Bristol Rovers (Am); Bristol City Apr 1921 27apps 12gls; Plymouth Argyle Jan 1924 6apps 4gls; Aberdare Athletic 19th Dec 1924 68apps 41gls; Guildford cs1926; Fulham Oct 1926 34apps 9gls; Rochdale cs1928 0apps; Caernarvon Athletic 29th Aug 1929; WREXHAM 15th Mar 1930; Burton Town Jun 1930;*
Honours; *Third Division South Championship Winner 1923; Welsh National League Division One Championship Winner 1930;*

A native of Bristol, Jack Smith started playing football for his local side, Victoria Albion, before signing for Bristol Rovers as an amateur. However, by April 1921 he had signed for neighbours Bristol City without having made a first team appearance for the Eastville club. It was while he was with City that he earned the nickname 'Smasher', because of his 'straight for goal methods'. He made his Football League debut for the Bristol 'Robins' in a 5-1 defeat at Derby in September 1921, going on to make a further nine League appearances and scoring three goals in a season which ended with City relegated. The following campaign Jack scored nine goals in eleven matches as the Ashton Gate club won the Third Division South Championship in some style. He remained with Bristol City until January 1924, adding another six appearances before his transfer to Third Division South side, Plymouth Argyle. Jack scored four goals in six League games for the 'Pilgrims', including a hat-trick against Bournemouth in a 4-0 home win in March 1924, as the Devon club finished runners-up in the League. In the summer of 1924 he toured Argentina with Argyle, but in December of the following season joined fellow Third Division South side Aberdare Athletic, in exchange for Walter Price. Jack was to enjoy the best spell of his career with Aberdare, scoring 41 goals in 68 games during the two years that he spent with the South Wales club. He signed for Guildford in the summer of 1926, before returning to League football with Fulham in October in a bid to solve their goalscoring problems. However, his touch deserted him at Craven Cottage, despite scoring on his debut in a 2-2 home draw with South Shields. Smith scored just eight more goals in 33 League games over the next two years for the 'Cottagers', and at the end of the 1927/28 season he left the London club to join Third Division North side Rochdale. However, he failed to record a first team appearance at Spotland, and returned to Wales to join Caernarvon Athletic in August 1929. He again became a free-scoring centre-forward for the 'Canaries', poaching many important goals, particularly in their run to the F.A.Cup Second Round proper, and became a vital member of the club's Welsh National League Division One Championship winning side. He had scored 58 goals by the time Wrexham signed him for a 'small fee' in March 1930, as a replacement for the departed Albert Mays. Jack made his debut for the 'Robins' in a 2-0 home defeat by Doncaster Rovers shortly after he had signed, but overall he failed to impress during his spell at the Racecourse. He only made a further five appearances before the end of the season, scoring two goals, both coming in the last match of the season, a 5-1 home win over Nelson. In the summer of 1930 Jack signed for Birmingham & District League side Burton Town, against whom he had been a major influence for Caernarvon in their two F.A.Cup encounters the previous season.

Season	League		F.A.Cup		Welsh Cup		Total	
	apps	gls	apps	gls	apps	gls	apps	gls
1929/30	6	2	-	-	-	-	6	2
	6	**2**	**-**	**-**	**-**	**-**	**6**	**2**

SMITH, Joseph Barry

1957 - 1958

Position; *Centre-Forward*
D.O.B; *15th March, 1934*
Birthplace; *South Kirby, Yorkshire*
Height; *5ft 11in* ***Weight;*** *12st 9lbs*
Debut; v. *Darlington (a) 24th August, 1957*
Total Appearances & Goals; *22 apps 15 gls*
Career; *Bradford United; Bradford Park Avenue; Farsley Celtic; Leeds United 10th Oct 1951 2apps 1gls; Bradford Park Avenue 27th May 1955 64apps 38gls; WREXHAM 1st June 1957; Stockport County 1st July 1958 17apps 5gls; Headington United cs1959; Oldham Athletic 20th Aug 1960 1app 0gls; Bangor City 9th Dec 1960; Southport 18th Aug 1961 0apps; Accrington Stanley 28th Oct 1961 3apps 0gls;*

Barry Smith played football for Shipley St.Walburga's School, and was chosen to represent Bradford Boys. Later, he turned out for Bradford United in the West Riding Youth League, from where he joined the ground staff at Bradford Park Avenue, playing in their Northern Intermediate League side. He was later released by the Park Avenue club and signed for Farsley Celtic. Still only 17 Barry was then snapped up by Leeds United, and later gave up his job as an apprentice plumber to sign professional forms for the Elland Road club in October 1951. It was almost twelve months before Barry made his Football League debut for Leeds at centre-forward, scoring in a 2-0 home win over Fulham. Just one more game for Leeds followed, a 1-0 home defeat against Leicester City in the same month. He remained on the Elland Road club's books until May 1955, two years of which were spent away on National Service with the Royal Artillery, based near Oswestry. Barry returned to Leeds following his demobilisation before joining Bradford Park Avenue in the summer of 1955. He went on to score 38 goals in 64 League matches in his two seasons with them. Barry was signed by fellow Third Division North side Wrexham in June 1957, making his debut in a 2-1 defeat at Darlington, and once again he found his scoring boots, returning ten goals from 18 League matches. Even so, his first team place was always under threat due to the presence at the club of fellow strikers Bernard Evans and Tommy Bannan. During his time at the Racecourse Smith was described as a 'very well built centre-forward who can also play on the left wing'. He was allowed to leave at the end of the season to join Stockport County, where he made his debut in the second match of the new campaign, a 3-3 draw at Bury. His stay at Edgeley Park lasted for just one year, in which he scored five goals in 17 League games, before moving on in the summer to link up with progressive non-league side Headington United (later renamed Oxford United). Barry enjoyed a season with Headington, returning to the Football League with Oldham Athletic in August 1960, though his stay at Boundary Park was to be short. He made just one League appearance for the 'Latics', a 1-1 home draw with Gillingham in September 1960, and by December he had returned to North Wales to join Bangor City, where he remained until the end of the season. A summer move to Southport then followed, but Barry failed to make a first team appearance for the 'Sandgrounders'. In October 1961 he joined Accrington Stanley where he appeared in three Football League games, though these appearances would eventually be scrubbed from the record books because of Stanley's resignation from the Football League in March 1962. He then drifted out of professional football, and into non-league circles. Barry was later known to have become a successful business man in the Bradford area, where he settled.

Season	League		F.A.Cup		Welsh Cup		Total	
	apps	gls	apps	gls	apps	gls	apps	gls
1957/58	18	10	1	0	3	5	22	15
	18	**10**	**1**	**0**	**3**	**5**	**22**	**15**

SMITH, Raymond James 1967 - 1972

Position; *Forward*
D.O.B; *18th April, 1943*
Birthplace; *Islington, London*
Height; *5ft 10in* ***Weight;*** *12st 7lbs*
Debut; v. *Luton Town (h) 19th August, 1967*
Total Appearances & Goals; *193/16 apps 70 gls*
Career; *Basildon Minors; Southend United Dec 1961 150apps 55gls; WREXHAM 4th Jul 1967 £8,000; Peterborough United 5th Jul 1972 £5,000 22apps 8gls; Bangor City;*
Honours; *Welsh Cup Winner 1972; Welsh Cup runner-up 1971; Division Four runner-up 1970;*

Although born in London Ray Smith moved to Essex at an early age with his family. He joined Basildon Minors, where his reputation as a rugged centre-forward soon spread. Little wonder, then, that Southend United manager Ted Fenton, moved quickly to sign him on amateur forms. Ray appeared for the 'A' team at Roots Hall before signing professional forms in December 1961. After a few matches for the reserves he stepped up to first team duty, making his Football League debut in a 1-0 home win over Newport County in February 1962. Ray clocked up a further seven League appearances that season, scoring one goal. Over the next five years he accumulated over 150 appearances for Southend, scoring more than fifty goals, and finishing as the club's leading scorer in 1966/67. In July 1967 former Southend manager Alvan Williams, then of Wrexham, returned to his old club and paid out a club record fee for Wrexham of £8,000 to take Ray to North Wales, together with Steve Ingle and Tony Beanland. He made his 'Robins' debut at home to Luton Town in August 1967, and got off to a scoring start with Wrexham's only goal in the 1-1 draw. Smith ended season as the club's leading scorer with 18 League goals. The following campaign saw his former team mate at Southend, John Neal, take over as manager at the Racecourse, and Smith continued to find the net, once again finishing as the club's leading scorer with fifteen. He developed a lethal strike partnership with Albert Kinsey during the 1969/70 season, as the pair scored 42 League goals between them to secure Wrexham promotion to the Third Division as runners-up to Chesterfield. The Denbighshire club's first season back in higher company proved to be one of consolidation, but Ray was struggling with niggling injuries, and when fit he found promising youngster Billy Ashcroft in good form. Ray did play in the Welsh Cup Final defeat by Cardiff City, but 1971/72 once again saw him in and out of the side, and he even played a few games in a central defensive position. The end of the season saw him play in his more formidable role of centre-forward in the Welsh Cup Final first leg victory over Cardiff City, while he substituted Arfon Griffiths in the second leg to ensure Wrexham's first ever victory since European football had been a reward for the competition winners. Even so, Ray was to miss out on the opportunity of playing European football, because he joined Peterborough United in July 1972 for a £5,000 fee, along with team-mate Bobby Park. His debut for the 'Posh' came in a 3-2 away defeat at Stockport, and he went on to record 22 League appearances, scoring eight goals. However, he was released at the end of the season, and returned to North Wales to join Bangor City. Ray later settled in the Wrexham area where he took up employment with Firestones on the Wrexham Industrial Estate. He was still employed with them at the time of writing, although they have subsequently changed their operating title to 'Owens Corning'.

Season	League		F.A.Cup		Welsh Cup		League Cup		Total	
	apps	gls	apps	gls	apps	gls	apps	gls	apps	gls
1967/68	44	18	1	0	2	0	1	1	48	19
1968/69	39	15	2	0	3	4	3	0	47	19
1969/70	42/1	15	4	2	2	1	4	0	52/1	18
1970/71	17/3	9	1	0	4	2	-	-	22/3	11
1971/72	19/10	3	1	0	3/1	0	1/1	0	24/12	3
	161/14	**60**	**9**	**2**	**14/1**	**7**	**9/1**	**1**	**193/16**	**70**

SNOW, George Edward Gardiner 1933 - 1940

Position; *Inside-Left*
D.O.B; *9th February, 1910*
Birthplace; *Newcastle-upon-Tyne, Tyne & Wear*
Died; *Hampstead, London A/M/J 1977*
Height; *5ft 10in* ***Weight;*** *12st 0lbs*
Debut; v. *Barnsley (a) 26th August, 1933*
Total Appearances & Goals; *268 apps 50 gls*
Career; *Walker Celtic; Leeds United Oct 1930 0apps; Rochdale Jun 1932 41apps 13gls; WREXHAM 15th June 1933 to Nov 1941 32apps 4gls;*

George Snow was brought up in the soccer hot bed of Newcastle. He was playing for the Shipbuilders works team, Walker Celtic, when he surprisingly attracted the attention of Leeds United, for whom he signed in October 1930. During his two years at Elland Road he failed to record a first team appearance, and in the summer of 1932, was transferred to Third Division North side Rochdale. George made his Football League debut for the Spotland club in the opening match of the new campaign, a 1-0 home defeat by Carlisle United. He went on to miss just one game that season, while managing to bag thirteen goals. Surprisingly, he left Spotland in the summer of 1933 to join fellow Third Division North side Wrexham, and thus began an eight year association with the North Wales club. George made his League debut for the 'Robins' at inside-left in a 3-0 defeat at Barnsley in the opening game of the 1933/34 season. He missed just three games that season, scoring seventeen goals from his inside-left position, a return bettered only by the phenomenal goalscorer Tommy Bamford, who had contributed a club record 44 League goals! Snow went on to serve the Racecourse club on a regular basis for another five seasons before World War Two disrupted his playing career. He was switched to play at left-half during 1935/36, where he was described as a 'real bustler' and 'an excellent half-back, who knew the full value of the through pass'. He gave the 'Robins' excellent service in both inside-left and half-back positions. Topping the club's scoring charts with 18 league goals in 1934/35, he also appeared in one of their biggest games of the 1930s, an F.A.Cup Third Round match against Manchester City in 1937, which the 'Sugar Bags' lost 3-1 following a determined performance. (The name 'Sugar Bags' was given to Wrexham at that time because their blue shirts with a white hoop around the chest resembled a bag of sugar!). World War Two finally put paid to his footballing career, by which time he had given sterling service to the North Wales club. Snow played in the opening three matches of the 1939/40 season before the Football League was suspended, though regionalised football was soon organised as it was said to 'keep up morale'. He continued to turn out in the re-organised West Division Regional League, where he made his final appearance for the club in November 1941, a 3-2 win over Tranmere Rovers. George is believed to have later settled in London, where he died in 1977 at the age of 67.

Season	League		F.A.Cup		Welsh Cup		N.S.C.		War League		War Cup		Total	
	apps	gls	apps	gls	apps	gls	apps	gls	apps	gls	apps	gls	apps	gls
1933/34	39	17	1	0	1	0	4	1	-	-	-	-	45	18
1934/35	42	18	2	0	2	0	2	0	-	-	-	-	48	18
1935/36	28	3	-	-	2	0	2	0	-	-	-	-	32	3
1936/37	34	1	3	0	1	0	1	0	-	-	-	-	39	1
1937/38	34	4	2	0	1	0	-	-	-	-	-	-	37	4
1938/39	30	2	1	0	2	0	1	0	-	-	-	-	34	2
1939/40	3*	0*	-	-	1	0	-	-	22	1	3	0	26	1
1940/41	-	-	-	-	-	-	-	-	8	3	-	-	8	3
	207	**45**	**9**	**0**	**9**	**0**	**10**	**1**	**30**	**4**	**3**	**0**	**268**	**50**

* = Not included in total as matches were made void.

SOLOMON, Jason Rafael
1996

Position; *Centre-Half*
D.O.B; *6th October, 1970*
Birthplace; *Welwyn Garden City, Hertfordshire*
Height; *6ft 0in* **Weight;** *12st 2lbs*
Debut v. *Millwall (a) 17th August, 1996*
Total Appearances & Goals; *4 apps 0 gls*
Career; *Watford Jul 1987, (Pro) Dec 1988 79/21apps 5gls; Peterborough United 13th Jan 1995 4apps 0gls (Loan); Wycombe Wanderers 17th Mar 1995 £10,000 11/2apps 1gls; WREXHAM Jul 1996; Fulham Nov 1996 1/3apps 0gls; Stevenage Borough Feb 1997 37/4apps 6gls; Aylesbury United Aug 1998;*
Honours; *Six England Youth International caps; F.A.Youth Cup Winner 1989;*

Jason Soloman showed enormous talent as a junior with his local side, Palshanger Yellows, where he was spotted by Watford. He signed for the 'Hornets' as a schoolboy in November 1984, and enrolled at the Lilleshall School of Excellence when he was 14 years-old. Jason spent almost two years at the School of Excellence in Shropshire and, on completion of his course there in July 1987, he rejoined Watford on Y.T.S. forms. He enjoyed two very successful years as an apprentice, earning selection for the England Youth side on six occasions, and helping Watford to win the F.A.Youth Cup as they beat Manchester City in the 1989 Final. The Watford side also included David James, who remained a close friend of Jason's after his move to Liverpool. Jason signed professional terms for the Hertfordshire club in December 1988, but had to wait until March 1991 before making his Football League debut at Port Vale. At that time Watford were struggling to remain in the old Second Division, but Jason, who was performing at left-back, went on to play his part in helping the 'Hornets' to escape the drop. Over the next few seasons he appeared regularly in the Watford first team, mostly in midfield, where he was a hard working player with a fierce shot. However, a change of manager found him playing mostly reserve team football, and in January 1995 was loaned out to Peterborough United where he made four League appearances in his four week spell. Wycombe Wanderers manager Martin O'Neill then came in for him just before the transfer deadline in March 1995 to sign him for £10,000. He made his debut for the Adams Park club in a home game with Birmingham City, but within a month O'Neill had resigned, and Alan Smith had taken over. This resulted in Jason being restricted to a handful of appearances during the 1995/96 season, and it came as no surprise when he was released in the summer. Solomon visited his friend David James at this time, and the Liverpool 'keeper contacted Wrexham manager Brian Flynn. He then offered Jason a trial at the Racecourse. He quickly made a good impression during the club's pre-season friendlies, and was handed his League debut for the 'Robins' at Millwall in the opening match of 1996/97. Solomon played alongside fellow new signing, Brian Carey, in the centre of defence, and he went on to make a total of four League and Cup appearances for the Racecourse club. However, with Tony Humes and Barry Jones also at his disposal Brian Flynn allowed Jason to move on in October. He joined Third Division Fulham, again for a trial period, where he made four League appearances, though again he was not offered terms. In February 1997 he signed for Conference League side, Stevenage Borough, who eventually finished the campaign in third position. He hit the national headlines with the 'Boro' during 1997/98, scoring one of the goals in their 2-1 F.A.Cup win at Swindon Town to earn a home tie with Premier League side Newcastle United. They held the 'Magpies' to a draw before making a brave exit from the competition in the replay at St.James' Park. Jason left Stevenage in the summer of 1998 to join Ryman's Premier League side Aylesbury United, where he began the 1998/99 season.

Season	League		F.A.Cup		League Cup		A.G.T.		Total	
	apps	gls	apps	gls	apps	gls	apps	gls	apps	gls
1996/97	2	0	-	-	2	0	-	-	4	0
	2	**0**	**-**	**-**	**2**	**0**	**-**	**-**	**4**	**0**

SOMERFIELD, Alfred George
1947

Position; *Outside-Right*
D.O.B; *22nd March, 1918*
Birthplace; *South Kirkby, Yorkshire*
Height; *5ft 10in* **Weight;** *10st 5lbs*
Debut; v. *Darlington (a) 7th June, 1947*
Total Appearances & Goals; *2 apps 1 gls*
Career; *Milnthorpe W.M.C; Frickley Colliery; Mansfield Town May 1938 15apps 6gls; Wolves Mar 1939 0apps, WW2 1app 1gls; Mansfield Town (WW2 Guest) 1941/42 2apps 1gls; Doncaster Rovers (WW2 Guest) 1942/43 2apps 0gls; Millwall (WW2 Guest) Aug 1943 6apps 0gls; Queens Park Rangers (WW2 Guest) 1943/44 20apps 5gls; Notts County (WW2 Guest) 1943/44 1app 0gls; Clapton Orient (WW2 Guest) 1944/45 3app 1gls; Crystal Palace (WW2 Guest) Aug 1944 22apps 14gls; Aldershot (WW2 Guest) 1945/46 7apps 3gls; Ipswich Town (WW2 Guest) 1945/46 1app 0gls; Queens Park Rangers (WW2 Guest) Sept 1945 8apps 1gls; WREXHAM Jun 1947; Crystal Palace Sept 1947 10apps 3gls;*
Honours; *Notts F.A.County Cup Winner 1939;*

Alf Somerfield first played for Milnthorpe W.M.C., but it was from his local side, Frickley Colliery in the Midland League that he was signed by Mansfield Town in May 1938. Alf broke into the 'Stags' first team in the following season, making his Football League debut as a centre-forward at Swindon Town in October, 1938, scoring one of the Mansfield goals in a 2-1 win. Thirteen more League appearances followed, in which he scored a further five goals, and his form soon began to attract the bigger club's. Eventually, he joined First Division Wolves in March 1939, in a deal that saw £500 and Ivan Flowers move in the opposite direction. However, World War Two had commenced before he had recorded a senior appearance at Molyneux, and brought the Football League to a halt. Somerfield did make one appearance for Wolves during the War period, a 3-1 away defeat at Leicester in a Midland Regional League match, when he scored the Wolves' goal. He completed six further appearances for Wolves, without scoring, as well as appearing as a 'guest' for a number of clubs including, Mansfield Town, Millwall, Crystal Palace, Aldershot, Clapton Orient, Ipswich Town, and Queens Park Rangers. Following the end of the hostilities he resumed his football career by joining Third Division North side Wrexham towards the end of the 1946/47 season. His debut for the 'Robins' came in June 1947, scoring the Racecourse club's goal in a 1-1 draw with Darlington. He then played in the final match of that long and weather disrupted season, at home to Tranmere Rovers on 14th June. In September 1947 Alf left Wrexham to join Crystal Palace, a club where he had enjoyed a very successful time during WW2. He made his debut for the 'Eagles' in a 1-1 home draw with Notts County in November 1947, and went on to make a further eleven League and Cup appearances, scoring three goals, before leaving Selhurst Park in the summer.

Season	League		F.A.Cup		Welsh Cup		Total	
	apps	gls	apps	gls	apps	gls	apps	gls
1947/48	2	1	-	-	-	-	2	1
	2	**1**	**-**	**-**	**-**		**2**	**1**

SOWDEN, Peter Tasker 1958 - 1959

Position; *Inside-Forward*
D.O.B; *1st May, 1929*
Birthplace; *Bradford, Yorkshire*
Height; *5ft 5in* ***Weight;*** *10st 10lbs*
Debut; v. *Swindon Town (a) 23rd August, 1958*
Total Appearances & Goals; *38 apps 4 gls*
Career; *Blackpool 14th June 1947 0apps; Bacup Borough 1948; Hull City 23rd Sept 1948 0apps; Elgin City cs1950; Aldershot 27th Oct 1950 4apps 0gls; Hull City 10th Aug 1951 0apps; Gillingham Aug 1952 134apps 27gls; Accrington Stanley 1st Sept 1956 54apps 13gls; WREXHAM 9th June 1958 £2,000; Chorley 16th Jul 1960; Great Harwood; Mossley cs1962; Rossendale United; Darwen 1967;*

Paddy Sowden began his nomadic football career at St.Bede's Grammar School in his native Bradford, and it was from here that he represented Yorkshire Schoolboys. He was still at school when he was spotted by a Blackpool scout, and joined the seaside club as a junior in 1946, signing professional terms in June 1947. Paddy failed to make a first team appearance at Bloomfield Road, and was released at the end of the 1947/48 season. He then moved into non-league football, joining Bacup Borough for the start of 48/49, but within a couple of months he was signed by Hull City in September 1948. However, Paddy's stay at Boothferry Park was short, as he was called up for his National Service with the Royal Engineers. During his two year stint he was based in Scotland, and the 'Tigers' allowed him to play for Elgin City in the Highland League when required. He moved South with the Army in 1951, and was based at Aldershot, where Hull City again agreed for Paddy to play for Aldershot when available. It was for the 'Shots' that he finally made his Football League debut, a 1-0 defeat at Leyton Orient in October 1950. Three further appearances for the Recreation Ground outfit followed before the end of his Call up. He then rejoined Hull City, but failed to make a first team appearance for the 'Tigers' before they released him at the end of the 1951/52 season. His football career really took off when he joined Third Division South side, Gillingham, enjoying four years with the Kent club for whom he scored on his debut against Newport County. He went on to record over 150 League and Cup games for the Priestfield club before turning down a new contract at the end of the 1955/56 season, as he wanted to move back North. In September 1956 Paddy got his wish, joining Accrington Stanley for a £4,000 fee. He became a regular in the 'Stanley' side during his first season at the club, but after nine matches of the 1957/58 season he was injured, and on recovery three months later he was unable to command a regular first team place. While at Peel Park Sowden had been described as 'only 5ft 5in, but squarely built, and a clever ball player with a deceptive body swerve, which made him a difficult man to tackle. He was on the small side for an inside-forward, but a great ball player.' During the summer of 1958 he was signed by Wrexham for £2,000, and looked forward to the club's first season in the newly organised Third Division. His debut came in the opening game of the season, a 1-0 defeat at Swindon. Paddy went on to become established as a regular in the 'Robins' team until September 1959, when he suffered an injury that was eventually to force him to quit professional football. Nevertheless, he continued playing non-league football after leaving the Racecourse in 1960, moving on to Chorley, Mossley, and Great Harwood - where he was appointed player/manager. He also played for Rossendale United and Darwen - again as player/manager - before taking charge at Horwich RMI. Paddy was then installed as youth team coach at Blackpool by manager Les Shannon. He spent three years in the position before leaving Bloomfield Road to take up an offer as assistant-manager to Harry Haslam at Luton Town in 1972. He helped the 'Hatters' to promotion in 1974, later joining Ron Atkinson at Cambridge United in a similar capacity in 1975. He was eventually given the job of general manager in 1977, leaving the 'U's' in 1980 to move to Canada and manage Vancouver Whitecaps for two years. On his return home he opened a health club and gymnasium in Biggleswade. Paddy later ran his own Sports business from his home in the Cambridge area, where he has settled.

Season	League		F.A.Cup		Welsh Cup		Total	
	apps	gls	apps	gls	apps	gls	apps	gls
1958/59	30	3	1	0	4	2	35	3
1959/60	8	1	-	-	-	-	8	1
	38	**4**	**1**	**0**	**4**	**2**	**43**	**4**

SPEED, Leslie 1946 - 1955

Position; *Full-Back*
D.O.B; *3rd October, 1923*
Birthplace; *Caergwrle, Denbighshire*
Height; *5ft 7in* ***Weight;*** *11st 11lbs*
Debut; v. *Carlisle United (a) 10th May, 1947*
Total Appearances & Goals; *241 apps 1 gls*
Career; *Portsmouth (WW2 Guest) 1944/45 1app 0gls; R.A.F; WREXHAM 9th April 1946, WW2 5apps 1gls; Stafford Rangers 1955; Holywell Town 13th Aug 1956; Pwllheli & District 12th Aug 1959; Holywell Town 16th Aug 1960;*
Honours; *Welsh Cup runner-up 1950; Two Third Division North representative appearances; Cheshire County League representative XI;*

Les Speed took up football at Hope Council School, and represented Flintshire Schoolboys until the end of his schooldays in 1938. In 1942 he joined the Royal Air Force, and after his initial training at R.A.F. Padgate was sent to R.A.F.Hendon. He played for both the Station XI and his Squadron XI, and was selected to play as a 'guest' for Portsmouth during this period. Les was later transferred to R.A.F.Netheravon on Salisbury Plains, and again turned out for his Station team as well as being chosen to play for Bomber Command. In 1944 he saw service in North Africa and Sicily before returning to Netheravon to be demobbed. During spells on home leave Les had appeared for Wrexham in the two legged F.A.Cup Third Round matches against Blackpool in January 1945. Following demobilisation he was offered the chance to join Portsmouth by the Fratton Park manager Jack Tinn, but Wrexham boss Tom Williams tabled similar terms, and his desire to return to North Wales saw Les join the 'Robins' in April 1946 for a £10 signing on fee! He was said to have developed into 'a rugged half-back, providing a quality so essential to the middle line- power, and was not afraid to supply a little robustness if necessary' during his time at the Racecourse, and he eventually became regarded as more of a utility player. Les played in most positions for Wrexham, including that of goalkeeper in one match. His most memorable game was the F.A.Cup Third Round tie against First Division Stoke City at the Victoria Ground, when Wrexham belied their League status with a rousing display, as they - unluckily - went down 2-1. Speed picked up a Welsh Cup runners'-up medal in 1950, after losing 4-1 to Swansea Town in the Final. He left the Racecourse in the summer of

1955 following 211 League appearances for the 'Robins', moving on to join Cheshire County League side Stafford Rangers as player/manager. In his ten years at the Racecourse, Les only ever scored one goal, in a Welsh Cup tie at Chester, which Wrexham lost 4-3 in December 1952. After leaving Stafford Rangers he joined Holywell Town, where he was eventually appointed player/manager in April 1957. Speed moved on to Pwllheli & District in August 1959, where he spent a season before another short spell with Holywell Town. He was invited to rejoin Wrexham as Youth team trainer in March 1963 by manager Ken Barnes, combining those duties with his full-time job as a Blacksmith, first at Llay Main Colliery, and then at Abenbury Brickworks. He was later employed at Firestones on the Wrexham Industrial Estate for 16 years, before being made redundant. He then began work with the Social Services until his retirement in 1988. Les is now settled in the Wrexham area.

Season	League		F.A.Cup		Welsh Cup		Total	
	apps	gls	apps	gls	apps	gls	apps	gls
1946/47	3	0	-	-	-	-	3	0
1947/48	22	0	-	-	3	0	25	0
1948/49	27	0	1	0	2	0	30	0
1949/50	42	0	3	0	5	0	50	0
1950/51	25	0	-	-	2	0	27	0
1951/52	29	0	-	-	1	1	30	1
1952/53	19	0	3	0	1	0	23	0
1953/54	15	0	5	0	1	0	21	0
1954/55	29	0	3	0	-	-	32	0
	211	**0**	**15**	**0**	**15**	**1**	**241**	**1**

SPENCER, Harold John 1950 - 1951

Position; *Half-Back*
D.O.B; *30th April, 1919*
Birthplace; *Burnley, Lancashire*
Height; *6ft 1in* ***Weight;*** *12st 12lbs*
Debut; v. *Mansfield Town (h) 19th August, 1950*
Total Appearances & Goals; *11 apps 0 gls*
Career; *Burnley Sept 1937 4apps 1gls, (WW2) 5apps 0gls; Crystal Palace (WW2 Guest) 1942/43 43apps 2gls; Torquay United (WW2 Guest) 1945/46 16apps 0gls; WREXHAM 21st Jul 1950; Portland United 1st Aug 1951; Fleetwood Town 1954;*
Honours; *Central League Championship Winner 1949;*

After representing Burnley Schoolboys Harold Spencer joined the ground staff of his home town club as a junior in 1935. He progressed through the ranks at Turf Moor to sign professional in September 1937, and he was just about ready for first team football when his career, like so many other players of this era, was cruelly interrupted by the outbreak of World War Two. He joined the Army in 1939, and, while stationed at Sudbury-on-Thames, appeared as a 'guest' player for both Crystal Palace and Torquay United in War League games. After his demobilisation from the Army in 1946 he considered a career with the Police, but eventually decided to continue playing football. He rejoined the 'Clarets', following the club's refusal to allow him a transfer to Crystal Palace.
Harry finally made his Football League debut for Burnley in the opening match of the 1946/47 season, a 1-1 home draw with Coventry City. He played in the following three games, scoring in a 2-0 away win at Birmingham, before finding himself back in the reserves. He continued as a valuable second team player at Turf Moor, and in September 1948 he was selected to represent a Central League XI against the Central League champions, Newcastle United. A year later Burnley themselves clinched the Central League title. Harry finally left Turf Moor in the summer of 1950, moving to North Wales and Third Division North side Wrexham. He made his debut for his new club at right-back in the opening game of the 1950/51 season, a 2-2 home draw with Mansfield Town. Despite his early promise, he found first team opportunities limited at the Racecourse, making just ten more senior appearances that season. Overall, his stay proved an unhappy one, as he refused to sign a new contract in the summer. In August 1951 Harry took up an appointment as player/manager of Portland United in Dorset, playing part-time in the Western League, whilst working for the Admiralty. He returned to the Burnley area in 1954, where he continued to play non-league football with Fleetwood for a short while. Following the end of his playing days, he became employed in the Engineering industry until his retirement in 1981, during which time he coached the Rolls Royce team. Harry settled in the Burnley area, where he was still residing at the time of writing.

Season	League		F.A.Cup		Welsh Cup		Total	
	apps	gls	apps	gls	apps	gls	apps	gls
1950/51	11	0	-	-	-	-	11	0
	11	**0**	**-**	**-**	**-**	**-**	**11**	**0**

SPINK, Dean Peter 1997 -

Position; *Centre-Foward*
D.O.B; *22nd January, 1967*
Birthplace; *Birmingham, West Midlands*
Height; *5ft 11in* ***Weight;*** *13st 8lbs*
Debut; v. *Sheffield United (h) 12th August, 1997 (Coca-Cola Cup)*
Total Appearances & Goals; *70/13 apps 12 gls*
Career; *Halesowen Town; Aston Villa 1st Jul 1989 £30,000 0apps; Scarborough 20th Nov 1989 (Loan) 3apps 2gls; Bury 1st Feb 1990 6apps 1gls (Loan); Shrewsbury Town 15th Mar 1990 £75,000 244/29apps 53gls; WREXHAM 11th Jul 1997 £65,000;*
Honours; *Welsh Invitation Cup Winner 1998; Auto Windscreen Shield runner-up 1996; West Midlands League Championship Winner 1986; Staffordshire Senior Cup winner 1989; Welsh Premier Cup Runners-up 1999;*

Dean Spink was signed by Aston Villa manager Graham Taylor from West Midland League side Halesowen Town in the summer of 1989 for a £30,000 fee at the relatively late age of 22. The role of part-time professional at Halesowen had been combined with his job as a window cleaner, having joined the West Midlands club straight from school. Dean represented both Lakey Star Secondary School and Maypole Comprehensive Schools, and earned selection for the South Birmingham Schools side. At Villa Park he initially played reserve team football before being loaned out to Fourth Division Scarborough for much needed Football League experience, and it was with the North Yorkshire that he in fact made his Football League debut in a 3-1 home defeat by York City. However, he followed this by scoring in each of his next two games before returning to the West Midlands, only to accept another loan spell, this time with Third Division Bury, for whom he made his debut in a scoreless home draw with Shrewsbury Town in February 1990. Shortly afterwards, Shrewsbury Town manager Ian McNeill signed him for the Shropshire club for £75,000, and he instantly repaid some of that fee by scoring on his debut, although Mansfield Town won 2-1. Dean went on to spend over seven years at the Gay Meadow, during which he helped the 'Shrews' to reach the Fifth Round of the F.A.Cup, where they lost 1-0 at home to Arsenal. The 1991/92 season saw him switched to play in the centre of defence, but couldn't prevent them from suffering relegation. Spink became a big favourite with the Shrewsbury supporters, and was described as 'very competitive and strong in the air, which makes him a danger at set pieces. He is more than happy playing up front as a good target man, although equally happy with the ball at his feet'. He was voted the Shrewsbury Town supporters' 'Player of the Year' in 1997, and was a very popular club captain. He left the Gay Meadow in the summer of 1997 in a move that upset the Shrewsbury Town faithful, as he joined their arch-enemies from over the border, Wrexham. Dean was signed to increase the 'Robins' attacking options, and made his debut at centre-forward in the opening game of the 1997/98 season in the blistering heat at Fulham. Despite Wrexham's domination of the game it wasn't a happy occasion for Dean as Wrexham lost 1-0. He went on to help the club to reach the verge of the play-off's, only to be denied a place by virtue of scoring one goal less than Fulham. He spent much of the first half of the 1998/99 campaign on the sub's bench, due to the popular signing of Welsh international Ian Rush, before an injury to Brian Carey saw Dean fill the breach at centre-half. It was in this position that he gave some impressive displays which earned the fans appreciation by being awarded the club's player of the season.

Season	League		F.A.Cup		League Cup		A.W.S.		W.I.C.		Total	
	apps	gls	apps	gls	apps	gls	apps	gls	apps	gls	apps	gls
1997/98	33/3	6	1/1	0	2	1	1	0	5	1	44/5	9
1998/99	26/8	3	4/1	0	0/1	0	5/1	0	8	0	43/11	3
	59/11	**9**	**5/2**	**0**	**2/1**	**1**	**5/1**	**0**	**13**	**1**	**87/16**	**12**

SPRUCE, George David 1950 - 1956

Position; *Centre-Half*
D.O.B; *3rd April, 1923*
Birthplace; *Chester, Cheshire*
Died; *Chester, 14th October 1998.*
Height; *5ft 11in* ***Weight;*** *11st 2lbs*
Debut; v. *Hartlepools United (h) 6th November, 1948.*
Total Appearances & Goals; *156 apps 4 gls*
Career; *Heath Rangers; WREXHAM 18th Oct 1948; Barnsley 28th May 1952 149apps 0gls; Chester Jul 1958 64apps 0gls; Runcorn cs1961; Prestatyn 24th Aug 1962;*
Honours; *Third Division North Championship Winner 1955; Welsh Cup runner-up 1950;*

George David Spruce was brought up in his native Chester and took up playing football while attending Love Street Central School, from where he represented Cheshire Schoolboys at all levels. It was during this time that he was invited to attend training sessions with Chester F.C., though no offer of an apprenticeship with the Sealand Road club materialised on leaving school. He joined local side, Heath Rangers, who played at Boughton Heath, while working as a bread delivery man. Professional clubs soon began to take an interest in him, and in August 1939 he received an invitation from Bolton Wanderers to go to Burnden Park for a trial. However, they did not pursue their interest because of the outbreak of World War Two a month later. During the conflict he enlisted in the Royal Navy, and spent most of the War at sea. When the hostilities finally ceased in 1945 George returned to his home in Chester and resumed playing for Heath Rangers. After some impressive performances in central defence Wrexham scout Joe Leach began to take an interest, and invited George to the Racecourse for a trial. When asked his age he told the Club that he was only 23, as he thought their interest would cool if they knew the truth. He was actually 25! During his trial period he played a couple of 'A' team games, followed by a spell in the reserves. He was thinking of returning to Heath Rangers when Peter Wilson, the club's regular centre-half, broke his leg. Ron Jackson covered at centre-half for three matches, but manager Tom Williams then turned to George for the home match against Hartlepools United in November 1948. Wrexham drew 2-2, and he went on to keep his place in the side for the rest of the season. Over the next three years George established himself as the 'Robins' regular centre-half, missing just a handful of games, and when Les McDowall was appointed manager in May 1950 he quickly appointed George as club captain. His consistent performances soon began to attract the attention of other clubs, and in May 1952 he was allowed to leave the Racecourse and join Second Division Barnsley for a fee of around £10,000.

During his time with Wrexham he had picked up a Welsh Cup runners'-up medal in 1950, when the 'Robins' lost to Swansea in the Final. He made his debut for the Oakwell club in September, in a 3-0 defeat at Nottingham Forest, but was to manage just five more appearances for the Yorkshire club that season as they suffered relegation. However, the following campaign saw him established as a regular in the Barnsley side, and in 1955 played his part in taking them back to the Second Division as they won the Third Division North Championship. During his time at Oakwell he was particularly unlucky with injuries, as he broke a leg against West Ham; broke an arm at Sheffield Wednesday; as well as breaking a toe and having a cartilage operation! Despite all those injuries he still managed to make over 150 League and Cup appearances for the 'Tykes'. In July 1958 George, 'a hard but fair central defender', was to leave Barnsley to join his home town club of Chester at the age of 35! He went on to complete over sixty League appearances for the 'Cestrians' before making his final Football League appearance for them in April 1961, a 3-0 home defeat by Darlington. He left Sealand Road in the summer of 1961, but continued playing non-league football for Cheshire County League side Runcorn. He spent one season with the 'Linnets' before joining Prestatyn in the Welsh League (North) in August 1962, enjoying one more term before finally hanging up his boots in 1963 at the age of 40. Spruce retained an involvement with the game by taking up refereeing around the local leagues in Chester, and finding employment with the Gas Board. He later became a taxi driver, retiring in 1988, and spent many happy hours of his retirement on the local greens in the Chester area, where he was a very successful bowler. His younger brother Phil also played League football for Wrexham during the 1950s. George passed away on 14th October 1998. He was 75.

Season	League		F.A.Cup		Welsh Cup		Total	
	apps	gls	apps	gls	apps	gls	apps	gls
1948/49	25	0	1	0	2	0	28	0
1949/50	39	1	3	0	4	1	46	2
1950/51	40	2	2	0	2	0	44	2
1951/52	31	0	3	0	4	0	38	0
	135	**3**	**9**	**0**	**12**	**1**	**156**	**4**

SPRUCE, Phillip Trevor 1950 - 1956

Position; *Half-Back*
D.O.B; *16th November, 1929*
Birthplace; *Chester, Cheshire*
Height; *5ft 10in* ***Weight;*** *11st 7lbs*
Debut; v. *Stockport County (a) 17th January, 1953*
Total Appearances & Goals; *24 apps 0 gls*
Career; *WREXHAM 7th Nov 1950; Rhyl 13th Jan 1956; Colwyn Bay 25th Jul 1962; Llandudno 30th Jun 1964; Colwyn Bay 30th Mar 1965; Llandudno 21st Dec 1966;*
Honours; *Welsh League (North) Championship Winner 1965;*

With his older brother already at the club Phil Spruce joined Wrexham in November 1950, although shortly afterwards he was called up for his

National Service with the Royal Air Force. He was stationed mostly at R.A.F.Uxbridge, which made him unavailable for most of the following two years until he was demobbed in December 1952. Following several reserve team outings, Phil was to make his Football League debut for the 'Robins' in January 1953, deputising for Les Speed at right-back in a 3-1defeat at Stockport County. Phil also played in the following match, a 1-0 home win over Tranmere Rovers, before returning to reserve team football in the Cheshire County League for the rest of the season. He had to wait until the September of the following season before he was handed another first team appearance, and then began a run of seven games as Ron Wynn's deputy at centre-half. They included the then club record Football League victory, a resounding 8-0 thrashing of Workington on the Racecourse. Towards the end of that season he added another twelve appearances at half-back, replacing Brian Jarvis. He failed to make the first XI throughout 1954/55, and managed just one more appearance for Wrexham's senior side, a 2-0 defeat at Chesterfield in November 1955, when he filled in at right-back in place of Albert Parker. Phil left the Racecourse in January 1956 and joined Cheshire County League side Rhyl, where he became an influential figure for a number of seasons at Belle Vue. He moved on to Colwyn Bay in the summer of 1962, where he spent two seasons before linking up with Llandudno. However, he returned to Colwyn Bay before the season had ended and assisted them to the Welsh League (North) title. He then moved back to Llandudno in December 1966. Phil eventually settled in his native city of Chester, and lived not far from his brother, George.

Season	League		F.A.Cup		Welsh Cup		Total	
	apps	gls	apps	gls	apps	gls	apps	gls
1952/53	2	0	-	-	-	-	2	0
1953/54	19	0	-	-	1	0	20	0
1955/56	1	0	-	-	-	-	1	0
	23	**0**	**-**	**-**	**1**	**0**	**24**	**0**

STACEY, Stephen Darrow

1966 - 1968

Position; *Left-Back*
D.O.B; *27th August, 1944*
Birthplace; *Bristol, Avon*
Height; *5ft 11in* ***Weight;*** *12st 6lbs*
Debut; v. *Southport (a) 26th February, 1966*
Total Appearances & Goals; *101/4apps 6 gls*
Career; *Highridge United; Sneyd Park; Bristol City Nov 1961 0apps; WREXHAM 25th Feb 1966; Ipswich Town 12th Sept 1968 £25,000 3apps 0gls; Chester Dec 1969 1app 0gls (Loan); Charlton Athletic 20th Jan 1970 (Loan) 1app 1gls; Bristol City 3rd Sept 1970 (Loan), 1st Oct 1970 £5,000 9apps 0gls; Exeter City Aug 1971 57/2apps 0gls; Bath City cs1973;*
Honours; *Welsh Cup runner-up 1967;*

Steve Stacey first played football for Fairfield Grammar School, where he was captain of both the intermediate and Senior XI teams. He also represented Bristol Boys, appearing at centre-forward, as well as turning out for junior side Highridge United. Eventually, he signed for his first senior side, Sneyd Park. Upon completing his education Steve joined Bristol City as an apprentice, progressing to sign professional in November 1961. He consistently scored 20-25 goals a season from his centre-forward berth for the reserve team, but his only first team game was a Welsh Cup match against Merthyr Tydfil at outside-right, though he did score in a 4-2 win. Soon after that game Steve switched to defence, remaining in that position until February 1966 when he was signed by Wrexham manager Jack Rowley. He was pitched straight into the 'Robins' first team, replacing Stuart Mason in a 2-2 draw at Southport, but couldn't prevent the club from ending the season 92nd in the Football League for the first time in it's history, which meant having to seek re-election. He missed just one game during the 1966/67 season, a Welsh Cup tie against Rhyl, and it was in that same competition that he helped Wrexham to reach the 1967 Final, where they lost to Cardiff City. He began the following campaign at centre-half, a position he held until December, while the 1968/69 season was only two months old when Ipswich Town paid out £25,000 to take him to Suffolk. During his time at the Racecourse he was described as 'a thoughtful player who likes nothing more than to move up into attack whenever the opportunity presents itself'. He made his debut for his new club a week later at home to Liverpool, though his stay at Portman Road proved to be a disappointment as he added just two more League appearances, although niggling injuries didn't help. In December 1969 he accepted the offer of a month's loan at Chester, making just one League appearance for them before returning to Ipswich. In January 1970 he accepted another month on loan with Charlton Athletic, where he made just one League appearance, a 2-1 defeat at home to Huddersfield Town. He actually scored the Charlton goal in that game, during a goal mouth scramble. Stacey stayed with Ipswich until September 1970, when he finally moved back to Bristol City. He made his second debut for City at right-back, in a 3-3 draw against Sheffield United, and remained in that position for the next eight games, though they proved to be his last as he had to be content with reserve team football for almost twelve months until signing for Exeter City on a free transfer in August 1971. He made his debut for the 'Grecians' in the opening game of the new season, a 4-0 defeat at Southport. Another thirty League appearances that season for Exeter were added, while he turned out in a further 29 League games during the following campaign joining Bath City in the summer of 1973. He then took up employment for a travel company in Bristol before deciding to accept an invitation to play football in Australia. Settling in Albany, Western Australia, Steve was accepted at Teachers' Training College, and later became a Recreation Officer with a local council until he managed the Recreation and Leisure facilities of three local authorities. He currently works for the Ministry of Education as second in charge of a Residential College in Albany. During this time Steve had played for and coached a couple of local teams, including a year at National level in Melbourne in the 1980s, after he had gained his full senior coaching badge in 1975. Steve also captained the Western Australia side against visiting British teams on a number of occasions, including Manchester United, Glasgow Rangers, and Middlesbrough. He also turned out for the team in the Marah Halim Cup tournament in Indonesia, beating South Korea 2-0 in the Final in 1975. Steve is now very much settled in Australia.

Season	League		F.A.Cup		Welsh Cup		League Cup		Total	
	apps	gls	apps	gls	apps	gls	apps	gls	apps	gls
1965/66	15	1	-	-	-	-	-	-	15	1
1966/67	46	2	2	0	5	0	1	0	54	2
1967/68	34/4	3	1	0	1	0	1	0	37/4	3
1968/69	6	0	-	-	-	-	3	0	9	0
	101/4	**6**	**3**	**0**	**6**	**0**	**5**	**0**	**115/4**	**6**

STANTON, Brian 1986

Position; *Midfield*
D.O.B; *7th February, 1956*
Birthplace; *Liverpool, Merseyside*
Height; *5ft 7in* **Weight;** *10st 7lbs*
Debut; v. *Chester City (a) 22nd March, 1986*
Total Appearances & Goals; *9 apps 0 gls*
Career; *New Brighton; Bury Oct 1975 72/11apps 14gls; Huddersfield Town 12th Sept 1979 £15,000 199/10apps 45gls; WREXHAM 21st Mar 1986 (Loan); Morecambe cs1986; Rochdale Dec 1986 42/7apps 4gls; Morecambe cs1988; Colne Dynamos; Royal Seaforth Veterans XI;*
Honours; *Fourth Division Championship Winner 1980;*

Brian Stanton was playing for New Brighton in the Cheshire County League when he joined Bury in October 1975 as an amateur, going on to sign professional for the 'Shakers' in March 1976. Brian did not make his Football League debut for the Gigg Lane club until January 1977, but went on to complete almost 100 League and Cup appearances before dropping a Division to join Huddersfield Town for a £15,000 fee in September 1979. He went straight into the side for his debut at Scunthorpe United, and made an immediate impact by scoring the 'Terriers' only goal in a 1-1 draw. Brian's first season at Leeds Road saw him prove his worth as an attacking midfield player with a knack of scoring spectacular goals. He helped Huddersfield to win the Fourth Division championship, and so exchange places with his former club, Bury, who had been relegated. After playing consistently in the 'Terriers' midfield over the next two years he enjoyed promotion back to the Second Division in 1983, as they finished third in the Division Three table. His most memorable match during that season was Huddersfield's 6-3 home win over local rivals Bradford City on New Year's Day 1983, when he scored four goals, three of which came in the space of six minutes. After six years at Leeds Road Stanton began to find the competition hotting up for a first team place in midfield, and in March 1986 he took up an offer to join Fourth Division Wrexham on loan, with a view to a permanent move. He made his debut for the 'Robins' in a 'derby' match at Chester, which ended in a 2-1 defeat, and added another seven League appearances, as well as a Welsh Cup semi-final appearance against Cardiff City, before returning to Yorkshire without being offered the chance of a move. At the end of the season he found himself released by the Leeds Road outfit, and drifted into non-league football with Northern Premier League side Morecambe. However, by December struggling Rochdale manager Eddie Gray resurrected his Football League career when he signed him for the Spotland club. Brian made his debut in a 1-1 draw at Scunthorpe, going on to complete over fifty League and Cup appearances for Rochdale until released by the club at the end of the 1987/88 season. He then rejoined Morecambe, and eventually played for Colne Dynamos. He later appeared in the local Leagues in Liverpool for the Royal Seaforth Veterans' XI.

Season	League		F.A.Cup		Welsh Cup		League Cup		F.R.T.		Total	
	apps	gls	apps	gls	apps	gls	apps	gls	apps	gls	apps	gls
1985/86	8	0	-	-	1	0	-	-	-	-	9	0
	8	**0**	**-**	**-**	**1**	**0**	**-**	**-**	**-**	**-**	**9**	**0**

STEEL, James William 1983 & 1984 - 1987

Position; *Centre-Forward*
D.O.B; *4th December, 1959*
Birthplace; *Dumfries, Dumfries & Galloway*
Height; *6ft 3in* **Weight;** *14st 0lbs*
Debut; v. *Portsmouth (h) 29th January, 1983*
Total Appearances & Goals; *230 apps 72 gls*
Career; *Greystoke Rovers; Oldham Athletic 20th Jun 1978 101/7apps 24gls; Wigan Athletic 11th Nov 1982 (Loan) 2apps 2gls; WREXHAM 26th Jan 1983 (Loan); Port Vale 17th Mar 1983 £10,000 27/1apps 6gls; WREXHAM 13th Jan 1984 £10,000; Tranmere Rovers 21st Nov 1987 £60,000 161/13apps 29gls;*
Honours; *Welsh Cup Winner 1986; Leyland DAF Cup Winner 1990; Welsh Cup runner-up 1984; Leyland DAF Cup runner-up 1991;*

Jim Steel was born in Dumfries, and began his football career with local junior side Greystoke Rovers. It was during his time with them that a team mate was invited to Oldham Athletic for a trial, and Jim agreed to travel

down to Boundary Park with him. Upon his arrival it was found that another hopeful had failed to turn up, so Steel was asked if he fancied a game! He did well enough to be offered apprentice terms with Oldham, which he signed at the tender age of 15. Steady progress through the 'Latics' youth and reserve sides followed, before he was given his first team chance in August 1978 at Cardiff City, and responded with two well taken goals in Oldham's 3-1 win. Jim went on to complete 108 League appearances for Oldham, scoring 24 goals, but the beginning of the 1982/83 season found him out of favour, and he was placed on the transfer list. He joined Wigan Athletic on loan in November 1982, and scored two goals in two games before returning to Boundary Park. In January 1983 Jim joined Wrexham on loan, and made his debut in a 2-0 home defeat against high flying Portsmouth. Despite this setback he soon endeared himself to the Racecourse faithful, scoring six goals in the following eight games. At the end of his second month on loan Port Vale moved in and paid £10,000 to take him to Vale Park. He would have signed for Wrexham given the opportunity, but due to the club's crippling financial situation manager Bobby Roberts couldn't afford the fee. Instead, he went on to help Vale clinch promotion to the Third Division, scoring both goals in Vale's 2-0 win at Stockport. 1983/84 saw John Rudge take over as manager at vale Park, and he allowed Steel to join Wrexham in January 1984, when Bobby Roberts finally raised the £10,000 required. Again the 'Robins' were struggling, but he was to assist the club to finish runners-up to Shrewsbury Town in the Welsh Cup Final, and thus qualify for Europe. The next season saw him help Wrexham to record an astounding win over F.C.Porto, notching the only goal in the 1-0 home leg win, before going to Portugal and secure a 4-3 defeat, which resulted in an away goals victory for the Welsh minnows. The next round saw the 'Robins' gallantly bow out to the Italians of A.S.Roma. Jim's performances against Porto impressed the Portuguese officials, and they later made an enquiry for his services. The following campaign saw Jim score the goals that earned Wrexham a 2-1 win over Kidderminster Harriers to lift the Welsh Cup, following a replay, and guarantee the club another European adventure. The draw was to see Wrexham take on, and beat, F.C.Zurrieq of Malta, to earn a plum draw with Real Zaragoza of Spain. This time the Racecourse club were to fall victim to the away goals rule, after drawing 0-0 in Spain and 2-2 at Wrexham. Steel's display against Zaragoza so impressed one of their officials that he recommended him to Spanish Second Division side Deportivo La Coruna, and at the end of the season he joined the Spanish club on loan as a temporary replacement for their striker who had broken his leg. Steel played five matches for the Spaniards, without scoring, and returned to Wrexham for the start of the 1987/88 season. He eventually left the Racecourse in November 1987, when Tranmere Rovers shelled out £60,000 for him. Although he had experienced some good times at the Racecourse, the club's League form was never particularly impressive throughout his four year stay. His transfer to Prenton Park proved to be a good move for him, as he helped Rovers to promotion in 1989 as Fourth Division runners-up. In 1990 he twice played at Wembley, when Tranmere won the Leyland DAF Cup, Jim scoring the winning goal in a 2-1 win over Bristol Rovers, and losing 2-0 to Notts County in the Third Division Play-Off Final. The following season, he appeared in the 3-2 defeat by Birmingham City in the Leyland DAF Cup Final, but he assisted Tranmere to promotion to the Second Division, beating Bolton Wanderers 1-0 in the Play-Off Final. Jim continued with Tranmere in the Second Division for a season, but at the end of 1991/92 retired from professional football altogether and took up employment as a Police Constable with the Merseyside Police, based on the Wirral. Jim continued to play football for the Police when time allowed, but he can also be seen on duty at Prenton Park on match days.

Season	League		F.A.Cup		Welsh Cup		Leagu Cup		F.R.T.		E.C.W.C.		Total	
	apps	gls	apps	gls	apps	gls	apps	gls	apps	gls	apps	gls	apps	gls
1982/83	9	6	-	-	-	-	-	-	-	-	-	-	9	6
1983/84	21	0	-	-	5	0	-	-	3	1	-	-	29	1
1984/85	45	14	1	0	3	0	2	0	2	0	4	1	57	15
1985/86	43	14	2	0	7	6	2	1	2	1	-	-	56	22
1986/87	37	17	3	1	4	1	4	1	4	1	4	1	56	22
1987/88	18	6	1	0	-	-	2	0	2	0	-	-	23	6
	173	**57**	**7**	**1**	**19**	**7**	**10**	**2**	**13**	**3**	**8**	**2**	**230**	**72**

STUBBS, Philip Eric Gordon — 1934 - 1935

Position; *Outside-Left*
D.O.B; *10th September, 1912*
Birthplace; *Chester, Cheshire*
Height; *5ft 11in* ***Weight;*** *12st 0lbs*
Debut; v. *New Brighton (h) 20th October, 1934*
Total Appearances & Goals; *28 apps 10 gls*
Career; *Winsford United; Nantwich; Bolton Wanderers Jan 1934 0apps; WREXHAM 5th Sept 1934; Nottingham Forest June 1935 22apps 6gls; Leicester City Nov 1936 74apps 14gls; Wrexham (WW2 Guest) Feb 1940 1app 1gls; Chester Sept 1939 (WW2 Guest) 27apps 1gls;*
Honours; *Second Division Championship Winner 1937;*

Eric Stubbs had played non-league football for Winsford and Nantwich before being discovered by Bolton Wanderers, to whom he was transferred for a 'fair fee' in January 1934. His stay at Burnden Park was to be short, however, as he signed for Wrexham in September of the same year, without having made a first team appearance for the 'Trotters'. He quickly settled in at the Racecourse, replacing Harry Waller at outside-left for his debut in a 3-0 home win over New Brighton in October. Eric kept his place in the side for the remainder of that season, playing on either flank, as he clocked up a total of 28 League appearances, scoring ten goals. It was said that, 'On his day is a fine marksman and speedy' and that he 'had an unusually big physique for a wing man.' His form had made the bigger clubs take notice, and in the close season of 1935 he signed for Second Division side Nottingham Forest. Eric made his debut for Forest in the opening game of the 1935/36 season, a 2-2 home draw with Bury. He went on to complete 22 League appearances for the City Ground club, before he was transferred to Leicester City in November 1936 as new manager Frank Womack's first major signing. At Filbert Street he helped to transform a rather mundane season into a convincing Second Division championship success. He established himself in the top flight with Leicester City for the next two seasons, making 74 League appearances for the 'Foxes' and scoring 14 goals before the Second World War disrupted his playing career. He played in the opening three League games of 39/40 season before the Football League was suspended, and returned to his home city of Chester. He turned out for Chester as football was resumed on a regional basis, appearing when possible during the hostilities. During this period he also made one 'guest' appearance for Wrexham, in a 4-1 defeat at New Brighton in February 1940, scoring the 'Robins' goal. Following the end of the conflict Eric signed for Chester in the transitional season of 1945/46, later taking up work as a Cheshire fruit farmer.

Season	League		F.A.Cup		Welsh Cup		N.S.C.		Total	
	apps	gls	apps	gls	apps	gls	apps	gls	apps	gls
1934/35	28	10	1	0	2	1	2	0	33	11
	28	**10**	**1**	**0**	**2**	**1**	**2**	**0**	**33**	**11**

STURRIDGE, Michael Alexandra — 1983

Position; *Forward*
D.O.B; *18th September, 1962*
Birthplace; *Birmingham, West Midlands*
Height; *5ft 11in* ***Weight;*** *11st 0lbs*
Debut; v. *Chesterfield (a) 17th December, 1983*
Total Appearances & Goals; *3/1 apps 0 gls*
Career; *Birmingham City Jun 1980 0apps; WREXHAM Dec 1983 (Loan); Kokkolan P.V. (Finland) Apr 1984; Bromsgrove Rovers Feb 1985; RoPS Rovaniemi (Finland) Jul 1985; Oldham Athletic 1985 (trial); Walsall 1985 (trial); Nuneaton Borough 1985/86; Cheltenham Town 1986/87; Redditch United 1988/89; Hednesford Town 1991;*

The eldest of the 'Sturridge' footballing brothers, Mike Sturridge joined Birmingham City straight from school in 1978. He had attended the Holte Comprehensive School in Aston, where he represented his school team, Aston Boys, West Midlands Boys, and an all-Birmingham Boys team, with whom he appeared in a tournament in Frankfurt, Germany. He also underwent trials for the England Schoolboy XI, progressing to a final pool of thirty, though he did not subsequently make the final eleven. Mike's early promise was soon noted by a number of Football League sides, but it was Birmingham whom he joined as an apprentice, thinking he had a better chance of making the grade with them. He continued to develop at St.Andrew's, and appeared in another tournament in Germany for the youth side, picking up the 'Player of the Tournament' trophy. He eventually signed professional with the 'Blues' in June 1980, but it was not until the 1981/82 season that he was to feature in the first team squad. He was told by manager Ron Saunders that he was to play in a vital end of season relegation battle with local rivals Wolves but, when he went to change, he found that he had been demoted to substitute for no apparent reason. Mike was totally disillusioned by this, but in December 1983 was given the opportunity to rekindle his appetite for the game with a loan spell at Wrexham. He made his Football League debut for the 'Robins' in a 1-1 draw at Chesterfield, when he stepped in at centre-forward for Andy Edwards. He played in the following match, a 2-0 win over Chester City on Boxing Day 1983, and added two more appearances before returning to Birmingham at the end of his month's loan. In the four games that he played for Wrexham Mike never appeared in a losing side. Having returned to St.Andrew's he was given the opportunity of another loan spell, this time with Hereford United, but after playing in just one reserve game he returned to Birmingham. At the end of the season he was released by the 'Blues' without having made a first team appearance. Despite a good offer to join Stourbridge Mike accepted an invitation to move to Finland, where he played for Kokkolan P.V.. However, he had only taken out a 12 month passport, and it expired with five games still to play! The club wished him to see out his contract, but he refused to stay, as he would then have been in the country illegally. Mike returned home, but that was far from the end of his troubles as the Finnish side withheld his registration until February 1985. He then joined Southern League side Bromsgrove Rovers, where he stayed until the end of the season, when he returned to Finland to play for RoPS Rovaniemi, which is close to Lapland. He came back to the UK when their season had ended in September, having trials with both Oldham Athletic and Walsall. He then drifted back into non-league football with Nuneaton Borough in 1985/86, but left after six weeks, along with Peter Shearer, to join Cheltenham Town. He later played non-league football for Redditch United, followed by a few games for Hednesford Town, before finally giving up the game in 1991. Mike, who still lives in the Birmingham area, has been employed at the Longbridge Rover plant in the City since 1990. His brothers, Dean and Simon, were still playing professional football at the beginning of 1998/99.

Season	League		F.A.Cup		Welsh Cup		League Cup		A.M.C.		Total	
	apps	gls	apps	gls	apps	gls	apps	gls	apps	gls	apps	gls
1983/84	3/1	0	-	-	-	-	-	-	-	-	3/1	0
	3/1	**0**	-	-	-	-	-	-	-	-	**3/1**	**0**

STYLES, Arthur John 1960 - 1961

Position; *Wing-Half*
D.O.B; *29th October, 1939*
Birthplace; *Smethwick, West Midlands*
Height; *5ft 10'1/2in* ***Weight;*** *12st 2lbs*
Debut; v. *Reading (a) 19th March, 1960*
Total Appearances & Goals; *20 apps 1 gls*
Career; *West Bromwich Albion (Am) Jul 1955; (Pro) 5th Nov 1956 1app 0gls; WREXHAM 16th Mar 1960; Hereford United Jul 1961; Kidderminster Harriers Jul 1963; Stourbridge (Player/coach) 1967; Halesowen Town 1968/69; Lye Town (Player/Manager) 1970;*
Honours; *Welsh Cup Winner 1960;*

While attending the James Watt Technical School in his native Smethwick Archie Styles represented both Staffordshire Schoolboys and Birmingham County Boys, and did well enough to earn selection for trials with the English Schools team. Even though Chelsea showed an interest in him, and Wolves had invited him to train with them as a schoolboy, he had no hesitation in signing as an apprentice for his local side, West Bromwich Albion, when the chance was offered in July1955. Archie made steady progress at the Hawthorns, and signed professional terms with the Albion in November 1956, a week after his 17th birthday. He made his way through the ranks and, at the end of the 1958/59 season, was selected to tour Canada and America, where Albion played nine matches between 22nd May and 10th June. The October of the following season saw him eventually make his Football League debut for the 'Baggies' in a 4-2 First Division defeat at Fulham, where he deputised for Jimmy Dudley at wing-half. It proved to be his one and only League appearance for Albion, as he left the Hawthorns on the transfer deadline in March 1960 to join Third Division Wrexham in a bid to try to prevent the 'Robins' eventual relegation. Archie added his debut for Wrexham in a 1-0 win at Reading, and made seven more appearances that season in the League, but he couldn't help them to avoid the drop. He did, however, feature in the 1960 Welsh Cup Final against Cardiff City, where Wrexham eventually lifted the trophy following a replay. Styles played in the first three games of the 1960/61 season, but eventually found himself in the reserves in the Cheshire County League, though he did manage seven more League and Cup appearances before the end of that campaign. He was described at the Racecourse as 'a strong rugged half-back, who has also appeared at inside-forward.' Archie was allowed to leave the Racecourse in the summer of 1961, and signed for Southern League side Hereford United as a part-time professional. This led him to take up employment as a sales representative for Henry Hope & Sons in Smethwick. Archie spent two years at Edgar Street, and played against Wrexham in a Welsh Cup Sixth Round tie in April 1963, which the 'Bulls' won 2-1. He switched to Kidderminster Harriers in the close season of 1963, where he spent a total of four years, during which he would help out with the training. A move to Stourbridge followed in 1967, and he spent about eighteen months with the 'Glassboys' before a knee injury kept him out of first team action for some time. Once fit he joined Halesowen Town, where he spent twelve months before announcing his retirement. He then took up coaching with Lye Town until the early 1970s. In 1982, Archie pulled on his boots again to turn out for the West Bromwich All Stars' side, and he continued to play for them until 1989, when he turned 50! Archie is now happily settled in the West Midlands at Lye, working as a Technical representative for a company involved with Architectural Glazing.

Season	League apps	League gls	F.A.Cup apps	F.A.Cup gls	Welsh Cup apps	Welsh Cup gls	League Cup apps	League Cup gls	Total apps	Total gls
1959/60	8	0	-	-	2	0	-	-	10	0
1960/61	8	0	-	-	1	1	1	0	10	1
	16	**0**	-	-	**3**	**1**	**1**	**0**	**20**	**1**

SUTTON, Melvyn Charles 1972 - 1982

Position; *Midfield*
D.O.B; *13th February, 1946*
Birthplace; *Birmingham, West Midlands*
Height; *5ft 10in* ***Weight;*** *10st 10lbs*
Debut; v. *Southend United (a) 12th August 1972*
Total Appearances & Goals; *461/8 apps 26 gls*
Career; *Aston Villa (Am) 1964 0apps; Cardiff City 1st Dec 1967 135/3apps 5gls; WREXHAM 1st Jul 1972 £15,000; Crewe Alexandra 5th Aug 1982 13apps 0gls;*
Honours; *Third Division Championship Winner 1978; Welsh Cup Winner 1970, 1971, 1975 & 1978; Welsh Cup runner-up 1972 & 1979;*

Mel Sutton joined Aston Villa as an amateur in 1964, but after three years in reserve team football he was allowed to leave Villa Park without having made a first team appearance. He joined Second Division Cardiff City in December 1967, but it was not until the following season that he was to make his Football League debut in a 1-0 home defeat by Charlton Athletic. Mel went on to establish himself in the 'Bluebirds' team, helping them to finish in a very creditable fifth place, and he made his European debut against FC Porto, although he missed the Welsh Cup Final victory over Swansea, despite having played in all the earlier rounds. The subsequent European campaign saw him pitted against Mjondalen I.F. of Norway and Goztepe Izmir of Turkey. At the end of the season he collected another Welsh Cup winners' medal as the 'Bluebirds' beat Chester 5-0 on aggregate, and the 1970/71 European adventure brought matches against P.O.Larnaca of Cyprus, Nantes of France, and the mighty Real Madrid in the Quarter-Finals. Once again, the Ninian Park club lifted the Welsh Cup, beating Wrexham 4-1 on aggregate, while 1971/72 saw the 'Bluebirds' defeated by Dynamo Berlin on the away goals rule. The South Wales club again reached the Welsh Cup Final, but this time they lost 3-2 on aggregate to Wrexham. During the summer of 1972 Mel signed for the North Wales club for a then club record fee paid of £15,000. He went straight into the 'Robins' team for the opening game of the season at Southend, and marked the occasion by scoring the only goal in a 1-0 win. He was on the mark again in his home debut against Watford, another 1-0 win. 'Sutty', as he was affectionately called, missed just three games that season, and played in the club's first ever European match against F.C.Zurich, as well as the second round games with Hajduk Split. His experience in Europe was a major asset in those games, with his hard running and precision passing bringing a new dimension to the Wrexham team, and the club went on to enjoy fabulous success throughout the ten years that 'Sutty' spent at the Racecourse. He became a key figure in a workmanlike midfield unit along with Arfon Griffiths and Mickey Thomas. The 1973/74 season saw Wrexham reach the Quarter-Finals of the F.A.Cup for the first time in the club's history, while the following campaign he played in the side that won back the Welsh Cup, beating his former club Cardiff City in the Final. In 1975/76 Mel played a significant part in helping Wrexham reach the Quarter-Finals of the European Cup-Winners' Cup, losing to the eventual winners of the competition, Anderlecht of Belgium, 2-1 on aggregate. The 'Robins' again featured in a number of giant-killing acts the following season, with memorable victories over Leicester City, Sunderland, and Spurs. In the

League the North Wales club almost won promotion to the Second Division for the first time in its history, but their bid failed despite needing just three points from their last five games. Manager John Neal left for Middlesbrough in the close season of 1976, and Arfon Griffiths was then put in charge. He quickly appointed Mel as his assistant, and together they finally led Wrexham to the promotion dream and the Third Division Championship in some style, as well as winning the Welsh Cup and reaching the Quarter-Finals of both the F.A. and League Cups. 'Sutty' continued to be a vital member of the 'Robins' midfield in their first assault on the Second Division, which was to be a season of consolidation. Wrexham also reached the Final of the Welsh Cup where they lost to Shrewsbury, although qualifying for Europe for the next season when they met Rijeka of Yugoslavia, who won 3-2 on aggregate. The end of the 1980/81 season saw Arfon Griffiths resign on a point of principle, after being told to cut one of his coaching staff - Mel, Mickey Evans, and George Showell. 'Sutty' was eventually appointed Wrexham's new manager, with Evans as his assistant, but the 1981/82 season was to be a long and arduous one as the 'Robins' struggled to retain their Second Division status. There was one bright spot, when Wrexham beat Brian Clough's Nottingham Forest 3-1 on their own ground in the F.A.Cup. With the club relegated to the Third Division Mel was relieved of his managerial duties. He then had a short spell playing for Crewe Alexandra under Arfon Griffiths, making thirteen League appearances without scoring, before hanging up his boots. Mel later moved to the Birmingham area, where he took over a newsagent's business, while keeping involved with football by scouting.

Season	League		F.A.Cup		Welsh Cup		League Cup		E.C.W.C.		Total	
	apps	gls	apps	gls	apps	gls	apps	gls	apps	gls	apps	gls
1972/73	44	5	2	0	1	0	2	0	4	1	53	6
1973/74	39	2	7	1	2	0	2	0	-	-	50	3
1974/75	33/1	2	1	0	5	2	1	0	-	-	40/1	4
1975/76	43/1	6	3	0	2/1	0	3	0	6	1	57/2	7
1976/77	44	2	6	0	3	0	5	0	-	-	58	2
1977/78	46	2	9	0	5	0	6	0	-	-	66	2
1978/79	39/2	0	1/2	0	4	0	3	0	2	0	49/4	0
1979/80	37/1	1	4	0	2	0	4	0	2	0	49/1	1
1980/81	30	1	5	0	3	0	1	0	-	-	39	1
	355/5	**21**	**38/2**	**1**	**27/1**	**2**	**27**	**0**	**14**	**2**	**461/8**	**26**

SYKES, **John** 1969 - 1970

Position; *Forward*
D.O.B; *2nd November, 1950*
Birthplace; *Huddersfield*
Height; *ft in* ***Weight;*** *st lbs*
Debut; v. *Workington (h) 5th May 1969*
Total Appearances & Goals; *1 app 0 gls*
Career; *Bradford Park Avenue Nov 1968 1app 0gls; WREXHAM 9th Jan 1969;*
Honours; *Northern Floodlit League Cup Winner 1970; Alves Cup Winner 1970;*

John Sykes was signed from school as an apprentice by Bradford Park Avenue, and went on to complete professional forms for the Yorkshire Club in November 1968. He made his Football League debut for Bradford before joining Wrexham in January 1969 in a part exchange deal that saw the experienced Ray Charnley move in the opposite direction. John went on to record his first team debut for Wrexham at home to Workington in the final game of the 1968/69 season, replacing Ian Moir at inside-forward as the 'Robins' went on to record a 1-0 victory. He remained at the Racecourse for one more season, although this was spent playing reserve team football for a very successful second XI as they won both the Northern Floodlit League Cup and the Alves Cup. He was released by manager John Neal, and is known to have later emigrated to Australia in March 1971.

Season	League		F.A.Cup		Welsh Cup		League Cup		Total	
	apps	gls	apps	gls	apps	gls	apps	gls	apps	gls
1968/69	1	0	-	-	-	-	-	-	1	0
	1	**0**	**-**	**-**	**-**	**-**	**-**	**-**	**1**	**0**

T

Mickey Thomas

TAPSCOTT, Eli John 1950 - 1956

Position; *Wing-Half*
D.O.B; *29th April, 1928*
Birthplace; *Plymouth, Devon*
Height; *5ft 7'1/2in* **Weight;** *11st 3lbs*
Debut; v. *Shrewsbury Town (h) 30th August, 1950*
Total Appearances & Goals; *192 apps 5 gls*
Career; *Brighton & Hove Albion 0apps; Leeds United March 1950 0apps; WREXHAM 25th May 1950; Yeovil Town cs1956; St.Austell; Holsworth 21st Sept 1960;*

Johnny Tapscott was the cousin of former Welsh international, Arsenal and Cardiff City forward, Derek Tapscott. As a schoolboy Johnny had represented Devon at Table Tennis, but it was football in which he went on to excel. Brighton & Hove Albion were the first club to recognise his potential, after he had been spotted playing in local football around his Plymouth home. He failed to break into the first team at the Goldstone Ground, and so moved North in March 1950 to try his luck with Leeds United. Again, however, he found that he could not make an impression on the Yorkshire club's senior squad, and just two months later he signed for Wrexham in May 1950. Soon after arriving at the Racecourse Johnny made his Football League debut in a 1-0 home win over Shrewsbury Town in the fourth game of the 1950/51 season. He laid claim to the inside-right shirt until the middle of October, when he was displaced by Eddie Beynon. However, the Wrexham manager Peter Jackson then converted Tapscott to a right-half, and it was in that position that he returned to the first team in March 1951 as a deputy for Stewart McCallum, remaining there until the end of season. The following year saw Johnny again having to be content with reserve team football, until Christmas 1951, after which he went on to enjoy considerable success. He eventually completed 172 League appearances for Wrexham and played in some of the club's memorable cup games of the 1950s against Stoke City, Orient, and his former side, Brighton. Sadly, injury was to bring Johnny's career to a premature end towards the close of the 1955/56 season, whereupon a testimonial match was arranged for him in April 1956 against a Select XI to help cushion the blow.

Season	League		F.A.Cup		Welsh Cup		Total	
	apps	gls	apps	gls	apps	gls	apps	gls
1950/51	22	1	-	-	-	-	22	1
1951/52	25	0	-	-	4	0	29	0
1952/53	45	1	3	0	1	0	49	1
1953/54	33	0	6	1	1	0	40	1
1954/55	35	2	-	-	4	0	39	2
1955/56	12	0	-	-	1	0	13	0
	172	**4**	**9**	**1**	**11**	**0**	**192**	**5**

TAYLOR, Edward Hallows 1928 - 1929

Position; *Goalkeeper*
D.O.B; *7th March, 1891*
Birthplace; *Liverpool, Merseyside*
Died; *Golcar, Huddersfield, 5th July, 1956*
Height; *5ft 8'1/2in* **Weight;** *11st 10lbs*
Debut; v. *Lincoln City (a) 3rd November, 1928*
Total Appearances & Goals; *25 apps 0 gls*
Career; *Marlborough Old Boys; Liverpool Balmoral; Oldham Athletic 27th Feb 1912 £30 86apps 0gls; Huddersfield Town 2nd June 1922 £1,950 119apps 0gls; Everton 12th Feb 1927 £1,650 40apps 0gls; Ashton National 14th Sept 1928; WREXHAM 3rd Nov 1928 to cs1929;*
Honours; *Eight Full England International caps; Two Football League Representative appearances; Football League Championship Winner 1924, 1926 & 1928;*

Ted Taylor was a relatively late newcomer to the Football League. He had played non-league football in goal for both Marlborough Old Boys and Liverpool Balmoral, from where he was signed by First Division Oldham Athletic in February 1912 for a fee of £30! Ted made his Football League debut for Oldham in the final match of the 1912/13 season, a scoreless home draw against Manchester United. He was to remain understudy to Howard Matthews for most of his time at Boundary Park, and made just 86 League appearances in the ten years that he spent with the 'Latics', although the First World War did limit his opportunities. Shortly after his benefit match with Manchester United, on 22nd April 1922, he was transferred to First Division Huddersfield Town for a fee of just under £2,000. Ted proved to be a good investment for the 'Terriers', as he helped them finish in 3rd place in his first season at Leeds Road. He missed just seven games the following season as Huddersfield won the First Division Championship. By this time Ted had been honoured with a call-up to the England squad in April 1923 against Scotland, in a 2-2 draw in Glasgow, while he went on to receive a total of eight full caps. He played in the first ten matches of the following season before he broke his leg in October 1924 at Maine Road against Manchester City, as the 'Terriers' went on to win the Championship for a second year in succession. He was back in goal for 1925/26, as Huddersfield captured a record third Championship. The following season Taylor was replaced in goal by Hugh Turner, and left Leeds Road in February 1927 to join Everton for a fee of £1,650. He went straight into the 'Toffee's' first team, making his debut in a 1-0 'derby' defeat against Liverpool, and kept his place in the side up to the end of the season to help Everton steer clear of the relegation zone, as they finished in 20th place. The following season couldn't have been more different, as Everton stormed to the First Division Championship, with Ted making 26 appearances. He had won his third Championship medal at the age of 37! In September 1928 Taylor joined his former Huddersfield team-mate, Ernie Islip, at Ashton National in the Cheshire County League. He remained there for just two months before he signed for Third Division North side Wrexham in November 1928, along with Ernie Islip. Ted went straight into goal, in place of George Greatrex, for his debut at Lincoln in a 1-1 draw, and completed a further 24 League appearances for Wrexham that season, playing his final match for the club against Hartlepool on the 6th April 1929. At the sprightly age of 38 years and 31 days Ted Taylor retired from playing football at the end of the season. He then returned to live in the Huddersfield area, where he died on 5th July 1956, at the age of 65.

Season	League		F.A.Cup		Welsh Cup		Total	
	apps	gls	apps	gls	apps	gls	apps	gls
1928/29	25	0	1	0	1	0	27	0
	25	**0**	**1**	**0**	**1**	**0**	**27**	**0**

TAYLOR, Jason Scott 1987 - 1989

Position; *Midfield*
D.O.B; *29th August, 1970*
Birthplace; *Mostyn, Flintshire*
Height; *5ft 9in* **Weight;** *11st 3lbs*
Debut; v. *Doncaster Rovers (a) 24th September, 1988*
Total Appearances & Goals; *0/1 apps 0 gls*
Career; *WREXHAM 1st Sept 1987; Bangor City June 1989; Brymbo Steelworks 1989/90; Gresford Athletic Feb 1990; Mold Alex August 1990;*
Honours; *Welsh Youth Cup Runner-up 1988 & 1989;*

Jason Taylor joined Wrexham as a Y.T.S. apprentice in September 1987, having already played for the Wrexham & District Schoolboys side. He played in the Wrexham youth team that secured two consecutive Welsh Youth Cup Finals, in 1988 and 1989, though they lost both to Cardiff City. His one and only first team appearance for the 'Robins' came in September 1988, as a substitute for Jon Bowden in a 2-2 draw at Doncaster Rovers. Jason was released by the club in June 1989, and joined Alliance Premier League side Bangor City during the close season. However, he was soon on the move again, leaving Farrar Road after having made just a couple of appearances. He then began playing local football for Brymbo Steelworks, and by February 1990 he had joined another Welsh National League side, Gresford Athletic. In August of the same year. Taylor joined Holywell Town and was appointed Club Captain in the Clubs first season in the new C-MRU Alliance League. His brother Chris, also played in the same side.

Season	League		F.A.Cup		Welsh Cup		League Cup		F.R.T.		Total	
	apps	gls	apps	gls	apps	gls	apps	gls	apps	gls	apps	gls
1988/89	0/1	0	-	-	-	-	-	-	-	-	0/1	0
	0/1	**0**	-	-	-	-	-	-	-	-	**0/1**	**0**

***TAYLOR,* Kenneth**

1970 - 1971

Position; *Right-Back*
D.O.B; *5th June, 1952*
Birthplace; *Porthmadog, Gwynedd*
Height; *5ft 8in* ***Weight;*** *10st 7lbs*
Debut; v. *Gillingham (h) 1st March, 1971*
Total Appearances & Goals; *1 app 0 gls*
Career; *Porthmadog; WREXHAM May 1970; Connah's Quay Nomads 14th Aug 1971; Porthmadog 29th Aug 1972; Nantlle Vale 15th Aug 1974;*
Honours; *Welsh Youth International;*

Ken Taylor came to the Racecourse as a 15 year-old junior from his home town club, Porthmadog, in July 1967 having been spotted playing for Caernarvonshire schoolboys. He went on to spend three years with Wrexham, working his way through the ranks to earn a professional contract in May 1970. During that time he had represented Wales at Youth level. After signing professional Ken found that his first team chances were very limited, due to the form of Steve Ingle, Stuart Mason, and Tommy Vansitart, though he did make his Football League debut on St.Davids Day 1971 against Gillingham on the Racecourse, when he replaced Steve Ingle. Wrexham lost the match 4-3, and it proved to be Taylor's only senior appearance in a Wrexham shirt. In the summer of 1971 he was informed by manager John Neal that he was to be released. Taylor then signed for Connah's Quay Nomads, where he was to spend the 1971/72 season before joining his town club of Porthmadog in the summer. He enjoyed two seasons at Y Traeth before joining Nantlle Vale in the summer of 1974. He later returned to the Wrexham area to play for a number of local sides. At the end of his playing days Ken settled in the Wrexham area, where he became employed by the Acumatic Filtration company in Llay.

Season	League		F.A.Cup		Welsh Cup		League Cup		Total	
	apps	gls	apps	gls	apps	gls	apps	gls	apps	gls
1970/71	1	0	-	-	-	-	-	-	1	0
	1	**0**	-	-	-	-	-	-	**1**	**0**

***TAYLOR,* Peter Mark Richard**

1992 - 1995

Position; *Forward/Midfield*
D.O.B; *20th November, 1964*
Birthplace; *Hartlepool*
Height; *5ft 7in* ***Weight;*** *11st 0lbs*
Debut; v. *Carlisle United (a) 24th March, 1992*
Total Appearances & Goals; *49/11 apps 9 gls*
Career; *Hartlepool United 16th Aug 1982 42/5apps 4gls; Crewe Alexandra 23rd Dec 1985 (Loan) 3apps 0gls; Blackpool 28th Aug 1986 104/15apps 43gls; Cardiff City 21st Dec 1990 (Loan) 6apps 3gls; WREXHAM 24th Mar 1992 £30,000; Retired 1995;*
Honours; *Third Division runner-up 1993;*

After leaving school Mark Taylor went to a local college to study for an OND in Structural Engineering. He played football on both Saturday and Sunday's during this time, and it was performances for his Sunday League side that attracted the attention of his local Football League club, Hartlepool United. He was invited along to Hartlepool for a trial, following which he signed part-time forms while he completed his college course. Once that was achieved Mark was given a full-time contract, and went on to make his Football League debut during the 1983/84 season. He spent four seasons with Hartlepool, during which he had a loan spell at Crewe Alexandra in December 1985, where he made three League appearances. Mark was released by Hartlepool at the end of the 1985/86 season, and despite having an offer to return to Crewe he decided to sign for Blackpool. He made a good start with the 'Seasiders', scoring 35 goals in 81 League matches in his first two seasons at Bloomfield Road. However, disaster was to follow when a knee injury sidelined him for 18 months. When fit enough to return to action he found that his senior opportunities were somewhat limited, so he took up the offer of a loan spell with Cardiff City in December 1990. Mark scored three goals in six matches for the Ninian Park club, before returning to Blackpool's first team. His efforts helped the 'Seasiders' reach the Play-Off Final at Wembley, where he scored in a penalty shoot-out as they lost to Torquay United. 1991/92 saw him again struggling to command a regular first team place, and in March 1992 was allowed to join Wrexham for £30,000. Mark made his debut in a 1-0 win at Carlisle, playing in his usual position of wide right midfield/winger. Even though he always gave his best at Wrexham Mark often found himself on the receiving end of some unpleasant barracking from the Racecourse terraces. His right sided position was not Wrexham's favourite line of attack during his time at the club, as Karl Connolly's abilities on the left wing often provided the more favourable - and eye catching - attacking option. Indeed when used more in a central attacking position he looked far more at home and with being more involved scored some useful goals. Taylor also suffered with his fair share of injuries, and they limited him to just 18 appearances in the promotion season of 92/93. He was back to his best throughout 1993/94, however, before a recurrence of his knee injury the following season, restricted him to just three appearances before announcing his premature retirement from League football. During his time at Wrexham Mark had prepared for a career after football by qualifying as a physiotherapist, and upon the departure of club physio Steve Wade was offered the position at Wrexham, which he accepted. However, in July 1995 he left the Racecourse to take up a similar position at Blackpool, as he still lived in the seaside town. Mark spent two seasons with the Bloomfield Road club before appointed physiotherapist at Premier League side Blackburn Rovers in the close season of 1997. Mark is still at Ewood Park at the time of writing.

Season	League		F.A.Cup		Welsh Cup		League Cup		F.R.T.		Total	
	apps	gls	apps	gls	apps	gls	apps	gls	apps	gls	apps	gls
1991/92	6/3	0	-	-	-	-	-	-	-	-	6/3	0
1992/93	13/6	2	1	0	2	1	1	0	1	0	18/6	3
1993/94	28/2	7	-	-	1	0	2	0	1	0	32/2	7
1994/95	3	0	-	-	-	-	1/1	0	-	-	4/1	0
	50/11	**9**	**1**	**0**	**3**	**1**	**4/1**	**0**	**2**	**0**	**60/12**	**10**

TAYLOR, Samuel 1930 - 1932

Position; *Inside-Left*
D.O.B; *20th November, 1902*
Birthplace; *Birmingham, West Midlands*
Died; *Birmingham, 8th October, 1975*
Height; *5ft 8in* ***Weight;*** *10st 7lbs*
Debut; v. *Southport (a) 30th August, 1930*
Total Appearances & Goals; *95 apps 36 gls*
Career; *Cradley Heath 1924/25; Birmingham Mar 1927 0apps; Stourbridge cs1927; Chesterfield Jun 1928 59apps 26gls; WREXHAM 10th May 1930; Walsall Jul 1932 20apps 4gls; Hereford Town Aug 1933;*
Honours; *Welsh Cup Winner 1931; Welsh Cup runner-up 1932; Birmingham & District League Championship Winner 1926;*

Sam Taylor had scored over 120 goals in three seasons for Birmingham & District League side Cradley Heath, and they won their League championship in 1926. This kind of form soon attracted the attention of the Football League clubs, and Birmingham signed the promising forward in 1926. Sam spent one season at St.Andrew's, but he failed to make an impression and was released in the summer without having made a first team appearance. He then signed for Birmingham & District League club Stourbridge, where his displays at inside-left once again caught the eye, and in June 1928 joined Third Division North Side, Chesterfield. He was pitched straight into the team for his Football League debut, against Wrexham on the Racecourse, where the home side triumphed 4-3. Taylor went on to spend two years at Saltergate, where he scored 26 goals in 59 League games before joining Wrexham in May 1930. He was brought to the Racecourse to replace the experienced Roland Woodhouse, and went straight into the side for the first game of 1930/31 at Southport, which ended in a 1-1 draw. He was virtually an ever-present throughout the two years that he spent at the Racecourse, missing just one League game - at Halifax in March 1932. He also collected a Welsh Cup winners' medal in 1931, when Wrexham beat Shrewsbury 7-0, adding a runners'-up medal in the same competition a year later as Swansea won 2-0. Sam was allowed to join Walsall in the summer of 1932, where he spent one season, making his debut in a 1-0 home win over Hull City in the opening match of the season. He registered four goals in 20 League games before returning to non-league football at the end of the season with Birmingham & District League side Hereford Town. After retiring from football Sam was employed by Gaskell & Chambers, where he worked alongside James Allen (Ex-Aston Villa, Portsmouth & England) and Arthur Johnson (Ex-Birmingham) producing 'Beer Engines' (Pumps) for Public Houses. He occasionally turned out for the firm in the Birmingham Works League, and they were a very successful side that won many trophies.

Season	League		F.A.Cup		Welsh Cup		Total	
	apps	gls	apps	gls	apps	gls	apps	gls
1930/31	42	16	3	1	4	4	49	21
1931/32	39	10	1	0	6	5	46	15
	81	**26**	**4**	**1**	**10**	**9**	**95**	**36**

THACKERAY, Andrew John 1988 - 1992

Position; *Midfield/Right-Back*
D.O.B; *13th February, 1968*
Birthplace; *Huddersfield, Yorkshire*
Height; *5ft 9in* ***Weight;*** *11st 0lbs*
Debut; v. *Exeter City (a) 27th August, 1988*
Total Appearances & Goals; *143/13 apps 14 gls*
Career; *Manchester City 15th Feb 1986 0apps; Huddersfield Town 1st Aug 1986 2apps 0gls; Newport County 27th Mar 1987 £5,000 53/1apps 4gls; WREXHAM 20th Jul 1988 £5,000; Rochdale 15th Jul 1992 £15,000 161/4apps 13gls; Halifax Town Jul 1997 37/1apps 5gls (GM 41apps 2gls; Nuneaton Borough Jun 1999;*
Honours; *Welsh Cup runner-up 1987, 1990 & 1991; F.A.Youth Cup Winner 1986; GM Conference League Championship Winner 1998;*

As a schoolboy in his native Huddersfield Andy Thackeray was regularly found playing as a striker for his local Schools' representative sides, and for West Yorkshire under-15 to 18 teams. It was as a forward that he was first offered schoolboy forms by Manchester City, and progressed quickly to an apprenticeship at Maine Road. During this time Andy played in Manchester City's F.A.Youth Cup winning side of 1986, alongside the likes of Paul Lake, Ian Brightwell, Steve Redmond, and Andy Hinchcliffe. He was sent-off in the first leg of that Final against Manchester United, along with Aiden Murphy of United, though both players were able to play in the second leg as City went on to record a 3-1 aggregate victory. Despite this success Andy found that he was to be released during the summer. It was then that his home town club, Huddersfield Town, came in, when manager Mick Buxton offered him a one year contract. He spent just under a season with the 'Terriers', making his Football League debut as a right-winger in a scoreless draw at Hull City in March 1987. He played in the following game, a 1-1 home draw with Sheffield United, before being sold to Newport County at the end of that month for £5,000. Andy became a regular at Somerton Park, where he was to switch to either full-back berths, or in midfield. However, these were desperate times at Newport, and at the end of the following season they crashed out of the Football League. Before 1988/89 had begun, Andy took up an offer to remain in the Football League by joining Fourth Division Wrexham for £5,000. He made his debut in a 2-0 win at Exeter, and played his part in helping the 'Robins' reach final of the play-offs, where they eventually lost to Orient. 89/90 season saw Andy and Wrexham reach the first Welsh Cup Final to be played at the National Stadium in Cardiff, where they lost 2-1 to Hereford, though they still qualified for Europe because there opponents were an English club. Thackeray featured in the victory over the Danish side Lyngby, following season which Wrexham drew Manchester United in the next round. He also reached yet another Welsh Cup Final, where Wrexham were beaten by Swansea, but overall it was a disappointing year as the 'Robins' finished bottom of the Football League. The 1991/92 season witnessed an amazing improvement in the club's health, with Andy playing in one of the greatest F.A.Cup upsets of all time as Wrexham beat the reigning Football League champions, Arsenal, 2-1 on the Racecourse. It was this game that signalled the change in Wrexham's fortunes, though the Yorkshire man was to play no further part in the revival as he was sold to Rochdale in the summer of 1992 for a bargain £15,000. He had been a consistent performer throughout his time at the Racecourse, comfortable either at right-back or in midfield. He had a good right foot, he was a good cross-field passer of the ball, and also liked to overlap. Thackeray immediately became a first team regular at Spotland, and was later made club captain. His reputation for consistency was maintained as Andy went on to make 165 League appearances, scoring 13 goals, before released in the summer of 1992.

He was quickly snapped up by Conference League side, Halifax Town, and went on to help the 'Shaymen' to win the championship in his first season, taking them back into the Football League after a five year absence. He returned to the Racecourse at the beginning of the 1998/99 season for a Worthington Cup tie which the 'Shaymen' won 2-0, although Wrexham were to go out on penalties after a second-leg comeback. At the end of that campaign Andy accepted a move to non-league Nuneaton Borough.

Season	League apps	League gls	F.A.Cup apps	F.A.Cup gls	Welsh Cup apps	Welsh Cup gls	League Cup apps	League Cup gls	F.R.T. apps	F.R.T. gls	E.C.W.C. apps	E.C.W.C. gls	Total apps	Total gls
1988/89	27/8	2	-	-	2/1	0	2	0	0/2	0	4*	0*	31/11*	2*
1989/90	29/5	7	-	-	5	1	2	0	1/1	0	-	-	37/6	8
1990/91	41	2	1	0	5	1	4	0	2	0	1	0	54	3
1991/92	42	3	5	0	3	1	2	1	5	0	-	-	57	5
	139/13	**14**	**6**	**0**	**15/1**	**3**	**10**	**1**	**8/3**	**0**	**5***	**0***	**183/17**	***18***

* = includes play-off matches.

THOMAS, Andrew 1995 - 1997

Position; *Defender*
D.O.B; *14th December 1977*
Birthplace; *Chester, Cheshire*
Height; *6ft 0in* ***Weight;*** *11st 3lbs*
Debut; v. *Petrolul Ploiesti (a) 24th August 1995 (E.C.W.C.)*
Total Appearances & Goals; *1 app 0 gls*
Career; *WREXHAM Jul 1994; Connah's Quay Nomads Jul 1997 70apps 3gls; Bangor City Jun 1999;*
Honours; *Welsh Youth International cap; Welsh non-league International cap; Welsh Cup runner-up 1998; Welsh Youth Cup Winner 1996;*

Andy Thomas represented his school, Hawarden High, and also turned out for St.David's on a Saturday in the Clwyd Youth League. He was selected for Flintshire Schoolboys at around this time, playing either in midfield or as a forward. Andy was first approached by Tranmere Rovers, where he spent a year towards the end of his school days. However, on completion of his education other clubs began to show an interest, the likes of Crewe, Preston, and Manchester United, but it was Wrexham who were first to offer him a YTS contract. Having agreed to sign for the Racecourse club he joined them in the summer of 1994, where he was soon switched to the centre of defence. During the 1994/95 season he was a member of the club's Youth team that enjoyed a good run in the F.A.Youth Cup eventually going out to Manchester United. The summer of 1995 saw Thomas enhance his career prospects as he was selected for the Welsh Youth team in a tournament in Northern Ireland, which they won by beating the hosts in the Final. Then, with Wrexham playing in the European Cup-Winners' Cup before the Football League season had begun, and lacking eligible Welsh senior players, Andy was named on the sub's bench for the home tie with Romanian Cup Winners, Petrolul Ploiesti. A freak injury to regular right-back Deryn Brace, before the second leg in Romania meant that he was called upon for his first team debut. In the hot sunshine, he didn't let himself or his team mates down, despite Wrexham losing 1-0. He then picked up further Youth honours for Wales, as well as a Welsh Youth Cup winners' medal in the 1996 Final, following a 3-2 win over Swansea City. It was enough to earn him a professional contract at the end of the season. However, he couldn't maintain the early promise, and was released at the end of 1996/97. Andy then signed for League of Wales side Connah's Quay Nomads in the summer, and went on to be an ever present in his first season with the 'Quaymen' with whom he is regarded as one of the best right-back's in the League of Wales, helping the 'Nomads' to reach the Final of the Welsh Cup, where they drew 1-1 with Bangor City before disappointingly losing 4-2 in a penalty shoot out. Andy continued to impress with the Deeside club, and having been an ever-present for the 1998/99 season, earned further international recognition by representing Wales in a non-league international against England at St.Albans. Andy signed for Bangor City in June 1999.

Season	League apps	League gls	F.A.Cup apps	F.A.Cup gls	Welsh Cup apps	Welsh Cup gls	League Cup apps	League Cup gls	F.R.T. apps	F.R.T. gls	E.C.W.C. apps	E.C.W.C. gls	Total apps	Total gls
1995/96	-	-	-	-	-	-	-	-	-	-	1	0	1	0
	-	**-**	**-**	**-**	**-**	**-**	**-**	**-**	**-**	**-**	**1**	**0**	**1**	**0**

THOMAS, Michael Reginald 1971 - 1978 & 1991 - 1993

Position; *Midfield*
D.O.B; *7th July, 1954*
Birthplace; *Mochdre, Denbighshire*
Height; *5ft 6in* ***Weight;*** *10st 7lbs*
Debut; v. *Bournemouth (a) 1st January, 1972*
Total Appearances & Goals; *331/16 apps 44 gls*
Career; *WREXHAM 28th Apr 1972; Manchester United 23rd Nov 1978 £300,000 90apps 11gls; Everton Aug 1981 £350,000 10apps 0gls; Brighton & Hove Albion Nov 1981 £350,000 18/2apps 0gls; Stoke City Aug 1982 £200,000 57apps 14gls; Chelsea Jan 1984 £75,000 43/1apps 9gls; West Bromwich Albion 26th Sept 1985 £100,000 20apps 0gls; Derby County 28th Mar 1986 9apps 0gls (Loan); Wichita Wings (USA) £35,000 Aug 1986; Shrewsbury Town Aug 1988 40apps 1gls; Leeds United Jun 1989 £10,000 3apps 0gls; Stoke City 20th Mar 1990 8apps 0gls (Loan); Stoke City Aug 1990 32/6apps 7gls; WREXHAM Jul 1991; Brymbo June 1994; Inter Cardiff Aug 1994; Porthmadog Sept 1994, (Player/Manager) Jan 1995-Jun 1995 29/1apps 0gls; Buckley Town Nov 1996; Mochdre Aug 1997; Amlwch Town Aug 1998;*
Honours; *51 Welsh International caps; One Welsh Under-23 International cap; Two Welsh under-21 International caps; Welsh Youth International cap; F.A.Cup runner-up 1979; Second Division Championship Winner 1984; Third Division Championship Winner 1978; Welsh Cup Winner 1972, 1975 & 1978; Welsh Youth Cup Winner 1971; P.F.A.Third Division XI 1978;*

What can one say about Mickey Thomas' football abilities that hasn't already been said? He was a tenacious midfield player, full of flair and eagerness, who would always give 100% wherever he played. However, his career was all too often offset by his problems off the field. Mickey's football career began with Wrexham, having been spotted playing for Conwy, Clwyd and North Wales Schoolboys. His all-action style of play and elusive runs down the flank finally helped Wrexham to gain promotion to the Second Division for the first time in the Club's history in 1978. Prior to that, he had played his part in the 'Robins' many Cup giant-killing exploits, both at home and abroad, helping them to reach the Quarter-Finals of the F.A.Cup in 1974 and 1978, as well as the Quarter-Finals of both the League Cup in 1978 and the European Cup-Winners' Cup in 1976. He also added three Welsh Cup winners' medals for good measure. Mickey won the first of his 51 Welsh international caps whilst with Wrexham, against West Germany at Cardiff in October 1976. After just a few months of playing Second Division football for the 'Robins' he was signed by Manchester United, in November 1978, for a then club record fee received of £300,000. He went on to play in the 1979 F.A.Cup Final, where United lost 3-2 to Arsenal, before leaving Old Trafford in July 1981 to join Everton in an exchange deal that saw John Gidman move in the opposite direction. However, Mickey's stay at Goodison Park was short-lived, as he made just ten appearances before being sold to Brighton & Hove Albion in November of the same year. He was beset with domestic problems during his time at the Goldstone Ground, absenting himself without leave on a number of occasions. He finally left Brighton in August 1982 to join Stoke City for £200,000. He later joined Chelsea, where he teamed up with former manager at Wrexham, John Neal, as well as his big mate, Joey Jones, and they all played major parts in taking Chelsea to the Second Division Championship in 1984. He later went on to have spells with West Bromwich Albion, Derby County, Wichita Wings in America, Shrewsbury Town, Leeds United and Stoke again, before finally returning to his spiritual home at Wrexham in August 1991. Mickey's second spell with

Wrexham proved to be just as fulfilling as his first, as he hit the national headlines with a superbly taken free-kick to pave the way towards knocking the Football League Champions, Arsenal, out of the F.A.Cup in January 1992. The following season saw him limited to just eight League appearances, due to injury, as Wrexham won promotion to the Second Division. However, Thomas's playing career came to an abrupt end in July 1993, when he was handed an eighteen month prison sentence for offences connected with counterfeit money. He was released from his prison sentence in April 1994, whereupon he continued to do what he did best........play football. He signed for Cymru Alliance League side Brymbo, though before the season had begun he had signed for League of Wales side Inter Cardiff, to help them in their UEFA Cup matches against Katowice of Poland. Mickey played in the home tie, but was refused permission by the authorities to travel for the second leg because he was still under licence and prohibited from leaving the country by Home Office regulations. After Inter's European adventure was over Thomas joined his former Wales and Wrexham playing colleague Ian Edwards, who was manager at League of Wales side Porthmadog, in September 1994. Edwards was dismissed in the following January, and Mickey was appointed as the club's new player/manager. He remained in that position until the summer of 1995, when he announced his resignation. He then played for both Buckley Town and Mochdre, before being granted a benefit match by Wrexham in July 1997. First Division Wolves provided the opposition, with Ian Rush and Vinnie Jones both turning out for Wrexham as 'guests'. A crowd of 4,315 assured Mike of a good pay day. He continued to play football along the North Wales Coast for his local side Mochdre until joining Ynys Mon based Welsh Alliance League side, Amlwch Town, as player/coach in the summer of 1998. He also turned out for Llandudno Town in the Cymru Alliance League that same season. Among his other ports of call have been West Shore Arabs F.C. and Conwy U. His son Arron had trials with Wrexham in Oct 97 (great left foot like his dad!) and scored the equaliser for the North Wales Coast F.A. U18s XI at Hampden Park in May 1998 against the Scottish Juniors. Now 17 he has appeared for Porthmadog and now Llandudno in the Cymru Alliance. A recent match report stated ....."Astute play set up Arron Thomas who arrowed a shot into the roof of the net from 25 yards!! Now, where have we seen that before!! His daughter is also a talented footballer and is a Welsh Womens International. Is often invited by T.V. Companies to summarise on various matches including B.B.C. Wales and Manchester United T.V. and is a great double act with Joey Jones at various football functions.

Season	League		F.A.Cup		Welsh Cup		League Cup		F.R.T.		E.C.W.C.		Total	
	apps	gls	apps	gls	apps	gls	apps	gls	apps	gls	apps	gls	apps	gls
1971/72	19/1	3	-	-	4	0	-	-	-	-	-	-	23/1	3
1972/73	23/3	0	1/1	1	-	-	2	0	-	-	4	0	30/4	1
1973/74	14/5	4	1/2	0	1	0	1	0	-	-	-	-	17/7	4
1974/75	29/2	5	-	-	2	1	-	-	-	-	-	-	31/2	6
1975/76	30	2	2	0	2	0	3	0	-	-	4	0	41	2
1976/77	45	6	6	0	4	0	5	2	-	-	-	-	60	8
1977/78	41/2	7	9	1	4	1	6	0	-	-	-	-	60/2	9
1978/79	16	6	-	-	-	-	3	0	-	-	2	0	21	6
1991/92	26	1	5	2	3	0	2	0	1	0	-	-	37	3
1992/93	8	1	1	0	1	0	1	0	-	-	-	-	11	1
	251/13	**35**	**25/3**	**5**	**21**	**2**	**23**	**2**	**1**	**0**	**10**	**0**	**331/16**	**44**

***THOMAS,* Robert Kenrick** 1961 - 1962

Position; *Wing-Half*
D.O.B; *23rd September, 1938*
Birthplace; *Nebo, Gwynedd*
Height; *5ft 8in* ***Weight;*** *11st 0lbs*
Debut; v. *Porthmadog (a) 31st January, 1962 (Welsh Cup)*
Total Appearances & Goals; *1 app 0 gls*
Career; *Nantlle Vale; Porthmadog; WREXHAM 5th May 1961; Bangor City 7th Jul 1962; Blaenau Ffestiniog 31st Aug 1963; Nantlle Vale 21st August 1964; Caernarvon Town 2nd Jun 1965; Nantlle Vale 30th Oct 1965; Caernarvon Town 2nd Aug 1971; Nantlle Vale 30th Jul 1973; Pwllheli & District 19th Jun 1975; Nantlle Vale;*
Honours; *Welsh League (North) Division One Championship Winner 1966;*

The son of a farmer, Rob Thomas played his early football for Penygroes Secondary School near Caernarvon, but at the age of fourteen made his debut in the tough learning school of the Welsh League North for Nantlle Vale against Holyhead. In a 14-1 defeat, Rob scored the Vale goal! After he left school he joined fellow Welsh League North side, Porthmadog, having been signed by three of the club's committee members at the age of 16 while shearing sheep on his father's farm! He spent five seasons with Porthmadog, during which time he was a reserve for the Welsh Amateur side, before his career took off when Porthmadog played Chester in a Welsh Cup match in February 1961. Chester won 2-1, but following that game he was approached by both Chester and Wrexham. He chose Wrexham because of another Caernarfon born player already on the books, Wyn Davies - and signed as an amateur in May 1961. His first team debut arrived in January 1962, when he replaced regular half-back George Evans for a Welsh Cup tie, ironically against his former club Porthmadog, which Wrexham won 2-0. However, it proved to be his only senior appearance, although he did play in a first team friendly against Bronshoj of Denmark, before released at the end of the season. Thomas was then signed as a full-time professional by former Welsh international Tommy G.Jones, who was the manager of Bangor City, though he was to miss the Farrar Road club's European Cup-Winners' Cup match with Naples because of an ankle injury. He eventually went on to appear for Caernarvon Town, Blaenau Ffestiniog, Pwllheli, and finally Nantlle Vale, where he was to play until he was 44 years-old! At Penygroes he played alongside the likes of Orig Williams and Idris (Tarw Nefyn) Evans, who were real tough characters and were feared opponents in North Wales Football. Rob quit the professional game when he left Bangor City, whereupon he took up employment with a local sand and gravel quarry company, as well as sheep farming the mountain slopes above Caernarfon, which is one of the great loves of his life.

Season	League		F.A.Cup		Welsh Cup		League Cup		Total	
	apps	gls	apps	gls	apps	gls	apps	gls	apps	gls
1961/62	-	-	-	-	1	0	-	-	1	0
	-	**-**	**-**	**-**	**1**	**0**	**-**	**-**	**1**	**0**

***THOMAS,* Steven** 1997 -

Position; *Midfielder*
D.O.B; *23rd June, 1979*
Birthplace; *Hartlepool, Durham*
Height; *5ft 10ins* ***Weight;*** *11st 12lbs*
Debut; v. *Newtown (a) 18th August 1997 (Welsh Invitation Trophy)*
Total Appearances & Goals; *4/6 apps 1 gls*
Career; *WREXHAM Jul 1997;*
Honours; *Welsh Youth International cap; Welsh Youth Cup Winner 1996; Welsh Youth Cup runner-up 1997;*

Brought up in his native Hartlepool Steve Thomas was introduced to Wrexham by his uncle, Mark Taylor, who was on the club's playing staff at the time. Steve had received offers from Hartlepool, Blackpool, and Sunderland, but decided on Wrexham and signed apprentice terms in the summer of 1995. In his first season at the Racecourse he earned a Welsh Youth Cup winners' medal, adding a runners'-up medal in the same competition the following season. It was in the summer of 1997 that Steve was eventually signed on professional terms, and having shown much promise he was given his first team opportunity for the club in August 1997, when he replaced Peter Ward in a 2-2 draw against Newtown in a Welsh Invitation Cup match. That season was also to see him capped by Wales at Youth level, qualification coming courtesy of his grandfather, who was born in Cardigan. He made one further senior appearance during the 1997/98 season, with a place in the starting line-up for the home game with Cardiff City, also in the Welsh Invitation Cup, which Wrexham lost 1-0 in October 1997. He then had to wait almost a year before being handed his next opportunity in the first team, making his Football League debut as a substitute for Kevin Russell, in a 1-0 home defeat by Stoke City in September 1998. Much is still expected of Steve, though he has suffered his fair share of injuries.

Season	League		F.A.Cup		League Cup		A.W.S.		W.I.C.		Total	
	apps	gls	apps	gls	apps	gls	apps	gls	apps	gls	apps	gls
1997/98	-	-	-	-	-	-	-	-	1/1	0	1/1	0
1998/99	1/4	0	-	-	-	-	-	-	2/1	1	3/5	1
	1/4	**0**	-	-	-	-	-	-	**3/2**	**1**	**4/6**	**1**

***THOMPSON,* Peter** 1955 - 1957

Position; *Centre-Forward*
Birthplace; *Blackhall Colliery, Durham*
Height; *5ft 10in* ***Weight;*** *12st 4lbs*
D.O.B; *16th February, 1936*
Debut; v. *Accrington Stanley (a) 19th November, 1955 (F.A.Cup)*
Total Appearances & Goals; *55 apps 30 gls*
Career; *Blackhall C.W; WREXHAM Nov 1955; Hartlepool United Jul 1957 47apps 17gls; Derby County Nov 1958 52apps 19gls; Bournemouth Jan 1962 39apps 14gls; Hartlepool United Sept 1963; Boston United cs1966; Scarborough;*
Honours; *Four England Amateur International caps; Welsh Cup Winner 1957;*

Peter Thompson attended the Henry Smith Grammar School in Blackhall, where only rugby was played. An all-round sportsman, he represented his school at the oval ball game, while playing soccer for a local junior side, Blackhall Dynamos. He was spotted by Middlesbrough, who invited him to join them on schoolboy forms, but his school refused him permission to do so. Upon completion of his education, Peter joined the Royal Air Force as a Physical Training Instructor, initially serving at St.Athans near Cardiff, where he played a few 'A' team games for Cardiff City before moving to R.A.F.Cosford, near Wolverhampton. It was whilst he was there that he was recommended to Wrexham by Keith Matthews, one of the club's players who was spending his two years' National Service in the R.A.F. Peter signed for the North Wales club on amateur terms in November 1955, and created a sensation when scoring 13 goals in his first four reserve team games in the Cheshire County League. Not surprisingly he didn't have to wait long for his first team debut, which came in an F.A.Cup first round match at Accrington, though Wrexham lost 3-1. Peter was injured after only ten minutes of his debut, following which he took no further part in the game, and because of the demands of the R.A.F. had to wait until the end of December before he was to get another chance. Then, he made his Football League debut in a 4-2 win over Crewe, and scored two of his side's goals. He played in the following four League games before having to return to the R.A.F., where he remained until September 1956. On leaving the Services Peter signed professional forms with Wrexham, by which time he had won four England amateur international caps, his debut coming in a 5-1 win over Wales at Peterborough. He became a regular in the side during the 1956/57 season, playing mainly at centre forward where he scored eighteen goals in 37 League games, and featured in the F.A.Cup match against Manchester United, when the biggest ever crowd gathered on the Racecourse witnessed a 5-0 victory for the famous 'Busby Babes'. Peter's goalscoring abilities were to help Wrexham reach the Welsh Cup Final for the first time since 1950, and he bagged one of the goals in the 2-1 win over Swansea Town at Ninian Park to bring the cup back to North Wales. Surprisingly, he decided to leave Wrexham in the close season of 1957 to return to his native North-East, where he joined Hartlepool United. He spent just over a year with the Pool, scoring 17 goals in 47 matches before joining Derby County in November 1958. Thompson had reasonable success with Derby, finishing as their leading goalscorer during the 1959/60 season, but was never assured of a regular first team place at the Baseball Ground, and when Bill Curry established himself Peter agreed to join Bournemouth for a £5,000 fee in January 1962. Thompson stayed a season on the south coast, scoring 14 goals in 39 League games before rejoining Hartlepool United in September 1963, where he was to remain until the end of 1965/66. Peter then moved into non-league football for both Boston United and Scarborough, during which time he trained to become a youth social worker and teacher. In doing so he gained an M.A. in Philosophy, going on to lecture in Secondary Teacher training at Sunderland Polytechnic College from 1975 until 1986. He eventually became a licensee at the Seagull Inn in his native Blackhall, near Hartlepool, where he now lives in retirement. Peter was a guest at the Grand Players Re-Union in September 1998.

Season	League		F.A.Cup		Welsh Cup		Total	
	apps	gls	apps	gls	apps	gls	apps	gls
1955/56	5	3	1	0	-	-	6	3
1956/67	37	18	7	4	5	5	49	27
	42	**21**	**8**	**4**	**5**	**5**	**55**	**30**

***THURNHAM,* Roy Thomas** 1961 - 1964

Position; *Half-Back*
D.O.B; *17th February, 1942*
Birthplace; *Macclesfield, Cheshire*
Height; *6ft 1in* ***Weight;*** *11st 7lbs*
Debut; v. *Hereford United (a) 18th April, 1963 (Welsh Cup)*
Total Appearances & Goals; *3 apps 0 gls*
Career; *Manchester City Jun 1960; WREXHAM 16th Jun 1961; George Cross, Melbourne May 1964;*

Roy Thurnham was a promising schoolboy footballer who played at centre-half for Manchester Schoolboys. He signed for Manchester City as an amateur upon leaving school, taking up work at a Manchester Shipping Office at the same time. His football career progressed well, and he left his office job to sign professional for the Maine Road club in June 1960. However, he spent just one more season at Maine Road, where he failed to make a first team appearance, before being given a free transfer in June 1961. Roy was then approached by former Manchester City player Ken Barnes, who had just been appointed as the new manager of Wrexham. Barnes signed the promising centre-half, and he went on to spend almost three years with Wrexham. His first team debut came towards the end of the 1962/63 season in a 2-1 Welsh Cup defeat at Hereford United, when he replaced the consistent Alan Fox at centre-half. He kept his place for the following two games, a 1-1 home draw with Reading, and a 3-0 home win over Halifax, before Fox returned to fitness and reclaimed his shirt. Thurnham spent one more season at the Racecourse, but failed to make another first team appearance, and was released in May 1964. He then decided to emigrate to Australia, where he continued to play football for George Cross in Melbourne.

Season	League		F.A.Cup		Welsh Cup		League Cup		Total	
	apps	gls	apps	gls	apps	gls	apps	gls	apps	gls
1962/63	2	0	-	-	1	0	-	-	3	0
	2	**0**	-	-	**1**	**0**	-	-	**3**	**0**

***TILSTON,* Thomas Arthur Anthony** 1952 - 1954

Position; *Inside-Forward*
D.O.B; *19th February, 1926*
Birthplace; *Chester*
Height; *5ft 11'1/2in* ***Weight;*** *12st 1lbs*
Debut; v. *Crewe Alexandra (h) 15th March, 1952*
Total Appearances & Goals; *89 apps 32 gls*
Career; *Chester Sept 1943 22apps 7gls; Tranmere Rovers Jun 1951 25apps 15gls; WREXHAM 15th Mar 1952; Crystal Palace 6th Feb 1954 58apps 13gls; Chelmsford City Jun 1956; Gravesend & Northfleet Oct 1957; Bedford Town Jul 1958; Bexleyheath & Welling Aug 1959;*

Tommy Tilston signed as a junior for his native Chester during the Second World War, but had to wait until August 1949 before he made his Football

League debut. His chance came in the opening game of 49/50, where he appeared at inside-forward in a 4-0 home defeat by Stockport County. Tommy had earlier made his first team debut in January 1949, a 6-0 Welsh Cup defeat inflicted by Wrexham at Sealand Road. He completed 22 League appearances for Chester, scoring seven goals, although frequently the butt of the Chester fans' criticism before he was transferred to Tranmere Rovers in June 1951. Tommy got off to a good start at Prenton Park by scoring twice on his debut in the opening game of the 1951/52 season, a 4-1 home win over Hartlepool United. However, despite registering fifteen goals in 25 League games, he had lost his place in the side by February, and a month later was allowed a transfer to another Third Division North side, Wrexham. Tilston went on to spend two fruitful years with Wrexham, which began by scoring on his debut in a 4-0 win over Crewe Alexandra. The 1952/53 season saw him become a part of Wrexham's great forward line of the 1950s, joining up with Billy Tunnicliffe, Tommy Bannan, Ron Hewitt and Glyn Hughes, and contributed seventeen goals in 43 League games as Wrexham finished third in the Third Division North - only three points behind the eventual champions, Oldham Athletic. In February 1954 Tommy was surprisingly allowed to leave the Racecourse, when he joined struggling Third Division South side Crystal Palace. He made his debut for the 'Eagles' in a scoreless draw with Aldershot, and went on to make 58 League appearances during his time at Selhurst Park, scoring 13 goals. He moved on in July 1956, joining Southern League side Chelmsford City, and later played for Gravesend & Northfleet, Bedford Town, and Bexleyheath & Welling. He is believed to have settled in the Chelmsford area.

Season	League		F.A.Cup		Welsh Cup		Total	
	apps	gls	apps	gls	apps	gls	apps	gls
1951/52	9	2	-	-	1	0	10	2
1952/53	43	17	3	1	1	1	47	19
1953/54	26	10	5	0	1	1	32	11
	78	**29**	**8**	**1**	**3**	**2**	**89**	**32**

TINNION, Brian

1969 - 1976

Position; *Forward*
D.O.B; *11th June, 1948*
Birthplace; *Workington, Cumbria*
Height; *5ft 8'1/2in* ***Weight;*** *11st 3lbs*
Debut; v. *Colchester United (h) 11th January, 1969*
Total Appearances & Goals; *316/19 apps 65 gls*
Career; *Workington Mar 1966 93/5apps 24gls; WREXHAM Jan 1969 £14,000; Chester Dec 1971 (Loan) 3apps 0gls; New York Cosmos 28th Apr 1976 £22,000; Hawaii Apr 1977; Detroit Apr 1978; Bangor City Nov 1978 (loan); Detroit;*
Honours; *England Youth international cap; Welsh Cup Winner 1972 & 1975; Division Four runner-up 1970;*

After leaving school Brian Tinnion took up an apprenticeship as an engine cleaner with British Rail before accepting professional terms with his hometown club, Workington. He had been with the Borough Park club as a junior, and during that time had earned international recognition by representing England at Youth level, playing in the same side as Stuart Mason. He made over 100 appearances for Workington before Wrexham manager John Neal splashed out a club record fee paid of £14,000 to capture the promising forward in January 1969. Brian made his 'Robins' debut in a 3-0 home defeat by Colchester United, replacing the departed Ray Charnley at centre-forward, and he remained in the side for the rest of the season. Tinnion missed most of the first half of the following season through illness and injury, but returned in January to help Wrexham win promotion to the Third Division. He had been converted from an inside-forward to right-winger by John Neal, and provided the crosses for Wrexham's potent strike force of Albert Kinsey and Ray Smith. Later he provided a similar service for Billy Ashcroft and Dave Smallman, starring for the 'Robins' in many of their memorable cup matches of the early 1970s, against the likes of Aston Villa, Southampton, Crystal Palace, Middlesbrough, Burnley, F.C.Zurich and Anderlecht. He also collected two Welsh Cup winners' medals with Wrexham in, 1972 and 1975, both victories earning the 'Robins' their place in Europe. In December 1971 he joined Chester for a month's loan, where he made three appearances, including a 2-1 home win over his former club - Workington - on his debut. Tinnion left the Racecourse club in the summer of 1976, having decided to go to the U.S.A. to join up with his former boss at Workington, Ken Furphy, then in charge of the progressive American side New York Cosmos. Furphy paid Wrexham £20,000 to secure his services, and Brian went on to appear for the Cosmos alongside many world class players, including, Franz Beckenbaur and Pele. He returned home in November 1978, during the American close season, when he had a short loan spell at Bangor City. After returning to America for the new season Brian eventually moved on to play for both Hawaii and Detroit, where he was to later become player/manager, helping his side win the championship, and finish leading scorer in 1983. Brian settled in Detroit and ran his own sports complex, designed to increase the awareness of the new 'indoor soccer' in the smaller states of the United States. A popular character at the Racecourse 'Budgie' as he was affectionately known, is always assured of a welcome whenever visiting the club.

Season	League		F.A.Cup		Welsh Cup		League Cup		E.C.W.C.		Total	
	apps	gls	apps	gls	apps	gls	apps	gls	apps	gls	apps	gls
1968/69	22	4	-	-	2	0	-	-	-	-	24	4
1969/70	19/5	5	0/2	0	0/1	0	-	-	-	-	19/8	5
1970/71	28/5	6	1	0	1/1	0	-	-	-	-	30/6	6
1971/72	28/2	5	0/1	0	4	2	3	0	-	-	35/3	7
1972/73	46	7	3	1	1	0	2	1	4	2	56	11
1973/74	46	13	7	1	2	0	2	0	-	-	57	14
1974/75	41/1	7	1	0	5	2	1	0	-	-	48/1	9
1975/76	35/1	7	3	0	2	2	2	0	5	0	47/1	9
	265/14	**54**	**15/3**	**2**	**17/2**	**6**	**10**	**1**	**9**	**2**	**316/19**	**65**

TOMS, William Edward

1923 - 1924

Position; *Inside-Forward*
D.O.B; *19th May, 1896*
Birthplace; *The Curragh,*
Height; *5ft 9in* ***Weight;*** *12st 0lbs*
Debut; v. *Rochdale (a) 27th October, 1923*
Total Appearances & Goals; *51 apps 11 gls*
Career; *Altrincham; Eccles Borough 1914; Southport Vulcan (WW1 Guest); Manchester United (Am) Sept 1919, (Pro) 16th Oct 1919 12apps 3gls; Plymouth Argyle 24th Sept 1920 £500 24apps 3gls; Oldham Athletic 6th July 1921 £250 20apps 5gls; Coventry City 3rd July 1922 £150 30 apps 18gls; Stockport County 5th June 1923 5apps 1gls; WREXHAM 24th Oct 1923; Crewe Alexandra Dec 1924 25apps 8gls; Great Harwood cs1925 until January 1926; Winsford United Aug 1926;*
Honours; *Welsh Cup Winner 1924;*

Billy Toms played his football for Altrincham and Eccles Borough prior to the First World War, during which he turned out for Southport Vulcan. It was following the end of the conflict that Billy was signed by Manchester United, having spent the War in the Army, where he had progressed to the rank of Lieutenant, and where he was awarded the Military Cross. Billy made his Football League debut for United in October 1919, in a 1-1 home draw with Middlesborough. He went on to score three goals in twelve League games for 'Boro' until joining Plymouth Argyle for £500 in September 1920. Toms went straight into Plymouth's team in a 3-1 home win over Gillingham, and remained at Home Park until the end of the season, when he returned north to join Oldham Athletic for a £250 fee, after scoring just three goals in 24 League games for the 'Pilgrims'. He spent just one year at Boundary Park, scoring five goals in twenty League games for the First Division side, where he was described as a 'Powerfully built, stocky inside-forward with a reputation as a sharp shooter. He was considered an asset to each side he played for.' The close season of 1922 saw him on the move again, when he joined Second Division Coventry City for a £150 fee. It was at Highfield Road that he began to find his goalscoring touch, as he recorded the 'Sky Blues' second ever hat-trick in a Football League match in a 7-1 victory over Wolves on Christmas Day 1922. However, he left Coventry at the end of the season after he had been suspended by the club for an 'undisclosed act of misconduct', along with Arthur Ormston. Billy joined Second Division Stockport County in June 1923 and played in their first five matches of the 1923/24 season, scoring one goal before losing his place in the side. It was then that Wrexham stepped in to secure his signature in October 1923. Billy was to spend over twelve months at the Racecourse, making his debut in a scoreless draw at Rochdale, and during his time was described as, 'a hefty forward, who does not draw back'. Playing at inside-forward, Toms helped the club reach the 1924 Welsh Cup Final, where Wrexham beat Merthyr 1-0 after a replay. He lost his place in the side to Jack Nock during 1924/25, and in December joined Crewe Alexandra for a short spell where he made his final Football League appearance in a 4-1 defeat at Lincoln in the final match of the campaign. He then dropped into non-league football with Great Harwood, followed by a spell with Winsford United. He was later known to have played for a factory side, C.W.S.Margarine Works.

Season	League		F.A.Cup		Welsh Cup		Total	
	apps	gls	apps	gls	apps	gls	apps	gls
1923/24	30	9	2	1	6	0	38	10
1924/25	12	1	1	0	-	-	13	1
	42	**10**	**3**	**1**	**6**	**0**	**51**	**11**

TUDOR, William Henry

1946 - 1949

Position; *Centre-Half*
D.O.B; *14th February, 1918*
Birthplace; *Shotton, Flintshire*
Died; *1965*
Height; *5ft 11in* ***Weight;*** *12st 2lbs*
Debut; v. *New Brighton (h) 31st August, 1946*
Total Appearances & Goals; *158 apps 6 gls*
Career; *Llanerch Celts; Lavender; West Bromwich Albion May 1935 31apps 0gls; WREXHAM 1939 (WW2 Guest) 88apps 4gls; Nottingham Forest (WW2 Guest) 1940/41 2apps 0gls; Darlington (WW2 Guest) 1943/44 2apps 0gls; Swindon Town (WW2 Guest) 1945/46 7apps 0gls; WREXHAM 16th May 1946; Bangor City Jul 1949; Pwllheli 2nd Aug 1950; Flint Town United 20th Jun 1951; Llandudno Junction 21st Feb 1952; Mancot 28th Aug 1952;*
Honours; *Welsh Schoolboy International cap;*

Billy Tudor showed plenty of promise as a footballer at both Shotton and Sealand Road Schools, from where he was chosen to represent Wales Schoolboys. After leaving School Billy joined Llanerch Celts, who were based in Rhosllanerchrugog, and later played for Lavender FC. It was there that he was spotted by West Bromwich Albion, the club his father had appeared for as a reserve. Billy went on to sign for Albion, initially as an amateur in April 1934, and then on professional terms twelve months later. He had to wait until September 1938 to make his debut, at Newcastle, but it turned out to be a disaster as Albion lost 5-1! Tudor must have impressed, however, as he kept his place in the side until the following April. The new season was less than a month old when Billy's career, and League football shuddered to a halt because of the outbreak of World War Two. During the conflict Billy turned out as a 'guest' player for a number of clubs, including Swindon Town, Nottingham Forest, Darlington, and Wrexham, where he spent the last three seasons of WW2 playing as a regular as it was close to his Shotton home. After the war Wrexham manager Tom Williams signed Billy from the Hawthorns club for a fee of £750 in May 1946. He then made his Football League debut for the North Wales club against New Brighton on the Racecourse in a 3-2 win, going on to play at centre-half for the 'Robins' on a permanent basis until missing the end of the 1947/48 season through injury. It was a season that saw Wrexham finish third, their highest League position since 1933. He managed just two League appearances in 1948/49, as the talent of George Spruce began to emerge. Tudor moved on to Bangor City in the summer of 1949, where he spent a season before linking up with Pwllheli, also for one year. He then had spells with Flint Town United, Llandudno Junction, and Mancot. Throughout his career Billy was regarded as a 'thoughtful player who always tried to make good use of the ball'. Sadly, he died in 1965, aged only 47.

Season	League		F.A.Cup		Welsh Cup		War League		War Cup		Total	
	apps	gls	apps	gls	apps	gls	apps	gls	apps	gls	apps	gls
1939/40	-	-	-	-	-	-	14	0	3	0	17	0
1943/44	-	-	-	-	-	-	22	0	-	-	22	0
1944/45	-	-	-	-	-	-	36	4	-	-	36	4
1945/46	-	-	-	-	-	-	16	0	2	0	18	0
1946/47	34	1	4	0	2	0	-	-	-	-	40	0
1947/48	20	1	2	0	1	0	-	-	-	-	23	0
1948/49	2	0	-	-	-	-	-	-	-	-	2	0
	56	**2**	**6**	**0**	**3**	**0**	**88**	**4**	**5**	**0**	**158**	**6**

TUNNEY, Edward Luton

1937 - 1952

Position; *Right/Left-Back*
D.O.B; *23rd September, 1915*
Birthplace; *Toxteth Park, Liverpool, Merseyside*
Height; *5ft 8in* ***Weight;*** *11st 0lbs*
Debut; v. *Bradford City (h) 13th November, 1937*
Total Appearances & Goals; *296 apps 0 gls*
Career; *Everton Aug 1936 0apps; WREXHAM 24th Sept 1937; Crystal Palace (WW2 Guest) 1943/44 4apps 0gls; Hartlepool United (WW2 Guest) 1943/44 16apps 0gls; Luton Town (WW2 Guest) 1944/45 41apps 0gls; Tranmere Rovers (WW2 Guest) 1944/45 3apps 0gls; Tottenham Hotspur (WW2 Guest) Mar 1945 1app 0gls; Winsford United 1952;*
Honours; *Welsh Cup runner-up 1950;*

Eddie Tunney began playing football at the Harrington Board School in his native Liverpool. He also represented the Liverpool Association of Boys' Clubs, the Yoik House Boys' Club, and both the Liverpool and Lancashire County F.A. sides. He left school at the age of 15, and took up training to become a compositor in the printing trade with Orford Bros in Liverpool city centre, and they kindly allowed him the time to play football. However, it wasn't until he was almost 21 years-old that Eddie was to sign for Everton as an amateur in 1935, before accepting semi-professional terms in August 1936. He failed to make a break through into the first team at Goodison Park, and in September 1937 was given the chance of regular first team football when he signed for Wrexham manager Captain James Logan. It was to be the beginning of a fifteen year association with the Racecourse club. He went straight into the 'Robins' team for his Football League debut at left-back, in place of Bill Bellamy, for the home match with Bradford City. He then became a permanent fixture in the Wrexham side, playing in either right or left back positions until the outbreak of World War Two, and featured in a 9-0 Welsh Cup win over Southport. Eddie played in the opening three matches of the 1939/40 season before all sport was suspended by the Government because of WW2. It was eventually decided to continue with the playing of football on a regionalised basis, as it was 'good for morale'.

Eddie then carried on with Wrexham until he joined the Army in 1941, becoming a Sergeant Instructor in the Physical Training Corps. This allowed him to play football when he could, and during the conflict 'guested' for Tranmere Rovers, Crystal Palace, Hartlepool United, and Luton Town, for whom he played in the last two seasons of WW2. Tunney also played one match for Tottenham Hotspur against Aldershot, who always had a strong side of 'guest' players during this period because of the barracks in the town. Spurs won the Football League South match 2-1. After WW2 had come to a successful conclusion Eddie became one of only four players to have played for Wrexham both before and after the hostilities. He also continued to work in the printing trade, with Brakells, spending a further six years at the Racecourse, remaining a first team regular until his final season at the Denbighshire club, 1951/52. He was described during this time as a 'tower of strength' in the Wrexham defence and of 'playing with consistency'. He appeared in all of the 'Robins' matches during the 1947/48 season, when the side just missed out on promotion to the Second Division, finishing in third place, and picked up a Welsh Cup runners'-up medal in 1950, when Wrexham lost 4-1 in the Final to Swansea Town. Before that game his loyalty to Wrexham Football Club had been rewarded, when he was granted a joint testimonial, along with Gib Bellis. Eddie's old club, Everton, provided the opposition in October 1949, and a crowd of 6,900 turned up to support these two stalwarts and to see Wrexham beat a weakened Everton side 4-1. Tunney remained with Wrexham until the summer of 1952, having made almost 300 appearances for the club, without scoring one goal! He continued playing football at non-league level for Winsford United in the Cheshire County League, whilst also taking steps to remain in the game by passing his F.A.Coaching badge. This enabled him to join the coaching staff at Tranmere Rovers, where he worked with their youth team for a number of years. He also taught Physical Training at the Yoik House Boys' Club, where he had begun playing football, while continuing to work in the print trade until his retirement in 1979 at the age of 64. Eddie settled in the Wirral area of Merseyside, and enjoyed immensely the re-union of former players in September 1998.

Season	League		F.A.Cup		Welsh Cup		War League		War Cup		Total	
	apps	gls	apps	gls	apps	gls	apps	gls	apps	gls	apps	gls
1937/38	26	0	2	0	1	0	-	-	-	-	29	0
1938/39	42	0	1	0	2	0	-	-	-	-	45	0
1939/40	-	-	-	-	-	-	14	0	3	0	17	0
1945/46	-	-	6	0	-	-	13	0	10	0	29	0
1946/47	18	0	4	0	1	0	-	-	-	-	23	0
1947/48	42	0	2	0	3	0	-	-	-	-	47	0
1948/49	36	0	1	0	2	0	-	-	-	-	39	0
1949/50	20	0	-	-	5	0	-	-	-	-	25	0
1950/51	35	0	2	0	2	0	-	-	-	-	39	0
1951/52	3	0	-	-	-	-	-	-	-	-	3	0
	222	**0**	**18**	**0**	**16**	**0**	**27**	**0**	**13**	**0**	**296**	**0**

TUNNICLIFFE, William Francis 1947 - 1953

Position; *Outside-Left*
D.O.B; *5th January, 1920*
Birthplace; *Stoke-on-Trent, Staffordshire*
Died; *Newcastle-under-Lyme, 24th March,1997.*
Height; *5ft 8'1/2in* ***Weight;*** *10st 0lbs*
Debut; v. *Halifax Town (a) 23rd August, 1948*
Total Appearances & Goals; *264 apps 90 gls*
Career; *Port Vale Jan 1937 3apps 0gls; Bournemouth Jul 1938 49apps 7gls; Port Vale (WW2 Guest) Oct 1939 19apps 10gls; Chester (WW2 Guest) Sept 1940 1app 0gls; Brighton H.A. (WW2 Guest) Sept 1941 5apps 2gls; Reading (WW2 Guest) 1942/43 3apps 0gls; Brentford (WW2 Guest) 1944/45 1app 0gls; WREXHAM 21st June 1947; Bradford City 21st Jan 1953 89apps 20gls; Stafford Rangers 1955/56; Congleton Aug 1956;*
Honours; *Welsh Cup runner-up 1950;*

Billy Tunnicliffe first played football for school team, Harpfield Boys, at Hartshill in his native Stoke-on-Trent. He also played for Staffordshire Schoolboys, and was invited for two trials for the England Schoolboys team at Salford and Stockton. After leaving school Billy was signed by Port Vale, where he combined working in the club offices with playing football for fifteen shillings (75p) a week! Billy went on to work his way through the ranks at Vale, making his Football League debut in February 1936 at the age of sixteen in a 2-1 home win over Rotherham United. He made a total of five first team appearances for the 'Burslem' Club before he left to join Bournemouth in July 1938. Tunnicliffe played just one season with the 'Cherries' before World War Two interrupted his career. He was enlisted in the Royal Army Service Corp, and served in Burma. Tunnicliffe managed only a handful of games for Bournemouth during the war, but did complete a few games as a 'guest' player for Port Vale, Chester, Brighton, Reading, Brentford, and Salisbury Corinthians during that period. He returned to Bournemouth after the hostilities, but by that time he had married, and his wife was home-sick. He asked for a transfer, and not surprisingly a number of clubs showed an interest in signing him. They included Aberdeen, Chester, Walsall, and Wrexham. It was the latter club who won the race in June 1948, signing him for a fee of around £1,000. He made his 'Robins' debut in the opening game of the 48/49 season, a 2-1 home win over Halifax Town, and scored one of the goals. Billy went on to become the idol of the Racecourse crowd, as he played a major part in helping the club to end the season in third place. He remained at the Racecourse until January 1953 when with Wrexham very

much still in the hunt for what would have been their first ever Third Division North Championship, he was surprisingly transferred to Bradford City for a four figure fee. During his time with the 'Robins' he missed just ten games in five and a half seasons, helping Wrexham to the 1950 Welsh Cup Final, where they lost 4-1 to Swansea Town, and voted the club's 'Player of the Year' for 1952. He also played in the memorable Third Round F.A.Cup tie at Stoke City, in which Wrexham so nearly overcame their First Division opposition. Billy was an old fashioned type of winger, who was described thus by a local reporter; 'To see him cut in from the wing and let fly was a joy to watch. He formed a brilliant partnership with Norman Sharp. Sharp made the bullets and Billy fired them. He was a consistent goalscorer for a winger.' At Bradford Billy scored on his debut in a 3-0 win over Stockport, and went on to collect twenty goals in 89 League games for the Valley Parade club before his release at the end of 54/55. He then signed for Cheshire County League side Stafford Rangers, for a season, followed by a short spell with another Cheshire County League side Congleton, before finally hanging up his boots. He later managed and coached his local side, Queen Street Boys, who played in the Staffordshire League. Billy died at Bradwell Nursing Home in Newcastle-under-Lyme in March 1997, aged 77.

Season	League		F.A.Cup		Welsh Cup		Total	
	apps	gls	apps	gls	apps	gls	apps	gls
1947/48	42	21	2	2	2	2	46	25
1948/49	42	11	1	0	2	2	45	13
1949/50	40	7	3	3	5	3	48	13
1950/51	45	13	2	0	2	1	49	14
1951/52	42	13	2	1	4	2	48	16
1952/53	25	9	3	0	-	-	28	9
	236	**74**	**13**	**6**	**15**	**10**	**264**	**90**

TURNER, Graham John 1965 - 1968

Position; *Central Defender*
D.O.B; *5th October, 1947*
Birthplace; *Ellesmere Port, Cheshire*
Height; *5ft 10in* ***Weight;*** *11st 13lbs*
Debut; v. *Torquay United (h) 28th April, 1965*
Total Appearances & Goals; *85 apps 0 gls*
Career; *WREXHAM 1st July 1965; Chester 12th Jan 1968 215/3apps 5gls; Shrewsbury Town 17th Jan 1973 £30,000 342/13apps 22gls;*
Honours; *England Youth International cap; Third Division Championship Winner 1979; Fourth Division runner-up 1975; Welsh Cup Winner 1977 & 1984; Welsh Cup runner-up 1970 & 1980; Welsh Youth Cup runner-up 1964;*

Graham Turner played football for Cambridge Road Primary and Stanney Lane Secondary Modern Schools in his native Ellesmere Port. He didn't collect any representative honours during this time, but showed enough early promise to be snapped up by Wrexham in 1963. It was while he was an apprentice with the Racecourse club that he was capped for the England Youth team, and this accelerated his prospects of a first team place. He made his Football League debut for the 'Robins' at the age of seventeen in the last match of 1964/65, replacing regular centre-back Ray Mielczarek in a 3-2 home defeat by Torquay United, and shortly afterwards was signed on professional terms by Wrexham. The following season saw him playing reserve team football until around January 1966, when Mielczarek was injured. Graham stepped in, and kept his place in the side until surprisingly transferred to neighbours Chester in January 1968, after manager Alvan Williams agreed an exchange deal that saw Turner swapped for Ian Moir and a fee. During his time at the Racecourse he had helped Wrexham to attain a creditable seventh place in 1967, a year after finishing 92nd in the Football League. He spent five years with Chester, completing 218 League games, and picking up a Welsh Cup runners'-up medal in 1970. In January 1973 he left Sealand Road to join Shrewsbury Town for a £30,000, where he went on to have considerable success. Turner helped the Shropshire club to promotion to the Third Division in 1975, and collected a Welsh Cup winners' medal in 1977, before being appointed as player/manager in November 1978. He then led Shrewsbury to the Third Division Championship in 1979, and to Welsh Cup victories in 1979 and 1984, as well as helping them twice reach the F.A.Cup Quarter-Finals. Graham's success at the Gay Meadow did not go unnoticed, and in July 1984 he was appointed the new manager of Aston Villa. He had a tough time at Villa, although he did take them to the League Cup semi-finals in 1986. However, after they had lost six of their opening seven matches at the start of the following season, Graham was relieved of his duties. He was not out of work for long, because just three weeks later, he was appointed the new manager of Wolves. They were languishing in the Fourth Division at the time, and were in dire financial difficulties. Turner began to resurrect a once great club, as he led them back to the Second Division, taking in the 1988 Sherpa Van Trophy at Wembley along the way. It was Wolves' desperation for Premier League football that finally led to his resignation as manager in March 1994. After a spell out of football Graham returned to management with Hereford United for the start of the 1995/96 season, but it was to be another tough job, under strict financial constraints, and despite his best efforts they couldn't avoid relegation to the Conference League at the end of 1996/97. He stayed at Edgar Street, and later led a consortium to take over at the club, where he is the Chief Executive at the time of writing. His son, Mark, also played League football for both Northampton Town and Hereford United.

Season	League		F.A.Cup		Welsh Cup		League Cup		Total	
	apps	gls	apps	gls	apps	gls	apps	gls	apps	gls
1964/65	1	0	-	-	-	-	-	-	1	0
1965/66	24	0	-	-	1	0	-	-	25	0
1966/67	34	0	2	0	4	0	-	-	40	0
1967/68	18	0	1	0	-	-	-	-	19	0
	77	**0**	**3**	**0**	**5**	**0**	**-**	**-**	**85**	**0**

Roly Ugolini

UGOLINI, Rolando 1957 - 1960

Position; *Goalkeeper*
D.O.B; *4th June, 1924*
Birthplace; *Lucca, Italy*
Height; *5ft 9in* **Weight;** *11st 13lbs*
Debut; v. *Darlington (a) 24th August, 1957*
Total Appearances & Goals; *93 apps 0 gls*
Career; *Lochee Harp; Glasgow Celtic Apr 1944 4apps 0gls; Middlesbrough May 1948 £7,000 320apps 0gls; WREXHAM 11th Jun 1957; Dundee United 18th Jun 1960;*

Rolando Ugolini was born in Lucca, the home of Italy's olive industry, in 1924. A year later he moved with his family to settle in Scotland, eventually becoming a nationalised Briton. With his Glasgow background it is no surprise that he spoke with a pronounced Scottish accent, and earned a big reputation as a goalkeeper in Scottish Junior football with both the St.Mary's and St.Anthony's Schools team. He was also selected for the West Lothian District Schools representative side. Roly then had two trial periods with Hearts, and also spent some time with Motherwell, Falkirk, and Dunfermline, but only ever wanted to play for one club........Glasgow Celtic. He realised his dream by signing for them in April 1944, and played in a number of War-time matches. Roly remained at Parkhead after the War had ended, where he found himself understudy to Scotland 'keeper Willie Millar. He managed just four Scottish League appearances for the 'Buoys' before he joined Middlesbrough in May 1948 for a £7,000 fee. Roly quickly established himself in the first team at Ayresome Park, despite conceding seven goals in his first pre-season practice match!, and earned himself the affectionate nickname of 'Rolando the Cat'. During his time at 'Boro' he was their regular 'keeper for eight seasons, missing just 16 matches as he completed 335 League and Cup appearances. Roly was described as 'possessing all the acrobatics of the continental 'keeper, plus the reliability associated of those who play for British teams.' He was a great character, too, who could perhaps be best described as being a bit like a Bruce Grobelaar of his day. Roly could send a dead ball well into the opponents half of the field, and also had safe handling. However, he lost his place in the 'Boro' first team towards the end of the 1955/56 season, and spent the following term playing reserve team football until he was signed by Wrexham manager Cliff Lloyd in June 1957 at the age of 33. Roly went straight into the 'Robins' first team in place of Billy Waters for the opening match of the season at Darlington, which ended in a 2-1 defeat. He enjoyed a three year stint at the Racecourse, during which he was the regular first team 'keeper until he losing his place to Charlie Hughes towards the end of the 1959/60 season. Roly helped Wrexham gain Third Division status in 1958, when the Third Division's North and South were amalgamated, although he missed out on the Welsh Cup Final that same season. At the end of the 1959/60 season, after having earlier broken his ankle, Ugolini decided to retire from football and return to Scotland. However, after only a few weeks he was persuaded to don the gloves again, when he signed for Dundee United for what was described as a 'small fee' paid to Wrexham. He spent two seasons with the Tannadice club, until retiring after having made 52 appearances. Released in May 1962 he assisted Berwick Rangers and Cowdenbeath in a few games before this time really calling it a day in September 1962! Throughout his footballing career Roly had been very popular with the supporters of all the clubs for whom he had played. After retiring from football he became a Turf Accountant building up a string of betting shops in Scotland, which he eventually sold. Roly settled in Edinburgh, where he was still residing at the time of writing.

Season	League		F.A.Cup		Welsh Cup		Total	
	apps	gls	apps	gls	apps	gls	apps	gls
1957/58	35	0	1	0	2	0	38	0
1958/59	31	0	1	0	3	0	35	0
1959/60	17	0	2	0	1	0	20	0
	83	**0**	**4**	**0**	**6**	**0**	**93**	**0**

VANSITTART, Thomas 1970 - 1974

Position; *Left-Back*
D.O.B; *23rd January, 1950*
Birthplace; *Merton, London*
Height; *5ft 10in* **Weight;** *11st 0lbs*
Debut; v. *Exeter City (a) 14th February, 1970*
Total Appearances & Goals; *99/2 apps 2 gls*
Career; *Crystal Palace Apr 1967 10/1apps 2gls; WREXHAM 13th Feb 1970 (Loan), 6th Jul 1970; Wimbledon Jul 1975; Walton & Hersham Jul 1976;*
Honours; *Welsh Cup runner-up 1971; Division Four runner-up 1970;*

Tommy Vansittart played for Morden Farm School, from where he was selected for representative football at Schoolboys' level for Merton & Morden, Wimbledon, St.Hellier, Sutton, Carlshalton, and Surrey. By this time he was training twice a week with Chelsea. However, when turning out for Surrey Schoolboys the youth team manager at Crystal Palace, Arthur Rowe, offered Tommy a three year apprenticeship, which he accepted. He then joined the Selhurst Park club upon leaving school at 15. That was in January 1966, and within two years of signing Vansittart, who played at centre-half at this time, was offered professional terms. During that period had been selected for trials with the England Youth team, and also captained the Palace youth side to the semi-finals of the F.A.Youth Cup, where they lost 3-1 on aggregate to Coventry City. Tommy had already made his Football League debut by then, in a 1-1 home draw with Carlisle United in March 1968, replacing the injured John McCormick at centre-half. McCormick returned after a couple of games, but Tommy was given further opportunities before the end of the season, and scored twice in a 6-0 win over Norwich City when he played in the forward line. It was another eighteen months before he was to figure in the 'Eagles' first team again, but in February 1970 was given the opportunity of regular first team football when Bert Head introduced him to the Wrexham manager, John Neal. He wanted to sign Tommy on loan to replace the injured Eddie May, as the 'Robins' were chasing promotion to the Third Division. Vansittart agreed to the move and made his debut in a 1-0 defeat at Exeter City. By the end of the month he had caught the promotion bug and remained at the Racecourse until the end of the season, going on to score the winner in the 3-2 home win over Grimsby Town that guaranteed Wrexham promotion. He returned to Selhurst Park in the summer, only to find that John Neal had offered Palace £10,000 for his services. He agreed to join the North Wales club permanently, and 1970/71 was to see him miss just one game as Wrexham finished in a very creditable ninth position. They also reached the Welsh Cup Final, losing 4-1 on aggregate to Cardiff City. The following year was to prove to be a disaster for Tommy, as he broke his right leg in a 2-2 draw at Rotherham United in November 1971. He was in plaster for thirteen months, and had two operations, until returning to first team action in September 1973 in a 3-2 home win over Southport. Over the next two seasons, however, he managed just five appearances. At the end of 74/75 he was informed by manager John Neal that he was to be released. He then returned to live in London, taking up work as an assistant cartage manager for a local transport firm, although he continued to play football for Wimbledon, who were still a non-league club at that time. 1976/77 found Tommy with Walton & Hersham for a year, followed by playing mostly Sunday League football for his local team, Crown Mead, although he did play a few games for Dorking in the F.A.Cup. He finally hung up his boots at the age of 33 after breaking his ankle. Tommy linked up again with his former Wrexham team-mate, Arfon Griffiths, when he was manager at Wrexham, to run the rule over southern teams who were due to play against the 'Robins'. He later moved to work for Bradbury & Wilkinson, a specialist printing firm producing the ink used in bank notes. In 1985, he ran in the Margate

Marathon, eventually settling in Crawley, Sussex, where he became employed as a storeman with Virgin at Gatwick Airport.

Season	League		F.A.Cup		Welsh Cup		League Cup		Total	
	apps	gls	apps	gls	apps	gls	apps	gls	apps	gls
1969/70	19/2	1	-	-	-	-	-	-	19/2	1
1970/71	45	0	1	0	5	1	2	0	53	2
1971/72	17	0	1	0	-	-	3	0	21	1
1972/73	3	0	-	-	1	0	-	-	4	0
1974/75	2	0	-	-	-	-	-	-	2	0
	86/2	**1**	**2**	**0**	**6**	**1**	**5**	**0**	**99/2**	**2**

VAUGHAN John 1985

Position; *Goalkeeper*
D.O.B; *26th June, 1964*
Birthplace; *Isleworth, London*
Height; *5ft 10in* ***Weight;*** *13st 1lbs*
Debut; v. *Chester City (h) 26th October, 1985*
Total Appearances & Goals; *4 apps 0 gls*
Career; *West Ham United 30th Jun 1982 0apps; Charlton Athletic 11th Mar 1985 6apps 0gls (Loan); Bristol Rovers 5th Sept 1985 6apps 0gls (Loan); WREXHAM 23rd Oct 1985 (Loan); Bristol City 4th Mar 1986 2apps 0gls (Loan); Fulham 21st Aug 1986 £12,500 44apps 0gls; Bristol City 21st Jan 1988 3apps 0gls (Loan); Cambridge United 6th Jun 1988 178apps 0gls; Charlton Athletic 5th Aug 1993 5/1apps 0gls; Preston North End 26th Jul 1994 65/1apps 0gls; Lincoln City Jun 1996 60apps 0gls; Colchester United 3rd Feb 1997 5apps 0gls (Loan);*
Honours; *Third Division Championship Winner 1996; F.A.Youth Cup Winner 1981; Southern Junior Floodlit Cup Winner (twice);*

John Vaughan was a very promising goalkeeper during his school days, playing for Hounslow Schools and Middlesex Schoolboys. His potential was spotted by West Ham United, who quickly signed him on apprentice terms, before he accepted a professional contract in June 1982. John never made a first team appearance for the 'Hammers', although he did pick up a F.A.Youth Cup winners' medal against Spurs in 1981 as well as two Southern Junior Floodlit Cup winners' medals. His first taste of League football came when he signed for Charlton Athletic on loan in March 1985, as cover for the injured Tony Lange. When Nicky John also joined the injury list John was called into the first team, making six appearances before he dislocated a finger in training, which led him to playing a couple of games in Charlton's reserves as an outfield player! Having returned to West Ham for the start of the 85/86 he then answered an emergency call from Bristol Rovers, whose regular 'keeper, Ron Green, was injured, and made another six League appearances for the 'Pirates' in his month's loan. Towards the end of October Vaughan was on the move again - this time to Wrexham, after Mike Hooper had been sold to Liverpool, leaving the club without any experienced cover. He made his 'Robins' debut in a 1-1 home draw with Chester, and managed three more games before returning to Upton Park. He then found himself back in reserve team football at West Ham, before another chance of first team football came along in March 1986 with a further loan spell, this time with Bristol City, where he made two League appearances. John finally left Upton Park in August 1986, when Fulham paid out £12,500 for his services. He will probably be best remembered at Craven Cottage as the 'keeper who let in ten goals in at Anfield! although he did make 44 League appearances for the club. In January 1988 John had another loan spell with Bristol City, where he completed three League games before returning to Fulham, only to find he was to be released in the summer. He then joined Cambridge United, where he finally began to show his true potential. He was a member of the Abbey Stadium outfit's side that won the 1990 Division Four Play-Off Final against Chesterfield at Wembley, and went on to make 178 League appearances in his five years with the 'U's'. In August 1993 he joined Charlton Athletic on a free transfer, acting mostly as cover for former 'Racecourse Robin', Mike Salmon, making just six League appearances before joining Preston North End in the close season of 1994. John spent two years at Deepdale, helping Preston gain promotion in 1996 as they won the Third Division Championship. However, he was released at the end of the season and joined Lincoln City, where he had competition for the 'keeper's shirt with Barry Richardson. In February 1997 he joined Colchester United on loan for five matches, before returning to Sincil Bank. 1997/98 saw him turn out in nineteen games for the 'Red Imps', as they gained promotion to the Second Division, but the following season saw Lincoln return straight back despite John's efforts.

Season	League		F.A.Cup		Welsh Cup		League Cup		F.R.T.		Total	
	apps	gls	apps	gls	apps	gls	apps	gls	apps	gls	apps	gls
1985/86	4	0	-	-	-	-	-	-	-	-	4	0
	4	**0**	**-**	**-**	**-**	**-**	**-**	**-**	**-**	**-**	**4**	**0**

VAUGHAN, William 1924 - 1925

Position; *Inside-Left*
D.O.B; *18th December, 1898*
Birthplace; *Willenhall, West Midlands*
Died; *Walsall, May 1976*
Height; *5ft 8in* ***Weight;*** *11st 0lbs*
Debut; *v. Halifax Town (a) 30th August, 1924*
Total Appearances & Goals; *11 apps 2 gls*
Career; *Willenhall; Bristol Rovers Sept 1919 6apps 1gls; Stafford Rangers; Merthyr Town 1922; Shrewsbury Town cs1923 24apps 8gls; WREXHAM 20th Aug 1924; Bilston United cs1925; Burton Town cs1926; Exeter City 13th May 1929 33apps 9gls; Merthyr Town 18th Jan 1928 9apps 4gls; Luton Town 26th Feb 1929 3apps 2gls; Brierley Hill Alliance 26th Jun 1929; Gresley Rovers Nov 1929; Exeter City Aug 1930 0apps; Bloxwich Strollers Oct 1930; Cheltenham Town 1932 2apps 3gls; Walsall Wood 14th Nov 1933; Winsford United 1934; Knotty Ash Athletic 9th Oct 1936;*
Honours; *Walsall Senior Cup Winner 1924;*

Billy Vaughan was a Boxing Champion during World War One, and it was not until after the conflict had ended that he took up a football career with Birmingham & District League side Willenhall. He was soon quickly signed up by Bristol Rovers, helping them secure a Football League place in the newly formed Third Division in 1920, though he actually made just six Football League appearances, his debut coming in a home defeat by Millwall. Billy later moved on to join Birmingham & District League side Stafford Rangers for a spell, before signing for Third Division South side Merthyr Town in 1922. After almost a year in South Wales he was back in the Birmingham & District League with Shrewsbury Town. He became a regular in their side and helped them finish the season as runners-up to Stourbridge, as well as winning the Walsall Senior Cup. His form with the Shropshire Club was good enough to attract the attention of Third Division North side Wrexham, and he joined them in the summer of 1924, much to the Shrews annoyance. He originally signed for the 'Robins' on English League forms, but Shrewsbury retained his Welsh League registration, preventing him from playing in the Racecourse club's reserve team. They, like Shrewsbury's second string, played in the Welsh League. Billy made his Football League debut for Wrexham in the first game of the 1924/25 season, a 3-1 defeat at Halifax. He then appeared in the following nine matches, all at inside-forward, in which he scored twice, one goal coming in a 1-0 win at Grimsby, and the other in a 3-1 home success over Hartlepools. However, Vaughan was to make just one more senior appearance for the 'Robins', a 5-0 defeat at Wigan. He then left the Racecourse in the summer of 1925 to join another Birmingham and District League side, Bilston United. After a year he signed for Burton Town, assisting them to finish as runners-up to Stourbridge in the Birmingham & District League, by scoring 27 goals. That kind of form saw Third Division South side Exeter City step in and sign him in May 1927. Billy made his debut for the 'Grecians' in the opening match of the season, a local 'derby' with Torquay which ended in a 1-1 draw, with Vaughan scoring the Exeter goal. He went on to add eight more goals in a further 32 League games for the Devon club, as they finished the season in a respectable eighth place. In the summer of 1928 Billy who had show he was not afraid to change clubs at regular intervals rejoined Merthyr Town, where he made nine League appearances, scoring four goals, moving on to Luton Town in February 1929. He made three League appearances for the 'Hatters', scoring two goals, one of which was on his debut in a 2-2 home draw with local rivals Watford. He remained at Kenilworth Road until the end of the season, before enjoying short spells with both Brierley Hill Alliance and Gresley Rovers eventually returning to Exeter City in August 1930. However, on this occasion he failed to make any impact, and in October returned to the Midlands to sign for Bloxwich Strollers. He then sampled non-league football with Cheltenham Town, Walsall Wood, Winsford United, and Knotty Ash Athletic in Liverpool.

During his nomadic career Billy had been described as 'of more than average ability, and performs his work with praiseworthy speed and thoroughness.' He settled in the Walsall area where he died in May 1976.

Season	League		F.A.Cup		Welsh Cup		Total	
	apps	gls	apps	gls	apps	gls	apps	gls
1924/25	11	2	-	-	-	-	11	2
	11	**2**	**-**	**-**	**-**	**-**	**11**	**2**

VINTER, Michael 1979 - 1982

Position; *Forward*
D.O.B; *23rd May, 1954*
Birthplace; *Boston, Lincolnshire*
Height; *5ft 9in* **Weight;** *11st 0lbs*
Debut; v. *West Ham United (h) 18th August, 1979*
Total Appearances & Goals; *116/15 apps 41 gls*
Career; *Boston; Notts County Mar 1972 £2,000 135/31apps 53gls; WREXHAM 15th Jun 1979 £150,000; Oxford United 2nd Aug 1982 £30,000 67/2apps 21gls; Mansfield Town 24th Aug 1984 £15,000 52/2apps 7gls; Newport County Aug 1986 30/2apps 7gls; Gainsborough Trinity cs1987; Boston United cs1988; Matlock Town cs1989; Oakham United (player/coach) cs1990; Hucknall Town (player/coach) Jun 1991; Sutton Town cs1992; Sneinton 1994;*
Honours; *Third Division Championship Winner 1984; Welsh Cup runner-up 1981;*

Mick Vinter was playing for his home town club, Boston, when he was spotted by Notts County manager, Jimmy Sirrel and his assistant Ron Fenton. At the time he was working as a letterpress printer, though he quickly decided to take up the offer of professional football with the 'Magpies'. He made his Football League debut as a substitute, replacing Ian Scanlon in the opening game of the 1972/73 season, a scoreless draw with Shrewsbury Town. He made three more appearances that season, as Notts County won promotion to the Second Division. It was not until 74/75 that he began to establish himself as a regular in the County first team. He finished each of his final three seasons at Meadow Lane as the club's leading goalscorer, before asking for a transfer as he thought his game was 'getting stale' after spending almost eight years with the Magpies. With the prospect of playing European football it was Wrexham manager Arfon Griffiths who persuaded Mick to join the Racecourse staff for a fee of around £150,000. He went straight into the first team for his debut in August 1979, against West Ham United on the Racecourse. Replacing the departed Bobby Shinton he got off to a great start by scoring the only goal of the match. He soon had his wish of playing in Europe, as the 'Robins' came up against the East Germans of 1.F.C.Magdeburg, although they lost 7-5 on aggregate. Mick also scored twice against Everton in an F.A.Cup match at Goodison Park that season, as Wrexham lost 5-2! He struggled to find the net on a regular basis over the next two seasons, although he did score in Wrexham's shock 3-1 F.A.Cup win at Brian Clough's Nottingham Forest. Mick left the Racecourse at the end of the 1981/82 season after the club had been relegated, although he bowed out in style by scoring a hat-trick in his final match, a 3-2 home win over Rotherham United He then joined Oxford United for a £30,000 fee, where he spent two years. During his time at the Manor Ground the club won the Third Division championship in 1984, and he played in the team that beat both Leeds United and Manchester United in the League Cup before losing to Everton in the Quarter-Finals. Mick moved on in the summer of 1984, when he joined Fourth Division Mansfield Town for a £15,000 fee. A two year stint at Field Mill took in another promotion campaign, in 1985/86, though his goalscoring ratio had taken a dip by the time he was released in the summer of 1986. Vinter then joined Newport County on trial in August 1986, and after impressing he signed for the Somerton Park club. He made 32 League appearances for the Gwent Club before deciding to quit League football at the end of the season because of a persistent pelvic injury, which restricted his mobility. Despite the setback, Mick continued to play non-league football with Gainsborough Trinity, followed by spells with Boston United, Matlock Town, Oakham United, Hucknall Town, and Sutton United. He was last known have played for Sneinton in the Notts Alliance, having settled in the Boston area. Mick Vinter was always alive to the half chance in his time with the Robins and scored a number of match winning goals, often late in the game. 'Poaching' was his trademark. Was known to be a Rep in the Nottingham area for Abbey Life Assurance Company in the early 1996's.

Season	League		F.A.Cup		Welsh Cup		League Cup		E.C.W.C		Total	
	apps	gls	apps	gls	apps	gls	apps	gls	apps	gls	apps	gls
1979/80	35	11	4	5	2	0	4	1	1	1	46	18
1980/81	31/6	9	0/2	0	3/1	2	2	1	-	-	36/9	12
1981/82	23/6	5	4	2	2	1	5	3	-	-	34/6	11
	89/12	**25**	**8/2**	**7**	**7/1**	**3**	**11**	**5**	**1**	**1**	**116/15**	**41**

Steve Watkin

WAINWRIGHT, Neil 1995 -1998

Position; *Winger/Midfield*
D.O.B; *4th November, 1977.*
Birthplace; *Warrington, Cheshire*
Height; *6ft 0ins* ***Weight;*** *11st 5lbs*
Debut; v. *Newtown (a) 18th August 1997 (Welsh Invitation Trophy)*
Total Appearances & Goals; *12/7 apps 3 gls*
Career; *WREXHAM 27th Mar 1997; Sunderland 18th Jun 1998 £100,000 0/2apps 0gls;*
Honours; *Pontins Premier League Championship Winner 1999; Welsh Youth Cup Winner 1996; Welsh Youth Cup runner-up 1994; Welsh National League Championship Winner 1996;*

Although born in Warrington, Cheshire, Neil Wainwright has lived almost all his life in Mold. It was with Mynydd Isa Youth Club that he was spotted and invited to train with the Chester School of Excellence, which has no connection with the city's football club at the Deva Stadium. From there Neil graduated to Crewe Alexandra, where he attended training sessions for several years. As Crewe deliberated over the offer of a YTS placement Wrexham's Youth Development Officer Mick Buxton stepped in, and signed the classy winger for the Racecourse club. Neil then made his way through the ranks at the Racecourse, signing professional in 1996, and underlining his undoubted potential when he was chosen to play in a pre-season home game against Everton. However, it was not until 1997/98 that he finally made the breakthrough into the first team, when he played in a Welsh Invitation Cup match at Newtown. Another couple of games in the same competition followed before he finally made his Football League debut - and celebrated in fine style, substituting Kevin Russell at Blackpool in December before scoring a stunning second goal in a 2-1 victory. Neil then secured a regular first team place for the next dozen games, becoming a firm favourite with the Wrexham fans, until a pulled ham-string at the end of February put him out of action for the rest of the season. He had just scored against Walsall on the Racecourse, when he sustained the injury and his absence from the remainder of the League programme was felt by many to be a significant factor in the club's subsequent failure to reach the play-off's by one goal. Despite this, he had already come to the attention of several higher Division clubs and, with his contract expired, he was soon to depart from the Racecourse, when he accepted terms with First Division side Sunderland in June 1998. Wrexham received a fee of £100,000 for Neil which with add-on clauses, could see the 'Robins' net up to £350,000 depending on his progress. Can play on either wing but prefers the left flank in order to cut inside and shoot with his better right foot. Has a good first touch, and loves taking on the opposition, helping to press the panic button and make things happen. With the Wear side club Neil could only manage two substitute appearances as they stormed to the First Division Championship, but was to gain success with the Stadium of Light club's second string winning a Pontins Premier League Championship medal.

Season	League		F.A.Cup		League Cup		A.W.S.		W.I.C.		Total	
	apps	gls	apps	gls	apps	gls	apps	gls	apps	gls	apps	gls
1997/98	7/4	3	1	0	-	-	1	0	3/3	0	12/7	3
	7/4	**3**	**1**	**0**	**-**	**-**	**1**	**0**	**3/3**	**0**	**12/7**	**3**

WALKER, Robert W. 1947 - 1948

Position; *Centre-Forward*
D.O.B; *21st May, 1922*
Birthplace; *Aberdeen,*
Height; *ft in* ***Weight;*** *st lbs*
Debut; v. *Crewe Alexandra (h) 6th March, 1948*
Total Appearances & Goals; *2 apps 0 gls*
Career; *Aberdeen; Bournemouth Nov 1946 2apps 2gls; WREXHAM 23rd June 1947;*

The Second World War interrupted Robert Walker's career after he had been on the books of his native city's club, Aberdeen. Following the end of the hostilities Robert signed for Bournemouth in November 1946 for a four figure fee, and remained with the 'Cherries' until the summer of 1947, by which time he had made his Football League debut in his accustomed centre-forward position. He made just one further appearance for Bournemouth, although he had scored two goals for the South Coast club in those two games. Impressive though these figures were, Robert was allowed to sign for Wrexham two days after his Dean Court team mate Billy Tunnicliffe had made the same move. Again, Walker was to find his opportunities limited, and was not until March 1948 that he finally made his first team debut for the 'Robins', appearing at half-back in place of Les Speed, against Crewe Alexandra in a 1-1 draw on the Racecourse. He played in the following match at Carlisle, a 2-1 win, but Speed then returned to the side to send Robert back to reserve team football. He remained with North Wales club until the end of that season, when it was said that he had moved back to Scotland for 'personal reasons'.

Season	League		F.A.Cup		Welsh Cup		Total	
	apps	gls	apps	gls	apps	gls	apps	gls
1947/48	2	0	-	-	-	-	2	0
	2	**0**	**-**	**-**	**-**	**-**	**2**	**0**

WALL, Thomas Peter 1965 - 1966

Position; *Full-Back*
D.O.B; *13th September, 1934*
Birthplace; *Westbury, Nr Shrewsbury, Shropshire*
Height; *5ft 9in* ***Weight;*** *11st 8lbs*
Debut; v. *Colchester United (h) 6th November, 1965*
Total Appearances & Goals; *16/7 apps 1 gls*
Career; *Shrewsbury Town Sept 1962 18apps 0gls; WREXHAM 6th Nov 1965 £3,000; Liverpool 7th Oct 1966 £26,000 (including Stuart Mason) 31apps 0gls; Crystal Palace 3rd Jun 1970 £35,000 167/10apps 4gls; Leyton Orient 15th Dec 1972 10apps 0gls (Loan); USA 1978;*
Honours; *Football League Division One runner-up 1969;*

Peter Wall attended Worthern Primary and Pontesbury Secondary Schools, near Shrewsbury, from where he represented Shropshire Schoolboys in both the English and Welsh School Shields. Upon completion of his education he became an apprentice electrician with Eddom and Rogers in Shrewsbury but, after only twelve months, the call of football was too great, and he joined Shrewsbury Town as an apprentice professional, progressing to sign full time on his eighteenth birthday in 1962. Peter made his first team debut for Shrewsbury against Wrexham on 28th December 1963, but on that occasion he was on the losing side, as the 'Robins' won 2-1. During his time with the Gay Meadow club he played in the first team during their 1964/65 F.A.Cup run, against Manchester City and Leeds United. However, he was unable to sustain a regular first team place, and so asked for a transfer. In November 1965 he was signed by Wrexham, for what later proved to be a bargain £3,000 fee. Although a full-back, Peter subsequently proved himself to be one of the most useful utility players on Wrexham's books. Even so, in his first year at the club the 'Robins' finished bottom of the Football League for the first time in their history, while he managed just a handful of appearances in the following season before both he and Stuart Mason were signed by Liverpool for a joint fee of £26,000 in October 1966. Although Stuart Mason later returned to Wrexham without making a first team appearance Peter had some useful runs in the Liverpool first XI making his League debut in front of the 'Kop' against

Burnley in a 3-1 win, when replacing Gerry Byrne at left-back. He then went on to complete 67/68, as the club's first choice in that position. He continued at left-back in the opening thirteen games of the following campaign, until replaced by Geoff Strong. He was then kept out of senior action until mid-way through the 1969/70 season, when he filled in for Tommy Smith, following which he was transferred to Crystal Palace in June 1970 for a £35,000 fee. Wall went on to make 177 League appearances for the South London club in eight years at Selhurst Park. In that time he experienced relegation twice - the First to the Second, and the Second to the Third Divisions - but did make seventeen appearances in their promotion season of 1977. Peter also appeared in every match of Palace's F.A.Cup run of 1976, which saw them reach the semi-finals before losing to Southampton. He had a spell on loan at Orient, from December 1972 until March 1973, where he made ten League appearances. Peter ended his Football League career at Selhurst Park in the summer of 1978, but crossed the Atlantic to continue playing in America. He later stepped up into management with California Surf, Phoenix Inferno, and L.A.Lazers. Peter settled in America, and he was last known to be residing in California in 1998.

Season	League		F.A.Cup		Welsh Cup		League Cup		Total	
	apps	gls	apps	gls	apps	gls	apps	gls	apps	gls
1965/66	12/6	1	1	0	-	-	-	-	13/6	1
1966/67	3/1	0	-	-	-	-	-	-	3/1	0
	15/7	**1**	**1**	**0**	**-**	**-**	**-**	**-**	**16/7**	**1**

WALLER, Henry W. 1932 - 1935

Position; *Outside-Left*
D.O.B; *2nd May, 1902*
Birthplace; *Willington, Durham*
Height; *5ft 8in* **Weight;** *10st 7lbs*
Debut; v. *Hartlepool United (a) 3rd September, 1932*
Total Appearances & Goals; *93 apps 33 gls*
Career; *Annfield Plain; Bury 1928; Torquay United Jun 1928 114apps 23gls; WREXHAM 30th Jul 1932; Wellington Town Jul 1935;*
Honours; *Welsh Cup runner-up 1933;*

In 1928 Harry Waller was playing for his local side, Annfield Plain, in County Durham when he was spotted by Bury, who then quickly signed him. However, he failed to make the grade at Gigg Lane, and so left to join Third Division South side Torquay United, in June of the same year. Harry had to wait until the end of September before making his Football League debut for the 'Gulls', at Crystal Palace in a 2-0 defeat. Playing mainly as a outside-left, although he was sometimes required to play on the right, Waller spent four seasons on the South Coast with Torquay, throughout which time he was a regular in the first team, scoring 23 goals in 114 League appearances. He transferred to Third Division North side Wrexham in the summer of 1932, where he made his debut in the third match of the 1932/33. He stepped into the side following a tragic injury to Billy Lanyon, who had broken his leg at Hull in the previous match. Lanyon's misfortune was Harry's opportunity to establish himself in the 'Robins' team, which he did for the next three seasons. During that time he helped the club finish runners-up in Division Three North, their best position since joining the Football League. He was also the provider of much of the ammunition for the great Tommy Bamford, although Harry also chipped in with sixteen League goals himself in that first season. He ended it by collecting a Welsh Cup runners'-up medal, when Wrexham lost 2-0 to local rivals Chester in the Final. The following season saw him once again providing Bamford with the crosses as he achieved the club's all-time scoring record with an amazing 44 goals in the League alone. However, by October of 1934/35 Harry had been ousted from the side by new signing Eric Stubbs, although he did return in January for a spell. It was the beginning of the end of Harry's career at the Racecourse, and he left the club in the close season of 1935 to join Birmingham and District League side Wellington Town.

Season	League		F.A.Cup		Welsh Cup		N.S.C.		Total	
	apps	gls	apps	gls	apps	gls	apps	gls	apps	gls
1932/33	39	16	3	0	6	3	-	-	48	19
1933/34	36	11	1	0	1	0	3	1	41	12
1934/35	18	6	-	-	-	-	1	0	19	6
	93	**33**	**4**	**0**	**7**	**3**	**4**	**1**	**108**	**37**

WALSH, David 1997 -

Position; *Goalkeeper*
D.O.B; *29th April, 1979*
Birthplace; *Wrexham, Denbighshire*
Height; *6ft 1in* **Weight;** *12st 5lbs*
Debut v. *Cardiff City (h) 27th April, 1999 (Welsh Premier Cup)*
Total Appearances & Goals; *2 apps 0 gls*
Career; *WREXHAM 1st July 1997 (Pro);*
Honours; *Welsh Youth International; Welsh Youth Cup Winner 1996; Welsh Premier Cup runner-up 1999; Welsh Youth Cup runner-up 1995;*

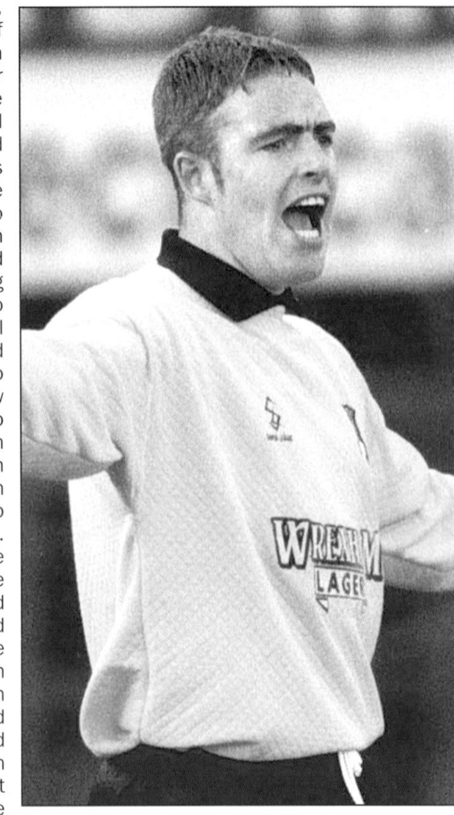

Born in Wrexham, David spent much of his early life in Mynydd Isa, near Mold, where he attended Bryn-Y-Baal Primary and Argoed High Schools. It was whilst there that he was also chosen to represent both Flintshire and Clwyd Schoolboys. During this time David also played for a local junior team called Bistre, but he was to leave them and follow his manager to Neston, who played in the Eastham Youth League, and for whom he was selected to represent the League. It was there that he played alongside Andy Griffiths and Julian Pepper, and where all three were spotted by Wrexham team youth coach Mick Buxton. David was eventually signed by Wrexham on schoolboy forms at the age of 15, despite interest from both Oldham Athletic and Tranmere Rovers. David was still on schoolboy forms when he played for the 'Robins' in the 1995 Welsh Youth Cup Final at Aberystwyth, although Wrexham lost 1-0 to Cardiff City in the Final. Having left school that summer, Walsh was signed by the Racecourse club on YTS terms, and won a Welsh youth Cup winners medal the following year when Wrexham beat Swansea 3-2 in the Final, which was played in the National Stadium in Cardiff as a prelude to the Welsh Cup Final between Barry Town and Llansantffraid. David was to progress at the Racecourse along with fellow YTS goalkeeper Leigh Edwards, both competing for the keepers' position, with the club usually alternating the two promising 'keepers every other game. During this period David was selected to represent the Welsh Youth team on a number of occasions, playing in the Milk Cup competition in Northern Ireland, where he played against the hosts, Russia and Turkey. He also played in a tournament in Italy against Slovakia, the United Arab Emirates and Italy themselves, as well as playing in the European Youth Championships against the likes of Norway and Holland. David was still only 17 when he was called into the Welsh under-21 squad for a European Championship game in Breda, Holland. Despite him being a regular in the under-21 squad ever since, he has found himself as understudy, first to Cardiff City 'keeper Pat Mountain, and then Blackburn Rovers' Anthony Williams, and he is still to be capped at this level. Walsh had progressed enough to sign professional forms with Wrexham in the summer of 1997, and has since worked hard in building himself up to be in a position to take over the number one spot. He finally made his first team debut in the Welsh Premier Cup semi-final in April 1999 against Cardiff City, in a 3-1 win on the Racecourse. David had been called into the side when loan signing Tommy Wright was away on international duty with Northern Ireland, and Mark Cartwright was out of favour having asked for a transfer. David was said to have had 'a highly competent debut', which was capped with him being named as the sponsors 'Man of the Match'. Much is expected of this promising 'keeper.

Season	League		F.A.Cup		W.P.C.		League Cup		A.W.S.		Total	
	apps	gls	apps	gls	apps	gls	apps	gls	apps	gls	apps	gls
1998/99	-	-	-	-	2	0	-	-	-	-	2	0
	-	**-**	**-**	**-**	**2**	**0**	**-**	**-**	**-**	**-**	**2**	**0**

WALTON, Mark Andrew 1993

Position; *Goalkeeper*
D.O.B; *1st June, 1969*
Birthplace; *Merthyr, Glamorgan*
Height; *6ft 2in* ***Weight;*** *13st 12lbs*
Debut; v. *Blackpool (h) 28th August, 1993*
Total Appearances & Goals; *6 apps 0 gls*
Career; *Swansea City Jul 1985 0apps; Mertyhr Tydfil; Luton Town 21st Feb 1987 0apps; Colchester United 5th Nov 1987 (Loan), 22nd Dec 1987 £15,000 40apps 0gls; Norwich City 15th Aug 1989 £75,000 22apps 0gls; WREXHAM 25th Aug 1993 (Loan); Dundee 27th Jan 1994 0apps; Bolton Wanderers 2nd Mar 1994 3apps 0gls; Merthyr Tydfil Nov 1994; Fakenham Town; Fulham 12th Aug 1996 40apps 0gls; Gillingham 5th Feb 1998 (Loan) 1app 0gls; Norwich City 25th Mar 1998 (Loan) 0apps; Brighton & Hove Albion Jul 1998 £25,000 19apps 0gls;*
Honours; *One Welsh Under-21 international Cap; Third Division runner-up 1997;*

Mark Walton was playing for Georgetown Boys' Club when Merthyr Tydfil offered him the chance to turn out for their Welsh League side at the age of 16. From there he was taken on by Swansea City as an apprentice in July 1983, where he was to spend just over a season before he joined Luton Town in February 1987. Mark spent almost a year at Kenilworth Road, without making a first team appearance, until Colchester United came in for him in November 1987. A fee of £18,000 exchanged hands, with Mark going straight into the first team for his Football League debut, replacing Graham Benstead in a Division Four home match with Wolves, which the 'U's' lost 1-0. Mark kept his place in the side, and turned out in another fourteen League games that season before Craig Forrest, on loan from Ipswich Town, replaced him. He did, however, return to play in the last couple of matches that season. Walton began the following campaign as the club's first choice 'keeper, and made 23 League appearances before losing his place in the side to another loan signing, Tom McAlister, from West Ham United. He had spent almost two years at Layer Road when his former manager at Colchester, Mike Walker, signed him for Norwich City in August 1989. A first team opportunity didn't materialise until April 1990; it arose when Bryan Gunn's wife went into labour!, allowing Mark to step in for the indisposed first choice 'keeper in a League match at Aston Villa, which ended in a 3-3 draw. Mark then had to wait almost twelve months before figuring in the first team again, when he played in the last four matches of 1990/91. In January 1992 Mark took over the 'keepers' shirt on merit from Gunn, as he helped the 'Canaries' to reach the F.A.Cup semi finals, where they lost to Sunderland at Hillsborough. He spent the whole of 1992/93 kicking his heels on the substitute's bench, and grabbed an opportunity of first team football by joining Wrexham at the beginning of 1993/94 - initially for a month's loan, with the prospect of the move becoming permanent. Mark made his debut in a 3-2 home defeat by Blackpool, and went on to complete five further League appearances before manager Brian Flynn made both Norwich City and Mark an offer. However, he turned it down and returned to Carrow Road. Before the season had ended Walton had been released by Norwich, and moved up to Scotland, where he joined Dundee. He failed to make a first team appearance, and so returned south of the border to join Bolton Wanderers, where he played three senior games. He then returned to his native South Wales in November 1994, when joining Conference League side Merthyr Tydfil, becoming a part-time professional, and taking up employment with Hoover, the club's main sponsors. He found it difficult to break into the first team at Penydarren Park, due to the consistency of Gary Wager. A keen cricketer in the summer months Mark represented Wales at Minor Counties level in June 1995, before he joined Southern League side Fakenham Town for the new football season. It was during his time with them that he was given a trial by Third Division side Fulham, and subsequently signed in August 1996. He helped the London club to promotion in his first season at Craven Cottage, but then found himself out of favour as Harrods owner, Mohammed Al Fayed, ploughed his money into the club. Among the many new arrivals were goalkeepers Andre Arendse - the South African international- and Maik Taylor, an expensive acquisition from Southampton. By February, Mark had been loaned out to fellow Second Division side Gillingham, where he made his debut in a live televised game at runaway League leaders, Watford. He helped the 'Gills' secure a 2-0 win in what proved to be his one and only game for the Kent Club. The following month he joined Norwich City on loan, as cover for first choice 'keeper, Andy Marshall. He finally moved permanently from Craven Cottage in the summer of 1998, joining Third Division Brighton & Hove Albion for a £25,000 fee. His father Ron Walton is Youth Development Officer at Swansea City.

Season	League apps	League gls	F.A.Cup apps	F.A.Cup gls	Welsh Cup apps	Welsh Cup gls	League Cup apps	League Cup gls	A.G.T. apps	A.G.T. gls	Total apps	Total gls
1993/94	6	0	-	-	-	-	-	-	-	-	6	0
	6	**0**	-	-	-	-	-	-	-	-	**6**	**0**

WARBURTON, George 1957 - 1960

Position; *Right-Back*
D.O.B; *13th September, 1934*
Birthplace; *Lodge, Nr.Wrexham, Denbighshire*
Height; *5ft 8in* ***Weight;*** *11st 7lbs*
Debut; v. *Bournemouth (h) 18th October, 1958*
Total Appearances & Goals; *24 apps 0 gls*
Career; *Pentre Broughton Y.C; Brymbo Steelworks 1950; WREXHAM (Am) 26th Mar 1956, (Pro) 19th Nov 1957; Barrow Aug 1960 14apps 0gls; Morecambe Jul 1961; Netherfield 1962/63; Holywell Town 26th Jan 1963; Colwyn Bay 26th Jun 1963; Blaenau Ffestiniog 26th Oct 1963;*
Honours; *Two Welsh Amateur International caps;*

George Warburton attended Black Lane School in Pentre Broughton, before moving on to Brymbo School, where he played for the school team. They had to play all their matches away, since they had no pitch! At this time he also played for Pentre Broughton Youth Club before leaving school at the age of 15 to begin working at the local Brymbo Steelworks. It was while playing for the Old Hearth Furness team in the inter-department games that he was signed by the works football team. He then played for their reserve team for the first twelve months, even though he had moved on to begin a five year apprenticeship as a mechanic at Kirbys in Wrexham. Following his promotion to the Brymbo Steelworks first team he had trials for the Welsh Amateur side, and both Tottenham Hotspur and Sheffield Wednesday took an interest in him before he signed amateur forms for Wrexham during the 1955/56 season. In September 1955 George left Kirbys to begin his National Service, in the No.1 Infantry Workshop, R.E.M.E.. During his first twelve months he played football for his regiment and for the Army Amateurs, and was chosen to play for the Welsh Amateur side against Scotland in a 2-2 draw at Hampden Park. At first he served at Tidworth, Devon, before being posted to Cyprus, where he played for his regiment team as they won the Minor Units Cup. Following the completion of his National Service in September 1957 Warburton arrived home to be called upon to play in a Welsh Amateur trial match between the North and the South, from which he was again chosen to play for Wales against England in an Amateur international at Bangor. In November 1957 George signed professional terms with Wrexham, although he was initially to act as full-back cover for Albert Parker and Aly McGowan. Their consistency forced George to bide his time until October 1958, when he replaced the injured Aly McGowan for eight matches, his debut coming in a 1-0 home win over Bournemouth. The following season, with Albert Parker having left the club, George began the season as the club's regular right-back. He completed fourteen games but, by the end of October the strong running full-back had lost his place in the side to Barry Wright. George then suffered a serious knee injury in a reserve team game at Buxton, from which he never really recovered. He managed just one more first team game, a Welsh Cup match against Abergavenny in April 1960. He was released at the end of the season, but was soon snapped up by Fourth Division, Barrow, following pre-season trial matches. He had earlier turned down the chance to join League newcomers Peterborough United, as he wanted to remain as a part-time pro, and continue working as a mechanic. George made fourteen League appearances for the Holker Street club during the 1960/61 season, but was released in the summer. He then joined non-league side Morecambe, before a series of short spells with Netherfield in the Lancashire League, followed by Holywell Town, Colwyn Bay and Blaenau Ffestiniog. He then hung up his boots, though it was a decision forced upon him by the state of his knee. By that time he had had his cartilage removed. Following the end of his football career George obtained employment at Brymbo Steelworks again in January 1963, as a overhead crane driver. He worked there for a couple of years before moving on to Vauxhall Motors, from where he went on to have a number of jobs before he retired, settling in the Wrexham area. A fine character, George was good enough to lead us on to a number of other former Robins.

Season	League		F.A.Cup		Welsh Cup		Total	
	apps	gls	apps	gls	apps	gls	apps	gls
1958/59	8	0	1	0	-	-	9	0
1959/60	14	0	-	-	1	0	15	0
	22	**0**	**1**	**0**	**1**	**0**	**24**	**0**

WARBURTON, John Salmon 1924 - 1925

Position; *Outside-Left*
D.O.B; *J/F/M, 1903*
Birthplace; *Crewe, Cheshire*
Height; *5ft 4in* **Weight;** *10st 5lbs*
Debut; v. *Rotherham County (h) 10th April, 1925*
Total Appearances & Goals; *1 app 0 gls*
Career; *Rhyl; Bangor City Jun 1923; Crewe Alexandra (trial); Mold Town Jul 1924; WREXHAM (Am) Nov 1924; Mold Town 1924/1925; Macclesfield Town Jun 1925; Congleton Town; Crewe Alexandra Jun 1928 2apps 0gls;*
Honours; *North Wales Coast F.A.Challenge Cup Winner 1925; North Wales Coast F.A. Representative XI 1923;*

John Warburton played for Rhyl, Bangor City and Mold Town in the Welsh League before he joined Wrexham, initially as an amateur, in November 1924 following the appointment of Mold's Charles Hewitt as the new manager at the Racecourse. An outside-left, John wasn't called upon to play a first team game for The 'Robins' until April 1925, when he stepped in for the injured Billy Graham in a 3-1 win over Rotherham County. It proved to be Warburton's one and only match for the Denbighshire club as he returned to Mold Town that same season, where he collected a North Wales Coast F.A.Challenge Cup winners' medal following their 2-0 win over Holyhead at Bangor, in which he scored one of the Mold goals. He later played for Cheshire County League side Congleton Town, from where he was to sign for Crewe Alexandra in June 1928. He made two Football League appearances for the 'Railwaymen', both in January 1929, in a 5-0 win at Ashington and then in a scoreless home draw with Bradford City. John left Gresty Road some time in 1929.

Season	League		F.A.Cup		Welsh Cup		Total	
	apps	gls	apps	gls	apps	gls	apps	gls
1924/25	1	0	-	-	-	-	1	0
	1	**0**	**-**	**-**	**-**	**-**	**1**	**0**

WARBURTON, Richard 1922 - 1923

Position; *Outside-Left*
D.O.B;
Birthplace;
Height; *ft in* **Weight;** *st lbs*
Debut; v. *Walsall (a) 10th February, 1923*
Total Appearances & Goals; *6 apps 1 gls*
Career; *Manchester City (Amateur) Apr 1922 0apps; WREXHAM Feb 1923; Rhos Athletic 21st Aug 1923; Mold Town Jun 1925;*

Richard Warburton was an amateur with Manchester City, where he failed to make a first team appearance before signing for Wrexham in February 1923, also as an amateur. He made his Football League debut for the 'Robins' that same month, replacing Matt Burton at outside-left in a 1-0 defeat at Walsall. Richard went on to make a further five appearances that season, scoring one goal in a 2-1 home win over Tranmere Rovers. He was released by the North Wales club during the close season of 1923, and joined Rhos Athletic for two years, before moving on to Mold Town in June 1925.

Season	League		F.A.Cup		Welsh Cup		Total	
	apps	gls	apps	gls	apps	gls	apps	gls
1922/23	6	1	-	-	-	-	6	1
	6	**1**	**-**	**-**	**-**	**-**	**6**	**1**

WARD, Ashley Stuart 1991

Position; *Forward*
D.O.B; *24th November, 1970*
Birthplace; *Middleton, Lancashire*
Height; *6ft 1in* **Weight;** *11st 7lbs*
Debut; v. *Doncaster Rovers (h) 12th January, 1991*
Total Appearances & Goals; *5 apps 2 gls*
Career; *Manchester City 5th Aug 1989 0/1apps 0gls; WREXHAM 10th Jan 1991 (loan); Leicester City 30th Jul 1991 £80,000 2/8apps 0gls; Blackpool 21st Nov 1992 (Loan) 2apps 1gls; Crewe Alex 1st Dec 1992 £80,000 58/3apps 25gls; Norwich City 8th Dec 1994 £500,000 53apps 18gls; Derby County 19th Mar 1996 £1,000,000 32/8apps 9gls; Barnsley 3rd Sept 1997 £1,300,000 45/1apps 20gls; Blackburn Rovers 29th Dec 1998 £4,250,000 17apps 5gls;*
Honours; *F.A.Youth Cup runner-up;*

Ashley Ward attended a Rugby Union playing Secondary Modern School in the Manchester area, but it was while he was playing for a local Sunday football league side that he was spotted by Manchester United. Even though he was able to play football only in his spare time Ashley was in great demand by a number of top football clubs, including Nottingham Forest and Blackburn Rovers, but it was United who won his signature when he joined them on associate schoolboy terms. However, Alex Ferguson took charge shortly afterwards, and decided to release the youngster. Ashley had more or less agreed to sign for Nottingham Forest when the former Wrexham manager Ken Barnes, who was chief scout at Manchester City, stepped in to sign him. After leaving school he joined City as an apprentice, and played in their Youth side that won the Lancashire Youth Cup, and reached the Final of the F.A.Youth Cup, where they lost to Watford, 2-1 on aggregate. Ward progressed to make several appearances on the sub's bench during the 1988/89 season, but it wasn't until after signing professional terms that he finally made his Football League debut. Inevitably it was as a substitute, in a 2-1 defeat at Southampton in December 1989. After overcoming a number of back, knee, and ankle injuries at Maine Road, Ward joined Wrexham on loan in January 1991, where he made his debut in a 2-1 home win over Doncaster Rovers, replacing Andy Preece in the side to score two delightful goals. He added four more League and Cup appearances for the 'Robins' before being taken off injured at Brentford in a Freight Rover Trophy match. He then returned to City, from where he was transferred to Leicester City at the end of the season for £80,000. He never really settled at Filbert Street, making just ten League appearances in twelve months. In November 1992 Ashley went on another loan spell, to Blackpool, appearing in just two League games when Crewe Alexandra stepped in to sign him for £80,000, before his loan spell with the 'Seasiders' had expired. His career really took off at Gresty Road, as he averaged practically a goal every other game, and it wasn't long before the Premier League clubs began to take notice. In December 1994 Crewe sold him to Norwich City for £500,000, and he got off to a great start by scoring twice on his debut, in a 3-0 home win over Chelsea. However, his efforts couldn't stop the 'Canaries' from being relegated, even though he ended the season as their top scorer with eight goals. The following term saw him finish as the club's joint scorer, along with Robert Fleck, with ten goals each. It had been a disappointing campaign for Norwich, and in the close season of 1996 Ward left Carrow Road to return to the Premiership, signing for newly-promoted Derby County for a £1,000,000 fee. He soon settled in at the Baseball Ground, helping the 'Rams' to finish in a very respectable twelfth position. The start of the 1997/98 season would see him play in Derby's inaugural match at their new Pride Park stadium, and he scored the first goal on the ground against Wimbledon. However, the strike was erased from the record books after the floodlights failed towards the end of the match which meant that the game had to be abandoned! At the beginning of September, following a home game against Barnsley, he signed for the Yorkshire side for £1,300,000, with an additional £250,000 payable if they avoided relegation. He made his debut for the 'Tykes' against Aston Villa, and went on to score eight goals for the Oakwell club as they bravely fought to maintain their Premier League status, though his efforts were not enough, as they were relegated at the end of the season. He made a return to the Premiership at Christmas 1998 when he became Blackburn Rovers Manager, Brian Kidd's first signing for £4.25 million, but couldn't help save the Ewood Park Club from relegation.

Season	League		F.A.Cup		Welsh Cup		League Cup		F.R.T.		Total	
	apps	gls	apps	gls	apps	gls	apps	gls	apps	gls	apps	gls
1990/91	4	2	-	-	1	0	-	-	1	0	6	2
	4	**2**	**-**	**-**	**1**	**0**	**-**	**-**	**1**	**0**	**6**	**2**

***WARD,* Peter** 1995 - 1999

Position; *Midfield*
D.O.B; *15th October, 1964*
Birthplace; *Durham*
Height; *5ft 10in* ***Weight;*** *11st 7lbs*
Debut; v. *Notts County (h) 12th August, 1995*
Total Appearances & Goals; *157/4 apps 18 gls*
Career; *Chester-le-Street; Huddersfield Town 7th Jan 1987 24/13apps 2gls; Rochdale 20th Jul or Sept 1989 83/1apps 10gls; Stockport County 6th Jun 1991 140/2apps 10gls; WREXHAM 10th Jul 1995;*
Honours; *Welsh Invitation Cup Winner 1998; Autoglass Cup runner-up 1992 & 1993;*

Peter Ward was playing for Chester-le-Street in his native County Durham when spotted by Huddersfield Town. He signed in January 1987 and made his Football League debut as a substitute for former 'Robin', Graham Cooper, in a 2-0 defeat at Oldham Athletic in February. Peter went on to spend two and a half years at Leeds Road, before he moved over the Pennines to Rochdale in September 1989. He made his debut for the Spotland club in a 2-1 home win over local rivals Burnley. He went on to become an influential figure in the Rochdale side that season, as they reached the F.A.Cup Fifth Round for the first time in the club's history, before being somewhat unfortunately beaten by the eventual finalists, Crystal Palace, at Selhurst Park. He made a total of 84 League appearances for Rochdale before joining Stockport County in the summer of 1991, in a player-plus-cash deal that saw Mark Payne move in the opposite direction. Ward made his debut for the 'Hatters' in a 5-0 home win over Swansea in August 1991, and went on to help County reach the Third Division play-off final, where they lost to Peterborough at Wembley. They also reached the Autoglass Cup Final that season, again at Wembley, once again ending up on the losing side, this time against Stoke City. Peter was made club captain for the following season as County once again reached the play-off's, where they lost to Port Vale in the semi-final. A couple of days later they returned to Wembley once again for yet more disappointment, as they lost to Port Vale in the Autoglass final. At Edgeley Park Peter was described as a 'tenacious battler'. He has a wonderful left-foot with the ability to direct long accurate passes, and has often made defenders pay dearly for conceding free-kicks on the edge of the penalty area. Highly respected at Stockport, he left the club at the end of a season that had also seen manager Danny Bergara's departure. During the summer of 1995 Wrexham manager Brian Flynn stepped in to sign Ward for £50,000, to add some much needed experience to the 'Robins' youthful midfield, addressing a problem that had been evident throughout much of the previous season. Peter made his debut in the opening game of 95/96, a 1-1 home draw with Notts County. He went on to help the club reach the verge of the play-off's in the following three season's being a vital member of the 'Robins' midfield engine room with his free-kicks causing concern among opposition goalkeepers. He also played a major part in helping Wrexham reach the Quarter-Finals of the F.A.Cup in 1997, and winning a Welsh Invitation Cup winners' medal in the first year of the competition in 1998. With Peter beginning to struggle during 1998/99 with niggling injuries, he found himself released at the end of the season.

Season	League		F.A.Cup		League Cup		A.G.T.		W.I.C.		Total	
	apps	gls	apps	gls	apps	gls	apps	gls	apps	gls	apps	gls
1995/96	33/1	6	4	0	1	0	1	1	-	-	39/1	7
1996/97	24	1	9	1	2	0	-	-	-	-	35	2
1997/98	35/2	6	4	0	2	0	1	0	7	1	49/2	7
1998/99	25	2	3	0	2	0	0/1	0	4	0	34/1	2
	117/3	**15**	**20**	**1**	**7**	**0**	**2/1**	**1**	**11**	**1**	**157/4**	**18**

***WARDLE,* Robert Ian** 1983

Position; *Goalkeeper*
D.O.B; *5th March, 1955*
Birthplace; *Halifax, Yorkshire*
Height; *5ft 11in* ***Weight;*** *11st 2lbs*
Debut; v. *Peterborough United (h) 3rd September, 1983*
Total Appearances & Goals; *14 apps 0 gls*
Career; *Bristol City Nov 1972 0apps; Shrewsbury Town Jul 1974 131apps 0gls; Liverpool Aug 1982 0apps; WREXHAM 1st Sept 1983 (Loan); Tranmere Rovers 25th Jul 1984 (Loan);*
Honours; *Third Division Championship Winner 1979; Welsh Cup Winner 1979; Welsh Cup runner-up 1980;*

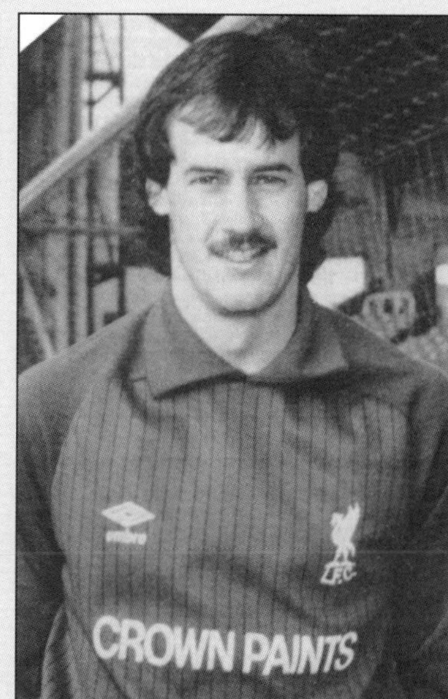

Although born in Halifax Bob Wardle was spotted by Bristol City, and signed as an apprentice upon leaving school. He progressed to sign professional terms with the Ashton Gate club in November 1972, and stayed with them for two seasons, playing reserve team football without making a first team appearance. He was released in the summer of 1974, whereupon he joined Shrewsbury Town in July. Another long stint in the reserve team, as deputy to Ken Mulhearn, was rewarded when he made his first team debut for the 'Shrews' at Wrexham, in a Welsh Cup semi-final in March 1975, which ended in a 2-1 defeat for the Shropshire side. He made another Welsh Cup appearance the following season, before completing his Football League debut in a 4-0 home win over Bradford City in November 1977. Although not the tallest of goalkeepers Wardle then went on to register 131 League appearances for the Gay Meadow outfit, picking up a Third Division championship and Welsh Cup winners' medals in 1979, and adding a runners-up medal in the Welsh Cup at the end of the following season. Liverpool were suitably impressed with his displays by this time, and in August 1982 he joined the Anfield club as cover for Ray Clemence. Bob spent his entire first season in the 'Reds' reserve team, and at the beginning of the 1983/84 season he took up an offer of a loan spell with Wrexham. Manager Bobby Roberts brought him to the Racecourse to replace the young and inexperienced Stuart Parker, who was still learning his trade. Bob made his debut for the 'Robins' in a 2-2 home draw with Peterborough United in only the second League match of the season, and went on to complete a further twelve League appearances in the two months that he spent at the Racecourse. His most notable achievement during his short spell was to save a penalty at Aldershot in a 1-1 draw. Bob returned to Liverpool in November, but he failed to make a first team appearance at Anfield before injury was to force him to retire prematurely from football in 1986. He was subsequently granted a testimonial by Shrewsbury Town, who played Liverpool.

Season	League		F.A.Cup		Welsh Cup		Leagu Cup		A.M.C.		Total	
	apps	gls	apps	gls	apps	gls	apps	gls	apps	gls	apps	gls
1983/84	13	0	-	-	-	-	1	0	-	-	14	0
	13	**0**	**-**	**-**	**-**	**-**	**1**	**0**	**-**	**-**	**14**	**0**

WATERS, William Anthony 1955 - 1960

Position; *Goalkeeper*
D.O.B; *19th September, 1931*
Birthplace; *Swansea, Glamorgan*
Height; *6ft 0in* **Weight;** *11st 11lbs*
Debut; v. *Oldham Athletic (h) 21st September, 1955*
Total Appearances & Goals; *119 apps 0 gls*
Career; *Hillsbro United; Blackpool Nov 1950 0apps; Southend United Nov 1953 0apps; Swansea Town 23rd Aug 1954 0apps; WREXHAM 14th Jun 1955; Millwall Jul 1960 5apps; Yiewsley Town cs1961; Merthyr Tydfil 6th Aug 1963; Llanelli Oct 1963; Haverfordwest County 17th Aug 1964; Llanelli 19th Sept 1964; Ton Pentre 10th Apr 1967; Llanelli 23rd Dec 1967;*
Honours; *Welsh Cup Winner 1957 & 1958;*

Billy Waters played his early football for Hafod Junior School, and later for Swansea Technical College. He became a goalkeeper during his schooldays, when the older boys would 'volunteer' him for the position, and he progressed sufficiently to represent Swansea Schoolboys as they won the Welsh Schools Shield in 1946. However, after leaving school he began working as an apprentice panel beater/coach maker. He played for local club Hillsbro United at the time, although also turning out for the Swansea Town Youth side when required. At the age of 19 he was spotted playing in local football by a Blackpool scout, who invited him for trials. Waters impressed and signed for the 'Seasiders' as a part-time professional in November 1950. However, he failed to break into the first team at Bloomfield Road, where the regular Scottish 'keeper at that time, George Farm, was firmly established as first choice. With his National Service looming Billy was released by Blackpool. He signed for Southend United during his two years' Army service in November 1953, but again failed to make a first team appearance and, following his demobilisation returned home to sign for Swansea Town in October 1954 on a monthly contract. Wrexham wanted to sign Billy at this time, but he remained with the 'Swans' until the end of the season - again without breaking into the first team. He finally agreed to sign for the North Wales club during the summer of 1955. He played for the reserve team in the Cheshire County League at first, but in September took over from Pat Egglestone to finally make his Football League debut in a 1-1 home draw with Oldham Athletic. He went on to spend a total of five seasons at the Racecourse, throughout which time he faced stiff competition for the goalkeeper's shirt from the likes of Pat Egglestone, Earl Godding, Roly Ugolini and Charlie Hughes. Even so, he picked up two Welsh Cup winners' medals during that time, the first against his home town club of Swansea in 1957, and the following season from a victory over local rivals Chester. He also took part in the famous F.A.Cup match of the 1950s against the Busby Babes of Manchester United, as well as having the distinction of saving penalties in three successive away matches. His career at the Racecourse came to an end when released at the end of the 1959/60 season, having made 99 League appearances. Waters received offers from a number of clubs before deciding to join Millwall, although he was to make just five League appearances in his one season at the 'Den'. They included a return to the Racecourse for a match that saw him end up on the winning side, 1-0. Upon leaving the Lions in the summer of 1961 he joined Southern League side Yiewsley Town, who later became Hillingdon Borough. He spent two years there before returning to South Wales to join Merthyr Tydfil. After only a month at Penydarren Park he joined Llanelli Town, which lasted around four seasons, although having a couple of short spells with Haverfordwest County and Ton Pentre during that time. He later took over as manager of the British Steelworks side in Llanelli where he worked, and remained at the Steelworks until he retired in 1990. Having settled in his native Swansea Waters later switched his allegiance to the oval ball game by becoming a frequent visitor to Dunvant Rugby club. Now settled in the Swansea area, Billy returned to North Wales for the Wrexham 'Get-together'/Re-union which was held recently.

Season	League		F.A.Cup		Welsh Cup		Total	
	apps	gls	apps	gls	apps	gls	apps	gls
1955/56	29	0	1	0	2	0	32	0
1956/57	42	0	7	0	5	0	54	0
1957/58	7	0	-	-	3	0	10	0
1958/59	13	0	-	-	1	0	14	0
1959/60	8	0	-	-	1	0	9	0
	99	**0**	**8**	**0**	**12**	**0**	**119**	**0**

WATKIN, Stephen 1989 - 1997

Position; *Forward*
D.O.B; *16th June, 1971*
Birthplace; *Wrexham, Denbighshire*
Height; *5ft 10in* **Weight;** *11st 10lbs*
Debut; v. *Torquay United (a) 16th October, 1990*
Total Appearances & Goals; *218/45 apps 78 gls*
Career; *WREXHAM 24th Jul 1989; Ngongotaya (New Zealand) 26th Mar 1990 (Loan); Swansea City 26th Sept 1997 £100,000 65/10apps 20gls;*
Honours; *Welsh 'B' international cap; Third Division runner-up 1993; Welsh Cup Winner 1995;*

Wrexham born Steve Watkin was first signed by his home town club as a schoolboy at the age of 15, having attended Acrefair Junior School and Dinas Bran Secondary School in Llangollen. He joined the famous Druids club as a 10 year-old, and played at each age level as a forward. His goalscoring feats were soon recognised and he gained selection, first for Wrexham & District, then Clwyd Schools, followed by North Wales Schoolboys, and this earned him a call up for the Welsh Schoolboys team. However, he didn't pick up a Welsh schoolboy cap, as he was a non-playing substitute. Upon leaving school he was offered Y.T.S. terms by Wrexham manager Dixie McNeil, but had an agreement to continue with his school studies, and went on to gain nine 'O' levels and two 'A' levels in Maths and Physics. Steve then turned down the offer of a University place to continue with his football career, and signed a one year professional contract with Wrexham in July 1989. The following season was spent in the club's reserve side, before he accepted the chance to jet off to New Zealand in the summer of 1990 to play for Second Division side Ngongotaya to gain more experience. As they were a part-time club Watkin combined playing football with working for a sports manufacturing company, but that obviously didn't affect his game as he scored 20 goals in as many games. Upon his return to Wrexham Steve signed a three month contract, and his Football League debut followed shortly afterwards, in October 1990, a 1-0 defeat at Torquay United. He went on to make eight more League appearances that season, but it was the following year, 1991/92, that saw his breakthrough into the first team on a regular basis. It was then that he made a name for himself, scoring the winning goal in the famous F.A.Cup match against the reigning Football League champions, Arsenal on a never to be forgotten day for Wrexham fan's everywhere. International recognition followed in March 1992, when he was selected to play for the Welsh 'B' side against Canada. He finished the year as the club's leading goalscorer with 13 League and Cup goals, and bettered that the following campaign, contributing eighteen goals in a lethal partnership with Gary Bennett to lead Wrexham to promotion to the Second Division. By this time he was firmly established as a regular in the forward line, where his ability to hold up the ball for his team mates proved invaluable. He

also possessed excellent ball control and made a significant contribution alongside Gary Bennett as the former Chester man continued to pile up the goals. Bennett summed up their relationship perfectly at the start of his second spell at the Racecourse, when he told Steve "Let's make it like it was. You do all the work and I'll score all the goals!" An in-form Steve Watkin is a player who will always lead the line well, but towards the end of 96/97 he struggled to maintain a regular first team place as his form dipped, and it was much the same at the beginning of 1997/98. In September, Third Division side Swansea City offered £100,000, and he reluctantly agreed to the move in a bid to revitalise his career. Steve made his debut for the 'Swans' the day after signing, in a 1-1 home draw with Leyton Orient, and returned to the Racecourse in October 1998 to score against his former club in a FAW Premier Cup match. He still remains very much a part of the first team set-up at the Vetch, helping the Swans' overcome West Ham in the F.A. Cup in January 1999 and narrowly missing out in the Third Division Play-Offs.

Season	League		F.A.Cup		Welsh Cup		League Cup		F.R.T.		E.C.W.C.		Total	
	apps	gls	apps	gls	apps	gls	apps	gls	apps	gls	apps	gls	apps	gls
1990/91	9	1	-	-	1	0	-	-	1	0	-	-	11	1
1991/92	24/4	8	5	5	2	0	-	-	2/1	0	-	-	33/5	13
1992/93	31/2	18	0/1	0	4	1	1	0	-	-	-	-	36/3	19
1993/94	39/1	9	2	1	2	1	4	0	2	0	-	-	49/1	11
1994/95	24/8	4	2/1	2	4/2	2	3/1	3	2	2	-	-	35/12	13
1995/96	16/13	7	2/1	1	-	-	1/1	1	1	0	2	0	22/15	9
1996/97	24/2	7	5/3	3	-	-	2	0	-	-	-	-	31/5	10
1997/98	0/3	1	-	-	-	-	0/1	0	-	-	-	-	1/4*	2*
	167/33	**55**	**16/6**	**12**	**13/2**	**4**	**11/3**	**4**	**8/1**	**2**	**2**	**0**	**218/45**	**78***

* = Includes 1app 1gls in Welsh Invitation Cup.

WEALE, Robert Henry

1933 - 1935

Position; *Outside-Right*
D.O.B; *9th November, 1903*
Birthplace; *Troed-y-Rhiw, Glamorgan*
Died; *Merthyr Tydfil, J/F/M 1970*
Height; *5ft 8in* ***Weight;*** *11st 6lbs*
Debut; v. *Southport (a) 8th April, 1933*
Total Appearances & Goals; *26 apps 4 gls*
Career; *Merthyr Vale; Luton Town (trial); West Ham United Mar 1925 3apps 0gls; Swindon Town Jun 1927 20apps 7gls; Southampton Dec 1928 £1,000 45apps 10gls; Boston Town Sept 1930 (trial); Cardiff City Oct 1930 6apps 0gls; Guildford City 1931; Newport County 12th Aug 1932 26apps 8gls; WREXHAM 15th Mar 1933 £1,000; Glentoran Aug 1935; Cheltenham Town 19th Aug 1935; Bath City 1936;*
Honours; *Welsh Cup Winner 1930; Welsh Schoolboy International;*

Bob Weale was a good schoolboy footballer and a sprinter, at which he won several medals. He was selected to represent Ebbw Vale Schoolboys at football, before being chosen for the Welsh Schoolboys team. Bob was playing for Merthyr Vale when invited for trials with Luton Town, and although they proved unsuccessful had shown enough promise to convince First Division West Ham United of his abilities, and they signed him in March 1925. He began playing for the 'Hammers' reserves in the Combination League, before progressing to make his Football League debut in October 1925, in a 1-0 home win over Notts County, where he played at outside-right. Bob also turned out in the next match, a 3-1 home defeat by Sheffield United, before making one more League appearance in a 3-1 defeat at Bury in December. He did not appear in the Upton Park club's first team again, and was allowed to join Swindon Town in the close season of 1927. Weale spent just over a season with the Wiltshire club, where he scored seven goals in twenty League outings, before Second Division Southampton paid out a club record fee of £1,000 for his services in December 1928. He was described as a 'fast, clever right-winger' during his time at the Dell, and soon showed his promise by scoring five goals in a three match spell from his outside-right position. However, the goals eventually began to dry up, and by the end of the term he had lost his first team place. In 1929 Bob's brother, Tom, had a trial with Southampton, and the 1929/30 season saw Bob restored to the first team, but once again he found himself out of favour by the end of the season after his form had become 'erratic'. In May 1930 he turned down Southampton's wage offer of £5.00 per week, rising to £8.00 when playing in the first team, in order to return to his native South Wales, as he signed for Second Division Cardiff City. His first team debut for the 'Bluebirds' came in the 1930 Welsh Cup Final against Rhyl, which had been held over from the previous season. Played in October Cardiff won 4-2, to earn Bob a Welsh Cup winners' medal. However, his League debut didn't follow until January, a 2-1 home win over Port Vale. He made just five more League appearances for Cardiff as they were relegated to the Third Division South at the end of the season. Weale then left Ninian Park and went into non-league football, playing first for Boston, then Guildford City, before joining Third Division South side Newport County, in the close season of 1932. Before the following campaign had ended he had been transferred to Wrexham, in March 1933 for a £1,000 fee, making his debut at Southport in a scoreless draw. He managed four more League outings, scoring once in a 1-1 draw at Doncaster, as Wrexham finished the season in second place their highest position since joining the Football League. Over the next two seasons Bob found his first team chances limited at the Racecourse, and in August 1935 joined Irish League side Glentoran on trial. However, he returned home within the same month and signed for Cheltenham Town. He later played for Bath City.

Season	League		F.A.Cup		Welsh Cup		N.S.C.		Total	
	apps	gls	apps	gls	apps	gls	apps	gls	apps	gls
1932/33	5	1	-	-	-	-	-	-	5	1
1933/34	6	3	-	-	-	-	1	0	7	3
1934/35	12	0	1	0	1	0	-	-	14	0
	23	**4**	**1**	**0**	**1**	**0**	**1**	**0**	**26**	**4**

WEAVER, Francis Robert

1925 - 1926

Position; *Centre-Forward*
D.O.B; *O/N/D, 1905*
Birthplace; *Chester, Cheshire*
Died; *Chester, J/A/S 1964*
Height; *5ft 10in* ***Weight;*** *11st 2lbs*
Debut; v. *Barrow (h) 3rd October, 1925*
Total Appearances & Goals; *1 app 0 gls*
Career; *Connah's Quay & Shotton; Colwyn Bay Aug 1923; Connah's Quay & Shotton 1923/24; Flint Town United cs1924; WREXHAM 1st May 1925; Mold Town Nov 1925; Whitchurch Jul 1927; WREXHAM 25th Feb 1928; Mold Town 8th Aug 1928; Connah's Quay & Shotton 14th Mar 1930; Oswestry Town Feb 1931;*
Honours; *Welsh Cup runner-up 1925;*

Frank Weaver was said to have been "ex-Colwyn Bay" when he signed for Flint Town in the close season of 1924, moving from Connah's Quay & Shotton. He reached the 1925 Welsh Cup Final with Flint, where he turned out against Wrexham in a 3-1 win for the Football League side. Despite the result Frank must have impressed, as he was signed by the Wrexham manager Charlie Hewitt at the end of the season, beating off Derby and Sunderland who had also shown interest in his signature. Frank joined the Racecourse club on amateur forms, with the agreement that he could continue playing for Flint in the Welsh League if he wasn't required by Wrexham. This arrangement was quite in order at the time, as Wrexham's first team played in an English League. Frank was finally called upon by Wrexham to make his Football League debut in October, replacing Ted Regan at centre-forward in a scoreless home draw against Barrow. That match proved to be Weaver's one and only game for the Denbighshire club, and a month later he also decided to leave Flint and join Mold Town. He later played for Whitchurch, and had a spell back at the Racecourse as first team cover, though he never made a senior appearance. He later returned to play for two of his former clubs, Mold Town and Connah's Quay & Shotton, before signing for Birmingham & District League side Oswestry Town in February 1931.

Season	League		F.A.Cup		Welsh Cup		Total	
	apps	gls	apps	gls	apps	gls	apps	gls
1925/26	1	0	-	-	-	-	1	0
	1	**0**	**-**	**-**	**-**	**-**	**1**	**0**

WEAVER, John Noel

1946 - 1947

Position; *Right-Back*
D.O.B; *26th November, 1924*
Birthplace; *Rhosrobin, Wrexham, Denbighshire*
Height; *5ft 8in* ***Weight;*** *11st 2lbs*
Debut; v. *Hull City (a) 16th November, 1946*
Total Appearances & Goals; *2 apps 0 gls*
Career; *Army; Fulham (WW2); WREXHAM 17th May 1946; Congleton Nov 1948; Blaenau Ffestiniog 23rd Jul 1951;*

John Weaver began playing football whilst at Rhosrobin Church School. He went on to represent the Wrexham & District Schoolboys side which eventually led to him sign as an amateur for Wrexham during the Second World War. During the hostilities he was enlisted in the Army, and moved down to South East London to assist with the clearance of Bomb damage. When there he appeared for Fulham, and could have signed for the Craven Cottage club at the end of the conflict, but preferred to return home to Wrexham. He was discharged from the Army in May 1946, and returned to North Wales where he was invited to sign professional for the Racecourse club. He went on to make his Football League debut in November 1946, replacing Cyril Jones at right-back in a 1-0 defeat at Hull City. His next appearance came at half-back in a 1-1 home draw with Southport the following month. However, he found his first team opportunities limited with the 'Robins', and that game proved to be his

last senior appearance for the club. He did continue to turn out for the reserve side until being allowed to join Cheshire County League side Congleton in November 1948. He later joined Blaenau Ffestiniog with whom he remained until 1953, when he had to retire from the game because of a persistent knee injury. Having served his time as a joiner during the War, John became employed with John McAlpine a firm he was to work for in various parts of the North West and North Wales as a Works Site Manager for over 25 years. A cousin to Welsh under-23 internationals Malcolm and Gordon Edwards, who both played for Bolton Wanderers in the 1950's and 1960's, Malcolm also appeared for Chester, Tranmere Rovers, and Barrow. John retired in the late 1980s, settling in Ruabon near Wrexham, where he was still residing at the time of writing.

Season	League		F.A.Cup		Welsh Cup		Total	
	apps	gls	apps	gls	apps	gls	apps	gls
1946/47	2	0	-	-	-	-	2	0
	2	**0**	**-**	**-**	**-**	**-**	**2**	**0**

WEBBER, Keith James — 1964 - 1966

Position; *Centre-Forward*
D.O.B; *5th January, 1943*
Birthplace; *Cardiff, Glamorgan*
Died; *Wrexham, September 1983*
Height; *5ft 9'1/2in* ***Weight;*** *12st 2lbs*
Debut; v. *Doncaster Rovers (h) 16th September, 1964*
Total Appearances & Goals; *86 apps 36 gls*
Career; *Barry Town; Everton Feb 1960 4apps 0gls; Brighton H.A. Apr 1963 £9,000 35apps 14gls; WREXHAM 14th Sept 1964 £4,500; Doncaster Rovers 15th Jun 1966 £6,000 63/4apps 18gls; Chester 4th Jun 1969 66/6apps 13gls; Stockport County Jul 1971 36/4apps 7gls; Morecambe; Northwich Victoria; Oswestry Town Aug 1973; Rhyl 16th Aug 1974;*
Honours; *Welsh Cup runners-up 1965 & 1970*

Keith Webber was a good all-round sportsman as a youngster. He was a Cardiff schools' sprint champion, and excelled at rugby, playing for Cardiff Boys and completing trials for the Welsh schools' team. However, it was the round ball game upon which he decided to concentrate, and began playing for Southern League Barry Town. There, he was spotted by a scout from Everton, and eventually signed for the Goodison Park club in February 1960 at the age of seventeen. Keith made his way through the ranks to complete his first team debut eight months later, in a 3-1 League Cup win over Walsall, and scored one of the goals. However, he was to manage just five more first team appearances for the 'Toffeemen', with his most memorable game coming against Liverpool in a Liverpool Senior Cup Final in front of a 54,000 crowd. In April 1963 Brighton & Hove Albion paid out £9,000 for Keith's services in a bid to stave off relegation to Division Four. He made his debut in a 1-0 home defeat by Bournemouth, but by the end of the season, he had been unable to prevent their slide into the basement. During his time at the Goldstone Ground, Webber was noted for his exceptional speed, all-out effort and a regular supply of goals. He ended 1963/64 as the club's second top scorer with fourteen League and Cup goals. However, the signing of Bobby Smith in the summer of 1964 saw Webber banished to reserve team football. Wrexham manager Ken Barnes then intervened in September 1964 and took him to the Racecourse for a bargain £4,500, though his 'Robins' career got off to a less than perfect start, when he injured an ankle in only his third match at Tranmere Rovers. It subsequently proved troublesome, and it was only towards the end of the season that he finally hit top form, when playing in the 1965 Welsh Cup Final, where Wrexham lost 3-0 to his native Cardiff City after a replay. 1965/66 was to be a bitter disappointment as Wrexham finished bottom of the Football League, and had to seek re-election for the first time in the club's history, Keith, though, had ended the campaign as the club's top scorer, having scored 22 League goals. However, an on-field altercation with another Wrexham player led to him being transferred to Doncaster Rovers for a £6,000 fee at the end of the season. He went on to spend three years at Belle Vue, where he finished joint top scorer in 1967/68, although the following season struggled to hold down a regular first team place. In June 1969 Keith left the South Yorkshire club to join Chester, with whom he played in another Welsh Cup Final in 1970, but found himself on the losing side once more, beaten again by Cardiff City, although he did finish as their top scorer with twelve League goals. Keith spent one more season at Sealand Road before joining Stockport County in July 1971, where he stayed for a year before leaving League football. He later moved around the non-league scene with spells at Morecambe, Northwich Victoria, Oswestry Town, and Rhyl, with whom he returned to the Racecourse in December 1974 for a Welsh Cup game which the North Wales Coast club lost 2-0. After retiring from football Webber became an insurance salesman and later the licensee of the Grosvenor Arms in Handbridge, Chester. He moved to the White Lion public house in Buckley in 1979, but left the licensed trade because of ill-health and took a job with a finance company. Tragically, Keith died of a heart attack at his Marford home in September 1983. He was just 40.

Season	League		F.A.Cup		Welsh Cup		League Cup		Total	
	apps	gls	apps	gls	apps	gls	apps	gls	apps	gls
1964/65	28	11	1	0	7	3	-	-	36	14
1965/66	45	22	2	0	1	0	2	0	50	22
	73	**33**	**3**	**0**	**8**	**0**	**2**	**0**	**86**	**36**

WEETMAN, Darran Graham — 1985 - 1986

Position; *Midfielder*
D.O.B; *7th June, 1968*
Birthplace; *Shrewsbury*
Height; *5ft 7in* ***Weight;*** *10st 7lbs*
Debut; v. *Halifax Town (a) 14th March, 1986*
Total Appearances & Goals; *1 app 0 gls*
Career; *WREXHAM Jun 1985; Morda United Aug 1986; Llansantffraid Aug 1992; Oswestry Town Jul 1993; Rhyl Jul 1996; Oswestry Town 1996/97;*
Honours; *Welsh National League Championship Winner 1995; Cymru Alliance League Championship Winner 1993 & 1996;*

Darran Weetman first began playing football at the Fitzalan Comprehensive School in Oswestry, where he was chosen to play for his school, Shropshire under-18's and Mid-Wales Youth sides. By this time he was a much sought-after youngster, having arranged trials with Shrewsbury Town, Aston Villa and West Brom. However, he had already undertaken a trial with Wrexham, and was contacted by the club's manager, Dixie McNeil, who invited him to sign apprentice terms upon leaving school. He progressed enough to be called up for his Football League debut in March 1986 at the age of seventeen replacing David Gregory in a 5-2 defeat at Halifax Town, though he was substituted by Steve Emery during the game. It proved to be his one and only first team appearance for Wrexham, as he was released at the end of the season. Darran then joined his local side, Morda United, who played in the Shropshire County League at the time, where he picked up three Championships', two Eccleston Cup, and two League Cup winners' medals. Weetman later left the Drill Field club to join progressive Cymru Alliance League side Llansantffraid, where he was also to earn League and Cup winners' medals. A move to the reformed Oswestry Town then saw him help the Park Hall club to the Welsh National League championship in only their second season. He had been appointed as player/coach to Ken Swinnerton in June 1994, following the shock resignation of the former Wrexham player Idris Pryce as manager. Promotion to the Cymru Alliance League brought the League title to the Shropshire club at the first attempt, but they were denied promotion to the League of Wales as they did not have any floodlights at that time. Darran added North-East Wales Cup, Cymru Alliance League Cup and Welsh National League Cup winners' medals to his collection during his time at Park Hall. After working for his father's haulage company for a number of years Weetman ended his playing career in 1997 upon taking up employment as a pipe fitter/welder for a North-East company. He is now required to travel the length and breadth of the country, though he still retains a base in the Oswestry area.

Season	League		F.A.Cup		Welsh Cup		League Cup		F.R.T.		Total	
	apps	gls	apps	gls	apps	gls	apps	gls	apps	gls	apps	gls
1985/86	1	0	-	-	-	-	-	-	-	-	1	0
	1	**0**	**-**	**-**	**-**	**-**	**-**	**-**	**-**	**-**	**1**	**0**

WELSH, William 1931

Position; *Inside-Right*
D.O.B; *2nd May, 1898*
Birthplace; *Douglas Water, Strathclyde*
Died; *Aviemore, 9th November, 1978*
Height; *5ft 8in* ***Weight;*** *11st 10lbs*
Debut; v. *Doncaster Rovers (h) 14th January, 1931*
Total Appearances & Goals; *11 apps 2 gls*
Career; *Technical College, Lanark; Douglas Water Thistle; Hearts cs1922; Dundee United 1925 57apps 17gls; Charlton Athletic 25th May 1927 £1,000 28apps 7gls; Wigan Borough 24th Dec 1928 £50 55apps 17gls; Southport 7th Mar 1930 11apps 3gls; Newport County 9th Jun 1930 6apps 0gls; Connah's Quay & Shotton 15th Nov 1930; WREXHAM 14th Jan 1931; Gateshead Jul 1931 58apps 22gls; Hartlepools United Jan 1934 3apps 0gls; Jarrow Jul 1936;*

Billy Welsh first played football as a goalkeeper for his Technical College in Lanark, where he had studied mining. He was a cousin to James Welsh, M.P., the Scottish poet and author. However, it was football that was Billy's passion, and was to progress in the game - not as a goalkeeper, but as an inside-forward. It was during a spell with his home town team Douglas Water Thistle, that he switched to the outfield position, and made such an impact that he was signed by Hearts in the summer of 1922. Billy spent almost three years at Tynecastle before joining Dundee United in 1925. He scored 17 goals in 57 Scottish League appearances for the Tannadice club before moving south at the end of 1926/27, to join Charlton Athletic for a £1,000 fee. He did well in his first season at the Valley, but made just four first team appearances in the ensuing campaign. 1929/30 didn't see him figure in the first team at all, and he was subsequently transferred to Wigan Borough for £50, though it was a fee that Charlton never received! and, three years after the transfer date, the club folded! Welsh stayed with Wigan until February 1930, playing in their best-ever season, 1928/29, which saw them finish fourth in the Third Division North. They also reached the Third Round of the F.A.Cup, where they lost 3-1 to Sheffield Wednesday in front of the biggest-ever attendance at Springfield Park, 30,443. Billy had scored 17 goals in 55 League games for Wigan until he was signed by Southport in March 1930. He then played in the final eleven matches of the season, scoring three goals, moving on to Third Division South side, Newport County in the summer. He made just six League appearances for the Somerton Park club before moving up to North Wales, and Welsh League side Connah's Quay & Shotton, in November 1930. His time with the Deeside Club proved to be even shorter, as he was quickly recruited by Wrexham in January 1931. Billy went straight into the first team, deputising for the injured Jack Hughes, in a 4-1 home win over Doncaster, but managed just eight more appearances before the end of the season. Another summer move, this time to Gateshead followed. It was here that Welsh was to enjoy the best goalscoring spell of his career, returning 22 goals from 58 League games. He was on the move again soon and Billy joined North-Eastern rivals Hartlepool in Jan 34, where he played in just three League games, without scoring, before finally leaving the Football League scene to join Jarrow in July 1936. During his playing career he was described as a 'well balanced goal scoring forward,' and was reputed to have scored 73 goals in 244 matches during his Scottish and English Leagues career. Billy later worked as a barman, winning a job-related award in 1966 at an hotel in Kingussie, in the Highlands of Scotland, where he settled.

Season	League		F.A.Cup		Welsh Cup		Total	
	apps	gls	apps	gls	apps	gls	apps	gls
1930/31	9	1	-	-	2	1	11	2
	9	**1**	**-**	**-**	**2**	**1**	**11**	**2**

WESTON, Donald Patrick 1959 - 1960 & 1966 - 1968

Position; *Inside-Forward*
D.O.B; *6th March, 1936.*
Birthplace; *New Houghton, Mansfield, Nottinghamshire*
Height; *5ft 7'1/2in* ***Weight;*** *10st 4lbs*
Debut; v. *Swindon Town (a) 23rd August, 1958*
Total Appearances & Goals; *84 apps 40 gls*
Career; *Army; WREXHAM (Am) May 1958, (Pro) 6th Jun 1959; Birmingham City 15th Jan 1960 £12,000 23apps 3gls; Rotherham United 22nd Dec 1960 £10,000 76apps 21gls; Leeds United Dec 1962 £18,000 68apps 24gls; Huddersfield Town Oct 1965 20/2apps 7gls; WREXHAM Dec 1966; Chester Jun 1968 1/2apps 0gls; Altrincham 1968/69; Bethesda Athletic 18th Aug 1969;*
Honours; *Second Division Championship Winner 1964; Football League Cup runner-up 1961; Welsh Cup runner-up 1967;*

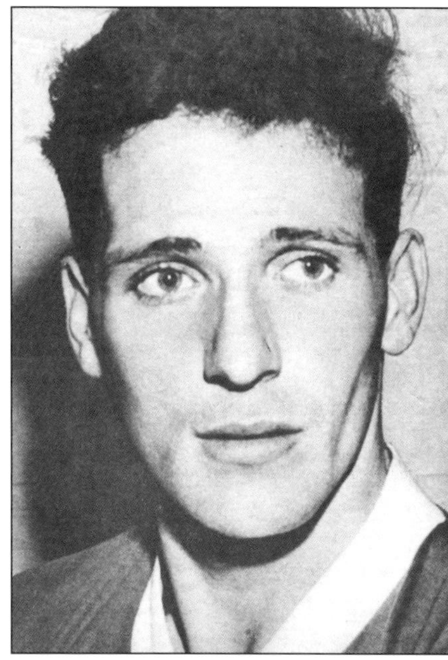

Brought up in the Mansfield area Don Weston was selected to represent East Derbyshire Schoolboys. However, he progressed no further in the game at that time, and upon leaving school took up employment as a coal miner. He continued to play football for his local side, Pleasley Imps, from where he turned out for Leeds United as an amateur, though he refused their offer of professional terms on 'personal grounds'. Shortly afterwards Don was called up for his National Service, serving with the 31st Training Regiment Royal Artillery and stationed at Kinmel Bay camp, near Rhyl. It was during this time that he was recommended to Wrexham, and they invited him to the Racecourse for trials which led to him signing amateur forms in May 1958. Weston made his Football League debut for the 'Robins' in the opening match of the 1958/59 season, a 1-0 defeat at Swindon, although he scored on his home debut in the following match, a 3-2 win over Notts County. During that season, one in which he scored 12 goals in 20 League and Cup games for the club whilst still serving with the Army, he once broke out of camp earning 14 days' confinement to barracks! Don had actually intended to make the Army his career, until he realised his potential as a footballer, and upon completion of his National Service in June 1959 signed professional terms with Wrexham. During the 1959/60 season he was described as having a 'devastating burst of speed, whose shooting power caused a sensation, and had a turn of foot like nobody's business'. He scored 16 goals in 28 League and Cup games that season before Birmingham City stepped in to pay a record fee received by Wrexham - £12,000 - for his signature. He made his 'Blues' debut in a 2-1 defeat against Manchester United at Old Trafford, but he struggled to score goals for his new club as frequently as he had been doing at the Racecourse, and in December 1960 he was sold to Rotherham United for £10,000. Don went on to play for the 'Millermen' in the first ever League Cup Final, where they lost 3-2 on aggregate to Aston Villa. He enjoyed almost two years at Millmoor, before Weston signed for Leeds United in December 1962 for an £18,000 fee. Don made an impressive start at Elland Road by scoring a hat-trick on his debut in a 3-1 home win over Stoke City, and finished the following season as the club's joint top scorer with 13 League goals, as Leeds won the Second Division championship. 1964/65 ended with Leeds as runners-up in their first season back in Division One, though the year ended in disappointment for Don as he was left out of the 1965 F.A.Cup Final side, Jim Storrie being preferred to partner Alan Peacock in attack. Despite this success Don found life harder in Division One, more so as a young Peter Lorimer began to breakthrough into the first team, and in October 1965 was transferred to Huddersfield Town. He made his debut in a scoreless draw with his former club, Rotherham United, but overall struggled to maintain a regular first team place during his time in Yorkshire. Soon after, Don returned to settle in the Mansfield area, where he worked as a car salesman. He has since run his own car sales business. He was also no mean Cricketer, turning out for his birthplace, New Houghton (Mansfield). He now enjoys Bowls. The Racecourse faithful were delighted when he returned to the club in Dec 66, as he was a great favourite with the crowd but although averaging nearly a goal every other game he was never quite the same second time around. After short spells with Chester and Altrincham Don finished off his playing career with a long stint at Welsh League North Club Bethesda Athletic.

Season	League		F.A.Cup		Welsh Cup		League Cup		Total	
	apps	gls	apps	gls	apps	gls	apps	gls	apps	gls
1958/59	17	8	-	-	3	4	-	-	20	12
1959/60	25	13	3	3	-	-	-	-	28	16
1966/67	13	6	-	-	4	1	-	-	17	7
1967/68	29	13	1	1	1	0	-	-	31	14
	84	**40**	**4**	**4**	**8**	**5**	**-**	**-**	**96**	**49**

WHITE, Alfred

1936 - 1937

Position; *Inside-Forward*
Birthplace; *Spennymoor, Durham*
D.O.B; *A/M/J 1909*
Height; *5ft 8in* **Weight;** *11st 4lbs*
Debut; v. *Darlington (a) 9th September, 1936*
Total Appearances & Goals; *25 apps 5 gls*
Career; *Spennymoor Juniors; Spennymoor United cs1927; Derby County Nov 1927 4apps 0gls; Bournemouth & Boscombe Athletic Oct 1931 125apps 35gls; WREXHAM 29th May 1936; Spennymoor United Jul 1937;*

Alf White was playing for his local club, Spennymoor United, as a promising 18 year-old when First Division Derby County took an interest in the young inside-forward, and signed him in November 1927. He went on to spend almost three years with the East Midlands club, making his Football League debut at centre-forward in January 1928, in a 4-0 defeat at Leicester. His next first team appearance came over two years later, when playing in a 1-0 home win over Grimsby Town in September 1930. Alf added one more game that season, a 2-1 home defeat by Middlesborough, while the following campaign saw his final appearance for the 'Rams' in a 3-2 defeat at Blackburn. He left the Baseball Ground in October 1931 to sign for Third Division South side Bournemouth. White went on to spend almost five years with the 'Cherries', making 131 League appearances and scoring 35 goals for the south coast club. He finally left Dean Court in May 1936, when he was transferred to Wrexham. His debut for the Racecourse club came in a 1-1 draw at Darlington in the third match of the 1936/37 season, when he replaced Ambrose Brown at inside-right. He then had a spell in the reserves, until replacing Jack Fryer at inside-left in a 6-0 win at Rochdale in October, with Alf scoring one of the goals. He kept his place in the side until February, when replaced by John Smith. Alf was to manage just three more League appearances for Wrexham before leaving the club at the end of the season. He then returned to the North-East to join his home town club, Spennymoor United, for the 1937/38 season. The Topical Times "Who's Who" of 1933 stated that he could play equally well on the wing.

Season	League		F.A.Cup		Welsh Cup		N.S.C.		Total	
	apps	gls	apps	gls	apps	gls	apps	gls	apps	gls
1936/37	21	5	3	0	-	-	1	0	25	5
	21	**5**	**3**	**0**	**-**	**-**	**1**	**0**	**25**	**5**

WHITE, William Henry

1961

Position; *Forward*
D.O.B; *13th October, 1936*
Birthplace; *Liverpool, Merseyside*
Height; *5ft 10in* **Weight;** *12 st 0lbs*
Debut; v. *Darlington (h) 15th March, 1961*
Total Appearances & Goals; *8 apps 0 gls*
Career; *Burnley Jan 1954 9apps 4gls; WREXHAM 14th Mar 1961; Chester Jul 1961 14apps 3gls; Halifax Town 1962;*

Billy White was spotted playing for Clubmoor Boys' Club in his native Liverpool, by Burnley, for whom he signed in January 1954 at the age of seventeen. After spending four years at Turf Moor he finally made his

Football League debut in a First Division match at West Bromwich Albion in December 1957, which ended in a 5-1 defeat. He fared much better in his second game, as he scored twice in a 3-2 win at Birmingham City. Billy went on to add a further seven League games, six of which came in Burnley's First Division Championship winning season of 1959/60, when he also scored two goals. His role was primarily as a deputy for Jimmy McIlroy or Jimmy Robson, with his 'clever ball control and accurate distribution ensuring that neither player was unduly missed'. White was to leave Turf Moor two days before the transfer deadline in March 1961, when he joined his former coach at Burnley, Billy Morris, then manager of Wrexham. He went straight into the Wrexham side at outside-right for a 3-1 home win over Darlington. A further seven League appearances were added before the end of the season, when he was surprisingly allowed to leave the Racecourse, joining Chester on a free transfer. Billy made his debut for Chester in the opening game of the 1961/62 season, a 1-0 home win over Oldham Athletic. He went on to complete another further twelve League appearances that season, scoring four goals, before being allowed to join Halifax Town in July 1962. However, he failed to make a first team appearance at the Shay, and he then dropped into non-league football.

Season	League		F.A.Cup		Welsh Cup		League Cup		Total	
	apps	gls	apps	gls	apps	gls	apps	gls	apps	gls
1960/61	8	0	-	-	-	-	-	-	8	0
	8	**0**	**-**	**-**	**-**	**-**	**-**	**-**	**8**	**0**

WHITEHOUSE, Brian

1962 - 1963

Position; *Inside-Forward*
D.O.B; *8th September, 1935*
Birthplace; *West Bromwich, West Midlands*
Height; *5ft $10\frac{1}{2}$in* **Weight;** *12st 0lbs*
Debut; v. *Oldham Athletic (a) 24th March, 1962*
Total Appearances & Goals; *54 apps 26 gls*
Career; *Vono Sports; West Bromwich Albion 20th Oct 1952 37apps 13gls; Norwich City £70,000 7th Mar 1960 41apps 14gls; WREXHAM 16th Mar 1962 £6,000; Crystal Palace 19th Nov 1963 £4,000 82apps 17gls; Charlton Athletic £8,000 11th Mar 1966 13apps 1gls; Leyton Orient 27th Jun 1966 £7,250 52apps 6gls;*
Honours; *Welsh Cup runner-up 1962;*

Brian Whitehouse attended the George Salter School in West Bromwich, and signed for local side Vono Sports. He was then snapped up by his local Football League side, West Bromwich Albion, signing apprentice forms on the 25th April 1950. He stepped up to the professional ranks two years later, going on to spend his two years' National Service with the Royal Artillery, stationed for some of that time at Oswestry. His Football League debut for Albion, came in a 1-1 draw at Portsmouth in April 1956. Although he was never a regular during his time at the Hawthorns Brian did score both of Albion's goals in the F.A.Cup semi-final draw with Aston Villa in March 1957. However, they lost the replay 1-0. In March 1960 he was transferred to Norwich City for £70,000, and scored the 'Canaries' first ever goal in the Football League Cup competition against Oldham. It was the beginning of a run which saw him acquire the reputation of a lucky talisman at Carrow Road, as the club lost just one of their games in which he had scored. Nevertheless, he was allowed to join Wrexham in March 1962, after then Racecourse manager Ken Barnes took an interest in him following an F.A.Cup match against Norwich in January. Whitehouse joined the 'Robins' at a time when they were chasing promotion and, playing at inside-forward alongside Ernie Phythian, he scored eight goals in eleven games to help Wrexham achieve their ambition. At the end of the season Brian played in the 1962 Welsh Cup Final, where Wrexham surprisingly lost to Bangor City, and during the next campaign played in the memorable F.A.Cup tie against Liverpool on the Racecourse, as he returned ten goals from 28 League games. Whitehouse left Wrexham in November 1963 to join Crystal Palace, and scored for his new club on his debut, in a 2-2 home draw with Hull. He then went on to help Palace secure promotion to the Second Division in 1964, before moving on to Charlton in March 1966 for an £8,000 fee. At the end of that season he switched to another London club, Leyton Orient, for a £7,250 transfer fee, with an agreement that Charlton would receive a further £250 if the 'O's ended the following season in the top six - they finished 14th! At the end of 67/68 Brian announced his retirement following problems arising from an Achilles tendon injury. During his career he had played in almost every position, including goalkeeper, and overall had a useful goal tally in both League and Cup competitions. Brian retained an involvement in the game by becoming trainer-coach at Luton Town, later being appointed assistant manager to Alec Stock in November 1968. He joined Arsenal as youth team coach in August 1969, and led the 'Gunners' to F.A.Youth Cup success in 1971. Whitehouse returned to his former club, West Bromwich Albion in July 1971, and was appointed temporary manager in April 1975 following the departure of Don Howe. In July 1975, he became first team coach to Johnny Giles, later serving under both Ronnie Allen and Ron Atkinson in the same capacity. He accompanied Atkinson to Manchester United in 1981, and later renewed the acquaintance at Villa Park, where they worked together until January 1995. Brian then teamed up yet again with 'Big Ron' at Coventry. Brian Whitehouse has now given over 30 years' magnificent service to the game.

Season	League		F.A.Cup		Welsh Cup		League Cup		Total	
	apps	gls	apps	gls	apps	gls	apps	gls	apps	gls
1961/62	11	8	-	-	3	1	-	-	14	9
1962/63	28	10	4	5	1	0	-	-	33	15
1963/64	6	1	-	-	-	-	1	1	7	2
	45	**19**	**4**	**5**	**4**	**1**	**1**	**1**	**54**	**26**

WHITLEY, Jeffrey — 1999

Position; *Midfield*
Birthplace; *Zambia*
Height; *5ft 9in* ***Weight;*** *11st 0lbs*
D.O.B; *28th January, 1979*
Debut v. *Colchester United (a) 15th January, 1999.*
Total Appearances & Goals; *10 apps 2 gls*
Career; *Manchester City 19th Feb 1996 (Pro) 27/21apps 3gls; WREXHAM 14th Jan 1999 (Loan);*
Honours; *Three Northern Ireland international caps; Northern Ireland 'B' international; Northern Ireland under-21 international; Second Division Play-Off winner 1999;*

Born in Zambia, Jeff Whitley moved to Britain when he was seven years-old, and was brought up, along with his elder brother Jim, in the Wrexham area. It was here that he played for local junior side Brickfield in the Wrexham Youth League, while also becoming a trainee with Manchester City at the age of 10. He was later signed on schoolboy forms by Wrexham, but shortly afterwards his family moved to Manchester, where he was to follow in his brother Jim's footsteps by signing Y.T.S. terms with Manchester City upon leaving school in July 1995. He went on to progress through the Youth ranks at Maine Road to sign professional in February 1996. By that time he had represented England at under-17 level, and had impressed enough to make his Football League debut, having made just two reserve team appearances. His debut against Barnsley in September 1996 was a 2-1 home defeat in which he was said to have 'excelled with a performance that had all the hallmarks of a future star'. Unfortunately in the last minute of that game he under-hit a back pass, that cost his side the points. This was quickly forgotten after a series of encouraging displays in the midst of a poor season for City, and he went on to play some very mature games, alternating between full and sub appearances to coax him along. His first senior goal for City came three months later, scoring the winner in a 3-2 home win over Bradford City. Although born in Zambia, Jeff was given the opportunity to play for Northern Ireland by the Irish manager, Lawrie McMenemy, qualifying due to his father being born in Belfast. He made his international debut in a convincing 3-0 victory against Belgium in Belfast in February 1997, when he came on as a substitute for his Manchester City team mate, Kevin Horlock. He has since made another two substitute appearance's, against Thailand in Bangkok on a summer tour in 1997, and then against Spain at Santander in a 4-1 defeat the following summer. Despite this early success, Jeff found his first team chances at Maine Road hard to come by during the 1997/98 season, when City were relegated to the Second Division for the first time in their history. Primarily a midfield player, Whitley, who has also played as a full-back/wing-back, was to find the following campaign much the same, but in January 1999 he accepted Wrexham manager Brian Flynn's offer of a loan spell with the Racecourse club. He made his 'Robins' debut at Colchester United in which he scored the first goal in a 3-1 win. Jeff was said to have been Wrexham's "best player on the night" by assistant manager, Kevin Reeves, who added that the talented midfielder "closes down his opponent quickly, gets in tackles, and is very aggressive, a real box to box player." After two months at the Racecourse Jeff was recalled by City manager Joe Royle to help in their promotion bid which was achieved with a win on penalties over Gillingham in the Play-Off final at Wembley.

Season	League		F.A.Cup		W.P.C.		League Cup		A.W.S.		Total	
	apps	gls	apps	gls	apps	gls	apps	gls	apps	gls	apps	gls
1998/99	9	2	-	-	1	0	-	-	-	-	10	2
	9	**2**	**-**	**-**	**1**	**0**	**-**	**-**	**-**	**-**	**10**	**2**

WHITTLE, Graham — 1971 - 1981

Position; *Forward*
D.O.B; *30th May, 1953*
Birthplace; *Liverpool, Merseyside*
Height; *5ft 9in* ***Weight;*** *10st 3lbs*
Debut; v. *Aston Villa (a) 1st May, 1971*
Total Appearances & Goals; *371/23 apps 117 gls*
Career; *WREXHAM 19th Jul 1971; Bangor City Aug 1981; Oswestry Town cs1982; Caersws 1982/83;*
Honours; *Third Division Championship Winner 1978; Welsh Cup Winner 1972, 1975 & 1978; Welsh Cup runner-up 1979; Welsh Youth Cup Winner 1971; Mid Wales League Championship Winner 1983;*

Graham Whittle was another product of Wrexham manager John Neal's successful youth policy, having been spotted playing football in his native City of Liverpool for Hartshill Boys' Club. He was invited for a trial at Burnley, where he played a few 'A' and 'B' team games for the 'Clarets', but they did not pursue their interest in him. At that time, John Neal had arranged a trial match on an old R.A.F. field behind Liverpool's training ground. From the hundreds of lads who turned up Graham was selected, along with Bob Scott, and they were both offered groundstaff terms. Graham's brother, Alan, had already made a name for himself by this time with Everton, and the youngster showed signs of following in his footsteps as he made his way through the junior ranks to sign professional for Wrexham in July 1971. By this time he had already made his Football League debut, which came in May 1971 at Aston Villa , as he was asked to deputise for

Arfon Griffiths in a memorable 4-3 victory. Graham went on to play a major role in Wrexham's rise to the Second Division, and starred in the club's many giant-killing encounters of the 1970s, as they reached the Quarter-Finals in 1974, and the last eight of the European Cup-Winners' Cup two years later, where they lost to the eventual winners, Anderlecht. Along the way he collected three Welsh Cup Winners' medals. He became a firm favourite with the Wrexham fans, due to his fierce determination, and big powerful shot which was feared by many a goalkeeper. He was never afraid to strike from any range, and scored many spectacular and memorable goals. It was once said of Graham, 'He can turn a game on one shot, and that makes him exceptional'. Combining with Billy Ashcroft to form a deadly strike partnership during the 1976/77 season he ended the campaign as the club's leading scorer with 28 goals, although it wasn't enough to secure promotion. The following season saw him form another lethal strike partnership with Dixie McNeil as the club galloped to the Third Division championship, with Graham scoring a hat-trick in the club's 7-1 demolition of Rotherham, the game that clinched promotion. Sadly, however, Whittle's career came to an end sooner than he had expected. A persistent knee injury eventually forced him to quit before his 28th birthday following advice from a specialist. He attempted to continue with Bangor City in the Northern Premier League, and it was during his year at Farrar Road that he was granted a testimonial match against Everton on the Racecourse. He later had a short spell with Oswestry Town, and also turned out for a while under his former team mate, Mickey Evans, at Caersws. Graham later turned to coaching with Lex XI, and worked as a milkman. He still lives in the Wrexham area.

Season	League		F.A.Cup		Welsh Cup		League Cup		E.C.W.C.		Total	
	apps	gls	apps	gls	apps	gls	apps	gls	apps	gls	apps	gls
1970/71	2	0	-	-	-	-	-	-	-	-	2	0
1971/72	35	4	3	3	5	2	-	-	-	-	43	9
1972/73	28/6	3	2	1	1	0	2	1	-	-	33/6	5
1973/74	41/2	10	6	0	3	1	1	1	-	-	51/2	11
1975/76	20	9	-	-	3	0	-	-	4	1	37	10
1976/77	43/1	28	6	3	4	2	3/2	2	-	-	56/3	35
1977/78	37	18	9	3	5	1	5	2	-	-	56	24
1978/79	22/4	7	-	-	4	0	2	1	2	0	30/4	8
1979/80	13/3	1	-	-	1	0	4	1	1/1	0	19/4	2
1980/81	1/1	0	-	-	-	-	0/2	0	-	-	1/3	0
	288/18	**91**	**27**	**11**	**31**	**7**	**18/4**	**7**	**7/1**	**1**	**371/23**	**117**

WILKINS, Raymond John Hamilton 1957 - 1959

Position; *Centre-Forward*
D.O.B; *16th August, 1928*
Birthplace; *Church Gresley, Leicestershire*
Height; *6ft 0in* ***Weight;*** *11st 0lbs*
Debut; v. *Chesterfield (a) 4th September, 1957*
Total Appearances & Goals; *4 apps 2 gls*
Career; *Loughborough College; Moira United; Derby County Jan 1950 30apps 11gls; Boston United cs1954; WREXHAM 19th May 1957; Oswestry Town Jun 1960; Macclesfield Town 6th Feb 1962; Pwllheli & District 7th Apr 1962; Gresley Rovers Sept 1962; Wilmorton and Alvaston;*
Honours; *North Wales Coast F.A.Challenge Cup Winner 1962;*

Ray Wilkins played football at school and then for Loughborough College, where he was studying to become a teacher. He then played for Moira United, where he was spotted by Derby County, and signed for the 'Rams' in January 1950. His Football League debut came a month later, as he lined up at centre-forward for a 2-2 home draw with Liverpool. Ray could not command a regular first team place in his four years with Derby, but did score eleven goals in the 30 League games that he played. He was described as a 'spirited centre-forward'. He was allowed to leave the Baseball ground in the close season of 1954, and joined non-league side, Boston United. It was with Boston that Ray returned to the Baseball Ground to play against Derby in a F.A.Cup match in December 1955, and the visitors shocked the 'Rams' with a 6-1 win! Wilkins remained with the Lincolnshire club for three seasons, where he combined playing with employment as a Physical Training Instructor at a Derby school. He returned to League football in May 1957, when he signed for Wrexham. At the same time he took up a similar teaching post at St.Davids' School in the town. Combining teaching with football he made his debut for Wrexham in September 1957 at Chesterfield, replacing Barry Smith at centre-forward. Although he marked the occasion with a goal, Wrexham lost 3-2. He appeared in just three more League and Cup games for the 'Robins', before being appointed player/coach of Wrexham's 'A' team in the summer of 1958. Ray was to join Cheshire County League side Oswestry Town in the summer of 1960, where he was to spend almost two seasons before joining Macclesfield Town in February 1962. However, he was only with the 'Silkmen' for two months before he returned to North Wales to play for Pwllheli & District, earning a North Wales Coast F.A.Challenge Cup winners' medal. In the summer of 1962 Wilkins returned to Derbyshire to teach, whereupon he signed for Gresley Rovers in September. He later played for Wilmorton & Alvaston, before taking over as manager of Crewton in July 1966. Ray later became headmaster at a Derby school. Also said to have excelled at Cricket.

Season	League		F.A.Cup		Welsh Cup		Total	
	apps	gls	apps	gls	apps	gls	apps	gls
1957/58	3	1	-	-	1	1	4	2
	3	**1**	**-**	**-**	**1**	**1**	**4**	**2**

WILKINSON, Algernon 1925 - 1926

Position; *Goalkeeper*
D.O.B; *21st January, 1894*
Birthplace; *Greasborough, Yorkshire*
Died; *Greasborough, J/F/M 1967*
Height; *5ft 10in* ***Weight;*** *11st 9lbs*
Debut; v. *Southport (h) 29th August, 1925*
Total Appearances & Goals; *35 apps 0 gls*
Career; *Rotherham County; Bradford City May 1919 12apps 0gls; Liverpool Jan 1923 0apps; Blackpool Sept 1924 5apps 0gls; Mold Town 7th Nov 1924; WREXHAM 8th May 1925; Flint Town 24th Sept 1926; Mold Town 22nd Aug 1927; Little Sutton Victoria Dec 1929;*
Honours; *Welsh League (North) Championship Winner 1925; North Wales Coast F.A.Challenge Cup Winner 1925;*

Algy Wilkinson was on the books of Rotherham County at the end of the Great War, when he was signed by First Division side Bradford City in May 1919. He went on to make his Football League debut between the posts for Bradford the following September in a 3-0 defeat at Derby. Algy spent almost four years at Valley Parade, mostly as understudy to Jock Ewart, which explains why he managed just twelve League appearances during that time. In January 1923 he was transferred to Liverpool, though he was never called upon to make a first team appearance throughout the eighteen months that he spent at Anfield, and was released at the end of the 1923/24 season. Wilkinson joined Second Division side Blackpool in September 1924, and made his debut for the 'Seasiders' that same month in a 5-0 home win over South Shields. He kept his place for the next four matches before being released shortly afterwards. He then switched to Welsh League (North) side Mold Town, where he earned a League Championship medal. Algy's form was quickly noted by Third Division North side Wrexham, who signed the 'keeper in May 1925. He took over from George Godding to make his League debut for the 'Robins' in the opening match of the 1925/26 season, a 3-2 home win over Southport, and kept his place throughout that season. However, following the signing of another 'keeper, the experienced Ted Robson, in the close season of 1927, Algy fell out of favour. He then joined Flint Town in September 1927, followed by a spell back at Mold Town, and later with Little Sutton Victoria.

Season	League		F.A.Cup		Welsh Cup		Total	
	apps	gls	apps	gls	apps	gls	apps	gls
1925/26	35	0	1	0	3	0	39	0
	35	**0**	**1**	**0**	**3**	**0**	**39**	**0**

WILLETT, Leonard William 1958 - 1960

Position; *Half-Back*
D.O.B; *17th September, 1940*
Birthplace; *Ruabon, Denbighshire*
Height; *5ft 8in* ***Weight;*** *10st 7lbs*
Debut; v. *Grimsby Town (a) 13th February, 1960*
Total Appearances & Goals; *1 app 0 gls*
Career; *Wolves 1956; WREXHAM 16th May 1958; Winsford United Jul 1960; Ellesmere Port Town cs1961; Ashton United cs1963; Caernarfon Town 8th Aug 1967; U.C.S.Lions (Australia) 1967; Merton Rovers (Australia); Germania (Australia); Newtown 1st Aug 1973;*
Honours; *Welsh Youth International; Welsh Schoolboy International;*

Len Willett played his early football for Rhosnesni, at the same time turning out for the National School in Wrexham. He later moved on to Denbighshire Technical College, from where he was selected to represent Wrexham Schoolboys, a team that he captained to both the quarter-finals

of the English Schools' Shield, and the final of the Welsh Schools Shield. He was eventually called up to play for Wales Schoolboys, against both Northern Ireland and England. With these early achievements it was no surprise that Len joined the groundstaff at Wolves in 1956, where he was to spend twelve months, during which he represented Wales at Youth level. However, he was allowed to leave Molineux in 1957 and to return home to Wrexham because of home-sickness. He began working for local electrical firm, Thornton's, whilst continuing to play football for Rhosddu in the Welsh National League. Willett stood out at this level, and before long Wrexham manager John Love signed him on professional terms in May 1958. He spent two years at the Racecourse, playing in his favourite half-back position, although mostly for the reserves, whom he helped to win the Cheshire Senior Cup as they beat Winsford United 7-2 on aggregate. Len finally made his first team debut in a mid-season friendly match against the Draconians in February 1960. He was chosen to make his Football League debut a week later at Grimsby Town, replacing Harvey Jones at half-back in a 3-1 defeat. Len's display was good enough to keep him in the first team frame for the rest of the season, and so it came as quite a surprise when it was announced that he was to be released at the end of the season. He joined Cheshire County League side Winsford United in July 1960, where he spent a year before moving on to Ellesmere Port Town in the summer of 1961. Len enjoyed two seasons here, helping them to reach the Third Round of the F.A.Cup before signing for Ashton United at the end of the 1962/63 campaign. He remained here until switching to Caernarfon Town for the start of 67/68. However, after just a few games for the Oval club Len decided to emigrate to Australia, where he joined U.C.S.Lions of Melbourne. He later played for Merton Rovers of Brisbane, from where he was chosen to captain Queensland in the Australian State Championships. It was with Merton that Willett won a Queensland First Division Championship medal, and also lifted the Aupol Cup, the Australian equivalent of the F.A.Cup. He later became the club's player/coach for a season before deciding to join Germania as player/manager. It was also at around this time that he was selected for the Australian National squad, although he never actually played. In the early 1970's, Len returned home to Wrexham, and continued his involvement with football by becoming player/manager of mid-Wales side, Newtown. After a little over a year he retired completely from football, due to persistent knee trouble. He returned to his trade of electrician, employed by Woolworths, before taking up an appointment as an electrical inspector for Chester City Council in 1974. He remained with them until ill health forced early retirement in 1991. Len, who still lives in Wrexham, is a frequent visitor to the Racecourse, where he has attended most home matches since 1974, having first watched Wrexham in 1948. A 'Robin' who has never deserted the nest!!

Season	League		F.A.Cup		Welsh Cup		Total	
	apps	gls	apps	gls	apps	gls	apps	gls
1959/60	1	0	-	-	-	-	1	0
	1	**0**	**-**	**-**	**-**	**-**	**1**	**0**

WILLIAMS, Alvan 1956 - 1957

Position; *Centre-Forward*
D.O.B; *21st November, 1932*
Birthplace; *Penmon, Anglesey, Gwynedd*
Height; *5ft 10in* ***Weight;*** *14st 0lbs*
Debut; v. *Chester (h) 18th August, 1956*
Total Appearances & Goals; *16 apps 7 gls*
Career; *Llangefni Town 1949; Bethesda Athletic cs1950; Bolton Wanderers cs1951; Stalybridge Celtic cs1954; Bury Dec 1954 2apps 1gls; WREXHAM 19th Jun 1956; Bradford Park Avenue 6th Jun 1957 92apps 21gls; Exeter City Aug 1960 19apps 1gls; Wigan Athletic cs1961 8apps 4gls; Bangor City 30th Dec 1961;*
Honours; *Welsh Cup Winner 1957;*

The son of a Vicar, Alvan Williams was born at Penmon Priory on Anglesey. He began playing football at Llangefni Grammar School on the island, either in goal or at centre-forward. It was in the latter position that he began playing for Llangefni Town after leaving school at 16. He spent a season with them before signing for Bethesda Athletic in the Welsh League, where he was to score regularly, prompting Bolton Wanderers to invite him for a trial. Following this Alvan was offered an apprenticeship and made his way through the Burnden Park 'B' and 'A' teams before being called up for his National Service. At this point he severed his connection with the Lancashire club altogether. He served in the Royal Artillery, spending his initial training at Oswestry before being posted to Woolwich, where he continued to play football for his regiment. However, football was not the only sport at which Alvan was to excel, as he became a competent amateur boxer during his Army days. After being demobbed Williams resumed his football career with Cheshire County League side Stalybridge Celtic, joining them in the summer of 1954. He had played only about a dozen games when invited for a trial by Bury, where he took part in a few 'A' team matches until offered a contract. He played mainly in the reserve team at Gigg Lane, but did make two Football League appearances, scoring one goal. At the end of 1955/56 he asked for a transfer, and returned to North Wales following an approach by Wrexham manager Cliff Lloyd. His debut for the 'Robins' came in the opening match of the 1956/57 season, a 2-2 draw with Chester on the Racecourse. Alvan spent just one season with Wrexham, during which he scored seven goals in sixteen matches, and appeared in the 1958 Welsh Cup Final victory over Swansea Town at Ninian Park. He also completed one game in goal for the reserves against Macclesfield Town, when Wrexham's recognised 'keeper failed to turn up! The summer of 1958 saw Alvan involved in an exchange deal, as he swapped places with Bradford Park Avenue's Barry Smith. He enjoyed three seasons with Bradford, scoring 21 goals in 92 League games before joining Exeter City in August 1960. A season with the 'Grecians', playing at centre-half, ended with a summer move to non-league side Wigan Athletic, scoring four goals in eight Cheshire County League games before joining Bangor City at Christmas 1961. He became assistant-manager to former Wrexham and Wales international, Tommy Jones, and the pair then led the Farrar Road club to Welsh Cup success and into Europe against Napoli. Alvan became a qualified F.A. coach, and soon after picking up his badge he joined Hartlepools United as coach to manager Bob Gurney. Still only 31, Williams replaced Gurney as manager in 1964, and lifted Hartlepools to a creditable mid-table position. In May 1965 he was appointed manager at Southend United, with the Roots Hall club relegated to Division Four at the end of his first year in charge. By April of the following campaign they had recovered to stand in fourth place in their Division, although Alvan had decided to become the new manager of Wrexham. The 'Shrimpers', in the mean time, missed out on promotion. Alvan then began to rebuild the North Wales club, and during the summer he brought in his trainer from Southend, John Neal, as well as a number of players. The club ended his first season in charge just six points adrift of a promotion spot, although the following season saw him resign following a contractual dispute with the directors. The foundations that he had laid were built upon by John Neal, appointed as his successor, who led the club to promotion the following season, and on to much success in the 1970's. After leaving Wrexham Alvan sought no further involvement in the game, returning to Anglesey where he converted an old vicarage into an hotel near Llangefni. He later operated a cafe business in Rhyl, and worked in Blackpool before managing a number of Public Houses in London. It was while he was at one of these that, along with two others, he was charged with the murder of a 19 year-old student, who they had ejected from the Robert Lee pub because of drunkenness. Alvan was found guilty of affray, and handed a suspended sentence. He later managed a number of licenced premises in the Birmingham area before returning to North Wales to take over the Ship Hotel in Bala. Now retired, Alvan remains settled in the Bala area. One of the great characters of football (sadly lacking in todays game!). Some of the stories to come out about Alvan are legendary, sadly they could never be repeated here!!

Season	League		F.A.Cup		Welsh Cup		Total	
	apps	gls	apps	gls	apps	gls	apps	gls
1956/57	13	7	-	-	3	0	16	7
	13	**7**	**-**	**-**	**3**	**0**	**16**	**7**

WILLIAMS, Derek 1954 - 1955

Position; *Goalkeeper*
D.O.B; *15th June, 1934*
Birthplace; *Mold, Flintshire*
Height; *6ft 1in* **Weight;** *13st 7lbs*
Debut; v. *Chester (a) 25th August, 1954*
Total Appearances & Goals; *12 apps 0 gls*
Career; *UCNW; Mold Alex; Manchester City May 1951 (Am) 1app 0gls; Mold Alex; Connah's Quay Nomads 1952/53; Bangor City 1953; Middlesex Wanderers 1954; WREXHAM 4th Aug 1954 (Am); Pwllheli 1955/56; Mold Alex 1955; Oldham Athletic 4th Sept 1956 (Am) 28apps 0gls; Chester Nomads 1963-1974;*
Honours; *11 Welsh Amateur International caps 1952-1955; 6 Welsh Youth International caps 1951-1953;*

Derek Williams certainly had a topsy-turvy career. Having signed amateur forms with Manchester City in May 1951 he hit the headlines in February 1952, when, as a 17 year-old schoolboy he replaced Bert Trautmann in goal in a scoreless draw against Blackpool at Maine Road. Derek's football career had begun at Mold Grammar School, where he captained the school side. At this time he played both as an outfield player and goalkeeper. He was chosen to represent Flintshire Schoolboys and was called up as reserve for the Welsh Schoolboys side in 1948/49. Derek was still at school when he began to play football for his local side, Mold Alexandra, turning out for them intermittently until 1955. He had trained with Wrexham as a schoolboy, though he never actually signed for the Club. The manager at that time, Les McDowall, left the Racecourse to return to his former club, Manchester City, and approached Derek who then signed for City on amateur forms in May 1951. It was for the Maine Road club that Williams was to make his Football League debut at the age of 17, playing against Blackpool who included Stan Matthews and Stan Mortenson in their side, which proved to be his only senior appearance. Having left school Derek continued his studies at the University College of North Wales in Bangor, and during this period was called upon to play for the Welsh Youth, Welsh Amateur, and both the Welsh and British Universities' teams, and despite interest in him from a number of Football League sides he decided to continue with his studies, though turning out as an amateur for both Connah's Quay Nomads and Bangor City. In the summer of 1954 he took part in a European Tour with the amateur representative side, Middlesex Wanderers, and on his return agreed to sign amateur terms for Wrexham. Derek went straight into the first team, replacing Pat Egglestone for the 'derby' match at Chester in the second game of 54/55. Despite a 1-0 defeat he kept his place in the side until October, when a nasty knee injury saw Earl Godding take over the 'keeper's position. He then went on to complete his studies, achieving a degree in mathematics eventually becoming a qualified Accountant. He continued to play amateur football when he could for both Bangor and Mold Alex, before he was to sign amateur terms for Oldham Athletic in September 1956. A 'tall, well built, brave goalkeeper', Derek Williams quickly established himself in Oldham's first team, but in February 1957 he became another footballer whose career was to be interrupted by National Service. Derek joined the Lancashire Fusiliers, completing his basic training at Bury Barracks, although he was rarely available for the 'Latics' after March 1957 having made a total of 28 League appearances by that time. Williams never made another first team appearance for Oldham, despite being a retained player with the club until 30th June 1959. His call-up would see him spend most of the two year period overseas, serving mostly in the Middle East attached to the British Embassy in Tripoli, Libya, with occasional spells of duty in Malta, Cyprus, Aden and the Emirates. Derek returned home at the end of his time in the Army whereupon he decided to turn his back on football and to take up Rugby Union, playing for Ruthin and progressing to represent both Denbighshire and North Wales. He did later return to the round ball game with Chester Nomads, one of the oldest amateur football teams in England, turning out for them until 1974 when he was forced to quit because of the knee injury picked up during his days with Wrexham. He later had a knee replacement, in 1991. During his football career he was described as a 'safe handler of the ball, either in the air or on the ground". Derek became an accountant, and for the past 25 years he has been a Financial Director and Company Secretary of an Anglo/Swiss Company, settling in the Chester area. He remains a supporter of Wrexham A.F.C., the club he has followed since a boy.

Season	League		F.A.Cup		Welsh Cup		Total	
	apps	gls	apps	gls	apps	gls	apps	gls
1954/55	12	0	-	-	-	-	12	0
	12	**0**	**-**	**-**	**-**	**-**	**12**	**0**

WILLIAMS, Edward Maelor Lloyd 1954 - 1955

Position; *Outside-Right*
D.O.B; *28th November 1935*
Birthplace; *Chester, Cheshire*
Height; *ft in* **Weight;** *st lbs*
Debut; v. *Oldham Athletic (h) 27th December, 1954*
Total Appearances & Goals; *1 app 0 gls*
Career; *Everton (Am) 0apps; Aston Villa Aug 1953 0apps; WREXHAM 11th Aug 1954; Caernarvon Town 3rd Aug 1957; Rhyl 7th Jul 1958; Witton Albion cs1959; Bangor City 19th Oct 1959; Bethesda Athletic 21st Dec 1959; Pwllheli & District 4th Feb 1960; Prestatyn 18th Aug 1960;*

Eddie Williams joined Everton as an amateur upon leaving school, only to be released at the end of the 1952/53 season. He was then snapped up on professional terms by Aston Villa in August 1953, and spent a year at Villa Park, though he failed to make a first team appearance, and was again released. It was then that he was signed by Peter Jackson for Third Division North side, Wrexham. After a number of reserve games Williams made his Football League debut at home to Oldham Athletic, replacing Glyn Hughes at outside-right in the 2-1 win. However, that proved to be his solitary senior outing for the Racecourse club, and again found himself out of favour at the end of the season. Eddie then joined Welsh League (North) side Caernarvon Town, going on to play for Rhyl, Witton Albion, Bangor City, Bethesda Athletic, Pwllheli & District, and Prestatyn.

Season	League		F.A.Cup		Welsh Cup		Total	
	apps	gls	apps	gls	apps	gls	apps	gls
1954/55	1	0	-	-	-	-	1	0
	1	**0**	**-**	**-**	**-**	**-**	**1**	**0**

WILLIAMS, Elfyn 1958 - 1959

Position; *Forward*
D.O.B; *25th September, 1939*
Birthplace; *Barmouth, Gwynedd*
Died; *1995*
Height; *5ft 9in* **Weight;** *11st 2lbs*
Debut; v. *Rochdale (a) 24th January, 1959*
Total Appearances & Goals; *1 app 0 gls*
Career; *Shrewsbury Town (Am) May 1957; Porthmadog 1957/58; WREXHAM 22nd Mar 1958; Crystal Palace Jul 1959 0apps; Porthmadog 24th Aug 1963;*

Elfyn had been an amateur with Shrewsbury Town, who had spotted him playing for Porthmadog in Welsh League football. He made nine appearances for the Gay Meadow club's reserve team before returning to the Traeth, from where Wrexham signed him in March 1958. By the following season Eddie was described as having 'played considerably well for the reserves, a player who adapted well to playing on any kind of surface. He was called up for his Football League debut in January 1959 at Rochdale, when regular outside-right Gren Jones was struck down with Lumbago.

The pitch at Spotland was likened to a skating rink: 'It was a game riddled with mistakes on a ground more suited to ice hockey, which included Elfyn missing a sitter from six yards, when he lifted the ball over the bar.' It proved to be his one and only first team appearance for the 'Robins', and was released at the end of the season. He was then signed by Crystal Palace during the close season, although he failed to make a first team appearance at Selhurst Park and eventually drifted into non-league football. Elfyn is known to have subsequently played again for Porthmadog. He passed away in 1995, aged 55.

Season	League		F.A.Cup		Welsh Cup		Total	
	apps	gls	apps	gls	apps	gls	apps	gls
1958/59	1	0	-	-	-	-	1	0
	1	**0**	**-**	**-**	**-**	**-**	**1**	**0**

WILLIAMS, Emlyn 1931 - 1935

Position; *Left-Back*
D.O.B; *15th January, 1912*
Birthplace; *Ynyshir, Maesteg, Glamorgan*
Height; *5ft 7'1/2in* ***Weight;*** *12st 0lbs*
Debut; v. *Rhyl (@ Chester) 20th April, 1932 (Welsh Cup)*
Total Appearances & Goals; *3 apps 0 gls*
Career; *Wrexham Nov 1931; Burton Town Jun 1935; Barnsley 6th Oct 1936 88apps 0gls; Preston North End 15th Jun 1939 62apps 0gls, WW2 33apps 0gls; Barnsley 21st Apr 1948 17apps 0gls; Accrington Stanley 24th Dec 1948 15apps 0gls;*
Honours; *Third Division North Championship Winner 1939; Birmingham & District League Championship Winner 1933 & 1934;*

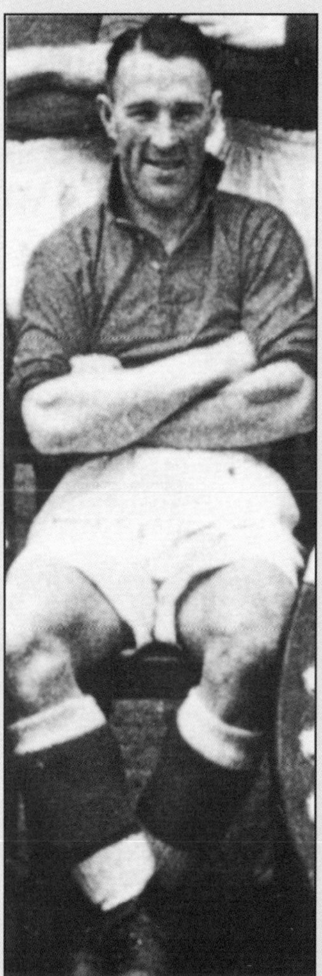

Emlyn Williams joined Wrexham on trial in November 1931. His first match saw him take the eye in a 3-1 home defeat in a Birmingham & District League match against Cradley Heath, when described as 'impressing with his good tackling'. He remained a regular in the reserve team for the rest of the season, before being called upon for his senior debut in a Welsh Cup semi-final match at Chester against Rhyl in April 1932. The match ended in a 3-3 draw, before Wrexham beat Rhyl 3-1 in the replay, though Emlyn was not selected for the second game. The following season found him again playing reserve team football, though he did make two first team appearances, both in the Welsh Cup: a 2-1 win at Bangor, and a 1-1 draw in the semi-final against Southport, who were beaten 3-1 in the replay. Despite his failure to secure a regular first team place he won two Birmingham & District League Championship medals with Wrexham's reserve side in both 1933 and 1934. This lack of first team opportunity eventually forced Emlyn to leave the Racecourse in the close season of 1935, after almost four seasons with the club. He joined Burton Town, spending a season with them, and impressing sufficiently to be signed by Second Division side Barnsley in October 1936. After some solid performances for Barnsley's reserve side, Emlyn was plunged into the first team for his belated Football League debut at Bradford Park Avenue in January 1937, a game which ended in a 2-1 defeat. He then established himself as the Oakwell club's regular full-back throughout both their relegation season of 1937/38, and their Third Division North championship success a year later. His performances were good enough to persuade First Division Preston North End to step in and sign him in the summer of 1939. However, his career at Deepdale was to be disrupted by World War Two. Emlyn returned to Preston at the end of the conflict, where he 'again' made his Football League debut for the club, going on to complete a total of 62 League appearances in almost two seasons before rejoining Barnsley in April 1948. However, his second spell at Oakwell was short-lived, as he accepted a move to Accrington Stanley in December of the same year as player/coach. Accrington had won only four of their 22 matches played when Emlyn arrived at Peel Park, and they were languishing near the bottom of the League. However, his arrival saw an immediate improvement, with a 2-0 win on his debut against third placed Doncaster Rovers. Having successfully helped to pull Accrington clear of the foot of the table Emlyn was disappointed to find his name on the open to transfer list at the end of the season.

Season	League		F.A.Cup		Welsh Cup		Total	
	apps	gls	apps	gls	apps	gls	apps	gls
1931/32	-	-	-	-	1	0	1	0
1932/33	-	-	-	-	2	0	2	0
	-	**-**	**-**	**-**	**3**	**0**	**3**	**0**

WILLIAMS, Eric R.T. 1925 - 1926

Position; *Centre-Half*
D.O.B;
Birthplace; *Wrexham, Denbighshire*
Height; *ft in* ***Weight;*** *st lbs*
Debut; v. *Chesterfield (a) 17th April, 1926*
Total Appearances & Goals; *1 app 0 gls*
Career; *Connah's Quay & Shotton; WREXHAM Apr 1926; Winsford United Aug 1927;*
Honours; *One Welsh Junior International Cap 1926;*

Eric Williams was signed as an amateur by Wrexham from Connah's Quay & Shotton in April 1926 to help out with an injury crisis prior to a Football League match at Chesterfield. He was called up to play at centre-half in the 3-1 defeat, having stepped in to deputise for Tommy Mathias. That match proved to be his only senior outing for the 'Robins' before returning to Connah's Quay & Shotton, where he had won a Welsh Junior international cap against Ireland. He later joined Cheshire County League side Winsford United for the 1926/27 season.

Season	League		F.A.Cup		Welsh Cup		Total	
	apps	gls	apps	gls	apps	gls	apps	gls
1925/26	1	0	-	-	-	-	1	0
	1	**0**	**-**	**-**	**-**	**-**	**1**	**0**

WILLIAMS, Everton Anthony 1973 - 1976

Position; *Forward*
D.O.B; *1st February, 1957*
Birthplace; *Blackrod, Jamaica*
Height; *5ft 10in* ***Weight;*** *12st 0lbs*
Debut; v. *Peterborough United (a) 24th September, 1975*
Total Appearances & Goals; *1/1 apps 0 gls*
Career; *WREXHAM Jul 1975; Rhyl cs1976; Bangor City Oct 1976; Rhyl 20th Aug 1977; Bangor City 1984/85; Oswestry Town 1986; Connah's Quay Nomads 1989/90;*
Honours; *Welsh Cup runner-up 1985;*

Everton Williams played for a very successful Oswestry Boys' High School side as they reached the Final of the English Schools Knock-Out Cup. He scored in every round on the way to the Final, but couldn't find the net in the Final against a school from Scunthorpe, which saw both teams share the Cup for six months apiece following a goalless draw. The competition had begun with over 700 schools taking part. Everton also represented the Shropshire Schoolboys side at this time, as well as turning out for Weston Rhyn during the 1974/75 season, as they won the Shropshire County League title. He had a trial with Derby County in July 1974 before agreeing to join Wrexham in the November of the same year, progressing to sign professional terms at the Racecourse in July 1975. His Football League debut came in the following season, when he came on as a substitute for Alan Dwyer in a 2-0 defeat at Peterborough United. He started the following game as a replacement for John Lyons in the 1-0 home win over Port Vale, though he was substituted later in the game by Billy Ashcroft. Despite this early promise Everton failed to make another senior appearance for the 'Robins', and was released at the end of that season. He then joined Northern Premier League side Rhyl for the start of the 1976/77 campaign, but by October he had joined Bangor City. He later went on to play for a number of North Wales sides, which included Rhyl and Bangor City again, where he was voted 'Player of the Year' in 1985. He also turned out for the Farrar Road club in the European Cup-Winners' Cup matches against the Spanish giants Athletico Madrid. Everton is later known to have played for both Oswestry Town and Connah's Quay Nomads before settling in the Chester area.

Season	League		F.A.Cup		Welsh Cup		League Cup		Total	
	apps	gls	apps	gls	apps	gls	apps	gls	apps	gls
1975/76	1/1	0	-	-	-	-	-	-	1/1	0
	1/1	**0**	**-**	**-**	**-**	**-**	**-**	**-**	**1/1**	**0**

WILLIAMS, Frank Harold 1923 - 1926

Position; *Outside-Right*
D.O.B; *10th March, 1906*
Birthplace; *Cefn-Y-Bedd, Denbighshire*
Died; *Trafford, Manchester, 11th December, 1982*
Height; *5ft 5in* ***Weight;*** *10st 5lbs*
Debut; v. *Lincoln City (a) 22nd December, 1923*
Total Appearances & Goals; *6 apps 0 gls*
Career; *Oak Alyn Rovers; WREXHAM Dec 1923; Preston North End Aug 1926; Port Vale Mar 1928 1app 0gls; Oswestry Town May 1929; Northern Nomads c1929; Rhyl Dec 1929; Ashton National Gas Jul 1930; Cross Street FC Jan 1931; Altrincham Mar 1931; Shrewsbury Town cs1932; Buxton cs1933;*
Honours; *One Welsh Amateur International cap; North Wales Coast F.A.Challenge Cup runner-up 1926;*

Frank Williams came from a footballing family, with two of his three brothers playing professional football: Jesse was a Welsh international, and played for Wrexham, Middlesbrough, and Orient, while Len represented both Bournemouth and Charlton. Frank was turning out for Oak Alyn Rovers when he was signed by Wrexham in December 1923, and he made his Football League debut for the 'Robins' that same month, in a 4-2 defeat at Lincoln while still only seventeen years-old. Frank lined up in that game on the right-wing, replacing Billy Harrison, while his brother Jesse occupied the left wing berth. He played in the following two matches before Harrison returned to the side. He had to wait until the following season for his next first team opportunity, when he made two more appearances. One more senior outing followed during 1925/26, a 3-0 home win over Durham in April 1926. Williams then joined Second Division Preston North End during the close season, where he spent almost eighteen months before signing for Port Vale in March 1928. He found his opportunities limited at Vale Park, and had to wait until the start of the following before being handed his debut, a 4-1 opening day defeat against Wolves. It proved to be Frank's first and last senior appearance for the Potteries club, as he spent the rest of the season in the reserve side before being released in May 1929. He then drifted into non-league football, where he played for Oswestry Town, Northern Nomads, Ashton National Gas, Cross Street FC, Altrincham, Shrewsbury Town, and Buxton - with whom he was to win a Welsh Amateur International cap against England in 1933. Frank had attended Chester College during that time, and eventually became a P.T.Master at a school in Altrincham. He then progressed to an appointment as Headmaster of a school in Manchester. Frank's son Chris became a Bishop in the Arctic.

Season	League		F.A.Cup		Welsh Cup		Total	
	apps	gls	apps	gls	apps	gls	apps	gls
1923/24	3	0	-	-	-	-	3	0
1924/25	2	0	-	-	-	-	2	0
1925/26	1	0	-	-	-	-	1	0
	6	**0**	**-**	**-**	**-**	**-**	**6**	**0**

WILLIAMS, Glyn 1947 - 1949

Position; *Full-Back*
D.O.B; *15th June, 1922.*
Birthplace; *Moss, Nr.Wrexham, Denbighshire*
Height; *5ft 9in* ***Weight;*** *11st 2lbs*
Debut; v. *Rochdale (h) 16th April, 1949*
Total Appearances & Goals; *4 apps 0 gls*
Career; *Rhosddu Chums; Hightown FC; WREXHAM 20th Jun 1947; Pwllheli 12th Nov 1949; Flint Town United 23rd Aug 1952; Bethesda Athletic 29th Jul 1959;*
Honours; *Welsh Cup Winner 1954; Five North Wales Coast F.A.representative caps; Welsh League (North) Championship Winner 1950, 1951, 1955, 1956 & 1957; North Wales Coast F.A.Challenge Cup Winner 1961; North Wales Coast F.A.Challenge Cup runner-up 1952 & 1954;*

Glyn Williams first played football for the Wrexham County School for Boys (Grove Park) in the 1930s. He also excelled at rugby at this time, again playing for his school team, but it was football that Glyn really enjoyed and he joined Rhosddu Chums and then Hightown FC. Glyn was called up into the Royal Air Force in 1942, but failed a medical to become a pilot because of 'unsafe for a pilot colour vision'! Instead he worked on ground service and served in India, where he played for his station team as they won the 'Delhi Area Cup' in 1945. After WW2 Williams was invited to play for the Wrexham 'A' and reserve teams by the club's manager Tom Williams and secretary Cliff Lloyd. He signed amateur forms with the Racecourse club, and was eventually handed his Football League debut in April 1949, when he replaced Eddie Tunney at right-back in a 2-0 home win over Rochdale. Glyn kept his place for the following three games before Tunney returned for the last match of the season. In the summer of 1949 Glyn enrolled at Teachers' Training College, where he went on to qualify as a teacher, but by November he had been informed by the new Wrexham manager Les McDowall that he did not fit in with his plans, and was released. He then signed for Welsh League (North) side Pwllheli. Having qualified as a teacher Glyn's first full-time post was in Rowley Regis, in the West Midlands, but in 1950 returned to take up an appointment at the Victoria Secondary Modern School in Wrexham. Playing under Tommy G.Jones, the ex-Wrexham and Wales player, Glyn won many trophies with Pwllheli, as well as being awarded the first of five caps for the North Wales Coast F.A. representative side against the Scottish Junior F.A. He left Pwllheli in the close season of 1952 to join Flint Town United. It was here that he enjoyed the best spell of his football career, as he helped Flint to win the Welsh Cup in 1954, with a 2-0 victory over Chester on the Racecourse in front of a crowd of almost 16,000. In the late 1950s Williams left Flint to join Bethesda Athletic, where he brought the curtain down on his football career. In 1960 Glyn, left the Victoria School, which closed, and went to teach at the newly opened Bryn Offa School. He remained there until 1982, when he retired. For many years he was connected with Wrexham Athletics' Club, serving as Chairman, and he's currently a vice-president of both Wrexham and Clwyd AAAs. Still living in the Wrexham area Glyn is also an active member of the Wrexham Hospital League of Friends where he also excels, liking nothing better than to help others.

Season	League		F.A.Cup		Welsh Cup		Total	
	apps	gls	apps	gls	apps	gls	apps	gls
1948/49	4	0	-	-	-	-	4	0
	4	**0**	**-**	**-**	**-**	**-**	**4**	**0**

WILLIAMS, George Graham 1964 - 1965

Position; *Outside-Left*
D.O.B; *31st December, 1936*
Birthplace; *Southsea, Nr.Wrexham, Denbighshire*
Height; *5ft 5in* ***Weight;*** *10st 4lbs*
Debut; v. *Notts County (h) 22nd August, 1964*
Total Appearances & Goals; *27 apps 7 gls*
Career; *Oswestry Town; Bradford City Aug 1955 9apps 2gls; Everton 9th Mar 1956 £5,000 31apps 6gls; Swansea Town 5th Feb 1959 89apps 20gls; WREXHAM 2nd Jul 1964; Glentoran Jan 1965 (Loan); Wellington Town cs1965; Tranmere Rovers Aug 1966 73apps 12gls; Port Vale Jul 1968 21/2apps 1gls; Runcorn 1969; Oswestry Town 26th Feb 1970;*
Honours; *Five Welsh International caps; Welsh Under-23 International; Welsh Schoolboy International cap; Welsh Cup Winner 1961; Welsh Cup runner-up 1965;*

Graham Williams was an exciting schoolboy prospect. He played for both Brynteg School and Wrexham Technical College, from where he represented Wrexham & District schoolboys, helping them to reach the semi-finals of the English Schools Shield, and to lift the Welsh Schools Shield. He also represented his country three times at Schoolboys level. It was at this time that he actually signed schoolboy forms for Spurs, who would send him 10 shillings a week for doing nothing! He also spent three weeks on trial with Wolves, at the end of which manager Stan Cullis told him that he was 'too small!' After leaving school Graham went on trial to Blackpool, who offered him a place on the ground staff. However, they wouldn't allow him to complete his apprenticeship as a joiner, so he signed for Wrexham on amateur terms and began playing for Oswestry Town. In February 1955 Wrexham manager Peter Jackson resigned, taking charge at Bradford City two weeks later. He then returned to his former club in August 1955 to sign 'Flicka', as he was affectionately known. His Football League debut for Bradford City came in a 1-1 draw at local rivals Bradford Park Avenue in front of a 20,000 crowd. Graham had spent less than eight months with the Yorkshire club, when Everton signed him in March 1956 for a £5,000 fee. He had clocked up just nine League appearances at Valley Parade. A bright future was predicted for him at Goodison Park, but his development was handicapped by having to complete his National Service with the Royal Engineers. He continued to play for Everton when he could during his two years, as well as representing the British Army XI on ten occasions. On being released from the Army 'Flicka' continued with Everton until February 1959, when he was transferred to Swansea Town, having made 31 League appearances for the 'Toffeemen' and scored six goals. He became an immediate favourite with the Vetch crowd, and won the first of his five full Welsh international caps at this time, when he played in a 5-1 victory against Northern Ireland. Although one of the smallest wingers in the League he was 'a brave, tricky and an elusive customer who was also admired for his bravery and willingness to take defenders on'. He collected a Welsh Cup winners' medal with Swansea in 1961, and the following season played in Europe against the East German side, Motor Jena. In February 1962 G.G. sustained a broken leg and this sidelined him for a long spell. Once fit, he agreed to a move back home to join Wrexham in July 1964. He re-established himself at the Racecourse, playing in 24 matches, and completed a two week loan spell with Glentoran in the New Year of 1965. This was followed by picking up a Welsh Cup runners'-up medal from a Final defeat against Cardiff City. However, he was allowed to leave the Racecourse at the end of the season, and he took up a good offer from Cheshire County League side Wellington Town, where he spent a season before returning to the Football League with Tranmere Rovers in August 1966. He spent two seasons at Prenton Park, where he helped the club to win promotion in his first season, and reach the Fifth Round of the F.A.Cup, losing 2-1 to Everton. In July 1968 'Flicka' joined Port Vale a year before drifting into non-league football with Runcorn, who were managed by the former Wrexham centre-forward, Jack Boothway. Later that season he returned to Oswestry Town, where he announced his retirement in the summer. Graham then returned to his job as a carpenter, and later became one of Denbighshire's most accomplished golfers. His son Phil also played League football for Crewe Alexandra, Wigan Athletic, and Chester, having served his apprenticeship with Arsenal. A popular character, Graham, who is now settled in the Wrexham area, can often be found playing on the local Golf courses.

Season	League apps	League gls	F.A.Cup apps	F.A.Cup gls	Welsh Cup apps	Welsh Cup gls	League Cup apps	League Cup gls	Total apps	Total gls
1964/65	24	6	-	-	2	1	1	0	27	7
	24	**6**	**-**	**-**	**2**	**1**	**1**	**0**	**27**	**7**

WILLIAMS, Jesse Thomas 1921 - 1924

Position; *Outside-Left*
D.O.B; *24th June, 1903*
Birthplace; *Cefn-Y-Bedd, Denbighshire*
Died; *Toronto, Canada, 20th October, 1972*
Height; *5ft 5in* ***Weight;*** *9st 6lbs*
Debut; v. *Darlington (a) 22nd September, 1923*
Total Appearances & Goals; *41 apps 3 gls*
Career; *Caergwrle FC; Oak Alyn Rovers; WREXHAM 23rd Jun 1923; Middlesbrough May1924 £600 37apps 8gls; Clapton Orient Jan 1928 32apps 3gls; Rhyl 11th Jul 1929; Ashton National Gas Jun 1930; Shrewsbury Town Aug 1931; Wellington Town Jul 1933; Colwyn Bay United Oct 1934*
Honours; *One Welsh International Cap 1925; Welsh Cup Winner 1924; Welsh Cup runner-up 1930; Welsh League Representative cap 1930;*

Jesse Williams was discovered by Wrexham playing in local football for Oak Alyn Rovers. He was recruited by the Racecourse club in 1923, and was described at the time as a 'diminutive, yet mercurial winger'. He made his Football League debut for the 'Robins' in September 1923, when he took the place of Ralph Lenny in a 3-0 defeat at Darlington. Despite the result Jesse went on to keep his place in the side for the rest of the season, one which he capped by picking up a Welsh Cup winners' medal following a 1-0 Final victory over Merthyr Town. His 'busy non-stop approach and delicate footwork' were a major feature of this skilful winger's game, who was also aptly described as a '5ft 5in bundle of energy'. His displays in a Wrexham shirt had not gone unnoticed, and was quickly signed up by Second Division Middlesbrough at the end of the season. Jesse made his League debut for his new club at the end of September, in a local 'derby' at South Shields which 'Boro won 1-0. He quickly established himself as a regular in the 'Boro side for the remainder of the season, and was rewarded with his international debut for Wales against, Ireland, which eventually proved to be his only cap. However, he was to make just ten more League appearances over the following three seasons, four of which came in 'Boro's' 1926/27 Second Division Championship campaign. In January 1928 Jesse was transferred to Second Division Clapton Orient, going straight into the first team for his debut in a 5-2 home defeat against Blackpool. He remained in the side for the rest of the season as Clapton narrowly avoided relegation. He played regularly throughout the first half of the following season, but with the team once again struggling to fight off relegation Williams played what proved to be his last match for the London club in January. At the end of the season the 'O's' were relegated, and Jesse was allowed to return home to North Wales, where he joined his brother Frank at Welsh League side Rhyl. Together they helped Rhyl to reach the 1930 Welsh Cup Final, where they gallantly lost 4-2 to Cardiff City after a replay. That season also saw Jesse selected for the Welsh League representative XI against the Cheshire County League. During the summer of 1930 both Jesse and Frank left Belle Vue to join Ashton National Gas. Jesse spent a year with them before moving on during the following summer to join Birmingham & District League side Shrewsbury Town. He spent two seasons at the Gay Meadow, joined by his brother Frank once again for the second of them. At the end of the 1932/33 campaign Jesse was transferred to Wellington Town, which was followed by a stint with Colwyn Bay United from October 1934 to 1937. After he had finished playing football Jesse retained an involvement with the game by becoming a football referee, and both he and his wife became fervent supporters and fund-raisers of Rhyl FC. He ran his own guest house in the seaside town, combining these duties with work as an undertaker before emigrating to Canada in 1959 to join his two sons. There, he was employed at the Toronto General Hospital until he retired. Jesse died in Toronto in 1972, aged 69.

Season	League		F.A.Cup		Welsh Cup		Total	
	apps	gls	apps	gls	apps	gls	apps	gls
1923/24	33	3	2	0	6	0	41	3
	33	**3**	**2**	**0**	**6**	**0**	**41**	**3**

WILLIAMS, John Dyfed — 1982 - 1983

Position; *Defender*
D.O.B; *22nd August, 1965*
Birthplace; *Pwllheli, Gwynedd*
Height; *5ft 11in* **Weight;** *11st 3lbs*
Debut; v. *Bradford City (h) 2nd April, 1983*
Total Appearances & Goals; *0/1 apps 0 gls*
Career; *WREXHAM Jul 1981; Bala Town cs1983; Porthmadog; Pwllheli;*
Honours; *Welsh Schoolboy International;*

Although born in Pwllheli, John Williams' family moved to Llanuwchllyn Y Bala in Gwynedd. He played for his school teams Ysgol O.M.Edwards and Ysgol Y Berwyn, both in Bala, from where he was to represent Merioneth, Gwynedd and North Wales Schoolboy teams. He also played for his local junior side Llanuwchllyn through the various age levels. In 1981, he was selected after numerous trial matches to represent the Welsh Schoolboys side against Belgium in Ostend, Eire in Merthyr, Scotland in Linlithgow, England in Cardiff and West Germany in Cwmbran, as well as the twelve Nations Tournament in France. In the meantime John had signed Associate Schoolboy forms with Wrexham and was playing regularly for the club's youth team. Upon leaving school in 1981 he agreed to sign as an apprentice professional, and it was still as an apprentice that he made his Football League debut at the age of seventeen against Bradford City on the Racecourse in April 1983, when replacing Steve Dowman as a substitute in a 4-0 home defeat. Although he continued playing for the youth team, it proved to be his only first team game for Wrexham, which wasn't helped by an injury to his left knee which resulted in four operations during his time at the Racecourse. The injury finally curtailed John's football career, as he was eventually released by Wrexham. He took up work as an upholsterer with his uncle, while he managed to continue to play football in the Welsh National League for Bala Town. He followed this by spells with both Porthmadog and Pwllheli. In 1988 he went to Australia, where he remained for two and a half years, before returning to live in London, where he ran in the London Marathon - finishing in the first 3,000 out of 36,000! In 1993 Williams returned to Australia where he still remains having settled in Sydney, working as a Video Operative and Editor. John's father John Eric Williams is a prominent figure in Welsh Culture, and was Director of Urdd Gobaith Cymru (Welsh League of Youth) between 1982 and 1996.

Season	League		F.A.Cup		Welsh Cup		League Cup		Total	
	apps	gls	apps	gls	apps	gls	apps	gls	apps	gls
1982/83	0/1	0	-	-	-	-	-	-	0/1	0
	0/1	**0**	-	-	-	-	-	-	**0/1**	**0**

WILLIAMS, John James — 1938 - 1939

Position; *Outside-Right*
D.O.B; *29th March, 1911*
Birthplace; *Aberdare*
Height; *5ft 7in* **Weight;** *10st 12lbs*
Debut; v. *Barnsley (h) 3rd December, 1938*
Total Appearances & Goals; *25 apps 4 gls*
Career; *Aberaman; Llanelli 8th Nov 1932; Huddersfield Town 29th Nov 1932 50apps 14gls; Aston Villa Nov 1935 £2,000 17apps 5gls; Ipswich Town Jul 1936 9apps; WREXHAM 28th Nov 1938, WW2 10apps 0gls; Colwyn Bay 5th Oct 1945; Runcorn 1947/48;*
Honours; *One Welsh International Cap; Southern League Championship Winner 1937; Cheshire County League Representative XI;*

Jack Williams played local football in his native South Wales for Aberaman and Llanelli before being recruited by First Division Huddersfield Town in November 1932. A short dark haired flanker, like so many other wingers more than made up for his build with guile and trickery. He went on to spend three seasons with the 'Terriers', making his Football League debut in February 1933 in a 1-0 home win over Sheffield United. Playing at outside-right he kept his place in the side for the rest of the season as Huddersfield finished in sixth position. The following campaign Jack add twelve League appearances as the 'Terriers' finished runners-up in the League to Arsenal. 1934/35 brought another nineteen League games before he left Leeds Road in the November of the following season to join First Division Aston Villa for a £2,000 fee. Williams got off to a great start at Villa Park by scoring two goals on his debut, a 4-0 home win over Stoke City, but even so couldn't prevent them from being relegated at the end of the season. He was then allowed to leave Villa Park to join progressive Southern League side Ipswich Town, where he made 35 appearances for the Suffolk club in his first season, helping them to clinch the Southern League Championship and election to the Football League Division Three South. Jack was then chosen to play in Ipswich Town's first ever Football League match in August 1938 against Southend United at Portman Road. He made eight more League appearances for Ipswich before a move to Wrexham in November 1938. Jack went straight into the 'Robins' first team at outside-right, at the expense of another former Villa player, Fred Goss, in a 1-1 home draw with Barnsley. He missed just one game that season and, at the end of it he was awarded international recognition when selected to play for Wales against France in Paris. However, his career, like many others, was to come to an abrupt halt with the outbreak of World War Two. He played in two of the opening three matches of the 1939/40 season before the Football League was suspended. When regional football was organised about a month later he continued to play for Wrexham throughout the War period, as and when the opportunity arose. At the end of WW2 he joined Welsh League (North) side Colwyn Bay for a short period before joining Cheshire County League side Runcorn, where he was called up to represent the League's XI against the Southern League. On his retirement from the game, Jack remained in the Wrexham area, where he was employed as a storekeeper for Hunt's Capacitors in the town, where he worked for many years.

Season	League		F.A.Cup		Welsh Cup		N.S.C.		Total	
	apps	gls	apps	gls	apps	gls	apps	gls	apps	gls
1938/39	25	4	-	-	2	2	3	0	30	6
	25	**4**	-	-	**2**	**2**	**3**	**0**	**30**	**6**

WILLIAMS, J.S. — 1921 - 1922

Position; *Outside-Left*
D.O.B;
Birthplace; *Broughton, Denbighshire*
Height; *5ft 10in* **Weight;** *10st 0lbs*
Debut; v. *Walsall (a) 27th December, 1921*
Total Appearances & Goals; *2 apps 0 gls*
Career; *Brymbo Green; Wrexham Dec 1921; Brymbo Green Jan 1921;*
Honours; *Flintshire Charity Cup Winner 1923;*

J.S.Williams was playing for Brymbo Green when signed by Wrexham as an amateur, along with his team mate Jonathan Evans, to help the club out of an injury crisis caused by injuries to both Ernie Lloyd and Reg Leck. They both made their Football League debuts in a 2-2 draw at Walsall over Christmas 1921, and Williams then made one more appearance for the club, in a 4-0 defeat at Nelson a week later, before Ernie Lloyd was fit to resume. Williams then returned to Brymbo Green, where he went on to collect a Flintshire Charity Cup winners' medal in 1923.

Season	League		F.A.Cup		Welsh Cup		Total	
	apps	gls	apps	gls	apps	gls	apps	gls
1921/22	2	0	-	-	-	-	2	0
	2	**0**	**-**	**-**	**-**	**-**	**2**	**0**

WILLIAMS, Leslie 1929 - 1931

Position; *Outside-Right*
D.O.B; *16th April, 1908*
Birthplace; *Wrexham, Denbighshire*
Died; *Wrexham, 8th March, 1985*
Height; *5ft 8in* ***Weight;*** *11st 2lbs*
Debut; v. *Doncaster Rovers (a) 16th November, 1929*
Total Appearances & Goals; *25 apps 4 gls*
Career; *Chester; WREXHAM (Am) Aug 1929, (Pro) 20th Apr 1930; Wolves Feb 1931 0apps; Gillingham Jul 1931 39apps 5gls; York City Jul 1932 7apps 0gls; Tranmere Rovers Nov 1933 (Month's Trial);*
Honours; *One Welsh international cap;*

Leslie Williams was one of 13 children, and attended the National School in Wrexham. One of his brothers, Harold, was considered to have been a better footballer, and Oldham Athletic were keen to sign him, but he had to stay at home and help to look after the large family. Leslie first joined Chester, who were a non-league side at that time, before Wrexham signed him during the close season of 1929. His first season at the Racecourse saw him make his Football League debut in November 1929 in a 4-2 defeat at Doncaster. An outside-right he had stepped in for left-winger George Wynne, with Archie Longmuir switching wings to accommodate Les. It was Longmuir who Williams replaced when he made six more League appearances towards the end of the season. The following year saw Leslie finally make a name for himself as he began the campaign as Wrexham's first choice outside-right. His form soon began to attract the bigger clubs; it was also noted by the Welsh international selectors, and in November 1930 he was called up into the full Wales international team for the match against England at Wrexham as an eleventh hour replacement for Elvet Collins, who had been forced to withdraw due to injury. Previews of the match had 'A.N.Other' in the outside-right position, and it was the unknown Williams who would fill the slot. Having completed just fifteen League matches for the 'Robins' he was to find that 'the proposition which he faced was too much.' Wales were beaten 4-0, and when Leslie returned he found that he had lost his place in the Wrexham side to Jackie Hughes. When at the Racecourse, he was described as being able to 'lead defenders a merry dance, but the received opinion was that he lacked pace and polish, and was in need of coaching.' Because of the form of the experienced Hughes Les was to add only two more League appearances for the 'Robins' before Wolves stepped in to sign him in February 1931. However, his stay at Molineux was short-lived, as he was allowed to join Division Three South side Gillingham in the summer of 1931 without having made a first team appearance for the West Midlands club. His 'Gills' debut came at Southend, in a 2-0 defeat in the opening match of the 1931/32 season. Les went on to record 39 League appearances, scoring five goals before he left the Kent club to move back North to sign for York City. A Press Report of the pre-season trial match stated "All the new men were impressive, especially Williams, who would appear to have solved the long-standing Wing problem". He made his debut for the 'Minstermen' in the first match of the season in a 1-0 defeat at Crewe, but it was to be a disappointing period for him, as he managed just six more League appearances before being released in the summer. It is not quite clear as to his immediate whereabouts then but he was invited over by Glentoran F.C. in Belfast around this time before joining Tranmere Rovers in November 1933 for a months trial at £3.10 shillings a match, but was released in January 1934. Leslie later returned to Wrexham, taking up employment at the Leather Works in the town, followed by working for Wrexham Maelor District Council, latterly as a Car Park Attendant.

Season	League		F.A.Cup		Welsh Cup		Total	
	apps	gls	apps	gls	apps	gls	apps	gls
1929/30	7	0	-	-	1	1	8	1
1930/31	17	3	-	-	-	-	17	3
	24	**3**	**-**	**-**	**1**	**1**	**25**	**4**

WILLIAMS, Michael 1975 - 1978

Position; *Midfielder*
D.O.B; *1st December, 1956*
Birthplace; *Bangor, Gwynedd*
Height; *5ft 9in* ***Weight;*** *10st 11lbs*
Debut; v. *Swindon Town (h) 26th April, 1975*
Total Appearances & Goals; *9 apps 0 gls*
Career; *WREXHAM Jun 1975; Bangor City (Loan) 26th Sept 1977; Bangor City cs1978;*
Honours*; Welsh Youth Cup Winner 1975;*

Mike Williams joined the groundstaff at Wrexham on apprentice terms upon leaving school in 1973. He went on to make his way through the youth ranks at the Racecourse, winning a Welsh Youth Cup winners' medal in 1975 when the 'Robins' youngsters beat Swansea City 3-0 in the Final. The last match of the 1974/75 season saw Mike record his Football League debut, a 2-1 home defeat by Swindon Town. He had been drafted into midfield as a replacement for Mel Sutton. Mike signed professional terms during the summer of 1975, but over the next two seasons he was to make just a handful of first team appearances as he acted as cover for a very successful midfield unit that included Sutton, Mickey Thomas, Graham Whittle, and Arfon Griffiths. He had a loan spell with Bangor City in September 1977, before being released at the end of the season. He was then signed permanently for the Farrar Road club, who then played in the Northern Premier League side. He is later believed to have changed his career options, and become a Policeman.

Season	League		F.A.Cup		Welsh Cup		League Cup		E.C.W.C.		Total	
	apps	gls	apps	gls	apps	gls	apps	gls	app	gls	app	gls
1974/75	2	0	-	-	-	-	-	-	-	-	2	0
1975/76	3	0	-	-	-	-	-	-	-	-	3	0
1976/77	3	0	-	-	1	0	-	-	-	-	4	0
	8	**0**	**-**	**-**	**1**	**0**	**-**	**-**	**-**	**-**	**9**	**0**

WILLIAMS, Michael 1984 - 1991

Position; *Defender*
D.O.B; *6th February, 1965*
Birthplace; *Mancot, Flintshire*
Height*; 5ft 10in* ***Weight;*** *10st 12lbs*
Debut; v. *Swindon Town (a) 25th August, 1985*
Total Appearances & Goals; *232/6 apps 5 gls*
Career; *Hawarden Rangers 1981; Chester 6th Feb 1983 30/4apps 4gls; WREXHAM Jul 1984;*
Honours; *Welsh Youth international; Welsh Cup Winner 1986; Welsh Cup runner-up 1988;*

Mike Williams played his early football for his school sides in his native Buckley, and it was during that time that he also competed in the Eastham League against sides from all over the Wirral. He did well enough to represent Wales at Schoolboy level, and was eventually spotted by Everton, completing schoolboy forms at the age of 14. Over the next two years he progressed to play for Wales at Youth level. Having played representative and 'B' team games for Everton in the Lancashire League, he was hopeful that he would sign as an apprentice at the Goodison Park club upon leaving school, but no such offer materialised, and he began the 1981/82 season playing for Hawarden Rangers. It was while he was playing for them that Chester's youth team coach, Cliff Sear, invited him along to Sealand Road for a trial, and impressed enough to sign for Chester as an apprentice. Mike progressed to make his Football League debut in May 1982, a 2-1 home defeat against Lincoln City, before signing professional terms on his eighteenth birthday. Although Chester were struggling at this time Williams was soon being tracked by other clubs, and was about to sign for John Neal at Chelsea when he suffered cartilage trouble. After recovering he found that he was surplus to Chester manager John McGrath's requirements, and was released in the summer of 1984. He was quickly snapped up by Wrexham manager Bobby Roberts on a free transfer. Although Mike made his Wrexham debut in the opening game of the 1984/85 season, substituting Kevin Rogers in a 2-1 defeat at Swindon, he didn't really establish himself in the first team until November. However, he went on to make his place in the side his own throughout his time at the Club, missing out only when injuries intervened - which in Mike's case - was disappointingly too often. In fact, it was a knee injury that was to force the end of his football career at the early age of just 26. He had completed three European campaigns for Wrexham, including the great win over F.C.Porto, and played a major part in the 'Robins' 1989 run to the play-off's, though he missed the two-legged final against Leyton Orient because of injury. He gained a Welsh Cup winners' medal in 1986, when Wrexham beat Kidderminster Harriers in the Final, and added a runners'-up medal in the same competition two years later, when Wrexham lost 2-0 to Cardiff City at Swansea. Mike was described as 'a fast and skilful defender, who should have played football at a higher level', but it was not to be, as his last three years with Wrexham saw him dogged by a persistent knee injury that failed to respond to surgery. He was forced to retire in the summer of 1991, but was awarded a testimonial match in April 1992, when Wrexham played against his former club Chester. A crowd of almost 2,000 turned up to pay tribute to Mike, as he played a cameo role in a game that ended 1-1. He later moved to Bradford, where he was employed as an assistant manager at the Yorkshire town's ice-rink, as well as maintaining a link with Wrexham by scouting for manager Brian Flynn. Mike has since settled in Hull where he works at the local Ice Rink.

Season	League		F.A.Cup		Welsh Cup		League Cup		F.R.T.		E.C.W.C.		Total	
	apps	gls	apps	gls	apps	gls	apps	gls	apps	gls	apps	gls	apps	gls
1984/85	23/4	0	-	-	2	0	-	-	2	1	2	0	29/4	1
1985/86	25/2	0	-	-	4	0	4	0	-	-	-	-	33/2	0
1986/87	42	1	3	0	5	0	4	0	4	0	4	0	62	1
1987/88	42	2	2	0	6	1	1	0	1	0	-	-	52	3
1988/89	27	0	2	0	3	0	-	-	4	0	-	-	36	0
1989/90	13	0	1	0	1	0	-	-	1	0	-	-	16	0
1990/91	-	-	-	-	-	-	1	0	-	-	3	0	4	0
	172/6	**3**	**8**	**0**	**21**	**1**	**10**	**0**	**12**	**1**	**9**	**0**	**232/6**	**5**

WILLIAMS, Peter Wesley

1978 - 1981

Position; *Forward*
D.O.B; *17th May, 1960*
Birthplace; *Hawarden, Flintshire*
Height; *5ft 8in* ***Weight;*** *10st 11lbs*
Debut; v. *Sheffield Wednesday (a) 3rd May, 1978*
Total Appearances & Goals; *5/6 apps 1 gls*
Career; *WREXHAM 15th Jul 1978; Bangor City May 1981; Johnstown Athletic;*
Honours; *Wales Under-21 International; Welsh Youth international; Welsh schoolboy international; Welsh Youth Cup Winner 1978; Northern Premier League Championship Winner 1982; Welsh Cup runner-up 1979;*

Peter Williams began playing football while attending the Grango School in Rhos and Ysgol Rhiwabon from where he was chosen to represent both Wrexham & District and Clwyd Schoolboys. He came to join Wrexham in unusual circumstances having turned up at the Racecourse to be a ball boy, but found that the club's 'B' team were short of players and he was invited to play for them! It was from that game that he progressed to the club's ground staff upon leaving school in 1976. He developed through the youth ranks at the Racecourse, picking up a Welsh Youth Cup winners' medal in 1978, when the 'Robins' beat Afan Lido 2-1 at Aberystwyth. He made his Football League debut before turning professional, in July 1978, in the last match of the 1977/78 season, one in which Wrexham were crowned Third Division champions. Manager Arfon Griffiths gave Peter, and two other youngsters - Steve Buxton and Steve Kenworthy - their first team debut's at Hillsborough against Sheffield Wednesday, which the 'Robins' lost 2-1. The following season brought international recognition when he played for Wales Under-21's against England at Swansea in February 1979, though England won 1-0, with a side that included Glenn Hoddle and Bryan Robson. At the end of that season he played in both leg's of the 1979 Welsh Cup Final, although Wrexham lost 2-1 on aggregate to Shrewsbury Town. Despite the result, the 'Robins' qualified for Europe by virtue of the opposition being an English club. Peter was to make most of his appearances for Wrexham's Second Division side as a substitute, scoring just one goal, in a 2-0 home win over Luton Town in March 1979. He played in both leg's of the European Cup-Winners' Cup matches with NK Rijeka of Yugoslavia, which the 'Robins' lost 3-2 on aggregate. With forwards like Dixie McNeil, Mick Vinter, Graham Whittle, Ian Edwards, and John Lyons at the club, he found his senior opportunities limited. He wasn't helped by a serious knee injury that forced him out of the reckoning for much of that season, which was followed by a broken leg in a Lancashire League game with Macclesfield Town, when he fell awkwardly following a fair tackle, though he continued to finish the game and return home. Having gone for a night out that same evening, the pain became so unbearable that he went to the hospital were he was diagnosed as having broken his leg! Following that injury, Peter was to make just one more appearance for the 'Robins' before his release in the summer of 1981. He then drifted into non-league football by signing for Northern Premier League side Bangor City, where he won a championship medal in his one season at Farrar Road, as well as helping the North Wales Coast club to reach the semi-finals of the Welsh Cup, where they just lost 2-1 on aggregate to First Division Swansea City. In the summer of 1982 he joined Welsh National League side Johnstown Athletic, where he spent almost five seasons before deciding to retire from playing after he broke his collar bone. Peter, who still resides in the Wrexham area, has been employed by Hoya Lens UK since 1993 as a coating technician for ophthalmic lenses.

Season	League		F.A.Cup		Welsh Cup		League Cup		E.C.W.C.		Total	
	apps	gls	apps	gls	apps	gls	apps	gls	apps	gls	apps	gls
1977/78	1	0	-	-	1	0	-	-	-	-	2	0
1978/79	3/3	1	-	-	1/1	0	0/3	0	1/	0	5/8	1
1979/80	1/2	0	-	-	-	-	-	-	-	-	1/2	0
1980/81	0/1	0	-	-	-	-	-	-	-	-	0/1	0
	5/6	**1**	**-**	**-**	**2/1**	**0**	**0/3**	**0**	**1/1**	**0**	**8/11**	**1**

WILLIAMS, Raymond 1951 - 1952

Position; *Right-Back*
D.O.B; *1st May, 1931*
Birthplace; *Bradley, Nr.Wrexham, Denbighshire*
Height; *ft in* ***Weight;*** *st lbs*
Debut; v. *Bradford Park Avenue (a) 1st September, 1951*
Total Appearances & Goals; *12 apps 0 gls*
Career; *Wrexham YC; Gresford; Holyhead Town cs1949; WREXHAM 29th May 1951; Holyhead Town 17th Aug 1953;*
Honours; *Welsh Youth International cap; Welsh League (North) Championship Winner 1950 & 1958; North Wales Coast F.A.Challenge Cup runner-up 1958 & 1959; Cookson Cup Winner 1950; North Wales Coast F.A. Representative XI 1956;*

Ray Williams played football for Rhosrobin and Gresford Schools, and upon completing his education he took up employment as a surface worker at Gresford Colliery. He did continue to play football for both Wrexham Youth Club and Gresford, and it was whilst he was turning out for Gresford that he made one appearance for Wales in a Boys' Club International against England in March 1949. That same season he was also chosen to play for Wales at Youth level against England, Scotland, and Ireland. By this time Wrexham had begun to take an interest in him, and he was invited to attend training sessions at the Racecourse. However, he began the 1949/50 season playing for Holyhead Town in the Welsh League North, and in his first season with the 'Harbourmen' helped them to win the North Wales Coast Amateur Cup, Cookson Cup, Elias Cup and the Welsh League (North) Division One Championship title. Ray impressed in the Holyhead defence, where he was described as 'a master of the sliding tackle', and following that campaign he was invited for trials with both Blackpool and Wolves. However, Wrexham had maintained an interest, and he finally signed for them in May 1951 on amateur terms. He didn't have long to wait before he made his Football League debut, which came in September as he replaced Eddie Tunney for an away match at Bradford Park Avenue. A 5-0 defeat didn't deter him, and he kept his place in the side for the next ten games before he was replaced by Les Speed. A bad leg injury then restricted his involvement with the first team for Wrexham before he was released at the end of the season. He returned to Holyhead, where he went on to win many honours with the 'Harbourmen', and stayed with them until the end of the 1960/61 season when he decided to hang up his boots, having become affectionately known to the Holyhead supporters as, 'Raymond Bach', his wholehearted approach winning many admirers. Upon ending his playing career he continued to work at Gresford Colliery, before moving on to Brymbo Steelworks, where he was employed for 23 years before its closure brought early retirement. Ray is now settled in the village of Coedpoeth, near Wrexham. As a keen gardener his efforts are something to be admired - Green fingers as well as good feet!!

Season	League		F.A.Cup		Welsh Cup		Total	
	apps	gls	apps	gls	apps	gls	apps	gls
1951/52	12	0	-	-	-	-	12	0
	12	**0**	**-**	**-**	**-**	**-**	**12**	**0**

WILLIAMS, Reginald Frank 1946 - 1948

Position; *Goalkeeper*
D.O.B; *12th March, 1917*
Birthplace; *Overton-on-Dee, Nr Wrexham, Denbighshire*
Died; *Marchwiel, Wrexham, 24th November 1978*
Height; *5ft 10in* ***Weight;*** *11st 7lbs*
Debut; v. *New Brighton (h) 31st August, 1946*
Total Appearances & Goals; *37 apps 0 gls*
Career; *Whitchurch; WREXHAM 30th Aug 1946; Halifax Town Aug 1948 0apps; South Liverpool Nov 1948; Oswestry Town 15th August 1949; Rhyl 12th Jan 1952; Ellesmere Port Town;*

Frank Williams joined Wrexham following World War Two , having served for six years with the Royal Engineers. He went on to make his Football League debut for the 'Robins' when he was almost 30 years old in the opening game of the 1946/47 season, a 3-2 home win over New Brighton. He kept his place in the side for the next seven games, following which he was replaced by Terry McNee. During his time at the Racecourse he earned the nickname 'Tiger' Williams, because of his cat-like stance and agility. 'Tiger' returned to the first team in January, only to lose his place again in March to Percy Lovett, before getting the nod for the last four games of the season. He began 1947/48 campaign as the Club's first choice 'keeper, and kept a clean sheet in a 1-0 win opening day victory at Halifax Town, but was eventually to find competition from both Geoff Atherton and Tom Bayley, and at the end of that season was released from the Racecourse. Frank then joined Halifax Town on a month's trial in August 1948, before he was to sign permanently for the 'Shaymen' in September. However, his stay at the 'Shay' was short-lived, because he was released in November without having made a first team appearance to join Cheshire County League side, South Liverpool. He is later known to have played in the same competition for Ellesmere Port Town, Rhyl, and Oswestry Town. Prior to World War Two Frank had attended the local school in his native Overton for whom he had played football. There, he had earned the nickname of 'Winkle', as he always wore the flower of the periwinkle when he went to school. This nickname stayed with him for the rest of his life. After he had left school 'Winkle' went to work on a farm, where he would work extra nights to free his Saturday afternoons so that he could play football for Whitchurch. He would then have to cycle the twelve miles between his home and the Shropshire club before playing! During this time he also became an expert ball room dancer. When the Second World War was declared he went to work at a Munitions factory, though he soon volunteered for the Army, becoming a driver/mechanic with the Royal Engineers. He was later promoted to corporal and took part in the D-Day landings in Normandy, and later in the occupation of Germany, when he played football for his company. After WW2, Frank was employed by a local plumber, as well as having his own small holding in Overton, where he was actively involved in the local community as a regular worshipper at the local church. He was also a keen cricketer, keeping wicket for many years. An active member of the Overton Branch of the Royal British Legion, he served as its chairman prior to his sudden death in November 1978 at a R.B.L. dinner at the Cross Lanes Hotel in Marchwiel. His wife Betty is a local Historian and has produced a publication on the district of Overton.

Season	League		F.A.Cup		Welsh Cup		Total	
	apps	gls	apps	gls	apps	gls	apps	gls
1946/47	17	0	-	-	-	-	17	0
1947/48	19	0	1	0	-	-	20	0
	36	**0**	**1**	**0**	**-**	**-**	**37**	**0**

WILLIAMS, Robert Daniel 1923 - 1924

Position; *Outside-Right*
D.O.B; *J/A/S 1902*
Birthplace; *Brymbo, Denbighshire*
Height; *5ft 6in* ***Weight;*** *10st 0lbs*
Debut; v. *New Brighton (a) 9th February, 1924*
Total Appearances & Goals; *3 apps 0 gls*
Career; *Rhos Church FC; Brymbo; WREXHAM (Am) Feb 1924; Brymbo Mar 1924; New Brighton (Trial) cs1924; Llandudno cs1924; Oswestry Town Mar 1926;*

Bob Williams had played local football for both Rhos Church and Brymbo. It was whilst he was playing for the latter that he was called up to sign for Wrexham as an amateur in February 1924 following an injury crisis at the Racecourse. Arthur Hughes was also signed at the same time, and they both made their Football League debuts in a scoreless draw at New Brighton, a day or so after joining the club. Bob was said to have made a 'fairly successful debut', and kept his place for the following two League games, both against Grimsby Town, and both ending in draws. He then played in a few reserve team games before returning to Brymbo at the end of March. He was offered a trial by another Football League side,

New Brighton, in the summer, but before the new season had began he had signed for Welsh League side Llandudno, where he remained until March 1926. Bob then moved on to Birmingham & District League side Oswestry Town.

Season	League		F.A.Cup		Welsh Cup		Total	
	apps	gls	apps	gls	apps	gls	apps	gls
1923/24	3	0	-	-	-	-	3	0
	3	**0**	**-**	**-**	**-**		**3**	**0**

WILLIAMS, Robert Raymond 1951

Position; *Inside-Forward*
D.O.B; *25th October, 1927*
Birthplace; *Liverpool, Merseyside*
Height; *ft in* ***Weight;*** *st lbs*
Debut; v. *Chester (a) 18th August, 1951*
Total Appearances & Goals; *7 apps 0 gls*
Career; *Liverpool Nov 1945 0apps; WREXHAM 14th Jun 1951; Shrewsbury Town 20th Oct 1951 5apps 0gls;*

Bob Williams joined Liverpool towards the end of the Second World War, and remained with the Anfield club until 1951. However, he failed to make a first team appearance during that time, and was released at the end of the 1950/51 season. He was then quickly snapped up by Wrexham manager Peter Jackson in June 1951. Bob made his Football League debut for the 'Robins' at inside-left in the opening match of the new season, a 2-1 defeat against Chester at Sealand Road. He kept his place in the side for the next five games, but was to manage just one more League appearance, at outside-right in a 3-0 defeat at Mansfield in September, before moving on to Third Division South side Shrewsbury Town in October. Williams and Eddie Beynon swapped places with Peter Fisher and Eric Hope in an exchange deal. Bob made his debut for Shrewsbury in the following game, a 2-0 home win over Port Vale, but he was to record just four more League appearances for the Gay Meadow club before his release at the end of the season.

Season	League		F.A.Cup		Welsh Cup		Total	
	apps	gls	apps	gls	apps	gls	apps	gls
1951/52	7	0	-	-	-	-	7	0
	7	**0**	**-**	**-**	**-**	**-**	**7**	**0**

WILLIAMS, Scott John 1991 - 1998

Position; *Defender/Midfield*
D.O.B; *7th August, 1974*
Birthplace; *Bangor, Gwynedd*
Height; *6ft 0in* ***Weight;*** *12st 0lbs*
Debut; v. *Doncaster Rovers (h) 5th September, 1992.*
Total Appearances & Goals; *30/9 apps 0 gls*
Career; *WREXHAM Jul 1991, (Pro) 2nd Jul 1993; Rochdale 3rd Jul 1998 0apps; Bangor City Nov 1998 16/1apps 1gls;*
Honours; *Welsh Under-21 International cap; Welsh Youth International cap; Welsh Schoolboy International cap; Welsh Youth Cup Winner 1992; Welsh Youth Cup runner-up 1993;*

Scott Williams first played football at Broughton Primary School, near Chester, eventually moving on to turn out for St.David's Secondary School in Saltney, where he was chosen to represent both Flintshire and Clwyd Schoolboys. It was whilst he was playing for the latter that he was spotted by a Leeds United scout, and invited for trials, following which he was signed on schoolboy forms at the age of 14. Prior to this Scott had been playing regular junior football for both Broughton Juniors and Broughton Super Saints. Shortly after signing for Leeds, Williams was capped by Wales at Schoolboy level, playing in the Victory Shield series against the other Home Countries. When it came to leaving school he was only offered a one year apprenticeship deal by Leeds, due to his birthday falling in August. He decided to turn this down and remain at school to study for his 'A' levels, though within a couple of months he had been signed by Wrexham on Y.T.S. forms, after turning down an approach from Oldham Athletic at the last moment. At the Racecourse Scott began to progress through the club's youth system, collecting a Welsh Youth Cup winners' and runners'-up medals, as well as gaining further international recognition by being selected for the Welsh Youth side. He was still on the Youth Training Scheme when he made his Football League debut at left-back in September 1992, replacing Phil Hardy in a 1-1 home draw against Doncaster Rovers. He also made one substitute appearance in the Welsh Cup that season, before he was signed on professional terms during the summer. The following season saw Scott becoming more involved with the first team, playing mainly in midfield, but also slotting into both full-back positions as and when required. Further international recognition came when he made his Welsh Under-21 debut against Moldova. This was followed by three more caps at this level against Germany and Bulgaria (twice). However, Scott had been plagued with injuries throughout his time at Wrexham, and the start of the 1995/96 season saw him sidelined with a serious back problem, which was to threaten his football career. However, he fought his way back to replace the injured Phil Hardy at left-back in March 1998, when he made three League appearances before Hardy returned. Despite Williams' return to fitness, he was informed that he was to be released by manager Brian Flynn at the end of the 1997/98 campaign. He then joined Third Division side Rochdale for the start of the 1998/99 season, initially on a three month contract, but he was subsequently released at the end of it. Scott then linked up with his home town club, League of Wales side Bangor City, in November 1998.

Season	League		F.A.Cup		Welsh Cup		League Cup		A.W.S.		E.C.W.C.		Total	
	apps	gls	apps	gls	apps	gls	apps	gls	apps	gls	apps	gls	apps	gls
1992/93	1	0	-	-	0/1	0	-	-	-	-	-	-	1/1	0
1993/94	11/3	0	-	-	0/1	0	1	0	1	0	-	-	13/4	0
1994/95	8/2	0	-	-	1	0	-	-	0/1	0	-	-	9/3	0
1996/97	3/1	0	-	-	-	-	-	-	-	-	-	-	3/1	0
1997/98	3	0	-	-	-	-	-	-	-	-	-	-	4*	0
	26/6	**0**	**-**	**-**	**1/2**	**0**	**1**	**0**	**1/1**	**0**	**-**	**-**	**30/9**	**0**

* = Includes 1app 0gls in Welsh Invitation Cup.

WILLIAMS, Stuart Grenville 1946 - 1951

Position; *Right-Back*
D.O.B; *9th July, 1930*
Birthplace; *Wrexham, Denbighshire*
Height; *5ft 9in* ***Weight;*** *12st 12lbs*
Debut; v. *Carlisle United (a) 1st September, 1949*
Total Appearances & Goals; *1 app 0 gls*
Career; *Victoria YC; WREXHAM Jul 1946; West Bromwich Albion Nov 1950 226apps 6gls; Southampton Sept 1962 £15,000 148/2apps 3gls; Released cs1966;*
Honours; *43 Welsh International caps; Football League First Division Championship runner-up 1954; Second Division runner-up 1966;*

The son of a Wrexham Football Club director Stuart Williams joined Wrexham straight from school, having been educated at Acton Park Junior and Grove Park Grammar Schools, from where he represented Wrexham & District Schoolboys. He also played for the Victoria Youth Club before signing for Wrexham as an amateur in July 1946. He progressed through the youth ranks at the Racecourse to make his Football League debut for the 'Robins' at the age of nineteen in September 1949, replacing Dennis Grainger at inside-right in a 1-0 away defeat at Carlisle United. A year later, however, Stuart was to leave the club, when he decided to take up work in insurance in the Midlands. He was given a trial at West Bromwich Albion in November 1950, and after impressing, signed a professional contract for the 'Baggies' in February 1951. His debut for Albion came a year later in a 3-0 defeat at Huddersfield Town, and shortly after he was converted from inside-forward to eventually become an international full-back. A Welsh debut followed in May 1954 against Austria in Vienna, and Stuart went on to represent Wales 33 times out of his total of 43 caps during his time at the Hawthorns, still an Albion club record for the most capped player whilst on their books. Also included in that total was making five appearances in the 1958 World Cup Finals in Sweden. 'A cool, consistently-fine right-back', he went on to give West Brom twelve years' sterling service, making 246 League and Cup appearances, when he was described as having a 'sure kick, splendid positional sense and a first rate temperament'. He finally left the Hawthorns in September 1962 to join Southampton for a £15,000 fee at the age of 32. Despite his advancing years Stuart went on to make 150 League appearances for the 'Saints', as well as representing Wales a further ten times. He picked up a Second Division championship runners'-up medal in 1966 with Southampton, before being released at the end of that season. In July 1966 he returned to West Brom as a coach, later becoming trainer at Aston Villa in 1970. He then had a spell in management, when he took charge of Payhaan in Tehran, Iran, before returning to Britain to become trainer/coach at Scottish League side Morton. He returned to the Dell as a coach in September 1971, later becoming assistant-manager to Ted Bates. In 1973 he took up a position as a scout with Carlisle United, before going back into management with Stavanger in Norway. He announced his retirement from football in 1975, settling in Southampton to become a representative with two tyre companies. Stuart then became manager of a transport company in 1987, before running his own 'Guest' House in Southampton, where he has since settled.

Season	League		F.A.Cup		Welsh Cup		Total	
	apps	gls	apps	gls	apps	gls	apps	gls
1949/50	1	0	-	-	-	-	1	0
	1	**0**	**-**	**-**	**-**	**-**	**1**	**0**

WILSON, Bevis Alan McLean,

1947 - 1951

Position; *Centre-Half*
D.O.B; *14th May, 1924*
Birthplace; *Eccles, Lancashire*
Died; *Barrow-in-Furness, 27th August, 1987*
Height; *5ft 11'1/2in* ***Weight;*** *11st 10lbs*
Debut; v. *Bradford City (h) 3rd September, 1947*
Total Appearances & Goals; *109 apps 0 gls*
Career; *WREXHAM 20th Jun 1947; Barrow 2nd Mar 1951 £2,000 309apps 1gls; Yeovil Town cs1960;*
Honours; *Welsh Cup runner-up 1950; Third Division North representative appearance.*

Peter Wilson was the son of a former County Cricketer. He was not christened Peter - he decided to give himself the name when he was a small child, and it stuck for the rest of his life. Though born in Eccles he was to be educated at Wrexham's Grove Park Grammar School, where he was more interested in Cricket and athletics, than he was in football, and was 'Victor Ludorum' at least twice, according to school magazines. Some of the records that he set during his schooldays stood for decades. Upon leaving school during the Second World War Peter was called up to serve in the Army, where he served for five years. In June 1947 at the age of 23, he was demobilised from the Army, and signed for Wrexham manager Tom Williams after having impressed at football during his Army days. He played in Wrexham's reserve side at first, but didn't have long to wait before making his Football League debut in September 1947, replacing Billy Tudor at centre-half in a 4-2 home win against Bradford City. He added a further 22 League appearances that season, as Wrexham finished third, their highest League position since 1933. Peter became a regular in the Wrexham team over the next two seasons, collecting a Welsh Cup runners'-up medal from a Final defeat against Swansea Town at Ninian Park, Cardiff. However, the 1950/51 season found him struggling to keep his first team place, as George Spruce gradually became Wrexham's regular centre-half. At the end of 50/51 he was transferred to fellow Third Division North side Barrow for a £2,000 fee. There, he switched positions, becoming a 'stylish type of full-back', and in his nine seasons with the Cumbrian side made 309 League appearances, during which time he was chosen to represent the Third Division North XI, to face their Southern counterparts. He was released by Barrow in the close season of 1960, whereupon he took up an offer to join Southern League side Yeovil Town, where he was to spend one season before deciding to end his playing career. Peter then returned to live in Barrow, where he joined the staff at V.S.E.L., where he remained in their employment until his sudden death in 1987, at the age of 63.

Season	League		F.A.Cup		Welsh Cup		Total	
	apps	gls	apps	gls	apps	gls	apps	gls
1947/48	23	0	-	-	2	0	25	0
1948/49	24	0	-	-	-	-	24	0
1949/50	41	0	2	0	5	0	48	0
1950/51	10	0	2	0	-	-	12	0
	98	**0**	**4**	**0**	**7**	**0**	**109**	**0**

WILSON, John

1937 - 1938

Position; *Outside-Right*
D.O.B;
Birthplace; *Rotherham, Yorkshire*
Height; *5ft 6in* ***Weight;*** *10st 8lbs*
Debut; v. *New Brighton (h) 4th September, 1937*
Total Appearances & Goals; *7 apps 0 gls*
Career; *Cradley Heath; Wolves 8th Sept 1936; WREXHAM 5th May 1937;*

John Wilson was signed by Wrexham manager Captain James Logan from First Division side Wolverhampton Wanderers in May 1937, although he had been playing for Birmingham & District League side Cradley Heath during the 1936/37 season while still on Wolves' books. Logan said of John on signing him, 'Although on the small side, he possesses great speed and ball control'. He made his Football League debut for the 'Robins' in the third match of the 1937/38 season, replacing Willie Ouchterlonie at outside-right in a 1-0 home defeat by New Brighton in September. One more appearance followed that same month, a 5-3 defeat at Darlington, before playing reserve team football until April, when he was recalled into the side for the injured Archie Burgon in a 2-0 home win over Halifax Town. During that spell John played in five games, the last a 2-0 home win over Accrington Stanley, which proved to be his final senior outing for the club before being released in the close season.

Season	League		F.A.Cup		Welsh Cup		N.S.C.		Total	
	apps	gls	apps	gls	apps	gls	apps	gls	apps	gls
1937/38	7	0	-	-	-	-	-	-	7	0
	7	**0**	**-**	**-**	**-**	**-**	**-**	**-**	**7**	**0**

WILSON, Mark

1998

Position; *Midfield*
D.O.B; *9th February, 1979.*
Birthplace; *Scunthorpe, Humberside*
Height; *6ft 0ins* ***Weight;*** *12st 2lbs*
Debut; v. *Burnley (a) 24th February, 1998.*
Total Appearances & Goals; *16/1 apps 7 gls*
Career; *Manchester United 9th Feb 1996; WREXHAM 23rd Feb 1998 (Loan);*
Honours; *England schoolboy international; Welsh Invitation Cup Winner 1998;*

Brought up in his home town of Scunthorpe Mark Wilson first began playing competitive football for his junior school side, at the same time turning out for a local youth club, Bottesford Town. When he stepped up to the Frederick Gough Secondary School he went on to represent both Scunthorpe and Humberside Boys before Grimsby Town spotted and signed him for their School of Excellence from the age of 13 to 15. His youth coach at Grimsby, Ian White, then nominated him for a place at the F.A.National Training School at Lilleshall, and after progressing through trials involving around 4,000 prospects he was invited to join the remaining 16 boys on a two year course. By that time, he had been invited for trials with virtually every Premier League - and several Football League Clubs, but it was Manchester United who won the race for his signature, and he signed a schoolboy contract upon going to Lilleshall. During his two years at the National Training School, Mark was called up to play for England Schoolboys, for whom he played at Wembley and also

in Berlin against Germany with around 10,000 British squaddies cheering them on. Mark crowned a memorable occasion by scoring the winning goal in the last minute to earn England a 3-2 victory. After leaving Lilleshall in 1995 he signed full-time for the Old Trafford club on YTS forms, progressing to sign a three year professional contract on his 17th birthday in February 1996. As he made his way through the ranks at United, Mark played in a 7-0 F.A.Youth Cup win over Wrexham at Old Trafford. He became a regular member of the Old Trafford 'A' team in the Lancashire League, before stepping up to the reserve side in the Pontin's League. In February 1998 he was handed the opportunity of regular first team football when Alex Ferguson allowed him to join Wrexham on loan to enhance his experience. His Football League debut came in dramatic style at Burnley, where the 'Robins' 'keeper, Mark Cartwright, was injured, and had to be replaced between the posts by midfielder Gareth Owen. Mark came on as a substitute, and led Wrexham to a 2-1 victory by scoring the winning goal. He remained at the Racecourse until the end of the season, during which time he scored four goals in 13 League games, which almost helped the North Wales club reach the promotion play-off's, only to miss out by one goal. However, he did win a Welsh Invitation Cup winners' medal, when Wrexham beat Cardiff City 2-1 in the Final on the Racecourse. The 'Robins' manager Brian Flynn said of him, "He has two good feet, he's quick, has good awareness and is not afraid of hard work. The role he plays for us allows him to get forward which suits him because he always looks like he is going to score goals. A player of those qualities can play at the highest level." At the end of the 1997/98 season Mark returned to Old Trafford, where he made his first team debut for the Old Trafford club in a Champions League game in Denmark against Brondby, a competition which United went on to win. He still remains a vital member of United's first team squad.

Season	League		F.A.Cup		League Cup		W.I.T.		A.W.S.		Total	
	apps	gls	apps	gls	apps	gls	apps	gls	apps	gls	apps	gls
1997/98	12/1	4	-	-	-	-	4	3	-	-	16/1	7
	12/1	**4**	**-**	**-**	**-**		**4**	**3**	**-**	**-**	**16/1**	**7**

WOOD, John Michael

1966 - 1968

Position; *Right-Back*
D.O.B; *9th September, 1948*
Birthplace; *Walsall Wood, Staffordshire*
Height; *5ft 10in* ***Weight;*** *11st 4lbs*
Debut; v. *Port Vale (h) 4th May, 1966*
Total Appearances & Goals; *6/4 apps 0 gls*
Career; *Blackburn Rovers (Trial); WREXHAM 7th Jul 1966; Rhyl 16th Jul 1968; Bethesda Athletic 30th Dec 1969; Nantlle Vale 26th May 1973; Prestatyn 7th Aug 1973; Pilkington FC 1977;*
Honours; *Welsh Cup runner-up 1967; Welsh Schoolboy international; Welsh League (North) Championship Winner 1971; North Wales Coast F.A.Challenge Cup runner-up 1971; Cookson Cup Winner;*

John Wood was born in Walsall Wood in Staffordshire, but moved with his Welsh family to North Wales in 1959 at the age of ten, as his father took up work in Rhyl. It was in North Wales that he first began to take an interest in football, and he played for his school teams at both Christchurch Primary and Rhyl Grammar Schools. He was chosen to represent Flintshire, North Wales and eventually Wales Schoolboys at under-15 level, for whom he played four times: against England at Chesterfield; Scotland at Cardiff; Northern Ireland at Swansea; and the Republic of Ireland at Bangor. It was whilst he was still at school that he began playing for Mostyn YMCA in the local Dyserth League, and from there he was invited to Blackburn Rovers for trials upon leaving school. They offered him amateur terms following a couple of trial sessions at Ewood Park, but he declined due to the travelling involved. He then went to college at Deeside, where he studied for an ONC in Business Studies, and while there that he joined Wrexham on amateur terms. He played for the 'A' and 'B' teams in the Welsh League (North), and Welsh National League, before stepping up to the reserve team in the Cheshire County League. However, before that season had ended, he had been called up to the first team, whilst still an amateur, replacing Stuart Mason in a 1-0 home win against Port Vale in May 1966. Soon after that match he was invited to sign a two year professional contract for the Club by manager Jack Rowley. The following season John played mostly reserve team football until around March, when he was called into the first team once again and made four more League appearances. His most memorable game for the 'Robins' came in the following month, when he played in the Welsh Cup Final first leg against Cardiff City on the Racecourse. He had been called into the side as a late replacement for Alec Lucas, who was injured. The match finished 2-2, but Wrexham lost the second leg 2-1, without John, as Alec Lucas was fit again. Just three more first team appearances followed in 1967/68, his last coming in January, a 1-0 Welsh Cup win over Bethesda Athletic on the Racecourse. At the end of that season manager Alvan Williams announced that John was to be released, whereupon he signed for Cheshire County League side Rhyl. He spent two seasons at Belle Vue, until signing for Bethesda Athletic in December 1969. John picked up a Welsh League(North) Championship medal, Cookson Cup, and North Wales Coast F.A.Challenge Cup runners'-up medals with Bethesda, later going on to play for both Nantlle Vale and Prestatyn, adding a Clwyd Premier League Championship medal. After four years he joined Pilkington FC, who played in the same League, and again won a championship medal. After he had finished playing professional football, he worked for Pilkingtons in their accounts department, and in sales marketing. He has also been employed by both Rogers & Jackson and Capitol Windows in a sales marketing capacity. He then took up a similar role with Seddon (Stoke) Ltd, based around the North Wales and Shropshire area. John is now settled in the North Wales area, at Kinmel Bay, near Rhyl. His son Lawrence Wood is a budding actor and a member of the Royal Shakespeare Company and has appeared on the Bill. Son-in-Law Paul Gray is manager with Welsh National League side Penley.

Season	League		F.A.Cup		Welsh Cup		League Cup		Total	
	apps	gls	apps	gls	apps	gls	apps	gls	apps	gls
1965/66	1	0	-	-	-	-	-	-	1	0
1966/67	1/3	0	-	-	1/1	0	-	-	2/4	0
1967/68	2	0	-	-	1	0	-	-	3	0
	4/3	**0**	**-**	**-**	**2/1**	**0**	**-**	**-**	**6/4**	**0**

WOOD, Ronald William

1949 - 1950

Position; *Inside-Forward*
D.O.B; *11th November, 1925*
Birthplace; *Manchester, Lancashire*
Height; *5ft 11in* ***Weight;*** *st lbs*
Debut; v. *Lincoln City (a) 24th December, 1949*
Total Appearances & Goals; *18 apps 6 gls*
Career; *Droylsden; WREXHAM 21st Nov 1949;*

Ron Wood was signed by Wrexham manager Les McDowall in November 1949 from Cheshire County League side, Droylsden, where he had impressed with his goalscoring exploits. He finally made his football League debut for the 'Robins' at the age of 24, in a 2-0 defeat at Lincoln City on Christmas Eve 1949. Despite that result Ron kept his place in the side, and went on to score four goals in five games, though he soon found himself out of favour when the goals dried up, and he was released at the end of the season. During his brief stay at the Racecourse he was described as 'a natural ball player with a fine sense of using open space'.

Season	League		F.A.Cup		Welsh Cup		Total	
	apps	gls	apps	gls	apps	gls	apps	gls
1949/50	16	5	-	-	2	1	18	6
	16	**5**	**-**	**-**	**2**	**1**	**18**	**6**

WOODHOUSE, Rowland 1927 - 1930

Position; *Inside-Forward*
D.O.B; *15th January, 1897*
Birthplace; *Leyland, Lancashire*
Died; *Leyland, 13th March, 1969*
Height; *5ft 7in* **Weight;** *11st 6lbs*
Debut; v. *Chesterfield (a) 27th August, 1927*
Total Appearances & Goals; *130 apps 27 gls*
Career; *Lancaster Town 1918; Preston North End Mar 1919 206apps 53gls; Everton May 1926 £650 2apps 0gls; WREXHAM 24th May, 1927; Halifax Town Jun 1930 12apps 2gls; Chorley cs1931;*
Honours; *F.A.Cup runner-up 1922;*

Rowland Woodhouse was spotted playing for Lancaster Town just after the First World War by Preston North End, and they signed the promising 22 year old inside-forward in March 1919. He went on to spend six seasons with the First Division club, making over 200 appearances, and playing in the 1922 F.A.Cup Final against Huddersfield Town, where the 'Lilywhites' lost 1-0. During his time at Deepdale he was described as 'always industrious, although apt to err through over eagerness', and that he was 'one of the smallest, lightest, and pluckiest forwards in the game' . In May 1926 he was transferred to Everton for a £650 fee, but his time at Goodison was spent playing mostly reserve team football. He made just two League appearances in the year that he spent there, his debut coming in a 3-3 draw at Blackburn in October, and his last appearance in December in a 5-1 defeat at Burnley. In May 1927 he was transferred to Wrexham, where he spent three seasons. Rowland made his 'Robins' debut in the opening match of the 1927/28 season in a 1-0 win at Chesterfield. That same season he starred in the Wrexham team that pitted its wits against First Division opposition for the first time in the club's history, when they were unlucky to lose 3-1 to Birmingham in the Fourth Round of the F.A.Cup. Woodhouse missed just one first team game that season, and was a regular member of the senior side throughout the following campaign, helping the club finish in third place, their highest position since joining the Football League. The 'Robins' again progressed to the Fourth Round of the F.A.Cup in 1929/30, where they lost 2-1 to Second Division Bradford City after a replay. In the summer Rowland was transferred to Halifax Town, where he spent a year before dropping into non-league football with Chorley. He announced his retirement from the playing side at the end of the 1933/34 season, and took up an appointment as trainer at Chorley. During his time with Wrexham he had been described as 'on the small side, but has plenty of energy. Stylish and looked on as the brains of the attack'.

Season	League		F.A.Cup		Welsh Cup		Total	
	apps	gls	apps	gls	apps	gls	apps	gls
1927/28	41	12	5	2	3	2	49	16
1928/29	36	6	1	0	-	-	37	6
1929/30	36	3	5	1	3	1	44	5
	113	**21**	**11**	**3**	**6**	**3**	**130**	**27**

WOOTTON, Leonard 1951 - 1952

Position; *Forward*
D.O.B; *13th June, 1925*
Birthplace; *Stoke-on-Trent, Staffordshire*
Died; *Hartshill, Stoke-on-Trent, 9th Sept, 1990.*
Height; *5ft 6in* **Weight;** *10st 7lbs*
Debut; v. *Barrow (h) 29th August, 1951*
Total Appearances & Goals; *23 apps 0 gls*
Career; *Everton (WW2) 1943/44 3app 0gls; Port Vale Aug 1945 10apps 1gls; Northwich Victoria Apr 1947; Queen of the South Dec 1949; WREXHAM 8th Aug 1951;*
Honours; *Scottish Division 'B' League Championship Winner 1951;*

Len Wootton signed for Third Division South side Port Vale after the Second World War. He had previously been on the books of Everton during WW2, when he made three appearances for the Goodison Park club. His Football League debut came in October 1946, when he lined up at inside-right in a 4-0 home defeat against Cardiff City. Despite that result Len kept his place in the side for the following nine games, during which he scored in a 2-1 win at Crystal Palace. However, he never made a another League appearance for Vale, and in April 1947 he was allowed to leave Vale Park to join Cheshire County League side Northwich Victoria. 'A fast tricky winger' Wootton soon became a big favourite of the Drill Field crowd, and his skills didn't go unnoticed as he signed for Scottish League Division 'A' side Queen of the South, in a bid to stop their slide into Division 'B'. However, he couldn't save the Dumfries club from relegation, though they bounced straight back at the end of the following season as Division 'B' champions. At the end of that campaign, Len was allowed to return to the Football League when he joined Third Division North side Wrexham in August 1951. He made his debut for the 'Robins' in a 4-2 home defeat against Barrow, playing at inside-forward. He was described as 'not the biggest of forwards', but he did score one of the Wrexham goals. Another nineteen League appearances followed, being told that his contract would not be renewed in the summer of 1952. Len later returned to Northwich Victoria, where he made twelve Cheshire County League appearances during the 1952/53 season.

Season	League		F.A.Cup		Welsh Cup		Total	
	apps	gls	apps	gls	apps	gls	apps	gls
1951/52	20	2	2	0	1	0	23	0
	20	**2**	**2**	**0**	**1**	**0**	**23**	**0**

WORTHINGTON, Gary Lee 1989 - 1991

Position; *Forward*
D.O.B; *10th November, 1966*
Birthplace; *Cleethorpes, Humberside*
Height; *5ft 10in* **Weight;** *10st 5lbs*
Debut; v. *Scarborough (a) 19th August, 1989*
Total Appearances & Goals; *90/4 apps 29 gls*
Career; *Manchester United Nov 1984; Huddersfield Town Jul 1986 0apps; Darlington Jul 1987 31/9apps 15gls; Wrexham Jun 1989 £15,000; Wigan Athletic 22nd Mar 1991 (Exchange for Ian Griffiths) 51/12apps 20gls; Exeter City Aug 1993 8/7apps 1gls; Doncaster Rovers 24th Mar 1994 8apps 2gls (Loan); Halifax Town Aug 1994 46/10apps 14gls; Dagenham & Redbridge Dec 1995 20apps 6gls; Halifax Town Aug 1996 19/8apps 1gls; Lancaster City Aug 1997;*
Honours; *England Youth International cap; Welsh Cup runner-up 1990;*

Gary is a member of the well known Worthington footballing family. Dave, his father, who played League football for Southend and Grimsby, and uncle the more famous Frank, who played for Bolton and Birmingham City, among many others, as well as representing England, and another Uncle, Bob, who also played League football. As a youngster, Gary signed for Manchester United on schoolboy forms at the age of 13. He went on to accept apprentice terms with the Old Trafford club upon leaving school in July 1983, and from there he stepped up to the professional ranks on his eighteenth birthday. Gary spent a further eighteen months with United before being released at the end of the 1985/86 season. He was soon fixed up when Huddersfield Town signed the promising youngster, but he failed to make any impression in his one season at Leeds Road, though his cause was hardly helped by the fact that he twice pulled up with a hamstring injury, and was then laid low with glandular fever, but despite these setbacks he was still released at the end of the season. Determined to remain in football he signed for Fourth Division Darlington, where he finally made his Football League debut. 15 goals in forty League games for the Feethams club followed, although at the end of his second season the club suffered relegation to the Conference League. Gary was

then sold to Fourth Division Wrexham for a £12,000 fee in June 1988, as a replacement for the departed crowd favourite, Kevin Russell. This made the task of settling in all the more harder, as much was expected of him. His debut came in the opening match of the 1989/90 season, a 2-1 defeat at Scarborough, and he marked the occasion by scoring the Wrexham goal. However, it proved to be a season of struggle, as Gary found himself in a similar situation to that at his previous club, with Wrexham fighting to preserve their Football League status. His two goals in an absolutely priceless 3-2 win over Colchester United in March went a long way to secure Wrexham's 'houdini' act, as they had been six points adrift at the beginning of the month. Gary picked up a Welsh Cup runners'-up medal at the end of the season, when Wrexham lost 2-1 to Hereford United in the first ever Welsh Cup Final to be played at the National Stadium in Cardiff, and he had the consolation of scoring the 'Robins' goal. There was little change in the club's situation throughout the following season: there was no money to buy new players, and Gary found himself playing alongside teenagers, who were being pitched in at the deep end, secure in the knowledge that there would be no relegation in the summer. As for Worthington, he had become a target for the boo-boys by this time, and manager Brian Flynn struck an exchange deal with Hereford United for Steve Lowndes, only for it to fall through when Lowndes couldn't agree terms. A similar deal was then arranged with Wigan Athletic, and Ian Griffiths moved to Wrexham in March 1991. Worthington made his debut for the 'Latics' as a substitute in a 1-0 home win over Crewe Alexandra, and went on to spend just over two years at Springfield Park, becoming a regular in the side until October 1992, although he then made just one more substitute appearance before the end of that season, when he was released. A move to Exeter City on a two year contract followed in the summer of 1993, but was placed on the transfer list with less than half his contract completed, as he couldn't settle. He had a loan spell with Doncaster Rovers in March 1994 before joining Conference League side Halifax Town in the summer of 1994. Gary remained at the Shay until December 1995, when he moved on to Dagenham & Redbridge in the same competition, although he returned to the Shay in the close season of 1996. He remained with them until the end of 96/97, when he joined Lancaster City in the Unibond Premier League where he ended his playing career. Gary now helps out with the coaching of youngsters at Manchester United, while he still resides in the Halifax area.

Season	League		F.A.Cup		Welsh Cup		League Cup		F.R.T.		E.C.W.C.		Total	
	apps	gls	apps	gls	apps	gls	apps	gls	apps	gls	apps	gls	apps	gls
1989/90	39/3	12	1	0	6	3	2	0	2	1	-	-	50/3	16
1990/91	29/1	6	1	0	2	4	4	2	2	1	2	0	40/1	13
	68/4	**18**	**2**	**0**	**8**	**7**	**6**	**2**	**4**	**2**	**2**	**0**	**90/4**	**29**

WRENCH, Mark Nicholas 1988 - 1990

Position; *Left-Back*
D.O.B; *27th September, 1969*
Birthplace; *Warrington, Cheshire*
Height; *5ft 10in* ***Weight;*** *11st 0lbs*
Debut; v. *Doncaster Rovers (a) 24th September, 1988*
Total Appearances & Goals; *5/1 apps 0 gls*
Career; *WREXHAM Sept 1988; Northwich Victoria Mar 1990 35/2apps 0gls; Hyde United 1991/92;*
Honours; *Staffordshire Senior Cup Winner 1990;*

Mark Wrench was another promising youngster to come to the Racecourse via Wrexham's youth network in the Merseyside area, having shown plenty of promise during his schooldays when he represented both Runcorn and Cheshire Schoolboys. He progressed to make his Football League debut at Doncaster Rovers in September 1988, the same month that he had signed professional terms. He made his bow as a substitute for Nigel Beaumont in the 2-2 draw, and then played in the next two matches at left-back in place of Darren Wright. He was to make just one further appearance that year, deputising again for Wright in a 1-0 defeat at York. Wrench made two more League appearances in the September of the following season, but they proved to be his last, as he was released in March 1990. He then signed for Conference League side Northwich Victoria, where he became the Vic's regular left-back for the next fifteen months. However, with just three more appearances at the beginning of 1991/92 he was on the move again, this time to Northern Premier League side Hyde United. Mark combined playing non-league football with his trade as an electrician.

Season	League		F.A.Cup		Welsh Cup		League Cup		F.R.T.		Total	
	apps	gls	apps	gls	apps	gls	apps	gls	apps	gls	apps	gls
1988/89	3/1	0	-	-	-	-	-	-	-	-	3/1	0
1989/90	2	0	-	-	-	-	-	-	-	-	2	0
	5/1	**0**	-	-	-	-	-	-	-	-	**5/1**	**0**

WRIGHT, Barry Albert 1959 - 1962

Position; *Left-Back*
D.O.B; *23rd July 1939*
Birthplace; *Gwersyllt, nr.Wrexham, Denbighshire*
Height; *5ft 8in* ***Weight;*** *10st 3lbs*
Debut; v. *Port Vale (h) 31st October, 1959*
Total Appearances & Goals; *13 apps 0 gls*
Career; *WREXHAM; Bolton Wanderers 1958; WREXHAM 15th May 1959; Chester Aug 1962 1app 0gls; Bangor City 29th Jul 1963; Oswestry Town Nov 1963; Caernarvon Town 15th Feb 1964; Nantlle Vale 3rd Aug 1965; Dolgellau & District 11th Sept 1965; Llandudno 24th Dec 1965; Pwllheli & District 22nd Jul 1966; Blaenau Ffestiniog 22nd Oct 1969; Barmouth & Dyffryn United 30th Dec 1971; Nantlle Vale 21st Nov 1974; Oswestry Town 1976/77;*
Honours; *North Wales Coast F.A.representative cap;*

Barry was a promising young footballer who played for Grove Park School and Wrexham & District Schoolboys. He was signed by Wrexham on schoolboy forms, and took his place in the club's 'Colts' team which involved playing for the Wrexham 'B' team in the Welsh National League. Upon leaving school Barry signed for Wrexham on amateur terms, progressing to the 'A' team in the Welsh League (North) and then to the reserves in the Cheshire County League, before he left Wrexham in 1958 to take up an offer from Bolton Wanderers. He spent a year at Burnden

Park before returning to the Racecourse, where he signed as a part-time professional in May 1959, combining football with work as a Water Board engineer. Wright played a few Cheshire County League games with the reserves before he was called up for his Football League debut at home to Port Vale in October 1959, replacing George Warburton at left-back in the 1-0 win. He kept his place in the side for the next seven League and Cup games before returning to reserve team football. Patience was then the name of the game, as he had to wait until January 1961 for his next opportunity, the delay being due to the consistent form of regular left-back, Aly McGowan. He added just two more appearances that season, while 1961/62 saw him manage just two outings in place of McGowan, who was a model of consistency as he helped the 'Robins' gain promotion to the Third Division. Barry had to be content with reserve team football for most of that season, at the end of which he was transferred to Chester. Again he found difficulty in breaking into the senior side, and didn't make his debut until December, when he stepped in to replace Colin Corbishley at half-back in a 1-0 home win over Gillingham. Despite this result it proved to be Wright's one and only first team game for Chester, who were eventually forced to apply for re-election. He left Sealand Road in the summer of 1963, dropping into non-league football with Bangor City. However, he was soon on the move again to Oswestry Town, where he had another short spell before linking up with Caernarvon Town. Barry then went on to spend the rest of his playing career in North Wales, turning out for a number of clubs that included Dolgellau & District, Nantlle Vale, Llandudno, Pwllheli & District, Blaenau Ffestiniog, Barmouth & Dyffryn United, and Oswestry Town (again). He returned to the Racecourse with Blaenau Ffestiniog, for a Welsh Cup match in January 1970, which saw Wrexham win by a solitary Ray Smith goal following a spirited performance by the visitors. Barry later managed Pwllheli & District in the 1970s. In March 1970 he was a member (along with Steve McCreath) of the North Wales Coast F.A. XI who defeated the scots on their own soil at Pittodrie (Home of Aberdeen) 4-3. He is now settled in the Wrexham area where he has become a very competent golfer winning many trophies.

Season	League		F.A.Cup		Welsh Cup		League Cup		Total	
	apps	gls	apps	gls	apps	gls	apps	gls	apps	gls
1959/60	6	0	2	0	-	-	-	-	8	0
1960/61	3	0	-	-	-	-	-	-	3	0
1961/62	2	0	-	-	-	-	-	-	2	0
	11	**0**	**2**	**0**	**-**	**-**	**-**	**-**	**13**	**0**

WRIGHT, Darren James

1986 - 1991

Position; *Left-Back*
D.O.B; *14th March, 1968*
Birthplace; *West Bromwich, West Midlands*
Height; *5ft 10in* ***Weight;*** *11st 4lbs*
Debut; v. *F.C.Zurrieq (a) 1st October, 1986 (E.C.W.C.)*
Total Appearances & Goals; *138/10 apps 9 gls*
Career; *Wolves Jul 1985; WREXHAM Jul 1986; Worcester City cs1991; Willenhall Town cs1992; Atherstone United Mar 1995; Cheltenham Town Oct 1995 £750 17/8apps 0gls; Stafford Rangers Jul 1998; Halesowen Town Jun 1999;*
Honours; *Welsh Cup runner-up 1988; England Semi-Professional International cap;*

Darren Wright was spotted playing for his local youth side in the West Bromwich League by Wolverhampton Wanderers. Having successfully completed his trial spell at Molineux he signed apprentice forms for the club, who were managed by Tommy Docherty at that time. Darren was still an apprentice when he made his Football League debut in a 3-1 defeat at Plymouth Argyle in September 1985. However, that proved to be his only game for Wolves as he was released in the summer of 1986 without being offered professional terms. Frank Upton, who was Wolves coach at that time, recommended Wright to Wrexham manager Dixie McNeil, who heeded the advice and signed the young full-back in July 1986. He found himself deployed mainly as a stand-in during his first season at the Racecourse, but he was to make his first team debut for the club in October 1986 when he came on as a substitute for Shaun Cunnington in a European Cup-Winners' Cup first round match against F.C.Zurrieq in Malta. His League debut followed shortly afterwards in a 4-2 win at Orient, though it was not until the following season that Darren established himself as a regular in the left-back position, particularly after Shaun Cunnington's transfer to Grimsby Town. He ended that season with a Welsh Cup runners'-up medal, as Wrexham lost 2-0 to Cardiff City in the Final at Swansea, and helped the 'Robins' reach the Third Division Play-off Final a year later against Leyton Orient. He had scored against Scunthorpe United in the semi-final, though Wrexham were to lose the final 2-1 on aggregate. The following season found Wright struggling with injury, which led him to miss the 1990 Welsh Cup Final against Hereford United in Cardiff's National Stadium. That summer Darren underwent an operation to remove a cyst, during which it was found that he had a torn cartilage. He then spent most of the following season in the treatment room, though he did make a second-half substitute appearance for Graham Cooper in the European Cup-Winners' Cup match in Lyngby, which Wrexham won 1-0. Darren worked hard regain his fitness, but he was reluctantly released by Wrexham at the age of 23 at the end of 1991, having failed in his bid to recover sufficiently to meet the demands of League football. Undeterred, and wanting to remain in the game, Wright joined Beazer Homes Premier Division side Worcester City, where he spent a year before joining West Midland League side Willenhall Town as player/coach in the close season of 1992. He enjoyed almost three years with

Willenhall, working under Chris Robinson, who he later followed to Atherstone United in March 1995. He remained with them until October 1995, when Robinson, who had earlier been appointed manager of Cheltenham Town, returned to his old club to sign Darren for a £750 fee. Robinson described him at that time as his 'on-the-pitch lieutenant', who he signed for his 'experience and good passing ability'. At Cheltenham Darren played his part in the club's promotion to the Conference League in 1997, where they ended their first season as runners-up to Halifax Town. They also reached the Fourth Round of the F.A.Cup, and the F.A.Trophy Final at Wembley, where they beat Southport 1-0, although Darren missed out on a final place. In the close season of 1998 he left Whaddon Road to join Stafford Rangers, where he spent a year before joining Halesowen Town in the summer of 1999. After he had finished playing full time professional football, Darren took up employment as a security guard.

Season	League		F.A.Cup		Welsh Cup		League Cup		F.R.T.		E.C.W.C.		Total	
	apps	gls	apps	gls	apps	gls	apps	gls	apps	gls	apps	gls	apps	gls
1986/87	13/1	0	-	-	1	0	0/1	0	3/1	1	0/1	0	17/4	1
1987/88	31/4	0	2	0	6	1	-	-	1/1	1	-	-	40/5	2
1988/89	37	2	2	0	3	2	2	0	4	0	-	-	52*	5*
1989/90	24	1	-	-	3	0	1	0	1	0	-	-	29	1
1990/91	-	-	-	-	-	-	-	-	-	-	0/1	0	0/1	0
	105/5	**3**	**4**	**0**	**13**	**3**	**3/1**	**0**	**9/2**	**2**	**0/2**	**0**	**138/10***	**9***

* = Includes 4apps & 1gls in Play-Off matches.

WRIGHT, Edgar

1931

Position; *Outside-Left*
D.O.B; *J/A/S 1910*
Birthplace; *Oakenholt, Flintshire*
Height; *ft in* ***Weight;*** *st lbs*
Debut; v. *Halifax Town (h) 31st January, 1931*
Total Appearances & Goals; *2 apps 0 gls*
Career; *Oakenholt; WREXHAM Jan 1931; Connah's Quay & Shotton cs1931;*

Edgar Wright was signed by Wrexham on amateur forms from Oakenholt FC, near Flint, in January 1931. He completed his first match for the club that same month in a reserve fixture against Flint Town, the game ending in a 2-1 win for Wrexham. Playing in his usual outside-left position Edgar was described as being the 'most convincing forward on the field'. Towards the end of the month he was given his Football League debut replacing Tommy Lewis at outside-left in a 3-2 home win over Halifax Town, a game in which he was said to have 'inspired hope in his skill to put the ball over in the centre'. He kept his place for the following match, a 2-2 home draw with Tranmere Rovers, but it proved to be his last first team appearance for the 'Robins' before he was allowed to leave the club at the end of the season. In the summer of 1931 he signed for Connah's Quay & Shotton.

Season	League		F.A.Cup		Welsh Cup		Total	
	apps	gls	apps	gls	apps	gls	apps	gls
1930/31	2	0	-	-	-	-	2	0
	2	**0**	**-**	**-**	**-**	**-**	**2**	**0**

WRIGHT, Stephen Peter
1983 - 1985

Position; *Defender*
D.O.B; *16th June, 1959*
Birthplace; *Clacton-on-Sea, Essex*
Height; *6ft 0in* **Weight;** *11st 0lbs*
Debut; v. *Bristol City (h) 16th September, 1983*
Total Appearances & Goals; *97 apps 1 gls*
Career; *Braintree Town; Colchester United Jun 1977 112/5apps 2gls; HJK Helsinki cs1981; Braintree Town Sept 1982; Lpafjard BK 1983; WREXHAM 14th Sept 1983; Torquay United Jul 1985 33apps 0gls; Crewe Alexandra Jul 1986 67/5apps 3gls; Rhyl cs1988; Chelmsford City cs1989; Wivenhoe Town Nov 1989; Clacton Town cs1993; Wivenhoe Town cs1995; Harwich & Parkeston Jul 1997;*
Honours; *Welsh Cup runner-up 1984; Vauxhall League Division One Championship Winner 1990; Eastern Counties League Championship Winner 1995;*

Steve Wright followed his father, Peter, into League football with Colchester United, where Wright senior had clocked up 245 appearances. Steve had left school to take up work as an upholsterer in Clacton, at the same time turning out for Colchester United reserves as a part-time player, but it wasn't long before the 'U's' moved to sign him on professional terms in June 1977. The following season saw him make his Football League debut, when he came on as a substitute in a 3-1 win at Carlisle in October 1977. Three more appearances that season followed before he became a regular in the side for the next two years, during which the 'U's reached the Fifth Round of the F.A.Cup in 1979, where they lost 1-0 at home to Manchester United. Steve contracted hepatitis during the summer of 1981 and it was December before he was able to return to first team action. He remained in the side until the end of the season, whereupon he was told that his services were no longer required at Layer Road. Wright then took up an offer to join Finnish League champions HJK Helsinki, for whom he played against Liverpool in a European Cup match. He later joined another Finnish club, Lpafjard BK, before returning home in the summer of 1983 to be handed a chance of returning to League football by his former Colchester boss Bobby Roberts, then manager at Wrexham. He went on to make his Football League debut for the 'Robins' in a 3-1 home win over Bristol City. 'Charlie', as he was more popularly known at Wrexham, became a first team fixture at the Racecourse for the next two seasons. He sampled European football, with that famous win over the Portuguese Cup winners F.C.Porto, followed by pitting his wits against the Italian giants of A.S.Roma, when he was described as having 'stood solid along with Jack Keay in keeping the talented A.S.Roma forwards at bay'. Despite having been a regular in the Wrexham side for two seasons Steve was allowed to leave the Racecourse by Dixie McNeil in the close season of 1985. He then joined David Webb's Torquay United, and made his debut in a 4-0 defeat at Scunthorpe United in the opening game of the 1985/86 season, one in which he played under three separate managers, and which ended with the 'Gulls' bottom of Division Four. He signed for Crewe Alexandra in the summer of 1986, where he made his debut in a 1-1 draw at Rochdale in the opening game of the 1986/87 season. Steve spent two years at Gresty Road, during which he made 72 League appearances and scored three goals before being released in the close season of 1988. He then returned to the Wrexham area, signing for Northern Premier League side Rhyl, while later taking over a public house in Acrefair, the Australia Arms. In 1989 Wright returned to Essex, where he took up a job with Britvic, continuing to play football for Chelmsford City for a short while before joining Wivenhoe Town in November 1989, and they won the Vauxhall League Division One title in his first season with them. He was appointed joint manager of Clacton Town in the close season of 1993, winning the Eastern Counties League championship in his second season with the club. A return to Wivenhoe Town in the close season of 1995 followed, where he spent two years until becoming joint manager of Dr.Marten's League First Division side Harwich & Parkeston in 1997. Steve is now employed as a district officer for a health care company. His son Jamie seems to be following in his grandfather's and dads footsteps, as the 9 year old is with Colchester United's School of Excellence.

Season	League		F.A.Cup		Welsh Cup		League Cup		F.R.T.		E.C.W.C.		Total	
	apps	gls	apps	gls	apps	gls	apps	gls	apps	gls	apps	gls	apps	gls
1983/84	37	0	1	0	7	0	-	-	1	0	-	-	46	0
1984/85	39	0	1	0	3	1	2	0	2	0	4	0	51	1
	76	**0**	**2**	**0**	**10**	**1**	**2**	**0**	**3**	**0**	**4**	**0**	**97**	**1**

WRIGHT, Thomas James
1999

Position; *Goalkeeper*
Birthplace; *Belfast*
D.O.B; *29th August, 1963*
Height; *6ft 1in* **Weight;** *14st 5lbs*
Debut; v. *Stoke City (a) 27th February, 1999.*
Total Appearances & Goals; *17 apps 0 gls*
Career; *Grange Rangers (Ballyclare); Brantwood (Belfast); Linfield Sept 1988; Newcastle United 27th Jan 1988 (Loan) & Mar 1988 £30,000 72/1apps 0gls; Hull City 14th Feb 1991 (Loan) 6apps 0gls; Nottingham Forest 24th Sept 1993 £450,000 11apps 0gls; Reading 4th Oct 1996 (Loan) 17apps 0gls; Manchester City 17th Jan 1997 (Loan) 5apps 0gls; Manchester City 3rd Mar 1997 £450,000 27apps 0gls; WREXHAM 25th Feb 1999 (Loan);*
Honours; *30 Northern Ireland international caps; One Northern Ireland Under-23 international cap; One Northern Ireland Under-21 international cap; First Division Championship Winner 1993; One Football League Representative cap 1993;*

As a youngster Tommy Wright was a proficient athlete being chosen for his country at the cross-country event, as well as becoming the All-Ireland champion from which he was offered a lucrative athletics scholarship in the United States. However, he chose to remain in Ireland and worked as a barman, although by this time he was also playing football on a regular basis. He had played for Grange Rangers in Ballyclare followed by a spell with Belfast side Brantwood from where he was signed up by Linfield in September 1988. Tommy played in the European Cup competition, but his time at Windsor Park was mostly spent as understudy to George Dunlop. Despite his time in Linfield reserves Wright did enough to bring him to the attention of Newcastle United who gave him the chance to prove his worth when he signed on loan for the 'Magpies' in January 1988. His stay at St.James' Park was extended when he was offered a full-time contract in March 1988, Linfield accepting £30,000 for their promising 'keeper. At St.James' Park Tommy found competition for a first team place coming from Dave Beasant, fellow Irishman Gary Kelly, and the ageing John Burridge. It was Beasant who Tommy replaced to make his Football League debut at Aston Villa in January 1989 in a 3-1 defeat, and this was followed by earning international recognition, when he made the first of his 30 caps for Northern Ireland in a 3-0 win over Malta at Windsor Park in May 1989. He was to regain the 'keepers position for the 1989/90 season before being sidelined through injury. A loan spell with Hull City in February 1991 was to see him bounce back to claim his place with the 'Magpies' for 1991/92, but he again suffered a further set-back through injury following a string of impressive performances. Pavel Srnicek was to take over in goal from Tommy as United won promotion to the Premier League the following year. The signing of another ex-Racecourse Robin, Mike Hooper, saw Tommy making just a fleeting appearance before Nottingham Forest manager, Frank Clark, paid out £450,000 for his services in September 1993. He made his debut for Forest debut in a 4-3 defeat at Bolton Wanderers having replaced Mark Crossley in goal. Tommy made nine further appearances for Forest that season as they won promotion to the Premier League, but his season was again disrupted by injury problems. He was to make just one further League appearance for Forest, although he did spend a three month loan spell with Reading during the 1996/97 season. At the end of that loan spell, he was taken on loan by Manchester City in January 1997, and after just five appearances his former manager at Forest, Frank Clark, re-signed him for £450,000. He again suffered with injury problems at the beginning of 1997/98, and when fit he found Martyn Margetson's form was to keep him out of the side. He did return to the side, but only to suffer a knee injury which finally ended his season, as City were to suffer relegation to the Second Division. The 1998/99 campaign saw Wrexham manager Brian Flynn requiring back-up for his only experienced goalkeeper Mark Cartwright, and it was to Wright that he turned, signing the highly experienced shot-stopper on loan in February 1999. 'Known for setting up attacks with quick throws and excellent long kicks', he made his debut for Wrexham in an impressive 3-1 win at Stoke City. Flynn was pleased with his performance, although Tommy was disappointed with not keeping a clean sheet. He went on to remain at the Racecourse on loan until the end of the season, helping to guide the 'Robins' to Second Division safety, although he missed the Welsh Premier Cup Final having been called back by Manchester City as cover for their Play-Off matches.

Season	League		F.A.Cup		W.P.C.		League Cup		A.W.S.		Total	
	apps	gls	apps	gls	apps	gls	apps	gls	apps	gls	apps	gls
1998/99	16	0	-	-	1	0	-	-	-	-	17	0
	16	**0**	-	-	**1**	**0**	-	-	-	-	**17**	**0**

WYLLIE, James

1950 - 1951

Position; *Inside-Forward*
D.O.B; *15th October, 1927*
Birthplace; *Saltcoats, Strathclyde*
Died; *Southport, 27th June 1992*
Height; *5ft 11in* ***Weight;*** *11st 3lbs*
Debut; v. *Bradford City (a) 2nd December, 1950*
Total Appearances & Goals; *22 apps 4 gls*
Career; *Ardeer Recreation c1942-1945; Bradford Park Avenue c1946 (Trial); Riccarton Bluebell c1948; Kilmarnock Dec 1948 1app 0gls; Southport 5th Jul 1950 15apps 1gls; WREXHAM 1st Dec 1950 £2,000; Kidderminster Harriers Jul 1951;*

James showed early promise as a footballer when he was selected to represent Ayrshire Schoolboys, and began playing football for Scottish Junior League side Ardeer Recreation during World War Two. Following the end of the conflict he took up the chance of joining Football League side Bradford Park Avenue, who were assembling players in readiness for the first season of the resumed Football League. Jimmy spent a month in Bradford before he returned home to Scotland to complete his time as a shipwright at Ardrossan. He continued playing football for Ardeer Recreation before linking up with another Scottish Junior League side, Riccarton Bluebell. It was whilst he was playing for them during the 1948/49 season that Scottish First Division side Kilmarnock signed him, but he was to make just one League appearance - against Dumbarton in March 1950 - when described as 'a good Kilmarnock reserve player, who gave a good account of himself'. Jimmy then moved south of the border to join Southport in July 1950, and his Football League debut came at right-half in the opening match of the 1950/51 season, a 1-0 home win over Carlisle United. However, Jimmy failed to maintain the early promise that he had shown, and by October he found himself out of favour. He left Haig Avenue to join Wrexham for a £2,000 fee in December 1950, having made just 15 League appearances for the 'Sandgrounders'. His stay in North Wales also proved to be short-lived following his debut at inside-left, replacing Eddie Beynon in a 5-3 defeat at Bradford City. Despite the result he kept his place until the end of April, when Beynon took over. Jimmy was described as 'a roving type of player, who covered a tremendous amount of ground during the course of a match, and was also not afraid of having a shot on goal' during his time at the Racecourse. He was released in the summer of 1951, but was then snapped up by Southern League side Kidderminster Harriers in July. He had spent over a season with Kidderminster when, during a 'derby' match with Worcester City on Boxing Day 1952, he suffered a broken leg, which effectively ended his playing career. Jimmy later returned to live in Scotland, where he worked as an assistant manager at Ardrossan shipyard until it closed in 1974. He was then employed by a Paisley engineering firm until he retired, whereupon he returned to settle in Southport, where he died in 1992.

Season	League		F.A.Cup		Welsh Cup		Total	
	apps	gls	apps	gls	apps	gls	apps	gls
1950/51	20	4	-	-	2	0	22	4
	20	**4**	-	-	**2**	**0**	**22**	**4**

WYNESS, William Dow

1934 - 1935

Position; *Centre-Forward*
D.O.B; *29th December, 1909*
Birthplace; *Monkwearmouth, Sunderland*
Died; *Sunderland, December 1998.*
Height; *5ft 8'1/2in* ***Weight;*** *11st 7lbs*
Debut; v. *Mansfield Town (h) 26th December, 1934*
Total Appearances & Goals; *2 apps 0 gls*
Career; *Hetton United; Southport Oct 1929 (trial); Hetton United; Crook Town cs1931; Aldershot Aug 1932; Blyth Spartans Jun 1933; Spennymoor United Oct 1933; WREXHAM 11th Jun 1934; Spennymoor United May 1935; Shrewsbury Town Jul 1935 36apps 19gls; Spennymoor United cs1936; South Shields cs1937; Sunderland Fire Brigade;*

Bill Wyness first played football at Stansfield Street and Thomas Street Schools in his native Sunderland, from where he also represented Sunderland Schoolboys. Eventually he began working at the shipyards as a heater for the riveters, though he continued to play football in his spare time for Hetton United. He was then offered the chance to join his elder brother George, who played League football for Chester, Rochdale, Gateshead and Notts County, for a trial at Southport in October 1929. However, his trial with the 'Sandgrounders' came to nothing, and he returned home to continue playing for Hetton United. In the close season of 1931 Wyness signed for North-Eastern League side Crook Town, who were a top non-league side in those days, causing many Cup upsets. It was in his first season with Crook that Bill helped them to another famous Cup victory, when they beat Third Division North side Stockport County 3-1. They then drew 0-0 at Aldershot before knocking them out of the competition 1-0 in the replay. Crook eventually lost 7-0 to First Division Leicester City at Filbert Street, in the Third Round. By that time Bill's prolific goalscoring had been noted by Third Division South side Aldershot, and he signed for the Recreation Ground side in the close season of 1932. He spent over twelve months with the 'Shots', although he failed to make a first team appearance, before returning home in the summer of 1933 to join Blyth Spartans. However, after a couple of months he signed for another North-Eastern League side, Spennymoor United. Once again the goals began to flow, tempting Third Division North side Wrexham to make a move for the prolific goalscorer in the close season of 1934. At first he found himself playing for the 'Robins' reserve team in the Birmingham & District League, where he continued to hit the target, though he was unable to make a breakthrough into the first team. In those days the club's centre and inside-forward positions were occupied by Archie Gardiner, George Snow, George Frewin, and Jack Fryer. Bill's patience finally paid off when he made his Football League debut on Boxing Day 1934, against Mansfield Town on the Racecourse. He played at inside-left, the position normally occupied by George Snow, who had been switched to centre-forward in place of the injured Archie Gardiner. Wrexham lost the game 3-1, and it proved to be Bill's one and only League appearance for Wrexham, although he did play in a Welsh Cup tie in March 1935, which Wrexham lost 6-0 at Swansea Town. He left the Racecourse at the end of the season, and returned home to rejoin Spennymoor United. However, the ink hadn't dried on the deal, when Birmingham & District League side Shrewsbury Town made an offer, which Spennymoor accepted before he had kicked a ball for them. He got off to a great start with the 'Shrews', scoring on his debut in a 6-1 win over Colwyn Bay. 19 goals in 36 League games followed that season, and he helped Shrewsbury reach the semi-finals of the Welsh Cup. At the end of the season Bill returned to the North-East, and to Spennymoor United once again. A year with them was followed by two seasons with South Shields before World War Two put a stop to his football career. After working in the shipyards Bill joined the Sunderland Fire Brigade on 22nd April 1940, serving with them throughout WW2 as Sunderland's industrial centre became a prime target for the enemy bombers. Wyness continued with the Fire Brigade after the conflict had ended, playing football in the local league and winning many trophies. He eventually retired from the Fire Brigade in 1964, when he was 55, upon which he was awarded both the Queen's Long Service and the Good Service Medals. Eight years later, he received a commendation for his 'courageous and resourceful conduct' in keeping a blaze in check at the Sunderland Telephone Exchange where he worked as a handyman. Bill who later suffered with Alzheimer's disease, died in Sunderland in December 1998. He was 88.

Season	League		F.A.Cup		Welsh Cup		Total	
	apps	gls	apps	gls	apps	gls	apps	gls
19934/35	1	0	-	-	1	0	2	0
	1	**0**	-	-	**1**	**0**	**2**	**0**

WYNN, Walter Ronald 1947 - 1956

Position; *Defender*
D.O.B; *2nd November, 1923.*
Birthplace; *Wrexham, Denbighshire*
Died; *Liverpool, 8th October, 1983.*
Height; *5ft 11in* **Weight;** *12st 6lbs*
Debut; v. *Barrow (a) 26th March, 1948.*
Total Appearances & Goals; *182 apps 12 gls*
Career; *Chester 1946 0apps; WREXHAM (Am) Dec 1947, (Pro) 22nd Apr 1948; Winsford United Jul 1956; Holywell Town 12th Jun 1957 to May 1961;*
Honours; *Welsh Cup runner-up 1950;*

Ron Wynn showed plenty of promise as a youngster, representing his school as well as Wrexham & District Schoolboys. Within weeks of his leaving school World War Two had begun, but Ron was too young to be enlisted at that time, and he had to wait two years before joining the Royal Navy. It was during this period that Ron played football in America for West New York, when his ship was docked in New York harbour whilst on protection duty in the Atlantic. After WW2 had ended Ronnie was signed by Chester, but he failed to make a first team appearance and was later released. Despite that setback, the former Aston Villa player Tom Gardner, who was playing for Wrexham at the time, recommended him to Racecourse manager Tom Williams, and he signed Ron as an amateur in December 1947. He played at centre-forward for the reserves at first, but was later switched to play at left-back, and it was in this position that he went on to impress sufficiently to be handed his Football League debut in a 1-1 draw at Barrow in March 1948. Ron signed professional terms the following month, yet in spite of some impressive performances it was not until the 1950/51 season that he became regarded as a first team regular. He went on to remain at the Racecourse until the end of the 1955/56 season, by which time he had shown his versatility by playing in around eight different positions!! He was best known as a 'wholehearted, hard-tackling, no-nonsense centre-back, but whatever shirt he wore, he would always give nothing less than his best'. It was also said that he was, 'hard as nails on the park, a tough determined performer- but not dirty'. Ron collected a Welsh Cup runner's-up medal with Wrexham in 1950, after losing 4-1 to Swansea Town in the Final at Ninian Park, Cardiff. He also played a big part in the club's epic Third Round F.A.Cup tie against First Division Stoke City in January 1953, which Wrexham narrowly lost 2-1. In April 1953, Ron was awarded a Benefit match for his loyal service, and it was Stoke City who sent a team in appreciation of Wrexham's efforts in that F.A.Cup encounter. However, there was no disputing the result of this meeting, as Wrexham lost 6-1! Wynn left the Racecourse during the summer of 1956, and joined Cheshire County League side Winsford United. A season with them was followed by a move to Welsh League side Holywell Town in June 1957. Ron played out his career with Holywell announcing his retirement in 1961. He then worked for a local Butchers in Wrexham, before obtaining employment with the Wrexham Lager Beer Company, whom he served for 15 years. It was later said of Ronnie that he was a 'Great Character, the sort that seems to be lacking from the game nowadays', and 'off the field he was as jovial a companion as one could have wished to meet, always quick witted and ready for a laugh. He was the life and soul of the party'. He was certainly one of the great characters of Wrexham Football Club.

Season	League		F.A.Cup		Welsh Cup		Total	
	apps	gls	apps	gls	apps	gls	apps	gls
1947/48	8	0	-	-	-	-	8	0
1948/49	6	0	-	-	-	-	6	0
1949/50	38	9	3	0	4	3	45	12
1950/51	10	1	-	-	-	-	10	1
1951/52	15	0	-	-	2	0	17	0
1952/53	26	0	3	0	1	0	30	0
1953/54	24	0	1	0	2	0	27	0
1954/55	27	2	-	-	4	0	31	2
1955/56	28	0	1	0	1	0	30	0
	182	**12**	**8**	**0**	**14**	**3**	**204**	**15**

WYNNE, George 1929 - 1930

Position; *Outside-Left*
D.O.B; *3rd May, 1910*
Birthplace; *Wrexham, Denbighshire*
Died; *Wrexham, 26th October, 1991.*
Height; *5ft 6in* **Weight;** *10st 7lbs*
Debut; v. *York City (h) 11th September, 1929*
Total Appearances & Goals; *9 apps 1 gls*
Career; *Flint Town 10th Jul 1928; Oak Alyn Rovers 7th Dec 1928; WREXHAM 28th Aug 1929; Colwyn Bay 17th Dec, 1948; Denbigh Town 7th Nov 1949 to May 1950;*

George Wynne joined Wrexham from local side Oak Alyn Rovers in the close season of 1929, having previously played for Flint Town. A month after signing for the Racecourse club, George was given his first team chance when he was called up to replace John Ascroft at outside-left for the home game with York City in September 1929. It proved to be a memorable occasion for him, as he scored the 'Robins' goal in a 1-1 draw. He kept his place in the side for the next game, a 2-0 home defeat by Port Vale, before being replaced by Ascroft. George went on to add six more League appearances for Wrexham that season, while his final appearance came in a Welsh Cup semi-final, 2-0 defeat by Cardiff City, on the Racecourse in April 1930. Wynne was then allowed to leave Wrexham at the end of the season. His career details are somewhat vague from this point, though it is known that he did resume playing football after World War Two, for Colwyn Bay and then Denbigh United. He later settled in the village of Caergwrle, near Wrexham. George Wynne passed away at Wrexham Maelor Hospital in 1991, aged 81.

Season	League		F.A.Cup		Welsh Cup		Total	
	apps	gls	apps	gls	apps	gls	apps	gls
1929/30	8	1	-	-	1	0	9	1
	8	**1**	**-**	**-**	**1**	**0**	**9**	**1**

YATES, Richard 1947 - 1948

Position; *Centre-Forward*
D.O.B; *6th June, 1921*
Birthplace; *Queensferry, Flintshire*
Died; *Deeside, J/A/S 1976*
Height; *5ft 11in* **Weight;** *11st 10lbs*
Debut; v. *Halifax Town (h), 20th December, 1947.*
Total Appearances & Goals; *34 apps 22 gls*
Career; *Wolves; Chester 23rd Aug 1939 (War time) 132apps 114gls; Tranmere Rovers (WW2 Guest) 1939/40 2apps 2gls WREXHAM (WW2 Guest) 1941 2apps 1gls; Charlton Athletic (WW2 Guest) 1944/45 2apps 1gls; Port Vale (WW2 Guest) 1944/45 1app 0gls; Reading (WW2 Guest) 1944/45 9apps 4gls; Bury (WW2 Guest) 1945/46 2apps 1gls; Rochdale (WW2 Guest) 1945/46 1app 0gls; Chester 52 apps 37 gls; WREXHAM 19th Dec 1947; Carlisle United 5th Nov 1948 16apps 9gls; New Brighton 10th Aug 1949 43apps 14gls; South Liverpool 9th December 1950; Flint Town United 14th Aug 1951; Colwyn Bay 31st Jan 1953; Bethesda Athletic 14th Mar 1953; Connah's Quay Albion 12th Oct 1953;*
Honours; *Welsh Cup Winner 1947; Welsh Schoolboy international cap;*

Dick Yates shone as a schoolboy footballer in Queensferry, and at the age of 14 was capped for Wales against Ireland, scoring three goals in the 4-0 win. Not long after this he was snapped up on amateur forms by Wolverhampton Wanderers, who were managed by Major Frank Buckley. At 15 he signed on the ground staff at Molineux, along with Billy Wright, Jimmy Mullen, and Dicky Dorsett. Dick stayed with Wolves for three years without making a first team appearance, and in August 1939 he moved nearer home when he signed for Third Division North side Chester. However, WW2 interrupted Dick's footballing career at Sealand Road, and he joined the R.A.F.. During his time in the Forces he turned out as a 'guest' player for several clubs, including Reading, Charlton, Port Vale, Bury, and Wrexham. It was whilst he was with Reading that Dick played against Arsenal at Highbury in front of a 45,000 crowd, and scored by out-jumping England international Bernard Joy. During WW2 Dick scored a total of 114 goals in 132 matches for Chester; they included 11 hat-tricks, and five goals in one match - a 6-1 win against New Brighton on Christmas Day 1941. At the end of the conflict Dick returned to play for Chester in one of their most successful sides. He made his Football League debut in the opening game of the 1946/47 season in a 4-4 draw at York, and though he was not on the score sheet that day went on to grab 36 League goals in just forty games that season. It was the sort of form that persuaded Sheffield Wednesday to enquire about him and two of his team mates, Tommy Burden and Tommy Astbury. Dick left Sealand Road in December 1948, having failed to reproduce his goalscoring exploits that season, and joined Wrexham for a four figure fee. He made an immediate impact at the Racecourse, by scoring a hat-trick on his debut in a 6-3 win against Halifax, contributing a number of important goals as Wrexham reached a very creditable third place in the Third Division North. Dick played ten games at the beginning of the following season, but by October had lost his place in the side to new signing Jack Boothway, and in November was allowed to leave the Racecourse. He then joined Carlisle United, again scoring on his debut in a 3-1 home win over Mansfield Town. He remained with the 'Cumbrians' until the end of the 1948/49 season, when he was allowed to return nearer home and join New Brighton. Dick was a 'Rakers' regular throughout that season, notching thirteen goals from 38 League games, including New Brighton's first hat-trick for two years against his former club, Carlisle. The following season saw Dick make just five appearances in what proved to be New Brighton's last ever in the Football League, although he left in December 1950 to join South Liverpool. Yates later went on to play for Flint Town United, Colwyn Bay, Bethesda Athletic, and Connah's Quay Albion. During his playing career he was described as 'a natural centre-forward with all the desired physical attributes, a powerful shot in either foot and great aerial ability in out jumping most defences', and as 'an even-time sprinter, who liked the long low through ball down the middle to enable him to use his speed to outpace the opposing defence.' Dick, who continued to live in the Queensferry area working as a pump attendant at John Summers steelworks in Shotton, passed away in 1976 at the age of 55.

Season	League		F.A.Cup		Welsh Cup		Total	
	apps	gls	apps	gls	apps	gls	apps	gls
1947/48	21	13	-	-	3	4	24	17
1948/49	10	5	-	-	-	-	10	5
	31	**18**	**-**	**-**	**3**	**4**	**34**	**22**

***YOUDS,* Edward Paul** 1990

Position; *Centre-Half*
D.O.B; *3rd May, 1970*
Birthplace; *Liverpool, Merseyside*
Height; *6ft 1in* ***Weight;*** *13st 3lbs*
Debut; v. *Hereford United (h) 10th February, 1990*
Total Appearances & Goals; *20 apps 2 gls*
Career; *Everton 10th June 1988 5/3apps 0gls; Cardiff City 29th Dec 1989 0/1app 0gls (Loan); WREXHAM 8th Feb 1990 (Loan); Ipswich Town 15th Nov 1991 £250,000 38/12apps 1gls; Bradford City 20th Dec 1994 (Loan), 17th Mar 1995 £150,000 85apps 8gls; Charlton Athletic 24th Mar 1998 £550,000 29/1apps 2gls;*
Honours; *First Division Play-Off Winner 1998;*

Eddie Youds came to the attention of the Everton scouts during his schooldays, and having joined the Goodison Park club straight from school went on to make his way through the junior ranks to sign professional in June 1988. He then progressed to regular Central League football for Everton's reserve side, before taking the opportunity to broaden his experience by going out on loan to Cardiff City in December 1989. His Football League debut came with the 'Bluebirds', as a substitute for Gareth Abraham in a 3-1 defeat at Bolton, though it proved to be his only appearance for Cardiff as he spent the rest of the time kicking his heels on the sub's bench. He returned to Everton when the month was over, but was soon heading for the Principality again when Wrexham manager Brian Flynn persuaded him to accept another loan spell. Wrexham were struggling to escape relegation to the Conference League at the time, and Eddie had been called upon to shore up the defence. He was plunged straight into the first team at centre-half against Hereford, when Joey Jones was suspended, and he remained in that position for the rest of the season, stabilising the defence and playing a major part in helping the club to avoid relegation. It was a contribution recognised by the presentation of a number of awards from various groups of the club's grateful fans. At the end of the season Eddie returned to Everton, for whom he went on to make his debut in a blue shirt as a substitute in a 1-0 defeat at Norwich in December 1990. His full debut came in the following game, a 1-0 home against Aston Villa, adding another six appearances before the end of the season. Youds had made just two League Cup appearances by the November of the following season, when Ipswich Town paid £250,000 to take him to Portman Road, but was to make just one League appearance for the Suffolk club, at Derby in a 1-0 defeat, as they went on to win the Second Division championship. The following season Ipswich become founder members of the newly-formed Premier League, and Eddie made a total of sixteen League appearances, while 93/94 saw him become a regular member of the Ipswich team. The following year found him struggling to maintain a regular first team place, and in December 1994 he took up an offer to join Bradford City on loan, making his debut in a 3-1 defeat at Rotherham on Boxing Day. Eddie remained at Valley Parade until March 1995, when he returned to Ipswich, but within a few days of his return to Portman Road Bradford City had agreed to pay £150,000 for his services. It was the following season that Youds was to play his part in the 'Bantams' reaching Wembley in the Final of the Second Division play-offs, where they beat Notts County 2-0. Youds was described at this time as a 'very strong and robust utility player, playing for Bradford at full-back, centre-half and in midfield where he created a good impression'. However, he was to miss all of 1996/97 through injury, before returning to action the following campaign. He continued to make a good impression, and in March 1998 was signed by promotion-chasing Charlton Athletic to strengthen their push for promotion, which was achieved by way of winning the First Division play-off final, where they beat Sunderland 7-6 on penalties after a 4-4 draw in one of the most exciting matches ever seen at Wembley Stadium. He became an important member of the Valley set-up in their bid to remain in the top flight.

Season	League		F.A.Cup		Welsh Cup		League Cup		F.R.T.		Total	
	apps	gls	apps	gls	apps	gls	apps	gls	apps	gls	apps	gls
1989/90	20	2	-	-	-	-	-	-	-	-	20	2
	20	**2**	**-**	**-**	**-**	**-**	**-**	**-**	**-**	**-**	**20**	**2**

ADDITIONS

BARRETT, Paul David 1999 -

Position; *Midfield*
Birthplace; *Newcastle-upon-Tyne,*
D.O.B; *13th April, 1978*
Height; *5ft 10'1/2in* ***Weight;*** *11st 4lbs*
Debut v. *Millwall (a) 27th March 1999*
Total Appearances & Goals; *10/2 apps 0 gls*
Career; *Newcastle United 20th Jun 1996 (Pro); WREXHAM 23rd Mar 1999;*
Honours; *England Youth International; Pontins League Division Three Championship Winner 1998; Pontins League Division Two Championship Winner 1999; Northern Intermediate League Championship Winner 1996;*

Newcastle born and bred, Paul Barrett played his early football for Moorside Comprehensive and Rutherford High Schools in the west end of the city, and it was during this time that he also played for Boys club's Montague B.C. and Walker Central B.C. with whom he won many trophies with both teams. It was during his education that he was also chosen to play for the City schoolboys side as well as Northumberland, before selection for the England Schoolboys team. Despite not winning a cap at this level Paul had began to attract the attention of many Premier and Football League sides. An offer to join the National School of Excellence at Lilleshall saw him turn down the chance, having received an offer to sign schoolboy forms with Newcastle United. This was followed in June 1998 by the offer of a two year YTS contract during which time he played in European Tournaments with Newcastle, as well as representing England at youth level against Scotland at Motherwell's Fir Park ground and at Yeovil's Huish Park. He won a Northern Intermediate League Championship medal in 1996, which was followed in the summer with Kevin Keegan offering him professional terms with the 'Magpies'. Paul then progressed enough to be selected for the substitute's bench for the UEFA Cup match with Metz in December 1996, which they won 2-0 (3-1 on aggregate), while he travelled as a squad member for the next round in Monaco. Despite hitting the fringe of the first team squad, Paul found it difficult to break into the first team with the club opting to sign a string of foreign stars. He won a Pontins League Division Three championship medal with the reserves in 1997/98, while the following season gained a Second Division championship medal. However, before that campaign had finished Barrett was given the chance of first team football with Wrexham, agreeing to sign a three year contract with the 'Robins' just before the transfer deadline in March 1999. He made his Football League debut as a substitute at Millwall, and soon earned himself a regular place in the 'Robins' midfield for the rest of the campaign. Paul is a very talented prospect, and one who has a bright future in the game.

Season	League		F.A.Cup		W.P.C.		League Cup		A.W.S.		Total	
	apps	gls	apps	gls	apps	gls	apps	gls	app	gls	app	gls
1998/99	8/2	0	-	-	2	0	-	-	-	-	10/2	0
	8/2	**0**	**-**	**-**	**2**	**0**	**-**	**-**	**-**	**-**	**10/2**	**0**

DEARDEN, Kevin Charles 1999 -

Position; *Goalkeeper*
Birthplace; *Luton, Bedfordshire*
D.O.B; *8th March, 1970*
Height; *5ft 11in* ***Weight;*** *13st 12lbs*
Debut v.
Total Appearances & Goals; ** apps * gls*
Career; *Tottenham Hotspur 5th Aug 1988 0/1apps 0gls; Cambridge United 9th Mar 1989 (Loan) 15apps 0gls; Hartlepool United 31st Aug 1989 (Loan) 10apps 0gls; Oxford United 1989/90 (Loan) 0apps; Swindon Town 23rd Mar 1990 (Loan) 1app 0gls; Peterborough United 24th Aug 1990 (Loan) 7apps 0gls; Hull City 10th Jan 1991 (Loan) 3apps 0gls; Rochdale 16th Aug 1991 (Loan) 2apps 0gls; Birmingham City 19th Mar 1992 (Loan) 12apps 0gls; Brentford 30th Sept 1993 198apps 0gls; Barnet 5th Feb 1999 (Loan) 1app 0gls; Huddersfield Town Mar 1999 (Loan) 0apps; WREXHAM 1st Jun 1999;*
Honours; *Third Division runner-up 1995;*

Kevin Dearden was signed by Tottenham Hotspur straight from school in the summer of 1986. He progressed enough between the sticks to sign professional terms with 'Spurs' in August 1988. With Norwegian Erik Thorstvedt the club's number one choice in goal, and Bobby Mimms as his understudy, Kevin still had some way to go before he was to figure in the first team. In March 1989 he was given the chance to enhance his experience. A number of loan moves followed, beginning with Fourth Division Cambridge United because of an injury to another former 'Robin' John Vaughan. Kevin made his Football League debut in a 3-0 win at Exeter, and went on to remain in the 'U's' goal until the end of that season. The new campaign saw Kevin accept another loan spell, this time with Hartlepool United, but this time it was not to be a happy time for him as he was twice in ten League games on the wrong end of 6-0 defeats! That loan spell ended in October, and he returned to White Hart Lane. A spell with Oxford as first team cover to Paul Kee saw him fail to make a first team appearance, but this was followed by another period with Swindon Town in March 1990. At the County Ground, Kevin stepped in to replace Fraser Digby for one game, a 2-1 win at Bournemouth before returning to 'Spurs'. 1990/91 saw Kevin once again called upon for a loan spell, this time with Peterborough United with whom he made his debut in the opening game of the season against Wrexham in a 0-0 draw on the Racecourse. Kevin made six further appearances for the 'Posh' before Paul Bradshaw took over. A spell with Hull City followed in January 1991, making his debut in a 1-0 home defeat to Sheffield Wednesday. Two further appearances were made before Tommy Wright was signed on a temporary basis from Newcastle United, later to play for Wrexham on loan. As for Kevin, he returned to White Hart Lane for the rest of that season, although the new campaign saw him join Rochdale on loan (by this time the 'Lone Ranger'), and play in the opening two League games of the season, a 1-1 draw with York and a 1-0 win over Lincoln - both at Spotland. He then remained with 'Spurs' until another spell came about in March with Birmingham City with whom he remained in goal until the end of the season, making twelve appearances. The 1992/93 season saw Ian Walker progress past Kevin and become understudy to the big Norwegian Thorstvedt. Despite this Kevin did make his one and only League appearance for 'Spurs' when he came on as a sub for Thorstvedt in a 1-1 draw at Chelsea in March 1993. Despite this Premier League appearance Dearden was allowed to leave White Hart Lane in September of the following season, accepting an offer to join the Third Division Brentford. Kevin stepped into the side to replace Dean Williams, and he remained as the 'Bees' number one choice 'keeper for the rest of the season. The following campaign saw him miss just three games as the West London club won promotion to the Second Division, with Kevin keeping an impressive 25 clean sheets. Described as an 'excellent shot-stopper', he will however always be remembered for a game at Bristol Rovers when he put the ball down for a 'Rovers' forward to dribble the ball into an empty net, as he heard a whistle, subsequently blamed on a spectator. The incident was later featured on 'Question of Sport'. Despite that set-back he remained a regular in goal for Brentford until the start of the 1998/99 season when he lost his place to Jason

Pearcy, which was followed with him being pushed to third in the queue with the signing of Andy Woodman from Northampton Town. In February he joined Barnet on loan, where he made just one appearance - a 5-2 defeat by Peterborough United. He was then signed by Huddersfield Town on loan to the end of the season as cover for Nico Vaesen, but failed to make a first team appearance. It was at the end of that campaign that Wrexham manager Brian Flynn stepped in to quickly snap up the experienced 'keeper on a two year contract.

ELLIOTT, Stuart Thomas 1999

Position; *Midfield*
Birthplace; *Willesden, London*
D.O.B; *27th August, 1977.*
Height; *5ft 9in* ***Weight;*** *12st 0lbs*
Debut v. *Wigan Athletic (h) 23rd March, 1999 (A.W.S. Northern Final)*
Total Appearances & Goals; *11/2 apps 0 gls*
Career; *Newcastle United 28th Aug 1995 0apps; Hull City 28th Feb 1997 (Loan) 3apps 0gls; Swindon Town 20th Feb 1998 (Loan) 1/1apps 0gls; Gillingham 23rd Oct 1998 (Loan) 4/1apps 0gls; Hartlepool United 29th Jan 1999 (Loan) 5apps 0gls; WREXHAM 22nd Mar 1999 (Loan);*
Honours; *Pontins League Division Three Championship Winner 1998; Pontins League Division Two Championship Winner 1999; Northern Intermediate League Championship Winner 1996; Welsh Premier Cup runner-up 1999;*

Stuart Elliott was regarded as an exciting prospect as a footballer from an early age. He played for his local junior club, Forest United in Kingsbury from the age of eight years-old until he was fifteen, and was only ten when he became attached to Arsenal with whom he remained until he was 15. He attended St.Mary's Secondary School in Hendon from where he was chosen to represent Barnet and Middlesex Schoolboys. It was whilst playing for his county side that Stuart was spotted by Newcastle scout Joe Vine, who recommended him to the Geordie club. Elliott was immediately invited for trials, and just two weeks later he signed YTS forms in July 1993. He made progress through the youth ranks at St.Jame's Park, and signed professional terms with the 'Magpies' in the summer of 1995. Kenny Dalglish took charge in January 1997, and in his first game against Southampton named Stuart as substitute although he never featured. Shortly after that game the 'tough abrasive defender' was loaned out to Hull City in February, and he made his Football League debut for the 'Tigers' at home to Northampton Town in a 1-1 draw which he capped by being sent-off in injury time!! He added two further League appearances before returning to Newcastle due to his suspension from the dismissal! Described as 'normally a centre-back, he has proved his versatility playing in a number of positions'. Stuart was appointed captain of the 'Magpies' second string for the 1997/98 season, though in February the opportunity of another loan spell materialised with First Division Swindon Town. He made an instant impression at the County Ground by scoring for the reserves, and was promptly promoted to the first team for his debut at home to Manchester City, but he could do little to prevent a 3-1 defeat. He was scheduled to stay with the Wiltshire club until the end of the season, but injury meant he returned to the north-east having added just one sub appearance. He recovered from that injury in time for the new campaign which saw Wrexham manager Brian Flynn make an £80,000 offer for the talented midfield/defender in October 1998. An agreement on terms was not forthcoming, and the Newcastle manager Ruud Gullit vetoed any chance of a loan deal. To add insult to Wrexham's disappointment, two days later Stuart was allowed to join Gillingham on loan. At Priestfield he made five League appearances before returning to Newcastle. At the end of January he joined Third Division Hartlepool United on a month's loan, with whom he also made five appearances in his month at the Victoria Ground. March 1999 saw Wrexham manager Brian Flynn finally get his man, when Stuart joined the 'Robins' on loan to the end of the season. He made his debut against Wigan Athletic in the second leg of the Autowindscreen Shield Northern Final. 2-0 down from the first leg, Wrexham gave a spirited performance which saw them go out fighting. Playing mainly as a midfield anchorman Stuart remained at the Racecourse until the end of the season, and helped Wrexham to reach the Welsh Premier Cup Final.

Season	League		F.A.Cup		W.P.C.		League Cup		A.W.S.		Total	
	apps	gls	apps	gls	apps	gls	apps	gls	app	gls	app	gls
1998/99	8/1	0	-	-	2/1	0	-	-	1	0	11/2	0
	8/1	**0**	-	-	**2/1**	**0**	-	-	**1**	**0**	**11/2**	**0**

LARKIN, Anthony Gerard 1975 - 1978

Position; *Centre-Half*
Birthplace; *Liverpool, Merseyside*
D.O.B; *12th January, 1956*
Height; *5ft 11in* ***Weight;*** *11st 12lbs*
Debut v. *Blyth Spartans (h) 13th May 1978 (Debenhams Cup Final)*
Total Appearances & Goals; *1/1 apps 0 gls*
Career; *WREXHAM 1st Jul 1975; Shrewsbury Town Jul 1978 54/1apps 0gls; Carlisle United Jul 1981 £7,000 47/2apps 2gls; Hereford United Mar 1983 28/7apps 2gls; Worcester City 1985; Dudley; Bridgnorth Town; Cinderford;*
Honours; *Third Division Championship Winner 1979; Welsh Cup Winner 1979; Third Division runner-up 1982; Debenhams Cup runner-up 1978;*

Included seperately due to only appearing in the first team in the 'friendly' Debenhams Cup Tournament. Tony Larkin represented the Liverpool Schoolboys side, and it was from here that he joined the ground staff at Everton. Despite his progress with the 'Toffeemen' he was allowed to leave Goodison Park in the summer of 1975. He was then offered the chance of professional football with Third Division Wrexham. During this time Tony, who played at centre-half for the 'Robins', found a first team place difficult to attain due to the consistency first of Eddie May, and then John Roberts. It wasn't until the end of the club's greatest ever season, 1977/78, that Tony was to feature in the first team. He was called into the side to replace Roberts and partner Wayne Cegielski in the centre of defence for the Debenhams Cup Final first leg with Blyth Spartans - the two teams that had gone the furthest in the F.A.Cup who did not have a bye to the Third round of that competition. The 'Robins' surprisingly lost 2-1 on the Racecourse to the north-east side, and in the second leg could only manage a 1-1 draw, with Tony coming on as a substitute for Steve Buxton. Despite these two appearances, Tony found himself released by the club in the summer, but he was soon to fix himself up with another club when he signed for Third Division Shrewsbury Town, managed by ex-'Robin' Graham Turner who Tony had met when he did his full F.A.coaching badge. It was with the 'Shrews' that Larkin was to make his Football League debut when he replaced Carlton Leonard at left-back in a 1-0 home win over Hull City towards the end of September. Tony went on to make a further 26 League appearances that season as the Gay Meadow club won the Third Division championship, reached the 6th round of the F.A.Cup, and won the Welsh Cup. Over the next two years Tony found himself in and out of the side, and at the end of the 1980/81 season he was allowed to leave the Shropshire club and join fellow Third Division side, Carlisle United. His first season with the 'Cumbrians' saw him gain further success when, playing alongside a 'Pop' Robson and a young Peter Beardsley, he helped the Brunton Park club to promotion, finishing the campaign as runners-up to Burnley on goal difference. The following season saw Tony turn out as a regular until Christmas when he lost his place in the side at centre-half to Dave Rushbury. By March Larkin was on the move when he signed for Hereford United, making debut in a 1-0 win at Hartlepool United. However, he couldn't help prevent the 'Bulls' from finishing 92nd in the Football League, and having to re-apply for election for the third time in four seasons. Over the next two years, Tony struggled to establish himself in the Hereford side after he suffered serious ligament damage in a clash with Mark Hateley who was

with Portsmouth at the time. Tony added just 25 appearances before leaving Edgar Street to become part-time with Worcester City. He undertook a teaching course at Hereford. He later turned out for Dudley, Bridgnorth, Cinderford, and spent three summers in America coaching and playing for Tulsa Roughnecks. Tony, who still lives in Hereford, has worked as a Leisure Co-ordinator and Mobility Instructor at the Royal National College for the Blind at Hereford. As part of his work there he has developed the 'Hoople' - a mobility aid for rough terrain which is comparable to the white stick used on normal ground. He also runs aerobic classes at the college, and was County F.A.coach for Hereford.

Season	League		F.A.Cup		Welsh Cup		League Cup		Debenhams Cup		Total	
	apps	gls	apps	gls	apps	gls	apps	gls	app	gls	app	gls
1977/78	-	-	-	-	-	-	-	-	1/1	0	1/1	0
	-	-	-	-	-	-	-	-	**1/1**	**0**	**1/1**	**0**

LOWE, David Anthony

1999 -

Position; *Forward*
Birthplace; *Liverpool, Merseyside*
D.O.B; *30th August, 1965*
Height; *5ft 10in* ***Weight;*** *11st 9lbs*
Debut v.
Total Appearances & Goals; ** apps * gls*
Career; *Wigan Athletic 1st Jun 1983 (Pro) 179/9apps 40gls; Ipswich Town 26th Jun 1987 £80,000 121/13apps 37gls; Port Vale 19th Mar 1992 (Loan) 8/1apps 2gls; Leicester City 13th Jul 1992 £250,000 68/26apps 22gls; Port Vale 18th Feb 1994 (Loan) 18/1apps 5gls; Wigan Athletic 28th Mar 1996 £125,000 85/22apps 26gls; WREXHAM 29th Jun 1999;*
Honours; *Freight Rover Trophy Winner 1985; Second Division Championship Winner 1992; Third Division Championship Winner 1997; Two England under-21 International caps; England Youth International cap;*

It was whilst playing schoolboy football in his native Liverpool that David Lowe was recommended by his school teacher to Wigan Athletic manager Harry McNally. He was immediately selected for the 'Latics' youth side, and after a week's training with the first team in which he kept scoring goals, he was offered an apprenticeship. It was still has an apprentice that David was to make his Football League debut, when Larry Lloyd was forced by injuries to play him in a 2-1 defeat at Reading in October 1982. He went on to earn international honours at youth level, and with Wigan he helped them reach the Freight Rover Trophy Final against Brentford at Wembley, scoring in the 3-1 win. After 221 League and Cup appearances for the Springfield Park club, he was signed by Ipswich Town for £80,000 in June 1987. David top scored in his first season with the Suffolk club, and earned under-21 honours with England, but he was to only play a peripheral role in their 1992 Second Division title success. A spell on loan with Second Division Port Vale in March 1992 saw him make nine League appearances and score two goals, though it wasn't enough to prevent Vale from being relegated. The summer of 1992 saw Leicester City manager Brian Little splash out £250,000 for his services, but he shattered his cheekbone in a pre-season friendly with Borussia Monchengladbach. He finally made his debut in a scoreless draw with Brentford as a substitute, soon becoming a regular with the 'Foxes'. However, he failed to make any impact at all in his second season at Filbert Street, and by February he accepted a further loan spell with Port Vale, with whom he remained until the end of the season, helping to aide the 'Valiants' promotion bid. He returned to Leicester in the summer, after the club had gained promotion to the Premier League following a 2-1 play-off win over Derby County. Dave featured 29 times in the Premier League that campaign, a season that was decidedly mixed: scoring and then being sent-off with Wimbledon's Vinnie Jones, and a week later coming on as sub against Spurs to score with a curled shot that was voted goal of the season by Leicester fan's. Described at Filbert Street as being 'a useful penalty-box predator who also likes to drag defensive cover wide, and plays well with his back to goal', David was to leave the 'Foxes' in March 1996, when he accepted a record transfer fee paid of £125,000 to rejoin Wigan Athletic. He then went on to help the 'Latics' win the Third Division title in 1997, and then finished the following season as their top scorer with 18 goals, as well as being voted the supporters 'Player of the Season'. 1998/99 saw David make just fifteen League appearances because of a lot of competition from some very expensive strikers. The 'Latics' reached the Second Division play-off's, and David participated in both legs of the play-off games against Manchester City, but failed to help Wigan reach the twin towers. Out of contract at the end of that season, David turned down an offer to remain on the coaching staff with the Lancashire club in order to continue playing. He accepted a two year contract with Wrexham, and manager Brian Flynn said on signing him, "David is an experienced striker, who has played at the highest level. He is a very, very good professional and very fit."

STEVENS, Ian David

1999 -

Position; *Forward*
Birthplace; *Malta*
D.O.B; *21st October, 1966*
Height; *5ft 10in* ***Weight;*** *12st 6lbs*
Debut v.
Total Appearances & Goals; ** apps * gls*
Career; *Preston North End 22nd Nov 1984 (Pro) 9/2apps 2gls; Lancaster City Aug 1986; Stockport County 27th Oct 1986 1/1apps 0gls; Lancaster City 27th Nov 1986; Bolton Wanderers 25th Mar 1987 26/21apps 7gls; Bury 3rd Jul 1991 100/10apps 38gls; Shrewsbury Town 11th Aug 1994 £20,000 94/17apps 37gls; Carlisle United 13th May 1997 £100,000 64/14apps 26gls; WREXHAM 30th Jun 1999;*
Honours; *Auto Windscreen Shield runner-up 1996;*

Ian Stevens signed for Preston North End on professional terms in November 1984 having spent two years as a trainee with the Deepdale club. He eventually made his Football League debut at York City in the last game of 1984/85, and celebrated by scoring the winning goal. Ian found it difficult to make the breakthrough into the first team with John Thomas and Gary Brazil preferred. He was to turn out in just ten further League games for the 'Lilywhites' before his release in the summer. He joined North West Counties League side Lancaster City in time for the new campaign, but by October he was given a further chance of professional football when he agreed non-contract terms with Stockport County. He immediately made his first team debut as substitute in a 1-0 defeat at Orient, but was to make just one more full appearance for 'County', a 3-1 defeat at Aldershot. He then rejoined Lancaster City where he was to remain until the following March, when he was snapped up by Bolton Wanderers. He was to spend just over four years at Burnden Park, though during that time he failed to command a regular first team place. He was given a free transfer in the summer of 1991, but was quickly snapped up by Third Division Bury. Ian became an instant success with the 'Shakers', finishing top scorer in his first two season's at Gigg Lane with 17 and 14 goals respectively. 1993/94 saw his goals dry up scoring just seven, and at the end of that campaign he was allowed to join Shrewsbury Town for £20,000. Described at this time as 'fast on the ball, and showing good control, he has a strong shot at distance and, despite a lack of height, good heading ability,' his first year at the Gay Meadow saw him fill in where required due to the 'Shrews' strike force of that time, Wayne Clarke and Dean Spink. 1995/96 saw him struggle to establish himself, but by the New Year he was a first team regular, scoring a hat-trick against Brighton and the winning goal against Bristol Rovers in the Southern Final of the Auto Windscreen Shield to earn the 'Shrews' a place at Wembley in the Final. However, a disappointing performance by the Shropshire club saw them lose 2-1 to Rotherham, but Ian picked himself up from that defeat to end the season as the club's leading scorer with twelve League goals. He again finished top scorer in 1996/97 with 17 League goals, and this was enough for Carlisle United to spend £100,000 for the out of contract goalscorer. His start at Brunton Park was disrupted by illness, and he didn't make his debut until October as a substitute at Burnley. His first goal for Carlisle was scored against Wrexham in a 2-2 draw in November, and despite his start with the 'Cumbrians' he was to go on and end the season as top scorer with 17 goals, which included a hat-trick against Bristol Rovers in January, the first hat-trick by a Carlisle player in the League since 1989, and the first at Brunton Park for over a decade. However, it wasn't enough to prevent them from relegation, and worse was to follow the next season when Carlisle were almost dumped out of the Football League, but thanks to on loan 'keeper Jimmy Glass scoring in the last minute to preserve their Football League status, and send Scarborough down. With Ian out of contract in the close season, he was quickly snapped up by Wrexham manager Brian Flynn, who described Stevens as an "experienced striker, and every time he played against us has caused us problems."

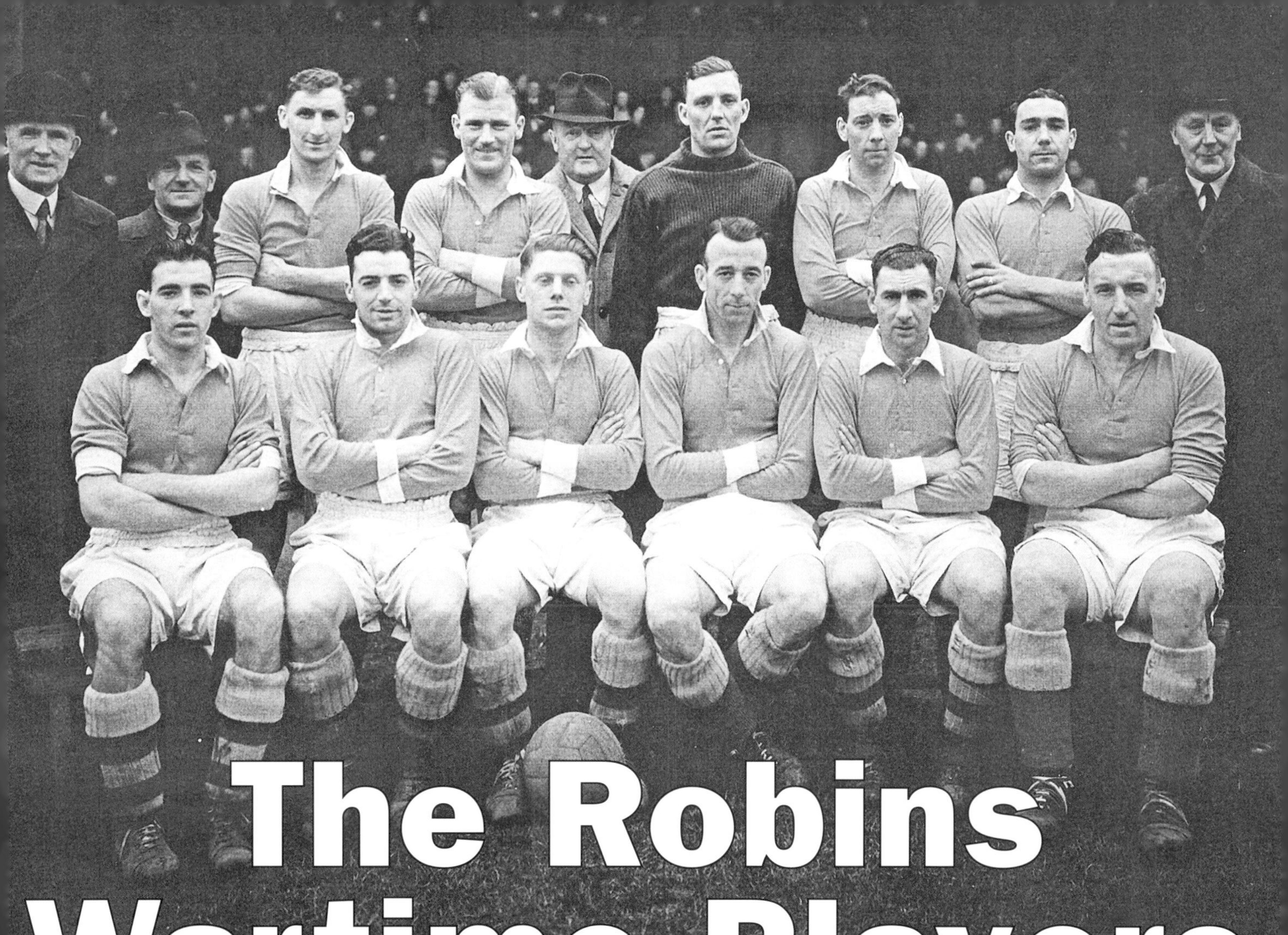

The Robins Wartime Players

The 1939/40 season was only three matches old when the British Government declared war on Adolf Hitler's Germany on 3rd September 1939. Any assembly of crowds was immediately banned until further notice, and this included all Football League games.

In October 1939 the Government decided that football should continue in some capacity as it was 'good for morale'. Friendly matches were introduced at first, and Wrexham played against Chester on the Racecourse, followed by a return match at Chester. Two games against Tranmere Rovers followed before football was reorganised into Regional Leagues. Wrexham were placed in the West Division, which included such teams as Chester and Tranmere Rovers, as well as Liverpool and Everton and the two Manchester clubs.

Unlike the First World War, when the club closed down from 1915 to 1919, the 'Robins' continued to operate throughout the conflict although it was a struggle at times; club Chairman Mr.John Hughes was on the verge of closing the club down at one point, though manager Mr.Tom Williams persuaded him to carry on.

The War period saw many players called up for the Forces and other services. Commitment to 'King and Country' took many players away from the area, though - by the same token - many were brought to the Racecourse. Due to travelling restrictions being placed it was almost impossible for clubs to field their own teams, so a 'guest player' system evolved where a club could draw upon the services of any player, registered or not, who could travel to its ground and back within the same day. There were no restrictions placed upon the number of 'guests' appearing in one match.

This period was to see many famous internationals turn out for Wrexham, as the club were in a key geographical position with a number of nearby military bases: Hightown Barracks in Wrexham; Horsley Hall in Marford; Kinmel Bay Camp at Rhyl; Nesscliffe Camp, near Oswestry; Park Hall Camp in Oswestry; RAF Tern Hill; and Dale Barracks in Chester - to name but a few.

Wrexham competed in the Football League Regional (West Division) for 1939/40, the Football League Regional (North Division) from 1940/41 until the end of 1944/45, while the club's last war-time season, 1945/46, found them in the Third Division North West League. The club also competed during this period in the League War Cup (1939-1946), the Welsh Cup (1939/40), the Lancashire Cup (1940/41 & 1945/46), and the F.A.Cup (1945/46).

These emergency competitions continued until life had returned to normal a year after the War had ended, in 1946.

This section gives brief biographical details of the 196 players who made appearances for Wrexham Association Football Club only in these war-time competitions. The war-time players who also made peace-time appearances are included in the main Racecourse Robins section.

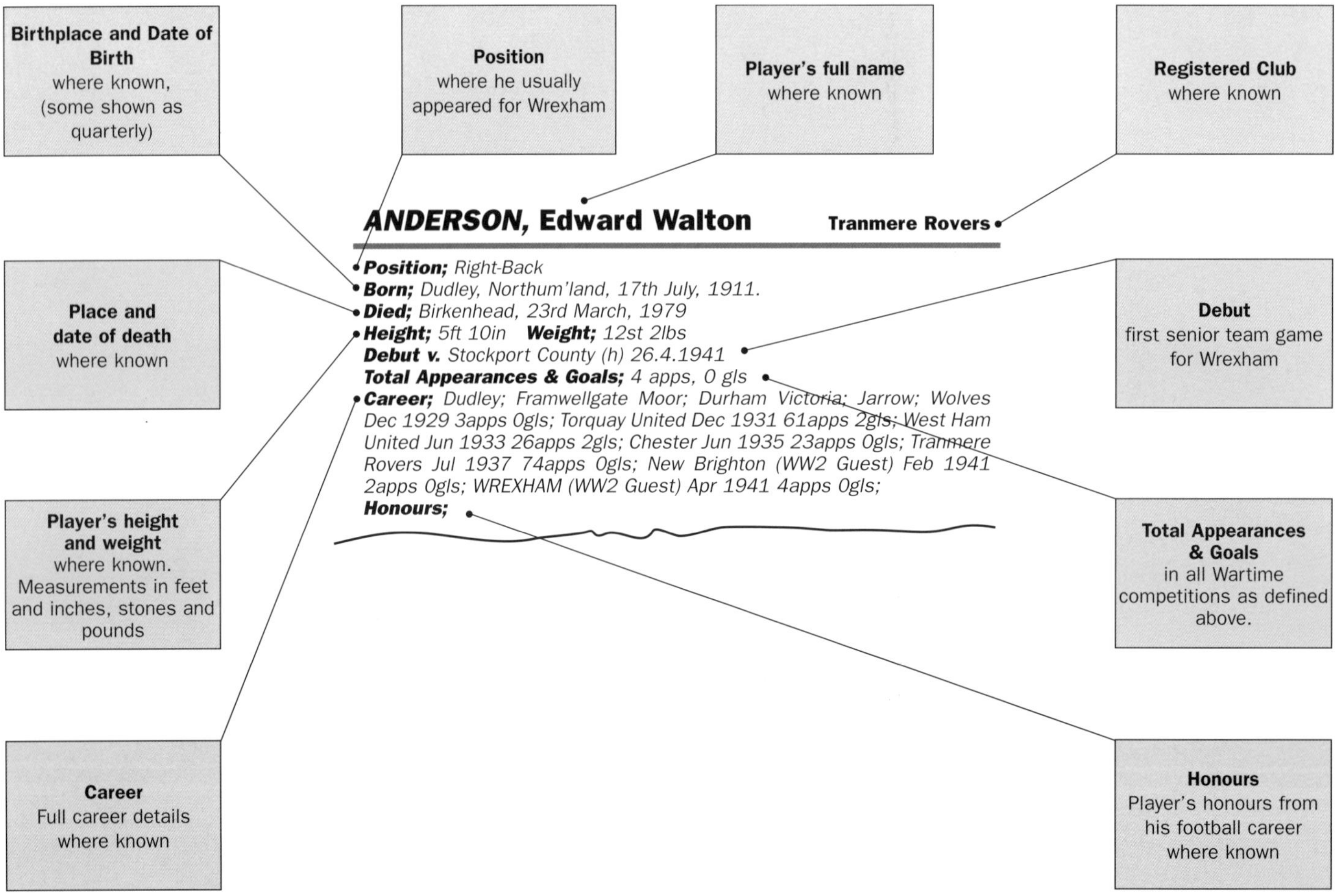

ANDERSON, A.J. — Third Lanark

Position: *Outside-Left*
Born;
Debut; v. *Chester (h) 22.3.1941*
Total Games: *4 apps, 1 gls*
Career: *Third Lanark; Tranmere Rovers (WW2 Guest) 1940/41 4apps 0gls; WREXHAM (WW2 Guest) Mar 1941 4apps 1gls; Everton (WW2 Guest) Sept 1941 41apps 8gls; Crewe Alexandra (WW2 Guest) 1942/3 12apps 3gls;*

A member of the now defunct Scottish League side Third Lanark prior to World War Two. He had appeared as a 'guest' for Tranmere Rovers before making his debut for Wrexham in a 5-2 home win over Chester in March 1941, scoring one of the 'Robins' goals. He added three more appearances for the club, also turning out as a 'guest' for both Everton and Crewe Alexandra.

ANDERSON, Edward Walton — Tranmere Rovers

Position; *Right-Back*
Born; *Dudley, Northum'land, 17th July, 1911.*
Died; *Birkenhead, 23rd March, 1979*
Height; *5ft 10in* ***Weight;*** *12st 2lbs*
Debut v. *Stockport County (h) 26.4.1941*
Total Appearances & Goals; *4 apps, 0 gls*
Career; *Dudley; Framwellgate Moor; Durham Victoria; Jarrow; Wolves Dec 1929 3apps 0gls; Torquay United Dec 1931 61apps 2gls; West Ham United Jun 1933 26apps 2gls; Chester Jun 1935 23apps 0gls; Tranmere Rovers Jul 1937 74apps 0gls; New Brighton (WW2 Guest) Feb 1941 2apps 0gls; WREXHAM (WW2 Guest) Apr 1941 4apps 0gls;*

A miner with big broad shoulders. He was coming to the end of his football career when World War Two broke out, having already appeared for Wolves, Torquay United, West Ham United, Chester, and Tranmere Rovers. He had previously turned out for New Brighton as a 'guest', making his first appearance for Wrexham in a 3-0 home win over Stockport County in April 1941. Three further appearances followed. After the end of WW2 he joined the coaching staff at Tranmere Rovers, later working in a similar capacity with Stockport County.

ANDERSON, J. Douglas

Position; *Right-Back*
Born; *Scotland*
Height: *5ft 11* ***Weight;*** *11st 4lbs*
Debut v. *Chester (h) 22.3.1941*
Total Appearances & Goals; *2 apps, 0 gls*
Career; *Aberdeen; Hibernian; Dundee United; Brentford (WW2) 1939/40 3apps 0gls; WREXHAM (WW2 Guest) Mar 1941 2apps 0gls; New Brighton Apr 1941 1app 0gls;*

Had played for Brentford in the first season of war-time football, and joined Wrexham in March 1941 when he made his debut in a 5-2 home win over Chester at right-back. He later played for New Brighton as a 'guest' player.

ANTONIO, George Rowlands — Stoke City

Position; *Inside-Forward*
Born; *Whitchurch, 20th November 1914.*
Died; *Oswestry, 2nd Jul 1997*
Height; *5ft 9 1/2in* ***Weight;*** *11st 5lbs*
Debut v. *New Brighton (a) 10.2.1940*
Career; *Oswestry Technical College; Oswestry Town; Stoke City Feb 1936 £200 84apps 13gls; WREXHAM (WW2 Guest) Feb 1940 6apps 2gls; Nottingham Forest (WW2 Guest) Mar 1940 9apps 3gls; York City (WW2 Guest) 1939/40 1app 0gls; Notts County (WW2 Guest) Sept 1942 24apps 7gls; Leeds United (WW2 Guest) 1943/44 10apps 5gls; Aldershot (WW2 Guest) 1943/44 18apps 7gls; Clapton Orient (WW2 Guest) 1944/45 2apps 0gls; Ipswich Town (WW2 Guest) 1945/46 3apps 0gls; Norwich City (WW2 Guest) 1945/46 2apps 2gls; Derby County Mar 1947 £5,000 18apps 2gls; Doncaster Rovers Oct 1948 £7,000 34apps 7gls; Mansfield Town Oct 1949 67apps 2gls; Oswestry Town Jul 1951 (Player/Manager); Wellington Town Jul 1954 (Player/Coach), Jan 1955 (Player/Manager); Stafford Rangers Sept 1957 (Player/Manager); Oswestry Town Jul 1958 (Player/Coach), Jun 1959 (Player/Manager); Berriew 1963 (Player/Manager);*
Honours; *Third Division North runner-up 1951;*

Christened George Rowlands, he added the surname of the Italian family who adopted him. A skilful and scheming inside-forward who had considerable experience with Stoke City and Derby County. He was with Stoke when WW2 began, whereupon he enlisted in the Army, appearing as a 'guest' for Nottingham Forest, Aldershot, York City, Notts County, Leeds United, Orient, Ipswich, Norwich, and Wrexham. He made six appearances for the 'Robins' during this period, his first in a 4-1 defeat at New Brighton in February 1940. After the hostilities had ended he resumed his football career with Stoke City, going on to play for Derby, Doncaster, and Mansfield, where he announced his retirement from the professional game. He later played for and managed a number of non-league sides: Oswestry Town, Wellington Town, Stafford Rangers, and Berriew before settling in Oswestry, where he passed away in July 1997, aged 82. He had been selected to play for Wales when he was at Stoke in 1937/38, until discovered to have been born on the wrong side of the border!

ARMITAGE, Lewis G. — Rotherham United

Position: *Forward*
Born; *Hull, 15th December 1921*
Height; *6ft 0in* ***Weight;*** *12st 0lbs*
Debut v. *Manchester City (a) 4.10.1941*
Total Games: *2 apps, 0 gls*
Career: *Rotherham United Dec 1940 6apps 2gls; WREXHAM (WW2 Guest) Oct 1941 2apps 0gls; Bristol City (WW2 Guest) 1942/43 1app 0gls; York City (WW2 Guest) 1945/46 2apps 0gls; Grimsby Town Jan 1948 8apps 2gls;*

Lewis Armitage joined Rotherham United during World War Two, signing for the Millmoor club in December 1940, before making his debut for Wrexham as a 'guest' in October 1941 in a 2-0 defeat at Manchester City. He added one more appearance for the 'Robins' in the following game, a 2-2 draw with New Brighton. Further outings as a 'guest' for both Bristol City and York City followed, before eventually returning to Rotherham United for the beginning of the new Football League season in 1946. Lewis made his debut in January 1947 in a 4-3 defeat at Darlington. He completed another fourteen appearances, scoring nine goals before he was transferred to Grimsby Town in January 1948 for a club record fee paid of £4,500. However, he was to make just eight League appearances, scoring two goals, in his short time with the 'Mariners' as he suffered an injury that was to end his career following a collision with the Manchester United goalkeeper. Regarded as a 'versatile forward, able to adapt to any position in the front line'.

ARMSTRONG, Matthew W. — Aberdeen

Position; *Centre-Forward*
Born; *Newton Stewart, Wigtownshire, 12th November 1911.*
Height; *5ft 8'1/2in* ***Weight;*** *10st 12lbs*
Debut v. *Blackpool (h) 31.3.1945*
Total Games: *9 apps, 7 gls*
Honours; *Three Scottish International caps; Three Scottish League Representative caps; Scottish Cup runner-up 1937;*
Port Glasgow Juniors; Aberdeen 191apps 137gls; Chelsea (WW2 Guest) 1939/40 1app 0gls; Clapton Orient (WW2 Guest) 1940/41 41apps 27gls; Brentford (WW2 Guest) 1942/43 3apps 1gls; West Bromwich Albion (WW2 Guest) Aug 1943 8apps 1gls; Walsall (WW2 Guest) Oct 1944 10apps 6gls; WREXHAM (WW2 Guest) Mar 1945 9apps 7gls; Chester (WW2 Guest) 1944/45 8apps 7gls; Accrington Stanley (WW2 Guest) 1944/45 2apps 2gls;

A Scottish international, who was a prolific goalscorer for Aberdeen before World War Two interrupted his football career. At Pittodrie he was said to have had a telepathic understanding with fellow Scottish cap, Willie Mills. Matt was to spend much of the WW2 period south of the border, where he appeared for many Football League sides as a 'guest'. He first played for Wrexham in March 1945, making his debut in a 2-2 home draw with Blackpool, and added eight more appearances for the 'Robins' in which he scored seven goals. Noted as a fine 'leader of the line'

ARTHUR, John — Everton

Position; *Outside-Right*
Born; *Edenfield, 14th December, 1917.*
Died; *Edenfield, 19th November, 1986.*
Height; *5ft 8in* **Weight;** *10st 6lbs*
Debut v. *Bradford City (a) 4.5.1946*
Total Appearances & Goals; *1 app, 1 goal*
Career; *Blackburn Rovers (Am) Mar 1936 0apps; Everton (Am) Aug 1936, (Pro) Sept 1936; 0apps; Stockport County May 1938 2apps 0gls; Everton Nov 1940 0apps, WW2 13apps 1gls; WREXHAM (WW2 Guest) May 1946 1app 1gls; Chester May 1946 24apps 3gls; Rochdale Apr 1947 170apps 25gls;*

Jackie Arthur began his career with Blackburn Rovers, but left Ewood Park without having made a first team appearance at the end of 1937/38. He then signed for Stockport County, making his Football League debut in a 2-1 home defeat by Rochdale in April 1939. One more League appearance followed before WW2 was to interrupt his playing career. He appeared as a 'guest' for both Everton and Wrexham during this period, and scored in his one and only war-time appearance for the 'Robins', a 4-2 defeat at Bradford City in May 1946. After the conflict Jackie continued his football career with Chester, before joining Rochdale almost a year later, where he made 170 League appearances. He retired from playing in 1953 and became a member of the training staff at Spotland. He was said to have 'modelled his play on Tom Finney.'

ASHTON, Roger William — Wrexham

Position; *Goalkeeper*
Born; *Llanidloes, 16th August, 1921.*
Died; *Neath, July 1985.*
Height; *5ft 9in* **Weight;** *12st 0lbs.*
Debut v. *Bolton Wanderers (a) 25.3.1944*
Total Appearances & Goals; *28 apps, 0 gls*
Career; *WREXHAM 22nd Dec 1945, (WW2) 28apps 0gls; Cardiff City Apr 1948 1apps 0gls; Bath City; Newport County Dec 1949 11apps 0gls; Merthyr Tydfil; Newport County Dec 1950; Milford United Oct 1951; Headington United; Barry Town c1952;*

'Roy', as he was popularly known, first played for Wrexham in March 1944 in a 1-1 draw at Bolton Wanderers. He made a total of 25 appearances during WW2, signing professional terms for the 'Robins' in December 1945. However, he struggled to make a breakthrough into the first team at the Racecourse after the War had ended, and in April 1948 he joined Cardiff City, where he made his Football League debut in the last match of the 1947/48 season, a 2-1 win at Barnsley. It proved to be his only appearance for the 'Bluebirds', and he dropped into non-league football with Bath City. He did return to the Football League in December 1949, signing for Newport County, but made only eleven League appearances for the Somerton Park club. He later played non-league football for Milford United, Headington United and Barry Town, where he suffered a broken leg in 1952.

ASTBURY, Thomas Arthur — Chester

Position; *Inside-Right*
Born; *Buckley, 9th February, 1920.*
Died; *Queensferry 19th October 1993.*
Height; *5ft 6in* **Weight;** *10st 4lbs*
Debut v. *Manchester United (h) 13.5.1940*
Total Appearances & Goals; *3 apps, 1 goal*
Career; *Bistre N.P.School; Buckley; Mold Alex; Chester May 1938 303apps 38gls, WW2 232apps 56gls; WREXHAM (WW2 Guest) May 1940 3apps 1gls; Everton (WW2 Guest) Apr 1944 1app 0gls; Manchester United (WW2 Guest) May 1945 1app 0gls;*
Honours; *Welsh Cup Winner 1947; Three War-time international caps;*

A loyal servant to Chester F.C., Tommy Astbury was signed by the 'Cestrians' from local football in North Wales prior to WW2. He went on to make a total of 533 appearances for Chester, including War-time appearances. During the conflict he also turned out as a 'guest' for Manchester United, Everton, and Wrexham with whom he enjoyed three outings: the first, in May 1940, came in a 3-2 home win over Manchester United, followed by a 2-1 win at Everton. His final appearance for the club was in March 1941, a 3-2 defeat at Blackburn Rovers, in which he scored one of the Wrexham goals. During the hostilities he was capped three times by Wales in War-time internationals against Western Command in 1942, and England (twice) in 1945. After the War Tom continued with Chester until 1954, during which time he collected a Welsh Cup winners' medal from the 1947 Final, when Chester beat Merthyr Tydfil. Throughout his career he was described as 'a bit on the small side, but a player of exceptional ability'. On retiring from playing he was appointed part-time coach with Chester, combining these duties with his job as a Sales Representative for a Builders' Merchant.

ATKINSON, William N. — Wrexham

Position; *Forward*
Born;
Debut v. *Stockport County (h) 25.10.1941*
Total Games: *6 apps, 7 gls*
Career: *WREXHAM 24th Oct 1941 6apps 7gls*

Bill Atkinson was a reserve team player who was called up for his 'Robins' debut against Stockport County in October 1941, and he made a very impressive start by scoring four goals in a 6-1 home win. He continued to score goals by notching three more in the next four games.

BAKER, Frank — Stoke City

Position; *Inside-Forward*
Born; *Stoke-on-Trent, 22nd October 1918.*
Died; *Blurton, Stoke-on-Trent, 13th November 1989.*
Height; *5ft 7in* **Weight;** *10st 8lbs.*
Debut v. *Liverpool (h) 25.11.1939*
Total Appearances & Goals; *1 app, 0 gls*
Career; *Port Vale (Am) Jul 1935 0apps; Stoke City May 1936 162apps 32gls, WW2 19apps 1gls; WREXHAM (WW2 Guest) Nov 1939 1apps 0gls;*
Honours; *Irish Cup Winner;*

Initially a left winger Frank Baker played for Port Vale reserves as an amateur, continuing in his job as a laundry van driver. However, it was Stoke who obtained his signature as a professional in May 1936, and he made his League debut for the 'Potteries' club in a 1-1 draw at home to Liverpool on Boxing Day 1936. He eventually replaced England international Joe Johnson in the 'Potters' team, before WW2 disrupted his career. Frank spent part of the war in Belfast playing for Linfield, where he picked up an Irish Cup Winners' medal, and earning selection for the Irish League XI. He also turned out for Wrexham during this period as a 'guest', making just one appearance in November 1939, a 2-1 win over Liverpool on the Racecourse. After WW2 had ceased, he resumed his career with Stoke City, where he remained until 1951 when injury forced his retirement, having twice suffered a broken leg. He later operated a fish and chip shop in Fenton for many years, and managed local side Foley, followed by coaching Stoke City's 'A' team.

BARRETT, James William — West Ham United

Position; *Centre-Half*
Born; *Stratford, London, 19th Jan, 1907.*
Died; *Southwark,25th November, 1970.*
Height; *5ft 11in* **Weight;** *14st 0lbs*
Debut v. *Wolves (a) 14.2.1942*
Total Appearances & Goals; *1 app, 0 gls*
Career; *Park School; Fairbairn House Lads; West Ham United May 1923 442apps 49gls, WW2 67apps 14gls; WREXHAM (WW2 Guest) Feb 1942 1app 0gls; Watford (WW2 Guest) 1942/43 1app 0gls; Bradford City (WW2 Guest) Jan 1943 11apps 2gls; Hartlepool United 1943/44 33apps 3gls; Crystal Palace (WW2 Guest) Feb 1945 1app 0gls;*
Honours; *1 England international cap; England schoolboy international; English Schools Shield runner-up 1921;*

Jim Barrett, or 'Tiny' as he was affectionately nicknamed during his time with West Ham because of his rather 'large bulk', was an all-round sportsman during his schooldays. He was a Boxing champ, first class swimmer, and played football for his school team, going on to represent West Ham Schoolboys. In those days Jim was a forward, playing for England, and scoring against Scotland. He signed professional for West Ham in 1923 at the age of 16, and made his debut in a 1-1 draw at Tottenham in April 1925. However, he had to wait until the following season before establishing himself as a regular in the heart of the 'Hammers' defence'!, where he enjoyed a marathon spell. He accumulated 442 League appearances, making one appearance for England, although it was short lived as he was injured after just eight minutes of the October 1928 match against Northern Ireland at Goodison Park. 'Tiny' was an adaptable footballer and played in several positions for West Ham, hence his 49 goals. WW2 effectively brought his top-flight career to an end, though it was during this period that he turned out in one game for Wrexham, a 4-1 defeat at Wolves in February 1942. After his playing career was over he coached the juniors at Upton Park, and had the satisfaction of seeing his son, Jim Junior, graduate to the West Ham first team where he made 85 League appearances. During his career Jim was said to have had 'a large frame which often intimidated opponents' and he was 'able to turn defence into attack quickly'.

BELL, Robert Charles — Tranmere Rovers

Position; *Centre-Forward*
Born; *Birkenhead, 10th April, 1911*
Died; *Todmorden, 25th December, 1988.*
Height; *5ft 10in* ***Weight;*** *10st 8lbs*
Debut v. *Stockport County (h) 13.4.1940*
Total Games: *3 apps, 3 gls*
Career: *Charlton Athletic; Tranmere Rovers (Am) Apr 1930, (Pro) Mar 1932; Everton Mar 1936 (Exchange deal of Archie Clark & £2,000), 14apps 9gls; (WW2) 1939/40 9apps 5gls; Tranmere Rovers (WW2 Guest) 1939/40 7apps 4gls; WREXHAM (WW2 Guest) Apr 1940 3apps 3gls;*

'Bunny' Bell, as he was more popularly known, set a Third Division North record of scoring nine goals in one game for Tranmere Rovers in a 13-4 home win over Oldham Athletic on 26th December 1935. Three months later he signed for Everton in an exchange deal that saw Archie Clark and £2,000 go to Prenton Park. 'Bunny' made just 14 League appearances in his three and a half years at Goodison Park, yet he scored nine goals. WW2 was to virtually end his football career, although he did play War-time football for Everton as well as making three appearances as a 'guest' for Wrexham. His first appearance for the 'Robins' came in a League War Cup match in April 1940, a 3-0 home win against Stockport County, in which he scored two of the Wrexham goals. He played in two more games for the club that season, a 1-1 home draw with Wolves, and a 4-2 home win, again, over Stockport County, in which he scored one of the goals. Following the end of his football career had ended 'Bunny' worked as a shipping clerk in Liverpool, later running his own grocer's shop in Birkenhead.

BIDEWELL, Sidney Henry — Chelsea

Position; *Centre-Forward*
Born; *Watford, 6th June, 1918.*
Debut v. *Manchester City (h) 10.5.1941*
Total Appearances & Goals; *1 app, 0 gls*
Career; *St.Albans; Wealdstone; Chelsea May 1937 4apps 2gls, WW2 23apps 1gls; WREXHAM (WW2 Guest) May 1941 1app 0gls; Southampton (WW2 Guest) Jan 1942 7apps 1gls; Gravesend & Northfleet cs1946 to 1948;*
Honours; *F.A.XI v. Oxford University;*

Described as a 'forceful attacker Sid Bidewell played non-league football for St.Albans and Wealdstone before signing for Chelsea in May 1937. He made a sensational debut for the 'Pensioners', when he scored twice against Huddersfield Town in a 3-1 home win. Stiff competition for the centre-forward position saw him make just three more League appearances before WW2 began. During this time Sid served with the Army, and played his one game for Wrexham as a 'guest' in May 1941, a scoreless home draw with Manchester City. He also turned out as a 'guest' for Southampton before continuing his football career with Southern League side Gravesend & Northfleet after the War.

BIRKETT, Wilfred — Everton

Position; *Goalkeeper*
Born; *Haydock, 26th June 1922.*
Died; *Haydock, 24th December 1993.*
Height; *5ft 9 1/2in* ***Weight;*** *11st 2lbs.*
Debut v. *Crewe Alexandra (h) 19.2.1944*
Total Appearances & Goals; *12 apps, 0 gls*
Career; *Haydock Cricket & Bowling Club; Everton (Am) 27th Aug 1942, (Pro) 2nd Feb 1944 0apps, WW2 11apps 0gls; Tranmere Rovers (WW2 Guest) 1943/44 11apps 0gls; WREXHAM (WW2 Guest) Feb 1944 12apps 0gls; Southport (WW2 Guest) 1944/45 24apps 0gls; Southport 4th Nov 1946 162apps 0gls; Shrewsbury Town 23rd Jul 1952 20apps 0gls; Southport 3rd Jul 1953 15apps 0gls;*

A 'spectacular and daring goalkeeper' Wilf Birkett signed for Everton during WW2. It was also at this time that he played for Wrexham as a 'guest', making twelve appearances, the first of which came in a 1-0 win at Crewe in February 1944. Wilf also 'guested' during this period for Southport, the club he was to join following the end of the War. His Football League debut for the 'Sandgrounders' in a 2-2 home draw with Barrow in November 1946, was the first of 162 League appearances for the club. He was said to have been at his best when Southport were 'up against it'. One of the game's characters Wilf left Haig Avenue to join Shrewsbury Town in the summer of 1952, but after just one season with the Gay Meadow club he returned to Southport where he spent a year before being forced to retire by a persistent shoulder injury. He remained at Haig Avenue for four more years as assistant trainer before moving on to Wigan Athletic as first team trainer, a position he held for twelve years - during which he was called out of retirement in an emergency to play for Wigan at Gateshead in an F.A.Cup match. He was also employed at this time with the Parks Department of Ashton UDC.

BLUNT, Edwin — Northampton Town

Position; *Inside-Forward*
Born; *Brindley Ford, Stoke-on-Trent, 21st May 1918.*
Died; *Hartshill, 20th September 1993*
Height; *5ft 8in* ***Weight;*** *11st 2lbs.*
Debut v. *Stockport County (h) 30.11.1940*
Total Appearances & Goals; *44 apps, 15 gls*
Career; *Lichfield Town; Port Vale Mar 1937; Northampton Town May 1937 87apps 2gls; Port Vale (WW2 Guest) Nov 1939 18apps 1gls; WREXHAM (WW2 Guest) Nov 1940 44apps 15gls; Stoke City (WW2 Guest) Jun 1941 23apps 0gls; Crewe Alexandra (WW2 Guest) 1942/43 39apps 9gls; Bury (WW2 Guest) 1944/45 35apps 5gls; Accrington Stanley Jul 1949 9apps 1gls;*

Eddie Blunt was signed by Port Vale from Lichfield City as an amateur, but was released two months later without having made a first team appearance. Despite this set back he was quickly snapped up by Northampton Town, where he made his Football League debut in March 1938, a 1-0 home win over Aldershot. It was not until the following season that he was able to command a regular first team place before WW2 intervened to ruin yet another promising career as he was still only 21 years old. During WW2 Eddie appeared as a 'guest' for Port Vale, Stoke City, Crewe Alexandra, Bury, Wolves, Stafford Rangers, and

Wrexham, where he was to spend much of the 1940/41 and 1942/43 seasons. His first appearance for the 'Robins' came in a 2-2 home draw with Stockport County in November 1940, in which he scored one of the Wrexham goals. Eddie returned to Northampton Town after the War, re-establishing himself in the 'Cobblers' first team, before eventually losing his place. He joined Accrington Stanley in July 1949 following trials, but left in February 1950, having completed just nine League appearances for the Peel Park club.

BOYES, Walter Edward — Everton

Position; *Outside-Left*
Born; *Killamarsh, Sheffield, 5th January, 1913.*
Died; *Sheffield, 16th September, 1960*
Height; *5ft 6in* ***Weight;*** *10st 8lbs.*
Debut v. *Everton (h) 7.4.1945*
Total Appearances & Goals; *1 app, 0 gls*
Career; *Netherthorpe Council School; Woodhouse Mills United; West Bromwich Albion (Am) Feb 1931, (Pro) Mar 1931 151apps 35gls; Everton Feb 1938 66apps 11gls, WW2 121apps 29gls; Middlesbrough (WW2 Guest) Oct 1941 2apps 0gls; Newcastle United (WW2 Guest) Feb 1942 2apps 0gls; Leeds United (WW2 Guest) 1942/43 30apps 8gls; Sunderland (WW2 Guest) 1942/43 3apps 1gls; Clapton Orient (WW2 Guest) 1942/43 5apps 0gls; Brentford (WW2 Guest) 1942/43 2apps 0gls; Millwall (WW2 Guest) Jan 1942 1app 0gls; Aldershot (WW2 Guest) 1943/44 3apps 0gls; Manchester United (WW2 Guest) Feb 1945 1app 0gls; Preston North End (WW2 Guest) 1944/45 1app 0gls; WREXHAM (WW2 Guest) Apr 1945 1app 0gls; Notts County Aug 1949 (Player/Coach) 3apps 1gls; Scunthorpe United Aug 1950 13apps 2gls; Retford Town (Player/Manager) 1953;*
Honours; *4 England International caps; Football League Championship 1939; F.A.Cup runner-up 1935;*

A spirited little footballer, who was perhaps best known as an orthodox outside-left, Walter Boyes was a purposeful player with an accurate shot, and was quick off the mark. He once scored 17 goals in one game during his Sheffield schooldays, before being snapped up as an amateur by West Bromwich Albion in February 1931. He made his Football League debut for Albion in November 1931 in a 3-0 home win over Aston Villa, and went on to play in the 1935 F.A.Cup Final defeat by Sheffield Wednesday. He was transferred to Everton prior to WW2, assisting them to the League championship, as well as adding two more England caps to the pair that he had been awarded whilst with Albion. During WW2 he played for many clubs as a 'guest', including Aldershot, Brentford, Clapton Orient, Leeds United, Manchester United, Middlesbrough, Millwall, Newcastle United, Preston North End, Sunderland, and Wrexham - for whom he made just one appearance in April 1945, a 2-1 home defeat against his own club, Everton! He also represented the Northern Command during WW2. After hanging up his boots he became a schoolmaster at Oakwood Collegiate School in Sheffield, though he remained in football by becoming manager of Hyde United in April 1958, later taking up the post of trainer at Swansea Town in 1959. However, he was forced to resign from that position in June 1960 due to ill-health, and passed away in September at the young age of 47. His success at football was made all the more remarkable by the fact that he had one leg an inch shorter than the other, but he could cross the ball with perfect accuracy and shoot with tremendous power.

BRADBURY, Thomas — Wrexham

Position; *Inside-Left*
Born;
Debut v. *New Brighton (h) 26.8.1939*
Total Appearances & Goals; *6 apps, 0 gls*
Career; *Derby County 0apps; WREXHAM 13th May 1939 6apps 0gls, WW2 2apps 0gls; Crewe Alexandra 1939/40 4apps 0gls.*

Tom Bradbury joined Wrexham in the close season of 1939 from Derby County, prior to the outbreak of WW2. He played at inside-left in the opening match of the 1939/40 season, a 2-0 home win over New Brighton, and again in the same position for the next two League games before football was suspended following the outbreak of WW2. With regionalised football then organised to replace the Football League Tom turned out just twice more for the 'Robins', towards the end of November and at beginning of December. The first match ended in a 7-0 defeat at Crewe, and his second in a 1-0 defeat at Port Vale. He is later believed to have played for Crewe Alexandra during the same season, making four appearances

BREMNER, Gordon Hutton — Arsenal

Position; *Inside-Forward*
Born; *Glasgow, 12th November, 1917*
Height; *5ft 8in* ***Weight;*** *10st 2lbs*
Debut v. *Liverpool (h) 6.9.1941*
Total Appearances & Goals; *106 apps, 36 gls*
Career; *Cartha Athletic (Glasgow); Arsenal 3rd March 1937 15apps 4gls; Chester (WW2 Guest) 1940/41 26apps 9gls; WREXHAM (WW2 Guest) Sept 1941 106apps 36gls; Tranmere Rovers (WW2 Guest) 1941/42 1app 0gls; Blackburn Rovers (WW2 Guest) Apr 1942 5apps 2gls; Preston North End (WW2 Guest) 1941/42 8apps 1gls; Fulham (WW2 Guest) 1945/46 1app 0gls; Motherwell Feb 1946;*
Honours; *Two Scottish War-time International caps; London Combination League Champions 1938 & 1939;*

Gordon Bremner joined Arsenal in March 1937 from Scottish Junior side Cartha Athletic, but was not to make his League debut for the 'Gunners' until April 1938, when he scored his side's only goal in a 1-0 win at Leeds United. He made fourteen more League appearances, scoring three times, for the 'Gunners', but played mostly reserve team football during his time at Highbury, although he did win two Combination League championship medals in 1938 and 1939. WW2 then intervened to disrupt his football career. He served as a sergeant in the Army during this period, and represented the Northern Command at football. It was also during this time that he appeared for Wrexham as a 'guest', clocking up 106 War-time appearances for the club, and scoring 36 goals. He made his first appearance in the second match of the 1941/42 season, a 5-3 home win over Liverpool, and he scored one of the goals. A very popular player with the Racecourse faithful Gordon continued with the 'Robins' until the end of the 1944/45 season, rarely missing a game. However, after WW2 had ended he decided against a return to Arsenal, and instead moved back to Scotland following his demobilisation to sign for Motherwell in February 1946, where his brother Thomas Hutton Bremner had also played.

BRIDGES, Harold — Tranmere Rovers

Position; *Inside-Left*
Born; *Burton-on-Trent, 30th June, 1915.*
Died; *Stockport, March, 1989*
Debut v. *Chester (a) 9.3.1940*
Total Appearances & Goals; *1 app, 0 gls*
Career; *Burton Town; Manchester City Apr 1937 0apps; Tranmere Rovers Jul 1939 33apps 9gls, WW2 31apps 15gls; WREXHAM (WW2 Guest) Mar 1940 1app 0gls; Crewe Alexandra (WW2 Guest) 1944/45 1app 1gls; Ashton National (Gas) cs1948;*

Harry Bridges was on Manchester City's books before signing for Tranmere Rovers in the close season of 1939. He made his Football League debut for the Prenton Park club in the opening game of the 1939/40 season, scoring in the 3-1 home win over Rotherham United, which was to be scratched from the record books just over a week later as his football career, like so many others, came to a grinding halt with the outbreak of WW2. During this period he turned out as a 'guest' for both Crewe Alexandra and Wrexham, making just one appearance for the 'Robins' in March 1940, a 4-1 defeat at Chester. Following WW2 Harry picked up what was left of his Football League career with Tranmere Rovers, finally making his Football League debut in the opening game of the 1946/47 season, a 4-1 home defeat by Rotherham United. He remained with the Birkenhead club until the end of 1947/48, before dropping into non-league football with Ashton National (Gas).

BRIGGS, Frank — Wrexham

Position; *Wing-Half*
Born; *Salford, 1st February, 1917.*
Died; *Bury, 11th April, 1984.*
Height; *5ft 8in* ***Weight;*** *10st 10lbs*
Debut v. *New Brighton (h) 26.8.1939*
Total Appearances & Goals; *27 apps, 0 gls*
Career; *Port Vale (Am) Nov 1937, (Pro) Dec 1937 8apps 0gls; Aston Villa May 1938 0apps; WREXHAM 17th May 1939 2apps 0gls, WW2 25apps 0gls; Oswestry Town;*

Frank Briggs made his Football League debut for Port Vale in a 1-1 draw at Rochdale in December 1937, and added just seven more appearances for Vale before being released at the end of that season. He joined Aston Villa where he spent the 1938/39 season with the club's reserves. Having failed to make a first team appearance at Villa Park Frank signed for Wrexham in the close season of 1939. He made his debut at half-back in the opening two games of the new 1939/40 season, a 2-0 home win over New Brighton and a 1-0 defeat at Rochdale. League football was temporarily suspended upon the outbreak of War. With the introduction of regional leagues Frank continued to play for the 'Robins' when he could, making 25 appearances during the conflict. When the conflict finally ceased he resumed his football career in non-league football with Birmingham League side Oswestry Town.

BRIGHAM, Harold — Stoke City

Position; *Right-Back*
Born; *Selby, 19th November, 1914.*
Died; *York, May 1978.*
Height; *5ft 9in* ***Weight;*** *11st 4lbs*
Debut v. *Chester (a) 12.4.1941*
Total Appearances & Goals; *2 apps, 0 gls*
Career; *Bolton Wanderers (Am) 0apps; Frickley Colliery; Stoke City May 1936 104apps 0gls; WREXHAM (WW2 Guest) Apr 1941 2apps 0gls; Chester (WW2 Guest) 1940/41 1app 1gls; Derby County (WW2 Guest) Nov 1943 11apps 0gls; Nottingham Forest Nov 1946 £4,000 35apps 2gls; York City Jul 1948 56apps 5gls; Gainsborough Trinity cs1950;*

Stoke City manager Bob McGrory beat off a number of League clubs to sign Harry Brigham from Frickley Colliery in May 1936. He had previously been on Bolton Wanderers books as an amateur, but went on to make his Football League debut with Stoke on Boxing Day 1936, in a 1-1 draw with Liverpool. He quickly established himself in the 'Potters' side, and was described by the media as the 'most coveted player in the Midlands' at the time. He continued to turn out for Stoke right through WW2, as well as appearing as a 'guest' for both Chester and Wrexham. His two appearances for the 'Robins' came in April 1941, when he played in a 1-1 draw at Chester, followed by a 5-0 defeat at Manchester City. At the conclusion of the War he left the Victoria Ground to take up an offer from Nottingham Forest in November 1946. He remained with Forest until the close season of 1948 when he joined York City, spending two seasons with the Bootham Crescent club, later sampling non-league football with Gainsborough Trinity.

BROWN, Victor Charles — Chester

Position; *Right-Back*
Born; *Bedford, 26th July, 1907.*
Died; *Northampton, J/F/M 1971.*
Height; *5ft 11'1/2in* ***Weight;*** *12st 0lbs*
Debut v. *Manchester United (h) 13.5.1940*
Total Appearances & Goals; *1 app, 0 gls*
Career; *Bedford Town; Leeds United Aug 1929 1app 0gls; Coventry City Jun 1933 100apps 0gls; Chester Jun 1939; Chester (WW2 Guest) 1939/40 34apps 0gls; WREXHAM (WW2 Guest) May 1940 1app 0gls; New Brighton (WW2 Guest) Mar 1941 1app 0gls;*
Honours; *Third Division South Championship Winner 1936;*

Vic Brown was signed by Leeds United from Bedford Town in the close season of 1929. In four years at Elland Road he managed just one first team appearance, a 3-1 home defeat by Leicester City in February 1931. His lack of first team opportunities was due to the consistency of the Milburn brothers, George and Jack. Vic finally left Leeds in June 1933 to join Coventry City, where his talents finally emerged as he went on to skipper the 'Sky Blues' to the Third Division South championship in 1935/36. Vic left Highfield Road in the summer of 1939 to join Chester, following approaches from a number of clubs that included Bristol Rovers, Northampton Town, Walsall, Lincoln City, and Accrington Stanley. His career with Chester was to come to an abrupt halt with the outbreak of WW2, and he made his one and only appearance for Wrexham as a 'guest' in a 3-2 win over Manchester United on the Racecourse in May 1940. Vic also appeared for New Brighton during this period. He later played for Haarlem in Holland, before returning home to join the coaching staff at Coventry City.

BRYAN, William J. — Wrexham

Position; *Goalkeeper*
Born; *Toll Bar, Doncaster, O/N/D 1912.*
Died; *1944, Killed in Action.*
Height; *5ft 10in* ***Weight;*** *9st 13lbs*
Debut v. *New Brighton (h) 26.8.1939*
Total Appearances & Goals; *24 apps, 0 gls*
Career; *Sunderland Aug 1934 0apps; Walsall Jun 1935 9apps 0gls; Southend United May 1936 7apps 0gls; Swindon Town Jul 1937 22apps 0gls; Wrexham 29th Jun 1939 3apps 0gls, (WW2) 21apps 0gls;*

Bill Bryan was signed by Wrexham from Swindon Town in the close season of 1939 to replace the departed Welsh international 'keeper, George Poland. He made his debut in the opening match of the 1939/40 season, a 2-0 home win over New Brighton. He appeared in the following two games before the outbreak of WW2. Bill never played another game for the 'Robins' until the 1940/41 season, when he returned to the Racecourse to make 21 appearances during that season. Sadly, Bill was reported to have been killed in action in 1944.

BURKINSHAW, George Allen — Barnsley

Position; *Centre-Half*
Born; *Barnsley, 1st October, 1922.*
Died; *Barnsley, J/A/S 1982*
Height; *5ft 11in* ***Weight;*** *11st 12lbs*
Debut v. *Rotherham United (h) 30.3.1946*
Total Appearances & Goals; *4 apps, 0goals*
Career; *Woolley Colliery; Barnsley Mar 1942 0apps, WW2 50apps 0gls; Bradford City (WW2 Guest) Dec 1945 1app 0gls; Wrexham (WW2 Guest) Mar 1946 4apps 0gls; Carlisle United Sept 1946 25apps 0gls; Barnsley Jun 1947 0apps; Bradford City Nov 1948 12apps 0gls; Goole Town cs1949;*

George Burkinshaw was signed by Barnsley during WW2 from local side Woolley Colliery. As well as playing for the Oakwell club during this period he also turned out as a 'guest' for Bradford City and Wrexham, where he made four appearances during the 1945/46 season. The first of these came in March 1946, a 2-0 home defeat by Rotherham United. After WW2 had ended George resumed his Football League career with Carlisle United, where he made his League debut in October 1946 in a 3-2 home win over New Brighton. He remained with the 'Cumbrians' for the rest of that season, rejoining Barnsley in the summer of 1947. He failed to make any further impression at Oakwell, and left in November 1948 without having made a first team appearance to join Bradford City. George made twelve League appearances for the 'Bantams', leaving the club at the end of the 1947/48 season to move into non-league circles with Goole Town.

BURNETT, George Gordon — Everton

Position; *Goalkeeper*
Born; *Liverpool, 11th February, 1920.*
Died; *Birkenhead, 29th April, 1985.*
Height; *5ft 10in* **Weight;** *12st 0lbs*
Debut v. *Walsall (a) 28.2.1942*
Total Appearances & Goals; *5 apps, 0 gls*
Career; *Litherland Boys Club; Everton (Am) 9th May 1938, (Pro) 16th Sept 1938 47apps 0gls, WW2 182apps 0gls; Millwall (WW2 Guest) 1940/41 18apps 0gls; Wrexham (WW2 Guest) Feb 1942 5apps 0gls; Tranmere Rovers (WW2 Guest) 1942/43 1app 0gls; Manchester United (WW2 Guest) Jan 1943 1app 0gls; Oldham Athletic 6th Oct 1951 £2,000 100apps 0gls; Ellesmere Port cs1955;*
Honours; *Third Division North Championship Winner 1953;*

George Burnett had limited opportunities with Everton before the outbreak of WW2 due to the form of Ted Sagar between the posts, but during the War period he played regularly for the 'Toffeemen' as well as making 'guest' appearances for Millwall, Tranmere Rovers, Manchester United and Wrexham. He made five appearances for the 'Robins', the first in February 1942, a 2-0 defeat at Walsall. Following the end of the War George resumed his career at Goodison Park, but over the next five years he was to make just 47 League appearances before joining Oldham Athletic in October 1951. At Boundary Park he was described as a 'cool and thoroughly capable 'keeper, who inspired confidence in those around him', and won a Third Division North championship medal with the 'Latics' in 1953. He left the Lancashire club in the summer of 1955 to join Cheshire County League side Ellesmere Port Town, before hanging up his boots to become a licensee in Chester.

BUTT, Leonard — Blackburn Rovers

Position; *Inside-Forward*
Born; *Wilmslow, 26th August, 1910.*
Died; *Macclesfield, June 1994.*
Height; *5ft 6in* **Weight;** *11st 3lbs.*
Debut v. *Tranmere Rovers (h) 21.12.1940*
Total Appearances & Goals; *2 apps, 5 gls*
Career; *Wilmslow Albion; Ashton National; Stockport County (Am) Jun 1928, (Pro) Aug 1928 8apps 1gls; Macclesfield Town May 1932; Huddersfield Town May 1935 67apps 11gls; Blackburn Rovers Jan 1937 110apps 44gls, (WW2) 53apps 35gls; Manchester United (WW2 Guest) Nov 1939 13apps 11gls; Wrexham (WW2 Guest) Dec 1940 2apps 5gls; Huddersfield Town (WW2 Guest) May 1941 6apps 3gls; Manchester City (WW2 Guest) May 1942 1app 0gls; York City (WW2 Guest) 1941/42 1app 0gls; Chelsea (WW2 Guest) Sept 1942 1app 0gls; Aldershot (WW2 Guest) 1943/44 3apps 0gls; Stockport County (WW2 Guest) Apr 1944 2apps 0gls; York City Jan 1947 25apps* 2gls; Mansfield Town Oct 1947 15apps 4gls; Mossley Jun 1948;
Honours; *Second Division Championship Winner 1939; League War Cup runner-up 1940; Cheshire County League Championship Winner 1932 & 1933; Cheshire Senior Cup Winner 1935;*

Les Butt was a diminutive, scheming inside-forward who was verging on international honours with Blackburn Rovers when War broke out. During WW2 he appeared as a 'guest' for Manchester United, Huddersfield Town, Manchester City, York City, Chelsea, Aldershot, Stockport County, and Wrexham, for whom he scored two goals on his debut in a 5-1 home win over Tranmere Rovers in December 1940. He followed that with a hat-trick in a 5-2 home win over Chester in March 1941. After the War Len resumed his playing career with Blackburn Rovers, signing for York City in January 1947. He went on to play for Mansfield Town and still holds the record as the oldest player to have turned out in a League match for Mansfield Town at 37 years 228 days. Upon leaving the 'Stags' in the summer of 1948 he became player/coach with Cheshire County League side Mossley. He was later a sculptor's assistant, and latterly worked at Macclesfield Town Hall.

CARVER,

Position; *Wing-Half*
Born;
Debut v. *Stoke City (h) 13.9.1941*
Total Appearances & Goals; *1 app, 0 gls*
Career; *Wrexham (WW2 Guest) Sept 1941 1app 0gls; Leicester City (WW2 Guest) 1942/43 1app 0gls;*

Carver made his one and only appearance for Wrexham at wing-half in a 7-1 home defeat by Stoke City in September 1941 .

CASE, D. — Wrexham

Position; *Forward*
Born;
Debut v. *Manchester United (a) 16.12.1944*
Total Appearances & Goals; *1 app, 0 gls*
Career; *Wrexham (WW2 Guest) Dec 1944 1app 0gls;*

Case was an amateur who was given a trial by Wrexham during WW2. He made his solitary appearance for the club in December 1944 in a 1-0 defeat against Manchester United, the game having been staged at Maine Road due to the extensive bomb damage at Old Trafford.

CATON, William C. — Stoke City

Position; *Inside-Forward*
Born; *Stoke-on-Trent, 11th September, 1924.*
Height; *5ft 8in* **Weight;** *12st 0lbs*
Debut v. *Crewe Alexandra (a) 25.12.1942*
Total Appearances & Goals; *7 apps, 0 gls*
Career; *Stoke United; Stoke City Sept 1941 0apps, WW2 22apps 2gls; Wrexham (WW2 Guest) Dec 1942 7apps 0gls; Carlisle United Apr 1950 64apps 16gls; Chesterfield Oct 1952 7apps 0gls; Worcester City; Crewe Alexandra Jul 1954 38apps 8gls;*

Bill Caton joined Stoke City from local side Stoke United during WW2. It was during the conflict that he also turned out for Wrexham as a 'guest', making his debut against Crewe Alexandra on Christmas Day 1942 in a game where the 'Robins' were over blessed with festive generosity as the visitors won 8-2!! Bill went on to make six more appearances for the Racecourse club. He returned to the Victoria Ground after the hostilities had ended but failed to make a first team appearance, moving to Carlisle in April 1950. Originally an inside-left, he dropped back to left-half on joining the 'Cumbrians', and where he finally made his Football League debut in a 5-1 home win over Chester, and he capped the occasion with a goals. Bill later turned out for Chesterfield, Worcester City and Crewe Alexandra.

CLARK, Gordon Vincent — Manchester City

Position; *Right-Back*
Born; *Gainsborough, 15th June 1914.*
Died; *Sheffield, October 1997*
Height; *5ft 7 1/2in* **Weight;** *11st 13lb*
Debut v. *Manchester City (a) 4.10.1941*
Total Appearances & Goals; *1 app, 0 gls*
Career; *Highgate School; Goldthorpe United; Crystal Palace (Trial); Denaby United; Manchester City 22nd Jan 1936 55apps 0gls, WW2 180apps 0gls; Stockport County (WW2 Guest) Nov 1939 4apps 0gls; Wrexham (WW2 Guest) Oct 1941 1app 0gls; Hyde United Apr 1947; Waterford Aug 1947;*

Gordon Clark had a trial with Crystal Palace, though nothing came of it, and whilst playing for Denaby United he was invited for another trial with Manchester City, for whom he eventually signed in January 1936. Gordon made his Football League debut the following season in a 4-0 home win over Leeds United, and he had just begun to establish himself in the City first team when WW2 broke out. He became a regular in the City line-up, making almost 200 War-time appearances while serving in the R.A.F.. Gordon made a 'guest' appearance for Wrexham, when he helped them out after they turned up at Maine Road a player short in October 1941. City won the game 2-0. After WW2 had ended he continued his career at Maine Road before joining Cheshire County League side Hyde United towards the end of 1946/47. He remained with them until the close season, crossing over to Ireland to join Waterford as player/manager, a position he held until 1950 when he was appointed manager of Distillery. However, this time his stay was short-lived, as he was appointed manager of Aldershot in May 1950. He remained in charge at the Recreation Ground until the early part of the 1955/56 season when he resigned to take up the position of chief scout with West Bromwich Albion. He gained a reputation as a great judge of ability, and was soon appointed assistant manager to Vic Buckingham. Following Vic's departure Gordon was appointed manager at the Hawthorns in June 1959. Albion finished fifth in his first season in charge, and tenth the following year. He resigned half way through 1961/62, rejoining Buckingham at Sheffield Wednesday as his assistant manager. He left Hillsborough in 1964 to take up an appointment as boss at Peterborough United in April, leading them to the Quarter-Finals of the FA Cup in 1965, and to the semi-finals of the League Cup in 1966. Gordon walked out on the 'Posh' in September 1967, and later joined Arsenal as Chief Scout, which was followed ten years later by an appointment as assistant manager to Bobby Campbell at Fulham in April 1977. The following year he took up an offer of coach at Philadelphia Fury before returning to the UK in 1979 to become assistant manager at Queens Park Rangers.

CLEGG, Donald — Huddersfield Town

Position; *Goalkeeper*
Born; *Huddersfield, 2nd June, 1921.*
Height; *5ft 10in* ***Weight;*** *11st 6lbs*
Debut v. *Stockport County (h) 7.11.42*
Total Appearances & Goals; *12 apps, 0 gls*
Career; *ICI; Huddersfield Town May 1940 3apps 0gls, WW2 55apps 0gls; Wrexham (WW2 Guest) Nov 1942 & 6th Feb 1943 12apps 0gls; Bradford City (WW2 Guest) Mar 1943 3apps 0gls; Bury Jul 1948 15apps 0gls; Stoke City Jun 1950 2apps 0gls; Rossendale;*

Don Clegg joined Huddersfield Town in May 1940, and in November 1942 appeared for Wrexham in a 7-1 home win over Stockport County. However, the 'Robins' were subsequently fined the grand sum of £3.00 for failing to ascertain through the proper channels that Don had already signed amateur forms for Huddersfield Town. He had failed to reveal this to the Racecourse management, and was promptly fined the same amount as the club! He eventually signed full-time for Wrexham in February 1943, although he returned to First Division Huddersfield Town in time for the recommencement of the new Football League season in 1946. His League debut for the 'Terriers' came in January 1947, a 2-1 home defeat by Portsmouth. Don made two further appearances before moving to Bury in the summer of 1948. He later had a short spell with Stoke City before drifting into non-league football with Rossendale United.

COEN, Lawrence R.W. — CoventryCity

Position; *Outside-Left*
Born; *Lowestoft, 4th December, 1914.*
Died; *Dudley, June 1972*
Height; *5ft 9in* ***Weight;*** *10st 12lbs*
Debut v. *Manchester City (h) 24.2.1940*
Total Appearances & Goals; *11 apps, 5 gls*
Career; *Lowestoft Junior School; Milford Haven 1930; West Bromwich Albion (Am) Aug 1932, (Pro) Oct 1932 7apps 4gls; Coventry City 1938 £1,000 20apps 3gls; Wrexham (WW2 Guest) Feb 1940 11apps 5gls; Nottingham Forest (WW2 Guest) 1944/45 1app 0gls; Notts County (WW2 Guest) 1944/45 15apps 2gls; Stockport County (WW2 Guest) Aug 1945 3apps 1gls; South Liverpool Aug 1948; Dudley Town cs1951;*
Honours; *England Junior International;*

'Lol' Coen joined West Bromwich Albion in August 1932 on amateur terms, and went on to sign professional for them two months later. He then had to wait until February 1937 before making his Football League debut in a 2-1 home defeat by Charlton Athletic. However, he was transferred to Coventry City in 1938 for £1,000, and was playing for them when World War Two broke out. He joined the R.A.F. - Lol won the D.F.C. during the conflict - although he was able to play football whenever he was at home. It was at the outset of the War that he joined Wrexham as a 'guest', completing eleven War-time appearances, the first of which came in a 3-2 home win over Manchester City in February 1940. During the conflict he also appeared for Nottingham Forest, Notts County, and Stockport County, during which he was described as having 'fair control, whose easy running action deluded many opposing defenders. He was swift and made for goal, pretty smart over 30-40 yards'. He continued with Coventry after the conflict had ended, eventually going into non-league football with South Liverpool in 1948 and later Dudley Town.

COLE, Cyril — Wrexham

Position; *Centre-Half*
Born; *Rhosllanerchrugog, Nr. Wrexham, 19th September 1920.*
Height; *5ft 9'1/2in* ***Weight;*** *12st 8lbs*
Debut v. *Stockport County (h) 25.10.41*
Total Appearances & Goals; *5 apps, 0 gls*
Career; *Penycae; Llanerch Celts; Wrexham (WW2) Oct 1941 5apps 0gls; Machynlleth 1948/49; Blaenau Ffestiniog 1951/52; Aberystwyth Town 1951/52;*
Honours; *Cambrian Coast League & Cup; Welsh League South Division Two Champions 1952;*

Cyril Cole first played football for the Grango School XI in his native Rhos. He moved on to Penycae in the Chums League at 15, before taking up employment at the Hafod Colliery near Wrexham. He later played for Llanerch Celts, where he had trials for the Welsh Amateur team, before he was taken to the Racecourse by his neighbour Cyril Jones - who played more games during the conflict for Wrexham than any other player. Cyril Cole was signed there and then, and he made his debut against Stockport County in October 1941. His chance came out of the blue, as he had just finished a shift at the colliery and his wife met him off the bus to tell him that he was playing! Wrexham won 6-1 and he remained in the side for the following match a 2-2 draw at Stockport. He made one more appearance that season, in a 4-2 defeat at Tranmere. A story which illustrates the nature of the game during the War years concerns a visit made by Wrexham to Liverpool. Cyril had travelled to Merseyside for the match, only to be asked to stand down upon his arrival at the ground as the club had managed to secure the services of another player who had just been posted to the area by the RAF!! He made two further appearances for the first team in the following campaign, an 8-2 home defeat by Crewe Alexandra on Christmas Day 1942, and a 4-0 defeat at Tranmere Rovers in March 1943. Cyril's brother, Eddie, also played for Wrexham's reserves around this time, and he was also on the books of Bolton Wanderers. After the War Cyril went on to turn out for Machynlleth, Blaenau Ffestiniog, and Aberystwyth Town before hanging up his boots in 1955 at the age of 35. He went on to work in the pits for forty years at both Hafod and Gresford Collieries.

COLLINS, Anthony J. — Wrexham

Position; *Outside-Right*
Born; *Rhos, Nr.Wrexham.*
Debut v. *Tranmere Rovers (h) 3.3.45*
Total Appearances & Goals; *7 apps, 0 gls*
Career; *Wrexham (WW2 Guest) Mar 1945 7apps 0gls*

Tony Collins is the younger brother of George Collins. He joined Wrexham during the Second World War, and made his debut for the club in a 2-1 home win over Tranmere Rovers in March 1945. He found his first team opportunities limited, mainly because of the quality of the 'guest' players that appeared for the club during this period. Just six more appearances followed.

COLLINS, George Ernest — Wrexham

Position; *Inside/Outside-Right*
Born; *Rhos, Nr.Wrexham*
Debut v. *Liverpool (a) 5.9.1942*
Total Appearances & Goals; *28 apps, 7 gls*
Career; *Wrexham (WW2 Guest) Sept 1942 28apps 7gls; Chester (WW2 Guest) Mar 1943 1app 0gls; Sunderland (WW2 Guest) Nov 1943 17apps 4gls; Luton Town (WW2 Guest) 1944/45 6apps 0gls;*

The older brother of Tony, George Collins made his debut for Wrexham in the second match of the 1942/43 season, a 4-0 defeat at Liverpool. He went on to add a further 27 appearances during the hostilities, and also completed one 'guest' appearance for Chester in a 3-2 home defeat by Stoke City in November 1943. He also 'guested' for both Sunderland and Luton Town, making his debut for the 'Rokerites' in a 3-1 defeat by local rivals Newcastle United, although he did gain revenge by scoring two goals in a 3-0 home win over 'The Magpies' on New Year's Day.

COOK, Willie — Everton

Position; *Right-Back*
Born; *Coleraine, 20th November, 1909.*
Died; *Fazackerley, April 1993.*
Height; *5ft 7 1/2in* **Weight;** *12st 12lbs*
Debut v. *Liverpool (h) 25.11.1939*
Total Appearances & Goals; *32 apps, 4 gls*
Career; *Port Glasgow Juniors 1928; Celtic Feb 1930 101apps 0gls; Everton Dec 1932 £3,000 225apps 5gls; Wrexham (WW2 Guest) Nov 1939 32apps 4gls; Aldershot (WW2 Guest) 1939/40 5apps 0gls; Chester (WW2 Guest) 1939/40 1app 0gls; Liverpool (WW2 Guest) Aug 1941 2apps 1gls; Southport (WW2 Guest) 1944/45 5apps 0gls; Wrexham Oct 1945; Ellesmere Port Town Jul 1946; Rhyl (Player/manager) Oct 1946;*
Honours; *15 Northern Ireland International caps; Scottish Cup Winner 1931; F.A.Cup Winner 1933;*

Willie Cook is one of an elite band of players to have earned Cup winners' medals in both England and Scotland, with Everton and Celtic. A Irish international with fifteen caps he for played for Aldershot, Liverpool, Chester, Southport, and Wrexham during WW2. His 'Robins' debut came in a 2-1 home win over Liverpool in November 1939, and went on to complete 32 appearances, scoring four goals for the Racecourse club. He signed for Wrexham in October 1945, when his playing career was coming to an end, though he did not manage an appearance in a Football League game for the club, as he signed for Cheshire County League side Ellesmere Port Town. He was later appointed player/manager at Rhyl in October 1946, and remained with the 'Lilywhites' until 1947 when he moved to Norway as coach to SK Brann (Bergen). A return home in February 1948 followed his appointment as coach at Sunderland, where he spent four years. In 1952 Willie moved to Peru where he was appointed National coach to the Peruvian FA in Lima. He was appointed Northern Ireland Youth team coach in January 1954, and later managed Portadown. In 1955 he became the national coach of Iraq before returning home a year later to take over as manager of Wigan Athletic. He later became team coach at Norwich City. Known to have always pushed cotton wool into his boots before a game.

COOPER, John — Wrexham

Position; *Centre-Half*
Born; *Rhosllanerchrugog*
Debut v. *Walsall 10.3.1945*
Total Appearances & Goals; *5 apps, 0 gls*
Career; *Wrexham (WW2 Guest) Mar 1945 5apps 0gls; Oswestry Town 1946;*

A reserve team player who was a teacher at Rhos and Llay Junior School, John Cooper was called upon for his Wrexham debut in March 1945 in a 1-0 home win against Walsall. He completed three more appearances that season before making his final first team appearance for the club in a 3-2 home win over Southport in November 1945. John later turned out for Oswestry Town, and went on to become the Headmaster of a school in Rhayader, where he also played for Machynlleth F.C. while based in Mid-Wales.

COOPER, Thomas — Liverpool

Position; *Right-Back*
Born; *Fenton, Stoke-on-Trent, 9th April, 1905.*
Died; *Aldeburgh, 25th June, 1940.*
Height; *5ft 9 1/2in* **Weight;** *12st 2lbs*
Debut v. *Manchester City (a) 28th October 1939*
Total Appearances & Goals; *3 apps, 0 gls*
Career; Longton; Trentham; Port Vale Aug 1924 £20 32apps 0gls; Derby County Mar 1926 £2,500 248apps 1gls; Liverpool Dec 1934 £7,500 150apps 0gls; Wrexham (WW2 Guest) Oct 1939 3apps 0gls;
Honours; *15 England International caps (1928-1935); 1 Football League Representative cap;*

A former miner who went on to play for England, Tom Cooper was a 'skilful and polished defender whose only alleged weakness was his heading'. Known as 'Snowy', he captained Derby and Liverpool as well as England, and was said to have 'few peers as a defender'. It was also said of Tom that he was, 'an excellent tackler who showed keen awareness and superb anticipation, while his distribution brought him to the attention of the England selectors'. He made three appearances for Wrexham as a 'guest' during WW2: a 6-1 defeat at Manchester City, followed by a 4-4 draw with Stoke City and a 2-2 draw with Chester, both on the Racecourse. Sadly, Tom was killed in a motorcycle accident while serving with the Military Police in Suffolk in June 1940.

COPE, George — Crewe Alexandra

Position; Right-Back/Centre-Half
Born; *Crewe, 26th January, 1915.*
Died; *Congleton, November, 1988.*
Height; *5ft 10in* **Weight;** *12st 6lbs*
Debut v. *Blackburn Rovers (h) 5.4.1941*
Total Appearances & Goals; *4 apps, 0 gls*
Career; *Nantwich Town; Crewe Alexandra Aug 1936 14apps 0gls, (WW2) 1939/40 22apps 0gls; Wrexham (WW2 Guest) Apr 1941 4apps 0gls;*

George Cope is the father of Ron, who went on to play for Manchester United. He joined Crewe Alexandra from Nantwich Town in the close season of 1936, and made his Football League debut for Alex in a 2-0 defeat at Rochdale on Boxing Day 1936. He added a further thirteen League appearances for the 'Railwaymen' over the three seasons prior to World War Two, which was to disrupt his playing career. Cope continued playing for Crewe during this period, as well as appearing for Wrexham as a 'guest'. His first game for the Racecourse club came in April 1941, a 3-0 home win over Blackburn Rovers, followed by a 5-2 victory over Stoke City in the same month. George then added two more games for the 'Robins', the first a 5-2 defeat at Liverpool in the opening game of 1941/42, with the second - and last - coming in the next game, when Wrexham gained swift revenge with a 5-3 win over the Anfield Reds.

CROSSLEY, G.

Position; *Inside-Right*
Debut v. *Tranmere Rovers (a) 6.3.1943*
Total Appearances & Goals; *1 app, 0 gls*
Career; *Wrexham (WW2 Guest) Mar 1943 1app 0gls;*

Crossley made his one and only war-time appearance for Wrexham in a 4-0 defeat at Tranmere Rovers in March 1943, appearing in the side at inside-right.

CULLIS, Stanley — Wolves

Position; *Centre-Half*
Born; *Ellesmere Port, 25th October, 1916*
Height; *5ft 10in* **Weight;** *11st 7lbs.*
Debut v. *Stockport County (a) 6.1.1940*
Total Appearances & Goals; *4 apps, 0 gls*
Career; *Cambridge Road School; Ellesmere Port Wednesday; Bolton Wanderers (Am) Aug 1933; Ellesmere Port Wednesday Dec 1933; Wolves Feb 1934 152apps 0gls; Aldershot (WW2 Guest) 1939/40 38apps 0gls; Wrexham (WW2 Guest) Jan 1940 4apps 0gls; Liverpool (WW2 Guest) Aug 1940 8apps 0gls; Fulham (WW2 Guest) 1940/41 9apps 0gls;*
Honours; *12 England International caps; 20 War-time international caps; F.A.Cup runner-up 1939; Three Football League XI Representative caps;*

Stan Cullis was one of a rare breed, a footballer who achieved outstanding success as both a player and a manager. Furthermore, he did it with the same club. He joined Wolves in February 1934 from his local side, Ellesmere Port Wednesday, and made his Football League debut a year later in a 3-2 home defeat against Huddersfield Town. He went on to gain 12 England caps and make 152 League appearances for Wolves, playing in the 1939 F.A.Cup Final, during which he was described as 'a supreme centre-half who was dominant in the air, as hard as nails in the tackle and used the ball creatively. A natural leader he captained both Wolves and England.' World War Two was to interrupt his career, but during this period he appeared in twenty war-time internationals for England, forming a brilliant half-back line with Joe Mercer and Cliff Britton. However, he was to make just 31 appearances for Wolves during this time. Stan turned out for Wrexham during January 1939 in a 1-0 win at Stockport, before adding three more appearances for the 'Robins'. He also turned out as a 'guest' for Aldershot, Liverpool, and Fulham. After ending his playing days in May 1947 he became assistant to manager Ted Vizard, and replaced him as Wolves manager in 1948. He went on to guide the team in Old Gold to three Football League Championships, in 1954, 1958 and 1959; two F.A.Cup Final successes in 1949 and 1960; as well as leading them into Europe for the first time. He later managed Birmingham City before leaving football in 1970 to work in a photographic agency, though he retained a connection with the game by writing for a Midlands sports paper. He was appointed to the Midlands Sports Council in 1972.

DAVIES, G.R. — Wrexham

Position; *Goalkeeper*
Debut v. *Manchester City (a) 4.10.1941*
Total Appearances & Goals; *5 apps, 0 gls*
Career; *Wrexham (WW2 Guest) Oct 1941 5apps 0gls;*

Davies made his debut for Wrexham in a 2-0 defeat at Manchester City in October 1941, playing in goal in place of Cyril Sidlow. He then kept his place for the following four games.

DAVIES, Ivor — Wrexham

Position; *Half-Back*
Debut v. *Crewe Alexandra (h) 25.12.1943*
Total Appearances & Goals; *1 app, 0 gls*
Career; *Wrexham (WW2 Guest) Dec 1943 1app 0gls;*

Ivor Davies made his solitary appearance for Wrexham in a 2-1 home win over Crewe Alexandra on Christmas Day 1943, playing in the half-back line in place of Bob Savage.

DAVIES, Robert Griffith — Nottingham Forest

Position; *Centre-Half*
Born; *Blaenau Ffestiniog, 19th October, 1913.*
Died; *Nottingham, 10th May, 1978.*
Debut v. *Wolves (h) 24.2.1945*
Total Appearances & Goals; *1 app, 0 gls*
Career; *Blaenau Ffestiniog; Nottingham Forest Nov 1936 55apps 0gls; Notts County (WW2 Guest) 1939/40 1apps 0gls; Blackpool (WW2 Guest) Feb 1944 36apps 1gls; Wrexham (WW2 Guest) Feb 1945 1app 0gls; Leicester City (WW2 Guest) Oct 1945 2apps 0gls;*
Honours; *Six Wales War-time international caps;*

Bob Davies joined Nottingham Forest in November 1936 from Blaenau Ffestiniog, signing for them at the local railway station! He was just establishing himself in the Forest first team when WW2 began. During this period he had mixed fortunes: he was lucky to survive an incident in which his parachute failed to open while acting as a paratroops instructor in 1941, after making almost 300 jumps himself! Although never capped by Wales in peace time football he recovered sufficiently from two broken legs to add to his Welsh War-time international tally. During the conflict Bob, 'a big strong pivot and a dominant defender' turned out as a 'guest' for Blackpool, Rochdale, Notts County, Leicester City, and Wrexham - for whom he made one appearance in February 1945, a 1-1 home draw with Wolves. After the War ended he resumed his playing career with Nottingham Forest until 1947, when he became physio with Walsall. He eventually returned to Forest, where he remained on the training staff until 1974, and also worked as a Physio for Nottinghamshire C.C.C. during the summer. He gave almost forty years service to Nottingham Forest.

DAVIES, Thomas Clifford — Wrexham

Position; *Half-Back*
Debut v. *Everton (h) 15.11.1941*
Total Appearances & Goals; *3 apps, 0 gls*
Career; *Caergwrle; Wrexham 18th Aug 1939, WW2 3apps 0gls;*

Cliff Davies joined Wrexham at the beginning of 1939/40 from Caergwrle, but World War Two was to prevent him making any further progress at the Racecourse. He finally made his first team bow in November 1941, playing in the half-back line in a 4-0 home defeat by Everton. Cliff went on to add two further appearances that season, but they proved to be his only games for the 'Robins', as he found a first team place hard to come by because of the quality of the 'guest' players who were at the club at that particular time.

DEAN, George — Wrexham

Position; *Outside-Left*
Debut v. *Stockport County (h) 17.4.1943*
Total Appearances & Goals; *1 app, 0 gls*
Career; *Wrexham (WW2 Guest) Apr 1943 1app 0gls;*

George Dean made his one and only first team appearance for Wrexham against Stockport County on the Racecourse in April 1943, when the 'Robins' enjoyed a 6-3 win over the visitors. He played at outside-left in place of Ehud Rogers, but was replaced himself in the following game by George Collins. George Dean became trainer of the reserve team at the Racecourse around 1945.

DEARSON, Donald John — Birmingham

Position; *Inside-Forward/Half-Back*
Born; *Ynysybwl, 13th May 1914.*
Died; *Sheldon, Birmingham, 24th December, 1990.*
Height; *5ft 10in* ***Weight;*** *13st 3lbs.*
Debut v. *Manchester City (h) 10.5.1941*
Total Appearances & Goals; *1 app, 0 gls*
Career; *Llanwit Major Juniors; Barry Town Aug 1932; Birmingham Apr 1934 131apps 17gls, WW2 166apps 24gls; Nottingham Forest (WW2 Guest) 1940/41 2apps 1gls; Wrexham (WW2 Guest) May 1941 1app 0gls; Northampton Town (WW2 Guest) 1940/41 12apps 10gls; West Bromwich Albion (WW2 Guest) Mar 1943 4apps 1gls; Coventry City Feb 1947 84apps 10gls; Walsall Mar 1950 51apps 13gls; Nuneaton Borough 1951/52; Bilston United 1952/53;*
Honours; *3 Welsh International caps; 15 War-time Welsh international caps; Welsh Amateur International; Football League South Championship Winner 1946; Second Division Championship Winner 1948;*

A Welsh international who joined Birmingham in April 1934 from Barry Town. He was described as a 'truly grand footballer in every sense of the word. Don gave 101% each time he took the field at whatever level he played'. A Welsh international forward who 'guested' for Wrexham during the conflict where he made just one appearance in May 1941, a scoreless home draw with Manchester City. 'A clever, scheming type of inside-forward with a powerful shot', he also appeared as a 'guest' for Northampton and West Brom during the hostilities. It was during this period that Don joined the Birmingham City Police, but he left after only nine weeks to take up work in the local BSA factory until the after the War ended. He then continued with Birmingham, winning a Football League South Championship medal in 1946. A move to Coventry City in February 1947, saw him lead them to the Second Division Championship in 1948, following which he went on to play for Walsall, Nuneaton, and Bilston United before ending his football career to go into greengrocery business in Yardley. He decided to sell up in 1967, whereupon he took up employment with British Leyland in Coventry.

DELLOW, Ronald William — Carlisle United

Position; *Outside-Right*
Born; *Crosby, 13th July, 1914.*
Height; *5ft 9in* **Weight;** *10st 5lbs.*
Debut v. *Chester (h) 28.8.1944*
Total Appearances & Goals; *6 apps, 2 gls*
Career; *Bootle Technical College; Bootle St.Marys; Bootle Celtic; Blackburn Rovers (Am) May 1933, (Pro) Aug 1933 0apps; Mansfield Town Jun 1934 24apps 10gls; Manchester City Jan 1935 £1,300 10apps 4gls; Tranmere Rovers Mar 1936 105apps 29gls; Carlisle United Aug 1939 16apps 5gls; Tranmere Rovers (WW2 Guest) 1939/40 1app 0gls; New Brighton (WW2 Guest) Aug 1940 52apps 7gls; Manchester City (WW2 Guest) Mar 1942 13apps 3gls; Everton (WW2 Guest) Oct 1942 13apps 5gls; Wrexham (WW2 Guest) Aug 1943 6apps 2gls; Southport (WW2 Guest) 1943/44 49apps 12gls; Blackburn Rovers (WW2 Guest) Sep 1945 2apps 0gls;*
Honours; *Third Division North Championship Winner 1938;*

A pacy goalscoring winger Ron Dellow came from a seafaring family, and served in the Merchant Navy before embarking on a football career with Blackburn Rovers. However, he failed to make a first team appearance for the Ewood Park club and joined Mansfield Town in June 1934, where his Football League debut came in a 2-1 home win over Rotherham United in September. He had made 24 appearances for the 'Stags' when Manchester City stepped in to sign him in January 1935 for a club record fee received of £1,300. He moved on to Tranmere Rovers just over a year later, winning a Third Division North championship medal in 1938. He had joined Carlisle United in the summer of 1939, when the war began. Ron appeared as a 'guest' for a number of clubs during the conflict including Tranmere, New Brighton, Manchester City, Everton, Southport, Blackburn Rovers, and Wrexham. He made his debut for Wrexham in a very pleasing 8-4 home win over local rivals Chester!, and went on to appear in five more games, scoring two goals. At the end of the hostilities Ron rejoined Carlisle before going to Ireland as player/manager of Ards in June 1947. He eventually settled in Holland, coaching a number of clubs including Hermes FC, H.B.S, Blauw Wit, Gooi, Heracles, Hilversum, and Vollendam, who he joined in November 1963 and remained as coach until May1969. He later worked for the Dutch F.A., continuing to coach for over twenty years, and not surprisingly marrying a Dutch girl along the way!

DERRICK, Albert Edward — Newport County

Position; *Inside-Right*
Born; *Newport, 8th September, 1908.*
Died; *Newport, 5th June, 1975.*
Height; *5ft 8in* **Weight;** *11st 0lbs*
Debut v. *Stockport County (h) 18.11.1944*
Total Appearances & Goals; *1 app, 0 gls*
Career; *Newport County (Am) Mar 1935, (Pro) 4th Oct 1935 125apps 48gls; Crewe Alexandra (WW2 Guest) 1943/44 3apps 0gls; Aberaman Athletic (WW2 Guest); Chester (WW2 Guest) 1944/45 4apps 1gls; Wrexham (WW2 Guest) Nov 1944 1app 0gls; Swindon Town 23rd Jan 1946 1app 0gls, (WW2) 17apps 6gls; Ebbw Vale 1947; Girlings FC;*

Having joined his local side Newport County as an amateur in March 1935, Albert Derrick progressed to sign professional six months later. He was the only local born player to appear in Newport's 1938/39 promotion-winning side, making 125 League appearances for the Somerton Park club and scoring a very impressive 48 goals until the Second World War intervened. He was noted at Newport as a 'persistent forward, who also appeared as a winger, whose virile methods brought him many goals'. As an Army reservist he was called up in 1939, and served for seven years, five of which were on the North-West Frontier. He did manage to play football when he could, and apart from Newport County, he also appeared as a 'guest' for Crewe, Aberaman, Chester, Swindon and Wrexham, as well as playing in many Army representative games during this period. This included selection for the British Army XI, although he was unable to play as he was on the 'high seas' at the time! He made one 'guest' appearance for Wrexham in November 1944, an 8-0 home win over Stockport County.

DEVLIN, John — Hibernian

Position; *Inside-Forward*
Born; *Airdrie, 11th December, 1917.*
Height; *5ft 9in* **Weight;** *11st 4lbs*
Debut v. *New Brighton (h) 2.11.1940*
Total Appearances & Goals; *14 apps, 3 gls*
Career; *Coatsdyke All Saints; Plains Juniors; Airdrie Juniors; Coltness United; Hibernian Aug 1939; Chester (WW2 Guest) 1939/40 1apps 0gls; Crewe Alexandra (WW2 Guest) 1940/1 1app 1gls; Wrexham (WW2 Guest) Nov 1940 14apps 3gls; Manchester City (WW2 Guest) Sep 1941 1app 0gls; Aldershot (WW2 Guest) 1942/43 1app 1gls; Fulham (WW2 Guest) 1943/44 4apps 3gls; Chelsea (WW2 Guest) Oct 1943 1app 0gls; Kilmarnock Mar 1946 £750; Walsall Dec 1947 £7,000 166apps 50gls; Bloxwich Strollers;*

John Devlin turned out for Wrexham during WW2 as a 'guest' when on the books of Scottish League side Hibernian, for whom he had played prior to the commencement of the hostilities. He served as an instructor with the Army Physical Training Corps, but still found time to appear as a 'guest' for Aldershot, Chester, Crewe, Manchester City, Chelsea, and Fulham. His first appearance for Wrexham came in a 4-2 home win over New Brighton in November 1940, and he scored one of the 'Robins' goals. He added a further nine appearances for that season, and four more during 1941/42. After the conflict was over he joined Kilmarnock, followed by a big money move to Walsall in December 1947. He gave the 'Saddlers' full value for their investment, performing with great aplomb in either an inside-forward berth or as a wing-half. Described as a 'charismatic footballer, skilful and versatile, with a fund of Caledonian craft put in for good measure.' He once scored five goals against Torquay United in September 1949. A great club man, Johnny left Walsall in 1952 and later played for Bloxwich Strollers. He eventually settled in the Walsall area.

DICKENSON, Albert — Northampton Town

Position; *Centre-Half*
Born; *Saltney Ferry, 10th February, 1914.*
Debut v. *New Brighton (h) 21.9.1940*
Total Appearances & Goals; *10 apps, 0 gls*
Career; *Everton (Am) Jul 1934, (Pro) Nov 1934 1app 0gls; Port Vale Sept 1936 5apps 0gls; Northampton Town Oct 1937 19apps 5gls; Chester (WW2 Guest) 1939/40 1app 0gls; Wrexham (WW2 Guest) Sept 1940 10apps 0gls;*

Albert Dickenson first joined Everton as an amateur, and signed professional forms in November 1934. He made one Football League appearance for the Goodison Park club in March 1935 at centre-forward in a 5-1 defeat at Portsmouth, after which he was allowed to join Port Vale in September 1936. Five appearances for Vale followed before he lost his place in the team through injury. He later played for Northampton Town until the conflict intervened. During this period Albert appeared as a 'guest' for both Chester and Wrexham, where he clocked up ten war-time appearances, the first coming in September 1940 at centre-half in a 5-0 home win over New Brighton. He made nine more appearances for the 'Robins' that same season.

DIX, Ronald William — Tottenham Hotspur

Position; *Inside-Left*
Born; *Bristol, 5th September, 1912.*
Died; *Bristol, 2nd April, 1998.*
Height; *5ft 9* **Weight;** *12st 7lbs*
Debut v. *Crewe Alexandra (a) 4.11.1944*
Total Appearances & Goals; *34 apps, 17 gls*
Career; *South Central School, Bedminster; Bristol Rovers (Am) Jul 1927, (Pro) Feb 1928 101apps 32gls; Blackburn Rovers 9th May 1932 £3,000 38apps 14gls; Aston Villa May 1933 97apps 30gls; Derby County Feb 1937 £4,875 94apps 35gls; Tottenham Hotspur Jun 1939 36apps 5gls, WW2 apps gls; Bristol City (WW2 Guest) Oct 1939 24apps 13gls; Chester (WW2 Guest) 1940/41 1app 0gls; Blackpool (WW2 Guest) Aug 1941 100apps 45gls; Bradford Park Avenue (WW2 Guest) 1944/45 9apps 2gls; Wrexham (WW2 Guest) Nov 1944 34apps 17gls; York City (WW2 Guest) 1944/45 15apps 7gls; Liverpool (WW2 Guest) Sep 1944 6apps 2gls; Reading Nov 1947 44apps 13gls to cs1949;*
Honours; *One England International cap; Two England schoolboy caps; Football League Representative XI; Football League North Cup Winner 1943 & runner-up 1944;*

Ron Dix earned a massive reputation as a schoolboy star, very much like Michael Owen in the late 1990s. He entered the record books in only his second League appearance for Bristol Rovers, when, by grabbing the opening goal in a 3-0 win over Norwich City, he became the youngest ever goalscorer in a Football League match. It is an achievement which has not subsequently been bettered. Having previously represented Bristol and Gloucestershire Schoolboys he went on to captain England Schools against both Scotland and Wales in 1937. Ron signed amateur forms for Bristol Rovers in May 1927 and made his debut in February 1928 against Charlton Athletic, claiming the record a week later at just 15 years and 180 days old. Professional terms followed on his eighteenth birthday, and he became a regular with the 'Pirates' until joining Blackburn Rovers in May 1932. He later played for Aston Villa and Derby County, where he was to represent the Football League in a 3-1 win over the Scottish League at Molineux, his first cap for England coming a week later against Norway. England won, and Ron scored the second goal early in the

second half, though it was to prove to be his only international cap for England. Ron dropped back into Division Two in June 1939, signing for Tottenham Hotspur for £8,000, and played in the opening three games of 1939/40 before war was declared. He had been described as a 'forward who made the ball do the work. Cleverly constructive and high quality.' He played frequently for Spurs during WW2, and also turned out as a 'guest' for Bristol City, Chester, Liverpool, Middlesbrough, York City, Wrexham, and Blackpool - winning a two legged North Cup Final in 1943 as the 'Tangerines' beat Sheffield Wednesday 3-1 on aggregate. His Wrexham debut came in a 1-0 win at Crewe in November 1944, and he added a further 33 appearances, scoring seventeen goals, over his two seasons with the club, proving very popular with the Racecourse crowd. On resumption of the Football League Ron continued his career with Spurs before joining Reading in November 1947. After retiring from the game he ran a children's clothes shop in Bedminster, combining this with his role as a part-time football reporter with the 'Bristol Evening Post'. He died in April 1998, aged 85.

DOLBY,

Position; *Half-Back*
Debut v. *Stoke City (a) 28.11.1942*
Total Appearances & Goals; *1 app, 0 gls*
Career; *Wrexham (WW2 Guest) Nov 1942 1app 0gls;*

Dolby made just one WW2 appearance for Wrexham at Stoke City in November 1942 in a 2-0 defeat, stepping in as cover in the half-back line.

DOUGLAS, David N. — Leicester City

Position; *Outside-Left*
Born; *Selby*
Debut v. *Southport (h) 5.5.1945*
Total Appearances & Goals; *2 apps, 0 gls*
Career; *Leicester City Oct 1944 to May 1946 3apps 1gls; Wrexham (WW2 Guest) May 1945 2apps 0gls;*

David Douglas was serving in the R.A.F. when Leicester City signed him in October 1944. He made just three appearances and scored one goal for the 'Foxes' before his release in May 1946. During the WW2 period, he turned out as a 'guest' for Wrexham in the last two games of the 1944/45 season: his debut came against Southport in a 2-0 home win, and he followed this by playing in the next match, the return game against the 'Sandgrounders', which Wrexham won 5-1.

DRISCOLL, John Henry — Wellington Town

Position; *Inside-Left*
Born; *Grays, Essex, J/A/S 1909*
Height; *5ft 9in* ***Weight;*** *10st 0lbs*
Debut v. *Chester 20.2.1943*
Total Appearances & Goals; *1 app, 0 gls*
Career; *Rodington FC; Oakengates Town; Oswestry Town Aug 1932; Shrewsbury Town Oct 1933; West Bromwich Albion Nov 1934; Sheffield Wednesday May 1937 5apps 2gls; Wellington Town Jun 1938; Wrexham (WW2 Guest) Feb 1943 1app 0gls;*
Honours; *Welsh Cup Winner 1940;*

John had played Birmingham League football for both Oswestry Town and Shrewsbury Town when he was signed by West Bromwich Albion in November 1934. However, he failed to make a first team appearance at the Hawthorns, and left to join Sheffield Wednesday in May 1937. His Football League debut for the 'Owls' came in a 1-0 defeat against Manchester United at Old Trafford, and he kept his place for the next game, scoring the only goal in a 1-0 win at Coventry. Just three more appearances for Wednesday followed, and at the end of the campaign he left Hillsborough to join another Birmingham League side, Wellington Town, and he was still at the Bucks Head when WW2 broke out. It was during this period that John made one appearance for Wrexham as a 'guest' player, a 3-0 defeat at Chester in February 1943.

DUGDALE, T.C.

Position; *Goalkeeper*
Debut v. *Crewe Alexandra (h) 30.1.1943*
Total Appearances & Goals; *1 app, 0 gls*
Career; *Wrexham (WW2 Guest) Jan 1943 1app 0gls;*

Dugdale made just one appearance in goal for Wrexham in January 1943, when he stepped into the side to replace Percy Lovett in a 1-0 home defeat by Crewe Alexandra.

DUNS, Leonard — Sunderland

Position; *Outside-Right*
Born; *Newcastle-on-Tyne, 26th Sept, 1916.*
Died; *Ponteland, Northumberland 20th April, 1989*
Height; *5ft 8'1/2in* ***Weight;*** *11st 9lbs*
Debut v. *Everton (a) 9.12.1944*
Total Appearances & Goals; *19 apps, 4 gls*
Career; *Newcastle West End; Sunderland 4th Sept 1933 215apps 45gls, WW2 4apps 1gls; Newcastle United (WW2 Guest) Oct 1939 30apps 3gls; Aldershot (WW2 Guest) 1939/40 13apps 6gls; Reading (WW2 Guest) 1941/42 9apps 0gls; Brentford (WW2 Guest) 1941/42 7apps 2gls; Bristol City (WW2 Guest) Apr 1942 1apps 0gls; Notts County (WW2 Guest) 1942/43 5apps 1gls; West Bromwich Albion (WW2 Guest) Sep 1943 13apps 5gls; Wrexham (WW2 Guest) Dec 1944 19apps 4gls; Retired May 1952;*
Honours; *F.A.Cup Winner 1937; Football League Championship 1936;*

Len Duns joined Sunderland in September 1933 from non-league side Newcastle West End. He made his Football League debut in a 2-2 draw at Portsmouth in November 1935, and went to collect a Football League Championship medal with the 'Rokerites' in 1936, adding an F.A.Cup winners' medal the following year. His career with Sunderland came to an abrupt halt in 1939 with the outbreak of WW2. It was during this period that he played as a 'guest' for Newcastle, Aldershot, Reading, Brentford, Bristol City, Notts County, West Bromwich Albion, and Wrexham. Len made his debut for the 'Robins' in a 2-2 draw at Everton, and he added another eleven appearances that season, with five more at the beginning of 1945/46. After the War Len resumed his career with Sunderland, until he hung up his boots at the end of the 1951/52 season. In 1951 he was described in the Footballers' Who's Who by Brian Glanville as a 'veteran right-winger, but still effective and progressive'.

EASTWOOD, Eric — Manchester City

Position; *Centre-Half*
Born; *Heywood, 24th March, 1916.*
Died; *Bolton, October 1991.*
Height; *5ft 9in* ***Weight;*** *11st 8lbs*
Debut v. *Chester (h) 23.2.1946*
Total Appearances & Goals; *3 apps, 0 gls*
Career; *Oxford Road School; Chorley Road Congregationals; Little Lever; Westhoughton; Heywood St.James; Manchester City 14th Mar 1935 14apps 3gls; Bolton Wanderers (WW2 Guest) 1939/40 29apps 0gls; Rochdale (WW2 Guest) 1940/41 3apps 1gls; Manchester United (WW2 Guest) May 1943 3apps 0gls; Wrexham (WW2 Guest) Feb 1946 3apps 0gls; Port Vale 27th Mar 1947 28apps 1gls;*

Eric Eastwood was the grandson of a Bolton Wanderers Director, and the son of Percy Eastwood, who played for Bolton, while his brother James turned out for both Crewe and Rochdale. At school Eric was a 100 yards' sprint champion and he also captained the Bolton Schoolboys' football team. He had two trials for England Schoolboys before signing for Manchester City in March 1935, although he had to wait until August 1938 for his Football League debut which came in City's 5-0 home win over Swansea Town. His career came to a sudden halt with the outbreak of WW2, and it was during the conflict that he appeared as a 'guest' for Bolton Wanderers, Manchester United, and Wrexham. He made three appearances for the Racecourse club , the first of which came in February 1946, a 2-0 home win over Chester. This was followed by two 2-1 victories over Rochdale, home and away. After the conflict had ended Eric returned to Maine Road to resume his career, but after just nine more League appearances he was allowed to sign for Port Vale. However, he was sidelined with groin muscle trouble throughout much of his time at Vale Park, and he made only sporadic appearances thereafter. He was given a free transfer in April 1950.

EDWARDS, George Robert — Aston Villa

Position; *Outside-Right*
Born; *Great Yarmouth, 7th April, 1918.*
Died; *Hockley Heath, Warwicks, 21st January, 1993.*
Height; *5ft 10 1/2in* ***Weight;*** *11st 6lbs*
Debut v. *Wolves (h) 20.4.1940*
Total Appearances & Goals; *2 apps, 1 goal*
Career; *Priory School; Yarmouth Caledonians; Norwich City 1st Apr 1936 9apps 1gls; Aston Villa 7th Jun 1938 138apps 34gls; Birmingham (WW2 Guest) Oct 1939 10apps 5gls; Norwich City (WW2 Guest) 1939/40 1app 0gls; Northampton Town (WW2 Guest) 1939/40 7apps 2gls; Walsall (WW2 Guest) Mar 1940 4apps 1gls; Wrexham (WW2 Guest) Apr 1940 2apps 1gls; Nottingham Forest (WW2 Guest) 1940/41 8apps 0gls; Notts County (WW2 Guest) 1940/41 16apps 2gls; Leicester City (WW2 Guest) 1945/46 1app 0gls; Bilston United Aug 1951; Yarmouth Town Aug 1955 to Sept 1955;*
Honours; *League North War Cup Winner 1944;*

Signed by Norwich as an amateur when he was still only sixteen. George Edwards made his Football League debut for the 'Canaries' in a 1-0 win at Burnley in the same month that he had joined the club. He spent two seasons at Carrow Road, adding another eight appearances before Aston Villa stepped in to sign him. George had appeared in the opening three games of the 1939/40 season for Villa when WW2 broke out, and during the hostilities he assisted a number of clubs as a 'guest', including Birmingham, Nottingham Forest, Notts County, Coventry City, Northampton Town, West Bromwich Albion, Walsall, and Wrexham. He made two appearances for the 'Robins', the first a 1-1 home draw with Wolves, followed by a 4-2 home win over Stockport County, when he found himself on the score sheet. George picked up a League North War Cup Winners' tankard with Villa, when they beat Blackpool in the two legged Final in 1944. At the conclusion of the War he continued with Villa, becoming leading scorer for three consecutive seasons between 1946 and 1948. He left Villa in the close season of 1951 and joined Bilston United, for whom he played until 1955 when he retired from football. George then operated a newsagents and sub-post office business in Birmingham, and also became a Director at Aston Villa.

ELLIS, John — Clapton Orient

Position; *Goalkeeper*
Born; *Tyldesbury, Lancashire 25th January, 1908.*
Died; *Tyldesbury, January, 1994.*
Height; *5ft 11'1/2in* ***Weight;*** *12st 0lbs*
Debut v. *Chester (h) 22.11.1941*
Total Appearances & Goals; *9 apps, 0 gls*
Career; *Tyldesbury United; Tyldesbury Juniors; Atherton; Winsford United; West Bromwich Albion (Am) May 1930 to Oct 1930 0apps; Wolves Feb 1931 26apps 0gls; Bristol Rovers 27th Jul 1934 86apps 0gls; Hull City 27th May 1938 31apps 0gls; Clapton Orient Jul 1939 0apps; Rochdale (WW2 Guest) 1939/40 2apps 0gls; Wrexham (WW2 Guest) Nov 1941 9apps 0gls; Stockport County (WW2 Guest) Sept 1944 2apps 0gls;*
Honours; *Division Three South Cup Winner 1935;*

John Ellis was playing Cheshire County League football for Winsford United when he was given a chance by West Bromwich Albion in May 1930, although soon released in the following October. He returned to Winsford and eventually earned a second chance of League football when Wolves signed him in February 1931. This time he seized his opportunity with both hands!, going on to make his Football League debut in a 4-1 defeat at Manchester City in November 1932. John remained at Molyneux until the end of 1933/34 when he moved on to Bristol Rovers. He picked up a Third Division South Cup winners' medal with the 'Pirates' in 1935, a year in which he was also the goalkeeper on the receiving end of Luton Town's record win of 12-0, which is also the Third Division South's record score. The 'Hatters' were certainly something of a bogey side for the 'keeper, as it was against them that he broke his collar bone in January 1935, and this forced him to miss Rovers' F.A.Cup tie against Manchester United. John was Rovers' regular 'keeper for 1935/36, when he was beaten 95 times, the most goals that any Rovers side had conceded in one season. He signed for Hull City in May 1938, and was between the posts when the 'Tigers' recorded their best ever victory, 11-1 over Carlisle United in January 1938. After 31 League outings for Hull he signed for Clapton Orient in the summer of 1939, and played in the 'O's' opening three games of the 1939/40 season before WW2 was to virtually put an end to his playing career. He did make 'guest' appearances during the conflict for Rochdale, Stockport and Wrexham, for whom he turned out nine times during the 1941/42 season. His 'Robins' debut came in a 1-1 home draw with Chester in November, though he also played in their 10-3 defeat at the hands of Manchester United! In those nine games for Wrexham he let in 40 goals! John served as an R.A.F. Policeman during WW2, and after the conflict had ended he became player/manager of Winsford United, and a scout with Leeds United.

EMMANUEL, Thomas D. — Southampton

Position; *Right-Back*
Born; *Treboeth, Swansea, 1st August 1915*
Height; *5ft 10in* ***Weight;*** *11st 8lbs*
Debut v. *Southport (h) 31/8/1940*
Total Appearances & Goals; *12 apps, 0 gls*
Career; *I.C.I.Works XI; Swansea Town Sept 1935 46apps 1gls; Southampton Sept 1938 £2,200 33apps 0gls; Wrexham (WW2 Guest) Aug 1940 12apps 0gls; Swindon Town (WW2 Guest) 1945/46 7apps 0gls; Llanelli 1946 to 1948;*

Tom Emmanuel was the older brother of David, who played for Swansea and Newport County. Tom spent three years with the Vetch Field club, where he made 46 appearances before signing for Southampton in September 1938 for a £2,200 fee. He looked set for a long future at the Dell when War broke out. During the conflict he saw service in Africa, Burma, India and Madasgar, but still managed to turn out as a 'guest' for both Swindon Town and Wrexham. Twelve appearances were clocked up for the North Wales club at the beginning of 1940/41, his debut coming in a 3-1 home win over Southport in August 1940. When normality returned Tom played for Llanelli for two seasons, and later worked as an inspector for the Swansea Bus Company for 25 years.

FAIRHURST, David Liddle — Hartlepool United

Position; *Left-Back*
Born; *Blyth, 20th July 1906.*
Died; *Solihull, 26th October, 1972.*
Height; *5ft 8in* ***Weight;*** *12st 7lbs.*
Debut v. *Chester (a) 4.9.1943*
Total Appearances & Goals; *2 apps, 0 gls*
Career; *New Deloval Villa; Blyth Spartans; Walsall Jun 1927 56apps 0gls; Newcastle United Mar 1929 £1,750 266apps 2gls; Hartlepool United cs1939; Wrexham (WW2 Guest) Sep 1943 2apps 0gls;*
Honours; *One England International cap; F.A.Cup Winner 1932;*

David Fairhurst hailed from Blyth, and followed in his father's footsteps by playing for Blyth Spartans. His brother William Shaw Fairhurst also played League football for Nelson, Northampton and Southport. However, it was Walsall where the former shipyard worker was to begin his own Football League career, signing for the Midlands club in 1927. He spent two years with the 'Saddlers', making his League debut in October 1927 in a 5-0 defeat at Swindon, and adding a further 55 League appearances before signing for Newcastle United in March 1929. The 'Sturdily built, and quite reliable fearless tackler' went on to spend a decade with the 'Magpies', picking up an England cap in 1934 against

France, and an F.A.Cup winners' medal from the 1932 Final against Arsenal. David left St.James' Park in the close season of 1939 to join Hartlepool United, playing in the first three matches of 1939/40. He continued to play football during the War years, and did not retire until he was almost 40. It was during this time that he appeared as a 'guest' for Wrexham, making two appearances in September 1943, a 3-3 draw at Chester, followed by an 8-0 hammering at Liverpool. After his playing career was over he became trainer with Birmingham City in July 1946.

FELLOWS, William James — Exeter City

Position; *Half-Back*
Born; *Bradford, 15th March 1910.*
Died; *Plymouth, November, 1987*
Height; *5ft 9 1/2in* ***Weight;*** *12st 0lb*
Debut v. *Tranmere Rovers (h) 13.3.1943*
Career; *Tavistock Town; Plymouth Argyle Jul 1927 5apps 0gls; Clapton Orient Jul 1933 78apps 1gls; Luton Town May 1935 110apps 3gls; Exeter City Jun 1938 56apps 1gls; Plymouth Argyle (WW2 Guest) Jan 1940 5apps 3gls; Wrexham (WW2 Guest) Mar 1943 1app 0gls; Tavistock Town 1947;*

Billy Fellows began his career with Tavistock Town before signing for Plymouth Argyle in July 1927. His Football League debut for the 'Pilgrims' came in a 2-1 win at Norwich City in April 1930, and four more League appearances for the Devon club followed before he was transferred to Clapton Orient in July 1933. After being an 'O's' regular for two seasons, Luton Town signed him in the summer of 1935, whereupon he became a permanent fixture in the 'Hatters' side for three seasons until signing for Exeter City in June 1938. Bill was an ever-present for the Devon side during 1938/39, but WW2 was to see the 'Grecians' close down until 1945. During the conflict he turned out for both Plymouth Argyle and Wrexham as a 'guest', making one appearance for the 'Robins' in March 1943, a 2-1 home win over Tranmere Rovers. After the War Billy resumed his playing career with Exeter City, adding another fourteen League appearances before rejoining Tavistock Town in 1947. He later ran two sports outfitters businesses in Tavistock.

FERRIER, Ronald Johnson — Oldham Athletic

Position; *Inside-Left*
Born; *Cleethorpes, 26th April, 1914.*
Died; *Cleethorpes, 11th October, 1991*
Height; *5ft 10'1/2in* ***Weight;*** *11st 6lbs*
Debut v. *New Brighton (h) 4.1.1941*
Total Appearances & Goals; *2 apps, 1 goal*
Career; *Grimsby Wanderers; Grimsby Town 13th May 1933 0apps; Manchester United 8th May 1935 18apps 4gls; Oldham Athletic 17th Mar 1938 45apps 25gls, WW2 70apps 47gls; Wrexham (WW2 Guest) Jan 1941 2apps 1gls; Grimsby Town (WW2 Guest) Nov 1941 19apps 12gls; Southampton (WW2 Guest) 1942/43 2apps 0gls; Reading (WW2 Guest) 1942/43 1app 0gls;Crystal Palace (WW2 Guest) Oct 1943 26apps 21gls; West Ham United (WW2 Guest) Jan 1945 1app 0gls; Plymouth Argyle (WW2 Guest) Sept 1945 1app 0gls; Lincoln City Aug 1947;*

Ron Ferrier joined Grimsby Town in May 1933, and though he failed to make a first team appearance in his two years at Blundell Park, Manchester United must have seen something to sign him in May 1935. He made his Football League debut for them in the second match of the season, a 3-0 home win over Charlton Athletic, when he lined up alongside former Wrexham goalscoring machine Tommy Bamford. Six more appearances followed for United as they went on to clinch the Second Division Championship, though in March 1936 he actually scored seven goals in a reserve team match against Bury. Ron completed a total of eighteen League appearances for United before he was signed by Oldham Athletic in March 1938 for a 'four-figure fee'. His clever stylish play soon made him a crowd favourite at Boundary Park, and a switch from inside-left to centre-forward saw him end the 1938/39 season as the club's leading scorer with 23 goals. He continued with Oldham for part of the War years, and also turned out as a 'guest' for Grimsby Town, Crystal Palace, Reading, Plymouth Argyle, Grimsby Town, West Ham United, Southampton, and Wrexham. Ron made two Lancashire Cup appearances for the 'Robins' in January 1941, his debut a 5-3 home defeat by New Brighton, followed by a 6-1 defeat in the return match though he had some consolation by scoring the Wrexham goal. He resumed his playing career with Oldham Athletic after the War, but managed just two appearances all season. He later spent some time on the coaching staff at Grimsby Town, before becoming player/coach with the Scunthorpe area side Lysaghts Sports in July 1950.

FOULKES, Reginald Ernest — Birmingham

Position; *Centre-Half*
Born; *Shrewsbury, 23rd February, 1923.*
Height; *6ft 0in* ***Weight;*** *12st 3lbs.*
Debut v. *New Brighton (a) 11.1.1941*
Total Appearances & Goals; *1 app, 0 gls*
Career; *Birmingham Mar 1940, WW2 21apps gls; Wrexham (WW2 Guest) Jan 1941 1app 0gls; Walsall Aug 1945 160apps 6gls, WW2 25apps 1gls; Norwich City May 1950 216apps 8gls; Wisbech (Player/manager) May 1956; Kings Lynn May 1957;*
Honours; *England Schoolboy International;*

Reg Foulkes played for Shrewsbury Schoolboys progressing to the England Schoolboys XI at the age of 14. He had trials with both Manchester United and Birmingham before signing for the latter in March 1940. 21 appearances followed for the 'Blues' during WW2, as well as turning out as a 'guest' for Wrexham. His solitary appearance for the 'Robins' came in January 1941, a 6-1 defeat at New Brighton. Following the end of the conflict he signed for Walsall in August 1945, and finally made his Football League debut for the 'Saddlers' in the opening game of the 1946/47 season, a 3-1 defeat at Southend. Reg went on to become a loyal servant to both Walsall and Norwich City who he joined in May 1950, and where his generalship in defence made him a resolute and determined captain. He later played for Wisbech Town and King's Lynn, ending his career as a permit player with Ceyms FC. Eventually he returned to settle in his native Shrewsbury.

FOXALL, Joseph Stanley — West Ham United

Position; *Outside-Right*
Born; *Crowle, Lincolnshire, 8th October, 1914.*
Died; *Barking, 12th August, 1991.*
Height; *5ft 11in* ***Weight;*** *11st 2lbs.*
Debut v. *Tranmere Rovers (h) 29.1.1944*
Total Appearances & Goals; *14 apps, 10 gls*
Career; *Gainsborough Trinity; West Ham United 1933/34 106apps 38gls, WW2 118apps 55gls; Charlton Athletic (WW2 Guest) 1941/42 1app 0gls; Grimsby Town (WW2 Guest) Apr 1942 5apps 1gls; Wrexham (WW2 Guest) Jan 1944 14apps 10gls;*
Honours; *League War Cup Winner 1940;*

Stan Foxall was signed from Gainsborough Trinity by West Ham United during the 1933/34 season. He took his time to establish himself in the 'Hammers' first team, having made his Football League debut in a 3-1 win at Bradford during September 1934. Stan was sometimes known as the 'Mystery Man' because of his unorthodox methods (occasionally bewildering his own team-mates!). Encouraged by manager Charlie Paynter to be more direct, Stan became a feared goalscorer, able to 'operate anywhere in the front line'. The War then intervened to disrupt Stan's career just after he had become a regular fixture in the Upton Park senior side. Even so, he continued to turn out for the East End club during the conflict, and he played in the League War Cup Final when

West Ham beat Blackburn Rovers at Wembley in 1940. knee injury. The War years also saw him 'guest' for Grimsby Town, Charlton Athletic, and Wrexham, where he played his first match in January 1944, a 2-0 home win over Tranmere Rovers. Another twelve appearances for the 'Robins' followed that season, in which he scored nine goals. His final appearance came in the opening match of the 1944/45 season, a 5-0 home win over Bury, and he signed off by scoring one of the Wrexham goals. Stan was forced to end his playing career shortly after that game after suffering a knee injury.

FRANKLIN, Cornelius — Stoke City

Position; *Centre-Half*
Born; *Stoke-on-Trent, 24th January, 1922.*
Died; *Stafford, 9th February, 1996.*
Height; *5ft 11in* ***Weight;*** *11st 4lb*
Debut v. *Chester (a) 16.5.1942*
Total Appearances & Goals; *5 apps, 0 gls*
Career; *Cannon Street School; Stoke Old Boys; Stoke City (Am) 1936, (Pro) Jan 1939 142apps 0gls; Wrexham (WW2 Guest) May 1942 5apps 0gls; Wolves (WW2 Guest) Dec 1942 1app 0gls; Lincoln City (WW2 Guest) 1945/46 3apps 0gls; Torquay United (WW2 Guest) 1945/46 1app 0gls; Santa Fe (Columbia) May 1950; Hull City Feb 1951 £22,500 95apps 0gls; Crewe Alexandra Feb 1956 £1,250 66apps 4gls; Stockport County Oct 1957 £1,250 20apps 0gls; Macclesfield Town 1958; Wellington Town Jul 1959 (Player/Coach); GKN Sankeys Wellington Jul 1960 (Player/Manager);*
Honours; *27 England International caps; 3 War-time England International caps; 5 Football League XI Representative caps; 2 England 'B' International caps;*

One of the stars of the immediate post war period, Neil Franklin was a centre-half of the highest skill and an unyielding defender. Neil, as he was better known, was further gifted with the ability to organise those around him into a committed and effective unit. He began his career with Stoke City, but before he had even kicked a football in jest, WW2 began. During the conflict he turned out as a 'guest' for Wolves, Lincoln, Torquay, Wrexham, and made three War-time international appearances for England. He had five outings with the 'Robins, the first of which ended in a 2-1 win at Chester in May 1942. When peace was restored he went on to enjoy a distinguished football career, which included a spell in Bogota with Santa Fe. However, upon returning home he found that he had been banned from the game for playing in Colombia. He never represented England again, although he was able to resume his League career with Hull, Crewe, Stockport, and Macclesfield. Damaged knee ligaments, sustained during his time at Hull, effectively ended his playing career as he could never recapture his best form after his recovery. Neil eventually tried his hand at management with non-league side Sankeys of Wellington. In 1963 he travelled to Cyprus to coach Appoel Nicosia for a short spell, before taking up an appointment as manager of Colchester United in November 1963. He spent five years in charge at Layer Road before eventually becoming a licensee in Oswaldtwistle.

FROST, Arthur Douglas — Newcastle United

Position; *Centre-Forward*
Born; *Liverpool, 1st December, 1915.*
Height; *5ft 11 1/2in* ***Weight;*** *12st 0lbs*
Debut v. *Chester (a) 16.05.42*
Total Appearances & Goals; *7 apps, 2 gls*
Career; *Army; New Brighton (Am) 23rd Jul 1938, (Pro) 19th Aug 1938 23apps 18gls; Newcastle United 4th Mar 1939 £2,515 5apps 1gls; New Brighton (WW2 Guest) Oct 1939 84apps 65gls; Wrexham (WW2 Guest) May 1942 7apps 2gls; Southport (WW2 Guest) 1942/3 12apps 6gls; Tranmere Rovers (WW2 Guest) 1942/43 8apps 3gls; Brighton H.A. (WW2 Guest) Feb 1945 3apps 1gls; South Liverpool 1946/47;*

Signed by New Brighton from the Army, where he had served with the South Lancashire Regiment. He was given his chance with the 'Rakers' and took it with great effect scoring 18 goals in 23 League games. Described as 'Cool and intelligent' Newcastle United quickly stepped in to sign the promising youngster. His time at St.James Park was cut short because of the War, however, he returned home during the conflict to 'guest' for a number of clubs including former club New Brighton, Southport, Tranmere Rovers, Brighton & Hove Albion, and Wrexham. His debut for the 'Robins' came in May 1942, a 2-1 win at Chester, and he was on target twice in a total seven appearances for the Racecourse club. After the war had ended Arthur played for South Liverpool.

FULLER, C. — Walthamstow

Position; *Half-Back*
Debut v. *Bury (a) 2.9.1944*
Total Appearances & Goals; *10 apps, 0 gls*
Career; *Walthamstow; Reading (WW2 Guest) 1942/43 1app 0gls; Fulham (WW2 Guest) 1943/44 1app 0gls; Wrexham (WW2 Guest) Sept 1944 10apps 0gls;*

Fuller was on the books of Walthamstow prior to the outbreak of World War Two. During this period he was a 'guest' for Reading, Fulham and Wrexham, for whom he turned out on ten occasions between September and November of 1944. Described as 'A clever classical half-back' he made his debut for the Racecourse club in a 3-1 win at Bury in only the second match of the 1944/45 season.

GAVIN, Charles — Arbroath

Position; *Half-Back*
Born; *Coatbridge*
Height; *5ft 9in* ***Weight;*** *11st 3lbs*
Debut v. *Bury (h) 26.8.1944*
Total Appearances & Goals; *12 apps, 1gls*
Career; *Glasgow Ashfield; Aberdeen; Arbroath; Wrexham (WW2 Guest) Aug 1944 12apps 1gls;*

Charlie Gavin joined Wrexham as a 'guest' during WW2, having played for Scottish League side Arbroath prior to the conflict. He made his debut for the North-East Wales club in the opening game of 1944/45, a 5-0 home win over Bury. Charlie went on to add another eleven further appearances for the 'Robins', his last coming in a 4-2 home defeat by Crewe Alexandra in the November of the same year. He was a member of the British Army XI in Berlin as the War came to an end.

GILL, Henry — Wrexham

Position; *Goalkeeper*
Debut v. *Manchester United (h) 12.12.1942*
Total Appearances & Goals; *1 app, 0 gls*
Career; *Wrexham 17th Dec 1942 1app 0gls;*

Henry Gill joined Wrexham as a trialist goalkeeper, making his debut in December 1942 as a replacement for Don Clegg. He lined up against Manchester United on the Racecourse, and the game which ended in a 5-2 defeat, proved to be his one and only appearance for the 'Robins'.

GLADWIN, George Willie E. — *Manchester United*

Position; *Half-Back*
Born; *Chesterfield, 28th March, 1907.*
Height; *5ft 7'1/2in* ***Weight;*** *12st 0lbs*
Debut v. *Blackburn Rovers (h) 28.9.1940*
Total Appearances & Goals; *1 app, 0 gls*
Career; *Worksop Town (Am) cs1926; Doncaster Rovers Aug 1930 226apps 22gls; Manchester United Feb 1937 £3,000 27apps 1gls; Barnsley (WW2 Guest) 1939/40 2apps 0gls; Wrexham (WW2 Guest) Sept 1940 1app 0gls; Doncaster Rovers (WW2 Guest) Jan 1942 5app 1gls;*
Honours; *Third Division North Championship Winner 1935;*

George was playing non-league football for Worksop Town when he signed for Doncaster Rovers in August 1930. He made his Football League debut for Doncaster in a 3-0 defeat at Wigan Borough in October 1930 and went on to complete over 250 appearances for the Belle Vue club, including a major part in the Third Division North Championship season of 1935, when he missed just three games. In February 1937 the 'small, but strongly built' player, who was regarded as a 'double' of Alex James, was signed by Manchester United. The former bricklayer clocked up 27 League appearances in over two seasons at Old Trafford, during which he was described as a 'fine acquisition. Developed into a capable wing-half or inside-forward'. His Football League career came to an abrupt halt with the outbreak of the War, although he then appeared as a 'guest' for Barnsley, Doncaster Rovers, and Wrexham. He made one appearance for the Racecourse club in September 1940, a 2-1 home win over Blackburn Rovers. George was wounded during the war forcing him to retire from the game.

GRAHAM, William — Norwich City

Position; *Inside-Left*
Born; *Hetton-Le-Hole, Durham, 3rd October, 1914.*
Died; *Clwyd, September 1996.*
Height; *5ft 9in* ***Weight;*** *10st 4lbs*
Debut v. *Manchester United (h) 13.12.1941*
Total Appearances & Goals; *15 apps, 9 gls*
Career; *Eppleton School; Houghton Secondary School; Hetton Juniors; Burnley (Trial) 1932; Blyth Spartans (Trial) 1932; Burnley Sept 1932 1app 0gls; Bury May 1935 74apps 2gls; Norwich City 3rd Feb 1939 17apps 4gls; Halifax Town (WW2 Guest) 1939/40 4apps 0gls; Wrexham (WW2 Guest) Dec 1941 15apps 9gls; Bury (WW2 Guest) 1943/44 2apps 0gls; Norwich City 1945/46 6apps 2gls; Barry Town Nov 1946; Holywell Town 1949;*

Bill Graham was a fine pre-war goalscorer, forming a productive partnership with Jack Acquroff at Bury, having made his Football League debut with Burnley. At Gigg Lane he was described as having 'the secret perpetual motion plus great positional awareness'. He joined Norwich City towards the end of the 1938/39 season, but - as with many others - WW2 was to effectively end his Football League career, although he continued to play football as a 'guest' during the conflict. He represented Halifax Town, Bury, Norwich City, and Wrexham, scoring on his debut for the 'Robins' in a 4-2 home defeat by Manchester United in December 1941. Another eleven appearances followed for the Racecourse club that season, in which he scored eight more goals, including a hat-trick in a 6-1 home win over Stockport in January 1942. He played in the opening four games of 1942/43, contributing one goal. Graham was to eventually settle in North Wales upon his retirement.

GRIFFITHS, David Thomas — Wrexham

Position; *Inside-Left*
Born; *New Broughton, Nr.Wrexham. 19th December, 1924.*
Height; *5ft 7in* ***Weight;*** *10st 4lbs*
Debut v. *Port Vale (a) 2.4.1945*
Total Games: *1 app, 1 gls*
Career; *New Broughton Y.C; Wrexham (WW2) Apr 1945 1app 1gls;*

David Griffiths turned out for New Broughton Youth Club in their 9-1 win in the Final of the Denbighshire Youth League Cup against Old Colwyn on Wrexham's Racecourse Ground in April 1943. After the match he was invited to join the 'Robins' by manager Tom Williams, and he went on to feature in many reserve team games during his time with the club. His performances eventually led to him being appointed captain of the reserve XI, and he also turned out in the Victory League against the likes of R.A.F.Tern Hill. His senior debut for the 'Robins' came at Port Vale in April 1945, where he scored in the 2-2 draw. A few days after that match David sustained a serious hamstring injury, which eventually restricted him to local football. He was a member of the renowned Rhos Male Voice Choir for over twenty years, and despite now living in retirement in Southsea David is still involved with Wrexham Football Club, taking the official team photograph every summer - a task that he has happily performed for many years. He is still a follower of the club, always supporting the team at the Racecourse Ground, and has not missed many games since the 1930s.

GRIFFITHS,

Position; *Inside-Left*
Debut v. *Wolves (a) 27.4.1940*
Total Appearances & Goals; *1 app, 0 gls*
Career; *Wrexham (WW2 Guest) Apr 1940 1app 0gls;*

Griffiths made his solitary senior appearance for the 'Robins' against Wolves in a League War Cup match in April 1940, playing in the inside-left position. The match ended in a 3-0 defeat for the Racecourse club.

GRIFFITHS, George J. — Wrexham

Position; *Goalkeeper*
Debut v. *Tranmere Rovers (a) 2.10.1943*
Total Appearances & Goals; *1 app, 0 gls*
Career; *Wrexham (WW2) Oct 1943 1app 0gls;*

George Griffiths stepped into the Wrexham side for regular goalkeeper Don Clegg in October 1943, making his one and only appearance for the 'Robins' in a disastrous 6-0 defeat at Tranmere Rovers.

GRIFFITHS, Harry Stanley — Port Vale

Position; *Half-Back*
Born; *Liverpool, 17th November 1912*
Died; *Stoke-on-Trent, 11th June 1981*
Height; *5ft 9in* ***Weight;*** *11st 3lbs*
Debut v. *West Bromwich Albion (a) 27.12.41*
Total Appearances & Goals; *7 app, 0 gls*
Career; *Everton Aug 1932 0apps; Port Vale May 1935 76apps 3gls, WW2 78apps 5gls; Wrexham (WW2 Guest) Dec 1941 7apps 0gls; Derby County (WW2 Guest) 1942/43 1app 0gls;*

An England Baseball International Harry Griffiths began his football career with Everton in August 1932, though he failed to make a first team appearance at Goodison Park and was allowed to join Port Vale in May 1935. He made his debut for Vale at centre-half in a 4-0 defeat at Sheffield United in October of the same year, and went on to remain with them until the outbreak of WW2. He then joined the Police force, although continuing to turn out for Vale and as a 'guest' for both Derby County and Wrexham. He made the first of seven appearances for the 'Robins' in December 1941, a 6-4 defeat at West Bromwich Albion and, playing in the half-back line, he added six more in the early part of 1942. Harry suffered a severe scalp wound after colliding with some railings whilst playing for Vale against Crewe at Vale Park in December 1944, and after receiving stitches he returned to the action wearing a black beret! He began the new season after the conflict in the Vale first team, but by October had lost his place. He was released at the end of the campaign, whereupon he continued with his career as a Police Officer.

GRIPTON, Ernest William — West Bromwich Albion

Position; *Centre-Half*
Born; *Princes End, Tipton, 2nd July, 1920.*
Died; *Tipton, J/F/M 1981.*
Height; *5ft 11in* ***Weight;*** *11st 6lbs.*
Debut v. *Rotherham United (a) 23.3.1946*
Total Appearances & Goals; *1 app, 0 gls*
Career; *Dartmouth Vics; Bush Rangers; Brownhills Albion; West Bromwich Albion (Am) Jun 1935, (Pro) Nov 1937 16apps 0gls, WW2 192apps 2gls; Wrexham (WW2 Guest) Mar 1946 1app 0gls; Luton Town Jun 1948 £3,000 3apps 0gls; Bournemouth Jul 1950 79apps 0gls; Worcester City Jun 1952;*

Billy Gripton was a formidable centre-half who was a dominant force in West Brom's defence for a number of years. His Football League appearances for Albion were affected by the conflict, but it was during this period that he made more appearances for the 'Baggies' than any other player. A 'hard, but fair, tackling centre-half, who was a superb tactician', he took over the pivotal role in the Albion team from ex-Wrexham player Billy Tudor. During WW2 Billy made his one and only appearance for the 'Robins' as a 'guest' player in March 1946, a 4-0 defeat at Rotherham. He left the 'Hawthorns' in June 1948 to join Luton Town for a £3,000 fee, where he spent two seasons, making just three appearances before moving on to Bournemouth in the summer of 1950. Billy enjoyed his time on the south coast, completing 79 appearances for the 'Cherries' before leaving Dean Court to return to the Midlands with non-league Worcester City. In 1956 he hung up his boots and became employed as groundsman at the Hawthorns Ground, West Bromwich. He was later appointed groundsman at Dudley Sports Centre in Tipton, and also acted as an adviser to Vono F.C.

HAINES, John Thomas William — Swansea Town

Position; *Inside-Forward*
Born; *Wickhamford, Nr.Evesham, 24th April, 1920.*
Died; *Worcester, 13th March, 1987.*
Height; *5ft 9in* **Weight;** *10st 11lbs.*
Debut v. *Bury (a) 14.3.1942*
Total Appearances & Goals; *1 app, 0 gls*
Career; *Badsey Council School; Evesham Grammar School; Evesham Town 1934; Cheltenham Town; Liverpool Nov 1937 0apps; Swansea Town Jun 1939 28apps 7gls, WW2 10apps 2gls; Wrexham (WW2 Guest) Mar 1942 1app 0gls; Doncaster Rovers (WW2 Guest) Mar 1943 2apps 0gls; Notts County (WW2 Guest) 1942/43 9apps 2gls; Bradford Park Avenue (WW2 Guest) 1943/44 1app 0gls; Lincoln City (WW2 Guest) 1943/44 47apps 24gls; Leicester City Jun 1947 12apps 3gls; West Bromwich Albion Mar 1948 59apps 23gls; Bradford Park Avenue Dec 1949 (£10,000) 136apps 34gls; Rochdale Sept 1953 (£2,000) 60apps 16gls; Chester Jul 1955 46apps 8gls; Wellington Town cs1957; Kidderminster Harriers cs1958; Evesham Town Oct 1958 to 1959/60;*
Honours; *One England International cap 1949;*

Jack Haines was signed by Liverpool from Cheltenham Town, but he failed to make a first team appearance at Anfield and was allowed to join Swansea Town in the close season of 1939. The War interrupted his Football League career, and during the conflict he served in the R.A.F. which meant he was able to turn out for many clubs as a 'guest'. This included one appearance for Wrexham in March 1942, in a 3-0 win at Bury. He resumed his career at the Vetch after the hostilities, finally making his Football League debut for the 'Swans'. He went on to appear for a number of clubs, although it was at West Bromwich Albion that he had his best spell, scoring 23 goals in 53 games. This kind of form earned him a call-up for the England national side against Switzerland in December 1948, and Jack scored two of the goals in a 6-0 win at Highbury. That same season he assisted Albion to promotion to the First Division, but was allowed to leave the Hawthorns during the following season to join Bradford Park Avenue. He played out his career in the lower reaches of the League with Rochdale and Chester before sampling non-league football with Wellington Town, Kidderminster Harriers and Evesham Town. At his peak Jack's forte was said to be 'excellent ball control and a powerful shot, but he suffered more than most with injuries'.

HAMPSON, Eric — Stoke City

Position; *Half-Back*
Born; *Norton, 11th November, 1921.*
Debut v.
Total Appearances & Goals; *1 app, 0 gls*
Career; *Summerbank FC; Stafford Rangers; Stoke City May 1939 8apps 0gls, WW2 24app 0gls; Wrexham (WW2 Guest) Mar 1941 1app 0gls; Stafford Rangers (player/manager);*

Eric Hampson was playing for Stafford Rangers when he was signed by Stoke City in May 1939. His Football League debut was still awaited when War was declared, though he did make the first of 24 war-time appearances for the 'Potters' that season. During the conflict he completed one game for Wrexham as a 'guest' in March 1941, a 3-2 defeat at Blackburn Rovers. Eric eventually resumed his career with Stoke City, although he did not make his Football League debut until January 1949, a 3-2 home defeat by Manchester City. He added another seven League appearances, and was later appointed player/manager of Stafford Rangers.

HANCOCKS, John — Walsall

Position; *Outside-Right/Left*
Born; *Oakengates, Telford, 30th April, 1919.*
Died; *Telford, 19th February, 1994.*
Height; *5ft 4in* **Weight;** *10st 0lbs*
Debut v. *Bury (h) 26.8.1944*
Total Appearances & Goals; *26 apps, 12 gls*
Career; *Oakengates Fellowship; Oakengates Town (Am) Oct 1937; Walsall Aug 1938 30apps 8gls, WW2 94apps 35gls; Chester (WW2 Guest) 1943/44 1app 0gls; Crewe Alexandra (WW2 Guest) 1943/44 5apps 3gls; Wrexham (WW2 Guest) Aug 1944 26apps 12gls; Nottingham Forest (WW2 Guest) 1945/46 1app 0gls; Wolves May 1946 £4,000 343apps 158gls; Wellington Town cs1957 player/manager; Cambridge United Jan 1960; Oswestry Town Jul 1960; GKN Sankeys Dec 1960;*
Honours; *3 England International caps; First Division Championship 1954; F.A.Cup Winner 1949; Football League XI Representative cap;*

During the first ten years of the golden Post-War period Johnny Hancocks was one of the game's finest goalscoring wingers. He wore a size two

boot, but could unleash shots of devastating power, especially from free-kicks. Equally comfortable on either flank he was quick, elusive, cunning and determined. He joined Walsall from Oakengates Town, and remained with the 'Saddlers until 1946 when he signed for Wolves. Johnny continued to play for Walsall during the conflict, and 'guested' for a number of clubs including Wrexham, making his 'Robins' debut in August 1944 in the opening game of the 1944/45 season, a 5-0 home win over Bury in which he scored one of the goals. He went on to turn out 26 times for the Racecourse club, scoring 12 goals, between 1944 and 1946. He served in the Army as a P.T. instructor, and played several times for the Western Command and Army sides before enjoying a distinguished career with Wolves, as well as being capped three times for England: against Switzerland, scoring twice; Wales; and Yugoslavia. In later years he worked for Maddock & Sons (Ironfounders) in his native Oakengates, where he settled. Johnny Hancocks was noted as 'a small man with a big heart - his ratio of goals for a winger was phenomenal'.

HANSON, Adolphe Jonathan — Chelsea

Position; *Outside-Left*
Born; *Bootle, 27th December, 1912.*
Died; *St.Helens, October 1993.*
Height; *5ft 9 1/2in* **Weight;** *11st 7lbs*
Debut v. *Liverpool (h) 17.5.1941*
Total Appearances & Goals; *1 app, 0 gls*
Career; *Bootle JOC; Everton (trial) cs1930, Jan 1931; Liverpool Nov 1931 166apps 50gls; Chelsea Jun 1938 £7,500 37apps 8gls; New Brighton (WW2 Guest) Oct 1939 49apps 37gls; Liverpool (WW2 Guest) May 1940 16apps 3gls; Wrexham (WW2 Guest) May 1941 1app 0gls; Chester (WW2 Guest) 1941/42 3apps 2gls; Manchester City (WW2 Guest) Nov 1943 1app 0gls; Bolton Wanderers (WW2 Guest) 1944/45 5apps 1gls; Crewe Alexandra (WW2 Guest) 1944/45 1app 0gls; Rochdale (WW2 Guest) 1944/45 17apps 11gls; Tranmere Rovers (WW2 Guest) 1944/45 27apps 11gls; Southport (WW2 Guest) 1945/46 13apps 4gls; South Liverpool (Player/manager) 1945; Shelbourne United (Player/manager 1946; Ellesmere Port Town (Player/manager) Feb 1949;*
Honours; *1 England War-time International caps;*

Alf Hanson was blessed with phenomenal pace, and starred for Liverpool in the 1930s, providing immaculate crosses from the left wing for Gordon Hodgson. His fifty goals in 166 League games was an excellent ratio for a winger, but in the close season of 1938 he was allowed to join Chelsea for the large fee of £7,500. After just one season with the London club War broke out, and he returned home to Liverpool, appearing as a 'guest' for a number of North-West based clubs, including Wrexham, for whom he made one appearance in May 1941, a 4-3 home win against his former club Liverpool. It was also during this time that he gained international recognition, playing for England against Scotland in a 3-2 defeat at St.James' Park Newcastle in February 1941. After the hostilities had ended Alf went on to become player/manager of South Liverpool, Ellesmere Port Town, and Shelbourne United in Ireland. A plumber by trade, he was the elder brother of Bolton 'keeper Stan Hanson.

HAYWARD, Aubrey — Wrexham

Position; *Outside-Left*
Born; *St.Martins, Shropshire*
Debut v. *Tranmere Rovers (h) 29.9.1945*
Total Appearances & Goals; *10 apps, 3 gls*
Career; *St.Martins; Wrexham (WW2 Guest) Sept 1945 10apps 3gls; Oswestry Town; St.Martins;*

Aubrey Hayward first joined Wrexham on trial as an 18 year-old from local side St.Martins. He signed for the Racecourse club during the 1945/46 season and made his debut in a 2-0 home win against Tranmere Rovers, when he scored what was described as a 'picture of a goal'. He was said to be 'on the small side, but he should make the grade'. Aubrey went on to complete a further nine appearances for the club before the end of WW2, scoring twice. Just as he was looking forward to the recommencement of the Third Division North for the 1946/47 season he was called up for service with the Royal Navy, and during his two years in the services he played for the Royal Navy XI all around the World. He returned to Wrexham briefly after his days at sea, but then decided on a career outside of football, running his own flooring contractor's business. He was involved in the game for a number of years with both Oswestry Town and his local side St.Martins, where he became a member of the Ifton Colliery Band, committee member and ex-trustee of the local Miners' Welfare club.

HAYWARD, Lionel Eric **Blackpool**

Position; *Centre-Half*
Born; *Newcastle-under-Lyme, 2nd August, 1917.*
Died; *Blackpool, A/M/J 1976.*
Height; *5ft 10'1/2in* ***Weight;*** *12st 2lbs*
Debut v. *Tranmere Rovers (h) 5.10.1940*
Total Appearances & Goals; *19 apps, 0 gls*
Career; *Hanley; Wardles; Port Vale Jul 1934 34apps 0gls; Blackpool May 1937 269apps 0gls, WW2 22apps 2gls; Wrexham (WW2 Guest) Oct 1940 19apps 0gls; Stoke City (WW2 Guest) Jun 1941 10apps 0gls; Luton Town (WW2 Guest) 1942/43 1app 0gls; Birmingham (WW2 Guest) Aug 1943 2apps 0gls; Crewe Alexandra (WW2 Guest) 1943/44 10apps 0gls; Walsall (WW2 Guest) Apr 1944 1apps 0gls;*
Honours; *F.A.Cup runner-up 1948 & 1951; Football League War Cup Winner 1943;*

Eric Hayward first joined Port Vale as an amateur, signing professional terms two months later, although he then failed to command a regular first team place, and was transferred to Blackpool May 1937. He became an established centre-half with the seaside club until War was declared, and although he continued to turn out for them during the conflict he also appeared as a 'guest' for a number of other clubs that included Stoke City, Wolves, Walsall, Birmingham City, Luton Town, and Wrexham. The first of his nineteen appearances for the 'Robins' came in October 1940, a 3-3 home draw with Tranmere Rovers. Eric was described a 'strong and skilful centre-half, who was utterly dependable, always there with last-ditch tackle or timely clearance'. He appeared for Blackpool in both the 1948 and 1951 F.A.Cup Finals as well as the 1943 War Cup Final. After ending his playing career with the 'Tangerines' he became assistant-manager to Ron Suart, and it was in that capacity that he helped nurture the likes of Alan Ball and Emlyn Hughes.

HEATH, W.

Position; *Centre-Forward*
Debut v. *Chester (a) 10.4.1944*
Total Appearances & Goals; *1 app, 0 gls*
Career; *Wrexham (WW2 Guest) Apr 1944 1app 0gls;*

Heath made his one and only appearance for Wrexham in a 2-2 draw at Chester in April 1944, when he played at centre-forward.

HEROD, Dennis J. **Stoke City**

Position; *Goalkeeper*
Born; *Stoke-on-Trent, 27th October, 1923.*
Height; *5ft 9in* ***Weight;*** *10st 4lbs*
Debut v. *Chester (a) 16.5.1942*
Total Appearances & Goals; *1 app, 0 gls*
Career; *Trent Vale United; Stoke City Jan 1941 191apps 1gls, WW2 133apps 0gls; Wrexham (WW2 Guest) May 1942 1app 0gls; Aldershot (WW2 Guest) 1942/43 9apps 0gls; Stockport County Jul 1953 £750 33apps 0gls;*

During the War Dennis Herod was handed his opportunity of a career in League football when he signed for Stoke City at the age of 17. He made over 120 war-time appearances between the sticks for the 'Potters', and it was during this time that he 'guested' for Wrexham. His one and only appearance came in a 2-1 'derby' win at Chester in May 1942. He also turned out for Aldershot during this period before being wounded during the conflict, though he recovered sufficiently to resume in goal for Stoke City following his demobilisation. The 'daring keeper' made Stoke's number one spot his own until the summer of 1953, when he left the Victoria Ground to join Stockport County. He remains the only goalkeeper to have scored in a first class game for Stoke when, following an injury in a game at Villa Park he continued on the wing and popped up to score his club's third goal in a 3-2 win! After his football career was over Dennis ventured into business as a greengrocer.

HEWITT, H.

Position; *Outside-Left*
Debut v. *Crewe Alexandra (a) 25.12.1942*
Total Appearances & Goals; *1 app, 1 goal*
Career; *Wrexham (WW2 Guest) Dec 1942 1app 1gls;*

Hewitt made his solitary appearance for Wrexham at Crewe Alexandra on Christmas Day 1942, and he scored one of the Wrexham goals in the 8-2 defeat!

HILL, A.E.

Position; *Outside-Left*
Debut v. *Stoke City (a) 28.11.1942*
Total Appearances & Goals; *1 app, 0 gls*
Career; *Wrexham (WW2 Guest) Nov 1942 1app 0gls;*

Hill recorded his only appearance for Wrexham in a 2-0 defeat at Stoke City in November 1942, when he played at outside left in place of McNee.

HILL, Frank Robert **Wrexham**

Position; *Wing-Half*
Born; *Forfar, 21st May, 1906.*
Died; *USA, 28th August, 1993.*
Height; *5ft 8in* ***Weight;*** *11st 9lbs*
Debut v. *Liverpool (h) 29.8.1942*
Total Appearances & Goals; *64 apps, 0 gls*
Career; *Forfar Athletic Jan 1925; Aberdeen Aug 1928; Arsenal 19th May 1932 £3,000 76apps 4gls; Blackpool Jun 1936 45apps 8gls; Southampton £2,200 Sept 1937 51apps 4gls; Wrexham (WW2) Aug 1942 64apps 0gls; Crewe Alexandra (WW2 Guest) 1943/44 1app 0gls; Crewe Alexandra Jul 1944 20apps 0gls;*
Honours; *3 Scottish International caps; One Scottish League XI Representative cap; First Division Championship 1933, 1934 & 1935; Charity Shield Winner 1934 & 1935; Charity Shield runner-up 1936;*

Nicknamed 'Tiger', Frank Hill won three Scottish caps whilst with Aberdeen, but failed to add to them following his move to England and Arsenal in May 1932. He did, however, collect three League Championship medals during his time at Highbury, although he was never regarded as a regular in the side. 'Tiger' later played for Southampton and Blackpool, before becoming assistant trainer with Preston in 1939. A Flight Lieutenant in the R.A.F., he served in India during WW2, and on returning to this country resumed playing football for Wrexham. 'Tiger' had made his first appearance for the 'Robins' in August 1942, a 4-3 home defeat by Liverpool in the opening game of the season. He continued to turn out for them occasionally until April 1944, when he accepted an appointment as player/manager of Crewe Alexandra for whom he was to continue playing until the age of 42. He remained as manager at Crewe until September 1948, and a month after leaving took charge of team affairs at Burnley, eventually becoming manager of Preston North End in August 1954. This was followed by a coaching stint in Baghdad in January 1957, before returning to take charge of Notts County in October 1958. He later managed Charlton Athletic from November 1961 to August 1965 when he became a scout with Manchester City.

HILLIARD, William Robert

Position; *Half-Back*
Debut v. *Manchester United (h) 4.12.1943*
Total Appearances & Goals; *12 apps, 0 gls*
Career; *Wrexham (WW2 Guest) Dec 1943 12apps 0gls; Southport (WW2 Guest) 1944/45 10apps 0gls; Barrow (WW2 Guest) 1945/46 4apps 0gls;*

Bill Hilliard made his first appearance for Wrexham in December 1943 in a 4-1 home defeat by Manchester United, when he stepped into the side at left-back. Most of his eleven further appearances for the club came as a member of the half-back line.

HINTON, Edward George Anthony — Distillery

Position; *Goalkeeper*
Born; *Belfast, 20th May, 1922.*
Died; *Belfast, 11th October, 1988.*
Height; *6ft 0'1/?in* **Weight;** *12st 11lbs.*
Debut v. *Tranmere Rovers (a) 6.3.1943*
Total Appearances & Goals; *1 app, 0 gls*
Career; *Grosvenor School; Glentoran (Am) 1937, (Pro) 1941; Distillery 1943; Wrexham 10th Mar 1943 1app 0gls; Notts County (WW2 Guest) 1943/44 1app 0gls; Swindon Town (WW2 Guest) 1945/46 1app 0gls; Fulham Aug 1946 82apps 0gls; Millwall Jul 1949 £1,500 91apps 0gls; Ballymena United Feb 1953; Bangor cs1953; Ballymena United Aug 1956;*
Honours; *7 Northern Ireland international caps; Irish Cup runner-up 1942; Second Division Championship 1949;*

Ted Hinton was a strongly built goalkeeper who dominated his penalty area. He played for Glentoran and Distillery, and joined Fulham after WW2 had ended. During the War he turned out once as a 'guest' for Wrexham in a 4-0 defeat at Tranmere Rovers in March 1943. He also 'guested' for both Notts County and Swindon Town before his move to Fulham. Ted spent three seasons at Craven Cottage, winning the first of his seven Northern Ireland caps in November 1946 in a 2-0 win over Scotland. He was involved in the first ten matches of Fulham's Second Division Championship season before being replaced by Doug Flack, and was then allowed to join London rivals Millwall at the end of that season. After three years at the Den, during which he completed 91 League appearances, Ted eventually returned to Ireland, where he continued to play in goal for both Ballymena United and Bangor.

HOLLIDAY, Frank — Wrexham

Position; *Inside-Right*
Born; *Wrexham*
Debut v. *Barrow (a) 1.1.1946*
Total Appearances & Goals; *2 apps, 0 gls*
Career; *Wrexham (WW2) Jan 1946 2apps 0gls;*

Frank Holliday was playing for Wrexham Boys' Club during the War when he was spotted and signed by manager Tom Williams. He completed a number of reserve team games before making his first team debut at inside-right on New Years Day 1946, replacing Fred Haycock in a 1-0 defeat at Barrow. Frank added just one more appearance for Wrexham, which came the following month in a 3-1 defeat at Southport. He was described as a 'scheming type of inside-forward, with good ball skills'.

HORSMAN, Leslie — Guiseley

Position; *Forward/Half-Back*
Born; *Burley-in-Wharfedale, 26th May, 1920.*
Height; *5ft 10in* **Weight;** *11st 10lbs*
Debut v. *Stockport County (h) .11.1943*
Total Appearances & Goals; *21 apps, 14 gls*
Career; *Guiseley; Wrexham (WW2 Guest) Nov 1943 21apps 14gls; Arsenal (WW2 Guest) Aug 1944 5apps 3gls; Bradford Park Avenue (WW2 Guest) 1944/45 1app 1gls; Bradford Park Avenue Jun 1945 239apps 18gls; Halifax Town Aug 1953 120apps 8gls;*

Les Horsman had played only local football for Guiseley before making his first appearance for Wrexham in November 1943 in a 4-1 home win over Stockport County, in which he scored one of the 'Robins' goals. He went on to add another twenty appearances for the club that season, scoring fourteen goals, including a hat-trick in his second game, a 4-1 home win over Stoke City. During the conflict he played for the Army XI, and was also invited to appear as a 'guest' for Arsenal, scoring on his debut in a 2-2 draw with Luton Town. He also turned out for Bradford Park Avenue, for whom he eventually signed as a professional at the end of the hostilities. He enjoyed over eight years with the West Yorkshire club, making over 250 League and Cup appearances. In the summer of 1953 he joined Halifax Town, where he clocked up over 100 games. In 1951 it was stated of him that he was 'now a strong centre-half, though Leslie is really a centre-forward'.

HORSMAN, William — Chester

Position; *Outside-Right*
Born; *Doncaster, c1902.*
Height; *5ft 8in* **Weight;** *11st 4lbs.*
Debut v. *Stoke City (h) .9.1941*
Total Appearances & Goals; *4 apps, 3 gls*
Career; *Doncaster Rovers; Hull City (Trial) Sept 1928; Selby Town; Birmingham Nov 1928 78apps 3gls; Chester Sept 1935 151apps 34gls, (WW2) 22apps 2gls; Wrexham (WW2 Guest) Sept 1941 4apps 3gls; Southport (WW2 Guest) 1945/46 3apps 0gls; Chester Nomads;*
Honours; *Third Division Northern Section Cup Winner 1936 & 1937;*

Billy Horsman made his Football League debut for Birmingham in a 3-1 defeat at Bury in March 1929, having previously played for Doncaster Rovers, Hull City and Selby Town. He went on to complete a further 77 League appearances for the 'Blues' helping them to the 1931 F.A.Cup Final against West Brom, where they lost 2-1, although he did not play in the Final. Billy left St.Andrew's in September 1935 to join Chester, where he made over 150 appearances, 'showing a goalscoring appetite which he had never displayed with Birmingham'. He remained at Sealand Road until the intervention of the War. This gave Bill the opportunity of playing for Wrexham as a 'guest', while serving in the R.A.F. He turned out four times for the 'Robins', the first of which came in September 1941, although it was to be a disastrous home debut as Wrexham lost 7-1 to Stoke City! He made up for this by scoring twice in the following match, also against Stoke, though the 'Robins' lost again, 5-2! Towards the end of WW2 Bill also 'guested' for Southport. He eventually settled in Chester, where he continued to play football for the well known amateur side Chester Nomads.

HOUGH, William Arthur — Blackburn Rovers

Position; *Right-Back*
Born; *Greenfield, Flintshire, 10th June, 1908.*
Died; *Preston, September 1988.*
Height; *5ft 8in* **Weight;** *12st 1lbs.*
Debut v. *Manchester City (a) 28.10.1939*
Total Appearances & Goals; 2 apps, 0 goals
Career; *Connah's Quay & Shotton; Holywell Arcadians; New Brighton (Am) 26th Aug 1930, (Pro) 11th Sept 1930 4apps 1gls; Preston North End 12th Dec 1930 69apps 0gls; Blackburn Rovers 11th Dec 1936 49apps 0gls, WW2 40apps 0gls; Wrexham (WW2 Guest) Oct 1939 1app 0gls;*
Honours; *Second Division Championship 1939; Football League War Cup runner-up 1940;*

Billy Hough was employed as a foundry worker while playing football for Connah's Quay & Shotton and Holywell Arcadians. He held the same job when he signed for New Brighton, and was unable to secure time off to make his League debut for the 'Rakers' at Halifax! However, he didn't have long to wait for his chance, which came in a 3-1 home win over Chesterfield in November 1930. He managed three more outings for New Brighton before signing for Preston North End the following month, and went on to assist the Deepdale club to promotion to the First Division in 1933/34 as runners-up to Grimsby Town. He went one better after joining Blackburn Rovers in December 1936, helping them to the Second Division Championship in 1939. Bill was described as 'strong, sure in recovery, sound in anticipation and safe in kicking.' WW2 was to see the Football League suspended, but Bill continued at Ewood Park, helping 'Rovers' to reach the Football League War Cup Final, where they lost to

West Ham United at Wembley in June 1940. He was to make just one appearance for Wrexham as a 'guest' during the conflict, turning out in only the second match of regionalised football at left-back in a 6-1 defeat by Manchester City in October 1939.

HOWARTH, Harold — Chester

Position; *Half-Back*
Born; *Little Hulton, 25th November, 1908.*
Height; *5ft 9'1/2in* ***Weight;*** *11st 7lbs.*
Died; *Bolton, 26th December, 1973.*
Debut v. *Blackburn Rovers (a) 29.3.1941*
Total Appearances & Goals; *2 apps, 0 gls*
Career; *Little Lever; Bolton Wanderers (Am) May 1928, (Pro) Aug 1928 59apps 0gls; Chester Feb 1935 176apps 6gls, (WW2) 96apps 4gls; Tranmere Rovers (WW2 Guest) 1939/40 2apps 0gls; Wrexham (WW2 Guest) Mar 1941 2apps 0gls; Southport Oct 1945, (WW2) 25apps 0gls, 0apps;*
Honours; *Third Division Northern Section Cup Winner 1936 & 1937;*

The only boy of five children Harry Howarth began playing local football for Little Lever, and was given a chance by Bolton Wanderers. He remained an amateur until completing his bricklaying apprenticeship, following which he turned professional with the 'Trotters'. Harry made his Football League debut for the Burnden Park club, and went on to clock up 59 League appearances before signing for Chester in February 1935. He was a regular with the Sealand Road club until the outbreak of WW2. He continued to play for Chester during this period, and made two 'guest' appearances for their over the border neighbours, Wrexham. His 'Robins' debut came at right-back in March 1941, in a 3-2 defeat at Blackburn Rovers. Harry's second outing was in the final match of 1940/41, a 3-3 draw with Stoke City. He also appeared as a 'guest' for Southport in the last season of WW2, before signing for them on a permanent basis in October 1945. Unfortunately he failed to make a Football League appearance for the 'Sandgrounders' and was later released. Harry was employed for Worsley Council as a bricklayer before becoming 'mine host' for many years at the 'Legs of Man' Public House in Bolton.

HUGHES, Alan — Wrexham

Position; *Outside-Right*
Debut v. *Liverpool (h) 29.8.1942*
Total Appearances & Goals; *2 apps, 0 gls*
Career; *Wrexham (WW2) Aug 1942 2apps 0gls;*

A local lad, Alan made the first of his two senior appearances for Wrexham in August 1942, playing at outside-right in a 4-3 home defeat by Liverpool in the opening match of the season. His second outing came two months later, again at outside-right in a 2-0 home defeat by Everton.

HUGHES, J.T. — Wrexham

Position; *Outside-Left*
Debut v. *Tranmere Rovers (a) 22.9.1945*
Total Appearances & Goals; *2 apps, 0 gls*
Career; *Wrexham (WW2) Sept 1945 2apps 0gls;*
Another local, Hughes made his debut for Wrexham at outside-left in a 3-2 win at Tranmere Rovers in September 1945. He added just one more appearance for the Racecourse club, a 1-1 home draw with Southport in February 1946.

HUGHES, Tom — Wrexham

Position; *Inside-Left*
Born; *St.Martins, Shropshire*
Debut v. *Walsall (h) 10.3.1945*
Total Appearances & Goals; *2 apps, 0 gls*
Career; *St.Martins; Wolves 1941/42; Wrexham (WW2) Mar 1945 2apps 0gls; Wellington Town 1946; Oswestry Town; Machynlleth; St.Martins; Ellesmere;*

Tom Hughes was working in Ifton Colliery during WW2, and playing local football for St.Martins when he was spotted and recommended to Wolves, who signed him in 1941/42. Due to the fact that mining came under the 'Essential Works Order' during the War, his application to join the Army was turned down, and had it been successful this would have enabled him to play more regularly for Wolves. At the beginning of the 1944/45 season, Wrexham manager Tom Williams signed the promising youngster. Although involved mostly in reserve football that season Tom made his first team debut in March 1945, appearing at inside-left in a 1-0 home win over Walsall. His second appearance came in a 4-1 defeat at Chester in December 1945. Misfortune was to strike shortly afterwards when he broke his collar bone, and this effectively ended his association with Wrexham. After the War Tom continued in non-league football for Wellington Town, Oswestry Town, Machynlleth, St.Martins and Ellesmere. He eventually became a Turf Accountant, and settled in the Shropshire village of St.Martins.

HUGHES, William Marshall — Birmingham

Position; *Left-Back/Centre-Half*
Born; *Carmarthen, 6th March, 1918.*
Died; *Birmingham, 16th June, 1981.*
Height; *5ft 10 1/2in* ***Weight;*** *12st 12lbs*
Debut v. *Stoke City (h) 21.11.1942*
Total Appearances & Goals; *9 apps, 2 gls*
Career; *Carmarthen Town; Llanelly Town; Archer Corinthians; Birmingham May 1935 104apps 0gls; Fulham (WW2 Guest) 1940/41 2apps 0gls; Wrexham (WW2 Guest) Nov 1942 9app 2gls; Chester (WW2 Guest) 1942/43 20apps 0gls; Swansea Town (WW2 Guest) 1942/43 1app 0gls; Luton Town Jul 1947 £11,000 31apps 0gls; Chelsea Mar 1948 £12,000 93apps 0gls; Hereford United Aug 1951; Flint Town Jan 1954 to 1955;*
Honours; *10 Welsh international caps 1938-1947; 14 War-time international caps; Great Britain XI Representative match 1947; Welsh Cup Winner 1954;*

Billy Hughes made his Football League debut for Birmingham in a 1-0 home defeat by Manchester City in January 1936 at the age of 17. Fellow full-back Cyril Trigg was also only 17, and they created a record as the League's youngest pair of full-backs. Described as a 'polished and skilful defender' he continued to star regularly for the 'Blues' until WW2 broke out. During the hostilities he switched to centre-half, and appeared as a 'guest' for a number of clubs including, Arsenal, Hearts, Chester, Q.P.R., West Ham United, and Wrexham. He made his 'Robins' debut in a 4-2 home defeat by Stoke City in November 1942, and added eight more appearances for the club in 1945. During the War he was selected for 14 war-time internationals for Wales, second only in number to Don Dearson. Billy resumed his career with Birmingham after the cease-fire, joining Luton Town for a club record fee of £11,000 in July 1947. He spent just one season with the 'Hatters' before signing for Chelsea. In 1951 he moved into non-league football with Hereford United, ending his career in the Welsh League (North) with Flint Town United, and helping them to a famous Welsh Cup victory in 1954. After ending his playing career he kept the Bluebell Inn at Halkyn, and acted as a scout for Chester. He later returned to the Midlands, becoming steward at the Wolseley Car Social Club.

ISHERWOOD, Dennis

Position; *Centre-Forward*
Born; *Northwich, 9th January, 1924.*
Died; *Stoke-on-Trent, February, 1974.*
Debut v. *Bury (a) 2.9.1944*
Total Appearances & Goals; *18 apps, 8 gls*
Career; *Rochdale (WW2 Guest) 1941/42 1app 0gls; Crewe Alexandra (WW2 Guest) 1942/43 4apps 1gls; Wolves (WW2 Guest) Sept 1943 2apps 2gls; Wrexham (WW2 Guest) Sept 1944 18apps 8gls; Port Vale (WW2 Guest) May 1945 1app 1gls; Chester Apr 1946 3apps 0gls, WW2 1app 0gls; Northwich Victoria; Wellington Town; Winsford United; Macclesfield Town; Runcorn; Congleton Town; Stafford Rangers;*

Dennis Isherwood was one young footballer among many affected by WW2, during which he appeared as a 'guest' for Rochdale, Crewe, Port Vale, Wolves, and Wrexham. He made an impressive debut for the 'Robins', scoring two of the goals in a 3-1 win at Bury in September 1944. Seventeen more appearances followed, in which he contributed eight goals before joining Chester after the conflict had ended. Dennis made his Football League debut for the Sealand Road club in a 5-1 defeat at Hartlepool in February 1947, and added two more outings before dropping into Cheshire County League football with a number of clubs including Northwich, Wellington, Winsford, Macclesfield, Runcorn and Congleton. He later became manager of Sandbach Ramblers.

JEFFERSON, Arthur — Queens Park Rangers

Position; *Left-Back*
Born; *Goldthorpe, Rotherham, 14th December, 1916.*
Died; *London, July 1998*
Height; *5ft 9in* **Weight;** *10st 8lbs.*
Debut v. *Chester (a) 15.1.1944*
Total Appearances & Goals; *37 apps, 0 gls*
Career; *Highgate School; Goldthorpe United; Preston North End May 1934 0apps; Manchester City Dec 1934 0apps; Peterborough United 1935; Queens Park Rangers Feb 1936 213apps 1gls, WW2 102apps 0gls; Southend United (WW2 Guest) 1939/40 1app 0gls; Chelsea (WW2 Guest) Feb 1942 3apps 0gls; Wrexham (WW2 Guest) Jan 1944 37apps 0gls; Aldershot (WW2 Guest) 1943/44 3apps 0gls; Aldershot Mar 1950 £1,500 170apps 0gls;*
Honours; *Third Division South Championship Winner 1948;*

Affectionately known as 'Rubber Legs' when he was at Q.P.R., Arthur Jefferson was totally committed to winning the ball, employing a great sliding tackle to assist his endeavours. Having previously been on the books of Preston, Manchester City and Peterborough, Arthur was with Q.P.R. at the outbreak of WW2. He made over 100 appearances for the Shepherds Bush club during this period, as well as 'guesting' for Aldershot and Wrexham. His debut for the Racecourse club came in a 3-1 win at Chester in January 1944, and he went on to add fifteen more appearances that season, 19 during 1944/45, and a further two at the beginning of 1945/46 in the Lancashire Cup. He was also selected for the Western Command representative side. After the conflict Arthur continued at Loftus Road until March 1950, when he was transferred to Aldershot, having captained the Londoners to their first ever promotion when they captured the Third Division South title in 1948. He spent five years at the Recreation Ground before retiring at 38. When his playing career was over Arthur returned to Shepherds Bush, running a Fish and Chip shop, with another former Q.P.R. player, 'Smudger' Smith, remaining a Loftus Road regular until late in life.

JONES, David — Carlisle United

Position; *Goalkeeper*
Born; *Blaenau Ffestiniog, 8th September, 1914.*
Height; *5ft 10in* **Weight;** *10st 0lbs.*
Debut v. *Liverpool (h) 29.8.1942*
Total Appearances & Goals; *10 apps, 0 gls*
Career; *Blaenau Ffestiniog; Everton (Am) Sept 1933 0apps; Colwyn Bay Utd; Stoke City Mar 1937 1app 0gls; Carlisle United May 1939 66apps 0gls to 1948; Stoke City (WW2 Guest) 20apps 0gls; Wrexham (WW2 Guest) Aug 1942 10apps 0gls; Burnley (WW2 Guest) 1941/42 1app 0gls; Northwich Victoria 1948;*

David Jones had been on the books of Everton as an amateur, but was not offered terms. He was later spotted by Stoke City playing in goal for Colwyn Bay United, and he made his one and only Football League appearance for the 'Potters' in the final match of 1938/39, a scoreless draw with Leeds United at Elland Road. He was signed by Carlisle United during the close season of 1939, appearing in the opening three matches of the new season before War was declared. He then returned to his native North Wales, and it was whilst he was 'back home' that he appeared for Wrexham as a 'guest'. His debut came in the opening match of the 1942/43 season, a 4-3 home defeat by Liverpool, and kept his place for the next nine games. He also 'guested' for Burnley before returning to Carlisle upon the resumption of League football. He remained with the 'Cumbrians' until 1948, when he joined Cheshire County League side Northwich Victoria.

JONES, Douglas

Position; *Forward*
Debut v. *Stoke City (a) 28.11.1942*
Total Appearances & Goals; *1 app, 0 gls*
Career; *Wrexham (WW2 Guest) Nov 1942 1app 0gls;*

Doug Jones made one appearance for Wrexham in November 1942 at centre-forward, replacing Norman Moore in a 2-0 defeat at Stoke City.

JONES, John Edward — Everton

Position; *Left-Back*
Born; *Bromborough, 3rd July, 1913.*
Died; *Sunderland, 26th January, 1995.*
Height; *5ft 9'1/2in* **Weight;** *10st 10lbs.*
Debut v. *Everton (h) 15.11.1941*
Total Appearances & Goals; *20 apps, 0 gls*
Career; *Bromborough Pool; Ellesmere Port Town; Everton Mar 1932 98apps 0gls, WW2 50apps 0gls; Tranmere Rovers (WW2 Guest) 1939/40 2apps 1gls;Wrexham (WW2 Guest) Nov 1941 20apps 0gls; Southport (WW2 Guest) 20apps 1gls; Wigan Athletic (WW2 Guest) Dec 1945; Sunderland 21st Dec 1945 24apps 0gls;*

Jack Jones began his football career as a centre-forward with Ellesmere Port Town, deciding upon a switch to left-back after signing for Everton in March 1932. In his new position he developed into one of the most astute and reliable full-backs of his day. He was still at Goodison Park when WW2 broke out, and it was during this period that he turned out as a 'guest' for Wrexham. His first appearance came in November 1941 against his own club, Everton, a game which ended in a 4-0 win for the 'Blues'. John clocked up another twelve appearances for the 'Robins' that season, and added seven more the following year. During this period he also appeared as a 'guest' for Tranmere Rovers, Southport and Wigan Athletic, moving to Sunderland in December 1945. Jack resumed his playing career at Roker Park after the conflict, appearing in 24 League games before calling it a day. He then took up an offer to become the 'Rokerites' assistant trainer.

JONES, John Thomas — Northampton Town

Position; *Goalkeeper*
Born; *Holywell, 25th November, 1916.*
Died; *Holywell, A/M/J 1978.*
Height; *5ft 8 1/2in* **Weight;** *11st 4lbs*
Debut v. *New Brighton (h) 21.10.1939*
Total Appearances & Goals; *29 apps, 0 gls*
Career; *Port Vale (Am) 7th Jul 1936, (Pro) 14th Dec 1936 3apps 0gls; Northampton Town May 1937 71apps 0gls; Wrexham (WW2 Guest) Oct 1939 29apps 0gls; Notts County (WW2 Guest) 1943/44 2apps 0gls; Hull City (WW2 Guest) Dec 1944 1app 0gls; Manchester City (WW2 Guest) Mar 1944 2apps 0gls; Rochdale (WW2 Guest) 1945/46 2apps 0gls; Oldham Athletic 4th Aug 1948 £250 22apps 0gls to Jul 1949;*
Honours; *Welsh Schoolboy International;*

John Jones joined Port Vale as an amateur in July 1936, turning professional in December of the same year. He made his first team debut a month later in a 2-0 F.A.Cup Third Round defeat at Sheffield Wednesday. Three further League appearances followed, but he was unable to command a regular first team spot, and left the club at the end of the season to join Northampton Town. Whilst with the 'Cobblers' he became known as 'Jones the cap', because of his notable headgear. Although on the short side for a 'keeper, he was 'agile, brave and daring almost to the point of recklessness'. John spent two seasons with Northampton, before his Football League career was disrupted by the hostilities. He immediately returned home to North Wales and, when football was resumed on a regional basis for the War years, he turned out for Wrexham as a 'guest'. His 'Robins' debut came in a 6-4 home win over New Brighton and he went on to add a further 21 appearances that campaign. Another seven appearances were clocked up over the next five years, as well as appearing as a 'guest' for Notts County, Hull City, Manchester City and Rochdale, before he returned to Northampton Town upon the resumption of League football. In August 1948 John joined Oldham Athletic, where he finished his Football League career.

JONES, Thomas William — Grimsby Town

Position; *Inside-Left*
Born; *Oakengates, 23rd March, 1907.*
Died; *Telford, 24th June, 1980.*
Height; *5ft 8'1/2in* ***Weight;*** *11st 0lbs.*
Debut v. *Tranmere Rovers (a) 3.10.1942*
Total Appearances & Goals; *4 apps, 0 gls*
Career; *Oakengates Town; Aston Villa (Trial); West Bromwich Albion (Trial) Jul 1929 0apps; Burnley Nov 1930 94apps 24gls; Blackpool Sept 1933 155apps 40gls; Grimsby Town Jul 1938 48apps 8gls, WW2 4apps 0gls; Wellington Town (WW2 Guest); Wrexham (WW2 Guest) Oct 1942 4apps 0gls; Crewe Alexandra (WW2 Guest) 1944/45 3apps 0gls;*
Honours; *Welsh Cup Winner 1940;*

The son of a pre-WW1 Wolves player, Tom was playing for Oakengates Town when granted trials at both Aston Villa and West Bromwich Albion. Nevertheless, it was for Burnley that he signed in November 1930, making his Football League debut in January 1931, a 4-1 defeat at Bradford. Tom remained at Turf Moor until September 1933, when he signed for Blackpool. He spent five years with the 'Seasiders', described as a 'schemer with craftsmanship, who knew a trick or two' before joining Grimsby Town in July 1938. He was still at Blundell Park when War threatened our shores, following which he became another player to turn out as a 'guest' for the Racecourse club. The first of his four appearances for the 'Robins' came in October 1942, a 4-4 draw at Tranmere, and he also took part in the 1940 Welsh Cup Final, lining up for Wellington Town in their 4-0 victory over Swansea Town. As well as his appearances for Wrexham he also 'guested' for Crewe Alexandra during this time.

JONES, Victor M. — Bath City

Position; *Inside-Right*
Debut v. *Everton (a) 30.10.1943*
Total Appearances & Goals; *3 apps, 0 gls*
Career; *Bath City; Rochdale (WW2 Guest) 1940/41 9apps 5gls; Wrexham (WW2 Guest) Oct 1943 3apps 0gls;*

Vic Jones was said to have been a player at Bath City when he turned out for Wrexham at inside-right against Everton at the end of October 1943. He also appeared in the following game, a 1-0 defeat at Stockport, before making his final appearance in a Wrexham shirt in April 1945, a 2-1 home defeat by Everton. During the conflict he also 'guested' for Rochdale.

KELLY, Gerard Michael — Southampton

Position; *Inside-Left*
Born; *Sunderland, 15th September, 1909.*
Died; *Ellesmere Port, February 1986.*
Height; *5ft 7'1/2in* ***Weight;*** *11st 4lbs*
Debut v. *Crewe Alexandra (h) 16.3.1940*
Total Appearances & Goals; *5 apps, 1 gls*
Career; *Castletown FC; Hylton Colliery Welfare; Sunderland 1927 0apps; Nelson Jun 1928 46apps 15gls; Huddersfield Town Oct 1929 £2,000 37apps 15gls; Charlton Athletic Mar 1932 £600 20apps 6gls; Chester Dec 1932 £285 73apps 27gls; Port Vale Jun 1936 20apps 2gls; Southampton Sept 1937 19apps 2gls; Wrexham (WW2 Guest) Mar 1940 5apps 1gls;*
Honours; *Welsh Cup Winner 1933; Welsh Cup runner-up 1935;*

Gerard Kelly was playing for his local side - Hylton Colliery - when he was signed by Sunderland in 1927. He failed to make the grade at Roker Park, and joined Third Division North side Nelson in June 1928 before going on to play League football for Huddersfield Town, Charlton Athletic, and Chester. He collected a Welsh Cup winners' medal whilst with the Sealand Road club, turning out against Wrexham in the 1933 Final, and scoring the first goal in Chester's 2-0 victory. He joined Port Vale in the summer of 1936, and had moved on to Southampton by the time that the Football League was brought to a halt in September 1939. Gerard continued to play football whenever he could during the hostilities, and turned out for Wrexham as a 'guest' in March 1940 in a 5-2 home win over Crewe Alexandra, notching one of the five goals. He added four more appearances for the 'Robins' before the end of the season.

KIRTON, John — Stoke City

Position; *Left-Half*
Born; *Rubislaw, Aberdeen, 4th March, 1916.*
Died; *Stoke-on-Trent, 13th March, 1996.*
Height; *5ft 10in* ***Weight;*** *10st 10lbs.*
Debut v. *Stoke City (a) 28.11.1942*
Total Appearances & Goals; *1 app, 0 gls*
Career; *St.Marchers; Banks O'Dee; Stoke City Nov 1935 162apps 2gls, WW2 72apps 2gls; Nottingham Forest (WW2 Guest) 1939/40 27apps 0gls; Wrexham (WW2 Guest) Nov 1942 1app 0gls; Notts County (WW2 Guest) 1942/43 18apps 0gls; Leeds United (WW2 Guest) 1943/44 6apps 0gls; Bradford City Jul 1953 8apps 0gls; Hinckley Athletic; Downings Tileries;*
Honours; *Scottish War-time International cap; Scottish Schoolboy International*

Like so many players of his era the War years took seven seasons out of John Kirton's football career. Given the consistency and ability that he had shown prior to the War with Stoke City he would have surely been a candidate for the club's all-time appearance record. He completed 72 games for Stoke during this period, and 'guested' once for Wrexham, against - of all clubs - Stoke City! Wrexham had turned up for the game a player short, and he agreed to turn out for the 'Robins', and it is perhaps no surprise that Stoke won 2-0! John earned international recognition during WW2, capped by Scotland against England at Wembley. Upon the resumption of League football John remained with the 'Potteries' club until 1953, when he joined Bradford City as player/coach. He made just eight appearances for the Valley Parade club before moving into non-league circles with Hinckley Athletic and Downings Tileries. He eventually settled in his adopted Stoke, taking up employment in the building trade.

LEA, George Isaac — Millwall

Position; *Left-Back/Half-Back*
Born; *Donnington Wood, Telford, 17th February, 1911.*
Died; *Dawley, Telford. 24th October, 1972.*
Height; *6ft 0in* ***Weight;*** *12st 8lbs*
Debut v. *Liverpool (h) 29.8.1942*
Total Appearances & Goals; *13 apps, 0 gls*
Career; *Oswestry Town (Pro) Sept 1930; Oakengates Town 1931; Birmingham May 1932 27apps 1gls; Millwall May 1937 37apps 0gls; Wellington Town (WW2 Guest) 1939/40; Wrexham (WW2 Guest) Aug 1942 13apps 0gls;*
Honours; *Division Three South Championship Winner 1937; Welsh Cup Winner 1940;*

George Lea began his senior football career playing in the Birmingham & District League for both Oswestry Town and Oakengates Town, before he signed for Birmingham in May 1932. His Football League debut came in the following October, a 2-1 home win over Sheffield Wednesday. After joining the 'Blues' he put on stones in weight and developed into a powerful left-back', yet he was never a regular in his five years at St.Andrew's, and moved on to Millwall in May 1937 where he won a Third Division South championship medal in his first season. During his time at 'The Den' he was described as a 'ninety minute player who could play anywhere in the middle line. An excellent striker of a dead ball and invariably took his side's free-kicks.' WW2 effectively put paid to his Football League career, although he did turn out during this period for both Wellington Town and Wrexham as a 'guest'. He played in the Shropshire side's Welsh Cup Final victory in 1940, when they beat Swansea Town 4-0, and he made his 'Robins' debut at left-back in the opening game of 1942/43, a 4-3 home defeat by Liverpool. He then went on to add another further twelve appearances that season for the Racecourse club. He later found fame as a breeder of racing pigeons, and was said to have Champion Jockey Sir Gordon Richards among his customers.

LEYLAND, John A. — Wrexham

Position; *Inside-Right*
Born; *St.Helens,*
Debut v. *Tranmere Rovers (a) 16.3.1946*
Total Appearances & Goals; *1 app, 0 gls*
Career; *Wrexham (WW2) Mar 1946 1app 0gls;*

John Leyland was signed by Wrexham manager Tom Williams, and had been playing reserve team football at the Racecourse when he was called up to make his one and only first team appearance in March 1946, replacing Fred Haycock at inside-right against Tranmere Rovers. The 'Robins' lost the match 3-2.

LIVINGSTONE, Archibald — Bury

Position; *Inside-Right*
Born; *Pencaitland, 15th November, 1915.*
Died; *Edinburgh, 12th August, 1961.*
Height; *5ft 8in* **Weight;** *11st 4lbs.*
Debut v. *Wolves (h) 16.1.1943*
Total Appearances & Goals; *56 apps, 20 gls*
Career; *Musselburgh Lewisvale c1932; Ormiston Primrose; Dundee; Newcastle United May 1935 £35 33apps 5gls; Bury Jun 1938 23apps 8gls, WW2 62apps 17gls; Leeds United (WW2 Guest) 2apps 0gls; York City (WW2 Guest) 1941/42 9apps 4gls; Wrexham (WW2 Guest) Jan 1943 56apps 20gls; Fulham (WW2 Guest) Feb 1944 4apps 2gls; Everton May 1946 4apps 2gls; Southport 17th Jun 1947 £1,000 23apps 2gls; Glenavon Aug 1948 (Player/Coach); Dundee 1949/50; Worksop Town;*
Honours; *Scottish War-time International;*

Archie Livingstone had played for Scottish League side Dundee before joining Newcastle United in May 1935. His Football League debut for the 'Magpies' came at Sheffield United in the November of the same year, and, despite scoring, he finished on the losing side as Newcastle were trounced 5-1. Archie clocked up 33 League appearances in his three seasons at St.James' Park before joining Bury in the summer of 1938. He left Gigg Lane after just over a season, whereupon WW2 broke out and he immediately enlisted with the Lancashire Fusiliers as a P.T.instructor. Curiously it was during the conflict that Archie's football career seemed to blossom, as he was selected for Scotland in a War-time international against England in 1943, and he also 'guested' for York City, Fulham, and Wrexham. He made a scoring debut for the 'Robins' in January 1943, a 3-3 home draw with Wolves, and went on to score seven goals in one game for the club, a 9-0 home win over Tranmere Rovers in September 1943 - a record which still stands to this day. Following the end of WW2 he joined Everton, but made only four League appearances for the 'Toffeemen' before signing for Southport. He failed to live up to his reputation at Haig Avenue, and moved across to Northern Ireland in 1948 to join Glenavon, concluding his career back in Scotland as player/coach with Dundee. After hanging up his boots Archie worked as a slater and plasterer in Ormiston, but suffered a recurrence of the Jaundice he had contracted in the Army at York, and passed away in Edinburgh's Eastern General Hospital at the age of just 45. At his peak he was noted as a 'nippy inside-forward, who would always have a crack at goal whenever the chance occurred'.

LLOYD, Clifford — Wrexham

Position; *Wing-Half*
Born; *Ellesmere Port, 14th November, 1916.*
Debut v. *Stockport County (h) 25.10.1941*
Total Appearances & Goals; *49 apps, 0 gls*
Career; *Liverpool 1935; Wrexham (WW2) Oct 1941 49apps 0gls; Fulham Dec 1943, WW2 48apps 0gls, 2apps 0gls; Margate Town 1949 (Player/Manager); Bristol Rovers May 1950 0apps;*

Not to be confused with the Cliff Lloyd who played for Wrexham prior to WW2, and who later became secretary and manager with the Racecourse club for a number of years, this Cliff Lloyd made a name for himself as secretary of the Professional Footballers' Association for many years. Having been on the books of Liverpool in 1935 Cliff made his debut for Wrexham in October 1941, a 6-1 home win over Stockport County. After the conflict he joined Second Division Fulham, for whom he had turned out as a 'guest' during WW2. He made his Football League debut in a 7-2 defeat at Bury, and played in the following game at West Ham, but they proved to his only League appearances for the Craven Cottage club. An appointment as player/manager at Margate Town followed in 1949, and, after a short spell with Bristol Rovers in 1950, he was appointed as a member of the PFA Management Committee. He retained that position until taking over as P.F.A. secretary in 1953, a position he was to hold until 1981. During his marathon stint he was involved, along with Jimmy Hill, in the successful bid to abolish of the maximum wage in the early 1960s.

LUNN, George — Aston Villa

Position; *Left-Back*
Born; *Bolton-upon-Dearne, Yorkshire, 28th June 1915.*
Debut v. *Wolves (h) 24.2.1945*
Total Appearances & Goals; *1 app, 0 gls*
Career; *Frickley Colliery; Aston Villa May 1938; Fulham (WW2 Guest) 1940/41 1app 0gls; Northampton Town (WW2 Guest) 1940/41 1app 0gls; Watford (WW2 Guest) 1940/41 1app 0gls; Clapton Orient (WW2 Guest) 1940/41 6apps 0gls; Doncaster Rovers (WW2 Guest) Jan 1943 1app 0gls; Chester (WW2 Guest) 1944/45 7apps 0gls; Southport (WW2 Guest) 1944/45 5apps 0gls; Wrexham (WW2 Guest) Feb 1945 1app 0gls; Stockport County (WW2 Guest) Feb 1945 1app 0gls; Rochdale (WW2 Guest) 1945/46 4apps 0gls; Birmingham City Sept 1946 0apps; Watford Oct 1947 5apps 0gls;*

George Lunn joined Aston Villa in May 1938 from non-league Frickley Colliery, but he failed to make a first team appearance at Villa Park before WW2 intervened. During the conflict he appeared as a 'guest' for a number of Football League clubs, including Fulham, Northampton Town, Clapton Orient, Doncaster Rovers, Chester, Southport, Stockport County, Rochdale, and Wrexham. Although recognised as a centre-half he made his debut at the Racecourse as a left-back in February 1945, a 1-1 draw with Wolves. Following the cease fire George signed for Birmingham City, but couldn't force his way through into the first team and so tried his luck in Ireland for the beginning of the 1947/48 season. However, he returned in October and joined Watford where he remained until the end of the season. He eventually made his Football League debut for the 'Hornets', although he was to add just four more League appearances. George then drifted into non-league football, although he did have a month's trial with Halifax Town in August 1950.

McAVOY, Douglas Haig — Kilmarnock

Position; *Inside-Left*
Born; *Kilmarnock, 29th November, 1918.*
Died; *Kilmarnock, 15th April, 1988.*
Height; *5ft 7in* **Weight;** *10st 0lbs*
Debut v. *New Brighton (a) 26.10.1940*
Total Appearances & Goals; *13 apps, 5 gls*
Career; *Kilmarnock Bentinck School; Kilmarnock Acas; Cumnock Juniors; Kilmarnock Aug 1936 63apps 14gls; Wrexham (WW2 Guest) Oct 1940 13apps 5gls; Liverpool Dec 1947 £7,000 2apps 0gls; Queen of the South Sept 1949;*
Honours; *Scottish Cup runner-up 1938;*

Doug McAvoy was a typical Scottish ball-winning footballer who made his reputation in the years leading up to WW2 with Kilmarnock, appearing for them in the 1938 Scottish Cup Final defeat by East Fife. When peace time football was suspended he was still with Kilmarnock, though during WW2 he 'guested' for a number of sides south of the border that included Wrexham. His 'Robins' debut came at the end of October 1940 in a 6-2 defeat at New Brighton, and another twelve appearances followed over the next two seasons, during which he scored five goals. Doug eventually resumed his career with Kilmarnock following the end of the hostilities, before he was signed by Liverpool in December 1947 for a £7,000 fee. He made his debut in front of the 'Kop' in January 1948 in a scoreless draw with Stoke City, but was to manage just one more appearance, a 1-1 draw with Chelsea in October 1948. In September 1949 he was allowed to return to Scotland with Queen of the South.

McGOVERN, Eric

Position; *Outside-Left*
Debut v. *Chester (a) 20.2.1943*
Total Appearances & Goals; *1 app, 0 gls*
Career; *Wrexham (WW2 Guest) Feb 1943 1app 0gls;*

Eric McGovern made his solitary appearance for Wrexham in February 1943, when he turned out as a 'guest' at outside-left in a 2-0 defeat at Chester.

McGRATTON, H.

Position; *Left-Back*
Debut v. *New Brighton (h) 4.1.1941*
Total Appearances & Goals; *3 apps, 0 gls*
Career; *Wrexham (WW2 Guest) Jan 1941 3apps 0gls;*

McGratton made his first appearance for Wrexham in a 5-3 home defeat by New Brighton in January 1941 in a Lancashire Cup match. Two further appearances followed in March: a 7-2 defeat at Liverpool, and a 5-2 home win over Chester.

McKENNAN, Peter Stuart — Partick Thistle

Position; *Inside-Forward*
Born; *Airdrie, 16th July, 1918.*
Died; *Dundonald, Ayrshire, 28th September, 1991.*
Height; *6ft 0in* **Weight;** *12st 0lbs.*
Debut v. *New Brighton (h) 21.10.1939*
Total Appearances & Goals; *1 app, 2 gls*
Career; *Whitburn Juniors; Edinburgh Juniors; Partick Thistle Jul 1935; Wrexham (WW2 Guest) Oct 1939 1app 2gls; Chelsea (WW2 Guest) Aug 1942 25apps 13gls; Brentford (WW2 Guest) 1943/44 20apps 14gls; West Bromwich Albion 30th Oct 1947 £10,650 11apps 4gls; Leicester City 12th Mar 1948 (Exchange for J.Haines and £6,000) 18apps 7gls; Brentford 18th Sept 1948 £7,000 24apps 6gls; Middlesbrough 19th May 1949 40apps 18gls; Oldham Athletic 24th Jul 1951 78apps 28gls; Coleraine 16th Jul 1954;*
Honours; Scottish League XI Representative cap; Irish League XI Representative cap; Third Division North Championship 1953;

Peter McKennan began his football career with Partick Thistle in his native Scotland a little over four years before WW2 began. AT the outset of the hostilities he became a sergeant-major in the Royal Welch Fusiliers, and, whilst serving in the Army, he appeared as a 'guest' for Wrexham in a 6-4 home win over New Brighton in October 1939. He marked the occasion by scoring two of the 'Robins' goals. During the conflict Peter also 'guested' for West Bromwich Albion, Chelsea, Brentford, and Glentoran in Northern Ireland, for whom he played throughout 1941, winning Irish League representative honours to add to his two pre-war Scottish representative caps. After WW2 had ended Peter remained in England, and played for Leicester City, Brentford, Middlesbrough, and Oldham Athletic - who he inspired to the Third Division North Championship in 1953. He then moved on to Coleraine as player/coach in July 1954. During his career Peter was described as a 'strong, forceful forward with magnificent ball control and a never say die spirit. A source of inspiration to those around him'.

McNEE, Christopher — Hamilton Academical

Position; *Outside-Left*
Born; *Glasgow*
Height; *5ft 7in* **Weight;** *11st 12lbs*
Debut v. *Everton (h) 17.10.1942*
Total Appearances & Goals; *12 apps, 3 gls*
Career; *Blantyre Vics; Hamilton Academical 1938/39; Wrexham (WW2 Guest) Oct 1942 12apps 3gls;*

Chris McNee made his first appearance for Wrexham at outside-left in a 2-0 home defeat by Everton in October 1942. He went on to add eleven more appearances for the club before the end of that season, scoring three goals. He had previously turned out for Scottish League side Hamilton Academical prior to the outbreak of WW2, they having spotted him playing in Scottish Junior football with Blantyre Vics..

MAJOR, Arthur — Crewe Alexandra

Position; *Wing-Half*
Debut v. *Crewe Alexandra (a) 7.12.1940*
Total Appearances & Goals; *1 app, 0 gls*
Career; *Notts County (Am) Mar 1933 0apps; Stalybridge Celtic; Crewe Alexandra (Am) May 1935, (Pro) Nov 1935 4apps 0gls, (WW2) 10apps 0gls; Wrexham (WW2 Guest) Dec 1940 1app 0gls;*

Arthur Major had once been on the books of Notts County, but his Football League debut came with Crewe Alexandra, to where he had moved from Stalybridge Celtic. He made his debut for the 'Railwaymen' against Wrexham on the Racecourse in December 1935 as the visitors ran out 1-0 winners, although he was to manage just three more games for them. His one and only appearance for Wrexham came as a 'guest' during WW2, when he lined up, co-incidentally, against Crewe Alexandra! in a 3-2 defeat at Gresty Road in December 1940.

MAKIN, George W. — Everton

Position; *Outside-Left*
Born; *Liverpool*
Debut v. *Wolves (h) 24.2.1945*
Total Appearances & Goals; *1 app, 0 gls*
Career; *Everton May 1943 (WW2) 22apps 4gls; Chester (WW2 Guest) 1943/44 2apps 0gls; Tranmere Rovers (WW2 Guest) 1943/44 4apps 0gls; Burnley (WW2 Guest) 1944/45 3apps 0gls; Southport (WW2 Guest) 1944/45 1app 0gls; Manchester United (WW2 Guest) Sept 1944 3apps 0gls; Stockport County (WW2 Guest) Jan 1945 1app 0gls; Wrexham (WW2 Guest) Feb 1945 1app 0gls; Crewe Alexandra (WW2 Guest) 1944/45 1app 0gls; Bury (WW2 Guest) 1945/46 1app 0gls; Pwllheli & District; Holyhead Town;*
Honours; *Welsh League (North) Championship winner 1951 & 1952; Cookson Cup winner 1952; Alves Cup winner 1952; North Wales Challenge Cup runner-up 1952; North Wales Coast Representative XI;*

George Makin began his career with Everton as a youngster during WW2, and it was during this time that he appeared as a 'guest' for a number of clubs in the North-West, including Chester, Tranmere Rovers, Burnley, Southport, Manchester United, Stockport County, Crewe Alexandra, Bury, and Wrexham. His solitary appearance for the 'Robins' came at outside-left in a 1-1 home draw with Wolves in February 1945. It is strange to record that inspite of the number of clubs that he played for during the conflict, he never actually went on to play League football. But, having failed to hit the high spots of the Football League he was certainly one of the 'stars' in the halcyon days of North Wales Coast football in the 1950s and early 1960s, when the Welsh League (North) was of the highest standard. He earned representative honours with the North Wales Coast F.A. side, appearing four times against the Scottish Juniors. He was also a member of the famous Pwllheli & District side in 1951/52; known as the 'Invincibles' they completed the season unbeaten in the League, they won both the Cookson and Alves Cups, and where finalists in the North Wales F.A.Challenge Cup. Former 'Racecourse Robin' T.G.Jones was the manager who guided them to all this success. George later turned out for Holyhead Town, where his stylish wing play was instrumental in bringing the 'Harbourmen' much success in League and Cup football. Provided much ammunition from the wing for prolific goalscorer Tommy Welsh to fire the bullets!!

MARTIN, John Rowland — Aston Villa

Position; *Inside-Left*
Born; *Hamstead, West Bromwich, 5th August, 1914.*
Height; *5ft 11in* **Weight;** *10st 10lbs.*
Debut v. *Chester (h) 11.11.1939*
Total Appearances & Goals; *6 apps, 1 goal*
Career; *Rugeley Grammar school; St.Marks College 1931; London Combined Colleges 1932; Hednesford Town Sept 1934; Aston Villa Dec 1934 81apps 22gls, WW2 40apps 12gls; Wrexham (WW2 Guest) Nov 1939 6apps 1gls; Birmingham (WW2 Guest) Dec 1939 2apps 0gls; Nottingham Forest (WW2 Guest) 1939/40 1app 0gls; Portsmouth (WW2 Guest) 1941/42 1app 0gls; Tottenham Hotspur (WW2 Guest) Sep 1942 42apps 14gls; Aldershot (WW2 Guest) 1943/44 1app 0gls;*
Honours; *Two England War-time international caps; England Amateur International; Football League Representative XI;*

John Martin's football career was yet another to be seriously disrupted by WW2. He had just established himself in the Aston Villa first team during the 1939/39 season, with performances hailing him as 'an inside-forward of the Corinthian kind, an outstanding success in 1938/39'. He had played in the opening three games of 1939/40 when the conflict began. John continued to play for Villa when he could, as well as appearing as a 'guest' for Nottingham Forest, Birmingham, Portsmouth, Spurs, Aldershot, and Wrexham. He made his debut for the 'Robins' at inside-left in a 2-2 home draw against Chester in November 1939, adding a further five appearances during 1939/40. During this period he was awarded international honours by England, playing in two War-time internationals against Scotland and Wales at Wrexham. Following the end of the hostilities John, who was described as a 'close and clever dribbler', took up where he had left off with Villa. He remained a regular at inside-forward at Villa Park until the 1948/49 season, when he lost his place, and eventually retired. During his time at Villa he continued in his profession as a schoolmaster at Hednesford, and was allowed to do his training in the evenings. He later became headmaster of Lilleworth Secondary Modern School in Hednesford, and also had a spell as manager of Hednesford Town.

MATTHEWS, Sir Stanley — Stoke City

Position; *Outside-Right*
Born; *Hanley, Stoke-on-Trent, 1st February, 1915.*
Height; *5ft 10in* ***Weight;*** *11st 8lbs.*
Debut v. *Crewe Alexandra (h) 14.12.1940*
Total Appearances & Goals; *1 app, 0 gls*
Career; *Stoke City Feb 1932 259apps 51gls; Crewe Alexandra (WW2 Guest) 1939/40 1app 0gls; Manchester United (WW2 Guest) Jun 1940 1app 0gls; Wrexham (WW2 Guest) Dec 1940 1app 0gls; Blackpool (WW2 Guest) Aug 1941 87apps 5gls; Arsenal (WW2 Guest) Jan 1945 1app 0gls; Blackpool May 1947 379apps 17gls; Stoke City Oct 1961 59apps 3gls;*
Honours; *54 England International caps; England Schoolboy International; 29 England War-time International caps; F.A.Cup Winner 1953; F.A.Cup runner-up 1948 & 1951; European Footballer of the Year 1956 (First player ever to be awarded the title); Footballer of the Year 1948 & 1963;*

What can one say about Stanley Matthews that hasn't already been said? Known as the 'Wizard of the Dribble' because of his tantalising ball skills on the right wing. He was awarded the CBE in 1957 for his services to football, and a knighthood followed in 1965. He played his last game for Stoke City at the age of 50, and then went on to occupy the hot-seat at Port Vale until 1968. He later managed Hibernians of Malta, and coached in South Africa, Australia, Canada and USA, before becoming President of Stoke City and Honorary vice-president of Blackpool. Sir Stanley had appeared for Wrexham as a 'guest' during the WW2 conflict in a 5-1 home win over Crewe Alexandra, although he failed to put his name on the score sheet. He also turned out as a 'Guest' for Manchester United, Crewe Alexandra, Blackpool and Arsenal. Along with Billy Meredith, who also played once for Wrexham in the 1890s, he was probably one of the greatest wingers of all time.

MEADE, T.

Position; *Left-Back*
Debut v. *Everton (h) 3.4.1943*
Total Appearances & Goals; *2 apps, 0 gls*
Career; *Newport County (WW2) 3apps 0gls; Wrexham (WW2 Guest) Apr 1943 2apps 0gls;*

Meade played War-time football for both Newport County and Wrexham, making his two appearances for the 'Robins' in April 1943. He turned out in both games at left-back, his debut coming in a 4-1 home win over Everton, followed by a 6-3 home success over Stockport County in the next match.

MILBURN, James — Leeds United

Position; *Right-Back*
Born; *Ashington, 21st September, 1919.*
Height; *5ft 6 3/4in* ***Weight;*** *11st 2lbs.*
Debut v. *New Brighton (a) 10.2.1940*
Total Appearances & Goals; *8 apps, 3 gls*
Career; *Ashington; Leeds United Oct 1936 208apps 15gls; Darlington (WW2 Guest) 1939/40 5apps 0gls; Wrexham (WW2 Guest) Feb 1940 38apps 3gls; Bradford City (WW2 Guest) Apr 1940 1app 0gls; Bradford Park Avenue Jun 1952 90apps 10gls;*

Jimmy Milburn was a younger brother of George and Jack, who were also at Leeds United, and he was also an uncle to the Charlton brothers. Jimmy, who was known as 'Iron Man' at Elland Road, and was described as 'a fierce tackler' beginning his football career with Ashington before a move to Leeds United in October 1936, although he didn't get his first team chance until the aborted 1939/40 season. During the conflict he appeared as a 'guest' for Darlington, Bradford City and Wrexham, making 38 appearances and scoring three goals for the Racecourse club. His 'Robins' debut came in a 4-1 defeat at New Brighton in February 1940, with his final appearance coming in a 2-1 home defeat by Everton in April 1945. During WW2 Jimmy served in India, and was later wounded in Belgium in 1944, although that did not stop him from serving with the Civil Defence. At the end of the conflict he resumed his football career with Leeds United, where he went on to make over 200 appearances before moving on to Bradford Park Avenue until he retired in the mid-fifties. As a player he was described as 'rather slight for a back, but his positional and all round competence make him a tough adversary for any winger'.

MOORE, Norman Woodliffe — Grimsby Town

Position; *Centre-Forward*
Born; *Grimsby, 15th October, 1915.*
Height; *5ft 10 1/2in* ***Weight;*** *11st 7lbs*
Debut v. *Tranmere Rovers (h) 20.12.1941*
Total Appearances & Goals; *8 apps, 13 gls*
Career; *Grimsby Town Mar 1939 7apps 1gls, WW2 8apps 3gls; Wrexham (WW2 Guest) Dec 1941 38apps 13gls; Aldershot (WW2 Guest) 1942/43 1app 0gls; Charlton Athletic (WW2 Guest) 1943/44 4apps 0gls; Luton Town (WW2 Guest) 1944/45 3apps 0gls; Crystal Palace (WW2 Guest) Oct 1944 3app 0gls; Fulham (WW2 Guest) 1944/45 1app 0gls; Norwich City (WW2 Guest) 1945/46 11apps 4gls; Hull City Apr 1947 81apps 46gls; Blackburn Rovers Mar 1950 £3,500 7apps 1gls; Bury Aug 1951 2apps 0gls; Goole Town Jul 1952; Wisbech;*
Honours; *Third Division North Championship Winner 1949; F.A.Representative XI 1949;*

Norman Moore was a member of a well known Grimsby footballing family - brother of Roy and uncle of Kevin, David and Andrew. He had been selected for Grimsby Schoolboys before beginning his professional football career at Blundell Park prior to the outbreak of WW2, having turned out for their junior sides. He remained on the 'Mariners' books until after the War had ended, during which he had appeared as a 'guest' for a number of Football League clubs, including Wrexham. At the Racecourse he made his debut in December 1940 in a 6-2 home defeat by Tranmere Rovers, and went on to make a total of 38 appearances, scoring thirteen goals for the 'Robins' during this period. After the War he had a short spell with Grimsby Town at Blundell Park before being given a free transfer. Norman then joined Humberside neighbours, Hull City, in April 1947, and was switched from playing at either inside-forward or wing-half positions to centre-forward with considerable success. He was the 'Tigers' top scorer for two consecutive seasons, and was described as having 'an exemplary work-rate, while his heading ability was outstanding', and his many goals became known as 'Norman conquests'. However, the 1949/50 season saw injuries disrupt his appearances and he joined Blackburn Rovers in the summer for £3,500. The move failed to rejuvenate him, and after eighteen months and just seven appearances he joined Bury, which again proved unfruitful. He then dropped into non-league football with Goole Town and Wisbech. Norman later left the game to take up employment with a firm of paper merchants before trying his hand at farming near North Kelsey.

MORGAN, Gwyn — Wrexham

Position; *Left-Back*
Died; *Rhosllanerchrugog, 1997*
Debut v. *Tranmere Rovers (a) 25.12.1941*
Total Appearances & Goals; *2 apps, 0 gls*
Career; *Wrexham (WW2 Guest) Dec 1941 2apps 0gls; Johnstown United 1948/49; Liverpool Marine cs1950; Lovells Athletic cs1951;*
Honours; *13 Welsh Amateur International caps*

A local boy from Rhos, Gwyn Morgan was presented with his first team opportunity at Wrexham on Christmas Day 1941, making his debut at left-back in a 4-2 defeat at Tranmere Rovers. Serving in the Royal Navy during the conflict, his next appearance for the 'Robins' came almost two years later, when he appeared at right-back against Manchester United in a 4-1 defeat on the Racecourse. After the hostilities had ended he turned out for Johnstown United, with whom he won the first of his thirteen Welsh Amateur international caps in 1948/49 against England. He joined Liverpool Marine for the 1949/50 season, where he spent two years before moving to South Wales to find work, where he turned out for Lovells Athletic. Gwyn is known to have passed away in 1997 in Rhos.

***MORRIS,* John** — Manchester United

Position; *Inside-Forward*
Born; *Radcliffe, Lancashire, 27th September, 1923.*
Height; *5ft 7'3/4in* ***Weight;*** *10st 8lbs*
Debut v. *Manchester United (a) 6.12.1941*
Total Appearances & Goals; *1 app, 0 gls*
Career; *Manchester United Mar 1941 83apps 32gls, WW2 apps gls; Wrexham (WW2 Guest) Dec 1941 1app 0gls; Bolton Wanderers (WW2 Guest); Charlton Athletic (WW2 Guest); Derby County Mar 1949 £23,850 130apps 44gls; Leicester City Oct 1952 £20,000 206apps 33gls; Corby Town May 1958 (Player/manager); Kettering Town cs1961 (Player/manager);*
Honours; *3 England International caps; F.A.Cup Winner 1948; 5 Football League Representative XI apps; Second Division Championship Winner 1954;*

Johnny Morris was on the books at Old Trafford from the age of 15, but world events would disrupt his football career. He played much of his early football during the conflict as a 'guest' for Bolton Wanderers, Charlton Athletic, and Wrexham, as well as Manchester United. Johnny served with the Royal Armoured Corps as a tank crew member, although he did not enlist until 1942, when he was 18. He made just one appearance for Wrexham in December 1941, playing in his outside-right position against his own club Manchester United, in the 'Robins' heaviest war-time defeat, 10-3. Described as a 'skilful, thoughtful dribbler, and blessed with a thunderous shot' he went on to help United win the F.A.Cup in 1948, and to play in the first of his five Football League representative appearances. In March 1949 he then commanded a British record transfer fee of £24,500 from Derby County, going on to win three England caps and scoring three goals for his country. Morris signed for Leicester City in October 1952, helping them to win the Second Division championship two years later. By this time he had begun to play at right-half, where he was said 'to have the ability to open up the game'. In May 1958 he left Filbert Street to take over as player/manager of Corby Town, later followed by a similar position at Kettering Town. John also managed Great Harwood and Oswestry Town. His younger brother, William, had a brief spell in League football with Rochdale. John later became a newsagent in Derby.

***MOSS,* Amos** — Aston Villa

Position; *Wing-Half*
Born; *Birmingham, 28th August, 1921.*
Height; *6ft 0'1/2in* ***Weight;*** *11st 8lbs.*
Debut v. *Tranmere Rovers (h) 23.9.1944*
Total Appearances & Goals; *2 app, 0 gls*
Birmingham Boys Club; Aston Villa May 1939 102apps 5gls, WW2 5apps 0gls; Leeds United (WW2 Guest) 1942/43 8apps 0gls; Wrexham (WW2 Guest) Sept 1944 1app 0gls; Clapton Orient (WW2 Guest) 1945/46 3apps 0gls; Kettering Town cs1956; Wisbech Town; Kidderminster Harriers (Player/Coach) Aug 1961; Rugby Town (Player/Coach) 1962;

Younger brother of Frank, whose father, Frank senior, also played for Aston Villa between 1914 and 1929. A Birmingham & District Schools' player Amos Moss joined Villa from Birmingham Boys' Club in May 1939. Unfortunately, before he could kick a ball for Villa, WW2 had broken out and his career was put on hold. It was during this period that Amos turned out as a 'guest' for Wrexham, making one appearance for the club in a 1-0 home win over Tranmere Rovers in September 1944. Eventually, Amos made his Football League debut alongside his brother in the Villa defence on Christmas Day 1946, a 2-2 home draw with Huddersfield Town. He remained with Villa for ten years after the cease-fire, although making just 102 League appearances in that time, before dropping into non-league circles with Kettering Town, Wisbech Town, Kidderminster Harriers as player/coach, and Rugby Town in a similar capacity. He retired from playing in 1963. At Villa he was described as a 'powerfully built half-back, but never holding down a regular first team place'.

***MOSS,* Frank** — Aston Villa

Position; *Centre-Half*
Born; *Aston, Birmingham, 16th September, 1917.*
Died; *Looe, Cornwall May 1997.*
Height; *5ft 11in* ***Weight;*** *11st 6lbs.*
Debut v. *Stockport County (h) 4.5.1940*
Total Appearances & Goals; *1 app, 0 gls*
Career; *Cowper Street School; Ryland Road School; St.Clements School; Worcester Nondescripts; Worcester City (Am) Aug 1933; Wolves (Trial); Sheffield Wednesday (Am) Nov 1935, (Pro) May 1936 22apps 0gls; Aston Villa May 1938 £2,000 296apps 3gls, (WW2) 12apps 0gls; Birmingham City (WW2 Guest) Feb 1940 2apps 0gls; Wrexham (WW2 Guest) May 1940 1app 0gls; Northampton Town (WW2 Guest) 1939/40 12apps 1gls;*

Frank Moss Junior was a resourceful centre-half: Tommy Lawton once said of him "I never got a kick when Frank was marking me - a great player, hard but fair." He was playing for Worcester Nondescripts when he was invited for trials with Wolves, but it was Sheffield Wednesday who gave him his first taste of League football, joining them in November 1935. He spent almost three years at Hillsborough before linking up with his father's team, Aston Villa, at the end of 1937/38. He became a permanent fixture at Villa Park until June 1955, clocking up 297 League appearances, a record which would undoubtedly been more impressive had he not missed seven seasons due to the War. During the hostilities he served as a signalman with the Royal Navy, operating on Gun Boats and Destroyers in the Middle-East. He would turn out for Villa when he could during this time, and he also appeared as a 'guest' for Birmingham, Northampton Town, and Wrexham. Frank made just one appearance for the 'Robins', at wing-half in a 4-2 home win over Stockport County in May 1940. Noted as a 'strong, resourceful player, who was at his best when pitched in against quality attackers,' his football career came to an end following a tackle by Manchester United's Duncan Edwards, although he did attempt a brief comeback before the curtain finally came down on a splendid career. He later coached the youngsters at Villa Park during the 1955/56 season, but left football altogether to concentrate on his newsagents' business in Kingstanding, which he operated from 1940 to 1958. Frank later retired to live in the Cornish resort of Looe.

***MUIR,* M.**

Position; *Outside-Right*
Debut v. *Stockport County (h) 7.11.1942*
Total Appearances & Goals; *6 apps, 3 gls*
Career; *Wrexham (WW2 Guest) Nov 1942 6apps 3gls; Rochdale (WW2) 1944/45 15apps 0gls;*

Muir made his debut for Wrexham at outside-right in a 7-1 home win over Stockport County during November 1942, scoring one of the goals. Five more appearances were added that season, in which he scored two goals. He also made fifteen appearances for Rochdale during the 1944/45 season.

***MULLIGAN,* Edward**

Position; *Centre-Forward*
Debut v. *Chester (h) 21.9.1944*
Total Appearances & Goals; *app, 0 gls*
Career; *Rochdale (WW2 Guest) 1943/44 3apps 0gls; Walsall (WW2 Guest) 1943/44 2apps 0gls;*
Wrexham (WW2 Guest) Sept 1944 1app 0gls;

Eddie made his one and only appearance for Wrexham at centre-forward in a 1-1 home draw with Chester in September 1944. He had previously registered war-time appearances for both Rochdale and Walsall.

NEWSOME, Robinson — West Bromwich Albion

Position; *Inside-Left*
Born; *Hebden Bridge, 25th September, 1919.*
Debut v. *Southport (a) 12.5.1945*
Total Appearances & Goals; *1 app, 0 gls*
Career; *Willington Boys Club; Congleton Town 1937; West Bromwich Albion Mar 1939 0apps, WW2 34apps 18gls; Manchester United (WW2 Guest) Apr 1943 1app 0gls; Burnley (WW2 Guest) 1942/43 2apps 0gls; Chester (WW2 Guest) 1943/44 31apps 11gls; Walsall (WW2 Guest) Mar 1941 27apps 9gls; Wrexham (WW2 Guest) May 1945 1app 0gls; Norwich City (WW2 Guest) 1945/46 13apps 11gls; Coventry City Jun 1947 £1,500 7apps 2gls; Hereford United cs1948; Brierley Hill Alliance cs1949; Dudley Town cs1950; Gornal Wood cs1953 to cs1955;*

Bobbie Newsome was on the books of West Bromwich Albion when WW2 commenced. He made his Albion debut during the conflict, as well as appearing for a number of other clubs during this period, including Burnley, Manchester United, Chester, Walsall, Norwich City and Wrexham. Bobbie made his solitary appearance for the 'Robins' in a 5-1 win at Southport, scoring one of the goals in the club's final match of the 1944/45 season. After WW2 had ended he resumed his playing career with Albion, but failed to make a League appearance and left the Hawthorns in the close season of 1947 to join Coventry City. At Highfield Road he finally made his Football League debut ....against West Bromwich Albion!! It was not to be a happy debut however, as he ended up on the losing side, 3-1. He did gain some consolation from a 1-0 win in his next match. Bobbie left the 'Sky Blues' in the summer of 1948, and drifted into non-league football with Hereford United, Brierley Hill Alliance, Dudley Town and Gornal Wood. During his football career he was described as a 'utility player, direct and sharp near goal'.

OAKLEY, Maurice — Wrexham

Position; *Centre-Forward*
Debut v. *Southport (a) 10.11.1945*
Total Appearances & Goals; *1 app, 0 gls*
Career; *Wrexham (WW2 Guest) Nov 1945 1app 0gls;*

Maurice Oakley was a Wrexham reserve team player who was brought into the 'Robins' side at centre-forward for his one first team appearance in November 1945, a 2-2 draw at Southport.

OWEN, Arthur — Tranmere Rovers

Position; *Left-Back*
Born; *c1911*
Debut v. *Stoke City (h) 2.6.1941*
Career; *Hoylake; Tranmere Rovers (Am) Sept 1936, (Pro) Nov 1936 11apps 0gls; Wrexham (WW2 Guest) Jun 1941 1app 0gls;*

Arthur Owen was playing local football for Hoylake when he was signed by Tranmere Rovers as an amateur in September 1936, before stepping up to the professional ranks two months later. His Football League debut came in January 1937, when he turned out in a 1-0 defeat at Southport. Arthur added another ten senior appearances for the Prenton Park club before WW2 was to interrupt his career. During the conflict Arthur 'guested' once for Wrexham, at left-back, in a 3-3 home draw against Stoke City in the final game of the 1940/41 season.

PARK, John B. — Newcastle United

Postion; *Outside-Right*
Born; *Douglas Water, Strathclyde. 7th October, 1913.*
Height; *5ft 9in* ***Weight;*** *11st 8lbs*
Debut v. *Tranmere Rovers (h) 21.12.1940*
Total Appearances & Goals; *18 apps, 9 gls*
Career; *Douglas Water Thistle; Hamilton Academical Apr 1933; Newcastle United Apr 1936 £1,800 60apps 11gls, WW2 12apps 2gls; Chester (WW2 Guest) 1939/40 1app 0gls; Wrexham (WW2 Guest) Dec 1940 18apps 9gls;*

John Park played for his local side before joining Hamilton Academical in April 1933, and after three years he had made sufficient impact for Newcastle to take him over the border for a £1,800 transfer fee. John made his 'Magpies' debut in the early part of the 1936/37 season, in a 3-0 win at Bradford Park Avenue. He went on to add a further 59 League appearances, in which he was described as an 'enthusiastic, robust player whose methods were not always scientific. Tough and uncompromising.' WW2 interrupted his playing career, although he continued with Newcastle as well as appearing as a 'guest' for both Chester and Wrexham. He made his first appearance for the 'Robins' at outside-right in December 1940, a 5-1 home win over Tranmere Rovers, scoring two of the goals. John went on to complete seventeen more appearances until October 1941, scoring another seven goals. He later became an engineer after his football career had ended.

PAYNE, E.G.H. — Swansea Town

Position; *Inside-Left*
Debut v. *Chester (h) 27.2.1943*
Total Appearances & Goals; *2 apps, 0 gls*
Career; *Swansea Town; Chester (WW2 Guest) 1941/42 4apps 0gls; Wrexham (WW2 Guest) Feb 1943 2apps 0gls; York City (WW2 Guest) 1945/46 1app 0gls;*

Payne was on the books of Swansea Town prior to the outbreak of WW2. It was during this period that he appeared as a 'guest' for Chester, York City, and Wrexham. He made two appearances for the Racecourse club, his debut coming at inside-left in a 3-2 home win over Chester in February 1943, followed by appearing in a 4-1 home success over Everton two months later.

PILLING, James Henry

Position; *Outside-Right*
Debut v. *Manchester United (a) 11.12.1943*
Total Appearances & Goals; *13 apps, 1 goal*
Career; *Wrexham (WW2 Guest) Dec 1943 13apps 1gls;*

Jimmy Pilling made his debut for Wrexham in December 1943, appearing at outside-right in a 5-0 defeat at Manchester United. He went on to add another dozen appearances for the 'Robins' over the next eighteen months, scoring one goal in a 3-0 win at Stockport County in November 1944.

PRESDEE, H.G.

Position; *Outside-Left*
Debut v. *Tranmere Rovers (a) 6.3.1943*
Total Appearances & Goals; *2 apps, 0 gls*
Career; *Cardiff City (WW2 Guest) 1941/42 1app 0gls; Wrexham (WW2 Guest) Mar 1943 2apps 0gls;*

Presdee had appeared as a 'guest' for Cardiff City prior to his two appearances for Wrexham in March 1943. They were both against Tranmere Rovers at outside-left: his debut came at Prenton Park, where the 'Robins' disappointingly lost 4-0, before they redeemed themselves in the following game with a 2-1 victory over the 'Prentonians' on the Racecourse.

PRITCHARD, F.J. — Cardiff City

Position; *Goalkeeper*
Debut v. *Everton (a) 8.11.1941*
Total Appearances & Goals; *2 apps, 0 gls*
Career; *Cardiff City 1939/40 28apps 0gls; Wrexham (WW2 Guest) Nov 1941 2apps 0gls;*

Jackie Pritchard had played most of the 1940/41 season for Cardiff City, during which he also turned out for Wrexham as a 'guest' in November. Both of his two games were against Everton: the first, at Goodison Park, ended in a 3-1 defeat, before the return game on the Racecourse saw the 'Toffeemen' return home with an even more convincing 4-0 victory.

PRITTY, George — Nottingham Forest

Position; *Wing-Half*
Born; *Aston, Birmingham, 4th March, 1915.*
Height; *5ft 11in* ***Weight;*** *11st 0lbs.*
Debut v. *Chester (a) 16.5.42*
Total Appearances & Goals; *2 apps, 0 gls*
Career; *Metro Old Boys; Aston Villa May 1933 3apps 0gls; Nottingham Forest Dec 1938 49apps 1gls, WW2 2apps 0gls; Wrexham (WW2 Guest) May 1942 2apps 0gls;*

George Pritty began his career with Aston Villa, making his Football

League debut in March 1937 in a 4-0 home win over Blackpool. He added two more appearances for Villa before signing for Nottingham Forest in December 1938. At the City Ground he went straight into the first team for his debut, a 1-0 win at Sheffield United, and remained a regular in the side until the outbreak of WW2. Described as 'hardy and resolute; stocky in build', George was to make his first appearance for Wrexham towards the end of the 1941/42 season in a 2-1 win at Chester in May, followed by a 4-0 home defeat in the next match, also against Chester. Upon the resumption of League football in 1946 George returned to Nottingham Forest, where he remained until the end of 1947/48.

PRYDDERCH, Ivor — Wrexham

Position; *Centre-Forward*
Born; *Rhosllanerchrugog, Nr.Wrexham, 20th May, 1916.*
Height; *5ft 8in* ***Weight;*** *11st 0lbs*
Debut v. *Manchester City (h) 27.9.1941*
Total Appearances & Goals; *1 app, 0 gls*
Career; *Druids United; Wrexham; Crewe Alexandra; Caergwrle; Plas Bennion; Stryd Issa; Wrexham (WW2 Guest) Sept 1941 1app 0gls;*

Ivor Prydderch first began playing football for the Grango School in Rhos, and became qualified as a bricklayer. During this time he played football for the well known Welsh non-league side Druids, as well as being on the books of both Wrexham and Crewe Alexandra. During the conflict he was registered with Wrexham as an amateur, playing in many friendlies against various regiments and local clubs in the Wrexham Victory League. He made his only first team appearance for the 'Robins' in September 1941, when he was called up at centre-forward for a 5-3 home defeat by Manchester City. However, his opportunities were limited due to the many quality players who were stationed nearby. Ivor enlisted in the Royal Air Force in 1942, and he played for his station camps at Abingdon (Oxfordshire), Valley (Ynys Mon), and Stonaway (Scottish Highlands). He was also to appear for local teams Caergwrle, Plas Bennion and Stryd Issa. After the conflict had ended he continued in his work as a bricklayer, remaining in the trade until his retirement. Ivor still resides in the Wrexham area at the time of writing (February 1999), while his sons and grandsons have all appeared in local football and are all keen followers of the 'Robins'.

PURTON, B — Wrexham

Position; *Half-Back*
Debut v. *Port Vale (a) 17.3.1945*
Total Appearances & Goals; *2 apps, 0 gls*
Career; *Wrexham (WW2) Mar 1945 2apps 0gls; Oswestry 1946;*

An amateur noted as a useful half back, Purton was a reserve called into the first team for a match at Port Vale in March 1945, where Wrexham drew 1-1. He was to make one further appearance for the 'Robins', also at Port Vale in the following month, when the game again ended all square, this time 2-2. Later joined Oswestry in the Birmingham and District League.

REECE, Thomas Samuel — Crystal Palace

Position; *Wing-Half*
Born; *Wolverhampton, 17th May, 1919.*
Died; *Wolverhampton, May 1990.*
Height; *5ft 8 /2in* ***Weight;*** *11st 8lbs*
Debut v. *Southport (a) 12.10.1940*
Total Appearances & Goals; *1 app, 0 gls*
Career; *Wolves Jul 1937 0apps; Crystal Palace 14th Sept 1938 76apps 5gls, WW2 15apps 0gls; Wrexham (WW2 Guest) Oct 1940 1app 0gls; Watford (WW2 Guest) 1941/42 1app 0gls; Wolves (WW2 Guest) 1942/43 1app 0gls; Brighton H.A. (WW2 Guest) 1944/45 32apps 2gls; Kidderminster Harriers cs1948;*

Tommy Reece was initially on the books of Wolves, but he failed to make a first team appearance at Molyneux and moved on to Crystal Palace in September 1938. It was with the 'Eagles' that he made his Football League debut, a 4-1 defeat at Watford in December 1938. He was not a regular in the Palace side, and WW2 further disrupted his progress at Selhurst Park. During the hostilities he appeared as a 'guest' for a number of clubs, including Watford, Wolves, Brighton, and Wrexham. He turned out just once for the 'Robins', at Southport in October 1940, but ended up on the losing side as Wrexham were beaten 6-2. As life returned to normal Tom resumed his playing career with Crystal Palace, where he was described as 'a good ball player who gave his forwards the kind of passes that a good wing-half should.' He left Selhurst Park in the summer of 1948, and joined Kidderminster Harriers.

REDFERN, William Joseph — Derby County

Position; *Inside-Right*
Born; *Connah's Quay, 15th September 1910*
Height; *5ft 11'1/2in* ***Weight;*** *12st 0lbs*
Died; *Connah's Quay, September 1988*
Debut v. *New Brighton (h) 21.10.1939*
Total Appearances & Goals; *63 apps, 34 gls*
Career; *Holwell Arcadians; Bangor City; Liverpool Marine; Newry Town; Luton Town Sept 1937 41apps 19gls; Derby County Aug 1939 0apps; Wrexham (WW2 Guest) Oct 1939 63apps 34gls; Chester (WW2 Guest) 1940/41 4apps 1gls;*
Honours; *One War-time Welsh international cap;*

Billy Redfern had played non-league football for a number of clubs when he returned from Newry Town in Ireland to join Luton Town in September 1937. An inside-forward, Billy made his Football League debut for the 'Hatters' and went on to record 41 appearances, scoring nineteen goals, before he was signed by First Division Derby County in the summer of 1939. He made his debut for the 'Rams' in the second match of the season, a 2-0 home win over Portsmouth, where he scored, but his career came to a sudden halt when WW2 broke out. Billy immediately returned home to Connah's Quay, and when football resumed a month or so later on a regional basis he began playing for Wrexham, scoring on his debut in a 6-4 home win over New Brighton. He was also chosen to represent Wales at this time in a War-time international against England on the Racecourse in November 1939, when the home side lost 3-2. Billy went on to become a crowd favourite at the Racecourse, as his 'brilliant footwork, and accurate marksmanship made him a forward to fear.' He spent the first three seasons of WW2 turning out for Wrexham when he could, scoring 34 goals in 63 games, as well as playing four games for Chester as a 'guest'. A latecomer to League football, he was said to be 'tall, with an unusual style'. At one time he worked as a Barber, but later traded as a Butcher before opening his own Grocery business in Connah's Quay.

REEDER, George

Position; *Goalkeeper*
Debut v. *Chester (h) 25.5.1942*
Total Appearances & Goals; *2 apps, 0 gls*
Career; *Wrexham (WW2 Guest) May 1942 2apps 0gls;*
George Reeder was a goalkeeper who made his first appearance for Wrexham in the final match of the 1941/42 season. It was not to be a happy debut, however, as the 'Robins' suffered a 4-0 defeat at the hands of local rivals Chester. He added one more game between the sticks for the North Wales club, when he turned out in a 4-2 home defeat by Stoke City in November 1942.

REID, Cyril Haig — Merthyr Tydfil

Position; *Goalkeeper*
Debut v. *Bolton Wanderers (h) 18.3.1944*
Total Appearances & Goals; *1 app, 0 gls*
Career; Wrexham (WW2 Guest) Mar 1944 1app 0gls; Merthyr Tydfil;
Honours; *Welsh Cup Winner 1949; Welsh Cup runner-up 1947;*

More popularly known as 'Tiger' Cyril Reid made his one and only 'guest' appearance in goal for Wrexham in a 3-3 home draw with Bolton Wanderers in March 1944. He was later to appear in two Welsh Cup Finals for Merthyr Tydfil, as they lost 2-1 to Chester after a replay in 1947, before lifting the trophy two years later with a 2-0 Final victory over Swansea Town. Cyril had played a major part in this success by saving a penalty with the game deadlocked at 0-0.

REID, J — Old Kingstonians

Position; *Centre-Forward*
Debut v. *Everton (a) 30.10.1943*
Total Appearances & Goals; *1 app, 1 gls*
Career; *Old Kingstonians; Wrexham (WW2 Guest) Oct 1943 1app 1gls;*

Described as originating from London based non-league club Old Kingstonian, Reid made his one and only appearance for Wrexham at centre-forward in a 4-2 defeat at Everton in October 1943, when he scored one of the 'Robins' goals.

REVELL, Charles — Charlton Athletic

Position; *Forward*
Born; *Belvedere, 5th June, 1919.*
Height; *5ft 10in* **Weight;** *11st 4lbs*
Debut v. *Tranmere Rovers (h) 29.1.1944*
Total Appearances & Goals; *12 apps, 12 gls*
Career; *Callenders Athletic; Tottenham Hotspur Jan 1937; Gravesend & Northfleet; Charlton Athletic 8th May 1939 104apps 15gls; Fulham (WW2 Guest) 1940/41 14apps 5gls; Tottenham Hotspur (WW2 Guest) Mar 1942 1app 1gls; Bury (WW2 Guest) 1943/44 12apps 10gls; Birmingham (WW2 Guest) Sept 1943 1app 0gls; Wrexham (WW2 Guest) Jan 1944 12apps 12gls; Blackpool (WW2 Guest) Dec 1944 3apps 0gls; Derby County Mar 1951 £3,000 22apps 2gls; Eynesbury Rovers Jun 1952 (Player/Manager);*
Honours; *Football League South Cup Winner 1944;*

Charlie Revell began his senior football career with Callenders Athletic, where he scored an incredible 140 goals in a single season - including thirteen in one match from the wing! He was soon snapped up by Tottenham Hotspur in January 1937, but spent most of his time playing for Gravesend & Northfleet, a nursery side of the London club. Charlie remained on 'Spurs' books until he was signed by Charlton Athletic in May 1939. The new season was only a month old when WW2 intervened. Charlie then enlisted in the Royal Air Force as a fitter, and he appeared for the R.A.F. against the Army in an Inter-Forces' representative game at Wembley, scoring twice. He also turned out for a number of clubs as a 'guest', including Fulham, Spurs, Birmingham, Blackpool, and Wrexham. He impressed during his time with the North Wales club, scoring twelve goals in as many games, although he didn't hit the target on his debut, a 2-0 home win over Tranmere Rovers in January 1944. Charlie's best performance came in a 4-0 home win over Crewe Alexandra in April 1944, where he scored all four goals. He collected a Football League South Cup winners' medal in 1944 when he scored twice in Charlton's 3-1 win over Chelsea. After WW2 had ceased he resumed his career at the Valley, and later joined Derby County in March 1951. Eighteen months at the Baseball ground ended with a return south to take up an appointment as player/manager of Eynesbury Rovers. He later managed Edgware Town (1955-1957); served as player/coach with Canterbury City reserves (Aug 1957); took over as manager of Erith and Belvedere (Jun 1958); and followed that with a coaching position at Crystal Palace. He later scouted for Charlton Athletic for five years. Charlie was employed by London County Council as a Play-Centre Supervisor. A qualified coach at football, cricket, tennis, swimming, and basketball he later became a Sports Master at a school in Bexleyheath.

ROBERTS, Edward — Coventry City

Position; *Centre-Forward*
Born; *Chesterfield, 2nd November, 1916.*
Height; *5ft 9in* **Weight;** *11st 0lbs*
Debut v. *Chester (h) 16.9.1944*
Total Appearances & Goals; *2 apps, 1 goal*
Career; *Lea Mission; Glapwell Colliery; Derby County Apr 1934 4apps 0gls; Coventry City Mar 1937 212apps 85gls; Bristol City (WW2 Guest) Oct 1940 57apps 45gls; Wrexham (WW2 Guest) Sept 1944 2apps 1gls; Kings Lynn cs1952; Banbury Spencer 1953;*

Ted Roberts was playing for local side Glapwell Colliery when he was spotted by Derby County, for whom he signed in 1934. He spent three years with the 'Rams', making his Football League debut in a 3-0 win over West Brom in 1936. Ted kept his place for the next three matches before returning to reserve team football, and eventually moved on to Coventry City in March 1937. He became established as a regular in the 'Sky Blues' line-up until WW2 broke out. At the age of 23, as with so many others, his best years as a footballer were lost, although it was during this period that he appeared for Wrexham as a 'guest' in September 1944. He made his first appearance in a 1-1 home draw with Chester, when he scored the 'Robins' goal, and his second - and last - game came in a 1-0 home win over Tranmere Rovers. With football finally returning to normality Ted returned to Coventry, where he became a regular in the senior side for six seasons, averaging a goal every other game, with his strength lying in his heading ability. He left Highfield Road at the end of 1951/52, dropping into non-league football with Kings Lynn, and then with Banbury Spencer. He returned to Coventry in the late 1950s as assistant-coach before becoming trainer-coach under Billy Frith. Ted later worked in local industry for Rolls Royce. His son, Dudley, played for the 'Sky Blues' in the mid-1960s.

ROBERTS, John Edgar — Port Vale

Position; *Centre-Forward*
Born; *Anfield, 20th October, 1907.*
Died; *Cape Town, South Africa, 1st June, 1985.*
Height; *5ft 8'1/2in* **Weight;** *11st 2lbs*
Debut v. *Stoke City (h) 4.11.1939*
Total Appearances & Goals; *7 apps, 7 gls*
Career; *Holt Secondary School; Marine; Orrell; Blundell Sands; Northern Nomads; Southport 11th Nov 1931 18apps 8gls; Liverpool (Am) May 1933, (Pro) Nov 1933 1app 0gls; Wigan Athletic Jun 1934; Port Vale 12th Dec 1935 95apps 56gls; Wrexham (WW2 Guest) Nov 1939 7apps 7gls;*
Honours; *England Amateur International;*

Jack Roberts, or 'Nipper' as he was nicknamed, left Holt Secondary School in Liverpool to play non-league football for Marine, Orrell, Blundell Sands and Northern Nomads before joining Southport in November 1931. It was for the 'Sandgrounders' that he made his Football League debut in November 1931, in a 1-1 draw against Chester. 1932/33 was to be the most memorable season of his career, as he scored eight goals in twelve games to earn a call-up for the England Amateur team against Scotland, and he celebrated in style by scoring the game's winning goal. He was signed by Liverpool in the close season of 1933, but managed just one League appearance before returning to non-league football with Wigan Athletic. He had considerable success with the 'Latics', scoring 54 goals in 57 games, which secured him a move back to the Football League with Port Vale. 56 goals in 95 League games followed for Vale before the six years of conflict interrupted his football career. During this period he appeared as a 'guest' for Wrexham, making an impressive debut by scoring a hat-trick in a 4-4 draw with Stoke City on the Racecourse in November 1939. Six more appearances for the 'Robins' were added before January 1940, when he scored four goals. Eventually, Jack enlisted with the Irish Guards, but was captured in Tunisia. He attracted widespread attention when escaping from a P.O.W. camp in Italy, walking 400 miles to freedom despite a broken neck! Following the end of the War, Jack emigrated to South Africa, working as a printer in Rhodesia and Zambia until he passed away in Cape Town in June 1985. A lifelong Everton fan his ashes were returned home to Liverpool and scattered on Goodison Park. As a young man he had captained England at Baseball.

ROBERTS, L.H. — Wrexham

Position; *Half-Back*
Debut v. *Stoke City (a) 20.9.1941*
Total Appearances & Goals; *2 apps, 0 gls*
Career; *Wrexham (WW2 Guest) Sept 1941 2apps 0gls;*

Roberts made his first team debut for Wrexham in September 1941 in a 5-2 defeat at Stoke City. Just one further appearance for the 'Robins' was added, another defeat - 4-2 at Tranmere Rovers - in April 1942.

RUGMAN, K. — Manchester City

Position; *Outside-Left*
Debut v. *Stockport County (a) 23.11.1940*
Total Appearances & Goals; *1 app, 0 gls*
Career; *Manchester City; Wrexham (WW2 Guest) Nov 1940 1app 0gls; Crewe Alexandra (WW2 Guest) 1940/41 1app 0gls;*

Rugman was on the books of Manchester City when he made just one 'guest' appearance for Wrexham in a 2-1 defeat at Stockport County in November 1940. He also appeared as a 'guest' for Crewe Alexandra the same season.

SALE, Thomas — Stoke City

Position; *Centre-Forward*
Born; *Stoke-on-Trent, 30th April, 1910.*
Died; *Stafford, 10th November, 1990.*
Height; *5ft 11in* ***Weight;*** *12st 0lbs*
Debut v. *Manchester City (a) 19.4.1941*
Total Appearances & Goals; *1 app, 0 gls*
Career; *Stoke St.Peters; Stoke City (Am) Aug 1929, (Pro) May 1930 162apps 75gls; Blackburn Rovers Mar 1936 £6,000 65apps 25gls; Stoke City Mar 1938 £3,000 42apps 23gls; Wrexham (WW2 Guest) Apr 1941 1app 0gls; Northwich Victoria Feb 1947; Hednesford Town;*
Honours; *1933 Second Division Championship Winner;*

Tommy Sale was a pottery worker playing for Stoke St.Peters when he was signed by Stoke City in August 1929. He was a 'bustling type of forward who could mould his game to any of the forward positions'. Quickly establishing himself in the team Tommy became a prolific scorer with Stoke, helping them to win the Second Division title in 1933. He was signed by Blackburn Rovers in March 1936, but when his goals started to dry up two years later Stoke bought him back for half the sum, and he quickly regained his scoring form. Sale continued to play football when he could during the War period, and in fact scored 180 war-time goals for Stoke. He also made one 'guest' appearance for Wrexham, in a rather disappointing 5-0 defeat at Manchester City in April 1941. Following the cease-fire Tommy, by now 35, found competition for places harder than ever, and in 1947 he left the Victoria Ground to join Northwich Victoria, followed by a spell with Hednesford Town. He later worked for Michelin in Stoke, coaching their football team for a short time.

SCREEN, John — Wrexham

Position; *Left-Back*
Born; *Oldbury, 3rd January, 1915.*
Height; *5ft 9in* ***Weight;*** *11st 6lbs*
Debut v. *New Brighton (h) 26th August 1939*
Total Appearances & Goals; *15 apps, 0 gls*
Career; *Smethwick Highfield; West Bromwich Albion May 1934 1app 0gls; Wrexham 2nd Jul 1939 £250 3apps 0gls, WW2 12apps 0gls; Walsall (WW2 Guest) Sept 1945 7apps 0gls; Banbury Spencer 1947;*
Honours; *England Junior International 1934;*

Jack Screen had made his one and only Football League appearance with West Bromwich Albion in January 1935, a 6-3 home win over Middlesbrough. Disappointingly, he failed to make any further impression on the 'Baggies' first team and was allowed to leave the Hawthorns in the close season of 1939. He signed for Wrexham, and made his debut in the opening game of the 1939/40 season, a 2-0 win over New Brighton. Jack played in the next two games before War was declared and all football suspended. As regionalised league's were introduced, Jack remained at the Racecourse, although enjoying just twelve War-time outings with the club. He did turn out seven times for Walsall as a 'guest' during this period, and after the conflict had ended he played non-league football for Banbury Spencer, later becoming trainer at Walsall, and eventually coach at Wolves.

SHEPHERD, Arthur Leslie

Position; *Winger*
Born; *Liverpool, 11th May, 1922.*
Height; *5ft 8in* ***Weight;*** *11st 0lbs*
Total Appearances & Goals; *2 apps, 1 goal*
Career; *Wrexham (WW2 Guest) Feb 1946 2apps 1gls; Liverpool 22nd Apr 1946 0apps; New Brighton 10th Aug 1949 30apps 10gls; South Liverpool Aug 1951;*

Arthur Shepherd was the younger brother of Liverpool full back Bill. Arthur was described as 'a strong go-ahead type of player with plenty of punch near goal'. It was prior to his joining Liverpool that he had impressed during the regional football of the WW2 period, when he played for Wrexham in a 2-0 home win over Chester in February 1946, scoring one of the 'Robins' goals. His second and final appearance for Wrexham came in the following month, a 2-0 home defeat by Rotherham, and within weeks he was signed by Liverpool. He spent over three years on the Anfield club's books, without making a first team outing, and he left in the summer of 1949 to join New Brighton. It was with the 'Rakers' that he finally made his Football League debut in the opening game of the 1949/50 season, a 1-0 win over Darlington in which he scored the only goal. Despite this early success Arthur was to find his first team appearances limited during 1950/51, and it proved to be the end of his Football League career as New Brighton failed to regain re-election to the Football League at the end of that season. He then drifted into non-league football with South Liverpool.

SIDLOW, Cyril — Wolves

Position; *Goalkeeper*
Born; *Colwyn Bay, 26th November, 1915.*
Height; *6ft 1in* ***Weight;*** *13st 10lbs*
Debut v. *Chester (h) 22.3.1941*
Total Appearances & Goals; *9 apps, 0 gls*
Career; *Colwyn Bay United 1931; Abergele Jan 1934; Colwyn Bay United Aug 1934; Flint Town United Nov 1934; Llandudno Town 1935; Wolves May 1937 4apps 0gls; Notts County (WW2 Guest) 1940/41 7apps 0gls; Wrexham (WW2 Guest) Mar 1941 9apps 0gls; Darlington (WW2 Guest) 1944/45 20apps 0gls; Hartlepool United (WW2 Guest) 1945/46 3apps 0gls; Burnley (WW2 Guest) 1945/46 2apps 0gls; Liverpool Feb 1946 £4,000 149apps 0gls; New Brighton Aug 1952; Wolves 1953 to 1955 0apps;*
Honours; *7 Welsh International caps; 9 Welsh Wartime international caps; Wales Amateur International; First Division Championship Winner 1947; F.A.Cup runner-up 1950; War League Cup Winner 1942; Welsh League (North) Championship Winner 1936; North Wales Coast F.A. XI;*

A young starlet who hit the headlines in North Wales coast circles in the 1930s, when appearing in goal for the North Wales Coast F.A. XI when just 16 in May 1932 at Dens Park, Dundee against the Scottish Juniors. Cyril Sidlow played for Abergele, Colwyn Bay, Flint, and Llandudno - with whom he won a Welsh League (North) championship medal in 1936. It was during his time at Llandudno that he was invited for a trial with Stoke City. Unfortunately, that came to nothing, but he was then signed by Wolves manager Major Frank Buckley in May 1937. He made his Football League debut for the 'Old Gold' side in April 1938, a 3-2 home win over Birmingham, turning out three more times in the League before WW2 broke out. Cyril remained with Wolves during this period, as well as assisting several other clubs as a 'guest' player, including Notts County, Darlington, Burnley, Hartlepools United, and Wrexham. He made nine war-time appearances for the Racecourse club, his first coming in a 5-2 home win over Chester in March 1941. During the conflict Cyril served with the Duke of Wellington's Regiment as a corporal, and was stationed in the North of England for a while. After the War had ended he was signed by Liverpool, where he collected a First Division Championship medal in 1947, being described as having 'outstanding reflexes, was agile, quick off his line, but a trifle casual on occasions'. He was one of the first 'keepers to adopt the practice of throwing the ball out to an unmarked colleague rather than kicking it forward. In 1952 he dropped into non-league football with New Brighton, eventually joining the coaching staff at Molyneux. Cyril later returned to the Building trade as a carpenter, at which he had become qualified prior to taking up professional football.

SIMMONDS, George

Position; Inside-Right
Born; *Islington, London,*
Debut v. *Everton (a) 14.4.1945*
Total Appearances & Goals; *2 apps, 1 gls*
Career; *Wrexham 11th Apr 1945 2apps 1gls;*

Londoner George Simmonds made his first team debut for Wrexham in a 5-3 defeat at Everton in April 1945, scoring one of the 'Robins' goals. He also featured in the following match, a 2-2 home draw with Chester, but that proved to be his last game for the North-East Wales club.

SIMMS, Hedley Arthur — Wellington Town

Position; *Centre-Forward*
Born; *Jacksdale, Nottinghamshire, 4th June, 1913.*
Died; *Backford, Chester, 10th November, 1993.*
Debut v. *Manchester United (h) 12.12.1942*
Total Appearances & Goals; *50 apps, 20 gls*
Career; *Northern Nomads; Chester (Am) Mar 1935 1app 1gls; Northern Nomads Aug 1935; Wellington Town 1936; Chester (WW2 Guest) 1939/40 1app 1gls; West Bromwich Albion (WW2 Guest) Nov 1942 1app 0gls; Wrexham (WW2 Guest) Dec 1942 50apps 20gls; Crewe Alexandra (WW2 Guest) 1943/44 1app 0gls; Southport (WW2 Guest) 1944/45 19apps 5gls;*
Honours; *England Amateur International 1935; Welsh Cup Winner 1940;*

Educated at the Queen Elizabeth School, Kirby Lonsdale, Hedley Simms played cricket for Boughton Hall and actually made two appearances for Cheshire County Cricket Club in 1939. He was also a promising footballer, and made his one and only Football League appearance for Chester in a 2-1 home win over Walsall in March 1935, scoring one of the goals. Despite that early success he left Sealand Road to join progressive amateur side Northern Nomads. He later joined Birmingham & District League team Wellington Town, with whom he picked up a Welsh Cup winners' medal in the 1940 Final, after beating Swansea Town 4-0. During WW2 Hedley served as a sergeant in the R.A.F., but that did not stop him from turning out as a 'guest' for Chester, West Brom, Crewe, Southport, and Wrexham - where he clocked up 50 appearances. His 'Robins' debut came in December 1942, a 5-2 home defeat by Manchester United, although he did score one of the Wrexham goals. At the end of the hostilities he was awarded a Benefit match by Wellington Town, in April 1946, in recognition of his ten seasons' of service to the club. Appropriately Wrexham provided the opposition. It was said of Simms, 'Straight as a die, always a gentleman'.

SMITH, Arthur — Wrexham

Position; *Outside-Left*
Height; *5ft 6in* ***Weight;*** *10st 7lbs*
Debut v. *Everton (h) 3.4.1943*
Total Appearances & Goals; *7 apps, 3 gls*
Career; *Wrexham (WW2 Guest) Apr 1943 7apps 3gls;*

A Yorkshireman who came to live in the Rhos area, Arthur Smith took up work at the local Hafod Colliery. He began playing football in the local Leagues before making his first appearance for Wrexham during WW2 as a 'guest'. His debut came in a 4-1 home win against Everton in April 1943, and he grabbed one of his side's goals. Six more outings followed, in which he scored another two goals, both in a 5-3 defeat by Crewe Alexandra in December 1943. He was described as an 'outside-left who stayed on the wing and could take his opponents on.'

SMITH, Basil Raymond — Wrexham

Position; *Goalkeeper*
Debut v. *Chester (h) 26.4.1943*
Total Appearances & Goals; *7 apps, 0 gls*
Career; *Northampton Town (WW2 Guest) 1939/40 1app 0gls; Wrexham (WW2) Apr 1943 7apps 0gls;*

Custodian Basil Smith signed for Wrexham on the day that he made his first appearance for the club in the final match of the 1942/43 season, when the 'Robins' romped to a 3-1 victory against Chester on the Racecourse. He then went on to add six more appearances for the club in the first half of the 1943/44 season.

SMITH, Clement — Stoke City

Position; *Centre-Forward*
Born; *Wath-upon-Deane, J/A/S 1910.*
Height; *5ft 7'1/2in* ***Weight;*** *11st 3lbs*
Debut v. *Crewe Alexandra (h) 14.12.1940*
Total Appearances & Goals; *1 app, 3 gls*
Career; *South Kirkby; Halifax Town May 1935 55apps 0gls; Chester Jul 1937 26apps 3gls; Stoke City March 1938 £2,000 25apps 7gls, WW2 10apps 4gls; Crewe Alexandra (WW2 Guest) 1939/40 7apps 2gls; Halifax Town (WW2 Guest) 1939/40 2apps 1gls; Southampton (WW2 Guest) 1939/40 10apps 2gls; Wrexham (WW2 Guest) Dec 1940 1app 3gls; Fulham (WW2 Guest) 1940/41 1app 0gls;*

Clem Smith made his Football League debut for Halifax Town, and went on to spend two seasons at the Shay before signing for Chester in the summer of 1937. The manager at Sealand Road, Alex Raisbeck, had previously been in charge at Halifax. Eighteen months later he joined Stoke City for a £2,000 fee, and remained with the 'Potters' until the outbreak of WW2, during which he turned out for a number of clubs as a 'guest'. It was said of him at Stoke that, 'what he lacked in inches he made up for in cleverness; a particularly good shot for a small man.' Clem was to make his one and only war time appearance for Wrexham in a 5-1 home win over Crewe Alexandra in December 1941, when he created a big impression by scoring a hat-trick. He also appeared for Crewe Alexandra, Halifax Town, Southampton, and Fulham during this period. 'Also a capable player at inside-forward.'

SMITH, L. — Swansea Town

Position; *Forward*
Debut v. *Chester (h) 28.8.1943*
Total Appearances & Goals; *4 apps, 3 gls*
Career; *Swansea Town; Wrexham (WW2 Guest) Aug 1943 4apps 3gls;*

A Swansea Town player, Smith scored two goals in his first game as a 'guest' for Wrexham, as the 'Robins' thrashed neighbours Chester 8-4 on the Racecourse in the opening match of the 1943/44 season. He added one more goal in his next three games for the North East Wales outfit, though they proved to be his last for the club.

SPRINGTHORPE, Terence Alfred — Wolves

Position; *Left-Back*
Born; *Draycott, 4th December, 1923.*
Height; *5ft 8 1/2in* ***Weight;*** *11st 10lbs*
Debut v. *New Brighton (a) 15.2.1941*
Total Appearances & Goals; *2 apps, 0 gls*
Career; *Wolves Dec 1940 35apps 0gls, WW2 9apps 0gls; Wrexham (WW2 Guest) Feb 1941 2apps 0gls; Cardiff City (WW2 Guest) 1940/41 1app 0gls; Leicester City (WW2 Guest) 1941/42 1app 0gls; Coventry City Dec 1950 12apps 0gls;*
Honours; *F.A.Cup Winner 1949; USA International cap;*

Although Terry signed for Wolves during WW2 he appeared as a 'guest' for Wrexham, Cardiff City, and Leicester City during this period. He made two appearances for the 'Robins', both in February 1941, and both against New Brighton in the League War Cup. His debut came in a 2-1 away defeat, while the return match saw New Brighton triumph 8-5 on the Racecourse. Following the end of the hostilities Springthorpe went on to make his Football League debut for Wolves in March 1947, in a 1-1 home draw with Sheffield United. 34 more League appearances followed, and collected an F.A.Cup winners' medal from Wolves' 1949 3-1 Wembley victory over Leicester City. He was transferred to Coventry City in December 1950, and made twelve League appearances for the 'Sky Blues' before going to America in the summer of 1951. Terry played for the U.S.A. against England in New York in June 1953, although he finished on the losing side as England gained revenge for their embarrassing 1950 World Cup defeat with a 6-3 victory.

SPROSTON, Bert — Manchester City

Position; *Right-Back*
Born; *Elworth, Nr.Sandbach, 22nd June, 1915.*
Height; *5ft 9in* ***Weight;*** *12st 0lbs*
Debut v. *Everton (a) 22.5.1940*

Total Appearances & Goals; *1 app, 0 gls*
Career; *Elworth CofE School; Sandbach Council School; Wheelock Village; Middlewich Athletic; Sandbach Ramblers; Huddersfield Town (trial); Leeds United Jun 1933 130apps 1gls; Tottenham Hotspur Jun 1938 £9,500 9apps 0gls; Manchester City Nov 1938 £10,000 125apps 5gls, WW2 31apps 0gls; Aldershot (WW2 Guest) 1939/40 1app 0gls; Wrexham (WW2 Guest) May 1940 1app 0gls; Millwall (WW2 Guest) Mar 1942 11apps 6gls; Ashton United Aug 1950;*
Honours; *11 England International caps 1937-1939; Second Division Championship Winner 1947; Four Football League XI Representative apps; 2 England Wartime International caps;*

Bert Sproston was signed by Leeds United as a 17 year-old from Sandbach Ramblers, and went on to make almost 150 appearances for the Elland Road club, his debut coming in a 1-1 draw at Chelsea in December 1933. During his time at Leeds he also won the first of his eleven England caps, against Wales in 1937. However, with the Yorkshiremen desperately short of money they sold Bert to Tottenham Hotspur in June 1938 for £9,500. His spell in London proved to be an unhappy one, as he struggled to settle in the South, and with the season only a few months old he accepted an offer to move back North, signing for Manchester City for another substantial fee. Sproston actually travelled to play against City with his Spurs' team-mates, and completed his transfer to Maine Road on the eve of the game, thus playing 'against' his old club on the following day! He saw out the season with City, but then WW2 broke out with the new campaign just weeks old. During this period he appeared for Wrexham as a 'guest', making just one appearance in the final match of 1939/40, a 2-1 win at Everton. Bert saw active service with the Army in India, and returned to Manchester City after the conflict had ended, where he went on to win a Second Division Championship medal in 1947. He remained at Maine Road until the end of the 1949/50 season, when he moved on to Ashton United. Bert later became trainer with Bolton Wanderers in July 1951, and eventually worked as a scout for the same club until well into the 1980s. He was noted as a star of the late 1930s, described as 'strong in the tackle, with an ability to recover quickly.'

STEARN, A.D. — Luton Town

Position; *Inside-Forward*
Debut v. *Stockport County (h) 17.4.1943*
Total Appearances & Goals; *1 app, 1 gls*
Career; *Luton Town; Wrexham (WW2 Guest) Apr 1943 1app 1gls*

Described as being 'ex-Luton', Stearn made his one and only appearance for Wrexham in April 1943, a 6-3 home win over Stockport County when he scored one of the goals.

STEEN, Alan William — Wolves

Position; *Outside-Right*
Born; *Crewe, 26th June, 1922.*
Debut v. *Liverpool (a) 8.3.1941*
Total Appearances & Goals; *18 apps, 8 gls*
Career; *Wolves (Am) May 1938, (Pro) Mar 1939 1apps 1gls; Notts County (WW2 Guest) 1940/41 3apps 0gls; Bolton Wanderers (WW2 Guest) 1941/42 2apps 0gls; Wrexham (WW2 Guest) Mar 1941 18apps 8gls; Luton Town May 1946 10apps 0gls; Aldershot Jun 1949 10apps 0gls; Rochdale Jun 1950 45apps 8gls; Carlisle United Dec 1951 16app 2gls;*

Alan Steen joined Wolves prior to WW2 and made his Football League debut for them in March 1939 as a 16 year-old in a 3-0 win over Manchester United. He celebrated the occasion by scoring one of the Wolves' goals. WW2 put a halt to his progress at Molyneux, although he did play for Wolves during this period - as he did for a number of clubs as a 'guest'. One of these teams was Wrexham, his 'Robins' debut coming in March 1941 at Anfield against Liverpool. The match ended in a 7-2 defeat for the visitors, though he did score one of their goals. Alan went on to add a further seventeen appearances, scoring another seven goals for Wrexham, his last appearance at Everton in a 3-1 defeat in November 1941. He spent two years of the conflict held as a Prisoner of War in Germany. When peace has been restored he signed for Luton Town in May 1946 with a high reputation. However, he managed just ten appearances for the 'Hatters' in three seasons, and in the summer of 1949 left Kenilworth Road to join Aldershot. He spent one season with the 'Shots', making ten League appearances before a similar spell with Rochdale, eventually moving on to Carlisle United in December 1951. Alan then drifted into non-league football for the 1952/53 season.

STEVENS, George Leopold — Crewe Alexandra

Position; *Centre-Forward*
Born; *Port Sunlight, 18th March, 1910.*
Height; *5ft 8'1/2in* ***Weight;*** *10st 6lbs*
Died; *Blackpool, 22nd September, 1987.*
Debut v. *Liverpool (a) 30.8.1942*
Total Appearances & Goals; *2 apps, 0 gls*
Career; *Wallasey Trams; New Brighton (Am) 5th Dec 1930, (Pro) 29th Jan 1931 54apps 33gls; Everton 11th Jun 1932 £600 2apps 0gls; Southend United 3rd Nov 1933 £100 72apps 45gls; Stockport County 13th Jun 1936 £150 28apps 9gls; Crewe Alexandra 11th Jul 1938 23apps 23gls, WW2 1939-43 40apps 29gls; Stoke City (WW2 Guest) May 1941 1app 0gls; Wrexham (WW2 Guest) Aug 1941 2apps 0gls; Oldham Athletic (WW2 Guest) Sept 1943 2apps 1gls; Crewe Alexandra (WW2 Guest) 1945/46 2apps 2gls;*
Honours; *Third Division North Championship Winner 1937;*

One of 13 children Leo Stevens was working as a Wallasey Tram Conductor, and playing for his works side, when he was signed by New Brighton on amateur forms in December 1930. He was plunged straight into the 'Rakers' first team, and rose to the occasion by scoring twice in a 2-1 home win over Rochdale. This slim fair-haired opportunist went on to finish the next two seasons as the clubs' top scorer. He was signed by Everton in the summer of 1932, but made only two appearances during the 1932/33 season as he found himself playing understudy to the legendary Dixie Dean. Leo left Goodison Park in the close season of 1933 to join Southend United, where he spent three seasons before returning North to sign for Stockport County. He picked up a Third Division North Championship medal in his first season at Edgeley Park. Just one more season with 'County' followed before a move to Crewe Alexandra. He scored 23 goals in the same number of League games for the 'Railwaymen', before WW2 intervened to disrupt his playing career. Leo continued playing during the conflict, turning out as a 'guest' for Stoke City, Oldham Athletic, Crewe, and Wrexham. His 'Robins' debut came in the opening match of the 1941/42 season, a 5-2 defeat at Liverpool, and this was followed by another 5-2 defeat, this time at Stoke City in the following month. Like so many other players during this period, WW2 effectively put an end to Leo's promising footballing career.

STUTTARD, John Ellis — Plymouth Argyle

Position; *Wing-Half*
Born; *Burnley, 24th April, 1920.*
Height; *5ft 9in* ***Weight;*** *11st 0lbs*
Died; *Burnley, 1984.*
Debut v. *Everton (a) 10.10.1942*
Total Appearances & Goals; *38 apps, 0 gls*
Career; *Burnley (Am) Feb 1938 0apps; Plymouth Argyle Sept 1938 29apps 1gls, WW2 5apps 1gls; Swansea Town (WW2 Guest) 1939/40 1app 0gls; Bournemouth (WW2 Guest) 1940/41 7apps 0gls; Wrexham (WW2 Guest) Oct 1942 38apps 0gls; Luton Town (WW2 Guest) 1943/44 10apps 0gls; Torquay United Sept 1947 82apps 0gls; Bideford Jul 1951; Sete (France) Jul 1952;*

Ellis Stuttard began his football career as an amateur with Burnley before signing for Plymouth Argyle in September 1938. He made his Football League debut for the 'Pilgrims' in a scoreless home draw against West Ham United in March 1939. However, his playing career was then soon disrupted by the outbreak of WW2, and it was during this period that Ellis appeared for Wrexham as a 'guest'. He made his debut in a 2-1 defeat at Everton in October 1940, and went on to add a further 37 war-time appearances for the 'Robins', his final game being a 3-0 win at Tranmere Rovers in January 1944. He also appeared as a 'guest' for Swansea Town, Bournemouth, and Luton Town during this time. After the war had ended Ellis resumed his career with Plymouth, but he was soon to move on, joining Torquay United in September 1947. He spent four seasons at Plainmoor before dropping into non-league football for a year with Bideford, before ending his playing career in France with Sete. He eventually returned home to take up a job as assistant-trainer at Swindon Town, followed by a spell as the club's Chief Scout, before returning to Plymouth Argyle in a similar position, taking over as manager in November 1961. After a disastrous start to the 1963/64 season, he stepped down to assistant-manager, before becoming Chief Scout at Exeter City in December 1964. He was subsequently appointed manager of the 'Grecians' in February 1965, although success eluded him and he resigned in June 1966. Ellis was then taken back to Plymouth by Billy Bingham as Chief Scout in 1968, and again assumed the helm of the Home Park club in March 1970. He held the position until October 1972, when he reverted to his Chief Scout role, a position he held until 1982 when he was declared redundant by the 'Pilgrims' as an economy measure.

SWAIN, John Sanderson — Scunthorpe & Lindsey United

Position; *Outside-Left*
Born; *Grimsby*
Height; *5ft 7in* **Weight;** *10st 9lbs*
Debut v. *Chester (h) 25.5.1942*
Total Appearances & Goals; *1 app, 0 gls*
Career; *Grimsby Town (Am) Jul 1936, (Pro) Sept 1936 22apps 6gls; Scunthorpe & Lindsey United Jul 1939; Wrexham (WW2 Guest) May 1942 1app 0gls;*

Jack Swain showed great promise as both a footballer and a cricketer while at school. He joined Grimsby Town as an amateur from college in July 1936, and signed professional forms two months later. His debut came in the November of the same year, in a 2-0 defeat at Sheffield Wednesday. Jack could not command a regular first team place at Blundell Park over the following three seasons, however, and in the summer of 1939 he moved on to Scunthorpe & Lindsey United, then a Midland League side. WW2 then intervened, and he joined the Army for the duration of the conflict, although he did manage to play some football during this time as a 'guest'. He turned out in just one game for Wrexham, a 4-0 home defeat by Chester in May 1942. After the War Jack became a football referee, progressing via the Midland League to the Football League. He also became a journalist by profession, and was a founder member of the local hospitals' sports broadcasting team that regularly covered Grimsby Town's home games at Blundell Park.

SWINNERTON, K.S.

Position; *Centre- Forward*
Debut v. *Everton (h) 15.11.1941*
Total Appearances & Goals; *1 app, 0 gls*
Career; *Wrexham (WW2 Guest) Nov 1941 1app 0gls;*

Swinnerton made his solitary first team appearance for Wrexham during War-time football, when he turned out at centre-forward in a 4-0 home defeat by Everton in November 1941.

TAYLOR, N.

Position; *Wing-Half*
Debut v. *Tranmere Rovers (h) 9.12.1939*
Total Appearances & Goals; *2 apps, 0 gls*
Career; *Wrexham (WW2 Guest) Dec 1939 2apps 0gls;*

Taylor made his Wrexham debut in a 5-0 home win over Tranmere Rovers in December 1939. It was followed by his second and final appearance in the next game, a 5-1 defeat against Manchester United at Old Trafford.

TENNANT, John Willie — Stoke City

Position; *Left-Back*
Born; *Newcastle-on-Tyne 3rd August, 1907.*
Died; *Liverpool, J/F/M 1978*
Height; *5ft 8'1/2in* **Weight;** *11st 10lbs*
Debut v. *Everton (a) 22.5.1940*
Total Appearances & Goals; *1 app, 0 gls*
Washington Colliery; Stoke City Apr 1928 1app 0gls; Torquay United cs1932 42apps 0gls; Liverpool May 1933 39apps 0gls; Bolton Wanderers Jan 1936 £2,750 105apps 1gls; Stoke City Nov 1938 £2,500 26apps 0gls; Liverpool (WW2 Guest) Nov 1939 15apps 1gls; Wrexham (WW2 Guest) May 1940 1app 0gls; Southport (WW2 Guest) 1942/43 5apps 0gls;

Jack Tennant played in goal as a schoolboy, though he was impressing as a forward when he was signed by Stoke City from Washington Colliery during the 1927/28 season. At the time he was employed as a Miner. Jack had previously played for Newcastle's reserves at right-back before leading the Washington side's attack. However, he was not to make his League debut for Stoke until over two years later, in a 2-1 win at Charlton Athletic in October 1930. It proved to be his only League appearance for the 'Potteries' club, as he was allowed to join Torquay United in the summer of 1932. A year in Devon ended with Liverpool stepping in to sign the fast improving full-back, and he spent three seasons at Anfield before joining Bolton Wanderers for £2,750 in January 1936. After almost two years with the Burnden Park club he returned to Stoke in November 1938, and he was with the Potters when WW2 broke out in September 1939. During this period Jack turned out for Wrexham as a 'guest', making his one and only appearance in the last match of the 1939/40 season, a 2-1 win at Everton. He also 'guested' for both Liverpool and Southport, the War bringing an end to his playing career. He was described as 'an adaptable player who could appear in many positions.'

THOMAS, David S. Lyn — Swansea Town

Position; *Inside-Right*
Born; *Swansea, 19th September, 1920.*
Height; *5ft 9in* **Weight;** *11st 6lbs*
Debut v. *Chester (h) 27.2.1943*
Total Appearances & Goals; *5 apps, 2 gls*
Career; *Abergregon Juniors; Swansea Town Oct 1942; Wrexham (WW2 Guest) Feb 1943 5apps 2gls; Blackpool (WW2 Guest) 1944/45 1app 0gls; Accrington Stanley (WW2 Guest) 1945/46 6apps 1gls; Swindon Town (WW2 Guest) 1945/46 6apps 3gls; Brighton & Hove Albion Jun 1947 13apps 4gls; Folkestone May 1949;*
Honours; *Welsh schoolboy international;*

Lyn Thomas was signed by Swansea Town during WW2 from Abergregon Juniors in October 1942. At school he had earned selection for the Welsh schoolboys' side against both England and Ireland, before becoming yet another example of WW2 putting a halt to a promising football career. During the conflict he appeared as a 'guest' for Blackpool, Accrington, Swindon, and Wrexham. He made five appearances for the Racecourse club, the first a 3-2 home win over Chester in February 1943, in which he scored two of the Wrexham goals. His final outing came in a 3-1 home defeat by Everton in the October of the following season. Following the end of the hostilities Lyn resumed his career with Swansea, but he failed to make a first team appearance and joined Brighton & Hove Albion in the summer of 1947. He finally made his Football League debut for the Goldstone Ground club in August, in a 3-2 win at Watford, but managed to add just twelve more appearances before his release at the end of the 1948/49 season. He then drifted into non-league football with Southern League side Folkestone.

THOMAS, Gwyn — Wrexham

Position; *Outside-Left*
Debut v. *Accrington Stanley (h) 15.9.1945*
Total Appearances & Goals; *1 app, 0 gls*
Career; *Wrexham (WW2) Sep 1945 1app 0gls;*
Gwyn Thomas was on Wrexham's books towards the end of World War Two, and he made his only competitive first team appearance for the 'Robins' in a 1-0 win over Accrington Stanley in September 1945 on the Racecourse.

TIMMS, B.

Position; *Forward*
Debut v. *New Brighton (a) 15.2.1941*
Total Appearances & Goals; *7 apps, 5 gls*
Career; *Wrexham (WW2 Guest) Feb 1941 7apps 5gls;*
Timms made his debut for Wrexham in a 2-1 defeat at New Brighton, a League War Cup match, and he scored the 'Robins' goal. He went on to make six more appearances for the Racecourse club before the season had ended, adding another four goals.

TRACEY, Chris Patrick — Morton

Position; *Outside-Left*
Born; *Glasgow, 17th August, 1909.*
Height; *5ft 5in* **Weight;** *10st 0lbs*
Debut v. *Tranmere Rovers (h) 25.9.1943*
Total Appearances & Goals; *2 apps, 0 gls*
Career; *Douglas Water Thistle Jun 1929; Kirkmuirhill Juniors Feb 1930; Watford May 1930 3apps 1gls; Morton Nov 1931; Kings Park Jan 1932;*

Morecambe Apr 1933; Newry Town; Bacup Borough Aug 1936; Morton Aug 1939; Wrexham (WW2 Guest) Sept 1943 2apps 0gls; Hartlepools United (WW2 Guest) 1943/44 1app 0gls; Lincoln City (WW2 Guest) 1945/46 1app 0gls; Luton Town Aug 1945;

A small and clever winger Charlie Tracey played junior football in his native Scotland before moving south of the border to join Watford in May 1930. He made his Football League debut for the 'Hornets' in a 1-0 victory against Thames United, and finished on the winning side in both of his two other games for the club. He returned to Scotland after one season with Watford, playing non-league football for King's Park. Charlie crossed the border again in April 1933 to join Morecambe, followed by spells with Bacup Borough, and Newry Town in Ireland. A move back to Scotland in the summer of 1939 saw him link up with Scottish League side Morton, before WW2 intervened to disrupt his career with the Greenock club. During the conflict he appeared as a 'guest' for both Hartlepools United and Wrexham, making two appearances for the 'Robins' in September 1943. The first came in a 9-0 home win over Tranmere Rovers, in which Archie Livingstone scored seven of the goals, and this was followed by the return match, a 6-0 win.........for Tranmere!! In August 1945 Charlie signed for Luton Town, but never played in a Football League match for the 'Hatters'.

TRENTHAM, Douglas Herbert — Everton

Position; *Outside-Left*
Born; *Chirbury, Shropshire, 2nd November, 1917.*
Height; *5ft 9'1/2in* ***Weight;*** *10st 4lbs*
Debut v. *Southport (h) 31.8.1940*
Total Appearances & Goals; *3 apps, 1 goal*
Career; *Mickle Trafford FC; Everton Dec 1936 16apps 7gls, (WW2) 1app 0gls; Wrexham (WW2 Guest) Aug 1940 3apps 1gls; Stockport County (WW2 Guest) Sept 1945 4app 0gls; Ellesmere Port Town Aug 1949;*

Doug Trentham was the younger brother of West Brom's Bert. Doug was signed by Everton from Mickle Trafford in December 1936, and made his Football League debut in a 1-0 defeat at Blackpool in September 1937. The war years saw Doug turn out for Wrexham as a 'guest'. He made the first of his three appearances for the 'Robins' in the opening game of 1940/41, a 3-1 home win over Southport, and he followed this by scoring in a 5-0 home victory over New Brighton in the next game. His final appearance came at the end of October, in a 6-2 defeat at New Brighton. Doug also 'guested' for Stockport County in September 1945, before resuming his career at Goodison Park at the end of the conflict. In August 1949 he dropped into non-league football with Cheshire County League side Ellesmere Port Town.

TURNER, Arthur Owen — Birmingham

Position; *Centre-Half*
Born; *Chesterton, 1st April, 1909.*
Died; *Sheffield, 12th January, 1994.*
Height; *5ft 11in* ***Weight;*** *12st 10lbs.*
Debut v. *Liverpool (a) 30.8.1941*
Total Appearances & Goals; *31 apps, 2 gls*
Career; *Woolstanton PSA; Downings' Tileries c1928; Woolstanton PSA c1929; Stoke City (Am) 28th Nov 1930, (Pro) 12th Feb 1931 291apps 17gls; Birmingham Jan 1939 £6,000 39apps 0gls, WW2 23apps 0gls; Bristol Rovers (WW2 Guest) 1939/40 1app 0gls; Crewe Alexandra (WW2 Guest) 1939/40 20apps 4gls; Stoke City (WW2 Guest) Mar 1941 11apps 0gls; Wrexham (WW2 Guest) Aug 1941 31apps 2gls; Southport 30th Jan 1948 28apps 0gls;*
Honours; *Second Division Championship Winner 1933;*

Despite leaving school at 13 Arthur Turner was signed as an amateur by Stoke City in November 1930. Within three years he had become established as an ever-present in the Stoke side that won the Second Division championship, and he later skippered the side. Arthur left Stoke in January 1939 to join Birmingham for £6,000, but the War put the brakes on his career with the 'Blues'. During the interim period he turned out as a 'guest' for Crewe Alexandra, while employed at the town's Rolls Royce factory. He also made 31 appearances for Wrexham, his debut coming in a 5-2 defeat at Liverpool in the opening game of the 1941/42 season. He avenged that defeat in the following match, scoring in a 5-3 win over..........Liverpool! When peace was restored Arthur resumed his career with Birmingham, leading the side to the Football League South Championship in the last season of War-time football. The 'Blues' also reached the semi-finals of the F.A.Cup before he moved on to Southport in January 1948, at the age of almost 39. He was immediately installed as captain at Haig Avenue and helped to transform a struggling side by bolstering the defence to achieve an unprecedented 13 match unbeaten run. Arthur was described as 'a resolute, no frills defender. Superb in the air and no slouch on the ground.' In October 1948 he was appointed manager of Crewe Alexandra, enjoying a three year spell in charge at Gresty Road, before taking up the post of assistant-manager at Stoke City in 1952. In 1950 he had accepted the offer to become the new manager of Wrexham, replacing Les McDowall who had left for Manchester City, but the directors of Crewe Alexandra refused to release him, and he resumed his job in charge of at Gresty Road. His second love was cricket, and he was always amongst the runs with Silverdale Cricket Club in North Staffordshire. He was appointed manager of Birmingham City in November 1954, a position he filled until September 1958, while his next stop was as manager of Headington United in January 1959, leading them to the Southern League title in both 1961 and 1962. Then, as Oxford United, he helped them to gain election into the Football League as a replacement for the defunct Accrington Stanley. He led the Manor Ground club to promotion in 1965, followed by the Third Division Championship in 1968. He stepped down as manager in February 1969 to become the club's General Manager, a position he held until 1972. Arthur later worked as Chief Scout for Rotherham United, followed by a similar position with Sheffield United until July 1981.

TUTIN, Arthur — Stoke City

Position; *Wing-Half*
Born; *Coundon, County Durham, A/M/J 1907.*
Height; *5ft 7in* ***Weight;*** *10st 4lbs*
Debut v. *Liverpool (a) 30.8.1941*
Total Appearances & Goals; *4 apps, 0 gls*
Career; *Shildon; Newton Aycliffe; Ferryhill Athletic; Bishop Auckland; Consett; Chilton Colliery; Spennymoor United; Sheffield Wednesday (Trial) Nov 1930; Bradford (Trial); Crook Town; Aldershot 1932 12apps 0gls; Stoke City Nov 1933 £500 183apps 15gls, WW2 9apps 0gls; Crewe Alexandra (WW2 Guest) 1939/40 38apps 0gls; Wrexham (WW2 Guest) Aug 1941 4apps 0gls;*

Arthur Tutin played non-league football in his native North-East, and attended trials with both Sheffield Wednesday and Bradford Park Avenue in a bid to break into League football. However, it was not until 1932 that he finally achieved his ambition when he joined Football League newcomers Aldershot, making his debut in only their second ever Football League game, a 2-2 draw at Queens Park Rangers. Although never a regular with the 'Shots', Stoke City saw enough to sign him in November 1933 for £500. He went on to become a consistent wing-half who was a delight to watch, in what has often been described as Stoke's best ever half-back line of Tutin, Arthur Turner and Frank Soo. WW2 effectively put paid to his Football League career, though he continued to play throughout the conflict as a 'guest' with both Crewe Alexandra and Wrexham. Arthur made four appearances for the 'Robins' in the opening four matches of the 1941/42 season, his debut ending in a disappointing 5-2 defeat at Liverpool.

WAINWRIGHT, George — Wrexham

Position; *Outside-Left*
Born; *Wrexham*
Debut v. *Crewe Alexandra (a) 17.11.1945*
Total Appearances & Goals; *2 apps, 0 gls*
Career; *Wrexham (WW2) Nov 1945 2apps 0gls;*

George Wainwright was a reserve team player at the Racecourse who was called into the side for the two F.A.Cup First Round matches with Crewe Alexandra in November 1945. This was the only season in which the F.A.Cup competition has been played over two legs. George made his debut for the 'Robins' in the first leg, a 2-1 defeat, while the second leg saw him score one of the Wrexham goals in the 3-0 win on the Racecourse, as the 'Robins' progressed to the Second Round, 4-2 on aggregate.

WALLBANKS, James — Reading

Position; *Wing-Half*
Born; *Platts Bridge, Nr.Wigan, 12th September, 1909.*
Died; *Reading, 28th October, 1979.*
Height; *5ft 9in* **Weight;** *11st 10lbs*
Debut v. *Liverpool (h) 6.9.1941*
Total Appearances & Goals; *24 apps, 1 goal*
Career; *Annfield Plain; Barnsley (Am) Mar 1929, (Pro) Oct 1930 11apps 0gls; Norwich City 11th May 1931 3apps 0gls; Northampton Town Aug 1932 2apps 0gls; Wigan Athletic Feb 1934; Millwall Jun 1934 88apps 0gls; Reading Oct 1938 47apps 1gls; Millwall (WW2 Guest) Aug 1940 18apps 0gls; Wrexham (WW2 Guest) Sept 1941 24apps 1gls; Fulham (WW2 Guest) 1943/44 1app 0gls; Sunderland (WW2 Guest) 1944/45 2apps 0gls;*

Jimmy Wallbanks came from a remarkable family of footballing brothers. Including himself, five played League football: Fred for Bury - Chesterfield, Bradford City, West Ham, and Nottingham Forest; Horace - for Aberdeen, Grimsby, and Luton; Harold - for Fulham, Southend, and Workington; and John - for Barnsley, Chester, and Bradford City. A hard working player, James played League football for Barnsley, Norwich, Northampton Town, Millwall, and Reading before WW2 brought his Football League career to a standstill. During this period he continued to play when he could, appearing as a 'guest' for Sunderland, Fulham, and Wrexham. He made his 'Robins' debut in the second match of 1941/42, a 5-3 home win over Liverpool, and went on to add a further 23 appearances that season, scoring one goal in a 2-2 home draw with New Brighton in October 1941. Jimmy later became trainer at Carlisle United, later taking up similar posts with his former clubs Millwall and Reading, and also enjoyed a spell as player/manager of Ramsgate.

WARING, Thomas — Bath City

Position; *Centre-Forward*
Born; *Birkenhead, 12th October, 1906.*
Died; *Liverpool, 20th December, 1980.*
Height; *6ft 1'1/2in* **Weight;** *13st 4lbs.*
Debut v. *Liverpool (h) 17.5.1941*
Total Appearances & Goals; *11 apps, 10 gls*
Career; *Birkenhead Schoolboys; Tranmere Celtic 1921; Tranmere Rovers (Am) 16th Feb 1926, (Pro) 29th Feb 1926; Aston Villa 17th Feb 1928 £4,750 216apps 159gls; Barnsley 2nd Dec 1935 18apps 4gls; Wolves 23rd Jul 1936 10apps 3gls; Tranmere Rovers 16th Oct 1936 74apps 42gls; Accrington Stanley 10th Nov 1938 22apps 10gls; Bath City Jul 1939; New Brighton (WW2 Guest) Oct 1939 80apps 52gls; Wrexham (WW2 Guest) May 1941 11apps 10gls; Everton (WW2 Guest) Mar 1942 2apps 1gls; Crewe Alexandra (WW2 Guest) 1942/43 22apps 8gls; South Liverpool; Ellesmere Port Town 1945/46; Graysons; Birkenhead Dockers; Harrowby FC;*
Honours; *5 England International caps 1931-1932; Third Division North Championship Winner 1938;*

Thomas or 'Pongo' Waring as he was more popularly known, having earned the nickname at school in Birkenhead, began playing senior football with Tranmere Rovers. He succeeded the legendary Dixie Dean at Prenton Park, and in early 1928 he scored six goals in an 11-1 League victory against Durham City. A month later he was signed by Aston Villa for £4,750. Over 23,000 saw him make his debut for Villa, and he went on to enjoy a very successful spell at Villa Park, scoring 159 goals in 216 League appearances, including a club record haul of 49 goals during the 1930/31 season. He was dubbed the 'Gay Cavalier' at Villa Park, though other nicknames of the period - 'Birkenhead Bombardier' and the 'Claret and Blue Torpedo' - more accurately reflected his potential in front of goal. He left Villa in 1935 to join Barnsley, much to the annoyance of the Villa faithful. However, he spent little time at Oakwell, moving on to Wolves in July 1936, although his spell at Molyneux was even shorter. His career turned full circle in October 1936, when he rejoined Tranmere Rovers, leading them to the Third Division North Championship in 1938. He was on the move again in November 1938, when he joined Accrington Stanley, and this proved to be his last fling with League football. As a player he was described as a 'very fine footballer, tall and long standing, with a penchant for scoring easily.' Other assessments portrayed him as a 'colourful character, not without controversy', and this was perhaps best illustrated when he was reprimanded by the Accrington Directors following an incident on the way home from a League game with Barnsley on Boxing Day 1938, when a bottle of whisky went missing from the trainers baggage!! Nevertheless, he remained with the club until the end of the season, whereupon he moved South to join progressive non-league side Bath City. His time in the West Country was disrupted by the outbreak of WW2, and it was during this period that 'Pongo' appeared as a 'guest' for Everton, New Brighton, Crewe, and Wrexham. He scored ten goals in eleven games for the 'Robins', even though he was nearing the end of his playing career. His debut saw him score twice in a 4-3 home win over Liverpool in May 1941. Following the end of the conflict he resumed his playing career in non-league football with South Liverpool and then Ellesmere Port Town, combining this with employment at the Merseyside docks.

WATSON, Willie — Huddersfield Town

Position; *Outside-Left*
Born; *Bolton-on-Dearne, 3rd March, 1920.*
Height; *5ft 8'1/2in* **Weight;** *11st 4lbs*
Debut v. *Liverpool (a) 7.10.1944*
Total Appearances & Goals; *13 apps, 3 gls*
Career; *Stile Common School; Paddock Council School; Boyds Hall Grammar School; Huddersfield Town Oct 1937 11apps 0gls, WW2 87apps 39gls; Nottingham Forest (WW2 Guest) 1943/44 1app 0gls; Wrexham (WW2 Guest) Oct 1944 13apps 3gls; Burnley (WW2 Guest) 1944/45 2apps 0gls; Brentford (WW2 Guest) 1945/46 1app 1gls; Sunderland 12th Apr 1946 £8,000 211apps 15gls; Halifax Town 5th Nov 1954 33apps 1gls;*
Honours; *4 England International caps 1950-1951; 3 England 'B' International caps; 1 England War-time International cap; 23 England Test Matches 1953-1958;*

Willie Watson is one of the select few to have been capped by England at both football and cricket. He began his football career with Huddersfield Town prior to WW2, and in 1939 he joined Yorkshire CCC - shortly before events in Europe brought all sporting pastimes to an abrupt halt. He continued playing for Huddersfield throughout the War when time allowed, as well as turning out as a 'guest' for Nottingham Forest, Burnley, Brentford, and Wrexham. Willie made his debut for the Racecourse club at Anfield in an impressive 3-0 win over Liverpool in October 1944, and went on to add a further twelve appearances, scoring three goals. He signed for Sunderland in April 1946, in readiness for the new Football League season, following the restoration of peace, where he was converted from a progressive and lively outside-left into an accomplished right-half, 'adroit at winning the ball and perceptive in feeding his attack'. He remained at Roker Park until 1954, by which time he had clocked up over 200 League appearances, he also played four times for England, his

debut coming in a 9-2 win over Northern Ireland at Maine Road in November 1949. His cricket career had also begun to blossom by this time, and he was awarded his County cap by Yorkshire in 1949, going on to appear in 22 Test matches for England. A left handed bat he made 25,670 first class runs, and in 1953 his great innings helped England to save the Test series against Australia. In November 1954 Willie tried his hand at football management, as player/manager of Halifax Town, but he did not achieve much success, and left in April 1956 to concentrate upon his cricket. Willie became assistant-secretary of Leicestershire CCC in December 1957, whom he had previously captained. He also became an England Selector, and was player/manager of the MCC touring party to East Africa in 1963. In September 1964 he returned to football as manager of Halifax Town, but they had to reapply for re-election to Division Four at the end of his first season. It came as something of a surprise therefore, when he was appointed as manager of Bradford City in April 1966, yet he answered his critics by laying the foundations for a promotion-winning side, only to leave before he could achieve his goal. He had been invited to take over as chief administrator of the famous Wanderers club in Johannesburg. Willie spent six years in that position before taking over a poultry farm in South Africa until his retirement in 1986. He was the son of another former Huddersfield Town player, William Watson, who won three League championships and two F.A.Cup medals with the Leeds Road club when they were a major force in the game.

WEAVER, Samuel — Chelsea

Position; *Wing-Half*
Born; *Pilsley, Derbyshire, 8th February, 1909.*
Died; *Mansfield, 15th April, 1985.*
Height; *5ft 9in* ***Weight;*** *11st 7lbs.*
Debut v. *Rochdale (h) 25.8.1945*
Total Appearances & Goals; *12 apps, 3 gls*
Career; *Sutton Town; Hull City Mar 1928 £50 48apps 5gls; Newcastle United Nov 1929 £2,500 204apps 41gls; Chelsea Aug 1936 £4,166 116apps 4gls, WW2 83apps 11gls; Southampton (WW2 Guest) 1939/40 1app 0gls; Fulham (WW2 Guest) 1939/40 6apps 0gls; Notts County (WW2 Guest) 1942/43 1app 1gls; Derby County (WW2 Guest) Oct 1942 25apps 3gls; Clapton Orient (WW2 Guest) 1943/44 2apps 0gls; West Ham United (WW2 Guest) 1943/44 1app 0gls; Mansfield Town (WW2 Guest) 1943/44 1app 0gls; Leeds United (WW2 Guest) 1944/45 27apps 2gls; Wrexham (WW2 Guest) Aug 1945 12apps 3gls; Stockport County Dec 1945 2apps 0gls, WW2 22apps 6gls;*
Honours; *3 England International caps; F.A.Cup Winner 1932;*

Sam Weaver was signed by Hull City for £50 from non-league Sutton Town, and was described at the time as having 'all the qualities to make the complete wing-half. He was strong in the tackle, and had vision and ability in setting his own attack on the move, having the confidence and skill to pursue an opening for himself'. His form for Hull had the scouts queuing up to see him, and Newcastle United won the race for his signature in November 1929, snapping him up for £2,500. It was on Tyneside that he developed his propelling throw-in, and he eventually won his first of three England caps in 1932, the same year that he assisted Newcastle to the F.A.Cup Final where they beat Arsenal. In 1934 the 'Magpies' were relegated, and although he remained at St.James' Park for two more seasons he signed for Chelsea in August 1936. Sam stayed with the 'Pensioners' until 1945, although WW2 interrupted his career at Stamford Bridge. During the conflict he appeared as a 'guest' for Fulham, Southampton, Notts County, Derby County, Clapton Orient, West Ham United, Mansfield Town, Leeds United, and Wrexham. His debut for the North Wales club came in the opening match of 1945/46, a 4-1 home win over Rochdale. He went on to make eleven more appearances for Wrexham before signing permanently for Stockport County in December 1945. Sam remained at Edgeley Park until the summer of 1947, when he took up an offer to join the training staff at Elland Road. He later held a similar job with both Millwall (from June 1949 to January 1954), and Bromley for a short spell, before joining Mansfield Town in September 1955. He went on to spend 25 years in various capacities at Field Mill, including that of manager between June 1958 and January 1960. During his football career he spent the summer months as a lower order batsman and left-arm bowler with Somerset. He was also a masseur with Derbyshire CCC at one time.

WHEATLEY, Harold Joseph — Port Vale

Position; *Inside-Right*
Born; *Eastham, 9th May, 1920.*
Debut v. *Manchester City (h) 21.10.1944*
Total Appearances & Goals; *5 apps, 0 gls*
Ellesmere Port Town; Port Vale Mar 1938 2apps 0gls; Ellesmere Port Town (WW2 Guest); Wrexham (WW2 Guest) Oct 1944 5apps 0gls; Stockport County (WW2 Guest) Dec 1944 1app 0gls; Chester (WW2 Guest) 1944/45 1app 0gls; Shrewsbury Town Sept 1946 7apps 0gls;
Honours; *Welsh Cup runner-up 1948; Midland League Championship Winner 1948;*

Joe Wheatley first came to prominence as a versatile inside-right or right-half for Ellesmere Port Town, and joined Port Vale as an amateur in March 1938. He signed professional forms a month later, although it was not until 1938/39 that he made his Football League debut in a 1-0 defeat at Clapton Orient. He added just one more League appearance for Vale before the War. During the conflict he appeared as a 'guest' for Ellesmere Port Town, Stockport County, Chester, and Wrexham. The first of his five appearances for the 'Robins' was made during the 1944/45 season, a 1-1 home draw with Manchester City in October 1944. Joe left Vale Park when he was transferred to Shrewsbury Town in the summer of 1946, where he collected a Midland League Championship medal in 1948. The Shropshire club also reached the Welsh Cup Final in the same year where they were beaten by Lovells Athletic. At the end of the 1949/50 season Joe was awarded a benefit match, along with Jack Butler, against a Football League XI, not knowing that Shrewsbury Town were to be elected to the Football League during the summer. Joe played in the 'Shrews' inaugural match at fellow League newcomers Scunthorpe United, which ended in a scoreless draw. However, he was to manage just seven more League appearances for Shrewsbury before losing his place. It was a particularly sad ending for this crowd favourite, whose skilful play just seemed to lack that extra pace demanded by League football.

WITCOMB, Douglas Frank — West Bromwich Albion

Position; *Wing-Half*
Born; *Cwm, Ebbw Vale, 18th April, 1918*
Height; *5ft 7in* ***Height;*** *11st 4lbs*
Debut v. *Manchester City (h) 24.2.1940*
Total Appearances & Goals; *2 apps, 0 gls*
Career; *Cwm Villa; Tottenham Hotspur; Northfleet; Enfield; West Bromwich Albion Oct 1937 55apps 3gls; Wrexham (WW2 Guest) Feb 1940 2apps 0gls; West Bromwich Albion (WW2) 1939/40 14apps 4gls; Grimsby Town (WW2 Guest) 1940/41 8apps 1gls; Leicester City (WW2 Guest) May 1941 1app 0gls; Swansea Town (WW2 Guest) 1941/42 5apps 0gls; Lovells Athletic (WW2 Guest); Newport County (WW2 Guest) 1945/46 1app 0gls; Sheffield Wednesday Mar 1947 £6,500 224apps 12gls; Newport County Nov 1953 25apps 0gls; Llandudno Town Aug 1954; Redditch Oct 1955.*
Honours; *Three Welsh International caps; Seven War-time International caps; Second Division Championship Winner 1952; Second Division runner-up 1950.*

Welsh international Doug Witcomb made two 'guest' appearances for Wrexham, the first of which came in a 3-2 home win over Manchester City in February 1940, A month later he made his second and last appearance for the 'Robins' in a 4-1 defeat at Chester. He had worked in the pits from the age of 14 up to the time that he was taken from his home in Ebbw Vale along with Ron Burgess, to join Tottenham Hotspur. They had both previously earned selection for the Ebbw Vale Schools side. Doug spent most of his time at 'Spurs' playing for the club's nursery side at Northfleet, and he also turned out for Enfield. He later fell ill and the Spurs Doctor sent him back to South Wales, stating that he was not strong enough for full-time football. Desperate to prove the Doctor wrong he signed for West Bromwich Albion in October 1937,

and went on to record 55 League appearances for the 'Baggies', forming an all-Welsh half-back line with Jimmy Murphy and his mate Billy Tudor - also a former 'Racecourse Robin'. At the 'Hawthorns' he was described as 'a wing-half or inside-forward of enormous talent; a quick and cunning distributor of timely passes, and a player with a powerful shot in his right foot'. Including WW2 he spent almost ten years with West Brom, winning ten Welsh caps (seven of which were War-time caps), and in 1939 he represented an All-British XI against the Football League at Wolverhampton. During the hostilities he served with the Royal Air Force, and turned out as a 'guest' for Leicester City, Grimsby Town, Leicester City, Lovells Athletic, Swansea Town, and Newport County in addition to his games for Wrexham. Doug returned to the 'Hawthorns' after the conflict and remained with the Albion until 1947 when he signed for Sheffield Wednesday, assisting them to promotion from Division Two in 1950 and again in 1952. He returned to his native South Wales in November 1953 to join Newport County. He later played non-league football for Llandudno Town, where he was had a short spell, "They made a big mistake in asking me, and I made a big mistake in accepting!" A transfer to Redditch followed, where he settled, taking up employment for High Duty Alloys and turning out for their Works XI, winning several trophies alongside his 16 year old son. There is a tragic postscript to Doug Witcomb however, as in August 1997, when he was nearing his 80s, he disappeared from his home in Redditch, having become depressed whilst caring for his ill wife. He hasn't been seen since, although he was reputed to have been seen near his former home in South Wales, where an unidentified body was recovered from the River Usk in the same month. His family were convinced that it was Doug, but three subsequent D.N.A. tests proved inconclusive. Doug was a very good footballer and a genuinely decent man, and this is how he will be remembered by everyone who knew him.

WHITE, Frederick — Sheffield United

Position; *Goalkeeper*
Born; *Wolverhampton, 5th December, 1916.*
Height; *6ft 1'1/2in* ***Weight;*** *12st 7lbs.*
Debut v. *Chester (h) 11.11.1939*
Total Appearances & Goals; *2 apps, 0 gls*
Honours; *Everton May 1935 0apps; Sheffield United May 1937 44apps 0gls, WW2 130apps 0gls; Wrexham (WW2 Guest) Nov 1939 2apps 0gls; Rotherham United (WW2 Guest) 1939/40 1app 0gls; Mansfield Town (WW2 Guest) 1944/45 4apps 0gls; Lincoln City Jun 1950 £200 42apps 0gls; Gainsborough Trinity Aug 1951;*

Fred White was signed by Everton from Wolverhampton junior football in May 1935, but he couldn't force his way into the senior side during his two years at Goodison Park, and so moved on to Sheffield United in May 1937. He went on to make 44 League appearances for the Bramall Lane club, even though his stay was disrupted by WW2. He did, however, complete a further 130 games for United during this period. He also turned out as a 'guest' for Rotherham United, Mansfield Town, and Wrexham, where he made his debut in a 2-2 home draw with Chester in November 1939. Fred also played in the following match for the 'Robins', but it proved to be his final swan-song for the club, as Wrexham lost 7-0 at Crewe! He continued to keep goal for the 'Blades' during the Post-War years, until May 1950, when he joined Lincoln City for £200. Described as a 'goalkeeper who gives confidence' Fred was the 'Red Imps' first choice 'keeper for the 1950/51 season, absent only through injury, though he left Sincil Bank in the summer to drop into non-league football with Gainsborough Trinity. After his involvement with the full time game had ended, Fred worked as a salesman in the building trade. He latterly scouted for several clubs managed by former Lincoln player Jim Smith.

WHITE, Frank Robert Henry — Preston North End

Position; *Outside-Left*
Born; *Wilncote, 14th April, 1911*
Died; *Lichfield, March 1987.*
Height; *5ft 6in* ***Weight;*** *10st 6lbs.*
Debut v. *Chester (a) 29.11.1941*
Total Appearances & Goals; *20 apps, 7 gls*
Career; *Tamworth Juniors; Stoneware Ltd, Tamworth 1930; Birmingham (Am) Sept 1931, (Pro) Oct 1932 147apps 46gls; Preston North End Dec 1938 19apps 10gls, WW2 6apps 0gls; Wrexham (WW2 Guest) Nov 1941 20apps 7gls; Aldershot (WW2 Guest) Jan 1944 7apps 1gls; Walsall (WW2 Guest) Aug 1944 8apps 1gls; Birmingham (WW2 Guest) Dec 1944 14apps 6gls; Redditch United Aug 1948;*

Frank White signed for Birmingham from Tamworth & District League side Stoneware Limited, having been spotted by 'Blues' goalkeeper Harry Hibbs. Although he had been appearing as an outside-left Birmingham initially deployed him at left-half, but he was best suited to the left-wing role where his career flourished. Frank made his Football League debut in a 1-0 defeat at Liverpool in April 1933, and during his time at St.Andrews' he was described as 'quick on the ball, and gave his partner ideal passes.' He spent just over five years in the Midlands before joining Preston North End in December 1938, scoring ten goals in 19 outings for the 'Lilywhites' before WW2 put a stop to his Football League career. During the conflict Frank appeared as a 'guest' for a number of clubs including Aldershot, Walsall, Birmingham, and Wrexham, where he made his debut in a 2-2 draw at Chester in November 1941. He went on to make a further nineteen appearances for the 'Robins', scoring seven goals, his final performance coming in March 1944, a 3-3 home draw with Bolton Wanderers. In the immediate Post-War years he joined up with his former Birmingham team mate, and ex-Wrexham player Charles Wilson-Jones at Redditch United, where he continued to play until 1950, when he retired. Frank later undertook coaching duties at his former club, Tamworth.

WHITELAW, David Logan — Gillingham

Position; *Goalkeeper*
Born; *Anderston, Glasgow, 9th August, 1909.*
Height; *6ft 0'1/2in* ***Weight;*** *14st 2lbs*
Debut v. *Everton (h) 23.10.1943*
Total Appearances & Goals; *61 apps, 0 gls*
Career; *Hill of Beath Star; Cadder United; Bristol City Jun 1930 12apps 0gls; Southend United Jul 1931 92apps 0gls; Gillingham Jul 1935 114apps 0gls; Bournemouth (WW2 Guest) 1940/41 1app 0gls; Wrexham (WW2 Guest) 26th Oct 1943 61apps 0gls; Chester (WW2 Guest) 1945/46 1app 0gls;*
Scottish-born David Whitelaw played local football in Glasgow before he was signed by Bristol City in June 1930. It was for the South West club that he made his Football League debut in November 1930, a 4-1 defeat at Reading. He was allowed to leave the 'Robins' at the end of that campaign, whereupon he was quickly snapped up by Southend United. The 'big weighty Scot' went on to spend four years with the 'Shrimpers', making 92 League appearances until his transfer to Gillingham in July 1935. He remained at Priestfield until WW2 intervened, where he clocked up over 100 appearances for the 'Gills'. During the conflict Dave appeared as a 'guest' for Bournemouth, Chester, and Wrexham. He made his debut between the sticks for the Racecourse club in a 3-1 home defeat by Everton in October 1943, and went on to add a further 60 appearances for the 'Robins' during the final three years of WW2. His final outing came in a 3-2 home defeat by Crewe Alexandra on Boxing Day 1945.

WILLIAMS, G. — Wrexham

Position; *Right-Back*
Total Appearances & Goals; *Wrexham (WW2 Guest) Jan 1941 1app 0gls;*

An amateur with Wrexham who made one War time appearance for the club in a Lancashire Cup tie in January 1941, playing at right-back in a 6-1 defeat at New Brighton.

WOODBURN, James — Newcastle United

Position; *Left-Half*
Born; *Rutherglen, 29th January, 1917.*
Died; *Leeds, 2nd January, 1978.*
Height; *5ft 9in* ***Weight;*** *10st 6lbs.*
Debut v. *Crewe Alexandra (h) 16.11.1940*
Total Appearances & Goals; *5 apps, 0 gls*
Career; *Kilsyth Emmet; Coltness United; Newcastle United Feb 1938 £100 44aps 4gls, (WW2) 46apps 4gls; Wrexham (WW2 Guest) Nov 1940 5apps 0gls; Gateshead Sept 1948 £750 132apps 10gls;*

Jim Woodburn joined Newcastle United from his local side, Coltness United, in February 1938, but it was not until October of the following season that he made his Football League debut in a 1-0 defeat at Coventry. With the outbreak of WW2 Jim was to turn out for Wrexham as a 'guest'. He made his debut in November 1940, a 3-1 home win over Crewe Alexandra, and he added four more appearances during that season. After WW2 had ended football entered its 'Golden Age', and Jimmy resumed his career at St.James' Park, where he remained until

September 1948. Noted as a 'fine utility player, who had fine awareness and positive sense' he was transferred to fellow North-East side Gateshead for £750, and he went on to become a regular in their side for a number of seasons. He recorded 132 League appearances, scoring ten goals for the Redhough Park club, as well as undertaking coaching duties. He retired in 1952 and began teaching in Durham. His father was a goalkeeper with St.Mirren.

WOODMAN, John Albert Edward — Wrexham

Position; *Centre-Forward*
Born; *Bristol, 9th July 1914.*
Died; *Bristol, 16th January, 1984.*
Height; *5ft 10in* ***Weight;*** *11st 12lbs*
Debut v. *New Brighton (h) 26.8.1939*
Total Appearances & Goals; *3 apps, 0 gls*
Career; *Windmill Hill School; Melrose FC; Bristol Rovers May 1935 39apps 21gls; Preston North End Jul 1937 £500 0apps; Swindon Town May 1938 £250 0apps; Wrexham 23rd Jun 1939;*

John Woodman was signed from local football by Bristol Rovers in May 1935, and went on to make his Football League debut at centre-forward in a scoreless draw at Cardiff City in the second match of the 1935/36 season. His goalscoring prowess eventually saw him average a goal in every other game, as well as scoring in a record seven consecutive games between January and February 1936. However, he found himself out of favour at the beginning of the 1936/37 season and, even though he did win his place back, Preston North End signed him for £500 in the summer of 1937. Unfortunately, he failed to make a first team appearance at Deepdale and joined Swindon Town a year later. Again he failed to make an impression, and it was then that he joined Wrexham in the summer of 1939. He got off to a good start with the North Walians, scoring on his debut in a 2-0 home victory against New Brighton on the opening day of the 1939/40 season. John played in the next two matches, but when the Football League was abandoned following the outbreak of WW2, he returned immediately to his home in the Bristol area.

WORSLEY, Herbert — Fulham

Position; *Outside-Right*
Born; *Stockport, 20th September, 1911.*
Died; *Denton, 25th June, 1971.*
Height; *5ft 7in* ***Weight;*** *10st 7lbs*
Debut v. *Oldham Athletic (a) 13.10.1945*
Total Appearances & Goals; *2 apps, 0 gls*
Career; *Altrincham; Manchester North End 1930; Bolton Wanderers (Am) Oct 1931; Manchester North End; Leeds United (Am) Aug 1932, (Pro) Jan 1934 3apps 0gls; Fulham Jun 1935 106apps 16gls, WW2 7apps 0gls; Stockport County (WW2 Guest) Aug 1942 65apps 18gls; Bury (WW2 Guest) 1944/45 15apps 0gls; Wrexham (WW2 Guest) Oct 1945 2apps 0gls*

Herbert Worsley's early career had seen him move around a number of non-league sides, although he did have a spell with Bolton Wanderers as an amateur. Leeds United were to be the club for whom he made his Football League debut, although it turned out to be a disaster as they lost 8-1 at Stoke City. He made two further appearances for the Elland Road club before he was allowed to join Fulham in June 1935. In his first season with them he helped the 'Cottagers' to reach the semi-finals of the F.A.Cup, and he was described at Craven Cottage as 'a skilful, speedy winger who became a firm favourite with the Fulham crowd during his time on the banks of the Thames'. He continued to play throughout the War years, also 'guesting' for a number of other clubs, including Stockport

County, Bury, and Wrexham. He made the first of his two appearances for the 'Robins' in October 1945, a scoreless draw at Oldham Athletic, followed by a 2-1 win over Stockport Count

WRIGHT, Horace Raymond — Wolves

Position; *Inside-Left*
Born; *Pontefract, 6th September, 1918.*
Died; *Luton, August 1987.*
Debut v. *Tranmere Rovers (h) 5.10.1940*
Total Appearances & Goals; *apps, 0 gls*
Career; *Woodbourne Athletic; Wolves Sept 1937 8apps 1gls, WW2 8apps 6gls; Wrexham (WW2 Guest) Oct 1940 3apps 0gls; Leeds United (WW2 Guest) Sept 1943 3apps 0gls; Exeter City Jul 1946 55apps 11gls; Yeovil Town 1948;*

Horace Wright made his Football League debut for Wolves in April 1938 in fine style, as they beat Leicester City 10-1 in a First Division match. The result still stands as Wolves' record League win. He made seven more League appearances for Wolves before War was declared in September 1939. During the conflict Horace turned out for Wrexham three times as a 'guest', the first of which came in a 3-3 home draw with Tranmere Rovers in October 1940. With peace restored Horace resumed his Football League career with Exeter City. He made a good start, by scoring on his debut in a 1-1 'derby' draw against Torquay United, and went on to spend two seasons with the 'Grecians' before drifting into non-league football with Yeovil Town in 1948.

Managers at the Racecourse

Wrexham Association Football Club were chosen by a Selection Committee until the club appointed their first recognised manager in November 1924. He was Charlie Hewitt and twenty further managers have been appointed since, the longest serving being the club's current manager, Brian Flynn. The following are the twelve managers who never actually played a recognised first team game for the club - The careers of the other nine managers are included in the players section.

HEWITT, Charles William — Nov 1924 - May 1926

Birthplace; *Greatham, Cleveland.*
D.O.B; *10th April, 1884.*
Died; *Darlington, Durham, 31st December, 1966.*
Height; *5ft 6in* **Weight;** *11st 4lbs (1911)*
First Game in Charge v. *Walsall (h) 10th November, 1924.*
Total Games in Charge; *79*
Career in Football; *Billingham Schools; West Hartlepool; Middlesbrough 1904 33apps 12gls; Tottenham Hotspur May 1906 30apps 11gls; Liverpool cs1907 16 apps 6gls; West Bromwich Albion Apr 1908 60apps 26gls; Spennymoor United May 1910; Crystal Palace 1910 £125; Hartlepool United 1919; Mold Town (Manager); WREXHAM (Manager) Nov 1924; Flint Town (Manager) 1927; Connah's Quay & Shotton (Manager) May 1928; Chester (Manager) May 1930; Millwall (Manager) Apr 1936-Apr 1940; Leyton Orient (Manager) Jan 1946-Apr 1948; Millwall (Manager) Aug 1948-Jan 1956;*
Honours; *Third Division South Championship Winner 1938; Welsh Cup Winner 1925, 1929 & 1933; Welsh National League (North) Championship Winner 1929; Cheshire County League Championship runner-up 1931;*

Charlie Hewitt began his football career in his native North East. He was playing for West Hartlepool when snapped up by First Division Middlesbrough some time in 1904. Hewitt went on to make his Football League debut at outside-right in a 3-2 defeat at Manchester City in February 1905. He was to remain with 'Boro' until the end of the 1905/06 season, when moving to London to join progressive Southern League side, Tottenham Hotspur. Charlie spent a season with 'Spurs', where he was switched to inside-right. After an impressive twelve months with the 'Lilywhites', in which they beat Blackburn Rovers in the F.A.Cup, he was signed by First Division Liverpool in the close season of 1907. He made an immediate impact by scoring in the opening game of the new season, a 3-1 defeat at Nottingham Forest. Despite this he was soon to lose his place in the first team and in April 1908 was allowed to leave Anfield and join Second Division West Bromwich Albion, appearing in their last match of the season, a 3-1 home win over Fulham. He spent the next two seasons as a regular at the Hawthorns, before returning to the North East in May 1910 to sign for Spennymoor United. His time here was short, as he returned to London to join another Southern League side, Crystal Palace. Hewitt remained on the books of the Selhurst Park club until 1919, although his stay was interrupted by the outbreak of World War One, during which he served on a Destroyer. After WW1 had ended Charlie returned to the North East, signing for Hartlepool United. He was later to take up his first managerial post in North Wales, with Welsh National League (North) side Mold Town. He made such an impression with them that he was snapped up by Wrexham to become the Club's first ever manager, the team having previously been chosen by a selection committee. A trained accountant Hewitt was appointed by the club's directors at a board meeting held on 29th October 1924, although he was not to take up the post until 10th November because he had first to relinquish his position with Mold. Hewitt was not to enjoy much success at the Racecourse, 16th place in the Third Division North at the end of his first season in charge, although he did have some cause for celebration when Wrexham beat Flint Town in the Welsh Cup final of 1925. The following season the club fared no better, ending it in 19th position, and following the appointment of a new chairman, Alfred McAlpine, Hewitt was replaced by a return to the old selection committee system. Despite this set-back, he was soon back in management, when he was appointed the new boss of Flint Town. He stayed at Flint until 7th May 1928, when he took charge of their local rivals, Connah's Quay & Shotton. He remained in that job for two seasons, with much success, helping them to win the Welsh National League (North) in 1929 as well as lifting the Welsh Cup when they beat Cardiff City in the final. Following this, he was appointed manager of Cheshire League side, Chester, in May 1930. Hewitt was given a free hand to build a successful team at Chester, and in his first season guided them to the runners-up spot, followed by election to the Football League. Hewitt was to spend five more seasons at Sealand Road, winning the Welsh Cup in 1933 including a 2-0 win over Wrexham. However, on 1st April 1936 he resigned to take up a similar position in London with Third Division South side, Millwall. He enjoyed instant success at the Den, leading the 'Lions' to the F.A.Cup Semi-final in 1936/37, the first ever Third Division club to achieve this feat, while the following season he led the 'Lions' to the Third Division South championship and promotion to the Second Division. War was again to interrupt his career, with the outbreak of World War Two, although he was to resign from his post of manager at the Den in the summer of 1940, after being investigated by the F.A. over alleged illegal payments to players. Because of his experience in WW1 he was made captain of a troop ship, on which he served throughout WW2. Following the end of the conflict he took up another football managerial position, this time with Leyton Orient, being appointed on 1st January 1946 and becoming the highest wage earner in the Club's history. After just nine months his 'stormy' stay at Brisbane Road came to an end when he resigned, due to lack of money for new players, although a week later he was persuaded to return. A lack of success on the field finally saw him quit again in April 1948. Four months later he returned to a bomb-damaged 'Den' as manager of Millwall, following their relegation from the Second Division. Hewitt set about rebuilding the team, but his second spell at the Den was not to be nowhere near as successful as his first, despite finishing runners-up to Bristol Rovers in 1953. He was shown the door in January 1956, although later to win a court case for unfair dismissal, and awarded £4,500 damages in July 1957. At this point he decided to retire from the game. Hewitt, who in May 1954 was presented with a F.A.long service medal for twenty years in the game, died in 1966 aged 82. During his career he had been described as a 'man of many words, abrasive, direct and autocratic. He was probably the last of the Football League managers in the showman tradition. Either loved or hated by his players, he was a man who would not mince his words, had high ideals and expected success through his own hard work and also from those around him'.

BAYNES, John Henly — Oct 1929 - Dec 1931

Birthplace; *Oldham, Lancashire.*
D.O.B; *18th February, 1888.*
Died; *Wrexham, Denbighshire, 14th December, 1931.*
Height; *ft in* **Weight;** *st lbs*
First Game in Charge v. *Gateshead (a) 19th October, 1929.*
Total Games in Charge; *107*
Career in Football; *Rotherham County; Mansfield Town (Manager) 1st May 1923-30th Apr 1926; Nottingham Forest (Secretary/Coach) Jun 1926-Jun 1929; WREXHAM (Manager) 17th Oct 1929;*
Honours; *Welsh Cup Winner 1931; Midland Counties League Championship Winner 1912, 1913, 1914, 1915, 1924 & 1925; Midland Counties League Championship runner-up 1926; Nottinghamshire FA Senior Cup Winner 1926;*

Following the departure of Charlie Hewitt as Wrexham's first ever manager, the team was chosen by a selection committee for the following three years, before the board of directors decided to appoint another manager. This time they chose Jack Baynes who, had it not been for his untimely death, could have produced a side capable of achieving the club's goal of reaching the Second Division. Baynes, who had not played football professionally, became an office boy with Midland Counties League side, Rotherham Town. With an uncanny eye for a good player and a budding talent, it was as an office boy that he spotted and signed his first player when still only 17 years-old!! He was appointed the Club's assistant manager before reaching the end of his teens!, becoming player/manager in his twenties, and leading Rotherham Town to four successive Midland Counties League championships between 1911/12 and 1914/15, although by that time the club were in financial difficulties which eventually forced them to cease operations. In 1916 Baynes was called away to join the Army in World War One, but was to return to join the newly named Rotherham County, who had won election to the Football League Division Two following their achievements in the Midland Counties League. In May 1923, Baynes was appointed manager of Midland Counties League side Mansfield Town, a job he was to hold for three very

successful seasons. Baynes' job title at Field Mill was 'secretary-manager', having full responsibility for the players in addition to the secretarial work, although the directors would still choose the team. His three-year spell with the 'Stags' was to see him become the club's most successful manager, leading Mansfield to two consecutive Midland Counties League championships, and a Nottinghamshire F.A.Senior Cup win in his final season, as well as guiding them to the first round proper of the F.A.Cup in each of those three campaigns. Baynes resigned as manager of Mansfield Town on 30th April 1926, following the completion of his contract. By that time he had been approached by Second Division side Nottingham Forest to become secretary/coach, although he had full control of team affairs. Forest were in the doldrums, having lost their First Division status, and their committee were looking to Baynes to rectify matters. Although unable to lead Forest back to the First Division he did unearth some very useful talent. He took them to fifth place in the Second Division in his first season at the City ground, though this was to be followed by two rather mediocre campaigns, and he left them in June 1929. A little over four months later, he returned to football, when he was chosen from over 80 applicants as the new manager of Third Division North side Wrexham on 17th October. When he took over at the Racecourse the club had won just two of their opening eleven matches of the season. Wrexham continued to struggle under Baynes, in spite of the introduction of new faces like William Dickie and George Bell, and they finished the campaign in a disappointing 17th position. The 1930/31 season saw him bring in experienced players like Ralph Burkinshaw, Jack Mustard, John Donoghue and Sam Taylor, adding to the likes of promising youngsters Tommy Bamford, Billie Rogers and Jack Hughes. The combination of youth and experience prompted much improvement in the Wrexham side as they made a push for promotion, though they ended their programme in fourth place, four points away from eventual champions Chesterfield. Consolation came in the Welsh Cup final, with a 7-0 hammering of Shrewsbury Town. They made a reasonable start to the 1931/32 campaign, but the team were soon to find themselves having to play without Baynes' guidance as he was admitted to Chester Royal Infirmary in early September for 'operative treatment'. After many anxious weeks he seemed to be making steady progress and he was to return home. However, three weeks later he suffered a relapse and was moved to Croesnewydd Hospital in Wrexham, where he passed away on 14th December 1931, aged only 43. The former Welsh international and Wrexham player, the Revd. Hywel Davies led the service at Jack Baynes' funeral.

BLACKBURN, Robert Ernest

Jan 1932 - Jan 1937

Birthplace; *Crawshaw Booth, nr. Rossendale, Lancashire.*
D.O.B; *23rd April, 1892.*
Died; *Birkenhead, Merseyside, 13th July 1964.*
Height; *5ft 10in* ***Weight;*** *12st 0lbs (1919)*
First Game in Charge v. *Southport (a) 30th January, 1932.*
Total Games in Charge; *241*
Career in Football; *Loveclough FC; Manchester Y.C.; Army Football (Royal Medical Corps); Aston Villa Apr 1919 32apps 0gls; Bradford City May 1922 40 apps 0gls; Accrington Stanley (Trainer) Aug 1924, (Manager) Nov 1924; WREXHAM (Manager) 25th Jan 1932; Hull City (Manager) 26th Dec 1937-Jan 1946; Tranmere Rovers (Manager) Sept 1946; (Secretary) May 1955-1959;*
Honours; *Welsh Cup runner-up 1932 & 1933; Third Division North Championship runner-up 1933;*

Ernie Blackburn began playing football for Burnley & District League side, Loveclough FC, followed by Manchester Youth Club. It was around this time that he was a member of the St.John's Ambulance Brigade and when World War One broke out volunteered for the Royal Army Medical Corps, seeing active service in France from August 1914 until April 1919. During this time he managed to play Army football whenever time allowed, and it was through his Army involvment that he came to the attention of Aston Villa. Upon his demobilisation, Blackburn signed for Villa, on the recommendation of their centre-forward, Harry Hampton, who Ernie had become acquainted with while serving at GHQ. Blackburn made his Football League debut for Villa in the opening match of 1919/20, the first season following the end of WW1. He played at right-back a 2-1 defeat at Sunderland, though he was to make just seven more League appearances that season, missing out on Villa's F.A.Cup final win over Huddersfield Town. Over the next two campaigns he again found first team opportunities hard to come by, and at the end of 1921/22 took up an offer to join Second Division Bradford City. Playing in his usual full-back position Blackburn was to make forty League appearances for the Valley Parade club before he was forced to retire due to a series of injuries which eventually took their toll. He remained in the game, joining Accrington Stanley as trainer in August 1924. However, four months after moving to Peel Park manager Sam Pilkington resigned and, following abortive efforts to appoint Harry Hadley as the new manager they turned to Ernie Blackburn. Throughout his reign at Peel Park Blackburn worked under the burden of serious financial problems, which made it impossible for him to build a settled side. During his eight and a half seasons with 'Stanley' they managed a top ten position just once, but whilst Ernie maintained control of the day to day running of the club team selection rested with a committee of directors. Though used in an advisory capacity Blackburn was never given sole responsibility. On 13th January 1932 he was handed the opportunity to become the new manager of fellow Third Division North side, Wrexham, when the club's board of directors offered him the position. He accepted, and took up the post twelve days later, eventually leading the club to its most successful period of pre-war football. His first season saw the club finish in a mid-table position of tenth, although they did reach the Final of the Welsh Cup, but lost 2-0 after a replay to Swansea Town. There followed a vast improvement the next campaign, finishing as runners-up to Hull City, just two points adrift of the 'Tigers'. 'The Robins' also had to be content with runners-up medals in the Welsh Cup again, as they lost 2-0 to Charlie Hewitt's Chester in the final. Three and a half lean years followed, as the club's finances forced Blackburn to sell the likes of Tommy Bamford, Billy Bryant and Tommy Lewis. In December 1937, he was given the chance to take over as manager of fellow Third Division North side Hull City, following lengthy negotiations with the Wrexham directors. The fresh challenge appealed to Ernie, and he resigned as Wrexham boss to take over at Anably Road. The parting of ways was amicable, and Wrexham's Supporters' Association presented him with a clock as an expression of gratitude for his services to the football club. He brought a financial astuteness to Hull, which was absolutely essential in view of the state of the club's finances. His ability to transform non-League recruits into quality players effectively saved the club from extinction in 1938, whilst also helping the club to finish in a very respectable third place. Blackburn remained in charge of the 'Tigers' throughout WW2, but after the hostilities had ended the directors decided not to retain him, and he departed before the new Football League season had begun. He was not out of the game long as another Third Division North club, Tranmere Rovers, stepped in to appoint him as their new manager. He brought many fine players to the Birkenhead club, but was unable to lead 'Rovers' to promotion in the nine years that he was in charge at Prenton Park. In May 1955 he relinquished his duties of manager and became the club secretary, a position that he held for four years until retiring in 1959. Throughout his managerial career Ernie Blackburn won a reputation as a hard worker, a fine judge of a player, and skilled at balancing the books. He settled in Birkenhead before his death in July 1964, aged 72.

***LOGAN*, James Henry** Jan 1937 - May 1938

Birthplace; *Dunbar, Lothian.*
D.O.B; *11th October, 1885.*
Height; *6ft 1in* ***Weight;*** *13st 0lbs (1910)*
First Game in Charge v. *Oldham Athletic (h) 30th January, 1937.*
Total Games in Charge; *66*
Career in Football; *St.Bernard's; Bradford City Apr 1905 5apps 1gls; Chesterfield Aug 1906 94apps 9gls; Bradford Park Avenue cs1909 59apps 3gls; Raith Rovers 1912; joined the Army 1916; Raith Rovers (Manager) 1918-1928 & Dec 1930; WREXHAM (Manager) 29th Jan 1937-May 1938;*
Honours; *Scottish Junior International;*

'Captain' Jimmy Logan was signed by Second Division Bradford City from Scottish Junior side St.Bernard's in April 1905, with whom he had gained international recognition as a Scottish junior international. He went on to make his Football League debut the following season in a scoreless draw with Manchester United at Old Trafford in October. He featured in the following two games, scoring on his home debut in a 2-0 win over Glossop, before being recalled to the side the following month -to play in goal!! However, it wasn't to be the best of games for Jimmy, as Bradford lost 6-1 at West Brom. He was allowed to leave during the close season of 1906 and join Second Division Chesterfield. Jimmy's brother, Peter, went on to play in over 300 games for Bradford City between 1908 and 1925. As for Jimmy he soon established himself in the 'Spireites' side, but by February he had been switched to playing in the centre of defence, a position that he was to hold for the next two seasons at Saltergate. They were hardly successful times however, and at the end of 1908/09 the club failed to gain re-election to the Football League. This saw Jimmy leave Chesterfield and return to Bradford, this time joining the Park Avenue club. He spent three seasons with them before returning to Scotland, teaming up with Raith Rovers. He enjoyed three years with the Kirkcaldy club before the outbreak of World War One, when he enlisted, with the rest of the Raith Rovers team, in the so-called Sportsmen Battalion of the Royal Scots. He joined up as a private, rising to the rank of captain before he was demobbed in 1919. After WW1 had ended Logan rejoined Raith, and was appointed team manager. They were good times at Raith; the 1921/22 season saw them finish third in the Scottish League, behind Celtic and Rangers, with a side that contained probably the best ever forward-line the club had produced -Bell, Miller, Jennings, James and Archibald. The star performer was Alex James, who was eventually sold to Preston North End for £3,250 in September 1925 and who won eight caps for Scotland. Logan remained in charge of Raith for ten years, leaving the club in 1929. He was then to take up the running of a public house in Kerriemuir, although he did have a second spell as manager of Raith Rovers following his appointment in December 1930. In January 1937 Captain James Logan applied for the job of manager of Third Division North side Wrexham. He was accepted for the post, later appointing former England international Arthur Cowell as his assistant in the close season of 1937. By that time Logan had helped Wrexham finish the season in a respectable eighth position. With Cowell at his side the club introduced new recruits in Bill Bellamy, George Burditt and James Raven, but they could not improve on the club's previous season's position, finishing in a very disappointing tenth place. With one game of the 1938/39 season remaining Logan resigned from his position as manager, though he agreed to stay on and take charge of the club's final match at Hartlepool.

***COWELL*, Arthur** Jun 1938 - Sept 1938

Birthplace; *Blackburn, Lancashire.*
D.O.B; *20th May, 1886.*
Died; *Lower Darwen, Lancashire, 12th February, 1959.*
Height; *5ft 7in* ***Weight;*** *10st 4lbs*
First Game in Charge v. *Southport (a) 27th August, 1938.*
Total Games in Charge; *7*
Career in Football; *Blackburn St.Peters; Nelson 1904; Blackburn Rovers May 1905 280apps 0gls, (WW1) 15apps 0gls, (Trainer) cs1920; WREXHAM (Trainer) May 1937, (Manager) Jun 1938-Sept 1938;*
Honours; *One England International cap; One Football League Representative cap; Football League Championship Winner 1912 & 1914;*

A cousin to England international Albert Houlker, Arthur Cowell was playing local football in his native Blackburn, for a Sunday School XI Blackburn St.Peters, when he was signed by Lancashire Combination League side Nelson in 1904. After almost a season he was transferred to First Division Blackburn Rovers in May 1905. He made his Football League debut on 23rd September 1905 at right-back, in a 1-1 draw at Notts County. So began one of the finest full-back partnerships in the long history of Blackburn Rovers, as Arthur and Bob Crompton remained the full-back pairing at Ewood Park until the outbreak of the First World War. During that time they helped 'Rovers' win the First Division championship twice, in 1912 and 1914, whilst also reaching the semi-finals of the F.A.Cup in 1911 and 1912. Although Crompton was a permanent fixture in the England side at that time Arthur was to win just one full cap, in 1910, against Ireland in Belfast in a 1-1 draw. It was said of Arthur 'despite his size, Cowell was a relentless tackler and, having won possession, his distribution often set up many threatening counter-attacks. He possessed the speed which enabled him to cover any gaps which occurred in the Rovers defence'. It was also said of him, 'Cowell complemented the play of Crompton perfectly with doggedness and polish' and that he was a 'masterful back, using resource as an aid to skill'. His playing career suffered because of WW1, although he did manage to play a number of games for 'Rovers'. Having kept himself reasonably fit he returned to the Blackburn side for the 1919/20 campaign, although he was to make just one further League appearance in a scoreless draw at Derby in December 1919. A serious injury that season forced him to accept his playing days were over, and he took up an appointment as the club's trainer. Cowell remained at Ewood Park in that position until the summer of 1937, when he was invited by Wrexham manager Captain James Logan to become his assistant at the Racecourse. Arthur was to see Logan resign at the end of the 1937/38 campaign, and the Wrexham board of directors immediately turned to him to take over in June 1938. However, his reign as manager was to be brief, resigning following just seven games in charge after a 1-0 home win over Rochdale, due to a disagreement with the directors who had appointed him. He later returned to the Blackburn area, where he was to run newsagents' shops in both Kirkham and Darwen.

***MORGAN*, Thomas Myatt** Apr 1939 - Mar 1942

Birthplace; *Stoke-on-Trent*
D.O.B; *O/N/D 1884*
Died; *Stoke-on-Trent, Staffordshire, 26th August 1943.*
Height; *ft in* ***Weight;*** *st lbs*
First Game in Charge v. *Darlington (a) 7th April, 1939.*
Total Games in Charge; *95*
Career in Football; *Etruria Church; Goldenhill Villa; Tunstall Park; Goldenhill Wanderers; Port Vale cs1910, (Manager) Oct 1929, (Assistant Secretary) Jun 1932, (Manager) Dec 1937; WREXHAM (Manager) Apr 1939-Mar 1942;*
Honours; *Third Division North Championship Winner 1930;*

A 'Potteries' man Tom Morgan played local football for Etruria Church,

Goldenhill Villa, Tunstall Park and Goldenhill Wanderers before he was signed by Port Vale in the close season of 1910. At that time they competed in the North Staffordshire & District League. He made his first team debut in a Burslem Park Cup match at inside-right in a 4-2 win over Audley, scoring twice. Tom made four more appearances for Vale before he was forced to retire through injury in the Spring of 1911. He then took up work for Vale's administrative staff, acting as a scout, assistant secretary and reserve team manager before finally appointed first team manager In October 1929. He was to guide Vale to the Third Division North championship in his first season in charge, their 67 points creating a new record at the time. The following season he led Vale to fifth in Division Two, their highest ever League position, yet in June 1932 he was relieved of his post and reverted to the role of assistant secretary. However, the Port Vale directors called upon Morgan once again in December 1937, when he was promoted to secretary-manager. Despite his appointment, to the surprise of the Vale directors, he applied for the post of secretary-manager of Wrexham Football Club in March 1939, and out of 29 applicants was given the opportunity to take charge of team affairs on 3rd April 1939, after the Port Vale directors finally gave their approval to the move. Morgan had been highly regarded at Vale Park, and was to leave the club with 'sincere regret'. At the Racecourse he took over from Tommy Griffiths, who had been working as caretaker-manager since Arthur Cowell's shock resignation. Morgan took charge for the last six games of the 1938/39 season, when the club finished in 14th position. He prepared for the new 1939/40 season with five new signings: Bill Bryan, John Screen, Frank Briggs, John Woodman and Tom Bradbury. All five made their debut's in the opening three games of the new season, before the Football League was suspended due to the outbreak of World War Two. Morgan remained as manager when regionalised football was introduced, and it was during the early part of the War that all the club's records and documents were destroyed in a house fire at his home. During the conflict, Morgan was to have many international players at his disposal, but he was to eventually resign from his managerial position in March 1942, returning to settle in the 'Potteries'. Shortly afterwards he passed away at Heywood Hospital, Stoke-on-Trent, in August 1943.

WILLIAMS, Thomas Watson — Apr 1942 - Feb 1949

Birthplace; *Rhyl, Flintshire*
D.O.B; *1897*
Died; *Wrexham, Denbighshire, 8th April, 1961.*
Height; *ft in* ***Weight;*** *st lbs*
First Game in Charge v. *Chester (a) 16th May 1942 (War League).*
Total Games in Charge; *287 (Including War League)*
Career in Football; *WREXHAM (Manager) 20th Apr 1942 to 24th Feb 1949;*

Although born in Rhyl Tom Williams' family soon moved to Wrexham, where he became devoted to the local football club. Surprisingly, although he had an unerring eye for football talent, he never actually played the game seriously. He had scouted for Burnley, Blackburn Rovers and Wrexham prior to World War Two, and it was during the WW2 period that he was given his first managerial opportunity, taking up an appointment as assistant manager to Tom Morgan. Following Morgan's resignation at the end of March 1942 the club turned to Williams, appointing him in the hot seat. These were difficult times for Wrexham Football Club, and it was Williams' influence that was to keep the club alive when chairman John Hughes suggested that the club should be closed until after the war had ended as they were in debt to the tune of £8,000. 'Big Tom', as he was popularly known, pleaded with his chairman and the bank manager to keep the club running, and his persuasive powers did the trick. Wrexham supporters of that era will not forget 'the team that Tom built', as it included many international and well known players of the time, Johnny Hancocks, Stan Cullis, Ronnie Dix, Arthur Jefferson, Jackie Milburn, Gordon Bremner and Stanley Matthews to name but a few. All paraded their talents on the Racecourse. Williams transformed Wrexham from a 'Cinderella' Third Division club into a 'dream' team that could more than hold its own against the likes of Liverpool, Everton, Manchester United etc. With the War at an end Williams was to continue as the club's manager and prepare for the recommencement of the new Football League campaign, 1946/47. The famous 'guest' players left their adopted club as Williams was to begin to rebuild. He signed a number of experienced players who, were by now, coming to the end of the their careers -players like Tom Gardner, Joe Lloyd, Fred Haycock, Billy Tudor and Ehud Rogers- and led the club to a very respectable seventh position in the first Post-War season. He followed this by finishing in third place at the end of the next season, Wrexham's best since 1933. 1948/49 would see Williams surprisingly asked to resign, following an internal dispute at a board meeting on 23rd February 1949, but 'Big Tom' adamantly refused. The following day he turned up at the ground as usual, but was told that his employment had been terminated, even though his contract did not expire until 1950. Following his departure two of the club's directors also resigned. Williams bought a sports shop in Chester Street, Wrexham, and continued his involvement in football by scouting for Liverpool. His love for Wrexham never waned, and he was later to become Chairman of the Supporters' Association. In 1960, following the departure of John Love as manager, the Wrexham goalkeeper Roly Ugolini led a deputation of players asking for 'Big Tom' to apply for the job. He did, but never received a reply! In April 1961, when Billy Morris vacated his managerial position, the Supporters' Association advocated the reappointment of Williams as manager, but again the board of directors looked elsewhere and appointed Ken Barnes. Four months later, on 8th April 1961, Tom Williams died whilst on a business trip in Acton, Wrexham. A former Wrexham director, Alderman William Dodman, who had resigned in protest at Williams' dismissal in 1949, said of him, "Tom Williams was highly respected everywhere. He always said that his dismissal by Wrexham was an injustice and I agree with him. If the club had been left in his hands, I think Wrexham would have been a Second Division side long ago. He managed the club during the war without pay and got a team together that could and did hold its own against the best in the country. His heart was always with Wrexham AFC and once said that he would go back for nothing."

McDOWALL, Les — 4th May 1949 to May 1950

See Players Who's Who Section
First Game in Charge v. *Southport (a) 7th May, 1949.*
Total Games in Charge; *51*

JACKSON, Wilbert — Nov 1950 - Feb 1955

Birthplace; *Luddendon Foot, nr. Halifax, Yorkshire.*
D.O.B; *25th August, 1904*
Died; *Shipley, Yorkshire, 9th May, 1986.*
Height; *5ft 11in* ***Weight;*** *10st 10lbs (1929)*
First Game in Charge v. *Bradford City (a) 9th December, 1950.*
Total Games in Charge; *224*
Career in Football; *Luddendon Foot; Hebden Bridge; Stoke City Apr 1924 72apps 1gls; Congleton Town; Southend United Jul 1934; Stoke City (Assistant Manager) cs1935; WREXHAM (Manager) 20th Nov 1950; Bradford City (Manager) Feb 1955-Mar 1961; Stoke City (Scout) 1961; Bradford City (Scout) 1969;*
Honours; *Third Division North Championship Winner 1926/27*

Although christened Wilbert Jackson, for reasons unknown he became known as 'Peter'! He began playing football for his local side, Luddendon Foot, followed by a spell at Hebden Bridge where he was spotted and signed by Second Division Stoke City in April 1924. He made his Football League debut in October of the following season in a 2-0 win at Clapton Orient, playing at centre-half. Peter went on to spend ten seasons at the Victoria Ground, during which time he was to make just 72 League appearances, 15 in their Third Division North championship season of 1926/27. He finally left Stoke in the summer of 1934 when he signed for Third Division South side Southend United. He made his debut for the 'Shrimps' in September in a 3-2 defeat at Aldershot, but was to make just two more League appearances that season as he again found himself having to be content with mainly reserve team football. At the end of the

1934/35 campaign he left the Essex club, to take up an offer to become assistant-manager to his former Stoke City team-mate, Bob McGrory, who was managing the 'Potteries' club. Peter remained at the Victoria Ground until 20th November 1950 when he was given the opportunity of stepping into the managerial seat of Third Division North side, Wrexham. His first job at the Racecourse was to stabilise the club's fortunes, and in attempting to do so made Football League history by giving debuts to his twin sons, David and Peter, during 1954/55. Jackson's best season with 'The Robins' was 1952/53, leading them to third place in the League, finishing only three points behind the champions, Oldham Athletic. That same season he returned to the Victoria Ground with his Wrexham side for a third round F.A.Cup match against his former club, when Wrexham so nearly caused an upset in front of a crowd of 36,636, Stoke eventually winning 2-1. Jackson resigned as the Wrexham manager on 16th February 1955, and two weeks later was appointed the new manager of Bradford City, which proved to be a turning point for the struggling Third Division North club as he brought a steadying hand and an air of confidence to Valley Parade. His two sons accompanied him from Wrexham and, in his third season in charge, Bradford enjoyed their best campaign since the war when they finished in third place, therefore qualifying for the newly formed Third Division. However, life at that level was to be one constant struggle and following relegation in 1960/61, Peter Jackson was relieved of his managerial duties. The 1959/60 season had seen him take Bradford to the fifth round of the F.A.Cup, when they had beaten Everton before losing to First Division Burnley after a replay. On leaving Valley Parade he returned to Stoke City in a scouting position, before returning to Bradford City in March 1969 in a similar position. A Freemason, belonging to Baildon Corinthian Lodge, he was also a sidesman at St.Margaret's Church at Frizinghall, nr.Bradford, where he was to settle. Peter Jackson, senior, died in hospital in Shipley on 9th May 1986. He was 81.

LLOYD, Cliff — Feb 1955 to Oct 1957

See Players Who's Who Section
First Game in Charge v. *Swansea Town (a) 17th February, 1955 (Welsh Cup).*
Total Games in Charge; *142 (Not including games as caretaker-manager)*

LOVE, John T. DFC — Dec 1957 - Oct 1959

Birthplace; *Edinburgh, Mid-Lothian.*
D.O.B; *18th March, 1924*
Height; *6ft 1in* ***Weight;*** *13st 1lbs*
First Game in Charge v. *Accrington Stanley (a) 14th December, 1957.*
Total Games in Charge; *101*
Career in Football; *Leith Athletic 1941; Hibernian; Leith Athletic 1947; Albion Rovers 13th Feb 1948; Nottingham Forest Feb 1949 £7,000 59apps 21gls; Llanelli (Player/Manager) 1952/53; Walsall (Player/Assistant-Manager) Mar 1953, (Manager) Sept 1955; WREXHAM (Manager) Dec 1957-Nov 1959;*
Honours; *Welsh Cup Winner 1958; Third Division South Championship Winner 1951; Scottish League Division Two runner-up 1948;*

John Love began playing football for his local side, Leith Athletic, during the Second World War, when he also appeared for Edinburgh side, Hibernian. At the age of 18 he enlisted with the Royal Air Force, serving as a flight-lieutenant. During his service he was initially a pilot with Bomber Command, later becoming a glider pilot. He was decorated with the Distinguished Flying Cross (DFC) for his part in the Crossing of the Rhine operation, during which he suffered a shrapnel wound. After WW2 John resumed playing football for Leith Athletic, before signing for Scottish Second Division side Albion Rovers during 1947/48. He played for them alongside Jock Stein, and helped guide them to promotion by finishing runners-up. He was watched by a number of English Leag,ue sides at the start of the following season, and in February 1949 was signed by Second Division side Nottingham Forest for a £7,000 fee, in a bid to stop their slide towards relegation. Love made his Football League debut at Luton, playing at inside-right in the 4-3 defeat. Despite scoring seven goals in thirteen games he couldn't prevent Forest from going down. The following season they finished fourth, before finally winning the Third Division South championship in 1950/51. Love surprisingly left Forest in 1952 to take up an appointment at Southern League side Llanelli as player/manager. He eventually returned to the Football League scene in March 1955 when Walsall manager, Major Frank Buckley, appointed him as his player/assistant-manager. Love made his Walsall debut in a 2-2 draw at Swindon. Following Buckley's resignation as manager in September 1955, the Walsall board of directors turned to Love to take over the vacant position. He steered the 'Saddlers' clear of the re-election zone, after four successive applications, but he was to quit playing himself because of injury and concentrate on management. The following campaign saw Walsall finish in 15th place. The 1957/58 season found Love in need of a fresh challenge, and when he was offered the managerial position at Wrexham in December 1957, he accepted. That season was, of course, the last of the Northern and Southern sections of the Third Divisions and Wrexham needed to finish in the top half of the table to qualify for the new 'national' Third Division. The club were fifth from bottom when Love took charge, but he was to lead them up the table and into the Third Division by finishing the season in 12th place, the last available position. 1958/59 was a season of consolidation, as Wrexham struggled to finish in 18th place. 1959/60 saw 'The Robins win just five of their opening twenty games and, with the club lying in 21st position, Love offered his resignation on 2nd November. It was accepted by the board of directors, who appointed Cliff Lloyd as caretaker-manager until the end of the season, when the club were relegated to the Fourth Division for the first time. As for Love, he went on to manage a number of 'minor' clubs.

MORRIS, William — Jun 1960-Apr 1961 & Mar 1965-Oct 1965

Birthplace; *Llandulas, nr. Colwyn Bay, Denbighshire.*
D.O.B; *30th July, 1918.*
Height; *5ft 6in* ***Weight;*** *10st 11lbs (1950)*
First Game in Charge v. *Peterborough United (a) 20th August, 1960.*
Total Games in Charge; *89*
Career in Football; *Old Colwyn Youth; Llandudno Town 1938; Burnley Jan 1939 211apps 47gls, (WW2) 25apps 15gls; WREXHAM (WW2 Guest) Nov 1939 23apps 1gls; Burnley ('A' team Trainer) 1952, (Trainer/Coach) cs1954; WREXHAM (Manager) Jun 1960-May 1961, (Manager) Mar 1965-24th Oct 1965;*
Honours; *Five Welsh International caps; One War-time Welsh International cap; F.A.Cup runner-up 1947; Second Division runner-up 1947;*

Billy Morris began playing football while at school in both Llandulas and Abergele. He left school in 1934, and took up work at Slaters car dealers in their paint shop in Abergele. He continued to play the game, turning out for Llandulas, Abergele, Colwyn Bay and then Llandudno in 1938. During his time with the latter he attended two Welsh Amateur international trials, thereby attracting the attention of Football League clubs. It was Second Division Burnley who were the first to recognise his potential, and Billy signed for the 'Clarets' in January 1939. 'A neat inside-forward with immaculate ball control' he went straight into the first team at inside-right for his debut in a 3-0 home win over Norwich City, keeping his place in the side until World War Two intervened. Billy enlisted in the Royal Welch Fusiliers, completing his initial training at the Hightown Barracks in Wrexham, during which time he turned out as a 'guest' for Wrexham. His first game was against Liverpool on the Racecourse in November 1939, Wrexham winning 2-1. He went on to make 23 appearances for the 'Robins' until May 1941. Billy was later posted overseas to serve in both India and Burma, attaining the rank of sergeant. Whilst serving in Kohima, Burma in 1944 his unit was ambushed, and Billy was shot by a Japanese bullet which passed straight through his neck. He made a full recovery and despite the conflict he still found time to play football, turning out for his divisional team in Rangoon, whom he once captained in a match that was kicked off by Gracie Fields! After the conflict had ended Billy returned home, where he took up playing again for Burnley,

helping them to promotion to the First Division in 1947, and also to the F.A.Cup final in the same season, where they lost 1-0 to Charlton Athletic after extra-time. Ten days prior to that game Billy won the first of his five Welsh international caps when he played for Wales in a 2-1 defeat by Northern Ireland in Belfast. At Turf Moor Billy was described as an 'elusive player, difficult to mark, a man who had a knack for finishing half-chances inside the six yard box, simply because he was in the right place at the right time'. His football career finally came to an end during the 1952/53 season, as he suffered from malaria which he had contracted during the war, and it had begun to affect his legs and hip with arthritis. He was then offered a coaching position, followed by his appointment as 'A' team trainer working with the youth players. Morris remained in that position until 1960, when he was released by Burnley to take up the manager's job at Wrexham. He was to spend just one season at the helm, as the club finished in 16th position, although the initial season of the League Cup competition saw Wrexham beat Blackburn Rovers on their way to the quarter-finals, where they lost to Aston Villa, the eventual winners. At the end of the season Morris resigned as manager because of his worsening hip problem. He left football altogether, opening a boarding house in Llandudno which he ran until receiving a phone call from the Wrexham chairman, Fred Tomlinson in March 1965, asking him to return as manager, following the departure of Ken Barnes. He returned in time to lead Wrexham to the Welsh Cup Final, where they lost to Cardiff City after a replay. In 1965/66 Wrexham won just three of their opening 14 matches and, after a 4-1 home defeat by Stockport County on 24th October 1965, Morris was relieved of his duties. He then ran a grocers and off-licence shop in Lysfaen, which he let his wife run, while he became employed by the Isle of Man Steamship Company. He later worked for the local council before retiring in 1976. He has since had both his hips replaced, and still resides in the Colwyn Bay area.

BARNES, Ken — May 1961 to Feb 1965

See Players Who's Who Section
First Game in Charge v. *Millwall (a) 19th August, 1961.*
Total Games in Charge; *20*

ROWLEY, John Frederick — Jan 1966 - Apr 1967

Birthplace; *Wolverhampton.*
D.O.B; *7th October, 1920.*
Died; *Ashton, Lancashire, 27th June, 1998.*
Height; *5ft 9in* ***Weight;*** *11st 7lbs (1936)*
First Game in Charge v. *Barnsley (h) 8th January, 1966.*
Total Games in Charge; *66*
Career in Football; *Dudley Old Boys; Wolverhampton Wanderers Nov 1935; Cradley Heath (Loan) 1936; Bournemouth Feb 1937 22apps 12gls; Manchester United Oct 1937 £3,500 380apps 182gls, (WW2) 79apps 100gls; Tottenham Hotspur (WW2 Guest); Wolverhampton Wanderers (WW2 Guest); Distillery (WW2 Guest); Plymouth Argyle (Player/Manager) Feb 1955-Mar 1960 56apps 14gls; Oldham Athletic (Manager) Jul 1960-May 1963; Ajax Amsterdam (Coach) Aug 1963-Jul 1964; WREXHAM (Manager) Jan 1966; Bradford Park Avenue (Manager) Apr 1967; Oldham Athletic (Manager) Oct 1968-Dec 1969;*
Honours; *Six England International caps; One War-time England International cap; One 'B' England International cap; Football League Representative cap; Football League Championship Winner 1952; Football League Championship runner-up 1947, 1948, 1949 & 1951; Division Two runner-up 1938; F.A.Cup Winner 1948; Football League War Cup Winner 1942; Division Three Championship Winner 1959; Division Four Championship runner-up 1963;*

Described as 'one of the finest centre-forwards of the post-war era' Jack was playing for Dudley Old Boys when signed by his home town club, Wolverhampton Wanderers, in November 1935. However, he failed to make a first team appearance for the Molineux club and was loaned out to Birmingham League side Cradley Heath in 1936, before being allowed to join Bournemouth on a free transfer in February 1937. He was plunged straight into the 'Cherries' first team in a 1-1 draw at Walsall, going on to score 12 goals in 22 appearances, which persuaded Manchester United to step in and pay Bournemouth a then club record fee received of £3,500 in October 1937. He made his debut in the same week against Sheffield Wednesday, but felt that he was not quite ready for Second Division football and asked to be dropped. Six weeks later he returned, and scored four of United's five goals against Swansea Town. At Old Trafford he teamed up with ex-Wrexham players Tommy Bamford and Bill Bryant, and together they led United back to the First Division, with Rowley playing in the outside-left position. During WW2 he served in France as an anti-tank gunner in the South Staffordshire Infantry, although he did manage to play football when he could. As a 'guest' he turned out for: Wolverhampton Wanderers (winning a War League Cup winners' medal in 1942); Tottenham Hotspur; and Irish League side, Distillery. His goalscoring exploits over this period - he scored eight goals in one match for Wolves, and seven in one game for Spurs - earned him a war-time international cap against Wales in 1944. He resumed his career with Manchester United after the War, now playing at centre-forward, he continued to score goals, finishing leading goalscorer for United in each of the first four Post-War seasons. He won an F.A.Cup winners' medal in 1948, as United beat Blackpool 4-2, with Jack scoring twice. In 1952 he finally won a Football League Championship medal, again finishing leading goalscorer with 30 goals. Dubbed 'Gunner' because of his net-bulging shooting he netted 208 goals in 422 games for United, figures which do not include the WW2 period. He won the first of his six full England caps in 1948, but his best game was against Northern Ireland in 1949 when scoring four of his six England goals. He was described during his time at United as 'not having much finesse, but very direct'. He finally left Old Trafford in February 1955 when given the opportunity to take his first step into management, joining Second Division Plymouth Argyle on a free transfer to become their player/manager. Argyle were struggling to avoid relegation at the time, but in his first game in charge led them to their first away win of the season, 3-2 at Fulham. By the end of the campaign they had picked up enough points to edge clear of the drop zone, but a year later Rowley and the Argyle fans suffered major disappointment as the 'Pilgrims' slipped into Division Three South. In similar circumstances many clubs would have sacrificed their manager, but Rowley was given the opportunity to rebuild, and it paid off when he led them to the Third Division South championship. However, Rowley was to leave Home Park suddenly in the close season of 1960 amid much boardroom unrest. He then took up an offer to become the manager of Fourth Division side, Oldham Athletic. It took Rowley three seasons to build a promotion-winning side, which came in 1962/63 when the 'Latics' finished runners-up. Three days after winning promotion Rowley was to make a sudden departure as the 'Latics' board demanded his resignation after 'internal dissention'. He soon accepted an invitation to join Ajax Amsterdam as coach in August 1963, where he was to spend one season. He returned to Football League management in January 1966 when he was appointed the new manager of Wrexham. The 'Robins' were languishing near the foot of Division Four at this time, and he was unable to stop the rot as the club finished the season bottom of the Football League, forcing them to seek re-election for the first and only time in their history. The following season saw a vast improvement, as Rowley brought in the experienced 'keeper, John Schofield; Don Weston; and George Showell, and they finished in a very creditable seventh position. However, before the season had ended Rowley surprisingly decided to quit the Racecourse and join Bradford Park Avenue in April 1967, taking with him his assistant Ken Roberts. He spent almost eighteen months at Park Avenue, but again walked out to take on a second spell as manager of Oldham Athletic in October 1968. This time he inherited a side that was bottom of the Third Division, and was powerless to prevent their eventual relegation. After five consecutive defeats spanning November and December 1969 he was relieved of his managerial duties at Boundary Park. He then concentrated on running his newsagents business which he had started in Buckstones Road, Shaw, near Oldham, in 1962. Jack Rowley passed away at the Downshaw Lodge Nursing Home in Ashton in June 1998. He was 77. Had the War not robbed Jack of six years at his peak, there is no telling what his final goal tally might have been, and may have even beaten brother, Arthur's own Football League record of the most Football League goals scored in a career, 434, while playing for Fulham, Leicester City and Shrewsbury Town.

WILLIAMS, Alvan, — Apr 1967 to Sept 1968

See Players Who's Who Section
First Game in Charge v. *Crewe Alexandra (a) 22nd April, 1967.*
Total Games in Charge; *69*

NEAL, John — Sept 1968 - May 1977

D.O.B; *3rd April, 1932.*
Birthplace; *Silksworth, County Durham.*
Height; *5ft 8in* ***Weight;*** *10st 10lbs (1963)*
First Game in Charge v. *Barnsley (h) 8th January, 1966.*
Total Games in Charge; *500*
Career in Football; *Silksworth Colliery Welfare Juniors; Hull City Aug 1949 60apps 1gls; King's Lynn Jul 1956; Swindon Town 6th Jul 1957 91apps 2gls; Aston Villa 28th Jul 1959 £6,000 96apps 0gls; Southend United 23rd Nov 1962;-Jun 1967 101apps 1gls; WREXHAM (Trainer) Aug 1967, (Manager) Sept 1968; Middlesbrough (Manager) May 1977; Chelsea May 1981-Jun 1985;*
Honours; *Second Division Championship Winner 1960 & 1984; Football League Cup Winner 1960; Fourth Division Championship runner-up 1970; Welsh Cup Winner 1972 & 1975; Third Division South Representative cap;*

John Neal was playing football for his local side, Silksworth Colliery Welfare Juniors, when spotted and signed by Second Division Hull City in August 1949 at the age of 17. It was said at the time that he seemed to 'have a fine future ahead of him.' He progressed to make his Football League debut in April 1950, playing at left-back in a 1-1 home draw with Luton Town in a Hull side that included both Don Revie and Raich Carter. Due to his National Service (he served as a clerk with the Royal Air Force) Neal would not appear in the first team for Hull again until November 1952, and it wasn't until the 1953/54 season that he was to have a decent run in the first team. Neal went on to make sixty League appearances for the 'Tigers' before he was released in the close season of 1956. He then signed for non-League side Kings Lynn, where he spent one season. His Football League career was resurrected by Swindon Town, still playing at left-back, he was made club captain, and completed 91 appearances in the two seasons that he spent at the County Ground. Aston Villa manager Joe Mercer signed Neal, regarded as one of the best full-back's in the lower divisions at the time, in the close season of 1959 for a fee of £6,000 to strengthen his defence following relegation from the First Division. Neal made his debut for Villa against boyhood idols, Sunderland, in August 1959, missing just one League game as Villa stormed to the Second Division championship. The following season saw him switch to outside-left, and it was in that position that he collected a Football League Cup winners' medal as Villa beat Rotherham United in the first ever final of that competition played over two legs. Villa had beaten Wrexham on the way. He then returned to playing at full-back, but his first team chances became limited towards the end of 1961/62. Neal finally left Villa Park to join Third Division Southend United in November 1962, going straight into the team for his debut in a 2-2 draw at Barnsley. He completed a further three seasons before he retired from playing, and was given a coaching position by manager Alvan Williams. In April 1967 Williams left Southend to take up a position as manager of Wrexham, and later invited Neal to join him as his first team trainer, an offer which he was accepted. He spent just over a season in that position before Williams resigned after falling out with his directors and, following his departure, Neal was offered the vacant position. His first signing cost Wrexham a then club record fee, £14,000, for former England Youth International Brian Tinnion. Wrexham finished in ninth place in his first season at the helm, but the following season, 1969/70, was to see him lead Wrexham to promotion. Over the next seven years, John Neal transformed Wrexham Football Club, reaping the benefits of his youth policy during the early to mid-1970s as the club produced players like Mickey Thomas, Joey Jones, David Smallman, Billy Ashcroft, Alan Dwyer, Graham Whittle and many more promising youngsters. He brought the Welsh Cup back to Wrexham for the first time in twelve years in 1972, and this led to 'The Robins' first ever experience of European football in the Cup-Winners' Cup. The Racecourse ground also improved dramatically with the impressive Yale Stand built at a cost of £100,000, which included some of the best changing facilities in the lower divisions at that time, whilst the floodlights were also greatly improved to give TV much clearer pictures. The 1973/74 season saw him guide Wrexham to the quarter-finals of the F.A.Cup for the first time in the club's history, with many memorable victories along the way against Malcolm Allison's Crystal Palace at Selhurst Park; Jack Charlton's unbeaten Middlesbrough on the Racecourse; and Lawrie McMenemy's Southampton at the Dell; before unluckily losing 1-0 at Turf Moor to First Division Burnley. He led the club to Welsh Cup victory for a second time in 1975, and the following season saw Wrexham reach the quarter-finals of the European Cup-Winners' Cup, where they went out 2-1 on aggregate to the eventual winners of the competition, Anderlecht of Belgium. Perhaps the most significant season of them all was the 1976/77 campaign, when Neal led 'The Robins' to the verge of promotion to the Second Division for the first time ever, only to fall at the last hurdle with two home defeats in the final two home games. It was a hard pill to swallow for many Wrexham fans, but worse was to follow when John Neal quit his post of manager of Wrexham shortly afterwards to take over the reins at First Division Middlesbrough. At Ayresome Park he was said to have 'instilled an attacking flair into the team', but he came under some criticism for dismantling the 'team that Jack (Charlton) built'. One of his first signings at 'Boro was Billy Ashcroft, from Wrexham. 'Regarded as one of the quiet men of football', Neal went on to spend four years at Ayresome Park, before leaving in the summer of 1981 following a disagreement with the 'Boro board over the sale of Craig Johnston to Liverpool. He was not unemployed for long however, as Ken Bates quickly stepped to instal him as Second Division Chelsea's new manager in place of Geoff Hurst. His first season in charge almost saw the 'Pensioners' relegated to the Third Division for the first time in their history, but he eventually led them back to the First Division in 1984 as champions of Division Two, having signed three of his old boys from Wrexham: Joey Jones, Mickey Thomas and Eddie Niedzwiecki. Following heart surgery in 1984, it was announced that Neal would move 'upstairs' to a boardroom position a year later, while John Hollins, who had been serving under Neal, was promoted to manager. Many thought that his retirement from management was premature. Since then he has worked for a number of clubs in a scouting capacity, as well as for Wales during Mike Smiths managership. John Neal is now settled in the Wrexham area, where he can often be seen on the many golf courses in the area.

GRIFFITHS, Arfon MBE, — May 1977 to May 1981

See Players Who's Who Section
First Game in Charge v. *Stockport County (h) 13th August, 1977.*
Total Games in Charge; *220*

SUTTON, Mel — Jun 1981 to May 1982

See Players Who's Who Section
First Game in Charge v. *Queens Park Rangers (h) 29th August, 1981.*
Total Games in Charge; *53*

ROBERTS, Bobby — Jun 1982 - Mar 1985

See Players Who's Who Section
First Game in Charge v. *Cardiff City (a) 28th August, 1982.*
Total Games in Charge; *158*

McNEIL, Dixie

May 1985 - Oct 1989

See Players Who's Who Section
First Game in Charge v. *Bury (a) 4th May, 1985.*
Total Games in Charge; *264*

FLYNN, Brian

Nov 1989 -

See Players Who's Who Section
First Game in Charge v. *Hartlepool United (a) 4th November, 1989.*
Total Games in Charge; *585*

Wrexham Managers' Football League Record

Name	P	W	D	L	F	A	Pts
Brian Flynn	438	156	126	156	594	609	594
Dixie McNeil	201	76	54	71	305	274	282
Bobby Roberts	124	30	36	58	163	207	126
Mel Sutton	41	10	11	20	37	54	41*
Arfon Griffiths	172	63	49	60	206	181	175
John Neal	405	171	108	126	599	483	450
Alvan Williams	61	25	16	20	89	71	66
Jack Rowley	59	19	23	17	103	97	61
Billy Morris+	73	23	12	38	98	111	58
Ken Barnes	169	69	31	69	322	313	169
John Love	91	30	24	37	125	157	84
Cliff Lloyd	124	44	29	51	206	191	117
Peter Jackson	196	78	38	80	307	307	194
Les McDowall	43	10	12	21	39	57	32
Tom Williams	113	51	25	37	180	151	127
Tom Morgan	6	3	1	2	11	7	7
Arthur Cowell	7	3	0	4	8	11	6
Captain James Logan	60	21	18	21	82	85	60
Ernie Blackburn	206	95	38	73	414	330	228
Jack Baynes	91	39	21	31	172	154	101
Charlie Hewitt	70	21	16	33	105	132	58
Caretaker Managers	124	47	29	48	181	222	130
Selection Committee	268	98	69	101	374	397	265
TOTAL	**3,142**	**1,182**	**786**	**1,174**	**4,720**	**4,601**	

* = Three points for a win began in 1981/82
\+ = Billy Morris' two spells as manager in total.

Caretaker Managers

Name	P	W	D	L	F	A	Pts
George Showell	11	6	2	3	15	11	20
Cliff Lloyd	74	24	20	30	97	129	68
Ralph Burkinshaw	7	3	1	3	12	17	7
Tommy Griffiths	29	11	6	12	47	61	28
Dixie McNeil	1	1	0	0	3	2	3
Ted Robinson	2	2	0	0	7	2	4

The Robins Records and Reference

Chairmen of Wrexham Association Football Club, Limited

Robert Lewis Ellis
1912 - 1915

Harry Herbert Woodville
1919 - 1922

Julian Alfred Soames
1922 - 1923

Dr. Samuel Edwards-Jones
1923 - 1932

John Hughes
1932 - 1933, 1935 - 1936 & 1938 - 1948

George William Turner
1933 - 1935

Herbert John Pritchard
1936 - 1937

Dr. Arthur Lloyd Davies
1937 - 1938

Thomas Edward Williams
1948 - 1949

Edward Partin
1949 - 1950

Wilfred Alfred Madeley
1950 - 1952

Joseph Thomas Davies
1952 - 1955

Thomas Stanley
1955 - 1958

Eric Anthony McMahon
1958 - 1961 & 1968 - 1973

Hugh Godfrey Phillips
1961 - 1965

Frederick James Tomlinson
1965 - 1966 & 1973 - 1984

William Harold Evans
1966 - 1968

William Pryce Griffiths
1984 - 1986 & 1988 -

Gordon Mytton
1986 - 1988

Note that the club was run by committee until becoming a limited company on 20th August 1912.

Between 1915 and 1919 the club was closed down because of World War One.

Directors of Wrexham Association Football Club, Limited

** indicates original member of the board*

Service	Director	Profession
1912 - 1915	Robert Lewis Ellis*	Clerk
1912 - 1915 & 1930 - 1934	William Henry Parry*	Licensed Victualler
1912 - 1925	John Gardham Lowe*	Gas Fitter
1912 - 1922 & 1924 - 1925	Harry Herbert Woodville*	Auctioneer
1912 - 1921	William Clare Harrison*	Licensed Victualler
1912 - 1922	Thomas Henry Jones*	Artist
1912 - 1913	John William Edwards*	Monumental Mason
1912 - 1913 & 1925 - 1940	James Alexander Mackie*	Clerk & Company Secretary
1913 - 1939 & 1945 - 1946	Thomas Samuel Clutton	Coal Merchant
1913 - 1915	George Latimer	Licensed Victualler
1913 - 1927 & 1932 - 1936	Horace Blew	Licensed Victualler
1919 - 1920	Wilmer Rogers	Colliery Clerk
1919 - 1924	Julian Alfred Soames	Brewer
1919 - 1921	Thomas Holland Bushby	Brewery Manager
1920 - 1923	William Lloyd Jenkins	Draper
1921 - 1923	George Thomas Davies	Corn Merchant
1921 - 1924	William Holland	Farmer
1921 - 1922 & 1924 - 1932	Thomas Roberts	Tobacconist
1922 - 1931	Arthur Moffatt	Accountant
1922 - 1923 & 1924 - 1933	Dr. Samuel Edwards-Jones	Surgeon
1923 - 1932	John Roberts	Licensed Victualler
1923 - 1925	Norman Wilson	Newspaper Representative
1924 - 1928, 1939 - 1946 & 1949 - 1955	George William Turner	Wholesale Merchant
1925 - 1947	John Hughes	Building Contractor
1927 - 1930	David Henry Leslie	Gentleman
1931 - 1935	Arthur Davies	Building Contractor
1932 - 1946	Herbert John Pritchard	Coal Merchant
1933 - 1938	Dr. Arthur Lloyd Davies	Surgeon
1934 - 1936	Edward Williams	Company Secretary & Manager
1935 - 1938	Frank E. Evans	Accountant
1936 - 1938	William Ferris Humphreys	Builder
1937 - 1946	Victor Henry Thornton Dyke Dennis	Farmer
1938 - 1948	Edward Alfred Cross	Draper
1938 - 1951	Edward Partin	Secretary & Political Agent
1938 - 1953	William Alfred Madeley	Licensed Victualler
1941 - 1966	Thomas Edward Williams	Milk Purveyor
1945 - 1949	Harold Benjamin Davenport	Miller
1946 - 1970	Joseph Thomas Davies	Grocer
1946 - 1949	William Dodman	Boot Maker
1946 - 1947	John Frederick Michael Mowat	Brewer
1947 - 1951	Arthur Barritt	Company Director of the Clwydian Cafe, Rhyl
1947 - 1959	Thomas Stanley	Garage Proprietor
1948 - 1956 & 1983 - 1989	Francis Edwin Wellum	Company Director / Electrical Engineer
1949 - 1950	Thomas Percival Griffiths	Licensed Victualler
1950 - 1976	Eric Anthony McMahon	Fishmonger
1951 - 1960	Iorwerth Evans	Building Contractor
1953 - 1982	Hugh Godfrey Phillips	Coach Proprietor
1954 - 1965	John R. Nicholas	
1955 - 1981	Thomas Harold Dodd	Wholesale Confectioner
1956 - 1991	Fredrick James Tomlinson	Farmer
1959 - 1960	Frank Elford William Blew	Mechanic
1960 - 1972	Nicholas Edwards	
1960 - 1971	William Harold Evans	Butcher
1967 - 1970	Kenneth A. Edwards	
1968 - 1981	Alexander William Gaade	Company Managing Director
1970 - 1982	Geoffrey Morrris	Estate Agent
1974 - 1977	Charles Edward Roberts	Company Director
1974 - 1983	Robert Edward Arthur Clark	Chartered Accountant
1976 - 1981	Anthony Morris	Estate Agent
1977 -	William Pryce Griffiths	Wholesale Newspapers
1981 - 1990	Gordon Mytton	Property Developer
1981 - 1984	Wyn Jones	Builder
1982 - 1990	Neville Dickens	Managing Director
1982 - 1983	Steve Freudmann	Travel Agent
1982 - 1983 & 1985 - 1999	Barry Williams	Insurance Broker
1982 - 1990	Joe Scott	Managing Director
1983 -	Colin Griffiths	Company Director Wholesale Newspapers
1983 - 1990	George Dickens	Managing Director
1985 -	David Leslie Rhodes	Wholesale Baker & Company Director
1990 -	Stephen Francis Mackreth	Printer
1990 - 1991	Dai Wood	Retail Confectioner
1990 - 1999	Carmello Gino Paletta	Wholesale Confectioner
1995 -	Phillip Griffiths	Senior Manager
1998 -	Babs De Rosa	Administrator

Players with 200 or more League Appearances

1	Arfon Griffiths	585/6	19	Gren Jones	241
2	Alf Jones	503	20	Billy Tunnicliffe	236
3	Gareth Davies	482/7	21	Ron Hewitt	231
4	Aly McGowan	408	22	Fred Davis	230
5	Mickey Evans	368/15	23	Steve Buxton	179/50
6	Joey Jones	378/1	24	Peter Jones	226/1
7	Mel Sutton	355/5	25	Tommy Bannan	226
8	Karl Connolly	259/14	26	Archie Longmuir	223
9	Alan Fox	350	27	Eddie Tunney	220
10	Eddie May	330/4	28	Billy Ashcroft	196/23
11	Graham Whittle	331/19	29	Albert Parker	216
12	Phil Hardy	295/3	30	Kevin Russell	195/18
13	Gareth Owen	245/43	31	Andy Marriott	213
14	Brian Tinnion	265/14	32	Les Speed	211
15	Brian Lloyd	266	33	Steve Watkin	167/33
16	Mickey Thomas	251/13	34	Wayne Phillips	184/24
17	Albert Kinsey	245/8	35	George Snow	207
18	Neil Salathiel	243/1	36	Tommy Bamford	204

Players with 100 or more consecutive appearances in all competitions

(Date given is the first game of the sequence)

Player	Date	No. of games
Brian Lloyd	04/03/72	312
Alf Jones	30/08/30	232
Alan Fox	03/10/59	200
Andy Marriott	09/10/93	182
Bobby Shinton	21/08/76	167
Alf Jones	03/10/25	159
Gareth Davies	17/01/76	127
Brian Tinnion	19/02/72	121
Jimmy Hamilton	30/09/33	107

Players with 100 or more consecutive appearances in Football League games only

(Date given is the first game of the sequence)

Player	Date	No. of games
Brian Lloyd	04/03/72	248
Alf Jones	30/08/30	201
Alan Fox	03/10/59	165
Andy Marriott	09/10/93	143
Alf Jones	03/10/25	138
Gareth Davies	17/01/76	135
Bobby Shinton	21/08/76	122
Brian Tinnion	19/02/72	122
Billy Tunnicliffe	23/08/47	115

Top Twenty Oldest Known Players

Player	Yrs	Dys	Opponents for last game
1. Bobby Roberts	43	88	v. Worcester City (h) 29/11/1983
2. Lot Jones	39	??	v. Tranmere Rovers (h) 22/04/1922
3. Bert Goode	39	204	v. Flint Town (h) 03/03/1926
4. Jimmy Case	38	355	v. Colchester United (h) 08/05/1993
5. Dai Davies	38	329	v. Brymbo Steelworks (h) 24/02/1987
6. Dixie McNeil	38	328	v. Notts County (h) 10/12/1985
7. Billy Cope	38	133	v. Durham City (a) 07/04/1923
8. Ted Taylor	38	30	v. Hartlepools United (a) 06/04/1929
9. Mel Pejic	38	2	v. Hull City (a) 29/04/1995
10. Ehud Rogers	37	348	v. Barrow (h) 28/09/1946
11. Arfon Griffiths	37	267	v. Millwall (a) 17/05/1979
12. Ted Robson	37	257	v. Halifax Town (h) 05/05/1928
13. Ian Rush	37	215	v. Barry Town (h) 23/05/1999
14. Tommy Matthias	37	127	v. Merthyr Town (h) 14/03/1928
15. Billy Harrison	37	125	v. Merthyr Town (h) 01/05/1924
16. Les McDowall	37	32	v. Grantham (h) 26/11/1949
17. Brian Flynn	37	22	v. Doncaster Rovers (h) 03/04/1992
18. Tom Gardner	36	333	v. Southport (a) 26/04/1947
19. Joey Jones	36	264	v. Chesterfield (h) 23/11/1991
20. John Schofield	36	236	v. Brentford (h) 02/10/1967

Top Twenty Youngest Known Debutants

Player	Yrs	Dys	Opponents
1. Ken Roberts	15	158	v. Bradford P.A. (a) 01/09/1951
2. Dennis Griffiths	16	201	v. Tranmere Rovers (h) 01/03/1952
3. Jonathan Cross	16	252	v. Crewe Alexandra (a) 09/11/1991
4. Kevin Jones	16	264	v. Manchester Utd (h) 07/11/1990
5. David Palmer	16	275	v. Porthmadog (h) 18/12/1978
6. Shaun Cunnington	16	348	v. Bristol Rovers (a) 18/12/1982
7. Tommy Griffiths	17	31	v. Tranmere Rovers (a) 24/03/1923
8. Earl Godding	17	18	v. Bradford P.A.(h) 24/01/1953
9. Phil Hardy	17	26	v. Hartlepool United (h) 05/05/1990
10. Tommy Millington	17	33	v. Brymbo Green (h) 14/02/1923
11. Mark Emmerson	17	52	v. Preston North End (a) 28/09/1982
12. Arfon Griffiths	17	84	v. Darlington (h) 15/11/1958
13. Darren Baker	17	89	v. Plymouth Argyle (a) 25/09/1982
14. Rob Lunt	17	91	v. Halifax Town (h) 12/03/1991
15. Roger Preece	17	100	v. Exeter City (a) 21/02/1987
16. Ron Roberts	17	135	v. Llandudno (h) 27/01/1960
17. Andy Edwards	17	156	v. Shrewsbury Town (h) 31/08/1982
18. Lee Jones	17	162	v. Manchester United (h) 07/11/1990
19. Mike McBurney	17	168	v. Plymouth Argyle (a) 27/02/1971
20. Mark Morris	17	177	v. Exeter City (a) 25/01/1986

Top Ten Youngest known goalscorers

Player	Yrs	Dys	Opponents
1. Darren Baker	17	115	v. Doncaster Rovers (a) 19/10/1982
2. Jonathan Cross	17	173	v. Rochdale (h) 22/08/92
3. Mike McBurney	17	193	v. Oswestry Town (a) 24/03/1971
4. Mickey Thomas	17	234	v. Bolton Wanderers (h) 26/02/1972
5. Bernard Evans	17	254	v. Bradford City (a) 15/09/1954
6. David Jackson	17	259	v. Grimsby Town (a) 09/10/1954
7. Peter Jackson	17	273	v. Rochdale (a) 23/10/1954
8. Lee Jones	17	274	v. Rochdale (h) 09/03/1991
9. John Muldoon	17	315	v. Bournemouth (h) 02/10/1982
10. Roger Preece	17	327	v. Swansea City (a) 02/05/1987

Top Ten Oldest Known Debutants

Player	Yrs	Dys	Opponents
1. Bobby Roberts	43	88	v. Worcester City (h) 29/11/1983
2. Lot Jones	39	??	v. Halifax Town (h) 18/03/1922
3. Jimmy Case	38	287	v. Bury (a) 27/02/1993
4. Bill Cope	37	274	v. Grimsby Town (a) 26/08/1922
5. Ted Taylor	37	241	v. Lincoln City (a) 03/11/1928
6. Les McDowall	37	10	v. Gateshead (a) 05/11/1949
7. Ian Rush	36	292	v. Reading (h) 08/08/1998
8. Billy Harrison	36	241	v. Ashington (h) 25/08/23
9. Tom Gardner	36	95	v. New Brighton (h) 31/08/46
10. Ernie Islip	36	17	v. Accrington Stanley (a) 17/11/1928

Leading League Goalscorers with 40 goals or more

Player		Goals
1	Tommy Bamford	174
2	Arfon Griffiths	120
3	Ron Hewitt	95
4	Graham Whittle	91
5	Albert Kinsey	84
6	Tommy Bannan	83
7	Gary Bennett	82
8	Karl Connolly	79
9	Billy Tunnicliffe	74
10	Billy Ashcroft	72
11	Ray Smith	60
12	Mike Metcalf	58
13	Jim Steel	57
14	Jack Boothway	55
15	Steve Watkin	55
16	Dixie McNeil	54
17	Brian Tinnion	54
18	Sammy McMillan	52
19	Kevin Russell	52
20	Bernard Evans	47
21	Steve Buxton	46
22	George Snow	45
23	Ernie Phythian	44
24	Albert Mays	41
25	Harold Lapham	40
26	Tommy Lewis	40
27	Don Weston	40

Players to have scored three hat-tricks or more

15	Tommy Bamford	3	Albert Mays
6	Gary Bennett	3	Mike Metcalf
4	Jack Boothway	3	Ray Smith
4	Bill Cotton	3	Samuel Taylor
3	Peter Baines	3	Graham Whittle
3	Karl Connolly		

Players who have managed a Premier/Football League club

Player	Club	Period	
Ken Barnes	Wrexham	1961	1965
Jimmy Case	Brighton & Hove Albion	1995	1996
Malcolm Crosby	Sunderland	1992	1993
Brian Flynn	Wrexham	1989	
Arfon Griffiths	Wrexham	1977	1981
	Crewe Alexandra	1981	1982
Jake King	Shrewsbury Town	1997	
Cliff Lloyd	Wrexham	1955	1957
Les McDowall	Wrexham	1949	1950
	Manchester City	1950	1963
	Oldham Athletic	1963	1965
Dixie McNeil	Wrexham	1985	1989
Eddie May	Cardiff City	1991	1994
	Cardiff City	1995	1995
	Torquay United	1995	1996
	Brentford	1997	1998
Bobby Roberts	Colchester United	1975	1982
	Wrexham	1982	1985
Ken Roberts	Chester	1968	1976
Mel Sutton	Wrexham	1981	1982
Graham Turner	Shrewsbury Town	1978	1984
	Aston Villa	1984	1986
	Wolves	1986	1994
	Hereford United	1995	
Alvan Williams	Hartlepool United	1964	1965
	Southend United	1965	1967
	Wrexham	1967	1968

Top Ten Oldest known goalscorers

Player	Yrs	Dys	Opponents
1. Lot Jones	39	??	v. Halifax Town (h) 18/03/1922
2. Bert Goode	39	74	v. Accrington Stanley (h) 24/10/1925
3. Arfon Griffiths	37	117	v. Porthmadog (h) 18/12/1978
4. Tom Gardner	36	312	v. Hartlepools United (h) 05/04/1947
5. Tommy Matthias	36	150	v. Crewe Alexandra (h) 06/04/1927
6. Gordon Davies	36	140	v. Hereford Utd (a) 26/12/1991
7. Joey Jones	36	40	v. Lincoln City (h) 13/04/1991
8. Ernie Islip	36	17	v. Accrington Stanley (a) 17/11/1929
9. Ken Barnes	35	351	v. Bradford City (h) 20/02/1965
10. Dixie McNeil	35	224	v. Cardiff City (a) 28/08/1982

Players to have top scored more than once (League & Cup)

5	Tommy Bamford	2	Harold Lapham
4	Tommy Bannan	2	Mike Metcalf
4	Karl Connolly	2	Billy Redfern
3	Gary Bennett	2	Kevin Russell
3	Bill Cotton	2	Ray Smith
3	Albert Kinsey	2	Jim Steel
3	Dixie McNeil	2	Billy Tunnicliffe
3	David Smallman	2	Keith Webber
2	Billy Ashcroft		
2	Jack Boothway		

Player of the Year 'The Jack Williams Trophy'

Year	Winner
1975/76	Brian Lloyd
1976/77	Graham Whittle
1977/78	Gareth Davies
1978/79	John Roberts
1979/80	Dixie McNeil
1980/81	Steve Fox
1981/82	Eddie Niedzwiecki
1982/83	Robbie Savage
1983/84	David Gregory
1984/85	Jack Keay
1985/86	Mike Williams
1986/87	Mike Williams
1987/88	Kevin Russell
1988/89	Kevin Russell
1989/90	Nigel Beaumont
1990/91	Mark Morris
1991/92	Andy Thackeray
1992/93	Tony Humes
1993/94	Gary Bennett
1994/95	Gary Bennett
1995/96	Wayne Phillips
1996/97	Andy Marriott
1997/98	Brian Carey
1998/99	Dean Spink

Young Player of the Year

Year	Winner
1983/84	Shaun Cunnington
1984/85	Andy Edwards
1985/86	Shaun Cunnington
1986/87	Roger Preece
1987/88	Darren Wright
1988/89	Darren Wright
1989/90	Gareth Owen
1990/91	Gareth Owen
1991/92	Phil Hardy
1992/93	Jonathan Cross
1993/94	David Brammer
1994/95	Bryan Hughes
1995/96	Mark McGregor
1996/97	Mark McGregor
1997/98	Neil Roberts
1998/99	Robin Gibson

Football League Top Goalscorers

Season	Goals	Player	Season	Goals	Player
1921/22	12	Bill Cotton & Matt Burton	1960/61	22	Mike Metcalf
1922/23	15	Bill Cotton	1961/62	20	Mike Metcalf
1923/24	20	Bill Cotton	1962/63	15	Brian Whitehouse & Ron Barnes
1924/25	15	Jimmy Jones	1963/64	20	Ernie Phythian
1925/26	14	James Lyons & Jack Nock	1964/65	18	Keith Webber
1926/27	19	James Smith	1965/66	22	Keith Webber
1927/28	17	Gordon Gunson	1966/67	22	Sammy McMillan
1928/29	33	Albert Mays	1967/68	19	Ray Smith
1929/30	29	Tommy Bamford	1968/69	19	Ray Smith
1930/31	45	Tommy Bamford	1969/70	29	Albert Kinsey
1931/32	34	Tommy Bamford	1970/71	17	Albert Kinsey
1932/33	40	Tommy Bamford	1971/72	11	Albert Kinsey & Eddie May
1933/34	50	Tommy Bamford	1972/73	15	David Smallman & Billy Ashcroft
1934/35	18	George Snow	1973/74	16	David Smallman
1935/36	25	Charles McCartney	1974/75	20	David Smallman
1936/37	24	Harold Lapham	1975/76	19	Billy Ashcroft
1937/38	16	Harold Lapham	1976/77	35	Graham Whittle
1938/39	29	George Burditt	1977/78	25	Dixie McNeil
1939/40	16	Ehud Rogers	1978/79	15	John Lyons
1940/41	19	Billy Redfern	1979/80	21	Dixie McNeil
1941/42	14	Billy Redfern	1980/81	20	Dixie McNeil
1942/43	12	Norman Moore	1981/82	15	Ian Edwards
1943/44	20	Gordon Bremner	1982/83	13	Steve Buxton & Robbie Savage
1944/45	27	Peter Baines	1983/84	24	David Gregory
1945/46	6	Fred Haycock	1984/85	15	Jim Steel
1946/47	25	Jack Boothway	1985/86	24	Steve Charles
1947/48	25	Billy Tunnicliffe	1986/87	22	Jim Steel
1948/49	17	Jack Boothway	1987/88	25	Kevin Russell
1949/50	13	Billy Tunnicliffe	1988/89	27	Kevin Russell
1950/51	15	Frank Fidler	1989/90	16	Gary Worthington
1951/52	16	Ron Hewitt	1990/91	15	Chris Armstrong
1952/53	22	Tommy Bannan	1991/92	13	Steve Watkin
1953/54	18	Tommy Bannan	1992/93	23	Gary Bennett
1954/55	19	Tommy Bannan	1993/94	39	Gary Bennett
1955/56	17	Elfed Evans	1994/95	47	Gary Bennett
1956/57	29	Ron Hewitt	1995/96	21	Karl Connolly
1957/58	15	Barry Smith	1996/97	15	Karl Connolly
1958/59	17	Tommy Bannan	1997/98	14	Karl Connolly
1959/60	16	Don Weston	1998/99	11	Karl Connolly

Players scoring 20 or more goals in a season (includes all Competitions)

Goals	Player	Season	Goals	Player	Season
50	Tommy Bamford	1933/34	23	Gary Bennett	1992/93
47	Gary Bennett	1994/95	23	Karl Connolly	1998/99
40	Tommy Bamford	1932/33	22	George Frewin	1932/33
39	Gary Bennett	1993/94	22	Tommy Bannan	1952/53
35	Graham Whittle	1976/77	22	Mike Metcalf	1960/61
34	Tommy Bamford	1931/32	22	Keith Webber	1965/66
33	Albert Mays	1928/29	22	Sammy McMillan	1966/67
29	Tommy Bamford	1929/30	22	Bobby Shinton	1976/77
29	George Burditt	1938/39	22	Jim Steel	1985/86
29	Ron Hewitt	1956/57	22	Jim Steel	1986/87
29	Albert Kinsey	1969/70	21	Tommy Bamford	1930/31
27	Peter Baines	1944/45	21	Samuel Taylor	1930/31
27	Peter Thompson	1956/57	21	Dixie McNeil	1979/80
27	Kevin Russell	1988/89	21	Steve Watkin	1992/93
25	Charles McCartney	1935/36	21	Karl Connolly	1995/96
25	Jack Boothway	1946/47	20	Bill Cotton	1923/24
25	Billy Tunnicliffe	1947/48	20	Archie Burgon	1936/37
25	Dixie McNeil	1977/78	20	Gordon Bremner	1943/44
25	Kevin Russell	1987/88	20	John Anderson	1956/57
24	Harold Lapham	1936/37	20	Mike Metcalf	1961/62
24	Bobby Shinton	1977/78	20	Ernie Phythian	1963/64
24	Graham Whittle	1977/78	20	David Smallman	1974/75
24	David Gregory	1983/84	20	Dixie McNeil	1980/81
24	Steve Charles	1985/86			

Players scoring in five or more consecutive games in the Football League

(Date shown is the start of sequence)

Games	Goals	Player	Date	Games	Goals	Player	Date
9	12	Tommy Bamford	07/02/31	5	6	Clive Colbridge	13/10/64
9	11	Kevin Russell	19/03/88	5	6	Albert Mays	08/09/28
6	10	Tommy Bamford	05/04/30	5	6	Ray Smith	25/10/69
5	10	Tommy Bamford	04/02/34	6	6	Steve Charles	17/08/85
5	9	Tommy Bamford	11/04/34	6	6	Don Weston	29/08/59
5	8	Stan Bennion	26/08/61	5	5	Archie Burgon	26/09/36

Football League Ever-Presents

Season	Players	Season	Players
1921/22	None	1960/61	Fred Davis & Alan Fox
1922/23	None	1961/62	Alan Fox
1923/24	Alf Jones	1962/63	Peter Jones
1924/25	None	1963/64	None
1925/26	None	1964/65	None
1926/27	Alf Jones	1965/66	None
1927/28	Alf Jones	1966/67	John Schofield & Steve Stacey
1928/29	George Bellis, Gordon Gunson & Billie Rogers	1967/68	None
1929/30	None	1968/69	None
1930/31	Alf Jones	1969/70	Albert Kinsey
1931/32	Alf Jones	1970/71	None
1932/33	John Brown & Alf Jones	1971/72	Eddie May
1933/34	Alf Jones	1972/73	Brian Lloyd & Brian Tinnion
1934/35	James Hamilton & George Snow	1973/74	David Fogg, Brian Lloyd & Brian Tinnion
1935/36	None	1974/75	Mickey Evans & Brian Lloyd
1936/37	James Hamilton	1975/76	Brian Lloyd & Eddie May
1937/38	Pat McMahon	1976/77	Gareth Davies, Brian Lloyd & Bobby Shinton
1938/39	Eddie Tunney	1977/78	Gareth Davies, Bobby Shinton & Mel Sutton
1939/40	None	1978/79	None
1940/41	Billy Redfern	1979/80	None
1941/42	None	1980/81	Dai Davies
1942/43	Cyril Jones	1981/82	Eddie Niedzwiecki
1943/44	None	1982/83	None
1944/45	Cyril Jones	1983/84	None
1945/46	Gib Bellis	1984/85	None
1946/47	None	1985/86	Barry Horne
1947/48	Eddie Tunney & Billy Tunnicliffe	1986/87	Shaun Cunnington & Barry Horne
1948/49	Dennis Grainger, Ron Jackson & Billy Tunnicliffe	1987/88	None
1949/50	Archie Ferguson & Les Speed	1988/89	Kevin Russell
1950/51	None	1989/90	None
1951/52	None	1990/91	None
1952/53	None	1991/92	Andy Thackeray & Phil Hardy
1953/54	None	1992/93	Barry Jones
1954/55	None	1993/94	None
1955/56	None	1994/95	Andy Marriott
1956/57	None	1995/96	Andy Marriott
1957/58	None	1996/97	None
1958/59	Alan Fox	1997/98	None
1959/60	Aly McGowan	1998/99	None

Players who have won a Football League Championship medal

Name	Club & Year
Phil Boersma	Liverpool 1973
Tom Boyle	Burnley 1921
Jimmy Case	Liverpool 1976, 1977, 1979 & 1980
Joey Jones	Liverpool 1977
Alan Kennedy	Liverpool 1979, 1980, 1982, 1982 & 1984
Ian Rush	Liverpool 1982, 1983, 1984, 1986 & 1990
Ted Taylor	Huddersfield Town 1924 & 1926 & Everton 1928

Players who have won a F.A.Cup Winners medal

Name	Club & Year
Ken Barnes	Manchester City 1956
Tom Boyle	Burnley 1914
David Gaskell	Manchester United 1963
William Harrison	Wolves 1908
Barry Horne	Everton 1995
Ernie Islip	Huddersfield Town 1922
Billy Myerscough	Aston Villa 1957
Ian Rush	Liverpool 1986, 1989 & 1992
George Showell	Wolves 1960

Players who have won a European Cup Winners medal

Name	Club & Year
Jimmy Case	Liverpool 1977, 1978 & 1981
Alan Kennedy	Liverpool 1981 & 1984
Joey Jones	Liverpool 1977
Ian Rush	Liverpool 1984

Players who have won a Football League Cup Winners medal

Name	Club & Year
Frank Carrodus	Aston Villa 1975
Jimmy Case	Liverpool 1981
Colin Green	Birmingham City 1963
Alan Kennedy	Liverpool 1981, 1982, 1983 & 1984
Ian Rush	Liverpool 1981, 1982, 1983, 1984 & 1995
John Schofield	Birmingham City 1963

Players who have won a UEFA Cup Winners medal

Name	Club & Year
Phil Boersma	Liverpool 1973
Jimmy Case	Liverpool 1976

Wrexham's Hat-trick Heroes Since 1921

Player	Goals	Date	Opponents & Score	Competition
Eric Regan	3	05-11-21	Chesterfield (h) 6-1	FL D3(N)
Bill Cotton	3	05-11-21	Chesterfield (h) 6-1	FL D3(N)
Bill Cotton	3	14-02-23	Brymbo Green (h) 5-0	WC R5
Bill Cotton	3	25-08-23	Ashington (h) 4-0	FL D3(N)
Bill Cotton	3	01-12-23	Port Vale (h) 5-1	FAC Q5
James Jones	3	14-03-25	Wigan Borough (h) 6-2	FL D3(N)
Jack Nock	3	14-03-25	Wigan Borough (h) 6-2	FL D3(N)
Archie Longmuir	3	24-10-25	Accrington Stan. (h) 5-6	FL D3(N)
James Lyons	3	06-02-26	Nelson (h) 3-2	FL D3(N)
Archie Longmuir	3	13-11-26	Accrington Stanley (h)	FL D3(N)
Harry Lovatt	3	15-01-27	Chesterfield (a) 3-1	FL D3(N)
Billie Rogers	4	09-03-27	Llandudno (a) 4-1	WC R5
Roland Woodhouse	3	01-10-27	Nelson (h) 5-2	FL D3(N)
Cecil Smith	3	05-11-27	Ashington (h) 5-1	FL D3(N)
Gordon Gunson	3	04-02-28	Barrow (h) 5-0	FL D3(N)
Albert Mays	4	25-08-28	Chesterfield (h) 4-3	FL D3(N)
Albert Mays	4	05-01-29	Barrow (h) 5-0	FL D3(N)
Albert Mays	3	26-01-29	Ashington (h) 4-0	FL D3(N)
Tommy Bamford	4	28-09-29	Rochdale (h) 8-0	FL D3(N)
John Ashcroft	3	03-05-30	Nelson (h) 5-1	FL D3(N)
Tommy Lewis	4	20-09-30	Crewe Alexandra (h) 7-0	FL D3(N)
Tommy Bamford	3	13-12-30	Wellington Town (a) 4-2	FAC R2
Samuel Taylor	3	25-04-31	Nelson (h) 5-1	FL D3(N)
Samuel Taylor	3	05-09-31	Rochdale (h) 4-0	FL D3(N)
Tommy Bamford	3	12-09-31	Doncaster Rovs. (a) 4-2	FL D3(N)
Tommy Bamford	3	30-12-31	Chester (a) 5-2	FL D3(N)
Bernard Parden	3	16-01-32	Rochdale (a) 4-2	FL D3(N)
Samuel Taylor	3	05-03-32	Shrewsbury Town (h) 4-2	WC R6
Tommy Bamford	4	26-03-32	Walsall (h) 5-1	FL D3(N)
Tommy Bamford	3	17-12-32	Accrington Stan. (a) 3-5	FL D3(N)
Tommy Bamford	3	31-12-32	Barnsley (a) 3-5	FL D3(N)
Tommy Lewis	3	07-01-33	Hartlepool Utd. (h) 8-1	FL D3(N)
Tommy Bamford	3	18-02-33	Gateshead (h) 5-1	FL D3(N)
Tommy Bamford	3	01-03-33	Rotherham Utd. (h) 5-1	FL D3(N)
Tommy Bamford	3	01-09-33	Mansfield Town (h) 5-0	FL D3(N)
Tommy Bamford	4	21-10-33	Doncaster Rov. (a) 4-1	FL D3(N)
Tommy Bamford	3	17-02-34	Gateshead (a) 3-0	FL D3(N)
Tommy Bamford	5	17-03-34	Carlisle United (h) 8-1	FL D3(N)
Tommy Bamford	3	28-04-34	Walsall (h) 4-2	FL D3(N)
Archie Gardiner	3	03-11-34	Darlington (h) 4-0	FL D3(N)
Charles McCartney	3	12-10-35	Tranmere Rovers (h) 4-0	FL D3(N)
Archie Burgon	3	19-12-36	Crewe Alex. (h) 5-0	FL D3(N)
Harold Lapham	4	29-03-37	Gateshead (h) 6-0	FL D3(N)
Harold Lapham	3	13-09-37	Hartlepool Utd. (h) 6-3	FL D3(N)
George Burditt	3	03-09-38	Doncaster Rov. (h) 3-0	FL D3(N)
John Roberts	3	04-11-39	Stoke City (h) 4-4	WW2
Billy Redfern	3	05-10-40	Tranmere Rovers (h) 3-3	WW2
Clem Smith	3	14-12-40	Crewe Alexandra (h) 5-1	WW2
Billy Redfern	3	22-02-41	New Brighton (h) 5-8	WW2
Len Butt	3	22-03-41	Chester (h) 5-2	WW2
Billy Atkinson	4	25-10-41	Stockport Cty. (h) 6-1	WW2
Billy Graham	3	10-01-42	Stockport Cty. (h) 6-1	WW2
Norman Moore	4	07-11-42	Stockport Cty. (h) 7-1	WW2
Ehud Rogers	3	03-04-43	Everton (h) 4-1	WW2
Peter Baines	3	17-04-43	Stockport Cty. (h) 6-3	WW2
Gordon Bremner	4	28-08-43	Chester (h) 8-4	WW2
Archie Livingstone	7	25-09-43	Tranmere Rov. (h) 9-0	WW2
Lee Horsman	3	20-11-43	Stoke City (h) 4-1	WW2
Gordon Bremner	3	01-01-44	Liverpool (h) 4-2	WW2
Charlie Revell	3	19-02-44	Crewe Alex. (h) 5-2	WW2
Charlie Revell	4	29-04-44	Crewe Alex. (h) 4-0	WW2
Peter Baines	4	18-11-44	Stockport Cty. (h) 8-0	WW2
Peter Baines	3	03-02-45	Crewe Alex. (a) 3-3	WW2
Ronnie Dix	3	10-02-45	Crewe Alex. (h) 6-1	WW2
Johnny Hancocks	3	12-05-45	Southport (a) 5-1	WW2
Fred Haycock	3	12-01-46	Tranmere Rovers (h) 7-3	WW2
Jack Boothway	3	09-11-46	Darlington (h) 7-1	FL D3(N)
Jack Boothway	4	30-11-46	Marine (h) 5-0	FAC R1
Jack Boothway	3	19-04-47	Lincoln City (h) 4-1	FL D3(N)
Dick Yates	3	20-12-47	Halifax Town (h) 6-3	FL D3(N)
Dick Yates	3	14-01-48	Penrhyn Quarry (a) 6-2	WC R5
Dennis Grainger	3	17-04-48	Tranmere Rovers (h) 6-0	FL D3(N)
Jack Boothway	3	27-08-49	Lincoln City (h) 4-0	FL D3(N)
Ron Wynn	3	11-02-50	Rochdale (a) 3-0	FL D3(N)
Billy Tunnicliffe	3	26-09-51	Chester (h) 3-2	FL D3(N)
Eric Hope	3	26-01-52	Rochdale (a) 5-1	FL D3(N)
Tommy Tilston	3	06-09-52	Stockport Cty. (h) 5-2	FL D3(N)
Tommy Tilston	3	12-09-53	Grimsby Town (h) 4-0	FL D3(N)
Tommy Bannan	3	24-10-53	Workington (h) 8-0	FL D3(N)
Eric Betts	3	24-10-53	Workington (h) 8-0	FL D3(N)
Eric Betts	3	24-08-55	Bradford City (a) 3-4	FL D3(N)
Ron Hewitt	3	15-09-56	Barrow (h) 5-0	FL D3(N)
Bernard Evans	3	29-12-56	Bradford Pk. Ave. (a) 4-0	FL D3(N)
Brian Griffiths	3	12-01-57	Darlington (h) 5-0	FL D3(N)
Ron Hewitt	3	13-04-57	Carlisle United (h) 6-4	FL D3(N)
Peter Thompson	3	19-04-57	Crewe Alex. (h) 5-0	FL D3(N)
Grenville Jones	3	28-09-57	Hull City (h) 6-0	FL D3(N)
Tommy Bannan	3	29-01-58	Flint Town Utd. (h) 7-0	WC R5
Barry Smith	3	29-01-58	Flint Town Utd. (h) 7-0	WC R5
Don Weston	3	04-03-59	Merthyr Tydfil (h) 5-0	WC R6r
Bernard Evans	3	29-04-59	Hull City (h) 5-1	FL D3
Bernard Evans	3	27-01-60	Llandudno (h) 4-0	WC R5
Mike Metcalf	3	14-12-60	Blackburn Rov. (h) 3-1	LC R3r
Mike Metcalf	3	18-10-61	Doncaster Rov. (h) 3-1	FL D4
Wyn Davies	3	03-03-62	Hartlepool Utd. (h) 10-1	FL D4
Ron Barnes	3	03-03-62	Hartlepool Utd. (h) 10-1	FL D4
Roy Ambler	3	03-03-62	Hartlepool Utd. (h) 10-1	FL D4
Ernie Phythian	3	06-10-62	Millwall (h) 5-1	FL D3
Mike Metcalf	3	21-09-63	Millwall (a) 4-1	FL D3
Ernie Phythian	3	07-03-64	Notts County (h) 4-0	FL D3
Martyn King	3	12-10-64	Aldershot (h) 4-0	FL D4
Sammy McMillan	3	02-10-65	Aldershot (h) 4-0	FL D4
Martyn King	3	31-11-65	South Liverpool (h) 4-1	FAC R1
Keith Webber	3	08-01-66	Barnsley (h) 6-3	FL D4
Keith Webber	3	14-01-66	Stockport Cty. (a) 4-2	FL D4
Sammy McMillan	3	15-08-66	Bradford Pk. Ave. (h) 6-0	FL D4
Mickey Evans	3	28-01-67	Rhyl (h) 5-0	WC R5
Ray Smith	3	16-10-67	Southend United (h) 4-1	FL D4
Ray Smith	3	18-03-69	Exeter City (a) 3-5	FL D4
Albert Kinsey	3	06-09-69	York City (h) 4-0	FL D4
Ray Smith	3	06-10-69	Colchester Utd. (h) 4-2	FL D4
Albert Kinsey	3	06-04-70	Bradford Pk. Ave. (h) 4-0	FL D4
David Smallman	3	22-11-72	Darlington (h) 5-0	FAC R1r
Brian Tinnion	3	08-09-73	Southport (h) 3-2	FL D3
Arfon Griffiths	3	22-12-73	Hereford Utd. (h) 5-0	FL D3
Geoff Davies	3	23-01-74	Blaenau Ffestiniog (h) 6-3	WC R4
Brian Tinnion	3	20-04-74	Plymouth Argyle (h) 5-2	FL D3
Mickey Thomas	3	28-09-74	Plymouth Argyle (h) 5-1	FL D3
David Smallman	3	08-03-75	Aldershot (h) 4-0	FL D3
Stuart Lee	3	12-01-76	Llanidloes (h) 8-0	WC R4
Billy Ashcroft	4	11-09-76	Chesterfield (a) 6-0	FL D3
Bobby Shinton	3	20-11-76	Gateshead (h) 6-0	FAC R1
Graham Whittle	3	27-12-76	Chester (h) 4-2	FL D3
Graham Whittle	4	27-03-78	Carlisle Utd. (a) 4-1	FL D3
Graham Whittle	3	22-04-78	Rotherham Utd. (h) 7-1	FL D3
John Lyons	3	09-12-78	West Ham Utd. (h) 4-3	FL D2
Ian Edwards	3	17-12-79	Connah's Q. Nom. (h) 5-0	WC R4
Mick Vinter	3	05-01-80	Charlton Ath. (h) 6-0	FAC R3
Dixie McNeil	3	18-11-80	Pwllheli (h) 6-0	WC R3
Mick Vinter	3	15-05-82	Rotherham Utd. (h) 3-2	FL D2
David Gregory	3	21-04-84	Tranmere Rov. (h) 5-1	FL D4
David Gregory	3	20-08-85	Rochdale (h) 4-0	LC R1
Andy Edwards	3	15-10-85	Cambridge Utd. (h) 6-2	FL D4
Jim Steel	3	14-10-86	Peterborough Utd. (h) 4-3	FL D4
Kevin Russell	3	22-03-88	Exeter City (h) 3-0	FL D4
Ollie Kearns	3	26-03-88	Newport County (h) 4-1	FL D4
Ollie Kearns	4	16-11-88	Lex XI (h) 8-0	WC R3
Kevin Russell	3	27-03-89	Burnley (h) 4-2	FL D4
Steve Watkin	3	16-11-91	Winsford Town (h) 5-2	FAC R1
Gary Bennett	3	10-10-92	Bury (h) 4-2	FL D4
Gary Bennett	3	14-09-93	Hull City (h) 3-0	FL D2
Gary Bennett	3	27-10-93	Carno (h) 6-1	WC R3
Gary Bennett	3	05-11-94	Wycombe W. (h) 4-1	FL D2
Gary Bennett	3	29-11-94	Bradford City (h) 6-1	AWS R2
Gary Bennett	3	14-01-95	Leyton Orient (h) 4-1	FL D2
Karl Connolly	3	30-09-95	Swindon Town (h) 4-3	FL D2
Karl Connolly	3	20-09-97	Luton Town (a) 5-2	FL D2
Karl Connolly	3	02-01-99	Scunthorpe Utd (h) 4-3	FAC R3

Wrexham's Goalscoring Substitutes Since 1965

Player	Goals	Date	Opponents & Score	Competition
Peter Wall	1	19-02-66	Doncaster R. (h) 4-3	FL D4
Haydn Jones	1	26-02-66	Southport (a) 2-2	FL D4
Geoff Lloyd	1	26-11-66	Chesterfield (h) 3-2	FAC R1
Mickey Evans	1	06-05-67	Rochdale (a) 3-1	FL D4
Steve Stacey	1	16-03-68	Aldershot (h) 2-1	FL D4
Mickey Evans	1	27-04-68	Notts County (h) 2-0	FL D4
Ray Charnley	1	07-12-68	Chesterfield (a) 1-2	FAC R2
Stuart Mason	1	02-09-69	Charlton Athletic (a) 2-0	FLC R2
Steve Ingle	1	28-03-70	Crewe Alexandra (h) 2-2	FL D4
Ray Smith	1	26-12-70	Port Vale (a) 3-0	FL D3
Billy Ashcroft	1	22-02-71	Bradford City (h) 2-0	FL D3
Albert Kinsey	1	11-09-71	York City (a) 1-1	FL D3
Ray Smith	1	08-03-72	Barnsley (a) 1-2	FL D3
Roger Mostyn	1	11-04-72	Swansea City (a) 2-0	FL D3
Billy Ashcroft	1	10-10-73	Norwich City (a) 2-6	FLC R2
Graham Whittle	2	22-12-73	Hereford United (h) 5-0	FL D3
Billy Ashcroft	1	04-01-75	Charlton Ath. (a) 1-1	FL D3
John Lyons	1	26-04-75	Swindon Town (h) 1-2	FL D3
John Lyons	1	22-08-78	Fulham (a) 1-0	FL D2
John Lyons	1	30-09-78	Cardiff City (h) 1-2	FL D2
Graham Whittle	1	28-02-79	Sheffield United (h) 4-0	FL D2
Steve Buxton	1	10-03-79	Blackburn Rovers (h) 2-1	FL D2
John Lyons	1	14-04-79	Preston N. E. (h) 2-1	FL D2
Graham Whittle	1	17-05-79	Millwall (a) 2-2	FL D2
Graham Whittle	1	20-10-79	Shrewsbury T. (a) 1-3	FL D2
John Muldoon	1	02-10-82	Bournemouth (h) 1-0	FL D3
Andy Edwards	1	06-09-83	Rochdale (h) 5-1	FL D4
Steve Buxton	1	25-02-84	Bury (h) 3-0	FL D4
John Muldoon	1	28-04-84	Northampton T. (a) 3-3	Fl D4
Vernon Keep	1	29-01-85	Wigan Ath. (h) 2-2	FRT
Steve Buxton	2	11-03-86	Rochdale (h) 2-0	FL D4
Steve Buxton	1	25-03-86	Aldershot (h) 4-1	FL D4
Steve Buxton	1	24-09-86	Portsmouth (h) 1-2	FLC R2
Steve Buxton	1	05-11-86	Real Zaragoza (h) 2-2	ECWC R2
Steve Massey	2	25-11-86	Tranmere R. (h) 6-1	FRT
James Slater	1	24.11.87	Ruthin Town (h) 3-0	WC R3
Steve Massey	1	27-02-88	Leyton Orient (a) 1-2	FL D4
Geoff Hunter	1	16-09-88	Colchester Utd. (h) 2-2	FL D4
Graham Cooper	1	19-11-88	Runcorn (h) 2-2	FAC R1
Ollie Kearns	1	26.12.88	Burnley (a) 3-1	FL D4
Chris Armstrong	1	22-09-90	Darlington (h) 1-1	FL D4
David O'Gorman	1	09-01-91	Ammanford T. (a) 5-0	WC R4
Geoff Hunter	1	19-01-91	Peterborough Utd. (h) 2-2	FL D4
Gareth Owen	1	19-02-91	Stroud (a) 2-1	WC R5
Chris Armstrong	1	19-02-91	Stroud (a) 2-1	WC R5
Steve Watkin	1	21-09-91	York City (a) 2-2	FL D4
Gordon Davies	1	29-10-91	Bangor City (h) 3-2	WC R3
Lee Jones	1	29-10-91	Bangor City (h) 3-2	WC R3
Lee Jones	1	25-01-92	West Ham Utd. (a) 2-2	FAC R1
Gareth Owen	1	15-02-92	Halifax Town (h) 2-0	FL D4
Lee Jones	1	02-05-92	Halifax Town (h) 2-0	FL D4
John Paskin	1	02-05-92	Burnley (a) 2-1	FL D4
John Paskin	1	17-10-92	Carlisle Utd. (a) 2-0	FL D4
John Paskin	2	23-01-93	Walsall (h) 3-1	FL D4
John Paskin	1	20-02-93	Gillingham (h) 2-0	FL D4
John Paskin	1	24-04-93	Carlisle Utd. (h) 3-1	FL D4
John Paskin	1	17-08-93	Crewe Alex. (a) 1-0	CCC R1
John Paskin	1	21-09-93	Nottingham F. (h) 3-3	CCC R2
David Brammer	1	12-02-94	Huddersfield T. (h)	FL D2
Gareth Owen	1	19-03-94	Barnet (a) 2-1	FL D2
David Brammer	1	16-04-94	Brighton & Hove (h) 1-3	FL D2
Jonathan Cross	1	24-09-95	Blackpool (a) 1-2	FL D2
Steve Watkin	1	12-11-94	Stockport Cty. (h) 1-0	FAC R1
Jonathan Cross	1	28-01-95	Manchester Utd. (a) 2-5	FAC R4
Steve Watkin	1	02-09-95	Bristol Rovers (a) 2-1	FL D2
Steve Watkin	1	05-09-95	Stockport Cty. (h) 2-2	CCC R1
Steve Watkin	2	18-11-95	Rotherham Utd. (h) 7-0	FL D2
Steve Morris	1	30-03-96	York City (h) 2-3	FL D2
Craig Skinner	1	03-09-96	Huddersfield T. (h) 1-2	CCC R1
Karl Connolly	1	19-10-96	Bournemouth (h) 2-0	FL D2
Gareth Owen	1	02-11-96	Chesterfield (h) 3-2	FL D2
Steve Watkin	1	07-12-96	Scunthorpe Utd. (h) 2-2	FAC R2
Steve Watkin	1	17-12-96	Scunthorpe Utd. (a) 3-2	FAC R2r
Kevin Russell	1	25-01-97	West Ham Utd. (a) 1-0	FAC R3r
Steve Morris	1	15-04-97	Bristol City (a) 1-2	FL D2
Steve Watkin	1	13-09-97	Bristol City (h) 2-1	FL D2
Martyn Chalk	1	25-10-97	Preston N. E. (a) 1-0	FL D2
Neil Wainwright	1	28-12-97	Blackpool (a) 2-1	FL D2
Martyn Chalk	1	20-01-98	Merthyr Tydfil (a) 2-0	WIC
Mark Wilson	1	24-02-98	Burnley (a) 2-1	FL D2
Karl Connolly	1	07-03-98	Carlisle United (h) 2-2	FL D2
Karl Connolly	1	02-05-98	Southend United (a) 3-1	FL D2
Gareth Owen	1	17-05-98	Cardiff City (h) 2-1	WIC Final
Neil Roberts	1	15-08-98	Colchester Utd. (h) 2-4	FL D2
Karl Connolly	1	25-08-98	Barry Town (a) 2-3	WPC
Jake Edwards	1	09-12-98	Macclesfield Town (a) 1-0	AWS R1
Robin Gibson	1	02-03-99	Northampton Town (h) 2-0	FL D2
Jake Edwards	1	23-03-99	Wigan Athletic (h) 2-3	AWS NF
Andy Morrell	1	10-05-99	Cardiff City (a) 1-2	WPC SF

The Robins' Full Internationals

* = Substitute x = goalscorer Numbers in brackets are total number of caps achieved which include other clubs

Tommy Bamford (Wales)
5 appearances (5)

25.10.1930	Scotland	1-1	Glasgow x
22.11.1930	England	0-4	Wrexham
22.04.1931	Ireland	3-2	Wrexham
05.12.1931	Ireland	0-4	Belfast
25.05.1933	France	1-1	Paris

Horace Blew (Wales)
22 appearances (22)

04.03.1899	Ireland	0-1	Belfast
18.03.1899	Scotland	0-6	Wrexham
20.03.1899	England	0-4	Bristol
22.02.1902	Ireland	0-3	Cardiff
15.03.1902	Scotland	1-5	Greenock
02.03.1903	England	1-2	Portsmouth
09.03.1903	Scotland	0-1	Cardiff
29.02.1904	England	2-2	Wrexham
12.03.1904	Scotland	1-1	Dundee
21.03.1904	Ireland	0-1	Bangor
06.03.1905	Scotland	3-1	Wrexham
08.04.1905	Ireland	2-2	Belfast
03.03.1906	Scotland	2-0	Edinburgh
19.03.1906	England	0-1	Cardiff
02.04.1906	Ireland	4-4	Wrexham
04.03.1907	Scotland	1-0	Wrexham
07.03.1908	Scotland	1-2	Dundee
16.03.1908	England	1-7	Wrexham
11.04.1908	Ireland	0-1	Aberdare
01.03.1909	Scotland	3-2	Wrexham
15.03.1909	England	0-2	Nottingham
14.03.1910	England	0-1	Cardiff

Tom Boden (Wales)
1 appearance (1)

15.03.1880	England	2-3	Wrexham

Tom Burke (Wales)
5 appearances (8)

03.02.1883	England	0-5	Kennington Oval
29.03.1884	Scotland	1-4	Glasgow
14.03.1885	England	1-1	Blackburn
23.03.1885	Scotland	1-8	Wrexham
11.04.1885	Ireland	8-2	Belfast x

Les Cartwright (Wales)
2 appearances (7)

18.04.1978	Iran	1-0	Tehran*
25.10.1978	Malta	7-0	Wrexham

Wynne Crompton (Wales)
3 appearances (3)

25.10.1930	Scotland	1-1	Glasgow
22.11.1930	England	0-4	Wrexham
22.04.1931	Ireland	3-2	Wrexham

Edwin Cross (Wales)
2 appearances (2)

25.03.1876	Scotland	0-4	Glasgow
05.03.1877	Scotland	0-2	Wrexham

Alf Davies (Wales)
2 appearances (2)

25.03.1876	Scotland	0-4	Glasgow
05.03.1877	Scotland	0-2	Wrexham

Alfred Owen Davies (Wales)
1 appearance (9)

15.04.1889	Scotland	0-0	Wrexham

Dai Davies (Wales)
28 appearances (52)

12.10.1977	Scotland	0-4	Anfield, Liverpool
16.11.1977	Czechoslovakia	0-1	Prague
14.12.1977	West Germany	1-1	Dortmund
18.04.1978	Iran	1-0	Tehran
13.05.1978	England	1-3	Cardiff
17.05.1978	Scotland	1-1	Glasgow
19.05.1978	Northern Ireland	1-0	Wrexham
25.10.1978	Malta	7-0	Wrexham
29.11.1978	Turkey	1-0	Wrexham
02.05.1979	West Germany	0-2	Wrexham
19.05.1979	Scotland	3-0	Cardiff
23.05.1979	England	0-0	Wembley
25.05.1979	Northern Ireland	1-1	Belfast
02.06.1979	Malta	2-0	Valletta
11.09.1979	Rep. of Ireland	2-1	Swansea
17.10.1979	West Germany	1-5	Cologne
21.11.1979	Turkey	0-1	Izmir
17.05.1980	England	4-1	Wrexham
21.05.1980	Scotland	0-1	Glasgow
23.05.1980	Northern Ireland	0-1	Cardiff
02.06.1980	Iceland	4-0	Reykjavik
15.10.1980	Turkey	4-0	Cardiff
19.11.1980	Czechoslovakia	1-0	Cardiff
24.02.1981	Rep. of Ireland	3-1	Dublin
25.03.1981	Turkey	1-0	Ankara
16.05.1981	Scotland	2-0	Swansea
20.05.1981	England	0-0	Wembley
30.05.1981	Russia	0-0	Wrexham

Gareth Davies (Wales)
3 appearances (3)

18.04.1978	Iran	1-0	Tehran
13.05.1978	England	1-3	Cardiff
19.05.1978	Northern Ireland	1-0	Wrexham

Revd. Hywel Davies (Wales)
1 appearance (1)

04.02.1928	Ireland	2-1	Belfast

James Davies (Wales)
1 appearance (1)

23.03.1878	Scotland	0-9	Glasgow

John Davies (Wales)
1 appearance (1)

07.04.1878	Scotland	0-3	Wrexham

Llew Davies (Wales)
11 appearances (13)

23.02.1907	Ireland	3-2	Belfast
05.03.1910	Scotland	0-1	Kilmarnock
14.03.1910	England	0-1	Cardiff
11.04.1910	Ireland	4-1	Wrexham
02.03.1912	Scotland	0-1	Edinburgh
11.03.1912	England	0-2	Wrexham
23.04.1912	Ireland	2-3	Cardiff
18.01.1913	Ireland	1-0	Belfast
03.03.1913	Scotland	0-0	Wrexham
17.03.1913	England	3-4	Bristol
19.01.1914	Ireland	1-2	Wrexham

Oswald Davies (Wales)
1 appearance (1)

22.03.1890	Scotland	0-5	Paisley

Robert Davies (Wales)
3 appearances (3)

17.03.1883	Ireland	1-1	Belfast
09.02.1884	Ireland	6-0	Wrexham
11.04.1885	Ireland	8-2	Belfast

Robert Davies (Wales)
2 appearances (2)

27.02.1892	Ireland	1-1	Bangor
05.05.1892	England	0-2	Wrexham

Walter Davies (Wales)
1 appearance (1)

09.02.1884	Ireland	6-0	Wrexham

William Davies (Wales)
2 appearances (11)

28.03.1903	Ireland	0-2	Belfast
08.04.1905	Ireland	2-2	Belfast

Charles Edwards (Wales)
1 appearance (1)

23.03.1878	Scotland	0-9	Glasgow

Ian Edwards (Wales)
1 appearance (4)

21.11.1979	Turkey	0-1	Izmir*

Robert Ernest Evans (Wales)
2 appearances (10)

03.03.1906	Scotland	2-0	Edinburgh
19.03.1906	England	0-1	Cardiff

Robert Owen Evans (Wales)
4 appearances (10)

22.02.1902	Ireland	0-3	Cardiff
02.03.1903	England	1-2	Portsmouth
09.03.1903	Scotland	0-1	Cardiff
28.03.1903	Ireland	0-2	Belfast

John Arthur Eyton-Jones (Wales)
4 appearances (4)

17.03.1883	Ireland	1-1	Belfast
09.02.1884	Ireland	6-0	Wrexham
17.03.1884	England	0-4	Wrexham
29.03.1884	Scotland	1-4	Glasgow

Dick Finnegan (Wales)
1 appearance (1)

01.02.1930	Ireland	0-7	Belfast

Sam Gillam (Wales)
2 appearances (5)

27.04.1889	Ireland	3-1	Belfast
08.02.1890	Ireland	5-2	Shrewsbury

George Glascodine (Wales)
1 appearance (1)

18.01.1879	England	1-2	Kennington Oval

George Godding (Wales)
2 appearances (2)

17.03.1923	Scotland	0-2	Glasgow
14.04.1923	Ireland	0-3	Wrexham

Arfon Griffiths (Wales)
17 appearances (17)

21.04.1971	Czechoslovakia	1-3	Swansea*
04.09.1974	Austria	1-2	Vienna x
30.10.1974	Hungary	2-0	Cardiff x
20.11.1974	Luxembourg	5-0	Swansea x
16.04.1975	Hungary	2-1	Budapest
01.05.1975	Luxembourg	3-1	Luxembourg
21.05.1975	England	2-2	Wembley x
23.05.1975	Northern Ireland	0-1	Belfast
19.11.1975	Austria	1-0	Wrexham x
24.03.1976	England	1-2	Wrexham
24.04.1976	Yugoslavia	0-2	Zagreb
06.05.1976	Scotland	1-3	Glasgow x
08.05.1976	England	0-1	Cardiff*
14.05.1976	Northern Ireland	1-0	Swansea
22.05.1976	Yugoslavia	1-1	Cardiff
06.10.1976	West Germany	0-2	Cardiff
17.11.1976	Scotland	0-1	Glasgow

Llewelyn Griffiths (Wales)
1 appearance (1)

15.03.1902	Scotland	0-1	Greenock

Billy Harrison (Wales)
5 appearances (5)

20.03.1899	England	0-4	Bristol
03.02.1900	Scotland	2-5	Aberdeen
24.02.1900	Ireland	2-0	Llandudno
26.03.1900	England	1-1	Cardiff
23.03.1901	Ireland	1-0	Belfast

Abel Hayes (Wales)
2 appearances (2)

08.02.1890	Ireland	5-2	Shrewsbury
24.02.1894	Ireland	4-1	Swansea

Tom Hewitt (Wales)
3 appearances (8)

The Robins' Full Internationals (cont.)

28.01.1911	Ireland	2-1	Belfast
06.03.1911	Scotland	2-2	Cardiff
13.03.1911	England	0-3	Millwall

Ted Hughes (Wales)
4 appearances (16)

03.03.1906	Scotland	2-0	Edinburgh
02.03.1912	Scotland	0-1	Edinburgh
11.03.1912	England	0-2	Wrexham
23.04.1912	Ireland	2-3	Cardiff

Barry Hunter (Northern Ireland)
6 appearances (11)

26.04.1995	Latvia	1-0	Riga
03.09.1995	Portugal	1-1	Opporto
11.10.1995	Liechtenstein	4-0	Eschen
15.11.1995	Austria	5-3	Belfast
24.04.1996	Sweden	1-2	Belfast
29.05.1996	Germany	1-1	Belfast

Gordon Jones (Wales)
2 appearances (2)

23.02.1907	Ireland	3-2	Belfast
04.03.1907	Scotland	1-0	Wrexham

James Jones (Wales)
1 appearance (1)

18.04.1925	Ireland	0-0	Wrexham

Joey Jones (Wales)
29 appearances (72)

25.10.1978	Malta	7-0	Wrexham
29.11.1978	Turkey	1-0	Wrexham
02.05.1979	West Germany	0-2	Wrexham
19.05.1979	Scotland	3-0	Cardiff
23.05.1979	England	0-0	Wembley
25.05.1979	Northern Ireland	1-1	Belfast
02.06.1979	Malta	2-0	Valletta
11.09.1979	Rep. of Ireland	2-1	Swansea
17.10.1979	West Germany	1-5	Cologne
21.11.1979	Turkey	0-1	Izmir
17.05.1980	England	4-1	Wrexham
21.05.1980	Scotland	0-1	Glasgow
23.05.1980	Northern Ireland	0-1	Cardiff
02.06.1980	Iceland	4-0	Reykjavik
15.10.1980	Turkey	4-0	Cardiff
24.02.1981	Rep. of Ireland	3-1	Dublin
25.03.1981	Turkey	1-0	Ankara
16.05.1981	Scotland	2-0	Swansea
20.05.1981	England	0-0	Wembley
30.05.1981	Russia	0-0	Wrexham
09.09.1981	Czechoslovakia	0-2	Prague
14.10.1981	Iceland	2-2	Swansea
18.11.1981	Russia	0-3	Tblisi
24.03.1982	Spain	1-1	Valencia
27.04.1982	England	0-1	Cardiff
24.05.1982	Scotland	0-1	Glasgow
27.05.1982	Northern Ireland	3-0	Wrexham
02.06.1982	France	1-0	Toulouse
22.09.1982	Norway	1-0	Swansea

Sam Jones (Wales)
1 appearance (1)

12.03.1887	Ireland	1-4	Belfast

Samuel Jones (Wales)
2 appearances (6)

18.03.1893	Scotland	0-8	Wrexham
05.04.1893	Ireland	3-4	Belfast

Fred Kelly (Wales)
2 appearances (3)

04.03.1899	Ireland	0-1	Belfast
18.03.1899	Scotland	0-6	Wrexham

Arthur Lea (Wales)
4 appearances (4)

23.02.1889	England	1-4	Stoke
07.02.1891	Ireland	2-7	Belfast
21.03.1891	Scotland	3-4	Wrexham
05.04.1893	Ireland	3-4	Belfast

Ben Lewis (Wales)
7 appearances (10)

27.02.1892	Ireland	1-1	Bangor x
05.05.1892	England	0-2	Wrexham
26.03.1892	Scotland	1-6	Edinburgh x
13.03.1893	England	0-6	Stoke
24.02.1894	Ireland	4-1	Swansea
12.03.1894	England	1-5	Wrexham
24.03.1894	Scotland	2-5	Kilmarnock

Thomas Lewis (Wales)
2 appearances (2)

26.02.1881	England	1-0	Blackburn
14.03.1881	Scotland	1-5	Wrexham

Brian Lloyd (Wales)
3 appearances (3)

19.11.1975	Austria	1-0	Wrexham
24.03.1976	England	1-2	Wrexham
06.05.1976	Scotland	1-3	Glasgow

Jimmy Lloyd (Wales)
1 appearance (2)

07.04.1879	Scotland	0-3	Wrexham

Albert Lumberg (Wales)
3 appearances (4)

02.02.1929	Ireland	2-2	Wrexham
26.10.1929	Scotland	2-4	Cardiff
20.10.1929	England	0-6	Stamford Bridge

Andy Marriott (Wales)
4 appearances (4)

24.04.1996	Switzerland	0-2	Lugano
27.05.1997	Scotland	1-0	Kilmarnock
11.10.1997	Belgium	2-3	Brussels
11.11.1997	Brazil	0-3	Brasilia*
06.03.1998	Tunisia	0-4	Tunis

Tommy Matthias (Wales)
12 appearances (12)

28.02.1914	Scotland	0-0	Glasgow
16.03.1914	England	0-2	Cardiff
14.02.1920	Ireland	2-2	Belfast
26.02.1920	Scotland	1-1	Cardiff
15.03.1920	England	2-1	Highbury
12.02.1921	Scotland	1-2	Aberdeen
14.03.1921	England	0-0	Cardiff
09.04.1921	Ireland	2-1	Swansea
04.02.1922	Scotland	2-1	Wrexham
13.03.1922	England	0-1	Liverpool
01.04.1922	Ireland	1-1	Belfast
17.03.1923	Scotland	0-2	Glasgow

Albert Mays (Wales)
1 appearance (1)

02.02.1929	Ireland	2-2	Wrexham x

Tom McCarthy (Wales)
1 appearance (1)

27.04.1889	Ireland	3-1	Belfast

Tracey Morgan (Wales)
1 appearance (1)

08.04.1905	Ireland	2-2	Belfast

Joe Owens (Wales)
1 appearance (1)

15.03.1902	Scotland	1-5	Greenock

Harry Phoenix (Wales)
1 appearance (1)

25.03.1882	Scotland	0-5	Glasgow

George Poland (Wales)
2 appearances (2)

15.03.1939	Ireland	3-1	Wrexham
20.05.1939	France	1-2	Paris

David Powell (Wales)
1 appearance (11)

08.05.1968	West Germany	1-1	Cardiff

Haydn Price (Wales)
3 appearances (5)

01.03.1909	Scotland	3-2	Wrexham
15.03.1909	England	0-2	Nottingham
20.03.1909	Ireland	3-2	Belfast

John Price (Wales)
12 appearances (12)

05.03.1877	Scotland	0-2	Wrexham
23.03.1878	Scotland	0-9	Glasgow
18.01.1879	England	1-2	Kennington Oval
15.03.1880	England	2-3	Wrexham
27.03.1880	Scotland	1-5	Glasgow
26.02.1881	England	1-0	Blackburn
14.03.1881	Scotland	1-5	Wrexham
25.02.1882	Ireland	7-1	Wrexham xxxx
13.03.1882	England	5-3	Wrexham
25.03.1882	Scotland	0-5	Glasgow
12.03.1883	Scotland	0-3	Wrexham
17.03.1883	Ireland	1-1	Belfast

Harry Pugh (Wales)
4 appearances (7)

29.02.1896	Ireland	6-1	Wrexham x
21.03.1896	Scotland	0-4	Dundee
06.03.1897	Ireland	3-4	Belfast
20.03.1897	Scotland	2-2	Wrexham x

James Roberts (Wales)
2 appearances (2)

18.01.1913	Ireland	1-0	Belfast x
03.03.1913	Scotland	0-0	Wrexham

Bob Roberts (Wales)
2 appearances (2)

27.02.1886	Ireland	5-0	Wrexham
12.03.1887	Ireland	1-4	Belfast

Bill Roberts (Wales)
4 appearances (4)

27.02.1886	Ireland	5-0	Wrexham x
29.03.1886	England	1-3	Wrexham
10.04.1886	Scotland	1-4	Glasgow
12.03.1887	Ireland	1-4	Belfast

Joe Rogers (Wales)
3 appearances (3)

29.02.1896	Ireland	6-1	Wrexham
16.03.1896	England	1-9	Cardiff
21.03.1896	Scotland	0-4	Dundee

Billie Rogers (Wales)
2 appearances (2)

25.10.1930	Scotland	1-1	Glasgow
22.11.1930	England	0-4	Wrexham

Herbert Sissons (Wales)
3 appearances (3)

11.04.1885	Ireland	8-2	Belfast xxx
27.02.1886	Ireland	5-0	Wrexham x
10.04.1886	Scotland	1-4	Glasgow

David Smallman (Wales)
3 appearances (7)

11.05.1874	England	0-2	Cardiff*
14.05.1874	Scotland	0-2	Glasgow*
18.05.1974	Northern Ireland	1-0	Wrexham x

John Taylor (Wales)
1 appearance (1)

28.03.1898	England	0-3	Wrexham

George Thomas (Wales)
2 appearances (2)

14.03.1885	England	1-1	Blackburn
23.03.1885	Scotland	1-8	Wrexham

Mickey Thomas (Wales)
12 appearances (51)

06.10.1976	West Germany	0-2	Cardiff
17.11.1976	Scotland	0-1	Glasgow
30.03.1977	Czechoslovakia	3-0	Wrexham*

The Robins' Full Internationals (cont.)

28.05.1977	Scotland	0-0	Wrexham*
03.06.1977	Northern Ireland	1-1	Belfast*
20.09.1977	Kuwait	0-0	Kuwait City*
12.10.1977	Scotland	0-2	Anfield, Liverpool
16.11.1977	Czechoslovakia	0-1	Prague
18.04.1978	Iran	1-0	Tehran
13.05.1978	England	1-3	Cardiff
19.05.1978	Northern Ireland	1-0	Wrexham*
25.10.1978	Malta	7-0	Wrexham x

Harry Trainer (Wales)
3 appearances (3)

16.03.1895	Ireland	1-4	Belfast xx
18.03.1895	England	1-4	Queens Club, Kensington
23.03.1895	Scotland	2-2	Wrexham

Joe Turner (Wales)
1 appearance (1)

05.05.1892	England	0-2	Wrexham

Dick Turner (Wales)
2 appearances (2)

07.02.1891	Ireland	2-7	Belfast
07.03.1891	England	1-4	Sunderland

Bill Turner (Wales)
5 appearances (5)

26.02.1887	England	0-4	Kennington Oval
12.03.1887	Ireland	1-4	Belfast
22.03.1890	Scotland	0-5	Paisley
07.03.1891	England	1-4	Sunderland
21.03.1891	Scotland	3-4	Wrexham

Joby Wilding (Wales)
6 appearances (9)

14.03.1885	England	1-1	Blackburn x
23.03.1885	Scotland	1-8	Wrexham
11.04.1885	Ireland	8-2	Belfast
20.03.1909	Ireland	5-0	Wrexham x
29.03.1886	England	1-3	Wrexham
26.03.1892	Scotland	1-6	Edinburgh

George Williams (Wales)
1 appearance (1)

23.02.1907	Ireland	3-2	Belfast

Jack Williams (Wales)
1 appearance (1)

21.05.1939	France	1-2	Paris

Leslie Williams (Wales)
1 appearances (1)

22.11.1930	England	0-4	Wrexham

George Wynn (Wales)
3 appearances (11)

01.03.1909	Scotland	3-2	Wrexham
15.03.1909	England	0-2	Nottingham
20.03.1909	Ireland	3-2	Belfast

'B' International Appearances by Wrexham Players

Phil Hardy (Republic of Ireland)
1 appearance (1)

09.02.99	F.A.I National League XI	4-3	Bray

Barry Hunter (Northern Ireland)
1 appearance (2)

10.05.93	England	2-4	Sheffield *

Gareth Owen (Wales)
1 appearance (1)

18.03.92	Canada Olympic XI	1-1	Wrexham

Neil Roberts (Wales)
1 appearance (1)

09.02.99	Northern Ireland	1-0	Wrexham *

Steve Watkin (Wales)
2 appearances (2)

18.03.92	Canada Olympic XI	1-1	Wrexham
02.02.94	Scotland	2-1	Wrexham

Under-23 International Appearances by Wrexham Players

Gareth Davies (Wales)
4 appearances (4)

01.10.69	England	0-2	Bristol
14.01.70	Scotland	1-1	Aberdeen
02.12.70	England	0-0	Wrexham
13.01.71	Scotland	1-0	Swansea

Mickey Evans (Wales)
2 appearances (2)

22.02.67 Northern Ireland 1-2 Belfast
(Match abandoned after 73 minutes - waterlogged)

02.12.70	England	0-0	Wrexham

Alan Fox (Wales)
1 appearance (1)

25.11.59	Scotland	1-1	Wrexham

Arfon Griffiths (Wales)
1 appearance (4)

04.12.63	Scotland	3-1	Wrexham

Joey Jones (Wales)
3 appearances (4)

27.02.74	Scotland	0-3	Aberdeen
21.01.75	England	0-2	Wrexham
25.02.75	Scotland	2-0	Swansea

Alec Lucas (Wales)
1 appearance (1)

30.11.66	Scotland	0-6	Wrexham

David Powell (Wales)
4 appearances (4)

01.11.67	England	1-2	Swansea
22.02.67	Northern Ireland	1-2	Belfast
02.10.68	England	1-3	Wrexham
20.03.68	Northern Ireland	0-1	Cardiff

Ron Roberts (Wales)
2 appearances (2)

06.12.61	Scotland	0-0	Wrexham
07.02.62	Northern Ireland	0-0	Belfast

David Smallman (Wales)
4 appearances (5)

29.11.72	England	0-2	Wrexham
14.03.73	Scotland	1-2	Swansea
27.02.74	Scotland	0-3	Aberdeen
21.01.75	England	0-2	Wrexham

Mickey Thomas (Wales)
1 appearances (1)

04.02.76	Scotland	2-3	Wrexham

Under-21 International Appearances by Wrexham Players

Deryn Brace (Wales)
5 appearances (5)

15.11.94	Georgia	2-1	Tbilisi
13.12.94	Bulgaria	1-1	Swansea
28.03.95	Bulgaria	1-3	Plovdiv
30.08.96	San Marino	4-0	Barry
04.10.96	Holland	0-2	Cardiff

Wayne Cegielski (Wales)
1 appearances (1)

09.02.77	Scotland	2-3	Edinburgh*

Kieron Durkan (Republic of Ireland)
3 appearances (3)

27.03.95	England	0-2	Dalymount Park
10.06.95	Austria	3-0	home x
10.10.95	Latvia	1-0	home

Phil Hardy (Republic of Ireland)
9 appearances (9)

23.03.93	Germany	0-8	away
26.05.93	Albania	1-1	Tirana
12.10.93	Spain	0-2	home
27.03.95	England	0-2	Dalymount Park
06.09.94	Latvia	1-1	away
25.04.95	Portugal	1-1	Richmond Park
10.06.95	Austria	3-0	home x
10.10.95	Latvia	1-0	home
14.11.95	Portugal	1-3	away

Frank Jones (Wales)
1 appearance (1)

09.09.80	Holland	2-0	Dordrecht

Gareth Owen (Wales)
8 appearances (8)

05.12.90	England	0-0	Tranmere*
30.05.91	Poland	2-1	Warsaw
15.05.92	Romania	3-2	Bucharest
13.10.92	Cyprus	4-2	Larnaca
17.11.92	Belgium	1-3	Kortjrik
30.03.93	Belgium	0-0	Cardiff
13.10.93	Cyprus	6-2	Cwmbran
16.11.93	Romania	1-2	Ebbw Vale

Steve Pugh (Wales)
2 appearances (2)

17.11.92	Belgium	1-3	Kortjrik*
30.03.93	Belgium	0-0	Cardiff*

John Roberts (Wales)
1 appearance (1)

15.12.76	England	0-0	Wolverhampton

Neil Roberts (Wales)
2 appearance (2)

04.09.98	Italy	1-2	Wrexham
17.11.98	Portugal	0-3	Braganca

Mickey Thomas (Wales)
1 appearances (1)

08.02.78	Scotland	1-0	Chester

Scott Williams (Wales)
4 appearances (4)

11.10.94	Moldova	0-1	Kishinev
15.11.94	Georgia	2-1	Tbilisi
13.12.94	Bulgaria	1-1	Swansea
28.03.95	Bulgaria	1-3	Plovdiv

Wrexham Players in Debut Order

Player	Debut	Last Game
1921/22		
Burton, Matt	27-08-21	05-05-23
Cotton, Bill	27-08-21	03-05-24
Edwards, Noel	27-08-21	03-04-26
Ellis, Jack	27-08-21	18-03-22
Foster, Bert	27-08-21	12-11-21
Godding, George	27-08-21	23-01-26
Goode, Bert	27-08-21	03-03-26
Griffiths, Bob	27-08-21	27-08-21
Lloyd, Ernie	27-08-21	06-05-22
Matthias, Tommy	27-08-21	14-03-28
Simpson, Bobby	27-08-21	06-05-22
Leck, Reg	08-09-21	18-02-22
Moorwood, Jack	08-09-21	27-10-23
Roberts, Ed	08-09-21	17-03-23
Settle, John	15-10-21	03-02-23
Regan, Ted	29-10-21	05-05-28
Elvidge, Clive	05-11-21	06-05-22
Blew, Horace	12-11-21	18-12-26
Jones, Gordon	26-11-21	26-11-21
Evans, John	27-12-21	02-01-22
Williams, J.S.	27-12-21	02-01-22
Matthews, Herbert	31-12-21	07-01-22
Northam, Cyril	07-01-22	06-05-22
Jones, Lot	18-03-22	22-04-22
Murphy, Les	18-03-22	18-03-22
1922/23		
Cope, Billy	26-08-22	07-04-23
Jones, Jack	26-08-22	29-03-24
Rowlands, Stan	26-08-22	07-04-23
Savage, George	26-08-22	02-05-25
Sheldon, Alf	26-08-22	05-05-23
Holmes, George	16-09-22	28-04-23
Roberts, Jas	23-09-22	18-11-23
Jackson, Billy	28-10-22	03-05-24
Moffat, Andy	04-11-22	12-03-23
Jones, Percy	06-01-23	06-01-23
Davies, John	10-02-23	10-02-23
Warburton, Richard	10-02-23	24-03-23
Millington, Tom	14-02-23	19-04-24
Finnigan, Dick	17-03-23	05-03-32
Griffiths, Tommy	24-03-23	17-05-41
1923/24		
Boyle, Tom	25-08-23	19-09-23
Harrison, Billy	25-08-23	01-05-24
Jones, Alf	25-08-23	13-04-36
Lenney, Ralph	25-08-23	06-03-24
Pugh, James	25-08-23	14-03-25
Williams, Jesse	22-09-23	03-05-24
Meigh, Tom	20-10-23	03-11-23
Toms, Billy	27-10-23	29-11-24
Matthews, Billy	03-11-23	25-04-25
Houston, Billy	22-12-23	12-04-24
Williams, Frank	22-12-23	24-04-26
Hughes, Arthur	09-02-24	23-02-24
Robinson, Billy	09-02-24	09-02-24
Williams, Bob	09-02-24	23-02-24
Bird, Jesse	21-04-24	08-11-24
1924/25		
Longmuir, Archie	30-08-24	26-04-30
Lovelady, Eddie	30-08-24	15-11-24
Vaughan, Billy	30-08-24	08-11-24
Howard, Fred	30-08-24	01-10-24
Hodgkinson, Bob	01-10-24	02-05-27
Jones, Frank	25-10-24	19-03-27
Nock, Jack	15-11-24	01-05-26
Jones, James	22-11-24	13-03-26
Davies, Hywel	06-12-24	12-11-27
Miles, Bob	13-12-24	03-01-25
Pitt, Howard	26-12-24	17-04-26
Lumberg, Albert	01-01-25	03-05-30
Large, Bert	17-01-25	17-01-25
Connell, Bill	21-02-25	28-03-25
Davies, Johnathan	28-03-25	28-03-25
Warburton, John	10-04-25	10-04-25
Mathias, Albert	02-05-25	02-05-25
1925/26		
Bailey, Rowland	29-08-25	17-10-25
Beevor, Alfred	29-08-25	08-10-27
Lyons, James	29-08-25	01-05-26
Parker, Tom	29-08-25	01-05-26
Wilkinson, Algernon	29-08-25	01-05-26
Holland, Jack	05-09-25	05-12-25
Bennett, Ted	16-09-25	01-05-26
Weaver, Frank	03-10-25	03-10-25
Roberts, Frank	28-11-25	24-04-26
Keetley, Joe	05-12-25	09-01-26
Williams, Eric	17-04-26	17-04-26
Lawrence, Eddie	24-04-26	05-05-28
Brown, Bill	28-04-26	28-04-26
1926/27		
Appleyard, George	28-08-26	11-09-26
Graham, Bob	28-08-26	03-05-30
Gunson, Gordon	28-08-26	07-03-36
Robson, Ted	28-08-26	05-05-28
Smith, James	28-08-26	14-04-28
Miles, Uriah	11-09-26	27-11-26
Lovatt, Harry	04-12-26	09-03-27
Jones, Price	22-01-27	22-01-27
Smith, Cecil	19-02-27	05-05-28
Bertram, ?	09-03-27	09-03-27
1927/28		
Bellis, George	27-08-27	04-05-29
Woodhouse, Rowland	27-08-27	03-05-30
Rogers, Billie	10-09-27	07-05-32
Condon, Bernard	15-10-27	22-10-27
Harris, Billy	15-10-27	17-03-28
Crompton, Wynne	22-10-27	23-01-32
Bingham, Harry	03-12-27	28-04-28
Jones, Bob	18-02-28	22-02-28
Evans, Arthur	25-02-28	27-02-28
Lucas, Arthur	07-03-28	17-03-28
Read, Ted	07-04-28	03-05-30
1928/29		
Greatrex, George	25-08-28	01-02-30
Mays, Albert	25-08-28	01-03-30
Hudson, Bob	25-08-28	26-04-30
Taylor, Ted	03-11-28	06-04-29
Islip, Ernie	17-11-28	30-03-29
Neal, John	23-03-29	09-11-29
Bamford, Tommy	30-03-29	02-09-44
1929/30		
Ascroft, John	31-08-29	03-05-30
Ross, Bob	31-08-29	21-04-30
Richards, Jack	04-09-29	14-09-29
Jones, Os	07-09-29	22-04-32
Richards, Iorwerth	11-09-29	14-09-29
Wynne, George	11-09-29	23-04-30
Baker, Norman	05-10-29	05-10-29
Dickie, Bill	16-11-29	22-03-30
Williams, Les	16-11-29	27-12-30
Bell, George	23-11-29	21-04-30
Rooney, Walter	23-11-29	21-04-30
Smith, John	22-03-30	03-05-30
Hughes, Jack	23-04-30	02-02-46
1930/31		
Burkinshaw, Ralph	30-08-30	16-04-32
Buxton, Arthur	30-08-30	28-12-40
Donoghue, John	30-08-30	30-04-32
Lewis, Tommy	30-08-30	10-10-42
Mustard, Jack	30-08-30	27-02-36
Taylor, Sam	30-08-30	07-05-32
Clayton, John	03-09-30	07-05-32
Parden, Bernard	11-10-30	30-01-32
Jackson, Horace	25-10-30	25-10-30
Hill, Albert	22-11-30	17-01-31
Lawrence, Matt	26-12-30	28-08-37
Rigby, Norman	03-01-31	31-01-31
Bamford, Walter	14-01-31	14-01-31
Welsh, Billy	14-01-31	14-03-31
Wright, Edgar	31-01-31	07-02-31
1931/32		
Brown, John	05-09-31	23-09-33
Ferguson, Chris	05-09-31	02-01-32
Burrows, Wilf	30-09-31	17-12-32
Prince, Jack	14-11-31	05-12-31
Adams, Ted	19-12-31	18-09-43
Jones, Arthur	19-12-31	07-05-32
Price, Cyril	16-01-32	23-01-32
Williams, Emlyn	20-04-32	03-04-33
1932/33		
Beck, Harry	27-08-32	16-04-34
Bulling, Jim	27-08-32	23-11-35
Frewin, George	27-08-32	13-04-36
Lanyon, Bill	27-08-32	29-08-32
McKenna, Frank	27-08-32	03-04-33
Findlay, Alex	27-08-32	13-02-35
Wilson-Jones, Charles		03-09-32
30-01-43		
Littlehales, Harry	03-09-32	24-09-32
Waller, Harry	03-09-32	16-03-35
Molloy, Tom	17-09-32	17-09-32
McMahon, Hugh	15-10-32	10-04-36
Weale, Bob	08-04-33	29-04-35
1933/34		
McCabe, Barney	26-08-33	11-11-33
Snow, George	26-08-33	28-09-40
Hamilton, Jimmy	02-09-33	28-08-37
Shonaken, John	09-09-33	09-09-33
Foster, Bob	30-09-33	28-04-34
Fryer, Jack	30-09-33	10-10-36
Bryant, Bill	07-10-33	20-10-34
Foyne, John	07-10-33	07-10-33
Lewis, Jack	23-12-33	12-02-38
Smallwood, Fred	14-04-34	22-11-41
Richards, David	16-04-34	10-04-36
1934/35		
Stubbs, Eric	20-10-34	10-02-40
Gardiner, Archie	27-10-34	13-04-36
Rogers, Ehud	27-10-34	28-09-46
Wyness, Bill	26-12-34	18-03-35
Rice, James	01-01-35	04-05-35
Evans, Vic	18-03-35	09-02-38
Manuel, Percy	06-04-35	13-04-35
McMahon, Pat	22-04-35	04-11-39
1935/36		
McCartney, Charles	31-08-35	12-04-37
Jones, Herbert	11-09-35	17-04-37
Jeavons, Bill	18-09-35	26-10-35
Burgon, Archie	02-11-35	06-05-39
Postin, Eli	23-11-35	25-04-36
Jones, Ron	30-11-35	13-10-45
Jones, T.G.	28-12-35	27-04-46
1936/37		
Brown, Ambrose	29-08-36	17-04-37
Bryant,Cliff	29-08-36	27-03-37
Mitchell, Adam	29-08-36	24-04-37
White, Alf	09-09-36	19-04-37
Readett, Harold	26-09-36	26-09-36
Lapham, Harold	10-10-36	06-05-39
Barrow, Bill	21-10-36	19-04-37
Smith, John	20-02-37	24-04-37
Phillips, Dai	03-04-37	17-09-38
Robertson, Hugh	17-04-37	20-11-37
1937/38		
Fraser, Nathan	28-08-37	19-02-38
Raven, James	28-08-37	06-10-45
Barnard, Sid	01-09-37	04-09-37
Bellamy, Bill	01-09-37	08-01-44
Breakwell, Tom	01-09-37	19-02-38
Odell, Walter	01-09-37	06-05-39

Wrexham Players in Debut Order (cont.)

Player	Debut	Last Game
Ouchterlonie, Willie	01-09-37	23-10-37
Wilson, John	04-09-37	30-04-38
Burditt, George	13-11-37	15-04-39
Tunney, Eddie	13-11-37	29-08-51
Mathias, James	05-02-38	02-09-40
Lloyd, Cliff	05-03-38	Unknown*
McAleer, Joe	19-03-38	30-04-38
1938/39		
Adamson, Bob	27-08-38	22-04-39
Poland, George	27-08-38	22-04-39
Smith, James A.	27-08-38	18-02-39
Bellis, Gib	29-08-38	18-04-49
Lloyd, Jackie	17-09-38	17-01-42
Goss, Fred	01-10-38	24-12-38
Nelson, Albert	01-10-38	29-08-39
Savage, Bob	03-12-38	22-01-44
Williams, Jack	03-12-38	30-08-41
Davies, Tom	10-12-38	10-12-38
Roberts, Walter	31-12-38	01-05-48
1939/40		
Bradbury, Tom	26-08-39	02-12-39
Briggs, Frank	26-08-39	04-05-46
Brown, Albert	26-08-39	31-05-47
Bryan, William	26-08-39	02-09-39
Screen, John	26-08-39	28-08-43
Woodman, John	26-08-39	02-09-40
Jones, John Thomas	21-10-39	24-02-45
McKennan, Peter	21-10-39	21-10-39
Redfern, Billy	21-10-39	25-05-42
Cooper, Tom	28-10-39	11-11-39
Hough, Bill	28-10-39	28-10-39
Roberts, John	04-11-39	06-01-40
Martin, John	11-11-39	13-04-40
White, Fred	11-11-39	18-11-39
Baker, Frank	25-11-39	25-11-39
Cook, Billy	25-11-39	09-01-46
Morris, Billy	25-11-39	10-05-41
Taylor, N	09-12-39	23-12-39
Cullis, Stan	06-01-40	23-03-40
Antonio, George	10-02-40	04-11-44
Milburn, James	10-02-40	07-04-45
Coen, Lawrence	24-02-40	06-04-40
Witcombe, Doug	24-02-40	09-03-40
Bridges, Harry	09-03-40	09-03-40
Kelsall, Charlie	16-03-40	13-10-51
Kelly, Gerard	16-03-40	27-04-40
Bell, Bob 'Bunny'	13-04-40	04-05-40
Edwards, George	20-04-40	04-05-40
Moss, Frank	04-05-40	04-05-40
Astbury, Tommy	13-05-40	29-03-41
Sproston, Bert	22-05-40	22-05-40
Tennant, John	22-05-40	22-05-40
1940/41		
Emmanuel, Tom	31-08-40	07-12-40
Trentham, Doug	31-08-40	26-10-40
Dickenson, Albert	21-09-40	22-02-41
Gladwin, George	28-09-40	28-09-40
Hayward, Lionel	05-10-40	02-06-41
Wright, Horace	05-10-40	14-02-42
Reece, Tom	12-10-40	12-10-40
McAvoy, Doug	26-10-40	06-04-42
Devlin, John	02-11-40	06-12-41
Woodburn, James	16-11-40	08-03-41
Rugman, K	23-11-40	23-11-40
Blunt, Edwin	30-11-40	03-04-43
Major, Arthur	07-12-40	07-12-40
Matthews, Stanley	14-12-40	14-12-40
Park, John	14-12-40	04-10-41
Smith, Clem	14-12-40	14-12-40
Butt, Leonard	21-12-40	22-03-41
Ferrier, Ron	04-01-41	11-01-41
McGratton, H	04-01-41	22-03-41
Foulkes, Reg	11-01-41	11-01-41
Williams, G	11-01-41	11-01-41
Springthorpe, Terry	15-02-41	22-02-41
Timms, B	15-02-41	26-04-41
Steen, Alan	15-02-41	15-02-41
Jones, Norman	08-03-41	11-01-47
Anderson, A	22-03-41	19-04-41
Anderson, J.Doug	22-03-41	02-06-41
Sidlow, Cyril	22-03-41	27-09-41
Hampson, Eric	29-03-41	29-03-41
Howarth, Harold	29-03-41	02-06-41
Cope, George	05-04-41	06-09-41
Brigham, Harry	12-04-41	19-04-41
Sale, Tommy	19-04-41	19-04-41
Anderson, Eddie	26-04-41	17-05-41
Bidewell, Sid	10-05-41	10-05-41
Dearson, Don	10-05-41	10-05-41
Hanson, Adolph	17-05-41	17-05-41
Waring, 'Pongo'	17-05-41	31-10-42
Owen, Arthur	02-06-41	02-06-41
Yates, Dick	02-06-41	09-10-48
1941/42		
Stevens, George	30-08-41	20-09-41
Turner, Arthur	30-08-41	26-09-42
Tutin, Arthur	30-08-41	20-09-41
Bremner, Gordon	06-09-41	21-04-45
Wallbanks, James	06-09-41	16-05-42
Carver,	13-09-41	13-09-41
Horsman, Bill	13-09-41	04-10-41
Roberts, L	20-09-41	06-04-42
Prydderch, Ivor	27-09-41	27-09-41
Armitage, Lewis	04-10-41	11-10-41
Clark, Gordon	04-10-41	04-10-41
Davies, G	04-10-41	01-11-41
Atkinson, Bill	25-10-41	29-11-41
Cole, Cyril	25-10-41	25-12-41
Lloyd, Cliff	25-10-41	Unknown*
Pritchard, F	08-11-41	15-11-41
Davies, Cyril	15-11-41	17-01-42
Jones, John Edward	15-11-41	19-12-42
Swinnerton, K	15-11-41	15-11-41
Ellis, John	22-11-41	17-01-42
White, Frank	29-11-41	18-03-44
Morris, John	06-12-41	06-12-41
Jones, D.O.	20-12-41	20-12-41
Moore, Norman	20-12-41	26-04-43
Morgan, Gwyn	25-12-41	04-12-43
Griffiths, Harry	27-12-41	25-05-42
Burnett, George	07-02-42	03-04-43
Barrett, Jim	14-02-42	14-02-42
Haines, John	14-03-42	14-03-42
Lovatt, Percy	14-03-42	15-05-47
Franklin, Neil	16-05-42	17-02-45
Frost, Arthur	16-05-42	10-10-42
Herod, Dennis	16-05-42	16-05-42
Hewitt, H	16-05-42	16-05-42
Pritty, George	16-05-42	25-05-42
Reeder, George	25-05-42	21-11-42
Swain, John	25-05-42	25-05-42
1942/43		
Hill, Frank	29-08-42	29-04-44
Hughes, Alan	29-08-42	17-10-42
Jones, David	29-08-42	31-10-42
Lea, George	29-08-42	27-02-43
Collins, George	05-09-42	30-12-44
Stuttard, Ellis	10-10-42	22-01-44
McNee, Chris	17-10-42	23-01-43
Clegg, Don	07-11-42	25-09-43
Muir, M	07-11-42	13-02-43
Hughes, Billy	21-11-42	10-02-45
Dolby,	28-11-42	28-11-42
Hill, A	28-11-42	28-11-42
Jones, Doug	28-11-42	28-11-42
Kirton, John	28-11-42	28-11-42
Gill, Henry	12-12-42	12-12-42
Simms, Hedley	12-12-42	12-05-45
Caton, Bill	25-12-42	18-09-43
Livingstone, Archie	16-01-43	09-12-44
Dugdale, T	30-01-43	30-01-43
Driscoll, John	20-02-43	20-02-43
McGovern, Eric	20-02-43	20-02-43
Payne, E	27-02-43	03-04-43
Thomas, David	27-02-43	23-10-43
Crossley, G	06-03-43	06-03-43
Hinton, Ted	06-03-43	06-03-43
Presdee, H	06-03-43	13-03-43
Fellowes, Bill	13-03-43	13-03-43
Meade, T	03-04-43	17-04-43
Smith, Arthur	03-04-43	03-03-45
Baines, Peter	17-04-43	04-10-46
Dean, George	17-04-43	17-04-43
Stearn, A	17-04-43	17-04-43
Smith, Basil	26-04-43	18-12-43
1943/44		
Dellow, Robert	28-08-43	02-10-43
Smith, L	28-08-43	18-09-43
Fairhurst, David	04-09-43	11-09-43
Tracey, Chris	25-09-43	02-10-43
Griffiths, George	02-10-43	02-10-43
Whitelaw, David	23-10-43	26-12-45
Jones, Vic	30-10-43	07-04-43
Reid, J	30-10-43	30-10-43
Malam, Albert	13-11-43	25-12-46
Hilliard, Bill	04-12-43	23-09-44
Pilling, Jimmy	11-12-43	10-02-45
Davies, Ivor	25-12-43	25-12-43
Jefferson, Arthur	15-01-44	12-05-45
Foxall, Stan	29-01-44	26-08-44
Revell, Charlie	29-01-44	30-09-44
Birkett, Wilf	26-02-44	04-05-46
Reid, Cyril	18-03-44	18-03-44
Ashton, Roy	25-03-44	16-02-46
Heath, W	10-04-44	10-04-44
1944/45		
Gavin, Charles	26-08-44	11-11-44
Hancocks, Johnny	26-08-44	03-11-44
Fuller, C	02-09-44	11-11-44
Isherwood, Dennis	02-09-44	01-12-45
Mulligan, Eddie	16-09-44	16-09-44
Roberts, Eddie	16-09-44	23-09-44
Watson, Willie	07-10-44	08-09-45
Wheatley, Harold	21-10-44	21-10-44
Dix, Ronnie	04-11-44	20-10-45
Hewitt, Len	11-11-44	25-01-47
Derrick, Albert	18-11-44	18-11-44
Duns, Leslie	09-12-44	13-10-45
Case, D	16-12-44	16-12-44
Davies, Bob	24-02-45	24-02-45
Lunn, George	24-02-45	24-02-45
Makin, George	24-02-45	24-02-45
Collins, Tony	03-03-45	08-12-45
Hughes, Tom	10-03-45	01-12-45
Purton, B	17-03-45	02-04-45
Armstrong, Matt	31-03-45	27-10-45
Griffiths, David	02-04-45	02-04-45
Boyes, Walter	07-04-45	07-04-45
Cooper, John	21-04-45	27-10-45
Douglas, David	05-05-45	12-05-45
Newsome, Rob	12-05-45	12-05-45
1945/46		
Weaver, Sam	25-08-45	10-11-45
Jackson, Ron	01-09-45	17-12-49
McLarty, Jesse	01-09-45	27-09-47
Thomas, Gwyn	15-09-45	15-09-45
Hayward, Aubrey	29-09-45	01-01-46
Cook, Billy	13-10-45	09-01-46
Worsley, Herbert	13-10-45	20-10-45
Oakley, Maurice	10-11-45	10-11-45
Wainwright, George	17-11-45	24-11-45
Mortimer, John	24-11-45	09-10-48
Gardner, Tom	22-12-45	26-04-47
Haycock, Fred	22-12-45	18-09-46
Speed, Les	26-12-45	23-04-55
Holliday, Frank	01-01-46	09-02-46
Eastwood, Eric	01-01-46	09-03-46
Shepherd, Arthur	23-02-46	30-03-46
Archibald, Murray	16-03-46	28-09-46
Leyland, John	16-03-46	16-03-46
Gripton, Ernie	23-03-46	23-03-46
Burkinshaw, George	30-03-46	04-05-46
Arthur, Jackie	04-05-46	04-05-46

Wrexham Players in Debut Order (cont.)

Player	Debut	Last Game
1946/47		
Lloyd, Joe	31-08-46	12-04-47
Pritchard, Vince	31-08-46	10-09-49
Williams, Frank	31-08-46	03-04-48
Sharp, Norman	18-09-46	31-12-49
McNee, Terry	28-09-46	25-12-46
Boothway, Jack	02-11-46	10-04-50
Weaver, John	16-11-46	21-12-46
Leyfield, John	25-12-46	14-01-50
Roberts, Stan	25-12-46	14-01-48
Hollis, Harry	05-04-47	05-04-47
Beynon, Eddie	03-05-47	18-08-51
McIlvenny, Eddie	10-05-47	17-09-47
Jones, Jack	27-05-47	06-03-48
McGinn, Frank	07-06-47	14-06-47
Sommerfield, Alfred	07-06-47	14-06-47
1947/48		
Tunnicliffe, Billy	23-08-47	17-01-53
Wilson, Peter	03-09-47	26-12-50
Bayley, Tom	04-10-47	06-03-48
Atherton, Geoff	22-11-47	18-09-48
Grainger, Dennis	06-12-47	02-05-51
Walker, Robert	06-03-48	13-03-48
Wynn, Ron	26-03-48	04-02-56
1948/49		
Ferguson, Archie	21-08-48	17-01-53
Rowell, Fred	21-08-48	29-04-50
Mawson, Ron	25-09-48	19-02-49
Spruce, George	06-11-48	01-05-52
Sharpe, Fred	04-12-48	04-12-48
Williams, Glyn	16-04-49	04-05-49
1949/50		
Graham, John	20-08-49	11-04-52
Williams, Stuart	01-09-49	01-09-49
Rowland, Len	14-09-49	26-08-50
McDowall, Les	05-11-49	26-11-49
Ellis, Ken	24-12-49	25-03-50
Wood, Ron	24-12-49	07-04-50
McLaughlin, Bob	21-01-50	29-04-50
Edwards, David	04-03-50	04-03-50
1950/51		
Donaldson, Les	19-08-50	05-09-51
Fidler, Frank	19-08-50	20-10-51
McCallum, Stewart	19-08-50	31-01-53
Spencer, Harry	19-08-50	02-05-51
Hayes, Bill	26-08-50	23-04-51
Johnson, Brian	26-08-50	01-01-52
McAdam, David	26-08-50	03-02-51
Griffiths, Estyn	30-08-50	15-09-51
Tapscott, Eli Johnny	30-08-50	04-02-56
Hilton, Jack	06-09-50	31-03-51
Jones, George	14-10-50	28-12-53
Lawrence, Cyril	14-10-50	14-04-52
Grieves, Dick	21-12-50	21-12-50
Wyllie, Jim	02-12-50	18-04-51
Grainger, Colin	24-02-51	11-04-53
Roberts, Dilwyn	30-04-51	30-04-51
1951/52		
Bannan, Tommy	18-08-51	25-04-59
Hewitt, Ron	18-08-51	29-02-60
Jessop, Bill	18-08-51	28-04-52
Kirkby, Jock	18-08-51	30-08-52
Williams, Bob	18-08-51	15-09-52
Connor, Bob	29-08-51	10-04-54
Wootton, Len	29-08-51	16-02-52
McWhinnie, Archie	01-09-51	05-09-51
Roberts, Ken	01-09-51	01-09-51
Williams, Ray	01-09-51	01-01-52
Fisher, Peter	01-09-51	27-02-54
Hope, Eric	2010-51	19-04-54
Parker, Albert	10-11-51	29-04-59
Griffiths, Dennis	01-03-52	31-08-57
Bonner, Bernard	08-03-52	08-03-52
Tilston, Tommy	15-03-52	30-01-54
1952/53		
Capper, Jack	23-08-52	26-03-55
Hughes, Glyn	23-08-52	23-04-55
Richards, Gordon	27-09-52	29-01-58
Heggie, Bill	18-10-52	06-11-55
McMillan, George	25-10-52	25-10-52
Spruce, Phil	17-01-53	12-11-55
Matthews, Keith	21-01-53	08-01-55
Godding, Earl	24-01-53	27-08-58
Griffiths, Brian	06-04-53	02-11-57
1953/54		
McGowan, Aly	15-08-53	05-04-65
Gwatkin, Phil	26-08-53	11-02-56
Betts, Eric	10-10-53	07-01-56
Jones, Tecwyn	07-11-53	27-02-54
Jarvis, Brian	16-01-54	25-04-59
Samuals, Les	06-03-54	06-11-55
Fox, Alan	12-04-54	11-03-64
1954/55		
Williams, Derek	25-08-54	01-01-55
Green, Bill	28-08-54	30-04-57
Evans, Bernard	15-09-54	01-10-60
Jackson, David	07-10-54	11-12-54
Jackson, Peter	07-10-54	11-12-54
Rowley, Arthur	04-12-54	20-10-56
Williams, Eddie	27-12-54	27-12-54
1955/56		
Bannister, Keith	20-08-55	08-10-55
Davis, Fred	20-08-55	29-04-61
Evans, Elfed	20-08-55	20-10-56
Littler, Eric	20-08-55	27-12-55
Waters, Billy	21-09-55	04-04-60
Evans, Dennis	12-11-55	16-04-58
Thompson, Peter	19-11-55	30-04-57
1956/57		
Anderson, Johnny	18-08-56	25-09-61
Jones, David	18-08-56	22-04-59
Williams, Alvan	18-08-56	30-04-57
Jones, Gren	22-08-56	11-04-61
Morgans, Gwyn	27-08-56	29-01-58
McNab, Tom	16-03-57	07-03-59
1957/58		
Dallas, Willie	24-08-57	12-04-58
McTurk, John	24-08-57	21-09-57
Smith, Barry	24-08-57	26-03-58
Ugolini, Roly	24-08-57	09-04-60
Dignam, Joe	24-08-57	19-10-57
Wilkins, Ray	04-09-57	05-03-58
Evans, George	19-10-57	23-05-63
Metcalf, Mike	19-10-57	14-12-63
Jones, Ken	02-11-57	02-01-60
Murray, Ken	22-02-58	04-04-59
1958/59		
Brown, Peter	23-08-58	16-04-60
Sowden, Paddy	23-08-58	26-09-59
Weston, Don	23-08-58	27-04-68
Warburton, George	18-10-58	04-04-60
Griffiths, Arfon	15-11-58	18-12-78
Williams, Elfyn	24-01-59	28-01-59
Beesley, Eric	28-01-59	28-01-59
1959/60		
Fenton, Ewan	22-08-59	29-02-60
Scott, Bert	25-08-59	29-08-59
Pryce, Idris	29-08-59	05-09-59
Porter, George	07-09-59	07-09-59
Hughes, Charlie	23-09-59	04-02-61
Bennion, Stan	30-09-59	15-09-62
Proctor, David	31-10-59	14-11-59
Wright, Barry	31-10-59	25-09-61
Jones, Harvey	28-11-59	23-04-60
Roberts, Ron	27-01-60	17-11-62
Hunter, Reg	06-02-60	18-11-61
Salisbury, Gareth	13-02-60	03-02-62
Willett, Len	13-02-60	13-02-60
Holland, Reg	05-03-60	27-12-65
Harbetson, Ron	09-03-60	27-12-60
Styles, Archie	19-03-60	03-04-61
Jones, Peter	30-04-60	16-05-66
1960/61		
Johnson, Arthur	20-08-60	10-01-62
Davies, Wyn	25-08-60	03-03-62
McCreadie, Harvey	12-11-60	22-03-61
Morris, Elfed	11-03-61	30-03-62
White, Bill	15-03-61	11-04-61
Bennett, Terry	22-03-61	22-03-61
1961/62		
Barnes, Ken	19-08-61	27-02-65
Barnes, Ron	19-08-61	27-08-63
Jones, Tecwyn Lloyd	10-10-61	29-08-64
Ambler, Roy	11-11-61	22-09-62
Keelan, Kevin	09-12-61	23-05-63
Hughes, Derek	13-01-62	13-01-62
Thomas, Rob	31-01-62	31-01-62
Colbridge, Clive	17-02-62	12-04-65
Phythian, Ernie	10-03-62	28-04-65
Whitehouse, Brian	24-03-62	02-11-63
Anderson, Tommy	28-03-62	15-12-62
1962/63		
Bellett, Wally	15-12-62	26-12-62
Simpkins, Ken	15-12-62	27-08-63
Parrish, Don	13-04-63	29-10-65
Thurnham, Roy	18-04-63	01-05-63
Powell, David	11-05-63	27-08-68
1963/64		
Morrall, Terry	24-08-63	17-04-65
Myerscough, Billy	24-08-63	25-04-64
Jones, John	31-08-63	17-02-64
Owen, Aled	31-08-63	11-03-64
Fleet, Steve	11-09-63	05-01-66
Lambert, David	11-09-63	21-12-63
Bent, Graham	12-10-63	19-09-64
Mayers, Derek	26-10-63	18-04-64
Robertson, Eddie	26-10-63	25-04-64
McGill, Jim	30-10-63	25-04-64
Dunlop, Albert	02-11-63	12-04-65
Johnson, Eric	21-12-63	28-08-65
Gillespie, Norrie	21-12-63	03-04-64
McMillan, Sammy	26-12-63	16-09-67
1964/65		
McClelland, Joe	22-08-64	27-02-65
Williams, Graham	22-08-64	17-04-65
Lambourne, Dennis	05-09-64	18-11-65
Jones, Alan	08-09-64	12-09-64
Webber, Keith	16-09-64	16-05-66
King, Martyn	03-10-64	10-05-66
Mielczarek, Ray	19-10-64	25-09-67
Jones, Haydn	20-03-65	26-02-66
Butt, Bobby	19-04-65	27-04-65
Smith, John	19-04-65	10-05-66
Campbell, David	24-04-65	06-05-67
Turner, Graham	28-04-65	30-12-68
1965/66		
Lucas, Alec	21-08-65	16-05-67
Roberts, Cledwyn	21-08-65	21-08-65
Harding, David	23-08-65	05-03-66
Wall, Peter	06-11-65	01-10-66
Rawlins, David	13-11-65	20-11-65
Hannigan, Ben	10-12-65	10-05-66
Edwards, Johnny	27-12-65	27-12-65
Mason, Stuart	01-01-66	27-04-73
Beighton, Graham	08-01-66	16-05-66
Lloyd, John	08-01-66	26-04-67
Hughes, Ian	05-02-66	30-04-66
Stacey, Steve	26-02-66	09-09-68
Kinsey, Albert	05-03-66	13-01-73
Wood, John	04-05-66	24-01-68

Wrexham Players in Debut Order (cont.)

Player	Debut	Last Game
1966/67		
Carrick, David	20-08-66	16-03-68
Evans, Mickey	20-08-66	26-12-78
McLoughlin, Tony	20-08-66	19-08-67
Oldfield, Terry	20-08-66	03-05-67
Schofield, John	20-08-66	02-10-67
Grant, David	08-10-66	06-05-67
Lloyd, Geoff	08-10-66	26-04-67
Showell, George	02-12-66	04-05-68
Booth, Ray	27-03-67	31-03-69
Jones, Phil	16-05-67	16-05-67
1967/68		
Beanland, Tony	19-08-67	28-04-69
Bradbury, Terry	19-08-67	28-04-69
Ingle, Steve	19-08-67	01-04-72
Smith, Ray	19-08-67	01-05-72
Kinsella, Pat	23-08-67	23-08-67
Livsey, Gordon	09-09-67	16-01-71
Bermingham, Alan	02-10-67	10-10-70
Reeves, Dennis	09-12-67	12-04-69
Moir, Ian	20-01-68	21-04-75
Davies, Gareth	24-02-68	30-10-82
Jones, Graham	24-01-68	09-03-68
1968/69		
Charnley, Ray	10-08-68	04-01-69
May, Eddie	10-08-68	29-04-76
Purdie, Bernard	02-11-68	02-03-70
Tinnion, Brian	11-01-69	21-04-76
Mackreth, Steve	05-04-69	21-04-69
Duncan, Joey	05-05-69	05-05-69
Sykes, John	05-05-69	05-05-69
1969/70		
Gaskell, David	09-08-69	26-02-72
Park, Bobby	09-08-69	03-04-72
Price, Brian	12-01-70	12-01-70
Vansitart, Tom	14-02-70	21-04-75
Boersma, Phil	21-03-70	27-04-70
1970/71		
Provan, Andy	15-08-70	01-05-72
Ashcroft, Billy	03-10-70	27-08-77
Green, Colin	23-01-71	13-02-71
Fogg, David	24-02-71	05-04-76
Hughes, David	01-03-71	01-03-71
Taylor, Ken	01-03-71	01-03-71
Whittle, Graham	01-05-71	15-11-80
Scott, Bob	07-05-71	04-02-86
1971/72		
Lloyd, Brian	29-08-71	20-08-77
McBurney, Mike	02-10-71	17-03-73
Thomas, Mickey	01-01-72	14-11-92
Mostyn, Roger	05-02-72	12-10-73
Loughlin, John	11-03-72	25-03-72
1972/73		
Sutton, Mel	12-08-72	06-03-81
Smallman, David	05-09-72	08-03-75
Jones, Joey	13-01-73	23-11-91
1973/74		
Davies, Geoff	20-10-73	08-03-76
Dwyer, Alan	23-01-74	04-05-81
1974/75		
Hill, Alan	04-01-75	17-05-83
Lyons, John	22-03-75	17-05-79
Williams, Mike	26-04-75	30-04-77
1975/76		
Kelly, Jimmy	20-09-75	18-10-75
Williams, Everton	24-09-75	27-09-75
Lee, Stuart	29-11-75	17-01-78
1976/77		
Roberts, John	21-08-76	03-05-80
Shinton, Bobby	21-08-76	17-05-79
Cegielski, Wayne	18-12-76	15-05-82
McLoughlin, John	26-04-77	26-04-77
1977/78		
Cartwright, Les	13-08-77	07-11-81
Niedzwiecki, Eddie	22-08-77	17-05-83
Davies, Dai	24-09-77	24-02-87
McNeil, Dixie	24-09-77	10-12-85
Williams, Peter	21-03-78	31-03-81
Buxton, Steve	03-05-78	03-02-90
Kenworthy, Steve	03-05-78	18-03-80
Tony Larkin	13-05-78	18-05-78
1978/79		
Palmer, David	18-12-78	18-12-78
Fox, Steve	26-12-78	25-09-82
Giles, David	26-12-78	10-11-79
Jones, Frank	07-05-79	29-11-86
Roberts, Ian	07-05-79	26-12-79
Edwards, Elfyn	24-05-79	24-05-79
1979/80		
Vinter, Mick	18-08-79	15-05-82
Darracott, Terry	15-09-79	01-03-80
Edwards, Ian	03-11-79	08-05-82
Carrodus, Frank	15-12-79	15-05-82
Arkwright, Ian	15-03-80	05-05-84
1980/81		
Salathiel, Neil	25-10-80	05-05-90
Dowman, Steve	06-03-81	14-05-83
Jones, Steve	31-03-81	20-02-82
1981/82		
Hunt, Simon	05-09-81	21-05-84
Bater, Phil	12-09-81	13-09-83
Ronson, Billy	10-10-81	15-05-82
Jones, Mark	09-02-82	09-02-82
Leman, Dennis	20-02-82	11-05-82
1982/83		
Gregory, David	28-08-82	18-05-86
Edwards, Andy	31-08-82	21-05-86
Keay, Jack	07-09-82	03-05-86
King, Jake	11-09-82	17-11-84
Baker, Darren	25-09-82	14-04-84
Emmerson, Mark	28-09-82	04-04-83
Humphries, Steve	28-09-82	02-10-82
Muldoon, John	28-09-82	10-12-85
Evans, Medwyn	16-10-82	12-05-84
Savage, Robbie	23-10-82	17-05-83
Parker, Stuart	01-12-82	16-03-85
Brand, Drew	04-12-82	04-12-82
Cunnington, Shaun	18-12-82	13-02-88
Bremner, Kevin	01-01-83	22-01-83
Steel, Jim	29-01-83	14-11-87
Williams, John	02-04-83	02-04-83
Jones, Steve	15-10-83	25-05-84
1983/84		
Heath, Seamus	27-08-83	05-05-84
Coleman, Phil	03-09-83	17-12-83
Wardle, Bob	03-09-83	01-11-83
Wright, Steve	16-09-83	11-05-85
Roberts, Bobby	29-11-83	29-11-83
Sturridge, Mike	17-12-83	31-12-83
Millington, Grenville	31-12-83	24-03-84
Sinclair, Ron	21-03-84	25-05-84
1984/85		
Horne, Barry	25-08-84	09-05-87
Rogers, Kevin	25-08-84	06-05-85
Williams, Mike	25-08-84	09-10-90
Nicoll, Paul	01-09-84	04-09-84
Pugh, Gary	04-09-84	20-10-84
Reilly, David	04-09-84	06-05-85
Crosby, Malcolm	08-09-84	06-10-84
Sander, Chris	22-09-84	03-11-84
Charles, Steve	03-11-84	09-05-87
Comstive, Paul	24-11-84	09-05-87
Houghton, Peter	24-11-84	29-12-84
Keep, Vernon	27-11-84	23-02-85
Hooper, Mike	13-02-84	19-10-85
1985/86		
Emery, Steve	17-08-85	14-03-86
Hencher, Nick	20-08-85	20-10-87
Vaughan, John	26-10-85	09-11-85
Keen, Mike	16-11-85	01-01-86
Mooney, Brian	13-12-85	01-02-86
Brignull, Phil	20-12-85	18-01-86
Ferguson, Don	11-01-86	03-05-86
Morris, Mark	25-01-86	06-10-93
Chadwick, Simon	08-03-86	11-03-86
Weetman, Darren	14-03-86	14-03-86
Stanton, Brian	22-03-86	19-04-86
1986/87		
Conroy, Mike	23-08-86	25-04-87
Cooke, Joe	23-08-86	01-03-88
Emson, Paul	23-08-86	20-02-88
Massey, Steve	23-08-86	17-05-88
Pearce, Chris	23-08-86	21-02-87
Preece, Roger	17-09-86	07-04-90
Wright, Darren	01-10-86	03-10-90
Haigh, Ian	25-11-86	25-11-86
Diamond, Barry	24-01-87	14-02-87
Heyes, Darren	24-01-87	31-01-87
Powell, David	28-02-87	03-03-87
Salmon, Mike	07-03-87	03-06-89
Oghani, George	14-03-87	11-04-87
1987/88		
Carter, Mike	15-08-87	24-05-89
Hinnigan, Joe	15-08-87	23-02-88
Hunter, Geoff	15-08-87	20-04-91
Russell, Kevin	15-08-87	
Bowden, Jon	18-08-87	14-09-91
Harvey, Jim	12-09-87	03-10-87
Slater, Jamie	03-10-87	24-11-87
Alleyne, Rob	24-10-87	01-01-88
Fairbrother, Ian	24-10-87	12-12-87
Scott, Steve	06-11-87	24-11-87
Kearns, Ollie	26-12-87	02-12-89
Flynn, Brian	20-02-88	03-04-92
1988/89		
Beaumont, Nigel	27-08-88	20-12-91
Cooper, Graham	27-08-88	18-12-90
Thackeray, Andy	27-08-88	02-05-92
Taylor, Jason	24-09-88	24-09-88
Wrench, Mark	24-09-88	05-09-89
Lane, Martin	08-10-88	05-11-88
Raynor, Paul	22-10-88	12-11-88
Jones, Paul	27-03-89	15-04-89
Filson, Martin	01-05-89	05-09-89
1989/90		
O'Keefe Vince	19-08-89	02-05-92
Reck, Sean	19-08-89	24-11-90
Worthington, Gary	19-08-89	16-03-91
Armstrong, Chris	29-08-89	04-05-91
Barnes, Robbie	02-09-89	29-09-90
Owen, Gareth	11-11-89	
Lee, Tony	09-12-89	09-12-89
Madden, Craig	06-01-90	24-02-90
Jones, Rob	26-01-90	20-04-91
Phillips, Wayne	10-02-90	31-01-98
Sertori, Mark	10-02-90	07-05-94
Youds, Eddie	10-02-90	05-05-90
Morgan, Steve	27-03-90	13-05-90
Kennedy, Alan	21-03-90	27-10-90
Preece, Andy	30-03-90	03-12-91
Hardy, Phil	05-03-90	
1990/91		
Watkin, Steve	16-10-90	20-09-97
Jones, Kevin	07-11-90	26-04-94
Jones, Lee	07-11-90	01-03-97
O'Gorman, David	09-11-90	07-05-91
Kelly, James	24-11-90	09-04-94
Ward, Ashley	12-01-91	21-02-91
Carey, Brian	19-01-91	

Wrexham Players in Debut Order (cont.)

Player	Debut	Last Game
Lunt, Rob	12-03-91	28-12-91
Griffiths, Ian	22-03-91	21-09-91
Murray, Joey	30-03-91	19-05-91
1991/92		
Connolly, Karl	17-08-91	
Davies, Gordon	17-08-91	04-02-92
Durkan, Kieron	03-09-91	13-02-96
Phillips, Stewart	03-09-91	07-09-91
Skipper, Peter	03-09-91	07-09-91
Marshall, Colin	28-09-91	12-10-91
Cross, Jonathan	09-11-91	16-12-97
Pejic, Mel	11-01-92	29-04-95
Jones, David	11-02-92	14-03-92
Paskin, John	22-02-92	22-02-94
Ireland, Simon	14-03-92	03-04-92
Lewis, Dudley	21-03-92	02-05-92
Taylor, Mark	24-03-92	04-02-94
Humes, Tony	28-03-92	
Knight, Craig	28-04-92	28-04-92
1992/93		
Esdaille, David	18-08-92	14-11-92
Hughes, Ken	18-08-92	16-01-93
Jones, Barry	18-08-92	05-12-97
Bennett, Gary	25-08-92	26-04-97
Williams, Scott	05-09-92	21-03-98
Pugh, Steve	03-10-92	27-12-94
Brammer, David	10-10-92	23-03-99
Lake, Mike	30-10-92	20-08-94
Case, Jimmy	27-02-93	08-05-93
1993/94		
Hunter, Barry	24-08-93	04-05-96
Walton, Mark	28-08-93	18-09-93
Marriott, Andy	09-10-93	02-05-98
Hughes, Bryan	22-01-94	09-03-97
Brace, Deryn	30-04-94	
1994/95		
Richardson, Nick	22-10-94	05-11-94
Quigley, Mike	18-02-95	04-03-95
Barnes, Richard	29-04-95	24-08-95
Coady, Lewis	17-04-95	22-04-95
McGregor, Mark	06-05-95	
1995/96		
Skinner, Craig	12-08-95	01-12-98
Ward, Peter	12-08-95	02-03-99
Morris, Steve	15-08-95	26-05-97
Chalk, Martyn	20-02-96	
1996/97		
Soloman, Jason	17-08-96	03-09-96
Cartwright, Mark	02-11-96	
Roberts, Paul	26-12-96	04-01-97
Ridler, David	15-03-97	
Jones, Paul	28-03-97	15-04-97
1997/98		
Spink, Dean	12-08-97	
Thomas, Steve	18-08-97	
Wainwright, Neil	18-08-97	05-05-98
Roberts, Neil	27-09-97	
Kelly, Ray	04-10-97	13-04-98
Ince, Clayton	16-12-97	16-12-97
Basham, Steve	07-02-98	24-03-98
Wilson, Mark	24-02-98	17-05-98
1998/99		
Rush, Ian	08-08-98	23-05-99
Rishworth, Steve	01-09-98	12-09-98
Roberts, Steve	27-10-98	
Cooke, Terry	31-10-98	09-01-99
Edwards, Jake	08-12-98	
Robin Gibson	05-01-99	
Andy Morrell	05-01-99	
Carl Griffiths	15-01-99	13-02-99
Jeff Whitley	15-01-99	13-03-99
Tommy Wright	27-02-99	10-05-99
Stuart Elliott	23-03-98	23-05-99
Paul Barrett	27-03-99	
David Walsh	27-04-99	

* As there were two Cliff Lloyd's who turned out for the club during WW2, it is unclear when either one of them made their final appearance for the club.

Wrexham Goalkeepers

This is a list of all Wrexham goalkeepers to have played for the club since joining the Football League in 1921. They are listed in most appearance order and show the ratio of goals conceded per game and the number of clean sheets that they kept.

	Goalkeeper	Total apps	Goals conc	Ratio per game	Clean Sheets League	Clean Sheets Cup	Clean Sheets Total
1	Brian Lloyd	333	419	1.26	88	24	112
2	Andy Marriott	261	330	1.26	59	18	77
3	Dai Davies	199	210	1.06	42	43	85
4	George Godding	186	255	1.37	47	12	59
5	Eddie Niedzwiecki	141	200	1.42	29	9	38
6	Archie Ferguson	140	195	1.39	33	5	38
7	Mark Morris	138	206	1.49	26	10	36
8	Pat McMahon	126	189	1.50	36	2	38
9	Mike Salmon	126	166	1.32	29	6	35
10	Billy Waters	119	185	1.55	23	5	28
11	Dick Finnigan	118	194	1.64	17	9	26
12	Vince O'Keefe	108	163	1.51	19	12	31
13	David Gaskell	107	165	1.54	24	8	32
14	Ted Adams	99	153	1.55	23	0	23
15	Steve Fleet	96	199	2.07	12	3	15
16	Pat Egglestone	95	135	1.42	27	2	29
17	Roly Ugolini	93	160	1.72	16	3	19
18	Gordon Livsey	90	99	1.10	31	1	32
19	Bob Connor	88	131	1.49	17	4	21
20	Ted Robson	83	139	1.67	16	3	19
21	Kevin Keelan	80	128	1.60	11	4	15
22	John Schofield	62	95	1.53	11	2	13
23	Arthur Johnson	61	67	1.10	19	2	21
24	Stuart Parker	51	91	1.78	9	4	13
25	Mark Cartwright	46	63	1.37	8	9	17
26	Charlie Hughes	44	75	1.70	6	4	10
27	George Poland	44	81	1.84	11	1	12
28	Chris Pearce	41	48	1.17	8	6	14
29	Algernon Wilkinson	39	76	1.95	5	0	5
30	Mike Hooper	38	52	1.37	9	1	10
31	Frank Williams	37	38	1.03	11	0	11
32	Wilf Burrows	35	55	1.57	9	2	11
33	Bert Foster	35	55	1.57	3	1	4
34	Ted Taylor	27	40	1.48	6	0	6
35	Earl Godding	24	46	1.92	5	0	5
36	Graham Beighton	23	51	2.22	1	0	1
37	Alan Jones	23	41	1.78	3	2	5
38	Don Ferguson	22	31	1.41	6	0	6
39	Geoff Atherton	21	30	1.43	6	1	7
40	Herbert Jones	20	45	2.25	2	0	2
41	Albert Dunlop	18	42	2.33	4	1	5
42	George Greatrex	17	37	2.18	1	0	1
43	Dennis Reeves	17	34	2.00	2	1	3
44	Ron Sinclair	16	23	1.44	0	3	3
45	Tommy Wright	16	17	1.06	4	0	4
46	Bill Hayes	15	25	1.67	3	0	3
47	Terry McNee	15	19	1.27	3	1	4
48	Percy Lovett	14	23	1.64	1	0	1
49	Grenville Millington	14	21	1.50	2	1	3
50	Bob Wardle	14	22	1.57	2	1	3
51	Derek Williams	12	18	1.50	0	0	0
52	Bill Connell	10	19	1.90	1	0	1
53	Ken Hughes	10	22	2.20	1	0	1
54	Mike Keen	8	20	2.50	0	0	0
55	Tom Bayley	7	13	1.86	0	0	0
56	Ron Mawson	7	12	1.71	2	0	2
57	Mark Walton	6	10	1.67	2	0	2
58	Chris Sander	5	11	2.20	0	0	0
59	Ken Simpkins	5	15	3.00	0	0	0
60	Arthur Smith	5	6	1.20	2	0	2
61	Arthur Lucas	4	6	1.50	1	0	1
62	John Vaughan	4	6	1.50	0	0	0
63	Darren Heyes	3	4	1.33	0	0	0
64	Jack Prince	3	4	1.33	0	0	0
65	Arthur Evans	2	5	2.50	1	0	1
66	Steve Humphries	2	3	1.50	1	0	1
67	Neville Jones	2	3	1.50	0	0	0
68	David Powell	2	3	1.50	0	0	0
69	Norman Rigby	2	3	1.50	0	0	0
70	Terry Bennett	1	3	3.00	0	0	0
71	Drew Brand	1	4	4.00	0	0	0
72	John Edwards	1	6	6.00	0	0	0
73	Ian Haigh	1	1	1.00	0	0	0
74	Clayton Ince	1	0	0.00	0	1	1
75	Les Murphy	1	1	1.00	0	0	0
76	Bobby Roberts	1	1	1.00	0	0	0
	Total	**3781**	**5563**	**1.47**	**796**	**227**	**1023**

Connections

This section shows player links between Wrexham and other prominent clubs $ Indicates War time guest

Aberdare Athletic
Alfred Beevor
Jimmy Jones
Lot Jones
Bill Lanyon
Jack Smith

Aberdeen
Billy Jackson
Archie Longmuir$
George McMillan
Robert Walker$

Aberystwyth Town
Chris Sander

Accrington Stanley
Dick Finnigan
Bob Foster
Bill Heggie
Billy Jeavons
Joe Keetley
Harold Lapham
Harvey McCreadie
Chris Pearce
Bert Scott
Barry Smith
Paddy Sowden
Emlyn Williams

Airdrie
Tommy Bannan

Albion Rovers
Hugh McMahon
John McTurk
James Rice

Aldershot
Phil Coleman
Malcolm Crosby
Stewart Phillips
Fred Rowell
Alf Somerfield$
Paddy Sowden

Alloa Athletic
Joe Dignam
James Rice
Bert Scott

Altrincham
Bill Bryant
Steve Buxton
David Carrick
Frank Carrodus
Clive Colbridge
Elfyn Edwards
David Esdaille
Steve Fleet
Len Hewitt
Reg Holland
David Jackson
Peter Jackson
Brian Jarvis
Peter Jones
Mickey Metcalf
Don Weston
Frank Williams

Arbroath
Joe McAleer

Arsenal
Arfon Griffiths
Jimmy Harvey
John Roberts
Ehud Rogers

Ashington
Ron Harbetson
Bill Harris

Aston Villa
Frank Carrodus
Tom Gardner
Bert Goode
Fred Goss
John Graham
Tom Griffiths
Fred Haycock
Kevin Keelan
Terry Morrall
Billy Myerscough
Bobby Park
Ken Roberts
Jack Williams

Aylesbury United
Andy Preece
Jason Soloman

Ayr United
Jimmy Hamilton

Bangor City
John Ascroft
Darren Baker
Alan Bermingham
Eric Betts
Eddie Beynon
Wilf Burrows
Arthur Buxton
Steve Buxton
David Campbell
Les Cartwright
Dai Davies
Jonathan Davies
Wyn Davies
Arthur Evans
Dennis Evans
Medwyn Evans
Martin Filson
Dennis Grainger
David Grant
Dennis Griffiths
Gordon Gunson
Ian Haigh
Harry Hollis
Derek Hughes
Steve Humphries
Reg Hunter
David E.Jones
Frank Jones
Kevin Jones
Steve W.Jones
Steve Kenworthy
Craig Knight
Dennis Lambourne
Herbie Large
Brian Lloyd
Cliff Lloyd
Jackie Lloyd
Eddie Lovelady
Alec Lucas
John Lyons
Jim McGill
Stuart Mason
Mickey Metcalf
Jack Moorwood
Roger Mostyn
Aled Owen
Dai Phillips
Brian Price
Jimmy Pugh
Steve Pugh
Bernard Purdie
Billie Rogers
Eli Roberts
Paul Roberts
Neil Salathiel
Gareth Salisbury
John Settle
David Smallman
Barry Smith
Cecil Smith
Jim Smith
Ray Smith
Jason Taylor
Andy Thomas
Robin Thomas
Brian Tinnion
Billy Tudor
John Warburton
Graham Whittle
Alvan Williams
Eddie Williams
Everton Williams
Mike Williams
Peter Williams
Scott Williams
Barry Wright

Barnet
Kevin Dearden
Steve Humphries

Barnsley
George Appleyard
Tommy Boyle
Colin Marshall
Andy Provan
Billy Ronson
George Spruce
Ashley Ward
Emlyn Williams

Barrow
Ted Adams
Tommy Anderson
Tommy Bannan
Harry Beck
Barry Diamond
Jack Holland
Alan Kennedy
Harold Lapham
John McLaughlin
Tom McNab
Billy Matthews
Willie Ouchterlonie
David Proctor
George Warburton
Peter Wilson

Barry Town
Bill Barrow
Bernard Condon
David Giles
David O'Gorman
Chris Pearce
Chris Sander
Keith Webber

Bath City
Bernard Condon
Bob Connor
Martin Filson
Roger Mostyn
Andy Provan
Steve Stacey
Bob Weale

Belfast Celtic
John Donoghue
George Frewin
Leslie Murphy
Ted Regan

Berwick Rangers
Norrie Gillespie

Birmingham City
Keith Bannister
Kevin Bremner
Frank Carrodus
Terry Cooke
Kevin Dearden
Steve Fox
David Giles
Colin Green
Barry Horne
Bryan Hughes
Ernie Islip
John Paskin
John Roberts
Kevin Rogers
Billy Ronson
John Schofield
Alf Sheldon$
Don Weston
Charles Wilson-Jones

Blackburn Rovers
Jack Boothway$
Cliff Bryant
Paul Comstive
Tom Gardner$
David Gregory
Simon Ireland
Arthur Johnson
Cyril Jones$
Harold Lapham
Archie Longmuir
Andy Marriott
Vince O'Keefe
Jack Richards
Mike Salmon
Craig Skinner
Ashley Ward

Blackpool
Ron Barnes
Drew Brand
Wayne Cegielski
Ray Charnley
Mike Conroy
Wyn Davies
Ewan Fenton
Tom Gardner$
Tommy Lewis
Hugh McMahon
Craig Madden
Ian Moir
Vince O'Keefe
Andy Preece
Billy Ronson
Mark Taylor
Ashley Ward
Algy Wilkinson
Charles Wilson-Jones$

Bolton Wanderers
Mike Carter
Paul Comstive
Wyn Davies
Bob Foster$
Tom Griffiths
Jack Hughes
Gordon Jones
Stuart Lee
Mike McBurney
George Oghani
Ernie Phythian
Dai Richards
Mike Salmon
Robbie Savage
Mark Walton

Boston United
Steve Charles
Martin Filson
Ken Simpkins
Peter Thompson
Mick Vinter
Ray Wilkins

Bournemouth
Tommy Anderson
Bill Barrow
George Bellis
Jimmy Case
Frank Fidler
Eddie Lawrence
Jim McGill
Steve Massey
Walter Roberts
Fred Rowell
Kevin Russell
Robbie Savage
Cecil Smith
Peter Thompson
Billy Tunnicliffe
Robert Walker
Alf White

Bradford City
Nigel Beaumont
Bill Bryant$
Ralph Burkinshaw
Bob Connor
Joe Cooke
Pat Egglestone
Alan Fox
John Graham
Ron Harbetson
Harry Hollis$
Steve Ingle
Ernie Islip
David Jackson
Peter Jackson
Harry Lovatt
Frank McGinn$
Adam Mitchell
Chris Pearce
Les Samuels
Robbie Savage
Billy Tunnicliffe
Algy Wilkinson
Graham Williams
Eddie Youds

Bradford P.A.
Roy Ambler
Tony Beanland
Tommy Breakwell
Ray Charnley
Ian Hughes
Jack Hughes
Tommy Lewis
Geoff Lloyd
Billy Matthews
Barry Smith
John Sykes
Alvan Williams

Brentford
Phil Bater
Kevin Dearden
Tecwyn Jones
George Poland$
James Raven
Billy Tunnicliffe$

Brighton H.A.
Kevin Bremner
Jimmy Case
Harry Hollis$
Albert Lumberg
Jimmy Pugh
Mickey Thomas
Billy Tunnicliffe$
Mark Walton
Keith Webber

Bristol City
Jimmy Harvey
Mike Hooper
Billy Matthews
Albert Mays
George Showell
Ron Sinclair
Jack Smith
Steve Stacey
John Vaughan

Bristol Rovers
Phil Bater
Cliff Bryant
Alex Findlay
Terry Oldfield
Eli Postin
James Raven
Paul Raynor
John Vaughan

Brymbo
Nigel Beaumont
Andy Edwards
Jonathan Evans
David Jones
Price Jones
Rob Jones
Steve Kenworthy
Herbie Large
Brian Lloyd
Cliff Lloyd
Jackie Lloyd
Tecwyn Lloyd-Jones
Stuart Parker
Gary Pugh
Dilwyn Roberts
Jason Taylor
Mickey Thomas
George Warburton
J.S.Williams
R.D.Williams
Charles Wilson-Jones

Burnley
Ted Adams
George Bellis
Tommy Boyle
Paul Comstive
Brian Flynn
Tom Gardner
Billy Jeavons
Andy Marriott
Albert Mays
Brian Mooney
Jack Mustard
George Oghani
Chris Pearce
Harold Readett
Kevin Russell
Les Samuels
Cecil Smith
Harry Spencer
Bill White

Burton
Harry Beck
Elfed Evans
Bob Hodgkinson
Billy Jeavons
Dennis Leman
Arthur Lucas
David McAdam
Barney McCabe
David Richards
Jack Smith
Bill Vaughan
Emlyn Williams
Les Williams

Connections

Bury
Ralph Burkinshaw
Frank Carrodus
David Esdaille
Ian Fairbrother
Brian Flynn
Bob Foster
David Gregory
Steve Kenworthy
Craig Madden
Derek Mayers
Vince O'Keefe
John Paskin
Andy Preece
Nick Richardson
Eddie Robertson
Mark Sertori
Dean Spink
Brian Stanton
Ian Stevens
Alvan Williams
Dick Yates$

Caernarfon Town
Darren Baker
Gib Bellis
Harry Bingham
David Campbell
Lewis Coady
Geoff Davies
Wyn Davies
Les Donaldson
Andy Edwards
Mark Emmerson
Bernard Evans
Elfed Evans
Martin Filson
Bill Green
Brian Griffiths
Dennis Griffiths
Estyn Griffiths
Ian Haigh
Seamus Heath
Nick Hencher
Ron Hewitt
Charlie Hughes
Glyn Hughes
Reg Hunter
Alan Jones
David Jones
Frank Jones
Harvey Jones
Haydn Jones
Mark Jones
Arthur Lucas
Mike McBurney
Ray Mielczarek
Elfed Morris
John Mortimer
Wayne Phillips
David Rawlins
John Settle
Jack Smith
John Smith
Robin Thomas
Len Willett
Eddie Williams
Barry Wright

Cambridge United
Les Cartwright
Kevin Dearden
Steve Dowman
John Lyons
Steve Massey
Bobby Shinton
Paul Raynor
John Vaughan

Cardiff City
Phil Bater
Phil Brignull
Elfed Evans
Brian Flynn
David Giles
Ron Hewitt
Steve Humphries
Jimmy Jones
John A.Jones
Jake King
Bob McLaughlin
Jack Nock
George Poland
Eli Postin
David Powell
Nick Richardson
Billy Ronson
Kevin Russell
Chris Sander
Cecil Smith
Jim Smith
Mel Sutton
Mark Taylor
Bob Weale
Eddie Youds

Carlisle United
Bert Adamson
Gordon Bell
Archie Burgon
John Clayton
Jimmy Hamilton
Jack Holland
Tony Larkin
Ralph Lenney
Charlie McCartney
George Oghani
Robert Ross
Ted Savage$
Ian Stevens
Dick Yates

Celtic
Mike Conroy
John Donoghue
Archie Longmuir
Rolando Ugolini

Charlton Athletic
Steve Dowman
Harry Hollis$
Mike Salmon
Steve Stacey
John Vaughan
Bill Welsh
Brian Whitehouse
Dick Yates$
Eddie Youds

Chelsea
Terry Bradbury
Gordon Davies
Chris Ferguson
Joey Jones
Eddie Niedzwiecki
Ted Savage$
Mickey Thomas

Chelmsford City
Wally Bellett
Phil Coleman
Estyn Griffiths
Ben Hannigan
Tecwyn Jones
Tommy Tilston
Steve Wright

Cheltenham Town
Cliff Bryant
Alex Findlay
Sean Reck
Mike Sturridge
Bill Vaughan
Bob Weale
Darren Wright

Chester
Ted Adams$
John Anderson
Geoff Atherton$
Wally Bellett
Gary Bennett
Stan Bennion
Harry Bingham
Terry Bradbury
Bill Bryant$
Jack Capper
Paul Comstive
Jonathan Cross
Geoff Davies
Ian Edwards
Ken Ellis
George Evans
Dick Finnigan
Steve Fox
Bert Goode
Bob Griffiths
Brian Griffiths
Jimmy Hamilton
Ron Hewitt
Joe Hinnigan
Reg Holland
Harry Hollis$
Peter Houghton
Jack Hughes
Horace Jackson
Arthur Johnson
Alf Jones
Frank Jones
Gordon Jones
Harvey Jones
Martin Lane
Jack Leyfield
Gordon Livsey
Brian Lloyd
Ernie Lloyd
Jim McGill
Jesse McLarty$
Tony McLoughlin
Sammy McMillan
Stuart Mason
Tommy Mathias
Billy Matthews
Mickey Metcalf
Gren Millington
Ian Moir
Elfed Morris
Billy Myerscough
Roger Preece
Andy Provan
Bernard Purdie
Dennis Reeves
Gordon Richards
Jack Richards
Nick Richardson
Frank Roberts
Bill Robinson
Ian Rush
Mike Salmon
John Settle
Norman Sharp$
Bobby Simpson
Ron Sinclair
Fred Smallwood
George Spruce
Steve Stacey
Eric Stubbs$
Tommy Tilston
Brian Tinnion
Billy Tunnicliffe$
Graham Turner
Keith Webber
Don Weston
Bill White
Les Williams
Mike Williams
Barry Wright
Dick Yates

Chesterfield
Robert Alleyne
Keith Bannister
Ambrose Brown
John Clayton
Hywel Davies
Jack Hughes
Billy Jeavons
Albert Malam
Gareth Salisbury
Sam Taylor

Cliftonville
Jon Cross
Seamus Heath
James Kelly1

Colchester United
Kevin Bremner
Phil Coleman
Steve Dowman
Martyn King
Tecwyn Lloyd Jones
John Lyons
Andy Marriott
Bobby Roberts
Gareth Salisbury
John Vaughan
Mark Walton
Steve Wright

Colwyn Bay
John Anderson
Geoff Atherton
Gib Bellis
Wilf Burrows
Lewis Coady
Gareth Davies
Fred Davis
Dennis Evans
George Evans
Dick Finnigan
John Foyne
Earl Godding
Estyn Griffiths
Bill Harris
Harry Hollis
Reg Hunter
Brian Jarvis
Alan Jones
David E.Jones
Ken Jones
Neville Jones
Percy Jones
Brian Lloyd
Jesse McLarty
Albert Malam
Keith Matthews
Billy Matthews
Ian Moir
Steve Morgan
Gwyn Morgans
Elfed Morris
John Neal
George Porter
Idris Pryce
Ted Regan
Cledwyn Roberts
Dilwyn Roberts
David Smallman
Phil Spruce
George Warburton
Frank Weaver
Jack Williams
Jesse Williams
George Wynne
Dick Yates

Connah's Quay
Ted Adams
Geoff Atherton
Norman Baker
Jesse Bird
Ray Booth
Matt Burton
Bobby Butt
Lewis Coady
Bill Cotton
Bill Dickie
Jack Ellis
Ken Ellis
Dick Finnigan
Steve Futcher
Harry Hollis
Derek Hughes
Frank Jones
Gordon Jones
Os Jones
Paul Jones
Vernon Keep
Herbie Large
Joe Lloyd
Alec Lucas
Albert Lumberg
Mickey Metcalf
Uriah Miles
Cyril Northam
David O'Gorman
Ted Regan
Ken Taylor
Andrew Thomas
Frank Weaver
Bill Welsh
Eric Williams
Everton Williams
Edgar Wright
Dick Yates

Conwy United
Darren Baker
Alan Bermingham
Andy Edwards
Frank Jones
Mark Jones
Vernon Keep
Brian Price
Eli Roberts

Cork City
Brian Carey
Mike Conroy
Ben Hannigan
John Schofield

Coventry City
Eric Betts
Les Cartwright
Ron Hewitt
Martin Lane
Billy Myerscough
Jimmy Pugh$
Robert Ross
Robert Ross
Billy Toms

Cowdenbeath
John Donoghue
Archie Longmuir
Hugh McMahon
Adam Mitchell

Crewe Alexandra
Peter Baines
Eric Betts
Jack Boothway
Drew Brand
Clive Colbridge
Billy Connell
Bill Cotton
Wyn Davies
Billy Harrison
Jimmy Harvey
Jack Holland
Billy Houston
Geoff Hunter
David E.Jones
Lee Jones
Os Jones
Jack Jones
Norman Jones$
Ron Jones$
Steve A.Jones
Albert Kinsey
Jack Lewis$
Tommy Lewis$
Eric Littler
Tecwyn Lloyd Jones
Harry Lovatt
Jim McGill
Albert Malam$
Stuart Mason
Tommy Millington
Jack Mustard
Albert Parker
Jack Prince
Bernard Purdie
James Roberts
Stan Roberts$
Alf Rowlands
Arthur Rowley
Neil Salathiel
Les Samuels
Bob Scott
Mel Sutton
Mark Taylor
Billy Toms
John Warburton
Ashley Ward
Steve Wright

Crystal Palace
Chris Armstrong
Eric Betts$
Wyn Davies
Ian Edwards
David Giles
Ken Hughes
Ken Jones
John Loughlan
George Poland$
Andy Preece
Alf Somerfield
Harry Spencer$
Tommy Tilston
Eddie Tunney$
Tom Vansitart
Peter Wall
Brian Whitehouse

Cwmbran Town
Kevin Rogers

Dagenham & Redbridge
Gary Worthington

Darlington
Gordon Bell
Jimmy Case
Paul Emson
Bob Graham
Ron Harbetson
Ron Hewitt
Steve Ingle
Barney McCabe
Charlie McCartney
Ken Murray
Walter Odell$
Peter Skipper
Billy Tudor$
Gary Worthington

Connections

Derby County
Martyn Chalk
Steve Emery
Paul Emson
Jimmy Lyons
Mickey Thomas
Peter Thompson
Ashley Ward
Alf White
Ray Wilkins

Derry City
Seamus Heath
Jack Keay
Jake King

Doncaster Rovers
Tommy Anderson
Rowland Bailey
George Burditt
Lewis Coady
David Esdaille
Archie Ferguson
Brian Flynn
Colin Grainger
Dennis Grainger$
Steve Humphries
Simon Ireland
Jack Jones
Joe Keetley
Hugh McMahon
Albert Malam
Stuart Mason
Adam Mitchell
Cyril Price
Alf Somerfield$
Keith Webber
Gary Worthington

Druids United
David Campbell
Derek Hughes
Ian Hughes
Lot Jones
Percy Jones
Herbie Large
Eddie Lawrence
Steve Mackreth
E.D.Roberts

Dumbarton
Barry Diamond
Nathan Fraser
Vince Pritchard

Dundalk
Alan Fox
Ben Hannigan

Dundee
Bert Adamson
John Anderson
Kevin Bremner

Dundee United
Bert Adamson
Dick Grieve
Willie Ouchterlonie
Rolando Ugolini
Bill Welsh

Dunfermline Athletic
Bernard Bonner
Archie Ferguson
Andrew Moffatt
Bert Scott

Durham City
Gordon Bell

East Fife
Bert Adamson
Andrew Moffatt

East Stirlingshire
Tom McNab

Ellesmere Port Town
Geoff Atherton
Bobby Butt
Bill Hayes
Derek Hughes
Alan Jones
Harvey Jones
Jack Jones
John A.Jones
Jack Leyfield
Terry McNee
John Mortimer
Don Parrish
Stan Roberts
Walter Roberts
Eddie Robertson

Everton
Jack Boothway$
Drew Brand
Terry Darracott
Dai Davies
Albert Dunlop
Colin Green
Tom Griffiths
Barry Horne
Billy Jackson
T.G.Jones
Tommy Lewis
Derek Mayers
Tommy Millington
Andrew Moffatt
James Roberts
Bill Robinson
Ehud Rogers$
Walter Rooney
David Smallman
Bobby Simpson
Ted Taylor
Mickey Thomas
Graham Williams
Rowland Woodhouse
Len Wootton$

Exeter City
John Anderson
George Appleyard
Phil Coleman
Joe Cooke
Wynne Crompton
John A.Jones
Dixie McNeil
Vince O'Keefe
Les Samuels
Steve Stacey
Bill Vaughan
Alvan Williams
Gary Worthington

Falkirk
Harry Hollis$
Robert Ross

Flint Town United
Drew Brand
Steve Buxton
Billy Connell
Andy Edwards
Jack Ellis
Ken Ellis
Dennis Grainger
Dennis Griffiths
Harry Hollis
Frank Jones
Gordon Jones
Kevin Jones
Mark Jones
Rob Jones
Vernon Keep
Craig Knight
Tony Lee
Ernie Lloyd
James Mathias
Jack Nock
Vince Pritchard
Billie Rogers
Neil Salathiel
Billy Tudor
Frank Weaver
Algy Wilkinson
Glyn Williams
George Wynne
Dick Yates

Forfar Athletic
Alex Smith

Fulham
Gordon Davies
Harry Hollis$
Bill Jessop$
Frank McKenna
Ted Regan
Ted Savage$
Jason Soloman
Jack Smith
John Vaughan
Mark Walton

Gateshead
Paul Emson
Ken Murray
Ted Robson
Bill Welsh

Gillingham
Kevin Bremner
Stuart Elliott
Joe Hinnigan
Fred Howard
Joe McAleer
Tommy Millington
Paddy Sowden
Mark Walton
Les Williams

Glentoran
Seamus Heath
Leslie Murphy
Bob Weale
Graham Williams

Gloucester City
Steve Emery
Alex Findlay

Grimsby Town
Peter Baines$
Shaun Cunnington
Paul Emson
Tom Gardner
Ron Harbetson
Frank McKenna

Halifax Town
Peter Baines$
Jimmy Case
Graham Cooper
Bill Cotton
Barry Diamond
Elfyn Edwards
Pat Egglestone
Martin Filson
Bob Graham
Darren Heyes
David Jackson
Arthur Johnson
Dudley Lewis
Albert Mays
John Molloy
Elfed Morris
Teddy Read
Nick Richardson
Mark Sertori
Ron Sinclair
Andy Thackeray
Rowland Woodhouse
Gary Worthington

Hamilton Academical
Joe Dignam
Archie Gardiner

Hartlepool United
Peter Baines
Tommy Bamford$
Geoff Davies
Kevin Dearden
Stuart Elliott
Alan Fox
Alan Kennedy
Gordon Livsey
Mike McBurney
Stewart McCallum
Bobby Park
Ernie Phythian
Bob Scott
Ken Simpkins
Fred Smallwood$
Mark Taylor
Peter Thompson
Eddie Tunney$
Bill Welsh

Haverfordwest Co
Chris Sander

Hearts
Les Donaldson$
Archie Gardiner
Stewart McCallum$
John Smith
Bill Welsh

Hednesford Town
James Kelly
Jimmy Lyons
Mike Sturridge

Hereford United
Drew Brand
Mike Carter
Wayne Cegielski
Jon Cross
Chris Elvidge
Steve Emery
Frank Fidler
Jimmy Harvey
Ron Hewitt
Ollie Kearns
Tony Larkin
Percy Lovett
Dixie McNeil
George Oghani
Mel Pejic
Stewart Phillips
Jimmy Pugh
Kevin Russell
Archie Styles
Sam Taylor

Hibernian
Mike Conroy
Joe McClelland
Harvey McCreadie
John J. Smith

Holyhead
Ray Booth
Les Donaldson
Dick Finnigan
Bob Griffiths
Harry Hollis
Fred Howard
Arthur Johnson
David E.Jones
R.T.Jones
Stewart McCallum
Keith Matthews
Aled Owen
John Settle
Ray Williams

Holywell Town
Richard Barnes
Gib Bellis
Eddie Beynon
Steve Buxton
Les Donaldson
Noel Edwards
Brian Griffiths
Glyn Hughes
George Jones
Kevin Jones
Mark Jones
Neville Jones
Norman Jones
Rob Jones
Vernon Keep
Charlie Kelsall
Craig Knight
Jesse McLarty
Gren Millington
Albert Parker
Jimmy Pugh
Neil Salathiel
Les Speed
George Warburton
Ron Wynn

Huddersfield Town
Graham Cooper
Barry Horne
Simon Ireland
Ernie Islip
Joey Jones
Dudley Lewis
Albert Malam
Ray Mielczarek
Bernard Purdie
Paul Raynor
Brian Stanton
Ted Taylor
Andy Thackeray
Peter Ward
Don Weston
Jack Williams

Hull City
Brian Cripsey
Kevin Dearden
Stuart Elliott
Jack Fryer
Tom Gardner
Bert Goode
Harry Hollis$
Matt Lawrence
Steve Massey
Mike Quigley
John Roberts
Peter Skipper
Tommy Wright

Hyde United
Jack Boothway
Barry Diamond
David Esdaille
Jack Hilton
David Jackson
Peter Jackson
Arthur Jones
David O'Gorman
George Oghani
Robert Ross
Mark Wrench

Inter Cardiff
Mickey Thomas

Ipswich Town
Tony Humes
David Lowe
Frank McGinn
Aled Owen
Alf Somerfield$
Steve Stacey
Jack Williams
Eddie Youds

Juventus
Ian Rush

Kettering Town
Bill Cotton
Paul Emson
Ron Jackson
Paul Jones
Ollie Kearns
Gordon Livsey
John Loughlan
Stewart McCallum
Paul Raynor

Kidderminster Harriers
Shaun Cunnington
Fred Haycock$
Ernie Islip
Kevin Keelan
James Kelly1
Gordon Livsey
Gareth Salisbury
Archie Styles
Charles Wilson-Jones
James Wyllie

Kilmarnock
James Wyllie

K.V.Kortijik
John Paskin

Leeds United
George Burditt$
Frank Fidler
Brian Flynn
Colin Grainger
Dennis Grainger
David McAdam
Derek Mayers
Leslie Murphy
George Poland$
Ian Rush
Norman Sharp$
Ron Sinclair
Barry Smith
Mickey Thomas
Don Weston

Leicester City
Robert Alleyne
Jack Brown
Jim Bulling
Brian Carey
Archie Gardiner
Fred Haycock$
Mike Hooper
Ron Jackson
Eric Littler
Harry Lovatt
David Lowe
Jack Nock
Bobby Roberts
Kevin Russell

Connections

Eric Stubbs
Ashley Ward

Lex XI
Nigel Beaumont
Alan Dwyer
Andy Edwards
Nick Hencher
Graham Jones
Mike Keen
Craig Knight
Brian Lloyd
Alec Lucas
Stuart Parker
Gary Pugh
Steve Scott
Jamie Slater
Jason Taylor

Leyton Orient
Tommy Anderson
Terry Bradbury
Mike Conroy
Wynne Crompton
David Giles
Carl Griffiths
Jack Holland
Eddie Lawrence
Albert Lumberg
Joe McAleer
Walter Odell$
Jimmy Pugh$
Paul Raynor
Billie Rogers
Alf Somerfield$
Peter Wall
Brian Whitehouse
Jesse Williams

Limerick
Tommy Anderson
Ewan Fenton
Brian Flynn
Alan Fox
Bill Hayes
Jake King

Lincoln City
Tommy Bannan
Jack Capper
Dennis Grainger$
Ron Harbetson
Seamus Heath
Eric Littler
Joe McAleer
Frank McGinn
Dixie McNeil
Harold Readett$
Ted Savage
Mark Sertori
John Vaughan

Linfield
Leslie Murphy
Tommy Wright

Liverpool
Peter Baines$
Phil Boersma
Jimmy Case
Tom Gardner
Bert Goode
Gordon Gunson
Fred Haycock$
Mike Hooper
Joey Jones
Lee Jones
Ron Jones
Joe Keetley
Alan Kennedy
John McLaughlin
Billy Matthews

Brian Mooney
George Poland$
Arthur Rowley
Ian Rush
Ted Savage$
Peter Wall

Llandudno
Rowland Bailey
Eddie Beynon
Frank Blew
Matt Burton
Gareth Davies
Noel Edwards
Dennis Evans
George Godding
Bob Hodgkinson
Billy Houston
Arthur Hughes
Reg Hunter
Frank Jones
Jack Jones
Neville Jones
Mark Jones
Price Jones
Herbie Large
Jesse McLarty
Elfed Morris
John Muldoon
John Neal
Idris Pryce
Eli Roberts
Phil Spruce
Mickey Thomas
R.D.Williams
Barry Wright

Luton Town
Phil Boersma
Jack Lewis
Harvey McCreadie
Tom Parker
Jimmy Pugh$
Harold Readett$
Gareth Salisbury
Eddie Tunney$
Bill Vaughan

Macclesfield Town
Frank Carrodus
Jonathan Davies
Kieron Durkan
Elfyn Edwards
Colin Grainger
Jack Hilton
Billy Houston
Peter Jackson
Os Jones
Mike Lake
Jack Leyfield
Harry Lovatt
Jim McGill
John Molloy
Billy Myerscough
Vince Pritchard
Teddy Read
Fred Smallwood
Cecil Smith
Ray Wilkins

Manchester City
Ken Barnes
Ted Bennett
Jack Boothway
Frank Carrodus
Terry Cooke
Gordon Davies
Wyn Davies
Dick Finnigan
Steve Fleet
Carl Griffiths
Fred Howard

Lot Jones
Ray Kelly
Stuart Lee
Dennis Leman
Les McDowall
Albert Malam$
Mike Quigley
Bobby Shinton
Ashley Ward
Jeff Whitley
Derek Williams
Charles Wilson-Jones$
Tommy Wright

Manchester United
Tommy Bamford
Bill Bryant
Terry Cooke
Wyn Davies
Frank Fidler$
Tom Gardner$
David Gaskell
Billy Harrison
Peter Jones
Albert Kinsey
Eddie McIlvenny
Sammy McMillan
Ian Moir
Jimmy Pugh
Ted Savage
Mickey Thomas
Billy Toms
Mark Wilson

Mansfield Town
Eric Betts
Albert Brown
Mike Carter
Steve Charles
John Clayton
Simon Ireland
Ken Murray
Bobby Roberts
Alf Somerfield
Mick Vinter
Charles Wilson-Jones$

Merthyr
Alfred Beevor
Phil Brignull
Gordon Davies
David Giles
George Holmes
Dennis Lambourne
Dudley Lewis
Albert Mays
Jack Nock
Dai Richards
Kevin Rogers
Bill Vaughan
Mark Walton
Billy Waters

Middlesbrough
Billy Ashcroft
Peter Baines$
Phil Boersma
Tom Griffiths
Dai Richards
Rolando Ugolini
Jesse Williams

Millwall
Chris Armstrong
Kevin Bremner
George Burditt
Phil Coleman
Dennis Grainger$
John Lyons
Jack Nock

Ted Savage$
Bobby Shinton
Alf Somerfield$
Billy Waters

Morecambe
Tony Beanland
Ray Charnley
Paul Comstive
Barry Diamond
Andy Edwards
Alan Kennedy
John Muldoon
Brian Stanton
George Warburton
Keith Webber

Morton
John Loughlan
John McTurk

Motherwell
Bobby Roberts

New Brighton
Ted Adams$
Peter Baines
Stan Bennion
Matt Burton
Arthur Buxton
George Greatrex
Phil Gwatkin
David Harding
Bill Heggie
Fred Howard
David Hughes
Arthur Johnson
Jack Jones
Charlie Kelsall$
Pat Kinsella
Albert Lumberg
Albert Malam
Billy Matthews
Gwyn Morgan
John Mortimer
Jack Mustard
Stan Roberts
Brian Stanton
Dick Yates

Nelson
Gordon Gunson
Bert Scott

New York Cosmos
Brian Tinnion

Newcastle United
Wyn Davies
Mike Hooper
Alan Kennedy
Ehud Rogers
Ian Rush
Bobby Shinton
Fred Smallwood$
Tommy Wright

Newport AFC
Stewart Phillips
Kevin Rogers

Newport County
Phil Brignull
Steve Dowman
Steve Emery
David Giles
Jack Holland
Glyn Hughes
Frank McKenna
Sean Reck
David Richards
Billie Rogers

Andy Thackeray
Mick Vinter
Bob Weale
Bill Welsh

Newtown
Steve Buxton
Andy Edwards
Jake King
John Muldoon
Neil Salathiel
David Smallman
Len Willett

Northampton Town
John Anderson
Ralph Burkinshaw
Wayne Cegielski
Peter Fisher
Wayne Cegielski
Peter Fisher
Bill Graham
Fred Haycock$
Harry Lovatt
Joe McAleer
Dixie McNeil
Steve Massey
Bobby Park
Andy Preece
John Roberts

Northwich Victoria
Robbie Barnes
Terry Bradbury
Steve Buxton
Wayne Cegielski
Graham Cooper
Geoff Davies
Gordon Davies
Les Donaldson
Mark Emmerson
Martin Filson
Phil Gwatkin
Seamus Heath
Ron Hewitt
Jack Hilton
Peter Houghton
Harvey McCreadie
Billy Matthews
John Mortimer
David O'Gorman
George Oghani
Jack Prince
David Proctor
Walter Rooney
Neil Salathiel
Bob Scott
Keith Webber
Len Wootton
Mark Wrench

Norwich City
Keith Bannister
Ron Barnes
Ted Bennett
John A.Jones
Kevin Keelan
Frank McKenna
David Proctor
Mark Walton
Ashley Ward
Brian Whitehouse

Nottingham Forest
Albert Brown
George Burditt
Jack Fryer
Fred Haycock$
Andy Marriott
Alf Rowlands
Eric Stubbs
Billy Tudor$

Charles Wilson-Jones
Tommy Wright

Notts County
Archie Burgon
Shaun Cunnington
Fred Haycock$
Eddie Lawrence
Harry Lovatt
Charlie McCartney
Albert Mays
Kevin Russell
Alf Somerfield$
Mick Vinter

Nuneaton Borough
Eric Betts
Jack Brown
Les Cartwright
Bill Dallas
Bill Jessop
Gordon Livsey
John Schofield
Mike Sturridge

Oldham Athletic
Eric Betts
Jon Bowden
Bill Cope
Bob Foster
Dennis Grainger
Steve Humphries
Brian Jarvis
Billy Jeavons
Bill Jessop
Arthur Jones
Archie Longmuir
Arthur Jones
Jim McGill
Steve Morgan
Ken Murray
Jack Prince
Harold Readett$
Bert Scott
Peter Skipper
Barry Smith
Jim Steel
Ted Taylor
Billy Toms
Derek Williams

Oswestry Town
Nigel Beaumont
Matt Burton
David Carrick
Wynne Crompton
Jonathan Davies
Alan Dwyer
Noel Edwards
Mark Emmerson
George Evans
Tom Gardner
Seamus Heath
Nick Hencher
Len Hewitt
Bob Hodgkinson
Alan Hill
Charlie Hughes
Derek Hughes
Ian Hughes
Jack Hughes
David E.Jones
Frank Jones
George Jones
Graham Jones
Ken Jones
Lot Jones
Os Jones
Steve W.Jones
Pat Kinsella
David Lambert
Bill Leeming

Connections

Cliff Lloyd
Geoff Lloyd
Alec Lucas
Sammy McMillan
Steve Mackreth
Stuart Mason
Billy Matthews
Gren Millington
Tommy Millington
Ian Moir
John Molloy
Roger Mostyn
John Muldoon
Jack Nock
Stuart Parker
George Porter
Vince Pritchard
Idris Pryce
Bernard Purdie
Iorwerth Richards
Ehud Rogers
Dilwyn Roberts
John Roberts
Ken Roberts
Ron Roberts
Alf Rowlands
Neil Salathiel
Steve Scott
David Smallman
Cecil Smith
John Smith
Keith Webber
Darren Weetman
Ray Wilkins
Frank Williams
Graham Williams
R.D.Williams
Barry Wright

Oxford United
Jack Capper
Joe Cooke
Bernard Evans
David Fogg
Ollie Kearns
Eddie McIlvenny
Sean Reck
Mike Salmon
Barry Smith
Mick Vinter

Partick Thistle
John Anderson
Jim McGill
Tom McNab

Peterborough United
Keith Bannister
Ron Barnes
Kevin Bremner
Joe Cooke
Kevin Dearden
David Gregory
Carl Griffiths
Bill Lanyon
Charlie McCartney
Steve Massey
Bobby Park
Kevin Russell
Ray Smith
Jason Soloman

Plymouth Argyle
Wally Bellett
Kevin Bremner
Mike Carter
Fred Haycock$
Albert Mays
Robert Ross
Craig Skinner
Jack Smith
Billy Toms

Port Vale
Jon Bowden
David Brammer
David Carrick
Wayne Cegielski
Bill Cope
Geoff Davies
Steve Fox
Colin Grainger
Carl Griffiths
Ian Griffiths
Billy Harrison
George Holmes
Geoff Hunter
Brian Lloyd
David Lowe
Chris Pearce
Jack Prince
Jim Steel
Billy Tunnicliffe
Frank Williams
Graham Williams
Len Wootton
Dick Yates$

Porthmadog
Richard Barnes
Ray Booth
Lewis Coady
Ian Edwards
Alan Jones
Cyril Jones
Haydn Jones
Martyn King
John Lloyd
Tecwyn Lloyd-Jones
Paul Nicoll
Brian Price
Gary Pugh
Steve Pugh
Paul Roberts
Ken Taylor
Robin Thomas
Elfyn Williams
John Williams

Portsmouth
Ambrose Brown
David Gregory
Carl Griffiths
Barry Horne
John McLaughlin
Tom Parker
Ted Robson

Preston North End
Steve Basham
Gary Bennett
David Carrick
Ray Charnley
Tom Gardner$
Joe Hinnigan
Jack Holland
Peter Houghton
Bill Jessop
Derek Mayers
Brian Mooney
Jack Mustard
Paul Raynor
Ian Stevens
John Vaughan
Frank Williams
Emlyn Williams
Rowland Woodhouse

Queen of the South
Tommy Anderson
John McTurk
Len Wootton

Q.P.R.
Tommy Anderson

Bernard Evans
Chris Ferguson
Jack Mustard
Alf Somerfield$

Raith Rovers
Archie Ferguson
Willie Ouchterlonie

Reading
Kevin Bremner
Fred Davis
Barry Hunter
Ollie Kearns
Harry Littlehales
Sean Reck
Alf Rowlands
Bob Scott
Fred Smallwood
Billy Tunnicliffe$
Tommy Wright
Dick Yates$

Rhyl
Stan Bennion
Graham Bent
Ray Booth
Clive Colbridge
Fred Davis
Les Donaldson
Albert Dunlop
Mark Emmerson
Bernard Evans
Steve Fox
David Grant
Colin Green
Ian Haigh
Seamus Heath
Nick Hencher
Barry Horne
Charlie Hughes
David Hughes
Ian Hughes
Arthur Johnson
Brian Johnson
Eric Johnson
Frank Jones
Graham Jones
Haydn Jones
Herbert Jones
Mark Jones
Neville Jones
Rob Jones
Steve W.Jones
Pat Kinsella
Tony Lee
Brian Lloyd
Ernie Lloyd
Geoff Lloyd
John Lloyd
Albert Lumberg
Stewart McCallum
Joe McClelland
Terry McNee
Derek Mayers
Bob Miles
Gren Millington
John Molloy
John Mortimer
Bernard Parden
Don Parrish
Idris Pryce
Gary Pugh
David Reilly
Kevin Rogers
John Settle
Cecil Smith
Phil Spruce
Keith Webber
Darren Weetman
Eddie Williams
Everton Williams

Jesse Williams
John Wood
Steve Wright

Rochdale
John Anderson
Ron Barnes
Eric Betts
Jon Bowden
Tommy Breakwell$
David Carrick
Paul Comstive
Joe Cooke
Kevin Dearden
Barry Diamond
John Graham
Dick Grieve
Ian Griffiths
Jimmy Hamilton
Os Jones$
Cyril Lawrence
Joe McAleer
Albert Malam$
Stuart Mason
Uriah Miles
Steve Morgan
Chris Pearce
Jack Prince
Stan Roberts$
Ted Robson
Bob Scott
John Shonaken
George Snow
Brian Stanton
Andy Thackeray
Peter Ward
Scott Williams
Dick Yates$

Rotherham United
Dennis Grainger$
Ernie Islip$
Ray Mielczarek
Billy Myerscough
Don Weston
Algy Wilkinson$

Runcorn
John Ascroft
Frank Carrodus
Mark Cartwright
Alan Dwyer
Elfyn Edwards
George Greatrex
Peter Houghton
Billy Houston
Bob Hudson
Norman Jones
Steve W.Jones
Tony Lee
Arthur Lucas
Jesse McLarty
Albert Malam
Keith Matthews
Mark Morris
Steve Pugh
Walter Rooney
Ken Simpkins
John Smith
George Spruce
Graham Williams

Scarborough
Ralph Burkinshaw
Steve Charles
Gordon Livsey
Harry Lovatt
Colin Marshall
George Oghani
Dean Spink
Peter Thompson

Scunthorpe United
Alfred Beevor
Steve Charles
Darren Heyes
Dennis Leman
Cyril Price
Robert Ross
Mark Sertori
Peter Skipper

Sheffield United
Ralph Burkinshaw
Steve Charles
Colin Grainger
Dennis Grainger$
Mike Lake
David Powell

Sheffield Wednesday
Ralph Burkinshaw
George Holmes
Ernie Islip$
Dennis Leman

Shrewsbury Town
Roy Ambler
Eddie Beynon
Kevin Bremner
Jim Bulling
Wilf Burrows
Pat Egglestone
Chris Elvidge
Peter Fisher
Bob Griffiths
Carl Griffiths
Eric Hope
Ken Hughes
Billy Jeavons
Jack Keay
Jake King
Tony Larkin
Percy Lovett
Tommy Mathias
Ian Moir
Terry Morrall
John Paskin
Roger Preece
Jack Prince
Dean Spink
Ian Stevens
Mickey Thomas
Graham Turner
Bill Vaughan
Peter Wall
Bob Wardle
Bob Williams
Frank Williams
Jesse Williams
Bill Wyness

South Liverpool
Bill Cotton
David Grant
Ian Haigh
Joe Hinnigan
Peter Houghton
Derek Hughes
Gordon Jones
Jesse McLarty
Albert Parker
Alf Rowlands
Frank Williams
Dick Yates

South Shields
Ralph Burkinshaw
Bill Harris
Ralph Lenney
Jack Mustard
Bill Wyness

Southampton
Peter Brown

Jimmy Case
Bob Foster
Bert Goode$
Barry Horne
Bob McLaughlin
Fred Smallwood
Bob Weale
Stuart Williams

Southend United
Bill Barrow
Tony Beanland
Gary Bennett
Terry Bradbury
Les Cartwright
Barry Hunter
Steve Ingle
Lot Jones
Brian Lloyd
Sammy McMillan
Eddie May
Jack Mustard
Ray Smith

Southport
Ted Adams
Roy Ambler
Tony Beanland
George Bellis
Paul Comstive
Bill Dickie
Elfyn Edwards
Elfed Evans
Tom Gardner$
Steve Ingle
Billy Jeavons
Os Jones
Jack Leyfield
Stewart McCallum
Albert Malam$
Gwyn Morgan
Terry Morrall
Steve Morris
Roger Preece
Andy Provan
Harold Readett$
Ted Savage$
John Shonaken
Bill Welsh
James Wyllie

St.Johnstone
Hugh Robertson
Aly McGowan

St.Mirren
Tommy Anderson
Bill Dallas
Pat McMahon
John McTurk
Andy Provan

Stafford Rangers
Ken Barnes
Robbie Barnes
Harry Beck
Terry Bennett
Billy Houston
Steve Humphries
Ken Jones
Paul Jones
Harry Lovatt
Idris Pryce
Ron Roberts
Peter Skipper
Les Speed
Billy Tunnicliffe
Bill Vaughan
Darren Wright

Stalybridge Celtic
Roy Ambler

Connections

Bill Bryant
David Carrick
Steve Charles
Martin Filson
David Gardner
Steve Morgan
Harold Readett
Les Samuels
Cecil Smith
Alvan Williams

Stenhousmuir
Robert Ross

Stevenage Borough
Paul Raynor
Jason Soloman

Stirling Albion
Joe Dignam
John McTurk

Stockport County
Tommy Anderson
Graham Beighton
Bill Bryant$
Steve Buxton
Martyn Chalk
Wyn Davies
Barry Diamond
Kieron Durkan
Alan Dwyer
Dick Finnigan
Steve Fleet
Harry Hollis$
Steve Ingle
Bill Jessop
Peter Jones
T.G.Jones$
Kevin Keelan
Pat Kinsella
Stuart Lee
Brian Lloyd
Ernie Lloyd
Albert Lumberg
Sammy McMillan
Steve Massey
Billy Matthews
George Oghani
John Paskin
Wayne Phillips
Andy Preece
Len Rowland
Mike Salmon
Les Samuels
Mark Sertori
Barry Smith
Ian Stevens
Billy Toms
Peter Ward
Keith Webber

Stoke City
Jack Boothway$
Matt Burton
Bill Cope
David Gregory
Billy Harrison$
Jock Kirkby
Hugh McMahon
Pat McMahon$
Jack Moorwood
Mel Pejic
Kevin Russell
Robbie Savage
Ron Sinclair
Mickey Thomas

Sunderland
Terry Cooke
Shaun Cunnington
Nathan Fraser$
Colin Grainger
Gordon Gunson
Joe Hinnigan
Alan Kennedy
Les McDowall
Andy Marriott
Brian Mooney
Ted Robson
Fred Smallwood$
Neil Wainwright

Swansea City
Tommy Bamford
Gordon Bell
Ted Bennett
Phil Boersma
Bernard Condon
Dai Davies
David Giles
Jack Holland
T.G.Jones$
Dudley Lewis
Joe Lloyd
Eddie May
David O'Gorman
Stewart Phillips
Paul Raynor
John Roberts
Ted Robson
Ehud Rogers
Chris Sander
Steve Watkin
Graham Williams

Swindon Town
Mike Carter
Kevin Dearden
Stuart Elliott
Gordon Gunson
Billy Tudor$
Bob Weale

Telford United
Robert Alleyne
Nigel Beaumont
Steve Buxton
Ken Hughes
Steve Humphries
Roger Preece
Neil Salathiel

Third Lanark
John Donoghue

Ton Pentre
Jimmy Jones
Kevin Rogers
Billy Waters

Torquay United
Tommy Anderson
Ian Arkwright
Ron Barnes
Elfed Evans
Bill Hayes
Jimmy Jones
Dudley Lewis
Vince O'Keefe
Andy Provan
Harry Spencer$
Harry Waller
Steve Wright

Tottenham Hotspur
Chris Armstrong
Archie Burgon
Kevin Dearden
Gordon Jones
Walter Odell
Aled Owen
Eddie Tunney$

Tranmere Rovers
Billy Ashcroft
Wally Bellett
Gary Bennett
George Bellis$
Wilf Burrows
Dai Davies
Elfyn Edwards
Jack Ellis
Bernard Evans
Dennis Evans
Bob Foster$
Nathan Fraser
Bob Griffiths
Ian Griffiths
Phil Gwatkin
Jimmy Harvey
Seamus Heath
David Jackson
Peter Jackson
Gordon Jones$
Lee Jones
Os Jones
Pat Kinsella
Reg Leck
Harry Littlehales
Mike McBurney
Albert Malam$
James Roberts
Ron Roberts
Eddie Robertson
Bill Robinson$
Alf Rowlands
Arthur Rowley
Jim Steel
Tommy Tilston
Eddie Tunney$
Graham Williams
Dick Yates$

Walsall
Harry Beck
Eric Betts
Dennis Grainger$
Bill Green
Fred Haycock$
Ron Hewitt
Bill Jessop$
Paul Jones
Ollie Kearns
James Kelly1
James Kelly2
Martin Lane
Bill Lanyon
Albert Mays
Billy Myerscough
Bobby Shinton
Ron Sinclair
Peter Skipper
Sam Taylor

Watford
Tommy Anderson
Os Jones
Ted Robson
Jason Soloman

Wellington Town
George Bellis
Eddie Beynon
Arthur Buxton
Jonathan Davies
Tom Gardner
Bill Green
Frank Jones
Alf Edwards
Alf Sheldon
Harry Waller
Graham Williams
Jesse Williams

Welshpool
Terry Bennett
Fred Howard
Graham Jones
Mike McBurney
Alf Rowlands

West Bromwich Albion
Shaun Cunnington
Ian Edwards
Elfed Evans
Gren Jones
Craig Madden
Andy Marriott
John Paskin
Stewart Phillips
David Powell (GK)
George Savage
Archie Styles
Mickey Thomas
Billy Tudor
Brian Whitehouse
Stuart Williams
Charles Wilson-Jones$

West Ham United
Eric Betts
Phil Brignull
Bill Cope
Ernie Islip$
Pat McMahon
Ted Savage$
Bob Weale

Weymouth
Terry Bradbury
Phil Brignull
Gordon Livsey
Andy Preece
Fred Rowell
Bobby Shinton

Wigan Athletic
Gary Bennett
Paul Comstive
Geoff Davies
David Gaskell
John Graham
Ian Griffiths
Joe Hinnigan
Peter Houghton
Alan Kennedy
Pat Kinsella
Albert Kinsey
David Lowe
Tony McLoughlin
Dennis Reeves
Peter Skipper
Jim Steel
Alvan Williams
Gary Worthington

Wigan Borough
Barney McCabe
Norman Rigby
Cecil Smith
Bill Welsh

Wimbledon
Geoff Davies
John Loughlan
Tom Vansitart

Winsford United
Elfyn Edwards
Mark Emmerson
David Esdaille
Dick Finnigan
John Foyne
Bill Heggie
Alf Jones
George Jones
Tony Lee
Jack Leyfield
Ernie Lloyd
Albert Lumberg
John Molloy
Don Parrish
Walter Roberts
Len Rowland
Eric Stubbs
Billy Toms
Eddie Tunney
Bill Vaughan
Len Willett
Ron Wynn

Witton Albion
Ken Barnes
Drew Brand
David Carrick
David Esdaille
Frank Fidler
David Gardner
Ron Hewitt
Brian Jarvis
Brian Johnson
Alan Jones
John A.Jones
David Lambert
John Lloyd
Billy Matthews
Keith Matthews
Mickey Metcalf
Uriah Miles
Gren Millington
John Molloy
Mark Sertori
Eddie Williams

Wolves
Ian Arkwright
George Bellis
Bill Bryant
Billy Harrison
Fred Haycock$
Albert Hill
Paul Jones
Joe Keetley
James Kelly
Jimmy Kelly
Albert Lumberg
John Paskin
George Showell
Alf Somerfield$

Worcester City
Les Cartwright
Wayne Cegielski
Billy Jeavons
Jimmy Jones
John A.Jones
Norman Jones
Martin Lane
Barney McCabe
Stewart Phillips
Andy Preece
Alf Sheldon
Bobby Shinton
Jim Smith
Darren Wright

Workington
John Ascroft
Clive Colbridge
Earl Godding
Bob Graham
Gordon Livsey
Stewart McCallum
Robert Ross
Len Rowland
Brian Tinnion

Wycombe Wanderers
Jason Soloman

Yeovil
Bill Cotton
Frank Fidler
Bob McLaughlin
Tommy Millington
Ken Murray
Peter Wilson

York City
Roy Ambler
Harry Beck
Wilf Burrows
Clive Colbridge
Graham Cooper
Malcolm Crosby
Barry Jones
Barney McCabe
Charlie McCartney
Craig Madden
Andy Provan
Ted Savage$
Craig Skinner
Les Williams

Wrexham F.C. Players 1890 - 1921

The following is a list of players to have played for Wrexham Football Club between 1890 and 1921. The appearances and goals shown are those from the Combination League (CL), Welsh League (WL), and the Birmingham & District League (BL). F.A.Cup (FAC) and Welsh Cup (WC) appearances and goals are also listed from that period only.
(If you can help with the forenames or with any other information on these players careers, then we would like to hear from you)

		Appearances/Goals				
Name	**Seasons with club**	**CL**	**WL**	**BL**	**FAC**	**WC**
Allman,	1909 - 1910			33-15	1-0	5-4
Antwiss,	1913 - 1914			3-1		1-0
Atherton,	1903 - 1904	1-0				
Ball, William	1893 - 1896	13-0	33-0		10-0	8-0
Barker,	1910 - 1911			5-4	1-1	
Beckett-Lloyd,	1903 - 1904	3-0				
Beeston, H	1894 - 1895		8-0			3-0
Bell,	1919 - 1920			2 0		
Berry, Arthur	1906 - 1910 & 1911 - 1914			58-18	6-0	7-3
Bickley, E	1919 - 1920			1-0		
Billington,	1898 - 1899 & 1905 - 1906			1-0		
Bishop, A	1920 - 1921			7-0	7-0	7-0
Blackburn,	1914 - 1915			11-2		1-0
Blactin,	1905 - 1906			6-0		
Blew, Frank	1919 -			13-0		2-0
Blew, Horace	1897 - 1911	138-2		84-1	27-0	34-0
Blytheway, George	1906 - 1907 & 1906 - 1910			57-22	6-4	9-2
Bond,	1890 - 1891	1-0				
Boxley, Fred	1919 - 1920			34-0	3-0	5-0
Bradshaw,	1906 - 1907			2-0	3-0	
Brammall	1908 - 1909			2-0		
Brewer,	1899 - 1900	1-0				
Brookes,	1901 - 1902	14-3			3-1	2-1
Brown,	1891 - 1892	1-0				
Burke, Thomas	1891 - 1892					
Butler, John	1893 - 1894	16-9			3-2	
Butterton,	1919 - 1920			5-5		1-0
Cafferty, M	1890 - 1891	2-0				
Caffikey,	1890 - 1891	1-0				
Caldow,	1913 - 1914			1-0		
Cane, J	1901 - 1903 & 1905 - 1906	30-5		1-0	3-1	4-0
Catherall,	1912 - 1913			4-0	4-1	
Cawthra, F	1913 - 1914			7-4		
Challinor,	1898 - 1900	26-8			3-1	4-3
Challoner,	1905 - 1906			1-0		
Chapple, Ernest	1906 - 1909			40-0	8-0	5-0
Charleston,	1919 - 1921			2-0		
Clarke, E	1906 - 1908			4-3		
Clutton,	1908 - 1909			1-0		
Coffin,	1911 - 1912			1-0		
Collins, W	1893 - 1896	3-0	12-2		3-0	
Cook, Arthur F	1910 - 1911			34-0	2-0	4-0
Cook, Fred C	1908 - 1915			171-11	20-4	23-4
Cooper,	1898 - 1899	1-0				
Corbett, B	1907 - 1908			4-0	1-0	
Corfield, Sam	1909 - 1911			65-6	3-2	9-1
Coventry,	1906 - 1907			5-0	4-0	
Dargie, Arthur	1907 - 1909			3-2		
Davies,	1907 - 1908			2-0		
Davies, A	1898 - 1899	4-1				
Davies, Arthur	1902 - 1905	3-0				
Davies, C	1914 - 1915			32-1	6-1	5-1
Davies, David 'Dai'	1900 - 1907	110-2		51-0	10-0	16-1
Davies, D	1912 - 1915			2-0	1-0	
Davies, F	1911 - 1912			1-2	2-1	
Davies, G	1890 - 1891	1-0				
Davies, George	1914 - 1915			34-12	6-5	5-1
Davies, J	1890 - 1891	3-0				1-0
Davies, J. 'Ned'	1890 - 1891	2-0				
Davies, J.T.	1903 - 1904	1-0				
Davies, John Wilson	1897 - 1899	2-1				1-0
Davies, Llewelyn Charles	1900 - 1903 & 1904 - 1920	58-5		233-10	38-0	45-1
Davies, Oswald	1890 - 1892	2-0			1-0	4-1
Davies, P	1903 - 1904	1-0				
Davies, Robert O.	1890 - 1894	56-9	16-3		9-1	10-6
Davies, T	1903 - 1904					
Davies, Thomas Charles	1896 -1899					

		Appearances/Goals				
Name	**Seasons with club**	**CL**	**WL**	**BL**	**FAC**	**WC**
Davies, Walter	1910 - 1913			29-8	2-2	4-4
Davies, William	1902 - 1905	50-35		3-2	8-13	
Dawson,	1892 - 1893	2-0				
Dawson,	1906 - 1907			14-2	2-0	1-0
Depledge,	1911 - 1912			3-0		
Devaney, George A.	1910 - 1915			154-0	22-0	19-0
Dillon,	1911 - 1912			6-0	2-0	
Dodd,	1892 - 1893	1-0				
Dodd, Albert	1908 - 1909			1-0	1-0	
Douglas, W	1914 - 1915			28-13	2-0	3-2
Eaborn,	1890 - 1891	1-0				
Edwards, Hugh	1903 - 1905	4-0				
Edwards, L	1892 - 1894	18-0			1-0	3-0
Edwards, Lem	1912 - 1913			2-0		
Edwards, Noel	1919 -			59-27	9-7	10-4
Edwards, W	1891 - 1892	1-0				
Ellis, Arthur Edward	1890 - 1898	69-0	25-1		13-0	22-0
Ellis, M.Jack	1919 -			31-0	4-0	5-0
Elm,	1912 - 1913			1-0		
Evans, Albert	1906 - 1908			1-0		
Evans, Arthur	1906 - 1909			8-1		1-0
Evans, F.T.	1890 - 1891	2-0			1-0	
Evans,	1894 - 1895		1-0			
Evans,	1908 - 1909			1-0		
Evans, Jabez	1920 - 1921			7-0	4-0	
Evans, John	1906 - 1909			7-0		
Evans, Percy	1909 - 1912			36-6	1-0	5-1
Evans, Robert Owen	1899 - 1903	68-0			7-0	8-0
Evans, R.H.	1905 - 1906			1-0		
Evans, Richard	1905 - 1906			7-2		
Evans, Robert Ernest	1905 - 1906			28-4		3-1
Evison, J	1890 - 1891	1-0				
Evison,	1905 - 1906				1-0	
Fenner, William Edward	1909 - 1910 & 1913 - 1915			64-3	7-0	11-0
Fisher, W	1890 - 1891 & 1892 - 1894	8-0				1-0
Flemming,	1912 - 1914			4-0		2-0
Forkin,	1907 - 1908				1-0	
Forsyth,	1912 - 1913			1-0		
Foster, Bert	1919 -			47-5	3-2	6-0
Fowler,	1905 - 1907			19-0	1-0	
Freeman, J	1905 - 1907			31-20	2-0	1-3
Gallagher,	1913 - 1914			9-0		1-0
Garrett,	1897 - 1899	23-6				2-1
Gillam, Sam	1890 - 1892	2-0				
Gittins, C	1891 - 1892	2-0				
Godding, George	1919 - 1920				2-0	
Godfrey, E	1890 - 1891					1-0
Goode, Bert	1910 - 1911 & 1913 -			163-78	21-17	27-29
Goodwin, Tommy	1907 - 1908			1-0	1-0	
Goodwin,	1913 - 1914			1-0		
Gordon, Tommy	1899 - 1907	129-68		46-15	15-8	20-10
Gough,	1892 - 1893	1-0				
Grainger, Harry	1893 - 1894 & 1898 - 1903	93-14			10-2	13-1
Greaves,	1911 - 1912			1-0		
Green,	1904 - 1905	1-0				
Green,	1911 - 1912			2-2		
Griffiths,	1909 - 1910			2-0		
Griffiths, A	1912 - 1914			24-3	5-0	1-0
Griffiths, E	1896 - 1897	2-0				
Griffiths, George	1903 - 1905 & 1906 - 1908	3-2		1-0		
Griffiths, Llew	1899 - 1908	119-62		55-24	17-5	17-11
Griffiths, R	1902 - 1903	1-0				
Griffiths, Robert	1919 - 1920			33-0	5-1	5-0
Griffiths, W	1904 - 1905	1-1				
Grindley,	1904 - 1905	1-0				
Grundy,	1904 - 1905	7-1				
Hancock,	1909 - 1910			28-0	1-0	5-0
Harrison, William Clare	1891 - 1892, 1893 - 1904 & 1905 - 1906	127-16	27-19		21-8	21-5
Harwood,	1911 - 1912			2-0		
Hayes, Abel	1890 - 1894	68-7	15-1		9-1	16-1
Hesketh, William	1903 - 1907	48-5		44-0	5-0	8-0
Hewitt, E	1897 - 1898	3-1				1-0
Hewitt, Thomas John	1910 - 1911			23-0	2-0	2-0
Holmes, F	1890 - 1891	4-1				1-0
Hoskins, E	1913 - 1914			6-2	2-2	
Huffadine, Ernie	1906 - 1915			297-7	38-1	36-1

Name	Seasons with club	Appearances/Goals CL	WL	BL	FAC	WC
Hughes,	1920 - 1921			1-2		
Hughes, A	1912 - 1913			1-0	1-0	
Hughes, Arthur	1905 - 1909			39-9	3-1	4-0
Hughes, Edward	1911 - 1912 & 1913 - 1915			38-13	8-2	4-1
Hughes, Edwin	1903 - 1906	31-3		26-8	3-0	7-1
Hughes, Francis	1910 - 1915			72-0	13-0	7-0
Hughes, John	1891 - 1899	42-16	19-19		6-0	12-8
Hughes, Jack	1906 - 1909			56-0	5-0	5-0
Hughes, J	1903 - 1904	18-1			1-0	1-0
Hughes, J.L.	1903 - 1904	8-0				
Hughes,	1901 - 1902	23-13			4-1	6-1
Hughes, Richard	1903 - 1906 & 1907 - 1908	21-10		1-0	5-0	4-0
Hughes, S	1912 - 1913			2-1		
Hughes, S	1919 - 1920			3-0		
Hughes, W	1903 - 1904	1-0				
Humphreys, Harry	1896 - 1897	2-0				
Humphreys,	1911 - 1912			1-0		
Hunter, W	1893 - 1894	4-0			1-0	
Husbands, Ted	1908 - 1910			46-0	3-0	9-0
Hutsby,	1911 - 1912			16-0	5-0	
Jackson,	1903 - 1904	5-2				
James, Edwin	1893 - 1894	3-0			1-1	
Jardine, David	1896 - 1902	80-1			9-0	12-0
Jardine, David	1914 - 1921			52-14	5-0	8-0
Jenkins,	1892 - 1893	1-0				
Jones, Ben	1919 - 1920			1-0	1-3	
Jones, C	1891 - 1892	2-0				
Jones, C	1910 - 1911			3-2	2-0	
Jones, E	1890 - 1891	1-0				
Jones, E	1902 - 1903	4-1				
Jones, Elias	1893 - 1894	13-0	1-0		3-0	2-0
Jones, Emlyn	1909 - 1910 & 1913 - 1914			10-0		
Jones, F	1920 - 1921			3-1		
Jones, Frank	1914 - 1915			8-0		
Jones, Glyn	1909 - 1910			2-0		
Jones, Gordon	1906 - 1907			30-8	5-3	3-2
Jones, H	1920 - 1921			1-0		
Jones, Harry	1909 - 1910			6-1		
Jones, Howell	1904 - 1906	3-3		7-0	1-0	
Jones, John Evan	1892 - 1893 & 1894 - 1898	42-0	2-0		6-0	11-0
Jones, J	1900 - 1903	28-14			2-0	3-2
Jones, J.B.	1902 - 1903	1-0				
Jones, J.E.	1896 - 1898	10-2			1-0	
Jones, Jeffrey	1908 - 1909			1-0		
Jones, Owen	1906 - 1907			2-2	1-0	
Jones, Percy	1919 - 1920			1-1		
Jones, R	1890 - 1892	1-0				1-0
Jones, R	1899 - 1900	1-0				
Jones, Reg	1913 - 1914			19-5	2-1	4-1
Jones, Reg	1919 - 1921			32-15	4-3	5-0
Jones, Sam	1891 - 1893	38-0			4-0	8-0
Jones, S	1910 - 1911			2-0		
Jones, T	1890 - 1892	3-0				
Jones, T	1906 - 1908 & 1911 - 1915			24-2		4-4
Jones, Trevor	1919 - 1921			33-0	5-0	5-0
Jones, Victor	1907 - 1908			1-0	1-0	
Jones, William John	1898 - 1900	16-10			2-0	
Jones, W	1912 - 1913			3-1		
Kelly, Frederick Charles	1897 - 1901	61-14			9-4	8-2
Kelly, G	1891 - 1892	1-0				
Kenyon, E	1910 - 1911				1-0	
Kyffin, Pryce	1890 - 1893	5-0				
Lappin,	1911 - 1912			5-1		
Lea, Arthur	1890 - 1894	56-16	13-3		7-2	14-5
Lewis, Benjamin	1891 - 1894 & 1896 - 1899	88-30	16-12		15-8	12-7
Lewis, J	1919 - 1920			1-1		
Lewis, Jack	1891 - 1892	1-0				
Lewis, Jonathan	1897 - 1899 & 1903 - 1904	23-10			3-0	3-1
Lewis, Oswald	1911 - 1912			6-0		
Lewis, S	1919 - 1920			10-3	3-0	
Lipsham, J	1913 - 1914			32-6	4-0	5-1
Littlehales,	1897 - 1898	1-0				
Lloyd, A	1905 - 1906			3-0		
Lloyd, W	1896 - 1897	2-0				
Lumberg, Albert	1900 - 1901	1-0				

Name	Seasons with club	Appearances/Goals CL	WL	BL	FAC	WC
Mason, J	1906 - 1907 & 1908 - 1912			44-19	3-4	8-4
Matthews, Herbert	1920 - 1921			3-1	1-0	1-0
Mathias,	1890 - 1892	2-0				
Mathias, G	1914 - 1915			2-0		
Mathias, John	1901 - 1902	1-0				
Matthias, Thomas James	1912 -			166-14	23-2	24-3
McAlister,	1909 - 1910			14-3	1-0	
McGuffe,	1911 - 1912			1-0	2-0	
Meredith, William Henry	1893 - 1894	1-0				
Millward,	1907 - 1908			4-1		
Mitchell, Joey	1898 - 1902, 1904 - 1905, 1910 - 1911 & 1912 - 1913	12-8		5-0	2-0	1-0
Morgan, Tracey	1904 - 1907 & 1909 - 1910	25-0		33-0	3-0	8-0
Morris, Charles Richard	1911 - 1913			22-0	2-0	2-0
Morris, J	1919 - 1921			4-0		
Morris, Llew	1908 - 1910 & 1913 - 1914			13-0		1-0
Moss, Ellis	1901 - 1903 & 1906 - 1907	3-0		1-0		
Moss, T	1905 - 1907			2-0	1-0	
Murphy, Leslie	1920 -			33-0	3-0	5-0
Murray,	1910 - 1911			9-0		2-0
Myatt,	1907 - 1908			27-3	1-0	3-2
Oakes,	1914 - 1915			2-0		
Ollerhead, J	1890 - 1891	1-0				
Osborne,	1911 - 1912			5-5		
Owen,	1919 - 1920			18-10	4-1	2-2
Owen, Elias	1890 - 1891	1-0				
Owen, George	1893 - 1894	17-2			2-0	
Owen, J	1890 - 1891	7-0				1-0
Owen, Trevor	1891 - 1896	35-9	24-12		9-2	6-2
Owens, Joe	1899 - 1906	122-43		6-0	11-2	15-6
Owens, T	1914 - 1915			13-3		2-1
Parry, E	1919 - 1920			2-0		
Parry, J	1891 - 1892	9-5			2-2	3-1
Parry, J	1905 - 1906 & 1907 - 1908			1-0	1-0	
Pedley, Jack	1910 - 1911			23-5		4-0
Percival, Joe	1906 - 1908			50-0	8-0	3-0
Peters,	1911 - 1912			1-0	1-0	
Pickering, John	1920 - 1921			11-1		2-0
Pike, Walter	1908 - 1910			8-2	1-1	
Pitt, E	1911 - 1912			3-4	3-1	
Potts,	1900 - 1901	2-0				
Pountley,	1890 - 1891	1-0				
Pountney,	1892 - 1893 & 1899 - 1903	69-38			10-4	7-5
Povah,	1897 - 1900	48-1			5-0	5-0
Powell,	1892 - 1893	2-0				
Price, Haydn	1908 - 1909			26-5	8-4	4-3
Pritchard, S	1892 - 1893	6-2			1-0	3-2
Pritchard, W	1891 - 1892	9-4				4-0
Pryce-Jones, Trevor	1890 - 1891	2-1			1-0	
Pugh, A	1893 - 1894	1-0				
Pugh, David Henry	1895 - 1897	15-8	12-6		4-2	7-4
Pugh, Joe	1891 - 1893	18-7			1-0	2-0
Randles,	1892 - 1893	1-0				
Rankin, Bruce	1908 - 1909			22-7	2-1	3-3
Rathbone, S	1920 - 1921			1-0		
Reid,	1908 - 1909			2-0		
Reid,	1912 - 1914			4-2		1-0
Reynolds,	1898 - 1899	3-0				
Richards,	1911 - 1912			1-0		
Riddell,	1910 - 1911			2-0		
Roberts, A	1914 - 1915			1-0		
Roberts, Arthur	1890 - 1891	2-0				
Roberts, Charles	1890 - 1891	1-0				
Roberts, E.D.	1919 -			63-8	9-0	10-1
Roberts, Elias	1905 - 1906			10-5		
Roberts, Frank	1919 - 1921			23-1	5-0	4-1
Roberts, Jack	1910 - 1913			69-42	10-14	6-7
Roberts, Jas	1910 - 1913			60-8	2-0	3-0
Roberts, Jos	1890 - 1891	11-2			1-2	3-1
Roberts, Robert	1890 - 1894	42-0	3-0		2-0	6-0
Roberts, Thomas	1907 - 1909			6-2	1-0	1-0
Roberts, W	1890 - 1892	2-0				2-2
Roberts,	1902 - 1903	1-0				
Robinson, Ted	1894 - 1907	194-16	16-1	35-0	24-1	33-3
Robinson, W	1900 - 1901	1-0				

Name	Seasons with club	CL	WL	BL	FAC	WC
		Appearances/Goals				
Rogers,	1909 - 1910			4-0		
Rogers, Joseph P.	1895 - 1896 & 1897 - 1902	68-0	12-0		12-0	11-0
Rowlands,	1899 - 1900	1-0				
Rowlands, Alfred Stanley	1912 - 1913			30-18	5-2	1-0
Rowlands, M	1910 - 1911			1-1		
Samuels, Edward	1891 - 1896	35-1	24-0		9-0	11-0
Samuels, S	1911 - 1913			25-11	1-1	2-1
Shallcroft, George	1893 - 1894 & 1896 - 1898	8-0				
Shaw, J	1902 - 1904 & 1906 - 1907	19-4		3-0	1-0	2-0
Shepherd,	1909 - 1910			10-6	1-0	
Simmonds,	1919 - 1920			1-0		
Simpson, Robert	1919 -			60-0	6-0	10-0
Smith,	1919 - 1920			1-0		
Smith, Alfred	1906 - 1909			71-45	12-11	11-7
Smith, T	1903 - 1904 & 1905 - 1906	1-0			1-0	
Stevens, F	1912 - 1913			4-2		
Stockton, C	1904 - 1908	2-0		66-10	4-1	8-4
Stokes, Frank	1890 - 1894 & 1895 - 1897	21-0	12-1		2-0	7-0
Stuart,	1912 - 1913			13-6	2-0	1-0
Sutherland,	1920 - 1921			1-0	1-0	
Tattum,	1898 - 1899	1-0				
Taylor, J	1919 - 1921			29-21		6-8
Taylor, John	1896 - 1898	37-1			5-0	7-0
Thomas, C	1890 - 1891	2-0				
Thomas, Evan	1903 - 1905 & 1906 - 1907	9-0		13-0		4-0
Townsend,	1896 - 1897	1-0				
Trainer, Harry	1894 - 1895		10-17		3-3	3-0
Turner, Joseph Hudson	1890 - 1892	34-15			2-0	9-7
Turner, Richard E.	1890 - 1892	15-0			2-0	3-0
Turner, William Haighton	1890 - 1892	18-11			1-0	8-5
Uren, Harold	1905 - 1906, 1908 - 1909 & 1913 - 1914			38-9	9-3	8-5
Walton, T	1892 - 1894	4-0				
Welfare, Harry	1911 - 1912			1-0		
Wesley,	1913 - 1914			1-0		
Westley,	1903 - 1904	8-0				1-0
Wheeler,	1892 - 1893	1-0			1-0	
Wilding, Joby	1890 - 1893 & 1897 - 1898	24-5			3-1	
Wilding, T	1892 - 1893 & 1897 - 1898	2-0				
Williams,	1920 - 1921				1-0	
Williams, Alf	1892 - 1894 & 1895 - 1899	32-8	12-7		4-1	10-4
Williams, D	1911 - 1912				1-0	
Williams, Evan	1890 - 1894	63-7			7-0	13-2
Williams, E	1905 - 1906				1-0	
Williams, George Owen	1906 - 1908			47-1	6-0	5-0
Williams, J	1899 - 1900	1-0				
Williams, J	1903 - 1904	5-0			1-0	
Williams, J	1908 - 1909			2-0		
Williams, J	1913 - 1915			6-0		
Williams, Pryce	1907 - 1909 & 1910 - 1915			209-8	30-5	26-4
Williams, R	1904 - 1906	8-0		7-4		
Williams, S	1905 - 1906			2-0	1-0	
Woodville, Harry	1897 - 1899	4-0				
Wray, Arthur	1920 - 1921			1-0		
Wynne, George Arthur	1908 - 1909			28-16	8-8	5-4
Wynne-Owen, H	1913 - 1914			1-0		
Yuill,	1908 - 1909 & 1910 - 1911			2-0		1-0

Subscribers

1. Wrexham Association Football Club
2. Football Association of Wales
3. Football League
4. Association of Football Statisticians
5. Joey Jones (Wrexham AFC)
6. Gareth M.Davies
7. Peter Jones
8. John R.Boyle (Wrexham) Ltd.
9. David Griffiths
10. Mark D.Griffiths
11. Allan Thomas (Wrexham A.F.C. Commercial Manager)
12. Dorothy & David Davies
13. Sarah Nia Davies
14. Gareth Peter Jones
15. Karen & Peter Jones
16. Neville & Josie Jones
17. David M. & Linda Jones
18. John & Pam Bolton
19. John Humphreys
20. John Humphreys (Llanymynech)
21. David Roberts
22. Jim Creasy
23. Pamela Waldron & Family
24. Jim Evans
25. Brian G. Davies
26. Geraint Parry
27. Simon Jones
28. Paul Jones
29. Bill Mulcahy - Australian Reds
30. Peter Roberts
31. Howard Austin
32. E.S.Roberts
33. Gavin & Daniel Evans - T.S.G.
34. Shaun Williams
35. Peter Davies -Red Passion Fanzine
36. Eifion Pugh
37. Gary S. Coombes
38. Dave & John Mainwaring
39. Adrian Dafydd Griffith
40. Winston Connah
41. Paul Davies
42. Nigel Wynn
43. Darren Spilsted
44. Patrick J. Davies
45. Paula Austin
46. Ian Frazer Jones
47. Michael Fisher
48. Darren Morris
49. Simon Roberts
50. M.V.G.Beynon
51. Mike Griffiths (Llay)
52. Jamie, Chelsea & Christian Slater
53. Phil Rogers
54. Andrew Rogers
55. Kevin Williams (Cochion Rhuddlan)
56. Mark Drury
57. Steve L.Turner
58. Neil Sanderson
59. David Owens (Rhostyllen)
60. David Ithell Kelly
61. Colin Bithell
62. Gilbert Roberts
63. Barry Dean Lewis
64. Taff Williams
65. Ken Peters
66. Roy Edwards
67. Wayne Williams
68. Jason Lewis
69. Steve Calton
70. John Gavin Gibson
71. Andy Artell
72. Nick Coleman
73. Eddie & Dorren Griffiths
74. Stephen K.Clare
75. Max Wiecko
76. Paul Acton
77. Geoff & Daniel Griffiths
78. Mark Griffiths
79. Mark Clemence
80. Andrew Clemence

81 W.D.Phillips

82. Revd J.Gareth Griffiths
83. Paul Lindsay
84. Mark Hayes
85. Kim Davies
86. Dyfan Wyn Owen
87. Paul Elson
88. Chas Sumner
89. Leon Owen Taraborelli
90. Stephen Lloyd
91. J.R.Ringrose
92. Clifford Hope
93. John Musgrove
94. Michael Parton
95. Donald Noble
96. L.A.Zammit
97. Mervyn H.Davies
98. Michael Clarke
99. T.I.Roberts 'Jacko' (Fron Male Voice Choir)
100. Richard Hill 'Manchester Reds'
101. Derek Hyde
102. Richard Waddington
103. Michael Grayson
104. Ron Sinclair
105. Steve Emms
106. David Keats
107. Alan Hill (Wrexham AFC 1973-1983)
108. Raymond Shaw
109. Lloyd Edwards
110. Edward Tunney (Wrexham AFC 1937-1952)
111. Peter Williams
112. Moira & Frederick Furness
113. Graham Hewitt
114. Philip Glyn Jones
115. Alan Wells
116. Brian G.Williams
117. Ian Cox
118. Brian Rogers & Geraint Rogers
119. Mark Andrew Williams
120. Peter Cave
121. Monique Scott
122. Margaret Scott
123. P.A.Beatty
124. Neil A.Williams
125. Dave Windross (York City)
126. Sarah Dallimore
127. Nigel Evans
128. Arthur R.Mullett
129. Mark Simpson
130. Martin Richards
131. Paddy Sowden (Wrexham AFC 1958-1959)
132. Andy Mills
133. Matthew Adam Lamb
134. Derek Williams (Wrexham AFC 1954-1955)
135. Alan Butler
136. Kevin Arthur
137. Mark R.Wilcock
138. Robert Connor (Wrexham AFC 1951-1954)
139. Gareth, Stuart & Dominic Grainger (Grandsons of Dennis - Wrexham AFC 1947-1951)
140. David & Sue Jones
141. James Llewellyn Moore
142. Trevor Robert Morris
143. M.James
144. John William Lloyd
145. Stephen Parrott
146. Reg & Mair Parrott
147. Robert Parrott
148. Robert Broughton
149. The Webbed Robin
150. Mark Thompson
151. Stephen Kieran Byrne
152. David E.Reeves
153. Duncan Watt
154. Roger Wash
155. Paul Sleeman
156. Michael Featherstone
157. Stephen Hardy
158. John Meredith Williams (T.A.B.)
159. Howard Smith
160. Gordon Small
161. Nick Jones
162. Darran Jones
163. Fred & Andrew Ridgeway
164. Dave McPherson
165. Geoff Allman
166. Jonny Stokkeland
167. Clifford Roberts
168. Bill Seddon
169. Andrew Wright
170. Cliff Grounds
171. Stuart Roberts
172. Dean Williams
173. Paul Vincent Tharme
174. R.E.A.Clark
175. Colin R.Davies
176. Phil Hollow (Plymouth Argyle)
177. Colin Bewley
178. Mike Hegarty
179. Mark Barnes
180. Michael Barnes
181. Paul & Stephen Matthias
182. Roy Ambler (Wrexham AFC 1961-1962)
183. David Parry-Jones
184. Phil Williams
185. Rhodri Charles
186. Mark Beresford
187. Tim Kendrick-Jones
188. Kevin Jones
189. Terry Frost
190. Gareth Hughes (Abergele)
191. Martin Fox
192. Nathan Fennah (Age 11 years, Hawarden)
193. T.R.Morris
194. Rob Davies (Cochion Wyddgrug)
195. Arwyn Jones (Yr Wyddgrug)
196. John Lewis
197. Richard Stocken
198. Brian Lloyd Hughes
199. Stephen Fowles
200. Alan Hindley
201. James, David & Andrew Jones
202. Geraint Lloyd
203. Gareth Topham

Subscribers

204. Douglas Lamming
205. B.H.Huxley
206. Stuart Harris
207. John V.Threlfall
208. Henry Richard Jones
209. David Ray Roberts (Birmingham Reds)
210. Steve Hughes
211. Geraint Owen (Gez) Hughes
212. Adrian Allen
213. James Baird Nicholson
214. M.J.Collins
215. Hywel Wyn Roberts
216. Joseph T.Gibson
217. Alan, Liz, Cathryn, Gareth & Megan
218. W.Trefor Roberts
219. D.S.Morris
220. J.E.Matthias
221. E.C.Griffiths
222. Robert James Rennie
223. Mark Antony Ellis
224. David E.Griffiths
225. R.Goodwin/A.N.Other
226. Mr.Alex Philp
227. Christopher Jones
228. Richard Varker
229. David W.O.Ellis - In Exile (Northwich)
230. Andrew Davies
231. Richard Wells
232. Wayne Jones (Amlwch)
233. Tony Williams
234. Christer Svensson
235. Robert David Griffiths
236. Allan Allcock
237. Ray Williams
238. Dave Evans (Morfa Nefyn)
239. Peris & Robert Edwards
240. Nigel Davies
241. Robert Ince
242. Alan Fox (Tredegar)
243. Nick Griffiths
244. Robert Parry
245. Richard Parry
246. Mr.G.S.Hudson
247. Wyn Gray Thomas (Caernarfon Town)
248. J.M.Baines
249. A.J.Price
250. Tim Blent
251. Tim Hughes
252. James William Cole
253. Gwyn, Evelyn & Rhys Roberts (Dolgellau)
254. Vernon A.Jones
255. In Memory of Ernie Jones
256. Geoffrey Ellis
257. Terry Smith
258. Geoffrey Owen Darkins
259. Stephen R.Daulby
260. Russell H.Jones
261. S.R. 'Roddy' Owen (Ex-Rhos)
262. Douglas Stuart Jones
263. Huw Adrian Jones
264. Ben Williams
265. Jennifer & Mark Parry
266. Michael G.Davies
267. Sarah Jones
268. Delwyn Williams (Del Caergeiliog)
269. B.Gareth Collins
270. Wrexham Library & Information Service
271. Wrexham Library & Information Service
272. Wrexham Library & Information Service
273. Wrexham Library & Information Service
274. Cyngor Gwynedd Gwasanaeth Llyfgell (Gwynedd County Library Service)
275. Cyngor Gwynedd Gwasanaeth Llyfrgell (Gwynedd County Library Service)
276. Cyngor Gwynedd Gwasanaeth Llyfrgell (Gwynedd County Library Service)
277. Cyngor Gwynedd Gwasanaeth Llyfrgell (Gwynedd County Library Service)
278. Cyngor Gwynedd Gwasanaeth Llyfrgell (Gwynedd County Library Service)
279. Cyngor Gwynedd Gwasanaeth Llyfrgell (Gwynedd County Library Service)
280. Cyngor Sir Ynys Mon/Isle of Anglesey County Council (Library Dept)
281. Cyngor Sir Ynys Mon/Isle of Anglesey County Council (Library Dept)
282. Mark Stuart (Holyhead Hotspur)
283. Lloydie (Coedpoeth)
284. Jason Lee Thomas (Caernarfon)
285. Will Williams (Caergybi)
286. Gari Pritchard (Valley)
287. Eric J, David & Brian (LlainGochi Holyhead) To Dad from Cara.
288. Elwyn Jones
289. Berwyn Jones (Johnstown)
290. Gareth Carman
291. Darren Denby
292. Kevin Roberts
293. Gareth Hill
294. Charles & George Ducker
295. David Alan Smith (Bridgend Reds)
296. Brian Evans
297. Philip Dexter
298. Conwy Library & Information Service Cultural Services Dept,
299. Denbighshire County Council Shropshire Libraries
300. Flintshire Library & Information Service
301. Flintshire Library & Information Service
302. Andy Thomas (Buckley)
303. Liverpool Library & Information Service
304. National Library of Wales (Llyfrgell Genedlaethol Cymru, Aberystwyth)
305. National Library of Wales (Llyfrgell Genedlaethol Cymru, Aberystwyth)
306. Denbighshire Library & Information Service
307. Denbighshire Library & Information Service
308. Powys Library Service
309. Cheshire Libraries & Archive Service
310. Cheshire Libraries & Archive Service
311. Cheshire Libraries & Archive Service
312. Steve Bates
313. Paul Valentine (Rhos Reds)
314. J.Culley
315. Michael Holland
316. Ian A.Evans
317. Glyn Williams (Wrexham AFC 1947-1949)
318. Ian Glyn Williams (Bristol)
319. Janet D.Gallimore (Leominster)
320. Ian Herbert
321. Peter Herbert
322. Dave Rawlins (Wrexham AFC 1959-1966)
323. A.Gilmour
324. Alan Jones (Wrexham AFC 1964-1966)
325. Arthur Jones (Mold)
326. Barry Jones (London Reds)
327. Mark Waters
328. Maria Rookyard
329. Stephen Pryce
330. Bert Goode (Son of former Wrexham player)
331. Malcolm Lloyd (Son of Joe Lloyd, Wrexham A.F.C. 1946-1947)
332. Adrian Clark (Shropshire Reds)
333. Steve Gurner
334. Gwilym Williams (Coedpoeth/Buckley/Slough)
335. Glynn Davies Williams
336. Alexander Hunt
337. Kevin Griffiths
338. Peter Smith
339. Glyn & Gareth Hayes
340. Paul Lloyd Williams (Buckley) Forever Loyal
341. M.Dethier Jean Michel
342. David J.Brooker
343. Kelly Verity Bishop & David Bishop
344. Darryl Edwards
345. Jim Harber
346. Mark Harber
347. Huw Griffiths (Wrecsam)
348. Andrew & Jacob Dylan Colley
349. Mrs.Betty Williams (Overton-on-Dee)
350. Phillip Wynford Hughes (Ontario)
351. John Griffiths (Mold)
352. John Williams & Richard Williams
353. David Jones (Oswestry)
354. David, Jan & Lauren Smith
355. Tim Sarsfield
356. Harvey Jones (Wrexham A.F.C. 1959-1960)
357. Phil Turner (Wrexham)
358. Ray Davies (Wetherby)
359. Alun Owen
360. Malcolm K.Davies (Adlink Advertising)
361. Ian Moir (Wrexham AFC 1968-1972 & 1973-1975)
362. Stuart Mason (Wrexham AFC 1964-1966 & 1968-1973)
363. Wrexham AFC Supporters Club
364. Shropshire Reds Wrexham AFC S.C.
365. London Reds Wrexham AFC S.C.
366. Vale of Clwyd Reds Wrexham AFC S.C.
367. Ynys Mon Reds Wrexham AFC S.C.
368. Terry Thompson
369. Alun Jones
370. Michael Wason (Clive)
371. Ian Garland - Caernarfon Town
372. Keith 'Fuzzy' Jones
373. Dennis Jones (Wem)
374. Bob & Gaynor Lowe
375. Peter Baxter
376. S.Metcalfe
377. Eric Beesley (Wrexham AFC 1957-1959)
378. Peter L.Mills
379. Roger Triggs
380. Mrs Annie Ferguson
381. Mr.J.Hurley
382. Brian Griffiths (Wrexham AFC 1952-1958)
383. Mrs.J.Roberts
384. Martin Jarred
385. R.I.Jones
386. Tomos Michael Hedd Jones
387. Graham Williams (Wrexham Lager Club)
388. Mark Griffiths (Rhiwabon)
389. Jamie Robert Lowe
390. Robyn & Lauren Evans (Borras Park)
391. Paul Atherton (Manchester City)
392. Steve Trinick (Manchester City)
393. Engraving Services Ltd;
394. Geraint Cooper (Solihul)